ENCYCLOPEDIA
OF MORMONISM

EDITORIAL BOARD

ENCYCLOPEDIA
OF MORMONISM

Edited by
Daniel H. Ludlow

Volume 2

*The History, Scripture, Doctrine, and Procedure
of The Church of Jesus Christ of Latter-day Saints*

Macmillan Publishing Company
New York

Maxwell Macmillan Canada
Toronto

Maxwell Macmillan International
New York   Oxford   Singapore   Sydney

Copyright © 1992 by Macmillan Publishing Company
A Division of Macmillan, Inc.

Macmillan Publishing Company
866 Third Avenue, New York, NY 10022

Maxwell Macmillan Canada, Inc.
1200 Eglinton Avenue East, Suite 200, Don Mills, Ontario M3C 3N1

Library of Congress Catalog Card No.:91–34255

Printed in the United States of America

printing number
  4 5 6 7 8 9 10

Macmillan Inc. is part of the Maxwell Communication
Group of Companies.

Library of Congress Cataloging-in-Publication Data

Encyclopedia of Mormonism/edited by Daniel H. Ludlow.
     p.   cm.
   Includes bibliographical references and index.
   ISBN 0-02-879605-5 (4 vol. set).—ISBN 0-02-904040-X (5 vol.
set).—ISBN 0-02-879600-4 (v. 1)
   1. Church of Jesus Christ of Latter-Day Saints—Encyclopedias.
2. Mormon Church—Encyclopedias.   3. Mormons—Encyclopedias.
I. Ludlow, Daniel H.
BX8605.5.E62   1992
289.3′03—dc20   91–34255
                                                         CIP

E

EARTH

Latter-day Saints believe that God created this earth to provide his children, the human race, with the opportunity to receive physical bodies and to hear and accept his gospel that they might be prepared for life with him on a celestialized earth hereafter. They also believe that this earth eventually will become a celestial, glorified world. Jesus Christ, under direction of God the Father, was the creator of the earth and all things in it (John 1:1–3). Creation was first a spirit creation followed by a physical creation of the planet and life on it. One LDS scholar observed, "The Latter-day Saints are the only Bible-oriented people who have always been taught that things were happening long, long before Adam appeared on the scene" (*CWHN* 1:49). Because God created the earth for these eternal purposes, Latter-day Saints view its natural resources and life forms as a sacred STEWARDSHIP to be used in ways that will ensure their availability for all succeeding generations. Latter-day scriptures also teach of a plurality of WORLDS. In itself this is not a unique concept among the religions of the world, but the LDS doctrine is distinctive (Crowe, pp. 241–46).

THE AGE OF THE EARTH. The scriptures do not say how old the earth is, and the Church has taken no official stand on this question (*Old Testament*, pp. 28–29). Nor does the Church consider it to be a central issue for salvation.

Discussions of the age of the earth feature three separate and distinct interpretations of the word "day" in the CREATION ACCOUNTS. Very few Latter-day Saints hold to the theory that the days of creation were twenty-four hours long. Some have attempted to accommodate scientific theories to scriptural accounts of creation by extending creation day lengths to one thousand years each. Support for this view has been found in scriptures suggesting "one day is with the Lord as a thousand years" (2 Pet. 3:8; cf. Abr. 3:2–4; 5:13; Facsimile No. 2).

But because even seven thousand years fails to approximate the billions of years suggested by contemporary scientific accounts, many Latter-day Saints have emphasized the possibility that the scriptural days of creation may have been vastly greater time periods. They point to the fact that "the Hebrew word for *day* . . . can also be used in the sense of an indeterminate length of time," and to Abraham's account of creation in which he "says that the Gods *called* the creation periods days" (*Old Testament*, pp. 28–29; see Eyring; Abr. 4:5, 8).

THE ORIGIN AND DESTINY OF THE EARTH. Joseph SMITH wrote, "We believe . . . that the earth will be renewed and receive its paradisiacal glory" (A of F 10). LDS revelation declares that the earth is destined to become a celestial body fit for the abode of the most exalted or celestial beings (D&C 88:18–20, 25–26). This is a unique departure from the traditional Christian beliefs that HEAVEN is the dwelling place for all saved beings, and that after fulfilling its useful role the earth will become uninhabited, or be destroyed. Doctrine and Covenants 130:9 teaches that finally the earth will become sanctified and immortalized, and be made crystal-like. The "sea of glass" spoken of in Revelation 4:6 "is the earth, in its sanctified, immortal, and eternal state" (D&C 77:1). Elder James E. Talmage wrote of this earthly regeneration: "In regard to the revealed word concerning the regeneration of earth, and the acquirement of a celestial glory by our planet, science has nothing to offer either by way of support or contradiction" (AF, p. 381).

Latter-day Saints understand the entire history of the earth to be directly linked to its role in God's plan of salvation for his children, his work and glory, "to bring to pass the immortality and eternal life of man" (Moses 1:39). The earth was created as a paradise. Because of the FALL OF ADAM and EVE, it was transformed to a telestial state, or the present mortal earth. This interval will end with the return of the Savior, after which the earth will be changed to a terrestrial state and prepared during the Millennium for its final transformation into a celestial sphere after the Millennium (D&C 88:18–19). The ancient Nephite concept derived from Christ's teachings to them includes the idea that before the final judgment the earth will be "rolled together as a scroll, and the elements [will] melt with fervent heat" (Morm. 9:2), "and the heavens and the earth [shall] pass away" (3 Ne. 26:3). This historical account is linear, marked by unique, important events that link the theological and physical history of the earth, that is, creation, fall, renewal at the second coming of Christ, and final glory.

Against the backdrop of this progressive history is the constancy of spiritual and physical law immanently affecting succeeding generations of God's children on earth. In this context President John TAYLOR said, "Change succeeds change in human affairs, but the laws of God in everything are correct and true; in every stage and phase of nature, everything on the earth, in the waters and in the atmosphere is governed by unchangeable, eternal laws" (*Gospel Kingdom*, p. 70, Salt Lake City, 1987; *see* LAW).

THE GREAT FLOOD. The Old Testament records a flood that was just over fifteen cubits (sometimes assumed to be about twenty-six feet) deep and covered the entire landscape: "And all the high hills, that were under the whole heaven, were covered" (Gen. 7:19). Scientifically this account leaves many questions unanswered, especially how a measurable depth could cover mountains. Elder John A. Widtsoe, writing in 1943, offered this perspective:

> The fact remains that the exact nature of the flood is not known. We set up assumptions, based upon our best knowledge, but can go no further. We should remember that when inspired writers deal with historical incidents they relate that which they have seen or that which may have been told them, unless indeed the past is opened to them by revelation.
>
> The details in the story of the flood are undoubtedly drawn from the experiences of the writer. Under a downpour of rain, likened to the opening of the heavens, a destructive torrent twenty-six feet deep or deeper would easily be formed. The writer of Genesis made a faithful report of the facts known to him concerning the flood. In other localities the depth of the water might have been more or less. In fact, the details of the flood are not known to us [Widtsoe, p. 127].

SPECIAL CONCERNS OF LATTER-DAY SAINTS. President Brigham YOUNG taught: "The whole object of the creation of this world is to exalt the intelligences that are placed upon it, that they may live, endure, and increase for ever and ever. We are not here to quarrel and contend about the things of this world, but we are here to subdue and beautify it" (*JD* 7:290). Viewing themselves as tenants upon the earth, Latter-day Saints regard its resources as a sacred trust from God for the use of all while upon the earth: "I, the Lord . . . make every man accountable, as a steward over earthly blessings, which I have made and prepared for my creatures" (D&C 104:13). The earth was created by Christ for specific purposes: "We will take of these materials, and we will make an earth whereon these may dwell; and we will prove them herewith, to see if they will do all things whatsoever the Lord their God shall command them" (Abr. 3:24–25). President Brigham Young taught that the dominion God gives human beings is designed to test them, enabling them to show to themselves, to their fellow beings, and to God just how they would act if entrusted with God's power (Nibley, 1978, p. 90; *see* PURPOSE OF EARTH LIFE).

Brigham Young supervised the relocation of the Church to the American West, which in the late 1840s was sparsely inhabited. His strong commitment to preservation of the environment and wise use of all natural resources influenced early Church colonizing efforts. Such prudence and wisdom in the use of land, water, air, and living things are still encouraged throughout the Church. In modern days of widespread concern for preserving the fragile relationships between the earth and its biosphere, Brigham Young's counsel remains vital:

> There is a great work for the Saints to do. Progress, and improve upon, and make beautiful everything around you. Cultivate the earth and cultivate your minds. Build cities, adorn your habitations, make gardens, orchards, and vineyards, and render the earth so pleasant that when you look upon your labours you may do so with pleasure, and that angels may delight to come and visit your beautiful locations [JD 8:83].

BIBLIOGRAPHY

Cracroft, Paul. "How Old Is the Earth?" *IE* 67 (Oct. 1964):827–30, 852.

Crowe, M. J. *Extraterrestrial Life Debate 1750–1900.* Cambridge, U.K., 1986.

Eyring, Henry. "The Gospel and the Age of the Earth." *IE* 68 (July 1965):608–609, 626, 628.

Jeffery, Duane E. "Seers, Savants and Evolution: The Uncomfortable Interface." *Dialogue* 8, nos. 3/4 (1973):41–75.

Jones, Albert. "Is Mother Earth Growing Old?" *IE* 13 (May 1910):639–43.

Nibley, Hugh W. "Before Adam." In *CWHN* 1:49–85.

———. "Brigham Young on the Environment." In *To the Glory of God*, ed. T. Madsen and C. Tate, pp. 3–29. Salt Lake City, 1972.

———. "Man's Dominion." *New Era* 2 (Oct. 1972):24–31.

———. "Subduing the Earth." In *Nibley on the Timely and the Timeless*, ed. T. Madsen, pp. 85–99. Provo, Utah, 1978.

———. "Treasures in the Heavens." In *CWHN* 1:171–214.

Old Testament: Genesis–2 Samuel [Religion 301] Student Manual, 2nd ed., rev. Salt Lake City, 1981.

Pratt, Orson. *JD* 16:324–25.

Smith, Joseph Fielding. *Man: His Origin and Destiny.* Salt Lake City, 1954.

Talmage, James E. "Prophecy as the Forerunner of Science—An Instance." *IE* 7 (May 1904):481–88.

Widtsoe, John A. *Evidences and Reconciliations.* Salt Lake City, 1987.

MORRIS S. PETERSEN

EASTER

Easter is the Christian holiday celebrating the resurrection of Jesus Christ. After Christ died on the cross, his body was placed in a sepulcher, where it remained, separated from his SPIRIT, until his resurrection, when his spirit and his body were reunited. Latter-day Saints affirm and testify that Jesus Christ was resurrected and lives today with a glorified and perfected body of flesh and bone. Following his resurrection, Jesus appeared first to Mary Magdalene and then to other disciples. Some were not convinced of his resurrection, believing that his appearances were those of an unembodied spirit. Jesus assured them, "Behold my hands and my feet, that it is I myself: handle me, and see; for a spirit hath not flesh and bones, as ye see me have" (Luke 24:39). He then ate fish and honey in their presence, further dispelling their doubt.

Easter is a celebration not only of the resurrection of Christ but also of the universal resurrection. Because of the ATONEMENT of Jesus Christ, all people will be resurrected. Their bodies and spirits will be reunited, never to be separated again. Latter-day Saints know the truth of Paul's statement, "But now is Christ risen from the dead, and become the firstfruits of them that slept. . . . For as in Adam all die, even so in Christ shall all be made alive" (1 Cor. 15:20; cf. Alma 11:42–45).

Latter-day Saints conduct Easter Sunday services but do not follow the religious observances of Ash Wednesday, Lent, or Holy Week. LDS Easter services traditionally review New Testament and Book of Mormon accounts of Christ's crucifixion, his resurrection, and surrounding events. For these services, chapels are often decorated with white lilies and other symbols of life. Ward choirs frequently present Easter cantatas, and congregations sing Easter hymns. As at services on other Sundays, the emblems of the sacrament (see COMMUNION) are passed to the congregation.

Some LDS families include Easter bunnies and eggs in their family festivities for the delight of children. Such traditions are not officially discouraged, though they have no religious significance to Latter-day Saints. The focus of the holiday is religious. For Latter-day Saints, Easter is a celebration of the promise of eternal life through Christ. They share the conviction of Job, "For I know that my redeemer liveth, and that he shall stand at the latter day upon the earth: And though after my skin worms destroy this body, yet in my flesh shall I see God" (Job 19:25–26).

BIBLIOGRAPHY

Kimball, Spencer W. "The Real Meaning of Easter." *Instructor* 93 (Apr. 1958):100–101.

MARY ELLEN STEWART JAMISON

ECONOMIC AID

Economic aid offered by the Church to needy people in various countries is intended to promote the well-being of individuals and families. In addition to temporary welfare assistance given by the Church to its members and to a variety of emergency and HUMANITARIAN SERVICES, the Church has rendered longer-term economic aid to many groups in a variety of nations. Church members are taught that family well-being depends upon, among other things, the means to provide food, clothing, and shelter. Just as individual members are taught to acquire skills necessary for this economic well-being (see EMERGENCY PREPAREDNESS; SELF-SUFFICIENCY), the Church encourages nations to provide economic opportunity for their citizens and to establish an economic atmosphere wherein individual skills can be used for the benefit of families and the nation.

The Church has not established political criteria for selecting recipients of its economic aid. Joseph SMITH echoed the counsel of the Savior to feed the hungry and clothe the naked (Matt. 25:35–40; T&S 3 [Mar. 1842]:732).

Many of the humanitarian projects supported by the Church have had a monetary component to them. In addition to the food and blankets sent to many peoples in Europe after World War II, money was sent to purchase land and buildings to be used for longer-term relief. In 1983, the Church sent emergency food and clothing to both Colombia (earthquake) and Tahiti (hurricane), and Church funds also were used to provide building materials for those whose homes had been devastated ("News of the Church," Ensign 13 [June 1983]:77). Similarly, aid to both Armenia and Africa included funds for economic development in addition to monies used for more immediate relief. As part of the 1989 aid to Armenia following earthquakes in the region, materials and tools were donated by the Church to allow craftsmen to rebuild homes and businesses (The Daily Universe, Dec. 6, 1989, Provo, Utah, p. 2). And in the $10 million aid to Africa in 1985 and 1986, approximately one-third of the funds were used to support long-term economic development projects (Ferguson, pp. 10–15). For example, in concert with Africare, some of the funds were used to construct dams, develop irrigation and other water projects, and train farmers in Ethiopia. Economic aid from the Church also supported vocational school develop-

ment and marketing cooperatives in the Sudan, and agricultural rehabilitation in Chad, Niger, and Cameroon ("News of the Church," Ensign 15 [Nov. 1985]:109). Special funds also have been used to support local self-sufficiency enterprises, literacy and health services, and agricultural development in Kenya, Zimbabwe, Mozambique, Zaire, Ghana, Mali, Nigeria, Chad, and in Central and South America.

One of the more extensive and systematic resources to provide Church economic aid has been the Ezra Taft Benson Agriculture and Food Institute located at BRIGHAM YOUNG UNIVERSITY. This institute, founded in 1975, was commissioned to raise the quality of life through improved nutrition and introduction of more effective agricultural practices. The institute conducts research, teaches, and carries out agricultural projects in countries around the world. It is well known for its development and promotion of small-scale food-growing projects that have been effective particularly in Bolivia, Ecuador, Guatemala, and Mexico. The Benson Institute conducts nutrition assessments and training; has developed, for small-scale farms, appropriate technology in developing countries (tractors, solar-powered water pumps and grain grinders, and wind-driven water pumps); trains students from developing countries; and has entered into several agreements with governments of developing countries to assist them in their agricultural development efforts. The institute collects and sends abroad medical and agricultural equipment and coordinates volunteers who wish to live in a country for varying periods of time to help with health, nutrition, and agricultural development (see various issues of the semi-annual Benson Institute Review).

In 1977, E. W. Thrasher donated $14 million as an endowment to the Church to be used to benefit the health of children throughout the world. A member of the PRESIDING BISHOPRIC of the Church is chairman of the executive committee of the Thrasher Research Fund. The fund has expended millions of dollars since 1977 to support research in nutrition and infectious diseases and to promote the health of children, primarily in developing countries. In one instance, the fund ran a project in a small village in Nigeria to demonstrate that low-cost appropriate health care technology and knowledge can be transferred to local residents (see Annual Reports of the Thrasher Research Fund, Salt Lake City, Utah).

BIBLIOGRAPHY

Benson Institute. *Benson Institute Review.* Provo, Utah, 1984.

Ferguson, Isaac C. "Freely Given." *Ensign* 18 (Aug. 1988): 10–15.

"News of the Church." *Ensign* 13 (June 1983):77.

"News of the Church." *Ensign* 15 (Nov. 1985):109.

STANLEY A. TAYLOR

ECONOMIC HISTORY OF THE CHURCH

From their beginnings Latter-day Saints have regarded economic welfare as an indispensable part of religion. An 1830 revelation received by Joseph SMITH stated, "Verily I say unto you, that all things unto me are spiritual, and not at any time have I given unto you a law which was temporal" (D&C 29:34–35). Accepted as part of the revealed word of God, this principle implied that every aspect of life had to do with spirituality and things eternal. For President Brigham YOUNG, who led the Church in the West for thirty years, this revelation meant that "in the mind of God there is no such a thing as dividing spiritual from temporal, or temporal from spiritual; for they are one in the Lord" (*JD* 11:18).

> We cannot talk about spiritual things without connecting with them temporal things, neither can we talk about temporal things without connecting spiritual things with them. . . . We, as Latter-day Saints, really expect, look for and we will not be satisfied with anything short of being governed and controled by the word of the Lord in all of our acts, both spiritual and temporal. If we do not live for this, we do not live to be one with Christ [*JD* 10:329].

Emphasis on economics was strengthened and supported by the social and economic experiences of the early Saints. Two early decisions were extremely important. The first was to move the headquarters and body of the Church from New York to KIRTLAND, OHIO, and to MISSOURI. This meant that leaders had to devise ways of helping poor members move westward. The move also involved Church leaders in buying land and formulating plans for community development (*see* CITY PLANNING), and in initiating financial enterprises and industries to provide employment. As the germ of the KINGDOM OF GOD, the Church was to gather and organize its members, settle them, and

The first Utah gold coins were minted in September 1849. Designed by Brigham Young, John Taylor, and John Kay, the obverse reads, "Holiness to the Lord," with a crown emblem of the priesthood over an All-Seeing Eye of Jehovah. On the reverse is "G.S.L.C.P.G." (Great Salt Lake City Pure Gold) and two clasped hands. Reprinted by permission from Alvin Rust, *Mormon and Utah Coin and Currency* (Salt Lake City, 1984).

assist them in creating an advanced society. Ultimately, according to LDS belief, the Church must establish ZION, the literal and earthly kingdom of God over which Christ will one day rule in person.

The second decision came as a reaction to PERSECUTION. Church leaders assumed responsibility for coping with persecution and looking after the welfare of its persecuted members. Persecutions thus created cohesiveness and community identity. They also necessitated frequent remov-

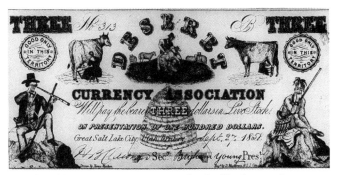

From 1857 to 1860, paper currency backed by livestock was printed over the signature of Brigham Young. These notes provided a medium of exchange for domestic growth and to finance the defense against the Utah Expedition. Brigham Young won a lawsuit in 1859 when the U.S. marshal confiscated the printing plates. Nearly all of these notes were redeemed by 1860. Reprinted by permission from Alvin Rust, *Mormon and Utah Coin and Currency* (Salt Lake City, 1984).

Zion's Cooperative Mercantile Institution (ZCMI) in Salt Lake City, c. 1880, was the parent outlet of what eventually became a territory-wide cooperative system. The cast-iron storefront has recently been restored. Photographer: Charles R. Savage.

als, forcing the Church to organize for the migrations and, in a new home, again purchase land and initiate industries. Above all, persecution prevented the rise of individualism and class distinction and diminished the surplus wealth that would have created a barrier between the rich and the less fortunate.

These experiences, and the social, intellectual, and religious origins of the Church, led to the development of a set of economic ideals and institutions that became a more or less permanent aspect of Latter-day Saint belief and practice, and made the LDS community a unique group in frontier America. The intimate association of religion with economic activity produced a planning and community concern that made possible a more just and permanent society than existed elsewhere in the West. These early LDS economic goals can be summarized under four headings: (1) ecclesiastical promotion of economic growth and development, often called "building the Kingdom of God"; (2) ecclesiastical sponsorship of group economic independence and self-sufficiency; (3) cooperation and organized group activity for attaining these goals; and (4) achievement and maintenance of economic equality.

PROMOTION OF ECONOMIC GROWTH. An early revelation called for the gathering "of mine elect"

and declared that "the decree hath gone forth from the Father that they shall be gathered in unto one place upon the face of this land" (D&C 29:7-8). Thus gathered, they could build the kingdom of God and prepare for the Millennium to come.

This policy of "accumulating people" as a prerequisite to building the kingdom was implemented, beginning in the 1830s, by the development of a large and effective missionary system and an overseas emigration service (see IMMIGRATION AND EMIGRATION), and by the establishment of a series of Zions or gathering places. This emigration system assisted 5,000 European converts in migrating to NAUVOO, ILLINOIS, and, beginning in 1846, organized 16,000 persons in and around Nauvoo to make the great trek to WINTER QUARTERS, Nebraska, and later to the SALT LAKE VALLEY. The PERPETUAL EMIGRATING FUND company alone assisted in transporting some 26,000 immigrants to the West between 1852 and 1887, when Congress dissolved it (see ANTIPOLYGAMY LEGISLATION). By 1890 Church agents had directed the migration of 83,000 European members to the Salt Lake Valley. The system efficiently converted donations of cattle, grain, and other produce into passenger fares, covered wagons, and oxen. Scholars have regarded the Church's arrangements as perhaps the best system of regulated immigration in U.S. history.

Often immigrants newly arrived in Salt Lake City were first put to work building the kingdom by means of a public works system. Centered on TEMPLE SQUARE in Salt Lake City, the Church Department of Public Works provided employment for immigrants during their first winter in the Salt Lake Valley. They added such useful structures to the commonwealth as roads, walls, meetinghouses, railroads, telegraph lines, canals, the SALT LAKE THEATRE, and the famous SALT LAKE TEMPLE and TABERNACLE.

New arrivals were soon dispatched in organized companies to settle in outlying agricultural villages (see COLONIZATION). Rights and property in these villages were allocated and regulated to ensure the highest possible development of resources. The governing principle, one of STEWARDSHIP, was consistent with the heavenly instruction of 1830 that declared: "Every man shall be made accountable unto me, a steward over his own property" (D&C 42:32). Each was to have property sufficient to support his family, while any surplus belonged to the Lord's storehouse. Property rights were granted conditionally and were not protected if the owner refused to utilize or develop the property. Indeed, the first pronouncement of President Brigham Young regarding government of the infant pioneer colony in the Salt Lake Valley included the following stipulation:

> No man will be suffered to cut up his lot and sell a part to speculate out of his brethren. Each man must keep his lot whole, for the Lord has given it to us without price. . . . Every man should have his land measured off to him for city and farming purposes, what he could till. He might till as he pleased, but he should be industrious and take care of it [Arrington, 1958, p. 46].

This policy seems to have been adhered to. The speculative withholding of land from use was prohibited, and the purchase or appropriation of town lots simply for the sake of the increase in value was prevented. Hoarding money was also against Church rules.

After the settlement of villages and the determination of property rights, the Saints were to proceed with the orderly development of local resources. Making the waste places blossom as the rose and the earth yield abundantly was more than an economic necessity: It was a form of religious activity. One early leader noted that the LDS religion consisted of digging water ditches as well as undergoing water baptism; religious duty encompassed both the redemption of man's home (the earth) and of his soul. The earth, as the future abiding place of God's people, was to be made productive and fruitful, transformed into a virtual Garden of Eden. "The Lord has done his share of the work," Brigham Young told them. "He has surrounded us with the elements containing wheat, meat, flax, wool, silk, fruit, and everything with which to build up, beautify and glorify the Zion of the last days." "It is now our business," he concluded, "to mould these elements to our wants and necessities, according to the knowledge we now have and the wisdom we can obtain from the heavens through our faithfulness." Only in this way "will the Lord bring again Zion upon the earth, and in no other" (JD 9:283–84).

The acceptance of this stewardship principle of resource development explains the passionate and devoted efforts of Latter-day Saints to develop the resources of the Great Basin to their fullest extent.

ECONOMIC INDEPENDENCE. The goal of LDS colonization and resource development, and of the Mormon village, was economic independence: The LDS commonwealth was to be financially and economically self-sufficient. A revealed "law" of the Church established this principle in 1831: "Let all thy garments be plain, and their beauty the beauty of the work of thine own hands" (D&C 42:40). An-

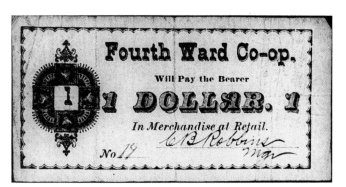

The first cooperative in Utah was founded by Lorenzo Snow in Brigham City in 1864. Using the Rochdale system of cooperation from England, the idea soon spread throughout Utah Territory. Scrip, such as this Logan Fourth Ward note, was issued by these co-ops to facilitate trade. Reprinted by permission from Alvin Rust, *Mormon and Utah Coin and Currency* (Salt Lake City, 1984).

Brigham Young's Cotton and Woolen Factory, located at the mouth of Parley's Canyon, east of Salt Lake City. This mill, one of several opened along the Wasatch front, began operation in 1863 and closed two years later in order to relocate the machinery in southern Utah. Photograph: A. J. Russell.

other revelation directed that they were to "contract no debts with the world" (D&C 64:27).

The principles of this revelation were applied often and broadly. In the Great Basin, the Latter-day Saints were asked to manufacture their own iron, produce their own cotton, spin their own silk, and grind their own grain—all without borrowing from "outsiders." It was reasoned that self-sufficiency was a practical policy because God had blessed each region with the resources necessary for the use of the people and the development of that region. As a result of the application of this principle, the Great Basin was the only major region of the United States whose early development was largely accomplished without outside capital.

Officially sponsored projects for self-sufficiency included an iron mission, consisting of about 200 families called by the Church who devoted strenuous efforts to develop the iron and coal resources near Cedar City; a sugar mission, in which several hundred people were united in the 1850s in an effort to establish the sugar-beet industry in Utah; a lead mission, in which some fifty men were called to work lead mines near Las Vegas, Nevada, to provide lead for paint and bul-

lets; a cotton mission, which sent more than a thousand families to southern Utah to raise cotton, olives, grapes, indigo, grain sorghum, and figs; silk missions, which involved the growing of mulberry trees and establishment of a silk industry in every suitable community; and a flax mission, a wool mission, and even a winery to provide wine for the holy SACRAMENT.

UNITY AND COOPERATION. Qualities required to execute successfully the economic program of the Church were unity of its members and the ability to organize for the pursuit of economic goals. This meant Churchwide cooperation. The seminal revelation enjoining unity was received in January 1831: "I say unto you, be one; and if ye are not one, ye are not mine" (D&C 38:27). This group spirit was induced both by the belief that unity was a Christian virtue and by the trying times that LDS pioneers experienced in their efforts to establish an independent commonwealth. Group solidarity and a strong central organization symbolized this effort. Whether they were migrating, building forts, digging ditches, or constructing mills, participants in the sublime task of building the kingdom were to submit themselves to the direction of God's leaders and display a spirit of willing cooperation.

As is well known, Brigham Young developed unified action and combined endeavor. He instituted cooperative arrangements for migration, colonization, construction, agriculture, mining, manufacturing, merchandising and, in fact, for every realm of economic activity.

EQUALITY. In "working out the temporal salvation of Zion," to use a common expression of the day, the formulators of Church policy focused primary attention on production and on the better management of available human and natural resources. Nevertheless, influenced by Christian principles, by its own necessities, and by the democratic concepts of Jacksonian America, early Mormonism was distinctly egalitarian in theology and economics. This had significant influences on Church policies and practices in the Great Basin.

The LDS doctrine of equality was formulated early. "If ye are not equal in earthly things, ye cannot be equal in obtaining heavenly things," read one March 1832 revelation (D&C 78:6), and, from the beginning, there was an earnest attempt to conduct business in this spirit of equality. When New York converts to the young Church began to arrive at the newly established gathering place of Kirtland, Ohio, in May 1831, the governing principle for the allotment of land and other properties was that every man receive "equal according to his family, according to their circumstances," and that all "receive alike, that ye may be one" (D&C 51:3, 9). Similarly, a revelation in Ohio instructed the Saints that "in your temporal things you shall be equal, and this not grudgingly, otherwise the abundance of the manifestations of the Spirit shall be withheld" (D&C 70:14). Similar instructions accompanied the stewardship system tried in Jackson County, Missouri: "And you are to be equal, or in other words, you are to have equal claims on the properties, for the benefit of managing . . . your stewardships, every man according to his wants and his needs, inasmuch as his wants are just" (D&C 82:17).

The core of the policy was reflected in the system of immigration (the more well-to-do were encouraged to donate means to assist in the immigration of poorer converts), the construction of public works (those with a surplus were expected to contribute), the allotment of land and water (parceled out equally to all by means of community draw-

The Maxwell automobile was manufactured in Salt Lake City in the early twentieth century by independent entrepreneurs. Photographer: Charles Ellis Johnson. Courtesy Rare Books and Manuscripts, Brigham Young University.

ings), and the initiation of many cooperative village stores and industries. But the influence of the ideal of equality was still wider. It led to several attempts to completely reorganize society and put economic affairs on a more egalitarian basis. Communities holding to these ideals were attempted by the Latter-day Saints in Ohio and Missouri (see CONSECRATION) and in more than 150 communities in the Far West, from Paris, Idaho, on the north, to Bunkerville, Nevada, and Joseph City, Arizona, on the south (see UNITED ORDERS). These cooperative communities were characterized by a high degree of economic equality and, although most of them lasted only a short time, their influence on LDS thought and self-conception is evident still.

It is fair to say that the Church could have gone much further in achieving its economic goals if the federal government had not intervened to prevent it. The UTAH EXPEDITION of 1857–1858, the Anti-Bigamy Act of 1862, the antipolygamy legislation of the late 1860s and the 1870s, and, even more, the hostile Edmunds Act, passed in 1882, and the Edmunds-Tucker Act of 1887—all of these undercut new Church economic activity, and forced the Church to withdraw from many existing activities.

By a strange coincidence of history, however, the Panic of 1891, ushering in the more severe Panic of 1893 and depression of the 1890s, helped reverse this trend. Utah, whose agriculture and mining industries were marginal, suffered more severely than many states; unemployment and low farm incomes were disturbing realities. In this crisis, Church leaders used all the resources at their command—including assets confiscated earlier by the federal government but now returned—to expand and improve the Great Basin economy. Their concerted efforts helped launch many new and successful industries. With an investment of about $500,000, the manufacture of sugar was re-initiated; another $500,000 financed the beginnings of the hydroelectric power industry in the West; some $250,000 was expended on the development of a salt industry on the shores of Great Salt Lake. To provide employment, the Saltair recreation resort was constructed. Railroads were projected, canals built, new colonies started—in short, Church leaders did everything possible to expand the economic base of the Great Basin and surrounding regions.

This expansion of economic activity was disturbing to national political and business leaders, who used the SMOOT HEARINGS of 1903–1907 to force the Church to sell most of its business interests. Holdings in the sugar and salt industries, in

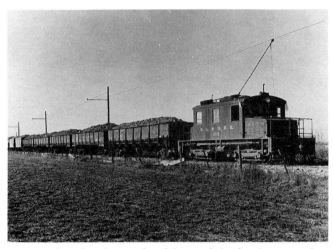

The Church owned and financed the development of an extensive sugar beet industry in Utah and Idaho. U and I Sugar Company resulted in 1907 from a merger, and various railroad companies, some wholly or partially owned by the Church or its leaders, served the intermountain area in the late nineteenth and early twentieth centuries. The Utah Railroad Company and the Salt Lake and Utah Railroad, shown here loaded with sugar beets, ran the Orem Line in the 1920s. Courtesy Rare Books and Manuscripts, Brigham Young University.

railroad and hydroelectric power, in coal and iron lands, in the telegraph system—these and others were sold to eastern capitalists. For the next decade and more, Utah's economy came to resemble that of other states in the Rocky Mountain region.

By mid-twentieth century, national sentiment was more sympathetic to Church-sponsored endeavors. Since the Great Depression of the 1930s, and especially since World War II, through the welfare services plan and other enterprises, the economic ideals of the founding generation have again been more actively pursued. Nonetheless, growing needs, especially outside North America, have required refocusing on areas central to the mission of the Church. As in the past, TITHING and other donations remain the key to the Church's active economic involvement. In the last half of the twentieth century, increasing emphasis has been placed on extending the full program of the Church, including temples, to members throughout the world. As "building the kingdom" has become increasingly international, the construction and maintenance of meetinghouses and temples in many lands have dominated Church finances. While the Church has invested in media facilities, including a SATELLITE COMMUNICATIONS SYSTEM, and expanded international microfilming of genealogical records (and a network of FAMILY HISTORY LIBRARIES to make the records available throughout the world), it has divested itself of many holdings that primarily benefited only Latter-day Saints in America's Mountain West.

At the end of the 1980s, the Church began implementing new budgeting arrangements that move toward greater equality. Divorcing funding levels from levels of contributions, these arrangements guarantee the funding of facilities and activities at a modest level for all Church members while limiting the amount the more affluent local units may spend. Also, with a growing worldwide membership, efforts at economic independence have increasingly focused on individual (family) self-sufficiency, and on aiding members everywhere to improve their economic situation and prepare for emergencies. Nonetheless, efforts to expand the reach and impact of the Church's welfare services and disaster relief programs also continue.

Though the present-day Church plays a direct role in economic development less often than it did in the pioneer economy, the fundamental ideals of self-sufficiency, unity and cooperation, and equality still characterize LDS economic goals. Latter-day Saints look forward to a more prosperous and just world even as they continue their efforts to establish institutions capable of blessing the lives of men and women as one essential preparation for the second coming of Christ.

[*See also* Kirtland Economy; Nauvoo Economy; Pioneer Economy.]

BIBLIOGRAPHY

Arrington, Leonard J. *Great Basin Kingdom: An Economic History of the Latter-day Saints, 1830–1900.* Cambridge, Mass., 1958.

———. "Religion and Economics in Mormon History." *BYU Studies* 3 (Spring-Summer 1961):15–33.

Arrington, Leonard J.; Feramorz Y. Fox; and Dean L. May. *Building the City of God: Community and Cooperation Among the Mormons.* Salt Lake City, 1976.

LEONARD J. ARRINGTON

EDMUNDS ACT OF 1882

See: Antipolygamy Legislation

EDMUNDS-TUCKER ACT OF 1887

See: Antipolygamy Legislation

EDUCATION

[*This entry discusses:*

Attitudes Toward Education
Educational Attainment

See also Academies; Brigham Young University; Church Educational System; Intellectual History; Schools; Social and Cultural History.]

ATTITUDES TOWARD EDUCATION

The ARTICLES OF FAITH underscore the deep and fundamental role that knowledge plays in the teachings of The Church of Jesus Christ of Latter-day Saints: "If there is anything virtuous, lovely, or of good report or praiseworthy, we seek after these things" (A of F 13). Speaking of the LDS commitment to learning and education, M. Lynn Bennion wrote: "It is doubtful if there is an organization in existence that more completely directs the educational development of its people than does the Mormon Church. The educational program of the Church today is a consistent expansion of the theories promulgated by its founders" (Bennion, p. 2).

The educational ideas and practices of the Church grew directly out of certain revelations received by Joseph SMITH that emphasize the eternal nature of knowledge and the vital role learning plays in the spiritual, moral, and intellectual development of mankind. For example: "It is impossible for a man to be saved in ignorance" (D&C 131:6) of his eternal nature and role. "The glory of God is intelligence, or, in other words, light and truth" (D&C 93:36). "Whatever principle of intelligence we attain unto in this life, it will rise with us in the resurrection. And if a person gains more knowledge and intelligence in this life through his diligence and obedience than another, he will have so much the advantage in the world to come" (D&C 130:18–19). "Knowledge saves a man, and in the world of spirits a man cannot be exalted but by knowledge" (*TPJS*, p. 357). An often-quoted statement from the Book of Mormon reads: "To be learned is good if they hearken unto the counsels of God" (2 Ne. 9:29). In June 1831 Joseph Smith received a revelation concerning "selecting and writing books for schools in this church" (D&C 55:4), and another on December 27, 1832, establishing the broad missions of education in the Church:

And I give unto you a commandment that you shall teach one another the doctrine of the kingdom. Teach ye diligently and my grace shall attend you, that you may be instructed more perfectly in theory, in principle, in doctrine, in the law of the gospel, in all things that pertain unto the kingdom of God, that are expedient for you to understand; of things both in heaven and in the earth, and under the earth; things which have been, things which are, things which must shortly come to pass; things which are at home, things which are abroad; the wars and the perplexities of the nations, and the judgments which are on the land; and a knowledge also of countries and of kingdoms—that ye may be prepared in all things [D&C 88:77–80].

The Church has been built on the conviction that eternal progress depends upon righteous living and growth in knowledge, religious and secular. "Indeed, the necessity of learning is probably the most frequently-repeated theme of modern-day revelations" (L. Arrington, "The Founding of the L.D.S. Institutes of Religion," *Dialogue* 2 [Summer 1967]:137).

Dedication of the Brigham Young Academy Building, Provo, Utah, January 1892. Led by outgoing Principal Karl G. Maeser, the faculty and student body marched up J street (University Avenue) to dedicate the new building, to honor Maeser, and to install Professor Benjamin Cluff, Jr., as the new principal. Courtesy Rare Books and Manuscripts, Brigham Young University.

Joseph Smith and many of the early Mormon pioneers came from a New England Puritan background, with its reverence for knowledge and learning (Salisbury, p. 258). The LDS outlook assumes the perfectibility of man and his ability to progress to ever-higher moral, spiritual, and intellectual levels. In this philosophy, moreover, knowledge of every kind is useful in man's attempt to realize himself in this world and the next. "It is the application of knowledge for the spiritual welfare of man that constitutes the Mormon ideal of education" (Bennion, p. 125). The early leaders of the Church, therefore, saw little ultimate division between correct secular and religious learning. Broad in scope and spiritual in intent, LDS educational philosophy tends to fuse the secular with the religious because, in the LDS context, the two are part of one seamless web (Bennion, pp. 120–23).

In 1833, Joseph Smith founded the Church's first educational effort, the SCHOOL OF THE PROPHETS, in Kirtland, Ohio. That school was de-voted to the study of history, political science, languages (including Hebrew), literature, and theology. Its main purpose was to prepare Church leaders to magnify their callings as missionaries to warn all people and testify of the gospel (D&C 88:80–81). It also set an example of adult learning that was followed "in Missouri, Illinois, and Utah, where parents joined their children in the pursuit of knowledge" (Bennion, p. 10).

In 1840, Joseph Smith sought the incorporation of the City of Nauvoo, Illinois, and along with it authority to establish a university. The NAUVOO CHARTER included authority to "establish and organize an institution of learning within the limits of the city, for the teaching of the arts, sciences and learned professions, to be called the 'University of the City of Nauvoo'" (quoted in Salisbury, p. 269).

The first academic year in Nauvoo was that of 1841–42. The university probably was among the first municipal universities in the United States (Rich, p. 10); it was certainly an optimistic and ambitious undertaking. The curriculum included languages (German, French, Latin, Greek, and Hebrew), mathematics, chemistry and geology, literature, and history; but "the data are too scant to reveal the scholastic rating of the instruction given. It was probably superior to the average secondary work of the time. The faculty represented considerable scholarship and indeed was a rather remarkable group to be found in a frontier city" (Bennion, p. 25).

The murder of Joseph Smith in 1844 abruptly ended the dream of the University of the City of Nauvoo and set in motion the difficult journey to the Great Basin. Despite the hardships, education was not forgotten. Brigham YOUNG instructed the migrating Saints to bring with them

> at least a copy of every valuable treatise on education—every book, map, chart, or diagram that may contain interesting, useful, and attractive matter, to gain the attention of children, and cause them to love to learn to read; and, also every historical, mathematical, philosophical, geographical, geological, astronomical, scientific, practical, and all other variety of useful and interesting writings, maps, etc., to present to the General Church Recorder, when they shall arrive at their destination, from which important and interesting matter may be gleaned to compile the most valuable works, on every science and subject, for the benefit of the rising generation [*MS* 10 (1848):85].

The charter of the University of the City of Nauvoo served as the foundation for the UNIVERSITY OF DESERET (now the University of Utah), established by Brigham Young in Salt Lake City in 1850. "Education," he once told this school's Board of Regents, "is the power to think clearly, the power to act well in the world's work, and the power to appreciate life" (Bennion, p. 115). He advised: "A good school teacher is one of the most essential members in society" (*JD* 10:225).

In 1851 the territorial legislature granted a charter providing for "establishment and regulation of schools" (Bennion, p. 40), but for some years the struggle for survival eclipsed the effort to establish a formal system of education. Utah's first schools were private, paid for by parents or by adult students, and classes took place during either the day or the evening, depending on local needs, interests, and resources (Rich, pp. 13, 17–18). Attendance rose and fell with the seasons and the demands of an agricultural society in which human labor was scarce and precious. Curricula varied as

well, often depending on the academic strengths or interests of the teacher; some schools offered traditional subjects, others more practical pursuits such as carpentry or masonry. The existence of these frontier schools was always precarious and their operation intermittent (Rich, p. 18), but they were an eloquent and often moving testimony to the commitment of early Mormon pioneers to education, demanding as they did considerable sacrifice of scarce time and resources.

Brigham Young's philosophy of education was practical and pragmatic, but he was not opposed, as has sometimes been assumed, to liberal education; he simply felt it was overstressed in the educational environment of his day (Bennion, p. 107). "Will education feed and clothe you, keep you warm on a cold day, or enable you to build a house? Not at all. Should we cry down education on this account? No. What is it for? The improvement of the mind; to instruct us in all arts and sciences, in the history of the world, in the laws of nations; to enable us to understand the laws and principles of life, and how to be useful while we live" (*JD* 14:83). He believed that "every art and science known and studied by the children of men is comprised within the Gospel" (*JD* 12:257).

President Young's educational philosophy was further enhanced by Karl G. Maeser, a German educator who joined the Church and immigrated

Beginning with Joseph Smith, all Church leaders have encouraged education. This Pioneer Day float in the 1950s celebrates the first school in Utah, which opened with nine pupils on October 17, 1847, three months after the pioneers arrived in Salt Lake Valley. Photographer: Albert Wilkes. Courtesy Nelson Wadsworth.

Karl G. Maeser (1828–1901), a German educator who joined the LDS Church and moved to Utah in 1860, was appointed the second principal of Brigham Young Academy, later Brigham Young University, in 1876.

to Salt Lake City in 1860. In 1876 Brigham Young appointed Maeser the principal of the Brigham Young Academy in Provo (*see* ACADEMIES). "The development of the Academy movement and the direction of Church policies in education were largely determined by this German educator" (Bennion, p. 117). His approach to education included a belief that "knowledge should be supported by corresponding moral qualities. The formation of character depends upon the nature of the moral training which accompanies intellectual advancement" (Maeser, p. 43). He maintained that religion was "the fundamental principle of education" and was its "most effective motive power" (Maeser, p. 56). His influential and widely circulated syllabus, *School and Fireside* (1898), clearly identified the critical functions of education as preparing people for practical life in the family and in the nation and inculcating fundamental principles of spiritual development.

In the early pioneer days, most schools in Utah Territory were LDS Church schools, and religion was an integral part of the curriculum. With the increasing diversification of Utah's population and the passage of the Edmunds-Tucker Act in 1887, which had the effect of prohibiting the teaching of religion in public schools, the Church looked for other means of assuring spiritual instruction for its young people. Between 1890 and 1929, the Church sponsored special religion classes conducted in ward meetinghouses for children in the first to the ninth grades in a movement that was "the first effort of the Mormons to supplement (but not to replace) secular education"; it was "America's first experiment in providing separate weekday religious training for public school children" (Quinn, p. 379).

This endeavor grew into the CHURCH EDUCATIONAL SYSTEM, which consists of several levels. First is SEMINARY, a daily religious education program held in a seminary building near the school for grades nine through twelve that provides for the study of the Book of Mormon, Old Testament, New Testament, and Doctrine and Covenants/Church History. Second, INSTITUTES of religion adjacent to campuses serve students enrolled in postsecondary programs by offering religion classes, usually scheduled twice a week to fit in with college schedules. Third, the Church sponsors four institutions of higher education: BRIGHAM YOUNG UNIVERSITY in Provo, Utah; BRIGHAM YOUNG UNIVERSITY—HAWAII in Laie, Hawaii; RICKS COLLEGE in Rexburg, Idaho; and LDS BUSINESS COLLEGE in Salt Lake City. In addition, in Mexico and the Pacific, the Church sponsors seven elementary schools, thirteen middle schools, and nine secondary schools that provide both secular and religious training.

In 1988–1989, the Church's educational system extended to 90 countries or territories and served about 250,000 seminary students, 124,500 institute students, 37,600 students in Church colleges and universities, and 9,300 students in other Church schools. The system employs over 4,100 full- and part-time employees, in addition to 15,000 members who are called to teach in the seminary and institute programs.

In sum, the attitude of the Church toward education is unusual in several respects. First, the Church is distinctive in the degree to which its members, child and adult alike, participate in the many educational activities of the Church: "As a people we believe in education—the gathering of knowledge and the training of the mind. The Church itself is really an educational institution. Traditionally, we are an education-loving people" (Widtsoe, 1944, p. 666). Second, its commitment

A Church-sponsored school, the Mapusaga High School, American Samoa, 10th and 11th grades, 1961–1962.

is to education as an essential component of religious life: "Every life coheres around certain fundamental core ideas. . . . The fact that [God] has promised further revelation is to me a challenge to keep an open mind and be prepared to follow wherever my search for truth may lead" (Brown, 1969, p. 11). Third, it holds a deep conviction that knowledge has an eternal dimension because it advances man's agency and progress here and in the world to come: "Both creative science and revealed religion find their fullest and truest expression in the climate of freedom. . . . Be unafraid of new ideas for they are as steppingstones to progress. You will, of course, respect the opinions of others but be unafraid to dissent—if you are informed" (Brown, 1958, p. 2–3). Fourth, it is insistent that secular and spiritual learning are not at odds but in harmony with each other: Latter-day Saints do not emphasize "the spiritual education of man to the neglect of his intellectual and physical education. . . . It is not a case of esteeming intellectual and physical education less, but of esteeming spiritual education more" (Roberts, pp. 122–23). "Secular knowledge is to be *desired*" as a tool in the hands of the righteous, but "spiritual knowledge is a *necessity*" (S. Kimball, *Faith Precedes the Miracle*, p. 280).

BIBLIOGRAPHY

Bennion, Milton Lynn. *Mormonism and Education*. Salt Lake City, 1939.

Brown, Hugh B. "An Eternal Quest—Freedom of the Mind." *BYU Speeches of the Year*, May 13, 1969.

———. "What Is Man and What He May Become." *BYU Speeches of the Year*, March 25, 1958.

Clark, J. Reuben, Jr. "The Charted Course of the Church in Education." Provo, Utah, 1936.

Clark, Marden J. "On the Mormon Commitment to Education." *Dialogue* 7 (Winter 1972):11–19.

Gardner, David P., and Jeffrey R. Holland. "Education in Zion: Intellectual Inquiry and Revealed Truth." *Sunstone* 6 (Jan.–Feb. 1981):59–61.

Kimball, Spencer W. "Second Century Address." *BYU Studies* 16 (Summer 1976):445–57.

Maeser, Karl G. *School and Fireside*. Utah, 1898.

Nibley, Hugh W. "Educating the Saints," and "Zeal without Knowledge." In *Nibley on the Timely and the Timeless*, ed. T. Madsen, pp. 229–77. Provo, Utah, 1978.

Quinn, D. Michael. "Utah's Educational Innovation: LDS Religion Classes, 1890–1929." *Utah Historical Quarterly* 43 (1975):379–89.

Rich, Wendell O. *Distinctive Teachings of the Restoration*, pp. 7–34, 161–88. Salt Lake City, 1962.

Roberts, B. H. "The Mormon Point of View in Education." *IE* 2 (Dec. 1898):119–26.

Salisbury, H. S. "History of Education in the Church of Jesus Christ of Latter Day Saints." *Journal of History* 15 (July 1922):257–81.

Widtsoe, John A. "The Returning Soldier." *IE* 47 (Nov. 1944):666, 701–702.

Young, Brigham. *Discourses of Brigham Young*, comp. John A. Widtsoe, pp. 245–63. Salt Lake City, 1978.

DAVID P. GARDNER

EDUCATIONAL ATTAINMENT

Latter-day Saints have a significantly higher level of educational attainment than does the population of the United States as a whole. Contrary to the norm for other religious denominations, members of The Church of Jesus Christ of Latter-day Saints who have earned advanced academic degrees are more likely to be deeply involved in religious practices and activity in the Church, both from a personal standpoint and in rendering service in their Church.

These phenomena may be the result of the doctrinal emphasis on learning and education that is so prevalent in the Church. Latter-day Saints are taught from early childhood that they must read and ponder the scriptures (*see* SCRIPTURE STUDY). The high priority given education in the lives of most Latter-day Saints has its roots in specific scriptures in the Bible, the Book of Mormon, the Doctrine and Covenants, and the Pearl of Great Price, which assure the Saints that "to be learned is good if they hearken unto the counsels of God" (2 Ne. 9:29).

Latter-day Saints are taught that what they learn in this life will go with them into eternity (D&C 130:18–19), that all truth and knowledge are available to each individual to acquire. They are gifts from God, but each individual must be worthy of them through diligent effort to learn. From birth to death, Church members hear from the pulpit, learn in Church meetings, and read in the scriptures that each individual must learn and grow in talent and ability. A quick rejoinder to a Mormon youth who might complain of finding nothing interesting or challenging to do is to read the scriptures, study from the great books, and follow the commandment to better oneself. This should be done not only for today and tomorrow but for eternity, since what one learns is a possession that never leaves. Latter-day Saints are taught that, although they cannot take their wealth or earthly goods with them into the next life, all of what they learn will be an everlasting possession.

The establishment of schools and colleges has been a priority since the founding of the Church.

Only three years after the organization of the Church in 1830, the Prophet Joseph Smith established the SCHOOL OF THE PROPHETS in Kirtland, Ohio. Only seven months after the arrival of the pioneers in the Great Salt Lake Valley, a university was established (*see* UNIVERSITY OF DESERET). Throughout the history of the Church, schools were established in Ohio, Missouri, Illinois, and Utah and in virtually every other location where the Saints have settled.

In Utah, where a large majority of the population are members of the Church, youth respond to scriptural precepts that stress the importance of learning by enrolling in high numbers in high school advanced placement courses that offer college-level credit. According to the annual report published in 1989 by the U.S. Department of Education, Utah ranked first among all the fifty states in the percentage of its high school seniors who took advanced placement courses (U.S. Department of Education State Education Performance Chart, 1989), in spite of the fact that Utah ranks among the lowest states in average expenditure per pupil.

Another factor motivating LDS youth to qualify for college credit while still in high school is the strong expectation in most of their families that they will serve as missionaries for the Church. With college being interrupted for missionary service, some of the time lost from pursuing a college degree can be recovered through heavy participation in advanced placement programs offered in high school.

Motivation to reach higher levels of education extends beyond the family and the scriptures. Outstanding accomplishments and milestone events in educational attainment are recognized from the pulpit in Church meetings where local leaders highlight distinguished academic accomplishments. The *Deseret News*, the daily newspaper published by the Church, adds to this momentum by sponsoring an annual "Sterling Scholars" program, which highlights outstanding student accomplishments in public high schools. This program features the best scholars in various fields of study at the high school level, culminating with photographs and biographical stories on semifinalists and finalists.

Because of their commitment to education, Latter-day Saints complete more schooling than the United States population as a whole (Albrecht and Heaton, p. 49). While 53.5 percent of Mormon males and 44.3 percent of Mormon females have at least some education beyond high school, only 36.5 percent of the males and 27.7 percent of the females in the U.S. population as a whole have any college-level education after high school.

Albrecht and Heaton also found that this traditionally high level of educational attainment among Latter-day Saints has not resulted in a decrease in their religious commitment. National survey data published by the Princeton Religious Research Center (1982) indicate the opposite result concerning the impact of higher education for the nation as a whole: the higher the level of educational attainment, the lower the level of religious zeal. The Princeton Center data suggest that it is generally quite difficult for academically preoccupied individuals to hold a view of the world that is at the same time both religious and scholarly. But, according to the research of Albrecht and Heaton (1984, pp. 43–57), LDS intellectuals have less often been caught in this dilemma. In these studies religiosity was measured in terms of making financial contributions, rendering services, and attending Church meetings.

BIBLIOGRAPHY

Albrecht, Stan L., and Tim B. Heaton. "Secularization, Higher Education, and Religiosity." *Review of Religious Research* 26 (Sept. 1984):43–58.

Princeton Religious Research Center. *Religion in America.* Princeton, N.J., 1982.

United States Department of Education. State Education Statistics: Student Performance Chart. Washington, D.C., 1989.

TERRELL H. BELL

ELDER, MELCHIZEDEK PRIESTHOOD

"Elder" is an office in the MELCHIZEDEK PRIESTHOOD of The Church of Jesus Christ of Latter-day Saints to which worthy male members may be ordained at the age of eighteen or older. The name elder is also used as a general title for all bearers of that priesthood, regardless of the specific PRIESTHOOD OFFICE they hold (D&C 20:38; cf. 1 Pet. 5:1; 2 Jn. 1:1; 3 Jn. 1:1).

In May 1829 Joseph SMITH and Oliver COWDERY were promised by John the Baptist, who had conferred the Aaronic Priesthood on them, that they would "in due time" become the first and second elders of the Church (JS—H 1:72; *HC* 1:40–41). Soon thereafter, they prayed for further information:

> We had not long been engaged in solemn and fervent prayer, when the word of the Lord came unto us in the chamber, commanding us that I should ordain Oliver Cowdery to be an Elder in the Church of Jesus Christ; and that he also should ordain me to the same office; and then to ordain others, as it should be made known unto us from time to time. We were, however, commanded to defer this our ordination until such time as it should be practicable to have our brethren, who had been and who should be baptized, assembled together [*HC* 1:60–61; cf. JS—H 1:72].

These particular ordinations were performed at the ORGANIZATION OF THE CHURCH, April 6, 1830 (D&C 20:1–4).

The duties of elders are to be "standing ministers" (D&C 124:137) to watch over the Church, help administer its affairs, teach, and counsel. They have the AUTHORITY to confer the GIFT OF THE HOLY GHOST by the LAYING ON OF HANDS and to give BLESSINGS, including HEALING THE SICK. Elders may perform all functions of the Aaronic Priesthood, including baptizing and administering the sacrament. They have authority under the direction of ward BISHOPS or STAKE PRESIDENTS to confer either the Aaronic or the Melchizedek Priesthood upon worthy recipients, and to ordain them to be deacons, teachers, PRIESTS, and other elders. Elders may serve as MISSIONARIES (see D&C 20:38–50, 70; 42:12, 44) and may be called to various other positions of leadership or service. In the October 1904 general conference, President Joseph F. Smith said that the elders are to be "standing ministers at home; to be ready at the call of the presiding officers of the Church and the stakes, to labor in the ministry at home, and to officiate in any calling that may be required of them, whether it be to work in the temples, or to labor in the ministry at home, or whether it be to go out into the world, along with the Seventies, to preach the Gospel" (*CR* [Oct. 1904]:4). In areas where the Church is not fully organized, members meet together in BRANCHES under the jurisdiction of a presiding elder, called a branch president (*see* ORGANIZATION: CONTEMPORARY).

All elders residing in any ward are organized into a quorum of up to ninety-six members (D&C 107:89). They are led by a president, two counselors, and a secretary, called from the quorum members by the stake president. The elders' quorum presidency reports to the stake president, but for all, local activity and service remain under the operating jurisdiction of the bishop of the ward. The elders meet as a quorum at least each Sunday. They are responsible to fellowship one another and to assist in administering the programs and activities of the quorum, ward, and stake, with the intent to lift and improve the condition of humankind (see WELFARE SERVICES). Elders are directed by revelation to function in a spirit of love, gentleness, patient persuasion, and righteousness (D&C 121:41–46).

The LDS use of "elder" differs from the use of the term in those societies where it refers to the older people who exert influence and authority in the community because of their age, status, wisdom, experience, and character, or by appointment of the group. The term was common to ancient societies such as those in Egypt, Midian, and Moab (Gen. 50:7; Num. 22:7). Elders (i.e., the zeqenim, the "old ones") were prominent leaders of the Israelite tribes during the Exodus (Ex. 4:29). They apparently assisted Moses in administering justice (Lev. 4:13–21; 9:1; Num. 16:25), and some were evidently authorized to participate in sacred religious ceremonies (Ex. 24:9–11; Num. 11:16–26). After the conquest of Canaan, the civic authority of elders increased, and they assisted in the government of the tribal communities. They served in accepting a king (2 Sam. 3:17–21; 5:3) and in other community and religious functions (1 Kgs. 8:1–3; 20:7–8). Scores of such functions are mentioned throughout the historical books of the Old Testament. With the prophet Ezekiel, these elders provided the primary leadership during the captivity in Babylon (605 B.C.; e.g., Ezek. 8:1; 14:1–5). Many years after the return from exile, the chief priests, scribes, and elders composed the Sanhedrin, the governing council of Judah. A local council of twenty-three elders governed each community. In New Testament times, elders were appointed as ecclesiastical leaders for each of the local Christian congregations (Acts 14:23; 15:6; 20:17–28; Titus 1:5; James 5:14; 1 Pet. 5:1–4). They associated with the apostles in the councils and governance of the Church, and functioned among their Christian brethren in ways similar to the Jewish Sanhedrin (Acts 11:30; 15:2; 16:4; 21:18). From among the elders of good repute, "overseers" or "bishops" may have been chosen (Acts 20:17–28; Titus 1:5–9; cf. 1 Tim. 3:1–7).

BIBLIOGRAPHY

Davies, G. Henton. "Elder in the Old Testament." Interpreter's Dictionary of the Bible, Vol. 2, pp. 72–73. Nashville, Tenn., 1962.

McConkie, Bruce R. Only an Elder. Salt Lake City, 1978.

Shepherd, M. H., Jr. "Elder in the New Testament." Interpreter's Dictionary of the Bible, Vol. 2, pp. 73–75. Nashville, Tenn., 1962.

Widtsoe, John A. Priesthood and Church Government, rev. ed. Salt Lake City, 1954.

R. RICHARD VETTERLI

ELECT OF GOD

The elect of God are those who are heirs to all that the Father has. Although the faithful have always been the elect of God, even before Abraham, the present concept that God elects or chooses individuals or groups to whom he makes promises of eternal SALVATION, and in turn requires of them certain obligations, has its roots in the COVENANT God made with ABRAHAM. In ancient times Abraham's descendants were considered the elect, especially through Isaac and Jacob (Israel). For disobedience, the Israelites were eventually scattered throughout the world. However, God has not forgotten his covenant with their fathers. Biblical, Book of Mormon, and latter-day prophets have declared that ultimately the Israelite people will be gathered from their dispersion and restored to favor with God (cf. Amos 9:13–15). All persons who are not literally of Israel can be brought into the elect lineage of Abraham by the LAW OF ADOPTION when they accept the gospel (Abr. 2:10; D&C 84:33–34; Gal. 3:26–29; 4:5–7).

The GOSPEL of Jesus Christ, restored to the earth through the Prophet Joseph SMITH, inaugurated the RESTORATION and the gathering of the elect from the four quarters of the earth (D&C 33:6; 110:11). When scattered children of Israel hear the gospel message of SALVATION, they are invited to come into the fold of Christ, his Church, by REPENTANCE, BAPTISM, and receiving the HOLY GHOST by the LAYING-ON OF HANDS (MD, p. 201).

To enjoy the fulness of the covenant BLESSINGS and the eternal felicity of God in the presence of Abraham, Isaac, and Jacob, the elect must be faithful in keeping all the covenants required of them by the Lord. Some may choose not to be so devoted, whereas others pursue such excellence in faithfulness that their CALLING AND ELECTION are made sure (cf. 2 Pet. 1:10). These become "the elect according to the covenant" (JS—M 1:22) and are made partakers of the same eternal reward that was extended to Abraham. That is, they are assured of EXALTATION in God's presence with Abraham, Isaac, and Jacob (Luke 13:28; D&C 132:29–32, 37).

BIBLIOGRAPHY

Richards, LeGrand. *Israel, Do You Know!* Salt Lake City, 1954.

ARTHUR A. BAILEY

ELIAS

Elias is both a name and a title and has four meanings: (1) Elias was a man, presumably of Abraham's time, who "committed the dispensation of Abraham"—which included the blessings of God's covenant with Abraham—to the Prophet Joseph SMITH and Oliver COWDERY on April 3, 1836, in the KIRTLAND TEMPLE (D&C 110:12); nothing more is known about this man. (2) "Elias" appears in the New Testament as the Greek transliteration of the Hebrew name ELIJAH (e.g., Matt. 17:3; James 5:17–18). (3) A forerunner in building God's kingdom is called "an Elias" (*TPJS*, pp. 335–36). (4) A prophet who helps restore something of particular importance is also referred to as an "Elias" (cf. JST Matt. 17:13–14). In scripture, therefore, the name Elias may refer to a preparer, a forerunner, a restorer, to Elias himself, or to Elijah.

Individuals who have acted as forerunners or restorers include Jesus Christ (JST John 1:21–28); Noah as Gabriel (D&C 27:6–7; *TPJS*, p. 157); John the Baptist (Luke 1:17); John the Revelator (D&C 77:9, 14); Adam as Michael, Moroni$_2$, and Peter, James, and John (D&C 27:5–13; 128:20–21); and Joseph Smith (D&C 1:17–18; *TPJS*, p. 335). Each of these may be considered an Elias.

Preparatory work in the Church is primarily associated with the AARONIC PRIESTHOOD; but when performed by the MELCHIZEDEK PRIESTHOOD, it is done under the spirit and power of Elijah (*TPJS*, pp. 336–37). In this connection, the keys given by Elias in the Kirtland Temple (D&C 110:12) were specifically for the ABRAHAMIC COVENANT.

GEORGE A. HORTON, JR.

ELIAS, SPIRIT OF

The "spirit of Elias" is a LDS concept that refers to the preparatory power that initiates gospel RESTORATION following periods of APOSTASY. The Prophet Joseph SMITH explained, "The spirit of Elias is to prepare the way for a greater revelation of God, which is the Priesthood of Elias, or the Priesthood unto which Aaron was ordained. And when God sends a man into the world to prepare for a greater work, holding the keys of the power of Elias, it was called the doctrine of Elias, even from the early ages of the world. . . . We find the Apostles endowed with greater power than John [the Baptist]: their office was more under the spirit and power of Elijah than Elias" (*TPJS*, pp. 335–36).

JOHN THE BAPTIST was the forerunner of Jesus Christ in the MERIDIAN OF TIME (Matt. 11:12–14; 17:12; JST John 1:21–24). He "was ordained by the angel of God . . . to make straight the way of the Lord before the face of his people, to prepare them for the coming of the Lord" (D&C 84:28). By authority of the AARONIC PRIESTHOOD, John preached repentance and baptism for the remission of sins, in preparation for the coming of one mightier who would baptize with the HOLY GHOST.

On May 15, 1829, John the Baptist, as a resurrected being, ordained Joseph Smith and Oliver COWDERY to the Aaronic Priesthood preparatory to Christ's SECOND COMING. Describing this ordination, Joseph Smith stated:

> An angel . . . laid his hands upon my head, and ordained me to a Priest after the order of Aaron, and to hold the keys of this Priesthood, which office was to preach repentance and baptism for the remission of sins, and also to baptize. But I was informed that this office did not extend to the laying on of hands for the giving of the Holy Ghost; that office was a greater work, and was to be given afterward; but that my ordination was a preparatory work, or a going before, which was the spirit of Elias [*TPJS*, p. 335].

Later, PETER, JAMES, and JOHN conferred upon Joseph Smith and Oliver Cowdery the MELCHIZEDEK PRIESTHOOD (D&C 27:12), and still later (April 3, 1836) ELIJAH conferred additional keys upon them (D&C 110:13–16).

Joseph Smith further explained:

> The spirit of Elias is first, Elijah second, and Messiah last. Elias is a forerunner to prepare the way,

and the spirit and power of Elijah is to come after, holding the keys of power, building the Temple to the capstone, placing the seals of the Melchizedek Priesthood upon the house of Israel, and making all things ready; then Messiah comes to His Temple, which is last of all. . . . Elijah was to come and prepare the way and build up the kingdom before the coming of the great day of the Lord, although the spirit of Elias might begin it [*TPJS*, pp. 335, 340].

A. JAMES HUDSON

ELIJAH

[*Because of Elijah's prophesied role (Mal. 4:5–6), he has become the subject of tradition and legend, as the article* Ancient Sources *explains. Moreover, as expressed in the companion essay,* LDS Sources, *Latter-day Saint teaching illuminates Elijah's latter-day roles as well as the fulfillment of prophetic expectations associated with him.*]

LDS SOURCES

During a divine manifestation to the youthful Joseph SMITH on the evening of September 21, 1823, the angel MORONI quoted Malachi 4:5–6, a prophecy that concerns Elijah's activities in the latter days. Moroni's rendering, which differs from the current biblical text, outlines and clarifies Elijah's prophesied role:

> Behold, I will reveal unto you the Priesthood, by the hand of Elijah the prophet, before the coming of the great and dreadful day of the Lord. And he shall plant in the hearts of the children the promises made to the fathers, and the hearts of the children shall turn to their fathers. If it were not so, the whole earth would be utterly wasted at his coming [JS—H 1:38–39; D&C 2].

Malachi's prophecy anticipates that Elijah would play an important role "before the coming of the great and dreadful day of the Lord" (Mal. 4:5). Elijah was endowed with the priesthood power of God. With this power, he declared to King Ahab that no rain would fall upon the land (1 Kgs. 17:1). Accordingly, the heavens were sealed and ancient Israel experienced a disastrous drought for three and a half years. When Elijah was carried up into heaven in a fiery chariot, his earthly mission appeared to have ended. But the sealing power that he exercised marked only the beginning of his responsibility regarding this eternal priesthood power.

At the conclusion of his mortal life, Elijah was translated; that is, he experienced some type of change from mortality without experiencing mortal death (*see* TRANSLATED BEINGS). Latter-day Saints conclude that a major reason for Elijah's translation was to enable him to return to the earth to confer KEYS of authority on the three chief apostles before Jesus' crucifixion and resurrection (*see* MOUNT OF TRANSFIGURATION). Since spirits cannot lay hands on mortal beings (D&C 129), and since Moses and Elijah could not return as resurrected beings because Jesus was the first to be resurrected (Packer, p. 109; cf. *TPJS*, p. 191), the need for the translation of Elijah and Moses is evident. On the Mount of Transfiguration (Matt. 17:1–9), Elijah specifically restored the priesthood keys of sealing, the power that binds and validates in the heavens all ordinances performed on the earth (cf. *TPJS*, p. 338).

On April 3, 1836, in a vision to Joseph Smith and Oliver COWDERY in the newly completed KIRTLAND TEMPLE, Elijah appeared and announced that the time had come when Malachi's prophecy was to be fulfilled. He committed the sealing keys of the priesthood to Joseph Smith and Oliver Cowdery (D&C 110:13–16). This restoration was necessary so that the sealing ordinances and covenants of God could be administered in righteousness upon the earth (*DS* 2:117). Joseph Smith explained:

> The spirit, power, and calling of Elijah is, that ye have power to hold the key of the revelations, ordinances, oracles, powers and endowments of the fulness of the Melchizedek Priesthood and of the kingdom of God on the earth; and to receive, obtain, and perform all the ordinances belonging to the kingdom of God. . . . What you seal on earth, by the keys of Elijah, is sealed in heaven; and this is the power of Elijah [*TPJS*, pp. 337–38].

Through the sealing power of the priesthood, men and women may be sealed to each other in marriage for all eternity in one of the temples of God. In addition, children may be sealed to their parents forever. Thus the family organization continues eternally (Sperry, p. 139).

Because many have died without either a knowledge of saving gospel principles or the opportunity to receive priesthood ordinances, the latter-day mission of Elijah made it possible to have these sealing ordinances performed vicariously on the earth for those who have died, thus giving all an opportunity for salvation (cf. *DS* 2:118–19). The Prophet Joseph Smith offered the following explanation:

> The spirit of Elijah is to come, the Gospel to be established, . . . and the Saints to come up as saviors on Mount Zion. But how are they to become saviors on Mount Zion? By building their temples, erecting their baptismal fonts, and going forth and receiving all the ordinances, baptisms, confirmations, washings, anointings, ordinations and sealing powers upon their heads, in behalf of all their progenitors who are dead, and redeem them; . . . and herein is the chain that binds the hearts of the fathers to the children and the children to the fathers, which fulfills the mission of Elijah [*TPJS*, p. 330].

When Latter-day Saints speak of the spirit of Elijah (*see* ELIJAH, SPIRIT OF), they mean at least two things. First, the promise of salvation made to the fathers has been renewed to the modern Church (JS—H 1:38–39; D&C 27:9–10). Second, the hearts of men and women have extensively turned to their fathers, as is evident in the dramatic growth in the number of genealogical societies, libraries, and individual genealogical or family history research organizations throughout much of the world. The spirit of Elijah has motivated thousands to make considerable investment in both money and time to search out the records of family ancestors and bring these records together to form a family history (*DS* 2:123–27; *see* GENEALOGY). In addition to numerous family history centers, the Church has built many temples where sacred priesthood saving ordinances may be performed for both the living and the dead (*see* SALVATION OF THE DEAD).

BIBLIOGRAPHY

Packer, Boyd K. *The Holy Temple.* Salt Lake City, 1980.

Smith, Joseph Fielding. *DS* 2:100–128. Salt Lake City, 1955.

Sperry, Sidney B. *The Spirit of the Old Testament.* Salt Lake City, 1970.

Widtsoe, John A. "Elijah, The Tishbite." *Utah Genealogical and Historical Magazine* 27 (Apr. 1936):53–60.

FRANKLIN D. DAY

ANCIENT SOURCES

Elijah in Jewish tradition was an Israelite prophet who was active in the northern kingdom during the reigns of King Ahab (and his consort Jezebel) and King Ahaziah (9th cent. B.C.). His name may be a cognomen: Eli-yahu (YHWH, or Jehovah, is God),

expressing the main emphasis of his prophetic ministry: the exclusive and pure worship of YHWH, and uncompromising opposition to the Canaanite pagan cult of Baal. His activities are described in 1 Kings 17–2 Kings 2, and account for his becoming in Jewish tradition the symbol of uncompromising religious zeal. The latter came to a dramatic climax in his confrontation with the priests of Baal, after a long period of drought which Elijah had prophesied would come as punishment for the idolatrous Baal-worship, on Mount Carmel. (The Catholic monastic order of Carmelites, taking Elijah's ascetic life in the desert as a model, considers him as its spiritual father.) Unlike the later "literary" prophets, Elijah is also described as a worker of miracles, but he shares with them the strong emphasis on social justice, as evidenced by his other great clash with the king and queen in the matter of Naboth's vineyard (1 Kgs. 21), which the royal couple desired for themselves.

According to the biblical account, Elijah did not die an ordinary death but was taken up into heaven in a whirlwind by a chariot of fire drawn by horses of fire. Hence, unlike other prophets, a large number of legends and beliefs concerning him developed. He is said to return frequently to earth, usually in the guise of a poor peasant, beggar, or even Gentile and—unrecognized—to help those in distress or danger, disappearing as suddenly as he appeared. A chair is set and a cup of wine poured for Elijah at every Passover celebration. He is also believed to be present at every circumcision ceremony, and a special chair ("Elijah's chair") for his invisible presence is placed next to that of the godfather holding the male baby. This particular belief may be due to two factors: Elijah's angelic status (having ascended to heaven) and the prophet Malachi's reference to him (Mal. 3:1) as the "angel of the covenant." In Jewish usage the term *berith* ("covenant") signifies more specifically the "covenant of circumcision" (cf. Gen. 17:9–10). Elijah also plays an important role in Jewish mysticism, where he appears as a celestial messenger revealing divine mysteries.

More important, however, than all the other aspects is Elijah's eschatological role in Jewish tradition. How and why this role developed is difficult to reconstruct, but by the time of Malachi, one of the last Old Testament prophets, some such beliefs seem to have already been in existence: "Behold, I will send you Elijah the prophet before the coming of the great and dreadful day of the Lord"

(Mal. 4:5). Elijah gradually assumed the role of precursor of the Messiah and the messenger announcing his advent. Some of the contemporaries of Jesus (cf. Matt. 16:13–14) seem to have thought that he might be Elijah (Matt. 11:14; 17:10–13) in a manner that suggests that John the Baptist, as the forerunner and announcer of the Messiah, was Elijah (namely, fulfilled his eschatological function). Later apocryphal writings (e.g., *The Apocalypse of Elijah*) connect the "revelations" concerning the last things they report with Elijah. Elements from the Jewish Elijah traditions and legends were also adopted and developed in different ways by Islam.

BIBLIOGRAPHY

"Elijah." *Encyclopaedia Judaica*, Vol. 6. Jerusalem, 1972.

Postbiblical Jewish sources are conveniently collected in Louis Ginzberg, *Legends of the Jews*, Vol. 6, 3rd reprint. Philadelphia, Pennsylvania, 1967, pp. 133–35 (under "Elijah"). A very good summary can be found in M. J. Stiassny, "Le Prophète Élie dans le Judaïsme," in *Élie le Prophète*, Études Carmélitaines, Vol. 2 (1956):199–255.

For Islamic traditions, see "Ilyas" and "al-Khadir" in *Encyclopaedia of Islam*.

R. J. ZVI WERBLOWSKY

ELIJAH, SPIRIT OF

For members of The Church of Jesus Christ of Latter-day Saints, the spirit of Elijah is the spirit of family kinship and unity. It is the spirit that motivates the concern to search out ancestral family members through FAMILY HISTORY; and, on their behalf, to perform proxy baptisms, temple ENDOWMENTS, AND SEALING ordinances (HC 6:252). This is seen as fulfillment of the prophecy of Malachi that in the last days Elijah "will turn the heart [in Hebrew, the innermost part, as the soul, the affections] of the fathers to the children, and the heart of the children to their fathers" (Mal. 4:5–6).

The appearance of Elijah to the Prophet Joseph SMITH and Oliver COWDERY in the KIRTLAND TEMPLE in 1836 inaugurated anew this spirit (D&C 110:13). The spirit of Elijah is active in the impetus anyone feels toward finding and cherishing family members and family ties past and present. In the global sense, the spirit of Elijah is the spirit of love that may eventually overcome all human family estrangements. Then the priesthood power can bind generations together in eternal family rela-

tionships and "*seal* the children to the fathers and fathers to the children" within the gospel of Jesus Christ (*WJS*, p. 329).

BIBLIOGRAPHY

Smith, Joseph Fielding. "Elijah the Prophet and His Mission." *Utah Genealogical and Historical Magazine* 12 (Jan. 1921): 1–20.

MARY FINLAYSON

ELOHIM

Elohim (God; gods; Heavenly Father) is the plural form of the singular noun 'eloah (compare Arabic *Allah*) in the Hebrew Bible, where it is used 2,570 times as compared to 57 times for its singular. But as one commentator has noted, why this "plural form for 'God' is used has not yet been explained satisfactorily" (Botterweck, Vol. 1, p. 272).

SINGULAR USAGE. Elohim appears in the Hebrew Bible as a common noun identifying Israel's God: "In the beginning God ['elohim] created [singular verb] the heaven and the earth" (Gen. 1:1). It was also frequently used interchangeably with Jehovah, the proper name for Israel's God: "And Jacob said, O God ['elohim] of my father Abraham, . . . the LORD [Jehovah] which saidst unto me, Return unto thy country" (Gen. 32:9; *see also* JEHOVAH, JESUS CHRIST).

Latter-day Saints use the name Elohim in a more restrictive sense as a proper name-title identifying the Father in Heaven (see GOD THE FATHER). The First Presidency of the Church has written, "God the Eternal Father, whom we designate by the exalted name-title 'Elohim,' is the literal Parent of our Lord and Savior Jesus Christ, and of the spirits of the human race" (*MFP* 5:26; *see also* Doctrinal Expositions of the First Presidency, "The Father and the Son," appendices, Vol. 4).

PLURAL USAGE. Ancient Israelites used 'elohim also as a proper plural form to refer to gods of nations other than Israel. At such times, the accompanying verbs and adjectives used were also plural. "Thou shalt have no other gods before me" (Ex. 20:3; here "other" is a plural adjective).

Occasionally, Latter-day Saints use Elohim in its plural sense as a common noun to refer to the plurality of gods known to exist (*TPJS*, pp. 371–74). However, despite their belief that many lords and gods exist in addition to Elohim, Jehovah, and the HOLY GHOST (D&C 121:28–32), they follow the example of Jesus and Paul, who worshiped the Father in Heaven (Matt. 19:17; 1 Cor. 8:4–6).

BIBLIOGRAPHY

Botterweck, G. Johannes, and Helmer Ringgren, eds. "Elohim." In *Theological Dictionary of the Old Testament,* rev. ed., Vol. 1, pp. 267–84. Grand Rapids, Mich., 1977.

KEITH H. MESERVY

EMERGENCY PREPAREDNESS

Latter-day Saints are taught to prepare for potential problems. Since the gospel is concerned with mankind's temporal as well as spiritual welfare, the Church considers any potential emergency that would adversely affect the quality of life or produce suffering to be a cause for advance preparation. This includes natural disasters, unemployment, disease, injuries, and other circumstances that could threaten life or personal well-being. The Church teaches its members to prepare for such emergencies.

The rationale for emergency preparedness is that by living providently and by acquiring in advance the skills and resources necessary to cope effectively with difficulties, Latter-day Saints can minimize or avoid the suffering that accompanies the unexpected. They can also have the sense of security and peace of mind (D&C 38:30) that are essential to spiritual development. They are also taught to work toward SELF-SUFFICIENCY—to provide adequately for themselves, to assist those in need, and to avoid unnecessary dependence upon the efforts or resources of others. They are told to put aside something when times are good so that they can care for themselves and others when times are bad. For Latter-day Saints, preparing for emergencies is more akin to saving for a "rainy day" than surviving "doomsday" (Kimball, p. 78).

For more than a hundred years, Church leaders have taught the members to store grain and other essentials that would sustain life in times of drought or famine (*Essentials of Home Production and Storage,* p. 17). The current guidelines for home storage are intended to apply internationally. They include having a supply of food, clothing, and, where possible, the fuel necessary to sustain life for one year (Benson, p. 33). Church

This LDS farm wife was photographed with her home-bottled produce (1940) as part of a U.S. Farm Security Administration project, which sent three photographers to rural Utah during 1936–1941. Many Latter-day Saints continue the tradition of canning home-grown food, following Church counsel to be prepared for all kinds of emergencies. Photographer: Russell Lee. Courtesy of the Library of Congress (37282-D).

guidance states, "We have never laid down an exact formula for what anybody should store. Perhaps if we think not in terms of a year's supply of what we ordinarily would use, and think more in terms of what it would take to keep us alive in case we didn't have anything else to eat, that last would be very easy to put in storage for a year" (*Essentials*, p. 6).

Home gardens, canning, and sewing have long been encouraged among the women by the RELIEF SOCIETY through homemaking lessons and workdays. Latter-day Saints are counseled to seek education and training opportunities that prepare them to adapt to changes in the working world, to avoid personal indebtedness, to maintain good health by eating and exercising properly, to learn first aid, and to know how to protect their lives and possessions against fire, flood, and theft. They are counseled to obtain life, medical, and property insurance where it is available. They are also urged to avoid panic buying, purchasing emergency resources on credit, pursuing fads, and giving official endorsement to specific brands, suppliers, or techniques.

Institutionally, the Church practices the principles of preparedness. Under the aegis of its

WELFARE SERVICES, the Church's WELFARE FARMS, canneries, and BISHOP'S STOREHOUSES grow, process, and distribute commodities for consumption by those in need in the Church. These facilities maintain approximately a year's supply of inventory, in both production supplies and finished goods. Church-owned grain reserves are stored to help provide needs from harvest to harvest, with a suitable margin for some who may come into need during more prolonged economic downturns. The Church does not attempt, however, to maintain emergency storage for its entire membership. Long-term security against catastrophic emergencies depends upon the faithful preparation of individual members and families throughout the world.

Consistent preparedness has enabled the Church to participate in humanitarian projects to relieve suffering resulting from such catastrophes as World War II, the rupture of the Teton Dam in Idaho in 1976, food shortages in Poland in 1982, flooding in Brazil in 1983, earthquakes in Mexico City in 1985, hurricanes in the Caribbean and South Carolina in 1989, and other natural and man-made disasters.

Ecclesiastical units of the Church (wards, stakes, regions, and areas) are directed to prepare and maintain a written emergency response plan. The scope and level of detail contained in the plans vary, depending upon the nature and severity of emergencies likely to occur in each area. Emergency response plans generally address leadership and communication issues, reporting procedures, the location and extent of resources available for emergency response efforts, guidelines for the use of Church buildings as shelters, and the names and addresses of emergency-response specialists.

The presiding officers of all Church units are encouraged to coordinate emergency planning and response efforts with appropriate community agencies. The importance of good citizenship by all Church members in times of need is axiomatic.

BIBLIOGRAPHY

Benson, Ezra Taft. "Prepare for the Days of Tribulation." *Ensign* 10 (Nov. 1980):32–34.

Essentials of Home Production and Storage. Salt Lake City, 1979.

Kimball, Spencer W. "Welfare Services: The Gospel in Action." *Ensign* 7 (Nov. 1977):76–79.

FRANK D. RICHARDSON

ENDLESS AND ETERNAL

The terms "endless" and "eternal" have at least two connotations each in The Church of Jesus Christ of Latter-day Saints. They are used both as adjectives and as nouns. The adjectival forms, fitting the more traditional viewpoint, denote a concept of time without beginning or end. In a second, less familiar usage, the phrase "endless and eternal" functions as a noun, another name for God (Moses 1:3; 7:35)—in the manner of "Alpha and Omega," or "the Beginning and the End."

In a revelation dated March 1830 (now D&C 19), the Prophet Joseph SMITH learned that phrases such as "endless punishment" and "eternal life" have qualitative as well as quantitative implications. The word "endless," for example, has sometimes been employed by God for greater impact "that it might work upon the hearts of the children of men" (D&C 19:7). Consequently, the term "endless punishment" may or may not imply a duration of time—that there will be no end to such punishment—but it clearly does imply that the punishment (or blessing) is associated with the Eternal One. "Eternal punishment is God's punishment. Endless punishment is God's punishment" (D&C 19:11–12). In like manner, the concept of eternal life referred to in scripture (e.g., John 17:3) implies more than life lasting forever; it also connotes a quality of life like that of God, as well as life with God (DS 2:8, 228).

BIBLIOGRAPHY

Doxey, Roy W., comp. *Latter-day Prophets and the Doctrine and Covenants*, Vol. 1, pp. 204–208. Salt Lake City, 1963.

Ludlow, Daniel H. *A Companion to Your Study of the Doctrine and Covenants*, Vol. 1, p. 142. Salt Lake City, 1978.

ARTHUR R. BASSETT

ENDOWMENT

An endowment generally is a gift, but in a specialized sense it is a course of instruction, ORDINANCES, and COVENANTS given only in dedicated TEMPLES of The Church of Jesus Christ of Latter-day Saints. The words "to endow" (from the Greek *enduein*), as used in the New Testament, mean to dress, clothe, put on garments, put on attributes, or receive virtue. Christ instructed his apostles to tarry at Jerusalem "until ye be endued with power from on high" (Luke 24:49), a promise fulfilled, at least in part, on the day of Pentecost (Acts 2). In modern times, a similar revelation was given: "I gave unto you a commandment that you should build a house, in the which house I design to endow those whom I have chosen with power on high; for this is the promise of the Father unto you; therefore I command you to tarry, even as mine apostles at Jerusalem" (D&C 95:8–9).

Though there had been preliminary and preparatory spiritual outpourings upon Latter-day Saints in Ohio and Missouri, the endowment in its full sense was not received until the Nauvoo Temple era. As he introduced temple ordinances in 1842 at Nauvoo, the Prophet Joseph SMITH taught that these were "of things spiritual, and to be received only by the spiritual minded" (*TPJS*, p. 237). The endowment was necessary, he said, to organize the Church fully, that the Saints might be organized according to the laws of God, and, as the dedicatory prayer of the Kirtland Temple petitioned, that they would "be prepared to obtain every needful thing" (D&C 109:15). The endowment was designed to give "a comprehensive view of our condition and true relation to God" (*TPJS*, p. 324), "to prepare the disciples for their missions in the world" (p. 274), to prevent being "overcome by . . . evils" (p. 259), to enable them to "secure the fulness of those blessings which have been prepared for the Church of the Firstborn" (p. 237).

The endowment of "power from on high" in modern temples has four main aspects. First is the preparatory ordinance, a ceremonial WASHING AND ANOINTING, after which the temple patron dons the sacred clothing of the temple.

Second is a course of instruction by lectures and representations. These include a recital of the most prominent events of the Creation, a figurative depiction of the advent of Adam and Eve and of every man and every woman, the entry of Adam and Eve into the GARDEN OF EDEN, the consequent expulsion from the garden, their condition in the world, and their receiving of the PLAN OF SALVATION leading to the return to the presence of God (Talmage, pp. 83–84). The endowment instructions utilize every human faculty so that the meaning of the gospel may be clarified through art, drama, and symbols. All participants wear white temple robes symbolizing purity and the equality of all persons before God the Father and his Son Jesus Christ. The temple becomes a house of revelation whereby one is instructed more perfectly "in

theory, in principle, and in doctrine" (D&C 97:14). "This completeness of survey and expounding of the gospel plan makes temple worship one of the most effective methods of refreshing the memory concerning the entire structure of the gospel" (Widtsoe, 1986, p. 5).

Third is making covenants. The temple endowment is seen as the unfolding or culmination of the covenants made at BAPTISM. Temple covenants give "tests by which one's willingness and fitness for righteousness may be known" (Widtsoe, p. 335). They include the "covenant and promise to observe the law of strict virtue and chastity, to be charitable, benevolent, tolerant and pure; to devote both talent and material means to the spread of truth and the uplifting of the [human] race; to maintain devotion to the cause of truth; and to seek in every way to contribute to the great preparation that the earth may be made ready to receive . . . Jesus Christ" (Talmage, p. 84). One also promises to keep these covenants sacred and to "trifle not with sacred things" (D&C 6:12).

Fourth is a sense of divine presence. In the dedicatory prayer of the temple at Kirtland, Ohio, the Prophet Joseph Smith pleaded "that all people who shall enter upon the threshold of the Lord's house may feel thy power, and feel constrained to acknowledge that thou hast sanctified it, and that it is thy house, a place of thy holiness" (D&C 109:13). Of temples built by sacrifice to the name of the Lord Jesus Christ, dedicated by his authority, and reverenced in his Spirit, the promise is given, "My name shall be here; and I will manifest myself to my people in mercy in this holy house" (D&C 110:8). In the temples there is an "aura of deity" manifest to the worthy (Kimball, pp. 534–35). Through the temple endowment, one may seek "a fulness of the Holy Ghost" (D&C 109:15). Temple ordinances are seen as a means for receiving inspiration and instruction through the Holy Spirit, and for preparing to return to the presence of God.

In Nauvoo, the Prophet Joseph taught for the first time that it is the privilege of Latter-day Saints to act as agents in behalf of their kindred dead. After receiving their own temple endowment, Latter-day Saints return to the temple frequently to participate in the endowment ceremony as proxies for, and in behalf of, deceased persons. Consistent with the law of agency, it is believed that those so served have complete freedom in the spirit world to accept or reject the spiritual blessing thus proffered them (*HC* 5:350).

[*See also* Baptism for the Dead; Salvation of the Dead; Temple Ordinances.]

BIBLIOGRAPHY

Kimball, Spencer W. *Teachings of Spencer W. Kimball*, ed. Edward L. Kimball. Salt Lake City, 1982.

Packer, Boyd K. *The Holy Temple*. Salt Lake City, 1980.

Talmage, James E. *House of the Lord*. Salt Lake City, 1968.

Widtsoe, John A. *Priesthood and Church Government*. Salt Lake City, 1939.

———. *Temple Worship*. Salt Lake City, 1986.

ALMA P. BURTON

ENDOWMENT HOUSES

An endowment house is a building or place where certain temple ordinances may be administered, outside of the temple itself. MOSES erected a tabernacle in the wilderness as a "temporary temple"; by analogy, so did the Prophet Joseph SMITH. Before the NAUVOO TEMPLE was completed, the large upper room of Joseph Smith's red-brick store building in NAUVOO, Illinois, was used to confer the first TEMPLE ORDINANCES on a few leaders of the Church on May 4, 1842, and then on their wives. These ordinances, called ENDOWMENTS, consisted of a course of instruction and rites that included prayers, washings, anointings, and the making of COVENANTS with the Lord Jesus Christ.

The Endowment House, c. 1888, in the northwest corner of Temple Square, Salt Lake City. Ordinances for the living, but not for the dead, were performed in this building until 1889 when it was torn down. Photographer: C. R. Savage.

The Latter-day Saints occasionally used a mountaintop as their temporary temple, and President Brigham YOUNG dedicated Ensign Peak, a hill just north of Salt Lake City, Utah, as a "natural temple." Though Brigham Young designated a temple site in Salt Lake Valley on July 28, 1847, just four days after his arrival, the temple took forty years to build. In the meantime, the upper floor of the Council House, Salt Lake City's first public building, served 2,222 members of the Church as their endowment house between February 21, 1851, and May 5, 1855.

A more permanent endowment house, designed by Truman O. Angell, Church architect, was soon built on the northwest corner of TEMPLE SQUARE. Brigham Young named it "The House of the Lord." It was dedicated on May 5, 1855, by Heber C. Kimball. The main structure was a two-story building 34 feet by 44 feet, with small one-story extensions on both ends. The first floor had a room for WASHING AND ANOINTING, and also "garden," "world," and "terrestrial" rooms. The upper floor was the "celestial room," with an adjacent SEALING room.

On the average, 25 to 30 endowments were given daily, for a total of 54,170 in the thirty-four years it was used. And an average of 2,500 marriages were also performed annually. In addition, the endowment house served as a place for special PRAYER CIRCLES and the SETTING APART and instruction of newly called MISSIONARIES.

As the SALT LAKE TEMPLE neared completion, the endowment house was torn down in November 1889. The Salt Lake Temple was dedicated April 6, 1893. A long-anticipated holy place for temple ordinances was then permanently established in Salt Lake City.

BIBLIOGRAPHY

Cowan, Richard O. *Temples to Dot the Earth*. Salt Lake City, 1989.

Lund, A. William. "History of the Salt Lake Endowment House." *IE* 39 (Apr. 1936):213.

LAMAR C. BERRETT

ENDURING TO THE END

Enduring to the end, or remaining faithful to the laws and ORDINANCES of the GOSPEL OF JESUS CHRIST throughout life, is a fundamental requirement for SALVATION in the KINGDOM OF GOD. This belief distinguishes Latter-day Saints from many other Christian denominations, which teach that salvation is given to all who simply believe and confess that Jesus is the Christ. Latter-day Saints believe that to be saved a person must have faith in Jesus Christ, demonstrate REPENTANCE of sins, submit to BAPTISM by immersion, and receive the GIFT OF THE HOLY GHOST by the LAYING-ON OF HANDS by those holding the true PRIESTHOOD authority, and then remain faithful to all COVENANTS, continue in RIGHTEOUSNESS, and endure faithfully to the end of mortal life (Heb. 3:6–14; 6:4–15; Mark 13:13). This enduring faithfulness makes it possible for a person to receive fully the GRACE of Christ. The Doctrine and Covenants states, "If you keep my commandments and endure to the end you shall have eternal life, which gift is the greatest of all the gifts of God" (D&C 14:7).

The Book of Mormon prophet NEPHI₁ taught the principle of enduring to the end as a requirement of salvation: "After ye have repented of your sins, and witnessed unto the Father that ye are willing to keep my commandments, by the baptism of water, and have received the baptism of fire and of the Holy Ghost, . . . and after this should deny me, it would have been better for you not to have known me. . . . He that endureth to the end, the same shall be saved" (2 Ne. 31:14–15; cf. Heb. 6:4–6). As Nephi explains, enduring to the end involves having faith, hope, and charity; faithfully following the example of Jesus Christ; and always abounding in good works (cf. Alma 7:23–24): "Unless a man shall endure to the end, in following the example of the Son of the living God, he cannot be saved. . . . Wherefore, ye must press forward with a steadfastness in Christ, having a perfect brightness of hope, and a love of God and of all men. Wherefore, if ye shall press forward, feasting upon the word of Christ, and endure to the end, . . . ye shall have eternal life" (2 Ne. 31:16, 20).

Enduring to the end includes being willing and prepared to endure faithfully the trials of life, as did Job, Stephen (Acts 7), PAUL (2 Tim. 4:5–7), PETER (1 Pet. 1–4), and MORONI₂ (Moroni 1:1–3). The Lord spoke this reassurance to the Prophet Joseph SMITH after several months of incarceration in LIBERTY JAIL: "My son, peace be unto thy soul; thine adversity and thine afflictions shall be but a small moment; And then, if thou endure it well, God shall exalt thee on high; thou shalt triumph over all thy foes" (D&C 121:7–8).

BIBLIOGRAPHY

Ashton, Marvin J. "If Thou Endure It Well." *Ensign* 14 (Nov. 1984):20–22.

Maxwell, Neal A. "Endure It Well." *Ensign* 20 (May 1990):33–35.

JOHN M. MADSEN

ENOCH

[*In three parts, this entry discusses Enoch, his visions, prophetic leadership, and significance.*]

LDS SOURCES

Enoch holds a prominent place in Latter-day Saint scripture and tradition as a PROPHET, SEER, and builder of ZION. The Bible states that "Enoch walked with God: and he was not; for God took him" (Gen. 5:21–24). In revelations to Joseph SMITH much additional information is given about Enoch, his knowledge of the sanctifying atonement of Christ, the visions he saw of the future of the world, the messages he proclaimed, the wickedness he opposed, the miracles he worked, the priesthood ordinances he performed, and the promises he received from the premortal Lord Jesus Christ (*see* BOOK OF MOSES). Enoch and his city of Zion are powerful symbols among the Latter-day Saints, affirming that supreme RIGHTEOUSNESS can be attained on earth as it is in heaven.

MOSES 6–7 IN THE PEARL OF GREAT PRICE. Enoch was the seventh in a chain of patriarchs extending back to ADAM (Moses 6:10–22). Adam's grandson Enos had fled with "the residue of the people of God" from a wicked land called Shulon into "a land of promise," which Enos named after his son, Cainan (6:17). The text implies that Enoch was born in this "land of righteousness" (6:41). Following the example of Adam and Eve, Enoch's father taught him "in all the ways of God" (6:21, 41; cf. 5:12).

When Enoch was said to be "but a lad" (although he was possibly over 65—Moses 6:25, 31), he was called to preach repentance to the wicked: "The Spirit of God descended out of heaven, and abode upon him" (6:26–30). Like other prophets, Enoch felt profoundly inadequate to the task: "All the people hate me; for I am slow of speech" (6:31–34; cf. 1:25–26; Ex. 4:10–12; Jer. 1:4–10; Isa. 6:1–10). The Lord instructed Enoch to anoint his eyes with clay and wash them, whereupon he saw a vision of "the spirits that God had created; and . . . things which were not visible to the natural eye" (Moses 6:35–36). The word "seer" thus applies to him.

Enoch then went forth preaching in the hills and high places, but the people took offense and considered him "a wild man" (6:37–38). One man named Mahijah was bold enough to ask Enoch who he was and whence he had come. Enoch then explained his vision of heaven and his understanding of the fall of Adam; he taught how humans after the Fall had become carnal and devilish by worshiping Satan, but how according to the plan of salvation they may repent and become "sons of God" through the blood of Jesus Christ, the Only Begotten Son of the Man of Holiness (6:42–7:1).

As Enoch continued his ministry, he told of another vision he had received in which he stood upon a mountain and saw the Lord face to face. The Lord showed Enoch the judgments of war and the barrenness that would come upon the wicked and commanded Enoch again to preach repentance and baptism in the name of the Father, Son, and Holy Ghost (7:2–11).

Enoch brought a large body of converts to the GOSPEL OF JESUS CHRIST, but his success did not come without fierce opposition (7:12–13). The enemies of the righteous mobilized against them. The scriptural account describes miracles of extraordinary power. By Enoch's words, "the earth trembled, and the mountains fled, . . . and rivers of water were turned out of their course" (7:13). Stricken by fear, Enoch's enemies and the giants of the land stood far off, and "the Lord came and dwelt with his people, and they dwelt in righteousness" (7:17).

Under Enoch's inspired leadership, the faithful achieved an extraordinary unity of heart and mind. Loving obedience to the laws of Christ was maintained; a state of economic equality was realized, and "there was no poor among them" (7:18). The spiritual unity of Enoch's people took on physical dimensions through the construction of a city "that was called the City of Holiness, even Zion" (7:19). Their lives were based on "the order of him who was without beginning of days or end of years [Jesus Christ]" (6:67), and "after the order of the covenant which God made with Enoch" (JST Gen. 14:27). This unique community matured over a period of 365 years, after which it was received up into heaven. Fulfilling his covenant to preserve the lineage of Enoch upon the earth, the Lord left behind Enoch's son, Methuselah, and grandson,

Lamech (Moses 8:2, 5). Lamech's son NOAH was born four years after the city of Enoch was taken into heaven.

In a third vision, Enoch beheld "all the inhabitants of the earth" (7:21). In this panoramic revelation, he witnessed the wickedness and violence in the days of Noah; he saw Satan laughing, with a great chain in his hand, and the Lord weeping over his creations, for mankind had rejected God and had become "without affection" (7:33). Enoch saw the atoning sacrifice of Jesus Christ (7:47–48) and received a promise that "a remnant of his seed should always be found among all nations" (7:52). Finally, he saw the joyous reunion of his city with a latter-day Zion built in anticipation of Jesus' second coming (7:63–67).

According to the biblical account, Enoch lived 365 years (Gen. 5:23); according to the book of Moses, 430 years (8:1; i.e., 365 plus 65, which was Enoch's age when he begat Methuselah and was ordained).

DOCTRINE AND COVENANTS 76, 84, 107. Enoch's rapid rise to spiritual maturity is indicated by the fact that he received the priesthood before his father and grandfather. The priesthood held by Enoch is described in several passages in the Doctrine and Covenants. He was ordained at age twenty-five under the hand of Adam. His priesthood was "after the holiest order of God," holding "the key of the mysteries of the kingdom, even the key of the knowledge of God" (D&C 84:15–19). The scriptures confirm that Enoch "saw the Lord, and he walked with him, and was before his face continually" (D&C 107:48–49). Indicative of Enoch's eternal priesthood station, heirs of the CELESTIAL KINGDOM are described as "priests of the Most High, after the order of Melchizedek, which was after the order of Enoch, which was after the order of the Only Begotten Son" (D&C 76:57).

Enoch received two blessings from Adam: one when he was ordained to the priesthood, the other 240 years later at the council of ADAM-ONDI-AHMAN, which seems to be more of a public blessing (D&C 107:48, 53). All the patriarchs in Enoch's ancestral line were present at this final reunion of Adam's righteous posterity, and Adam prophesied the future of his descendants "unto the latest generation" (107:56). These prophecies were written in the BOOK OF ENOCH.

ENOCH AND THE LATTER-DAY SAINTS. Latter-day Saints believe that Enoch's righteousness was grounded on the same gospel principles that apply in all dispensations and eternally. For this reason, Latter-day Saints feel a spiritual kinship with Enoch and his people: Enoch's Zion represents every spiritual ideal for which Latter-day Saints strive. Called to build a modern Zion, the prophet and seer Joseph Smith used the name Enoch as one of the code names for himself in early editions of the Doctrine and Covenants. An economic system designed to promote material and spiritual equality within the Church, the Order of Enoch (*see* UNITED ORDER), has been implemented at various times in Church history. Church members look toward the day when the righteous will build the counterpart of Enoch's City of Holiness, the New Jerusalem, in Jackson County, Missouri. Missionaries around the world preach repentance, for the earth is to be cleansed by fire, as it was with the flood that followed Enoch's ministry. Church members anticipate the return of Enoch's city from above to be reunited with the Zion beneath (Moses 7:58), when the earth will rest under the millennial reign of Jesus Christ.

BIBLIOGRAPHY

Maxwell, Neal A. *Of One Heart: The Glory of the City of Enoch.* Salt Lake City, 1975.

Millet, Robert L. "Enoch and His City (Moses 6, 7)." In *Studies in Scripture*, Vol. 2, pp. 131–44. Salt Lake City, 1985.

Nibley, Hugh W. *Enoch the Prophet.* In CWHN 2.

Ricks, Stephen D. "The Narrative Call Pattern in the Prophetic Commission of Enoch (Moses 6)." *BYU Studies* 26 (Fall 1986):97–105.

RULON D. EAMES

ANCIENT SOURCES

According to Genesis 5:22–25, "Enoch walked with God after the birth of Methuselah three hundred years, and had other sons and daughters. Thus all the days of Enoch were three hundred and sixty-five years. Enoch walked with God; and he was not, for God took him" (RSV).

Enoch, the father of Methuselah and great-grandfather of Noah, was honored by Jews and Christians because of the following reasons: (1) Genesis 5 says that he lived 365 years, a number attractive to Jews who were arguing for cultic alignment with the solar calendar (*1 Enoch*). (2) He "walked with God" and therefore pleased God and was perfect (*Wisdom of Solomon* 4:13). (3) He did not die—"God took him"—and hence would return from heaven (*1 Enoch* 14:21–24) to bring to fruition God's promises for his people. (4) He was "seventh" (seven is a perfect number) after Adam (Gen. 5; *1 Enoch* 93:3; Jude 14). Enoch is declared by "an angel" to be "the Son of man" (*1 Enoch* 71:14). He alone has seen everything (*1 Enoch* 19). He will reprimand the fallen angels (*1 Enoch* 14), reveal everything (*1 Enoch* 91), intercede for humans (*1 Enoch* 15:2), and bring eternal peace into the world that is to come, as indicated at creation, since righteousness never forsakes him (*1 Enoch* 71:14–17).

BOOKS OF ENOCH. It is clear that early Jews and Christians honored the books of Enoch. The most ancient of these are excerpted in what is now called 1 (Ethiopic) Enoch. In the estimation of most experts today, all the documents preserved in 1 Enoch are Jewish and antedate the destruction of Jerusalem in A.D. 70. In probable chronological order these books of Enoch are as follows: *The Book of Astronomy* (*1 Enoch* 72–82) describes the movement of the sun, the reception of its light by the moon (73:7, 78:10), and the divinely ordained solar calendar. *The Book of the Watchers* (*1 Enoch* 1–36) is a composite work consisting of the Parables of Enoch (1–5), the Watchers (6–16), and Enoch's journeys (17–19 and 20–36); the main purpose of this compilation is to explain that evil entered into this world because of the fall of angels (cf. Gen. 6). *The Book of Dream Visions* (*1 Enoch* 83–90) contains a Vision of the Deluge (83–84) and an Animal Apocalypse (85–90), which describes the history of the world from before the Flood until the appearance of "one great horn," who is probably Judas Maccabeus. *The Epistle of Enoch* (*1 Enoch* 91–105; 106–107 is probably from the lost book of Noah, and 108 is a later addition) is addressed against the affluent sinners (94:8–9; 95:3; 96:4–8; 97:8–10), contains an older review of history (the Apocalypse of Weeks, *1 Enoch* 93:1–10, and 91:11–17, which is misplaced), and exhorts the righteous to continue in their hope (104) and to walk in the way of righteousness and avoid the way of wickedness. *The Similitudes of Enoch* (*1 Enoch* 36–71) is one of the most brilliant theological documents of Judaism before Jerusalem's destruction in 70 A.D; it describes the future appearance of the Messiah, the Righteous One, the Elect One, and the Son of Man, and tends to equate them as one figure, who is eventually revealed to be Enoch. Related to the books of Enoch is the *Book of the Giants*, which is preserved in Qumranic fragments that date from the first century B.C.

2 Enoch is one of the most difficult Jewish writings to date and to understand because it is preserved only in medieval Slavonic manuscripts. It was beloved by the Bogomils, who were shaped by ancient Jewish sources but who also created or reshaped ancient documents. Many scholars trace *2 Enoch* back to a Jew who lived before A.D. 100. After an introduction in which he informs his sons of his impending assumption, Enoch describes his ascent through the seven heavens (3–21). Then the Lord reveals secrets to Enoch (22–38), who admonishes his sons (39–66) and is translated into the highest heaven (67; chap. 68 is extant only in the long recension). The apocalypse concludes with a description of Melchizedek's miraculous birth from Sophanima, who has died. He is then taken into paradise by the archangel Michael and will return at the end of time to be the head of the priests (69–73).

3 Enoch in its present form is a medieval Jewish work; but it may go back to an earlier document and certainly preserves very ancient traditions. The forty-eight chapters of *3 Enoch* contain cosmological information, especially regarding the heavenly world of God's throne and chariot. The archangel Metatron informs the seer Ishmael that he is Enoch, who has been transformed into an angel.

THE EXIT OF ENOCH. Despite the fact that the author of Jude (verse 9) quoted from *1 Enoch* as prophecy and that the Ethiopian church has canonized the book and celebrated numerous other works that interpret it, the books of Enoch fell out of favor in mainstream Judaism and Christianity. With the compilation of the Mishnah by Rabbi Judah around A.D. 200 and the tendency to denigrate apocalypticism, Enoch fell out of favor. Hillel and his school were the norm for rabbinics. With the closing of the Christian canon, as a result of the emergence of the Holy Roman Empire in the fourth century, the books of Enoch were branded as extracanonical, and the veneration once given to the wise scribe Enoch was transferred to, or reserved for, Jesus Christ.

BIBLIOGRAPHY

Black, M., with J. C. VanderKam. *The Book of Enoch or 1 Enoch: A New English Edition.* Leiden, 1985.

Charles, R. H. *The Book of Enoch or 1 Enoch.* Oxford, 1912.

Charlesworth, J. H. *The Old Testament Pseudepigrapha,* 2 vols. Garden City, N.Y., 1983, 1985. (Contains introductions, translations, and notes to 1 Enoch, 2 Enoch, and 3 Enoch).

Knibb, M., with E. Ullendorff. *The Ethiopic Book of Enoch: A New Edition in the Light of the Aramaic Dead Sea Fragments,* 2 vols. Oxford, 1978.

Milik, J. T., with M. Black. *The Books of Enoch: Aramaic Fragments of Qumrân Cave 4.* Oxford, 1976.

VanderKam, J. C. *Enoch and the Growth of an Apocalyptic Tradition.* Washington, D.C., 1984.

JAMES H. CHARLESWORTH

BOOK OF ENOCH

The book of Enoch is one of the ancient writings that Latter-day Saints anticipate receiving sometime in the future (*see* SCRIPTURE: FORTHCOMING SCRIPTURE). This is not to be confused with the pseudepigraphic books of Enoch, which nevertheless have garnered the interest of some Latter-day Saints since at least 1840 (Pratt, p. 61). In Doctrine & Covenants 107:53–57, reference is made to a meeting of Adam's righteous posterity held at ADAM-ONDI-AHMAN three years before Adam's death. The influence of the Holy Spirit was manifested powerfully in prophecy as Adam blessed his posterity. While these verses give a précis of what happened, many more things were "written in the book of Enoch, and are to be testified of in due time" (D&C 107:57). Speaking of this book in December 1877, Elder Orson Pratt said, "When we get that, I think we shall know a great deal about the ante-diluvians of whom at present we know so little" (*JD* 19:218). An extract from the prophecy of Enoch was revealed and published in the BOOK OF MOSES (chaps. 6–7), the latter chapter being published in the *The Evening and The Morning Star* of August 1832 (*HC* 1:130–31).

BIBLIOGRAPHY

Pratt, Parley P. "The Apocryphal Book of Enoch." *MS* 1 (July 1840):61.

LEWIS R. CHURCH

ENOS

See: Book of Mormon: Overview

ENSIGN

Since 1971 the full title of the official monthly magazine for the English-speaking adult members of the Church is *The Ensign of The Church of Jesus*

Christ of Latter-day Saints. Printed in ten regular issues and two general conference issues (May and November), the *Ensign* is the publication link between Church headquarters and its adult members and friends, serving as a general-interest magazine, house organ, and instructional guide. It replaced the *Improvement Era, Instructor,* and the *Relief Society Magazine* in serving members of the Church eighteen years and older.

The word "ensign" is rich in meaning. The King James Bible translators used it to mean a signal, sign, identifying symbol, standard, or banner. Hence, we read the biblical prophecy that in the last days the Lord would "set up an ensign for the nations" (Isa. 11:12), a standard to which Israel and the righteous of all nations might gather in preparation for the Millennium (Isa. 5:26; 18:3; 31:6–9; 49:22; 62:10; Zech. 9:16). In latter-day scriptures, "ensign" symbolizes such "standards" as the new and everlasting covenant (D&C 45:9), the gospel of salvation (D&C 49:8–9; 2 Ne. 29:2), the latter-day ZION (D&C 64:41–43), and The Church of Jesus Christ of Latter-day Saints (D&C 115:4–6).

The *Ensign* magazine proposes to strengthen the faith of members of the Church, to promulgate gospel truths, and to keep members abreast of Church policies, programs, and happenings. In addition to publishing the conference issues, it provides a monthly First Presidency message, used also in HOME TEACHING; a monthly Relief Society VISITING TEACHING message; articles on scripture, doctrine, and member experiences and testimonies; and support articles for individuals, couples, parents, and local Church leaders and teachers.

Circulation in 1971 was 300,000; in 1990 it was 615,000, nearly a 4 percent annual gain, reflecting Church growth trends. All its editors since Doyle L. Green (1971–1976) have been general authorities: Dean L. Larsen (1976–1978), James E. Faust (1978–1979), M. Russell Ballard (1979–1984), Carlos E. Asay (1984–1986), Joseph B. Wirthlin (1986), Hugh W. Pinnock (1987–1989), and Rex D. Pinegar (1989–). Jay M. Todd has been the managing editor since 1972.

BIBLIOGRAPHY

Editorial. *Ensign* 1 (Jan. 1971):97.

Green, Doyle L. "The Church and Its Magazines." *Ensign* 1 (Jan. 1971):12–15.

JAY M. TODD

EPHRAIM

Ephraim was the son of Joseph and Asenath and the younger brother of Manasseh (Gen. 41:50–52). According to the Bible, when Joseph brought his two sons to his father, Jacob, for a blessing, Ephraim received the birthright blessing in place of Manasseh (Gen. 48:13–20), one of the departures noted in the Bible from the custom of bestowing on the firstborn son the special privileges that belonged to him by right of primogeniture. The Lord continued to acknowledge Ephraim's blessing centuries later when he said, "I am a father to Israel, and Ephraim is my firstborn" (Jer. 31:9; cf. 1 Chr. 5:1–2). Ephraim's descendants will continue in significant roles. The Book of Mormon records that Joseph of old "obtained a promise of the Lord, that out of the fruit of his loins the Lord God would raise up a righteous branch unto the house of Israel . . . to be remembered in the covenants of the Lord" (2 Ne. 3:5). Further, a "choice seer" would arise from Joseph's descendants who would "do a work for the fruit of [Joseph's] loins, his brethren, which shall be of great worth unto them, even to the bringing of them to the knowledge of the covenants which I [the Lord] have made with thy fathers" (2 Ne. 3:7). Many Latter-day Saints believe that they are of the branch of Ephraim, of whom Joseph prophesied (2 Ne. 3:5–16; D&C 133:30–34) and that the Prophet Joseph SMITH is the "choice seer" (3 Ne. 3:6).

Because of their rebellion against the Lord many centuries ago, Ephraim's descendants were scattered among the Gentile nations, along with members of the other tribes, beginning with the fall of the northern kingdom of Israel c. 722 B.C. (2 Kgs. 17:5–6; *see also* ISRAEL: SCATTERING OF ISRAEL and ISRAEL: LOST TRIBES OF ISRAEL).

In the LAST DAYS, Ephraim's descendants have the privilege and responsibility to bear the message of the RESTORATION of the gospel to the world and to gather scattered Israel (D&C 113:3–6). "We believe in the literal gathering of Israel and in the restoration of the Ten Tribes; that Zion (the New Jerusalem) will be built upon the American continent" (A of F 10; cf. Deut. 4:27–31; 28; 29; 30; 3 Ne. 20–21). The keys of gathering Israel were committed to the Prophet Joseph Smith by MOSES on April 3, 1836, in the KIRTLAND TEMPLE (D&C 110:11). Many of Ephraim's descendants are being gathered first, for they have the responsibility of preparing the way for the gathering of the other tribes (D&C 113). "And they [others of the tribes of Israel] shall bring forth their rich treasures unto the children of Ephraim, my servants . . . and there shall they fall down and be crowned with glory, even in Zion, by the hands of the servants of the Lord, even the children of Ephraim, and they shall be filled with songs of everlasting joy" (D&C 133:30–33; *see also* ISRAEL: GATHERING OF ISRAEL).

One of the tools to be used in the gathering is the Book of Mormon, also known among Latter-day Saints as the stick of Joseph or the stick of Ephraim (Ezek. 37:15–19; 2 Ne. 3:12; D&C 27:5). It is to play an important part in convincing LAMANITES, Jews, and Gentiles that Jesus is the MESSIAH and that God does remember his covenant people (*see* BOOK OF MORMON: TITLE PAGE).

For Latter-day Saints, identification of a person's lineage in latter-day COVENANT ISRAEL is made under the hands of inspired PATRIARCHS through PATRIARCHAL BLESSINGS that declare lineage. Elder John A. Widtsoe, an Apostle, declared, "In giving a blessing the patriarch may declare our lineage—that is, that we are of Israel, therefore of the family of Abraham, and of a specific tribe of Jacob. In the great majority of cases, Latter-day Saints are of the tribe of Ephraim, the tribe to which has been committed the leadership of the Latter-day work. Whether this lineage is of blood or adoption it does not matter" (p. 73; cf. Abr. 2:10).

The patriarchal blessings of most Latter-day Saints indicate that they are literal, blood descendants of ABRAHAM and of Israel. Those who are not literal descendants are adopted into the family of Abraham when they receive BAPTISM and CONFIRMATION (*see* LAW OF ADOPTION). They are then entitled to all the rights and privileges of heirs (*TPJS*, pp. 149–50). This doctrine of adoption was understood by ancient prophets and apostles (e.g., Rom. 11; 1 Ne. 10:14; Jacob 5; cf. D&C 84:33–34).

BIBLIOGRAPHY

McConkie, Bruce R. *A New Witness of the Articles of Faith*, pp. 541–75. Salt Lake City, 1985.

Smith, Joseph Fielding. *DS* 3:244–64.

Widtsoe, John A. *Evidences and Reconciliations*, pp. 72–77. Salt Lake City, 1943.

BRIAN L. SMITH

EPISTEMOLOGY

Epistemology is the branch of philosophy dealing with the nature and scope of knowledge. The Church of Jesus Christ of Latter-day Saints has no uniform position on the classical issues of epistemology, such as the relationship of the sources of knowledge, theories of truth, and modes of verification, but the superiority of knowing by revelation from God is commonly cited from the scriptures.

The word "knowledge" is used in different ways and has different meanings in different cultures. Different kinds of knowledge may be independent of each other.

The Western philosophical tradition, like Western thought generally, emphasizes knowledge in the sense of knowing facts. But this emphasis may not be appropriate, especially from a gospel perspective. Some scriptures teach that other kinds of knowledge may be more important. Thus, Jesus prays, "This is life eternal, that they might know thee the only true God, and Jesus Christ, whom thou hast sent" (John 17:3). This is knowledge by acquaintance more than "knowledge about" (cf. JST Matt. 7:32–33). There are also indications that factual knowledge alone is not sufficient for salvation: "But be ye doers of the word, and not hearers only" (James 1:22). At the request of President Spencer W. KIMBALL, a prophet, the words in a LDS children's hymn were changed from "Teach me all that I must know" to "Teach me all that I must do," because it is not enough just to know; one must do the will of the Lord.

A related gospel theme is that knowing comes from doing. "If any man will do his will, he shall know of the doctrine, whether it be of God, or whether I speak of myself" (John 7:17). The Prophet Joseph SMITH taught, "We cannot keep all the commandments without first knowing them, and we cannot expect to know all, or more than we now know unless we comply with or keep those we have already received" (*TPJS*, p. 256).

In formal philosophy, "knowing," in the sense of knowing facts, is often defined to mean true belief together with good reasons. In other words, a person knows some statement X if and only if that person believes X, and if X is true, and if the person has good reasons for believing X. The European-American philosophical tradition recognizes two kinds of reasons that support the claim to know: rational argument and empirical evidence. Within the Church these are tacitly accepted as sources of knowledge, sometimes even of religious knowledge. For example, after reviewing the traditional arguments for the existence of God, James E. Talmage observed that some were "at least strongly corroborative" of God's existence (*AF*, p. 29).

However, there is a continuing tradition, based on the scriptures and reinforced by modern Church leaders, that specifically religious knowledge requires a different and distinctively spiritual source. "We believe that no man can know that Jesus is the Christ, but by the Holy Ghost. We believe in [the gift of the Holy Ghost] in all its fulness, and power, and greatness, and glory" (*TPJS*, p. 243; D&C 76:114–16). It is widely accepted by Latter-day Saints that gospel knowledge must ultimately be obtained by spiritual rather than exclusively rational or empirical means (e.g., 1 Cor. 12:3). Thus, in The Church of Jesus Christ of Latter-day Saints, there is no clear counterpart to the Roman Catholic tradition of natural theology.

One of the most suggestive and frequently cited scriptures in LDS teaching makes the point: "And by the power of the Holy Ghost ye may know the truth of all things" (Moro. 10:4–5). This scripture is usually taken to apply to all knowledge. This suggests that both rational argument and empirical evidence, the two traditional approaches to knowledge, can be either supplanted by or encompassed within spiritual knowledge. Of course, the scripture does not say that knowledge comes only by the Holy Ghost. Yet, within the Church, it is often held that what might be thought of as secular learning, for example, modern scientific knowledge, is directly associated with the RESTORATION of the gospel and is rooted in divine inspiration throughout the world.

[*See also* Faith in Jesus Christ; Prophets; Reason and Revelation; Science and Religion.]

K. CODELL CARTER

EQUALITY

Equality among persons is understood by Latter-day Saints as essential to divine LOVE, which explains and justifies all other ethical virtues and principles (Matt. 22:37–40). All persons are of equal value in the sight of God. Each person (of every nation and every race) is as precious to him as another (2 Ne. 26:33; Alma 26:37). From God all people will receive equivalent opportunities through Jesus Christ to attain ETERNAL LIFE, his greatest blessing (1 Ne. 17:33–35; Hel. 14:17; D&C 18:10–12). All who are worthy to become HEIRS of Christ will enjoy equality with him and with each other in the CELESTIAL KINGDOM (D&C 88:106–107).

Latter-day Saints believe that when people love as God requires them to love (John 15:9–12), having full and equal regard for one another, they can form a ZION society as directed by the Lord and enjoy in this world the type of equality that defines relations between persons in the celestial world (D&C 78:4–8; 105:4–5). References to equality in latter-day SCRIPTURES primarily concern the building of Zion and living according to celestial LAW. In Zion the people have "all things common among them" (3 Ne. 26:19; 4 Ne. 1:3; cf. D&C 82:17–18; 104:70). They have equal chances to develop their abilities and equal opportunity to realize them in the work of Zion, all contributing according to their individual strengths and talents (D&C 82:17–18; Alma 1:26). A Zion people labor together as equals by organizing themselves according to the principle of "equal power" (D&C 76:94–95; 78:5–7; 105:4–6). For example, on the local level "all things" are done according to the "counsel" and "consent" of the community (D&C 104:21). Each member has an equal role in giving counsel and an equal vote in giving consent (see COMMON CONSENT). But equality of power also defines the relations between members so that each is the center of decision and action in performing an individual stewardship within the community (D&C 82:17; 104:70–76).

Celestial law also requires that persons receive as equals that which is essential to survival and contributes to well-being. Consequently, in Zion there are "no poor among them" (Moses 7:18; 4 Ne. 1:3). This does not mean that every person receives the same amount. The "needs," "wants," and "circumstances" of individuals vary so that treatment of them must also vary to be equal in effect (D&C 51:3, 8; 42:33). Still, it is "not given that one should possess that which is above another." When such inequality exists, "the world lieth in sin" (D&C 49:20; cf. Alma 5:53–54), and "the abundance of the manifestations of the Spirit [are] withheld" (D&C 70:14).

A. D. SORENSEN

ETERNAL LIFE

The scriptures clearly state that eternal life comes from God through his son Jesus Christ (John 3:16; 14:6; Heb. 5:9; 2 Ne. 31:20–21; Alma 11:40; Ether 3:14; D&C 45:8), and is the "greatest of all the gifts of God" (D&C 14:7; see also EXALTATION; GODHOOD). To Latter-day Saints the phrase "eternal life" refers not only to everlasting life but also and more particularly to the quality of life God lives. Eternal life is available to all people who have lived on earth who accept this gift by their obedience to God's laws and ordinances.

God's work, and the source of his glory, is bringing to pass "the immortality and eternal life" of his children (Moses 1:39). In other words, God works to enable his children's return to his presence so that they may both live with him and live as he lives.

So allied is Christ with the Father that the scriptures sometimes define eternal life as "knowing" them: "This is life eternal, that they might know thee the only true God, and Jesus Christ, whom thou hast sent" (John 17:3; D&C 132:24).

Knowing Christ in this world comes by receiving him and his law (D&C 132:23–24). Jeremiah spoke for the Lord: "I will put my law in their inward parts, and write it in their hearts. . . . And they shall teach no more every man his neighbour . . . saying, Know the Lord: for they shall all know me" (Jer. 31:33–34). As stated in the Gospel of John, one begins to know Christ and his will by searching the scriptures, for, as Jesus affirmed, "they are they which testify of me" (John 5:39).

Having the law written in one's heart implies an acceptance that prompts action; indeed, the scriptures mention many actions that one must take in order to receive the gift of eternal life. To enter the path leading toward eternal life, one must exercise faith in Christ (John 3:36; 6:47; Moro. 7:41), repent, be baptized for the remission of one's sins (2 Ne. 31:17–18), and receive the gift of the Holy Ghost. The scriptures state that once on the path, the believer must strive to keep the COMMANDMENTS (2 Ne. 31:19–20; Alma 7:15–16)—that is, to do the works of RIGHTEOUSNESS (D&C 59:23), primary among which is charity (1 Cor. 13; Matt. 25:34–36). The believer must also ENDURE TO THE END (2 Ne. 31:20–21; D&C 50:5; cf. Paul's phrase "patient continuance in well doing," Rom. 2:7), and make covenants in connection with TEMPLE ORDINANCES (D&C 124:55; 128:12).

While in mortality, individuals may come to a stage of knowing the Father and the Son that allows the Lord to promise them eternal life. This occurrence is described in scripture as receiving the HOLY SPIRIT OF PROMISE (D&C 88:3–4) and the Second Comforter (John 14:16; D&C 88:2–4; see also JESUS CHRIST, SECOND COMFORTER); having the more sure word of prophecy (D&C 131:5); and having one's CALLING AND ELECTION made sure (2 Pet. 1:10; D&C 131:5).

God invites all people to seek and ask earnestly for eternal life, and reassures all who do so that they will not be given a stone (cf. Matt. 7:7–11). They are promised "revelation upon revelation, knowledge upon knowledge," which brings an understanding of "peaceable things—that which bringeth joy, that which bringeth life eternal" (D&C 42:61). Those who will receive eternal life in its fullest come forth in the first RESURRECTION (Mosiah 15:21–25) and inherit the highest degree of glory in the CELESTIAL KINGDOM (D&C 76:50–59; 88:4; 101:65).

The Prophet Joseph Smith was at a loss for words to capture the eternal splendor of God the Father and of his son Jesus Christ, "whose brightness and glory defy all description" (JS—H 1:17). Language can describe the glories of eternal life only inadequately through metaphors of overwhelmingly bright light or fire (Ex. 24:17; Acts 26:13–15; Rev. 21:23; 1 Ne. 1:8–10; D&C 110:1–4; cf. "shine as the brightness of the firmament," Dan. 12:3); pure truth (John 14:6; Ether 4:12; D&C 84:45–48; 93:36; Moses 7:29–40); glass or crystal (Rev. 4:6; D&C 130:9); and timelessness (Ps. 90:4; 2 Pet. 3:8; Rev. 10:6; Alma 40:8; D&C 88:110). Paul points out how far eternal life exceeds the descriptive ability of language when he says, "Eye hath not seen, nor ear heard, neither have entered into the heart of man, the things which God hath prepared for them that love him" (1 Cor. 2:9).

[See also Immortality and Eternal Life.]

BIBLIOGRAPHY

Monson, Thomas S. *Pathways to Perfection*. Salt Lake City, 1976.

CATHERINE CORMAN PARRY

ETERNAL LIVES, ETERNAL INCREASE

"Eternal lives" is a term that refers to the right and power to beget children after the resurrection, granted to those who are exalted in the highest degree of the CELESTIAL KINGDOM. This is an aspect of ETERNAL PROGRESSION. "In the celestial glory there are three heavens or degrees; and in order to obtain the highest, a man must enter into this order of the priesthood [meaning the new and everlasting covenant of marriage]; And if he does not, he cannot obtain it. He may enter into the other, but that is the end of his kingdom; he cannot have an increase" (D&C 131:1–4).

This distinctive doctrine of The Church of Jesus Christ of Latter-day Saints was taught by Joseph SMITH and was especially articulated on May 16–17, 1843, at Ramus, Illinois, where he often visited and preached. Conversing on spiritual topics with a small party of friends, the Prophet Joseph Smith shed light on the concept of eternal increase: "Except a man and his wife enter into an everlasting covenant and be married for eternity, while in this probation, by the power and authority of the Holy Priesthood, they will cease to increase when they die; that is, they will not have any children after the resurrection. But those who are married by the power and authority of the priesthood in this life, and continue without committing the sin against the Holy Ghost, will continue to increase and have children in the celestial glory" (*TPJS*, pp. 300–301). Doctrine and Covenants, section 131, is largely concerned with this subject, and was first included in 1876.

A husband and wife who are married in the new and everlasting covenant and sealed by the HOLY SPIRIT OF PROMISE under the proper PRIESTHOOD authority are promised that they shall inherit "thrones, kingdoms, principalities, and powers," and their "glory shall be a fulness and a continuation of the seeds forever and ever" (D&C 132:19). They are likened to gods, having no end. They share in the promises of eternal posterity made to ABRAHAM and SARAH: "Both in the world and out of the world should they continue as innumerable as the stars" (D&C 132:30).

Brigham YOUNG, in 1862, spoke of eternal lives, stating that the opportunity to become heirs to all things, and to become a "King of kings and Lord of lords, . . . is promised to the faithful, and are but so many stages in that ceaseless progression of eternal lives. . . . There will be no end to the increase of the faithful" (*JD* 10:5). He described such a situation as a pleasing one, creating happiness beyond mortal comprehension. In 1864 he elaborated: "In like manner, every faithful son of God, becomes, as it were, Adam to the race that springs from his loins, when they are embraced in the covenants and blessings of the Holy Priesthood . . . in the progress of eternal lives. . . . We have not yet received our kingdoms, neither will we, until we have finished our work on the earth, passed through the ordeals, are brought up by the power of the resurrection, and are crowned with glory and eternal lives" (*JD* 10:355).

Latter-day Saints believe that all worthy men and women, through righteous living and being sealed by the power of the priesthood, will in ETERNAL LIFE inherit, with ADAM and EVE, Abraham and Sarah, and all the faithful, those same blessings and enjoy a continuation of seeds forever, or eternal increase.

SHIRLEY S. RICKS

ETERNAL PROGRESSION

The principle of eternal progression cannot be precisely defined or comprehended, yet it is fundamental to the LDS worldview. The phrase "eternal progression" first occurs in the discourses of Brigham YOUNG. It embodies many concepts taught by Joseph SMITH, especially in his KING FOLLETT DISCOURSE. It is based on the proposition that "there is no such thing as principle, power, wisdom, knowledge, life, position, or anything that can be imagined, that remains stationary—they must increase or decrease" (Young, *JD* 1:350).

Progression takes many forms. In one sense, eternal progression refers to everything that people learn and experience by their choices as they progress from PREMORTAL LIFE, to MORTALITY, to postmortal spirit life, and to a resurrected state in the presence of God. Personal progression is possible in each of these states, but not the same kind of progression. Progression apparently occurred in the premortal life, for most spirits there chose to follow Christ and some were noble and great, while others chose to follow Lucifer. Entering mortality affords opportunities for further progression. Obtaining a PHYSICAL BODY is a crucial step, enabling a person to experience physical sensations of all kinds and to progress in knowledge and understanding, all of which will rise with the person in the Resurrection (D&C 130:18). Brigham Young taught that even in mortality, "We are in eternity" (*JD* 10:22), and the object of this existence is "to learn to enjoy more, and to increase in knowledge and experience" (*JD* 14:228). "When we have learned to live according to the full value of the life we now possess, we are prepared for further advancement in the scale of eternal progression—for a more glorious and exalted sphere" (*JD* 9:168).

Life is never static. "One must progress or retrograde. One cannot stand still. Activity is the law of growth, and growth, progress, is the law of life" (A. Bowen, in *Christ's Ideals for Living*, O. Tanner, ed., Salt Lake City, 1980, p. 368). A person's attitude about "'eternal progression' will largely determine his philosophy of life . . . exalting, increasing, expanding and extending broader and broader until we can know as we are known, see as we are seen" (Young, *JD* 16:165).

At the Resurrection and Judgment, people will be assigned a DEGREE OF GLORY. Further progress is believed possible within each degree. Marriage and family life, however, continue only in the CELESTIAL KINGDOM, allowing "eternal increase" through having spirit children (*see* ETERNAL LIVES, ETERNAL INCREASE). "All this and more that cannot enter into our hearts to conceive is promised to the faithful, and are but so many stages in that ceaseless progression of eternal lives" (Young, *JD* 10:5).

No official Church teaching attempts to specify all the ways in which God progresses in his exalted spheres; "there is no end to [His] works, neither to [His] words" (Moses 1:38). God's glory and power are enhanced as his children progress in glory and power (see Moses 1:39; Young, *JD* 10:5). Ideas have been advanced to explain how God might progress in knowledge and still be perfect and know all things (*see* FOREKNOWLEDGE OF GOD; OMNIPOTENT GOD).

The concept of eternal progression is a salient feature of the gospel of Jesus Christ, readily distinguishable from traditional Christian theology. The philosophical views of the Middle Ages were basically incompatible with such a concept, and the idea of progress that emerged in the eighteenth-century Enlightenment was that of social evolution (Bury, *The Idea of Progress*, London, 1932). The traditional Christian view has held that those in heaven enter "a state of eternal, inactive joy. In the presence of God they would worship him and sing praises to him eternally, but nothing more" (Widtsoe, p. 142). Latter-day Saints, however, constantly seek personal and righteous improvement not only by establishing ZION in this world, but by anticipating the continuation of progression eternally.

BIBLIOGRAPHY

Widtsoe, John A. "Is Progress Eternal or Is There Progress in Heaven?" *IE* 54 (Mar. 1951):142; see also *Evidences and Reconciliations*, pp. 179–85, Salt Lake City, 1960.

LISA RAMSEY ADAMS

ETHER

See: Book of Mormon: Book of Ether

ETHICS

The Church of Jesus Christ of Latter-day Saints is typically involved in three levels of ethical concern: the theory of values; the foundations of moral decision; and the integration of personal and professional codes of ethics, such as those relating to medical, military, or governmental service. The inner dynamism of the Church and its increasing involvement with a confluence of cultures point beyond closed ethical systems. Latter-day Saints espouse an ethic of divine approbation; to discern the will of God and receive assurance that one is acting under God's approval are the ceaseless quest of DISCIPLESHIP. This may be called Spirit-guided morality.

The scriptures affirm that questions of the good and the right are intertwined with questions of the holy and with the primal Jewish-Christian imperative "Be ye holy for I am holy" (1 Pet. 1:16; cf. Lev. 11:44). Daily tensions between the sacred and the secular are part of the ethical dilemma, and Latter-day Saints seek help from the scriptures and classical sources.

Philosophers often distinguish two approaches to ethics: teleology and deontology. The teleological approach appraises the morality of an act by its relation to an end or purpose, while the deontological approach understands morality primarily in terms of duty or response to law. In Christian ethics, these views have proved difficult to reconcile. For Latter-day Saints, however, both obedience to divine imperatives and pursuit of ultimate happiness are correlative elements in the maturation of human beings. The conflict between duty and desire is overcome as one grows closer to God through faith and service and finds joy in upholding divine counsels and commandments.

Ethicists likewise contrast performance and motive in the religious life. Rabbinical tradition, for example, emphasizes the continuous study and scrupulous observance of Torah, while Reformation Protestantism stresses motive. Again, Latter-day Saints reject this perennial division; both are crucial in the religious life. "Ye shall know them by their fruits" (Matt. 7:16). Grace transforms men toward a Christlike nature. But purity of heart is manifest in scripture study and vigorous service; thus, mastery of law and inner change go hand in hand as components of discipleship and joyful living.

Classical Christian thought encourages the cultivation of habits and dispositions tied to both intellectual and moral virtues. Both ancient and modern revelations advocate such virtues as "knowledge, temperance, patience, brotherly kindness, godliness, charity, humility, diligence" (2 Pet. 1:5–7; cf. D&C 4:5), and all the Christlike attributes of the Sermon on the Mount. There are correlative warnings against besetting vices: pride, unrighteous dominion, lust, anger, unforgiveness, covetousness, idleness, halfheartedness. The Saints are constantly reminded to "seek not the things of this world but seek ye first to build up the kingdom of God and to establish his righteousness" (JST Matt. 6:38). NEPHI$_1$ and MORONI$_2$, both prophets of the Book of Mormon, teach, as does the apostle Paul, the importance of faith, hope, and charity, which is defined as "the pure love of Christ" (1 Cor. 13:1–13; 2 Ne. 31:20; Moro. 7:21–48).

Much ethical discussion today revolves around whether there are any external and binding sanctions for ethics and morality. In the theological context, there is the classical dilemma of whether God's will is right because he wills it or whether he wills it because it is right. Latter-day Saints are not committed to certain theories of natural law. Modern scriptures suggest that ethical laws and "bounds" and conditions exist independent of God (D&C 88:3–40; see LAW: DIVINE AND ETERNAL LAW). They also teach that God both institutes laws and adapts them (*TPJS*, p. 320). Both the meaning and the application of law in changing circumstances require revelation of the present will of God.

LDS ethics are neither extremely atomistic nor social-communitarian but recognize the importance of both the individual and social aspects of human existence. "And that same sociality which exists among us here will exist among us there [the eternal world], only it will be coupled with eternal glory, which glory we do not now enjoy" (D&C 130:2).

Ethical discussion often focuses on how one comes to know what is good or right. Appeals to intuition or conscience are opposed by radical conventionalism, which presumes that values are reducible to custom and that the mores of a given group or individual are not known (discovered) but simply preferred. Latter-day Saints respect conscience, and the scriptures reiterate that conscience must be refined and directed by the Holy Ghost. They consider ethical maturity to derive from experience; including religious experience; from rational and practical deliberation; and from the mandates, both general and specific, that recur in scripture and the counsels of the prophets.

BIBLIOGRAPHY

Hill, Donald G., Jr., ed. *Perspectives in Mormon Ethics*. Salt Lake City, 1983.

F. NEIL BRADY

EUROPE, THE CHURCH IN

[*This article discusses the establishment and growth of the Church in continental Europe. See separate articles on the Church in the* British Isles, *the* Middle East, *and* Scandinavia.]

The Protestant countries of Western Europe—Scandinavia, Switzerland, Germany, and the Netherlands—played a major role in the growth and success of the Church from the beginnings in

EUROPEAN AREAS

☐ Europe (168,000 members)

▨ United Kingdom/Ireland
   (152,000 members)

✪ Area Headquaters

◆ First Stake in Country

▟ Temple

✳ Membership less than 100

ICELAND
(200)

SWEDEN
(7,900)

FINLAND
(4,200)

NORWAY
(3,700)

Helsinki
1977

Oslo 1977

Stockholm
1975
1985

SCOTLAND
(22,000)

DENMARK
(4,300)

U.S.S.R.
(700)

N. IRELAND
(5,300)

Glasgow 1962

Belfast 1974

Copenhagen
1974

ENGLAND
(117,000)

POLAND
(200)

IRELAND
(2,800)

U.K.

Manchester 1960

Berlin 1961 ◆

Solihull

The
Hague
1961

NETH.
(7,000)

GERMANY
(38,100)

Frieburg
1985

WALES
(7,100)

Merthyr Tydfil 1975

BEL.
(4,400)

CZECHOSLOVAKIA ✳

London 1958

Brussels
1977

1987

✪ Frankfurt

Paris 1975 ◆

LUX. ✳

Vienna
1980

HUNGARY
(600)

ROMANIA ✳

FRANCE
(23,000)

Zurich 1961

AUSTRIA
(3,700)

Bern 1955

SWITZ.
(6,300)

Milan
1981

YUGOSLAVIA
(100)

BULGARIA ✳

SPAIN
(21,000)

ITALY
(14,000)

ALB. ✳

Lisbon
1981

Madrid 1982

PORTUGAL
(28,000)

GREECE
(200)

0   100   200   300   400   500

Scale in Miles

BYU Geography Department

the 1830s until well into the twentieth century. Along with the United States, Canada, and Great Britain, continental Europe provided most of the early LDS converts until around 1960, when successes in Latin America and Asia began to overshadow it as a source of new converts. Without the waves of European converts, many of whom emigrated to fill up the pioneer settlements of the Great Basin Kingdom (*see* COLONIZATION), the Church would, at best, have grown more slowly, been more insular and provincial.

That success in Europe was, however, geographically uneven. Early converts came overwhelmingly from the countries of the Protestant Reformation. Attempts were made as early as the 1850s to gain converts in France, Italy, Ireland, and Austria-Hungary, but results were meager and missionaries became discouraged. Real success in these and other Catholic countries would have to wait for the more open societies and attitudes of the twentieth century. LDS missionaries also found virtually no access to the Orthodox populations of Eastern Europe, whether in Russia, Greece, or the Balkans, and there were only a very few conversions of European Jews.

LDS converts came from many different Protestant denominations and sects, but most of them were religious "seekers" of one kind or another, sometimes already united in congregations like Timothy Mets's "New Lighters" in Holland in the early 1860s. Most of the seekers had studied the Bible and were looking for a church with apostles, prophets, and the spiritual gifts they had read about in the New Testament. They also tended to be discouraged with traditional doctrines and the behavior of churches and pastors, and longed for the assurance of communion with the spirit of God in preparation for Christ's imminent return.

Most European converts came from the middle, lower middle, and especially the working classes. One study which surveyed LDS immigrants to the United States between 1840 and 1869 found that only 11 percent were middle class, mostly artisans; the rest came overwhelmingly from the working classes. Early attempts were made by missionaries to interest such dignitaries as the queens and kings of various countries, but

these appeals fell on deaf ears and sometimes even led to the missionaries' banishment. Their preaching also had little resonance with the traditional nobility, the moneyed aristocracy, and an increasingly secular and powerful intelligentsia. Thus, cut off from "respectable" society, they went "to the poor like their Captain of old" (*Hymns*, 1985, No. 319), among whom they found believers. Only in the later twentieth century, as they had done in America, did European Latter-day Saints as a group begin to be part of the growing middle class as they received greater opportunities for higher education and financial success.

The new European Saints of the nineteenth century came from both rural and urban societies. Farmers, agricultural workers, and artisans joined with industrial workers and townspeople leaving the depressed countrysides and the slums of industrializing Europe for the kingdom of the Saints in what they and thousands of other emigrants believed was the promised land, the land of unlimited opportunity.

Some three years after the Church was established in Europe, it introduced the doctrine of the GATHERING, which encouraged the new members to gather to ZION. Before 1900 more than 91,600 heeded the call, and although after the turn of the century Church authorities began to discourage emigration, thousands more joined the ever-broadening stream of European immigrants to America. They scrimped and saved, sometimes for years—the average wait was ten years—to get the eighty to one hundred dollars needed to get from Liverpool to Salt Lake City. Saints from the Continent went to Liverpool, where, with British converts, they booked passage on large emigrant ships, such as the *Amazon, Nevada,* or *Monarch of the Sea.* They first landed in New Orleans for the trip upstream to Nauvoo, later they landed at New York, Philadelphia, or Boston, traveled by train to Omaha, and then journeyed by covered wagon or handcart the remaining 1,100 miles to Utah. For some the trip was better than tolerable; for many others, it was an ordeal endured only through faith and determination.

Seeing that most new converts were so poor that they could not emigrate without help, the

The Church of Jesus Christ of Latter-day Saints in Europe, including the British Isles and Scandinavia, as of January 1, 1991.

ÉTOILE DU DÉSERET

ORGANE DE L'ÉGLISE DE JÉSUS-CHRIST DES SAINTS-DES-DERNIERS-JOURS.

LA VÉRITÉ, L'INTELLIGENCE, LA VERTU ET LA FOI SONT UNIES.

SI VOUS M'AIMEZ, GARDEZ MES COMMANDEMENTS. (JEAN, XIV, 15.)

Il y a déjà quelque temps j'ai eu l'occasion de publier un récit abrégé de l'origine, des progrès, de l'établissement, des persécutions, de la foi et de la doctrine de l'Eglise de Jésus-Christ des Saints-des-Derniers-Jours. Je me proposais de publier quelque autre ouvrage analogue donnant plus de particularités sur notre doctrine, notre organisation et notre position actuelle. Mais, après réflexion, et après m'être concerté avec mes amis, j'ai pensé qu'il serait préférable, pour l'accomplissement de mes desseins, de prendre la forme d'un recueil.

Conséquemment, nous ferons paraitre de temps à autre un cahier pareil à celui-ci, qui non-seulement réalisera le but que je me proposais, mais en outre donnera les nouvelles que nous sommes à même de recevoir de la

Elder John Taylor, one of the first LDS missionaries in continental Europe, began the French publication *Etoile du Deseret* ("Star of Deseret"). Courtesy Rare Books and Manuscripts, Brigham Young University.

Church, in 1849, set up the PERPETUAL EMIGRATING FUND which allowed thousands of Saints to borrow the money to emigrate and then repay the fund after they were settled in the American West. After the completion of the transcontinental railroad in 1869, the journey was not so arduous because the railroad brought emigrants directly to Zion.

European LDS emigration peaked in the 1850s and 1860s, although a fairly constant stream, especially of Germans, continued after the turmoil of both world wars. They all became part of the "melting pot," with few Saints returning to their native lands.

The European members turned out to be exceptionally good pioneers. Most brought with them solid religious conviction and faith, an unusually strong work ethic, usable and practiced skills derived from the quality artisanship of Europe, and a desire to blend into their new society and surroundings. They also brought a deep respect for Church leaders as God's chosen servants, a willingness to settle where they were called, and a desire to help promote the missionary cause, especially in their native lands. They were persuasive recruiters of their fellow countrymen to the new LDS settlements. Many met incoming emigrant trains to take settlers to their new paradise.

Besides laborers and skilled craftsmen, there were also businessmen and entrepreneurs and teachers; there were women trained as midwives and a few as doctors. Europe also produced poets, journalists, artists, architects, photographers, musicians, and also dramatists. From their ranks arose a range of great leaders from GENERAL AUTHORITIES to missionaries—who usually labored in their homelands. Devout women and children who supported the Church, often at great sacrifice, carried out their own daily and Church duties. Most important, however, were the tens of thousands of less-known European Saints; Zion could not have done without them. Census figures give us some idea of their numbers. In 1880, out of a total Utah population of 143,863, almost 43,000, or 30 percent, were foreign-born. If children born in America to foreign-born members are included, the figure would exceed 60 percent.

Not all European converts to the Church immigrated to America, even in the peak years of the gathering. Some had families they could not and would not leave; others lacked faith and funds. Some drifted from the faith or could not find suitable marriage partners in it. Others succumbed to the extraordinary anti-Mormon pressures and persecutions that arose simultaneously almost everywhere with the arrival of the missionaries. Throughout Europe in the nineteenth and early twentieth centuries, Latter-day Saints, and especially missionaries, were at one time or another harassed, abused, vilified, stoned, jailed, and expelled; yet these same missionaries were simultaneously fed, clothed, housed, protected, and warned by generations of grateful and admiring members. In the nineteenth century, the Church was taken seriously, perhaps too seriously, by those in power. Many Europeans regarded the Church as a non-Christian American sect. Throughout Europe, where the marriage of church and state had been sanctified by tradition, political authority often took its cues on religious matters from a clergy made more vocal by declining influence.

Prominent Europeans visited Utah to get a firsthand view of this unusual and exotic LDS society. They admired the way the Saints had made the "desert . . . blossom as the rose" (Isa. 35:1), but found the people fanatical and their theology incomprehensible. Polygamy was considered especially uncivilized by Europeans, who viewed their own culture, especially near the end of the nineteenth century, as the apogee of civilization. For the European intelligentsia, the LDS Church was purely and distinctly an aberrational American phenomenon.

In spite of all this, the Church took hold in Europe, at least enough to strengthen the Church in America when strengthening was needed most, and also to lay a foundation for its own existence later on. Following their great successes in Great Britain in the 1830s and 1840s, the missionaries crossed the English Channel to work on the European mainland. The responses in Switzerland and Hamburg, Germany, were generally positive, with a foothold established in each of these areas. Less successful were the missions of Lorenzo SNOW in Italy and John TAYLOR in France, but even in those nations a few converts were made, from whom significant LDS posterities have grown. There was a slow but steady growth of the Church in Switzerland and Germany, especially after German unification in 1870. A mission was established in the Netherlands in the 1860s, and over the years thousands became Latter-day Saints and immigrated to Zion.

Results were not so encouraging in the huge Austro-Hungarian Empire of more than fifty million that sprawled over most of the map of East Central Europe. In 1865 President Brigham YOUNG sent one of the apostles, Orson Pratt, to open that empire to missionary work. Elder Pratt and his companion, William Riter, had little success, spending most of their time in jail. A later missionary, Thomas Biesinger, made scattered converts in Vienna and Prague; and a Hungarian convert, Misha Markow, traveled throughout most of the Balkan states and Russia, beginning in 1903, performing isolated baptisms and encountering ubiquitous opposition.

At the same time, attempts were made to breach the edges of the Islamic world in neighboring Turkey. A Swiss convert, Jacob Spori, established a mission there in 1884 with limited success (*see* MIDDLE EAST, THE CHURCH IN). After Spori baptized some Russians, Elder Francis M. Lyman, an apostle, and Joseph Cannon dedicated imperial Russia to preaching the gospel in 1903.

TWENTIETH CENTURY. For Europeans, Church members included, the dawning twentieth century would bring historic and cataclysmic changes. These included two devastating world wars with literally millions of casualties and a debilitating

depression in between, fascism and communism, the Cold War and Americanization, prosperity and the rebirth of Europe, and finally, by 1990, the extension of freedom and democracy to most of the people of the continent.

There were also significant changes in European LDS life. Emigration gradually declined, allowing the European population to grow and more permanent LDS congregations to emerge. New countries, first in the West, then later in the East, were opened to missionary work; and some, such as France, Belgium, and Italy, that had been opened but later closed, reopened and became more fruitful. Freedom of religion and the end of religious persecution spread as democracy overcame a variety of tyrannies. The discontinuance of polygamy and the accommodation to the broader palette of political realities in the world emphasizing the spiritual mission of the Church opened doors.

The defeat of Germany and the Central Powers in World War I, though viewed as a disaster for the people, did have a bit of a silver lining for the Church, especially in Central Europe. The coming of democracy to Germany and Austria permitted the return of missionaries. A vigorous branch was established in Vienna that would serve as a strong foundation for the Church in Austria. The rigors of war and defeat had produced a poverty and humility among the people that helped make them more receptive to the gospel message. Missionaries streamed into post-World War I Germany and,

Leipzig Relief Society (1907). Many residents of eastern Germany joined the Church in the late nineteenth and early twentieth century.

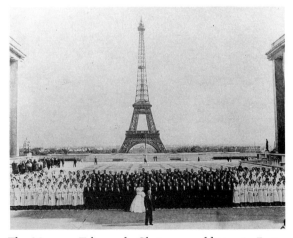

especially in the first years of the Weimar Republic, baptisms were at an all-time high. By 1930 there were more Latter-day Saints in Germany than in any other country outside the United States of America, and expectations ran high for continued growth.

The coming of Hitler to power changed life for the Church and its members, not only in Germany but eventually in the rest of Europe as well. Soon the omnipresent police state was making life in Germany more difficult for the Saints, especially the missionaries; many anticipated the Church would be closed down, but it never was. Both members and missionaries made every effort to get along with the regime while rejecting its excesses. What was important to them was to be able to continue to preach the gospel, to stay in the country, and to keep the branches together and prospering after so many years of struggle. Moreover, their numbers were small and they had little leverage with the regime. The Church grew slowly throughout Europe in the 1930s, and the growing tension in society made missionary work progressively more difficult.

In the fall of 1938, at the time of the Munich conference, missionaries were taken out of Germany temporarily; this became a valuable dress rehearsal for the situation a year later, when the Church was forced overnight to withdraw all missionaries from Germany and eventually from all of Europe. After European Mission President Thomas E. McKay left in April 1940, the local leaders of the Church units on the Continent were on their own throughout the war.

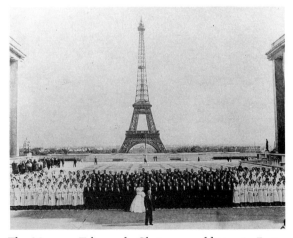

The Mormon Tabernacle Choir on world tour in Paris, 1955.

The cataclysm of World War II prompted Church leaders to send Elder Ezra Taft BENSON to Europe in 1946 to survey the damage, find the Saints, arrange for temporal help, and, most important, let them know that the Church cared about them. Elder Benson found decimated but devout congregations of Saints wherever he went, from England to Austria. He lamented over their circumstances and was inspired by their devotion. He also arranged for them to meet, and he set in motion the wheels that would bring the welfare supplies that had been accumulating in America to the needy in Europe. Years later, members vividly and gratefully remembered this mission of mercy and found in it hope and encouragement to face a difficult future; one non-Mormon German professor recalled having received his first pair of shoes after the war from the Mormons. Soon help began to pour in as CARE packages of relief supplies arrived from friends and fellow Saints in America. The Saints in the Netherlands, which had been invaded and occupied by Germany, sent potatoes. Trainloads of welfare supplies were sent from Utah to needy Mormons and non-Mormons alike. It was a great expression of Christianity in action, and the image of the Church in Europe began to change for the better as a result of its participation in this collective humanitarian effort.

Missionaries began to return to Europe as early as 1946. Soon missions were reestablished and some mission presidents had to locate scattered Saints, but others found things intact. Members met where they could, sometimes in bombed-out quarters, sometimes in members' apartments, and sometimes out in the open. A new mission was also established in Finland in 1947. During the first decade after the war, efforts focused again on the traditional interests of strengthening the Saints and gaining new ones.

Prior to the war, European members had never been able to attend a local Church temple. Many had been diligent in doing genealogical research, but unless they had immigrated to the United States or had been able to visit there, they had not had the opportunity to attend a temple and receive the blessings given only therein.

But all this was to change dramatically. Members in post-World War II Europe soon acquired all of the blessings and responsibilities of Saints in America. In 1952, a year after he became President of the Church, David O. MCKAY announced plans to build the first temple in Europe just outside of Bern, Switzerland. This temple was dedicated in September 1955; a second one was completed and opened near London in 1958. The building of these temples symbolized the inauguration of the new age for the Church in Europe. In the 1980s, the Church dedicated a temple in 1984 at Västerhaninge (near Stockholm), Sweden; in 1985 at Freiberg, then the German Democratic Republic (GDR); and in 1987 at Friedrichsdorf (near Frankfurt), then the Federal Republic of Germany.

Some other important changes were the creation of new missions and the establishment of Europe's first stake in 1961. In addition, the progress of secularization, with its emphasis on freedom of religion, the ecumenical spirit of Vatican II in the Roman Catholic Church, and the presence of American LDS service personnel helped to break down the traditional prejudices and make it possible for the Church to gain a real foothold in Italy, and later in Spain and Portugal. New vigor was experienced in France as baptisms increased; membership in France grew from 1,509 in 1960 to 8,606 in 1970. Most significant was the conviction that it was now possible to do missionary work among the Catholics of Western Europe in the same way, and with as encouraging results, as among Protestants.

The Saints became not only more numerous but also more prosperous and better educated; Europeans such as F. Enzio Busche (Germany), Charles A. Didier (Belgium), Derek A. Cuthbert (England), Jacob de Jager (the Netherlands), and Hans B. Ringger (Switzerland) were called as General Authorities. Stakes, wards, and new missions were organized with leadership essentially in local hands; European LDS youth were better educated in Church doctrine through the establishment of seminary and institute classes; a new and larger wave of missionaries from Europe joined the worldwide force; and Central and Eastern Europe were, especially after the political revolutions of 1989, opening their doors to the Church.

In Europe the image of the Latter-day Saints and the Church was changing. The coming of real democracy, with its basic human rights, including the freedom of religion; the pervasive influence of the United States as the primary defender of an exposed Europe in the Cold War; the mobility and growing prosperity that came to Europe; and the continuing growth of the Church generally gave it a more favorable press.

At the same time, the deepening Cold War made life progressively more difficult for some seven thousand Saints in the GDR. Strong anticommunist rhetoric from America, plus Russian influence and strong communist prejudices against churches and people of religious conviction, brought Latter-day Saints behind the Iron Curtain continued surveillance and harassment. The erection of the Berlin Wall in 1961 left them largely to their own devices, with only occasional visits by Church authorities from the West. Some, in order to make their peace with the new order, withdrew from Church fellowship, but a majority banded together to form a strong, cohesive LDS community.

In the 1960s, the Church began a vigorous program of building chapels for European congregations that helped to meet the needs of the Saints as well as to gain some respectability in society. By 1970 chapels dotted the Western European landscape; they attracted some positive outside attention and gave members a new sense of accomplishment. They also helped Saints begin to shed the "sect" image and mentality and to move more confidently into their various national societies after years of persecution and disrespect.

In an attempt to strengthen the LDS European youth, the seminary and institute programs of the Church were established in the early 1970s. These would help LDS families teach their children the gospel and prepare them for missions and lifetimes of service. Gradually, an increasing number of young men and women did serve missions. The 1970s also brought area conferences at which the European Saints were able to see how many of them there actually were and to be counseled anew by Church leaders to remain where they were and help strengthen the Church in their own areas.

EASTERN EUROPE. Prior to the 1960s, LDS success in Europe had been confined largely to the Protestant countries of Western Europe. A few converts, such as Janos Denndorfer, had been made in Hungary around the turn of the century, and a few others later in Czechoslovakia, but the turmoil of the first half of the twentieth century and the dropping of the Iron Curtain around Eastern Europe effectively precluded the early introduction of the gospel and Church into those countries.

In the 1960s, attempts were made to begin missionary work in Yugoslavia, but it was not until

The Swiss Temple in Zollikofen (near Bern, Switzerland, 1978) was dedicated in 1955 by President David O. McKay, with the Mormon Tabernacle Choir participating. This temple, built of white reinforced concrete with gold spire, was the first outside the United States and Canada. Courtesy Floyd Holdman.

Kresimir Cosic came to Brigham Young University, became a convert to the Church, and later was a basketball hero in his native country, that the Church could take hold there. A few missionaries were allowed to enter, but their opportunities to teach the people were circumscribed.

Vienna became the center of attempts by the Church to push into Central and Eastern Europe, much as it had been the capital of the polyglot Austro-Hungarian Empire of the nineteenth century. In the 1970s a few missionary couples were called to serve in Budapest, Hungary, and by the early 1980s they had established a branch comprised of more than one hundred capable, educated Hungarians. This gradual breakthrough almost exactly mirrored the gradual turning of Hungarian society and government away from the strict subservience to the Communist masters and toward the West.

For President Spencer W. Kimball, the need to preach the gospel everywhere in the world, especially in the large areas from which the Church had heretofore been excluded was a consuming passion. He had no political agenda. A major breakthrough came with the work of Ambassador David M. Kennedy in gaining official recognition of the Church in various areas and in the dedication of Poland for the preaching of the gospel by President Kimball in 1977. This represented a major change in Church policy toward communist governments and paved the way for even more significant opportunities in the late 1980s. It became the basis for a policy that allowed contacts with scattered Saints in Czechoslovakia and brought the Church recognition and respect from the communist leadership of the GDR, in all a breakthrough in that part of Europe. The most dramatic results of this changed relationship were the 1985 erection of the temple at Freiberg, GDR, wherein for the first time hundreds of lifelong Latter-day Saints were able to fulfill their dreams of temple worship, and the subsequent admission of LDS missionaries into the country for the first time in nearly forty years. In 1989 the first missionaries allowed to leave the GDR arrived in Salt Lake City to be sent throughout the world.

The nearly bloodless revolutions of 1989 presented the Church with an opportunity to begin a new epoch in Central and Eastern Europe. As the communist order crumbled and more democratic regimes were established in one country after another, one common demand was for freedom of religion. As a result, by the end of 1990 the Church in these countries existed under virtually the same conditions as in Western Europe and the United States. The reunification of Germany applied all of the rules of the Bonn Constitution to what had been the GDR. Missions have been established in Poland, Hungary, and Greece, and reestablished in Czechoslovakia. Leaders of these nations have welcomed Latter-day Saints because of their strong Judeo-Christian values and their wholesome families. Missionaries are currently proselytizing on a limited basis. Congregations of the Church have been officially recognized in the Soviet Union, and it has good prospects there, and in Yugoslavia, for the immediate future. Missionaries have been permitted into Romania and Bulgaria, the first significant breakthroughs in those countries. Thus, at the beginning of the 1990s, The Church of Jesus Christ of Latter-day Saints in Europe stands on a new threshold. Its major challenge, in both East and West, is to become better known and respected. Europeans are generally unaware of its dynamic worldwide growth, the nature of its teachings, or the quality of life it offers.

In Western Europe, the Church is growing slowly, with the exception of its clear success in Portugal, but a process of consolidation appears to be taking place. Strong second-, third-, and even fourth-generation LDS families are appearing everywhere. Church members are taking advantage of expanded opportunities for education, especially higher education, and are thus better able to contribute to and benefit from the prosperity of Western Europe. European Latter-day Saints are sending out more of their own as missionaries than ever before, and two and three generations of indigenous leaders are heading the Church in Europe.

Finally, from an LDS point of view, Europe is still divided. The Western countries are awash in secularism, prosperity, and religious apathy that pose a major challenge for the Church to find new ways to gain the interest and respect of these secular societies. For Central and Eastern Europe, the new decade and the coming new century will undoubtedly see thousands of new LDS converts and congregations. Perhaps even as the people in these countries have brought a new inspiration of freedom and human rights to the West, they will also bring a new spirit of religious desire that will benefit the Church.

BIBLIOGRAPHY

Babbel, Frederick W. *On Wings of Faith.* Salt Lake City, 1972.

"Encore of the Spirit," *Ensign* 21 (Oct. 1991): 32–53.

Sharffs, Gilbert W. *Mormonism in Germany.* Salt Lake City, 1970.

DOUGLAS F. TOBLER

EUTHANASIA

See: Death and Dying; Prolonging Life

EVANGELISTS

The sixth ARTICLE OF FAITH names evangelists together with APOSTLES, PROPHETS, and TEACHERS among the essential offices in the organization of the Church (cf. Eph. 4:11; Acts 21:8).

In an address on June 27, 1839, the Prophet Joseph SMITH identified the office of evangelist as a PATRIARCH, who as "the oldest man of the blood of Joseph or of the seed of Abraham" was to bless "the posterity of the Saints" as Jacob blessed his sons (*TPJS*, p. 151). This was the office of Patriarch to the Church. Evangelists, as patriarchs, had been ordained beginning in 1833, although not mentioned in REVELATION until 1835 (D&C 107:39–40).

Scholars have been unable to define precisely the role or office of the evangelist (Greek, *euaggelistēs*, "one bringing good tidings") in the NEW TESTAMENT. Apparently it was an office or activity that could be combined with the calling of BISHOP (2 Tim. 4:5). The sense of evangelist as an author of one of the canonical Gospels is late. The earliest known pagan and pre-Christian use of the term refers to a person who pronounced oracular statements (Kittel, 2:736).

Whatever the exact nature of the office, the early Christian evangelist was closely linked with apostles and prophets. He was viewed as one who carried on the work of the apostles, but always in a charismatic or prophetic office. One New Testament reference hints that Philip was an evangelist, and mentions his four daughters, who "did prophesy" (Acts 21:8–9).

BIBLIOGRAPHY

Kittel, R. *Theological Dictionary of The New Testament.* Grand Rapids, Mich., 1964.

R. DOUGLAS PHILLIPS

EVE

Eve, first woman of earthly creation, companion of ADAM, and mother and matriarch of the human race, is honored by Latter-day Saints as one of the most important, righteous, and heroic of all the human family. Eve's supreme gift to mankind, the opportunity of life on this earth, resulted from her choice to become mortal.

Eve, Adam, Abraham, and others were among the noble and great ones involved with the creation of the earth (Abr. 3:22–24; cf. McConkie, p. 59). God foreordained her and named her Eve, "the Mother of All Living"; in the GARDEN OF EDEN Adam called her Eve, reflecting that calling (Moses 4:26). She was created spiritually and physically in the same manner as was Adam (*MD*, p. 242). God called *their* name Adam, and "in the image of his own body, male and female, created he them" (Moses 6:9).

Eve and Adam faced a dilemma as they sought to obey God's commandments. They could not keep the primary commandment to have children as long as they remained nonmortals in the Garden (2 Ne. 2:22–23). The instruction not to eat of the tree of knowledge of good and evil, however, was uniquely modified with the words "nevertheless, thou mayest choose for thyself" (Moses 3:16–17), and becoming mortal was expressly stated as the consequence.

Satan was present to tempt Adam and Eve, much as he would try to thwart others in their divine missions: "And he sought also to beguile Eve, for he knew not the mind of God, wherefore he sought to destroy the world" (Moses 4:6; cf. Matt. 4:3–11; Moses 1:12–22; JS—H 1:15–16). Eve faced the choice between selfish ease and unselfishly facing tribulation and death (Widtsoe, p. 193). As befit her calling, she realized that there was no other way and deliberately chose mortal life so as to further the purpose of God and bring children into the world.

The Church of Jesus Christ of Latter-day Saints strongly affirms that in partaking of the fruit of the tree of knowledge of good and evil, Eve along with Adam acted in a manner pleasing to God and in accord with his ordained plan (see FALL OF ADAM). Brigham YOUNG explained: "The Lord knew they would do this and he had designed that they should" (JD 10:103). "We should never blame Mother Eve, not the least" (JD 13:145). Adam and Eve "accepted a great challenge. . . . They chose wisely in accordance with the heavenly law of love for others" (Widtsoe, p. 194). Afterward, in one of the earliest recorded statements in scripture, Eve recounted the PLAN OF SALVATION as she expounded on the joy prepared for humankind in eternity: "Were it not for our transgression we never should have had seed, and never should have known good and evil, and the joy of our redemption, and the eternal life which God giveth unto all the obedient" (Moses 5:10–11).

Loving parents in heaven prepared Eve and Adam for their roles in MORTALITY. After the Fall, God gave Adam and Eve the law of SACRIFICE so that they could obtain forgiveness of sins committed in mortality (Moses 5:5). He placed enmity (an abhorrence of evil) between Eve's seed and Satan and his followers (Moses 4:21). God granted to Eve the powers of motherhood, disclosing the difficult labor of childbirth. The Hebrew word rendered "sorrow" (Gen. 3:16–17) does not connote "sadness," but "labor," or "sweat," or "pain."

Adam and Eve were husband and wife. While in the Garden, God sealed them in eternal marriage (Gen. 2:22–24). God instructed Eve, "Thy desire shall be to thy husband, and he shall rule over thee" (Gen. 3:16). President Spencer W. KIMBALL explained that the Hebrew word translated as "rule" would better be understood as "'preside' because that's what he does" (Ensign [Mar. 1976]:72), and the husband presides only in righteousness (see FAMILY: TEACHINGS ABOUT). Correlatively, God introduced Eve to Adam in terms that are rendered into English by the phrase "an help meet for him"; these words mean "to be strong, to help, rescue, or save" and "to meet, to correspond to, to be equal," thus indicating that Eve was to be a strong, saving partner in righteousness (Gen. 2:18).

The Lord himself made coats of skins and clothed Adam and Eve (Moses 4:27). Eve bore unto Adam sons and daughters. She worked with Adam. They prayed to the Lord and heard his voice (Moses 5:4–5). They made "all things known" to their children and taught them to read, write, and to keep records of family remembrance (Moses 5:12; 6:5–6).

Eve is a "joint-participant with Adam in all his ministry, [and] will inherit jointly with him all the blessings appertaining to his high state of exaltation" (MD, p. 242). President Joseph F. SMITH saw her in vision in 1918: among the great and mighty ones in the celestial congregation of the righteous, he beheld "our glorious Mother Eve, with many of her faithful daughters who had lived through the ages and worshipped the true and living God" (D&C 138:39).

The fall of Eve and Adam is profoundly significant: they opened the way of mortality for all humankind, and they subjected themselves to death in order to make continued progression toward eternal life possible. Mother Eve bestowed upon her daughters and sons a heritage of honor, for she acted with wisdom, love, and unselfish sacrifice.

BIBLIOGRAPHY

McConkie, Bruce R. "Eve and the Fall." In Woman, pp. 57–68. Salt Lake City, 1979.

Nibley, Hugh W. "Patriarchy and Matriarchy." CWHN 1:87–114.

Smith, Joseph Fielding. "Was the Fall of Adam Necessary?" Answers to Gospel Questions, Vol. 4, pp. 79–83. Salt Lake City, 1963.

Widtsoe, John A. "Was the 'Fall' Inevitable?" Evidences and Reconciliations, pp. 192–95. Salt Lake City, 1987.

BEVERLY CAMPBELL

EVENING AND THE MORNING STAR, THE

The Evening and The Morning Star was the first newspaper of The Church of Jesus Christ of Latter-day Saints. It was published in fourteen eight-paged, double-columned monthly issues in Independence, Missouri, from June 1832 to July 1833. When the press in Missouri was destroyed by a mob, publication was resumed several months later in Kirtland, Ohio, with ten issues published from December 1833 to September 1834. W. W. (William Wines) Phelps, its editor in Missouri, printed in it a brief history of the Church, a number of LDS hymns, instructions to members of the Church, letters reporting its progress throughout the country, and many of the revelations received by the Prophet Joseph Smith. Oliver COWDERY, its editor in Ohio, printed reports and commentaries about the Saints' difficulties in Missouri and some of the doctrinal writings of Sidney RIGDON, a counselor in the First Presidency.

Because the circulation of the Missouri-printed *Star* was small and localized, Cowdery reprinted all the original twenty-four issues in Kirtland between January 1835 and October 1836, in a new sixteen-page format, with numerous grammatical improvements, and a few articles deleted. *The Evening and the Morning Star* was succeeded by the *Latter Day Saints' Messenger and Advocate* in October 1834 (HC 2:167).

[*See also* Messenger and Advocate.]

RONALD D. DENNIS

EVIL

[*The LDS concept of evil is also explained in the article on Devils. The following article discusses a view of the purposes of evil and presents an LDS response to traditional discussions of the problem of evil.*]

In ordinary discourse, the term "evil" has a very wide definition and, along with the term "bad," is used in English most often to refer to morally wrong intentions, choices, and actions of agents (moral evil); to the operations of nonhuman nature such as disease, earthquakes, volcanic eruptions, and tornadoes (natural evil); and to the human and animal pain and suffering (psychological evil) that moral and natural evils may cause. In more techni-cal philosophical discourse, it is applied also to inherent human limitations and defects (metaphysical evil).

The term is used with additional meanings in LDS scripture and discourse. In the Old Testament, the term is translated from the Hebrew term, *ra'*, and its cognates, whose applications range widely from (1) what tastes nasty or is ugly, displeasing, or sad, through (2) moral wickedness and the distress, misery, and tragedy that ensue from it, to (3) willful disobedience of God and his intentions for human beings. The latter two senses of the term predominate in the New Testament and in latter-day scriptures. Given its widely variant meanings, the precise meaning of evil must be ascertained from its context.

LDS scripture further illuminates biblical suggestions about God's purposes for his children and, thereby, helps to clarify one fundamental sense of evil. God disclosed to Moses: "This is my work and my glory—to bring to pass the immortality [resurrection, with everlasting bodily duration] and eternal life [Godlike quality or mode of being] of man" (Moses 1:39). Thus, anything inconsistent with, contrary to, or opposed to the achievement of these ends would be evil.

There seems to be no basis in latter-day scripture for either the privative or relativistic views of evil advocated by some philosophers. In the fifth century, St. Augustine, puzzled by the existence of evil in a world that was created by God, concluded that evil must not be a substance or a positive reality in its own right, but only the absence of good (*privatio boni*). Yet, in the Old and New Testaments, evil is depicted as menacingly real, a view shared by latter-day scripture. Nor is there any scriptural evidence that good and evil are simply matters of personal preference. Rejecting this kind of relativism, Proverbs declares, "There is a way which seemeth right unto a man, but the end thereof are the ways of death" (Prov. 14:12); and Isaiah warns, "Woe unto them that call evil good, and good evil; that put darkness for light, and light for darkness; that put bitter for sweet, and sweet for bitter!" (Isa. 5:20). Relativism is also rejected in latter-day scripture (2 Ne. 28:8).

Nonbelievers and believers alike often question why God would allow evil of any kind to exist. The question becomes especially acute within an Augustinian worldview that affirms God to be the ex nihilo or absolute creator of whatever exists other than himself. On that premise it appears that God is the *ultimate* source or cause of all evil, or, at least, a knowing accessory before the fact, and thus omniresponsible for all evils that occur.

Latter-day Saints reject the troublesome premise of creation ex nihilo (out of nothing), affirming rather that there are actualities that are coeternal with God. These coeternal actualities include INTELLIGENCES (sometimes perceived as primal selves or persons), chaotic matter (or mass energy), and laws and principles (perhaps best regarded as the properties and relations of matter and intelligences). Given this plurality of uncreated entities, it does not follow, within an LDS worldview, that God is the ultimate source of evil. Evil is traceable, alternatively, to the choices of other autonomous agents (such as Lucifer, the Devil) who are also coeternal with God, and, perhaps, even to recalcitrant properties of uncreated chaotic matter.

Though on the basis of latter-day revelation it is evident that God is neither the source nor the cause of either moral or natural evil, the question still arises as to why he does not prevent or eliminate it. The ancient philosopher Epicurus posed the problem in the form of a dilemma: Either God is unwilling to prevent the evil that occurs or he is unable to prevent it. If he is unable, then he is not omnipotent; if he is unwilling, then he is not perfectly good. Epicurus' statement of the dilemma is based on two assumptions: (1) a perfectly good being prevents all the evil it can; and (2) an omnipotent being can do anything and, hence, can prevent all evil.

From an LDS perspective the first assumption appears to be false. A perfectly good being would certainly wish to maximize the good, but if, in the nature of things, allowing an experience of evil were a necessary condition of achieving the greatest good, a perfectly good being would allow it. For example, it seems evident that the existence of OPPOSITION and TEMPTATION is a necessary condition for the expression of morally significant FREEDOM and the development of genuinely righteous personalities (see 2 Ne. 2:11–16; Moses 6:55).

Latter-day Saints would also reject the second assumption. Since there are realities that are coeternal with God, his omnipotence must be understood not as the power to bring about any state of affairs absolutely, but rather as the power to bring about any state of affairs consistent with the natures of coeternal realities. This insight makes possible an instrumentalist view of evil. With Epicurus' basic assumptions thus modified by latter-day revelation, it seems possible to construct a coherent LDS concept of the nature, use, and existence of evil (*see* THEODICY).

[*See also* Great and Abominable Church; Sin; War in Heaven.]

DAVID L. PAULSEN

EVOLUTION

The position of the Church on the origin of man was published by the First Presidency in 1909 and stated again by a different First Presidency in 1925:

> The Church of Jesus Christ of Latter-day Saints, basing its belief on divine revelation, ancient and modern, declares man to be the direct and lineal offspring of Deity. . . . Man is the child of God, formed in the divine image and endowed with divine attributes (*see* Appendix, "Doctrinal Expositions of the First Presidency").

The scriptures tell why man was created, but they do not tell how, though the Lord has promised that he will tell that when he comes again (D&C 101:32–33). In 1931, when there was intense discussion on the issue of organic evolution, the First Presidency of the Church, then consisting of Presidents Heber J. Grant, Anthony W. Ivins, and Charles W. Nibley, addressed all of the General Authorities of the Church on the matter, and concluded,

> Upon the fundamental doctrines of the Church we are all agreed. Our mission is to bear the message of the restored gospel to the world. Leave geology, biology, archaeology, and anthropology, no one of which has to do with the salvation of the souls of mankind, to scientific research, while we magnify our calling in the realm of the Church. . . .
>
> Upon one thing we should all be able to agree, namely, that Presidents Joseph F. Smith, John R. Winder, and Anthon H. Lund were right when they said: "Adam is the primal parent of our race" [First Presidency Minutes, Apr. 7, 1931].

WILLIAM E. EVENSON

EXALTATION

To Latter-day Saints, exaltation is a state that a person can attain in becoming like God—SALVATION in the ultimate sense (D&C 132:17). Latter-day Saints believe that all mankind (except the SONS OF PERDITION) will receive varying DEGREES OF GLORY in the AFTERLIFE. Exaltation is the greatest of all the gifts and attainments possible. It is available only in the highest degree of the CELESTIAL KINGDOM and is reserved for members of the CHURCH OF THE FIRSTBORN. This exalted status, called ETERNAL LIFE, is available to be received by a man and wife. It means not only living in God's presence, but receiving power to do as God does, including the power to bear children after the resurrection (*TPJS*, pp. 300–301; D&C 132:19). Blessings and privileges of exaltation require unwavering faith, repentance, and complete obedience to the GOSPEL OF JESUS CHRIST.

In a revelation to the Prophet Joseph SMITH, the Savior stated the following conditions: "Strait is the gate, and narrow the way that leadeth unto the exaltation and continuation of the lives, and few there be that find it, because ye receive me not in the world neither do ye know me" (D&C 132:22).

All Church ORDINANCES lead to exaltation, and the essential crowning ordinances are the ENDOWMENT and the eternal MARRIAGE covenant of the TEMPLE (D&C 131:1–4, 132).

MARGARET MCCONKIE POPE

EXCOMMUNICATION

See: Disciplinary Procedures

EXHIBITIONS AND WORLD'S FAIRS

From its beginnings, the Church has characteristically presented its message through personal contact or in small groups: Faith and testimony are interpersonal. The Church has placed extensive emphasis on the mass media, and in participating in exhibits such as world's fairs. In addition, in recent years these activities have provided the Church an opportunity to present the message of the gospel amid milestone presentations of the arts, the sciences, and industry. The witness of the

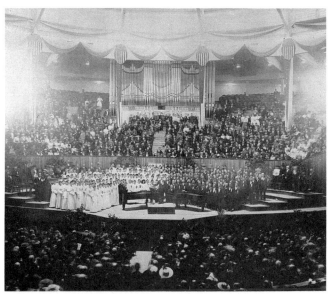

The Mormon Tabernacle Choir, under the direction of Evan Stephens, with soloists Robert C. Easton, Nellie Druce-Pugsley, and others, won second place in the competition for the Eisteddfod International Prize at the 1893 Columbian World's Fair in Chicago. Photographer: James H. Crockwell.

living and revealed Jesus Christ has been implicit in all Church exhibits, with two related themes given prominence: life's greatest questions—Where did I come from? Why am I here? What follows death?—and family values.

The first Church participation in a world's fair on a truly international scale was at the World's Columbian Exposition in Chicago in 1893, where the Mormon Tabernacle Choir won high honors in the choral competition. The Church later sponsored booths in several expositions and fairs, including the International Hygiene Exposition at Dresden, Germany, in 1930, and the Century of Progress Exposition in Chicago in 1933–1934. Exhibits were also mounted at international expositions held in San Diego in 1935–1936 and San Francisco in 1939–1940.

The Church's participation in the New York World's Fair in 1964 was a major effort. Its pavilion was a full-size replica of the three east towers of the Salt Lake Temple. Original paintings, the presentation of the film MAN'S SEARCH FOR HAPPINESS, and a replica of the Thorvaldson CHRISTUS STATUE were featured. A large staff of trained volunteer guides conducted tours and question-and-answer sessions for the more than six million visitors who came to the pavilion.

Exhibits have since been presented at fair pavilions in Montreal, Canada; Osaka, Japan; San Antonio, Texas; and Seattle, Washington. Some of the exhibit artifacts have since been placed in VISITORS CENTERS throughout the world.

RICHARD J. MARSHALL

EXTERMINATION ORDER

A military order signed by Missouri Governor Lilburn W. Boggs on October 27, 1838, directed that the Mormons be driven from the state or exterminated (*see* MISSOURI CONFLICT). Boggs's action was based on information brought to him that day by two citizens of Richmond, Missouri, concerning the Mormon–Missourian conflicts in northwest Missouri and on reports of the Battle of Crooked River, in which armed Mormons had clashed with a company of state militia on October 25.

Boggs, acting in his capacity as commander-in-chief of the Missouri militia, ordered General John B. Clark to march to Ray County with a division of militia to carry out operations against armed Mormons. The order described the Mormons as being in "open and avowed defiance of the laws, and of having made war upon the people of this State." It stated that "the Mormons must be treated as enemies, and must be exterminated or driven from the State if necessary for the public peace—their outrages are beyond all description."

A copy of the order reached General Samuel D. Lucas of the state militia by the time he encamped outside the LDS town of Far West, in Caldwell County, on October 31. Lucas gave a copy to the LDS Colonel George M. Hinkle and other Church representatives, to whom he dictated terms of surrender, and they showed it to Joseph SMITH. It was probably a significant factor in the Prophet's decision to surrender to Lucas.

Following Joseph Smith's surrender, arrest, and imprisonment, the governor's order was carried out by a combination of militia troops and vigilantes. It culminated in the forcible removal from Missouri of virtually all members of the Church during the winter and early spring of 1838–1839.

The legality and propriety of Boggs's order were vigorously debated in the Missouri legislature during its 1839 session. The order was supported by most northwest Missouri citizens, but was questioned or denounced by others. However, no determination of the order's legality was ever made.

On June 25, 1976, Governor Christopher S. Bond issued an executive order rescinding the Extermination Order, recognizing its legal invalidity and formally apologizing in behalf of the state of Missouri for the suffering it had caused the Latter-day Saints.

BIBLIOGRAPHY

"Document Containing the Correspondence, Orders, etc. in Relation to the Disturbances with the Mormons; and the Evidence Given before the Hon. Austin A. King." Office of the Boon's Lick Democrat, Fayette, Mo., 1841, p. 61 (contains full text of the order).

Gentry, Leland H. "A History of the Latter-day Saints in Northern Missouri from 1836 to 1839." Ph.D. diss., Brigham Young University, 1965.

LeSueur, Stephen C. *The 1838 Mormon War in Missouri.* Columbia, Mo., 1987.

DALE A. WHITMAN

EZEKIEL, PROPHECIES OF

The prophecies of Ezekiel (593–c. 570 B.C.) interest Latter-day Saints because they contain unique insights into aspects of God's saving work with his children, such as the responsibilities of a watchman or leader (chaps. 3, 33), the nature of personal AGENCY and ACCOUNTABILITY (chap. 18), divine mercy and forgiveness (chap. 18), and God's covenant relationships with Israel and Judah (chaps. 34–39). The principal attention of most Latter-day Saints to the book of Ezekiel focuses on chapters 34–48 because they shed light on God's latter-day work, including Israel's return to its land, the restoration of the land to full productivity, the rebuilding of the temple as a residence for God, and the appearance of important records that they identify with the Bible and Book of Mormon.

In chapter 34, Ezekiel described the scattering of Israelites among the nations of the earth as a leadership failure—Israel's "shepherds" had exploited rather than cared for the "sheep" (*see* ISRAEL: SCATTERING OF ISRAEL). Consequently, the Lord will become the Shepherd to seek out lost sheep and gather "them from the countries . . . to their own land" (34:11, 13). Finally a latter-day David will become their leader (34:24), the sterility of the land will be overcome (36:8–11), the Dead Sea will support fishing (47:1, 7–10), and Israel, as well as the nations, will know that the Lord is with them and "They shall know that I am the Lord" (34:23–28, 30).

Chapters 35–36 reflect the tensions that will develop when returning Israelites find their land inhabited by others who claim it as their own (35:10, 12, 15; 36:2–5). The Lord, however, promised that he would divide the land "by lot" among the returning Israelites for their inheritance, at the same time assuring any non-Israelites living in their midst that they, too, would be granted an "inheritance . . . among the tribes of Israel" (47:22 [13–23]).

The Lord emphasized how real this gathering would be (37:1–14). As in the Resurrection, scattered Israelites, like individual dry bones, might still hope to be formed into one body—with sinews and flesh, breath, and spirit—once more in their own land. The Resurrection thus serves as a metaphor of the gathering as well as a means whereby it will be accomplished, as promised by the Lord: "I will open your graves, and cause you to come up out of your graves, and bring you into the land of Israel" (37:12).

After Israelites gather and prosper, they will live peacefully in "unwalled villages," "at rest," dwelling "safely," "without walls" (38:11). At this point, they will be attacked by Gog, whose goal is to plunder their prosperous land. In the battles that follow, the Lord will refine Israel while bringing judgment against the nations—both those who attack Israel and those who live in distant lands (cf. Isa. 4:4; Zech. 12:2–3; 14:2–3; Zeph. 3:8; Ezek. 39:2–4, 6, 11, 21–24). Jerusalem will be rebuilt as a divine center, God's temple will be erected in their midst (chaps. 40–47), and he will reside there, so that Jerusalem will be "called Holy, for the Lord shall be there" (JST Ezek. 48:35).

In this gathering context, Ezekiel spoke of the unification of the so-called "sticks" of Judah and Ephraim (i.e., Israel), a joining that signals not only the beginning of the gathering of Israel (Ezek. 37:15–22; cf. 3 Ne. 20:46; 21:1–3, 7–13) but also the means by which the ultimate gathering—of peoples back to God—will be accomplished (cf. 1 Ne. 22:12; 2 Ne. 6:11).

Latter-day Saints identify Judah's record as the Bible and Ephraim's record as the Book of Mormon (D&C 27:5). They understand that when the Book of Mormon was translated and published, it became possible to join the two records. And since the stated purpose of the Book of Mormon is to convince "Jew and Gentile that Jesus is the Christ, the Eternal God, manifesting himself unto all nations" (title page of the Book of Mormon), they see this joining of testimonies as being a principal means whereby Israel will be brought back to God (*see* BOOK OF MORMON, BIBLICAL PROPHECIES ABOUT).

BIBLIOGRAPHY

Meservy, Keith H. "Ezekiel's Sticks and the Gathering of Israel." *Ensign* 17 (Feb. 1987):4–13.

Sperry, Sidney B. *The Voice of Israel's Prophets*, pp. 218–37. Salt Lake City, 1952.

KEITH H. MESERVY

EZIAS

Ezias was a prophet of Old Testament times whose prophecies were apparently recorded on the PLATES of brass, a record brought to the Western Hemisphere by the Book of Mormon prophet LEHI. Ezias was mentioned by NEPHI₂ (c. 22 B.C.) in a list of prophets who testified of the coming ministry and redemption of Christ (Hel. 8:13–20).

MELVIN J. THORNE

F

FAITH IN JESUS CHRIST

Faith in Jesus Christ is the first principle of the GOSPEL OF JESUS CHRIST (A of F 4). One who has this faith believes him to be the living Son of God, trusts in his goodness and power, repents of one's sins, and follows his guidance. Faith in the Lord Jesus Christ is awakened as individuals hear his gospel (Rom. 10:17). By faith they enter the gate of REPENTANCE and BAPTISM, and receive the GIFT OF THE HOLY GHOST, which leads to the way of life ordained by Christ (2 Ne. 31:9, 17–18). Those who respond are "alive in Christ because of [their] faith" (2 Ne. 25:25). Because God's way is the only way that leads to salvation, "it is impossible to please him" without faith (Heb. 11:6). Faith must precede miracles, signs, gifts of the Spirit, and righteousness, for "if there be no faith . . . God can do no miracle" (Ether 12:12). The Book of Mormon prophet MORONI₂ summarized these points:

> The Lord God prepareth the way that the residue of men may have faith in Christ, that the Holy Ghost may have place in their hearts, according to the power thereof; and after this manner bringeth to pass the Father, the covenants which he hath made unto the children of men. And Christ hath said: If ye will have faith in me ye shall have power to do whatsoever thing is expedient in me. And he hath said: Repent all ye ends of the earth, and come unto me, and be baptized in my name, and have faith in me, that ye may be saved [Moro. 7:32–34].

Although in common speech people speak of having faith in people, principles, or things, faith in its eternal sense is faith in, and only in, Jesus Christ. It is not sufficient to have faith in just anything; it must be focused on "the only true God, and Jesus Christ" whom he has sent (John 17:3). Having faith means having complete confidence in Jesus Christ alone to save humankind from sin and the finality of death. By his grace "are ye saved through faith" (Eph. 2:8). If "Christ be not risen," then "your faith is also vain" and "ye are yet in your sins" (1 Cor. 15:14, 17). To trust in the powers of this world is to "trust in the arm of flesh" and, in effect, to reject Christ and his gospel (2 Ne. 4:34).

Paul explained, "Now faith is the substance [or assurance] of things hoped for, the evidence [the demonstration or proof] of things not seen" (Heb. 11:1). Mortals must live by faith, since divine realities are veiled from their physical senses. The invisible truths of the gospel are made manifest by the Holy Spirit and are seen in the lives of people who live by faith, following the daily directions of that Spirit. Though most mortals have not seen the spiritual realities beyond this physical world, they can accept such premises in faith, based on personal spiritual witness(es) and the scriptural record of former and latter-day special witnesses whom God has called and who have experienced these realities firsthand.

True faith is belief plus action. Faith implies not only the mental assent or cognition of belief

Christ Healing the Blind Man, by Carl Heinrich Bloch (1834–1890; oil on copper plate; 20″ × 30″). Jesus heals a man blind from birth (John 9). Healings and other miracles are one manifestation of faith in the Lord Jesus Christ. Courtesy the Frederiksborg Museum, Hillerød, Denmark.

but also its implementation. Beliefs in things both spiritual and secular impel people to act. Failure to act on the teachings and commandments of Christ implies absence of faith in him. Faith in Jesus Christ impels people to act in behalf of Christ, to follow his example, to do his works. Jesus said, "Not every one that saith unto me, Lord, Lord, shall enter into the kingdom of heaven; but he that *doeth* the will of my Father which is in heaven" (Matt. 7:21; italics added). James further emphasized that "faith, if it hath not works, is dead, being alone. Yea, a man may say, Thou hast faith, and I have works: shew me thy faith without thy works, and I will shew thee my faith by my works" (James 2:17–18; *see also* GRACE).

Righteousness leads to greater faith, while sin and wickedness diminish faith. "The just [man] shall live by his faith" (Hab. 2:4). Violating the commandments of God brings a loss of the Spirit of the Lord and a loss of faith, for faith in Jesus Christ is incompatible with disobedience. The Book of Mormon prophet ALMA₂ characterized the words of Christ as a seed that is tested as people plant it

in their hearts and nourish it. If they desire to see the seed grow, they must give it room and nourish it with their faith. If it is a good seed, it will swell and grow, and they will know that it is good. However, if they neglect the seed, it will wither away. But if they will "nourish the word . . . by [their] faith with great diligence," it will grow into a tree of life, and they will taste its fruit, which is eternal life (Alma 32:26–43).

Faith may be nurtured and renewed through scripture study, prayer, and works consistent with the commandments of the gospel. Because those who act on faith, repent, and are baptized receive a remission of sins, they have reason to hope for eternal life (Moro. 7:41). With this hope, their faith in Jesus Christ further inspires individuals to minister to each other in CHARITY, even as Christ would have done (Moro. 7:44), for the "end of the commandment is charity out of . . . faith unfeigned" (1 Tim. 1:5). "Charity is the pure love of Christ, and it endureth forever" (Moro. 7:47). Thus, faith, or "steadfastness in Christ," enables people to ENDURE TO THE END, continuing in faith and charity (2 Ne. 31:20; 1 Tim. 2:15; D&C 20:29). True faith is enduring and leads to an assurance that one's efforts have not gone unnoticed and that God is pleased with one's attitude and effort to implement the principles of the gospel of Jesus Christ in one's personal life.

While Alma explained how faith leads to knowledge, modern LDS commentary also points out how certain kinds of knowledge strengthen faith (*MD*, pp. 261–67). The knowledge that God exists, a correct understanding of his character, and a reassurance that he approves of one's conduct can help one's faith "become perfect and fruitful, abounding in righteousness" ("Lectures on Faith," pp. 65–66; *see* LECTURES ON FAITH).

The restoration of the gospel in modern times was initiated by an act of faith by the youthful Joseph Smith. Reading the Bible, he was struck by the encouragement of James to all who lack wisdom that they should "ask in faith, nothing wavering" (James 1:6). The visions that came to Joseph Smith in answer to his prayers (*see* VISIONS OF JOSEPH SMITH) are evidence that prayers are "answered according to [one's] faith" (Mosiah 27:14). Though God delights to bless his children, he "first, [tries] their faith, . . . then shall the greater things be made manifest" (3 Ne. 26:9). But there will be "no witness until after the trial of your faith" (Ether 12:6), and "without faith you can do nothing" (D&C 8:10). "Signs come by faith, not by the will of men" (D&C 63:10).

Because faith involves the guidance of the Holy Ghost to individuals, it leads them by an invisible hand to "the unity of the faith" (Eph. 4:13). Through the strength of others and increased confidence in the Lord's way, faith provides a shield against the adversary (Eph. 6:16). Similarly, faith has been described as part of one's armor, serving as a "breastplate of faith and love" (1 Thes. 5:8) in protecting the faithful from evil.

BIBLIOGRAPHY

Benson, Ezra Taft. *The Teachings of Ezra Taft Benson*, pp. 65–69. Salt Lake City, 1988.

Kimball, Spencer W. *Faith Precedes the Miracle*. Salt Lake City, 1973.

"Lectures on Faith." In *The Lectures on Faith in Historical Perspective*, ed. L. Dahl and C. Tate, pp. 29–104. Provo, Utah, 1990.

DOUGLAS E. BRINLEY

FALL OF ADAM

Latter-day Saints recognize the fall of ADAM and EVE as an actual event that occurred in the GARDEN OF EDEN and has affected the entire earth and everyone in the human family. The Fall was a necessary step in the eternal progress of mankind and introduced the conditions that made the mission of Jesus Christ absolutely necessary for SALVATION. The four STANDARD WORKS and the teachings of many prominent leaders of the Church are the sources for the LDS doctrine of the Fall. These sources dwell at length on the beneficial effects of the Fall as part of God's "great plan of happiness" (Alma 42:8) for his children and testify that Adam and Eve are to be honored for their actions (*see* PLAN OF SALVATION; PURPOSE OF EARTH LIFE).

The creation of the earth was a multistep process in which the fall of Adam and Eve and their expulsion from the Garden of Eden were the final necessary steps in bringing about the mortal condition. Without the Fall, Adam and Eve would have had no children (2 Ne. 2:23); hence, the human family would not have come into existence upon this earth under the conditions and circumstances in the garden. The prophet LEHI explained, "Adam fell that men might be" (2 Ne. 2:25), and ENOCH declared, "Because that Adam fell, we are" (Moses 6:48).

After the Fall, Adam and Eve were taught the gospel of Jesus Christ and rejoiced in their situation. Adam blessed God, saying, "Because of my transgression my eyes are opened, and in this life I shall have joy, and again in the flesh I shall see God" (Moses 5:10). And Eve was glad, saying, "Were it not for our transgression we never should have had seed, and never should have known good and evil, and the joy of our redemption, and the eternal life which God giveth unto all the obedient" (Moses 5:11).

The Fall was not an accident, not an obstruction to God's plan, and not a wrong turn in the course of humanity. "The Lord . . . created the earth that it should be inhabited" by his children (1 Ne. 17:36), and since Adam and Eve would have had no children in their Edenic condition, the Fall was a benefit to mankind. It was part of the Father's plan, being both foreknown to him and essential to the human family. All these things were "done in the wisdom of him who knoweth all things" (2 Ne. 2:24).

The Fall brought two kinds of death upon Adam, Eve, and their posterity: the separation of the spirit and the physical body, which the scriptures call the "temporal death" (Alma 11:42–43); and being shut out of God's presence, which is called SPIRITUAL DEATH (2 Ne. 9:6; D&C 29:41). Jesus Christ redeems all mankind unconditionally from the two deaths brought by the fall of Adam (*see* ORIGINAL SIN), raises all mankind from the grave, and restores them to God's presence for a judgment (Hel. 14:16–17). The Atonement also redeems individuals from the consequences of their own sins on conditions of repentance.

The Book of Mormon explains, "The natural man is an enemy to God, and has been from the fall of Adam, and will be, forever and ever, unless he yields to the enticings of the Holy Spirit, and putteth off the natural man and becometh a saint through the atonement of Christ the Lord" (Mosiah 3:19; cf. Alma 22:14; 42:9–15). God "created Adam, and by Adam came the fall of man. And because of the fall of man came Jesus Christ, . . . and because of Jesus Christ came the redemption of man" (Morm. 9:12; cf. 2 Ne. 9:6).

The Doctrine and Covenants states that the Fall occurred as a result of transgression: "The devil tempted Adam, and he partook of the forbidden fruit and transgressed the commandment. . . . Wherefore, I, the Lord God, caused that he should be cast out from the Garden of Eden, from my presence, because of his transgression, wherein he became spiritually dead" (D&C 29:40–41). Thereafter, God sent angels to teach Adam and his seed "repentance and redemption, through faith on the name of mine Only Begotten Son" (D&C 29:42; cf. Moses 5:6–8).

The Fall was not a sin against chastity. Adam and Eve were "man and wife" and were commanded by God to multiply (Gen. 1:27–28; Moses 3:21–25; Abr. 5:14–19). Joseph Fielding SMITH, an apostle explained, "The transgression of Adam did *not* involve sex sin as some falsely believe and teach. Adam and Eve were married by the Lord while they were yet immortal beings in the Garden of Eden and before death entered the world" (*DS* 1:114–15; cf. *JC*, pp. 29–31).

An inseparable relationship between the fall of Adam and the ATONEMENT OF JESUS CHRIST is established in ancient and modern scripture. Paul's summation is, "For as in Adam all die, even so in Christ shall all be made alive" (1 Cor. 15:22). Latter-day revelation further emphasizes that Christ will redeem all things from death and the effects of the Fall.

The Prophet Joseph SMITH taught that Adam's role was "to open the way of the world" (*TPJS*, p. 12); thus, he was the first man to enter mortality, and the fall of Adam has a mortal effect upon the entire earth. The earth shall die (D&C 88:25–26), but through the atoning power of Jesus Christ "the earth will be renewed and receive its paradisiacal glory" (A of F 10). "All things shall become new, even the heaven and the earth, and all the fulness thereof, both men and beasts, the fowls of the air, and the fishes of the sea; and not one hair, neither mote, shall be lost, for it is the workmanship of mine hand" (D&C 29:24–25; cf. 101:24–26; Isa. 51:6).

As Lehi declared, "If Adam had not transgressed he would not have fallen, but he would have remained in the Garden of Eden. And all things which were created must have remained in the same state in which they were after they were created; and they must have remained forever, and had no end" (2 Ne. 2:22; cf. Moses 3:9). Various interpretations have been suggested concerning the nature of life on the earth before the Fall and how the Fall physically affected the world, but these go beyond the clearly stated doctrine of the Church. The Church and the scriptures are emphatic, however, that the Fall brought the two kinds of death to Adam and his posterity.

BIBLIOGRAPHY

McConkie, Joseph Fielding, and Robert L. Millet, eds. *The Man Adam*. Salt Lake City, 1990.

Packer, Boyd K. "The Law and the Light." In *The Book of Mormon: Jacob Through Words of Mormon, to Learn With Joy*, pp. 1–31. Provo, Utah, 1990.

Smith, Joseph Fielding. *Man, His Origin and Destiny*. Salt Lake City, 1954.

ROBERT J. MATTHEWS

FAMILY

[This entry consists of two articles:

Teachings About the Family
Family Life

The first article presents the major teachings about the family that tend to set Latter-day Saints apart from other people and focuses on latter-day scriptures and teachings of Church leaders. The second article provides a substantial explanation of the way in which families experience Church membership together, including the fact that the standard orientation of Church programs is toward families. The family is central to LDS theology, religion, society, and culture. In addition to the articles appearing below, see Children; Fatherhood; Marriage; Motherhood; *and* Mother in Israel. *Regarding specific Church policies and practices concerning the family, see* Abuse, Spouse and Child; Adoption of Children; Birth Control; Divorce; Family Home Evening; *and* Family Prayer.]*

TEACHINGS ABOUT THE FAMILY

The basic unit of The Church of Jesus Christ of Latter-day Saints is the family: "The home is the basis of a righteous life, and no other instrumentality can take its place nor fulfill its essential functions" (McKay, Preface). Within the family, people experience most of life's greatest joys and greatest sorrows. The family relationships of every person on earth are of cardinal importance, and of all the social organizations created for human beings, only the family is intended to continue into the next life.

FAMILIES ON EARTH ARE AN EXTENSION OF THE FAMILY OF GOD.   According to the LDS concept of the family, every person is a child of heavenly parents as well as mortal parents. Each individual was created spiritually and physically in the image of God and Christ (Moses 2:27; 3:5). The First Presidency has declared, "All men and women are in the similitude of the universal Father and Mother, and are literally the sons and daughters of Deity" (*MFP* 4:203). Everyone, before coming to this earth, lived with Heavenly Father and Heavenly Mother, and each was loved and taught by them as a member of their eternal family (*see* PREMORTAL LIFE). Birth unites the spirit with a physical body so that together they can "receive a fulness of joy" (D&C 93:33; cf. 2 Ne. 2:25).

MARRIAGE IS ORDAINED OF GOD. "Whoso forbiddeth to marry is not ordained of God, for marriage is ordained of God unto man" (D&C 49:15). The marriage sanctioned by God provides men and women with the opportunity to fulfill their divine potentials. "Neither is the man without the woman, neither the woman without the man, in the Lord" (1 Cor. 11:11). Husbands and wives are unique in some ways and free to develop their eternal gifts, yet as coequals in the sight of their heavenly parents they are one in the divine goals they pursue, in their devotion to eternal principles and ordinances, in their obedience to the Lord, and in their divine love for each other. When a man and woman who have been sealed together in a temple are united spiritually, mentally, emotionally, and physically, taking full responsibility for nurturing each other, they are truly married. Together they strive to emulate the prototype of the heavenly home from which they came. The Church teaches them to complement, support, and enrich one another.

THE FAMILY CAN BECOME AN ETERNAL UNIT. Worthy members can be sealed by the power of the PRIESTHOOD in holy TEMPLES for TIME AND ETERNITY either in or after marriage. At the time of their temple SEALING, both husband and wife enter "an order of the priesthood [called] the new and everlasting covenant of marriage" (D&C 131:1–4). Without worthiness and authority, a marriage cannot endure eternally and is "of no efficacy, virtue, or force in and after the resurrection from the dead" (D&C 132:7). If a husband and wife are faithful to their temple marriage, they will continue as co-creators in God's celestial kingdom through the eternities. They will administer the affairs of their family in unity with the guidance of the Holy Spirit. Regarding members of the Church not born into such homes or not married in this life through no fault of their own, President Spencer W. KIMBALL taught that those "who would have responded if they had [had] an appropriate oppor-

Church leaders encourage families to study the scriptures together. This photograph shows Elder John A. Widtsoe, a member of the Quorum of the Twelve Apostles, his wife Leah Eudora Dunford and two of their children reading the Bible. Photographer: Charles Ellis Johnson. Courtesy Rare Books and Manuscripts, Brigham Young University.

tunity—will receive all those blessings in the world to come" (Kimball, p. 295).

THE POWER TO CREATE LIFE IS A GIFT FROM GOD. Because the procreative powers come from God, sexual purity is spiritual and mental, as well as physical and emotional (*see* SEXUALITY). Jesus said, "Whosoever looketh on a woman, to lust after her, hath committed adultery already in his heart. Behold, I give unto you a commandment, that ye suffer none of these things to enter into your heart" (3 Ne. 12:28–29). CHASTITY is sacred (cf. Jacob 2:28).

PROCREATION IS A COMMANDMENT OF GOD. Through the sexual experience, husbands and wives enrich their marriage and create physical bodies for spirits to come to earth to achieve divine purposes. Latter-day Saints strive to create a home life dedicated to fulfilling these purposes. It is both a joy and a responsibility for parents to bring heavenly spirits into this world. Adam and Eve were commanded to "be fruitful, and multiply" (Gen. 1:22). Latter-day revelation has given the same instructions. Church members are taught not to postpone or refuse to have children for selfish or materialistic reasons. On questions such as how many children a couple will have, the spacing of children, and BIRTH CONTROL, Latter-day Saints are instructed to use their AGENCY, selecting a course as husband and wife in accordance with divine principles and seeking confirmation from the Holy Spirit.

PARENTS ARE RESPONSIBLE FOR TEACHING THEIR CHILDREN THE GOSPEL OF JESUS CHRIST. "Inasmuch as parents have children . . . that teach them not to understand the doctrine of repentance, faith in Christ the Son of the living God, and of baptism and the gift of the Holy Ghost . . . the sin be upon the heads of the parents. . . . And they shall also teach their children to pray, and to walk uprightly before the Lord" (D&C 68:25, 28). Parents are admonished to be examples to their children, realizing that their children are also their spirit brothers and sisters.

AN ENVIRONMENT OF LOVE IS NECESSARY FOR REARING CHILDREN. The spirit of a righteous home is love. The Lord said, "Thou shalt live together in love" (D&C 42:45)—love of heavenly parents, the Lord Jesus Christ, and the Holy Ghost; of husband and wife; and of parents for children, children for parents, and siblings for each other.

MAKING ONE'S HOME A PLACE OF PEACE AND JOY TAKES EFFORT. The effort that goes into making a peaceful home requires consistent planning, prayer, and cooperation. The Church encourages families to hold weekly FAMILY HOME EVENINGS, in which all members of the family study eternal gospel principles and ordinances and do things together that bring them joy. Two Church Presidents have stated, "The most important of the Lord's work [you] will ever do will be the work you do within the walls of your own homes" (Lee, p. 7), and "No other success can compensate for failure in the home" (McKay, p. iii).

WORTHY FAMILY MEMBERS LOOK FORWARD WITH FAITH AND HOPE TO ETERNAL FAMILY RELATIONSHIPS. Earthly families expect to live again as extended families with ancestors and descendants who have died. They become those "who received the testimony of Jesus, and believed on his name, . . . and are sealed by the Holy Spirit of promise, which the Father sheds forth upon all those who are just and true" (D&C 76: 51, 53).

THE RIGHTEOUS ARE BLESSED. All righteous individuals, who maintain personal worthiness, love, and faithfulness, are promised the RICHES OF ETERNITY, which include the eventual blessings of being sealed to other family members who also qualify for celestial blessings.

BIBLIOGRAPHY

Benson, Ezra Taft. *God, Family, Country: Our Three Great Loyalties*, pp. 167–273. Salt Lake City, 1974.

Kimball, Spencer W. *The Teachings of Spencer W. Kimball*, ed. Edward L. Kimball. Salt Lake City, 1982.

Lee, Harold B. *Strengthening the Home* (pamphlet). Salt Lake City, 1973.

McConkie, Oscar W., Jr. "LDS Concept of the Family." *Journal of the Collegium Aesculapium* 2 (July 1984):46–51.

McKay, David O. *Family Home Evening Manual*. Salt Lake City, 1965.

White, O. Kendall, Jr. "Ideology of the Family in Nineteenth-Century Mormonism." *Sociological Spectrum* 6 (1986):289–306.

REED H. BRADFORD

FAMILY LIFE

FAMILY DEMOGRAPHICS. The inherent emphasis on family in Latter-day Saint theology is expressed in demographic patterns that are different for Mormons compared to the general population. First, Mormon fertility rates have consistently been higher than national averages. Utah has traditionally had the highest fertility rate of any state in the Union due to the high percentage of Latter-day Saints in the state (approximately 70 percent).

Research shows that the larger than average family size among Latter-day Saints is not due to their reluctance to use various methods of birth control. Heaton and Calkins' research (1983) shows that in a national sample they are just as likely to use modern birth control methods as are the rest of the nation. But for Latter-day Saints, contraceptives often are not used until after child rearing has occurred and is used less frequently so that the desired larger family size can be obtained. Heaton concludes that the larger family size for Latter-day Saints is associated with beliefs of LDS parents regarding the value of having children, involvement with an LDS reference group, and socialization in a context which favors having children (1988, p. 112).

In the general population, as family size increases, so does coercive discipline. Affectional family relationships decrease. But research among Latter-day Saints shows an opposite pattern, with larger families reporting increased affectional relations (Thomas, 1983, p. 274).

Latter-day Saints consistently report lower than national average rates of premarital sexual experience, teenage pregnancy, and extramarital sexual experience (Heaton, 1988). Yet, research reported by Smith (1976) shows that inactive Mormons were changing toward more liberal sexual

Families, including young children, attend Church services together on Sunday. Joseph Freeman, Jr., of Kearns, Utah, was one of the first blacks ordained to the priesthood in 1978. Courtesy Doug Martin.

attitudes and behavior during the 1970s, even while active Latter-day Saints showed no movement toward more liberal attitudes or behavior. The percentages reporting no present premarital sexual activity by active Latter-day Saints actually increased between 1950 and 1972, from 95 percent to 98 percent for men and from 96 percent to 98 percent for women (pp. 79–81).

Current data show that a higher percent of Latter-day Saints will marry than does the general population. They will also marry younger, have a lower divorce rate, and remarry after divorce at a higher rate than is found in the general population (Heaton, 1988, pp. 110–11).

With respect to divorce, it is clear that the most religiously committed Latter-day Saints have divorce rates considerably lower than the inactive or noncommitted Church members, even though Utah is one of the mountain and western states which have generally had higher than national average divorce rates (Thomas, 1983, p. 277). Heaton and Goodman's research (1985) shows that of Latter-day Saints attending church regularly, 10 percent of men and 15 percent of women report divorce, compared to 21 percent of men and 26 percent of women who do not attend regularly. Also, among men with temple marriages, 5.4 percent reported divorce compared to 27.8 percent of the nontemple group. For women with temple marriages, 6.5 were divorced while 32.7 percent were divorced in nontemple marriages.

FAMILY ROLES AND THE CHURCH. With the emphasis upon family found within all of the organizations of the Church, from PRIMARY to PRIESTHOOD QUORUMS, the husband and wife become the main points of contact between family and Church. The wife's involvement with the Church will most likely emerge through PRIMARY and RELIEF SOCIETY activities. The husband's contact with the Church can emerge through almost any organization with the exception of the Relief Society, which is limited to women.

Since the Church is organized around a lay male priesthood, more positions of leadership are occupied by husbands than by wives. In addition, the reorganization of Church procedures and functions begun under the general heading of "priesthood correlation" reemphasized the role of the father in conducting family councils, which were seen as part of the councils designed to govern the Church extending all the way to the council of the

First Presidency. The family is seen as the most basic unit of the Church, and all Church programs are designed to strengthen the family.

Given the role of the priesthood in LDS Church government, as well as the teachings about the family, Latter-day Saints have been seen generally as encouraging traditional division of labor along gender lines within families, while at the same time emphasizing the authority of the father through priesthood lines. When researchers have asked about who should perform various functions within the family, Latter-day Saints have tended to score high on measures of traditional beliefs regarding who *ought* to do what in a family (Brinkerhoff and MacKie, 1988). However, in research that asks husbands and wives what they actually do in decision making within the family or how they carry out various duties (that traditionally were seen as belonging to either the husband or the wife), Latter-day Saints have consistently emerged as high on egalitarian measures (Thomas, 1983; Brinkerhoff and MacKie, 1983, 1988). These somewhat paradoxical patterns have not been adequately explained. A common explanation, namely that egalitarian pressures from the larger society is changing the behavior of LDS husbands and wives, is not a convincing one, in light of these recent research findings. Wuthnow advises those who study religious influence to keep a healthy

In the Family Circle, by Dennis Smith (1978, cast bronze), Nauvoo Monument to Women, LDS Church Visitors Center, Nauvoo, Illinois. This life-sized statue, one of thirteen commissioned by the Relief Society for the Nauvoo Monument to Women, carries the inscription: "And they shall also teach their children to pray, and to walk uprightly before the Lord" (D&C 68:28).

skepticism toward any description of religion "as a force in the service of social conservatism" (1973, p. 128). His advice seems especially relevant to this issue with LDS attitudes and beliefs.

In addition, while the Latter-day Saint father is given responsibility to lead the family, he is expected to do so in a manner which helps every family member grow and develop. LDS beliefs also emphasize the egalitarian nature of men-women relationships. LDS doctrine teaches that there is a MOTHER IN HEAVEN as well as a Father, that EVE's eating of the forbidden fruit furthered God's plan of salvation (*see* FALL OF ADAM), that women must perform certain essential priesthood ordinances in the temple, and that the highest order of the priesthood and the complete blessings of EXALTATION are available only to the married couple; neither can enter exaltation without the other.

This egalitarian relationship between men and women is symbolized in the LDS portrayal of relationships between Adam and Eve after their expulsion from the Garden of Eden. The two must earn their bread by the sweat of their brows and "Eve did labor with him" (Moses 5:1). They are both commanded to offer sacrifices, and they teach their children all these things (Moses 5:5, 12). Eve along with Adam mourns for the wickedness of their children, and they seek the Lord in prayer together (Moses 5:13–16). After receiving information from God, Eve in turn instructs Adam about some basic points of the gospel (Moses 5:11).

Another egalitarian emphasis emerges in temple ceremonies and ordinances. Without women performing sacred priesthood ordinances in the temple, the highest saving ordinances performed on earth by men and women could not be completed. This is symbolic of men–women relationships generally. Alone they remain incomplete while united man and woman develop their highest divine potential.

PARENTAL BELIEFS AND FAMILY BEHAVIOR. Family commitment is deemed crucial for both husbands and wives, although the wife typically bears the greater responsibility for management of the home and the nurturing of the children. Thomas (1988) studied a sample of LDS parents and documented that the degree to which husbands and wives shared in their child-rearing duties was the second strongest influence on marital satisfaction. More recent research (Thomas and

Cornwall, 1990) has documented that it is the wife's marital satisfaction that is highly correlated with shared child-rearing, while the husband's marital satisfaction is unrelated to shared child rearing. This finding corroborates a long-standing general pattern in family research which shows that what happens in family life is more central to a wife's definition of satisfaction than a husband's. It also points to the need for LDS husbands to realize that their increased involvement in child care will be one of the best contributions they can make to their wife's marital satisfaction. Also, those families that score high on the measure of home religious observance (FAMILY PRAYER, SCRIPTURE READING, and family council) also report the highest amount of shared child-rearing.

In related findings, whether the couple had been married in the temple was the best indicator of whether the family would carry out their home religious observance. These data support the conclusion that temple marriage is related to family behaviors which include more home religious activities, increased husband involvement in shared child-rearing activities, and thus increased marital satisfaction.

The emphasis among Latter-day Saints on family often can lead to greater involvement with members of the extended family. The Church encourages families to organize across generations to foster FAMILY HISTORY and genealogical work deemed essential to the family's well-being in eternity. Such work is often discussed at family reunions. However, there is not good comparative research available to know to what degree LDS families are different from or similar to other families on extended family interaction.

THE CHURCH AND FAMILY FUNCTIONING. These demographic realities mean that generally LDS families are larger, are more likely to avoid divorce, are characterized by religious commitment and activities centered around child-rearing, and require great financial resources. In addition to providing financially for the family, running the household, and rearing children, adults usually have one or more Church CALLINGS that may involve extensive time in service to others. And, since the number of LDS women who are employed outside the home is virtually equal to the national average in the United States (see Mason, p. 103; Heaton, 1986, p. 184, 190), making home a first priority is a genuine challenge. As children

grow, parents are encouraged to include them in doing household tasks, with the goal that the resulting skills and attitudes which they develop can contribute to the quality of family life, as well as prepare them for confidence and competence in the world external to the family. Church leaders are encouraged to minimize the time they and other members spend in their callings and to safeguard family time from constant intruding influences.

Sometimes the focus of Church activities on the two-parent family belies the truth that not all members are in a stage of life where they can rear children with a committed mate. Those who never married, are divorced, are widowed, are single parents, or are married to non-Latter-day Saints are always in LDS WARDS and, ideally, they are included in the community of Saints. Priesthood quorums and the Relief Society are charged both to integrate such families into ward activities as well as provide for special needs. And, when members of any family become involved in such activities as drug abuse, divorce, or family violence, the Church intends that leaders provide a network of emotional support, prevention, and rehabilitation.

BIBLIOGRAPHY

Bahr, Howard M.; S. J. Condie; and K. L. Goodman. *Life in Large Families*. Washington, D.C., 1982.

Brinkerhoff, Merlin B., and Marlene MacKie. "Religious Sources of Gender Traditionalism." In *The Religion and Family Connection: Social Science Perspectives*, ed. D. Thomas, pp. 232–57. Provo, Utah, 1988.

Heaton, Tim B. "The Demography of Utah Mormons." In *Utah in Demographic Perspective*, ed. T. Martin; T. Heaton; and S. Bahr, pp. 181–93. Salt Lake City, 1986.

———. "Four C's of the Mormon Family: Chastity, Conjugality, Children, and Chauvinism." In *The Religion and Family Connection: Social Science Perspectives*, ed. D. Thomas, pp. 107–24. Provo, Utah, 1988.

———, and S. Calkins. "Family Size and Contraceptive Use among Mormons: 1965–75." *Review of Religious Research* 25, no. 2 (1983):103–14.

———, and Kristen L. Goodman. "Religions and Family Formation." *Review of Religious Research* 26, no. 4 (1985):343–59.

Lee, Harold B. *Strengthening the Home*. Salt Lake City, 1973, (pamphlet).

Mason, Jerry. "Family Economics." In *Utah in Demographic Perspective*, ed. T. Martin; T. Heaton; and S. Bahr, pp. 91–109. Salt Lake City, Utah, 1986.

Smith, W. E. "Mormon Sex Standards on College Campuses, or Deal Us Out of the Sexual Revolution." *Dialogue* 10, no. 2 (1976):76–81.

Thomas, Darwin L. "Future Prospects for Religion and Family Studies: the Mormon Case." In *The Religion and Family Connection: Social Science Perspectives*, ed. D. Thomas, pp. 357–82. Provo, Utah, 1988.

————. "Family in the Mormon Experience." In *Families and Religions: Conflict and Change in Modern Society*, ed. W. D'Antonio, and J. Aldous, pp. 267–88. Beverly Hills, Calif., 1983.

————, and Marie Cornwall. "The Religion and Family Interface: Theoretical and Empirical Explorations." Paper presented at the XII World Congress of Sociology, International Sociological Assn., Madrid, Spain, July, 13, 1990.

Wuthnow, R. "Religious Commitment and Conservatism: In Search of an Elusive Relationship." In *Religion in Sociological Perspective*, ed. C. Glock. Belmont, Calif., 1973.

DARWIN L. THOMAS

FAMILY HISTORY CENTERS

Family History Centers are extensions of the FAMILY HISTORY LIBRARY in Salt Lake City, Utah. The first center opened in 1964. Originally, they were known as branch genealogical libraries. When the Genealogical Library became the Family History Library in 1987, the branches became Family History Centers. In 1990 there were over 1,500 such centers in 49 countries.

Located most often in LDS stake centers, Family History Centers are open to the public, generally twenty hours per week, staffed entirely by volunteers. There is no charge, but space is often limited. At a Family History Center, researchers have access to the Family History Library's microfilm copies of family history records, which can be lent to the center for a specified time. Many local centers also have significant collections of genealogical source material on microfiche, and some have their own collections of research materials specific to their area.

At a Family History Center, patrons find many of the same research tools that are available at the central Family History Library, including microfiche editions of the Family History Library Catalog, the INTERNATIONAL GENEALOGICAL INDEX™ (IGI), the FAMILY REGISTRY™, and a series of instructional handouts that describe how to do research in the United States and many other countries. Many centers also provide access to FAMILYSEARCH™, a computer system that organizes data and simplifies the task of family history research.

Addresses of worldwide Family History Centers are available from the Family History Library.

V. BEN BLOXHAM

FAMILY HISTORY, GENEALOGY

The terms "family history" and "genealogy" are synonymous for Latter-day Saints. Dallin H. Oaks, a member of the Quorum of Twelve Apostles, said, "The process by which we identify our place in our eternal family is called genealogy. Genealogy is family history" (Regional Representatives Seminar, April 3, 1987). To emphasize the family nature of genealogy, the First Presidency in 1987 changed the name of the Genealogical Department to the Family History Department and the name of the Genealogical Library to the FAMILY HISTORY LIBRARY.

LDS interest in family history is based on the fundamental doctrines of SALVATION, AGENCY, and EXALTATION. It is the plan of God that all persons shall have the opportunity to hear the gospel of Jesus Christ and receive the saving ordinances, regardless of when they lived on earth. If they do not hear the gospel preached through the Lord's authorized servants in this life, they will hear it in the SPIRIT WORLD after death. Latter-day Saints identify their ancestors and arrange for baptism and other ordinances to be performed by proxy—that is, with a living person standing in for the deceased person—in a temple. This is not an optional function of LDS belief; it is, rather, a commandment of God. As Elder Oaks further explained, "We are not hobbyists in genealogy work. We do family history work in order to provide the ordinances of salvation for the living and the dead" (1989, p. 6; *see also* SALVATION OF THE DEAD).

Members of the Church were instructed in the sacred role of family history work in 1894, when President Wilford WOODRUFF declared, "We want the Latter day Saints from this time to trace their genealogies as far as they can, and to be sealed to their fathers and mothers. Have children sealed to their parents, and run this chain through as far as you can get it. . . . This is the will of the Lord to this people" (p. 543; *see also* SEALING). The purpose of family history, President Woodruff explained, is to obtain names and statistical data so that TEMPLE ORDINANCES can be performed in behalf of deceased ancestors who did not have the opportunity to hear the restored gospel during mortal life. He taught on another occasion that "we have got to enter into those temples and redeem our dead—not only the dead of our own family, but the dead of the whole spirit world" (*JD* 21:192).

Fundamental to the doctrine of the salvation of the dead is the exercise of agency. When persons die, their spirits continue living in the post-mortal spirit world and are capable of making choices. Latter-day Saints perform BAPTISMS FOR THE DEAD so that those who live as spirits may choose whether or not to accept baptism in the true Church of Jesus Christ in the spirit world. If they do not accept the baptism, it is of no effect. The same is true of the other saving ordinances that members perform in the temples in behalf of the dead.

Love is the central motivation for family history work. Identifying ancestors and performing saving ordinances for them are an expression of love. It is the spirit and power of Elijah, who gave the keys of this power to Joseph Smith in the Kirtland Temple in 1836, to "turn the hearts of the fathers to the children, and the children to the fathers" (D&C 110:15; see also Mal. 4:5–6; JS—H 1:39; D&C 2:2). The desire to discover one's ancestors and complete temple ordinances for them is sometimes referred to as the Spirit of Elijah (*see* ELIJAH, SPIRIT OF). President Joseph Fielding SMITH associated family history and temple work with love for mankind, declaring that laboring on behalf of the dead is "a work that enlarges the soul of man, broadens his views regarding the welfare of his fellowman, and plants in his heart a love for all the children of our Heavenly Father. There is no work equal to that in the temple for the dead in teaching a man to love his neighbor as himself" (p. 3).

In response to President Woodruff's teaching regarding family history responsibilities, Latter-day Saints organized the GENEALOGICAL SOCIETY OF UTAH in Salt Lake City in 1894. Over the years, the society, through the Family History Library and its worldwide network of more than 1,500 family history centers, has become a major support of the Church's efforts to provide instruction in family history through research information (first in book form and later in microfilm and then in compact disc) and through making available a

skilled staff to assist researchers to identify their ancestors.

Interest in family history is not limited to Latter-day Saints. There has been remarkable growth of interest in genealogy and family history dating from about 1836, when Elijah committed the keys to the Prophet Joseph Smith. In many countries, thousands of people have joined genealogical and historical societies, and more than half of the patrons of the Family History Library and its associated Family History Centers are members of other faiths. The Church has joined in cooperative efforts with hundreds of genealogical and family history societies, archives, and libraries in identifying family history records and preserving the information found in them (*see* WORLD CONFERENCES ON RECORDS).

Modern technology has played a significant role in the advance of family history in the second half of the twentieth century. The Church has developed an extensive worldwide microfilming program. Since 1938, it has done microfilming in more than a hundred countries, and has accumulated more than 1.3 billion exposures with approximately 8 billion names. Microfilm records have provided the basis for dramatic expansion of family history research. They have enabled rapid growth of the collections of the Family History Library and has made possible both the distribution of family history information to the Church's Family History Centers and the NAME EXTRACTION PROGRAMS that have allowed the extensive automation of family history information contained in the FAMILYSEARCH® computer system.

As a result, doing family history research has never been easier than it now is. Through FamilySearch, patrons of the Family History Library and Family History Centers have access to the 147 million names in the INTERNATIONAL GENEALOGICAL INDEX™ and the growing 9.67-million-name lineage-linked Ancestral File™. As name extraction programs convert information from paper records (such as the 1880 U.S. Federal Census and the 1881 British Census) and as people from around the world contribute information to the Ancestral File, the computer resources associated with FamilySearch will make identifying one's ancestors a much simpler task.

The Church teaches that members' family history duties are threefold. First, they must develop a desire to help redeem the dead. As members gain a testimony of the principle of salvation of the dead, they feel a personal responsibility to help. They also care about those in the spirit world who are waiting for temple ordinances to be performed.

Second, they must determine what to do. Every Latter-day Saint can do something to further the family history work. Dallin H. Oaks counseled, "Our effort is not to compel everyone to do everything, but to encourage everyone to do something" (1989, p. 6). Accordingly, Latter-day Saints are encouraged to participate in activities relating to the salvation of the dead. What and how much a member does depend on personal circumstances and abilities, what one's family may have already accomplished, individual guidance from the Spirit, and direction from Church leaders. Activities include identifying one's ancestors and performing temple ordinances for them, participating in family organizations, serving in the Name Extraction Program, keeping a personal journal, preparing personal and family histories, and accepting Church callings in temple and family history service. Identifying ancestors of the first few generations usually does not require extensive library research or sophisticated research tools. The beginning of family history research usually involves checking known family records (see JOURNALS), consulting family members either orally or by letter, and looking at readily available public records, such as birth certificates. Identifying ancestors beyond the first few generations usually requires the resources of libraries, computer tools available with systems like FamilySearch, and expert help. Family organizations enable members to pool information and resources to further the family history work. The Name Extraction Program enables persons to convert information found on microfilm copies of paper records—parish registers, census rolls, and so forth—to a computer format to become part of FamilySearch files or to supply needed names to the temples.

Third, members must continue to serve. The work of the Family History Department will not be complete until every name is recorded and every ordinance performed.

BIBLIOGRAPHY

Come unto Christ Through Temple Ordinances and Covenants, 2nd ed. Salt Lake City, 1988.

Greenwood, Val D. *The Researcher's Guide to American Genealogy,* 2nd ed. Baltimore, 1990.

Instructions for Priesthood Leaders on Temple and Family History Work. Salt Lake City, 1990.

Oaks, Dallin H. "Family History: 'In Wisdom and Order'." *Ensign* 19 (June 1989):6–8.

Smith, Joseph Fielding. *Church News* (Oct. 24, 1970):3.

Woodruff, Wilford. *Deseret Weekly* (April 21, 1894):543.

DAVID H. PRATT

FAMILY HISTORY LIBRARY

The Family History Library in Salt Lake City, supports the LDS practice of family history research that identifies forebears and makes possible the temple work leading to SALVATION OF THE DEAD. It provides services and resources that enable Latter-day Saints and others to identify and learn more about their ancestors. It is also a developmental center where new resources and programs are perfected and made available to Church members worldwide through FAMILY HISTORY CENTERS.

On November 13, 1894, the GENEALOGICAL SOCIETY OF UTAH was organized. One of its purposes was the "establishing and maintaining [of] a genealogical library for the use and benefit of its members and others" (Minutes of the Genealogical Society of Utah, Nov. 13, 1894). From its modest beginnings in an upstairs room of the Church Historian's Office with about 300 books, the collection has grown and its facilities have changed commensurately, so that in 1990 the library occupied a modern five-story building which housed 200,000 books, 300,000 microfiches, and more than 1.6 million rolls of microfilm, making it the largest library of its kind in the world.

During its first fifty years, the library was open only to dues-paying members. In 1944 it was incorporated under the administration of the Church, and its resources were made available to the public. In 1989, the library had 813,000 visitors. Genealogists, historians, demographers, geneticists, and other researchers from many countries travel to Salt Lake City to utilize the wealth of information available in the library. They are attracted by its collections, the expertise of the staff, and the nearly 700 classes offered annually in research sources and methodology.

The biggest attraction is the microfilm collection. Since 1938, the Genealogical Society of Utah and its successor organization, the LDS Church

Family History Department, have been preserving copies of original documents on microfilm. In 1990 the library sponsored approximately 200 microfilming projects in various parts of the world. These efforts have added microfilmed copies of more than 5 million manuscripts to the library's collections. The microfilms show the original records of births, marriages, and deaths; military records; censuses; wills; notaries' records; cemetery records; and other kinds of documents that describe people and families from the past. Other resources include compiled genealogies, local histories, old maps, city directories, and name indexes. The largest collections are from countries in North America and Europe, with substantial collections from Latin America. The library has also acquired written and oral materials from Asia, Africa, Australia, and the islands of the Pacific Ocean.

Computer terminals give patrons access to the FAMILYSEARCH^{TM} system, which guides researchers into the Family History Library Catalog, the INTERNATIONAL GENEALOGICAL INDEX^{TM} (IGI), and ANCESTRAL FILE®. These computer files of family history information are stored on compact discs. The compact-disc edition of the catalog provides access to books and microfilms that contain original records, reference sources, and family histories and genealogies.

Library visitors can also learn how to use PERSONAL ANCESTRAL FILE®. This computer program enables families to manage family history records on their personal computers. In addition, users can easily exchange genealogical information with others who have compatible computer programs or with Ancestral File.

Another resource is the FAMILY REGISTRY^{TM}. This service helps both individuals and family organizations to share with others information they may have about deceased individuals and to ask for information about an ancestor who is currently the subject of their research. Library visitors have access to microfiche records listing the ancestors and family organizations that have been registered. This file eases coordination of research with others who may share the same family lines.

At the Family History Library professional genealogical reference consultants, library attendants, and hundreds of volunteers serve library visitors. They are trained to guide patrons to sources identifying their families and to help them interpret the information in these books and docu-

The Church's Family History Library (c.1988) houses the world's largest collection of genealogical records. More than 2,000 people come here daily to research their family histories. The five-floor library opened in Salt Lake City in 1985. Photographer: Marty Mayo.

ments. Staff members are multilingual and can read handwriting from many countries and time periods.

BIBLIOGRAPHY

Cerny, Johni, and Wendy Elliott, eds., *The Library: A Guide to the LDS Family History Library.* Salt Lake City, 1988.

Mayfield, David M. "The Genealogical Library of The Church of Jesus Christ of Latter-day Saints." *Library Trends* 32 (Summer 1983):111–27.

RAYMOND S. WRIGHT, III

FAMILY HOME EVENING

Family home evening is a weekly observance of Latter-day Saints for spiritual training and social activity, usually held on Monday evenings. In 1915, the FIRST PRESIDENCY of the Church wrote: "We advise and urge the inauguration of a 'Home Evening' throughout the Church, at which time fathers and mothers may gather their boys and girls about them in the home and teach them the word of the Lord. . . . This 'Home Evening' should be devoted to prayer, singing hymns, songs, instrumental music, scripture-reading, family topics and specific instruction on the principles of the Gospel, and on the ethical problems of life, as well as the duties and obligation of children to parents, the home, the Church, society, and the Nation"

An LDS family meets together for family home evening (Tokyo, 1986). Latter-day prophets encourage families to gather in their homes weekly to discuss and experience the gospel and build family unity. The Church provides a resource manual that families can use to prepare discussions. Courtesy Floyd Holdman.

(*IE* 18 [June 1915]:733). To assist parents in their STEWARDSHIP, the first home evening manual was prepared that same year and distributed to members of the Church.

This emphasis on home gospel instruction echoes the call of prophets throughout the ages who have instructed parents to teach their children diligently of love and to bring them up in the nurture and admonition of the Lord (Deut. 6:5–7; Eph. 6:4). The Prophet Joseph SMITH received revelations that admonish parents to "bring up your children in light and truth" (D&C 93:40) and to teach them "to understand the doctrine of repentance, faith in Christ the Son of the living God, and of baptism and the gift of the Holy Ghost" (D&C 68:25) and "to pray, and to walk uprightly before the Lord" (D&C 68:28). President Brigham YOUNG urged parents to take time to "call their families together . . . and teach them the principles of the gospel" (*MFP* 2:288).

Between 1915 and the 1960s, a large proportion of Church membership shifted from a family-centered rural population to an urban one. With that change came renewed emphasis from the First Presidency on the importance of the family. In general conference, April 1964, President David O. MCKAY reminded parents that "No other success can compensate for failure in the home" (*IE* 67 [June 1964]:445). In 1965, the weekly family home evening program was more fully implemented, and a lesson manual was given each family to aid

parents in teaching their children. Families were encouraged to participate in a home night once each week, which could consist of scripture reading, singing, and activities suited to the ages of the children. In 1966, STAKES were urged to set aside a regular night for family home evening and to avoid scheduling Church activities on that night. In 1970, Monday evening was designated as family home evening, Churchwide, with no competing ecclesiastical functions to be held. Revised home evening manuals, with suggested weekly lessons and activities, were provided from 1965 to 1984.

In 1985, a *Family Home Evening Resource Book*, designed to be used for a decade, was introduced. It provided broader resource material for gospel instruction and additional ideas for family activities, and was designed to be adapted for use by single adults, couples, single-parent families, and families with children of all ages. In 1987, a family home evening video supplement was made available. Nineteen video vignettes were included, treating important educational and moral topics.

A typical family home evening might proceed as follows: A parent or older child, whose turn it is to plan the lesson, selects a lesson, such as "Heavenly Father Provided Us a Savior," from the *Family Home Evening Resource Book*. After an opening hymn and prayer, the lesson material, adapted to the needs and interest level of the family members, is presented. After the lesson the family discusses family schedules, family business, and special concerns. A family activity follows that helps strengthen bonds of love among family members. This could be any activity that the family enjoys doing together, such as playing a game, helping the needy, gardening, or attending a cultural event. Following the activity, the family kneels together in family prayer and then often enjoys refreshments. Single adults or others who live alone may join as a group to participate in family home evening activities, or they may observe appropriately modified weekly activities individually. Home evening activities allow for considerable variation in the desires and needs of each family or group. Always, however, the emphasis is spiritual enrichment.

Family home evening is intended to be a regular event that helps parents teach, protect, and prepare children for responsible living. Family councils, personal parent interviews, scripture reading, serving or playing together, family prayer, and meaningful family home evenings all help to build quality family relationships. Families who do these things are promised that "love at home and obedience to parents will increase, and faith will develop in the hearts of the youth of Israel, and they will gain power to combat [the] evil influences and temptations" that beset them (*Family Home Evening Manual*, 1965, p. v).

BIBLIOGRAPHY

Johnson, Sherrie. "Using the New Family Home Evening Resource Book." *Ensign* 14 (Jan. 1984):6–9.

Kimball, Spencer W. "Home: The Place to Save Society." *Ensign* 5 (Jan. 1975):3–10.

Lee, Harold B. "Priesthood Correlation and the Home Evening." *IE* 67 (Dec. 1964):1077–81.

———. "The Home Evening." *IE* 70 (Jan. 1967):22–23.

Lynn, Wayne B. "Better Home Evenings." *Ensign* 20 (June 1990):22–25.

JAMES P. MITCHELL
TERRI TANNER MITCHELL

FAMILY ORGANIZATIONS

Latter-day Saints think of families with respect to both this life and the next. They strive to organize family groups at the individual family level and in extended family relationships and organizations.

Family organizations provide social and familial support, historical awareness, instruction, and genealogical information necessary to bind generations together by temple ordinances (*see* FAMILY HISTORY; TEMPLE ORDINANCES).

From the early days of the Church, LDS families have regularly established family organizations, held reunions, and worked to make strong family identity. In 1978 the Church asked all families to organize themselves at three levels: immediate families, grandparent families, and ancestral families.

The immediate family consists of husband and wife, and begins when they are married. Later, if a couple is blessed with children, the size and concerns of this unit grow. When the children marry and have children of their own, the grandparent organization is initiated. Beyond that, each family is ideally involved in an ancestral organization, which consists of all the descendants of an earlier common progenitors couple.

The immediate family holds FAMILY HOME EVENINGS and family councils, encourages and assists in missionary work, family preparedness, family history, temple work, and teaching the gospel, and provides cultural and social activities for its members. The grandparent organization is involved in similar activities, but is also concerned

Platt and Wilma Ward (front row), with their children (second row), their children's spouses (third row), grandchildren and great-grandchildren (1988). Family reunions draw the extended family together to support and sustain family traditions and values. Courtesy Craig Law.

with family reunions, which include the grandparents' children and grandchildren. The purpose of the ancestral organization is to coordinate genealogical activity on common lines. Such organizations frequently raise money for family history research, publish family histories, and generally direct the activities of the larger family.

Many families use the ancestral organization as a repository of photographs, journals, family histories, and other materials that might be used by family members or general researchers as they prepare their own histories. Some families occasionally have an ancestral family reunion, but more usually they have representatives who meet to coordinate family history and genealogical activities. Some may be organized as nonprofit corporations or trusts that may be recognized as charitable organizations if their purposes are limited to religious activities.

The benefits of a family organization can be significant. One benefit is that involvement with family organizations increases one's sense of identity and heritage. For example, in a recent survey of university students who were LDS, Catholic, Protestant, or of no particular religion, the number of ancestors' names and origins known by the LDS students was significantly higher than for the other groups.

BIBLIOGRAPHY

Benson, Ezra Taft. "Worthy of All Acceptation." *Ensign* 8 (Nov. 1978):30–32.

Jacobson, Cardell K.; Phillip R. Kunz; and Melanie W. Conlin. "Extended Family Ties: Genealogical Researchers." In S. Bahr and E. Peterson, eds., *Aging and the Family.* Lexington, Mass., 1989.

PHILLIP R. KUNZ

FAMILY PRAYER

It is considered a duty and privilege by Latter-day Saint parents to lead their children in regular family prayer. The scriptural basis for this practice is seen in the Book of Mormon. As the Savior was teaching the Nephites, he said, "Pray in your families unto the Father, always in my name, that your wives and your children may be blessed" (3 Ne. 18:21). President Ezra Taft BENSON has said, "Family prayer is . . . the means to acknowledge appreciation for blessings and to humbly recognize

A Guatemalan family kneels in their home for family prayer (1989). Latter-day prophets encourage families to draw closer to God and to each other through daily family prayer (see 3 Ne. 18:21). Courtesy Craig Dimond.

dependence on Almighty God for strength, sustenance, and support" (*CR* [April 1984] p. 7).

Ideal circumstances find the LDS family kneeling in prayer twice daily, morning and evening. As family members grow older and engage in an increasing variety of activities, finding a convenient time for all members to be present for group prayer is often difficult. Some never meet the challenge, whereas others hold prayer and SCRIPTURE STUDY early in the morning when they are less likely to be interrupted. Another common time for group prayer is just before breakfast and dinner.

Family prayer affords the opportunity for both children and parents to lead in prayer, one at one family prayer and another at the next. Most prayers thank the Lord for blessings received (see THANKSGIVING) and on behalf of the family petition for desired blessings. Challenges facing family members and friends are often placed before Father in Heaven in united supplication. Specific concerns for the well-being of each family member can be enumerated. Sometimes the family fasts and joins in family prayer on behalf of family members, friends, neighbors, or others who are ill or in special need of the Lord's blessings.

Family prayer allows individuals and families to focus attention and affection on God. It builds faith and loyalty within the family and epitomizes Christ-centered family WORSHIP. Family prayer affords the opportunity to offer praise to God and gratitude for daily blessings as well as for the Savior's mission, example, and love. Church members believe that the benefits of daily family prayer include family UNITY, strength in the Lord, freeing the heart of evil inclinations, tender moments of divine communication, and an understanding of God's relationship to his children.

Many members who live alone participate in a family prayer experience by choosing to pray aloud for family members and others. They may also join family home evening groups or other friends and associates for regular group prayer.

BIBLIOGRAPHY

Groberg, John H. "The Power of Family Prayer." *Ensign* 12 (May 1982):50–52.

Hinckley, Gordon B. "The Force of Family Prayer." *IE* 66 (June 1963):528–32.

Kimball, Spencer W. "Family Prayer." In *Prayer*, pp. 84–87. Salt Lake City, 1977.

Perry, L. Tom. "Our Father Which Art in Heaven." *Ensign* 13 (Nov. 1983):11–13.

BRUCE L. OLSEN

FAMILY REGISTRY™

Family Registry is a service provided by the Family History Department of The Church of Jesus Christ of Latter-day Saints to help people who are doing research on the same family lines to cooperate with one another and share results, thus avoiding unnecessary duplication of effort and expense. This service provides a way for individuals and family organizations to ask for information about an ancestor who is currently the subject of their research or to share with others information they may have about deceased individuals.

The Family Registry has an alphabetical list of the surnames being researched, together with the names and addresses of persons who have registered. The index is updated periodically and published on microfiche. The January 1990 edition

contained 287,000 names. Those who register are expected to respond to others who wish to coordinate research efforts. The Family Registry index can be personally searched by anyone at the FAMILY HISTORY LIBRARY in Salt Lake City, Utah, or at more than 1,500 FAMILY HISTORY CENTERS or other libraries that participate in offering this service. There is no charge for registration or for searching the index.

BIBLIOGRAPHY

"A New Tool for Genealogists." *Church News* (Dec. 18, 1983):12.

Nichols, Elizabeth L. "The Family Registry." *Genealogy Digest* 16 (Summer 1985):26–31.

JOHN C. JARMAN

FAMILYSEARCH™

FamilySearch™ is an automated computer system that simplifies the task of family history research. The FamilySearch system includes search-and-retrieval programs designed to work on personal computers and computer files of family history information. FamilySearch was developed by the Family History Department of The Church of Jesus Christ of Latter-day Saints.

The information in each file is distributed on compact discs, each capable of storing the equivalent of about 320,000 pages of text. They are read by computers equipped with a compact-disc player and with the FamilySearch software.

FamilySearch is available to the public at the FAMILY HISTORY LIBRARY in Salt Lake City and over time will be distributed to FAMILY HISTORY CENTERS affiliated with the library.

FamilySearch's primary purpose is to help members of the Church identify their ancestors and complete TEMPLE ORDINANCES for them. The power of the program, together with the large files available to it, make FamilySearch a valuable research tool.

When the system was introduced in 1990, it included the following files:

1. The Family History Library Catalog, which has been available for many years in a microfiche edition in the Family History Library in Salt Lake City and in family history centers, describes the collection of the library and provides help in locat-

ing the book, microfilm, or other research tool a patron may need. The automated edition simplifies use of the catalog.

2. The INTERNATIONAL GENEALOGICAL INDEX (IGI), which has been available for many years in a microfiche edition. The automated edition gives information about deceased persons for whom temple ordinances have been performed. It also lists birth, christening, and marriage dates and temple ordinance information.

3. Ancestral File™ is a family-linked file containing genealogies contributed by members of the Church since 1979. Many other genealogies have also been included, and additional contributions of family history information are welcomed.

Other files will be added to FamilySearch as they become available.

BIBLIOGRAPHY

"FamilySearch™ Software," Attachment, First Presidency Letter, April 2, 1990.

Mayfield, David M., and A. Gregory Brown. "FamilySearch." *Genealogical Computing* 10 (1990):1.

L. REYNOLDS CAHOON

FARMS MANAGEMENT CORPORATION

See: Business: Church Participation in Business

FAR WEST, MISSOURI

Far West, Caldwell County, Missouri, was settled in 1836 as Latter-day Saints sought a home and refuge from persecution in Clay County. It became the county seat, with an estimated 3,000 to 5,000 inhabitants. Far West is important to LDS history because that is where the following happened: (1) a temple site was dedicated and the cornerstones laid; (2) seven revelations now published in the Doctrine and Covenants (113, 114, 115, 117, 118, 119, 120) were received; (3) Joseph F. SMITH, sixth president of the Church, was born (November 13, 1838); (4) the Quorum of the Twelve Apostles officially left from for a mission to Great Britain; (5) a stake of Zion was organized; (6) Joseph SMITH and his family lived (beginning March 14, 1838); (7) and for a short time the headquarters of the Church was located.

Among the notable revelations in the Doctrine and Covenants received at Far West and vicinity are: the proper NAME OF THE CHURCH was given (115:4); four new members of the Twelve Apostles were named and the Twelve as a quorum were called to serve an overseas mission (118:1–6); and the law of TITHING was explained (119, 120).

Joseph Smith and other Church leaders were arrested in Far West on October 31, 1838, by the state militia and taken to Independence, then to Richmond, and from there to Liberty, Missouri, where they were imprisoned. While the Prophet was in prison during the winter and spring of 1838–1839, the Latter-day Saints were driven from Far West and other Missouri sites under Governor Boggs's EXTERMINATION ORDER and relocated in Illinois.

The Church still has interest in Far West and has erected appropriate monuments at the temple site.

[*See also* History of the Church: c. 1831–1844; Missions of the Twelve to British Isles; Missouri.]

BIBLIOGRAPHY

Cannon, Donald Q., and Lyndon W. Cook. *Far West Record.* Salt Lake City, 1983.

Gentry, Leland H. "A History of the Latter-day Saints in Northern Missouri from 1836 to 1839." Ph.D. diss., Brigham Young University, 1965.

LARRY C. PORTER

FASTING

The practice of periodic abstinence from food and drink for devotional purposes has been documented since early times. The Bible and the Book of Mormon attest to fasting in its several forms, public or private, institutionalized or spontaneous. In a revelation to the Prophet Joseph Smith, the Lord commanded the Latter-day Saints to "continue in prayer and fasting from this time forth" (D&C 88:76).

Church members fast together generally on the first Sunday of each month, in preparation for FAST AND TESTIMONY MEETING. They usually abstain from food and drink for two consecutive meals, attend Church services, and donate a FAST OFFERING for the care of the needy. Additionally, an individual, family, or congregation may fast for a specific cause such as one who is sick or otherwise afflicted. An individual may desire the intimate communication with deity engendered by a prayerful fast when preparing for a difficult task or significant change in the circumstances of life. A person may fast when seeking spiritual enlightenment or guidance in decision making, strength to overcome weakness or endure trial, comfort in sorrow, or help at other times of special need.

General principles of the fast include prayerful preparation concerning the subject of the fast and frequent contemplation and meditation throughout to achieve oneness in purpose and spirit with the Lord; a quiet, humble, and cheerful conduct befitting one seeking blessing or spiritual enlightenment (Matt. 6:16–18; cf. 3 Ne. 13:16–18); and a prayer of gratitude and thanksgiving when ending the fast.

Rich blessings are promised to those who fast and help the needy (Isa. 58:8–9). Self-control, communion with the Lord, and spiritual strength and power accompany compliance with the law. The spirit of the fast is aptly represented in latter-day scripture: "Verily, this is fasting and prayer, or in other words, rejoicing and prayer" (D&C 59:14).

BIBLIOGRAPHY

Ricks, Stephen D. "Fasting in the Bible and Book of Mormon." In *Book of Mormon: The Keystone Scripture*, ed. Paul R. Cheesman. Provo, Utah, 1988, pp. 127-36.

Smith, Joseph F. *Gospel Doctrine*, 10th ed. Salt Lake City, 1956.

DAWN M. HILLS

FAST OFFERINGS

The first Sunday of each month is designated as a Fast Sunday, and Latter-day Saints are asked to fast for twenty-four hours and donate at least the value of the meals not eaten as fast offerings. Fast offerings are cash or in-kind donations given to the BISHOP to help the needy following a short period of fasting.

The concept of fast offerings appears as early as the time of Isaiah, who encouraged people to fast and "deal thy bread to the hungry" and to "bring the poor that are cast out to thy house" when fasting (Isa. 58:7). Fasting was also practiced in the postapostolic Church, in which several early Christian fathers advised that "to help the poor with the food saved, fasting is a good work" (Kittel, Vol. 4, p. 934). By the mid-second century some

churches held twice-weekly voluntary fasts, and leaders collected funds for the poor following weekly worship services (Swenson, pp. 373–78).

The Prophet Joseph SMITH, instituted the practice of collecting fast offerings for the poor in KIRTLAND, OHIO (*JD* 12:115), where Church members had begun gathering in the early 1830s. Later, on May 17, 1845, in Nauvoo, Illinois, the QUORUM OF THE TWELVE APOSTLES sent a general letter to the Church defining "the principles of fasts," stating:

> Let this be an example to all saints, and there will never be any lack for bread: When the poor are starving, let those who have, fast one day and give what they otherwise would have eaten to the bishops for the poor, and everyone will abound for a long time; and this is one great and important principle of fasts approved of the Lord. And so long as the saints will all live to this principle with glad hearts and cheerful countenances they will always have an abundance [*HC* 7:413].

During the exodus from Nauvoo the pioneers seldom observed a common fast day but often were asked to give to the poor. It appears that the giving of regular fast day donations was reinstituted in the Salt Lake Valley during the drought of 1855–1856. Of that period George A. Smith wrote:

> In all these times of scarcity . . . measures were taken to supply those who were unable to furnish themselves. A fast day was proclaimed for the church on the first Thursday of each month, and the food saved in that way distributed among the poor; and thousands of persons, who had abundance of bread put their families on rations, in order to save the same for those who could not otherwise obtain it [*CHC* 4:109–110].

Since that time, the observation of a monthly fast of two meals on the first Sunday of each month and the donation of fast offerings have become regular practices in the Church. In the pioneer economy most donations—both tithing and fast offerings—were of food or livestock, and members took donations to the local tithing office or BISHOP'S STOREHOUSE. The goods were then distributed to the needy. Today, fast offerings usually consist of cash. Aaronic Priesthood DEACONS often serve as agents of the bishop in collecting fast donations.

WARDS and STAKES are encouraged to be self-reliant in caring for their poor. Bishops are instructed to seek out those in need and to provide them with life's essentials. Surplus fast offering funds in stakes are forwarded to Church headquarters, where they are redistributed to areas of greatest need.

Special fasts are occasionally proclaimed by the FIRST PRESIDENCY when urgent needs arise. Such was the case on May 15, 1845, when "enough was contributed to supply the wants of the poor until harvest" (*HC* 7:411). In 1985, Church members observed two special fast days and donated $10,465,000 to hunger relief and community development projects in Africa, South America, and elsewhere (*see* HUMANITARIAN SERVICES).

Historically, fast offerings have seldom been sufficient to provide for all the welfare needs of the Church, and shortages have been met from general Church funds. The counsel of Church President Spencer W. KIMBALL remains in effect: "I think that when we are affluent, as many of us are, that we ought to be very, very generous. . . . I think we should . . . give, instead of the amount we saved by our two meals of fasting, perhaps much, much more—ten times more where we are in a position to do it" (*CR* [Apr. 1974], p. 184).

BIBLIOGRAPHY

Kittel, Gerhard, ed. THEOLOGICAL DICTIONARY OF THE NEW TESTAMENT, Vol. 4, pp. 924–35. Grand Rapids, Mich., 1964.

Swenson, Russel B. "Welfare Work in the Early Christian Church." *Instructor* 82 (Aug. 1947):373–78.

ISAAC C. FERGUSON

FAST AND TESTIMONY MEETING

An LDS fast and testimony meeting is normally held on the first Sunday of each month, where faithful members of the Church are invited to bear a verbal witness of their feelings of the gospel of Jesus Christ. The meeting usually follows a fast by the members, usually from at least two consecutive meals and from liquids also. The fast is officially broken by partaking of the SACRAMENT of the Lord's Supper. In modern scripture, fasting is described as "rejoicing and prayer" (D&C 59:14), which implies that it is more than just abstaining from food. That tone of devotion is also the feeling associated with contributing fast offerings, giving the equivalent cost of the meals, or more, to be used for the poor. The fast and testimony meeting becomes the locus of spiritual sensitivity and contrition, of concentration on the things of God.

A member of the BISHOPRIC or branch presidency conducts the fast and testimony meeting. Usually it begins with an opening hymn and an invocation or prayer, which may be followed by the naming and blessing of newborn children and the confirming of recently baptized members of the Church.

After the sacrament has been administered, the person conducting the meeting expresses his testimony, then invites the members of the congregation of all ages to do likewise. Sometimes they stand in place to speak; at other times they come forward to the pulpit. Each one arises, as prompted by the Spirit, and addresses the congregation extemporaneously. In this setting feelings of profoundest concern are often expressed: appreciation of good family relationships, thanksgiving for the blessings of the gospel, recognition of significant changes in lives, and the fruits of obedience. A faith-promoting experience may be shared or a witness given regarding a point of doctrine or attesting divine inspiration. Such expressions are usually concluded by a prayer or petition in the name of the Lord. The experience is at once enlightening, sobering, and moving. Tears are not uncommon amid acknowledgment of weaknesses and efforts to improve, along with gratitude for divine goodness.

Rarely are such individual expressions longer than five or six minutes. Thus a number of children and adults generally participate in a meeting, which usually lasts a little more than an hour, but may be extended or shortened at the discretion of the presiding officer. In any given year a majority of the membership of the Church, young and old, will have participated in this earnest form of witness on fast Sunday.

One precedent for formal testimony bearing was set at the dedication of the KIRTLAND TEMPLE. On that occasion several stood and, under the outpouring of the Spirit, spoke of things they had seen and felt. In Kirtland it was customary to hold fast meetings on Thursday afternoons. Since 1896 these meetings have usually been held on Sunday.

MARY JOLLEY

FATE

Fate, as usually interpreted, is the antithesis of self-determination and responsibility. Latter-day Saints reject on scriptural grounds all appeals to precausation whether as "fate," "the stars," "blind chance," or even the PREDESTINATION of man by God. Fate in these forms implies a precaused outcome of one's life. Instead, man is seen as having innate autonomies and capacities—the gift of AGENCY—that the divine will guarantees all men: "I the Lord God make you free, therefore ye are free indeed: and the law also maketh you free" (D&C 98:8; cf. 2 Ne. 2:25–27; Alma 12:31; Moses 4:3). People are free to choose obedience or disobedience, good or evil, and most other aspects of their lives, and they are accountable for their choices. The belief that all is fated, stifles, discourages, and hinders the progress and growth possible for the children of God. Fate is considered a negative term in the gospel. Even one's own momentous decisions influence one's so-called fate or destiny only as long as the decisions are maintained. The GOSPEL OF JESUS CHRIST opens to all mankind the opportunity to rise above chance fate in this life and choose eternal life with God.

BIBLIOGRAPHY

The Church of Jesus Christ of Latter-day Saints. *Gospel Principles*. Salt Lake City, 1978, pp. 18–21.

GERALD E. JONES

FATHERHOOD

LDS fathers have primary responsibility for providing spiritual and physical support for all other family members (D&C 68:25, 28; 75:28). Giving Christlike service as a husband and father is the most important work a man can perform during mortality. Far more than mere procreation, fatherhood entails the lifelong care of children and loving support of their mother. Elder Theodore Tuttle wrote that for husbands to be effective fathers they should strive to learn and express those attributes they understand Heavenly Father to possess (pp. 66–68).

Latter-day Saints view parenthood as the highest and most sacred calling from God to his children on earth. Mothers and fathers are taught to labor together in faith and love to bring children into the world, to care for them, and to teach them the gospel of Jesus Christ so that they may receive eternal life, thus as parents following the example of their Father and Mother in Heaven (D&C 93:40). Through sacred covenants with God and with each other, men and women establish in this life families that have the potential to endure forever.

Fatherhood is best represented in men who unselfishly cherish and befriend their wives and promote their children's happiness and righteousness. This includes nurturing and expressing love, establishing obedience of their children through firmness and warmth, and teaching the gospel in home and Church settings. Fathers are also encouraged to lead by example (Benson, 1985).

Boys and men are taught the characteristics that exemplify loving and responsible fathers. As part of the Primary organization curricula, songs and lessons teach children to admire their fathers and to associate manhood and fatherhood with the characteristics of Christ. As members of a PRIESTHOOD QUORUM, young men are taught self-reliance, self-mastery, achievement, honor and respect for women, and chastity. Youth activities, Church sermons, and family programs also emphasize the importance of service to and sacrifice for others as part of fatherhood. Adult men are exposed to continuing emphasis on fatherhood. Formal instruction in Melchizedek Priesthood quorums is often aimed at motivating and inspiring men to esteem women as fellow children of the Father of all human beings, to observe strict marital fidelity, to give appropriate emphasis to the needs of children, and to learn skills that promote happy and successful lives for all family members.

Men in leadership positions are admonished not to neglect their family duties. When necessary,

LDS fathers lead, teach, play with, and counsel their children as part of their indispensable participation in family life. For Latter-day Saints, no calling or role surpasses a father's personal obligation to guide his children in righteousness. Courtesy Floyd Holdman (Tokyo, 1986).

men may be released from demanding Church positions in order to give appropriate time to their families. Fathers are taught to spend time with their families; to bring the family together in frequent prayer, scripture study, and family meetings; and to teach children to keep God's commandments, to work, and to respect others (Mosiah 4:14–15; 3 Ne. 18:21).

[*See also* Father's Blessings; Lifestyle; Marriage; Men, Roles of; Motherhood.]

BIBLIOGRAPHY

Benson, Ezra Taft. "Worthy Fathers, Worthy Sons." *Ensign* 15 (Nov. 1985):35–37.

Father, Consider Your Ways (pamphlet). Salt Lake City, 1978.

Perry, L. Tom. "Train Up a Child." *Ensign* 18 (Nov. 1988):73–75.

"The Role of the Father in the Home." In *Seek to Obtain My Word: Melchizedek Priesthood Personal Study Guide 1989*, pp. 199–204. Salt Lake City, 1988.

Tanner, N. Eldon. "Fatherhood." *Ensign* 7 (June 1977):2–5.

Tuttle, A. Theodore. "The Role of Fathers." *Ensign* 4 (Jan. 1974):66–68.

A. LYNN SCORESBY

FATHERS' BLESSINGS

Fathers' blessings are given by the power of the MELCHIZEDEK PRIESTHOOD following the pattern of the ancient PATRIARCHS, such as ADAM, NOAH, ABRAHAM, Isaac, Jacob, LEHI, MOSIAH, ALMA$_2$, and MORMON. All gave blessings to their children. Adam's final blessing upon several of his descendants is described in Doctrine and Covenants 107:53–57. So significant was the ORDINANCE on that occasion that "the Lord appeared unto them, and they rose up and blessed Adam" (*TPJS*, p. 38).

For the earthly blessing to be honored in heaven, it is necessary that a father has been baptized, has received the HOLY GHOST, and bears the Melchizedek Priesthood. Through these ordinances and COVENANTS, the father may claim the powers of heaven to guide his thoughts and ratify his words. To give such a blessing, the father places his hands upon the head of his child, and assures the child by word and spirit that the blessing, spoken by a loving parent, comes with divine approval and INSPIRATION.

The father may give blessings when requested by his wife or children or when he feels their need.

A father, assisted by other men who hold the Melchizedek Priesthood, gives his infant child a name and a father's blessing during a sacrament meeting (c. 1975; see D&C 20:70). Fathers may also bless their children at other times of need. Courtesy Doug Martin.

He does not force a blessing on anyone, for that would conflict both with the law of AGENCY and the spirit of LOVE. There is no ideal frequency for such blessings, only as the needs of the person and the whisperings of the Spirit suggest. A father will find performing this sacred ordinance easier if his relationships with his children are gentle and kind. If there is a conflict between father and child, it may be necessary to reconcile it before attempting the blessing.

A father's blessing is both an ordinance authorized by God and an action that draws father and child together even as it reassures a mother, who sees her husband spiritually minister to their child. It is a symbolic and official godlike act of pure love.

BIBLIOGRAPHY

"Fathers Blessings and Patriarchal Blessings." *Melchizedek Priesthood Personal Study Guide*, p. 43. Salt Lake City, 1988.

VICTOR L. BROWN, JR.

FAYETTE, NEW YORK

The township of Fayette, New York, is located in Seneca County between Seneca and Cayuga lakes.

The Church of Jesus Christ of Latter-day Saints was organized in the log cabin of Peter Whitmer, Sr., approximately 4.7 miles northwest of the village of Fayette and 3 miles southwest of modern Waterloo, New York (*see* ORGANIZATION OF THE CHURCH [1830]).

Joseph SMITH first came to Fayette in the spring of 1829, when David WHITMER, who knew Oliver COWDERY, invited him and the Prophet to come to his father's house from HARMONY, PENNSYLVANIA, to complete the translation of the Book of Mormon. They arrived in Fayette the first week of June and completed the translation by the end of June. They also preached occasionally in the area, baptizing many converts. Joseph Smith received five REVELATIONS in Fayette during that month (D&C 14–18). Soon after the translation was completed, Whitmer, Cowdery, and Martin HARRIS testified that they were shown the plates by a heavenly messenger near the Whitmer home (*see* BOOK OF MORMON WITNESSES).

In April 1830, the Prophet received a revelation instructing him to organize the Church on APRIL 6, which was accomplished in the home of Peter Whitmer, Sr. (D&C 20–21). In the days and months that followed, many meetings were held in the general area of Fayette and more converts were baptized. The first general conference of the Church was held in Fayette on June 9, 1830.

Because of renewed opposition in Harmony, Pennsylvania, where Joseph and his wife, Emma, had returned after the Church was organized, they moved again to the Whitmer home in Fayette, living there from August 1830 to January 1831. In those months, Joseph continued the work of his inspired translation of the Bible (*see* JOSEPH SMITH TRANSLATION OF THE BIBLE [JST]), part of which was later published as the BOOK OF MOSES; he also received thirteen additional revelations (D&C 28–40). The second general conference was held in Fayette on September 26, 1830.

In December 1830 and January 1831, revelations were received instructing the Latter-day Saints to move to Ohio to a more friendly environment (D&C 37:1–3; 38:31–32), where LDS missionaries had made many converts. Joseph and Emma Smith left Fayette in the latter part of January 1831, and most of the remaining members left later that spring and summer.

Today the Church has built a VISITORS CENTER, a chapel, and a replica of the Whitmer log cabin on the old Whitmer farm.

Reconstructed log home at the site of the Peter Whitmer, Sr., home in Fayette, New York. Here the Book of Mormon translation was completed, the testimony of the Three Witnesses was signed (June, 1829), and the Church was organized on April 6, 1830. Twenty revelations in the Doctrine and Covenants were received here. Courtesy LaMar C. Berrett.

BIBLIOGRAPHY

Porter, Larry C. "A Study of the Origins of The Church of Jesus Christ of Latter-day Saints in the States of New York and Pennsylvania, 1816–1831." Ph.D. diss., Brigham Young University, 1971.

LAMAR E. GARRARD

FEAR OF GOD

In ancient SCRIPTURE the phrase "fear of God" typically signified faith, reverence, and trust. Fear of God, so defined and felt, tends to diminish other forms of fear that arise in the absence of genuine faith. Thus, modern REVELATION admonishes against fearing to do good (D&C 6:33), fearing enemies (D&C 122:9; 136:17), fearing Satan (Moses 1:20), and fearing death (D&C 101:36). An undergirding principle permeates Latter-day Saint practice: "If ye are prepared ye shall not fear" (D&C 38:30). In the spiritual realm, unpreparedness can lead to what the scriptures call "a certain fearful looking for of judgment" (Heb. 10:27).

Latter-day Saints are sometimes described, because of an assumed overemphasis on works, as living in "fear and trembling." The phrase is Paul's (Phil. 2:12). Actually, Mormons aspire to follow Paul's teaching and practice to be "anxiously engaged in a good cause," but that anxiety is related to freedom and responsibility (see D&C 58:27).

They strive to find and fulfill their CALLINGS and fear to fall short of the divine purpose in their lives. They are constantly charged to magnify their callings and not to be weary in well-doing. Modern revelation promises that on condition of "persuasion, by long-suffering, by gentleness and meekness, and by love unfeigned" (D&C 121:41), "[their] confidence [shall] wax strong in the presence of God" (D&C 121:45). This parallels the promise of John: "Perfect love casteth out fear" (1 Jn. 4:18).

JOHN R. CHRISTIANSEN

FELLOWSHIPPING MEMBERS

Latter-day Saints consider themselves brothers and sisters (*see* BROTHERHOOD and SISTERHOOD) responsible to help one another. Their informal

A New Zealand Church member is greeted with the traditional "hongi" by John Shaw Welch, president of the LDS Maori Agricultural College (1917). Friendship, understanding, kindness, love, and service are fostered in Latter-day Saint communities through personal fellowshipping and social activities. Courtesy Edith W. Morgan.

acts of friendship and kindness foster congeniality within the Church and assist new members as they move into its social context. In addition, the Church has developed some practices specifically intended to help integrate new members.

After baptism, the full-time and stake missionaries present to new members a series of lessons entitled *Discussions for New Members*. Home teachers also teach them and help them become part of the local Church unit. The BISHOPRIC, priesthood quorum, and auxiliary leaders also help converts feel welcome. New members are encouraged to attend Church meetings and participate in other scheduled ward activities. Converts are also invited to accept Church CALLINGS (such as teaching a class or serving in an administrative capacity). Women are welcomed into RELIEF SOCIETY activities, and girls into YOUNG WOMEN; male adults and teenagers receive the PRIESTHOOD and begin functioning in their priesthood responsibilities. Newly baptized members grow in love for the gospel as they serve others. After one year of membership, worthy adult members are encouraged to attend the TEMPLE, where they receive TEMPLE ORDINANCES that bind families together as eternal units.

[*See also* Conversion; Joining the Church; Membership.]

BIBLIOGRAPHY
Discussions for New Members. Salt Lake City, 1987.

LYNN REED PAYNE

FEMINISM

Feminism is the philosophical belief that advocates the equality of women and men and seeks to remove inequities and to redress injustices against women. Far from a monolithic ideology, feminist theory embraces a variety of views on the nature of women and argues for a pluralistic vision of the world that regards as equally important the experiences of women of all races and classes.

In the United States, "feminism" has been an umbrella term encompassing a coalition of those women and men who share a devotion to the cause of women's rights but who often differ on specific goals and tactics. Personal, religious, and political values all influence which reforms and measures a specific feminist will support.

The doctrine of The Church of Jesus Christ of Latter-day Saints converges in some areas with the ideals of feminism and diverges in others. It insists on the absolute spiritual equality of women and men, proclaiming that "all are alike unto God," both "black and white, bond and free, male and female" (2 Ne. 26:33; Gal. 3:28). GIFTS OF THE SPIRIT are given equally to men and women: "And now, he imparteth his word by angels unto men, yea, not only men but women also" (Alma 32:23). LDS principles argue unequivocally for the development of the full potential of each person, regardless of gender.

So central is the equality of all humankind to Christ's message that during his earthly ministry Christ openly rejected cultural proscriptions that relegated women to an inferior spiritual and political status. He recognized women's spirits and intellects; he taught them directly (Luke 10:38–42); he identified himself as the Messiah to a woman, the first such affirmation recorded in the New Testament (John 4:26); he healed women (Matt. 15:22–28) and raised a woman from the dead (Luke 8:49–56). After his resurrection, he appeared first to a woman, whom he asked to tell his apostles of the glorious event (John 20:11–18), although according to Jewish law women were not considered competent as legal witnesses.

Such equality of women and men is based on the celestial model of heavenly parents, both Father and Mother, who share "all power" and have "all things . . . subject unto them" (D&C 132:20) and who invite their children to emulate their example of perfect love and unity and become as they are. Mormons are taught that righteous power, held by heavenly parents and shared with their children, is never coercive but is characterized "by persuasion, by long-suffering, by gentleness and meekness, and by love unfeigned" (D&C 121:41). While the implications of these expansive beliefs are always subject to individual implementation, Mormon women and men have found in these doctrines sources of spiritual strength, including the desire to know more about MOTHER IN HEAVEN.

LDS doctrine is, however, at odds with several versions of feminism, including those that emphasize female sufficiency apart from men. Because Church doctrine stresses the necessity of overcoming differences and forging a celestial unity between husband and wife in order to achieve EXALTATION (cf. 1 Cor. 11:11), the radical feminist critique of the family as an institution of repression for women and the call for its replacement find little support among Latter-day Saints. While individual families may be repressive and dysfunctional, most Latter-day Saints believe that the defect is not inherent in the structure. Indeed, the family is viewed as the source of both men's and women's greatest work and joy, not only on earth but also in eternity.

BIBLIOGRAPHY

Beecher, Maureen Ursenbach, and Lavina Fielding Anderson, eds. *Sisters in Spirit: Mormon Women in Historical and Cultural Perspective.* Urbana, Ill., 1987.

Dialogue 6 (Summer 1971) and 14 (Winter 1981). Both issues have a number of essays on women in the Church.

Donovan, Josephine. *Feminist Theory: The Intellectual Traditions of American Feminism.* New York, 1985.

MARY STOVALL RICHARDS

FINANCES OF THE CHURCH

The financial strength of The Church of Jesus Christ of Latter-day Saints derives primarily from the commitment of its members to the scriptural principle of TITHING and other forms of voluntary contributions and service. The collection and disbursement of all funds are carefully managed according to standard procedures worldwide and under the direct supervision of the FIRST PRESIDENCY. The Church also maintains limited business investments and financial reserves as part of its larger strategy for supporting expanding ecclesiastical programs. The handling of all funds is regularly audited in accordance with sound financial practices.

Latter-day Saints take seriously the commandment to pay tithing and the Lord's promises as given in the Old Testament:

> Will a man rob God? Yet ye have robbed me. But ye say, Wherein have we robbed thee? In tithes and offerings. Ye are cursed with a curse: for ye have robbed me, even this whole nation. Bring ye all the tithes into the storehouse, that there may be meat in mine house, and prove me now herewith, saith the Lord of hosts, if I will not open you the windows of heaven, and pour you out a blessing, that there shall not be room enough to receive it [Mal. 3:8–10].

This law of finance for God's Church has been reiterated in latter-day scripture. In 1838 the Lord emphasized this important law in a revelation to the Prophet Joseph SMITH and defined tithing as "one-tenth of all their interest [income] annually" (D&C 119:4).

The years preceding the turn of the century were financially difficult for the young, struggling Church because of the 1890s depression and the escheat of Church funds during the long antipolygamy campaign of the federal government. In May 1899 the aged Lorenzo SNOW, President of the Church, traveled from Salt Lake City to St. George, Utah, to comfort members whose lands had been plagued with severe drought. Streams and wells had dried up, and they faced starvation. During this visit President Snow was inspired to invoke the words of Malachi and promise the Saints in their dire and destitute circumstances that if they would pay an honest tithing, the "windows of heaven would be opened." The Saints responded, the rains came, and the people were blessed (Cowan, pp. 15–18).

From this event, the principle of tithing received renewed emphasis throughout the Church. Members responded with increased commitment and faith, and within a few years, the Church was financially sound, and has remained so since. Through the faith and sacrifices of its members, the Church has been able to sustain steady worldwide growth. Latter-day Saints regard the payment of tithing as a privilege and often tell of spiritual and financial blessings that have come through obedience to this law.

In addition to paying tithing, members may contribute to several specially designated funds (see FINANCIAL CONTRIBUTIONS). On the first Sunday of each month, members fast for two meals and contribute, at a minimum, the cash equivalent of two meals to a FAST OFFERING fund, used exclusively to provide assistance to the poor and needy. MISSIONARY support is primarily a family responsibility. Since January 1, 1991, the monthly cost to missionaries and their families has been standardized to the average monthly expense of missionaries worldwide. However, members are also encouraged to contribute to assist those missionaries who have insufficient finances.

FINANCIAL ADMINISTRATION. Sound cash management procedures are used in the collection and disbursement of funds. Tithing is contributed at the local WARD or BRANCH and is remitted to designated Church headquarters. AREA or regional offices around the world collect and disburse funds as directed by the presiding officers at Church headquarters.

Fast offering funds are collected in the wards, where they are first used to care for the needy in the ward. Surplus fast offerings not required for use in the local areas are sent to Church headquarters or area offices. Any deficits from the care of the poor in the local unit are supplemented from general surplus fast offerings. Thus, a local BISHOP has the means to take care of his ward's welfare needs.

On July 8, 1838, a revelation was received by the Prophet Joseph Smith making known the method for the disbursement of tithing received by the Church: "Verily, thus saith the Lord, the time is now come, that it [tithing] shall be disposed of by a council, composed of the First Presidency of my Church, and of the bishop and his council, and by my high council" (D&C 120:1).

Subsequently, the Council on the Disposition of Tithes, consisting of the First Presidency of the Church, the QUORUM OF TWELVE APOSTLES, and the PRESIDING BISHOPRIC, was established. This council meets regularly and oversees the expenditures of all Church funds worldwide. It approves budgets and financial strategy and establishes financial policy.

Two subcommittees of the Council on the Disposition of Tithes are the Budget Committee and the Appropriations Committee. Both committees consist of the First Presidency, selected members of the Quorum of the Twelve Apostles, and members of the Presiding Bishopric.

The Church Budget Office provides staff support to the First Presidency and gives overall administrative direction to the preparation of the annual Church budget. At the beginning of each annual budgeting cycle, budget guidelines are given to Church administrative department heads, international offices, missions, temples, and other units. Within these guidelines, budgets are constructed at the lowest levels of accountability and scrupulously reviewed through various levels of management and councils. The Budget Committee meets periodically to provide in-depth budget review and to formulate budget recommendations to the Council on the Disposition of Tithes.

The Appropriations Committee meets each week. All expenditure requests throughout the world, except those few which have been delegated to a lower level of administration by the

Council on the Disposition of Tithes, are reviewed, checked to make certain the request is within budget, and appropriated. Expenditures that have been delegated are reported to the committee.

FINANCIAL CONTROLS. Financial controls are administered through the use of financial policy, budgeting, organization structure, and regular, comprehensive audits. Key financial policy comes from the Council on the Disposition of Tithes. Additional financial policy and procedure directives are issued by the Finance and Records Department, which, under the direction of the First Presidency and the Presiding Bishopric, is responsible for the administration of treasury accounting/controllership, taxation, and risk-management functions.

The Church has an Audit Committee composed of experienced businessmen who are not associated with the Church as employees or General Authorities. This committee reports directly to the First Presidency of the Church and works closely with the Finance and Records Department and the Auditing Department to ensure strict adherence to ethical principles and rigid financial policies and procedures. The Auditing Department also reports directly to the First Presidency of the Church and thus maintains its independence from all other departments. Its staff of certified public accountants performs ongoing audits of finance, operation, and computer systems for Church departments and other Church-controlled organizations. Responses to all audits are required and are monitored.

PARTICIPATION AND INVESTMENTS IN BUSINESS. The First Presidency has established other boards and committees to oversee the management of the Church's investments and reserves (see BUSINESS: CHURCH PARTICIPATION IN). Each of these key committees is chaired either by a member of the First Presidency or by another appointed General Authority.

The Investment Policy Committee is chaired by the First Presidency and includes the president of the Council of the Twelve, other members of the Twelve as appointed, and the Presiding Bishopric. Its purpose is to establish investment policy and strategy and to review key investment decisions.

The Deseret Management Corporation (DMC) is a corporation with its own board of directors. DMC functions as a holding company for most of the commercial businesses owned by the Church. These companies pay all taxes that are paid by commercial corporations. Some properties are also held for reasons other than investment. In addition to protecting the surroundings of sacred properties, such investments may be maintained to support the ecclesiastical efforts of the Church.

The Church still holds a few properties that were originally established to support commerce in LDS communities (see ECONOMIC HISTORY OF THE CHURCH). However, as a result of an evaluation of these holdings and their contributions to its mission, the Church has divested many such holdings.

BIBLIOGRAPHY

Cowan, Richard O. *The Church in the Twentieth Century.* Salt Lake City, 1985.

Doxey, Roy W. *Tithing: The Lord's Law.* Salt Lake City, 1976.

RICHARD C. EDGLEY
WILFORD G. EDLING

FINANCIAL CONTRIBUTIONS

Members of the Church may make financial contributions in several ways, including payment of TITHING, donation of FAST OFFERINGS, and contributions to missionary work. Each kind of contribution is directed to a specific purpose and is based on admonitions in both ancient and modern scriptures (Mal. 3:8; D&C 119:4; cf. 2 Chr. 3:5–12; Rom. 15:26).

The payment of tithing is expected of each member regardless of age, income level, or circumstance. Faithful Latter-day Saints contribute one-tenth of their income annually to the Church. Members consider these tithing funds to be sacred monies, and leaders carefully administer their expenditures at each level of Church organization. Tithing is used to pay most of the operating expenses of the Church and also now funds the construction of buildings, including meetinghouses and temples.

Fast offerings are a second kind of financial contribution expected of all Church members. Once each month Church members are to abstain from food for at least two meals and contribute the cash equivalent of the savings as a "fast offering" to assist the poor and needy. These contributions are dispersed on both a local and Churchwide basis;

they are shared as needed throughout the Church and are available to local bishops for the aid of needy persons in their wards. In extraordinary circumstances, as in the case of the 1985 Ethiopian famine, the Church has called a special fast to raise relief funds for a specific disaster (*see* ECONOMIC AID; HUMANITARIAN SERVICE). For many years, the value of the two meals foregone during the fast determined the amount of the monthly fast offering contribution. Today Church leaders suggest that the amount of the voluntary offering be associated less with the value of the two meals and more with ability to respond generously to need.

A third kind of contribution made by Church members supports missionary work, a major activity of the Church that is financed largely by individual families. Young men and women can be "called" on missions, usually at the ages of nineteen and twenty-one, respectively, and are responsible for most of their own financial support, including food, rent, clothes, and local transportation. Major travel expenses and medical care are provided from Church funds. Parents and Church leaders urge young people to begin earning and saving money for their missions at an early age. Contributions from parents, family members, and friends supplement the missionaries' own funds to make up the total financial support required. Beginning in 1991, support for missionaries called from North American stakes is donated directly to the Church at uniform rates, but redistributed by the Church to missionaries according to varying costs of living in different areas of missionary service. Married couples may also be called to serve missions, and they, too, are responsible for their own financial support.

Members confidentially submit tithing and other donations to their local BISHOPS. Each ward bishop receives tithing and then remits it to central Church offices. Assisted by financial clerks, bishops provide contribution slips to donors and maintain complete records. They also review contribution summaries confidentially with each member once a year. Contribution records are forwarded to Church headquarters in accordance with uniform practices. Stake officers conduct regular audits of these records and practices.

Bishops, assisted by other ward leaders, prepare and submit annual ward budgets to be approved by stake presidents (*see* WARD BUDGET). Funding levels are determined by the membership and activity level of the ward. One outcome of this procedure is that local expenditures are determined by local need and not by the resources of members in a particular ward.

Until 1990, ward operating budgets were mostly dependent on contributions from local members made in addition to regular tithes, fast offerings, and missionary fund contributions. Youth and adult activities, instructional manuals and equipment, and building maintenance were funded locally. Since 1990, in North American stakes tithing paid by Church members is used to fund all local programs, activities, and maintenance of physical facilities. Members perform some maintenance functions as a voluntary service.

The method of funding construction of Church buildings has also varied considerably over time. For many years, the building of meetinghouses was financed largely through contributions from the local members who would use the building. These building fund contributions were made in addition to the tithes, fast offerings, and missionary funds contributed by Church members. Building fund monies could be raised through request (assessment of members), through a variety of fund-raising projects (dinners, socials, etc.), and sometimes through donations of labor and materials (*see* BUILDING PROGRAM). Temples, which are buildings for special religious ceremonies, were financed for many years in much the same manner as local meetinghouses. Now meetinghouses and temples are constructed largely out of tithing funds.

Because the Church has no professional clergy, it is administered at every level through LAY PARTICIPATION AND LEADERSHIP, and officials other than the General Authorities contribute their time and talents without remuneration. Thus, events such as weddings, funerals, and baptisms are conducted by the lay ministry in Church-owned buildings at no charge to the member for services or facilities. Because the General Authorities are obliged to leave their regular employment for full-time Church service, they receive a modest living allowance provided from income on Church investments.

STEPHEN D. NADAULD

FINE ARTS

[*Historically, the fine arts have been important to Latter-day Saints, who have encouraged participation in, and provided support for, art, dance, drama, litera-*

ture, music, and public speaking. For articles about LDS fine arts, see Angel Moroni Statue; Architecture; Art; Artists, Visual; Christus Statue; Folk Art; Material Culture; Sculptors; *and* Symbols. *On dance, see* Dance. *On drama, see* Cumorah Pageant; Drama; Pageants; Polynesian Cultural Center; *and* Salt Lake Theatre. *On literature, see the entry* Literature *with articles on* Drama, Novels, Personal Essays, Poetry, *and* Short Stories. *On music, see* Hymns and Hymnody; Mormon Tabernacle Choir; Mormon Youth Symphony and Chorus; *and* Tabernacle Organ. *On public speaking, see* Public Speaking.]

FIRESIDES

Firesides are informal gatherings of Church members and friends, often in homes or other congenial surroundings, as if around a fire. The premises are that the home is sacred ground and that all members are to "teach one another" and share experiences and training, that "all may be edified of all and that every man may have an equal privilege" (cf. D&C 88:122). Typically, firesides feature a single speaker reporting new developments, insights, or interesting experiences.

Religious firesides exhibit ties to the ancient fascination of the warmth and protection of a fire. In LDS life, firesides may be traceable to the exodus across the plains. After an arduous day of travel, the PIONEERS in the evening would arrange their wagons in a circle, and gather around the campfire to pray, sing, share their spiritual experiences, and rejoice in the progress and blessings of the day. Eliza R. SNOW wrote a typical song of this exodus:

> The camp, the camp—its numbers swell—
> Shout! Shout! O camp of Israel!
> The king, the Lord of hosts is near,
> His armies guard our front and rear [Journal of Eliza R. Snow].

In this spirit, one journal records, "It verily seemed that the glory of God rested down on the wagons and overspread the prairie."

Holding firesides has become a common Sunday evening practice for socializing, fellowshipping, and learning. WARDS, STAKES, or REGIONS commonly sponsor firesides. They are frequently a forum for returned MISSIONARIES presenting cultural insights from their mission experiences, often with the use of slides, tapes, photos, and so forth.

By extension of the term, there are "morningsides" for high-school SEMINARY students who

attend religious classes before school, and "noonsides" for some who want to add meaningful religious moments to their lunch hour. Multistake firesides with large audiences are regularly held at BRIGHAM YOUNG UNIVERSITY. Some satellite broadcasts beamed throughout the world from the Salt Lake TABERNACLE and featuring presentations from the general Church leaders are also called firesides.

In all firesides, essential elements prevail: prayer, music, the spoken word, and sometimes special activities or workshops. All in all, they encourage lay participation, sharing, and free expression, and lead to deeper comprehension of one's heritage, both religious and cultural, and a "knowledge of history and of countries and of kingdoms" (D&C 93:53; 88:79).

BIBLIOGRAPHY

Journal of Eliza R. Snow. Bancroft Library, UC Berkeley.

RONALD W. PATRICK

FIRSTBORN OF GOD

See: Jesus Christ: Names and Titles of

FIRST ESTATE

First estate refers to the unspecified period of time otherwise known as PREMORTAL LIFE. The words "first estate" in Jude 1:6 are the King James translation of the Greek *arché.* In other English versions the word is translated as "principality," "domain," "dominion," "appointed spheres," "responsibilities," and "original rank." In the context of Jude 1:6 each of these implies that certain intelligent beings existed in significant positions in the pre-earth life and fell from their favored status with God.

Latter-day Saints believe that all MANKIND were begotten as individual spirit children of God, with individual agency, prior to being born into MORTALITY. Using this agency, a third part of these spirits followed Lucifer and rebelled against God and the PLAN OF SALVATION that God proposed to bring about the eventual EXALTATION of his children through the atoning sacrifice of Jesus Christ. Because of their rebellion, these spirits "kept not their first estate" (Jude 1:6) and were subsequently cast out of heaven, being denied the opportunity of having a mortal body on this earth (D&C 29:36–38; Moses 4:1–4; Abr. 3:26–28; cf. Rev. 12:4, 7–9). All the remaining spirits proved themselves sufficiently faithful to be permitted the privilege of experiencing earth life with a PHYSICAL BODY (Abr. 3:22–26).

[*See also* Birth; Second Estate.]

ALEXANDER L. BAUGH

FIRST PRESIDENCY

The First Presidency is the governing body of and highest ranking quorum in The Church of Jesus Christ of Latter-day Saints. Its AUTHORITY, duties, and responsibilities extend over every person and all matters in the Church. This quorum usually consists of three persons—the PRESIDENT OF THE CHURCH and two counselors selected by the President. Joseph SMITH, the first President, called more than two men to assist him. Other Presidents have occasionally also used this practice of additional counselors as needed. Most recently, Spencer W. KIMBALL was assisted at times by three counselors.

The First Presidency was established in March 1832, two years after the founding of the Church. Jesse Gause and Sidney RIGDON were called to be counselors to Joseph Smith. Gause served in this position only until that December, when he proved unfaithful and was excommunicated. The calling was subsequently given to Frederick G. Williams, who was ordained on March 18, 1833 (D&C 81, 90). Further direction pertaining to the organization of the First Presidency was given in a revelation on priesthood in 1835. Three men were to be chosen and appointed, and ordained to that office by the QUORUM OF THE TWELVE APOSTLES, "and upheld by the confidence, faith, and prayer of the church" (D&C 107:22).

Latter-day Saints believe that the New Testament APOSTLES—PETER, JAMES, and JOHN— comprised a first presidency with Peter as the presiding officer, and with James and John as counselors. As an ancient first presidency, they functioned in a manner similar to the First Presidency today. For instance, the Bible describes occasions when Jesus dealt with Peter alone (Matt. 18:19; Luke 24:34), and others when the three apostles were involved (Matt. 17:1–3; 26:37–39; Mark 5:37–42). These passages suggest that the roles of these three men were different from the roles of the other apostles. As a first presidency, Peter, James, and John possessed the special authority to give Joseph Smith and Oliver COWDERY the KEYS of ministry in the DISPENSATION OF THE FULNESS OF TIMES. It is these keys that control the exercise of the priesthood by all others in the vital functions of the Church in modern times.

Members of the First Presidency are not co-equal. The authority rests solely with the President, the counselors having a subordinate role, with the first counselor having precedence over the second counselor. In the absence of the President, the counselors preside in meetings with the Council or Quorum of the Twelve Apostles and other GENERAL AUTHORITIES, and in the conferences of the Church. If the President is ill and unable to carry out all his functions, the counselors

President Wilford Woodruff (center), with second counselor Joseph F. Smith (right) and first counselor George Q. Cannon (left), at the time of the dedication of the Salt Lake Temple, April 6, 1893. John F. Bennett Collection. Photographer: Charles Ellis Johnson. Courtesy the Utah State Historical Society.

may conduct the affairs of the Church under his direction. In such a case, the counselors operate in close consultation with the President of the Council of the Twelve. However, the President of the Church remains the final authority.

The selection of the counselors is the prerogative of the President. A new President may or may not choose to retain the counselors of his predecessor. The counselors are usually apostles, but in a few cases men have been called who were not ordained apostles, the first such being Sidney Rigdon (1832) and Frederick G. Williams (1833). More recently, Thorpe B. Isaacson was called in 1965 to serve in the First Presidency under David O. McKay. In some cases, the counselors have been apostles but not members of the Twelve, such as Alvin R. Dyer, another counselor to President McKay.

The general membership of the Church votes to sustain the First Presidency but does not elect them. Because members of the Church believe that the calling and authority of the First Presidency come from God, their vote is one of COMMON CONSENT, to ratify or oppose a selection that has already been made.

Doctrine and Covenants 107:9 states, "The Presidency of the High Priesthood, after the order of Melchizedek, have a right to officiate in all the offices in the church." As the highest level of authority, the Quorum of the First Presidency has the ultimate power of appointment, presidency, interpretation of DOCTRINE, and all other matters pertaining to the Church. Thus, all other quorums, councils, and organizations of the Church operate under the authority of this quorum.

Affairs administered directly by the First Presidency have included planning general and area conferences and solemn assemblies; budgeting, auditing, educational, historical, personnel, and other general Church departments; and temples. All other matters are administered by the Council of the Twelve, the PRESIDING BISHOPRIC, or the SEVENTY, under the direction of the First Presidency.

In the First Presidency, the decision making is to be unanimous. Close and careful consultation between the President and his counselors helps to assure a consensus (Hinckley, p. 50).

The First Presidency normally meets at least weekly as a unit, then in joint session with the Quorum of the Twelve Apostles to consider matters needing their attention. It is in this COUNCIL

The First Presidency in 1985: President Ezra Taft Benson (center), first counselor Gordon B. Hinckley (left), and second counselor Thomas S. Monson (right). The President of the Church has at least two counselors, who together with him form the First Presidency, which presides over the Church.

OF THE FIRST PRESIDENCY AND THE QUORUM OF THE TWELVE APOSTLES that any changes in administration or policy for the Church are considered and approved.

The First Presidency also meets weekly with the Presiding Bishopric. Meetings are held each month with all the General Authorities, where they are informed about any changes in programs or procedures. In addition, the First Presidency meets as needed with other councils, boards, and groups to which various responsibilities have been delegated.

Upon the death of the President, the Quorum of the First Presidency is automatically dissolved and the ultimate authority of the Church passes immediately to the Twelve, with the presiding officer being the President of the Quorum of the Twelve Apostles. The counselors, if they are apostles, return to their respective positions in that quorum according to seniority of appointment. The First Presidency is reconstituted at the calling of a new President, who in every instance has been the President of the Quorum of the Twelve Apostles, and then he selects his own counselors. Once this is accomplished, supreme authority returns to the First Presidency.

BIBLIOGRAPHY

Hinckley, Gordon B. "In . . . Counsellors There Is Safety." *Ensign* 20 (Nov. 1990):48–51.

Article of Faith Number 4, by Michael Clane Graves (1982, acrylic on canvas). The first principles of the gospel, here represented geometrically, are faith in the Lord Jesus Christ, repentance, baptism by immersion for the remission of sins, and laying on of hands for the gift of the Holy Ghost. Courtesy Museum of Fine Arts, Brigham Young University.

Tanner, N. Eldon. "The Administration of the Church." *Ensign* 9 (Nov. 1979):42–48.

J. LYNN ENGLAND
W. KEITH WARNER

FIRST PRINCIPLES OF THE GOSPEL

The first principles and ordinances of the gospel are "first, Faith in the Lord Jesus Christ; second, Repentance; third, Baptism by immersion for the remission of sins; fourth, Laying on of hands for the gift of the Holy Ghost" (A of F 4). The resurrected Savior taught that these principles constitute his "gospel": "Repent, all ye ends of the earth, and come unto me and be baptized in my name, that ye may be sanctified by the reception of the Holy Ghost, that ye may stand spotless before me at the last day. Verily, verily, I say unto you, this is my gospel" (3 Ne. 27:20–21; cf. Acts 2:37–38). These four principles prepare one to *enter* the "strait and narrow path which leads to eternal life" (2 Ne. 31:17–18).

First, faith in Jesus Christ often begins with a desire to believe (Alma 32:26–28), which may be kindled by hearing or reading others' true testimonies of Christ and his atonement. One nourishes faith by patient obedience to God's commandments. Faith then grows through a process that includes REPENTANCE, baptism for REMISSION OF SINS, increased confidence in Christ, and eventually a Christlike nature (Hafen, pp. 141–200).

Repentance involves (1) realization of guilt; (2) godly sorrow and suffering; (3) confession for relief from the hurtful effects of sin; (4) restitution, as far as it is possible; (5) replacement of sin with obedience to God's requirements; and (6) acceptance of Christ's atoning sacrifice. Through the Atonement, if one repents, Christ's mercy satisfies the demands of justice.

Baptism, the third principle and first essential ordinance, is the fruit of repentance and is required of all who would be saved in the KINGDOM OF GOD (John 3:3–5; cf. 2 Ne. 9:23). Baptism has several purposes. It is a symbolic washing and cleansing of sins and is prerequisite to membership in the Church. When followed by the reception of the Holy Ghost, it is the doorway to personal SANCTIFICATION (Moro. 6:1–4). The prescribed method of baptism is by immersion in water by a PRIEST in the AARONIC PRIESTHOOD or by one who holds the MELCHIZEDEK PRIESTHOOD. "The symbolism of the rite is preserved in no other form" (*AF*, p. 137).

Being "born of the Spirit," or receiving the GIFT OF THE HOLY GHOST, entitles one to the continual help, guidance, and comfort of the Holy Ghost. "The special office of the Holy Ghost is to enlighten and ennoble the mind, to purify and sanctify the soul, to incite to good works, and to reveal the things of God" (*AF*, p. 167). When asked how the Church differed from the other religions of the day, Joseph Smith replied that "we differed in mode of baptism, and the gift of the Holy Ghost . . . [and] that all other considerations [of differences from other churches] were contained in the gift of the Holy Ghost" (*HC* 4:42). The gift of the Holy Ghost is conferred by the LAYING-ON OF HANDS by a holder of the Melchizedek Priesthood.

Summarizing the process from faith and repentance to sanctification, the Book of Mormon prophet Mormon stated, "And the first fruits of repentance is baptism; and baptism cometh by faith unto the fulfilling the commandments; and the fulfilling the commandments bringeth remission of sins; and the remission of sins bringeth meekness, and lowliness of heart; and because of meekness and lowliness of heart cometh the visitation of the Holy Ghost, which Comforter filleth with hope and perfect love, which love endureth by diligence unto prayer, until the end shall come, when all the saints shall dwell with God" (Moro. 8:25–26).

These four principles and ordinances of the gospel are "first" because they both initiate and enable the process of development from a spiritual rebirth to a divine nature.

BIBLIOGRAPHY

Hafen, Bruce C. *The Broken Heart: Applying the Atonement to Life's Experiences.* Salt Lake City, 1989.

Kimball, Spencer W. *The Miracle of Forgiveness.* Salt Lake City, 1969.

MARIE KARTCHNER HAFEN

FIRST VISION

The First Vision of the Prophet Joseph SMITH is the beginning point, the fountainhead, of the RESTORATION of the gospel in this DISPENSATION. This theophany occurred in a grove near Palmyra, New York, in the spring of 1820.

Joseph's narratives record that when he was in his twelfth year he began to sense the need for redemption and investigated several religious groups. A short time after his family moved to Manchester, New York, he witnessed unusual religious excitement in the area, bringing divisions of allegiance in his community and family. As converts began filing off to one faith and another, he observed that their professed good feelings for each other were lost in "a strife of words and a contest about opinions" (*JS—H* 1:5–8). Confused and concerned, he asked himself, "If any one of them be right which is it? And how shall I know it?" (Backman, pp. 156, 162, 168; Jessee, p. 198).

Searching the scriptures, Joseph was influenced by an admonition to prayer in the epistle of JAMES. "If any of you lack wisdom, let him ask of God" (James 1:5). "Never," he later recalled, "did any passage of scripture come with more power to the heart of man than this did at this time to mine" (*JS—H* 1:12). He retired to a secluded grove near his father's log-cabin farmhouse and knelt in prayer (Backman, p. 156).

A struggle with a satanic influence followed, but with divine help he survived it. As he continued to call upon God, he records, "I saw a pillar of light exactly over my head, above the brightness of the sun, which descended gradually until it fell upon me." Immediately he was delivered from oppressive darkness (JS—H 1:16). Within the light, he saw two personages "whose brightness and glory defy all description" and who "exactly resembled each other in features and likeness" (JS—H 1:17; WENTWORTH LETTER, Backman, p. 169). One of them spoke his name, pointed to the other, and said, "This is My Beloved Son. Hear Him!" (JS—H 1:17). In what followed, Joseph learned that through Christ, who had taken upon himself the SINS of mankind, he was forgiven of his sins. "Behold I am the Lord of glory. I was crucified for the world that all those who believe on my name may have eternal life" (Backman, p. 157). He was also assured of the reality and imminence of

First Vision, by Gary E. Smith (1979, oil on canvas, 24″ × 30″). Unable to determine for himself what church or sect was right, fourteen-year-old Joseph Smith determined to ask God. Following his prayer, he recorded, "I saw two Personages, whose brightness and glory defy all description, standing above me in the air. One of them spake unto me, calling me by name and said, pointing to the other—*This is My Beloved Son. Hear Him!*" (JS–H 1:17). Courtesy Blaine T. Hudson.

Christ's second coming "to bring to pass that which [hath] been spoken by the mouth of the prophets and apostles" (Backman, pp. 157, 167, 169; Jessee, p. 6). When he recovered himself, Joseph asked which church he should join and was told to join none because they all taught "incorrect doctrines"; they had a form of godliness, but "denied the power thereof" (cf. 2 Tim. 3:5). Further, he was told "that the fulness of the gospel should at some future time be made known unto me" (JS—H 1:17–20; Backman, pp. 163, 169; Jessee, p. 213). As he left the grove, he recalled, "My soul was filled with love," and for many days "I could rejoice with great joy and the Lord was with me" (Backman, p. 157).

Joseph's tranquillity was short-lived. At first, except from his family, he met only contempt from those who learned of his experience. He had not anticipated the bitter denunciations that this event would call forth.

On several occasions between 1832 and 1842, the young Prophet wrote or dictated accounts of the vision, each in a different setting, the last two for publication. Each record omits or adds some details. In 1832, for example, Joseph Smith wrote that prior to his First Vision he searched the scriptures and concluded that no society taught New Testament Christianity (Backman, p. 156; Jessee, p. 5). In the 1838 account he notes that he often said to himself, "Who of all these parties are right; or, are they all wrong together?" Later in this same account he parenthetically adds "(for at this time it had never entered into my heart that all were wrong)" (JS—H 1:10, 18; Jessee, pp. 198, 200).

Latter-day Saints regard this vision as authentic and revelatory of the nature of God. In the biblical and scriptural context, they see it as parallel to the VISIONS of MOSES or the theophanies recorded in the Book of Mormon. Joseph himself compared his experiences in and after the vision to those of PAUL (JS—H 1:24; *TPJS*, p. 151).

LDS teaching is, in the words of Stephen L Richards (a former counselor in the FIRST PRESIDENCY), "steeped in the verity of the First Vision." It undergirds the doctrine of an anthropomorphic God and theomorphic man, of the relationships of the persons of the Godhead, and of continual REVELATION. Mormon prayers, hymns, forms of worship, and eschatology are all rooted in this understanding. It renews the witness of the Hebrew prophets that visions are not the least but the most reliable mortal access to the divine; that

the majesty, glory, and power of God are "beyond description"; that the biblical record of face-to-face communion with God is more than a strained metaphor. It confirms the New Testament testimony of the apostles that GOD THE FATHER and JESUS CHRIST are separate persons who manifest themselves as they are to the sons and daughters of God; and that the Son is in the similitude of the Father, and the Father in the similitude of the Son.

[*See also* Visions of Joseph Smith, Jr.; Religious Experience.]

BIBLIOGRAPHY

Backman, Milton V., Jr. *Joseph Smith's First Vision*. Salt Lake City, 1980.

Smith, Joseph. *The Personal Writings of Joseph Smith*, comp. and ed. Dean C. Jessee. Salt Lake City, 1984.

MILTON V. BACKMAN, JR.

FOLK ART

Through a combination of religious and western American metaphors and images, the whole saga of the Church has been artistically represented, from its origins in 1820 in a grove near Palmyra, New York, to the present. Songs and stories about the migration to Utah and the colonization of the Great Basin, anecdotal biographies of Church leaders, folklore incidents of faith, and the miraculous and sometimes comical struggles of the pioneer Saints form integral parts of LDS culture (*see* ART IN MORMONISM). Mormon folk art perpetuates a sense of inclusiveness and serves to bind Latter-day Saints together and help define who they are. Overwhelmingly, Mormon folk art has been the work of a faithful, pragmatic people.

For Latter-day Saint artists, the migration west was "the worst of times and the best of times." Driven from Nauvoo, they faced the prospect of building a new Zion, a home in the mountains. Their folk art is richly expressive of connections to their past and of their unique experience on the frontier. When one pioneer woman, Bathsheba SMITH, packed her trunk for the journey into western territory, she carefully selected what to take and what to leave behind. Deep in the corner of her single trunk she placed her paints, paper, and brushes wrapped in cloth. She added her lace-making tools and fibers to make the beautiful delicate lace for which she was famous. These tools of art she placed beneath the folds of a quilt made by her mother for her wedding day.

In a concrete sense, Bathsheba Smith was blending the old and the new by preserving the past and welcoming the future. When she once again took up her paints, this time in Utah, she would paint the story of the journey. Pioneer artist C. C. A. Christensen would do likewise, chronicling a story that would figure prominently in the folk art of the Mormon people. William Clayton would immortalize the faith of the pioneers in the words of a hymn: "Come, come, ye Saints, no toil nor labor fear; but with joy wend your way."

Mormon folk art was practical—functional, yet often beautiful and decorative. The imagery of

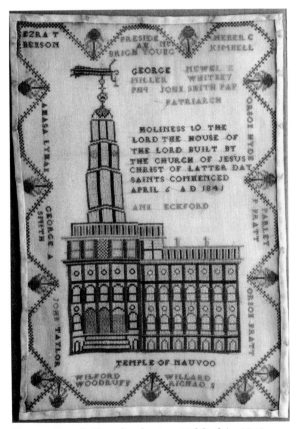

Nauvoo Temple Sampler, by Ann Eckford (c. 1846, embroidered cross stitch, 15″ × 20″). The names of the members of the Quorum of the Twelve Apostles as constituted in 1846 surround this cross stitch representation of the Nauvoo Temple. George Miller is also shown as president of the High Priests quorum (PHP), Bishop Newel K. Whitney as president of the Aaronic Priesthood (PAP), and stake president John Smith as patriarch. Church Museum of History and Art.

the LDS pioneer quilt reflected a western preoccupation with the natural environment. Pine trees, oaks, and mountain laurels had always been favored quilt motifs, but new images, notably the sego lily and the BEEHIVE, told of the work of the Mormon pioneers in Deseret.

The beehive appears in every genre of Mormon folk art—quilts, paintings, sculptures, architecture, and gravestones. The stonework of nineteenth-century Mormon culture is a rich statement of popular values, legends, and religion. A strong visual connection exists between pioneer gravestone imagery and New England tombstone art. But the cemeteries of small towns throughout Utah speak also of the unique LDS belief system and pioneer heritage. In addition to traditional motifs, religious emblems associated with the outside of temples flourished in this lively local art form.

One need not travel far into rural Utah to notice the distinctive folk architecture that existed among the Saints. The most common design was the "I" house, or old "Nauvoo style" house. It was a tall two-story house with a chimney at each gable end and usually a symmetrical arrangement of doors and windows at the front. Larger homes were constructed by connecting two or three I houses together to create a "T," "L," or "H" house. The most common indigenous building material was adobe, a local unfired brick produced by a mixture of mud and straw.

Distinct Mormon folklore also reflected the Latter-day Saint belief system. Stories of visits from the THREE NEPHITES often served as spiritual landmarks for the teller, and Elder J. Golden Kimball became a sort of folk hero through stories about his experiences and wit. Like quilts, Mormon folklore had a very specific function: usually it sought to enhance the faith and the sense of spirit of its audience. The story of the migration of the Mormon pioneers and the building of Zion became almost a kind of modern-day scripture.

Early twentieth-century LDS women continued the pioneer tradition of their mothers. Their RELIEF SOCIETY "workdays" became the institutional means for preserving folk art traditions. The emphasis on homemaking reflected a respect for traditional art forms that were displayed in quilting, fine sewing, and other household arts and crafts. Homemaking day became a monthly social event as Relief Society sisters met in a group for home crafts, homemaking lessons, and supper. The result was sometimes a somewhat modern-day

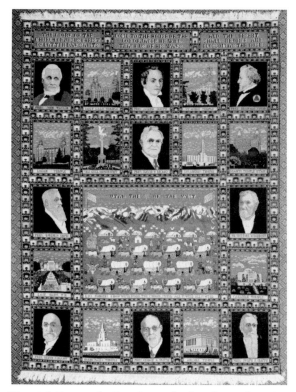

Pictorial Rug with Temples and Church Leaders, by Reuben and Mary Ouzounian (c. 1955; wool, cotton, silk, goat hair; 270 cm × 360 cm). Armenian Latter-day Saints living in Aleppo (now Haleb), Syria, completed this rug during their long and uncertain wait for visas permitting them to join Church members in Utah. Among the motifs are the Rocky Mountains under American flags, covered wagons recalling earlier pioneers, and representations of the temples and Church presidents to that date. Church Museum of History and Art.

version of Mormon folk art, different from the more personal expression of nineteenth-century women.

In the mid-twentieth century the Church often adopted an institutional method of preserving past art forms. The Church-wide dance festivals held into the 1970s brought young people together from across the world to share in an evening of the celebration of folk dance forms. Similarly, roadshows gave expression to local members' talents in miniplays that often depicted pioneer heritage values and customs (*see* DRAMA). Musicals like *My Turn on Earth* and *Saturday's Warrior* in much the same way as nineteenth-century folklore perpetuated folk traditions about premortal exis-

tence and the significance of life on earth (*see* MUSIC).

Twentieth-century Mormon folk art also reflects a faithful people as the story of the founding events and of the pioneers continues to figure prominently in every type of folk art. In general, it features respect for traditional art forms and mass participation. Folk art forms now flourishing in many different cultures have been welcomed as personal expressions of the testimony and love of Church members around the world.

[*See also* Folklore; Material Culture.]

BIBLIOGRAPHY

Brunvand, Jan Harold. *A Guide for Collectors of Folklore in Utah.* Salt Lake City, 1971.

Cannon, Hal. *The Grand Beehive.* Salt Lake City, 1980.

Fox, Sandi. *Quilts in Utah.* Salt Lake City, 1987.

MARTHA SONNTAG BRADLEY

FOLKLORE

Mormon folklore comprises that part of the Church's cultural heritage which Latter-day Saints pass on from person to person and from generation to generation, not through written documents or formal instruction but through the spoken word or customary example. That is, someone will listen to tales told at home or at a Church meeting about the sufferings of the Mormon pioneers and then will repeat these accounts to others; or a young girl will watch and then assist her grandmother make "temple quilts" (quilts on which the form of the Mormon temple in which a couple is married is stitched) for the marriages of each grandchild, and in the process will eventually learn to make her own quilts; or each evening children will be gathered by their parents into family prayer and then one day will continue the practice in their own families.

The materials of Mormon folklore fall roughly into three broad categories. First are things people make with words (from songs and stories of grandparents struggling to establish a New Zion in the harsh Great Basin Kingdom, to contemporary accounts of God's providential hand guiding "the affairs of the saints" and directing the efforts of missionaries in an ever-expanding church, to humorous tales that caricature Mormon foibles and ease the pressures of "being in the world but not of it"). Second are things people make with their hands (from traditional implements, such as the Mormon hay derrick, to homemade "quiet books" designed to keep small children constructively occupied during church meetings, to home preserves and special holiday foods, to a decorative family Book of Remembrance [*see* MATERIAL CULTURE]). And third are things people make with their actions (from "creative dating" practices of youth, to special family celebrations of birth and baptismal dates, to family genealogical meetings, to church and community celebrations of traditional holidays from Thanksgiving to Pioneer Day).

This listing of examples focuses very consciously on the word "make," because the categories of Mormon folklore are dynamic rather than static. Each recounting of a miraculous healing, each quilting of a familiar log-cabin pattern, each performance of a family birthday game is in every instance a new act of creation that speaks from both the past and the present. They speak from the past because the forms are traditional and recurring, having been developed by the LDS community over decades. They speak from the present because the forms are constantly reshaped to fit the needs of contemporary Latter-day Saints and to reflect contemporary values and concerns.

Because of this constant regeneration and reshaping of older forms, Mormon folklore lies not at the periphery but at the center of LDS culture. It is not, as is sometimes thought, simply a survival from the past kept alive primarily by older, less educated, and agrarian Church members; rather, it is a vital, functioning force in the lives of all Latter-day Saints. Further, as the Church continues to grow and change, new forms of folklore that speak more directly to present needs will sometimes replace the old. For just as Latter-day Saints in the pioneer era generated and transmitted folklore in response to the circumstances of their lives, so, too, contemporary Latter-day Saints will create and pass along folklore as they react to the strains and stresses, the joys and the sorrows of their lives. For example, converts to the Church living in the mission fields, away from church centers in the mountain West, may be little moved by tales of pioneer suffering and may know little of earlier stories of the providential saving of the pioneers' crops from swarms of locusts or of the legends of the THREE NEPHITES; but they will know and tell stories of their own miraculous conversions and of

the ridicule and suffering they endure, with the help of God, as they struggle to survive as the only Latter-day Saints in sometimes unfriendly and often hostile communities.

Properly to understand the Latter-day Saints, one must know their folklore—must see how it bolsters their faith, builds a sense of community, ties them to the past, and provides them an escape through humor from pressures that might otherwise be their undoing. Especially, one must understand Mormon folklore in order to understand the Mormon ethos. This is so because people tell stories about those events that interest them most or participate in customary practices that are most important to them. Because these stories and practices depend on the spoken word or on voluntary participation for their survival, those that fail to appeal broadly to a Mormon value center, a common body of LDS attitudes and beliefs, will simply cease to exist. Those that persist, therefore, serve as an excellent barometer for prevailing Mormon cultural and religious values.

In a number of Utah and western towns a Mormon temple, usually built on a hill or in the center of the valley, dominates the landscape, symbolizing for all who pass by the religious values that originally brought LDS settlers to the region. In towns and valleys surrounding the temples, in Sunday School classes, in family gatherings, among friends, the descendants and converts of these settlers relate stories that tell of the price paid for blessings now enjoyed, that give evidence of the providential hand of God in the lives of the faithful, that lift sagging spirits, bolster courage, promote obedience and give hope for the eventual and ultimate victory of Zion. The stories give a glimpse of this rich and ever-growing body of narratives, the lore of faith.

The question remains whether narratives embodying these values are really "true"—and, concomitantly, if they are not true, what is their ultimate value? Although the stories frequently are based on actual events, their details clearly change as they are passed along by word of mouth. These changes, however, do not occur randomly; they are dictated by cultural determinants. As stories are transmitted from person to person, they are often changed, usually unconsciously, to express the new tellers' beliefs and to meet their needs. Because folk narratives mirror and reinforce these beliefs, and because the beliefs are themselves historical facts, moving people to action more handily than the realities on which they are based, they can yield valuable historical data. But it is more profitable to turn to them for other reasons, to view them not as history but as literature, and to discover in them not the ledger-book truths of actual events but expression of the people's heart and mind. To a greater or lesser degree, Mormon folk stories may or may not be factually accurate. But as keys to understanding the Latter-day Saints and their church, they are always true.

BIBLIOGRAPHY

For studies in Mormon folklore see Austin Fife and Alta Fife, *Saints of Sage and Saddle: Folklore Among the Mormons* (Bloomington, Ind., 1956); and William A. Wilson, "The Study of Mormon Folklore: An Uncertain Mirror for Truth," *Dialogue* 22 (Winter 1989):95–110.

For bibliographic references see Jill Terry, "Exploring Belief and Custom: The Study of Mormon Folklore," *Utah Folklife Newsletter* 23 (Winter 1989):1–4; and William A. Wilson, "A Bibliography of Studies in Mormon Folklore," *Utah Historical Quarterly* 44 (1976):389–94.

WILLIAM A. WILSON

FOLLOWING THE BRETHREN

Latter-day Saints believe that God gives REVELATIONS to living PROPHETS and that their words, when so inspired, are to be received as his (D&C 1:38). It has therefore become common in the Church to say that Christ and his prophets are as one because they represent him (cf. John 17:21–23). This means that prophets, as agents of Christ, announce his gospel, and are one with him in teaching, testimony, and purpose (*see* UNITY). Thus, the scriptural injunction to follow Jesus and the baptismal COVENANT to obey his commandments also require following his prophets.

Among Latter-day Saints the injunction to "follow the Brethren" derives from this requirement of obedience to Jesus and to prophetic instruction. In this context, "the Brethren" are the GENERAL AUTHORITIES, particularly the FIRST PRESIDENCY and the QUORUM OF THE TWELVE APOSTLES, who are formally sustained as prophets, seers, and revelators. The principle involved can be extended to include local priesthood leaders such as PRIESTHOOD QUORUM presidencies, BISHOPS and STAKE PRESIDENTS, and the presidencies of the women's auxiliary organizations— RELIEF SOCIETY, YOUNG WOMEN, and PRIMARY— within their respective jurisdictions. This exten-

sion of the principle to all Church leaders at every level is based on the recognition that all officers in the Church are entitled to revelation in their CALLINGS and on the assumption that they are in harmony with the Brethren. Referring specifically to the prophet who is currently President of the Church, the Lord has instructed members to "give heed unto all his words and commandments which he shall give unto you as he receiveth them, walking in all holiness before me; For his word ye shall receive, as if from mine own mouth, in all patience and faith" (D&C 21:4–5).

Latter-day Saints claim a variety of blessings from following prophetic instruction. Not only does following the Brethren unite the Saints, enabling them to advance the purposes of the RESTORATION more effectively, but it also allows them to receive the rewards of such obedience, which include the GIFTS OF THE SPIRIT.

Following the Brethren, however, does not imply blind obedience, for every member of the Church is entitled to an individual witness of the Holy Spirit that the leadership of the Church is inspired by God. For this reason, following the living prophet obliges members to live worthy to receive personal inspiration and revelation. It gives contemporary meaning to MOSES' desire that "all the Lord's people" be prophets and thus recipients of inspiration (Num. 11:29), and to the Savior's saying that all should "live by every word that proceedeth forth from the mouth of God" (D&C 84:44; Deut. 8:3; Matt. 4:4).

Because Church members are entitled to divine confirmation of prophetic declarations, there is no teaching among Latter-day Saints of "prophetic infallibility." As Joseph SMITH taught, "a prophet was a prophet only when . . . acting as such" (*TPJS*, p. 278). Prophets have personal and private opinions, and they are "subject to like passions," as all people are (see James 5:17; Mosiah 2:10–11). However, when acting under the influence of the Holy Spirit in the prophetic role, "whatsoever they shall speak . . . shall be the will of the Lord" (D&C 68:3–4; *see* SCRIPTURE). As the Savior told Joseph Smith, "He that receiveth my servants receiveth me; and he that receiveth me receiveth my Father" (D&C 84:36–37; see also Matt. 10:40; 3 Ne. 28:34).

BIBLIOGRAPHY

Christiansen, ElRay L. "Sustaining the Authorities of the Church." *Relief Society Magazine* 44 (Feb. 1957):76–79.

Packer, Boyd K. "Follow the Brethren." *Speeches of the Year*, pp. 1–10. Provo, Utah, 1965.

Stapley, Delbert L. "Respect for Authority." *IE* 60 (Dec. 1957):914–15, 938.

MARK L. MCCONKIE

FOREKNOWLEDGE OF GOD

Modern scripture speaks unequivocally of the foreknowledge of God: "All things are present before mine eyes" (D&C 38:2). It affirms that God has a fulness of truth, a "knowledge of things as they are, and as they were, and as they *are to come*" (D&C 93:24, emphasis added).

Divine foreknowledge includes the power to know even the thoughts and intents of the human heart: "There is none else save God that knowest thy thoughts and the intents of thy heart" (D&C 6:16). Divine foreknowledge is at least, in part, knowledge of his own purposive plans for the cosmos and for humankind, plans that "cannot be frustrated, neither can they come to naught" (D&C 3:1). "Known unto God are all his works from the beginning of the world" (Acts 15:18; Abr. 2:8). These include the conditions of the plan of salvation. For example, "God did elect or predestinate that all those who would be saved, should be saved in Christ Jesus, and through obedience to the Gospel" (*TPJS*, p. 189). It is likewise foreknown that all humankind will die, be resurrected, and be brought to judgment.

In scripture, the root terms for divine knowing connote more than a subject-object, cognitive relationship; they imply a close, direct, participative, affective awareness. Divine foreknowledge is the knowledge of a Heavenly Father, not knowledge of a metaphysical abstraction. Scriptures that speak of divine foreknowledge emphasize God's understanding of an experience with his people and their destiny rather than the content and logic of that knowledge. Anyone seeking to understand divine foreknowledge must begin by recognizing that scripture does not directly address the question as it has been formulated in philosophy and theology, where the emphasis is on the content and logic of knowledge. The scriptures are explicit that God knows all and that we can trust him. They have not been explicit about what that means philosophically or theologically. Consequently, short of new revelation, any answer to the theological question of God's foreknowledge can be only speculative.

In an attempt to reconcile divine foreknowledge and human freedom, major Jewish and Christian theologians and philosophers have offered three alternatives. In the first, both horns of the dilemma are affirmed: "Everything is foreseen, and freedom of choice is given." This is the position of Rabbi Akiba and Maimonides (Aboth 3, 19; Yad, Teshuvah 5:5), as well as of Augustine and Anselm (*City of God* 5.9–10; *The Harmony of the Foreknowledge, the Predestination, and the Grace of God with Free Choice* 1.3). Maimonides argues that though it is logically impossible for human foreknowledge of one's actions to be compatible with freedom, God's foreknowledge, which is of a different and mysterious kind, is compatible with freedom.

In the second, God's foreknowledge is limited. Since people are free, God knows the possibilities and probabilities of human choice, but not the inevitabilities. God is omniscient in knowing all that can be known; but not in knowing beforehand exactly how people will use their freedom, since that cannot be known because future, contingent events do not exist. This is the view of the Talmudist Gersonides (Levi Ben Gershon, 1288–1344; Milhamot Adonai, III, 6) and, with some modifications, of Charles Hartshorne and process philosophers.

In the third, humans are not genuinely free. Freedom is an illusion that arises from human ignorance of divine cause and necessity. All that individuals do is actually determined and predetermined. God both pre-knows and pre-causes all that occurs. This is the view of Spinoza and Calvin.

Historically, most Latter-day Saints have taken the first general position: everything is foreseen and freedom remains. Some have taken the second, that God's foreknowledge is not absolute. The third alternative, that human freedom is illusory, is incompatible with LDS belief in genuine free agency and responsibility. Praise and blame, accountability and judgment, are meaningless unless humans are free. Any doctrine of foreknowledge that undercuts this principle violates the spirit and letter of LDS scripture.

Consequently divine foreknowledge, however it is finally defined, is not PREDESTINATION. What God foresees is not, for that reason, divinely caused, even though it is in some sense known (Talmage, p. 317). Divine foreknowledge is the background of *foreordination*. But, again, foreordination is not pre-causation. Rather, "foreordination is a conditional bestowal of a role, a responsibility, or a blessing which, likewise, foresees but does not fix the outcome" (Maxwell, p. 71).

BIBLIOGRAPHY

Hartshorne, Charles, and William L. Reese. *Philosophers Speak of God*. Chicago, 1953.

Maxwell, Neal A. "A More Determined Discipleship." *Ensign* 9 (Feb. 1979):69–73.

Talmage, James E. *The Vitality of Mormonism*, pp. 317 ff. Boston, 1919.

JAMES E. FAULCONER

FOREORDINATION

Foreordination is the premortal selection of individuals to come forth in MORTALITY at specified times, under certain conditions, and to fulfill predesignated responsibilities. In LDS interpretation, "foreordained" does not mean predetermined (*see* PREDESTINATION). It is the outcome of voluntary choice, not the violation or abrogation of it. The idea of preexistence and premortal preparation for earth life is hinted at in biblical sources, and evidence of it appears in some early Jewish-Christian sources. But it has been less prominent in later thought.

ABRAHAM was told that he was included among the valiant SPIRITS and was therefore chosen or *foreordained* before his birth to be a leader in God's kingdom on earth (Abr. 3:22–23). The Lord likewise informed Jeremiah, "Before I formed thee in the belly I knew thee; and . . . I ordained thee a prophet unto the nations" (Jer. 1:5). Alma$_2$ taught that priests belonging to a "holy order" were foreordained "according to the foreknowledge of God, on account of their exceeding faith and good works" (Alma 13:1, 3). The Prophet Joseph SMITH concluded that "every man who has a calling to minister to the inhabitants of the world was ordained to that very purpose in the Grand Council of heaven before this world was" (*TPJS*, p. 365). And in addition to these foreordinations to priesthood callings, many spirits may have been foreordained to specific nations and generations, which Paul characterized as the "bounds of habitation" (Acts 17:26), as well as to families and to varied assignments, work, or missions on earth.

While each of these selections is ultimately based on the omniscience and foreknowledge of God, several factors may influence one's earthly circumstances. Foreordination comes as a blessing or reward for premortal righteousness and valiant commitment to Jesus Christ. BIRTH into the house of ISRAEL and heirship to all the blessings of Abraham, Isaac, and Jacob are often seen as the birthright of dedicated souls (see Eph. 1:4–5; Rom. 9:4). These rights and blessings may still be obtained by any and all who elect to receive them, whether in this life or the next. People sooner or later will manifest, as Elder B. H. Roberts, of the Seventy, taught, "the strength of that intelligence and nobility to which their spirits had attained in the heavenly kingdom before they took bodies upon earth" (T. Madsen, *Defender of the Faith* [Salt Lake City, 1980], p. 2). The Doctrine and Covenants teaches that men and women may come to God through RIGHTEOUSNESS and diligence and thus become numbered with those who are "sons [and daughters] of Moses and of Aaron and the seed of Abraham, and the church and kingdom, and the elect of God" (D&C 84:34).

Through faithfulness on earth, whatever one's premortal foreordination or prior covenants, one may, as PAUL taught, become "adopted" into the favored lineage: "They are not all Israel, which are of Israel" (Rom. 9:6). Many, that is, may be foreordained to high missions in mortality, but may, through sin, rebellion, or sloth, fail in their foreordinations and give up their blessings. Obedience to the COVENANTS and ORDINANCES of the gospel is a primary factor in determining ultimate election to the chosen lineage.

Latter-day Saints further believe that the times, places, and circumstances of birth into mortality may be the outcome of former covenants and decisions as well as that which would be best, in divine wisdom, to provide both opportunities and challenges for the individual's growth and development. Additionally, foreordination may also be based on God's own purposes and plans to bless all of his children. The specifics of these factors remain unclear. As a result, a person's premortal character can never be judged by his or her present station in life. Some of the most bitter and arduous circumstances may be, in the perspective of eternity, the most blessed, and perhaps even the situations that men and women elected and agreed to enter. Foreordination does not preclude the exercise of agency. Foreordination is a *conditional* preappointment to or bestowal of certain blessings and responsibilities.

Following Augustine and Calvin, some have interpreted the word "predestine" in Romans 8:29–30 and Ephesians 1:4–5 as meaning divine precausation. In this view, God is the ultimate causal agent, whereas man is always and only an effect. Latter-day Saints reject this interpretation. They believe that neither the Greek nor related scriptural sources lead to this view. Paul's usage of this term refers to being foreordained to divine sonship through Christ. Furthermore, since God knows "all things, for all things are present before [his] eyes" (D&C 38:1–2), he anticipates our choices. However, he does not make the choices for us. Knowing our potential, he foreordains those who will help to bring about his purposes. Latter-day Saints extend this concept to embrace foreordination to any divinely appointed ministry or function.

BIBLIOGRAPHY

Maxwell, Neal A. "Meeting the Challenges of Today." *Speeches of the Year*, pp. 149–56. Provo, Utah, 1978.

Top, Brent L. *The Life Before.* Salt Lake City, 1988.

Winston, David. "Preexistence in the Wisdom of Solomon and Mormon Sources." In *Reflections on Mormonism*, ed. Truman Madsen, pp. 13–35. Salt Lake City, 1978.

BRENT L. TOP

FORGERIES OF HISTORICAL DOCUMENTS

The possibility of forgery must be considered by all historians as they ponder their evidence and by archivists as they build their collections. Forged Dutch colonial documents have been found in New York, and forgeries of Lone Star Republic documents have been identified in Texas.

One of the most famous forgeries in LDS history is the alleged "Joseph Smith Revelation" appointing James J. Strang his successor. It was created in the 1840s, probably by Strang, and is now located at the Beinecke Library at Yale University. The motives of Strang, who hoped to succeed Joseph Smith, were clear. Equally apparent were the reasons for the forgery of a pamphlet attributed to Joseph Smith's early associate, Oliver COWDERY. *Defense in a Rehearsal of My Grounds for Separating Myself from the Latter Day Saints*, supposedly written in Ohio in 1839, first appeared in an anti-Mormon publication in 1906 (Anderson, pp. 20–21). Others have attempted forgeries for money, ego, or the desire to influence or alter history.

The Hofmann forgeries of the 1980s have raised questions about some historical documents related to early Latter-day Saint history. In their search for new sources for information about the Church's formative period, historians were fascinated by the seemingly endless cache of historical documents supposedly located by Mark Hofmann. These documents purported to illuminate such topics as Joseph Smith's reception and translation of the records known as the Book of Mormon and the selection of his successor in Church leadership. Many, if not most, "Hofmann documents" turned out to be skillful forgeries. Hofmann had built a paper fortune from document dealing and duplicity, but when he was unable to produce additional promised documents for clients, he murdered a Salt Lake City businessman and the wife of an acquaintance in 1985. The subsequent investigation led to his arrest, confession of murder and forgery, and life sentence in the Utah State Prison.

The story of the Hofmann forgeries is the subject of several books and numerous articles. The case has deeply embarrassed both historians and the dealers and collectors who handled his documents. It has also prompted greater caution and healthy skepticism about the validity of purported historical documents of unknown background or provenance.

Documents that have been maintained in the official custody of a church or government agency throughout their life cycle should be considered more reliable than "newly found" documents. Scholars and archivists should be especially wary of those documents whose provenance is unclear. In all cases new and startling evidence must be critically evaluated against the standard of known and reliable documents.

BIBLIOGRAPHY

Anderson, Richard L. "The Second Witness of Priesthood." *IE* 71 [Sept. 1968]:15–16, 18, 20–22, 24.

Jessee, Dean C. "New Documents and Mormon Beginnings." *BYU Studies* 24 (Fall 1984):392–428.

Sillitoe, Linda, and Allen Roberts. *Salamander: The Story of the Mormon Forgery Murders.* Salt Lake City, 1988.

Whittaker, David J. "The Hofmann Maze: A Book Review Essay with a Chronology and Bibliography of the Hofmann Case." *BYU Studies* 29 (Winter 1989):67–124.

MAX J. EVANS

FORGIVENESS

See: Remission of Sins

FOX, RUTH MAY

Ruth May Fox (1853–1958) devoted many years to the Young Ladies' Mutual Improvement Association (YWMIA; in 1977 YOUNG WOMEN), serving as president from 1929 to 1937, following her tenure as first counselor to President Martha Horne Tingey from 1905 to 1929. Vibrant and spirited, Ruth May Fox was a woman of great strength and refined features. A poet and songwriter, she wrote the text to "Carry On," a hymn traditionally associated with the Mutual Improvement Association; it was introduced and featured at that association's June conference in 1930. She was an advocate of

Ruth May Fox (1853–1958), third general president of the Young Ladies' Mutual Improvement Association, served from 1929 to 1937. From the Utah State Historical Society collection. Courtesy Nelson Wadsworth.

woman suffrage and education, evidenced in part by her sponsorship of the Traveling Library Program and her focus on self-education.

Ruth May Fox was born November 16, 1853, in Westbury, Wiltshire, England, the daughter of Mary Ann Harding and James May. Five months later, her parents joined the LDS Church. After her mother's death in 1855, her father was called to be a traveling elder for the Church, causing her to live with various LDS families and relatives until she was approximately eight years old, when her father took her to Yorkshire, where he was employed. Around 1865 he emigrated to America, where Ruth joined him a few months later, and soon after, he remarried. The family lived in the Philadelphia area for two years, during which time she worked in factories to earn enough money to help finance their journey to Utah.

In July 1867 the Mays started for Utah, first traveling to North Platte, Nebraska. After securing supplies for their journey, they had only enough money to buy one yoke of cattle, so they shared a wagon with another family and walked most of the way to Utah.

Ruth worked in the Deseret (Salt Lake City) and Ogden Woolen Mills, where her father was a carder, and used her earnings to help purchase the family home. She then attended John Morgan's College in Salt Lake City for four months, which ended her formal education. When her father returned to Salt Lake City and started his own mill, she helped him operate the heavy equipment.

On May 8, 1873, when she was nineteen and he was twenty, she married Jesse Williams Fox, Jr.; they were blessed with twelve children. Ruth and Jesse prospered in the early years of their marriage, but met financial difficulties around 1888. Soon after, Jesse took a second wife, without any forewarning to Ruth. He eventually lost his business, accumulated large debts, and lost the family home. The two families lived separately, and as Jesse lived with the other household, Ruth was largely left to her own resources to survive. In 1900 she and her children ran the Saint Omer Boarding House to supplement their income; in 1914 she began work as a typist for the YWMIA. She lived with her children from 1914 until her death in 1958, resuming housekeeping only to nurse her husband through illnesses in 1921 and from 1927 until his death in 1928.

Among Ruth May Fox's lifelong beliefs was a strong commitment to suffrage for women. She was active in the Utah Woman Suffrage Association and the Republican party and helped draft the suffrage clause of the Utah Constitution. She served as president of the Utah Woman's Press Club, treasurer of the Utah Woman Suffrage Association, chairman of the Salt Lake County Second Precinct Ladies' Republican Club, and board member of the Deseret Agricultural and Manufacturing Society and of Traveler's Aid Society. She died on April 12, 1958, in Salt Lake City at the age of 104.

BIBLIOGRAPHY

"Ruth May Fox (1853–1967 [sic])." In Kenneth W. Godfrey, Audrey M. Godfrey, and Jill Mulvay-Derr, eds., *Women's Voices: An Untold History of the Latter-day Saints, 1830–1900.* Salt Lake City, 1982.

Thatcher, Linda. "'I Care Nothing for Politics': Ruth May Fox, Forgotten Suffragist." *Utah Historical Quarterly* 49 (Summer 1981):239–53.

LINDA THATCHER

FREEDOM

The gospel of Jesus Christ does not represent freedom merely as a philosophic concept or abstract possibility, but establishes it at the foundations of the creation of the world and as the fundamental condition of God's dealings with his children. As a general expression the word "freedom" refers to AGENCY, liberty, independence, and autonomy. Freedom, or the genuine possibility of choosing, necessarily defines the most basic condition of human beings in the temporal world.

Latter-day Saint scriptures teach that the premortal life was an environment of choice in which God proposed to his spirit children a PLAN OF SALVATION for their growth and advancement (see Job 38:6–7; 2 Ne. 2:17; D&C 29:36; Abr. 3:22–28). In earth life, with bodies of flesh and bone and vast new possibilities of action, God's children would be free to make choices within the whole spectrum of good and evil. They would also experience the necessary consequences of those choices. "And we will take of these materials, and we will make an earth whereon these may dwell; And we will prove them herewith, to see if they will do all things whatsoever the Lord their God shall command them" (Abr. 3:24–25).

God promised those who would do his will that they would be redeemed from their errors and

sins and gain eternal life. Satan opposed the Father's plan, aware that this more extensive freedom involved the risk of spiritual death, where some would be separated from the Father by their sins, would not repent, and thus could not return to dwell in his kingdom. To avert such a separation, Satan proposed an environment without freedom and hence without sin. Consequently, all would return to the Father, but without moral improvement or advancement (*see* DEVIL). The "honor" for their return would belong to Satan (Isa. 14:13; Moses 4:1).

A majority of God's spirit children joyfully elected freedom over bondage, knowledge over ignorance, advancement over stagnation, and even danger over security; so the temporal world was created, with freedom as its unconditional ground. The temporal world is an environment of choices and thus of moral action and ACCOUNTABILITY as people are summoned to do the will of God. Men and women may not evade or escape their freedom, for reality always appears as a set of choices informed by some kind of understanding of good, the outcome of which defines in some measure the course of human events. The Book of Mormon says of this decision,

> Wherefore, men are free according to the flesh; and all things are given them which are expedient unto man. And they are free to choose liberty and eternal life, through the great Mediator of all men, or to choose captivity and death, according to the captivity and power of the devil; for he seeketh that all men might be miserable like unto himself [2 Ne. 2:27].

FREEDOM AND HUMAN CHOICE. Latter-day Saints understand, however, that not all of God's children will find themselves in situations of equal freedom. All people are born into a world created by the acts and beliefs of those who lived before them. These differences are preserved in the traditions, institutions, and practices that have been handed down. While God gives everyone the LIGHT OF CHRIST that draws each to the good, the traditions and practices into which some are born may conceal the truth and lead such people into harmful and sinful acts. For these, God will have mercy (Alma 9:15–16).

Still others are born into situations where the truth is widely known and the opportunity to do good is broadly available. Yet they do evil in the face of the truth and thus create consequences that reduce their choices, distance themselves from the Spirit of God, and bring upon themselves unhappiness, destruction, and the darkness of Satan's power (Gal. 5:13–25). Furthermore, they do not suffer alone from the consequences of their choices. The ill-used freedom of some can result in the undeserved suffering of others, and while this is unjust, the risk of unwarranted suffering is necessarily present in a world where evil exists. Nevertheless, this condition too serves God's purpose, for some adversity humbles people before God (Alma 32:12–16). Through earthly trials men and women are tried and tested, but thereby progress and unfold the talents and gifts that God has given them (2 Ne. 2:11; Alma 62:41; D&C 122:1–9). When a whole people choose darkness over light, however, they create a legacy of confinement for following generations that sometimes has to be divinely corrected (e.g., Gen. 6:5–7; Lev. 18:24–30; Moses 8:22–30; Hel. 10:11–12).

On the other hand, those who choose good are made more free by a larger presence of the HOLY GHOST in their lives, and a greater power to know and do God's will (John 7:16–18; 8:29–32; Alma 19:33). Therefore, the good choices of some can bless the lives of others. As a consequence of the righteous works of a few (see Gal. 5–6), previously limited lives can expand to enjoy new and positive opportunities, while old injustices and grievances are brought to settlement. In the measure that the institutions and beliefs of a people embody truth and virtue and oppose corruption and depravity, an environment of greater freedom develops. A fulness is achieved when God establishes his kingdom on earth and reveals to humankind knowledge, power, gifts, and ordinances that open up the way to complete salvation and exaltation. The city of Enoch, as well as the righteous people living in America for 200 years after the visit of the resurrected Savior (see 4 Ne. 1), established high-water marks in the history of human freedom. In this sense, then, God not only calls individuals to live righteous lives, but summons them as his people to make covenants with him and to justly exercise his power as a community of the faithful. Freedom, therefore, should not be seen as merely a possibility of individuals, for it opens up to its fulness only within the kingdom of the righteous (see D&C 138, esp. verse 18).

FREEDOM AND GOVERNMENT. The scriptures further teach that God instituted governments to bless humankind on the earth (*see* CONSTITUTION OF THE UNITED STATES OF AMERICA; POLITICS: POLITICAL TEACHINGS). Good government must do more than preserve order; it must protect freedom, ensure justice, and secure the general welfare. "And the law of the land which is constitutional, supporting that principle of freedom in maintaining rights and privileges, belongs to all mankind, and is justifiable before me" (D&C 98:5; *see* CONSTITUTIONAL LAW). God proclaims, "I, the Lord God, make you free, therefore ye are free indeed; and the law also maketh you free" (D&C 98:8). The law protects individuals and their liberties from the arbitrary and deleterious acts of others. The genuine rule of law requires that all be equally subject to rules that are prospective, widely known, and publicly arrived at through mechanisms of government that have been and continue to be consensually agreed upon. The law secures peace by proscribing choices injurious to others, ensures justice by holding all accountable to the law in accordance with fair procedures, and secures the general welfare through the passage of laws that regulate and coordinate social intercourse to the benefit of all. In exchange for these advantages, citizens must fulfill their obligations to sustain and support the government. In the end, the environment of freedom is enhanced and expanded through good government.

Nevertheless, governments are often oppressive and act to restrict freedom and establish privileges for the few by arbitrarily setting up public rules and applying them unevenly without proper safeguards. The abuse of political power is most offensive and bondage nearly complete when freedom of conscience and its expression in free speech are restricted and the right to worship God openly according to one's own beliefs is abridged. In the end, Latter-day Saints believe that the claims of government should be limited to its own proper domain and not allowed to encroach upon the province of freedom to act according to moral conscience. To avoid such political evil, Latter-day Saints are encouraged not only to support constitutional government and the processes it establishes but also to work for laws that bring about freedom and encourage virtue. In this larger sense, the scriptures summon those who follow Jesus to go the extra mile, to give more than they receive, to do good without thought of what they might gain in return. Thus, as citizens, Latter-day Saints are obligated to go beyond the pursuit of self-interest; they are committed to serve others, to bring about

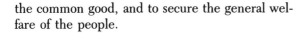

the common good, and to secure the general welfare of the people.

BIBLIOGRAPHY

Oaks, Dallin H. "Free Agency and Freedom." In *The Book of Mormon: Second Nephi, The Doctrinal Structure*, ed. M. Nyman and C. Tate, pp. 1–17. Salt Lake City, 1989.

DAVID E. BOHN

FREEMASONRY IN NAUVOO

The introduction of Freemasonry in NAUVOO had both political and religious implications. When Illinois Grand Master Abraham Jonas visited Nauvoo on March 15, 1842, to install the Nauvoo Masonic Lodge, he inaugurated an era of difficulty with other Illinois Masons and introduced to Nauvoo ancient ritual bearing some similarity to the LDS temple ordinances (*see* FREEMASONRY AND THE TEMPLE).

Regular Masonic procedure calls for an existing lodge to sponsor each new proposed lodge. Early in the summer of 1841, several Latter-day Saints who were Masons, including Lucius N. Scovil, a key figure in Nauvoo Freemasonry, asked Bodley Lodge No. 1, in Quincy, Illinois, to request that the Illinois Grand Lodge appoint certain individuals as officers of a Nauvoo lodge. Indicating that the persons named were unknown in Quincy as Masons, the lodge returned the letter with instructions for further action.

Less than a year later, Nauvoo had a lodge without the normal sponsorship. Grand Master Jonas apparently waived the rule and granted Nauvoo a "special dispensation" to organize. He also made Joseph SMITH and his counselor, Sidney RIGDON, "Masons at sight." Some believe that Jonas was willing to follow this course because he envisioned the growing Mormon vote supporting his own political ambitions (*see* NAUVOO POLITICS). Although the action may have endeared him to some Latter-day Saints, it antagonized other Masons. Joseph Smith had reason to expect that the Saints might benefit from the network of friendship and support normally associated with the fraternal organization, but instead, the Nauvoo Lodge only produced friction.

Jonas published an account of the March 15 installation of the Nauvoo Lodge in his newspaper, *Columbia Advocate*. "Never in my life did I witness a better dressed or more orderly and well-behaved assemblage," he wrote (*HC* 4:565–66). During the installation ceremonies, held in the grove near the temple site, Joseph Smith officiated as Grand Chaplain. That evening, with the Masons assembled in his office, the Prophet received the first degree of Freemasonry. Nauvoo Masons then commenced weekly early morning meetings.

In August 1842, Bodley Lodge No. 1 protested the granting of a dispensation to the Nauvoo Lodge, resulting in a temporary suspension of activities. An investigation found that approximately three hundred Latter-day Saints had become Masons during the brief existence of the lodge, but found no irregularities warranting dissolution. The Grand Lodge not only authorized reinstatement of the Nauvoo Lodge but subsequently granted dispensations for other lodges nearby made up principally of Latter-day Saints. Eventually nearly 1,500 LDS men became associated with Illinois Freemasonry, including many members of the Church's governing priesthood bodies—this at a time when the total number of non-LDS Masons in Illinois lodges barely reached 150.

As long-time rivals of Nauvoo for political and economic ascendancy, neighboring Masons feared and resisted Mormon domination of Freemasonry. Charging the Nauvoo Lodge with balloting for more than one applicant at a time, receiving applicants into the fraternity on the basis that they reform in the future, and making Joseph Smith a Master Mason on sight, enemies forced an investigation in October 1843. The Grand Lodge summoned Nauvoo officials to Jacksonville, Illinois. Armed with pertinent books and papers, Lucius Scovil and Henry G. Sherwood answered the allegations. Though the examining committee reported that everything appeared to be in order, it expressed fear that there *might* be something wrong, and recommended a year's suspension. At this point, Grand Master Jonas, in an impassioned speech, declared that the books of the Nauvoo Lodge were the best-kept he had seen and stated his conviction that but for the fact that the Nauvoo Lodge was composed of Mormons, it would stand as the highest lodge in the state. A committee was appointed to make a thorough investigation in Nauvoo. Though the committee reported no wrongdoing, the Nauvoo Lodge was again suspended. The injunction was later removed, but the Nauvoo Lodge continued to lack the support of its fellow Masons.

In April 1844, the Nauvoo Lodge dedicated a new Masonic hall. By this time, the lodge had been severed from the Grand Lodge and one Illinois Mason had been expelled from his lodge for attending the dedication. The Nauvoo Lodge continued its activities in the newly built hall until April 10, 1845, when Brigham YOUNG advised Lucius Scovil to suspend the work of the Masons in Nauvoo. Only a few additional meetings were held prior to the Latter-day Saints' departure for the Great Basin in 1846.

Joseph Smith participated minimally in Freemasonry and, as far as is known, attended the Nauvoo Masonic Lodge on only three occasions. Nonetheless, LDS Masons commented on his mastery of its orders, tenets, and principles and of his understanding of the allegorical symbolism of its instructions.

Most scholars who have looked carefully at the Nauvoo Masonic Lodge agree that it was more victim than villain. All agree that widespread anti-Mormon feelings and the extensive hatred of Latter-day Saints by local rivals, and not irregularities or misconduct, caused the controversy with regard to the Masonic Lodge in Nauvoo.

BIBLIOGRAPHY

Hogan, Mervin B. "Mormonism and Freemasonry: The Illinois Episode." In *Little Masonic Library*, ed. Silas H. Shepherd, Lionel Vibert, and Roscoe Pound, Vol. 2, pp. 267–326. Richmond, Va., 1977.

Ivins, Anthony W. *The Relationship of "Mormonism" and Freemasonry.* Salt Lake City, 1934.

McGavin, E. Cecil. *Mormonism and Masonry.* Salt Lake City, 1954.

KENNETH W. GODFREY

FREEMASONRY AND THE TEMPLE

Students of both Mormonism and Freemasonry have pondered possible relationships between Masonic rites and the LDS TEMPLE ceremony. Although some argue that Joseph SMITH borrowed elements of Freemasonry in developing the temple ceremony, the ENDOWMENT is more congruous with LDS scriptures (especially the BOOK OF ABRAHAM and the BOOK OF MOSES) and ancient ritual than with Freemasonry. Latter-day Saints view the ORDINANCES as a revealed restoration of ancient temple ceremony and only incidentally related to Freemasonry. The two are not antithetical, however, nor do they threaten each other, and nei-

ther institution discourages research regarding the ancient origins of their two ceremonies.

Many sacred ceremonies existed in the ancient world. Modified over centuries, these rituals existed in some form among ancient Egyptians, Coptic Christians, Israelites, and Masons, and in the Catholic and Protestant liturgies. Common elements include the wearing of special clothing, ritualistic speech, the dramatization of archetypal themes, instruction, and the use of symbolic gestures. One theme common to many—found in the Egyptian Book of the Dead, the Egyptian pyramid texts, and Coptic PRAYER CIRCLES, for example—is man's journey through life and his quest, following death, to successfully pass the sentinels guarding the entrance to eternal bliss with the gods. Though these ceremonies vary greatly, significant common points raise the possibility of a common remote source.

The Egyptian pyramid texts, for example, feature six main themes: (1) emphasis on a primordial written document behind the rites; (2) purification (including anointing, lustration, and clothing); (3) the Creation (resurrection and awakening texts); (4) the garden (including tree and ritual meal motifs); (5) travel (protection, a ferryman, and Osirian texts); and (6) ascension (including victory, coronation, admission to heavenly company, and Horus texts). Like such ancient ceremonies, the LDS temple endowment presents aspects of these themes in figurative terms. It, too, presents, not a picture of immediate reality, but a model setting forth the pattern of human life on earth and the divine plan of which it is part.

Masonic ceremonies are also allegorical, depicting life's states—youth, manhood, and old age—each with its associated burdens and challenges, followed by death and hoped-for immortality. There is no universal agreement concerning when Freemasonry began. Some historians trace the order's origin to Solomon, Enoch, or even Adam. Others argue that while some Masonic symbolism may be ancient, as an institution it began in the Middle Ages or later.

Though in this DISPENSATION the LDS endowment dates from Kirtland and Nauvoo (see KIRTLAND TEMPLE; NAUVOO TEMPLE), Latter-day Saints believe that temple ordinances are as old as man and that the essentials of the GOSPEL OF JESUS CHRIST, including its necessary ritual and teachings, were first revealed to Adam. These saving principles and ordinances were subsequently revealed to SETH; NOAH; MELCHIZEDEK; ABRAHAM, and each prophet to whom the priesthood was given, including PETER. Latter-day Saints believe that the ordinances performed in LDS temples today replicate rituals that were part of God's teachings from the beginning.

The Prophet Joseph Smith suggested that the endowment and Freemasonry in part emanated from the same ancient spring. Thus, some Nauvoo Masons thought of the endowment as a restoration of a ritual only imperfectly preserved in Freemasonry and viewed Joseph Smith as a master of the underlying principles and allegorical symbolism (Heber C. Kimball to Parley P. Pratt, June 17, 1842, Church Archives). The philosophy and major tenets of Freemasonry are not fundamentally incompatible with the teaching, theology, and doctrines of the Latter-day Saints. Both emphasize morality, sacrifice, CONSECRATION, and service, and both condemn selfishness, sin, and greed. Furthermore, the aim of Masonic ritual is to instruct—to make truth available so that man can follow it.

Resemblances between the two rituals are limited to a small proportion of actions and words; indeed, some find that the LDS endowment has more similarities with the Pyramid texts and the Coptic documents than with Freemasonry. Even where the two rituals share symbolism, the fabric of meanings is different. In addition to creation and life themes, one similarity is that both call for the participants to make COVENANTS. Yet, the endowment alone ties covenants to eternal blessings and to Jesus Christ. The Masonic ceremony does not emphasize PRIESTHOOD or the need to be commissioned by God to represent him. The active participation of God in the world and in men's lives is a distinctly LDS temple motif. While Masons believe in an undefined, impersonal God, everything in the LDS endowment emanates from, or is directed to, God who is a personage and man's eternal Father. The endowment looks to the eternities and to eternal lives, but Freemasonry is earthbound, pervaded by human legend and hope for something better.

Freemasonry is a fraternal society, and in its ritual all promises, oaths, and agreements are made between members. In the temple endowment all covenants are between the individual and God. In Freemasonry, testing, grading, penalizing, or sentencing accords with the rules of the fraternity or membership votes. In the endow-

ment, God alone is the judge. Within Freemasonry, rank and promotions are of great importance, while in the LDS temple rites there are no distinctions: all participants stand equal before God. The clash between good and evil, including SATAN's role, is essential to, and vividly depicted in, the endowment, but is largely absent from Masonic rites. Temple ceremonies emphasize SALVATION FOR THE DEAD through vicarious ordinance work, such as BAPTISM FOR THE DEAD; nothing in Masonic ritual allows for proxies acting on behalf of the dead. Women participate in all aspects of LDS temple rites; though Freemasonry has women's auxiliaries, Masonic ritual excludes them. The endowment's inclusion of females underscores perhaps the most fundamental difference between the two rites: LDS temple rites unite husbands and wives, and their children, in eternal families (*see* ETERNAL LIVES; MARRIAGE). Latter-day Saint SEALINGS would be completely out of place in the context of Masonic ceremonies.

Thus, Latter-day Saints see their temple ordinances as fundamentally different from Masonic and other rituals and think of similarities as remnants from an ancient original.

BIBLIOGRAPHY

Ivins, Anthony W. *The Relationship of "Mormonism" and Freemasonry.* Salt Lake City, 1934.

Madsen, Truman G., ed. *The Temple in Antiquity.* Provo, Utah, 1984.

Nibley, Hugh W. *The Message of the Joseph Smith Papyri: An Egyptian Endowment.* Salt Lake City, 1975.

Packer, Boyd K. *The Holy Temple.* Salt Lake City, 1980.

Shepherd, Silas H.; Lionel Vibert; and Roscoe Pound, eds. *Little Masonic Library,* 5 vols. Richmond, Va., 1977, esp. Mervin B. Hogan, "Mormonism and Freemasonry: The Illinois Episode," Vol. 2, pp. 267–326.

KENNETH W. GODFREY

FRIEND, THE

Published monthly since January 1971 for children to age twelve, the *Friend* replaced the CHILDREN'S FRIEND, which was published from 1902 through 1970. The goal of the *Friend* is to reach the children of the Church directly, even those not involved with the PRIMARY, by presenting the gospel "while reinforcing the values of the stable homes" (Anderson, p. 13). It attempts to fulfill this goal by printing contemporary, historical, scriptural, and imaginative stories, often with pictures; recipes and crafts; games and pencil activities such as hidden pictures, scriptural matching, and connect-the-dots drawings; a calendar for the month; stories of Church leaders and other inspiring people; suggestions for reading; specials for the holidays; "Friend to Friend" discussions with Church leaders; and "Messages from the First Presidency" or from other GENERAL AUTHORITIES.

Keenly aware of the challenges facing children in the 1990s, the *Friend* tries to fill their needs and help parents as they raise their children in the very difficult modern world. The *Friend* attempts to meet President Spencer W. KIMBALL's challenge "to support the parents in teaching their children to pray and walk uprightly before the Lord" (Oman and Madsen, p. 39).

The editors of the *Friend* have been Lucile Reading (1971–1982) and Vivian Paulsen (1982–).

BIBLIOGRAPHY

Anderson, Lavina Fielding. "The Church and Children." *Ensign* 8 (Apr. 1978):6–13.

Hinckley, Gordon B. "A Friend for Every Child." *IE* 73 (Dec. 1970):97–98.

Oman, Susan, and Carol Madsen. "100 Years of Primary." *Ensign* 8 (Apr. 1978):32–39.

ELIZABETH WAHLQUIST

FULNESS OF THE GOSPEL

The phrase "fulness of the gospel" refers to the whole doctrine of redemption demonstrated and taught in the ministry and life of Jesus Christ. It "consists in those laws, doctrines, ordinances, powers, and authorities needed to enable men to gain the fulness of salvation" (*MD*, p. 333).

Fulness is a term sometimes used in the scriptures to describe Christ himself, regarding both his stature as the Son of God and what he offered mankind. John, in bearing witness of the Savior, said, "And of his fulness have all we received, and grace for grace" (John 1:16). To receive the fulness the Savior offered is to accept him as the one who made salvation possible for all through the Atonement and to follow his teachings. Thus, to experience a fulness of joy requires one to keep God's commandments (D&C 93:27).

Christ himself declared the fulness of his gospel: "For I came down from heaven, not to do mine own will, but the will of him that sent me. And this is the Father's will . . . , that every one which seeth the Son, and believeth on him, may have everlasting life; and I will raise him up at the last day" (John 6:38–40).

Latter-day Saints believe that every PROPHET, from whatever DISPENSATION, prophesied of Christ. But the phrase fulness of the gospel implies that periods have occurred when the gospel was not on the earth in its fulness, either in doctrine or in ordinance. The Book of Mormon was described by a heavenly messenger to Joseph Smith in 1820 as "giving an account of the former inhabitants of this continent," and "the fulness of the everlasting Gospel was contained in it, as delivered by the Savior" (JS—H 1:34).

President Ezra Taft BENSON explains: "The Book of Mormon contains the fulness of the gospel of Jesus Christ (D&C 20:9). That does not mean it contains every teaching, every doctrine ever revealed. Rather, it means that in the Book of Mormon we will find the fulness of those doctrines required for our salvation. And they are taught plainly and simply so that even children can learn the ways of salvation and exaltation" (Benson, pp. 18–19).

NEPHI₁, a Book of Mormon prophet living centuries before the coming of Christ, indicated that the fulness of the gospel would not always be on the earth. In a vision of the Lord's future ministry, he saw that parts of the gospel would be altered and tampered with. Nephi wrote, speaking of the Bible, "When it proceeded forth from the mouth of a Jew it contained the fulness of the gospel of the Lord, of whom the twelve apostles bear record." But men have taken away from the Bible "many parts which are plain and most precious; and also many covenants of the Lord have they taken away," which resulted in a loss of the gospel (cf. 1 Ne. 13:24–29).

Latter-day Saints believe that this apostasy and corruption of the scriptures necessitated a later restoration of the fulness of the gospel through prophets called of God. This restoration began with the FIRST VISION of 1820 to the Prophet Joseph Smith and continued with subsequent revelations, including modern SCRIPTURE and priesthood AUTHORITY, which remain today in The Church of Jesus Christ of Latter-day Saints.

[*See also* Restoration of All Things; Restoration of the Gospel of Jesus Christ.]

BIBLIOGRAPHY

Benson, Ezra Taft. *A Witness and a Warning.* Salt Lake City, 1988.

DEAN B. FARNSWORTH

"FUNDAMENTALISTS"

"Mormon Fundamentalism" denotes the beliefs and practices of contemporary SCHISMATIC GROUPS that claim to follow all the teachings of the Prophet Joseph SMITH. They often style themselves believers in the "fulness of the gospel," which they assert must include PLURAL MARRIAGE and sometimes the UNITED ORDER.

The Fundamentalist movement began after the issuance of the MANIFESTO of 1890, which publicly declared an official end to plural marriage in The Church of Jesus Christ of Latter-day Saints. The period from 1890 to 1904 was one of confusion for some over the application and extent of the ban on new plural marriages in the Church. For example, since the Manifesto referred to "marriages violative of the law of the land," some felt the prohibition did not apply outside the United States. In 1904 the Manifesto was therefore officially and publicly proclaimed to be worldwide in jurisdiction and overall scope.

Following this second pronouncement, unyielding Fundamentalists continued to hold that God requires all "true" believers to abide by the principle of polygamy, irrespective of Church mandate. This insistence has separated Fundamentalists from mainstream Mormonism. In the 1920s, Lorin C. Woolley of Centerville, Utah, claimed God had authorized him to perpetuate plural marriage, saying he received this commission while a young man in 1886 through the ministration of Jesus Christ, John TAYLOR, and Joseph Smith. His assertion further polarized the Fundamentalists and the Church.

Some Fundamentalists of the 1920s rejected Woolley's claims to authority and went their separate ways. Charles Kingston settled in Bountiful, Utah, and set up a type of united order community that persists as a relatively closed society. Alma Dayer LeBaron moved to Mesa, Arizona, and eventually to Juarez, Mexico, laying the groundwork for the Church of the Firstborn of the Fulness of Times and offshoots such as the Church of the Lamb of God. Other Fundamentalists have broken away through the years, making various religious claims.

Despite these defections, the majority of Fundamentalists remained an organized group, showing small but steady gains in adherents. In the mid-1930s, a united order colony was established in an isolated community near the Utah-Arizona border called Short Creek, now Colorado City, Arizona. Property was held in a trust called the United Effort. This colony has become a haven for many Fundamentalists, although a majority of their followers still reside in the Salt Lake City area.

In the mid-1940s, Utah and Arizona law officials raided the Short Creek community and broke up polygamous families, putting husbands in jail and children in foster homes. Fundamentalist leaders remained in state prison until September 24, 1945 (the fifty-fifth anniversary of the Woodruff Manifesto), when they issued a public statement indicating their intention to cease ignoring the law of the land. They returned to their families and refrained from violating the law for a time.

A few years later, a major schism in the Colorado City group occurred over the question of priesthood authority and the right to rule. Joseph Musser (the ostensible leader of the group), Rulon Allred, his brothers, and a few others broke away and started their own group, which has grown to about 2,000 members through conversion and births and is now known as the United Apostolic Brethren. In 1976, Rulon Allred, then leader of the group, was murdered, evidently by a plural wife of Ervil LeBaron, of the Church of the Lamb of God. Owen Allred replaced his brother as leader. The Colorado City group reorganized, with Leroy Johnson assuming leadership, and in 1990 was one of the largest fundamentalist groups, numbering in the thousands. Upon Johnson's death (Nov. 25, 1986, at Hilldale, Utah) a power struggle ensued; schisms continue in the Colorado City group over authority and legal title to property.

Fundamentalists claim to believe in the four LDS STANDARD WORKS, the early history of the Church, and the prophets of the RESTORATION up to, and including, John Taylor. Fundamentalist doctrines of priesthood presidency are derived from a unique interpretation of Doctrine and Covenants section 84, which they claim refers to a priesthood council or hierarchy of seven men designated as "high priest" apostles. Various claims to succession have led to the current schisms in these groups. Many independent Fundamentalists believe the claims to authority of the two main groups are flawed; they thus live and believe apart from those groups.

The thread that binds all Fundamentalists together is their belief that the LDS Church has improperly changed doctrines and practices. One independent Fundamentalist published a book listing ninety-five purported changes, thus mimicking Martin Luther's ninety-five theses. Prominent among these criticisms are the abrogation of plural marriage, cessation of living the united order, alleged loss of revelation to the Church since 1890, purported forfeiture of keys of the priesthood due to termination of the practice of plural marriage, supposed repudiation of "true" knowledge of the GODHEAD, changes in the method of missionary work (failure to preach without purse or scrip), asserted corruption of temple garments and ordinances, cessation of the gathering of Israel to Utah, changing the method of priesthood conferral, and allowing all worthy male members of the Church to hold the priesthood, regardless of race.

BIBLIOGRAPHY

Anderson, J. Max. *The Polygamy Story: Fiction and Fact*. Salt Lake City, 1977.

Kraut, Ogden. *Ninety-five Theses*. Dugway, Utah, n.d.

Truth Magazine. Salt Lake City, 1935–1956.

J. MAX ANDERSON

G

GABRIEL

See: Angels

GAMBLING

The Church of Jesus Christ of Latter-day Saints condemns gambling, games of chance, and lotteries as moral evils and admonishes its members not to participate in them in any form. Gambling is based on the morally wrong philosophy of getting something for nothing, of taking money without giving fair value in exchange. Not only is gambling morally wrong, but it is also bad economics for customers. The lavish gambling centers around the world stand as ample evidence that the chances of winning are weighted heavily in favor of the establishment and against the bettor. This same remoteness of winning is part of state-run lotteries. The chance of purchasing a winning ticket in one 1990 state lottery was noted by the news media as 1 in 14 million. The Church considers lotteries as gambling, and the First Presidency has asked Latter-day Saints not to participate in them and to oppose establishing them in their states:

> There can be no question about the moral ramifications of gambling, including government-sponsored lotteries. Public lotteries are advocated as a means of relieving the burden of taxation. It has been dem-

onstrated, however, that all too often lotteries only add to the problems of the financially disadvantaged by taking money from them and giving nothing of value in return. The poor and the elderly become victims of the inducements that are held out to purchase lottery tickets on the remote chance of winning a substantial prize. It is sad to see governments now promoting what they once enacted laws to forbid. We urge members of the Church to join with others with similar concerns in opposing the legalization of gambling and government-sponsorship of lotteries [*Church News*, Oct. 5, 1986, p. 4].

BIBLIOGRAPHY

Oaks, Dallin H. "Gambling—Morally Wrong and Politically Unwise." *Ensign* 17 (June 1987):69–75.

CHARLES D. TATE, JR.

GARDEN OF EDEN

The significance of the Garden of Eden is fundamental among the beliefs of The Church of Jesus Christ of Latter-day Saints and is referred to in each of the STANDARD WORKS. As one of the final steps in the Creation, God planted a garden eastward in Eden and placed in it varieties of animals and plants (Gen. 2:8–9). It was an idyllic environment, without enmity among living things and without death. ADAM and Eve were given dominion over all things and directed to cultivate and beautify the garden (Gen. 2:15). However, in this pristine condition, Adam and Eve would have had no children (2 Ne. 2:22–25; Moses 5:11).

God placed the tree of knowledge of good and evil in the midst of the garden and gave Adam and Eve their AGENCY whether to partake of its fruit (Moses 7:32). Unless they ate, they would remain forever in the garden, limited in their ability to progress and without posterity. However, while partaking would bring opportunity to bear children and to learn good from evil by experience, including sorrow, pain, and death, they would be exiled temporarily from the presence of God. The decision of Eve and Adam to transgress a commandment of God and partake of the fruit of the tree brought mortality and death to them and to their posterity; for it made possible the human family upon the earth (2 Ne. 2:25). The FALL OF ADAM also made the ATONEMENT OF JESUS CHRIST necessary.

Neither biblical records nor secular history and archaeological research identify the dimensions or the location of the garden in terms of the present-day surface of the earth. Latter-day revelation specifies that as a mortal, Adam lived at ADAM-ONDI-AHMAN in what is now Daviess County, Missouri (D&C 107:53–56; 116:1; 117:8). Several early LDS leaders, among them Brigham YOUNG and Heber C. KIMBALL, stated that the Prophet Joseph SMITH taught them that the Garden of Eden was located in what is now Jackson County, Missouri (*JD* 10:235; cf. 11:336–7; *DS* 3:74).

BIBLIOGRAPHY

Cowley, Matthias F. *Wilford Woodruff*, p. 481. Salt Lake City, 1964.

GRAHAM W. DOXEY

GARDEN OF GETHSEMANE

See: Gethsemane

GARMENTS

The word "garment" has distinctive meanings to Latter-day Saints. The white undergarment worn by those members who have received the ORDINANCE of the temple ENDOWMENT is a ceremonial one. All adults who enter the temple are required to wear it. In LDS TEMPLES, men and women who receive priesthood ordinances wear this undergarment and other priestly robes. The garment is worn at all times, but the robes are worn only in the temple. Having made COVENANTS of righteousness, the members wear the garment under their regular clothing for the rest of their lives, day and night, partially to remind them of the sacred covenants they have made with God.

The white garment symbolizes purity and helps assure modesty, respect for the attributes of God, and, to the degree it is honored, a token of what PAUL regarded as taking upon one the whole armor of God (Eph. 6:13; cf. D&C 27:15). It is an outward expression of an inward covenant, and symbolizes Christlike attributes in one's mission in life. Garments bear several simple marks of orientation toward the gospel principles of OBEDIENCE, TRUTH, life, and DISCIPLESHIP in Christ.

An agency of the Church manufactures these garments in contemporary, comfortable, and lightweight fabrics. They are available for purchase through Church DISTRIBUTION CENTERS.

SCRIPTURE, as well as legends from many lands and cultures, points toward the significance of sacral clothing. A biblical tradition teaches that ADAM and EVE, prior to their expulsion from Eden, wore sacred clothing. "Unto Adam also and to his wife did the Lord God make coats of skins, and clothed them" (Gen. 3:21). These were given in a context of REPENTANCE and forgiveness, and of offering SACRIFICE and making covenants.

In antiquity, priestly vestments were part of widespread tradition. The Targums (Aramaic paraphrases of the Old Testament) teach that these garments were "precious garments" or "glorious garments" or "garments of honor." Rabbi Eleazer called them "coats of glory." A rabbinic source asks: "And what were those garments?" The answer is, "The vestments of the High Priesthood, with which the Almighty clothed them because Adam was the world's first-born" (Kasher, *Encyclopedia of Biblical Interpretation*, Vol. 1, p. 137). In MOSES' time those who officiated in the Tabernacle wore a certain kind of garment: "And [Moses] put upon [Aaron] the coat, and girded him with the girdle, and clothed him with the robe, and put the ephod upon him, and he girded him with the curious girdle of the ephod, and bound it unto him therewith" (Lev. 8:7; see Testament of Levi 8). Latter-day Saints similarly wear temple garments in connection with their priesthood functions.

The clergy and many of the committed in almost all major faiths wear special clothing. For Latter-day Saints, among whom there is no professional ministry, men and women from all walks of life share in the CALLINGS, responsibilities, and blessings of the priesthood. Their sacred clothing, representing covenants with God, is worn under rather than outside their street clothes.

In a Messianic passage Isaiah declared: "I will greatly rejoice in the Lord, my soul shall be joyful in my God; for he hath clothed me with the garments of salvation, he hath covered me with the robe of righteousness" (Isa. 61:10). In the current dispensation, the principle has been reaffirmed in prophetic idiom: "Zion must increase in beauty, . . . and put on her beautiful garments" (D&C 82:14). Latter-day Saints believe that all such clothing is symbolic of the submission, sanctification, and spotless purity of those who desire to serve God and Christ and ultimately regain their eternal presence (D&C 61:34; 135:5).

BIBLIOGRAPHY

Nibley, Hugh W. *Sacred Vestments*, 38 pages. Provo, Utah, 1984.

Packer, Boyd K. *The Holy Temple.* Salt Lake City, 1980.

EVELYN T. MARSHALL

GATES, SUSA YOUNG

Susa (Susan, Susannah) Gates was born on March 18, 1856, in Salt Lake City. A writer, publisher, advocate for women's achievements, educator, missionary, genealogist, temple worker, wife, and mother of thirteen children, she was fond of saying, "Keep busy in the face of discouragement" (Person, p. 208).

The second daughter of Brigham Young's twenty-second wife, Lucy Bigelow Young, Susa Young has been called "the most versatile and prolific LDS writer ever to take up the pen in defense of her religion" (Cracroft, p. 73). Following private education that included music and ballet, she entered the University of Deseret at age thirteen. The next year she became co-editor of the *College Lantern*, possibly the first western college newspaper.

In 1872, at age sixteen, she married Dr. Alma Bailey Dunford; they had two children, Leah Eudora Dunford and Alma Bailey Dunford. The marriage ended in divorce in 1877. The next year,

Susa Young Gates (1856–1933), daughter of Brigham Young, was a leader, editor, trustee of Brigham Young University, active in the local and national women's organizations, and the mother of ten sons and three daughters. Courtesy Utah State Historical Society.

Susa entered BRIGHAM YOUNG ACADEMY in Provo and, while a student, founded the department of music and conducted a choir. During a trip to the Sandwich Islands (Hawaii), she renewed her acquaintance with Jacob F. Gates, whom she married on January 5, 1880. The success of their marriage has been attributed to their mutual respect for, and support of, one another's work. Only four of the eleven children born to this marriage survived to adulthood: Emma Lucy Gates Bowen, Brigham Cecil Gates, Harvey Harris (Hal) Gates, and Franklin Young Gates.

During the 1880s and 1890s, Susa Gates focused her energy on childbearing and child-rearing, missionary work, education, writing, and women's concerns. After completing a Church mission with her husband to the Sandwich Islands in 1889, she founded the *Young Woman's Journal*.

It was adopted as the official magazine for the Young Ladies Mutual Improvement Association (*see* YOUNG WOMEN) in 1897. She founded the Utah Woman's Press Club, became press chairman of the National Council of Women, and founded the RELIEF SOCIETY MAGAZINE, which she edited until 1922. She wrote biographies of Lydia Knight and of her father, Brigham Young, novels including *John Stevens' Courtship* and *The Prince of Ur*, a pamphlet entitled the "Teachings of Brigham Young," and a history of women in the Church, on which she was still working at the time of her death.

Concern for women's achievements was a prominent force in Susa Gates's life. During the 1890s, while she was most occupied with raising her own children, she became a charter member of the National Household Economic Association and was a representative to women's congresses in Denver, Washington, D.C., Toronto, and London, where she was invited to speak on the topic "Equal Moral Standards for Men and Women" and where she joined other women of the International Council, including Susan B. Anthony, for tea with Queen Victoria.

At the turn of the century, Susa suffered a nervous and physical breakdown. Ill for three years, she was forced to terminate a mission that she and her husband had begun in 1902. A priesthood blessing that promised her she would live to do temple work marked the beginning of her recovery. She underwent a year of intense spiritual introspection and later wrote of that period, "I disciplined my taste, my desires and my impulses— severely disciplining my appetite, my tongue, my acts . . . and how I prayed!" (Person, p. 212). While maintaining her commitments to family and women's advancement, she focused her energy on genealogy and temple work.

In 1906, Susa Young Gates organized genealogical departments in two newspapers, the *Inter Mountain Republican* and the *Deseret News*, and wrote columns for both papers over the next ten years. She produced instructional manuals for genealogists, devised a systematic index of names for the Church, and published the *Surname Book and Racial History*. In 1915, she introduced genealogical class work at the International Genealogy Conference in San Francisco and became head of the Research Department and Library of the Genealogical Society of Utah in 1923. She personally cataloged more than 16,000 names of the Young fam-

ily. She spent much time in the last years of her life doing ordinance work in the Salt Lake Temple with her husband. She died on May 27, 1933.

BIBLIOGRAPHY

Arrington, Leonard J. "Blessed Damozels: Women in Mormon History." *Dialogue* 6 (Summer 1971):22–31.

Cracroft, R. Paul. "Susa Young Gates: Her Life and Literary Work." Master's thesis, University of Utah, 1951.

Person, Carolyn W. D. "Susa Young Gates." In *Mormon Sisters: Women in Early Utah*, ed. Claudia L. Bushman, pp. 198-223. Cambridge, Mass., 1976.

LOUISE PLUMMER

GATHERING

For Latter-day Saints, the gathering of ISRAEL involves bringing together the heirs of the covenant to designated places where they can enjoy the blessings of temples (*see* ABRAHAMIC COVENANT; COVENANT ISRAEL; PROMISED LAND). Latter-day Saints believe in "the literal gathering of Israel" and hold that, along with a vital future role for the Old World Jerusalem, "Zion (the New Jerusalem) will be built upon the American continent" (A of F 10). Church members still look for an eventual temple and permanent headquarters to be built in ZION, a NEW JERUSALEM in Missouri.

Early Latter-day Saints first encountered the concept of a New Jerusalem separate from the Old World Jerusalem in Book of Mormon prophecies that the land of America was to be "the place of the New Jerusalem" (3 Ne. 20:22; Ether 13:3). More information came in September 1830, soon after the Church was organized, when a revelation mentioned building a New Jerusalem near the Missouri River at a location soon to be revealed (D&C 28:9). Another revelation that same month enjoined the Saints to "bring to pass the gathering of [the Lord's] elect," suggesting both the work of missionaries and the physical gathering of the faithful to a designated location. It also stressed that the Saints should be "gathered in unto one place" (D&C 29:7–8).

In NAUVOO, Joseph SMITH taught that "in any age of the world" the object of gathering the people of God was the same—"to build unto the Lord an house whereby he could reveal unto his people the ordinances" of his temple (*WJS*, p. 212). The gathering was necessary to build a temple, and a temple was a prerequisite for the establishment of

Zion. Consequently, at each of the Saints' headquarters gathering places, a temple site was designated, and in KIRTLAND, Nauvoo, and Salt Lake City, temples were constructed. Gathering also provided a refuge, a place for mutual protection and spiritual reinforcement and instruction. It strengthened LDS communities and brought economic and political benefits as well (see CITY PLANNING).

The Kirtland area in northeastern Ohio was the first gathering place. But when converts from New York arrived there in May 1831, they learned that Ohio would be a gathering place only "for a little season" (D&C 51:16). Some left that same year for Missouri once it was revealed that Zion was to be built in Jackson County, Missouri, a land "appointed and consecrated for the gathering of the saints" (D&C 57:1–3; see also MISSOURI: LDS COMMUNITIES IN JACKSON AND CLAY COUNTIES).

For the following seven years the Church had two gathering places—Ohio, the site of the Saints' first temple, and Missouri, the site of the City of Zion. However, in 1838, less than two years after the dedication of the KIRTLAND TEMPLE, opposition drove the Ohio faithful from that temple-city. The persecution in Missouri that earlier had forced the Saints from Jackson County now forced them from their new headquarters in Far West, Missouri, before temples could be built (see MISSOURI CONFLICT). Between 1839 and 1846, Latter-day Saints gathered by the thousands at Nauvoo, Illinois, where they again completed a temple before leaving, in the face of violence, for a gathering place in the Rocky Mountains (see SALT LAKE VALLEY; WESTWARD MIGRATION).

Although the major current purposes for gathering the faithful into a single place have been accomplished, belief in the necessity of gathering the elect continues. Members in all parts of the world are now encouraged to remain in their own communities and "build Zion" in their own wards and stakes (see IMMIGRATION AND EMIGRATION). Temples have now been built in many countries, and missionaries further the establishment of Zion by gathering "the pure in heart" (D&C 97:21) to the stakes of Zion throughout the world.

BIBLIOGRAPHY

Cook, Lyndon, and Andrew Ehat, eds. Words of Joseph Smith, pp. 209–216. Provo, Utah, 1980.

RONALD D. DENNIS

GENEALOGICAL SOCIETY OF UTAH

The Genealogical Society of Utah, organized in 1894, became The Genealogical Society of The Church of Jesus Christ of Latter-day Saints in 1944. In 1976 it became The Genealogical Department, and in 1987 the name was changed to The Family History Department. Each name change brought renewed emphasis and expanded resources to further the search for ancestors. The name Genealogical Society still continues as the microfilm section of the Family History Department of the Church.

The central purpose of the organization is expressed in a statement by Elder Joseph Fielding SMITH: "Salvation for the dead is the system whereunder those who would have accepted the gospel in this life, had they been permitted to hear it, will have the chance to accept it in the spirit world, and will then be entitled to all the blessings which passed them by in mortality" (DS 2:100–196). Provisions have been made, therefore, for the living to provide, vicariously, ordinances of salvation for their deceased family forebears and friends. This cannot be done without information about the dead.

In April 1894, President Wilford WOODRUFF said, "We want the Latter-day Saints from this time to trace their genealogies as far as they can, and to be sealed to their fathers and mothers . . . and run this chain as far as you can get it" (Durham, p. 157). On November 13, 1894, the FIRST PRESIDENCY of the Church authorized the organization of the Genealogical Society of Utah as an aid to genealogical research, and appointed Franklin D. Richards president. Of this beginning Archibald F. Bennett, a later executive secretary, gave the following historical summary: "It was to be benevolent, educational, and religious in purpose— benevolent in gathering together into a library books that would help the people trace their ancestry; educational in teaching the people how to trace their ancestry . . . ; religious in that they would do all in their power to encourage the people to perform in the temples all the necessary ordinances" (Genealogical Society of Utah, minutes, Nov. 13, 1894, Genealogical Department of the Church).

Some of the widely known facilities and resources that have been established over the past century to facilitate these purposes are: (1) the

FAMILY HISTORY LIBRARY at Salt Lake City; (2) the extensive collection of microfilmed and microfiche records of family history; and (3) the INTERNATIONAL GENEALOGICAL INDEX™ (IGI).

1. The Family History Library is the largest of its kind in the world. Patrons come from all over the globe to search for information about past generations. More than 1,000 branches of this library have been established in forty-three countries to make these records available to all who are interested.

2. The microfilm and microfiche collection is continually expanding. From 1938 to the present, irreplaceable records have been preserved on microfilms. Some 1.5 million rolls of microfilm and approximately 200,000 microfiche containing the names of an estimated 1.5 billion deceased people are now available to researchers.

3. The IGI includes names and vital statistics of millions of people who lived between the early 1500s and 1875 in some ninety countries, alphabetized by surname and arranged geographically. Millions of names are added each year. This index is accessible on microfiche and is computerized.

These and other resources have aided millions of researchers in finding their "roots," and have made possible the performance of TEMPLE ORDINANCES for millions who lived and died without that opportunity.

The continued commitment to identify ancestors and provide temple ordinances for them which began in this dispensation with divine revelations to the Prophet Joseph SMITH, and was furthered by the organization of the Genealogical Society of Utah, and has enabled millions of genealogists throughout the world to develop a strong association between family history and The Church of Jesus Christ of Latter-day Saints.

BIBLIOGRAPHY

Durham, G. Homer, ed. *Discourses of Wilford Woodruff*, p. 157. Salt Lake City, 1946.

GEORGE D. DURRANT

GENEALOGY

[*Genealogy is a record of lineage showing the descent of a person or family from an ancestor or ancestors. Searching for and compiling genealogical information*

are sacred responsibilities to Latter-day Saints. Therefore, extensive activity is conducted by the Church and by members to obtain and record vital statistical information, to compile family histories, and to strengthen family ties both on earth and in the hereafter. In LDS doctrine the family is of eternal significance. Thus, three major purposes of compiling genealogical records are to identify one's roots, to perform saving ordinances in a temple for persons who did not receive them in mortal life, and to seal individuals together for eternity as families.

Articles relating to this subject are Ancestral File; Baptism for the Dead; Book of Remembrance; Born in the Covenant; Elijah, Spirit of; Family; Family History; Family History Centers; Family History Library; Family Organizations; Family Registry; FamilySearch; Genealogical Society of Utah; Granite Mountain Record Vault; International Genealogical Index (IGI); Name Extraction Program; Personal Ancestral File; Salvation of the Dead; Sealing; Temple Ordinances; Temples; World Conferences on Records.]

GENERAL AUTHORITIES

General Authorities are men called to serve at the highest levels of leadership in The Church of Jesus Christ of Latter-day Saints. As general PRIESTHOOD officers of the Church, they have Churchwide rather than local stewardship and may receive assignments anywhere in the world. In order of precedence, the General Authorities include the FIRST PRESIDENCY, QUORUM OF THE TWELVE APOSTLES, quorums of the SEVENTY, and PRESIDING BISHOPRIC (see ORGANIZATION). First Presidency members and the senior member of the Quorum of the Twelve are addressed as "President." The Twelve Apostles and members of the quorums of the Seventy are addressed as "Elder." Members of the Presiding Bishopric are addressed as "Bishop." As a group, they are often referred to as "the Brethren."

Like all who serve in the Church, these men are lay leaders and do not solicit their assignments. They are "called of God, by prophecy, and by the laying on of hands by those who are in authority" (A of F 5; *see* LAY PARTICIPATION AND LEADERSHIP). They are called by a member of the First Presidency; subsequently, their names are presented to the Church MEMBERSHIP for a sustaining vote each year during general conference and in WARD and STAKE conferences.

Members of the First Presidency and Quorum of the Twelve are sustained as PROPHETS, SEERS,

AND REVELATORS. They are commissioned to be special witnesses of Jesus Christ and his Church, and together with the Seventy they are to bear witness of him and "to build up the church, and regulate all the affairs of the same in all nations" (D&C 107:21–26, 33–35).

As assigned, General Authorities may travel throughout the world to preach the gospel, train and instruct local leaders and members, preside at stake conferences, organize new stakes, call and set apart new STAKE PRESIDENCIES, and generally look after the interests of the Church. They may also be called upon to address the Church membership at General Conference.

In addition, General Authorities fulfill administrative responsibilities at Church headquarters, directly overseeing the Church's efforts in such areas as MISSIONARY work, Church history, FAMILY HISTORY (genealogy), TEMPLE WORSHIP, priesthood, FINANCES and RECORD KEEPING, curriculum, PUBLIC COMMUNICATIONS, and the BUILDING PROGRAM. Some serve on the Church Board of Education, overseeing the CHURCH EDUCATIONAL SYSTEM and sitting on boards of trustees for Church-owned colleges and BRIGHAM YOUNG UNIVERSITY.

General Authorities, particularly members of the quorums of the Seventy, may be assigned to live away from Church headquarters for a time and serve in AREA PRESIDENCIES, presiding over regions and stakes in those areas. Occasionally some are called as MISSION PRESIDENTS or TEMPLE PRESIDENTS, although non-General Authorities most often serve in these positions.

Wives and children of General Authorities may be called to serve in regular Church assignments in their home wards and stakes. Wives of General Authorities who are serving in area presidencies may be called to assist with AUXILIARY ORGANIZATIONS such as the PRIMARY, YOUNG WOMEN, and RELIEF SOCIETY in the countries where their husbands are serving. General Authorities themselves are not called to serve in the local organizations.

The general presidencies and boards of the Church's auxiliary organizations are sustained as general officers of the Church, but they are not General Authorities. They are set apart for a time as general officers for their specific auxiliary organization.

Unlike local leaders, who maintain their normal vocations while serving in Church assign-

First Presidency (1925–1931). Left to right: First counselor Anthony W. Ivins, President Heber J. Grant, and second counselor Charles W. Nibley.

ments, General Authorities set aside their careers to devote their full time to the ministry of their office. The living allowance given General Authorities rarely if ever equals the earnings they sacrifice to serve full-time in the Church.

Members of the First Presidency and Quorum of the Twelve serve for life. Other General Authorities serve either until limited by age or health or for temporary periods. They may be released or receive emeritus status. After their service they return to ward and stake responsibilities.

Calls from one group to another are possible. For example, any General Authority may be called to serve in the First Presidency or Quorum of the Twelve, although previous service as a General Authority is not a prerequisite for these positions. Men from many nations have been called to serve as General Authorities.

Life as a General Authority demands great sacrifices of time and energy. It requires heavy involvement in decision making and continual travel away from home and family. But the work is rewarding. "I have witnessed the miracles that come with faith," said President Gordon B. Hinckley when serving as Second Counselor in the First Presidency. "I have seen the evidences of true goodness and greatness in men and women living under a great variety of circumstances. I have observed in a very intimate and wonderful way the workings of the power of the Almighty among his children" (p. 7).

There is striking UNITY among the General Authorities, which is at least partly due to decision making by COMMON CONSENT. "The General Authorities are all individuals, each with his own per-

General Authorities hold general authority over the Church. Quorum of the Twelve Apostles (1921–1931): Seated (left to right): Rudger Clawson, Reed Smoot, George Albert Smith, George Franklin Richards, Orson F. Whitney, David O. McKay. Standing (left to right): Joseph Fielding Smith, James E. Talmage, Stephen L Richards, Richard R. Lyman, Melvin J. Ballard, John A. Widtsoe.

sonality," said President Hinckley. "Each brings to his responsibilities a wide variety of experience and background. When matters come up for discussion in the leading councils of the Church, each is free to express his views. As one observes that interesting process at work, it is fascinating to witness the power of the Holy Spirit influence these men. Initial differences, never sharp but nonetheless perceptible, soften and meld into an expression of unity" (p. 6).

Although they have general administrative authority and are entitled to INSPIRATION regarding the governing of Church affairs, General Authorities respect the right each member of the Church has to receive personal REVELATION. The Lord told Joseph SMITH that the gospel was restored so "that every man [and woman] might speak in the name of God" (D&C 1:20).

General Authorities are men who, through years of experience in Church service, have proven to be faithful, effective, and devoted leaders and servants. As witnesses of the Lord and as general officers of the Church, they are trusted, loved, and respected throughout the Church.

[*See also* Following the Brethren.]

BIBLIOGRAPHY

Arrington, Leonard J., ed. *The Presidents of the Church: Biographical Essays.* Salt Lake City, 1986.

Flake, Lawrence R. *Mighty Men of Zion: General Authorities of the Last Dispensation.* Salt Lake City, 1974.

Hinckley, Gordon B. "He Slumbers Not, nor Sleeps." *Ensign* 13 (May 1983):5–8.

Presidents of the Church: "They That Move the Cause of Zion." Salt Lake City, 1979.

Tanner, N. Eldon. "The Administration of the Church." *Ensign* 9 (Nov. 1979):42–48.

Updated information on newly called General Authorities is available in the *Deseret News Church Almanac,* published biennially.

MARVIN K. GARDNER

GENERAL HANDBOOK OF INSTRUCTIONS

The *General Handbook of Instructions* is the official book of instruction for Church leaders, mainly STAKE PRESIDENTS and BISHOPS. Church leaders who receive the handbook include GENERAL AUTHORITIES, Church department heads, general auxiliary presidencies, temple presidents, and officers in stakes, wards, missions, districts, and branches. It is a handbook of Church policy and practices, not doctrine. The FIRST PRESIDENCY and QUORUM OF THE TWELVE APOSTLES prepare the handbook to provide uniform procedures and methods for local leaders as they minister to the members and direct Church affairs in their areas throughout the world. Other Church handbooks, such as those for PRIESTHOOD and AUXILIARY ORGANIZATIONS, are based on the *General Handbook of Instructions.*

Handbooks have included such things as instruction on (1) Church administration and meetings; (2) calling members to Church positions and releasing them from such calls; (3) ordaining members to priesthood offices; (4) performing ORDINANCES and giving BLESSINGS; (5) doing sacred temple work, and family history; (6) responding to calls for missionary service; (7) keeping records, reports, and accounting for finances; (8) applying Church discipline; and (9) implementing Church policies on such matters as buildings and property, moral issues, and medical and health issues.

The first edition of the handbook was a fourteen-page booklet of shirt-pocket size published in 1899. It instructed stake and ward leaders in how to receive, process, and account for members' tithing, most of which was farm produce and livestock rather than money. The Church revised the handbook annually until 1910 and, thereafter, about every five years. The most significant and constant change that has prompted the revisions has been the growth of the Church from 271,681 members in 1899 to more than 7 million in 1990. Other factors that have prompted revisions include the shift in North American members from an agrarian to an urban society, the immigration of converts, the Depression of the 1930s, the wars in the twentieth century, the increase of sensitive social issues, and the transitions from a membership centered in Utah to a membership in North America, and ultimately, to an international Church. Between revisions, letters from the First Presidency to local leaders and items in the priesthood *Bulletin* update instructions in the handbook.

The handbook is written in terms of principles, as far as possible, rather than explicit directions. Local leaders apply the principles in their stakes, wards, and branches as they are directed by spiritual inspiration.

The *General Handbook of Instructions* is preeminent among Church publications in both its preparation and its use as an authoritative guide for local Church leaders.

FRANK O. MAY, JR.

GENTILES

[In the Bible, the Hebrew and Greek words translated into English as "Gentile" signified other peoples; i.e., "not Israelite" and later "not Jewish." For Latter-day Saints, "Gentile" generally means "not Latter-day Saint," although the meaning also extends to include "not Jewish" and "not Lamanite." These latter senses are rooted partly in scripture, where the distinction between Gentiles and Israelites or Jews is firmly maintained, and partly in the language adopted by early leaders of The Church of Jesus Christ of Latter-day Saints. In the LDS scriptural view, Gentiles play an important role in the restoration of the gospel in the latter days (1 Ne. 13:38–39; 22:6–11; 3 Ne. 21:1–6) and in the latter-day work of gathering Israel (1 Ne. 22:12; 3 Ne. 21:6, 22–29). For discussions related to this topic, see Abrahamic Covenant; Gentiles, Fulness of; Israel: Gathering of Israel; and Law of Adoption.]

GENTILES, FULNESS OF

The "fulness of the Gentiles" is a term for a doctrine taught in the New Testament, the Book of Mormon, and the Doctrine and Covenants. It refers to a process whereby, after Jesus' ministry among his Jewish countrymen, the gospel was preached to Gentiles in the MERIDIAN OF TIME. Jesus told his Jewish listeners that the kingdom of God would be taken from them "and given to a nation bringing forth the fruits thereof" (Matt. 21:43). He also said that many Gentiles would sit down in the kingdom of heaven with Abraham, Isaac, and Jacob (Matt. 8:5–12). Paul taught that in his day the Gentiles would be given an opportunity to receive the gospel, be adopted into the house of Israel, and receive the blessings of the covenant people (Rom. 9–11), concluding that "blindness in part is happened to Israel, until the fulness of the Gentiles be come in" (Rom. 11:25).

Jesus prophesied the destruction of Jerusalem and the dispersion of the people of Judah among all nations "until the times of the Gentiles be fulfilled" (Luke 21:24; JST Luke 21:24, 32). As latter-day revelation makes clear, "the times" of the Gentiles refers to the time when the fulness of the gospel will come among them (D&C 45:24–28). Latter-day revelation further teaches that in the last days the restored gospel will "go forth unto the ends of the earth, unto the Gentiles first, and then, behold, and lo, they shall turn unto the Jews" (D&C 90:9–11), so "that all who will hear may hear" (D&C 1:11) and "all the families of the earth be blessed" (Abr. 2:11). When the Gentiles reject the gospel, "the times of the Gentiles [will] be fulfilled" (D&C 45:29–30).

In 1823 the angel Moroni told Joseph Smith "that the fulness of the Gentiles was soon to come in" (JS—H 1:41). During the ministry of the resurrected Jesus among Book of Mormon peoples, he foretold the coming forth of the restored gospel among the Gentiles and warned that when they reject the fulness of his gospel and are lifted up in pride and all manner of wickedness, he will take his gospel from among them (3 Ne. 16:7–10). After they reject the gospel, it will be offered to the house of Israel (3 Ne. 16:11–12). Thus, Gentiles who have accepted the gospel will be numbered with Israel and escape the judgments that are to come upon the wicked (3 Ne. 16:13–14). In the dispensation of the fulness of times, the Gentiles will have been first to receive the gospel, and the first (Israel) will be the last (cf. 1 Ne. 13:42; *MD*, pp. 721–22).

BIBLIOGRAPHY

Nyman, Monte S. *An Ensign to All People*, pp. 49–56. Salt Lake City, 1987.

MONTE S. NYMAN

GETHSEMANE

The name Gethsemane (derived from Hebrew "oil press") is mentioned twice in the Bible, both in the New Testament (Matt. 26:36; Mark 14:32); in each case, it is called a "place" (Greek *chōrion*, "piece of land") to which Jesus Christ and his apostles re-

tired after their last supper together. The fourth gospel calls the area "a garden" (John 18:1). For Latter-day Saints, Gethsemane was the scene of Jesus' greatest agony, even surpassing that which he suffered on the cross, an understanding supported by Mark's description of Jesus' experience (Mark 14:33–39).

According to Luke 22:43–44, Jesus' anguish was so deep that "his sweat was as it were great drops of blood falling down to the ground," an observation that harmonizes with the view that Jesus suffered most in Gethsemane during his ATONEMENT. Even though these verses are missing in some of the earliest extant manuscripts of Luke's gospel, their content is confirmed in modern revelation (e.g., D&C 19:18). The evidence for Jesus' extreme agony in Gethsemane is buttressed by a prophecy in the Book of Mormon and a statement by the resurrected Savior recorded in the Doctrine and Covenants. About 125 B.C., a Book of Mormon king, BENJAMIN, recounted in an important address a prophecy of the coming MESSIAH spoken to him by an angel during the previous night. Concerning the Messiah's mortal experience, the angel declared that "he shall suffer temptations, and pain of body, hunger, thirst, and fatigue, even more than man can suffer, except it be unto death; for behold, blood cometh from every pore, so great shall be his anguish for the wickedness and the abominations of his people" (Mosiah 3:7). The Doctrine and Covenants gives the following poignant words of the resurrected Jesus: "Behold, I, God, have suffered these things for all, that they might not suffer if they would repent; . . . which suffering caused myself, even God, the greatest of all, to tremble because of pain, and to bleed at every pore, and to suffer both body and spirit" (D&C 19:16, 18).

Modern LDS leaders have emphasized that Jesus' most challenging experience came in Gethsemane. Speaking in a general conference of the Church in 1982, Marion G. Romney, a member of the FIRST PRESIDENCY, observed that Jesus suffered "the pains of all men, which he did, principally, in Gethsemane, the scene of his great agony" (*Ensign* 12 [May 1982]:6). Church President Ezra Taft BENSON wrote that "it was in Gethsemane that Jesus took on Himself the sins of the world, in Gethsemane that His pain was equivalent to the cumulative burden of all men, in Gethsemane that He descended below all things so that all could repent and come to Him" (Benson, p. 7).

While tradition locates Gethsemane on the lower slopes of the Mount of Olives, the exact spot remains unknown. Luke associates it with the Mount of Olives (Luke 22:39), and John notes that it lay across the Kidron brook (John 18:1), which flows from the north along Jerusalem's east side. The particular use of "place" (Greek *topos*) to describe the spot in the gospels of Luke and John suggests that the location was bound up with Jesus' destiny and consequently possesses a sacred character (Luke 22:40; John 18:2). It was a spot that Jesus and his disciples customarily visited (Luke 22:39), which allowed Judas and the others to find him on the night of his arrest (John 18:2).

BIBLIOGRAPHY

Benson, Ezra Taft. *Come Unto Christ*. Salt Lake City, 1983.

Maxwell, Neal A. "The New Testament—A Matchless Portrait of the Savior." *Ensign* 16 (Dec. 1986):20–27.

Wilkinson, John. *Jerusalem as Jesus Knew It*, pp. 125–31. London, 1978.

S. KENT BROWN

GIFT OF THE HOLY GHOST

The gift of the HOLY GHOST is the right or privilege of receiving divine manifestations, spiritual gifts, and direction from the Holy Ghost. This gift is conferred upon members of the Church by the LAYING ON OF HANDS following BAPTISM. It is considered one of the essential ORDINANCES of the GOSPEL OF JESUS CHRIST and an absolute prerequisite of SALVATION.

The Holy Ghost is the third member of the GODHEAD, while the gift of the Holy Ghost consists of the privilege to receive inspiration, manifestations, and other spiritual gifts and blessings from that member of the Godhead (*TPJS*, p. 199). Among the most important spiritual blessings associated with the gift of the Holy Ghost is the sanctifying or cleansing power of the Holy Ghost, whereby men and women are BORN OF GOD. Through this BAPTISM OF FIRE AND OF THE HOLY GHOST, individual hearts and desires are cleansed and spirits made pure as the culmination of the process of repentance and baptism (2 Ne. 31:13, 17; 3 Ne. 27:20). Other important manifestations of the Holy Ghost include bearing witness of Jesus Christ and of divine truths, providing spiritual guidance and warning as appropriate, and enabling discernment of right and wrong.

The gift of the Holy Ghost is understood to be the key to all of the "spiritual gifts" found in the Church, including the gifts of PROPHECY and REVELATION, of healing, of speaking in tongues, and of the translation and interpretation of tongues. These distinctive GIFTS OF THE SPIRIT normally are manifested only among those who have received the gift of the Holy Ghost and who qualify by their needs and their worthiness for such divine assistance, even as the original apostles of Christ received these gifts only after the Holy Ghost came upon them on the Day of Pentecost (Acts 2:1–17).

In LDS practice, the gift of the Holy Ghost is given by the laying-on of hands as indicated in the New Testament (see Acts 8:17–18; 19:2–6; 2 Tim. 1:6; Heb. 6:2), normally immediately following or within a few days of the baptism by water. A bearer of the Melchizedek Priesthood (usually joined by a few others holding the same priesthood) lays his hands upon the head of the newly baptized member, calls the person by name, confirms him or her a member of the Church, and says, "Receive the Holy Ghost." The exact wording of this ordinance is not prescribed, but it always involves the CONFIRMATION of MEMBERSHIP, the bestowal of the gift of the Holy Ghost, and a reference to the priesthood authority by which the ordinance is performed. These basic components of the ordinance often are followed by a verbal BLESSING that offers counsel and direction to the new member. In proxy TEMPLE ORDINANCE work for deceased persons, the same basic confirmation follows the ordinance of baptism for the dead.

The New Testament account of how the Saints in Samaria received the gift of the Holy Ghost makes clear that bestowal of this gift requires a higher AUTHORITY than is needed for performing baptisms (see Acts 8:14–17).

When Jesus Christ visited the Nephites, he first gave authority to baptize (3 Ne. 11:22), and in a subsequent visit he gave authority to bestow the Holy Ghost, as he touched and spoke to each of the twelve disciples individually (3 Ne. 18:36–37). Whereas baptisms can be performed by priests in the Aaronic Priesthood, the Holy Ghost can be conferred only by bearers of the higher or Melchizedek Priesthood (Moro. 2:2; JS—H 1:70). JOHN THE BAPTIST referred to this fundamental distinction between the two priesthoods: "I indeed baptize you with water unto repentance: but he that cometh after me is mightier than I . . . he shall baptize you with the Holy Ghost, and with fire" (Matt. 3:11).

The gift of the Holy Ghost is formally bestowed upon an individual only once, but the spiritual benefits associated with this gift can and should be continuous during a lifetime. Latter-day Saints are taught to strive to live so as to have the Holy Ghost as a "constant companion" to strengthen them and help them choose the right (D&C 121:46). The granting of the gift alone, however, does not insure these inspirations. The actual reception of the Holy Ghost is conditional upon the humility, faith, and worthiness of the individual who has had the gift bestowed on him or her. President Joseph F. SMITH taught that the gift of the Holy Ghost confers upon worthy and desirous members "the right to receive . . . the power and light of truth of the Holy Ghost, although [they] may often be left to [their] own spirit and judgment" (GD, pp. 60–61).

The gift of the Holy Ghost is referred to by the Prophet Joseph SMITH as one of the basic principles and ordinances of the gospel, being integrally linked to faith in Jesus Christ, repentance, and baptism by immersion for the REMISSION OF SINS (see FIRST PRINCIPLES OF THE GOSPEL; A of F 4). Together these four constitute the "first principles" of the gospel of Jesus Christ (see GOSPEL OF JESUS CHRIST; 3 Ne. 27:19–21) and the only means whereby men and women can be cleansed of all sin—to become pure and spotless and worthy to enter the presence of God.

The Holy Ghost continues to aid in the process of spiritual purification through "the baptism by fire," which has been described in these words: "By the power of the Holy Ghost—who is the Sanctifier (3 Ne. 27:19–21)—dross, iniquity, carnality, sensuality, and every evil thing is burned out of the repentant soul as if by fire; the cleansed person becomes literally a new creature of the Holy Ghost. . . . He is born again" (MD, p. 73). The Savior referred to this spiritual rebirth when he told Nicodemus, "Except a man be born of water and of the Spirit, he cannot enter into the kingdom of God" (John 3:5).

A single experience of being "born again" does not alone insure salvation. It is also necessary for a person to "endure to the end," an essential element of the gospel of Christ (2 Ne. 31:20; 3 Ne. 27:16–17). The prophet Nephi$_1$ taught that

ENDURING TO THE END requires that one "feast upon the words of Christ," following the guidance of the Holy Ghost in "all things what ye should do" (2 Ne. 32:3–5). The gift of the Holy Ghost thus ensures that divine guidance and spiritual renewal take place throughout one's life, provided that the requisite repentance and humility are manifested.

BIBLIOGRAPHY

Lampe, G. W. H. "Holy Spirit." In *The Interpreter's Dictionary of the Bible*, Vol. 2, pp. 626–39. Nashville, Tenn., 1962.

Shepherd, M. H., Jr. "Hands, Laying on of." In *The Interpreter's Dictionary of the Bible*, Vol. 2, pp. 521–22. Nashville, Tenn., 1962.

Talmage, James E. *AF*, pp. 157–70.

BRUCE DOUGLAS PORTER

GIFTS OF THE SPIRIT

The seventh Article of Faith of The Church of Jesus Christ of Latter-day Saints reads: "We believe in the gift of tongues, prophecy, revelation, visions, healing, interpretation of tongues, and so forth." All such heavenly endowments come as gifts of the Spirit—that is, through the grace of God and the operation and power of the HOLY GHOST. As prerequisites to obtaining such gifts, a person must receive the ordinances of baptism and the bestowal of the GIFT OF THE HOLY GHOST from an authorized priesthood holder, must earnestly seek to obtain the gift or gifts, and must make sincere efforts to keep the Lord's COMMANDMENTS.

Clearly the Spirit can grant any gift that would fill a particular need; hence, no exhaustive list is possible, but many gifts have been promised the Church. Through the New Testament, readers are familiar with the six specified above: the two related to the gifts of tongues and their interpretation, or the power to speak in a language not previously learned and the ability to interpret such speech; the gift of prophecy, exhibited sometimes in the predictive sense but more often in the sense that "the testimony of Jesus is the spirit of prophecy" (Rev. 19:10); revelation, or the heaven-inspired receipt of knowledge, wisdom, or direction; visions, or visual spiritual manifestations such as PROPHETS have received in all ages and as Joel predicted for many others in the latter days (Joel 2:28–29); healing, or the power to "lay hands on the sick" that they may recover (Mark 16:18).

Scripturally, gifts of the Spirit are among the signs that "follow them that believe" (Mark 16:17). Eager to receive such promised gifts but lacking in understanding, some of the early converts to the Church (1831–32) became caught up in "spiritual" excesses that were common to revivalist campground meetings, with which they were familiar. In early days in KIRTLAND, OHIO, the Prophet Joseph SMITH observed, "many false spirits were introduced . . . many ridiculous things were entered into . . . [that would] cause the Spirit of God to be withdrawn" (TPJS, pp. 213–14). In congregations around Kirtland, Parley P. PRATT specifically noted "disgusting" spiritual operations, "unseemly gestures," people falling "into ecstasies, and . . . drawn into contortions . . . fits" (Pratt, p. 61). Joseph Smith condemned such practices as unnatural and without useful purpose, since they communicated no intelligence (TPJS, pp. 204, 214). Thus dissociating the Church from the spiritual extravagances of frontier Christianity, the authorities moved swiftly against such erroneous practices, reclaiming those members whom they could and excommunicating those who persisted in their error.

In the doctrinal unfolding of the infant Church, Joseph Smith received revelations relating to spiritual gifts, notably that of March 8, 1831 (now D&C 46). Having first warned against deception by false spirits, the revelation set out the gifts much as PAUL and MORONI₂ did for the first-century and the Nephite churches, respectively (see 1 Cor. 12; Moroni 10). Mentioned besides the six above were knowledge; wisdom; faith to be healed; the working of MIRACLES; knowledge of the ways in which gifts may be administered; and the DISCERNMENT of spirits, whether they are of God or of the devil. Listed too was the gift of the Spirit's witness of Jesus Christ and his atonement for the sins of the world, and, for some, the gift of believing the words of one who declares that witness (D&C 46:14).

The revelation promises at least one gift to every faithful Latter-day Saint. Bishops and other presiding officers, by virtue of their CALLINGS to watch over the Church, may receive multiple gifts, including the special gift of discernment to detect false from true spirits. On the latter point, Joseph Smith cautioned about "the common error of considering all supernatural manifestations to be of God," warning that evil spirits as well as heavenly ones can, for example, speak in tongues and inter-

pret them; and that in their deception they may even give recognition to the Savior and his authorized servants (TPJS, pp. 206–13, 229; also Luke 4:33–35; Acts 16:16–18).

Many early LDS journals recount experiences with spiritual gifts: In 1830 Newel Knight saw a vision of heaven apparently similar to what the martyr Stephen described ("Newel Knight's Journal," pp. 52–53). In Kirtland in 1831, Chloe Smith, who had been languishing near death, was instantly restored to health under Joseph Smith's ministration (Pratt, pp. 66–67). At a meeting in Ontario, Canada, in 1833, Lydia Bailey (later Knight) spoke in tongues (Journal History, Oct. 19, 1833). Following Heber C. Kimball's prophetic promise in 1836 that a son would be born to Parley and Thankful Pratt, childless after ten years of marriage, a son was born a year later (Pratt, pp. 130–31, 165). Then as now, both leaders and the general membership were blessed with such gifts.

Gifts of the Spirit are to be sought for their beneficial effect rather than for their remarkable character (see 1 Cor. 14). In fact, as Joseph Smith observed, only one or two of the gifts are visible when in operation. In its commonly understood sense, the gift of tongues is one such, but President Joseph F. SMITH stressed its more practical aspect: "I needed the gift of tongues once, and the Lord gave it to me. I was in a foreign land, sent to preach the gospel to a people whose language I could not understand. Then I sought earnestly for the gift of tongues, and by this gift and by study, in a hundred days after landing upon those islands I could talk to the people in their language as I now talk to you in my native tongue. This was a gift that was worthy of the gospel. There was a purpose in it" (Smith, p. 201). In this way, the gift is frequently enjoyed by LDS missionaries today.

Throughout the world, Latter-day Saints report a variety of spiritual gifts in the normal course of their lives. Faithful members commonly receive through the Spirit the gift of the testimony of Jesus Christ and his restored gospel—and those individual testimonies constitute the strength of the Church; the gift of knowledge of spiritual things is enjoyed widely; daily, PRIESTHOOD bearers lay hands on the heads of sick family members or friends, as requested (see James 5:14–15), and bring them heaven's healing powers, frequently with instant effect; men, women, and young persons receive revelation as needed for the benefit of themselves, their families, or those whom they serve in Church callings. Virtually all of these activities and others of comparable spiritual significance go on in the privacy of home and heart without any public awareness of them.

All spiritual gifts are needed in the Church (1 Cor. 12), but that some are more to be desired than others is evident from Paul's writings: One is to seek the best gifts. Of special significance for all who desire "a more excellent way" (1 Cor. 12:31) is to receive and develop the gift of CHARITY. This "pure love of Christ" is a fundamental mark of true DISCIPLESHIP, a prerequisite to ETERNAL LIFE, and a quality one is therefore to pray and work for with all energy of heart (Moroni 7:47–48; 10:21; Ether 12:34). Paul's masterful exposition on charity (1 Cor. 13) further defines this attribute and confirms love as the great commandment and the Christian's crucial need. Disciples are to manifest this gift and also desire others (1 Cor. 14:1), working by the power of God and by the gifts of the Spirit (Moro. 10:25).

BIBLIOGRAPHY

"Newel Knight's Journal." In *Scraps of Biography*. Salt Lake City, 1883.

Pratt, Parley P. *Autobiography of Parley Parker Pratt.* Salt Lake City, 1967.

Smith, Joseph F. *Gospel Doctrine.* Salt Lake City, 1977.

H. GEORGE BICKERSTAFF

GOD

Latter-day Saints declare, "We believe in God, the Eternal Father, and in His Son, Jesus Christ, and in the Holy Ghost" (A of F 1). Joseph SMITH offered the following clarification: "The Father has a body of flesh and bones as tangible as man's; the Son also; but the Holy Ghost has not a body of flesh and bones, but is a personage of Spirit" (D&C 130:22; see GOD THE FATHER; HOLY GHOST; JESUS CHRIST).

The Father, Son, and Holy Ghost are three separate and distinct beings who constitute one GODHEAD. Generally speaking, the Father is the Creator, the Son is the Redeemer, and the Holy Ghost is the Comforter and Testifier (cf. *MFP* 5:26–34; *TPJS*, p. 190). Many scriptural passages illustrate the distinct character of the members of the Godhead. For example, at the baptism of Jesus, while he was in the water, the Father's voice was heard from heaven, and the Holy Ghost descended "like a dove" and rested upon the Son (Matt. 3:13–17; see JESUS CHRIST: BAPTISM). All three persons were manifested separately and simultaneously. Also, Jesus said, "My Father is greater than I" (John 14:28), and in another place declared, "The Father judgeth no man, but hath committed all judgment unto the Son" (John 5:22). Further, Jesus pointed to the Father and himself as two separate witnesses of the divinity of his work (John 5:32–37; 8:12–18). On the MOUNT OF TRANSFIGURATION the heavenly Father identified the mortal Jesus to Peter, James, and John as "my beloved Son" (Matt. 17:5). Moreover, the Son often prayed to his Father. In Gethsemane he prayed to the Father while in deep anguish (Mark 14:32–39; cf. Luke 22:40–46; D&C 19:16–19), and on the cross he cried out to the Father, "My God, my God, why hast thou forsaken me?" (Matt. 27:46; Mark 15:34; cf. Ps. 22:1). All of these passages clearly show that the Father is a being distinct from the Son. Although they are one in mind and purpose, they are two separate individuals and bear testimony of one another (cf. 3 Ne. 11:7–11).

The way in which the Godhead is one is illustrated by Jesus' prayer that his disciples would be one, even as he and the Father are one (John 17:21–22; cf. 3 Ne. 11:27, 32–36; 28:10–11). Here he was praying for his disciples' unity of mind, purpose, and testimony, not for the merger of their identities into a single being. He prayed that they would be one in desire, purpose, and objective, exactly as he and his Father are (*TPJS*, p. 372; see UNITY).

The Father, as God, is omnipotent, omniscient, and, through his spirit, omnipresent (see LIGHT OF CHRIST). He is merciful and gracious, slow to anger, abundant in goodness. His course is one eternal round. He is a God of truth and no respecter of persons. He personifies love.

Though Latter-day Saints extensively use the scriptures to learn about God, their fundamental knowledge concerning him is based upon the Prophet Joseph Smith's FIRST VISION, the Prophet's subsequent revelatory experiences, and individual personal REVELATION. While mankind may reason or speculate concerning the existence of God, and his nature, the principal way by which they can know about God is dependent upon his revealing himself to them (see TESTIMONY OF JESUS CHRIST).

Before A.D. 325, the date of the first Christian ecumenical council at Nicaea, the nature of God was debated by philosophers and people of faith.

Since then, the concept of God has been the subject of ecumenical councils, philosophical discussions, and creeds. None of these is the source of the LDS understanding of God. To be sure, many classical arguments for the existence of God have been advanced, including the ontological arguments of Anselm, the five "proofs" of St. Thomas Aquinas, the teleological argument of Descartes, the ethical argument of Leibniz, and the postulates of practical reason of Kant. As impressive as any of these might be as achievements of the human intellect, none of them is the source of faith in God for Latter-day Saints, whose faith is based upon personal testimony grounded in personal experience (see EPISTEMOLOGY; FAITH; REASON AND REVELATION).

The last chapter of the Book of Mormon records this promise: "And when ye shall receive these things [of God], I would exhort you that ye would ask God, the Eternal Father, in the name of Christ, if these things are not true; and if ye shall ask with a sincere heart, with real intent, having faith in Christ, he will manifest the truth of it unto you, by the power of the Holy Ghost. And by the power of the Holy Ghost ye may know the truth of all things" (Moro. 10:4–5). The personal witness that one receives in answer to prayer is called a TESTIMONY. Latter-day Saints teach that through this source a person can receive a sure witness that God lives, a confirmation regarding the various principles that the scriptures teach, and clarification where it is needed.

Belief in God, or a measure of faith in him, is essential to finding the reality of his existence. Inasmuch as God exists, and human beings are his children, it is important for men and women to know these facts because such knowledge is a component of ETERNAL LIFE (John 17:3). Individuals need to know that they are themselves eternal beings, that they are dependent upon God for their earthly existence (cf. Mosiah 2:21), and that their future condition depends on how they relate to God and keep his commandments (see COMMANDMENTS; OBEDIENCE).

God loves his children and has provided the means for them to realize their divine potential (see GODHOOD). God has given humankind the program for his children as a whole (see PLAN OF SALVATION), and through the gift of the Holy Ghost he gives special guidance to individuals as they seek it (see INSPIRATION). God revealed his will to prophets in ancient times and to apostles in the MERIDIAN OF TIME, and he continues to reveal

himself to living prophets and apostles in the latter days.

Learning of God's existence creates the desire to know him, and know what he would have one do or be. As one's faith and knowledge of God increase, one desires more and more to keep God's commandments and feel close to him (see FAITH). The Prophet Joseph Smith taught that knowing the true character of God forms the basis for the faith that leads to salvation (Lectures on Faith 4:1; see LECTURES ON FAITH). Jesus promised that the Comforter, or Holy Ghost, would be sent to one who keeps God's commandments (John 14:26). The ideal is to enjoy that influence continuously.

The Prophet Joseph Smith said, "It is the first principle of the Gospel to know for a certainty the character of God, and to know that we may converse with him as one man converses with another, and that he was once a man like us: yea, that God himself, the Father of us all, dwelt on an earth, the same as Jesus Christ himself did" (TPJS, pp. 345–46). Further, "God himself was once as we are now, and is an exalted man, and sits enthroned in yonder heavens! That is the great secret. If the veil were rent today, and the great God who holds this world in its orbit, and who upholds all worlds and all things by his power, was to make himself visible,—I say, if you were to see him today, you would see him like a man in form—like yourselves in all the person, image, and very form as a man; for Adam was created in the very fashion, image and likeness of God, and received instruction from, and walked, talked and conversed with him, as one man talks and communes with another" (TPJS, p. 345).

Thus, all humans must learn from God who they are, where they came from, why they are on earth, where they are going, and what their eternal potential is, by studying the scriptures and receiving personal revelation. All things center in God.

BIBLIOGRAPHY

"The Father and the Son: A Doctrinal Exposition by the First Presidency and the Twelve." MFP 5:26–34.

Kimball, Spencer W. The Teachings of Spencer W. Kimball, ed. Edward L. Kimball. Salt Lake City, 1982.

McConkie, Bruce R. A New Witness for the Articles of Faith. Salt Lake City, 1985.

Smith, Joseph Fielding. DS 1:1–55. Salt Lake City, 1954.

Talmage, James E. AF, pp. 29–51. Salt Lake City, 1965.

DAVID H. YARN, JR.

GOD, ATTRIBUTES OF

See: God; God the Father; Godhood; Lectures on Faith

GOD THE FATHER

[*This entry is composed of four articles*:

Overview
Names and Titles
Glory of God
Work and Glory of God

The first article is an introduction to doctrines about God the Father and the sources where they may be found. The second article lists the main names and titles by which God is known in LDS scripture. The third article offers a brief discussion of the Glory of God. *The concluding article in this entry elaborates on the concept of the purposes of God in relation to mankind.*]

OVERVIEW

Latter-day Saints commonly refer to God the Eternal Father as Elohim, a Hebrew plural (*'elohim*) meaning *God* or *gods*, and to his Son Jesus Christ as Jehovah (*see* ELOHIM; JEHOVAH, JESUS CHRIST). Distinguishing between the persons of the Father and the Son is not possible with more ambiguous terms like "God"; therefore, referring to the Father as "Elohim" is a useful convention as long as one remembers that in some passages of the Hebrew Bible the title *'elohim* does not refer exclusively to the person of God the Father. A less ambiguous term for God the Father in LDS parlance might be "Ahman" (cf. D&C 78:15, 20), which, according to Elder Orson PRATT, is a name of the Father (*JD* 2:342).

In Church theology, the doctrine of the nature of God is established more clearly by the First Vision of the Prophet Joseph SMITH than by anything else. Here, Joseph Smith saw for himself that the Father and the Son were two separate and distinct beings, each possessing a body in whose image and likeness mortals are created. For Latter-day Saints, no theological or philosophical propositions about God can override the primary experience of the Prophet (*see* FIRST VISION).

In one sense, it creates a slight distortion to focus on one member of the Godhead and discuss his characteristics in isolation from those of the other two, for Father, Son, and Holy Ghost are one in mind, one in purpose, and one in character (John 10:30; 17:11, 21–23). Most of what can be said of the Father is also true of the Son and vice versa. The Prophet Joseph Smith said that the Son does nothing for which the Father is not the exemplar (*TPJS*, p. 312; cf. John 5:19–20).

Yet God the Father is not one in substance with the Son or the Holy Spirit, but is a separate being. The Father existed prior to the Son and the Holy Ghost and is the source of their divinity. In classical terms, LDS theology is subordinationist; that is, it views the Son and the Holy Ghost as subordinate to and dependent upon God the Eternal Father. They are his offspring. Thus Joseph Smith referred to the Father as "God the first" to emphasize his priority in the Godhead (*TPJS*, p. 190). The Son and the Holy Spirit were "in the beginning, with God," but the Father alone existed before the beginning of the universe as it is known. He is ultimately the source of all things and the Father of all things, for in the beginning he begot the Son, and through the instrumentality of his agent, the Son, the Father accomplished the creation of all things.

Latter-day Saints perceive the Father as an exalted Man in the most literal, anthropomorphic terms. They do not view the language of Genesis as allegorical; human beings are created in the form and image of a God who has a physical form and image (Gen. 1:26). The Prophet Joseph Smith explained, "The Father has a body of flesh and bones as tangible as man's; the Son also; but the Holy Ghost has not a body of flesh and bones, but is a personage of Spirit" (D&C 130:22). Thus, "God is a Spirit" (John 4:24) in the sense that the Holy Ghost, the member of the Godhead who deals most often and most directly with humans, is a God and a spirit, but God the Father and God the Son are spirits with physical, resurrected bodies. Latter-day Saints deny the abstract nature of God the Father and affirm that he is a concrete being, that he possesses a physical body, and that he is in space and time. They further reject any idea that God the Father is "totally other," unknowable, or incomprehensible. In LDS doctrine, knowing the Father and the Son is a prerequisite to eternal life (John 17:3; D&C 88:49). In the opinion of many Latter-day Saints, the concept of an abstract, incomprehensible deity constitutes an intrusion of Greek philosophical categories upon the biblical record.

The Father, Elohim, is called the Father because he is the literal father of the spirits of mortals (Heb. 12:9). This paternity is not allegorical. All individual human spirits were begotten (not created from nothing or made) by the Father in a premortal state, where they lived and were nurtured by Heavenly Parents. These spirit children of the Father come to earth to receive mortal bodies; there is a literal family relationship among humankind. Joseph Smith taught, "If men do not comprehend the character of God, they do not comprehend themselves" (*TPJS*, p. 343). Gods and humans represent a single divine lineage, the same species of being, although they and he are at different stages of progress. This doctrine is stated concisely in a well-known couplet by President Lorenzo SNOW: "As man now is, God once was: as God now is, man may be" (*see* GODHOOD). This principle is clearly demonstrated in the person of Jesus Christ, a God who became mortal, and yet a God like whom mortals may become (Rom. 8:29; 2 Cor. 3:18). But the maxim is true of the Father as well. As the Prophet Joseph Smith said, "God himself was once as we are now, and is an exalted man, and sits enthroned in yonder heavens! That is the great secret" (*TPJS*, p. 345). Thus, the Father became the Father at some time before "the beginning" as humans know it, by experiencing a mortality similar to that experienced on earth. There has been speculation among some Latter-day Saints on the implications of this doctrine, but nothing has been revealed to the Church about conditions before the "beginning" as mortals know it. The important points of the doctrine for Latter-day Saints are that Gods and humans are the same species of being, but at different stages of development in a divine continuum, and that the heavenly Father and Mother are the heavenly pattern, model, and example of what mortals can become through obedience to the gospel (*see* MOTHER IN HEAVEN). Knowing that they are the literal offspring of Heavenly Parents and that they can become like those parents through the gospel of Jesus Christ is a wellspring of religious motivation. With God as the literal Father and with humans having the capacity to become like him, the basic religious questions "Where did I come from?," "Why am I here?," and What is my destiny?" are fundamentally answered.

Latter-day Saints also attribute omnipotence and omniscience to the Father. He knows all things relative to the universe in which mortals live and is himself the source and possessor of all true power manifest in it. This is part of what it means to be exalted, and this is why human beings may safely put their faith and trust in God the Father, an exalted being. Nevertheless, in most things dealing with this world, the Father works through a mediator, his Son, Jesus Christ. With few exceptions, scriptural references to God, or even to the Father, have Jesus Christ as the actual subject, for the Father is represented by his Son. On those few recorded occasions when the Father has plainly manifested himself, he has apparently limited his personal involvement to bearing witness of the Son, as at the baptism of Jesus (Matt. 3:17), at the transfiguration (Matt. 17:5), in his witness to the Nephites and Lamanites (3 Ne. 11:7), and in Joseph Smith's First Vision (JS—H 1:17). Christ is the agent of the Father, and since he alone, by his atonement, has made access to the Father possible, Latter-day Saints worship and pray to the Father and offer all other sacred performances to him in the name of the Son, Jesus Christ (Moses 5:8).

Another important personal attribute of the Father is his perfect love (1 Jn. 4:8). Because of this love, it is the nature of the Father to improve everything and everyone to the extent that they will allow. Out of preexisting chaos, matter unorganized, the Father created an orderly universe. Out of preexisting intelligence, he begat spirit children. Even those of his children who will not cooperate and obey, and who cannot therefore become like him, he still saves, if they will allow it, and places them in lesser kingdoms of glory (D&C 76:42–43; *see* SALVATION): "For behold, this is my work and my glory—to bring to pass the immortality and eternal life of man" (Moses 1:39). The love of the Father is not limited to those who worship and obey him, although their rewards will be greatest, but it is extended to all of his children. The Father's work, and his glory, is to love and to lift all of his children as far as they will allow him. Latter-day Saints believe it is the intention of the Father to make all human beings as happy as they possibly can be. To that end, the Father authored the PLAN OF SALVATION. The Father desires that all human beings be exalted like himself, receive the powers and the joys that he possesses, and experience a fulness of joy in eternity. The limiting factor is the degree to which humans, by exercising their faith and obedience and by making wise choices, will permit the Father to bless them in achieving this goal. Sometimes having faith in God means having faith that the Father's plan will do what it is designed to do—to bring maximum happiness to human beings. Nevertheless, Latter-day Saints believe, in contrast to some other views, that the Father will never violate individual agency by forcing his children to exaltation and happiness. Coercion in any degree, even in the form of predestination to the celestial kingdom, is abhorrent to the nature of the Father. All relationships to him or associations with him are voluntary.

BIBLIOGRAPHY

Cannon, Donald Q., and Larry E. Dahl. *The Prophet Joseph Smith's King Follett Discourse: A Six Column Comparison of Original Notes and Amalgamations.* Provo, Utah, 1983.

McConkie, Bruce R. *A New Witness for the Articles of Faith*, pp. 58-65. Salt Lake City, 1985.

Smith, Joseph Fielding. *DS*, Vol. 1, pp. 1–17.

STEPHEN E. ROBINSON

NAMES AND TITLES

Known names and titles of God the Eternal Father are limited in number, especially when compared to the names applied to Jesus Christ (see JESUS CHRIST, NAMES AND TITLES OF). Latter-day Saints understand the Godhead to consist of three separate individuals: the Father; Jesus Christ, his Son; and the Holy Ghost (D&C 130:22). Therefore, when the need exists to distinguish God the Father from the other two members of the Godhead, Church members select from the names found in scripture.

GOD. Among Latter-day Saints, the title "God" generally identifies God the Father. Occasionally, God may refer to the unified Godhead of the Father, Son, and Holy Ghost (cf. 2 Ne. 31:21; D&C 20:28) and at times to each member individually (*AF*, pp. 159–63). This characteristic makes the attempt to distinguish the Father from Jesus Christ in scripture very difficult at times. Significantly, Jesus' declarations that he and the Father are "one," and to know one is to know the other, indicate that the unity or "oneness" of the Godhead—in purpose and mind and testifying of one another—is of primary worth and seems to diminish the importance of making distinctions among its members. The scriptures teach that a person will come to know the Father by first knowing Christ (John 14:6–23; D&C 84:35–38; 93:1–22; 132:12). Jesus' instructions that his believers are to

be "one" with him as he is "one" with the Father are basic to his doctrine (cf. John 17:1–26; 3 Ne. 11:32–36).

FATHER, FATHER IN HEAVEN. The name-title "Father in Heaven" refers to the director of creation and Father of the spirits of all mankind (*MFP* 5:26–27). Jesus used the terms "my Father," "our Father," and "the Father" when teaching about and praying to his Father. The Aramaic word *'abba* (father) has carried over into English translations of the New Testament (Mark 14:36; Rom. 8:15; Gal. 4:6). In the Book of Mormon, the resurrected Jesus continually used the title "Father" when referring to the Father in Heaven (e.g., 3 Ne. 11:11; 19:20–23). In some instances, however, Father may refer to the Son (see JESUS CHRIST: FATHERHOOD AND SONSHIP). According to both the New Testament and Book of Mormon, faithful souls who are converted to Jesus Christ and who make personal covenants with him are spiritually reborn, becoming "his sons and his daughters" (e.g., Mosiah 5:7; cf. 1 Cor. 4:15; 2 Cor. 6:18; *MFP* 5:27–31).

GOD THE FATHER. The combination of the title "God" and the appellative "Father" specifies the Father of Jesus Christ and of all spirits. Latter-day Saints worship God the Father and Jesus Christ and pray to the Father in the name of Christ as directed by the Lord (D&C 88:64).

ELOHIM. The commonly used term for "God" or "gods" in the Hebrew Bible is *'elohim*, a plural form whose singular is *'eloah* or *'el* and has the meaning of "lofty one" or "exalted one." Early Church leaders adopted the policy of designating God the Father by the exalted name-title "Elohim" (cf. *MFP* 5:26; see ELOHIM; NAME OF GOD). This terminology has continued down to the present.

JEHOVAH, LORD, LORD GOD. The term "LORD," printed with capital letters in many English versions of the Old Testament, is a substitute for the name Jehovah (*yhwh* in the Hebrew Bible). Even though Latter-day Saints identify Jesus Christ as Jehovah (3 Ne. 15:3–5; cf. D&C 110:1–4; *see* JEHOVAH, JESUS CHRIST), they utilize the title "Lord" for both the Father and the Son, as is common throughout scripture. The title "Lord God" in the Hebrew Bible is a compound of *'elohim* preceded by either *yhwh* (Jehovah) or *adonai* (lord or master). This combined name-title refers mainly to Jehovah in the Old Testament. In the New Testament, the Book of Mormon, and in other latter-day scriptures, "Lord God" can mean either the Father (e.g., Moses 4:1–4) or the Son (Mosiah 3:21).

AHMAN. In two revelations to Joseph SMITH (D&C 78:20; 95:17), Jesus Christ referred to himself as "the Son Ahman," allowing the possibility that "Ahman" may be a word meaning God, and one of the names of the Father (see AHMAN). The name also appears in a compound place name, ADAM-ONDI-AHMAN (D&C 116:1; 117:8, 11).

MAN OF HOLINESS. Adam learned by revelation that one of the names of God the Father is "Man of Holiness" (Moses 6:57). Enoch also recorded God's words: "Behold, I am God; Man of Holiness is my name; Man of Counsel is my name; and Endless and Eternal is my name" (Moses 7:35; see ENDLESS AND ETERNAL).

In the Bible and latter-day scripture, other titles for God carry valuable meaning: "Father of Spirits," "God of all other Gods," "Endless," "The Living God," and "Lord of Sabaoth [Hebrew for "Hosts"], which is by interpretation, the creator of the first day, the beginning and the end" (D&C 95:7).

BIBLIOGRAPHY

Talmage, James E. AF. Salt Lake City, 1915.

GLADE L. BURGON

GLORY OF GOD

Glory is an intrinsic attribute and emanation of God, which LDS SCRIPTURES associate with divine law and with the power and Spirit that "proceedeth forth from the presence of God to fill the immensity of space" (D&C 88:7–13). Prominent terms for this "spirit of glory" (1 Pet. 4:14) are the Spirit of God, the HOLY SPIRIT, the Spirit of the Lord, the light of truth, the LIGHT OF CHRIST, and the Spirit of Christ. This all-pervading Spirit is so pure and refined that it is not perceptible to mortals under ordinary circumstances (D&C 131:7–8; TPJS, pp. 207, 301–332). Yet on occasion, the prophets testify, the innate glory has been visibly manifest as flaming spiritual fire (Ex. 24:17; Acts 2:3; Hel. 5:43–45; 3 Ne. 17:24; 19:13–14; HC 1:30–32). Moses and Jesus were transfigured by the same glorifying power (Ex. 34:29–35; Matt. 17:2).

Because glory radiates from God, he is described as "a consuming fire" (Deut. 4:24; cf. Isa. 33:14). God may withhold or conceal his glory (TPJS, pp. 162, 181, 325). But he may also radiate such transcendent light and heat that no mortal flesh can endure his presence (Mal. 4:1; D&C 133:41, 49; HC 1:17, 37). Only when clothed by the Spirit can anyone endure the glorious presence of God (Moses 1:2, 11; D&C 67:11).

The spirit of glory permeates God's creations (D&C 63:59; 88:41). Therefore, they are kingdoms of glory, and to behold any or the least of his creations is to behold a portion of his glory (Moses 1:5; Ps. 19:1; D&C 88:45–47; TPJS, p. 351). Since God's works are endless, his glory is ever-increasing (Abr. 3:12; Moses 1:38; 7:30). His "work and glory" are to bring to pass the immortality and eternal life of his children (Moses 1:39). As Jesus' submission to the will of his Father glorified both himself and his Father, so does the obedience of his children glorify both themselves and God (John 13:31; 17:1). Oneness with God is achieved through this relationship of glory (John 17:21–23; D&C 88:60).

The degree to which mortal men and women acquire and live the moral and spiritual principles of light and truth inherent in divine INTELLIGENCE determines the degree to which they will be filled with the glory of God when resurrected and, therefore, the sphere of glory they will inherit in eternity (D&C 88:22–32; 93:20, 28; 130:18–19; TPJS, p. 366).

RODNEY TURNER

WORK AND GLORY OF GOD

A revelation received by Moses between his experience at the burning bush (Ex. 3:1–4:17) and his return to Egypt (Ex. 4:20; cf. Moses 1:26) describes the work and glory of God as "to bring to pass the immortality and eternal life of man" (Moses 1:39). One of the most frequently quoted passages of scripture in LDS sermons, this declaration elucidates the chief object of God's actions on behalf of his children.

Earlier in this vision, Moses had "beheld many lands; and each land was called earth, and there were inhabitants on the face thereof" (Moses 1:29). Then the Lord told him that "as one earth shall pass away, and the heavens thereof even so shall another come; and there is no end to my works" (1:38). After receiving this expansive, orienting view of God's creations, Moses asked the

Lord, "Tell me, I pray thee, why these things are so, and by what thou madest them?" (1:30).

The Lord answered the first question by explaining that "this is my work and my glory—to bring to pass the immortality and eternal life of man" (Moses 1:39). Creating worlds and populating them with his children are major parts of God's "work." He creates EARTHS as dwelling places for his spirit children, where they receive physical bodies and learn to walk by faith. Whereas IMMORTALITY is never-ending life, ETERNAL LIFE means to become like God (*see* GODHOOD). Thus, God's "glory" consists in mankind's attainment of everlasting glory, the ultimate being eternal life.

In answer to Moses' second question (i.e., "by what thou madest them?"), the Lord stated that worlds were created by the power of the "Only Begotten Son, who is full of grace and truth" (Moses 1:32). This passage underscores the view that the creative acts of God, which include all inhabitable worlds (Moses 1:33; cf. John 1:1–2), are done through the Only Begotten as God's agent, and are done in grace and truth for the benefit of his children.

DENNIS L. LARGEY

GODHEAD

[*For discussions about the three members of the Godhead and their divine attributes and manifestations in the world, see* GOD; GOD THE FATHER; ELOHIM; MAN OF HOLINESS; JESUS CHRIST; HOLY GHOST; HOLY SPIRIT; GIFT OF THE HOLY GHOST; DOVE, SIGN OF. *See also* GODHOOD; ENDLESS AND ETERNAL; NAME OF GOD; INTELLIGENCE; FOREKNOWLEDGE OF GOD; OMNIPOTENT GOD, OMNIPRESENCE OF GOD, OMNISCIENCE OF GOD.]

Latter-day Saints believe in God the Father; his Son, Jesus Christ; and the Holy Ghost (A of F 1). These three Gods form the Godhead, which holds the keys of power over the universe. Each member of the Godhead is an independent personage, separate and distinct from the other two, the three being in perfect unity and harmony with each other (*AF*, chap. 2).

This knowledge concerning the Godhead derives primarily from the Bible and the revelations of the Prophet Joseph Smith (*see* SMITH, JOSEPH: TEACHINGS OF JOSEPH SMITH). For example, the three members of the Godhead were separately manifested at the baptism of Jesus (Matt. 3:16–17) and at the stoning of Stephen (Acts 7:55–56). Joseph Smith commented, "Peter and Stephen testify that they saw the Son of Man standing on the right hand of God. Any person that had seen the heavens opened knows that there are three personages in the heavens who hold the keys of power, and one presides over all" (*TPJS*, p. 312).

On June 16, 1844, in his last Sunday sermon before his martyrdom, Joseph Smith declared that "in all congregations" he had taught "the plurality of Gods" for fifteen years: "I have always declared God to be a distinct personage, Jesus Christ a separate and distinct personage from God the Father, and that the Holy Ghost was a distinct personage and a Spirit: and these three constitute three distinct personages and three Gods" (*TPJS*, p. 370). The two earliest surviving accounts of Joseph's FIRST VISION do not give details on the Godhead, but that he consistently taught that the Father and the Son were separate personages is clearly documentable in most periods of his life (e.g., D&C 76:23 [1832]; 137:3 [1836]; his First Vision, JS-H 1:17 [recorded 1838]; D&C 130:22 [1843]). While the fifth LECTURE ON FAITH (1834) does not identify the Holy Ghost as a "personage," it affirms that "the Father, Son, and Holy Spirit constitute the Godhead" (cf. Millet, pp. 223–34).

Although the three members of the Godhead are distinct personages, their Godhead is "one" in that all three are united in their thoughts, actions, and purpose, with each having a fulness of knowledge, truth, and power. Each is a God. This does not imply a mystical union of substance or personality. Joseph Smith taught:

Many men say there is one God; the Father, the Son and the Holy Ghost are only one God. I say that is a strange God anyhow—three in one, and one in three! It is a curious organization anyhow. "Father, I pray not for the world, but I pray for those that thou hast given me . . . that they may be one as we are." . . . I want to read the text to you myself—"I am agreed with the Father and the Father is agreed with me, and we are agreed as one." The Greek shows that it should be agreed. "Father, I pray for them which thou hast given me out of the world, . . . that they all may be agreed," and all come to dwell in unity [*TPJS*, p. 372; cf. John 17:9–11, 20–21; also cf. *WJS*, p. 380].

The unity prayed for in John 17 provides a model for the LDS understanding of the unity of the Godhead—one that is achieved among distinct individuals by unity of purpose, through faith, and by divine will and action. Joseph Smith taught that the Godhead was united by an "everlasting covenant [that] was made between [these] three personages before the organization of this earth" relevant to their administration to its inhabitants (*TPJS*, p. 190). The prime purpose of the Godhead and of all those united with them is "to bring to pass the immortality and eternal life of man" (Moses 1:39; Hinckley, p. 49–51).

Each member of the Godhead fulfills particular functions in relation to each of the others and to mankind. God the Father presides over the Godhead. He is the Father of all human spirits and of the physical body of Jesus Christ. The human body was formed in his image.

Jesus Christ, the Firstborn son of God the Father in the spirit and the Only Begotten son in the flesh, is the creative agent of the Godhead and the redeeming mediator between the Father and mankind. By him God created all things, and through him God revealed the laws of salvation. In him shall all be made alive, and through his atonement all mankind may be reconciled with the Father.

The Holy Ghost is a personage of spirit who bears witness to truth. The Father and the Holy Ghost bear witness of the Son, and the Son and the Holy Ghost bear witness of the Father (3 Ne. 11:32; cf. John 8:18). Through the Holy Ghost, revelations of the Father and of the Son are given.

The LDS doctrine of the Godhead differs from the various concepts of the Trinity. Several postbiblical trinitarian doctrines emerged in Christianity. This "dogmatic development took place gradually, against the background of the emanationist philosophy of Stoicism and Neoplatonism (including the mystical theology of the latter), and within the context of strict Jewish monotheism" (*ER* 15:54). Trinitarian doctrines sought to elevate God's oneness or unity, ultimately in some cases describing Jesus as *homoousious* (of the same substance) with the Father in order to preclude any claim that Jesus was not fully divine. LDS understanding, formulated by latter-day revelation through Joseph Smith, rejects the idea that Jesus or any other personage loses individuality by attaining Godhood or by standing in divine and eternal relationships with other exalted beings.

[*See also* Christology; Deification.]

BIBLIOGRAPHY

Hinckley, Gordon B. "The Father, Son, and Holy Ghost." *Ensign* 16 (Nov. 1986):49–51.

Millet, Robert L. "The Supreme Power over All Things: The Doctrine of the Godhead in the Lectures on Faith." In *The Lectures on Faith in Historical Perspective*, ed. L. Dahl and C. Tate, pp. 221–40. Provo, Utah, 1990.

Roberts, B. H. "The Doctrine of the Church in Respect of the Godhead." *IE* 1 (Aug. 1898):754–69.

PAUL E. DAHL

GODHOOD

Logically and naturally, the ultimate desire of a loving Supreme Being is to help his children enjoy all that he enjoys. For Latter-day Saints, the term "godhood" denotes the attainment of such a state—one of having all divine attributes and doing as God does and being as God is. Such a state is to be enjoyed by all exalted, embodied, intelligent beings (*see* DEIFICATION; ETERNAL PROGRESSION; EXALTATION; GOD; PERFECTION). The Church of Jesus Christ of Latter-day Saints teaches that all resurrected and perfected mortals become gods (cf. Gen. 3:22; Matt. 5:48). They will dwell again with GOD THE FATHER, and live and act like him in endless worlds of happiness, power, love, glory, and knowledge; above all, they will have the power of procreating endless lives. Latter-day Saints believe that Jesus Christ attained godhood (*see* CHRISTOLOGY) and that he marked the path and led the way for others likewise to become exalted divine beings by following him (cf. John 14:3).

The LDS conception of godhood is central to their understanding of why God creates and acts. Latter-day Saints believe in a God who "cleaves unto" other eternal INTELLIGENCES (D&C 88:40) and wants to make them happy. Joseph Smith observed, "Happiness is the object and design of our existence; and will be the end thereof, if we pursue the path that leads to it; and this path is virtue, uprightness, faithfulness, holiness, and keeping all the commandments of God" (*TPJS*, p. 255). Happiness is the goal of existence, and God created this world in order to promote happiness (2 Ne. 2:25). Because he loves the world, he gave his "only begotten Son" (John 3:16). God gives commandments to help mankind achieve happiness. Joseph Smith wrote: "In obedience there is joy and peace unspotted, unalloyed; and as God has designed our happiness—and the happiness of all His creatures, he never has—He never will institute an ordinance or give a commandment to His people that is not calculated in its nature to promote that happiness which He has designed, and which will not end in the greatest amount of good and glory to those who become the recipients of his law and ordinances" (*TPJS*, pp. 256–57). The Book of Mormon refers to God's plan of salvation as "the great plan of happiness" (Alma 42:8). In this sense, God creates in order to increase the total happiness in the universe.

As the Supreme Being in the universe, God has the greatest capacity for happiness. Thus, to maximize joy in others, God desires them to be as much like him as possible. "For behold, this is my work and my glory—to bring to pass the immortality and eternal life of man" (Moses 1:39; cf. Ps. 16:11). This latter-day scripture is understood to mean that God's goal is to help men and women share in the kind of eternal life he lives. Joseph Smith wrote: "God . . . was more intelligent, [and he] saw proper to institute laws whereby [his children] could have a privilege to advance like himself. The relationship we have with God places us in a situation to advance in knowledge. He has power to institute laws to instruct the weaker intelligences, that they may be exalted with himself, so that they might have one glory upon another, and all that knowledge, power, glory, and intelligence, which is requisite in order to save them in the world of spirits" (*TPJS*, p. 354).

All of God's spirit children have within them a divine nature with the potential to become like him. To become more like God, individuals must gain increased light and truth and follow all the commandments that God has given. They must know God (John 17:3; D&C 88:49) and see him (1 Jn. 3:2). Those who achieve this level of perfection will become joint-heirs with Christ: "For as many as are led by the Spirit of God, they are the sons of God. . . . And if children, then heirs; heirs of God, and joint-heirs with Christ; if so be that we suffer with him, that we may be also glorified together" (Rom. 8:14–17). "All that [the] Father hath" shall be given to them (D&C 84:37–38). In biblical terms, those who are worthy to share in all the power and glory that God himself has are called "gods": "Ye are gods; and all of you are children of the most High" (Ps. 82:6; John 10:34–38). Latter-day scriptures refer to several persons, including Abraham, Isaac, and Jacob, who once lived on earth and who are now resurrected beings and have become gods (D&C 132:37).

Most people are accustomed to using the term "God" to identify only one being, the Father. But the scriptures sometimes use the term to designate others as well. In this sense, while the faithful worship only one God in spirit and in truth, there exist other beings who have attained the necessary intelligence and righteousness to qualify for the title "god." Jesus Christ is a god and is a separate personage, distinct from God the Father (*see* GODHEAD).

People qualify themselves for this rank and degree of exaltation by bringing themselves fully in line with all that God has commanded them to do: "Here, then, is eternal life—to know the only wise and true God; and you have got to learn how to be Gods yourselves, and to be kings and priests to God, . . . namely, by going from one small degree to another, and from a small capacity to a great one; from grace to grace, from exaltation to exaltation, until you attain to the resurrection of the dead, and are able to dwell in everlasting burnings, and to sit in glory, as do those who sit enthroned in everlasting power" (*TPJS*, pp. 346–47).

Joseph Smith also wrote, "Every man who reigns in celestial glory is a God to his dominions" (*TPJS*, p. 374). This does not mean that any person ever would or could supplant God as the Supreme Being in the universe; but it does mean that through God's plan and with his help, all men and women have the capacity to participate in God's eternal work. People participate in this work by righteous living, by giving birth to children in mortality and helping them live righteous lives, and by bringing others to Christ. Moreover, Latter-day Saints believe that those who become gods will have the opportunity to participate even more fully in God's work of bringing eternal life to other beings. God is referred to as "Father in Heaven" because he is the father of all human spirits (Heb. 12:9; cf. Acts 17:29), imbuing them with divine potentials. Those who become like him will likewise contribute to this eternal process by adding further spirit offspring to the eternal family.

Latter-day Saints believe that God achieved his exalted rank by progressing much as man must progress and that God is a perfected and exalted man: "God himself was once as we are now, and is an exalted man, and sits enthroned in yonder heavens! That is the great secret. If the veil were rent today, and the great God who holds this world in its orbit, and who upholds all worlds and all things by his power, was to make himself visible,—I say, if you were to see him today, you would see him like a man in form—like yourselves in all the person, image, and very form as a man; for Adam was created in the very fashion, image and likeness of God, and received instruction from, and walked, talked and conversed with him, as one man talks and communes with another" (*TPJS*, p. 345).

Much of the LDS concept of godhood is expressed in a frequently cited aphorism written in 1840 by Lorenzo SNOW, fifth President of the Church. At the time, Snow was twenty-six years old, having been baptized four years earlier. He recorded in his journal that he attended a meeting in which Elder H. G. Sherwood explained the parable of the Savior regarding the husbandman who hired servants and sent them forth at different hours of the day to labor for him in his vineyard. Snow continued, as recorded in his sister's biography of him: "The Spirit of the Lord rested mightily upon me—the eyes of my understanding were opened, and I saw as clear as the sun at noonday, with wonder and astonishment, the pathway of God and man. I formed the following couplet which expresses the revelation, as it was shown me. . . . As man now is, God once was: As God now is, man may be" (Eliza R. Snow, p. 46).

BIBLIOGRAPHY

Snow, Eliza R. *Biography and Family Record of Lorenzo Snow.* Salt Lake City, 1884.

Snow, LeRoi C. "Devotion to a Divine Inspiration." *IE* 22 (1919):653–62.

Widtsoe, John A. *Evidences and Reconciliations*, pp. 65–67. Salt Lake City, 1960.

K. CODELL CARTER

GOLD PLATES

On September 21, 1823, the angel Moroni appeared to Joseph SMITH and instructed him about a record engraved on thin goldlike sheets. The record, written by MORONI₂, his father MORMON, and other ancient inhabitants of the Americas, was buried in a stone box in a hill not far from the Smith residence. Moroni eventually delivered these plates to Joseph, who translated and published

them as the Book of Mormon and returned them to Moroni. While the plates were in Joseph's keeping, others saw them, including eleven witnesses whose testimonies appear in all editions of the book. Various descriptions provided by eyewitnesses suggest that the plates may have been made of a gold alloy, measured about 6 inches by 8 inches (15.2 cm by 20.3 cm), were 6 inches (15.2 cm) thick, and weighed about 50 pounds (22.7 kg).

[*See also* Book of Mormon Plates and Records; Book of Mormon Translation by Joseph Smith; Book of Mormon Witnesses; Plates, Metal.]

GRANT R. HARDY

GOSPEL OF ABRAHAM

On April 3, 1836, the keys of the "dispensation of the gospel of Abraham" were committed to the Prophet Joseph SMITH and Oliver COWDERY in the Kirtland Temple as part of the RESTORATION OF ALL THINGS in the DISPENSATION OF THE FULNESS OF TIMES (D&C 110:12). It was promised that through latter-day recipients of the gospel and their seed, all generations who accept it shall be blessed (HC 2:434–36). This renewed the promise that was given anciently to Abraham (Gen. 12:1–3; Abr. 2:6, 9–11; cf. Gal. 3:7–9, 29).

Latter-day Saints teach that Adam, Enoch, Noah, Abraham and many others headed DISPENSATIONS OF THE GOSPEL. Divine blessings and commandments were bestowed appropriate to the circumstances of the faithful people of God in each dispensation.

The gospel dispensation of Abraham includes the PATRIARCHAL ORDER OF THE PRIESTHOOD and the eternal marriage covenant (D&C 131: 1–4; 132:28–30; *see also* MARRIAGE: ETERNAL MARRIAGE), by which the ABRAHAMIC COVENANT is perpetuated from generation to generation among the faithful. Abraham was given a promise of innumerable posterity both in the world and out of the world. This promise is renewed for all who obey the gospel of Jesus Christ and receive the priesthood covenant of celestial marriage, "and by this law is the continuation of the works of [the] Father" among mankind both in time and eternity (D&C 132:31–33). The restoration of all things included the restoration of the KEYS to Joseph Smith to make it possible in modern times for all who do the works of Abraham to inherit the covenant and blessings of Abraham.

[*See also* Seed of Abraham.]

JOEL A. FLAKE

GOSPEL OF JESUS CHRIST

[*This entry is discussed below under two headings:*

The Gospel in LDS Teaching

Etymological Considerations for "Gospel"

The first division outlines the Latter-day Saint conception of the gospel of Jesus Christ, the fundamental teaching of the Church, as it is presented in scripture and in the teachings of the modern prophets. The second explores the complex history of the term and its possible meanings, particularly in Greek-speaking New Testament times.]

THE GOSPEL IN LDS TEACHING

JESUS CHRIST and his APOSTLES and PROPHETS have repeatedly announced the "good news" or "gospel" that by coming to Christ, a person may be saved. The Father is the author of the gospel, but it is called the gospel of Jesus Christ because, in agreement with the Father's plan, Christ's ATONEMENT makes the gospel operative in human lives. Christ's gospel is the only true gospel, and "there shall be no other name given nor any other way nor means whereby salvation can come unto the children of men, only in and through the name of Christ, the Lord Omnipotent" (Mosiah 3:17; cf. Acts 4:12).

Even though Latter-day Saints use the term "gospel" in several ways, including traditional Christian usages, the Book of Mormon and other latter-day SCRIPTURES define it precisely as the way or means by which an individual can come to Christ. In all these scriptural passages, the gospel or DOCTRINE of Christ teaches that salvation is available through his authorized servants to all who will (1) believe in Christ; (2) repent of their SINS; (3) be baptized in water as a witness of their willingness to take his name upon them and keep his COMMANDMENTS; (4) receive the Holy Ghost by the LAYING-ON OF HANDS; and (5) endure to the end. All who obey these commandments and receive the BAPTISM OF FIRE AND OF THE HOLY GHOST and endure in faith, hope, and charity will be found guiltless at the last day and will enter into the kingdom of heaven (Alma 7:14–16, 24–25; Heb. 6:1–2).

THE PLAN OF SALVATION. President Brigham YOUNG taught that the "Gospel of the Son of God that has been revealed is a plan or system of laws and ordinances, by strict obedience to which the people who inhabit this earth are assured that they may return again into the presence of the Father and the Son" (*JD*, 13:233). The gospel of Jesus Christ is a key part of the PLAN OF SALVATION (or plan of redemption), which provides an opportunity for all people to obtain ETERNAL LIFE. Because of the FALL OF ADAM, which has passed upon all individuals by inheritance, all are subject to a PHYSICAL DEATH and a SPIRITUAL DEATH (2 Ne. 9:4–12; D&C 29:39–45; 1 Cor. 15:12–22) and cannot save themselves. God, the loving Father of all spirits, has declared that it is his work and glory "to bring to pass the immortality and eternal life of man" (Moses 1:39). For this purpose he provided a savior, Jesus Christ, who, because of his perfect LOVE, his sinlessness, and his being the Only Begotten of the Father in the flesh, was both willing and able to offer himself as a sacrifice for the sins of the world (John 3:16). Through his atonement, Christ redeemed all men, women, and children unconditionally from the two deaths occasioned by the transgression of Adam and Eve, and will also redeem them from their own sins, if they accept and obey his gospel (Moses 6:62; D&C 20:17–25; 76:40–53).

BASIC ELEMENTS. Modern revelations state that the Book of Mormon contains "the fulness of the gospel" (D&C 20:9; 27:5; 42:12). Of all the standard works, the Book of Mormon contains the most detailed exposition of the gospel. In three separate passages the basic elements of the gospel are explained by a prophet or by Jesus himself (2 Ne. 31:2–32:6; 3 Ne. 11:31–41; 27:13–21). Each of these passages is framed by the affirmation that "this is my doctrine" or "this is my gospel." The revelations to the Prophet Joseph SMITH confirm these Book of Mormon statements of the gospel in every detail (see D&C 18:17–23; 19:29–31; 20:25–29).

These core texts repeat the basic elements of the gospel message several times in slightly varied ways. Joseph SMITH referred to them in abbreviated form as "the first principles and ordinances of the Gospel" (A of F 4).

1. Faith. LDS teaching emphasizes FAITH IN JESUS CHRIST as the first principle of the gospel. The priority of faith is twofold. The individual who accepts the gospel must start with faith in Jesus Christ, believing in him and his power to save people from their sins. Without faith, no one would be strongly motivated to repent and to live the rest of the gospel principles. Faith is also fundamental to the other elements of the gospel in that each of them is dependent on acts of faith in important ways. In this sense, NEPHI₁ compares living the gospel to entering a strait and narrow path that leads to eternal life. The gate by which one can enter this path is repentance and baptism. With the guidance of the Holy Ghost, one can follow the path, exercising faith and enduring to the end. Thus, faith in Jesus Christ is a link between what one does to enter the gate and what must be done thereafter. One cannot have entered the gate by repenting and making baptismal covenants "save it were by the word of Christ with unshaken faith in him, relying wholly upon the merits of him who is mighty to save" (2 Ne. 31:19). After starting on this strait and narrow path, one cannot reach salvation except by "press[ing] forward with a steadfastness [faith] in Christ . . . feasting upon the word of Christ" (2 Ne. 31:20), which includes those things that the HOLY GHOST tells one to do (2 Ne. 32:3, 5).

2. Repentance. The centrality of faith is emphasized by the way the gospel is presented in the Book of Mormon, with faith usually mentioned in the center and the call to REPENTANCE at the first. Individuals must forsake their sins and offer up "a sacrifice . . . [of] a broken heart and a contrite spirit." This requires that the sinner come down into the depths of HUMILITY and become "as a little child" (3 Ne. 9:20–22).

3. Baptism. The gospel emphasizes the absolute need for baptism for those accountable and capable of sin. Like repentance, baptism is also a commandment, and candidates for salvation must be baptized in order to obey the commandment (see 2 Ne. 31:6–7).

This essential ordinance is a witness to the Father that the repentant individual has covenanted with God to keep his commandments and has taken upon himself or herself the name of Christ. Faith in Jesus Christ, repentance, and baptism are the gate by which one enters into the way that leads to eternal life (2 Ne. 31:13–15). Because infants are incapable of sin or of making such covenants, parents are instructed to prepare them for baptism by the time they reach eight years of age, the age of ACCOUNTABILITY established in revelation (D&C 68:25–28; see INFANT BAPTISM).

4. The Holy Ghost. While water baptism symbolizes purification and rising from death to life, the actual cleansing or REMISSION OF SINS comes by obedience, and as a gift from God "by fire and by the Holy Ghost" (2 Ne. 31:17; Matt. 3:11), by which the individual is BORN OF GOD, having become a "new creature" (Mosiah 27:24–26; 1 Pet. 1:23). This spiritual experience is a witness from the Father and the Son that the sacrifice of the penitent has been accepted. After Jesus had taught the Nephites and they were baptized, "the Holy Ghost did fall upon them, and they were filled with the Holy Ghost and with fire" (3 Ne. 19:13; cf. Acts 2:4).

The GIFT OF THE HOLY GHOST, administered by the laying on of hands by one having authority, includes the promise "If ye will enter in by the way, and receive the Holy Ghost, it will show unto you all things what ye should do" (2 Ne. 32:5). This gift is a constant companion by which the individual receives "the words of Christ" directly for guidance in his or her own life, in addition to inspired instruction from Church leaders (2 Ne. 32:3; see also John 14:26; 16:13).

5. Endure to the End. "Enduring to the end" is the scriptural phrase describing the subsequent life of a member of Christ's church who has embraced the first principles of the gospel and has entered the gate that leads to eternal life. Once on this strait and narrow path, the member must press forward in faith, and continue in obedience to all the commandments of God.

Faith is linked with hope and charity. Receiving a remission of sins generates a hope of salvation. This is more than a desire, and gives a feeling of assurance. Such hope grows continually brighter through the workings of the Holy Ghost if one is consistently obedient (Ether 12:4). Charity, the "pure love of Christ," is characteristic of those who obey the commandments (Moro. 7:3–4, 47). Such persons reflect to others the same kind of pure love that they experience from the Lord.

6. Salvation. In addition to receiving daily blessings, Jesus Christ promises that those who comply with all of the principles and ordinances will receive eternal life. As revealed to the Prophet Jo-

seph Smith, salvation entails becoming an HEIR to the fulness of the CELESTIAL KINGDOM (D&C 76:50–70).

All LDS standard works contain clear statements of the gospel of Jesus Christ (see D&C 10:63–70; 11:9–24; 19:29–32; 20:37; 33:10–13; 39:6; 68:25; Moses 5:14–15, 58; 6:50–53). Latter-day Saints find the same concept in many New Testament passages (Matt. 3:11; 24:13–14; Acts 2:38; 19:4–6; Rom. 1:16), although frequently only a few of the six key elements are specifically mentioned in any one passage. This is also true of the Book of Mormon. For example, the promise "They that believe in him shall be saved" (2 Ne. 2:9) may be understood as a merism (an abbreviation of a formula retaining only the first and last elements) that implicitly invokes all six components even though they are not mentioned individually. Another merism states that believing in Jesus and enduring to the end is life eternal (2 Ne. 33:4; cf. v. 9).

OTHER MEANINGS. Although emphasis is placed on truths necessary for salvation, LDS usage of the term "gospel" is not confined to the scriptural definition. Latter-day Saints commonly refer to the entire body of their religious beliefs as "the gospel." By the broadest interpretation, all TRUTH originating with God may be included within the gospel. President Joseph F. SMITH said:

> In the theological sense, the gospel means more than just the tidings of good news, with accompanying joy to the souls of men, for it embraces every principle of eternal truth. There is no fundamental principle, or truth anywhere in the universe, that is not embraced in the gospel of Jesus Christ, and it is not confined to the simple first principles, such as faith in God, repentance from sin, baptism for the remission of sins, and the laying on of hands for the gift of the Holy Ghost, although these are absolutely essential to salvation and exaltation in the kingdom of God [pp. 85–86].

Notwithstanding this wide range of meanings associated with the gospel, as President Smith explained, the saving truths encompassed by the first principles are indispensable and must be followed to obtain salvation. They are the central focus of the Church's teachings and practices. Latter-day Saints are under strict command to share the fundamental, first principles of the gospel with others so that all may have an equal chance to obtain salvation. Proselytizing efforts of individual members and full-time MISSIONARIES are intended to invite others to come to Christ through obedience to gospel principles and ordinances.

President Ezra Taft BENSON has similarly explained that "the gospel can be viewed from two perspectives. In the broadest sense, the gospel embraces all truth, all light, all revealed knowledge to mankind. In a more restrictive sense the gospel means the doctrine of the Fall . . . [and] atonement." Clarifying the restrictive sense, he explained:

> When the Savior referred to his gospel, He meant the . . . laws, covenants, and ordinances that men must comply with to work out their salvation. He meant faith in the Lord Jesus Christ, repentance from all sin, baptism by immersion by a legal administrator for the remission of our sins, and the receipt of the gift of the Holy Ghost, and finally he meant that one should be valiant in his testimony of Jesus until the end of his days. This is the gospel Jesus preached [p. 30].

Those who die without hearing the gospel while in MORTALITY will receive this opportunity in the SPIRIT WORLD. The necessary ordinances of baptism and the laying on of hands for the gift of the Holy Ghost will be performed on behalf of the dead by living members in Latter-day Saint TEMPLES. The deceased will decide for themselves whether to accept or reject the ordinances performed in their behalf (see SALVATION OF THE DEAD).

ETERNAL NATURE OF THE GOSPEL. Latter-day Saints believe that the gospel has always existed and will continue to exist throughout the eternities. The Prophet Joseph Smith said, "The great Jehovah contemplated the whole of the events connected with the earth, pertaining to the plan of salvation, before it rolled into existence, or ever 'the morning stars sang together' for joy" (*TPJS*, p. 220). The eternal nature of the gospel was also emphasized by President John TAYLOR, who declared that "the gospel is a living, abiding, eternal, and unchangeable principle that has existed coequal with God, and always will exist, while time and eternity endure, wherever it is developed and made manifest" (p. 88).

LDS scriptures explain that after the Lord had taught Adam and Eve the plan of salvation and the gospel (Moses 5:4–11), Adam was "caught away by the Spirit of the Lord" into the water where he was baptized. Following his baptism, the "Spirit of God descended upon him, and thus he was born of the Spirit" (Moses 6:48–68). In later describing this experience, Enoch explained that God called upon Adam with his own voice, teaching him the same gospel set out in other scriptures:

If thou wilt turn unto me, and hearken unto my voice, and believe, and repent of all thy transgressions, and be baptized, even in water, in the name of mine Only Begotten Son, who is full of grace and truth, which is Jesus Christ, the only name which shall be given under heaven, whereby salvation shall come unto the children of men, ye shall receive the gift of the Holy Ghost [Moses 6:52].

Latter-day scripture records that Adam and Eve taught their children the gospel, but that Satan came among them and persuaded some to love him more than God (Moses 5:13; see DEVIL). Thus it has been with the descendants of Adam and Eve, and in this situation, the Lord called upon people everywhere to believe in the Son and to repent of their sins that they might be saved. This gospel message was a "firm decree" sent forth "in the world, until the end thereof," and was preached from the beginning by ANGELS, by the voice of God, and by the Holy Ghost (Moses 5:12–15, 58–59).

Latter-day Saints understand the history of the world in terms of periods of faithfulness and of APOSTASY. Although there have been many times when the gospel of Jesus Christ has been lost from the earth, it has repeatedly been restored through prophets sent to declare new DISPENSATIONS OF THE GOSPEL. The gospel has been given to successive generations and will maintain its efficacy forever. The RESTORATION of the fulness of the gospel to Joseph Smith initiated the "last dispensation," or the DISPENSATION OF THE FULNESS OF TIMES, and he was promised that the gospel will never again be taken from the earth. The gospel of Jesus Christ continues to be the only means given under heaven whereby men and women can come to their Savior and be saved, and is the standard against which all people will be judged (see JUDGMENT DAY).

ETYMOLOGICAL CONSIDERATIONS FOR "GOSPEL"

The English word "gospel" is derived from the Old English godspel (god story). It was chosen by English translators of the NEW TESTAMENT as a translation of the Greek euaggelion (Latin, evangelium) or "good news." The term is used in the New Testament principally to refer to the message of salva-

tion through Jesus Christ, often referred to as the "gospel of Jesus Christ" (Mark 1:1) or the "gospel of the Kingdom of God" (Mark 1:14; Luke 8:1). The gospel or "good news" in the New Testament is the "glad tidings" to all that if they will come to Christ and keep his commandments, they will be saved (Matt. 7:21; Mark 16:15–16). PAUL uses euaggelion more than other New Testament writers, adopting both noun and verb forms of the Greek term. The practice of referring to written accounts of the life and ministry of Jesus as "gospels" arose among Christians in the first century and was well established by the second.

Although latter-day scriptures give a more definite and formulaic concept of the gospel, their teaching is consistent with and enhanced by scholarly reflections on the possible etymologies of the New Testament term. Both Hebrew and Greek antecedents occur in verb and derivative noun forms, the primary sense referring to the delivery of messages, particularly good news—victory in battle being a common example. This is expanded in Isaiah by application to the herald who announces the return of exiles to Jerusalem, proclaiming the good news of prosperity and deliverance and the kingship of Jehovah (Isaiah 52:7; see Friedrich, p. 708).

Ancient Greek usage of euaggelion included the ideas of liberation from enemies and deliverance from demonic powers. It can refer to oracular sayings, but more precisely to their fulfillment. This cluster of meanings made euaggelion an appropriate term for New Testament writers who understood the gospel as the means by which men can escape the evil powers of this world and as the fulfillment of ancient prophecies of a coming Messiah.

Religious usage of euaggelion before Christian times was common to the popular imperial cults in which the worship of Greek and Roman emperors was believed to bring wealth and power in various forms. When first used by Christians, this language must have been ironic, having the effect of forcing its hearers and readers to compare Caesar on his throne and Christ on the cross, and to make the corresponding choice between the universal pursuit of power and wealth (material benefits) in this world and the singular way of faith, repentance, and the Spirit taught by Jesus. This implicit comparison becomes explicit when three New Testament gospels report Jesus' instruction to "render unto Caesar the things that are Caesar's, and to

God the things that are God's" (Mark 12:17; cf. Matt. 22:21 and Luke 20:25). Paul uses the same irony when he calls the gospel a mystery (see Friedrich, pp. 712, 723–25; Eph. 6:19). The disappointment of some with Jesus as Messiah was precisely that he was not the kind of savior worshiped in the cults of emperors.

The Book of Mormon uses the terms "gospel" and "doctrine" interchangeably, in a way that is consistent with New Testament usage, at least to the extent that both imply communications that can be reduced to verbal statements (*see* DOCTRINE). The New Testament term "doctrine" (*didaskalia*) means "teaching" and refers either to the doctrine of Christ, or to the vain teachings of people or devils. Similarly, Book of Mormon writers use both "gospel" and "doctrine" to refer to a teaching that can be reduced to a set of statements or "points of . . . doctrine" (1 Ne. 15:14; Hel. 11:22).

BIBLIOGRAPHY

Benson, Ezra Taft. *Teachings of Ezra Taft Benson.* Salt Lake City, 1988.

Collins, Raymond F. "Gospel." *Encyclopedia of Religion,* Vol. 6, pp. 79–82. New York, 1987.

Friedrich, Gerhard. "Euaggelizomai, Euaggelion, . . ." In *Theological Dictionary of the New Testament,* Gerhard Kittel, ed., Vol. 2, pp. 707–737. Grand Rapids, Mich., 1964.

Nibley, Hugh. "Prophets and Glad Tidings." In *CWHN* 3: 259–67.

Piper, O. A. "Gospel," In *Interpreter's Dictionary of the Bible,* Vol. 2, pp. 442–48. Nashville, Tenn., 1962.

Roberts, B. H. *The Gospel: An Exposition of Its First Principles and Man's Relationship to Deity.* Salt Lake City, 1966.

Smith, Joseph F. *GD*, pp. 85–86, 95–106.

Talmage, James E. *AF*, pp. 52–170.

Taylor, John. *Gospel Kingdom,* Salt Lake City, 1964.

Yarn, David H., Jr. *The Gospel: God, Man, and Truth.* Salt Lake City, 1965.

NOEL B. REYNOLDS

GRACE

One of the most controversial issues in Christian theology is whether salvation is the free gift of unmerited grace or is earned through good WORKS. Paul's statement that "a man is justified by faith without the deeds of the law" (Rom. 3:28) is frequently cited to support the former view, while James's statement that "faith without works is dead" (James 2:20) is often quoted in favor of the latter view. The LDS doctrine that salvation requires *both* grace and works is a revealed yet commonsense reconciliation of these contradictory positions.

C. S. Lewis wrote that this dispute "does seem to me like asking which blade in a pair of scissors is most necessary" (p. 129). And in one way or another almost all Christian denominations ultimately accept the need for both grace and works, but the differences in meaning and emphasis among the various doctrinal traditions remain substantial.

LDS doctrine contains an affirmative sense of interaction between grace and works that is unique not only as to these concepts but also reflects the uniqueness of the restored gospel's view of man's nature, the FALL OF ADAM, the ATONEMENT, and the process of salvation. At the same time, the LDS view contains features that are similar to basic elements of some other traditions. For example, the LDS insistence that such works as ORDINANCES be performed with proper priesthood AUTHORITY resembles the Catholic teaching that its sacraments are the requisite channels of grace. Also the LDS emphasis on the indispensability of personal faith and REPENTANCE in a direct relationship with God echoes traditional Protestant teachings. The LDS position "is not a convenient eclecticism, but a repossession [through the Restoration] of a New Testament understanding that reconciles Paul and James" (Madsen, p. 175).

The Church's emphasis on personal responsibility and the need for self-disciplined obedience may seem to de-emphasize the role of Christ's grace; however, for Latter-day Saints, obedience is but one blade of the scissors. All of LDS theology also reflects the major premise of the Book of Mormon that without grace there is no salvation: "For we know that it is by grace that we are saved, after all we can do" (2 Ne. 25:23). The source of this grace is the atoning sacrifice of Jesus Christ: "Mercy cometh because of the atonement" (Alma 42:23).

The teachings of Christian theology since the Middle Ages are rooted in the belief that, primarily because of the effects of the Fall and original sin, humankind has an inherently evil nature. In both the Catholic and the Protestant traditions, only the grace of God can overcome this natural evil. Various Christian writers have disputed the extent to which the bestowal of grace completely overcomes man's dark nature. In the fifth century, reflecting his personal struggle with what he believed to be his own inherent evil nature, Augustine saw grace as the only escape from the evil of earthly pleasures and the influence of the worldly "city of man." In the thirteenth century Thomas Aquinas was more sanguine, recognizing the serious wounding caused by original sin, but also defending man's natural potential for good.

In the early sixteenth century, Martin Luther, through his reading of Paul and reacting against the sale of indulgences, concluded that faith, God's unilateral gift to chosen individuals, is the true source of grace and, therefore, of justification before God. Luther thus (perhaps unintentionally) broke the medieval church's control over grace, thereby unleashing the political force of the PROTESTANT REFORMATION. For Luther, man's individual effort can in no way "earn" or otherwise be part in the righteousness infused by grace. Even the good works demonstrated in a life of obedience to God are but the visible *effects* of grace. This idea later influenced the development of the Puritan ethic in America. John Calvin, Luther's contemporary, developed a complete doctrine of PREDESTINATION based on Luther's idea that God unilaterally chooses those on whom he bestows the gifts of faith and grace.

The Catholic response to Luther's challenge rejected predestination and reaffirmed both that grace is mediated by church sacraments and that grace cannot totally displace human AGENCY. At the same time, Catholic thought underscored the primacy of God's initiative. "Prevenient grace" operates upon the human will before one turns to God; yet, once touched by grace, one is still free to cooperate or not. The interaction between divine grace and human freedom is not totally clear; however, grace is increased as one obeys God's commandments, and grace raises one's natural good works to actions of supernatural value in a process of spiritual regeneration.

In recent years, some Protestant theologians have questioned the way an exclusive emphasis on unmerited grace negates a sense of personal responsibility. Dietrich Bonhoeffer, for example, condemned the idea of "cheap grace," which falsely supposes that because "the account has been paid in advance . . . everything can be had for nothing" (*The Cost of Discipleship*, 1963, p. 45). John MacArthur was concerned that contemporary evangelism promises sinners that they "can have eternal life yet continue to live in rebellion against

God" (*The Gospel According to Jesus*, 1988, pp. 15–16). And Paul Holmer wrote that stressing the dangers of works is "inappropriate if the listeners are not even trying! Most Church listeners are not in much danger of working their way into heaven" ("Law and Gospel Re-examined," *Theology Today* 10 [1953–54]:474).

Some Latter-day Saints have shared similar concerns about the limitations of a one-sided view of the grace-works controversy, just as they have shared the Catholic concern about a doctrine of grace that undercuts the fundamental nature of free will. Latter-day Saints see Paul's writing about the inadequacy of works and "the deeds of the law" (Rom. 3:27–28) as referring mainly to the inadequacy of the ritual works of the law of Moses, "which had been superseded by the higher requirements of the Gospel [of Jesus Christ]"; thus, Paul correctly regarded many of "the outward forms and ceremonies" of the law of Moses as "unessential works" (AF, p. 480). As the prophet ABINADI declared in the Book of Mormon (c. 150 B.C.), "Salvation doth not come by the law alone; and were it not for the atonement, which God himself shall make for the sins and iniquities of his people, . . . they must unavoidably perish, notwithstanding the law of Moses" (Mosiah 13:28).

In a broader sense, LDS devotion to the primary role of grace while concurrently emphasizing self-reliance stems from a unique doctrinal view of man's nature and destiny. As noted by Reformation scholar John Dillenberger, "In stressing human possibilities, Mormonism brought things into line, not by abandoning the centrality of grace but by insisting that the [real] powers of humanity . . . reflected the actual state of humanity as such. . . . Mormonism brought understanding to what had become an untenable problem within evangelicalism: how to reconcile the new power of humanity with the negative inherited views of humanity, without abandoning the necessity of grace." In this way, Dillenberger concluded, "perhaps Mormonism . . . is the authentic American theology, for the self-reliance of revivalist fundamentalist groups stood in marked contrast to their inherited conception of the misery of humanity" (p. 179).

In LDS teachings, the fall of Adam made Christ's redemption necessary, but not because the Fall by itself made man evil. Because of transgression, Adam and Eve were expelled from Eden into a world that was subject to death and evil influences. However, the Lord revealed to Adam upon his entry into mortality that "the Son of God hath atoned for original guilt"; therefore, Adam's children were not evil, but were "*whole* from the foundation of the world" (Moses 6:54). Thus, "every spirit of man was *innocent* in the beginning; and God having redeemed man from the fall, men became again, in their infant state, *innocent* before God" (D&C 93:38).

As the descendants of Adam and Eve then become accountable for their own sins at age eight, all of them taste sin as the result of their own free choice. "All have sinned, and come short of the glory of God" (Rom. 3:23). One whose cumulative experience leads her or him to love "Satan more than God" (Moses 5:28) will eventually become "carnal, sensual, and devilish" (Moses 5:13; 6:49) by nature. On the other hand, one who consciously accepts Christ's grace through the Atonement by faith, repentance, and baptism yields to "the enticings of the Holy Spirit, and putteth off the natural man and becometh a saint through the atonement of Christ the Lord" (Mosiah 3:19). In this way, the individual takes the initiative to accept the grace made available by the Atonement, exercising faith through a willing "desire to believe" (Alma 32:27). That desire is often kindled by hearing others bear testimony of Christ. When this word of Christ is planted and then nourished through obedience interacting with grace, as summarized below, the individual may "become a saint" by nature, thereby enjoying eternal (meaning godlike) life.

Grace is thus the source of three categories of blessings related to mankind's salvation. First, many blessings of grace are *unconditional*—free and unmerited gifts requiring no individual action. God's grace in this sense is a factor in the Creation, the Fall, the Atonement, and the plan of salvation. Specifically regarding the Fall, and despite death and other conditions resulting from Adam's transgression, Christ's grace has atoned for original sin and has assured the resurrection of all humankind: "We believe that men will be punished for their own sins, and not for Adam's transgression" (A of F 2).

Second, the Savior has also atoned *conditionally* for personal sins. The application of grace to personal sins is conditional because it is available only when an individual repents, which can be a demanding form of works. Because of this condition, mercy is able to satisfy the demands of justice

with neither mercy nor justice robbing the other. Personal repentance is therefore a *necessary* condition of salvation, but it is not by itself *sufficient* to assure salvation (*see* JUSTICE AND MERCY). In addition, one must accept the ordinances of BAPTISM and the LAYING ON OF HANDS to receive the GIFT OF THE HOLY GHOST, by which one is born again as the spirit child of Christ and may eventually become sanctified (cf. D&C 76:51–52; *see also* GOSPEL OF JESUS CHRIST).

Third, after one has received Christ's gospel of faith, repentance, and baptism unto forgiveness of sin, relying "wholly upon the merits of him who is mighty to save," one has only "entered in by the gate" to the "strait and narrow path which leads to eternal life" (2 Ne. 31:17–20). In this postbaptism stage of spiritual development, one's best efforts—further works—are required to "endure to the end" (2 Ne. 31:20). These efforts include obeying the Lord's commandments and receiving the higher ordinances performed in the temples, and continuing a repentance process as needed "to retain a remission of your sins" (Mosiah 4:12).

In the teachings of Martin Luther, such works of righteousness are not the result of personal initiative but are the spontaneous effects of the internal grace one has received, wholly the fruits of the gracious tree. In LDS doctrine by contrast, "men should . . . do many things of their own free will, and bring to pass much righteousness. For the power is in them, wherein they are agents unto themselves" (D&C 58:27–28). At the same time, individuals lack the capacity to develop a Christlike nature by their own effort. The perfecting attributes such as hope and charity are ultimately "bestowed upon all who are true followers . . . of Jesus Christ" (Moro. 7:48) by grace through his atonement. This interactive relationship between human and divine powers in LDS theology derives both from the significance it attaches to free will and from its optimism about the "fruits of the spirit" (Gal. 5:22–25) among the truly converted, "those who love me and keep all my commandments, *and* him that seeketh so to do" (D&C 46:9).

God bestows these additional, perfecting expressions of grace conditionally, as he does the grace that allows forgiveness of sin. They are given "after all we can do" (2 Ne. 25:23)—that is, in addition to our best efforts. In general, this condition is related less to obeying particular commandments than it is to one's fundamental spiritual character, such as "meekness and lowliness of heart" (Moro.

8:26) and possessing "a broken heart and a contrite spirit" (Ps. 51:17; 3 Ne. 9:20; Hafen, chap. 9). Or, as Moroni wrote at the end of the Book of Mormon, "If ye shall deny yourselves of all ungodliness, and love God with all your might, mind, and strength, then is his grace sufficient for you, that by his grace ye may be perfect in Christ; . . . then are ye sanctified in Christ by the grace of God, through the shedding of the blood of Christ" (Moro. 10:32–33).

BIBLIOGRAPHY

Dillenberger, John. "Grace and Works in Martin Luther and Joseph Smith." In *Reflections on Mormonism: Judaeo-Christian Parallels,* ed. Truman G. Madsen. Provo, Utah, 1978.

Hafen, Bruce C. *The Broken Heart: Applying the Atonement to Life's Experiences.* Salt Lake City, 1989.

Holmer, Paul L. "Law and Gospel Re-examined." *Theology Today* 10 (1953–1954):474.

Keller, Roger R. *Reformed Christians and Mormon Christians: Let's Talk!* Urbana, Ill., 1986.

Lewis, C. S. *Mere Christianity.* New York, 1943.

Madsen, Truman G. *Reflections on Mormonism,* p. 175. Provo, Utah, 1978.

McDonald, William, ed. "Grace." In *New Catholic Encyclopedia*, Vol. 6. New York, 1967.

Millet, Robert L. *By Grace Are We Saved.* Salt Lake City, 1989.

Rahner, Karl, ed. *The Teaching of the Catholic Church.* Regensburg, Germany, 1965.

BRUCE C. HAFEN

GRANITE MOUNTAIN RECORD VAULT

Since 1938, the GENEALOGICAL SOCIETY OF UTAH has been collecting genealogical and historical information on rolls of microfilm. The Granite Mountain Record Vault is the permanent repository for these microfilms. It is located about one mile from the mouth of Little Cottonwood Canyon in Utah's Wasatch Range, twenty miles southeast of downtown Salt Lake City.

The Vault, as it is commonly known, is a massive excavation reaching 600 feet into the north side of the canyon. Constructed between 1958 and 1963 at a cost of $2 million, it consists of two main areas. The office and laboratory section sits beneath an overhang of about 300 feet of granite and houses shipping and receiving docks, microfilm processing and evaluation stations, and administra-

The Granite Mountain Record Vault, carved from solid rock in the Wasatch Mountains near Salt Lake City, Utah, is the repository of millions of feet of microfilmed genealogical records from around the world (c. 1980).

tive offices. Under 700 feet of stone, the Vault proper is situated farther back in the mountain behind the laboratory section and consists of six chambers (each 190 feet long, 25 feet wide, and 25 feet high), which are accessed by one main entrance and two smaller passageways. Specially constructed Mosler doors weighing fourteen tons (at the main entrance) and nine tons (guarding the two smaller entrances) are designed to withstand a nuclear blast. In the six chambers, nature maintains constant humidity and temperature readings optimum for microfilm storage.

Each chamber contains banks of steel cabinets ten feet high. As of February 1991, approximately 1.7 million rolls of microfilm, in 16mm and 35mm formats, were housed in two of the six chambers. The collection increases by 40,000 rolls per year. Alternate media, such as optical disks with greater capacity for storage than microfilm, are being considered for use and may make further expansion of the Vault unnecessary.

The genealogical information contained on these microfilms is collected from churches, libraries, and governmental agencies and consists primarily of birth, marriage, and death registers; wills and probates; census reports; and other documents that can be used to establish individual identities. Latter-day Saints use such information to assemble family group charts and pedigrees for the purpose of binding together ancestral lines of kinship through sealing ordinances performed by proxy in temples. Such ordinances are considered essential for the SALVATION OF THE DEAD—that is, those who died without hearing the full message of the gospel of Jesus Christ.

BIBLIOGRAPHY

Schueler, Donald G. "Our Family Trees Have Roots in Utah's Mountain Vaults." *Smithsonian* 12 (Dec. 1981):86–95.

Shoumatoff, Alex. *The Mountain of Names: A History of the Human Family*. New York, 1985.

STEVEN W. BALDRIDGE

GRANT, HEBER J.

Heber J. Grant (1856–1945), seventh President of The Church of Jesus Christ of Latter-day Saints, was a business leader and a devoted follower of the GOSPEL OF JESUS CHRIST who used his talents in the service of his Church. As an APOSTLE, he was instrumental in preserving Mormonism's credit and reputation after the economic devastation of the Panic of 1893. As President, he was a model of strong character and an ambassador of goodwill to a world often hostile to the Latter-day Saints.

Born November 22, 1856, in Salt Lake City to Jedediah M. and Rachel Ridgeway Ivins Grant, Heber associated from a young age with Church and territorial leaders. His father served as Brigham YOUNG's counselor in the FIRST PRESIDENCY and as mayor of the city, and his mother enjoyed the society of the leading women of the LDS community.

Heber did not benefit from the association of his father directly. Jedediah Grant died nine days after Heber was born, the victim of "lung disease," and Rachel became the paramount influence in Heber's life. Prim and reserved, she came from a New Jersey family of merchants and devoted practitioners of religion. She joined the Church just prior to her twentieth birthday, in part because of the labors of the fiery missionary who later became her husband. In 1855, Rachel became one of Jedediah's plural wives.

After Jedediah's death, diminished means eventually forced Rachel and her son to move from the substantial Grant home on Main Street to a "widow's cabin" several blocks away. The change was wrenching. Declining the proffer of Church aid, Rachel supported the family by sewing and taking in boarders. Young Heber sat on the floor

many an evening and pumped the sewing machine treadle to relieve his weary mother.

The location of the Grants' new home placed them within the Salt Lake Thirteenth Ward, one of the largest and most culturally diverse LDS congregations in the territory, and so Heber enjoyed the best of frontier Mormonism. He was one of the few youths of the city to serve as a "block teacher," and at the unusually young age of fifteen he was ordained to the office of seventy in the priesthood.

In the absence of public schools, Rachel found the means to enroll her son in good private schools, beginning with Brigham Young's school at State and South Temple streets. Grant remembered himself as being good at mathematics, memorization, and recitation, but less gifted in gram-

Heber J. Grant (1856–1945), self-educated entrepreneur, was called as president of the Tooele Stake (west of Salt Lake City) when he was twenty-three years old and as an apostle at age twenty-five. Courtesy the Utah State Historical Society.

mar, spelling, and especially foreign languages. Following frontier practice, his class experience was limited; he left school at the age of sixteen.

When the Thirteenth Ward organized the first Young Men's Mutual Improvement Association (YMMIA) in 1875, Grant was called as a counselor to its president at age nineteen. The YMMIA's weekly sessions gave him a chance for study, self-improvement, and speech-making. On his own he read LDS and Protestant devotional literature, Samuel Smiles' chatbooks idealizing the self-made man, and books of readings filled with firm and traditional values. As a young man, he was an active member of the "Wasatch Literary Association," a high-spirited local group that met each Wednesday evening for cultural exercises. These might include declamations, lectures, debates, readings, musical renditions, and even small-scale theatrical productions. In later years he often acknowledged his debt to the "Wasatchers" for much of his cultural and intellectual training.

For several years business became Grant's preoccupation. In addition to selling insurance, he peddled books, found Utah retailers for a Chicago grocery house, performed tasks for the Deseret National Bank, and taught penmanship. With Brigham Young's support, he was appointed assistant cashier of the Church-owned Zion's Savings and Trust Company. Hard work began to pay dividends. A typical Utah wage earner might make $500 annually; in his early twenties, Grant earned ten times that amount. Soon he opened another insurance agency in Ogden and began to fulfill his hope of developing "home industry." With a partner, he purchased the Ogden Vinegar Works.

On October 30, 1880, Grant was called as president of the Tooele Stake, about twenty-five miles west of Salt Lake City. Not yet twenty-four years old, he presided over more than a half-dozen congregations, dispensing spiritual and temporal counsel to frontier-hardened and not always pliant settlers. Moreover, the area presented one special difficulty: with the opening of western Utah mines, non-Mormons had settled in the county and for a time wrested local political control from the Church.

To Grant's new challenges were added personal difficulties. He had married a longtime acquaintance from the Thirteenth Ward, Lucy Stringham, on November 1, 1877, three weeks before his twenty-first birthday. Shortly after the couple moved to Tooele, she developed a lingering stom-

Heber J. Grant and his first wife, Lucy Stringham Grant, on their tenth wedding anniversary in 1887, together with their five daughters, Rachel, Lucy, Florence, Edith, and Anna. Photographer: Charles R. Savage.

ach illness and related problems that twelve years later claimed her life. Not long after, his Salt Lake City businesses began to suffer from lack of attention. His Ogden vinegar factory burned, and he was underinsured.

Although he enjoyed ministering to his Tooele flock, his personal difficulties weighed heavily on him. He later admitted that during these years he felt so "blue" that he did not know what to "do or where to turn" (Grant to B. F. Grant, July 21, 1896, Grant Papers, LDS Archives). Under this burden, his six-foot, 140-pound frame almost gave way. The attending doctor pronounced a diagnosis of "nervous convulsions" and warned the young man that if he did not slow his pace he would certainly experience a "softening of the brain" (Grant typed diary, Nov. 1, 1887; Francis M. Lyman diary, Jan. 7, 15, 16, 23, 1882, Church Archives).

In 1882, less than two years after his arrival in Tooele and ten months after his nervous collapse,

Grant was asked to attend a council meeting in Church President John Taylor's office, where President Taylor announced a revelation filling two vacancies in the QUORUM OF THE TWELVE APOSTLES. As the document was read, Grant learned of his appointment to the quorum. He felt unprepared to serve in what he believed was such a high and important calling. He also wondered whether his relish for commerce properly mixed with religion. Grant's troubled "long night of the soul" was resolved during one of his first preaching tours. While traveling in Arizona, he had a spiritual manifestation that confirmed his call and put an end to his self-doubts. The epiphany also affirmed several blessings that Grant had received while a youth. On several occasions, Church leaders had prophesied his eventual high Church service.

During Grant's early service as an apostle, he concluded that wealth and money-making were honorable when dedicated to the common good, by which he meant two things: almsgiving and the founding of businesses to aid the Church and community. During his years as a young apostle, he did both. His gifts to friends and worthy purposes often took a third of his income. At a time when apostles commonly engaged in private activities, he was tireless in founding and developing "home institutions" to benefit the community. The enterprises included a Utah retail and wholesale business, a livery stable, two "home" insurance companies, a bank, a Salt Lake newspaper, the famed Salt Lake Theatre, the Utah Sugar Company, and a series of less prominent enterprises.

He was equally busy with Church assignments as a member of the Church Salary Committee, the Sunday School Board, and the Mutual Improvement superintendency. Twice he proselytized among the dangerous Yaqui Indians in Mexico, and his many tours to the Southwest earned him the title "the Arizona Apostle."

Grant eventually married three wives, who bore him twelve children. In addition to Lucy Stringham, he entered into plural marriage with Huldah Augusta Winters and Emily Wells. The three Grant wives were similar in many ways. Well educated for the times, all had taught school, and each descended from old pioneer families. "One's wealth consists in those whom he loves and serves and who love and serve him in return," he often said. Incessant travel took him away from the family, an absence he bridged by his long and sensitive personal letters. More than 50,000 letters are preserved in the Church archives, many of them to his children and grandchildren.

The Panic of 1893 caught both Grant and the Church overextended and eventually caused him to go to New York City to negotiate credit for himself and the Church. His loan brokering allowed him and the Church to remain solvent during the hard times of the 1890s, but the effects of the panic were severe for him personally; he lost his fortune and never fully recovered it.

As Utah and the Church entered the twentieth century, Grant's ministry changed. The growing Church required more and more of his time. He filled two foreign assignments, opening the Japanese Mission (1901–1903) and later presiding over the European Mission (1903–1905). On returning to the United States, he was assigned to supervise Church education, the Genealogical Society, and the Church magazine, the *Improvement Era*. He also still found time for community service, including assisting the cause of prohibition and directing World War I Liberty Bond drives.

In 1916 his seniority brought him to the presidency of the Quorum of Twelve Apostles. Two years later, Church President Joseph F. SMITH, on his deathbed, took Grant's hand and said, "The Lord bless you, my boy, the Lord bless you. You have got a great responsibility. Always remember that this is the Lord's work and not man's. The Lord is greater than any man. He knows whom he wants to lead his Church and never makes any mistake. The Lord bless you" (*CR*, Apr. 1941). On November 23, 1918, Heber J. Grant was sustained as President of the Church.

During his twenty-six-and-a-half-year administration—the Church's second longest—Church members grew familiar with the hardy, pioneer themes of President Grant's leadership. He repeatedly spoke of the need for charity, duty, honor, service, and work, and admonished the Saints to live modestly and to observe the prohibitions of the Church's health code, the Word of Wisdom. For Saints disoriented by the century's rapid social and cultural changes, President Grant's firm voice, ramrod-straight posture, and forceful—and sometimes sharp-tongued—delivery conveyed strength and resolution. He personified time-tested values.

After years of adverse Church publicity and misunderstanding, President Grant gladly accepted invitations to speak to non-Mormon groups throughout the United States, often traveling with his sole surviving wife, Augusta, in the hope of improving the image of the Church. He usually mixed personal reminiscence, business homilies, and a message about the Church. His influence was not limited to formal addresses. He cultivated personal contacts with business, cinema, media, and political leaders in the hope of presenting the Church in a more sympathetic light to the public at large. The production of such pro-LDS Hollywood films as *Union Pacific* and *Brigham Young* was partly due to his quiet influence. He promoted national tours by the Mormon Tabernacle Choir and supported the political activity of Utah senator and LDS apostle Reed Smoot, whose growing national influence brought favorable comment to Utah and the Church.

Faced with regional and then national economic depression during the late 1920s and the 1930s, the Grant administration had to cope with hard times. In keeping with the lessons learned during the depressed 1890s, President Grant trimmed Church expenses wherever he could; also his business experience, and particularly his eastern contacts, repeatedly helped to stabilize the Church financially. He advised a number of local businesses—both Mormon and non-Mormon concerns—without compensation, helping to pull them through the difficult times. Moreover, in 1936 the Church under his leadership sought to assist impoverished Latter-day Saints by establishing the Church Security Program, later renamed the Church Welfare Program, one of the major accomplishments of his administration (*see* WELFARE; WELFARE SERVICES). To help get it established, President Grant gave the program his large dry farm in western Utah, in which he had invested more than $80,000.

During his time as president, he dedicated three new temples: Laie, Hawaii (1919), Cardston, Canada (1923), and Mesa, Arizona (1927). Several hundred chapels were constructed, many in areas outside the Utah heartland. The Washington, D.C., chapel, dedicated in 1933, symbolized Church growth nationally.

Many of the characteristics of the Church in the twentieth century came into focus during President Grant's administration. Religious education received new emphasis with the establishment of an extensive seminary and institute program to provide a spiritual dimension in the education of the youth. Under his direction, Church leaders stressed sacrament meeting attendance, temple

On November 23, 1918, Heber J. Grant was sustained as the seventh President of the Church. His twenty-six year administration was noted for placing the Church on a sound financial basis, expanding the role of education in the Church, and establishing the modern Church welfare program. Photographer: Charles R. Savage.

activity, observance of the Word of Wisdom, family-history research, and monthly visits to Church members in their homes. To cope with the expansion of the Church, he called a new group of General Authorities, Assistants to the Twelve Apostles.

Near the end of his life and under his direction, the First Presidency addressed the moral perplexities of war. A statement issued at the beginning of World War II said, "The Church . . . cannot regard war as a righteous means of settling international disputes." Yet the statement urged allegiance to "constitutional law" and acceptance of national military service, whatever the nationality of Church members (*IE* 45 [May 1942]:348–49). The scrupulously neutral statement reflected President Grant's own reservations about American entrance into the conflict and his growing personal pacifism.

Members came to love President Grant's expansive ways. Until mounting burdens and declining health intervened, his office door was open to General Authorities, stake and local leaders, and even to members troubled with problems. He traveled widely throughout America and in 1937 heralded the Church's European centennial by touring the missions of Great Britain and western Europe, the second LDS President to venture across the Atlantic Ocean while in office. Seeking to personalize his presidency, he distributed thousands of homiletic books, personally autographing each and sometimes marking passages for emphasis. Recalling his mother's struggles, he freely gave of his personal means, particularly to widows, and established a missionary fund for his increasing progeny.

In 1940, while visiting Southern California, he suffered a series of strokes that slowed his pace and forced him to delegate active administration of the Church, relying primarily on J. Reuben Clark, Jr., his first counselor. President Grant died on May 14, 1945, at Salt Lake City.

During President Grant's administration Church membership doubled. He traveled more than 400,000 miles, filled 1,500 appointments, gave 1,250 sermons, and made 28 major addresses to state, national, civic, and professional groups. His greatest achievements, however, cannot be measured statistically. During almost sixty-five years of Church service, he helped transform the Church from a sequestered, misunderstood, pioneer faith to an accepted, vibrant religion of twentieth-century America.

BIBLIOGRAPHY

No modern, full-scale biography of Heber J. Grant exists. For admiring surveys, see Bryant S. Hinckley, *Heber J. Grant: Highlights in the Life of a Great Leader* (Salt Lake City, 1951); Francis M. Gibbons, *Heber J. Grant: Man of Steel, Prophet of God* (Salt Lake City, 1979); and Ronald W. Walker, "Heber J. Grant," in *The Presidents of the Church*, ed. Leonard J. Arrington (Salt Lake City, 1986).

For accounts of various events of Grant's life, see Ronald W. Walker, "Crisis in Zion: Heber J. Grant and the Panic of 1893," *Arizona and the West* 21 (Autumn 1979):257–78, reprinted in *Sunstone* 5 (Jan.–Feb. 1980):26–34; "Heber J. Grant and the Utah Loan and Trust Company," *Journal of Mormon History* 8 (1981):21–36; "Young Heber J. Grant: Entrepreneur Extraordinary," *The Twentieth Century American West*, Charles Redd Monographs in Western History, (1983):85–119; and "Young Heber J. Grant's Years of Passage," *BYU Studies* 24 (Spring 1984):131–49.

For his role in stabilizing Church finances in the early twentieth century, see Thomas G. Alexander, *Mormonism in Transition* (Urbana, Ill., 1986).

RONALD W. WALKER

GREAT AND ABOMINABLE CHURCH

The phrase "great and abominable church," which appears in an apocalyptic vision received by the Book of Mormon prophet NEPHI₁ in the sixth century B.C. (1 Ne. 13:6), refers to the church of the DEVIL and is understood by Latter-day Saints to be equivalent to the "great whore that sitteth upon many waters" described in Revelation 17:1. This "whore of all the earth" is identified by Nephi's brother JACOB as all those who are against God and who fight against ZION, in all periods of time (2 Ne. 10:16). Nephi did not write a detailed account of everything he saw in the VISION, as this responsibility was reserved for JOHN the apostle, who was to receive the same vision; however, Nephi repeatedly refers to its content and teachings, using various images and phrases (1 Ne. 13:4–9, 26–27, 34; 14:1–4, 9–17).

Like John, Nephi and Jacob describe persecutions that evil people will inflict on God's people, particularly in the LAST DAYS. The angel who explained the vision to Nephi emphasized that this great and abominable church would take away from the Bible and "the gospel of the Lamb many parts which are plain and most precious; and also many covenants of the Lord" (1 Ne. 13:26), causing men to "stumble" and giving Satan "great power" over them (1 Ne. 13:29; D&C 86:3; Robinson, "Early Christianity," p. 188). Though many Protestants, following the lead of Martin Luther, have linked this evil force described in Revelation 17 with the Roman Catholic church, the particular focus of these LDS and New Testament scriptures seems rather to be on earlier agents of APOSTASY in the Jewish and Christian traditions (see A. Clarke, *Clarke's Commentary*, Vol. 6, pp. 1036–38, Nashville, Tenn., 1977).

When Nephi speaks typologically rather than historically, he identifies all the enemies of the Saints with the church of the devil (1 Ne. 14:9–10; 2 Ne. 10:16). They are those from all nations and all time periods who desire "to get gain, and . . . power over the flesh, and . . . to become popular in the eyes of the world, . . . who seek the lusts of the flesh and the things of the world, and to do all manner of iniquity" (1 Ne. 22:23). Other scriptural terms related to the great and abominable church include "Babylon" and the "great harlot" (Rev. 17:5; 1 Ne. 22:13; D&C 1:16). Images of pride, greed, and covenant abandonment are associated with these terms, in sharp contrast to the church of God. The scriptures are consistent in warning people to flee from the church of evil and find refuge in the church of God (Jer. 51:6; Rev. 18:4; 1 Ne. 20:20; D&C 133:14; see also P. Minear, "Babylon," in *Interpreter's Dictionary of the Bible*, 1:338, Nashville, Tenn., 1962). The Book of Mormon image of a great and abominable church complements the biblical images of Babylon and the harlot.

The fate of the great and abominable church is described in both ancient and modern scriptures (Jer. 51:37; Rev. 18:21; 1 Ne. 14:15–16; 22:14; D&C 1:16): Though the nations of the earth will gather together against them, "the covenant people of the Lord, who were scattered upon all the face of the earth" are promised redemption even if it requires power sent down from heaven, as if by fire (1 Ne. 14:14; 22:17). When Jesus Christ returns, he will claim his own and reject those who have opposed him (Mal. 4:1–3; 2 Thes. 2:6–10; 1 Ne. 22:23–26; *see* JESUS CHRIST: SECOND COMING OF JESUS CHRIST). As the Savior institutes his millennial reign, great will be the fall of Babylon, the harlot, and the great and abominable church (Rev. 18; 2 Ne. 28:18), for every knee will bow and every tongue confess, with thankfulness, that Jesus is the Christ (Isa. 45:23; Mosiah 27:31).

BIBLIOGRAPHY

Nibley, Hugh W. "The Passing of the Primitive Church: Forty Variations on an Unpopular Theme." In *CWHN* 4:168–208.

———. "Prophecy in the Book of Mormon: The Three Periods." In *CWHN* 7:410–35.

Robinson, Stephen E. "Warring Against the Saints of God." *Ensign* 18 (Jan. 1988):34–39.

———. "Early Christianity and 1 Nephi 13–14." In *The Book of Mormon: First Nephi, The Doctrinal Foundation*, ed. M. Nyman and C. Tate, pp. 177–91. Provo, Utah, 1988.

DENNIS A. WRIGHT

H

HANDCART COMPANIES

The large backlog of needy LDS converts awaiting passage from Europe and reduced TITHING receipts at home persuaded Brigham YOUNG in 1855 to instruct that the "poor saints" sailing from Liverpool to New York and taking the train to Iowa City should thence "walk and draw their luggage" overland to Utah. In 1856 five such handcart companies were organized to make the 1,300-mile trip on foot from the western railroad terminus at Iowa City to Salt Lake City (*see* IMMIGRATION AND EMIGRATION; MORMON TRAIL).

Success seemed assured when the first two companies, totaling 486 immigrants pulling 96 handcarts, arrived safely in Salt Lake City on September 26, 1856. They accomplished the trek in under sixteen weeks. The third company, and presumably the last of the season, made up of 320 persons pulling 64 handcarts, arrived on October 2. But at that point the two remaining companies, totaling 980 people and 233 handcarts, were still on the way, having started dangerously late. One of these companies, under James G. Willie, left Iowa City on July 15, crossed Iowa to Florence (Omaha), Nebraska, then, after a week in Florence, headed out onto the plains. The last company, under Edward Martin, departed Florence on August 25. Three independent wagon compa-

nies, carrying 390 more immigrants, also started late.

A week after the departure of the Martin Company, Franklin D. Richards, an apostle who had organized the handcart effort as president of the European Mission, also departed Florence with sixteen other returning missionaries. This party, on horseback and in fast carriages, passed the Martin Company on September 7, the Willie Company on September 12, and arrived in Salt Lake City on October 4.

Richards's report that many more immigrants were coming was a shock: the late-starting immigrants would not be adequately clothed for the cold weather they would surely experience; they, like those in all previous lightly supplied handcart companies, would be perilously short of food; and, as they were unexpected, the last resupply wagons, which were routinely dispatched into the mountains to meet immigrant companies, had already returned.

Anticipating the worst, President Young mobilized men and women gathered for general conference and immediately ordered a massive rescue effort. A party of twenty-seven men, led by George D. Grant, left on October 7 with the first sixteen of what ultimately amounted to 200 wagons and teams. Several of the rescue party, including Grant, had been among the missionaries who had ridden in from the East five days before.

The Handcart Family, by Torlief Knaphus (1926, life-sized bronze), Temple Square, Salt Lake City. This statue on Temple Square commemorates the faith and sacrifice of 2,962 pioneers who walked from Iowa and Nebraska to Utah, pushing and pulling handcarts loaded with their provisions and belongings. Courtesy Utah State University.

Two weeks later, one of the earliest blizzards on record struck just as both the handcart companies and the independent wagon companies were entering the Rocky Mountains in central Wyoming. After several days of being lashed by the fierce blizzard, people in the exposed handcart companies began to die.

Grant's rescue party found the Willie Company on October 21—in a blinding snowstorm one day after they had run out of food. But the worst still lay ahead, when, after a day of rest and replenishment, the company had to struggle over the long and steep eastern approach to South Pass in the teeth of a northerly gale. Beyond the pass, the company, now amply fed and free to climb aboard empty supply wagons as they became available, moved quickly, arriving in Salt Lake City on November 9. Of the 404 still with the company, 68 died and many others suffered from severe frostbite and near starvation.

Those of the Martin Company, three-fourths of them women, children, and the elderly, suffered even more. When the storm hit on October 19, they made camp and spent nine days on reduced rations waiting out the storm. Grant's party, after leaving men and supplies with the Willie Company, plunged farther east through the snow with eight wagons in search of the Martin Company. A scouting party sent out ahead of the wagons found them 150 miles east of South Pass.

The company, already in a desperate condition, was ordered to break camp immediately. The supply wagons met them on the trail, but the provisions were not nearly enough and, after struggling 55 miles farther, the company once again went into camp near Devil's Gate to await the arrival of supplies.

In the meantime, the rescue effort began to disintegrate. Rescue teams held up several days by the raging storm turned back, fearing to go on and rationalizing that the immigrant trains and Grant's advance party had either decided to winter over or had perished in the storm.

The Martin Company remained in camp for five days. When no supplies came, the company, now deplorably weakened, was again forced out on the trail. It had suffered fifty-six dead before being found, and it was now losing people at an appalling rate.

Relief came barely in time. A messenger ordered back west by Grant reached and turned around some of the teams that had abandoned the rescue. At least thirty wagons reached the Martin Company just as it was about to attempt the same climb to South Pass that had so sorely tested the Willie Company. Starved, frozen, spent, their spirits crushed, and many unable to walk, the people had reached the breaking point.

But now warmed and fed, with those unable to walk riding in the wagons, the company moved rapidly on. The Martin Company, in a train of 104 wagons, finally arrived in Salt Lake City on November 30. Out of 576, at least 145 had died and, like the Willie Company, many were severely afflicted by frostbite and starvation.

Elements of the three independent wagon companies and the rescue effort straggled into Salt Lake City until mid-December—except for twenty men, under Daniel W. Jones, who remained for the winter at Devil's Gate to guard freight unloaded there by the independent wagon companies, in part to make room for exhausted members of the Martin Company. The Jones party suffered misery and starvation at Devil's Gate. At one point they were reduced to eating rawhide until friendly Indians gave them some buffalo meat.

The decision to send out the Willie and Martin companies so late in the season was extremely reckless. In mid-November President Brigham Young angrily reproved those who had authorized the late start or who had not ordered the several parties back to Florence when they still had the opportunity, charging "ignorance," "mismanagement," and "misconduct." Though terrible, the suffering could have been far worse. Had the rescue effort not been launched immediately—well before the storm struck—the handcart companies would probably have been totally destroyed.

Six more handcart companies crossed the plains after 1856. To demonstrate that the idea was still viable, seventy missionaries made the trip in the opposite direction in the spring of 1857. Five companies, totaling 1,076 immigrants with 223 handcarts, crossed west with little difficulty: two in 1857, one in 1859, and two in 1860. In all, 2,962 immigrants walked to Utah with handcarts. About 250 died along the way—all but about 30 of those in the Willie and Martin companies.

For Latter-day Saints, the handcart story, particularly the account of the Willie and Martin companies, has darkened the collective memory of the westering saga. But that episode is also remembered for the unparalleled gallantry exhibited by so many, immigrants and rescuers alike. Of particular note is the superb performance of the women; their courage and mettle contributed enormously to the eventual survival of both companies. It was at once the most ill-advised and tragic, the most heroic, and arguably the proudest single event in the Mormon pioneer experience.

BIBLIOGRAPHY

Cornwall, Rebecca, and Leonard J. Arrington. *Rescue of the 1856 Handcart Companies.* Vol. 11 of the Charles Redd Monographs in Western History. Provo, Utah 1981.

Hafen, LeRoy R., and Ann W. Hafen. *Handcarts to Zion: The Story of a Unique Western Migration, 1856–1860.* Vol. 14 of the Far West and the Rockies Historical Series. Glendale, Calif., 1960.

Stegner, Wallace. *The Gathering of Zion: The Story of the Mormon Trail.* New York, 1964.

HOWARD A. CHRISTY

HARMONY, PENNSYLVANIA

Harmony, Pennsylvania, is an important HISTORICAL SITE of The Church of Jesus Christ of

Handcart Company, by C. C. A. Christensen (1900, oil on canvas, 25″ × 38″). Two of the handcart pioneers , C. C. A. Christensen and his wife, sailed to the United States in 1857, made their way to Iowa City, purchased hickory handcarts, and set out on their walk to the Great Salt Lake Valley. Over thirty years later he painted this scene from the more than 1,300 mile journey. Church Museum of History and Art.

Latter-day Saints on the Susquehanna River in northeastern Pennsylvania. Significant events occurred there during the periodic residence of the Prophet Joseph SMITH from 1825 to 1830. Harmony was the home of Isaac Hale, father of Joseph Smith's wife, Emma Hale. Joseph Smith and his father boarded with Isaac Hale in 1825 while working on Josiah Stowell's mining project. In December 1827, Joseph and Emma moved to Harmony from Manchester, New York, to work on the translation of the PLATES of the BOOK OF MORMON. Eventually they bought a small farm and house, where most of the Book of Mormon was translated between April 7 and early June 1829. Nearby, on May 15, 1829, Joseph Smith and Oliver COWDERY received the AARONIC PRIESTHOOD from JOHN THE BAPTIST and were authorized to baptize each other. The first convert BAPTISM, that of Samuel H. Smith, took place there ten days later. Somewhere between Harmony and COLESVILLE, NEW YORK, PETER, JAMES, and JOHN restored the MELCHIZEDEK PRIESTHOOD. After the Church was organized in 1830, Joseph and Emma returned to Harmony and lived there through that summer. Fifteen REVELATIONS now found in the DOCTRINE AND COVENANTS were received in Harmony.

The Harmony in Church history refers to a township rather than the village of Harmony. The

The home of Joseph and Emma Hale Smith in Harmony, Pennsylvania, from 1827 to 1830. The lower center portion is the original home, where Emma gave birth to their first child, Alvin, who died the same day, June 15, 1828. Here Joseph received at least fifteen revelations (D&C 3–13, 24–27) and translated the lost 116 pages and a large portion of the Book of Mormon.

township boundary was changed in 1853, placing the Church site in present-day Oakland Township. The site of the Hale residence lies about a mile and a half west of present-day Oakland, Pennsylvania, in Susquehanna County, along the north side of Route 171.

Today the Church owns about 288 acres at the Harmony location. On a small landscaped triangular plot located between the highway and a railroad right-of-way, a granite and bronze monument dedicated in 1960 commemorates the restoration of the Aaronic Priesthood. The exact location of the restoration is not known (see AARONIC PRIESTHOOD: RESTORATION).

The house owned by Joseph and Emma Smith burned in 1919. The buried foundation is just west of the monument. The graves of Isaac and Elizabeth Hale and of an infant son born to Joseph and Emma are close to Route 171, in a public cemetery located east of the Church property.

BIBLIOGRAPHY

Porter, Larry C. "A Study of the Origins of The Church of Jesus Christ of Latter-day Saints in the States of New York and Pennsylvania, 1816–1831." Ph.D. diss., Brigham Young University, 1971.

HORACE H. CHRISTENSEN

HARRIS, MARTIN

Martin Harris (1783–1875), a New York farmer, was one of the Three Witnesses to the divine origin of the Book of Mormon. He also financed the first publication of the Book of Mormon in 1830 at a cost of $3,000 ·and later helped finance publication of the Book of Commandments.

Martin Harris was born May 18, 1783, in Easton (now Saratoga), Washington County, New York, and died July 10, 1875, in Clarkston, Cache County, Utah. On March 27, 1808, he married his first cousin, Lucy Harris. At least six children were born to the couple. In the War of 1812, Private Harris was a teamster in the Battle of Buffalo. By May 1814, at the Battle of Puttneyville, he was first sergeant in the Thirty-ninth New York Militia. He returned home an honored war veteran. He inherited 150 acres and by 1828 owned a total of 320 acres. His wife characterized him as industrious, attentive to domestic concerns, and an excellent provider and father.

Harris stood about five feet, eight inches tall; had a light complexion, blue eyes, and brown hair; and wore a Greek-style beard off the edge of his jaw and chin. When formally dressed, he wore a favorite gray suit and a large, stiff hat. Non-Mormon contemporaries extolled Harris's sincerity, honesty, memory, generosity, neighborliness, shrewd business practices, and civic spirit.

Harris promoted construction of the Erie Canal through Palmyra along a route that passed not far from his house. Palmyra's citizens elected him road overseer for seven years, and he was a member of Palmyra's vigilance committee. A Jeffersonian-Jacksonian Democrat, he was a believer in the value of homespun common sense. He favored gold and silver money and rejected paper currency. He distrusted banks, Federalists, and authoritarians. A Christian democratic activist, he admired ancient Greek culture and raised money for Greek Christians to fight the Turks.

Looking on himself as an unchurched Christian, Harris chose to follow God on his own. As a "restorationist," he looked for the return of biblical Christianity. He stated that "in the year 1818 . . . I was inspired of the Lord and taught of the Spirit that I should not join any church" (interview by Edward Stevenson, Sept. 4, 1870, Stevenson Microfilm Collection, Vol. 32, *HDC*).

Martin Harris met Joseph SMITH some time after 1816, when the Smith family moved to Pal-

Martin Harris (1783–1875) at about age eighty-seven. Harris gave financial support to Joseph Smith and for the publication of the Book of Mormon. He served as one of Joseph's scribes, became one of the Three Witnesses of the Book of Mormon, and testified of its truthfulness throughout his life. Charles W. Carter collection.

myra. By 1824, Joseph Smith, Sr., had told him about the angel Moroni's appearances and the golden plates, and in the fall of 1827, Martin consented to help publish the translation. He helped Joseph Smith protect the plates from thieves and financed the Prophet's move from Manchester to Harmony, Pennsylvania, when persecution intensified.

In February 1828, Harris visited Joseph Smith in Harmony and obtained a transcription and translation of characters from the plates. He took the two documents to "learned men" in Utica, Albany, and New York City, where Samuel Latham Mitchill and Charles Anthon examined the texts. Harris and Smith believed that these visits fulfilled a prophecy in Isaiah 29:11–14 concerning

a book to be translated by an unlearned man. Harris hoped that the scholars' comments would help win financial and religious support for the Book of Mormon in the community (*see* ANTHON TRANSCRIPT).

From April 12 to June 14, 1828, Martin Harris served as Joseph Smith's scribe, producing 116 manuscript pages. To gain family support, he persuaded Joseph to let him take the pages to Palmyra to show his family, and during a three-week period when he visited relatives, attended to business, and served jury duty, the 116 pages were stolen. It is reported that Lucy Harris said that she burned them. Ill and suffering the insecurity of progressive deafness, she reportedly feared that Palmyra's boycott of the Book of Mormon would lead to her and her husband's financial ruin. After the loss of the manuscript, Harris ceased his work as scribe.

In June 1829, Martin Harris, along with Joseph Smith, Oliver COWDERY, and David Whitmer, prayed and received no answer. Harris blamed himself for the failure and withdrew. The Prophet, Cowdery, and Whitmer prayed again and were shown the gold plates of the Book of Mormon by the angel Moroni. Subsequently, the angel appeared to Harris and Joseph Smith. In this vision, Harris heard the voice of God say that Joseph's translation was correct, and Jesus Christ commanded Harris to testify of what he had seen and heard. The testimony of the Three Witnesses is printed in the Book of Mormon (*see* BOOK OF MORMON WITNESSES).

When translation of the book was completed, Joseph Smith had trouble finding a printer who would undertake publication. The printers feared that local opposition would hurt sales. A Palmyra printer, Egbert B. Grandin, finally agreed to print the Book of Mormon after Harris agreed to mortgage some of his farm for $3,000 as security. On April 7, 1831, Harris sold part of his farm to pay the printing bill, though he may have had other reasons to part with this acreage than just to satisfy Grandin.

Martin Harris was present at the organization of the Church on April 6, 1830, and was baptized that day by Oliver Cowdery. In May 1831 he led fifty converts from Palmyra to Kirtland, Ohio. Lucy and their children remained in Palmyra, resulting in two households and periodic trips for Harris between the two locations.

In the summer of 1831, Harris accompanied Joseph Smith and others to Missouri to purchase property and designate the site for Zion, where the Saints were to gather. He was one of the first to be asked to live the "law of consecration," a divinely revealed plan for equalizing the distribution of property and providing for the poor. That year, he also helped supervise and finance Church publications.

Returning east in 1832, Harris and his brother Emer served a mission together, baptizing one hundred persons at Chenango Point (now Binghamton), New York. In January 1833, Martin Harris was imprisoned briefly in Springville, Pennsylvania, in an attempt to stop him from preaching.

Returning to Kirtland in January 1834, Harris became a member of the first high council of the Church. Later that year, he volunteered to go to Jackson County, Missouri, with ZION'S CAMP to assist persecuted Mormons. On February 14, 1835, in accord with an earlier revelation (D&C 18:37–38), "the three witnesses" selected the first QUORUM OF TWELVE APOSTLES.

In 1836, Harris attended the dedication of the Kirtland Temple. Later that summer Lucy Harris died. Harris married Caroline Young, Brigham YOUNG's niece, on November 1, 1836. The couple had seven children.

During 1837, a time of intense conflict within the Church, Harris clashed with Sidney Rigdon and refused to join the Church-sponsored Kirtland Safety Society, which was issuing paper money. Harris was released from the high council on September 3, 1837, and was excommunicated during the last week of December 1837. Although evidence exists that Harris's excommunication was never official, he accepted the action and subsequently applied for and was baptized on November 7, 1842.

When Brigham Young led the body of Latter-day Saints west, Harris went to England to bear witness of the Book of Mormon. The Strangites, a splinter group formed after Joseph Smith's death (*see* SCHISMATIC GROUPS), paid his expenses, though he did not believe or preach Strangite doctrine. In 1829, Harris had prophesied that the Book of Mormon would be preached in England, and he was eager to preach there himself. Returning to Kirtland, he prospered and acted as a self-appointed guide-caretaker of the deserted Kirtland Temple, listing himself in the 1860 census as "Mormon preacher."

Prior to 1856, LDS missionaries, some of whom had already gone to Utah, the Harris family,

and Brigham Young invited Martin and Caroline Harris to join the Saints in Utah. In the spring of 1856, Caroline and the children journeyed to Utah, but Harris remained in Kirtland until 1870. In 1860 he lived with George Harris, his son by Lucy. From 1865 to 1870, he supported himself by leasing ninety acres of land in Kirtland.

In 1869, efforts were renewed to bring Martin Harris to Utah. William H. Homer, Edward Stevenson, Brigham Young, and many other Latter-day Saints helped him financially to make the journey. Still active and vigorous at age eighty-seven, Martin Harris, accompanied by Edward Stevenson, arrived by train in Salt Lake City on August 30, 1870. He accepted rebaptism as evidence of his reaffirmation of faith on September 17, 1870, and, at Brigham Young's invitation, publicly testified of the Book of Mormon. He moved to Harrisville, then to Smithfield, Utah (where he saw Caroline and their son Martin Harris, Jr.), and in 1874 to Clarkston, Utah, where he died on July 10, 1875, after once more bearing testimony of the Book of Mormon.

Martin Harris inspired a folk-hero tradition that has lasted down to the present. In 1983 the Church's musical play *Martin Harris: The Man Who Knew* was produced in Clarkston. The play marked a fourth generation's rehearsal of Martin Harris's witness: "Yes, I did see the plates on which the Book of Mormon was written. I did see the angel, I did hear the voice of God, and I do know that Joseph Smith is a true Prophet of God, holding the keys of the Holy Priesthood" ("The Last Testimony of Martin Harris," recorded by William H. Homer in a statement sworn before J. W. Robinson, Apr. 9, 1927, *HDC*).

BIBLIOGRAPHY

Anderson, Richard Lloyd. *Investigating the Book of Mormon Witnesses.* Salt Lake City, 1981.

Gunnell, Wayne Cutler. "Martin Harris—Witness and Benefactor to the Book of Mormon." Master's thesis, Brigham Young University, 1955.

James, Rhett Stephens. *The Man Who Knew: The Early Years— A Play About Martin Harris, 1824–1830, and Annotated History of Martin Harris.* Salt Lake City, 1983.

Shelton, Scott R. "Martin Harris in Cache Valley—Events and Influences." Master's thesis, Utah State University, 1986.

Tuckett, Madge Harris, and Belle Harris Wilson. *The Martin Harris Story.* Provo, Utah, 1983.

RHETT STEPHENS JAMES

HAUN'S MILL MASSACRE

On October 30, 1838, segments of the Missouri militia attacked a settlement of Latter-day Saints at Jacob Haun's mill, located on Shoal Creek in eastern Caldwell County, Missouri. Because the attack was unprovoked in a time of truce, had no specific authorization, and was made by a vastly superior force with unusual brutality, it has come to be known as "The Haun's Mill Massacre." It was one incident in the conflict between the Missourians and the Latter-day Saints that resulted in the LDS expulsion from the state in 1839 (see MISSOURI CONFLICT).

Tensions had been building up ever since the Latter-day Saints began moving into Caldwell and Daviess counties in central Missouri in 1836. From August to October 1838, incidents of overt conflict had grown dramatically. Rumors abounded that the Mormons planned to "despoil" the Missourians and take their land. Specifically, some believed that the Haun's Mill's population threatened to spill over into non-Mormon Livingston County. Outbursts of violence led Governor Lilburn W. Boggs on October 27 to issue an "Extermination Order," demanding that the Latter-day Saints leave the state or be exterminated. It is uncertain whether this order was a catalyst for the attack, but it is clear that both the Latter-day Saints and the Missourians believed that their rights had been violated and their existence threatened.

Thirty to forty LDS families were at Haun's Mill when some 200 to 250 militia from Livingston, Daviess, and Carroll counties, acting under Colonel Thomas Jennings, marched against the village. Assuming that an earlier truce still held, the residents were surprised by the late afternoon attack. Church leader David Evans' call for "quarter" was ignored, and the villagers were forced to flee for safety. The Mormon women and children fled south across a stream into the woods, while the men gathered in the blacksmith shop, but found it a poor place for defense because the Missourians were able to fire through the widely spaced logs directly into the group huddled inside.

Seventeen Latter-day Saints and one friendly non-Mormon were killed. Another thirteen were wounded, including one woman and a seven-year-old boy. No Missouri militiamen were killed, though three were wounded. Certain deaths were particularly offensive to the Saints. Seventy-eight-

Millstone at the site of the Haun's Mill Massacre on October 30, 1838. Seventeen Mormon civilians were killed in the raid. Photographer: George E. Anderson (1907).

year-old Thomas McBride surrendered his musket to militiaman Jacob Rogers, who shot him, then hacked his body with a corn knife. William Reynolds discovered ten-year-old Sardius Smith hiding under the bellows and blew the top of the child's head off.

While women cared for the wounded, the men remained in hiding during the night. The dead were thrown into an unfinished well and lightly covered with dirt and straw. A few Missourians returned the next day, took plunder, and warned the remaining Saints to leave Missouri.

The 1838–39 Missouri judicial proceedings investigating the "Mormon War" largely ignored the events at Haun's Mill, but Latter-day Saints wrote numerous, bitter accounts. The Haun's Mill Massacre became embedded in the LDS psyche as an epitome of the cruel persecutions that they had endured.

BIBLIOGRAPHY

Blair, Alma R. "The Haun's Mill Massacre." *BYU Studies* 13 (Autumn 1972):62–67.

History of Caldwell and Livingston Counties, Missouri. St. Louis, 1886.

Johnson, Clark V. "Missouri Persecutions: The Petition of Isaac Leary." *BYU Studies* 23 (Winter 1983):94–103.

LeSueur, Stephen C. *The 1838 Mormon War in Missouri*. Columbia, Mo., 1987.

Times and Seasons 1 (1840):145–50.

ALMA R. BLAIR

HAWAII, THE CHURCH IN

The Church of Jesus Christ of Latter-day Saints has been in Hawaii since 1850, when Elder Charles C. Rich, an apostle, called ten LDS men from the gold mines of northern California to open missionary work in the Sandwich Islands, now Hawaii. Within several months five of the elders left the mission, but George Quayle Cannon, Henry William Bigler, James Keeler, William Farrer, and James Hawkins remained. Initial conversions came on the island of Maui, where the first branch was organized in the Kula District, near Pulehu, on August 6, 1851. The Church made remarkable headway, with more than 4,000 Hawaiian convert members in fifty-three branches by late 1854. By this time, several small schools were under way, meetinghouses were constructed, and the BOOK OF MORMON had been translated into the Hawaiian language by Elders Cannon and Farrer and Jonatana H. Napela, a local member. It was printed in 1855. In 1990, the 49,000 members of the Church in Hawaii, both native Hawaiian and others were found in thirteen stakes, constituting more than a hundred WARDS and BRANCHES. A TEMPLE has served members in Hawaii since November 1919.

Following the pattern established elsewhere, an attempt was made to gather the Hawaiian Saints to a local ZION. A village, called the City of Joseph, was established on the island of Lanai in 1854. However, the project failed, at least partly because of environmental conditions. In addition, with the most devoted Hawaiian members having moved to Lanai, the branches on other islands were weakened, and the Church fell into decline. This trend became severe when the Mainland missionary leaders were called back to Utah in 1858 because of the UTAH EXPEDITION.

This leadership vacuum opened the way for the adventurer Walter Murray Gibson to run the Church on Lanai and elsewhere as his personal political kingdom from September 1861 until 1864. He was excommunicated from the Church in April 1864 for introducing many false doctrines, including selling offices in the priesthood.

Shortly thereafter, President Brigham YOUNG sent Francis Asbury Hammond and George Nebeker to Hawaii to buy property for a new gathering place. On January 26, 1865, the Church purchased for $14,000, a 6,000-acre plantation at Laie on Oahu island for the spiritual and temporal welfare of the members. Laie remains the focal point of LDS activities in Hawaii though strong stakes have also developed in Honolulu and in other areas.

Since 1865, there have been five major developments in the history of the Church in Hawaii:

The Oahu Stake Samoan choir posed in the 1960s in front of the Hawaii Temple. This choir was one of several patterned after the Tabernacle Choir. The temple, dedicated November 27, 1919, is located at Laie, on the northeast shore of Oahu.

First, on June 1, 1915, President Joseph F. SMITH dedicated a site at Laie for the Hawaii Temple. Four and a half years later, on November 27, 1919, his successor, President Heber J. GRANT, dedicated the completed structure, the first LDS temple outside the North American continent.

Second, President Grant organized the Oahu Stake on June 30, 1935, with Ralph E. Woolley as president.

Third, for the benefit of the Japanese people in Hawaii, President Grant formed the Japanese Mission in Hawaii in 1937, with Hilton A. Robertson as president. Its name was changed to the Central Pacific Mission in 1942. By 1949 missionaries of the Japanese/Central Pacific Mission had baptized 671 Americans of Japanese ancestry into the Church, and thousands of others have joined the Church since then. Many of these converts and their children have held important positions in the Church. Adney Yoshio Komatsu was the first of that group to be called as a GENERAL AUTHORITY.

Fourth, in September 1955 the Church College of Hawaii was founded under the direction of President David O. MCKAY. Initially a junior college, it was made a four-year school in 1959 and

LDS congregation and meetinghouse in Hawaii, 1915. Mormon missionaries arrived in the Sandwich Islands in 1850.

was renamed Brigham Young University—Hawaii Campus in 1974. Two thousand students, mostly from the Pacific and the Asian Rim, attend.

Finally, the Church founded the POLYNESIAN CULTURAL CENTER at Laie in November 1963 to preserve and present the cultures of Polynesia and to provide employment for the college students. The center has grown to become Hawaii's number-one paid attraction, drawing nearly a million visitors a year.

BIBLIOGRAPHY

Britsch, R. Lanier. *Unto the Islands of the Sea: A History of the Latter-day Saint in the Pacific.* Salt Lake City, 1986.

———. *Mormona: The Mormons in Hawaii.* Laie, Hawaii, 1989.

R. LANIER BRITSCH

HEAD OF THE CHURCH

Members of The Church of Jesus Christ of Latter-day Saints believe that Jesus Christ is personally the Head of the Church, leading and guiding it by REVELATION (D&C 10:69; 3 Ne. 21:22).

According to the New Testament, God gave Jesus authority to be "the head over all things to the church" (Eph. 1:22; cf. 2:20; Col. 1:18). For Latter-day Saints, the restoration of the Church was similarly initiated in 1820 when God the Father, following an ancient pattern, appeared in vision with his Son Jesus Christ, who instructed Joseph SMITH (JS—H 1:17; see Matt. 3:17; 2 Pet. 1:17–18; 3 Ne. 11:7). The Savior gave information and counsel to Joseph on that and later occasions.

Latter-day Saints affirm that subsequent revelations to his prophets have verified that Christ was and is both the Head of the Church and the author of its restoration and development (JS—H 1:30–42; D&C 1:1; 20:1, 37). No mortal, including the PRESIDENT OF THE CHURCH, considers himself to be the head. In fact, the President and all Church leaders consider themselves servants called by Christ or his authorized agents to represent him by teaching, training, and edifying members of the Church and by taking the gospel message to those not in the Church.

BIBLIOGRAPHY

Faust, James E. "Continuous Revelation." *Ensign* 19 (Nov. 1989):8–10.

BURNS R. SABEY

HEALTH, ATTITUDES TOWARD

In light of modern revelation, Latter-day Saints believe that the PHYSICAL BODY and its health and well-being are an essential part of the gospel of Jesus Christ. One purpose of mortality is to acquire and care for a physical body that is united with a SPIRIT in a temporary union. The body is the house or tabernacle of each person's unique eternal spirit. At death, the body and the spirit are temporarily separated. One cannot fulfill his or her eternal potential, however, when the spirit and body are apart. In the RESURRECTION the spirit and the then-immortal body will become eternally reunited and inseparable.

The physical body is a gift from God. No mortal body is perfect; some persons are born with handicaps or serious disabilities. Nevertheless, in premortal life spirits looked forward with great anticipation to receiving a physical body. Latter-day Saints look upon the body as an essential component in the progress to become perfect, even as the Heavenly Father is perfect.

The health laws or commandments given in the scriptures are to teach mankind how to care for their bodies. Such laws have spiritual consequence. Obedience to health laws can enhance physical, mental, and spiritual well-being.

Latter-day Saints are counseled not to take harmful and habit-forming things into their bodies. Tobacco, alcoholic beverages, coffee, tea, and drugs are to be avoided. Fruits, vegetables, herbs, grains, and fish are good for the body; meats, however, should be used sparingly (see WORD OF WISDOM).

In addition, the Lord counseled, "Cease to be idle; cease to be unclean; . . . retire to thy bed early, . . . arise early, that your bodies and your minds may be invigorated" (D&C 88:124). Modern prophets have stressed that people should keep their bodies healthy.

Other principles, such as love, kindness, compassion, forgiveness, and charity, foster a healthy and positive mental perspective. A God-given moral code promotes good health and enduring family life by requiring CHASTITY before marriage and total fidelity within marriage.

Without a solid foundation of ethical values, including integrity, responsibility, self-esteem, and self-discipline, children and adults are in danger of being drawn to high-risk behaviors that impair both the body and the spirit. Mortality is a time for the spirit to constrain and discipline the body's appetites. The choices made on a day-to-day basis determine whether one is incapacitated by addictive substances, suffers from sexually transmitted diseases (including AIDS), dies prematurely from degenerative diseases, or suffers traumatic injury.

Thus, Latter-day Saints believe that God has mandated striving to achieve and maintain optimal health. A central purpose of mankind's creation is negated when one trivializes, through wrong choices, the sacredness of one's own body or the body of another. The apostle Paul declared, "What? Know ye not that your body is the temple of the Holy Ghost which is in you, which ye have of God, and ye are not your own?" (1 Cor. 6:19).

BIBLIOGRAPHY

McKay, David O. "The 'Whole' Man." *IE* 55 (Apr. 1953):221–22.

Smith, Barbara B. "Good Health—A Key to Joyous Living." *Ensign* 8 (Nov. 1978):77–78.

JAMES O. MASON

HEAVEN

Significant meanings of the word "heaven" are (1) the place where God resides (Matt. 6:9; Alma 18:30); (2) the eternal dwelling place of the righteous in the hereafter (Matt. 6:20; 1 Pet. 1:4); and (3) the type of life enjoyed by heavenly beings. A desire for heaven—to eventually live in a better world than the present one—is the basis of a hope that motivates Latter-day Saints (cf. Ether 12:4; D&C 25:10).

Although the specific word "heaven" is regularly used in the day-to-day literature of the Church, it is not as frequently used as it no doubt would be if there were not substitute terms. The revealed nomenclature involving the hereafter in latter-day scripture is precise in detailing the varied conditions that exist in the afterlife. Hence in LDS literature there are many words that refer to life beyond mortality, such as PARADISE, the CELESTIAL KINGDOM, the TERRESTRIAL KINGDOM, the TELESTIAL KINGDOM, or the DEGREES OF GLORY.

In the future, this earth will be renewed and receive a paradisiacal glory (A of F 10; Isa. 65:17–25; D&C 88:25–26). This change of the earth will be associated with the millennial reign of the Savior, and the earth will eventually become a "new heaven and a new earth" (D&C 29:23). The earth will ultimately be "like unto crystal and will be a Urim and Thummim to the inhabitants who dwell thereon" (D&C 130:9). When this occurs, both the Father and the Son will rule over this planet and those who dwell upon it. This earth will be a heaven to its celestial inhabitants. Speaking of conditions of the future life, the Prophet Joseph SMITH explained, "That same sociality which exists among us here will exist among us there, only it will be coupled with eternal glory, which glory we do not now enjoy" (D&C 130:2).

The doctrinal emphasis on the eternal nature of the family and the implementation of gospel principles into home and family relationships have frequently led leaders of the Church to characterize the faithful family as a foretaste of "heaven here on earth" (Monson, p. 69).

[*See also* Afterlife; Kingdom of God: In Heaven.]

BIBLIOGRAPHY

McDannell, Colleen, and Bernhard Lang. *Heaven: A History.* New Haven and London, 1988.

Monson, Thomas S. "Hallmarks of a Happy Home." *Ensign* 18 (Nov. 1988):69–72.

ARTHUR WALLACE

HEAVENLY FATHER

See: God the Father

HEAVENLY MOTHER

See: Mother in Heaven

HEBREWS, EPISTLE TO THE

Many passages in this New Testament letter have particular significance for Latter-day Saints. In general conferences of the Church, the most frequently cited scriptures from the book of Hebrews are those concerning the GODHEAD (Heb. 1:1–3; 12:9; 13:8); the obedient suffering of Jesus (Heb. 2:14–18; 4:15–16; 5:8–9; *see also* ATONEMENT); the eternal PRIESTHOOD of Jesus Christ (Heb. 7–8);

how one must be called by God in order to hold the priesthood (Heb. 5:1–4); the nature of true faith, which motivates people to righteous action (Heb. 11); going on "unto perfection" (Heb. 6:1); and enduring to the end (Heb. 12:4–11). These themes are essential pillars of the gospel of Jesus Christ.

The main point at the center of the epistle is that Jesus Christ is the eternal "high priest, who is set on the right hand of the throne of the Majesty in the heavens; a minister of the sanctuary, and of the true tabernacle" of God (Heb. 8:1–2). This theme is developed throughout the epistle, showing how eternal salvation comes through the greatness, sufficiency, and supremacy of Jesus Christ. The letter was written to devoted converts from Judaism to the early Christian church, who already understood the first principles of the gospel and had received its basic ordinances (Heb. 6:1–4). Step by step, it systematically strives to persuade them "to hold fast to their faith" (Buchanan, p. 266), to keep the covenant, and to realize the incomparable hope and irrevocable promises given to them by God through the sacrifice of Jesus Christ. With its explication of the Atonement in terms of priesthood, oaths, covenants, and temple imagery, this entire epistle resonates and harmonizes with LDS concepts and practices.

Chapter 1 begins by boldly declaring that Jesus is the sole mediator between God and all human beings; he is superior to, and supersedes, both prophets and angels. As a separate and distinct personage in the Godhead, he is the God of creation and the perfect revelation of GODHOOD for all time. He is the express image of his Father, both spiritually and physically; he alone purged the sins of mankind and sits on the right hand of God the Father (Heb. 1:1–3). The Father brought the Savior (who was his "firstbegotten" in the premortal existence) "into the world" (Heb. 1:6; cf. D&C 93:21; 1 Ne. 11:18). As the firstborn, Jesus is the heir of all things (Heb. 1:2), and those who are faithful become joint-heirs with him (*see* HEIRS).

Chapter 2 holds a strong warning to heed the word of God given through Jesus Christ (Heb. 2:1–4). The next world is in subjugation to Christ alone (Heb 2:5–10). God made him a little lower than "the gods" (taking the marginal reading of Ps. 8:4–6). Because God is the Father of all, even Christ is subject to him. Christ is second only to the Father, yet he is the spirit brother of mankind (Heb. 2:17). Like his brothers and sisters in mortality, he suffered temptation, but unlike them, he never sinned (Heb. 2:18; 4:15–16). Through this suffering, he learned obedience and gained compassion for all God's children.

The admonition of chapter 3 counsels people to contemplate the greatness of the Lord and to commit themselves to him. The total obedience shown by the Savior to his Father marks the way. The time for commitment is "today." The gospel is not always available to mankind, and so it is necessary to respond covenantally "this day," lest individuals be left like the rebellious Israelites to die in the deserts of their own lives (Heb. 3:7–17; cf. Josh. 24:14–25; Jacob 6:5–7; D&C 64:23–25).

Chapter 4, drawing in part upon Israelite temple symbolism, admonishes the Saints to enter into the rest of the Lord (Heb. 4:1, 11). This comes by believing, softening the heart, laboring, standing openly before God, relying on the compassion of Jesus the High Priest, and coming boldly to the mercy seat of God to find grace in time of need (Heb. 4:7, 11, 13, 15, 16).

Chapter 5 explains how Jesus obtained his authority to act as Israel's great High Priest. He did not presume to take this honor upon himself. As with Aaron, God chose him and bestowed authority upon him as "a priest for ever after the order of Melchisedec" (Heb. 5:6; Ps. 110:4).

Chapter 6 calls upon all members of the church to "lay hold upon the hope" of PERFECTION and ETERNAL LIFE, which has been extended to them by an immutable oath and covenant (Heb. 6:1, 13–20; *see also* OATH AND COVENANT OF THE PRIESTHOOD). Diligence in serving Christ will bring a full assurance of extraordinary promises, as God covenanted with ABRAHAM and promised him eternal increase (Heb. 6:13–14; cf. D&C 132:30). This hope, made possible in Christ, is an anchor for the soul, since God cannot lie. However, those who once have tasted the good word of God and have partaken of the Holy Ghost and then fall away and "crucify to themselves the Son of God afresh," the sin is so grievous that they cannot be renewed again unto repentance (Heb. 6:6–10).

God's promises to Abraham are extended to all who come unto Christ: Jesus was a priest after the order of MELCHIZEDEK, who was the priest who blessed Abraham, in whose loins was Levi. The superiority of Christ's Melchizedek priesthood over the Levitical priesthood and the LAW OF MOSES is developed in chapter 7. Melchizedek was a type of Christ. His priesthood was more endur-

ing than the Levitical priesthood, which was limited to blood lines and was not given with an oath and whose priests did not continue because of death and needed daily renewal (Heb. 7:3, 21, 23, 27). The Melchizedek order of priesthood, however, was directed by Jesus Christ, who, unlike the high priest under the law of Moses on the annual Day of Atonement (Lev. 16:4), did not need to "offer sacrifice for his own sins, for he knew no sins" (JST Heb. 7:26). His priesthood was *aparabatos*, meaning "permanent, unchangeable, and incomparable" (Heb. 7:24). No other priesthood will succeed it. It will be the permanent power of salvation and ETERNAL LIVES within Christ's church forever more (*TPJS*, pp. 166, 322).

As the great High Priest, Jesus offered himself as the eternal atoning sacrifice and became the mediator of this new and better covenant (Heb. 8:6), putting the law of God into the hearts of his people (Heb. 8:10; 10:16). The old law (of Moses), with its performances and sacrifices, had been fulfilled. Through the new covenant, God promised to remember the sins of the repentant no more (Heb. 10:17), and each Saint was challenged to enter into "a new and living way" through the blood of Christ (Heb. 10:15–20). Those who were willing to do so in patience and faith would be justified and receive the promise (Heb. 10:35–38).

Chapter 11 then concentrates on faith and its outward effects in the lives of Israel's spiritual heroes. Faith is the actual substance or substantiation or assurance (*hypostasis*) and the evidence or evincing (*elenchos*) of things not seen that are true (Heb. 11:1; Alma 32:21). True faith necessarily manifests itself in works of righteousness. Chapter 12 thus exhorts the faithful to endure the CHASTENING and correction of God, who is the Father of their spirits. By inheriting the blessings of eternity as sons of the living God, his Saints are able to come to the new Mount Zion, the heavenly Jerusalem, being made perfect, an assembly of "firstborns" (*prototokōn*), having inherited all with the Firstborn.

Chapter 13 concludes by noting that "marriage is honourable in all," and by counseling all to "let brotherly love continue," to "be without covetousness," and to be loyal to Jesus alone, "bearing his reproach, for here [on earth] have we no continuing city, but we seek one to come" (Heb. 13:1, 4–5, 13–14). Those who enter into this holy order and keep its covenants prepare themselves for eternal life, and fulfillment of the invocation that "the God of peace, that brought again from the dead our Lord Jesus, that great shepherd of the sheep, through the blood of the everlasting covenant, make you perfect in every good work to do his will" (Heb. 13:20–21).

BIBLIOGRAPHY

Anderson, Richard L. *Understanding Paul.* Salt Lake City, 1983.

Buchanan, George W. *To the Hebrews.* Garden City, N.Y., 1972.

Gentry, Leland H. "Let Us Go On unto Perfection: Paul's Message in the Book of Hebrews." In *Sidney B. Sperry Symposium,* pp. 135–44. Provo, Utah, 1983.

RICHARD D. DRAPER

HEIRS

[*This entry consists of two parts:* Heirs of God *and* Joint-Heirs with Christ. *The first part explains that by obedience to the commandments of God a person can become an heir of God. The second part emphasizes that the gospel of Jesus Christ also provides the way for one to become a joint-heir with Jesus Christ, and obtain the special inheritance of the Church of the Firstborn.*]

HEIRS OF GOD

The doctrine of becoming an heir of God through the gospel of Jesus Christ was noted by Paul (Rom. 8:14–17; Gal. 3:26–29; 4:1–7; *see also* CALLING AND ELECTION; CHURCH OF THE FIRSTBORN). In this connection, The Church of Jesus Christ of Latter-day Saints teaches that all humans are spirit sons and daughters of God, with the potential of inheriting all that the Father has (D&C 84:33–38). Every member of the human family is a child of God. However, through obedience to the gospel of Jesus Christ, including having faith, love, charity, and participating in TEMPLE ORDINANCES and SEALINGS, men and women can become heirs of God in a special way. Such persons are called the "children of Christ, his sons and his daughters," being "spiritually begotten" by him (Mosiah 5:7). They will be exalted in the CELESTIAL KINGDOM. Members of the Church make several COVENANTS with God, beginning with baptism and continuing through the temple ENDOWMENT and MARRIAGE, by which they promise to obey God's commandments and to consecrate to him all that they possess in order to become heirs through Christ in the Father's kingdom. Such may eventually be exalted by God and be given many divine powers, including ETERNAL INCREASE.

Promises of inheritance are extended also to those who die without a knowledge of the gospel, for they shall have opportunity in the SPIRIT WORLD to hear the message of redemption, and have the essential ordinances of the gospel performed in their behalf in the temples of the Church.

[*See also* Salvation of the Dead.]

JOSEPH GRANT STEVENSON

JOINT-HEIRS WITH CHRIST

Joint-heirs with Christ identifies those persons who attain the highest degree of the CELESTIAL KINGDOM. Latter-day Saints regard Jesus Christ as the firstborn spirit child of God the Father and the Only Begotten of the Father in the flesh. Because of this priority, he is the natural heir of the Father. Through strict obedience to the Father's will, progressing from grace to grace by obeying the gospel and its ORDINANCES and making the infinite ATONEMENT, Jesus became the Savior of all mankind and also heir to all that the Father has. Those who accept Jesus Christ as their redeemer, repent of their sins, obey the ordinances of the gospel, and live in willing obedience with the Holy Spirit as their guide, can also become heirs of God and joint-heirs with Jesus Christ. In the eternities, they can inherit the same truth, power, wisdom, glory, and EXALTATION possessed by God the Father and by the Son (see D&C 84:38).

The scriptures set forth the Father's plan of salvation for becoming joint-heirs with Christ. This includes taking the name of Christ upon oneself and living a Christlike life. Obeying the gospel means keeping the ordinances and ceremonies as well as living the moral law. Having started on the course of salvation, each individual is expected to continue to serve the Lord with a pure heart to the end of the mortal life. Through the GRACE of Jesus Christ and the blood that he shed, the willing and obedient are redeemed and sanctified.

All people are spirit children of God and recipients of his love, but only through accepting and living the gospel of Jesus Christ are individuals born again, spiritually begotten, and adopted into the family of God in a special relationship as the "sons and daughters" of Christ (Mosiah 5:7; Gal. 4:5–7; Rom. 8:14–17; *see also* BORN OF GOD; LAW

OF ADOPTION). Through the gospel, one becomes a joint-heir with Christ, a member of the CHURCH OF THE FIRSTBORN, and a partaker of the fulness of God's glory.

N. GAYLON HOPKINS

HELAMAN₁

The first Helaman noted in the Book of Mormon (c. 130 B.C.) was one of the three sons of BENJAMIN, king of the NEPHITES and the people of Zarahemla. He is mentioned only once in connection with his father's efforts to educate him and his brothers, MOSIAH₂ and Helorum. Benjamin taught them both the language of their fathers and the prophecies spoken by their fathers, "that thereby they might become men of understanding" (Mosiah 1:2).

MELVIN J. THORNE

HELAMAN₂

Helaman₂ (c. 100–57 B.C.) was a noted BOOK OF MORMON military commander and PROPHET. The eldest son of ALMA₂, he was brother to Shiblon and Corianton (Alma 31:7) and father to HELAMAN₃. He became a HIGH PRIEST (Alma 46:38) and was known for teaching REPENTANCE to his people.

While a young man, he remained behind during the mission of his father and brothers to the Zoramites (Alma 31:7), apparently to manage domestic and ecclesiastic affairs in Alma's absence. Later, his father gave him a special blessing, which is often quoted among Latter-day Saints, admonishing him to keep the commandments of God and promising that, if he did so, he would prosper in the land (Alma 36:30; 37:13). Helaman's father also instructed him to continue the record of his people and charged him with the sacred custody of the NEPHITE records, the plates of brass, the twenty-four plates of the JAREDITES, the interpreters, and the LIAHONA, that is, the divine compass that led LEHI's family to the new promised land in the western hemisphere (Alma 37:1–47). Before his father's death, Helaman recorded his father's prophecy concerning the final destruction of the Nephite people (45:9–14).

Although Helaman was known simply as one of "the high priests over the church" (Alma 46:6), apparently he was the chief priest because "Helaman and his brethren" (45:22–23; 46:1, 6; 62:45) or "Helaman and the high priests" (46:38) always performed the ecclesiastical functions; no other presiding high priest is named. When Helaman and his brothers attempted "to establish the church again in all the land" (45:22) after a protracted war with the LAMANITES (43–44), their action triggered civil unrest led by Amalickiah, which in turn embroiled the Nephites in one of their most devastating wars.

During Helaman's youth, a large number of Lamanite converts, called Ammonites (see BOOK OF MORMON PEOPLES), moved to the Nephite territory of Jershon (Alma 27). They swore an oath that they would never again take anyone's life (Alma 24:17–18). Later, when other Lamanites attacked their Nephite protectors, the Ammonites offered to break their oath in order to help the Nephite army defend their families and land. It was "Helaman and his brethren" who persuaded them not to break their covenant. They did welcome 2,060 Ammonite young men, who were not under their parents' oath, who volunteered to fight in the Nephite cause and chose Helaman to lead them (53:10–22). Accepting their invitation, he became both military leader and spiritual father, an observation found in Helaman's long letter to his commander MORONI₁ (Alma 56–58). While Helaman led these "stripling soldiers" (53:22) into many battles, none was killed, although all received wounds (56:56; 57:25; 58:39). These young men credited God with their protection and paid solemn tribute to their mothers who had trained them in faith (56:47). During Helaman's military campaign as leader of these young men, he won victory after victory, often capturing enemies without shedding blood. Exhibiting extraordinary ingenuity and character, he always acknowledged God's blessings in his successes (56:19; 57:35; 58:33).

After the war, Helaman returned home and spent his remaining years regulating the affairs of the Church, convincing "many people of their wickedness, which did cause them to repent of their sins and to be baptized unto the Lord their God" (Alma 62:45). An era of peace resulted from his final efforts. He died in 57 B.C.

PAUL R. CHEESMAN

HELMAN₃

Helaman₃, son of HELAMAN₂, was the record keeper and chief judge in the land of Zarahemla for the fourteen years prior to his death in 39 B.C. Little is known of his personal affairs. He was given charge of NEPHITE historical records by his uncle, Shiblon, in 53 B.C. (Alma 63:11–13), and the book of Helaman in the BOOK OF MORMON takes its name from him.

After the assassination of the chief judge Pacumeni in 50 B.C., Helaman was elected by the people to this highest national office. A murder plot against him was subsequently uncovered, and the would-be assassin, Kishkumen, was mortally wounded. The murderous band, led by Gadianton, escaped into the wilderness. Of Gadianton, MORMON wrote "In the end of this book [Book of Mormon] ye shall see that this Gadianton did prove the overthrow . . . of the people of Nephi" (Hel. 2:13; see also SECRET COMBINATIONS).

During the three-year period 48–46 B.C., a substantial number of people left Zarahemla— because of unspecified dissensions—and "went forth unto the land northward" (Hel. 3:3). So extensive was the migration that only a fraction of its impact could be discussed in Mormon's record (Hel. 3:14). Despite dissension, emigration, and war, "Helaman did fill the judgment-seat with justice and equity; yea, he did observe to keep the statutes, and the judgments, and the commandments of God; and he did do that which was right in the sight of God continually; and he did walk after the ways of his father, insomuch that he did prosper in the land" (3:20). During his tenure, tens of thousands of people were baptized into the church, even to the astonishment of the high priests and teachers (3:24–25). Through the force of his personality, Helaman maintained peace throughout two-thirds of his political career.

When Helaman died, he left the spiritual responsibilities and the sacred records in the hands of his son, NEPHI₂ (Hel. 3:37; 5:5–14; 16:25).

BIBLIOGRAPHY

Moss, James R. "Six Nephite Judges." Ensign 7 (Sept. 1977): 61–65.

CHRISTINE PURVES BAKER

HELL

The term "hell" as used in the King James Version of the Bible is the English translation of four words in the original biblical languages: Hebrew *sheol* and Greek *hades*, *geenna* (Heb. *gehenna*), and a noun implied in the verb *tartar*. These terms generally signify the abode of all the dead, whether righteous or disobedient, although *geenna* and *tartaróō* are associated with a place of punishment. The derivation and literal meaning of *sheol* are unknown, but words in Hebrew derived from it bear the idea of "hollowness."

Latter-day scriptures describe at least three senses of hell: (1) that condition of misery which may attend a person in mortality due to disobedience to divine law; (2) the miserable, but temporary, state of disobedient spirits in the SPIRIT WORLD awaiting the resurrection; (3) the permanent habitation of the SONS OF PERDITION, who suffer the second SPIRITUAL DEATH and remain in hell even after the resurrection.

Persons experiencing the first type of hell can be rescued from suffering through repentance and obedience to the laws and ORDINANCES of the gospel of Jesus Christ because of the ATONEMENT of Jesus Christ. The Savior suffered so that he could deliver everyone from hell (Alma 7:11–13; 33:23). Those who do not repent, however, may experience the pains of hell in this life as well as in the next (D&C 76:104; 1 Ne. 16:2; Alma 40:14). The Prophet Joseph SMITH described the true nature of hell: "A man is his own tormenter and his own condemner. Hence the saying, They shall go into the lake that burns with fire and brimstone. The torment of disappointment in the mind of man is as exquisite as a lake burning with fire and brimstone" (*TPJS*, p. 357). Thus, hell is both a place, a part of the world of spirits where suffering and sorrow occur, and a state of mind associated with remorseful realization of one's own sins (Mosiah 2:38; Alma 36:12–16).

A second type, a temporary hell of the postmortal spirit world, is also spoken of as a SPIRIT PRISON. Here, in preparation for the Resurrection, unrepentant spirits are cleansed through suffering that would have been obviated by the atonement of Christ had they repented during mortality (D&C 19:15–20; Alma 40:13–14). At the last resurrection this hell will give up its captive spirits. Many of these spirits will enter into the TELESTIAL KINGDOM in their resurrected state (2 Ne. 9:10–12;

D&C 76:84–89, 106; Rev. 20:13). References to an everlasting hell for these spirits are interpreted in light of the Doctrine and Covenants, which defines ENDLESS AND ETERNAL as referring not to the length of punishment, but rather referring to God's punishment because he is "endless" and "eternal" (19:4–13). Individual spirits will be cleansed, will cease to experience the fiery torment of mind, and will be resurrected with their physical bodies.

The Savior's reference to the "gates of hell" (Hades, or the spirit world; Matt. 16:18) indicates, among other things, that God's priesthood power will penetrate hell and redeem the repentant spirits there. Many have been, and many more will yet be, delivered from hell through hearing, repenting, and obeying the gospel of Jesus Christ in the spirit world after the death of the body. LDS doctrine emphasizes that after his mortal death Jesus Christ went to the spirit world and organized the teaching of the gospel there (D&C 138; cf. Luke 23:43; 1 Pet. 3:18–20). The Athanasian Creed and some forms of the "Apostles'" Creed state that Christ "descended into hell." LDS teaching is that Jesus entered the spirit world to extend his redemptive mission to those in hell, upon conditions of their repentance (see SALVATION OF THE DEAD).

A third meaning of "hell" (second spiritual death) refers to the realm of the devil and his angels, including those known as sons of perdition (2 Pet. 2:4; D&C 29:38; 88:113; Rev. 20:14). It is a place for those who cannot be cleansed by the Atonement because they committed the unforgivable and UNPARDONABLE SIN (1 Ne. 15:35; D&C 76:30–49). Only this hell continues to operate *after* the Resurrection and Judgment.

BIBLIOGRAPHY

"Descent of Christ into Hell." In *Oxford Dictionary of the Christian Church*, p. 395. New York, 1983.

Nibley, Hugh W. "Christ Among the Ruins." *Ensign* 13 (July 1983):14–19.

M. CATHERINE THOMAS

HIGH COUNCIL

A high council is a body of twelve HIGH PRIESTS who are called and set apart in each STAKE to assist and advise the STAKE PRESIDENCY under whom they serve.

Following the organization of the Church, in 1830, the Prophet Joseph SMITH served as the spiritual leader for the growing body of members. However, with the rapid growth in membership and a commitment to LAY PARTICIPATION AND LEADERSHIP, it soon became evident that a more extensive governing structure would be required. The FIRST PRESIDENCY was organized in 1832.

At a conference held in KIRTLAND, OHIO, on February 17, 1834, Joseph Smith established a standing stake high council composed of twelve high priests, with himself, Sidney RIGDON, and Frederick G. Williams comprising the First Presidency and also as the presidency of the Kirtland Stake. Later that year, a separate stake presidency and high council were organized in MISSOURI. They operated independent of the Kirtland council, except for cases that went from Missouri to Kirtland on appeal. These initial standing high councils became the prototype for future stake organizations as the Church continued to grow and expand. Following the organization in 1835 of the "traveling high council," or QUORUM OF THE TWELVE APOSTLES (D&C 107:33–36), stake high councils concerned themselves only with stake matters.

With continued Church growth, additional areas were organized into stakes under the direction of the First Presidency to provide a means of coordinating the spiritual activities of the local WARDS and BRANCHES. In each case, a three-member stake presidency, assisted by a twelve-member high council, was called to preside over the stake. Their authority was limited to the stake in which they functioned.

As in the Quorum (or Council) of the Twelve Apostles, a seniority system exists within a stake high council; as vacancies occur in the council, the stake presidency calls new members, and the oldest in term of service is recognized as the senior member.

Under the direction of the stake presidency, the high council has important executive, legislative, and judicial powers (see D&C 102). Members of the stake high council serve as advisers to the stake presidency on any matter about which the presidency might seek counsel, and they carry out specific assignments. For example, a high councilor may have an assignment to represent the stake presidency, to assist in the training of a new ward BISHOPRIC, to attend a ward's priesthood executive committee meetings and ward council meetings, or to train and advise ward MELCHI-ZEDEK PRIESTHOOD quorum leaders. He may be asked to report regularly to the stake presidency concerning the status of a particular ward. In addition, he may serve as a member of the stake Melchizedek Priesthood committee, which assists the stake presidency in installing, training, and advising Melchizedek Priesthood leaders. Other assignments that are generally given to a member of a high council include membership on the AARONIC PRIESTHOOD/Boy Scouting Committee; adviser to the stake YOUNG WOMEN organization; stake mission president; coordinator of stake WELFARE programs; coordinator for temple service and FAMILY HISTORY programs; stake EMERGENCY PREPAREDNESS director, or other such administrative roles. A high councilor will usually also be assigned to speak periodically in ward SACRAMENT MEETINGS under the direction of the stake presidency.

At regular meetings of the stake high council, the presidency presents matters of business to the council for its approval. Such matters may include endorsing an individual's name for an assignment in the stake organization, recommending a person as a potential ward bishop or counselor in a bishopric, or considering an individual for ordination to an office in the Melchizedek Priesthood. The stake president may also ask for discussion of particular issues, and high councilors may be asked to report on the status of their assignments.

As part of its judicial function, the high council serves as a disciplinary council when convened by the stake president to consider cases of serious transgression that affect the standing or fellowship of a Church member. Following the presentation of the facts of the case and due deliberation and prayer, a decision is rendered by the stake president and ratified by the stake high council (*see* DISCIPLINARY PROCEDURES).

DONOVAN E. FLEMING

HIGH PRIEST

The term "high priest" refers to an office in the MELCHIZEDEK PRIESTHOOD. Men must be ordained high priests to serve as BISHOPS, on high councils, or in STAKE PRESIDENCIES, or as GENERAL AUTHORITIES (*see* HIGH COUNCIL; PRIESTHOOD). Stake presidents may ordain high

priests for other reasons as well. When released from any of these callings, a high priest continues to be a member of the high priests quorum in his resident stake and to participate in the activities of his ward's high priests group (*see* PRIESTHOOD QUORUM).

The PRESIDENT OF THE CHURCH is the PRESIDING HIGH PRIEST in the Church (D&C 107:65–66), the president of the stake is the presiding high priest in the stake, and the bishop is the presiding high priest in the ward. Since 1956, stake presidencies have been serving as the presidencies of their respective stake high priests quorums. Each ward in a stake has a high priests group with a group leader and one or more assistants, as needed. Ward groups of high priests meet weekly to be instructed in their duties and in the principles of the gospel (D&C 124:134; J. Taylor in *JD* 23:219). During group meetings they also receive and report on assignments such as HOME TEACHING and volunteer service projects.

To be ordained a high priest, an ELDER must be recommended by the ward bishopric to the stake presidency. After approval by the stake presidency and high council, his name is presented to the general body of stake priesthood bearers for a sustaining vote after which he is ordained by or under the direction of the stake president.

The first ordinations to the office of high priest in The Church of Jesus Christ of Latter-day Saints were done at the fourth conference of the Church, held in June 1831 in Kirtland, Ohio. Twenty-three men were ordained at that time, including the Prophet Joseph Smith, who was ordained a high priest under the hands of Lyman Wight, who had been ordained to that office by the Prophet. Joseph Smith had received this authority earlier at the hands of Peter, James, and John (*see* MELCHIZEDEK PRIESTHOOD: RESTORATION OF). Current records do not specify when high priests were first organized as a quorum, but it apparently was before January 1836. For a period of time, high priests quorums were organized in each ward with their own presidencies, but in 1877 Brigham Young indicated that stake presidents had responsibility over these quorums. In December 1975 the First Presidency clarified details of the current arrangement under which ward high priests groups function as units of the stake high priests quorum, with the stake president as the president of the quorum and ward high priest group leaders functioning under his direction. As of 1989, there were approximately 246,000 high priests in the Church.

From Adam to Moses, righteous men holding the holy priesthood were ordained high priests. Adam, Enoch, Noah, Melchizedek, Abraham, Moses, and many others were all ordained high priests (D&C 107:53; Alma 13). After the time of Moses the Melchizedek Priesthood was generally withdrawn from the earth, except among the prophets, and the law functioned under the Aaronic Priesthood. Thus, under the LAW OF MOSES a high priest was the chief priest in the AARONIC PRIESTHOOD. He presided over all other priests in their functions and ordinances, particularly those of the temple. Only a direct descendant of the first-born son of AARON anointed to be the spiritual head of the people could become the high priest.

In the Book of Mormon, there were apparently no Levites or descendants of Aaron among the people. High priests were the presiding spiritual authorities and held the Melchizedek Priesthood (e.g., Alma 8:23; 30:20, 23).

In the epistle to the Hebrews, Paul declares Christ to be the promised high priest "after the order of Melchisedec," an order higher in authority than the Aaronic Priesthood and not dependent upon the Aaronic lineage (Heb. 5:4–6, 10; 7:3, 11, 14–15; Ps. 110:4). As the great high priest, Christ made an eternal sacrifice, once for all time and all people (Heb. 9:11–12), and he continues to preside over all the ordinances and the organization of the Church, which bears his name (see HEAD OF THE CHURCH).

BIBLIOGRAPHY

Cotton, J. Harry, and Alexander C. Purdy. *The Interpreter's Bible*, Vol. 11, pp. 637–708. New York, 1955.

Schrenk, Gottlob. "Priest, High Priest." *Theological Dictionary of the New Testament*, ed. G. Kittel, Vol. 3, pp. 257–83. Grand Rapids, Mich., 1965.

Widtsoe, John A. *Priesthood and Church Government*, rev. ed. Salt Lake City, 1954.

A. LEGRAND RICHARDS

HIRAM, OHIO

Hiram, Ohio, a small town twenty-five miles south and slightly east of KIRTLAND, OHIO, was the site of a large branch of The Church of Jesus Christ of Latter-day Saints in the 1830s and served for one year as home to the Prophet Joseph SMITH. John and Elsa Johnson, a prosperous farmer and his wife, residents in Hiram Township, welcomed Joseph, Emma, and their adopted twins to live with them in September 1831. Joseph had healed Elsa's arthritic arm several months earlier.

During the Smiths' stay, Joseph received an outpouring of fifteen of the revelations now published in the DOCTRINE AND COVENANTS. Section 1, known as the Preface, was given at one of many Church conferences held there. On February 16, 1832, Joseph and his scribe at this time, Sidney RIGDON, beheld a divine vision of the eternal worlds that forms the basis of Latter-day Saint understanding of life after death. In this vision (*see* DOCTRINE AND COVENANTS: SECTION 76) they reported seeing both God the Father and his Son Jesus Christ and bore witness of Jesus Christ: "He lives! For we saw him, even on the right hand of God" (verses 22–23). A Hiram conference in November 1831 voted to print all revelations received up to that date as the BOOK OF COMMANDMENTS.

On the cold night of March 24, 1832, a mob dragged Joseph and Sidney from their beds into a nearby meadow, beat them, and poured tar and feathers on their bodies (*HC* 1:261–65). Joseph and Sidney bore the marks of that night for the rest of their lives. Another consequence was the death of Joseph and Emma's adopted eleven-month-old son. Ill with the measles at the time, he was exposed to the cold and died five days later.

While living in Hiram, Joseph accomplished a significant portion of his translation of the Bible (*see* JOSEPH SMITH TRANSLATION OF THE BIBLE

The John Johnson home in Hiram, Ohio. Joseph Smith received several revelations here, including D&C 76, known as the Vision, about the degrees of glory in heaven. Courtesy LaMar C. Berrett.

[JST]). He left the area only once for a trip to Missouri and for several nearby preaching missions.

The Johnson home is now owned by the Church and is open as a VISITORS CENTER. The Hiram Ward meetinghouse stands nearby.

BIBLIOGRAPHY

Backman, Milton V., Jr. *The Heavens Resound*. Salt Lake City, 1983.

KARL RICKS ANDERSON

HISTORIANS, CHURCH

From its beginnings, the Church has considered RECORD KEEPING and history writing an imperative duty (D&C 123:1–7). The Book of Mormon, published in 1830, is a product of ancient records kept by command of God (1 Ne. 9:3, 5; Jacob 1:2; 3 Ne. 23:4, 11–13). Record keeping is also commanded by modern revelation (D&C 21:1; 47:3; 69:3; 72:5–6). Latter-day Saints write history not only to obey divine injunctions but also to combat false reports and to convert and edify future generations (*HC* 1:1; 2:199; 6:409).

Although most of the early commandments pertained to the keeping of "official" Church records, Latter-day Saints also apply them to individuals. Joseph SMITH and other prominent leaders set the example by keeping journals. Clerks and scribes recorded revelations, minutes of meetings, speeches, correspondence, blessings, and ordinances.

EARLY CHURCH HISTORIANS, 1830–1842. Record keeping and history writing were institutionalized with the appointment of Oliver COWDERY as the first Church Recorder when the Church was organized on April 6, 1830 (D&C 21:1). That the Prophet's closest associate and most capable scribe, who also served as second elder in the Church, should be called as Church Recorder is an indication of the importance attached to the position. According to his successor, Cowdery wrote the history of the Church up to mid-1831, when he was released; that early history has never been located. During his second term in office (1835–1837), Cowdery completed a series of eight historical letters that he had started publishing in the MESSENGER AND ADVOCATE in October 1834.

John Whitmer, one of the eight BOOK OF MORMON WITNESSES, served officially as Church recorder between 1831 and 1834 and, after his release, wrote unofficially until his excommunication in 1838. His history for 1831–1838 was published in 1908.

George W. Robinson, a son-in-law of Sidney RIGDON, became general recorder in 1837 (*HC* 2:513). He accompanied Joseph Smith in visiting Church settlements in northern Missouri and kept a brief record captioned "The Scriptory Book of Joseph Smith, Jr." Robinson was released in 1840 when he moved across the river from Nauvoo.

From 1838 to 1843 there was considerable overlapping in the service of Church recorders and historians. Little progress had been made on the Church annals, which, in part, were being written to help combat highly visible ANTI-MORMON PUBLICATIONS. In a flurry of activity to correct the situation, Joseph Smith had earlier minutes copied into the Far West Record, renewed efforts on his

Willard Richards (1804–54), ordained an apostle in 1840, was one of Joseph Smith's secretaries. He was appointed a Church historian in 1842 and general Church recorder in 1845. Engraving, c. 1853.

own history with the assistance of Sidney Rigdon, and called John Corrill and Elias Higbee as Church historians to work with Robinson.

Soon after his appointment, John Corrill chafed at criticism by the Prophet and chose to testify against his former associates in several legal proceedings, leading to his excommunication. To justify his break with the Church, he quickly wrote and published in 1839 the history that he never wrote as Church historian.

As a Church historian, Elias Higbee helped collect affidavits regarding the Saints' losses in Missouri, and in October 1839 he accompanied Joseph Smith and Sidney Rigdon to Washington, D.C., to present them to U.S. officials. After President Van Buren rebuffed them in February 1840, Higbee stayed on, trying unsuccessfully for a hearing before the Senate Judiciary Committee. His documents relating to this Washington mission, later incorporated in the "History of Joseph Smith," were his main contribution to Church history.

In 1840, twenty-eight-year-old Robert B. Thompson replaced Robinson as Church historian, but he had little time for history. He wrote in Joseph Smith's letter book, recorded patriarchal blessings, and served as city treasurer, clerk of the high council, and associate editor of the TIMES AND SEASONS. After Thompson died in 1841, James Sloan, an experienced clerk, served as historian, but within a year he was called on a mission to his native Ireland.

PIONEER CHURCH HISTORIANS, 1842–1900. After fluctuating changes in titles and personnel, the offices of Church recorder and Church historian merged and became stable with the appointment of Willard Richards in late 1842. He came to his literary duties singularly qualified and immediately brought new impetus and dignity to the position. Richards kept the Prophet's diary for him, wrote correspondence, compiled most of the "History of Joseph Smith" (see HISTORY OF THE CHURCH), and either recorded or supervised the recording of the Prophet's sermons, minutes of meetings, and ordinances performed in the Nauvoo Temple.

Richards's efforts provided continuity during the unsettled years of pioneer travel. With the help of his assistant, Thomas Bullock, he packed Church records in sturdy boxes for removal to the West. At Winter Quarters he set up a temporary Church Historian's Office in an octagonal cabin that also served as Church headquarters. In Utah he maintained the Historian's Office in his own home in Salt Lake City until his death on March 11, 1854.

No one seemed more qualified to complete the "History of Joseph Smith" than Joseph Smith's cousin George A. Smith, who was appointed as Church historian and general Church recorder on April 7, 1854. He had a modest building constructed across the street from Brigham YOUNG's office that served as the Historian's Office from 1856 to 1917. His main contributions were completing the "History of Joseph Smith" and directing the compilation of the "History of Brigham Young."

Albert Carrington, a graduate of Dartmouth College, Brigham Young's secretary, and editor of the *Deseret News*, was ordained an apostle and appointed historian in 1870. During Carrington's four-year term, work continued on the Manuscript History of Brigham Young. Orson PRATT, an apostle, was sixty-three years old when he was appointed Church historian in 1874 and never involved himself personally in writing Church history. He died in 1881.

Although Wilford WOODRUFF (1833–1898) served as Church historian from 1883 to 1889, he made his greatest contributions to Church history as assistant Church historian from 1856 to 1883. He was the prime motivator behind a project to publish a biography of each man who had served in the Quorum of the Twelve Apostles, and was instrumental in preparing the sermons of Joseph Smith for publication in the *History of the Church*. Woodruff's journals, which he kept with diligence from the time he joined the Church until a few weeks before his death, proved invaluable in compiling the histories of Joseph Smith and Brigham Young.

Franklin D. Richards, an apostle, served as an assistant Church historian for five years before becoming Church historian in 1889. He traveled to San Francisco to provide information for Hubert H. Bancroft, who was then preparing his histories of western states and territories. The resulting *History of Utah* (1890) was considered the most balanced and scholarly account of Church pioneer history to that time. Elder Richards energetically collected historical sources and authorized his assistant, Andrew Jenson, to travel extensively to gather materials. On his own initiative, Jenson had already undertaken historical projects beneficial to the Church before he was sustained as an assistant Church historian in 1897.

EARLY-TWENTIETH-CENTURY CHURCH HISTORIANS. Anthon H. Lund served from 1900 to 1921. An able and considerate administrator, he supervised significant projects, including moving the office and records in 1917 to the new Church Office Building. Andrew Jenson continued traveling to stakes and missions, gathering materials to compile a "manuscript history" of each; he also published thousands of biographical sketches. In 1906, when he was assigned responsibility for the "Journal History," Jenson began a retroactive compilation of sources in the form of annals extending back to 1830, a history that by 1932 had grown to 518 volumes. He also continued work on several private historical projects until his death in 1941.

Elder B. H. Roberts of the Seventy established himself as a historian with the publication of *The Life of John Taylor* (1892), *Outlines of Ecclesiastical History* (1893), *The Missouri Persecutions* (1900), and *The Rise and Fall of Nauvoo* (1900). In 1902 he was appointed assistant Church historian and assigned to edit and republish the *History of the Church*. He had completed six volumes by 1912, and a seventh in 1932, about a year before his death. While editing the *History of the Church*, Roberts also wrote "A History of the Mormon Church," which first appeared in monthly installments in the *Americana* magazine, 1909–1915. Later revised, these were published in 1930 as Roberts' COMPREHENSIVE HISTORY OF THE CHURCH.

Joseph Fielding SMITH began a sixty-nine-year association with the Historian's Office in 1901, when he was employed as an assistant to Andrew Jenson. As an assistant Church historian (1906–1921), he wrote several historical pamphlets and booklets, and as Church historian (1921–1970), he continued writing. His *Essentials in Church History* (1922) remained a standard until the 1980s. His two-volume *Church History and Modern Revelation* (1953) provided explanations about the antecedents and historical setting of many revelations published in the DOCTRINE AND COVENANTS. An apologist in the classical tradition, Elder Smith's philosophy of history has been widely influential within the Church.

RECENT CHURCH HISTORIANS. Joseph Fielding Smith worked to modernize operations of the His-

torian's Office. He improved standards for preserving, classifying, and managing archival materials; hired professional librarians and archivists; and helped plan a new four-story facility. As President of the Church, he appointed Elder Howard W. Hunter, an apostle, as Church historian (1970–1972). After consulting with professional historians and archivists, in 1972 Elder Hunter recommended a reorganization of the Historian's Office into a Historical Department with three divisions: a library for published materials, archives for manuscripts, and a division for research and writing.

Since Willard Richards, each Church historian and general Church recorder had been a member of the Quorum of the Twelve or First Presidency. That long-standing tradition was changed in 1972 when Leonard J. Arrington, a nationally prominent professional historian, was sustained in general conference as Church historian (1972–1977). His duties were also different from those of his predecessors: His main task was to produce scholarly works for publication. Earl E. Olson, Church archivist, was charged with gathering and preserving the materials of history; Donald T. Schmidt became librarian; and later Florence Jacobson headed an Arts and Sites Division. They all served under Managing Director Alvin R. Dyer, an Assistant to the Twelve. The Historical Department moved to enlarged quarters in November 1972. On May 17, 1976, Joseph Anderson, an Assistant to the Twelve, succeeded Elder Dyer as managing director.

With a corps of professional historians, Arrington promoted and directed the writing and publication of LDS history at an unprecedented rate. The division also assisted with acquisitions and conducted a dynamic oral history program.

The appointment of G. Homer Durham of the First Quorum of the Seventy as Managing Director in 1977 signaled a retrenchment in the Church's direct sponsorship of professional history writing. Several history writing projects were curtailed or abandoned. On June 26, 1980, the Church announced the establishment of the Joseph Fielding Smith Institute for Church History, which would be affiliated with BRIGHAM YOUNG UNIVERSITY. Arrington directed the new institute, and most of the professional historians associated with him transferred to the university. This placed the writing of history in a university setting, leaving the Historical Department to manage materials in its archives in support of scholarship without the responsibility of monitoring a genre of "official" Church history.

Elder G. Homer Durham was appointed as Church historian on February 8, 1982. During his administration Florence Jacobsen became a prime motivator in the establishment of a new MUSEUM of Church History and Art, which opened its doors in April 1984. The three divisions in the Historical Department were now the Archives, Library, and Museum. Following Durham, Elder Dean L. Larsen, of the Presidency of the Seventy, was sustained as Church historian and recorder (1985–1989). In 1989 John K. Carmack of the First Quorum of the Seventy, who had been serving under Elder Larsen since 1986, became the department's executive director.

BIBLIOGRAPHY

Bitton, Davis, and Leonard Arrington. *Mormons and Their Historians*. Salt Lake City, 1988.

Jenson, Andrew. *L.D.S. Biographical Encyclopedia*, 4 vols. Salt Lake City, 1901–1936.

Searle, Howard C. "Early Mormon Historiography." Ph.D. diss., University of California at Los Angeles, 1979.

HOWARD C. SEARLE

HISTORICAL SITES

The sites of historical importance to Latter-day Saints include those associated with Christianity in general (the Holy Land, Jerusalem, Bethlehem, Jordan River, Mount of Olives, etc.), as well as those directly related to LDS beliefs. The latter mainly include places in the United States associated with the founding and organization of The Church of Jesus Christ of Latter-day Saints and its subsequent migrations west. LDS historical sites are important to individual members because of the Church's emphasis on its history and cultural roots rather than as formal pilgrimage destinations (*see* HISTORY, SIGNIFICANCE TO LATTER-DAY SAINTS). Church members commonly visit these sites as tourists and, in the process, gain greater personal understanding of the history of the Church and its beliefs.

Many historical sites in the United States were obtained through the efforts of such individuals or entities as Joseph F. SMITH, Heber J. GRANT, Willard W. Bean, Wilford C. Wood, and the Corporation of the Presiding Bishopric of the LDS Church. Most of these sites have been restored to the time of the historical events and are staffed by local unpaid volunteers or missionaries.

VISITORS CENTERS are located at several sites, and are free and open to the public. Each location includes displays and literature explaining the site and its significance in Church history. One such site is the Joseph Smith Memorial in Sharon, Windsor County, Vermont. Joseph SMITH was born here on December 23, 1805. In 1905 the Church erected a 38.5-foot-high granite monument to commemorate the 38.5 years of his life. A full-time missionary couple live at the home.

Near the village of Palmyra, New York, in the township of Palmyra, is located the site of the log house in which the Smiths resided from 1817 to the early or mid-1820s, and again intermittently until late 1830. In the adjacent township of Manchester is the Smith family farm, existing frame home, SACRED GROVE, and also the hill CUMORAH only a few miles southeast of the home. The Sacred Grove is where the boy Joseph received his FIRST VISION, the initial event in the restoration of the Church. Latter-day Saints believe that the young Joseph Smith was directed by the angel Moroni to retrieve from the hill Cumorah the gold plates from which the Book of Mormon was translated. The first edition of the Book of Mormon was printed in the Grandin Press Building in Palmyra. A mile and one-half north of Palmyra is the farm of Martin Harris, a portion of which was sold to fi-

A stonemason prepares the base of the obelisk erected in 1905 at Joseph Smith's birthplace in the township of Sharon, Vermont. The inscription is taken from the Title Page of the Book of Mormon and emphasizes the Prophet's role as translator of the book.

LDS HISTORICAL SITES WITH FULL-TIME STAFF

Main Historic Dates	Place	Location
1805	Joseph Smith Memorial	Sharon, Vt.
1817–1818	Joseph Smith Farm	Manchester, N.Y.
1820	Sacred Grove	Manchester, N.Y.
1823–1827	Hill Cumorah	Manchester, N.Y.
1827–1831	Martin Harris Farm	Palmyra, N.Y.
1829–1830	Grandin Press Building	Palmyra, N.Y.
1829–1831	Peter Whitmer, Sr., Farm	Fayette, N.Y.
1831–1833	John Johnson Home	Hiram, Ohio
1831–1833	Independence Temple Site	Independence, Mo.
1831–1838	Newel K. Whitney Store	Kirtland, Ohio
1831–1838	Newel K. Whitney Home	Kirtland, Ohio
1836–1838	Kirtland Temple (RLDS owned and staffed)	Kirtland, Ohio
1838–1839	Liberty Jail	Liberty, Mo.
1839–1846	Nauvoo (LDS and RLDS sites)	Nauvoo, Ill.
1844	Carthage Jail	Carthage, Ill.
1846–1848	Winter Quarters	Omaha (Florence), Nebr.
1847	Temple Square	Salt Lake City, Utah
1847–1848	Mormon Battalion Duty Station	San Diego, Calif.
1854	Beehive House	Salt Lake City, Utah
1863–1869	Jacob Hamblin Home	Santa Clara, Utah
1867	Cove Fort	Cove Fort, Utah
1869–1877	Brigham Young Winter Home	St. George, Utah
1875 (Ded.)	St. George Tabernacle	St. George, Utah
1878 (Est.)	Thomas L. Kane Memorial Chapel	Kane, Pa.

nance the publication of the Book of Mormon. Thirty miles to the southeast is the Peter Whitmer farm in FAYETTE, NEW YORK, where the Church was formally organized in 1830. Yet another hundred miles southeast from Fayette is HARMONY, PENNSYLVANIA, where the majority of the Book of Mormon was translated by Joseph Smith and written down by Oliver Cowdery.

Joseph Smith moved his family to KIRTLAND, OHIO, in early 1831. They remained there until January 1838, when they fled to MISSOURI to escape mob violence. Events of importance in the life of Joseph Smith that occurred in Kirtland include receiving many revelations now found in the Doctrine and Covenants and the construction of the first Latter-day Saint temple. The WHITNEY STORE was the location of many of these events and has been restored. The KIRTLAND TEMPLE was dedicated on March 27, 1836. It is owned today by the REORGANIZED CHURCH OF JESUS CHRIST OF LATTER DAY SAINTS (RLDS).

At Independence, Jackson County, Missouri, an LDS visitors center is situated on a portion of the temple lot dedicated by Joseph Smith in 1831. Twelve miles to the north is LIBERTY JAIL in Clay County, Missouri, where Joseph was imprisoned from December 1, 1838, to April 6, 1839. Here he received sections 121–123 of the Doctrine and Covenants. The reconstructed remnant of the jail stands today as a reminder of the trials experienced by the Prophet for his beliefs, of the faithfulness of his followers (some of whom shared the jail with him), and of the suffering of his wife, Emma SMITH, and his children during the harsh winter while he was imprisoned. Northeast of Liberty are the historic sites of FAR WEST, in Caldwell County, Missouri, and ADAM-ONDI-AHMAN, in Daviess County, Missouri.

After TEMPLE SQUARE in Salt Lake City, NAUVOO is the second most visited historic location in the Church. Joseph Smith moved to the village of Commerce in Hancock County, Illinois, on May 10, 1839. Purchased by the Church, Commerce was renamed Nauvoo and became a major destination for converts to the Church, reaching a population in excess of 11,000 in 1845, and some 20,000

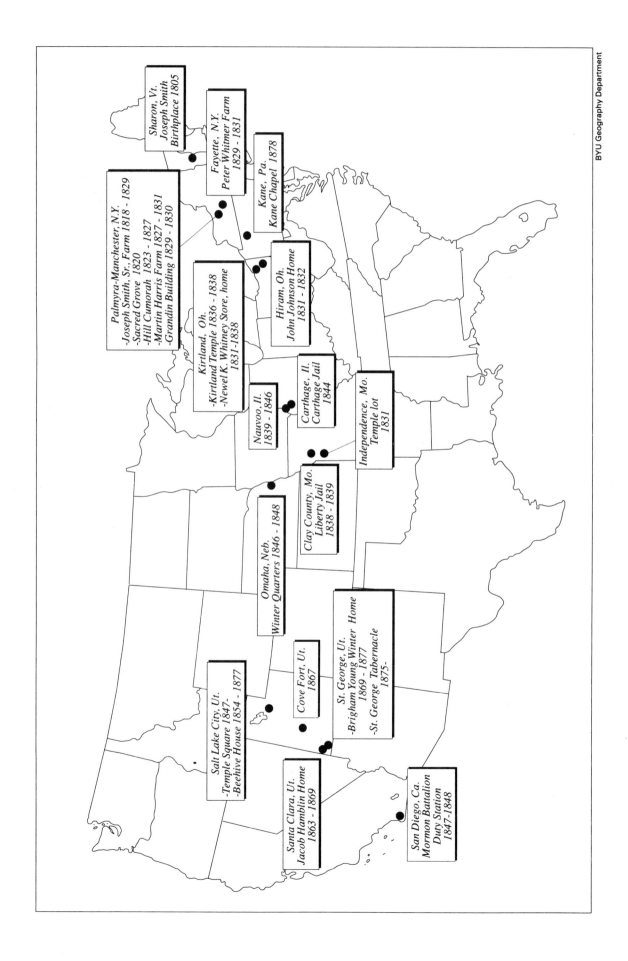

Sharon, Vt.
Joseph Smith
Birthplace 1805

Fayette, N.Y.
Peter Whitmer Farm
1829 - 1831

Kane, Pa.
Kane Chapel 1878

Palmyra-Manchester, N.Y.
-Joseph Smith, Sr., Farm 1818 - 1829
-Sacred Grove 1820
-Hill Cumorah 1823 - 1827
-Martin Harris Farm 1827 - 1831
-Grandin Building 1829 - 1830

Hiram, Oh.
John Johnson Home
1831 - 1832

Kirtland, Oh.
-Kirtland Temple 1836 - 1838
-Newel K. Whitney Store, home
1831-1838

Carthage, Il.
Carthage Jail
1844

Nauvoo, Il.
1839 - 1846

Independence, Mo.
Temple lot
1831

Clay County, Mo.
Liberty Jail
1838 - 1839

Omaha, Neb.
Winter Quarters 1846 - 1848

St. George, Ut.
-Brigham Young Winter Home
1869 - 1877
-St. George Tabernacle
1875-

Cove Fort, Ut.
1867

Salt Lake City, Ut.
-Temple Square 1847-
-Beehive House 1854 - 1877

Santa Clara, Ut.
Jacob Hamblin Home
1863 - 1869

San Diego, Ca.
Mormon Battalion
Duty Station
1847-1848

in the greater area. The Church has obtained a number of the buildings and sites owned by early members in Nauvoo and has restored or reconstructed them to show what life was like for the Saints in Nauvoo.

Near Nauvoo is the town of Carthage, the county seat for Hancock County. Here Joseph Smith was imprisoned on June 25, 1844, and murdered by a mob on June 27. Nauvoo and CARTHAGE JAIL are supervised by the Illinois Peoria Mission and full-time missionaries staff them.

Following the martyrdom, the Saints, under the direction of Brigham YOUNG, left Nauvoo in the winter of 1846, founding a number of temporary settlements en route to the West. WINTER QUARTERS, Nebraska (now Florence, a suburb of Omaha), on the west bank of the Missouri River, and Kanesville, Iowa (now COUNCIL BLUFFS), on the east bank, were the locations of a large settlement in the fall and winter of 1846–1847, remaining there until 1852. The Winter Quarters cemetery is all that remains of this historical site today.

The MORMON TRAIL to Utah has a number of monuments and historic sites. Salt Lake City has numerous historical sites. Temple Square with the temple, tabernacle, assembly hall, and visitors center is the most visited site in the Church. Other sites include "THIS IS THE PLACE" MONUMENT, the Beehive and Lion houses built and occupied by Brigham Young, and the nearby cemetery with his grave.

The Church also maintains three historic sites in St. George, Utah: the Brigham Young winter home, representing the LDS expansion southward along the valleys of the Intermountain West; the St. George Tabernacle, an epitome of the construction of large assembly halls in the major communities settled by Latter-day Saints; and the St. George Temple, the first temple completed in Utah. The temple's dedication in 1877 demonstrated the commitment of the Latter-day Saints to temple work and to establishing permanent communities in the Intermountain West. It is an important example of LDS architecture of the period. And in nearby Santa Clara stands the home of Jacob Hamblin, one of the earliest missionaries to the Indians in southern Utah.

These and other historic sites serve as reminders of the humble yet extraordinary beginnings of

Visitors center and monument near Sharon, Vermont, at the birthplace of the Prophet Joseph Smith. The obelisk rises 38.5 feet—one foot for each year of Joseph Smith's life. This cottage and monument were dedicated on December 23, 1905, the centennial anniversary of the Prophet's birth. Courtesy University of Utah.

the Church and of the sacrifices made by those individuals who committed their lives to follow its teachings.

BIBLIOGRAPHY

Burton, Alma P. *Mormon Trail from Vermont to Utah: A Guide to Historical Places of The Church of Jesus Christ of Latter-day Saints.* Salt Lake City, 1966.

Kimball, Stanley B. *Historic Sites and Markers Along the Mormon and Other Great Western Trails.* Urbana, Ill., 1988.

Oscarson, R. Don, and Stanley B. Kimball. *The Travellers' Guide to Historic Mormon America.* Salt Lake City, 1990, revised.

RICHARD H. JACKSON

HISTORY, SIGNIFICANCE TO LATTER-DAY SAINTS

History plays a vital role in LDS thought, where it joins with theology and practical religion to answer many of life's questions and to make daily life meaningful, intelligible, and worthwhile. God is seen as actively achieving his ultimate purposes

---

←— Church historical sites with visitors centers, 1990.

through events that make up history, while simultaneously allowing individuals the choice of working for or against his purposes.

Although Latter-day Saints do not have an officially stated philosophy of history, several basic ideas in LDS theology establish the significance of history.

1.   First is the nature of mankind. As God's literal spirit offspring, humans partake of divine attributes and destiny; they have the potential to attain GODHOOD. On the other hand, humanity is fallen and has become "carnal, sensual, and devilish" (Moses 5:13), with capacities for evil and degradation comparable with those of the devil himself. Hence, there is dramatic interest among Latter-day Saints in the broadest spectrum of human thoughts, words, and deeds.

2.   Second is an unequivocally positive commitment to life in this world (see PURPOSE OF EARTH LIFE). In LDS thought, a seamless web of individual being extends back in time to a self-conscious pre-earth life, and forward to the possibility and hope of eternal life in the presence of God. Prior choices and God's purposes have determined one's presence and place in this life; and, to a large extent, present choices will determine one's eternal future. In axioms such as "Men are, that they might have joy" (2 Ne. 2:25), LDS doctrine emphasizes the significance and goodness of the historical experience.

3.   Human freedom is required. In order to preserve human AGENCY, God does not break "across the line of history through the instrumentality of unmerited love," but he participates "in the historical process by inspiring men and co-operating with them in their efforts to improve the world's conditions" (Boyd, pp. 450, 453). Thus, God "directs and influences" the historical process, but he also respects the "centrality of freedom" for his children, something to which he is committed "partly by his nature and partly by his will" (Poll, pp. 33, 35).

4.   History itself is part of eternal truth. "Truth is knowledge of things as they are, and as they were, and as they are to come" (D&C 93:24; cf. 88:79). Thus, written records (including sacred histories) can encompass only a small portion of eternal reality, and even under optimum circumstances are incomplete and imperfect.

The LDS idea of history has much in common with that of Jews and Christians who believe in the living God-who-acts-in-history. Latter-day Saints view human history as the unfolding of God's plan of salvation for mankind (*Heilsgeschichte*), a view that dominated Western civilization until the eighteenth century. They generally agree with the traditional linear concept of history laid down in Augustine's *City of God*, although they place the eventual divine society on this earth (in a glorified and eternal physical state), not in an otherworldly dimension.

LDS faith is intertwined with historical events. Latter-day Saints essentially believe the literal biblical account of God's direct role in the Creation and of the fall of Adam and Eve—the proof of human freedom. A series of gospel DISPENSATIONS then unfolded. In each dispensation God's plan for mankind was revealed, only to be rejected eventually by chosen, but backsliding, human beings. The supreme set of events in history is the birth, ministry, death, and resurrection of Jesus Christ. This quintessentially Christian philosophy reaches its culmination in a hope, confidence, and preparation for Jesus' literal second coming, marking the end of this phase of the world's history. Latter-day Saints believe in a Christ-centered history and find power and reassurance in the fact that Jesus Christ became a real, historic person who endured mortality and its trials (Heb. 4:15–16). They add other elements to the Savior's historical reality. They believe that the resurrected Jesus appeared among the people of the Book of Mormon, and that God the Father and Jesus Christ appeared to Joseph SMITH in 1820 to open the last dispensation when the fulness of the gospel will be taught to all of the nations and people.

The foundations of the Church are grounded in a series of historic events, without which the Restoration would be incomprehensible and impotent. Joseph Smith recorded many visions and he received the gold plates from the angel Moroni, from which he translated the Book of Mormon. There followed many revelations to Joseph Smith and to the prophets who have succeeded him, revealing doctrines and applying eternal principles to existing historical and individual situations. That living prophets receive revelation from God, who is vitally interested in human needs in changing conditions, underscores the LDS view of God's continuing place in history.

That view is that God has played a role throughout ancient and modern history by foreordaining religious, political, scientific, and other leaders (e.g., Cyrus; see Isa. 44:28; Jer. 1:5). The great reformers (Luther, Calvin, Knox), discoverers such as COLUMBUS, and the authors of the CONSTITUTION OF THE UNITED STATES OF AMERICA were foreordained to prepare the way for the Restoration and to establish a new nation "conceived in liberty" that, like ancient Israel, was not chosen for special privilege but was to be a blessing to all mankind (Petersen, pp. 69–72; Backman, p. 724). This view was summarized by President Ezra Taft BENSON: "God, the Father of us all, uses the men of the earth, especially good men, to accomplish his purposes" (*Ensign* 2 [July 1972]:59).

God's role in the mundane details of history may be less obvious but more frequent than thought. Elder Bruce R. McConkie declared that the real history of the world "will show God's dealings with men, [and] the place the gospel has played in the rise and fall of nations" (*MD*, 1958, p. 327). Still, the record is incomplete; many important issues about historical injustices and catastrophes are yet to be explained by the God who acts in history, and what is not yet fully known in the macrocosmic realm is often explained in the meaningful experiences of individual people. God knows and cares about each human being. As with the larger world, God intervenes in individual lives at decisive moments, but also recognizes human autonomy and leaves the majority of life's decisions to individual choice.

God's role in human history should not, however, be taken to the extreme. His foreknowledge does not require predestination. Foreordination means that in his wisdom and foreknowledge God has called an individual to a role in the human drama if that person chooses to fill it. To Latter-day Saints, history is a combination of God's direction (which is neither "coercive [n]or continuous" [Poll, p. 33]) and divine intervention when that is indispensable to his purposes, with broad freedom of choice for humans within God's expansive framework. In this large realm of human freedom, the panorama of history has taken place. Here, political, social, economic, psychological, and other such forces largely hold sway, and thus are essential in explaining human choices and actions.

This historical view became an integral part of early LDS theology, of Joseph Smith's personal mission, of his vision of the Church's mission throughout the world, and of the anticipated second coming of Jesus Christ. All of this may also account in part for the meticulous attention given to RECORD KEEPING in the Church and by the prophets (*see* HISTORY OF THE CHURCH; HISTORIANS). All members of the Church are encouraged to write personal JOURNALS and FAMILY HISTORIES, and to make them a part of their extended families' sacred possessions.

In recent years the recognition of the Church by historians and sociologists as a distinctive new religion has generated broader interest in the writing and understanding of its history. But the writing of general history, especially religious history, has always had its difficulties. Surviving documents are limited and often inconsistent. Spiritual experiences are often kept private, and primarily lend themselves only to spiritual verification. Memories and lore are selective and fallible. Purposes, needs, audiences, historical fashions, and professional methods change from one decade to the next.

Traditional LDS historians, following their Jewish and early Christian predecessors, have tended to focus heavily on the hand of God in writing about Church and world history. Their histories are generally descriptive and declarative, sympathetic to the historical figures, and written mainly to inspire and build faith. According to William Mulder, "No where in Mormon recordkeeping can [one] escape the teleological, the didactic, the eschatological" (p. 17).

This view is countered by other historians, such as Fawn M. Brodie, who explicitly rejected the prophetic truth claims of the LDS faith and interpreted Joseph Smith and the Restoration wholly on the basis of modern naturalistic, historicist, and psychoanalytic methods. Their objective is typically to provide causal explanations by emphasizing the human aspects while rejecting divine involvement.

Most recent LDS historical scholarship represents a wide and changing spectrum. There is, as Henry Bawden advised, room for a number of perspectives and purposes. On the one hand, there is "faithful history," as expressed by Richard L. Bushman and others, in which the historian has a responsibility not only to consider the divine role but also to lead the kind of life that will permit the discernment of God's influence. For others, strictly empirical social-scientific and historicist methods suffice. Most historians of "Mormonism," however, LDS and non-LDS alike, recognize that both secular factors and spiritual claims can be taken seriously, while at the same time adhering to traditional canons of historical scholarship and addressing historical questions raised by contemporary issues.

[See also Biography and Autobiography.]

BIBLIOGRAPHY

Backman, Milton V., Jr. "Preliminaries to the Restoration." IE 61 (Oct.-Nov. 1958):722–24, 769–71, 773, 846–54.

Boyd, George T. "God in History." IE 64 (June 1961):380–81, 449–57.

Bushman, Richard L. "Faithful History." Dialogue 4 (Winter 1969):11–25.

Mulder, William. "Mormon Angles of Historical Vision: Some Maverick Reflections." Journal of Mormon History 3 (1976):13–22.

Petersen, Mark E. The Great Prologue. Salt Lake City, 1975.

Poll, Richard D. History and Faith. Salt Lake City, 1989.

DOUGLAS F. TOBLER
S. GEORGE ELLSWORTH

HISTORY OF THE CHURCH

[This entry discusses the history of the Church in the following six periods:

    c. 1820–1831, Background, Founding, New York Period

    c. 1831–1844, Ohio, Missouri, and Nauvoo Periods

    c. 1844–1877, Exodus and Early Utah Periods

    c. 1878–1898, Late Pioneer Utah Period

    c. 1898–1945, Transitions: Early-Twentieth-Century Period

    c. 1945–1990, Post–World War II International Era Period

In addition, several other articles cover the history of the Church in the light of specific historical disciplines or approaches: see Doctrine: Meaning, Source, and History; Economic History; Intellectual History; Legal and Judicial History; Politics: Political History; Social and Cultural History; and Church of Jesus Christ of Latter-day Saints, The.

Bibliographic sources relevant to all of these periods are: James B. Allen and Glen M. Leonard, The Story of the Latter-day Saints, Salt Lake City, 1976; Leonard J. Arrington and Davis Bitton, The Mormon Experience, New York, 1979; Church Education System, History in the Fulness of Times, Salt Lake City, 1989; and Joseph Fielding Smith, Essentials in Church History, Salt Lake City, 1950.]

C. 1820–1831, BACKGROUND, FOUNDING, NEW YORK PERIOD

[For other articles pertaining to the main events in the first period of Church History, see also First Vision; Moroni, Visitations of; various entries listed under Book of Mormon; articles on the restoration of the Aaronic Priesthood, of the Melchizedek Priesthood, and Organization of the Church, 1830.

Early biographical information can be found in articles on the Smith Family Ancestors, Joseph Smith, Emma Smith, and several other members of the Smith Family, in addition to Martin Harris, Oliver Cowdery, David Whitmer, and Sidney Rigdon. For a listing of Mormon sites and communities of this period, see New York, Early LDS Sites in.]

The establishment of The Church of Jesus Christ of Latter-day Saints began in the 1820s with events that occurred primarily in New York State. The Prophet Joseph SMITH received his FIRST VISION in 1820, obtained the GOLD PLATES of the Book of Mormon from the hill Cumorah in 1827, received priesthood authority in 1829, and officially organized the Church on April 6, 1830. By the time the Church left New York for Ohio early in 1831, it was organized and its basic direction was clearly established.

In its formative years, the infant Church learned above all to depend on revelation for direction. Joseph Smith, young and relatively unschooled, did not pretend to work out the doctrines of the new Church by himself. Direct revelations from God led him step by step. Perhaps the most revolutionary idea in the Church is its belief in Christian revelation beyond the Bible. Latter-day Saints have never doubted the inspiration of the Bible; it has been an essential standard from the beginning (see BIBLE: LDS BELIEF IN). Their experience led them to realize, however, that God also spoke to prophets who were not included in that conventional canon of scripture: the Book of Mormon showed them this (2 Ne. 29:10–14), and they heard Joseph Smith speak with the same authority as biblical apostles and prophets. Consequently, Latter-day Saints began to think of revelation in a new way, and the principle of continuing revelation greatly disturbed their fellow Christians, but from the beginning nothing was more basic to the Church.

Church history sites near Palmyra, N.Y., 1820–1831.

ences from the Enlightenment made it more difficult to embrace religious faith than when Congregationalism had predominated in New England. Joseph Smith's quest for salvation began with the question of which Church is true. This question was possibly thrust upon him by his parents' uncertainties and by the plurality of churches—Presbyterian, Baptist, Methodist, Quaker—in his own village.

Moved by evangelical revivals, Joseph Smith asked for direction from God about the true religion in the early spring of 1820. Although only fourteen, he had confidence in the biblical promise that he could get an answer (James 1:5). He went into the woods near his home, kneeled down, and prayed. In his accounts of the event, he testifies that the answer he received astonished him. Both God the Father and Jesus Christ appeared and told him to join none of the existing churches. He was assured that he was in good standing with God, told many things he could not write about, and then the vision closed, leaving him overcome. This revelation of the Father and the Son is considered by Latter-day Saints to be the opening event in the RESTORATION of the gospel.

For three and a half years Joseph received no further communication from the heavens. Wondering if he had disqualified himself through unworthiness, Joseph was praying on the evening of

Path leading from the Smith home to an area known as the Sacred Grove, south of Palmyra, New York. Photographed c. 1907. Photographer: George E. Anderson. Courtesy Nelson Wadsworth.

The history of the Church begins with the family of Joseph SMITH, Sr., and Lucy Mack SMITH, the Prophet's parents (see SMITH FAMILY), who, with thousands of other New Englanders, flooded into New York in the early nineteenth century looking for better land. They brought with them their Calvinist religious intensity, but with a zeal modified by the new conditions of life in republican and pluralistic America. They had long searched without success for a faith on which they could rely. The increasing number of Christian denominations and a host of new intellectual influ-

Church history sites in western New York, 1820–1831.

September 21, 1823, when to his astonishment, an angel appeared in the room and announced that he was MORONI and had come with instructions from God. He told Joseph about a record written on gold plates giving a history of the former inhabitants of the western continents. The resurrected Savior, Jesus Christ, had appeared to these people and had given them the fulness of the gospel. The angel said the plates were buried in a hill near Joseph's home. In the course of the night, the angel came three times, delivering the same basic message and adding a little more information each time. Although exhausted, Joseph went to the hill the next day and found the plates encased in a stone box just below the surface of the earth; but he was not allowed to remove them. The angel appeared again and told him he must come back again the following year on the same day, September 22. For the next four years, Joseph faithfully returned to that place in the same manner. Fi-

E. B. Grandin Press, on which pages of the first edition of the Book of Mormon were printed, August 1829 to March 1830, in Palmyra, New York.

nally, on September 22, 1827, he was allowed to take the plates into his possession (*see* MORONI, VISITATIONS OF).

The events of the four-year interval between 1823 and 1827 doubtless helped Joseph Smith to mature in preparation for the responsibilities and challenges that subsequently came to him. There is some evidence that his father was involved in treasure hunting, a common activity among poor New England farmers who hoped through the use of magic to discover buried money, and it was necessary for Joseph to extricate himself from the mistaken notions of that superstition. The angel told Joseph that one of the reasons for the delay in giving him the gold plates was that he had dwelt on their monetary worth (*PWJS*, p. 7). In November 1825, Joseph and his father worked briefly with a man named Josiah Stowell of SOUTH BAINBRIDGE (AFTON), NEW YORK, who believed a Spanish treasure was located in HARMONY, PENNSYLVANIA, near the Susquehannah River. The project failed, and the Smiths gradually separated themselves from the money-digging activities of their neighbors to concentrate on the religious mission described by the angel. As a happy outgrowth of the Harmony project, while working there Joseph met Emma Hale (*see* SMITH, EMMA HALE), whom he married on January 18, 1827. In the meantime, his older brother Alvin died; Joseph was arrested in 1826 as

a "glass looker" under a New York law that made it a crime "to tell fortunes, or where lost or stolen goods may be found" (see the legal definition of "Disorderly Persons," *The Justice's Manual*, Albany, New York, 1829, p. 144; *see also* SMITH JOSEPH: LEGAL TRIALS OF); and his parents lost their farm through their inability to make the last mortgage payment. These misfortunes, along with other experiences, deepened and strengthened the young man as he learned to discern between good and evil and to endure opposition.

After Joseph obtained the plates in 1827, curious and sometimes malicious neighbors in Manchester and Palmyra, New York, made it impossible to begin work on the translation. They ransacked the Smith house and barn, and only by constantly moving and concealing the plates could he keep them safe. He had been strictly warned

An early oil painting of the Prophet Joseph Smith (1805–1844). People who knew Joseph Smith personally commented that no picture could do him justice, for when he spoke compassion and power were evident, sometimes to the point that his countenance became visibly radiant. Artist unknown. Courtesy Library-Archives, Reorganized Church of Jesus Christ of Latter Day Saints.

not to show them to anyone, but that did not satisfy the curiosity seekers. Emma's brother, Alva, offered to help; he transported the pair with their belongings and the plates—hidden in a barrel of beans—125 miles to Harmony, Pennsylvania, where Emma's father lived. Joseph procured some acreage from his father-in-law, Isaac Hale, and a small house was provided. It was here that the translation began (*see* BOOK OF MORMON TRANSLATION BY JOSEPH SMITH).

A sympathetic neighbor from Palmyra, Martin HARRIS, took enough interest in the plates to visit Joseph in Harmony. With the plates, Joseph had received an instrument called interpreters, or a URIM AND THUMMIM, that enabled him to translate the characters engraved on the metal tablets. Joseph made copies of a few characters for Martin to take to language experts in Albany and New York City to verify Joseph's work. There is some confusion about what happened in these interviews, but Martin Harris was unequivocally satisfied (*see* ANTHON TRANSCRIPT). When he returned to Harmony, he offered to take the dictation as Joseph translated. Between April 12 and June 14, 1828, the two of them completed 116 pages of manuscript. At this point, Harris, who suffered from his wife's doubts about the existence of the plates, asked permission to show the manuscript to her and four other family members. With great reluctance Joseph Smith agreed. After hearing nothing from Martin for a number of weeks, Joseph went to his parents home in Manchester, New York, to confront him. Martin despairingly confessed that he could not find the manuscript. He had succumbed to pressure, shown the manuscript to neighbors beyond his agreement, and someone had stolen it (*see* MANUSCRIPT, LOST 116 PAGES).

On the occasion of the crisis, Joseph received a revelation through the Urim and Thummim in which the Lord severely rebuked him. He more than Martin was held responsible for the loss of the manuscript. "Behold, you should not have feared man more than God," he was told (D&C 3:7). Martin did no more transcribing for Joseph, and from that time until the spring of 1829, Joseph accomplished little on the translation. In April, Oliver COWDERY, a young schoolteacher who had boarded with the Smith family in Manchester, came to learn more about the Book of Mormon. Having himself received a vision of the Lord and the plates, he was persuaded that the work was divine and offered to serve as scribe (*PWJS*, p. 8).

Beginning on April 7, 1829, the two, Joseph and Oliver, worked together almost constantly until the translation was completed in June, a little more than two months later.

In the course of translating a portion of 3 Nephi that described the manner of baptism, Joseph and Oliver wondered about their own need for baptism. As had become customary with Joseph, he sought instruction from God. On May 15, 1829, while he and Oliver prayed, a heavenly messenger appeared to them. Identifying himself as John the Baptist, he conferred on them the Aaronic Priesthood, which gave them the authority to baptize (*see* AARONIC PRIESTHOOD: RESTORATION). With that newly received authority and under the direction of the angel, the two men baptized each other in the Susquehannah River. This revelation established an important principle in the Church: that divine ORDINANCES such as baptism can be performed only by persons who have received priesthood authority by ordination. John the Baptist told Joseph and Oliver they would later receive a second and higher priesthood called the Melchizedek Priesthood. Subsequently Peter, James, and John appeared to them on the banks of the Susquehannah River some place between Harmony and Colesville, New York, and ordained them APOSTLES (*see* MELCHIZEDEK PRIESTHOOD: RESTORATION).

By late May 1829, religious opposition against Joseph was growing in Harmony, and he and Oliver needed a calmer place to work. Oliver wrote to a friend, David WHITMER, who agreed to move them to his family's farm in FAYETTE, NEW YORK. Emma joined them in Fayette shortly afterward. A copyright was obtained for the Book of Mormon on June 11, 1829, and the translation soon was completed. As they completed the book, Joseph Smith learned through revelation that others would be allowed to see the golden plates. Witnesses were promised in the Book of Mormon itself, and Joseph's associates were eager to know who would have the privilege. Martin Harris, David Whitmer, and Oliver Cowdery were chosen, shown the plates by the angel Moroni, and heard the voice of God declaring to them that the work had been translated by the power of God. A few days later at Manchester, Joseph Smith was permitted to show the plates to eight other men. They examined the plates closely and lifted them with their hands. The statements of these two sets of witnesses were printed in the back pages of the 1830 edition of the

Book of Mormon and appear in the front pages of all recent editions (see BOOK OF MORMON WITNESSES).

Finding a printer to publish the Book of Mormon proved to be difficult. Palmyra people who were suspicious of Joseph Smith banded together to intimidate the local printer, Egbert B. Grandin, by threatening not to purchase copies. Others, like Martin's wife, Lucy Harris, challenged Joseph's financial motives. After contacting printers as far away as Rochester, Joseph persuaded Grandin to accept the job. Martin Harris's guarantee made the difference in Grandin's decision. On August 25, 1829, Harris mortgaged his farm, pledging to pay $3,000 for 5,000 copies. Joseph and Martin hoped to sell enough copies to raise at least $3,000, but in the end Martin had to sell 151 acres to fulfill his agreement. Typesetting began in August 1829, and finished copies were available March 26, 1830.

Publication of the Book of Mormon brought to a close the endeavor that had occupied Joseph Smith since receiving the plates in 1827. Meanwhile, the revelations he was receiving made clear that translating the Book of Mormon was not the end of his divine mission. He was also to organize a church. Samuel Smith had been baptized in Harmony in late May 1829; Hyrum SMITH, David and Peter Whitmer, Jr., and others were baptized in June in Seneca Lake. They had begun meeting together, and they had taught and tried to persuade all who requested information. On April 6, 1830, in the house of Peter Whitmer, Sr., in Fayette, New York, Joseph Smith organized the Church of Jesus Christ (see ORGANIZATION OF THE CHURCH, 1830; NAME OF THE CHURCH). Six men subscribed as members, and over fifty people were present. The group sustained two officers as leaders of the Church, Joseph Smith as first elder and Oliver Cowdery as second elder. Joseph was also given the titles of SEER, translator, and PROPHET. In addition, a revelation made provision for ordaining ELDERS, PRIESTS, TEACHERS, and DEACONS as a lay priesthood (see DOCTRINE AND COVENANTS: SECTIONS 20–22). Some of the lay persons present at the organization were ordained that day, and from the start, the Church made no provision for a special clerical order (see LAY PARTICIPATION AND LEADERSHIP).

Three clusters of believers were organized into branches of the fledgling Church soon after its organization—one in Fayette; another in Manchester at the old Smith home; and a third in COLESVILLE in southern New York, which was near the farm of Josiah Stowell (in Bainbridge Township, Chenango County), Joseph's onetime employer and a loyal supporter. Members of the Joseph Knight family, who had provided Joseph and his assistants food and clothing during the translation, lived in Colesville and were the nucleus of the branch there. Joseph and Emma moved back to their house in Harmony, but met with all three branches at prescribed quarterly conferences held at the Peter Whitmer farm in June and September 1830.

In the summer of 1830, troubles began to arise. Twice Joseph was put on trial as a "disorderly person." Both times he was acquitted. More disturbing to Joseph, some of his own followers questioned his authority and claimed revelations and prerogatives of their own. Hiram Page, ordained a teacher in June 1830 and a husband of Catherine Whitmer, wrote out a sheaf of revelations he claimed came from God. Although still young and inexperienced, Joseph sensed the confusion and danger of many voices trying to speak authoritatively. At the September conference in Fayette, Joseph received a revelation that established that only one person approved by COMMON CONSENT was to receive commandments and revelations for the entire Church (D&C 20:65; 28:1–3, 11–13). Hiram Page lacked that authorization. After hearing Joseph, the conference confirmed him as sole revelator for the Church (D&C 28:2; D. Cannon and L. Cook, eds., *Far West Record*, Salt Lake City, 1983, p. 3). This principle of revelation for the whole Church coming through the man sustained as the Prophet remains a practice of the Church to this day.

In the six months after the organization of the Church, converts were added in small numbers. Joseph Smith's brother Samuel went out with copies of the Book of Mormon to share with anyone interested. Joseph Smith, Sr., visited his brothers, sisters, and parents in St. Lawrence County, New York, where most of them lived, to tell them what had happened. Later conversions resulted from these expeditions, but very few at the time. Parley P. Pratt, a farmer from Ohio, believed that God led him to the house of Hyrum Smith, Joseph's brother, to find out about the Book of Mormon.

The most successful early missionary venture was launched in September and October 1830, when Oliver Cowdery, Peter Whitmer, Jr., Parley PRATT, and Ziba Peterson were called to teach the Indians (see LAMANITE MISSION). The Book of Mormon had special relevance for NATIVE AMERICANS because it was a religious record from ancient America, and the four were charged to take this message to the Indians who were assembling in the territory west of Missouri. The mission was notable as much for what was accomplished en route, however, as for the preaching to the Indians. After leaving New York, the missionaries stopped in the Mentor-Kirtland area of northeast Ohio near Pratt's former farm. Before joining the Church, Pratt had been associated with the Campbellite movement, which was forming into the Disciples of Christ church. This group believed in rigorously adhering to the teachings and practices of the New Testament church, sloughing off all later additions. The teachings of Joseph Smith appealed to many of them because his doctrines embodied for them a pure restoration of true Christianity. About 130 persons were converted, including the leading Campbellite preacher in the area, Sidney RIGDON. In a few weeks, the four missionaries nearly doubled the membership of the Church. They continued on to Indian country that winter, enduring severe hardships on their long trek on foot from St. Louis across Missouri. They found a land in western Missouri into which the Church would soon begin settling. They also taught among the Delaware and Shawnee Indians until government officials told them to stop because of a prohibition against proselytizing among the tribes.

Soon after the missionaries left Ohio for the West in December 1830, Sidney Rigdon left for New York, accompanied by Edward Partridge. They brought news of the conversions in Ohio and urged Joseph Smith and the membership to move there. Joseph was prepared to take the suggestion seriously because of revelations he received concerning the gathering of the Church (D&C 37:1–4; 38:31–33). Indeed, for the remainder of the century, converts to the Church would assemble at a central gathering place, first in Ohio, then in Missouri, in Illinois, and finally in Utah. Another revelation focused on the second coming of Jesus Christ and on the destructions to be visited upon the world before that event occurred. It said that before those tribulations, the people of God were to "be gathered in unto one place upon the face of this land" (D&C 29:8). A further revelation spoke of a city of ZION to be built somewhere in the West (D&C 28:9). These hints led Church members to realize that they would not remain long in New York.

When a revelation came in December 1830 (D&C 37) telling them to move to Ohio, it was accepted by most. At a conference on January 2, 1831, directions and an additional revelation (D&C 38) were given for the move. The Prophet, Emma, and a few others went ahead and arrived in KIRTLAND on February 1, 1831, to prepare for the arrival of others. The Colesville Branch, under Newel Knight; the Fayette Branch, under the Prophet's mother and Thomas Marsh; and the Manchester Branch, under Martin Harris, traveled to Ohio in separate companies during April and May 1831. By mid-May virtually all of the New York Mormons from the named branches were in Kirtland.

BIBLIOGRAPHY

Backman, Milton V., Jr. *Eyewitness Accounts of the Restoration*, rev. ed. Salt Lake City, 1986.

Bushman, Richard L. *Joseph Smith and the Beginnings of Mormonism*. Urbana, Ill., 1984.

Madsen, Truman, G., guest ed. *BYU Studies* 9 (Spring 1969):235–404 (entire issue devoted to LDS origins in New York).

Porter, Larry C. "A Study of the Origins of The Church of Jesus Christ of Latter-day Saints in the States of New York and Pennsylvania, 1816–1831." Ph.D. diss., Brigham Young University, 1971.

Smith, Lucy Mack. *History of Joseph Smith*, ed. Preston Nibley. Salt Lake City, 1958.

Whittaker, David J. "Sources on Mormon Origins in New York and Pennsylvania." *Mormon History Association Newsletter* no. 43 (Mar. 1980):8–12.

RICHARD L. BUSHMAN
LARRY C. PORTER

C. 1831–1844, OHIO, MISSOURI, AND NAUVOO PERIODS

[*This article focuses first on the Church in northeastern Ohio, where Kirtland served as Church headquarters, and in western Missouri. By 1839 the focus shifts to western Illinois, with Nauvoo the new headquarters city. For discussion of the difficulties that led to violence and finally expulsion from Missouri, see* Missouri Conflict.

This article outlines organizational and doctrinal developments and examines tensions and conflicts between the Saints and their neighbors, and within the Church itself. Many of these resulted from the attempt to build a tightly unified, sacral community that responded to continuing revelation within a larger society often hostile to these goals. The Prophet Joseph Smith, whose martyrdom ends this period, was a dominant figure; see articles under Smith, Joseph, *and* Visions of Joseph Smith. *The* Gathering *and* Temples *were central concerns; see* Kirtland Temple *and* Nauvoo Temple.]

In October 1830 four LDS missionaries on their way to preach to the Indians west of Missouri (*see* LAMANITE MISSION) introduced the restored gospel to the communities of northeastern Ohio. Before they resumed their journey, the missionaries baptized approximately 130 converts, organized the new members into small "branches," and appointed leaders over each group. Approximately thirty-five of these members lived in Kirtland, Ohio, a community directly east of what is today metropolitan Cleveland.

Sidney RIGDON, a restorationist preacher in that vicinity, joined the Church in November 1830 and notified Joseph Smith of the missionaries' success. As a result, the Prophet inquired of the Lord and recorded revelations (D&C 37:3; 38:32) calling the converts of the recently organized Church in New York to "assemble together at the Ohio." He and his family moved to Kirtland by early February 1831, and about two hundred New York Saints followed by summer, making northeastern Ohio the first LDS gathering place.

Most of the New York Saints and many of the earliest Ohio converts did not remain in Ohio. In the summer of 1831, Joseph Smith traveled to the Missouri frontier and identified Independence, Jackson County, Missouri, as a second gathering place. Latter-day Saints anticipated that a holy city, a NEW JERUSALEM, would be established in a new North American ZION, a city of refuge from tribulations that would afflict the wicked in the last days (D&C 29:7–9; 45:65–71; 57:1–3). Sidney Rigdon dedicated the land for gathering, and Joseph Smith designated the specific site where a temple would be built, and, after appointing others to supervise the gathering to Zion, returned to Ohio.

In HIRAM, OHIO, a rural farming community about thirty miles south of Kirtland, Joseph Smith worked on his inspired translation of the Bible (*see* JOSEPH SMITH TRANSLATION OF THE BIBLE [JST]), a project that served him as a school. Prayerfully seeking enlightenment about particular passages and doctrines frequently brought new revelation and understanding. After the Prophet and Sidney Rigdon, who was serving as his scribe, were beaten and tarred and feathered by a mob in March 1832, they and their families moved to Kirtland.

The two gathering places of the early 1830s each had a different purpose. Although Latter-day Saints migrated to the Missouri frontier to lay the foundations of a new Zion, the administrative headquarters of the Church, responsible for directing the missionary program and building the first temple, remained in Ohio. There was some competition between the two centers, with both needing resources and members and both wanting the presence of the Prophet Joseph Smith. But, as revelation made clear, the goals of the two were complementary: the promised "endowment from on high" associated with the KIRTLAND TEMPLE was a prerequisite for success in Zion (D&C 105:9–13, 33). Joseph Smith resided in Kirtland until 1838, keeping in touch with Missouri members by mail and messenger, and traveling there five times to instruct Church members on policies, programs, and beliefs.

In Jackson County, Latter-day Saints published two periodicals, the EVENING AND THE MORNING STAR and the *Upper Missouri Advertiser*, and attempted to establish a unique economic order based on CONSECRATION with assigned stewardship of property and other assets, as directed by revelations to Joseph Smith (*see* MISSOURI: LDS COMMUNITIES IN JACKSON AND CLAY COUNTIES). Disagreements about legal requirements and individual selfishness hampered implementation, but the basic impediment was that the Saints had too little capital and very little to consecrate. Still, some participants were inspired by the concepts involved, and the ideals behind the effort left a significant legacy (*see* UNITED ORDERS).

Although the Latter-day Saints migrated to western Missouri to build a city of peace and refuge, they encountered major hostility. Older settlers considered these newcomers a threat to their own patterns of living. Missourians complained that Mormons sought to influence slaves, that their "eastern" lifestyle was incompatible with the Missouri frontier, that they were an economic and political threat, that their friendship for the Indians threatened the region's security, and that they held unusual religious beliefs. These charges indicate a significant cultural clash between the LDS immigrants and older settlers. Rapid immigration of Latter-day Saints into Jackson County intensified the tensions, resulting in confrontation.

After violence erupted in the summer of 1833, Governor Daniel Dunklin sent a local militia into the area to establish peace. Assuming that the militia would protect all settlers, Latter-day Saints surrendered their arms to this military force. But other Missourians were not disarmed, leaving Church members defenseless. In early November 1833, mobs drove more than a thousand Latter-day Saints from Jackson County, forcing them to aban-

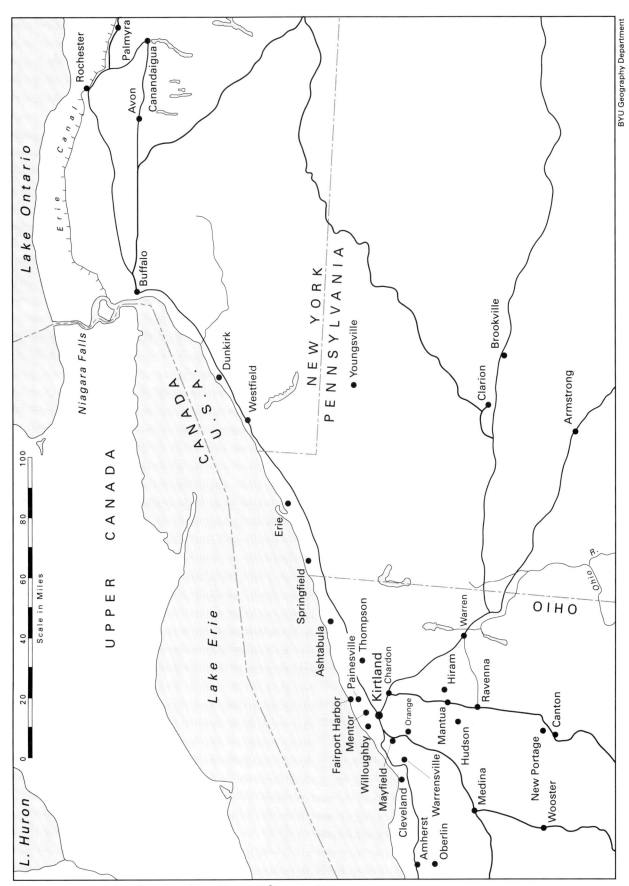

Western New York and eastern Ohio. Towns and routes, 1831.

BYU Geography Department

Overview of LDS historical sites, 1805–1900.

BYU Geography Department

Kirtland Temple, dedicated 1836. Building the Kirtland Temple was of central importance to the Saints in the mid-1830s, so that they could receive there the promised blessings from on high before taking the gospel to the ends of the earth. Photographed c. 1900. Courtesy Rare Books and Manuscripts, Brigham Young University.

deal, they had not assisted the Missouri Saints to return to their lands. They found fault with Joseph Smith's leadership, and the experience contributed to their later dissent. But for many participants, Zion's Camp was an unparalleled opportunity to live day and night with the Lord's prophet—reminiscent of ancient Israel under Moses. The experience bonded them to Joseph and to each other, and out of the crucible of Zion's Camp came many future LDS leaders. The two reactions reflected differing views about prophetic leadership and about how a society based on revelation and priesthood should be organized—differences that became more pronounced in later Kirtland.

The revelation disbanding Zion's Camp refocused attention on Ohio and on the necessity of completing the Kirtland Temple without delay (D&C 105). Before returning to Ohio, Joseph Smith organized a Missouri STAKE and appointed a presidency and HIGH COUNCIL, matching what he had done in Kirtland the February before. Soon, several Missouri Church leaders left for Kirtland to assist with temple construction.

All parties concerned had viewed the Saints' stay in Clay County, Missouri, as temporary. With a return to Jackson County now unlikely, pressures

don their homes and farms. Most of them escaped across the Missouri River to Clay County.

Between November 1833 and the summer of 1836, Clay County was the major gathering place for Latter-day Saints in Missouri. During these years, Church members tried but failed to secure redress for the loss of property in Jackson County. They also sought government protection for an attempt to return to their lands. In 1834, believing that Governor Dunklin had agreed to extend the assistance of state militia to reinforce their own efforts, Church members assembled a small paramilitary force from Ohio and elsewhere to accompany the Missouri refugees back to Jackson County. ZION'S CAMP, as the expedition was called, failed to obtain gubernatorial support and disbanded in June rather than initiate armed conflict.

Though it failed in its primary aim, Zion's Camp profoundly affected many participants and had lasting significance. For most, the hurried march from Ohio to Missouri, more than 800 miles in humid heat, was the most difficult physical challenge of their lives. Some had even greater difficulty with the realization that in spite of that or-

Joseph Smith's red brick store (1885; built, 1841; restored, 1978–1979) was an important building during the Nauvoo period. It was a center of social, economic, political, and religious activity. Joseph Smith's office and meeting room on the second floor became the headquarters of the Church, and the first endowments were given there. In 1842, the Relief Society was organized there. B. H. Roberts collection.

mounted for them to find another location. Urged by community leaders to leave before violence erupted, most Latter-day Saints migrated northward, establishing a new western headquarters at Far West, Missouri. Responding to this movement of thousands of Latter-day Saints into unsettled northwestern Missouri, the state legislature in late 1836 created two new counties, Caldwell and Daviess (*see* MISSOURI: LDS COMMUNITIES IN CALDWELL AND DAVIESS COUNTIES). Since most Latter-day Saints settled in Caldwell, it became known as the Mormon County.

Joseph Smith later taught that a primary purpose for the gathering of the faithful in any age was to build a house of the Lord wherein could be revealed the ordinances of his temple. As temple construction progressed, the LDS population in Kirtland multiplied from about 100 in 1832 to over 1,500 in 1836. Latter-day Saints migrated there from New England, New York, and elsewhere to assist in building the Lord's house, in which, they had been promised as early as January 1831, they would be "endowed with power from on high" (D&C 38:32).

In March 1836 the Kirtland Temple was completed and dedicated, and during the months before and after the dedication, the Saints enjoyed an unusual pentecostal season. In the temple, a week after its dedication, KEYS OF THE PRIESTHOOD were conferred on Joseph Smith and Oliver COWDERY in visitations by MOSES, ELIAS, and ELIJAH. Blessings and instructions received in the temple were particularly significant for missionaries (*see* MISSION), whose proselytizing travels from Kirtland during the 1830s ranged from Canada to the American South and, in 1837, to the British Isles, with extensive missionary work within Ohio.

While its headquarters remained in Kirtland, the Church experienced major doctrinal and administrative development. A number of the most significant revelations in the Doctrine and Covenants were received in the Kirtland and Hiram areas, including the vision of the Resurrection and the three DEGREES OF GLORY (D&C 76); the law of consecration and stewardship (D&C 42); the WORD OF WISDOM, sometimes called the Lord's law of health (D&C 89); revelations on the PRIESTHOOD and its organization (D&C 84, 107); and the coming of the MILLENNIUM (D&C 1, 29, 88, 133). Many of these revelations came in response to questions raised by Joseph Smith's translation of the Bible. Joseph Smith also received a revelation

relating to PLURAL MARRIAGE (D&C 132), but it was not recorded until 1843. The BOOK OF ABRAHAM, not published until 1842, resulted from the Prophet's acquisition in 1835 of a collection of mummies and PAPYRI from Egypt.

As growth required organizational development, a series of revelations directed the establishment of both local and general Church officers. These included the office of BISHOP in 1831, the FIRST PRESIDENCY of the Church in 1832, and a permanent HIGH COUNCIL in 1834. In February 1835 the QUORUM OF THE TWELVE APOSTLES and the Quorum of the SEVENTY were organized, selected principally from Zion's Camp veterans. Both quorums had responsibility for proselytizing. Though the Twelve were spoken of as second to the Presidency, their immediate assignments were to supervise the labors of the Seventy and to oversee the Church outside its organized stakes.

Revelation also directed officers of the Church to study widely in many fields of knowledge in preparation for their ministries and directed that a SCHOOL OF THE PROPHETS be organized for that purpose (D&C 88:77–80, 118–41). The attitudes and imperatives expressed in the revelation became influential not only in instituting that first Church-sponsored school but also in the Church's approach to learning and education throughout its subsequent history.

Publication of the *Evening and the Morning Star*, disrupted in Missouri by the expulsion from Jackson County, was resumed for nearly a year in Kirtland. The *Latter Day Saints'* MESSENGER AND ADVOCATE, successor to the *Star*, was the first Church periodical to publish some of Oliver Cowdery's letters dealing with the history of Joseph Smith. The Doctrine and Covenants, containing many of the revelations given to Joseph Smith, was published in Kirtland in 1835.

The promulgation of new doctrine and the establishment of a church hierarchy offended some Latter-day Saints who preferred the less complicated faith they had embraced in the Church's infancy. Those who did not share the Prophet Joseph Smith's vision of a new society organized under priesthood were also disturbed by the increased direction Church leaders gave members in temporal matters and by the Prophet's extensive involvement in economic affairs. The collapse of an unchartered Kirtland Safety Society that had been sponsored by Church leaders helped bring discontent to a head (*see* KIRTLAND ECONOMY). Lawsuits

Joseph Smith Directing the Nauvoo Legion, by John Hafen (1887, oil on canvas, 19″ × 25″). Joseph Smith in Nauvoo, with the Nauvoo Temple in the background (completed after his death). Joseph Smith was the central religious and political leader of the LDS community in Nauvoo, Illinois, and commander of the Nauvoo Legion. Courtesy Utah State Historical Society.

were filed against Joseph Smith, threats were made against his life, and against the lives of his most vigorous supporters, and a number of prominent Church members apostatized. In the midst of this turmoil, the Prophet sent some of his staunchest supporters as missionaries to the British Isles. There, in less than a year, they gained more than 1,500 converts and laid the groundwork for thousands more to follow (*see* MISSIONS OF THE TWELVE TO BRITISH ISLES).

By 1837, Latter-day Saints outnumbered other residents of Kirtland Township. That year, LDS candidates were elected to all major town offices except that of constable. Many Church members in Kirtland were relatively poor and lived in clusters of small temporary homes. Some non-Mormons became resentful of this influx of the poor and of Church leadership that seemed undemocratic and thus un-American. Economic and political rivalries developed, accompanied by

threats and some mob violence. Outside pressure mounted for the removal of the Mormons from Kirtland at the same time as bitter internal dissension plagued the Church. In January 1838, Joseph Smith, Sidney Rigdon, and other Church leaders whose lives had been threatened fled to western Missouri, followed gradually by most of the Latter-day Saint residents of Kirtland and vicinity.

In 1837–1838, LDS migration into western Missouri increased rapidly. This growth sparked increased agitation among neighbors who feared Mormon economic and political domination and who saw the influx as a threat to their way of life. Grievances that had been expressed by Jackson County citizens in 1833 were repeated and enlarged. Rumors and accusations became the basis for intolerant actions. Some insisted that since Caldwell County had been created for Mormons, Latter-day Saints were not to settle outside the borders of that county.

A daguerreotype of the Nauvoo Temple (c. 1846). The Latter-day Saints worked to complete this building and receive the ordinances of the temple before they left Nauvoo for the West. The temple was completed in 1846, burned by an arsonist in 1848, largely demolished by a tornado in 1850, and completely leveled in 1856 for safety reasons.

The decisive confrontation was sparked by a fight that erupted when ruffians attempted to prevent LDS voting at Gallatin, Daviess County. Exaggerated reports of this melee unloosed agitation that had been mounting and led to the formation of mobs determined to drive all Mormons from Daviess County. Mobs also threatened Latter-day Saints living in DeWitt, Carroll County, until, on October 11, 1838, they were forced to leave their homes and farms. As the refugees traveled to the LDS stronghold at Far West, they were continually harassed and several died.

After Governor Lilburn Boggs refused pleas to protect the DeWitt Saints, Church leaders mobilized the Caldwell County militia and prepared to protect themselves. Some members of the DANITES, originally organized to assist with Latter-day Saint community development, engaged in paramilitary activity, including burning the headquarters of mobbers at Gallatin and Millport who had threatened their destruction. Meanwhile, a local militia forced Latter-day Saints to leave their farms in Ray County and threatened to shoot Church members accused of being spies. Trying to prevent the threatened executions, a unit of the LDS Caldwell County militia engaged the Ray militia on October 25 at Crooked River. Men were killed on both sides, and wildly exaggerated rumors of marauding Mormons enflamed the countryside. On October 27, without investigating the charges and countercharges, Governor Boggs accused Church members of initiating hostilities and ordered the state militia to exterminate the Mormons or drive them from the state (see EXTERMINATION ORDER). Three days later, the HAUN'S MILL MASSACRE, in which more than two hundred militiamen attacked a tiny LDS settlement and brutally killed seventeen, underscored the likelihood that Boggs's order would be carried out literally.

Confronted by overwhelming militia forces, the Latter-day Saints surrendered at Far West and agreed to leave the state. Approximately 10,000 Church members were forced to leave Missouri, most in winter and amid intense hostility. Traveling eastward, they crossed the Mississippi River into Illinois. After suffering immense losses of property and some loss of life, in early 1839 most reached Quincy and other western Illinois communities whose residents offered aid and refuge.

Meanwhile, Church leaders in Missouri were arrested and charged with treason. Most were promptly released, but ten were imprisoned without trial during the winter of 1838–1839, some in RICHMOND JAIL and others in LIBERTY JAIL. During the Prophet Joseph's half-year stay in Liberty Jail, he wrote some of the most insightful and eloquent inspired writings of his career (D&C 121–23), and he emerged in April 1839 with a clear understanding of what must be done to complete his mission satisfactorily and a firm determination to do so.

The Saints arranged to purchase land for a new gathering place on both sides of a bend in the Mississippi River north of Quincy. Nauvoo, Illinois, superseded the fledgling community of Commerce and became Church headquarters. Many members also settled across the river in Lee County, Iowa.

Plagued by malaria, Nauvoo-area Saints sought to confront larger issues while still struggling to establish a viable community after the Missouri disaster. Attempting to obtain redress for Missouri losses, President Joseph Smith visited national political leaders in Washington, D.C., but the prevailing emphasis on states' rights precluded federal assistance. Despite illness and poverty, nine members of the Quorum of the Twelve Apostles fulfilled an assignment to proselytize in the British Isles. They arrived in England in early 1840 and during the next fifteen months saw nearly 5,000 converts join the approximately 1,500 they found on arrival. The following year, Orson Hyde, an apostle, visited Jerusalem and dedicated Palestine for the gathering of the Jews (see ISRAEL: GATHERING OF ISRAEL).

In England the Twelve launched the *Latter Day Saints' Millennial Star* and published a hymnal and a second edition of the Book of Mormon, founding in the process what became a major LDS publication center for the next half century. The Twelve initiated the emigration of LDS British converts to America in 1840, and during the next six years nearly 5,000 migrated to Nauvoo (see IMMIGRATION AND EMIGRATION). Under the leadership of Brigham Young, the Quorum of the Twelve became an effective administrative force during this mission. When they returned to Nauvoo, they were given new responsibilities. In August 1841, Joseph Smith announced that the Twelve now stood "next to the First Presidency," and their jurisdiction was expanded to include supervision of the Church's stakes as well as mission areas.

Draining the swamps and welcoming a growing number of settlers, the Saints in Nauvoo created a thriving community that eventually numbered nearly 12,000, rivaling Chicago as the largest city in Illinois. Construction and growth fueled the economy, cultural life thrived, and the Saints developed the most important religious community of their short history. Having learned from experience that they could not rely on the goodwill of others for protection, they sought institutional guarantees. In the NAUVOO CHARTERS the Illinois state legislature provided the protections of home rule, a municipal judiciary, and a city militia. Determined never again to be defenseless as they had been in Missouri, they built their chartered NAUVOO LEGION into the largest militia in Illinois.

To an unusual degree, Joseph Smith occupied a position of political as well as ecclesiastical power, serving at various times as city councilman, mayor, commanding general of the Nauvoo Legion, and editor of the leading local newspaper, the *Times and Seasons*. These positions gave him wide latitude to build a sacral society and to accomplish the things he felt most central to his mission.

After receiving additional priesthood keys in the Kirtland Temple in 1836, Joseph Smith looked to the day when he could complete his temple-related responsibilities and convey additional teachings and ordinances to the Saints. He emerged from Liberty Jail convinced that his time to do so was short and that Nauvoo would be his last opportunity. As soon as the Saints had regrouped and were secure in their new home, he began unfolding a set of additional teachings, ordinances, and organizational patterns—many of them temple-related—that further distanced the Saints from their own earlier notions and from the beliefs of their neighbors. This process began with an important revelation of January 1841 (D&C 124) that, among other things, launched the construction of the NAUVOO TEMPLE, and continued for more than three years. By April 1844, just three months before his death, the process was complete.

In Nauvoo Joseph Smith expounded on the nature of the GODHEAD and the origin and destiny of the human race, stressing the concept of ETERNAL PROGRESSION in conjunction with the PLAN OF SALVATION (*see* KING FOLLETT DISCOURSE). Teaching the universal availability of salvation, he introduced vicarious ordinances for deceased individuals, including BAPTISM FOR THE DEAD. Experiencing resistance to new doctrines and practices, yet driven by personal forebodings to avoid delay, the Prophet began in 1841–1842 to introduce PLURAL MARRIAGE and sacred temple ordinances (*see* ENDOWMENT) privately to a limited number of trusted associates, including members of the Quorum of the Twelve, who were later to deliver them to worthy members of the Church once the temple was complete.

Among the most important Nauvoo organizational developments was the March 1842 founding of the RELIEF SOCIETY, a benevolent, social, and religious organization for women (*see* RELIEF SOCIETY ORGANIZATION IN NAUVOO). The Relief Society provided women a structure to facilitate charitable work and sisterhood. More important, it brought women into close contact with priesthood organization and helped to prepare them for temple experiences to come. The Church's first WARDS, or basic congregational units, were founded in Nauvoo, and additional responsibilities for BISHOPS were defined. The COUNCIL OF FIFTY was the last organizational element set up by Joseph Smith. Though it played a useful practical role for several years after its March 1844 organization, its greatest importance was in providing a governmental model for the future kingdom of God on earth.

From the temple to the Council of Fifty, members of the Quorum of the Twelve Apostles stood by the Prophet as his closest advisers and assistants. Foreseeing the day when the Saints might need a more secure haven in the isolated West, in February 1844 Joseph Smith assigned the Twelve to lead an expedition to find such a location (*see* WESTWARD MIGRATION), but shortly put the project on hold. First, he wanted them to travel to the East on a more political mission. When inquiries to the presidential candidates in the approaching national election produced no one willing to defend Mormon rights, the Prophet Joseph Smith launched his own presidential campaign, providing a platform for making his views known and speaking out on behalf of his people. During their usual summer proselytizing, the Twelve and other supporters would travel in the East, combining preaching with electioneering. Before they left, about March 26, 1844, Joseph Smith made his "last charge" to the Twelve. He declared that he had now given them every priesthood key that he possessed and that it was their responsibility to shoulder the burden of the kingdom while he rested.

Before they returned from the East, he was murdered.

Although Nauvoo grew rapidly, progress on its most ambitious construction projects, the NAUVOO TEMPLE and the NAUVOO HOUSE hotel, lagged, in part because of a shortage of capital. Hopes to make Nauvoo a manufacturing center failed to materialize for the same reason (see NAUVOO ECONOMY). But the continued success of LDS proselytizing and the influx of immigrants, combined with LDS solidarity and industriousness, transformed Nauvoo into a formidable economic and political competitor to the other towns in Hancock County.

Neighbors unsympathetic to Nauvoo also had other complaints. The theocratic organization of the LDS community, with its apparent unity of purpose and its local autonomy, aroused resentment. The tendency for Latter-day Saints to vote as a bloc for local and state candidates who were most likely to benefit them alienated both Whigs and Democrats (see NAUVOO POLITICS). Nauvoo's strong militia aroused envy and distrust. The fact that the city's judicial system shielded Joseph Smith from prosecution provoked charges that he had placed himself beyond the law.

As these things increased the hostility of adversaries of the Church, Thomas Sharp, editor of a newspaper in nearby Warsaw, made his *Warsaw Signal* a voice for these concerns and took up a sustained crusade against Joseph Smith and Nauvoo. In the spring of 1844 several disgruntled former associates combined forces with anti-Mormons to mount an offensive against the Prophet from within Nauvoo itself. They published the *Nauvoo Expositor* newspaper, which attacked the Church and made inflammatory charges against Joseph Smith. The Nauvoo City Council declared the paper a public nuisance and ordered the sheriff to destroy it, an action that aroused the Prophet's enemies and provided the basis for his arrest. On June 27, 1844, Joseph and his brother Hyrum were murdered in the jail at the county seat, Carthage, while awaiting trial (see CARTHAGE JAIL; MARTYRDOM OF JOSEPH AND HYRUM SMITH).

The Prophet Joseph Smith established the doctrinal and organizational foundation of the modern Church and prepared Brigham Young and the Quorum of the Twelve Apostles to build on the foundation he had laid (see SUCCESSION IN THE PRESIDENCY). His ministry and his mission were complete.

BIBLIOGRAPHY

Allen, James B., and Glen M. Leonard. *The Story of the Latter-day Saints.* Salt Lake City, 1976.

Backman, Milton V., Jr. *The Heavens Resound.* Salt Lake City, 1983.

Flanders, Robert Bruce. *Nauvoo: Kingdom on the Mississippi.* Urbana, Ill., 1965.

Gentry, Leland H. "A History of the Latter-day Saints in Northern Missouri from 1836 to 1839." Ph.D. diss., Brigham Young University, 1965.

Hill, Marvin S. *Quest for Refuge.* Salt Lake City, 1989.

LeSueur, Stephen C. *The 1838 Mormon War in Missouri.* Columbia, Mo., 1987.

Pratt, Parley P. *Autobiography of Parley P. Pratt.* Salt Lake City, 1985.

Underwood, Grant. "Millenarianism and the Early Mormon Mind." *Journal of Mormon History* 9 (1982):41–51.

MILTON V. BACKMAN, JR.
RONALD K. ESPLIN

C. 1844–1877, EXODUS AND EARLY UTAH PERIODS

[*After outlining developments in Nauvoo, Illinois, following the martyrdom of Joseph Smith, this article traces the exodus from Nauvoo to the West. It then focuses primarily on the political and economic developments associated with establishing a new commonwealth in the Great Basin under Brigham Young's direction. It also reviews Church organization, plural marriage, and the building of temples.*

To understand daily life and what it meant to be a Latter-day Saint during this period, see Pioneer Life and Worship *and* Social and Cultural History. *For more on Church leadership and organization, see*: Organizational and Administrative History, Auxiliary Organizations, Sunday School, Retrenchment Association, Young Men. *For the Exodus*: Westward Migration; Mormon Trail; Historical Sites; Council Bluffs; Iowa, LDS Communities in; "This is the Place" Monument. *For the development of the Mormon commonwealth consult*: Agriculture; Economic History; Pioneer Economy; Immigration and Emigration; Handcart Companies; City Planning; Deseret Alphabet; Deseret University; Native Americans; *and articles on pioneer settlements in* Arizona, California, Colorado, Idaho, Nevada, New Mexico, *and* Wyoming. *See also* Politics: Political History *and* Woman Suffrage.]

The MARTYRDOM OF JOSEPH AND HYRUM SMITH on June 27, 1844, precipitated a major crisis. In the immediate aftermath and emotional shock of losing their founding prophet, many Latter-day Saints suffered a crisis of faith: Could *anyone* take his place? Would the Lord still be with the Church? Nor was it immediately clear to everyone *who* should lead: Would it be Sidney RIGDON, Joseph Smith's counselor in the First Presidency? The QUORUM OF THE TWELVE APOSTLES, led by Brigham YOUNG? Someone else? Whoever succeeded to leadership would face the challenge of resolving tensions within the Church and facing powerful adversaries without.

At the time of the assassination, most members of the Quorum of the Twelve were in the East on missions. Sidney Rigdon, who had left Nauvoo for Pittsburgh just before the martyrdom, returned August 3 and asserted a claim to lead as "Guardian." Three days later several of the Twelve, including Brigham Young, arrived just in time for an August 8 meeting already called to decide guardianship. Rigdon spoke first for his claims. He was followed by Brigham Young, who asserted the responsibility of the Twelve to lead the Church in Joseph's absence and to build on the foundation he had laid. The great majority voted to sustain the Twelve. Many claimed that Brigham Young was transfigured before them, speaking with the voice of the deceased prophet and appearing like him in person and manner.

The August 8 vote effectively settled the question of succession: no one else could make a persuasive claim of having either the authority or the full confidence of the Prophet. The vote sustained

Crossing the Mississippi on the Ice, by C. C. A. Christensen (late nineteenth century, tempera on canvas, 6′6″ × 9′9″). Forced by persecution from Nauvoo in early 1846, some Latter-day Saints crossed the Mississippi into Iowa during weather so bitterly cold that wagon trains could cross safely on the ice. Courtesy Museum of Fine Arts, Brigham Young University.

the Quorum of the Twelve, with Brigham Young at their head, as the leaders of the Church, but it did not immediately result in a new First Presidency; that would come later, after the Twelve had completed the Nauvoo Temple and located a new home for the Church in the West, responsibilities they felt an obligation to accomplish *as a quorum.* Nor did the vote satisfy those who longed for a way to be Latter-day Saints but without the Nauvoo innovations that they viewed as problematic and that the Twelve would continue—such things as the emphasis on TEMPLE, new doctrines including PLURAL MARRIAGE, and the unity of temporal and ecclesiastical concerns under the priesthood. Some of these briefly followed others who set themselves up as leaders, but many simply drifted away. Years later, some banded together as the REORGANIZED CHURCH OF JESUS CHRIST OF LATTER DAY SAINTS with emphasis and direction quite different from Joseph Smith in Nauvoo or the Twelve in the Great Basin (*see* SCHISMATIC GROUPS).

The first priorities of the Twelve were to complete the NAUVOO TEMPLE while privately preparing for the exodus to the West (*see* WESTWARD MIGRATION, PLANNING AND PROPHECY)—which they were committed to delay until the Saints received temple ORDINANCES. The Saints so rallied behind the temple that the capstone was in place by May 1845, and the edifice was ready for ordinance work by December. Eventually nearly 6,000 men and women received temple ordinances before leaving for the West. In the spring of 1845, with the temple nearing completion, Church leaders began preparations for the move West. In September, shortly after mob violence erupted against the outlying settlements around Nauvoo, the Twelve publicly announced that the Saints would all depart.

Brigham Young was supported in these endeavors by eight of the Twelve—the same who had served abroad under his direction in 1840–1841—and by members of the COUNCIL OF FIFTY. Organized in March 1844 by Joseph Smith, the Council of Fifty had been involved in two major activities prior to his death: secretly negotiating with the Republic of Texas for possible settlements there, and publicly campaigning to support Joseph Smith's candidacy for the U.S. presidency. More than seventy-five percent of the surviving members of the original Council of Fifty supported Brigham Young, but William Smith, John E. Page, Lyman Wight, all apostles, and Nauvoo Stake

Mormon pioneers pose in front of their wagons crossing the plains (c. 1866). Photographer: C. R. Savage. Courtesy Utah State Historical Society.

President William Marks dissented and were never reconciled either to the temple or to the Great Basin exodus and its implications. The Council of Fifty helped organize the exodus from Nauvoo and, in early Utah, helped establish an economic and political theocracy.

The exodus began in February 1846, before renewed hostilities erupted. All during the spring and summer, a flow of wagons moved out across the Iowa prairies. The Latter-day Saints were still unsettled in Iowa when a U.S. military officer arrived on June 26 with a requisition for 500 volunteers to serve in the campaign against Mexico. Though sometimes regarded as an oppressive trial imposed upon the refugee Mormons by the U.S. government, the call actually resulted from secret negotiations with U.S. President James Polk (see MORMON BATTALION). Though the battalion took 500 able-bodied men from their midst, it brought a much-needed $70,000, which was used to aid the families of the men and fund the general program of the exodus.

Because the evacuation of Nauvoo and the trek across Iowa had largely exhausted the travel season, the Saints prepared to winter on the Missouri River. They built temporary settlements at WINTER QUARTERS on the river's west bank, now Florence, Nebraska, a suburb of Omaha, and on the east bank at Kanesville, later COUNCIL BLUFFS, IOWA. There preparations continued for the great migration to the interior basins of North America. On January 14, 1847, Brigham Young announced a revelation that the Saints should be "organized into companies [of hundreds, fifties, and tens], with a covenant and promise to keep all the commandments . . . of the Lord our God" (D&C 136:2–3). On April 5, 1847, he led the first pioneer company, departing from Winter Quarters.

After a three-month journey, advance scouts entered the valley of the Great Salt Lake. Three days later, on July 24, 1847 (see PIONEER DAY), Brigham Young entered the valley. On July 28 he

Wagons circled at Independence Rock. Artist W. H. Jackson (1929). Independence Rock marked the beginning of the 96-mile route along Wyoming's Sweetwater River. Today, the graffiti of pioneers can still be seen carved in the rock. Courtesy Nelson Wadsworth.

designated a temple site and announced to the 157 pioneers that "this is the right spot," making it clear that he and the Saints intended a long stay in the vicinity of the Great Salt Lake.

After his return from Utah to Winter Quarters in October 1847, Brigham Young presented to the apostles the question of reorganizing the First Presidency. Although no written revelation explicitly authorized the Twelve to reorganize the presidency, many considered that right implicit in the 1835 revelation concerning the authority of that quorum in relation to the First Presidency (D&C 107:21–24). The Twelve sustained Brigham Young as President of the Church, with Heber C. Kimball and Willard Richards as his counselors, an action ratified by Church members later that month at a special conference at Kanesville, Iowa, and the following year in Salt Lake City.

Brigham Young, second President of the Church, led the Saints from Joseph Smith's death in 1844 until 1877. Known as "an American Moses," his life was dedicated to establishing Zion as revealed through the Prophet Joseph Smith and in meeting the changing needs of the Church for over thirty years. Brigham's dying words were "Joseph! Joseph! Joseph!"

In Utah, Brigham Young set out to fulfill Joseph Smith's dream of establishing a permanent refuge for the Saints. This included creating a political state in which the Church would play a dominant role. The theocratic nature of this government was indicated by the fact that a Church HIGH COUNCIL, presided over by Joseph Smith's uncle John Smith, conducted both religious and civil affairs in the SALT LAKE VALLEY from the fall of 1847 until the return of Brigham Young to the valley in September 1848, when the Twelve and the Council of Fifty assumed direction.

In the closing months of 1848, the Council of Fifty began deliberations toward establishing a more permanent government. Anticipating that the Great Basin would become United States territory, the Council debated the relative merits of petitioning Congress for territorial or statehood status. It opted first for a territory but soon after, in July 1849, following precedents in Texas and California, petitioned for statehood and began to organize the provisional State of Deseret (see DESERET, STATE OF). Brigham Young was elected Governor and other Church authorities comprised its executive and judicial branches and much of its legislative branch. The legislature convened in December 1849, and the State of Deseret functioned as an autonomous state within the national domain until March 28, 1851, when it was formally dissolved and superseded by UTAH TERRITORY, which had already been created as part of the national Compromise of 1850 (see also UTAH STATEHOOD).

The boundaries of the State of Deseret were vast, encompassing all of present Utah, most of Nevada and Arizona, more than one-third of California, and parts of Oregon, Idaho, Wyoming, Colorado, and New Mexico. To establish control of this domain, Brigham Young began a vigorous COLONIZATION program, which, before his death in 1877, founded nearly 400 settlements. An energetic system of proselytizing, particularly in the BRITISH ISLES and SCANDINAVIA, with thousands converted, of whom nearly 90,000 immigrated to Utah by the end of the century. The Church promoted, organized, and conducted this immigration. For the benefit of those who could not otherwise afford travel costs, the Church organized the PERPETUAL EMIGRATING FUND. Chartered in 1850 by the State of Deseret, for the next thirty-seven years the Perpetual Emigrating Fund Company raised funds and utilized Church resources to assist approximately 26,000 emigrants from Europe to the mountain West.

Engines from the Union Pacific Railroad (right) and the Central Pacific Railroad (left) met at Promontory Summit, Utah, on May 10, 1869, to commemorate the completion of the transcontinental railroad. The coming of the railroad made access to Utah easier, beginning an era of economic development but increased tension with non-Mormons. Courtesy Union Pacific Railroad Museum.

The State of Deseret was the closest the Church ever came to realizing the theocratic model previously outlined by Joseph Smith. Church authorities served in important civil positions. After federally appointed judges left the territory in 1851, probate courts, with BISHOPS as judges, were given jurisdiction over both civil and criminal cases. The intention was that LDS influence over the political life of the territory would eliminate the PERSECUTION that had repeatedly occurred. In later years the very success of this theocratic society would create less violent but ultimately more dangerous conflicts with American society (*see* POLITICS: POLITICAL HISTORY).

Inseparable from the prolonged conflict with the federal government was the LDS practice of PLURAL MARRIAGE. Although polygamy had been practiced privately prior to the exodus, Church leaders delayed public acknowledgment of its practice until 1852. In August of that year, at a special conference of the Church at Salt Lake City, Elder Orson Pratt, an apostle, officially announced plural marriage as a doctrine and practice of the Church. A lengthy revelation on MARRIAGE for eternity and on the plurality of wives, dictated by Joseph Smith on July 12, 1843, was published following this announcement (D&C 132). Viewing it as a religious obligation for faithful brethren to marry more wives than one, Latter-day Saints believed that polygamy was protected by constitutional guarantees of religious freedom. There were no federal laws against polygamy, and the territorial incorporation of the Church allowed it "to solemnize marriages compatible with the revelations of Jesus Christ" (Arrington and Quinn, p. 261). In some communities as much as twenty to twenty-five percent of the LDS population eventually lived in polygamous households, with most men who practiced polygamy having one to four plural wives.

For the first several years, life in their new western refuge seemed tenuous. A mild winter in 1847–1848 was followed by spring frosts and a discouraging summer. Then drought damaged and plagues of crickets devoured a good portion of the crops. Many believed that they saved a remnant of their crops only because of the miraculous intervention of great numbers of gulls that descended on the fields and devoured the crickets (*see* SEAGULLS, MIRACLE OF). After the lean winter of 1848–1849, however, the pioneers were able to raise enough in most years to see them through the winter. An unexpected bonanza came in 1849 when hundreds of travelers bound for the California gold fields came through Utah, eagerly trading scarce manufactured goods, exhausted animals, and even flour for local produce. The initial settlements by this time were well-enough established to begin colonization throughout the Rocky Mountain area.

The Saints founded dozens of colonies, at first primarily within the confines of present Utah. First settled was a core area extending north and south from the headquarters at Salt Lake City along the western edge of the mountains. The next colonies were in the higher mountain valleys of the region, such as the Cache and Heber valleys. Almost at the same time, other colonies were established in more distant areas, in response to particular needs, such as the founding of an iron industry (Parowan, Jan. 1851; Cedar City, Nov. 1851); establishing stations along immigration routes (San Bernardino, 1851; purchase of Fort Bridger, 1855); undertaking missions to the Indians (Fort Lemhi in present Idaho; Las Vegas, Nevada; Fort Supply in 1853 in present Wyoming; and the Elk Mountain Mission in east-central Utah, all in 1855); producing warm-climate crops, such as cotton and sugar (St. George, 1861); or, later, searching for a refuge for polygamous families.

The most common motive for colonization was the need to find land for a growing population of farmers, a need leading to settlement of most suitable sites in Utah by 1880 as well as others in northern Arizona, southwestern Colorado, northwestern New Mexico, western Wyoming, and southeastern Idaho. Often new areas were opened with a "mission" call (*see* CALLINGS), wherein established settlers were asked to undertake a Church-sponsored mission to found a colony. Once the mother colony was established, nearby areas were settled spontaneously as young people coming of age sought land to farm.

Ute Indians in Salt Lake City in 1869 on the road to a Grand Pow-wow, with the Zion's Cooperative Mercantile Institution (ZCMI) in the background. Photographer: Charles W. Carter.

The founding of a commonwealth in the West was not accomplished without conflicts and difficulties. A prolonged drought in 1855 was followed by a severe grasshopper infestation. The insecurities thus created may have helped feed the fire of the REFORMATION OF 1856–1857, a period of intense soul-searching and recommitment. The fiery and at times intemperate sermons of the Reformation had heightened pioneer anxieties when, early in 1857, believing exaggerated reports that the Mormons were in a state of rebellion, U.S. President James Buchanan secretly ordered 2,500 federal troops to Utah. Acting without the benefit of an investigation, Buchanan relieved Brigham Young as governor, a position to which Young had been reappointed even after the 1852 announcement of polygamy. Unfortunately, Buchanan did everything in secrecy, even stopping the mails to Utah to give the troops the advantage of surprise.

After receiving private confirmation of the government action, Brigham Young instructed all missionaries to return to Utah and ordered missions closed and the more isolated colonies abandoned. Accustomed to persecutions involving state militia, Latter-day Saints saw the advance of armed forces toward Utah as a prelude to plunder, rape, and slaughter. As they prepared for armed resistance, war hysteria swept the territory.

As advanced units of the UTAH EXPEDITION approached Fort Bridger, they encountered the Saints implementing a "scorched earth" policy of resistance. Mormon raiders seized and burned federal supply trains and destroyed the forage in front of the advancing troops. The timely arrival of heavy snows mired the army for the winter, allowing mediators, especially Thomas L. KANE, time to seek reconciliation. Meanwhile, President Young ordered northern Utah settlements abandoned and organized the "Move South." If the Latter-day Saints had to leave their refuge, they would leave the Great Basin as much a wilderness as they had found it. Negotiations succeeded by spring, just as the army started to move. Alfred Cumming was installed as governor, and on June 12, 1858, Brigham Young accepted a pardon for his supposed rebellion. Two weeks later, General Albert Sidney Johnston led his troops through a deserted Salt Lake City and established an isolated Camp Floyd forty miles to the southwest. The Utah War became fittingly known as Buchanan's Blunder.

A disastrous consequence of the war hysteria was the MOUNTAIN MEADOWS MASSACRE of September 1857, in which local officials in southern Utah joined with Indians to massacre a company of settlers en route to California. It is well documented that Brigham Young's command was to let the travelers pass through in peace, but his advice arrived too late to prevent the killing, and a locally orchestrated cover-up portrayed the crime as solely an Indian depredation. Responding to charges that whites were involved, President Young urged the new governor to investigate, but Governor Cumming maintained that if whites were involved they would be pardoned under the general amnesty granted in 1858. Eventually, as more information came to light, some of the principal participants were excommunicated from the Church and one, John D. Lee, was convicted in federal court and executed.

Though preoccupied by the Civil War, the federal government nonetheless demonstrated interest in Utah Territory. In 1862 Fort Douglas was established on the eastern edge of Salt Lake City, under the leadership of a dedicated anti-Mormon, Patrick Edward Connor. Connor and his troops were charged with guarding transportation routes, but they also published the aggressively anti-Mormon *Union Vedette*, encouraged mining, and promoted non-Mormon immigration to the territory. In 1863 Connor's troops attacked a group of Northern Shoshone Indians on the Bear River in the northern Cache Valley, killing some 250 men, women, and children.

The decade following the Utah War was one of general expansion for the Church. In 1862 Congress enacted a law prohibiting polygamy in the territories and disincorporating the Church, but the law went unenforced until after REYNOLDS V. UNITED STATES in 1879. Church immigrants continued to arrive by the thousands, and Brigham Young continued planting colonies to house them. The steady influx of non-Mormons to Utah and the construction of a transcontinental railroad, however, pointed toward future challenges to LDS domination of their Great Basin commonwealth.

The completion of the transcontinental railroad brought opportunities as well as challenges. Brigham Young had long anticipated the end of physical isolation and in some ways encouraged it. In 1852 and in 1854, the Saints petitioned Congress for a transcontinental railroad to pass through Utah. Such a railroad would simplify immigration and permit Church leaders to establish rail links connecting many distant colonies with Salt Lake

JOHN W. YOUNG
1876-1877

BRIGHAM YOUNG
1847-1877

DANIEL H. WELLS
1857-1877

THE FIRST PRESIDENCY
1876-1877

The First Presidency of the Church (1876–1877), at the time of Brigham Young's death in 1877. Left to right: John W. Young, President Brigham Young, Daniel H. Wells.

City. When the Pacific Railroad Act was passed on July 1, 1862, President Young subscribed for $10,000 worth of stock in the newly organized Union Pacific Railroad Company, of which he became a director in 1865.

Though the railroad made it easier for Church immigrants to reach Utah, it also encouraged non-Mormon immigration. The end of isolation likewise threatened Utah's economic and political independence. In order to build the local economy and postpone the establishment of a powerful non-Mormon business community, Church officials had long struggled to discourage the importation of eastern manufactured goods. They now launched a determined campaign to discourage the purchase of imported luxuries, including tea, coffee, alcohol, and tobacco, and Joseph Smith's 1833 revelation discouraging the use of these products was given added emphasis (see WORD OF WISDOM).

Despite Brigham Young's long opposition to the development of precious metal-mining in Utah, the approach of the railroad revived enthusiasm for harvesting Utah's mineral wealth. Under the direction of several prominent Church businessmen and intellectuals such as William Godbe, Edward W. Tullidge, and Eli B. Kelsey, a "New Movement" developed within the Church against what they referred to as "Priesthood Autocracy." These men wrote persuasive articles in the *Utah Magazine* urging the exploitation of Utah's mineral

resources in order to keep the industry in local (and therefore LDS) control. Envisioning a different result, Brigham Young denounced the "Godbeites" for inviting "Gentile" domination of Utah. Eventually, Godbe, whose doctrinal unorthodoxy posed an additional challenge, was excommunicated. Although Brigham Young rejected the Godbeite solution, he recognized the realities of the new economic situation and inaugurated a series of programs to reinforce spiritual solidarity and economic independence.

One part of Brigham Young's program involved the organization of the SCHOOL OF THE PROPHETS in 1867. The original School of the Prophets had been established by Joseph Smith in 1833 to provide adult education and prepare for the temple. In the Utah organization, adoption of an economic program accompanied discussions of theology. The Schools of the Prophets instructed landowners in methods of securing property titles, solicited contributions of labor and funds to finance branch railroads, established locally owned cooperative merchandising and manufacturing enterprises, urged the reduction of wages to allow greater exportation of Utah goods, organized boycotts of hostile Gentile establishments, and required that members pledge to observe the Word of Wisdom. The Schools also contracted with the Union Pacific and Central Pacific railroads to grade the transcontinental line in Utah, thus limiting the influx of non-Mormon laborers and providing cash revenue to Latter-day Saints. Within a few years, as economic conditions changed, these organizations gradually disappeared.

More permanent than the Schools of the Prophets were the organizations that Brigham Young established for the women and youth of the Church. Between the rebirth of the RELIEF SOCIETY in 1867 and Brigham Young's death a decade later, with General President Eliza R. SNOW assisting bishops in forming local organizations, the society spread to every Church settlement in the Great Basin. In addition to its charitable purposes, the Relief Society worked with the Schools of the Prophets in encouraging HOME INDUSTRY and discouraging the purchase of imports. Major achievements of the Relief Society included the beginning of a grain storage program, launching SILK CULTURE, founding the WOMAN'S EXPONENT, building Relief Society halls in most settlements, starting a commission store for home industries, and impressive support of women's medical training (see MATERNITY AND CHILD HEALTH CARE). Relief Society leaders were also active in WOMAN SUFFRAGE, and in 1870 Utah women were second to Wyoming women to receive the franchise.

In 1869 Brigham Young established an organization for young women with the unwieldy name "Young Ladies' Department of the Cooperative Retrenchment Association." He urged the girls to avoid all extravagances, and to "cease to build up the merchant who sends your money out of the Territory for fine clothes made in the East" (Susa Young Gates, *History of the Young Ladies Mutual Improvement Association of the Church*, p. 9 [Salt Lake City, 1911]). The Young Ladies' Mutual Improvement Association, as it was later named, became an organization primarily concerned with cultural, social, and religious activity (see YOUNG WOMEN; RETRENCHMENT ASSOCIATION).

After the completion of the transcontinental railroad in 1869, both Union Pacific and Central Pacific defaulted on their grading contracts. The losses to the Mormon economy were staggering: $500,000 in cash, and even greater aggregate losses to subcontractors, merchants, and laborers. In an effort to compensate for these losses, Church leaders sponsored railroads within the territory, using the half million dollars' worth of iron, construction equipment, and rolling stock that the bankrupt Union Pacific had used as a substitute payment on its obligations. Although these rail-

roads brought benefits to Utah, their success did not completely assuage the bitterness the Saints felt toward the initial setbacks with the transcontinental railroad.

In addition to intensifying his call for home manufacture and boycotts of non-Mormon merchants as the rails approached Utah, Brigham Young established a cooperative system of merchandising. In October 1868 he organized Zion's Cooperative Mercantile Institution (ZCMI) to "bring goods here and sell them as low as they can possibly be sold and let the profits be divided with the people at large" (Arden Olsen, *History of the Mormon Mercantile Cooperation in Utah*, p. 80 [Ph.D. diss., University of California, Berkeley, 1935]). With widespread support, the new department store became a profitable enterprise that continues as Salt Lake City's largest retailer. Branch stores were established in many communities, as were cooperative tanneries, gristmills, dairies, butcher shops, banks, iron works, sawmills, woolen mills, and cotton factories. These helped the Saints forestall for another decade the "outside" control that the arrival of the railroad presaged.

The remarkable success of the Cooperative Movement suggested to Brigham Young that a revival of "The United Order of Enoch," long his goal, might now be feasible. Inaugurated by Brigham Young during the winter of 1873–1874, the Order Movement had been inspired by a desire to emulate attempts to live the law of CONSECRATION in the 1830s and by the success of the Brigham City Cooperative. Under the direction of Elder Lorenzo SNOW, Brigham City had become eighty-five percent self-sufficient, conducting virtually all agriculture, construction, manufacturing, and trade in the surrounding area. Almost the entire population was employed in the various departments of the cooperative, and received their remuneration in products rather than cash. So successful was the Brigham City Cooperative that it was hardly affected by the financial Panic of 1873.

After Brigham Young launched the UNITED ORDER movement, more than 200 orders were established throughout Utah, southern Idaho, northern Arizona, and Nevada. Because he left the operation of these orders in local hands, several different types emerged. Some, like Orderville in southern Utah, were almost totally communal. In the larger cities, where tightly organized communal orders were impossible, separate ward congregations financed individual cooperative enterprises, such as farms or factories, and then exchanged products. The manifestations of the United Order of Enoch varied, but they represented a genuine effort of the people to become "one," as the early revelations had commanded. As with nearly all voluntary enterprises of this nature, these orders eventually disbanded due to internal strains and external pressures. The movement itself ended by 1877, although some orders, such as that at Orderville, continued for another decade.

Prior to his death in 1877, Brigham Young was able to see the fulfillment of one of his most sacred aspirations—the completion of a temple in Utah. The full significance of TEMPLES and their ordinances dated back to the Nauvoo period, when Joseph Smith introduced baptism for the dead, marriage for eternity, and a set of religious instructions and covenants called the ENDOWMENT. Since abandoning the Nauvoo Temple in 1846, Brigham Young dreamed of a temple in the West. Upon arriving in the valley he dedicated ground in Salt Lake City for such a temple, but the imposing structure took forty years to complete. In the meantime, a temporary ENDOWMENT HOUSE, constructed in 1855, provided a place for sacred ordinances. After deciding to build a less imposing structure in the south, Brigham Young dedicated the completed St. George Temple on April 6, 1877. In the decade following his death, two additional temples were built in Utah (Logan and Manti) before the Salt Lake Temple was finally dedicated in 1893.

After the St. George temple dedication, Brigham Young initiated a massive reorganization of the Church, primarily at the local level, clarifying and redefining priesthood responsibilities in the process. Every ward and stake was affected and most received new leadership.

By the time of his death on August 29, 1877, Brigham Young had brought the Latter-day Saints to an apex of growth in their mountain retreat and kingdom. His dying words, "Joseph! Joseph! Joseph!" were appropriate for one who had lived his life, as he frequently said, as an apostle of Jesus Christ and of Joseph Smith. In his sometimes unbending manner, Brigham Young had worked for more than forty years to attain the goals of Joseph Smith. The Saints had achieved a unified economic and political power, though they would soon be forced to bend in the face of unrelenting federal pressure. More important, by courageously facing their challenges and pursuing their dreams in the desert, they had become a strong and cohesive people of faith. Committed to gospel ideals regardless of the costs, they left a heritage that continues to inspire Latter-day Saints throughout the world.

BIBLIOGRAPHY

General works focusing on this period include Leonard J. Arrington, *Brigham Young, American Moses,* New York, 1985; and *Great Basin Kingdom,* Cambridge, Mass., 1958; Eugene E. Campbell, *Establishing Zion: The Mormon Church in the American West, 1847–1869,* Salt Lake City, 1988; Dean L. May, *Utah: A People's History,* Salt Lake City, 1987; and a brief account in Leonard J. Arrington and D. Michael Quinn, "The Latter-day Saints in the Far West, 1847–1900," in F. Mark McKiernan, Alma R. Blair, and Paul M. Edwards, eds., *The Restoration Movement: Essays in Mormon History,* Lawrence, Kans., 1973, pp. 257–70.

In addition to numerous relevant articles in the *Journal of Mormon History, BYU Studies, Dialogue, Sunstone,* and the *Utah Historical Quarterly,* see: Richard E. Bennett, *Mormons at the Missouri 1846–1852,* Norman, Okla., 1987, for the period leading to Utah settlement; Wallace Stegner's *The Gathering of Zion,* New York, 1964, a classic account of migration to Utah; Leonard J. Arrington, Feramorz Y. Fox, and Dean L. May, *Building the City of God: Community and Cooperation Among the Mormons,* Salt Lake City, 1976, which focuses on communitarianism; and Norman F. Furniss's *The Mormon Conflict, 1850–59,* New Haven, Conn., 1960, the best book-length study of the Utah War.

LEONARD J. ARRINGTON
DEAN L. MAY

C. 1878–1898, LATE PIONEER UTAH PERIOD

[*This article discusses a period of stress and adaptation following the death of Brigham Young as the Church confronted great pressures to conform to contemporary American mores. After presenting an overview of the period, the article considers organizational changes, economic programs, establishment of new LDS settlements, and missionary work, then focuses on the struggle over* Polygamy, *culminating in the* Manifesto of 1890 *announcing the official end of* Plural Marriage. *In the wake of the Manifesto came home rule for Utah (see* Utah Statehood), *expanded proselytizing, attempts to shore up religious education (see* Academies), *and more limited Church economic involvement (see* Pioneer Economy).

To understand daily life and what it meant to be a Latter-day Saint during this period, see Pioneer Life and Worship *and* Social and Cultural History. *For additional information on continued Church* Colonization *into new areas, see entries on pioneer settlements in* Mexico *and*

Canada, *and in* Arizona, Colorado, Idaho, Nevada, New Mexico, *and* Wyoming. *On developments related to plural marriage, see:* Legal and Judicial History; Antipolygamy Legislation; Reynolds v. United States; *and* Manifesto of 1890.]

During the 1878–1898 period of growth, severe problems, and pronounced changes, the Church met many challenges under Church Presidents John TAYLOR and Wilford WOODRUFF. The 1879 Supreme Court ruling upholding ANTIPOLYGAMY LEGISLATION introduced a decade of ever harsher enforcement of ever harsher laws. Facing governmental persecution and seeking "home rule" through statehood, the Church moved to end the practice of plural marriage and surrender its once firm control of Utah Territory's politics and economics. In the 1890s UTAH TERRITORY and its LDS residents embarked on the road to "Americanization."

Though this period was noted for its prolonged confrontation with the federal government, growth was also a striking characteristic. Church membership doubled (from 115,065 to 229,428), as did the number of stakes (20 to 40) and wards (252 to 516). LDS settlements extended into Mexico and Canada. As proselytizing efforts expanded, the number of missions increased (from 8 to 20).

Priesthood quorum work became more orderly and standardized. GENERAL AUTHORITIES regularly visited quarterly stake conferences and ward conferences. AUXILIARY ORGANIZATIONS became widely established in stakes and wards, and general-level auxiliary presidencies and boards were appointed. The Church also finished three new temples, bringing the total in Utah to four.

After President Young's death in August 1877, the QUORUM OF THE TWELVE APOSTLES did not immediately organize a new FIRST PRESIDENCY. John Taylor presided over the Church as president of the Twelve until October 1880. Under his leadership the Twelve completed the reorganization of wards and stakes that President Young had begun.

They also expanded auxiliary organizations. By 1880 the Twelve selected three of their own (Elders Wilford Woodruff, Joseph F. SMITH, and Moses Thatcher) to form a general superintendency of the Young Men's Mutual Improvement Association (YMMIA; *see* YOUNG MEN) and to supervise new central YMMIA boards or committees created first for counties and later for stakes. The Young Ladies' RETRENCHMENT ASSOCIATION became the Young Ladies' Mutual Improvement Association (YLMIA) in 1878, with boards established in the stakes beginning that year and a

Eagle Gate in Salt Lake City with the Beehive House in the background, c. 1900. Courtesy Rare Books and Manuscripts, Brigham Young University.

Churchwide organization beginning in 1880 with Elmina S. TAYLOR as president (see YOUNG WOMEN). The Primary Association, a new organization to benefit children, was started in 1878 in Farmington, Utah. After other wards copied the program, a Churchwide PRIMARY organization was created in 1880, headed by Louie B. Felt. RELIEF SOCIETY President Eliza R. SNOW continued to supervise all women's work in the Church, which now included YLMIA and Primary. Elder George Q. Cannon of the First Presidency continued as general superintendent of the SUNDAY SCHOOLS throughout this period. The Sunday Schools, Relief Society, and MIA were organized in the British Isles and Scandinavia beginning in the late 1870s and early 1880s.

Legal tangles surrounding the settlement of Brigham Young's estate became a bothersome problem for the Twelve. After federal legislation severely limited Church holdings, President Young had controlled a complicated mix of personal and Church property. His heirs and the Church finally settled the matter by compromise out of court in 1879.

In 1880, its fiftieth birthday, the Church proclaimed a Year of Jubilee, modeled on an ancient Hebrew custom, to give relief to the poor. It erased from the books an indebtedness of $802,000 to the PERPETUAL EMIGRATING FUND—half of the outstanding total. In addition to distributing cattle and sheep to the needy, authorities forgave the worthy poor half their unpaid tithing. The Relief Society also lent nearly 35,000 bushels of wheat from its storage bins to help drought-stricken farmers.

After directing the Church for three years, in October 1880 John Taylor and the Twelve again organized a First Presidency: John Taylor, President of the Church, and George Q. Cannon and Joseph F. Smith, who had previously served in the First Presidency under Brigham Young, as counselors.

Revelations to President Taylor in 1882 and 1883 prompted a reorganization of the SEVENTY. For the first time the seventy-six local quorums were organized on a geographic basis, enrolling all seventies within their respective boundaries. In addition, between 1884 and 1888, twenty-five new quorums were created. This reorganization revitalized the Seventy, and the number of seventies filling full-time missions increased as soon as the change was implemented.

This period also saw a growth in Church-related publications. Two new magazines served the youth: the CONTRIBUTOR (1879–1896) for young men and the YOUNG WOMAN'S JOURNAL (1889–1929) for young ladies. The *Morgenstjernen* (1882–1885), a historical publication in Danish, continued in English as *The Historical Record* (1886–1890). The Sunday School published its first music book (1884), and the Book of Mormon first appeared in a Swedish translation (1878). In 1880 the Church accepted by vote the Pearl of Great Price as scripture, giving the Church the fourth of its STANDARD WORKS. It also published, in 1879, editions of the Book of Mormon and Doctrine and Covenants, with Elder Orson Pratt's chapter and verse divisions, cross-references, and notes.

President Taylor also implemented a new economic program. Less rigidly structured than the earlier UNITED ORDERS, it struck a balance between private enterprise and group economic planning. Zion's Central Board of Trade fostered cooperative economic activity by promoting business, seeking new markets, providing information to farmers and manufacturers, preventing competition harmful to home industry, and sometimes regulating wages and prices. Stake boards of trade coordinated with the central agency. Unfortunately, by 1885 anti-Mormon crusades forced these boards of trade to disband. Pioneer and PRESIDING BISHOP Edward Hunter, who had served since the 1850s, died in 1883 and was replaced in 1884 by William B. Preston.

During the 1880s the Relief Society further developed programs that had begun in the 1870s: storing grain, maintaining ward Relief Society halls and commission stores, sponsoring nursing and midwifery education programs, overseeing the organizations for children and young women, watching over the spiritual well-being of LDS women, and improving the ongoing care of the poor. New developments included the 1882 opening of the DESERET HOSPITAL, Utah's second hospital and the first operated by the Church. The death of Eliza R. Snow in 1887 marked the end of an era for the Relief Society; in 1888 Zina Diantha H. YOUNG replaced her as president.

Despite severe problems, Church leaders remained committed to providing the blessings of temples to more of the Saints. To supplement the one functioning temple in St. George, President John Taylor dedicated Utah's second temple, at Logan, on May 17, 1884. Built primarily with donated money, materials, and labor, it cost an estimated $800,000. A third temple, in Manti, Utah, built at a cost close to $1 million, was dedicated in 1888 by Elder Lorenzo SNOW, a member of the Quorum of the Twelve. Work also continued on the larger Salt Lake Temple, begun in 1853, but not completed until 1893.

Colonization continued. Between 1876 and 1879, no fewer than 100 new LDS settlements were established outside Utah and more than 20 within the territory. LDS settlements in Arizona expanded rapidly. Stakes, formed in the vicinity of the Little Colorado River in 1878 and 1879, were absorbed into the newly created St. Johns and Snowflake stakes in 1887. Meanwhile, along the Gila and Salt rivers, the St. Joseph and Maricopa stakes were formed in 1883. New LDS settlements appeared in Nevada; in eastern Utah, where the Emery Stake was created in 1882; and in southeastern Utah and nearby parts of Colorado and New Mexico, where the San Juan Stake was formed in 1883. Many LDS converts from the southern states settled in the San Luis Valley in south-central Colorado, and in 1883 their settlements became the San Luis Stake.

Antipolygamy prosecution caused Church leaders to found colonies in Mexico and Canada, beyond the reach of U.S. laws. After President Taylor's 1885 visit to Mexico, hundreds of Saints poured into Chihuahua and established villages in a region that is still identified as Mexico's "Mormon Colonies" (*see* MEXICO, PIONEER SETTLEMENTS IN). These settlements at first were part of the Mexican Mission. Within a decade more than 3,000 Saints had moved in, more settlements were established, and in December 1895 the Juárez Stake was created to direct Saints in the Mexican colonies.

Under instructions from President Taylor, Cache Stake President Charles Ora Card located a place of refuge in southern Alberta in 1886 for Latter-day Saint colonists (*see* CANADA, PIONEER SETTLEMENTS IN). The next spring, arrivals from Utah founded Cardston, fourteen miles north of the United States border. Settlements sprang up nearby in Aetna (1888) and Mountain View (1893). In June 1895 the Alberta Stake became the first stake organized outside the United States (the Salt Lake Stake excepted, then in Mexican territory).

Missionary work produced impressive successes and brought frustrating problems. Between 1879 and 1889 the Church operated a small mis-

sion in Mexico that had about 242 converts. In New Zealand a branch was organized among the Maoris in 1883. In 1884 Jacob Spori opened the Turkish Mission, which included Palestine. Numbers of missionaries bound for Europe increased. The gathering to Utah of European converts continued, despite anti-Mormon publicity that prompted U.S. officials to ask European governments to stop Mormons from emigrating. That request was not granted.

After a Southern States Mission was organized in 1875, conversions occasionally provoked violence. Missionaries were driven from some communities, and in 1879 a Georgia mob shot and killed Elder Joseph Standing. At Cane Creek, Tennessee, in 1884, a mob murdered two missionaries and two residents who had shown an interest in the Church.

Wanting to see their history told fairly, Church leaders provided extensive information to California-based historian Hubert Howe Bancroft. Bancroft's *History of Utah* (1889) was one of the first non-LDS scholarly histories to treat the Church in a fair light.

In 1879 the Supreme Court upheld as constitutional the Anti-Bigamy Act of 1862, affirming the illegality of plural marriage (*see* REYNOLDS V. UNITED STATES). As new legislation was passed and prosecutions became more severe, polygamous husbands and fathers had four choices—give up their families, hide from the law, face prosecution, or leave the United States. Despite this crisis, President Taylor, declaring that when the laws of man and God conflict he would obey God, refused to desert his own plural families or to tell the other brethren to abandon theirs. Attacks on polygamy, often led by religious organizations, came from every direction. When national women's groups urged President Rutherford B. Hayes to prosecute Utah polygamists, 2,000 LDS women signed a resolution affirming that plural marriage was a religious practice protected under the Constitution.

Bitterness between the Saints and the GENTILES brewed nationally and within Utah. Public pressure led Congress to pass the Edmunds Act in 1882, which mandated up to five years' imprisonment and $500 fines for polygamy, and up to six months and $300 fines for unlawful cohabitation (*see* ANTIPOLYGAMY LEGISLATION). Persons practicing polygamy or unlawful cohabitation lost their civil rights to serve on juries, hold public office, and vote. The law created a board of five commissioners to handle voter registration and elections. It declared children born of polygamists before January 1, 1883, legitimate, and it gave the president power to grant amnesties at his discretion.

The Utah Commission began its work in 1882 by declaring that anyone who had ever practiced plural marriage, even before the 1862 anti-bigamy law, could not vote. Since the commission required voters to take a "test oath," swearing that they were not in violation of the law, within one year the law disfranchised more than 12,000 Latter-day Saints. In 1885, however, the U.S. Supreme Court ruled that this test oath was unconstitutional.

The judicial crusade against polygamists severely disrupted Church society in Utah, Idaho, and Arizona. Polygamous men and their families suffered greatly, as did the Church as an organization. Otherwise law-abiding husbands and fathers— and some wives and children—became fugitives in a Mormon "underground," frequently moving from place to place to escape federal marshals hunting "cohabs." Saints developed secret hiding places in homes, barns, and fields, codes to warn one another, and spotters to watch for the marshals. Federal "deps" (deputy marshals) adopted disguises as peddlers or census takers and hired their own spotters to question children and neighbors and to invade the privacy of homes. Bounties were offered for every cohab captured. Families suffered, particularly wives left to tend farms while their husbands were in hiding. Wives who refused to testify against their husbands were sent to prison. Men, women, and children suffered long periods of deprivation and fear.

In Utah between 1884 and 1893, 939 Saints went to prison for polygamy-related charges. In Idaho and Arizona the Saints suffered from similarly harsh prosecution. When Arizona prisons became crowded, cohabs were sent to a Detroit penitentiary. One Utahan, Edward M. Dalton, was killed by a pursuing deputy, which embittered the Saints against the government. So did a U.S. Supreme Court ruling that a man who stopped living with his wife but who provided her food and shelter was guilty of cohabitation.

The crusade disrupted normal Church activities significantly. President Taylor avoided arrest by traveling. In the last public sermon he preached, he criticized what he called a judicial

outrage, then went into hiding. Several apostles went into exile, taking special missions to remote areas in the West, Mexico, Canada, and Hawaii. Several others filled European missions and missions to Native Americans. Many stake presidents and bishops likewise tried to avoid arrest.

Between 1884 and 1887 general conferences were held in Provo, Logan, and Coalville, rather than in Salt Lake City, to help attenders avoid arrest. Few General Authorities attended. Elder Franklin D. Richards, an apostle who was immune from arrest because his plural wife had died, presided over some of the conferences. General epistles from President Taylor and President Cannon gave guidance to the conferences.

President Taylor directed the Church by letters. For more than two years President Taylor remained "underground," separated from most of his family and friends. He died in hiding in Kaysville, Utah, on July 25, 1887, after serving as a General Authority nearly forty-nine years. By the time of his death, nearly every settlement in Utah had been raided by federal marshals, hundreds of Saints had become refugees in Mexico or Canada, and nearly all the leaders were in hiding. At his funeral in Salt Lake City, he was honored for being a double martyr whose blood was shed in Carthage Jail with Joseph and Hyrum Smith and who then died in exile because of government persecution.

Once again the Council of the Twelve, led by senior apostle Wilford Woodruff, took the helm of the Church and steered the course, largely from the "underground," until they again established a First Presidency at general conference in April 1889. Elder Woodruff became Church President, and George Q. Cannon and Joseph F. Smith were his counselors. This would be the last time that the Twelve delayed reorganizing the First Presidency upon the death of the President. In December 1892, President Woodruff, indicating that prolonged delay was not pleasing to the Lord, instructed senior apostle Lorenzo Snow to reorganize immediately upon his death.

By 1887 national political leaders saw that the Church was not bending to the law, so Congress framed a tougher measure, the Edmunds-Tucker Act, designed to destroy the Church as a political and economic entity in order to force the Saints to abandon plural marriage. The law dissolved the Church as a legal corporation, required the forfeiture of all property in excess of $50,000, dissolved the Perpetual Emigrating Fund Company and claimed its property, and disbanded the NAUVOO LEGION (territorial militia). To aid prosecutions, the law required compulsory attendance of witnesses at trials and confirmed the legality of forcing wives to testify against husbands. County probate judges, who helped impanel juries, had to be appointed by the President of the United States. Federally appointed officers took control of schools. Probate courts certified all marriages. The act disinherited all children born of plural marriages one year or more after the act was passed. WOMAN SUFFRAGE was abolished and a new test oath was designed. No one could vote, serve on a jury, or hold public office without signing an oath pledging support of antipolygamy laws.

Federal lawmen zealously tried to arrest and imprison Church leaders. President Woodruff stayed in the underground, near St. George, Utah, directing the Church by letter and private meetings. George Q. Cannon, President Woodruff's first counselor, was arrested in February 1886, posted bail, and then escaped into hiding until 1888 when, with a more lenient judge on the bench, he gave himself up. He served 175 days in prison and paid a $450 fine. Allowed visitors in prison, he was able to conduct much Church and personal business. He supervised the Sunday Schools and finished writing a biography of Joseph Smith. His presence buoyed up the spirits of his fellow cohabs in the prison. Latter-day Saints regarded these prisoners as martyrs and gave them gala receptions when they were released.

Arrests were a problem, but most damaging to the Church were its inability to acquire and use funds to further its work and the loss of political rights. To protect $3 million worth of real and personal property from confiscation, the Church asked prominent members to assume ownership of certain properties as trustees. Nonprofit associations were created to hold property, including the three Utah temples. Ward and stake associations took over local meetinghouses, tithing houses, and Church livestock. Many stakes established ACADEMIES with the use of tithing that was returned to them by the Church.

Federal receivers confiscated about $800,000 worth of property not turned over to private parties or associations, then rented back certain properties to the Church, such as the Temple Block in Salt Lake City. Church leaders tested the constitu-

tionality of the confiscations, but in 1890 the Supreme Court upheld the new law by a 5–4 vote. The economic destruction of the Church seemed certain.

Matching this economic crusade was a political assault. With all women, thousands of LDS men, and all convert-immigrants disfranchised, anti-Mormon politicians won control of the Ogden and Salt Lake City governments. In Idaho practically all Church members were disfranchised by a test oath requiring them to state under oath that they did not believe in or belong to a church that believed in plural marriage. When the Supreme Court in 1890 upheld the Idaho test oath, anti-Mormons pushed the Cullom-Struble Bill in Congress that would disfranchise all Latter-day Saints everywhere (see LEGAL AND JUDICIAL HISTORY).

Economically crippled and with its members denied political rights, the Church faced a ruinous future unless its practice of plural marriage was stopped. President Woodruff consulted with leaders and prayed earnestly to know what to do. After receiving divine revelation, he issued the MANIFESTO on September 24, 1890, announcing an official end to plural marriage. "The Lord showed me by vision and revelation exactly what would take place if we did not stop this practice," President Woodruff later said. "He has told me exactly what to do, and what the result would be if we did not do it" (Deseret Evening News, Nov. 14, 1891). The Manifesto said that the Church had halted the teaching of plural marriage and was not allowing new plural marriages. President Woodruff said he would submit himself to the laws of the land and urged Church members to do the same. At general conference on October 6, 1890, the Church accepted the Manifesto. It was incorporated into the Doctrine and Covenants in 1908.

Speaking for the First Presidency, George Q. Cannon explained that a revelation from 1841 applied in 1890; it had instructed the Church that when "enemies come upon them and hinder them from performing that work, behold, it behooveth me to require that work no more at the hands of those . . . men, but to accept of their offerings" (D&C 124:49). Most Saints accepted the new direction, but not easily and not all. Indeed, a limited number of new plural marriages occurred in the next decade before Church leaders made it clear that all who persisted in the practice faced excommunication.

With the issuance of the Manifesto, hostilities ebbed and the Church entered a new era of cooperation. It was generally understood that husbands would not be required to reject their plural wives and their children, and local prosecutors became very lenient in punishing those charged with polygamy. U.S. President Benjamin Harrison, who in 1891 had visited Utah and shaken hands with President Woodruff, granted a limited amnesty to the Saints in 1893, followed by a general amnesty granted by U.S. President Grover Cleveland in 1894. After the Manifesto and the amnesties, General Authorities resumed their normal administrative duties.

Seeking statehood for Utah, Church leaders instructed Utah Saints to join the national political parties and become Democrats or Republicans. A Republican Congress passed an enabling act in 1894 that Democratic President Grover Cleveland signed. Utah wrote a new constitution that prohibited plural marriage and ensured the separation of church and state. On January 4, 1896, Utah became a state, nearly fifty years after President Brigham Young first sought that status (*see* UTAH STATEHOOD).

In 1896 General Authorities accepted a "political manifesto" stipulating that none of them would run for elected office without prior approval of their presiding Church authorities. When Elder Moses Thatcher, an apostle, refused to sign the document, he was dropped from the Quorum of the Twelve.

During the 1890s the Church missionary force nearly tripled. In the Pacific region, missionary work penetrated into Samoa in 1888 and Tonga in 1891. In 1898 the Australasian Mission was split into the Australian and the New Zealand missions. Some Hawaiian Saints immigrated to Utah and created a settlement at Iosepa in western Utah. Missionary work was resumed in California in 1892 and in the eastern United States in 1893. Proselytizing continued in Europe, though emigration from there declined by 50 percent in the 1890s compared with the 1880s. By the 1890s the Church, with its base in America secured and most good land in the West occupied, discouraged immigration and asked overseas converts to build up stakes in their homelands rather than gather to Zion.

The Edmunds-Tucker Act strengthened public schools, which excluded religious education. In response, the Church began holding afterschool religion classes in meetinghouses and established ACADEMIES or high schools in larger settlements. Between 1888 and 1891 thirty-one LDS academies were opened in Utah, Idaho, Arizona, Canada, and Mexico.

The 1890s saw Church women extending their reach and demonstrating their political rights. Continuing their affiliation with eastern women's movements, they became charter members of the National Council of Women and found their eastern associates to be important allies in their fight against disfranchisement. Relief Society–sponsored suffrage activities led to the inclusion of guaranteed woman suffrage in the 1895 Utah State Constitution.

After forty years, construction of the Salt Lake Temple was completed and dedicated in April 1893. Following a brief open house on April 5, the first opportunity for nonmembers to tour a temple, the sacred edifice was dedicated on April 6, forty years after the laying of the cornerstone. The dedicatory services were repeated between April 6 and May 18, and included five sessions reserved for children under the age for baptism; about 75,000 Latter-day Saints attended. Thereafter members of the Church entered the temple only to perform ORDINANCES for the living and the dead. The following year President Woodruff announced by revelation that LDS family groups no longer needed to be sealed to prominent priesthood leaders by adoption (*see* LAW OF ADOPTION), but that they should be sealed by lineage as far back in time as possible. As a result, members began pursuing GENEALOGY and performed sealing ordinances for ancestors several generations back. The Church created the GENEALOGICAL SOCIETY OF UTAH to assist researchers.

In 1893 the Salt Lake Tabernacle Choir, while on a major tour, sang at the Chicago World's Fair, winning second prize in an important contest. The entire First Presidency traveled with the choir, marking the first time a Church President had traveled east since the migration to the West nearly fifty years before. This performance was indicative of a new public image for the Church, though that same year the Church was denied representation in the World's Parliament of Religions, which also met in Chicago.

There were other significant developments under Wilford Woodruff's direction: in November 1896, the Church's monthly Fast Day was changed from the first Thursday to the first Sunday of each

Laying the capstone of the Salt Lake Temple, April 6, 1892. The temple was dedicated one year later. Photographers: Sainsbury and Johnson.

month, a practice that continues; in 1897, the custom of REBAPTISM was ended. In the same year, Wilford Woodruff, himself a pioneer of 1847, presided over a Churchwide commemoration of the first entrance into the Salt Lake Valley fifty years before. Salt Lake City celebrated with parades, programs, and the unveiling of a Brigham Young Monument.

During the 1890s the Church and Utah joined the American mainstream economically as well as politically. Many cooperative ventures became private, and most Church-controlled businesses were sold or started to compete as income-producing enterprises. But integration into the national economy was not painless. The earlier confiscation of properties and decrease in the payment of tithing caused by the antipolygamy crusade hurt the

Church severely, as did the national depression of 1893. Leaders were forced to borrow heavily from eastern financiers to pay debts and meet obligations, and by 1898 the Church's debts exceeded $1,250,000. However, despite debt and a national depression, the Church promoted and invested in such basic industries as beet sugar manufacturing, hydroelectric power, and selected mining and transportation ventures to help expand the economic base of the Great Basin and benefit Latter-day Saint communities (*see* ECONOMIC HISTORY).

With the ending of plural marriages, the achievement of statehood for Utah, and entrance into the American mainstream in terms of politics and finances, Latter-day Saints moved firmly into a new era. One measure of the change was Church response to the Spanish-American War in 1898:

the First Presidency encouraged LDS young men to support the national effort, thereby demonstrating LDS patriotism and loyalty.

President Wilford Woodruff died on September 2, 1898, in San Francisco, California, at the age of ninety-one. In accordance with his instructions, a new First Presidency was immediately named, with Elder Lorenzo Snow becoming the Church's fifth President.

BIBLIOGRAPHY

Alexander, Thomas G. *Mormonism in Transition: A History of the Latter-day Saints, 1890–1930.* Urbana and Chicago, 1986.

Arrington, Leonard J. *Great Basin Kingdom: An Economic History of the Latter-day Saints 1830–1900.* Lincoln, Neb., 1966.

Larson, Gustive O. *The "Americanization" of Utah for Statehood.* San Marino, Calif., 1971.

Lyman, Edward Leo. *Political Deliverance: The Mormon Quest for Utah Statehood.* Urbana and Chicago, 1986.

Roberts, B. H. *A Comprehensive History of The Church of Jesus Christ of Latter-day Saints, Century I,* Vol. 6. Provo, Utah, 1965 (reprint).

WILLIAM G. HARTLEY
GENE A. SESSIONS

C. 1898–1945, TRANSITIONS: EARLY-TWENTIETH-CENTURY PERIOD

[*At the turn of the century the Church's finances suffered from the lingering effects of the federal crusade against* Polygamy *and the public doubted that its recently declared cessation of* Plural Marriage *had indeed taken effect. After discussing developments in these two areas, this article looks at the Latter-day Saints' integration into the larger American society, including examining the Church's position on war and peace. It also reviews the efforts to systematize that accompanied the steady growth throughout this period.*

In addition to cross-references found in the text, relevant general articles include Organizational and Administrative History *and* Economic History. Centennial Observances *accompanied the Church's one-hundredth anniversary in 1930.* Lorenzo Snow, Joseph F. Smith, *and* Heber J. Grant *were Presidents of the Church during this period.*]

The Church entered the twentieth century beleaguered and isolated. The LDS experience hitherto had involved founding, exodus to the isolated American West, building there a spiritual and temporal KINGDOM OF GOD, and grappling with an unsympathetic and often hostile larger American community. The year 1898, however, was a watershed. Following the death of President Wilford WOODRUFF in September, Lorenzo SNOW (1898–1901) succeeded to office and began a series of changes aimed at renewal and redefinition. He, along with his successors President Joseph F. SMITH (1901–1918) and President Heber J. GRANT (1918–1945), reacted to the sweeping changes of the first half of the twentieth century and reached back to preserve old values in a rapidly changing world. The result by the middle of the century was a Church accepted by and integrated into American society, more vigorous and vital than anyone but its most stalwart defenders might have foreseen a half century earlier.

An immediate problem was finances. The antipolygamy crusade (*see* ANTIPOLYGAMY LEGISLATION) had severely impaired revenue and assets, first by incarcerating leaders who normally managed donations and second by seizing and mismanaging Church property. The Panic of 1893 and the resulting depression made the situation worse. In an effort to provide employment and stimulate the local economy, leaders had borrowed money to fund public works and business projects. President Snow quickly ended this practice. His administration slashed expenditures, sold nonessential property, and urged followers to increase their financial contributions.

He dramatically announced this new policy in a southern Utah preaching tour. In May 1899, speaking to assembled members in St. George, he promised that faithful compliance to the Church's longstanding TITHING code would bless members and at the same time free the Church from its debts. A year after President Snow's tithing emphasis, Church income doubled. Leaders also encouraged cash donations instead of in-kind commodities and instituted systematic spending and auditing procedures. Because of these reforms, by 1907 President Smith was able to announce that the Church at last had retired its debt. Annual tithing receipts stood at $1.8 million, in contrast to the Church's 1898 debt of $1.25 million. Moreover, the Church had property worth more than $10 million. The Church never again resorted to deficit spending, not even during the Great Depression.

President Snow's reforms did not preclude the holding of investment property or controlling of businesses by Church officers and directors (*see* ECONOMIC HISTORY). While some enterprises were divested, such as the Deseret Telegraph, the Utah Light and Railway Company, and the Saltair Resort at the Great Salt Lake, the Church particularly invested in concerns that advanced its social or institutional purposes. It retained the DESERET NEWS, and in the early 1920s leaders established one of the country's first radio stations, later known as KSL RADIO. The SALT LAKE THEATRE, the pioneer playhouse, was returned to the Church to provide sanctioned recreation—only to close at the onset of the Depression because of reduced box office revenues and what Church leaders thought were declining theatrical values.

Drawing on the precedent of the NAUVOO HOUSE, Salt Lake City's Hotel Utah was built to draw tourists from hostile non-Mormon hoteliers and enhance the Church's image. The Beneficial Life Insurance Company provided low-cost insurance. The Utah Sugar Company, transformed into the Utah–Idaho Sugar Company, continued to provide local farmers a market for their most important cash crop, while Zion's Cooperative Mercantile Institution (ZCMI) and Zion's Savings Bank & Trust attended the public with competitive retailing and banking services. This altruistic investment policy was also pursued on a broader level. Church leaders sat on the board of other corporations important to the region.

These investments and the social concerns they expressed harked back to the pioneer ideals of community concern and uplift. They were not the only remnant of the past. PLURAL MARRIAGE continued to be a troublesome issue for Latter-day Saints and focused national attention on the Church, particularly during the Snow and Smith administrations. Although many members believed that the 1890 MANIFESTO ended plural marriage, others interpreted the pronouncement as simply shifting the responsibility for practicing it from the Church to the individual. As a result, from 1890 to 1904 some plural marriages continued, though on a greatly reduced level. Moreover, while some husbands stopped living with plural wives, most felt a moral and spiritual obligation to continue caring for their families.

This confusion and ambiguity spilled over visibly into politics. In 1898 Elder B. H. Roberts, a member of the FIRST COUNCIL OF SEVENTY and the husband of three wives, was elected to the U.S. House of Representatives. The Salt Lake Ministerial Association and similar organizations elsewhere used Roberts's election to focus on continuing plural marriages, charging the Church with failure to abide by the agreements that had brought UTAH STATEHOOD. Anti-Roberts petitions

In 1898 the Church found itself saddled with large debts earlier incurred to finance water and irrigation projects, sugar beet and salt factories, power plants, railroads and the completion of the Salt Lake Temple. Lorenzo Snow became president of the Church on September 13, 1898, and took immediate steps to remove this financial burden. He emphasized payment of tithing and on December 1, 1898, issued these eleven-year six-percent bonds. Half of the bonds were redeemed within five years and the entire debt was retired in 1907.

containing seven million signatures flooded Congress and the House eventually refused Roberts his seat.

Still more serious was the case of Reed Smoot. The 1903 election of Smoot, a monogamous member of the Quorum of Twelve Apostles, to the U.S. Senate once more stirred national uproar. The Senate Committee on Privileges and Elections commenced hearings on Smoot in 1904 (*see* SMOOT HEARINGS), but Congress focused more often on the Church itself. Were church and state truly separate in Utah? Did the Church control the conduct of its members? Did it encourage polygamy and polygamous cohabitation? During the two-year investigation, President Joseph F. Smith and other leaders testified before the committee. Others, such as Matthias F. Cowley and John W. Taylor, suspected of performing plural marriages since the Manifesto, refused. To close the controversy and demonstrate the Church's willingness to make the question a matter of discipline, President Smith announced a "Second Manifesto" that expressly forbade future plural marriages. He also required the resignations of both Cowley and Taylor from the Council of the Twelve. In 1907 the Senate narrowly voted to allow Smoot to retain his seat.

Plural marriage still failed to recede entirely, even in the face of the now resolute policy of President Smith and later President Grant. Elders Cowley and Taylor, for instance, each received further discipline for additional plural marriage activity, the former being "disfellowshipped," while Taylor, after taking an additional plural wife, was excommunicated. Their conduct was similar to that of a growing number of former Mormons in the twentieth century. Styled FUNDAMENTALISTS, they accepted automatic excommunication rather than yield on plural marriage or discard other nineteenth-century practices. Unlike Latter-day Saints generally, who were strengthened by their belief in current prophetic revelation and therefore approached new times in new ways, the Fundamentalists faced the modern world by looking backward.

Nor did the plural marriage issue go away in the popular press. During the first decade of the twentieth century and even beyond, the Church

The laying of the cornerstone of the Church Offices (now called the Church Administration Building) at 47 East South Temple, Salt Lake City. The building was completed in 1917. Photographer: Albert Wilkes. Courtesy the Utah State Historical Society.

came under severe public scrutiny by muckrakers and political opponents in Utah. Newspapers, magazines, and cinema in both the United States and Europe focused on sensationalized (and often fictionalized) aspects of polygamy, depicted Church leaders as autocrats, and denounced the Church as un-American and un-Christian (*see* ANTI-MORMON PUBLICATIONS; STEREOTYPING OF MORMONS). Old charges of DANITE atrocities and BLOOD ATONEMENT resurfaced. In Utah the assault was led by two former U.S. Senators, Frank J. Cannon and Thomas Kearns, who used the *Salt Lake Tribune* to launch bitter attacks on Smoot and the Church and to support the American Party. This short-lived, anti-Mormon political party controlled Salt Lake City government from 1905 to 1911.

The Church attempted to meet the barrage of abuse even though the tide flowed strongly against it. Early efforts included promoting Saltair Resort and Salt Lake City's TEMPLE SQUARE as visitors centers. With the TABERNACLE ORGAN and MORMON TABERNACLE CHOIR as attractions, the latter site by 1905 annually drew 200,000 visitors. Attendance climbed steeply thereafter. When possible, leaders placed refutations in the muckraker publications. Moreover, a point-by-point rebuttal was read during the Church 1911 general conference. Perhaps the ablest and most enduring rejoinder came from B. H. Roberts. From 1909 to 1915, he issued a series of articles on Mormon history in the magazine *Americana*. These were later updated as Roberts's fair-minded, six-volume COMPREHENSIVE HISTORY OF THE CHURCH.

Increasingly men and women outside the Church also defended the Latter-day Saints. By 1900 C. C. Goodwin, a former editor of the anti-Mormon *Salt Lake Tribune* and longstanding critic, frankly labeled Mormons as successful, prosperous, and generally likable. Leading sociologist Richard T. Ely praised LDS group life. Morris R. Werner produced a Brigham YOUNG biography devoid of previous stereotypes and hostility. These path-breaking ventures were followed by others. By the late 1920s President Grant conceded that virtually anything the Church might request could be placed in the media. Indeed *Time Magazine* gave President Grant cover treatment, while Hollywood studios completed such favorable motion pictures as *Union Pacific* and *Brigham Young.*

In part the change in public attitude came from the integration of Church members into the

The First Presidency (1934–1945) on the steps of the Church Administration Building (c. 1942). President Heber J. Grant (center), first counselor J. Reuben Clark, Jr. (left), second counselor David O. McKay (right). Courtesy Edward L. Kimball.

larger American society. Nineteenth-century Latter-day Saints expanded their agricultural settlements throughout the mountain West and even into Canada and Mexico (*see* COLONIZATION), although their agrarian communities were often tightly knit, provincial enclaves. In contrast, as LDS outmigration continued in the twentieth century, Church members now rubbed shoulders with fellow Americans in urban settings. During the 1920s, for instance, the percentage of Latter-day Saints living in the intermountain West declined while those living on the American West Coast rose. In 1923 the Los Angeles Stake, the first modern stake outside the traditional Mormon cultural area, was created. Between 1919 and 1927 the number of Latter-day Saints in California increased from fewer than 2,000 to more than 20,000. The twentieth-century Church dispersion had begun, first with the migration of large numbers to the West Coast, then also with increasing volume to the East and Midwest.

Direct contact with neighbors lessened cultural, religious, and even emotional barriers, bringing Mormons and non-Mormons an increased appreciation for each other. The growing number of successful Americans who were also Latter-day Saints or Utah-born accelerated the process. Maud Adams was lionized for her widely popular stage portrayal of Peter Pan. Philo T. Farnsworth's inventions brought about television. Cyrus Dallin and Mahonri Young achieved distinction in the arts.

Latter-day Saints were particularly drawn to public affairs. Edgar B. Brossard became a member and then chairman of the United States Tariff Commission. J. Reuben Clark, Jr., rose in the higher levels of the State Department bureaucracy, finishing his government career as ambassador to Mexico. During the New Deal, Marriner S. Eccles was chairman of the Federal Reserve System. James H. Moyle served as assistant secretary of the treasury from 1917 to 1921, while William Spry was commissioner of public lands from 1921 to 1929. Heber M. Wells was the treasurer of the U.S. Shipping Board. Richard W. Young became a U.S. commissioner of the Philippines and returned from the First World War as Utah's first regular army general. For members of a once persecuted religious minority, each such personal success betokened the Church's growing acceptance and prestige. "Outsiders" were becoming "insiders."

Two Church members had disproportionate influence in shaping the Church's new image. One was Reed Smoot. Aloof, but honest and utterly tireless in his devotion to government duty and Church interests, Smoot remained in the Senate for thirty years. As chairman of the powerful Senate Finance Committee, he wielded major influence over American economic policy. More than any other Latter-day Saint in public service, he personified the Church, assuaging questions about its patriotism and integrity by his personality and presence.

The other was President Heber J. Grant. A businessman by inclination and early profession, President Grant's homespun ways and business-mindedness charmed an age given to commercial enterprise. Non-Mormons delighted particularly in his speeches. Concluding an address before the San Francisco Commonwealth Club, he was greeted with cries of "Go on! Go on!" When he

addressed the Second Dearborn Conference of Agriculture, Industry, and Science, the "Chemurgicians" twice gave him standing ovations. His public relations ministry included more than delivering speeches. He promoted tours of the Tabernacle Choir. He personally guided nationally prominent business and political leaders through Salt Lake City and cultivated their friendship. He visited U.S. Presidents Warren G. Harding, Calvin Coolidge, Herbert Hoover, and Franklin D. Roosevelt at the White House. While President Grant was respected by his own people, non-Mormons also liked and idealized him.

The Church's sturdy growth during the period reflected its more positive image. Membership more than tripled during the half century; from the years 1900 to 1945 totals grew from 268,331 to 979,454. Prior to 1898 the Church had organized 37 stakes (16 were discontinued); by 1945 another 116 had been added. The Church's missionary force changed and increased accordingly, growing younger, attracting more unmarried individuals, and after 1898, including an increasing number of young women. At the turn of the century, fewer than 900 missionaries were called annually; by 1940 there were 2,117.

Missionary work continued to be a major preoccupation. The most ambitious new mission was Japan, opened in 1901 by missionaries led by Elder Heber J. Grant, then an apostle. Three years later the Mexican mission was reopened. The 1920s saw more than 11,000 German-speaking converts, though most converts came from English-speaking areas: Great Britain, Canada, and the United States, with the Southern States Mission being the most successful. Unfortunately, there as elsewhere, missionaries were subject to acts of physical violence. At the beginning of the century, annual convert baptisms were 3,786; a half century later the total had reached 7,877.

The Church sought to make its proselytizing more effective. Instead of dispatching missionaries without "purse and scrip," most now were financially supported by their families or local congregations. Missionary training classes were organized at Church ACADEMIES and colleges. In the mid-1920s a Salt Lake City "Mission Home" for departing sisters and elders was inaugurated, where missionaries typically received lessons on proper diet, hygiene, etiquette, and especially missionary techniques and Church doctrine for two weeks. The era also produced new proselytizing tracts. Charles

W. Penrose wrote a series entitled *Rays of Living Light*, James Talmage completed the *Great Apostasy*, and Ben E. Rich authored *A Friendly Discussion*. To preserve a sense of its heritage and to help tell its story, the Church purchased sites of significance to its early history (*see* HISTORICAL SITES): the CARTHAGE JAIL in Illinois (1903), where Joseph Smith and his brother Hyrum had been killed; a part of the Independence, Missouri, temple site (1904); Joseph Smith's birthplace in Sharon, Vermont (1905–1907); and the Smith homestead in Manchester, New York (1907). At each of these locations, the Church eventually constructed VISITORS CENTERS.

Perhaps more than by expansion, the era was characterized by internal consolidation. Lorenzo Snow's succession to office was symptomatic. For the first time the accession of the senior-tenured apostle to the office of Church president was completed within days instead of the past interregnums of about three years (*see* SUCCESSION IN THE PRESIDENCY). Recognizing the Church's increasing complexity, President Snow urged General Authorities to devote their full time to their ministry. By 1941 the question no longer was simply leadership efficiency but expansion. "The rapid growth of the Church in recent times, the constantly increasing establishment of new Wards and Stakes . . . [and] the steadily pressing necessity for increasing our missions in numbers and efficiency," the First Presidency noted in 1941, "have built up an apostolic service of the greatest magnitude" (*CR* [Apr. 1941]:94–95). In response to these new requirements, five men were appointed ASSISTANTS TO THE TWELVE. In contrast to the short-term laity that continued to occupy most Church positions, "general" Church officers—about thirty in number—now received compensation and served full-time, lifelong ministries.

Priesthood governance was also altered. The first half of the century saw a steady decentralizing of decision making as stake and local leaders received enlarged authority. The Church reduced the size of stakes to make them more functional and placed new emphasis on "ward teaching" (*see* HOME TEACHING). With smaller districts and more boys and men assigned to teaching, the percentage of families receiving monthly visits grew from 20 percent in 1911 to 70 percent a decade later. Finally, in a major departure from pioneer practice, members were urged to take secular disputes to civil and criminal courts rather than to Church tribunals. Once a means of regulating social and economic issues, Church courts now concerned themselves exclusively with Church discipline.

PRIESTHOOD QUORUMS were strengthened. Priesthood meetings were now held weekly, with meeting quality improved by centrally generated lesson materials. President Joseph F. Smith in 1906 outlined a program of progressive priesthood advancement for male youth. Contingent on worthiness, young men received ordination to the office of DEACON at the age of twelve, TEACHER at fifteen, and PRIEST three years later. In turn, worthy men typically received the offices of ELDER and HIGH PRIEST, altering the nineteenth century dominance of the SEVENTY among adult men. In 1910 quorums of high priest and seventy were realigned to coincide with stake boundaries, allowing closer direction by local authorities.

The tendency toward consolidation was also manifest in the Church's AUXILIARY ORGANIZATIONS. Youth programs, once informal, diverse, and locally administered, increasingly yielded to centrally directed age group programs and unified curricula. The children's PRIMARY Association no longer served older youth, while the Young Men's Mutual Improvement Association (YMMIA) and its young women counterpart (YWMIA) included adolescents as young as twelve (*see* YOUNG MEN; YOUNG WOMEN). At first both the national Boy Scout and Campfire Girl programs were used for younger MIA members (*see* SCOUTING), but soon the latter was dropped in favor of an indigenous program. Activity programs received increasingly strong emphasis. With SUNDAY SCHOOL and now priesthood quorums providing doctrinal instruction, the MIA increasingly turned to DANCE, DRAMA, MUSIC, and SPORTS. Church headquarters produced a magazine for each auxiliary: The Primary had the CHILDREN'S FRIEND (1902) and the Sunday School the JUVENILE INSTRUCTOR (1900), later known as the INSTRUCTOR (1929). YMMIA had the IMPROVEMENT ERA (1897), YWMIA the YOUNG WOMAN'S JOURNAL (1889); in 1929 the two joined forces and the IMPROVEMENT ERA became the publication for both. Articles, curricula, and programs were periodically reviewed and correlated. For instance, a general Church Correlation Committee and the Social Advisory Committee combined to issue a pivotal and far-reaching report in 1921 (*see* CORRELATION).

The RELIEF SOCIETY experienced these same trends. Its first three twentieth-century presidents, Zina D. H. YOUNG (1888–1901), Bathsheba W. SMITH (1901–1910), and Emmeline B. WELLS (1910–1921), all remembered the Nauvoo organization. For them women's meetings were to be spontaneous, spiritually active, and locally determined. The new century, however, redefined their vision. In 1901 a few lesson outlines were provisionally provided. Twelve years later, with the recommendation of a Church correlation committee, Relief Society leaders adopted a uniform, prescribed curriculum. They also implemented uniform meeting days (Tuesday), record books, and a monthly message for the VISITING TEACHING women who made monthly home visits. In 1915 an official RELIEF SOCIETY MAGAZINE replaced the semi-independent WOMAN'S EXPONENT, a voice for Relief Society since 1872. While the First Presidency at first endorsed the continuation of female prayer healing—often undertaken in meetings on an impromptu basis—the practice dwindled and by mid-century was abolished. As a further sign of centralization under priesthood leadership, the Relief Society was housed in the Bishop's Building and increasingly received its direction from the PRESIDING BISHOPRIC rather than the FIRST PRESIDENCY. Though Relief Society had once played a role in developing and supervising the Primary and YWMIA, their supervision of the children's and youth auxiliaries ended.

The Relief Society's later presidents, Clarissa S. WILLIAMS (1921–1928), Louise Y. ROBISON (1928–1939), and Amy Brown LYMAN (1940–1945), cooperated in these changes. Speaking for modernism and efficiency, they and their advisory boards set aside such past tasks as HOME INDUSTRY, SILK CULTURE, and commission retailing in favor of community outreach; "scientific" or professionally trained social work; campaigns against alcohol, tobacco, and delinquency; and, during the Great Depression, public relief. The latter effort was crucial. "To the extent that Relief Society Organizations in Wards are operating in cooperation with Priesthood Quorums and Bishoprics," declared Elder Harold B. Lee, who led the Church's relief efforts, "just to that extent is there a security [welfare] program in that ward" (*Relief Society Magazine* 24 [Mar. 1937]:143). These efforts reflected the early-twentieth-century Mormon feminine ideal. Women were to uplift, soften, and assist. While women leaders continued to play an active role in the National and International Council of Women, the rank and file were less active in political, social, and professional roles than in homemaking.

Several doctrinal issues were clarified, another indication of systematization at work. From the early years of the Snow administration, Church authorities discussed how strictly the 1833 health revelation, the WORD OF WISDOM, should be obeyed. In 1921 the question was answered by making abstinence from alcohol, tobacco, tea, and coffee one of the standards for admission to TEMPLES. During the century's first three decades, the health code led most Latter-day Saints to support local, state, and national PROHIBITION.

In 1909 the First Presidency issued a statement designed to clarify the Church position on EVOLUTION. While the method of CREATION was not discussed, the declaration held that "Adam was the first man and that he was created in the image of God." The issue remained troublesome, however. Along with the question of higher biblical criticism, it led to the resignation of three Brigham Young University professors in 1911 and to extended private discussion among Church leaders two decades later.

In 1916 the First Presidency and Quorum of the Twelve issued a second important doctrinal exposition entitled "The Father and the Son." Apparently occasioned by anti-Mormon pamphleteering charging the Church leaders with conferring divinity on ADAM, the statement delineated the respective roles of the first two members of the GODHEAD. Shortly before his death, Joseph F. Smith received a vision of missionary work and spiritual existence in the afterlife, which was eventually included as Section 138 in the Doctrine and Covenants. In addition to specific matters, general LDS doctrine and history received systematic treatment, often for the first time, by such works as President Smith's *Gospel Doctrine*, Elder James E. Talmage's *Articles of Faith* and *Jesus the Christ*, and Elder B. H. Roberts's three-volume *New Witnesses for God*.

With its membership still predominantly American, the Church was especially affected by the events occurring in the United States during this period. Almost from the outset, President Grant's administration was beset with hard times. Farming and mining, two of Utah's main industries, slumped badly in the 1920s and especially in the 1930s during the Great Depression. President Grant carefully conserved Church finances, trimming expenditures and construction projects.

Using his contacts with national business and political leaders, he kept key Utah and Church-owned enterprises afloat. He was also concerned for the individual Saint. After careful preparation, he announced in 1936 the Church Welfare Program (*see* WELFARE SERVICES), which sought self-sufficiency and sustenance for the needy by simultaneously providing both work and needed commodities.

Despite difficult times, the Church maintained its primary functions. Just prior to the economic downturn, it completed an imposing five-story building in Salt Lake City. Temples were completed in Hawaii (1919); Cardston, Alberta, Canada (1923); and Mesa, Arizona (1927). Education also received attention. Between 1875 and 1911, the Church established thirty-four all-purpose ACADEMIES. However, as the century progressed, financial distress and the rising acceptance of public education brought changes, and many of the academies were closed or transferred to state control (*see also* EDUCATION). The Church, however, did not entirely surrender its educative

role. A released-time seminary program for high school students began in 1912 (*see* SEMINARIES), and during the 1920s, INSTITUTES OF RELIGION for college students were established, the first at the University of Idaho.

Twentieth-century wars and warfare demonstrated the distance the Church had traveled from nineteenth-century alienation and isolation. Latter-day Saints supported the Spanish-American War effort and U.S. involvement in the two twentieth-century world wars. In the former the First Presidency issued a statement affirming the loyalty of the Latter-day Saints and telegraphed local leaders to encourage enlistment. Utah became one of the first states to fill its initial quota. Involvement in World War I was even more substantial. At first uncertain of its proper role, the Church eventually helped Utahans oversubscribe the government's financial quota for the state. By September 1918 Utah had more than 18,000 men under arms, almost half of them volunteers. Participation in the Second World War was more dutiful, perhaps be-

The Quorum of the Twelve Apostles (1941–1943) on the steps of the Church Administration Building. Right to left: Rudger Clawson, [George Albert Smith—not present], George F. Richards, Joseph Fielding Smith, Stephen L Richards, Richard R. Lyman, John A. Widtsoe, Joseph F. Merrill, Charles A. Callis, Albert E. Bowen, Sylvester Q. Cannon, Harold B. Lee.

cause of the private misgivings of President Grant and his Counselor J. Reuben Clark over New Deal policymaking. Nevertheless, by April 1942, 6 percent of the total Church population served in the American forces or in defense-related industries; others served for Canada, Britain, and Germany.

While each conflict saw some pacifist currents and even opposition, the general tendency was supportive of the need to yield loyalty to constituted government. "The Church is and must be against war," the First Presidency declared in April 1942. Yet when "constitutional law . . . calls the manhood of the Church into the armed service of any country to which they owe allegiance, their highest civic duty requires that they heed that call" (*CR*, pp. 88–97; *see* WAR AND PEACE).

While documenting religiosity is difficult, statistics suggest the impact of the Church on the everyday life of its people. Meeting attendance showed sturdy growth throughout the era. In 1920 weekly average attendance at sacrament meeting was 16 percent; in 1930, 19 percent; in 1940, 23 percent; and 1950, 25 percent. Suggestive of Church family ideals, LDS birthrates exceeded the national average, as did marriage rates. No doubt the Church health code is reflected in the fact that in 1945 the LDS death rate was about half the national average.

A closer view of statistics reveals that in the decades of the early twentieth century the number of children born per LDS family declined, the age at time of marriage increased, and divorce ratios often mirrored national trends—lingering behind but moving in the same direction as national trends, as if assimilation were simply incomplete (*see* VITAL STATISTICS).

The half-century brought social, cultural, and political integration; growth and consolidation; and programs that redefined and reapplied earlier Church ideals. But the era also produced indications that Church members were not immune to such broad currents as secularism and even materialism. For observers, at mid-century basic questions remained: Could the Church preserve its traditional values and energy? Or would its journey into the modern world cost the movement its identity and mission?

BIBLIOGRAPHY

For general surveys of the period:

Alexander, Thomas G. *Mormonism in Transition: A History of the Latter-day Saints, 1890–1930.* Urbana, Ill., 1986.

Allen, James B., and Glen M. Leonard. *The Story of the Latter-day Saints.* Salt Lake City, 1976.

Arrington, Leonard J., and Davis Bitton. *The Mormon Experience.* New York, 1979.

Church Education System. *Church History in the Fulness of Times.* Salt Lake City, 1989.

Cowan, Richard O. *The Church in the Twentieth Century.* Salt Lake City, 1985.

Roberts, B. H. *A Comprehensive History of The Church of Jesus Christ of Latter-day Saints.* Salt Lake City, 1930.

For LDS programs, policies, and teachings during the period:

Alexander, Thomas G. "Between Revivalism and the Social Gospel: The Latter-day Saints Social Advisory Committee, 1916–1922." *BYU Studies* 23 (Winter 1983):19–39.

———. "The Reconstruction of Mormon Doctrine: From Joseph Smith to Progressive Theology." *Sunstone* 5 (July–Aug. 1980):24–33.

———. "'To Maintain Harmony': Adjusting to External and Internal Stress, 1890–1930." *Dialogue* 15 (Winter 1982): 44–58.

Hartley, William G. "The Priesthood Reform Movement, 1908–1922." *BYU Studies* 13 (Winter 1973):137–56.

Hefner, Loretta L. "This Decade Was Different: Relief Society's Social Services Department, 1919–1929." *Dialogue* 15 (Autumn 1982):64–73.

RONALD W. WALKER
RICHARD W. SADLER

C. 1945–1990, POST–WORLD WAR II INTERNATIONAL ERA PERIOD

[*Since World War II, the Church has enjoyed—and had to cope with—rapid international growth. After summarizing postwar revitalization and the attendant increases in membership, the article focuses on the adaptations that accompanied growth and internationalization. In surveying recent developments, it provides an introduction to the contemporary Church.*

For additional information about Church growth during this period, see Vital Statistics *and articles about the Church in* Africa; Asia, East; Asia, South and Southeast; Australia; British Isles; Canada; Europe; Hawaii; Mexico and Central America; Middle East; New Zealand; Oceania; Scandinavia; South America: Brazil; South America: North; South America: South; *and* West Indies. *For developments in organization and procedure, see* Organization: Organizational and Administrative History; Organization: Contemporary. *Consult also the biographies of those who served as Church President in this period: George Albert* Smith *(1945–1951); David O.* McKay *(1951–1970); Joseph Fielding* Smith *(1970–1972); Harold B.* Lee *(1972–1973); Spencer W.* Kimball *(1973–1985); and Ezra Taft* Benson *(1985–).*]

Throughout his life and ministry, President George Albert SMITH's prevailing message was one of love. It was fitting, therefore, that it was during his administration that goods were sent from America to Europe to help relieve the suffering of the Saints following World War II, especially those in Germany who had been devastated by war. In 1946 Ezra Taft BENSON, of the Council of the Twelve Apostles, directed the reopening of the European Mission and the Church's relief efforts there. He found branches disorganized, meetinghouses destroyed, and many members without homes. Most had lost possessions and everywhere there was pressing need for food and clothing. The Church's welfare services became a significant factor in the recovery of many Saints as well as some nonmembers.

Since the war had postponed everything from missionary work to building construction, it was necessary to reestablish and revitalize Church programs everywhere. The missionary force was rapidly rebuilt and hundreds of meetinghouses were constructed. Half of all the chapels in use in the mid-1950s were erected in the years following World War II, a period when more than half of all Church expenditures went for building projects.

BECOMING AN INTERNATIONAL CHURCH. The close of World War II marked the dawn of a new era in Church history in which a dominant theme was international growth. In 1947 Church membership reached one million, and by 1990 the total was over seven million. Growth was especially strong along America's West Coast, in Latin America, and, after 1978, in Africa. In 1950 the Church had 180 organized stakes, nearly half of them in Utah; in 1990 there were 1,700 stakes, with less than one-fourth in Utah. In 1950 the Church was organized in fewer than 50 nations or territories, but by 1990 it had expanded to 128. Less than 8 percent of the Church lived outside the United States and Canada in 1950, but forty years later this was approximately 35 percent. During the same period the number of missionaries grew from 6,000 to 40,000 and the number of TEMPLES increased from eight, only one of which was outside the United States, to forty-four, with twenty-three outside the United States.

This remarkable growth resulted from renewed efforts to fulfill the revelation given to Joseph Smith "that the kingdom . . . may become a great mountain and fill the whole earth" (D&C 109:72). Early in his administration President David O. MCKAY, the first to travel so extensively

as Church President, toured missions in Europe, Latin America, Africa, and the South Pacific, dedicating two temple sites in Europe and announcing that a temple would be built in New Zealand. In 1955 he declared that the Church must "put forth every effort within reason and practicability to place within reach of Church members in these distant missions every educational and spiritual privilege that the Church has to offer" (CR [Apr. 1955]:25). Building temples, increasing the number of missions, organizing stakes worldwide, persuading the Saints to build up Zion in their homelands rather than emigrate to America, and eventually putting Church leadership into the hands of each country's native people were all significant steps toward fulfilling that goal. In addition, increasing emphasis was placed on calling local missionaries who, in some areas, later essentially replaced American missionaries.

Growth did not come without its problems, however, not the least of which was sorting out which practices, teachings, and programs really constituted the essence of the gospel and which were reflections of the American culture in which the Church had grown. To open the eyes of members—particularly Americans—to the need for defining the gospel in terms of universal principles, Church leaders spoke out with increasing frequency. In 1971, for example, Elder Bruce R. McConkie reminded some American Saints that in New Testament times even the apostles were so indoctrinated with the idea that the plan of salvation was limited to a particular people that they found it difficult to take it to gentile nations, and he applied the lesson to the modern Church. He called upon American Saints to rise above their biases, though there would be "some struggles and some difficulties, some prejudices, and some uncertainties along the way." Other peoples, he noted, "have a different background than we have, which is of no moment to the Lord. . . . It is no different to have different social customs than it is to have different languages. . . . And the Lord knows all languages" (Palmer, pp. 143, 147). In 1987 Elder Boyd K. Packer reminded a group of Church leaders that "We can't move [into various countries] with a 1947 Utah Church! Could it be that we are not prepared to take the *gospel* because we are not prepared to take (and they are not prepared to receive) all of the things we have wrapped up with it as extra baggage?" (as quoted in *Dialogue* 21 [Fall 1988]:97). The goal was to ennoble

The Church of Jesus Christ of Latter-day Saints in the United States and Canada. Areas and membership as of January 1, 1991.

The Church of Jesus Christ of Latter-day Saints in the United States and Canada. First stake in each state or province, and temples with dedication date as of January 1, 1991. ⟶

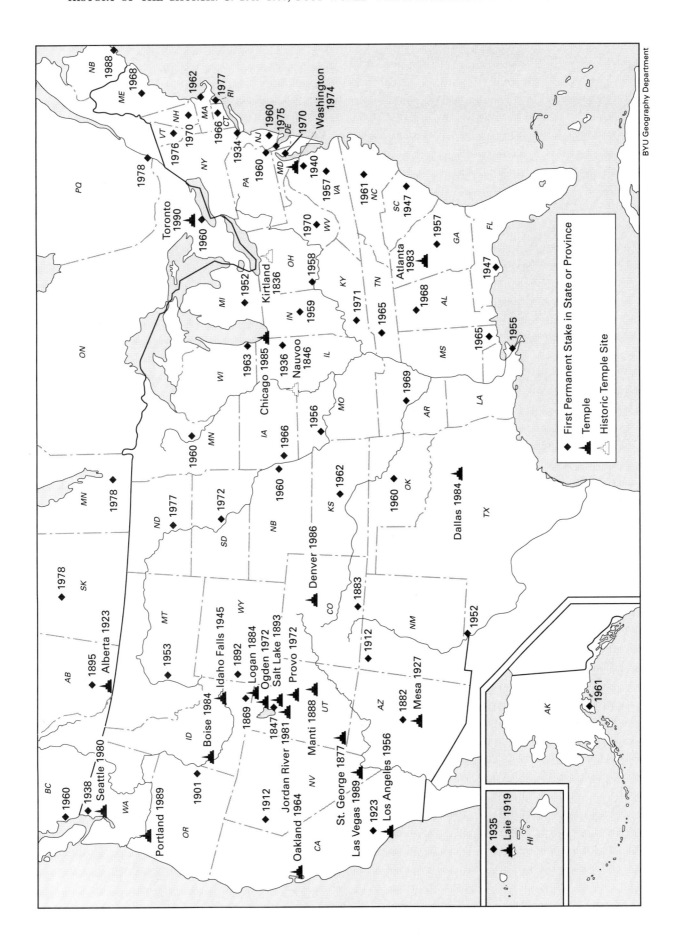

BYU Geography Department

First Permanent Stake in State or Province

Temple

Historic Temple Site

Elder Spencer W. Kimball puts his arms around President Harold B. Lee during a break at the Munich Area Conference, August 1973, four months before Lee died and Kimball became President. Courtesy Edward L. Kimball.

people of diverse cultures and perspectives to more fully find true brotherhood and sisterhood within the common spiritual bounds of the Church.

In 1974 President Spencer W. KIMBALL challenged members to "lengthen our stride" in carrying the gospel to all the earth, and urged them to pray that barriers might be removed. He appointed David M. Kennedy, former U.S. secretary of the treasury and ambassador-at-large, as the Church's international representative to work with governments in resolving problems that had hindered the Church's activities. In 1977 the Church was legally recognized in Poland, and in 1985 a temple was dedicated in the German Democratic Republic. The dramatic political revolutions of 1989–1990 opened other eastern bloc countries and led to the beginnings of LDS missionary work in the Soviet Union.

One of the far-reaching changes in the twentieth century was the revelation received by President Spencer W. Kimball in June 1978 extending priesthood blessings to all worthy male members. The result of long and earnest prayer, the revelation meant that "the long-promised day has come when every faithful, worthy man in the Church may receive the holy priesthood . . . without regard for race or color" (*see* DOCTRINE AND COVENANTS: DECLARATION—2). Without delay, worthy BLACKS were sealed in temples and many received assignments as missionaries and leaders. In Ghana and Nigeria, where blacks had been pleading for the establishment of the Church for years, the Church grew rapidly, but it also expanded in other areas with large black populations. The first black General Authority, Elder Helvécio Martins of Brazil, was sustained at the general conference of the Church in April 1990.

ADMINISTRATIVE CHANGES. Numerous administrative changes also reflected the demands of Church growth. In 1967 stakes were organized into REGIONS. Beginning in 1975, several regions were organized into AREAS, and by 1984 area presidencies, each consisting of three General Authorities, were assigned responsibility for stakes throughout the world.

In 1975 President Kimball announced the organization of the First Quorum of the SEVENTY, members of which were General Authorities of the Church and included the former ASSISTANTS TO THE TWELVE. In 1989 the Second Quorum of the Seventy was organized; these General Authorities serve for terms of three or five years. In 1978 the practice was begun of placing members of the Seventy on emeritus status for reasons of health or age, and the following year the PATRIARCH TO THE CHURCH also became an emeritus.

General Authorities also took steps to more effectively coordinate Church programs and, beginning in 1961, placed greater emphasis on "priesthood correlation" (*see* PRIESTHOOD; CORRELATION OF THE CHURCH). Under the chairmanship of Elder Harold B. Lee, committees at Church headquarters planned, prepared, and reviewed curricula and activities for all organizations or age groups. They defined more carefully the unique roles of each organization and eliminated unnecessary duplication. Leaders focused on the home as the most effective place for teaching and applying gospel principles. FAMILY HOME

The Salt Lake Temple, the twenty-eight-story Church Office Building, and former Hotel Utah Building (being renovated into Church offices, a chapel, and other facilities), c. 1989.

EVENING received renewed emphasis, and beginning in 1965 attractive manuals providing lesson helps were issued.

In the early 1970s there was also a consolidation of administrative responsibilities at Church headquarters. Agencies were grouped into several large departments, each under the jurisdiction of one or more General Authorities, with full-time professionals generally managing day-to-day operations. For example, the welfare, social services, and health programs were consolidated into a WELFARE SERVICES Department. A tangible symbol of this consolidation was the new twenty-eight-story Church office building in Salt Lake City, bringing most Church administrative units together. In 1970, functions of Aaronic Priesthood and the Young Men's Mutual Improvement Association were combined (see YOUNG MEN). In 1971 the publishing program was consolidated (see MAGAZINES). Magazines in other languages than English were unified in 1967, with standardized content except for local matters (see INTERNATIONAL MAGAZINES).

Other changes came as rapid international growth increased the travel and administrative load of Church leaders. In the 1970s STAKE PRESIDENTS were authorized to "set apart" full-time missionaries (see SETTING APART), ordain BISHOPS and PATRIARCHS, and dedicate chapels. General Authorities met in conference with individual stakes less frequently but, beginning in 1971, the Church began holding "area conferences," where a delegation of General Authorities met with the Saints gathered from geographic regions. In 1979 the number of stake conferences each year was reduced from four to two, and in the 1980s regional or multiregional conferences replaced area conferences (see CONFERENCES).

CHURCH EDUCATION. Between 1950 and 1990 total enrollment in the Church's educational programs increased from 38,400 to 442,500 (see CHURCH EDUCATIONAL SYSTEM). Full-time enrollment at BRIGHAM YOUNG UNIVERSITY soared from 5,400 in 1950 to nearly 25,000 by 1975, leading to an enrollment ceiling. Rather than devoting ever larger amounts to higher education, funds increasingly went to meet more basic needs associated with worldwide growth. The major expansion in enrollment came in the area of religious education. Since the early twentieth century, students in predominantly LDS communities had attended "released time" SEMINARY classes adjacent to their secondary schools. Beginning in California in the 1950s, "early morning" seminaries convened in church buildings near public secondary schools. After 1968, in areas where members were even more scattered, young people received "home study" seminary materials. The Church also increased the number of INSTITUTES of religion placed adjacent to college and university campuses. By 1990 seminary or institute programs were conducted in seventy-four nations or territories.

The Church also gave special attention to the religious life of college students. In 1956 the first student stake, with twelve wards, was organized on the Brigham Young University campus. This provided Church services that ministered directly to student needs and offered expanded opportunities for leadership. The plan spread to other areas where there were enough students to justify it. Subjective evidence suggested greater spiritual growth; and in such statistically measurable matters as temple marriage and attendance at meetings, student wards led the Church.

In some areas of the Pacific and Latin America, areas of particularly rapid Church growth where public education was not widely available, the Church returned to its earlier practice of establishing schools for religious instruction and to teach educational basics. It established forty elementary and secondary schools in Mexico, and established a junior college on the outskirts of Mexico City. As better public educational facilities developed, the Church closed many schools.

BUILDING PROGRAM. New congregations required new buildings. Even with two or three wards sharing most buildings, the Church found it necessary to complete more than one new MEETINGHOUSE every day. Potential costs were enormous, and in many areas the local Saints could not afford to raise their share.

One solution emerged when the Church encountered a labor shortage while erecting school buildings in the South Pacific. Beginning in 1950, it called young men as "building missionaries" to donate their labor for two years. As they completed buildings at a much lower cost, experienced builders taught them construction skills; labor missionaries also learned marketable skills from experienced builders. In the 1950s and 1960s building missionaries erected schools and chapels in the South Pacific, Latin America, Europe, and elsewhere. Later, in an effort to minimize construction and maintenance costs, the building department developed a series of standardized plans that could be adapted to different locations and expanded as needed.

Though general Church funds assisted with meetinghouses, local congregations were expected to contribute not only labor but also a significant portion of the money needed—in addition to paying regular tithes and offerings. With a view toward easing the financial burden on local congregations, the share borne by local Saints gradually diminished until, by 1989, local contribution was no longer required.

By the 1980s, new meetinghouses were generally smaller and sometimes more austere than earlier ones, but this approach allowed the Church to erect hundreds of chapels annually, and especially to provide badly needed meeting places in developing areas. It was also a move towards equality. Money that might have gone to build more expensive buildings in affluent areas instead provided comfortable places for worship throughout the Church.

TECHNOLOGY AND THE MODERN CHURCH. The Church actively seeks to harness the astonishing developments in modern technology to enhance its administrative capabilities and to aid in delivering its spiritual message. Since the Church installed its first computer in the Financial Department in 1962, it has made use of this technology in myriad ways, including in architectural design, a computerized membership record system, automated accounting, processing missionary papers, record keeping at both the general and local level, and in providing resources for historical and genealogical research.

Perhaps no Church activity has felt the impact of modern technology more than genealogical work. As Church membership grew, so did the need for more effective means of gathering and processing names for temple work. The Genealogical Department (now the Family History Department) microfilmed vital records from around the world, making them available in its library in Salt Lake City (*see* FAMILY HISTORY LIBRARY) and in hundreds of FAMILY HISTORY CENTERS throughout the world. In the 1960s, the Genealogical Department also began using the computer to organize names obtained from these records. Since 1978, designated Church members have been devoting four or more hours of weekly service "extracting" information from microfilms for the sake of temple work. The Family History Department also produced PERSONAL ANCESTRAL FILE, a widely used computerized genealogical program, and began making key genealogical data available on laser disks.

Technology touched the temple in other ways. Motion picture and video technology allowed temple instructions to be presented more efficiently and more effectively. Because this could be done in one room instead of the former series of four rooms, temples could be built smaller and thus were less expensive to construct, making it possible for more members throughout the world to have a temple nearby. The new technology also made it possible to present the ORDINANCES in several languages simultaneously, if necessary.

The effect of television on Church communications and the Church public image was also dramatic. General conferences of the Church were first broadcast on KSL Television in Salt Lake City in 1949, and by the mid-1960s one or more session of each conference were being televised coast-to-coast in the United States. In the 1980s the Church developed a SATELLITE COMMUNICATION SYSTEM connected to stake centers throughout the world so that Latter-day Saints could view both conference and other Church-initiated programs.

MISSIONARY WORK. By 1990 over two-thirds of the Church's annual growth came from convert baptisms. Approximately 30,000 of more than 40,000 full-time missionaries were young men ages nineteen to twenty-one; single women twenty-one years of age or older and couples who had reached retirement age made up most of the remainder.

Considerable attention was given to improving proselytizing techniques and abilities. After much experimentation, a systematic plan based on a series of regularized lesson discussions was officially adopted in the 1950s. After considerable refinement and modification, by 1990 the plan focused less on memorization on the part of the missionaries and more on their ability to rely on the Spirit in the presentation of outlined subject matter.

Missionaries were also given more effective training, especially in languages. In 1963 a Language Training Mission, later known as MISSIONARY TRAINING CENTER, was established near Brigham Young University, and five years later a similar program opened near the Church College of Hawaii (*see* BRIGHAM YOUNG UNIVERSITY: HAWAII CAMPUS). By 1990 missionaries were receiving intensive language and missionary training in fourteen missionary training centers around the world, though about 75 percent were attending the Provo center.

Innovations in the missionary program included encouraging more nonproselytizing activities and Christian service. In 1971, for instance, "health missionaries" began teaching the basics of nutrition, sanitation, and disease prevention, especially in developing countries. By 1990 all missionaries were urged to spend two to four hours a week in community service, in addition to proselytizing. Also, older missionary couples were often assigned to nonproselytizing Church service, including health and welfare work, leadership training, staffing VISITORS CENTERS and doing other public relations activities, assisting patrons in the Church's various family history centers, temple service missions, and teaching missions.

PUBLIC ISSUES AND SOCIAL CONCERNS. Though the Church attempted to distance itself from direct political involvement, Church leaders nevertheless from time to time declared official positions on moral issues. The First Presidency publicly lamented the growing flood of PORNOGRAPHY, the widespread practice of BIRTH CONTROL, and ABORTION, and the general decline in moral standards, including the rising number of DIVORCES and the increased prominence of HOMOSEXUALITY. In 1968 the Church became directly involved in Utah's political process by openly opposing liquor-by-the-drink. It has also made public pronouncements in favor of Sunday closing laws and state right-to-work laws and against state lotteries (*see* GAMBLING).

Amid the intense civil rights conflict that characterized the United States in the 1960s the First Presidency openly called for "full civil equality for all of God's children," and specifically urged Latter-day Saints to work for civil rights for blacks.

In the 1970s, as the controversy in America over women's rights escalated, the First Presidency took a public stance in favor of full equality before the law for women but, at the same time, publicly opposed the Equal Rights Amendment as anti-family. The First Presidency was also deeply concerned with the morality of the nuclear arms race and officially denounced it in 1980 and again in 1981 (see WAR AND PEACE).

In contrast to the early twentieth century when most Latter-day Saints lived in predominately rural settings, since mid-century, most have lived in urban centers. The hectic lifestyle in large cities created added emotional strains, and an array of attractions and temptations tended to pull family members in different directions. Responding to these and other needs, the Church instituted a series of social programs. Since 1919 the Relief Society had operated an adoption agency and provided foster homes for disadvantaged children. This was expanded. The INDIAN STUDENT PLACEMENT SERVICES, begun in the 1950s under the chairmanship of Elder Spencer W. Kimball, extended to thousands of NATIVE AMERICAN children the advantages of attending good schools while living in wholesome LDS family environments. A "youth guidance" program provided counseling to families in need. These three programs, required by law to employ licensed professional social workers, were combined in 1969 to form the Church's SOCIAL SERVICES Department. This department also sponsored youth day camps, programs for members in prison, and counseling for alcohol or drug abusers.

Church leaders also began to show more concern for the special needs of unmarried men and women. Whether divorced, widowed, or simply never married, their social and spiritual needs were often not being met through traditional Church activity oriented toward couples and families. In the 1970s special programs for young single adults as well as older singles were created under the auspices of the priesthood and Relief Society. Through self-directed councils at the ward, stake, and regional level, they participated in dances and other cultural activities and found broader opportunities to become acquainted with other members their own age who shared common interests. In addition, wards for young singles were organized, first in the Emigration Stake in Salt Lake City, and then in other areas.

RETURN TO BASICS. One of President Ezra Taft Benson's clarion calls to the Saints in the 1980s was to return to traditional values. In particular, he urged regular study of the Book of Mormon as a means to strengthen faith in Christ and to receive guidance in meeting contemporary challenges. His call, however, was only one manifestation of the efforts of modern Church leaders to respond to the ever-deepening challenges of the world and to lead the Saints in a return to basics.

In 1972 the adult Gospel Doctrine class in Sunday School began a systematic study of the STANDARD WORKS. The scriptures were the only texts, and they were to be studied in an eight-year (later four-year) rotation. Soon all Church curricula were tied to the scriptures. To support the curriculum and encourage individual scripture study, Church leaders supervised the publication of new editions of the standard works, each cross-referenced to the others. The Church publication of the King James Version of the Bible, in 1979, contained an important 800-page appendix that included a BIBLE DICTIONARY, a TOPICAL GUIDE to all the scriptures, maps, and extracts from the JOSEPH SMITH TRANSLATION OF THE BIBLE. In 1981 new editions of the other standard works appeared, including additional study helps.

The "return to basics" theme was echoed also in many other changes in Church policies and programs. In 1980 the Church meeting schedule was consolidated into a single three-hour block on Sundays, replacing the traditional schedule of priesthood meeting and SUNDAY SCHOOL in the morning, SACRAMENT MEETING in the late afternoon or evening, and auxiliary meetings during the week (see MEETINGS, MAJOR CHURCH). The move simplified transportation challenges for many members, but Church leaders emphasized that the central objective was to allow more time for families to study the scriptures or engage in other appropriate Sabbath activities together.

Beginning in 1990 in the United States and Canada and extended to other parts of the world in 1991, ward and stake budget donations were no longer required from members; all operating expenses of local units would be paid from tithes and offerings. The uniform system promoted greater equality, cutting many local operating budgets while increasing others (see FINANCES OF THE CHURCH; FINANCIAL CONTRIBUTIONS). In explaining the new policy, Elder Boyd K. Packer of the

Council of the Twelve called it an inspired "course correction," part of an overall effort to get back to basics (*Ensign* 10 [May 1990]:89–91). The metaphor could well be applied to much of what had happened since 1945.

Church members have generally accepted changes well, and have seen in them an opportunity for further spiritual growth. As a result, in 1990 the Church was moving more rapidly than ever before toward being able to accommodate diverse nationalities, language groups, and cultures. Church leaders continued to emphasize the traditional doctrines, but general conference addresses increasingly tended also to define Sainthood in terms of what Elder M. Russell Ballard characterized in April 1990, as the "small and simple things": love, service, home, family, and worship of the Savior (*Ensign* 10 [May 1990]:6–8). These are among the universals that constitute the essence of what it means to be a Latter-day Saint.

BIBLIOGRAPHY

Much has been written about this period in professional journals. A few broad treatments are mentioned in the introduction to this history section. See also Spencer J. Palmer, *The Expanding Church* (Salt Lake City, 1978). For additional information, consult the bibliographies accompanying the biographies of Church Presidents who served during this period: George Albert Smith, David O. McKay, Joseph Fielding Smith, Harold B. Lee, Spencer W. Kimball, and Ezra Taft Benson.

JAMES B. ALLEN
RICHARD O. COWAN

HISTORY OF THE CHURCH (HISTORY OF JOSEPH SMITH)

The seven-volume history of The Church of Jesus Christ of Latter-day Saints titled *History of the Church* covers less than two decades and might better be titled "The History of Joseph Smith." It is the official history of the Church's founding generation, still in print and still widely used. The motivation for compiling this early history was fourfold: (1) to obey a commandment of the Lord (D&C 21:1); (2) to preserve a record of the Church for later generations (*see* RECORD KEEPING); (3) to combat and correct ANTI-MORMON PUBLICATIONS; and (4) to provide a written record as a protection against false accusations and lawsuits (*see* SMITH, JOSEPH: TRIALS OF JOSEPH SMITH).

Although the responsibility for keeping a history of the Church was delegated to the Church recorder and historian, Joseph Smith was the prime motivator. He selected able men, gave them regular encouragement and instruction, and provided space for them in his home or store. Because of his lack of formal education, Joseph Smith depended on others to do most of the actual writing of both the sources and the completed history. More than two dozen scribes and writers are known to have assisted him.

After several early attempts, Joseph Smith and his clerk, James Mulholland, began this history at Commerce, Illinois, on June 10, 1839 (*HC* 3:375–77). Originally titled "The History of Joseph Smith," it began with a first-person account of Joseph Smith's early visions (*see* VISIONS OF JOSEPH SMITH), which had been written in the spring of 1838 (*HC* 3:25–26). Although little of the subsequent history was dictated or written by the Prophet himself, writers used his diaries where available and retained the first-person narrative style throughout.

A series of scribes, clerks, and Church historians labored sporadically on the history for nearly twenty years, through difficult periods of persecution, pioneer travel, and western colonization. Written as annals rather than narrative history, the manuscript version fills six large journals called the "Manuscript History of the Church." Willard Richards, appointed as Joseph Smith's "private Sect. & Historian" on December 21, 1842, compiled most of the history—over half after the death of Joseph Smith on June 27, 1844. With the assistance of his adopted son and clerk, Thomas Bullock, Richards completed the narrative to March 1, 1843, before his own death in 1854. It was left to George A. Smith, his successor as Church Historian, to compile the history of the MARTYRDOM OF JOSEPH AND HYRUM SMITH, expand notes of the Prophet's sermons, and continue the narrative into August 1844, when Brigham YOUNG was sustained to lead the Church.

The Church published this history serially in its periodicals, first in the TIMES AND SEASONS at Nauvoo and then in Salt Lake City's DESERET NEWS from 1852 to 1857. The seven-volume version published by the Church today is a product of the editing of B. H. Roberts of the Seventy, who worked intermittently on the project from 1902 to 1932. Because it quotes extensively from letters, minutes, and diaries of the day, the *History of the Church* has often been referred to as the *Documentary History of the Church*, or *DHC*.

Emphasizing the role of God in human affairs, this history falls within the Judeo-Christian tradition of "providential history." Because it was not written in a literary vacuum, it exhibits characteristics and flaws commonly found in the history and biography of its day: unacknowledged ghostwriting, edited sources, and a lack of balance. The most frequent distortion is the changing of an associate's third-person description of Joseph Smith's words and actions to a first-person account attributed to Joseph Smith, thereby conveying a false sense that he wrote it. Nonetheless, resting as it does on extensive documents from the period and compiled by persons who were eyewitnesses to the events, the factual content of the history has proven reliable.

BIBLIOGRAPHY

Jessee, Dean C. "The Writing of Joseph Smith's History." *BYU Studies* 11 (Summer 1971):439–73.

———. *The Personal Writings of Joseph Smith.* Salt Lake City, 1984.

———. *The Papers of Joseph Smith*, Vol. 1. Salt Lake City, 1989.

HOWARD C. SEARLE

HOLINESS

In LDS thought, as in most religions, it is God who invests a person, place, or object with holiness: "For I am able to make you holy, and your sins are forgiven you" (D&C 60:7). Thus the TEMPLES of the Church are said to be holy because they are dedicated to Deity who has manifested himself within them. Latter-day Saints speak of the SABBATH as holy because God has put his spirit into that day. The wooded area where Joseph SMITH received his FIRST VISION is spoken of as the SACRED GROVE because the Father and the Son appeared there. Marriage and other priesthood ORDINANCES are considered holy because God is directly and personally a party to such covenants. The scriptures are holy because they contain the word of God.

Although they infrequently use the term "holy" (an exception is in a beloved hymn which beseeches God, "More holiness give me"), Latter-day Saints strive for a measure of holiness and PERFECTION in MORTALITY: "Man may be perfect in his sphere; . . . individual perfection is relative. . . . The law of the Gospel is a perfect law and the sure effect of full obedience thereto is perfection" (Talmage, p. 169).

The process of becoming holy is based on three doctrines: JUSTIFICATION, which satisfies the demands of justice for the sins of the individual through the ATONEMENT OF JESUS CHRIST; purification, made possible by that same atonement and symbolized in the SACRAMENT of the bread and water, requiring the constant cleansing of oneself from earthly stains and imperfections; and SANCTIFICATION, the process of being made holy. Having

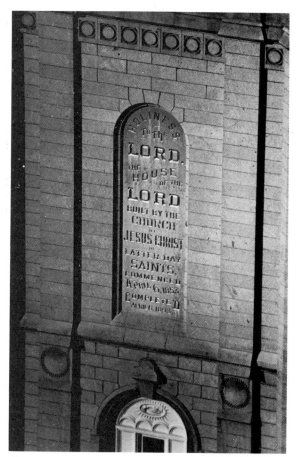

The eastern face of the Salt Lake Temple and of each LDS temple bears the inscription, "Holiness to the Lord." The phrase also appeared on doorknobs and other articles of daily use in Nauvoo and pioneer Utah, reflecting the prophecy in Zech. 14:20–21 that "in that day shall there be upon the bells of the horses, HOLINESS UNTO THE LORD . . . Yea, every pot in Jerusalem and Judah shall be holiness unto the Lord of hosts."

purified oneself of imperfections to the greatest degree possible, one is invested, over a lifetime, with holiness from God. ALMA₂ is an example of one recognized by God as holy (Alma 10:7–9).

These principles are summarized in the next to the last verse of the Book of Mormon: "And again, if ye by the grace of God are perfect in Christ, and deny not his power, then are ye sanctified in Christ by the grace of God, through the shedding of the blood of Christ, which is in the covenant of the Father unto the remission of your sins, that ye become holy, without spot" (Moro. 10:33).

BIBLIOGRAPHY

Lee, Harold B. *Stand Ye in Holy Places.* Salt Lake City, 1974.

Talmage, James E. *The Vitality of Mormonism*, p. 169. Boston, 1919.

ELOUISE M. BELL

HOLY GHOST

The Church of Jesus Christ of Latter-day Saints teaches that the Holy Ghost is a spirit man, a spirit son of GOD THE FATHER. It is fundamental Church doctrine that God is the Father of the spirits of all men and women, that Jesus is literally God's Son both in the spirit and in the flesh, and that the Holy Ghost is a personage of spirit separate and distinct from both the Father and the Son. The Holy Ghost is the third member of the Eternal GODHEAD, and is identified also as the HOLY SPIRIT, Spirit of God, Spirit of the Lord, and the COMFORTER. All three members of the Godhead were manifested at Jesus' baptism (Mark 1:9–12; *see also* DOVE, SIGN OF). Regarding them the Prophet Joseph SMITH taught: "The Father has a body of flesh and bones as tangible as man's; the Son also; but the Holy Ghost has not a body of flesh and bones, but is a personage of Spirit. Were it not so, the Holy Ghost could not dwell in us" (D&C 130:22). In a figurative sense, the Holy Ghost dwells in the hearts of the righteous Saints of all DISPENSATIONS (D&C 20:18–21).

Joseph Smith also stated that an "everlasting covenant was made between three personages before the organization of this earth, and relates to their dispensation of things to men on the earth; these personages . . . are called God the first, the

Creator; God the second, the Redeemer; and God the third, the witness or Testator" (*TPJS*, p. 190).

Latter-day Saints understand that by obedience to the laws and ORDINANCES of the gospel Adam received the Holy Ghost and thus learned that redemption from the Fall will come through Christ to all who accept him (Moses 5:6–9). Thus, the gospel was preached from the beginning, being declared by ANGELS, by the voice of God, and by the GIFT OF THE HOLY GHOST (Moses 5:58–59; cf. 2 Pet. 1:21). NEPHI₁ (c. 600 B.C.) testified that the Holy Ghost is "the gift of God unto all those who diligently seek him, as well in times of old as in the time that he should manifest himself unto the children of men. . . . For he that diligently seeketh shall find; and the mysteries of God shall be unfolded unto them, by the power of the Holy Ghost, as well in these times as in times of old, and as well in times of old as in times to come" (1 Ne. 10:17–19).

Joseph Smith taught that the influence of the Holy Ghost, which is the convincing power of God of the truth of the gospel, can be received before BAPTISM, but the gift, or constant companionship, of the Holy Ghost, which comes by the LAYING-ON OF HANDS, is obtained only after baptism (*TPJS*, p. 199). "You might as well baptize a bag of sand as a man," he said, "if not done in view of the remission of sins and getting of the Holy Ghost. Baptism by water is but half a baptism, and is good for nothing without the other half—that is, the baptism of the Holy Ghost" (*TPJS*, p. 314). Thus, a person is expected to receive the witness of the Holy Ghost to the truthfulness of the gospel of Jesus Christ, of scripture, and of the words of the living PROPHETS before baptism; the full outpouring of the Spirit does not come, however, until the person has complied with the command to be baptized. Only after baptism can the gift be conferred by one in AUTHORITY (Moro. 10:3–5; D&C 76:52). And even then the Holy Ghost cannot be received by someone who is not worthy of it, since the Holy Ghost will not dwell in the heart of an unrighteous person. Thus, the actual companionship of the Holy Ghost may be received immediately after baptism or at a subsequent time, when the one receiving the promise becomes a fit companion for that holy being. Should the individual cease thereafter to be clean and obedient, the Holy Ghost will withdraw (1 Cor. 3:16–17).

The Holy Ghost is a sanctifier. Because no unclean thing can dwell in a divine presence, the whole system of salvation centers on the process of sanctification; people are saved to the extent that they are sanctified. Sanctification and holiness are inseparable. "To be sanctified is to become clean, pure, and spotless; to be free from the blood and sins of the world; to become a new creature of the Holy Ghost, one whose body has been renewed by the rebirth of the Spirit. Sanctification is a state of saintliness, a state attained only by conformity to the laws and ordinances of the gospel" (*MD*, p. 675).

The Holy Ghost is a revelator. The Prophet Joseph Smith taught that "no man can receive the Holy Ghost without receiving revelations" (*TPJS*, p. 328). To enjoy the companionship of the Holy Ghost is to enjoy the spirit of REVELATION (D&C 8:2–3). Without revelation there can be no competent witness of Christ or his gospel (Rev. 19:10). The Holy Ghost is the source of all saving knowledge. Those who sincerely and prayerfully seek this knowledge are promised that everything expedient will be revealed to them (D&C 18:18). Nephi testified that Christ manifests himself "unto all those who believe in him, by the power of the Holy Ghost; yea, unto every nation, kindred, tongue, and people, working mighty miracles, signs, and wonders, among the children of men according to their faith" (2 Ne. 26:13; cf. 1 Cor. 2:11–13; D&C 76:116).

The Holy Ghost is a teacher. All who will be saved must be tutored by the Holy Ghost. The things of the Spirit can only be understood when taught and learned by the Spirit (D&C 50:11–24). The divine commission to teach the truths of salvation rests with the Holy Ghost. Jesus was filled with the power of the Holy Ghost (Luke 4:1). "He spake not as other men, neither could he be taught; for he needed not that any man should teach him" (JST Matt. 3:25). The Father gave Christ the Spirit without measure (John 3:34). Angels also speak by the power of the Holy Ghost (2 Ne. 32:3). Such is the standard for all who go forth in Christ's name. "Ye are not sent forth to be taught," the Savior said to the early Latter-day Saints, "but to teach the children of men the things which I have put into your hands by the power of my Spirit; and ye are to be taught from on high. Sanctify yourselves and ye shall be endowed with power, that ye may give even as I have spoken" (D&C 43:15–16).

Describing the influence of the Holy Ghost as it fell upon him and Oliver COWDERY, the Prophet Joseph Smith said, "We were filled with the Holy Ghost, and rejoiced in the God of our salvation. Our minds being now enlightened, we began to have the scriptures laid open to our understandings, and the true meaning and intention of their more mysterious passages revealed unto us in a manner which we never could attain to previously, nor ever before had thought of" (JS—H 1:73–74; cf. Alma 5:46). The Holy Ghost also brings to remembrance that which has previously been learned (John 14:26), directs that for which one should pray (D&C 46:30), and makes known what is to be spoken in preaching and teaching (D&C 84:85).

The Holy Ghost is the Comforter. A distinctive characteristic of the truths of salvation is that they are attended by a spirit of comfort and peace. It is the office of the Holy Ghost to lift burdens, give courage, strengthen faith, grant consolation, extend hope, and reveal whatever is needed to those having claim on his sacred companionship (Moses 6:61).

Jesus taught that no sin is greater than the sin against the Holy Ghost (Matt. 12:31–32). A latter-day revelation explains, "The blasphemy against the Holy Ghost, which shall not be forgiven in the world nor out of the world, is in that ye commit murder wherein ye shed innocent blood, and assent unto my death, after ye have received my new and everlasting covenant, saith the Lord God" (D&C 132:27). Joseph Smith observed further that such a one rejects the Son after the Father has revealed him, denies the truth, and defies the PLAN OF SALVATION. "From that time he begins to be an enemy. . . . He gets the spirit of the devil—the same spirit that they had who crucified the Lord of Life—the same spirit that sins against the Holy Ghost. You cannot save such persons; you cannot bring them to repentance; they make open war, like the devil, and awful is the consequence" (*TPJS*, p. 357–58; cf. D&C 76:31–38, 43–48; *see also* UNPARDONABLE SIN).

The Holy Ghost is such an uplifting power and source of necessary gospel knowledge that to have his constant companionship and influence is the greatest gift a person can receive in mortality (cf. D&C 121:46). It is reported that on one occasion, when the Prophet Joseph Smith was asked, "Wherein [the LDS Church] differed from the other religions of the day," he replied, that it was in "the gift of the Holy Ghost by the laying-on of hands, . . . [and] that all other considerations were contained in the gift of the Holy Ghost" (*HC* 4:42).

BIBLIOGRAPHY

McConkie, Bruce R. *A New Witness for the Articles of Faith*, chaps. 28–31. Salt Lake City, 1985.

McConkie, Joseph Fielding, and Robert L. Millet. *The Holy Ghost*. Salt Lake City, 1989.

JOSEPH FIELDING MCCONKIE

HOLY OF HOLIES

In ancient times, through divine instruction to Moses, the Holy of Holies was made the center of the tabernacle (Ex. 25–27). It was a fifteen-foot cube formed by hanging veils made of goat hair, ram skins, and other dyed skins. Some were embroidered with figures of cherubim in blue, purple, and scarlet. The Holy of Holies was designated as the repository for a chest called the ark of the covenant. This chest, constructed of gold-plated acacia wood, was the place of the stone tablets inscribed by the hand of God, and the resting place for the mercy seat. Fashioned in one piece of fine gold, this seat, with cherubim engraven above it, formed the visible throne for the presence of God. Once a year, on the day of atonement, the high priest entered the Holy of Holies and sprinkled sacrificial blood over the mercy seat as expiation for Israel's sins. Though the ark has disappeared, this ritual was continued in the temples of Zerubbabel and Herod.

A latter-day Holy of Holies has been dedicated in the great temple in Salt Lake City. It is a central chamber adjoining the celestial room. Beyond its sliding doors are six steps to similar doors, symbolic of the veil that guarded the Holy of Holies in ancient times. The sanctuary is of circular design with a domed ceiling. The appointments include inlaid wood, gold leaf, stained glass, and unique lighting. The presiding high priest, the President of the Church, controls access to this sanctuary.

BIBLIOGRAPHY

Encyclopedia Judaica, Vol. 15, cols. 681–82, 748–49. Jerusalem, 1971.

Talmage, James E. *House of the Lord*, pp. 162–63. Salt Lake City, 1974.

LYSLE R. CAHOON

HOLY SPIRIT

The Holy Spirit is a term often used to refer to the HOLY GHOST. In such cases the Holy Spirit is a personage. Ghost is an Old English word meaning spirit. The scriptures use this term to designate the third member of the GODHEAD (Alma 11:44) and to speak of the Spirit's power to testify (Alma 7:16), to grant knowledge (Alma 5:46; D&C 76:116), to persuade (Mosiah 3:19), to indicate remission of sins (D&C 55:1), and to sanctify (Alma 5:54). The term Holy Spirit is the core of the phrase HOLY SPIRIT OF PROMISE denoting the Holy Ghost's sanction of every ordinance performed in righteousness. The influence or spirit that emanates from Jesus Christ, which is also called the LIGHT OF CHRIST, is holy, but is neither the Holy Spirit nor a personage.

JERRY A. WILSON

HOLY SPIRIT OF PROMISE

The Holy Spirit of Promise is one of many descriptive name-titles of the HOLY GHOST and refers to a specific function of the Holy Ghost. In John 14:16, the Savior, who had been a comforter to his disciples, assured them that after his departure into heaven they would receive another comforter: "And I will pray the Father, and he shall give you another Comforter, that he may abide with you for ever." The next verse speaks of this Comforter as "the Spirit of truth," who "dwelleth with you, and shall be in you" (verse 17). The Lord subsequently identified this promised Comforter as the Holy Ghost (verse 26). Doctrine and Covenants 88:3 reiterates and clarifies: "Wherefore, I now send upon you another Comforter, even upon you my friends, that it may abide in your hearts, even the Holy Spirit of promise; which other Comforter is the same that I promised unto my disciples, as is recorded in the testimony of John."

The Holy Spirit of Promise is the power by which ordinances and other righteous acts performed on this earth, such as baptism and eternal marriage, are ratified, validated, and sealed in heaven as well as on earth. Paul taught the Ephesians that after acting on their faith in Christ they "were sealed with that holy Spirit of promise," which was the surety of their "inheritance until the redemption of the purchased possession" (Eph. 1:12–14). The SEALING of earthly COVENANTS and performances is conditional and depends upon the recipient's personal commitment and worthiness. If a person who has received the Holy Spirit of Promise subsequently becomes unrighteous, the seal is broken until full repentance and forgiveness occur (*DS* 1:55; 2:94–99).

The necessity of sealing by the Holy Ghost is emphasized in the following passage: "All covenants, contracts, bonds, obligations, oaths, vows, performances, connections, associations, or expectations, that are not made and entered into and sealed by the Holy Spirit of promise, . . . are of no efficacy, virtue, or force in and after the resurrection from the dead; for all contracts that are not made unto this end have an end when men are dead" (D&C 132:7). Earthly representatives of the Lord, such as bishops and elders may be deceived by an unworthy person, but no one can deceive the Holy Spirit, who will not ratify an ordinance received unworthily. This safeguard is attached to all blessings and covenants associated with the gospel of Jesus Christ.

The ultimate manifestation of the Holy Spirit of Promise is in connection with having one's CALLING AND ELECTION made sure—that is, receiving "the more sure word of prophecy" testifying that an individual is sealed up to ETERNAL LIFE (D&C 131:5). The Holy Spirit of Promise validates this blessing or seals it upon the person. Referring to the Holy Spirit of Promise the Lord says, "This Comforter is the promise which I give unto you of eternal life, even the glory of the celestial kingdom" (D&C 88:4; cf. *MD*, pp. 361–62).

BIBLIOGRAPHY

McConkie, Bruce R. *Doctrinal New Testament Commentary*, Vol. 3, pp. 333–37. Salt Lake City, 1973.

LAWRENCE R. FLAKE

HOME

[*"Home" refers to more than a dwelling for a family. Latter-day Saints consider the ideal home a sacred place where holiness can be lived and taught. It is where civilization is created, one family at a time, and where God's plan of salvation is taught to the next generation, by both example and precept. Home and family relationships can be eternal. Children are to be nurtured in an atmosphere of love. Homes are to be characterized by service, cooperation, and even sacrifice by and for each other. The ideal home can become a haven from worldliness, materialism, and selfishness. While living in a relationship of fidelity, parents are to make home commitments their first priority.*

Articles on the home environment are Abuse, Spouse and Child; Divorce; Family: Family Life; Fatherhood; Marriage; Maternity and Child Health Care; Men, Roles of; Mother in Israel; Motherhood; Women, Roles of; *and* Youth. *Articles related to children and adolescents in the home are* Adoption of Children; Birth; Born in the Covenant; Children; Dating and Courtship; *and* Sex Education. *Articles on parental responsibilities and home organization are* Birth Control; Book of Remembrance; Emergency Preparedness; Family History; Family Home Evening; Family Organizations; Family Prayer; Father's Blessing; Procreation; Sexuality; Values, Transmission of.]

HOME INDUSTRIES

From the earliest days of the Church, home industry, in one form or another, has been advocated among the Latter-day Saints. Included were the more common form of cottage industries and also both light and heavy manufacturing of most of the community's consumable goods. Home industry and manufacturing were to promote thrift and self-sufficiency among the members, to serve as a buffer against possible corrosive influences (greed, materialism, inequality), to provide employment for the poor, and to protect the Saints from persecution or to prepare them for further upheavals and expulsions such as had driven the Saints from state to state.

Home industries became Church policy in 1831, with the establishment of the LAW OF CONSECRATION, which continued in various forms through the nineteenth century (*see* UNITED ORDERS). From 1831 to 1838, the Church sought to provide material necessities for all according to need. The Saints were to limit consumption voluntarily and, when production exceeded demand, to give the surpluses to the Church. Members pledged time, labor, energy, ability, and material possessions for the good of the group. In pioneer Utah it was not unusual for men to be called on MISSIONS to devote full time to establish specific industries (*see* PIONEER ECONOMY).

As European converts immigrated to the UTAH TERRITORY during the 1850s, they were encouraged to bring designs and tools for use in manufacturing. Home industries thrived through an

The opening of the first creamery in Richfield, Utah, typical of many Mormon home industries and local businesses. Photographer: George E. Anderson. Courtesy Nelson Wadsworth.

abundance of skilled artisans among new immigrant converts. To support a self-sufficient regional economy (autarky), and to discourage a dependence on imports, the Saints developed an exchange economy. Leaders and members gave full patronage to home manufacturers, who were given preferential treatment and verbal support by leaders in Church CONFERENCES and in state legislative sessions.

Thus, in the Utah Territory, the Church, the government, and individuals were involved in a collective entrepreneurship that was supportive of immigration and public works programs. The mutual exchange of goods and labor among residents of the region developed the economic foundations of a commonwealth. Goods available in excess of personal needs were exported to bring money into the territory. This approach also involved dedication to building the KINGDOM OF GOD, so encouragement of home manufacture included caution against exorbitant profits and speculation.

The contributions of women were fundamental to making these economic strategies a success. President Brigham YOUNG encouraged women to study mathematics, accounting, and medicine, among other things, so that they could provide

clerking, bookkeeping, shop keeping, health care, and other professional services, thereby releasing the men to perform more strenuous physical labor (*JD* 13:61).

Both the poor and the not-so-poor were encouraged to live more frugally. Women learned not to waste anything of substance; and the desire, ideally, was for domestic and home manufacture to produce most necessary articles used for food, clothing, and shelter. Such industry was to sustain families religiously, politically, socially, and financially.

In 1867, the Church assigned to the RELIEF SOCIETY the responsibility of teaching the poor to provide for themselves. Female home manufacturing societies supported cottage industries that employed women and children and encouraged families to resist the purchasing of goods not made at home. The Relief Society became a major institutional sponsor of these self-sufficiency programs. For example, approximately 150 units of the Relief Society throughout the territory helped to raise silkworms and to reel and weave the filament produced for the fledgling silk industry (*see* SILK CULTURE). The need for production of materials not available locally engendered the establishment of substitute industries. Women experimented with the processing of such native plants as stinging nettle, milkweed, and red top grass for use as textiles.

Brigham Young and other leaders encouraged every branch of manufacture that could be adapted to the climate and the territory. A seemingly endless variety of products included downy beds, molasses, milk products, fruits, vegetables and grains, woolen and silk goods, woven rye and native grass products, all kinds of clothing articles, brooms, ink, leather, felt, alum, coppers, dyes, soap, matches, iron, school books, jewelry, perfume, paper, rope, harnesses, wagons, machinery, sacking, carpets, tools, sugar, flax, bonnets, and lumber.

In 1867–1869, home industries continued to be a major focus of both the Relief Society and the Young Women's RETRENCHMENT ASSOCIATION. These organizations helped to make homemade articles fashionable and to discourage the purchase of imported goods. The coming of the railroad in 1869 and the resultant influx of outside businesses required a redoubling of these efforts to preserve the independence of the local economy.

Village cooperatives were established to provide the exchange and distribution of the products of home industry. Zion's Cooperative Mercantile Institution (ZCMI) was a major institution for carrying out such strategies, and the department store followed a policy of preference for the home industries of Mormon manufacturers. In addition, STAKE Boards of Trade were organized to help the cause of home manufacture. As late as 1878, ZCMI had a published policy of providing what was needed for home consumption but exporting the best for profit.

The success of Mormon home industry depended upon geography, economics, and ideology. The expansion of the United States through migration, facilitated by the transcontinental railroad, brought about an effective end to autarky and to LDS protectionist philosophy. Ultimately, however, the economic policies of Brigham Young and the Church had affected all of the mountain West and provided a pattern of economic survival copied and adapted by some other groups as they settled in the Great Basin. Later, the ideals of self-sufficiency, cooperation, and preparedness were reemphasized during the Great Depression of the 1930s and resulted in the implementation of a Church WELFARE SERVICES program.

Today, cottage industries still are a source of income, usually secondary and on a small scale, for some LDS households. A retail outlet known as MORMON HANDICRAFT was established by the Church in 1937 to provide sale on consignment of high quality, hand-crafted products of household industries. In 1986 the DESERET BOOK COMPANY purchased Mormon Handicraft and presently operates the store, which is renowned for hand-sewn quilts, needlework, and other craft items.

In harmony with the ideals that originally spawned the advocacy of home industry, Latter-day Saints today are counseled to grow vegetable gardens, make or preserve whatever commodities they can, and avoid debt and materialism. Work (industry) is expected to be the "ruling principle" in the lives of the Saints, and sharing of one's resources in service to the poor is considered a hallmark virtue of a true Saint.

[*See also* Business: Church Participation in; Economic History; Self-Sufficiency; Stewardship; Welfare.]

BIBLIOGRAPHY

Arrington, Leonard J. *Great Basin Kingdom.* Cambridge, Mass., 1958.

Burgess-Olson, Vicky. *Family Structure and Dynamics in Early Utah Mormon Families 1847–1885.* Evanston, Ill., 1975.

Young, Brigham. *Discourses of Brigham Young,* ed. John A. Widtsoe. Salt Lake City, 1971.

MAXINE LEWIS ROWLEY

HOME TEACHING

Each ward of The Church of Jesus Christ of Latter-day Saints assigns priesthood holders as home teachers to visit the homes of members every month. They go in pairs; often a youth holding the AARONIC PRIESTHOOD accompanies an adult holding the MELCHIZEDEK PRIESTHOOD. Home teachers are called by their local priesthood quorum leaders and are typically assigned to visit between three and five families. They report on the needs and welfare of their assigned families in regularly scheduled interviews with their priesthood leaders. The home teaching program is a response to modern revelation commissioning those ordained to the priesthood to

teach, expound, exhort, baptize, and watch over the church . . . and visit the house of each member, and exhort them to pray vocally and in secret and attend to all family duties, . . . to watch over the church always, and be with and strengthen them; and see that there is no iniquity in the church, neither hardness with each other, neither lying, backbiting, nor evil speaking [D&C 20:42–54].

At one time called "acting teachers" (1909), the name was formally changed to "ward teachers" in 1912. However, for years before that time the effort was informally called "block teaching" because of the geographic way in which families were assigned (Hartley, pp. 375–98). In April 1963, the ward teaching program was expanded and renamed "home teaching," with emphasis "on the responsibilities of the entire priesthood to 'watch over the Church' as commanded in the early revelations—to be concerned with the whole family as a group and as individuals" (*IE* 66 [June 1963]:504).

In a Home Teachers Meeting during general conference in 1966, Marion G. Romney, then an apostle, instructed home teachers to live so that they could always enjoy the companionship of the Holy Ghost and act under his inspiration in their home teaching responsibilities and to encourage and inspire every family to make and keep the home a truly Latter-day Saint home.

In 1987 Church President Ezra Taft BENSON identified three basic guidelines to be followed by home teachers:

First, Church leaders are to encourage home teachers to know as well as possible the people they are called to teach. Home teachers need to be aware of individual attitudes, interests, and general welfare, working closely with the head of each family to meet the family's temporal and spiritual needs.

Second, the Church expects home teachers to deliver a short monthly message. When possible, messages are to come from the scriptures, particularly the Book of Mormon. Leaders are to instruct home teachers to prepare intellectually and spiritually, giving prayerful consideration to both the temporal and spiritual needs of each family as they prepare lessons. The companionship of the Holy Ghost is essential for successful home teaching, for "if ye receive not the Spirit ye shall not teach" (D&C 42:14). The Church instructs home teachers, therefore, to pray together before each visit, invoking the blessings of the Lord upon the family, and, where possible, to pray with family members at the conclusion of the visit.

Third, home teachers are to magnify their callings (Jacob 1:19) by rendering devoted service. This includes visiting each family early in the month, by appointment, and making additional visits as needed.

Organizationally, home teaching provides a system for effective Churchwide communication. Through stakes, wards, and home teachers, Church leaders have a direct line to every member and have the potential, if necessary, to communicate quickly with the total Church membership, via the local priesthood leaders.

Effective home teaching makes significant contributions to members' lives. Alert, insightful home teachers find various ways of rendering service, such as providing recognition for achievements; informing families of Church activities; assisting during family emergencies, including illness or death; strengthening and encouraging less active members; and arranging transportation. They serve as resources and share the burden of support that would otherwise be carried by the bishop.

As home teachers are called to work directly with families, they are often in a better position to help these family members than are other Church officers or teachers. As a result, home teaching is one of the most effective ways the Latter-day Saints manifest their commitment to "bear one another's burdens, that they may be light; . . . mourn with those that mourn; yea, and comfort those that stand in need of comfort, and stand as witnesses of God" (Mosiah 18:8–9).

BIBLIOGRAPHY

Benson, Ezra Taft. "To the Home Teachers of the Church." *Ensign* 17 (May 1987):48–51.

Cullimore, James A. "Home Teachers—Watchmen over the Church." *Ensign* 3 (Jan. 1973):124–26.

Hartley, William. "Ordained and Acting Teachers in the Lesser Priesthood, 1851-1883." *BYU Studies* 16 (Spring 1976):375–98.

Packer, Boyd K. "The Saints Securely Dwell." *Ensign* 3 (Jan. 1973):88–90.

R. WAYNE BOSS

HOMOSEXUALITY

God's teachings about human sexuality are clear, unambiguous, and consistent from Adam to the present. "God created man in his own image . . .

male and female created he them" (Gen. 1:27). "And the Gods said: Let us make an help meet for the man, for it is not good that the man should be alone, therefore we will form an help meet for him. . . . Therefore shall a man . . . cleave unto his wife, and they shall be one flesh" (Abr. 5:14–18). "Neither is the man without the woman, neither the woman without the man, in the Lord" (1 Cor. 11:11).

When two people of the same sex join in using their bodies for erotic purposes, this conduct is considered homosexual and sinful by The Church of Jesus Christ of Latter-day Saints, comparable to sexual relations between any unmarried persons. Masturbation is not condoned but is not considered homosexual.

People who persist in committing acts that violate divine law are subject to Church DISCIPLINARY COUNCILS to help them understand the damage they are doing to their eternal well-being. Particularly offensive is any conduct that harms others, especially those who because of their youth are vulnerable to seduction or coercion. The eternal laws that pertain to CHASTITY before marriage and personal purity within marriage apply to *all* sexual behavior. However, "marriage is not doctrinal therapy for homosexual relations" (Oaks, p. 10). The restored GOSPEL OF JESUS CHRIST exalts the relationship of husband and wife, as particularly illustrated in the TEMPLE ORDINANCES. From these doctrines, covenants, and ordinances, it is clear that any sexual relationship other than that between a legally wedded heterosexual husband and wife is sinful. The divine mandate of marriage between man and woman puts in perspective why homosexual acts are offensive to God. They repudiate the gift and the Giver of ETERNAL LIFE.

Recognizing that failure to keep the covenants of the gospel of Jesus Christ deprives a person of God's blessings, the Church offers counseling to help those who are troubled by homosexual thoughts or actions to learn to use their agency to live in accord with divine laws and thereby enjoy the rich blessings a benevolent Father offers to all his children, whatever their temptation or thoughts. "That has been the message of the Jewish and Christian prophets in all ages: repent. Abandon your sins; confess them; forsake them. And become acceptable to God" (Oaks, p. 7).

BIBLIOGRAPHY

Oaks, Dallin H. CBS-TV interview, Dec. 30, 1986, unpublished transcript.

Packer, Boyd K. "Covenants." *Ensign* 20 (Nov. 1990):84–86.

VICTOR L. BROWN, JR.

HOPE

The concept of hope plays a vital role in Latter-day Saint thought. Firmly centered in Christ and his resurrection, it is the "hope of eternal life" (Titus 1:2) repeatedly alluded to by Paul. It is the opposite of the despair found among those who are "without Christ, having no hope, and without God in the world" (Eph. 2:12). As the Book of Mormon prophet Moroni writes, "If ye have no hope, ye must needs be in despair" (Moro. 10:22). For those, however, who accept Christ's atonement and resurrection, there comes a "brightness of hope" (2 Ne. 31:20) through which all who believe in God "might with surety hope for a better world" (Ether 12:4).

The scriptures employ the term "hope" in a variety of ways. Some usages suggest desire, such as the statement in Article of Faith 13 that "we believe all things, we hope all things, we have endured many things, and hope to be able to endure all things." Others denote firm expectation, such as Paul's description of Abraham "who against hope believed in hope, that he might become the father of many nations" (Rom. 4:18). Still others make it an integral part of faith, such as the scriptural observations that "faith is the substance of things hoped for, the evidence of things not seen" (Heb. 11:1).

Regardless of their form, the individual variations of meaning all center on the confidence or trust in God that springs from knowledge that mankind is saved through the Atonement ("for we are saved by hope," Rom. 8:15). Hence, hope is inseparably connected with faith. Book of Mormon passages add insight to New Testament teachings by expanding on this interactive relationship: "How is it that ye can attain unto faith, save ye shall have hope?" (Moro. 7:40); "hope cometh of faith" (Ether 12:4); "without faith there cannot be any hope" (Moro. 7:42).

In combination with faith, hope leads to knowledge of the truth about Jesus Christ ("if ye have faith, ye hope for things which are not seen, which are true" [Alma 32:21]). It is also an essential attitude for individual salvation ("man must hope, or he cannot receive an inheritance in the place which thou hast prepared" [Ether 12:32]).

Paul's praise of "faith, hope, and charity" (1 Cor. 13:13) as basic Christian virtues expands understanding of these concepts with its intimation that faith and hope are prerequisites to developing charity—a Christlike love of others. This type of love cannot grow out of despair or disbelief. Using the same triadic concept, the Book of Mormon describes their relationship to repentance, baptism, and the Gift of the Holy Ghost, all required for salvation in the kingdom of God (2 Ne. 31:16–21). Hope is integral to the gospel formula: through steadfastness in Christ (faith), a perfect brightness of hope, and love of God (charity), the baptized can endure to the end and be saved. Having these attributes is also necessary for service in the Lord's kingdom: "If you have not faith, hope, and charity, you can do nothing" (D&C 18:19; cf. D&C 4:5).

Paul observed that the writings of ancient prophets were given "that we through patience and comfort of the scriptures might have hope" (Rom. 15:4; cf. Ps. 16:9; Prov. 10:28; 14:32; Jer. 17:7; Joel 3:16). The Prophet Joseph Smith claimed that Latter-day Saints "have the greatest hope . . . for our dead of any people on the earth" if they have died in the faith (*TPJS*, p. 359). He was referring to their possession of another testament of Christ (the Book of Mormon) and to additional latter-day scriptures that contain newly revealed truth about the purpose of mortal existence, the state of life after death, the eternity of the marriage covenant, and the plan of salvation generally. This additional knowledge gives Latter-day Saints special reason for hope in this life and for life in the worlds to come.

JAMES K. LYON

HOPE OF ISRAEL

The phrase "hope of Israel" appears three times in scripture: Jeremiah 14:8; 17:13; and Acts 28:20. These passages refer to Israel's Lord and Savior as the "hope of Israel." Latter-day Saints believe that all blessings or promises associated with this hope are dependent upon acceptance of, and obedience

to, Israel's God, Jesus Christ (*see* JEHOVAH, JESUS CHRIST).

The phrase "hope of Israel" also calls to mind the expected fulfillment of divine promises made to Abraham, Isaac, Jacob, and their posterity. The promises included an inheritance in the PROMISED LAND, combined with prosperity and peace—conditioned on their obedience—and an endless posterity that will continue "in the world and out of the world" (D&C 132:29–33; cf. Gen. 15:5; *see also* ABRAHAMIC COVENANT). Only through Jesus Christ and the latter-day RESTORATION of his Church will the fulfillment come of these promises made to the fathers (cf. 3 Ne. 20:10–46; Isa. 11:10–12; Jer. 14:8, 13; 1 Tim. 1:1; Titus 2:11–13).

In his defense before King Agrippa, Paul referred to this hope (Acts 26:6–8). Apparently Paul, as well as other prophets, believed that the full redemption of Israel can be realized only after the Resurrection, when Jesus Christ comes to rule in his millennial kingdom (cf. Acts 24:15; 28:20; Ps. 16:9–11; 37:1–11; Isa. 26:19; Ezek. 37:1–14).

For Latter-day Saints, the phrase "hope of Israel" is well known through the words of a familiar hymn (*Hymns*, 259) which characterize the youth of ZION as the "Hope of Israel." They are to "rise in might" and wield "the sword of truth and right" above hosts marshaled in "ranks of sin." If the youth willingly heed the call to battle against sin and error, remaining watchful and prayerful, they will see victory.

[*See also* Covenant Israel; Israel.]

JOHN M. MADSEN

HORNE, MARY ISABELLA

From 1870 to 1904 Mary Isabella Hales Horne (1818–1905) was president of the Senior Cooperative RETRENCHMENT ASSOCIATION, an organization that spearheaded a number of women's activities, including a Churchwide retrenchment from "worldly," or materialistic, pursuits in the 1870s, and a movement in support of plural marriage in the 1880s. During most of the three decades, she was also president of the Salt Lake Stake RELIEF SOCIETY and treasurer of the Central (later General) Board of Relief Society.

Mary Isabella Hales was born on November 20, 1818, in Rainham, Kent County, England. She

Mary Isabella Horne (1818–1905) was an original member of the Relief Society in 1842. She was Relief Society president in the Salt Lake Stake for 30 years. At the same time, she was president of the Senior Cooperative Retrenchment Association from 1870 to 1904.

was the oldest of seven children born to Stephen and Mary Ann Hales. Her father was a shoemaker and her mother a seamstress.

The Hales family immigrated to York (now Toronto), Canada, where Isabella met Joseph Horne at a Methodist camp meeting in 1834. They were married on May 9, 1836, and were baptized members of The Church of Jesus Christ of Latter-day Saints in July 1836 by Orson Hyde, an apostle. The newlyweds became friends of the Prophet Joseph SMITH, and both had a firm testimony of his prophetic calling. In 1838, they gathered with the Saints to Far West, Missouri, and subsequently suffered through the violent expulsion of the Saints from Missouri. They moved to Quincy and NAUVOO, Illinois, and then crossed the plains to the Salt Lake Valley in 1847. The Hornes had fifteen children, including three sets of twins.

In 1869 President Brigham YOUNG challenged Isabella Horne to encourage the women of the Church to spend less time preparing elegant meals and sewing fancy clothing, and more time nurturing their spiritual development. On February 10, 1870, the Senior Cooperative Retrenchment Association was formally organized, with Mary Isabella Horne as president. Under her direction, the association also supported local Relief Society, PRIMARY, and YOUNG WOMEN's organizations; the WOMAN'S EXPONENT; the 1876 centennial fair; and the UNITED ORDER. It also supported mass meetings in which resolutions were drafted in strong support of WOMAN SUFFRAGE.

In December 1877, Isabella Horne was called to preside over the Salt Lake Stake Relief Society. She served twenty-six years, directing a total of sixty-five WARD Relief Society presidencies. She presided over Relief Society sessions of the women's conferences of the stake, which were attended by many women from throughout the territory until the first general auxiliary conferences were inaugurated in 1889. She also instituted a nurse training program in the stake that was later adopted by Relief Society's general officers. In 1880 the Central Board of the Relief Society was organized and she was appointed treasurer, a position she held until 1901.

In addition to these assignments, Isabella Horne served as a member of the DESERET HOSPITAL committee (1882–1894); as a counselor to Zina D. H. YOUNG in the presidency of the Deseret Silk Association, established in 1876; and as president of the Women's Cooperative Mercantile and Manufacturing Institution from 1890 to 1905.

She died on August 25, 1905, at the age of eighty-six. At her death, Emmeline B. WELLS, another prominent leader among Utah women, said of her that she "was a born leader, a sort of General among women and indeed in this respect might surpass most men, of extraordinary ability. . . . A woman of great force of character, and wonderful ability, such a one as might stand at the head of a great institution and carry it on successfully. . . . Sister Horne can appropriately be called a stalwart, a champion for the rights of her own sex, and indeed for all mankind" [*Woman's Exponent* 36 (Apr. 1908):58].

BIBLIOGRAPHY

Horne, Mrs. Joseph. "Migration and Settlement of the Latter-day Saints." Typescript, 1884. Bancroft Library, University of California, Berkeley.

Kramer, Lyneve Wilson, and Eva Durrant Wilson. "Mary Isabella Hales Horne: Faithful Sister and Leader." *Ensign* 12 (Aug. 1982):63–66.

SUSAN ARRINGTON MADSEN

HOSANNA SHOUT

Among Latter-day Saints, the sacred ceremony of the Hosanna Shout is usually reserved for TEMPLE DEDICATIONS. It is given in the spirit of thanksgiving and petition, fulfilling the instruction to bless the name of the Lord with loud voices and "with a sound of rejoicing", with "hosannas to him that sitteth upon the throne forever" (D&C 19:37; 36:3; 39:19; 124:101).

When the ordinance of the WASHING OF FEET was introduced at Kirtland, shouts of hosanna were viewed as a sealing benediction on both private and quorum prayer and then on the dedicatory prayer. At prayer meetings in the KIRTLAND TEMPLE, the Saints sometimes used related phrases such as "Blessed is the name of the Most High God" and "Glory to God in the highest" (*HC* 2:386).

The Hosanna Shout is whole-souled, given to the full limit of one's strength. The congregation stands and in unison shouts the words "Hosanna, Hosanna, Hosanna to God and the Lamb. Amen, Amen, and Amen," repeating them three times. This is usually accompanied by the rhythmic waving of white handkerchiefs with uplifted hands. The epithet "Lamb" relates to the condescension and atonement of Jesus Christ.

The Hosanna Shout memorializes the preearthly COUNCIL IN HEAVEN, as "when . . . all the sons of God shouted for joy" (Job 38:7). It also recalls the hosannas and the waving of palm branches accorded the Messiah as he entered Jerusalem. And hosannas welcomed him as he appeared to the Nephites. President Lorenzo Snow taught that this shout will herald the Messiah when he comes in the glory of the Father (cf. 1 Thes. 4:16).

BIBLIOGRAPHY

Woodbury, Lael J. "The Origin and Uses of the Sacred Hosanna Shout." In *Sperry Lecture Series*. Provo, Utah, 1975.

LAEL J. WOODBURY

HOSPITALS

Members of The Church of Jesus Christ of Latter-day Saints have historically felt a responsibility to care for the physical well-being of fellow Church members and their neighbors. This early commitment was typified by the establishment of a board of health for the city of Nauvoo, Illinois, and a formal council of health in Salt Lake City in 1849. The Church has continued to sponsor health services through the operation of several hospitals and a welfare program.

In 1874, because of the high infant and maternity mortality rate, RELIEF SOCIETY president Eliza R. SNOW, with the support of Church President Brigham YOUNG, urged a number of women to obtain medical degrees at Eastern medical colleges. In 1882, under her direction, the DESERET HOSPITAL was established in Salt Lake City and staffed and administered primarily by Latter-day Saint women doctors. While it was highly regarded by the community and supported in part by the Relief Society and the RETRENCHMENT SOCIETY, it closed only eight years later because of inadequate funding.

Though the Deseret Hospital was short-lived, interest in having a hospital sponsored by the Church continued. In January 1905, the Dr. W. H. Groves LDS Hospital opened, also in Salt Lake City, becoming one of several denominational hospitals in the area. It was largely funded through a bequest of W. H. Groves, an LDS dentist who had come to Utah from Nottingham, England. The hospital, a five-story complex with eighty beds, was equipped with up-to-date medical equipment and innovations, including an elevator and a nurse-calling system. In 1924 the Cottonwood Maternity Hospital, a major facility in childbirth care, was established and was maintained thereafter for several years by the Cottonwood Stake Relief Society in Salt Lake County.

The Dr. W. H. Groves LDS Hospital in Salt Lake City, as it appeared when established in 1905, was one of a number of hospitals owned and operated by the LDS Church between 1882 and 1974.

LDS Hospital, the 571-bed successor to the Groves LDS Hospital, is regarded as one of the West's premier tertiary care centers. The hospital supports continuous physician and nursing education and is a leader in medical research, including the treatment of heart disease, organ transplants, respiratory disorders, and obstetrical care, and in its pioneering use of computers in health care, both clinically and administratively.

In 1911 May Anderson of the Primary Association recognized the need for a medical center to meet the unique needs of children. Her efforts, with support of general Primary president Louie B. Felt, led to the establishment of the children's ward at the LDS Hospital in 1913. In 1922 the Primary proposed that a separate facility be established, emphasizing the need for children to be treated by pediatric professionals. Consequently, the Church purchased and remodeled an old home in downtown Salt Lake City for use as the LDS Children's Convalescent Hospital, under the supervision of the Primary Association.

During the next twenty-five years, nearly 6,000 children were treated, and the hospital attracted pediatric specialists of national and international reputation. By 1937 this facility became inadequate, but not until after World War II were sufficient funds gathered to build a new one.

In 1922, to help support charity cases, Primary board member Nelle Talmage suggested an annual "Penny Day" when Church members would contribute pennies equaling their age. Children would contribute pennies on their birthdays. The program continues presently as the Pennies by the Inch campaign (a penny donated for each inch of the donor's height), which furthers the idea of children helping other children in need.

A new Primary Children's Hospital facility was completed in 1953, and its size was doubled in 1966. The LDS Hospital shortly thereafter closed its pediatric unit, shifting its care for infants and children to the Primary Children's Medical Center. In 1990 the Center moved to a larger facility at the University of Utah Medical Complex and has become one of the finest children's hospitals in the United States.

In 1963 the Church owned or administered fifteen hospitals in the intermountain area under the direction of the PRESIDING BISHOPRIC. In 1970 the Health Services Corporation of the Church was organized and a commissioner of health was appointed to oversee the rapidly expanding health needs of the Church and to unite the fifteen hospitals into a coordinated health care system. This system demanded increasing amounts of administrative time and financial commitment by the Church.

In 1974 the First Presidency announced that the Church's fifteen hospitals would be donated and turned over to a new nonprofit organization so that the Church could devote "the full effort of [its] Health Services . . . to the health needs of the worldwide Church." While noting that the hospitals were "a vigorous and financially viable enterprise," the First Presidency emphasized that "the operation of hospitals is not central to the mission of the Church." The First Presidency further indicated that with the expansion of the Church in many nations it was "difficult to justify the provision of curative services in a single, affluent, geographical locality" (news release, Sept. 6, 1974).

On April 1, 1975, the Presiding Bishopric signed the final divestiture agreement transferring ownership and management of LDS Hospital, Primary Children's Hospital, and thirteen other facilities to the new philanthropic organization. This nonprofit organization was named Intermountain Health Care. It is directed by a geographically and religiously diverse board of trustees. With the divestiture of the hospitals, the Church rapidly

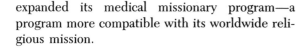

expanded its medical missionary program—a program more compatible with its worldwide religious mission.

BIBLIOGRAPHY

Bush, Lester E., Jr. "The Mormon Tradition." In *Caring and Curing*, ed. R. Numbers and D. Amundsen, pp. 397–420. New York, 1986.

DeWitt, Robert J. *Medicine and the Mormons*. Bountiful, Utah, 1981.

Josephson, Marba. "The Primary Children's Hospital." *IE* 55 (Oct. 1952):714–17, 734, 736, 738, 740, 742, 744–45.

WILLIAM N. JONES

HUMANITARIAN SERVICE

The Church of Jesus Christ of Latter-day Saints has a continuing commitment to relieve human suffering, to help eliminate life-threatening conditions, and to promote self-reliance among all people. Assistance is to be provided as Christian service, without regard to race, nationality, or religion. This obligation is an expression of scriptural counsel such as is found in the Book of Mormon:

> They did not send away any who were naked, or . . . hungry, or that were athirst, or that were sick, or that had not been nourished; and they did not set their hearts upon riches; therefore they were liberal to all, both old and young, both bond and free, both male and female, whether out of the church or in the church, having no respect to persons as to those who stood in need [Alma 1:30].

Church giving is possible because of donations by individual members, who honor the counsel of Joseph Smith regarding one's temporal obligation to others:

> Respecting how much a man . . . shall give annually we have no special instructions to give; he is to feed the hungry, to clothe the naked, to provide for the widow, to dry up the tear of the orphan, to comfort the afflicted, whether in this church or in any other, or in no church at all, wherever he finds them [*T&S* 3:732].

The Church has always felt a responsibility to "take care of its own" (*see* WELFARE SERVICES), but traditionally it has also reached out to the general population in times of need, both in North America and throughout the world. As early as 1851, just four years after reaching the Salt Lake Valley, Brig-ham YOUNG instituted a program of teaching Indians to farm by appointing three men as "farmers to the Indians." By 1857 more than 700 acres were under cultivation among the Indians (L. J. Arrington, *Brigham Young: American Moses*, New York, 1985, pp. 217–18).

The Church has responded to major world calamities according to its ability to give. In 1918 the U.S. House of Representatives formally expressed its appreciation to the RELIEF SOCIETY women of the Church "for . . . contributions of wheat to the Government for the use of the starving women and children of the allies, and for the use of our soldiers and sailors in the army and navy of the United States" (*IE* 21:917). The Relief Society had provided from its storage granaries more than 200,000 bushels of "first-class milling wheat" to the United States for the cause of human liberty and to save the lives of thousands who might have suffered for the lack of bread.

Even more extensive assistance to Europe during and after World War II was made possible in part because of a Church Welfare Services plan implemented in 1936. The plan taught members frugality and provident living and encouraged donations for the needy, which then would be available for emergencies and calamities.

President David O. MCKAY summarized the Church's actions during World War II: "We have given to the national Red Cross in Washington very large sums, and expect to add to these from time to time. Insofar as contributions toward foreign sufferers in war-ridden countries is concerned, we have sent considerable sums . . . to those countries to help our needy Church membership there and have made available for charitable purposes considerable local funds in those countries" (*MFP* 6:163–64).

Post–World War II humanitarian aid included ninety-two railway carloads of welfare supplies (about two thousand tons) sent to Europe from the Church in Salt Lake City. Ezra Taft BENSON, then a member of the QUORUM OF THE TWELVE APOSTLES, spent 1946 in Europe supervising the distribution of this aid, consisting mainly of food, clothing, utensils, and medical supplies. These goods were supplemented by a program in which Church members in North America sent tens of thousands of individual food and clothing parcels. While a primary objective of the Church's efforts was to assist Church members in Europe, generous amounts of food and clothing were given to local child-care and feeding programs (Babbel, pp. 168–69).

In 1953, a cooperative movement on the part of all Utah denominations collected relief supplies for Greece to relieve suffering caused by earthquakes. The United Churches Ionian Relief Committee was formed with Dr. J. Frank Robinson, president of Westminster College in Salt Lake City, as chairman. Among the denominations represented were the Greek Orthodox and Roman Catholic churches, the Jewish synagogues, and the Latter-day Saints. Expressing thanks to the Church for its efforts, Mr. John Tzounis, Greek consul in San Francisco, stated: "It is no secret, and I am thankful for this opportunity to stress the fact publicly, that the contribution of the Mormon Church was the greatest single contribution to the relief fund, not only in the United States, but the whole world over" ("President McKay Given Royal Award by King of Greece," *Deseret News*, Dec. 4, 1954, p. 2).

The Welfare Services Missionary Program was created in 1971, allowing service beyond emergency circumstances. Health professionals called as missionaries to various lands have provided training in hospitals, clinics, and community health organizations, as well as health education for the general population through seminars and workshops. Agricultural missionaries were added to the welfare missionary ranks in 1973, giving technical assistance to farmers in Central and South America, in the South Pacific, and on Indian reservations in the United States and Canada.

The Church's humanitarian response to the proliferation of refugees coming from Vietnam, Cambodia, and Laos in the 1970s began, through an agreement with the United Nations High Commission for Refugees (UNHCR), with a team of Welfare Services missionaries at the Phenot Nikom Refugee Camp in Thailand. From 1978 to the present, missionary teams have provided continuous training in English language and American culture for refugees bound for the United States at camps in Thailand, the Philippines, and Hong Kong.

By 1980, some 768 welfare missionaries (volunteers to give humanitarian aid) were serving in more than forty Church mission areas throughout the world. By 1990, more than 350 missionaries with specific professional backgrounds (nurses, doctors, educators, agricultural specialists) also were providing temporal assistance in many nations (including countries in eastern Europe), primarily in health, agriculture, and leadership development.

A severe drought and civil war in northeast Africa resulted in famine during 1984 and 1985. The FIRST PRESIDENCY and the Quorum of the Twelve "determined that Sunday, January 25, 1985, should be designated as the special fast day when our people will be invited to refrain from partaking two meals and contribute the equivalent value, or more, to the Church to assist those in need. All FAST OFFERING funds contributed on this day will be dedicated for the use of the victims of famine and other causes resulting in hunger and privation among people of Africa, and possibly in some other areas, . . . regardless of Church membership" (The First Presidency Letter to General and Local Priesthood Authorities, Jan. 11, 1985). This special fast day in the United States and Canada produced contributions from the Latter-day Saints of $6.4 million (Welfare Services Department, unpublished document).

The Church immediately collaborated with reputable organizations in providing temporal assistance to the famine-stricken populations of northeast Africa. Specific contributions of grain, tents, and trucks for transporting the needed goods were made to the International Committee of the Red Cross (ICRC) and Catholic Relief Services, valued at more than $3.5 million. Additional donations were made to Catholic Relief Services, CARE, and Africare for projects relating to longer-term relief in the same geographic region (*see* ECONOMIC AID).

Additional monies were later contributed to the ICRC and Catholic Relief Services for airlifting needed food to isolated populations in Ethiopia and the Sudan, where civil strife made trucking the goods impossible. The entire $6.4 million contributed during the first fast, as well as the accumulated interest, had been spent for assistance to Africa by the end of 1986. A second fast, also undertaken in 1985 in concert with a resolution by the U.S. Congress (The First Presidency Letter to General and Local Priesthood Authorities, Jan. 11, 1985), produced an additional $4 million to assist the needy. Special events such as these supplement regular, ongoing humanitarian efforts in the Church. Surpluses from the Welfare Services system are regularly contributed to charitable organizations in the form of food, clothing, and other in-kind household goods throughout the United States and internationally.

Most recently, more than twenty development projects have been sponsored by the Church in Africa (e.g., Kenya, Zimbabwe, Mozambique, Zaire, Chad, Mali, Nigeria, Ghana) as well as additional projects in Central and South America, Asia, and the United States.

BIBLIOGRAPHY

Babbel, Frederick W. *On Wings of Faith.* Salt Lake City, 1972.

Ballard, M. Russell. "Prepare to Serve." *Ensign* 15 (May 1985):41–43.

Benson, Ezra T. "Ministering to Needs through the Lord's Storehouse System." *Ensign* 7 (May 1977):82–84.

Ferguson, Isaac C. "Freely Given." *Ensign* 18 (Aug. 1988):10–15.

"Food for Destitute Greeks." *Deseret News* (Church Section), Feb. 20, 1954, pp. 8–9.

Hinckley, Gordon B. "The Victory over Death." *Ensign* 15 (May 1985):51–54, 59.

Pace, Glenn L. "Principles and Programs." *Ensign* 16 (May 1986):23–25.

Smith, Joseph F. "Our Duty to Humanity, to God and to Country." *IE* 20 (May 1917):645–56.

Times and Seasons 3 (Mar. 15, 1842):732.

ISAAC C. FERGUSON

HUMILITY

True humility is the recognition of one's imperfection that is acquired only as one joyfully, voluntarily, and quietly submits one's whole life to God's will (Micah 6:8; James 4:6; Mosiah 4:10; Morm. 5:24; Ether 6:17). This includes obeying in love his every commandment, repenting of sins, honoring with endurance his every COVENANT, and striving for greater PERFECTION with self-discipline. Humility can result only from faithful submission to the teachings of Jesus Christ. Seeds of humility can be experienced in spontaneous moments of overwhelming gratitude, awe, and reverence when individuals recognize God's hand in the beauty of a sunset, the power of a waterfall, the miracle of life, or the magnitude and glory of human creations. Thus humility is not only a state of being but a process of obeying and reconciling one's life to God's providence as it is made known through his scriptures, prophets, creations, and answers to prayer.

Those seeking to be humble are counseled to pursue knowledge of God's glory, to experience his goodness and love, to receive a REMISSION OF SINS, and to "retain in remembrance, the greatness of God, and your own nothingness, and his goodness and long-suffering towards you" (Mosiah 4:11).

The Church promotes understanding of humility by encouraging members to study the scriptures and writings of Church leaders who pair this virtue with other virtues such as being meek, patient, loving, and submissive (Mosiah 3:19); gentle, long-suffering, diligent in obeying God's commandments, and full of hope and charity (Alma 7:23, 24); faithful and prayerful (D&C 105:23); repentant (Moro. 8:10); wise (Alma 32:12); able to bear adversity and weaknesses (Ether 12:27); joyful and pure in heart (Hel. 3:35); knowledgeable (D&C 4:6); self-disciplined; and teachable and broken-hearted. A lifestyle void of humility exhibits undesirable qualities: PRIDE (Hel. 4:12); haughtiness (Isa. 2:11), wickedness (2 Ne. 28:14), guile (D&C 124:97), jealousy (D&C 67:10), evil (2 Chr. 36:12), hate, envy, anger, arrogance, inordinate ambition, fault-finding, and self-righteousness.

Latter-day Saints with a TESTIMONY pursue humility as a duty, believing it is God's will to seek this virtue. "God will have a humble people. We can either choose to be humble or we can be compelled to be humble" (Benson, 1989, p. 6). As the foundation for spiritual progress, humility disposes people to hear God's word, to be receptive to inspiration, revelation, and spiritual wisdom. It befits members to accept CALLINGS in the Church. Humility must accompany REPENTANCE before BAPTISM (D&C 20:37), approaching the divine with "a broken heart and contrite spirit" (2 Ne. 2:7; 3 Ne. 12:19; D&C 20:37). To seek humility is to ask it of God, to recognize it as fruit of a spiritual life (2 Chr. 33:12). Divine grace, strength, and forgiveness are promised to the humble (1 Pet. 5:5; 3 Ne. 4:33; Ether 9:35; D&C 1:28; 104:23). Scripture warns the proud of impending afflictions, temptations, and even destruction (Isa. 10:33; 2 Chr. 12:7; Mosiah 3:18; Morm. 5:24; D&C 5:28, 32). Adversity and weaknesses can humble individuals, bringing them closer to God. TRIALS often develop spirituality and humility. However, Church leaders emphasize that good conduct and humility without covenants and ORDINANCES will neither redeem nor exalt (Packer, p. 82).

Latter-day Saints are enjoined to imitate Jesus, who was meek and lowly, following not only his example and teachings but also those of his prophets as they walk in his footsteps. "Only Jesus Christ is uniquely qualified to provide that hope, that confidence and that strength to . . . rise above our human failings. To do that, we must . . . live by his laws and teachings" (Benson, 1983, p. 6). To become humble like Jesus, to become his disciples, individuals must take up their crosses, trust in him, approach perfection through wise choices, and submissively endure to the end (D&C 122:7). Christ's pattern of humility was unblemished. Though members aspire to this perfection, they are to keep perspective on their fallibility by balancing unfulfilled aspirations to emulate Christ with positive recognition of his gifts to them, of their worth as God's children, and of their progress toward humility over a lifetime. In the face of social pressures for self-interested individuality, the Church stresses selflessness and humility as keys for returning to God. Persons who would attain the fulness of the immortalizing promises of the ATONEMENT must persist in achieving humility in spite of obstacles and societal ethics that distract from this goal (Mosiah 3:19).

The desire for humility is nourished by an understanding acceptance of the greatness of the Savior's sacrifice to provide SALVATION and RESURRECTION for all. As people comprehend God's love for them, hearts and minds will be humbled and drawn into closer unity with him and with all fellow beings.

BIBLIOGRAPHY

Benson, Ezra Taft. "Jesus Christ: Our Savior and Redeemer." *Ensign* 13 (Nov. 1983):6–8.

———. "To the Elderly in the Church." *Ensign* 19 (May 1989):4–8.

Maxwell, Neal A. *Meek and Lowly.* Salt Lake City, 1987.

Packer, Boyd K. "The Only True Church." *Ensign* 15 (Nov. 1985):80–82.

ALICE T. CLARK

HUMOR

Although LDS doctrines, practices, and experiences have in some circles evoked a measure of scoffing and laughter over the years, only since the 1970s has a body of published humor dealing with the Mormon experience appeared. Institutionalized LDS humor divides roughly into an early period when the Church was the object of outsiders' jokes and a modern period when members have become able to laugh at themselves.

As with many minority groups, the first humor that dealt with the Church was created by antagonists to turn people away from it. Much of this humor took the form of cartoons in the popular press, and verses and parodies of popular or folk songs (Bunker and Bitton, 1983). These attacks were prevalent in nineteenth-century periodicals, and such noted writers as Mark Twain and Artemus Ward took aim at available targets like Brigham YOUNG and POLYGAMY.

From this early period, almost no pro-Mormon humor or humor regarding the Church created by the members of the Church themselves survives. While it is certain that members enjoyed humor, as evidenced in numerous JOURNALS and letters, little of it was apparently directed at their own experiences and cultural practices. This was particularly true of published material. Latter-day Saints were too involved with building a new way of life to indulge in frivolity or of anything that might appear to question their commitment. Humor, therefore, was incidental.

Around 1900 this attitude began to change, expressly in the talks of Elder J. Golden Kimball, of the Seventy. During his long tenure as a General Authority, his iconoclastic wit and biting sense of humor not only made the Saints love and quote him, but also helped them to see a lighter side of their often difficult existence.

Still, little in-group humor appeared in print before 1948, when Samuel W. Taylor's novel *Heaven Knows Why!* was published. Playing on the cultural patterns of typical small-town western Mormonism, the book gained limited success and recognition as an alternative selection of the Literary Guild, but it also caused a stir of discontent in the LDS community, hitting too close to home and seeming to ridicule not only lifestyle but also sacred doctrines. Because of its limited acceptance, it quickly dropped out of print.

A turning point seems to have come as a result of World War II, which brought outsiders into the almost exclusively LDS Rocky Mountain communities and spread members of the Church throughout the world. The resulting interchange showed both groups that in many ways they were not as different from each other as they had assumed, and allowed them to laugh at their common foibles and presumptions.

As the Church became better known as an American lifestyle, its members felt freer to find humor in their own cultural patterns and practices.

J. Golden Kimball, by Gordon N. Cope (1933, oil canvas, 31" × 24"). J. Golden Kimball (1853–1938), a member of the First Council of the Seventy from 1892 until his death, was known and loved for his frank, sometimes disturbing, wit and humor. Church Museum of History and Art.

Concurrently, its rapid growth created a larger audience for specifically LDS materials as well as an audience educated, sophisticated, and affluent enough to understand, enjoy, and buy them.

Taylor's book, reissued in 1979, now has enthusiastic readers, as have the works of cartoonists Calvin Grondahl and Pat Bagley. Jack Weyland's *A New Dawn* and Alma Yates's *The Miracle of Miss Willie* are among recent novels that depict LDS cultural idiosyncrasies. Parodies and spoofs aimed at the LDS audience include Orson Scott Card's *Saintspeak*, Carol Lynn Pearson's "notebooks," and numerous articles by Chris Crowe.

However, this growing acceptance of culturally bound humor has limitations. LDS DOCTRINES, ORDINANCES, and TEMPLE ceremonies are not usually the objects of humor, although unexpected or unorthodox responses to specific doctrines, particularly those by nonmembers or of

small children may be. Scandal or notoriety that might reflect on all members is not considered funny, but the everyday problems of family life, Church and missionary service, as well as the need to reconcile principles and practices, lend themselves well to humor. Latter-day Saints generally seem willing to laugh at themselves and their LIFESTYLE, but not at sacred things (*see* LIGHTMINDEDNESS).

BIBLIOGRAPHY

Bunker, Gary L. and Davis Bitton. *The Mormon Graphic Image, 1834–1914*. Salt Lake City, 1983.

Cracroft, Richard H. "The Humor of Mormon Seriousness." *Sunstone* (Jan. 1985):14–17.

Wilson, William A. "The Seriousness of Mormon Humor." *Sunstone* (Jan. 1985):8–13.

MARGARET P. BAKER

HYDE, ORSON

As a member of the first Twelve Apostles (1835) of the modern dispensation and the first missionary to take the message of the restored gospel to continental Europe and the Near East, Orson Hyde was closely allied with the rise and the development of the LDS Church. Born on January 8, 1805, in Oxford, New Haven County, Connecticut, he was raised in the care of Nathan Wheeler of Derby, Connecticut. In 1819, Hyde walked some six hundred miles to the town of KIRTLAND, OHIO, where Wheeler had purchased land. There he found employment as a clerk in the N. K. Whitney & Co. store. Continuously searching for deeper religious truths, he came under the influence of Sidney RIGDON, a Reformed Baptist minister, and embraced restorationist ideals advanced by Alexander Campbell and Sidney Rigdon.

When Oliver COWDERY and other missionaries to the Lamanites came through the Kirtland region in October–November 1830, Orson spoke against the "Mormon Bible," a position he changed after carefully examining the Book of Mormon. After three months of studying and pondering the doctrines taught by the Latter-day Saints, he was baptized in the Chagrin River on October 30, 1831, by Sidney Rigdon, who also had been converted (Barron, pp. 15–25).

A succession of missions followed Hyde's conversion. He and Hyrum Smith preached in Elyria

Orson Hyde (1805–1878), about 1853. He accepted the gospel in 1831 in Kirtland, Ohio, and was ordained an apostle in 1835. He was called to go to Jerusalem in 1840, and on October 24, 1841, dedicated the Holy Land for the gathering of Israel. Attributed to Marsena Cannon.

and Florence, Ohio, and in 1832 he joined Samuel Smith in journeying to the "eastern countries" of the United States. In 1833 he and John Gould were sent as Church emissaries to resolve difficulties in Jackson County, Missouri. He marched with ZION'S CAMP the following year. After returning to Ohio, he married Nancy Marinda Johnson in Kirtland, on September 4, 1834.

On February 15, 1835, Orson Hyde was ordained a member of the Quorum of the Twelve Apostles, and in 1837 he represented the Church in petitioning the Ohio state legislature for a bank charter for the Kirtland Safety Society. He went with Heber C. KIMBALL on the first mission to Great Britain (1837–1838). Their work led to the eventual conversion of thousands to the Mormon faith (see MISSIONS OF THE TWELVE TO THE BRITISH ISLES).

Hyde was in Far West, Missouri, by the summer of 1838, and in October he signed an affidavit against the Saints during the severe persecution of that period. John Taylor said that perhaps Hyde "had been sick with a violent fever" (*HC* 3:168). Whatever the reason, Hyde made things right with Joseph SMITH and in the spring of 1839 wrote to the Twelve in Illinois asking if he could return. Dropped from the Quorum of the Twelve on May 4, 1839, he was again sustained as an apostle on June 27, 1839.

Years before, it had been prophesied that Hyde "had a great work to perform among the Jews" (*HC* 4:106), and in 1840 he was directed to undertake a mission that took him to New York, London, Amsterdam, Constantinople (Istanbul), and Jerusalem, speaking to the Jewish communities wherever he could. On October 24, 1841, Elder Hyde climbed the Mount of Olives near Jerusalem and offered a prophetic prayer of dedication, asking the Lord to remove the "barrenness and sterility of this land" (Hyde, p. 21). He returned home via Cairo, Alexandria, Trieste, and Germany. In Germany he published the first LDS German tract, *Ein Ruf aus der Wüste* (A Cry out of the Wilderness; Frankfurt, 1842).

When the majority of the Saints left Nauvoo for Iowa Territory early in 1846, Orson Hyde was asked to remain behind to supervise the completion and dedication of the NAUVOO TEMPLE. Dedicatory services were conducted on April 30 and May 1, 1846. From 1846 to 1847 he presided over the British mission. When President Brigham YOUNG returned to the Salt Lake Valley in 1848, Hyde was placed in charge of the camps of Israel in the Midwest. He remained in Kanesville (Council Bluffs, Iowa) until 1852, publishing the *Frontier Guardian* (1849–1852).

In Utah, Elder Hyde was called to head the Carson Valley Nevada Mission in 1855. He returned to Salt Lake in 1857 because of the UTAH EXPEDITION. Further implementing his plan to have the Twelve Apostles preside over designated settlement areas, President Young called Elder Hyde to supervise settlement in the Sanpete-Sevier district of Utah in 1858.

At a meeting of the Twelve Apostles held in 1875, Brigham Young made a decision affecting Hyde's standing as the senior member of the Quorum. It was ruled that since he and Orson PRATT had briefly separated themselves from the Quorum in 1838 and 1842, respectively, they should lose their seniority to Elders John TAYLOR, Wilford WOODRUFF, and George A. Smith, who had been ordained during their time away (Durham, *Succession in the Church* [Salt Lake City, 1970], pp. 73–76). Because of that decision, John Taylor rather than Orson Hyde succeeded Brigham Young as President of the Church.

Following a lingering illness, Orson Hyde died at his home in Spring City, Utah, on November 28, 1878. With his passing the Church lost a noted missionary, colonizer, eloquent speaker, and devoted servant.

BIBLIOGRAPHY

Barron, Howard H. *Orson Hyde, Missionary, Apostle, Colonizer.* Bountiful, Utah, 1977.

Hill, Marvin S. "An Historical Study of the Life of Orson Hyde, Early Mormon Missionary and Apostle from 1805–1852." Master's thesis, Brigham Young University, 1955.

Hyde, Orson. *A Sketch of the Travels and Ministry of Elder Orson Hyde.* Salt Lake City, 1869.

HOWARD H. BARRON

HYMNS AND HYMNODY

Hymns have been central to the LDS tradition of worship from the earliest days of the Church. Latter-day Saints revere their hymnbook almost as scripture because of their belief that the first LDS hymnal had its origins in divine commandment. In July of 1830, only three months after the Church was organized, Joseph SMITH's wife Emma SMITH was instructed to "make a selection of sacred hymns . . . to be had in my church" (D&C 25:11). The resulting 1835 volume, *A Collection of Sacred Hymns, for the Church of the Latter Day Saints,* included among its ninety hymns a number of original, distinctively LDS texts. For example, two by the book's co-editor William W. Phelps, "The Spirit of God Like a Fire Is Burning" (*Hymns* 1985, No. 2) and "Now Let Us Rejoice" (*Hymns* 1985, No. 3) celebrate the RESTORATION of the latter-day Church. These and other original hymns were printed alongside well-known Protestant texts by such authors as Isaac Watts and Reginald Heber. A second hymnal, expanded to 304 hymns, was printed in Nauvoo in 1841.

Under the direction of Brigham YOUNG, Parley PRATT, and John TAYLOR, a volume familiarly known as the *Manchester Hymnal* was printed in Manchester, England, in 1840. Formally titled *A Collection of Sacred Hymns for the Church of Jesus Christ of Latter-day Saints in Europe,* this book served as the principal hymnbook of the English-speaking Saints for many decades. Converts from the BRITISH ISLES brought it with them when they traveled to join the main body of the Saints in Utah. New hymns, most of them American in origin, were added to each later edition, but the *Manchester Hymnal* continued to be published in England until 1890. By 1912 it had gone through twenty-five editions. Like Emma Smith's hymnal and most others of the time, it printed the texts but not the music.

Emma Smith had looked forward to the day when the Saints would be "blessed with a copious variety of the songs of Zion," as she wrote in the preface to the first hymnbook. Her hopes were fulfilled; early LDS hymn writers continued to add important original hymns on such distinctive doctrines as the PREMORTAL LIFE (Eliza R. SNOW, "O My Father," *Hymns* 1985, No. 292), the latter-day restoration (Parley P. Pratt, "An Angel from on High," *Hymns* 1985, No. 13), and the GATHERING of the Saints to Utah (William G. Mills, "Arise, O Glorious Zion," *Hymns* 1985, No. 40).

In 1886 President John Taylor called together a committee to provide a musical supplement to the *Manchester Hymnal.* The result was the *Latter-day Saints' Psalmody,* which was published in Salt Lake City in 1889 and went through six more editions. The *Psalmody* emphasized home composition, that is, new music that was written by such LDS composers as George Careless and Ebenezer Beesley to accompany the old texts in the *Manchester Hymnal.* For some of the longer texts in the *Psalmody,* only the first few verses were printed.

During the 1870s and 1880s the SUNDAY SCHOOL and PRIMARY organizations began to print hymns and songs, singly and in collections, for their own use. In 1873 the Sunday School began publishing Sunday School hymns in the JUVENILE INSTRUCTOR magazine, and in 1880, under the direction of Eliza R. Snow, the Primary published a volume of texts and a companion volume of tunes.

In earlier decades the line between official and unofficial hymnbooks was not clearly drawn, and some of the LDS hymnals were private undertakings. An unofficial hymnbook, *Songs of Zion,* compiled by German Ellsworth and published in Chicago, became extremely popular. It went through eleven editions between 1908 and 1925.

Deseret Sunday School Songs, published by the Sunday School in 1909, was intended as a Sunday School songbook rather than a general WORSHIP hymnal. However, because so many Latter-day Saints loved its gospel-song hymns, with their energetic rhythms and simple exhortative texts, several of its hymns have found a secure place among the Mormons. "Master, the Tempest Is Raging" (*Hymns* 1985, No. 105) and "Put Your Shoulder to the Wheel" (*Hymns* 1985, No. 252) are two examples. The 1927 *Latter-day Saint Hymns*, a volume of more dignified and traditional hymns, was intended to supplement *Deseret Sunday School Songs* as the hymnal for SACRAMENT MEETINGS.

Hymns: Church of Jesus Christ of Latter-day Saints, printed in 1948, replaced both the 1927 hymnbook and *Deseret Sunday School Songs*. Many Church members were disappointed, however, to find that the 1948 hymnal omitted some favorites from among those in the *Deseret Sunday School Songs* and other sources. Responding to popular preference, the Church printed a new edition in 1950, restoring such well-established hymns as "A Poor Wayfaring Man of Grief" (*Hymns* 1985, No. 29) and "Have I Done Any Good?" (*Hymns* 1985, No. 223).

The 1950 hymnal retained official status until 1985, when it was replaced by *Hymns of The Church of Jesus Christ of Latter-day Saints*. This hymnal, published 150 years after Emma Smith's first one, retains almost one-third of the hymns she originally chose—a remarkable tribute to her judgment and to the well-defined and enduring nature of the LDS hymn tradition. There is little that is revolutionary about the new hymnal but much that is significant. Its publication provided an opportunity to omit outdated or little-used hymns in favor of new material of high quality. In all, seventy hymns that were part of the 1950 hymnal were dropped in 1985, and ninety-two new or newly borrowed hymns were added, of which forty-four are LDS contributions wholly or in part. Hymns by present-day LDS contributors continue to reflect Church thinking and concerns: FASTING (Nos. 138, 139), home and family (Nos. 298, 300), MISSIONARY work (Nos. 253, 263), and so forth. Out of a total of 358 contributors, 168 are Latter-day Saints.

The 1985 hymnal shows that, as in the past, LDS hymnody embraces well-known material from other Christian traditions, for example, Martin Luther's "A Mighty Fortress" (No. 68) and Charles Wesley's "Rejoice, the Lord Is King!" (No.

66). Many of the hymns pair a Latter-say Saint text with a borrowed hymn tune, or an indigenous tune with a borrowed text. Tunes are again drawn from many sources: opera (Nos. 160, 196), popular songs of an earlier time (Nos. 34, 237), folk songs (Nos. 15, 284), and others. The selections overall, especially among the new hymns, reflect a strong denominational preference for traditional styles in both music and text. Because the custom of four-part congregational singing continues in most areas of the Church today, virtually all the hymns are printed with soprano, alto, tenor, and bass lines. Although a number of older gospel songs remain strong favorites, the ballad-type sacred song, important today in the congregational singing of some other denominations, has not found a place in Mormon hymnody.

A committee appointed by the General Authorities of the Church, and working under their guidance, recommended the hymns for the 1985 hymnbook. The goal was to include as many of superior artistic merit as possible while keeping in mind the preferences and needs of the general Church membership; a well-loved hymn ran little risk of being dropped, even if it did not meet high literary or musical standards. In the process of selecting and editing these hymns, certain issues that have become major points of discussion in other denominations presented far fewer difficulties. For example, male-oriented language with reference to GOD THE FATHER and Jesus Christ was retained, consistent with the LDS concept of them as male. In addition, Latter-day Saints seem fairly comfortable with military metaphors in their hymn texts, though some language dating from times of actual physical conflict, particularly in "Up, Awake, Ye Defenders of Zion" (No. 284), was edited to make it less bellicose. Certain other texts that originally focused on North America were altered to reflect the Church's overall worldwide mission (Nos. 91, 290).

The present hymnbook is divided into eleven sections: Hymns about the Restoration, Praise and THANKSGIVING, Prayer and Supplication, Sacrament, Easter, Christmas, Special Topics, Children's Songs, For Women, For Men, and Patriotic. The national anthems of the UNITED STATES OF AMERICA and the United Kingdom are included, and anthems for Canada, Australia, and New Zealand are available separately.

An eight-page appendix called "Using the Hymnbook" provides instructions for directors and organists. It is followed by seven indexes: Authors and Composers; Titles, Tunes, and Meters; Tune Names; Meters; Scriptures (an index correlating scriptural passages with hymn texts); Topics; and First Lines and Titles. Scripture references also appear with each hymn.

Subsequently, the Church Music Committee identified one hundred hymns from the 1985 hymnbook as the standard core of hymns to be published in other languages, with a list of fifty optional additional hymns. The remaining hymns in non-English hymnbooks reflect the choices and contributions of the members in the particular language areas. In this way the Church strives to preserve in its international hymnbooks a balance between Churchwide tradition and local preference.

The *Children's Songbook*, published in 1989, follows *The Children Sing* (1951) and *Sing with Me* (1969) as the official music resource for the Primary organization. With its straightforward messages and attractive melodies, its simplified accompaniments, and its many color illustrations, the *Chil-dren's Songbook* is intended to appeal directly to children as well as to their parents and teachers.

[*See also* the Appendix for a brief selection of important Latter-day Saint music.]

BIBLIOGRAPHY

Cornwall, J. Spencer. *Stories of Our Mormon Hymns*. Salt Lake City, 1975.

Davidson, Karen Lynn. *Our Latter-day Hymns: The Stories and the Messages*. Salt Lake City, 1988.

Macare, Helen Hanks. "The Singing Saints: A Study of the Mormon Hymnal, 1835–1950." Ph.D. diss., UCLA, 1961.

Moody, Michael F. "Contemporary Hymnody in The Church of Jesus Christ of Latter-day Saints." Ph.D. diss., University of Southern California, 1972.

Pyper, George D. *Stories of Latter-day Saint Hymns*. Salt Lake City, 1939.

Weight, Newell B. "An Historical Study of the Origins and Character of the Indigenous Hymn Tunes of the Latter-day Saints." D.M.A. diss., University of Southern California, 1961.

KAREN LYNN DAVIDSON

I

"I AM"

See: Jesus Christ, Names and Titles of

IDAHO, PIONEER SETTLEMENTS IN

Although the main thrust of Latter-day Saint COLONIZATION was to the south of Salt Lake City, Church members also established numerous settlements in the rich farm valleys of southern Idaho.

The first LDS excursion into Idaho followed President Brigham YOUNG's call of twenty-seven families to labor among the Indians in the Oregon Territory in 1855. The result was the founding of Fort Limhi on a tributary of the Salmon River near present-day Salmon, Idaho. As the U.S. Army approached Utah in 1857 (*see* UTAH EXPEDITION), conflict with local Indians erupted, two missionaries were killed, and, in 1858, the fort lost most of its stock. The settlers were called back to Salt Lake City and the colony was never reopened.

In 1860 the community of Franklin, near the present Utah-Idaho border, became the first permanent Anglo-American settlement in the future territory of Idaho. Indian problems plagued the settlement until the Battle Creek massacre, in which federal soldiers from Salt Lake City's Fort Douglas killed a large number of Indians in 1863.

Additional settlers went east from Cache Valley (Franklin was its northernmost town) over the mountains into the Bear Lake region in southeastern Idaho, opening the settlements of Paris, Bloomington, St. Charles, Ovid, Montpelier, Fish Haven, Liberty, and Bennington. Charles C. Rich, an apostle, oversaw these communities, which by 1864 included nearly seven hundred settlers. Latter-day Saints started additional settlements in the Idaho part of northern Cache Valley, Malad Valley, and Marsh Valley beginning in the 1860s, and in Gentile Valley in the 1870s.

Church members helped construct the railroad between Ogden, Utah, and Franklin, Idaho, in 1871–1874, and beginning in 1878, they helped extend the line farther into Idaho through Blackfoot and Idaho Falls (then called Eagle Rock) to Monida Pass, on the present-day Idaho-Montana border. Many Latter-day Saints homesteaded near the railroad and established such communities as Chesterfield, Egin Bench, and Rexburg. For the next two decades, Mormon settlements increasingly dotted the landscape for two hundred miles between Pocatello and Victor in the Teton Basin. By 1890, the Bannock Stake, centered in Rexburg, reported 3,861 members. Because the Snake River Valley was arid, LDS settlers devoted considerable energies to canal building. By 1910, more than one hundred canals operated in the Upper Snake River Valley, and LDS settlements were established

The first frame house north of Bear River (built in Marsh Valley, Idaho, 1873). William West Woodland (center) crossed the plains in 1847 and again as a guide in 1848; pictured here with his wife, some of his 14 children, two granddaughters, and a hired hand (c. 1897). Courtesy the Woodland family.

(Moreland, New Sweden, Thomas, Springfield, and Aberdeen) where there were canals.

Latter-day Saints also moved west from Pocatello. In 1879 William C. Martindale, from Tooele, Utah, explored the Goose Creek Valley and returned to Utah with a favorable report. Church families soon began homesteading areas that included Goose Creek and Raft River. Oakley, where the Oregon and California trails separated, became the central location of the colony.

LDS influence in Idaho in the nineteenth century was confined largely to the southeast, where the Saints were a majority in many settlements. In the twentieth century Latter-day Saints have become a significant minority in communities farther west, still primarily in the southern part of the state.

BIBLIOGRAPHY

Bitton, Davis. "Peopling the Upper Snake: The Second Wave of Mormon Settlement in Idaho." *Idaho Yesterdays* 23 (Summer 1979):47–52.

Campbell, Eugene E. *Establishing Zion: The Mormon Church in the American West.* Salt Lake City, 1988.

Rich, Russell R. *Land of the Sky-Blue Water: A History of the LDS Settlement of the Bear Lake Valley.* Provo, Utah, 1963.

Ricks, Joel E., ed. *The History of a Valley: Cache Valley, Utah-Idaho.* Logan, Utah, 1956.

ROBERT D. MARCUM

ILLINOIS, LDS COMMUNITIES IN

[*The Church was centered in western Illinois from 1839 to 1846. After their expulsion from Missouri in 1838–1839, Mormon refugees fled to Quincy, Springfield, and other locations in Illinois, where local residents gave them assistance. Church leaders purchased the village of Commerce and land in its vicinity, along with a large tract across the Mississippi River in Iowa. Commerce was renamed* Nauvoo *and became the principal LDS community of its time and one of the largest cities in Illinois.*

Numerous small settlements in the vicinity of Nauvoo fell within the city's sphere of influence (see Donald Q. Cannon, "Spokes on the Wheel: Early Latter-day Saints Settlements in Hancock County, Illinois," Ensign 16 [Feb. 1986]:62–68). The LDS town of Ramus (later Macedonia and now Webster), about twenty miles southeast of Nauvoo, became a Church stake, as did Lima, twenty-five miles south of Nauvoo. La Harpe, a few miles north of Ramus, also had a considerable LDS pop-

Paris, Idaho, Tabernacle in 1987. Designed by one of Brigham Young's sons, Joseph Don Carlos Young, this Romanesque pioneer building was constructed 1884–1889. The distinctive dark and light red sandstone was hauled by teams from canyons 18 miles away or pulled during the winter across the frozen Bear Lake. Courtesy Craig Law.

ulation. Warren, twenty miles southwest of Nauvoo, was a short-lived LDS community adjacent to Warsaw. Anti-Mormon violence focused on these outlying LDS communities and caused their evacuation in 1845.

In addition to several entries under Nauvoo, see Carthage Jail; Historical Sites; *and* Martyrdom of Joseph and Hyrum Smith. *Two articles include information on the Illinois period:* Joseph Smith, *and* History of the Church: c. 1831–1844 *and* c. 1844–1877.

For LDS immigration to Illinois and subsequent departure for the Rocky Mountains, see Immigration and Emigration *and* Westward Migration, Planning and Prophecy.]

IMMACULATE CONCEPTION

Immaculate conception is the belief of some Christians that from her conception in her mother's womb, Jesus' mother was free from ORIGINAL SIN.

Original sin holds that ADAM's sinful choice in the Garden of Eden, made for all his descendants, led to a hereditary sin incurred at conception by every human being and removed only by the sacraments of the church. From this view arose the concept of Mary's immaculate conception. By a unique grace, Mary was preserved from the stain of original sin, inheriting human nature without taint in order that she be a suitable mother for Jesus. This teaching was defined as obligatory dogma by Pope Pius IX in 1854.

Latter-day Saints accept neither the above doctrine of original sin nor the need for Mary's immaculate conception (*MD*, p. 375). Instead, they "believe that men will be punished for their own sins, and not for Adam's transgression" (A of F 2), because Jesus' ATONEMENT redeems all, including Mary, from the responsibility for Adam's trespass (Moro. 8:8). "God having redeemed man from the fall, men became again, in their infant state, innocent before God" (D&C 93:38). For Latter-day Saints, Mary was a choice servant selected by God to be the mother of Jesus.

BIBLIOGRAPHY

"Immaculate Conception." *New Catholic Encyclopedia*, Vol. 7, pp. 378–82. New York, 1967.

Watlington, Amanda G. *Official Catholic Teachings: Christ Our Lord.* Wilmington, 1978.

CONNIE LAMB

IMMIGRATION AND EMIGRATION

The immigration of tens of thousands of converts, first into America's Midwest and then into the mountain West, was a major part of the growth of the Church in the United States during the nineteenth century. So closely interrelated were proselytizing and the GATHERING of the faithful in the vicinity of Church headquarters that President Brigham YOUNG declared in 1860 that emigration "upon the first feasible opportunity, directly follows obedience to the first principles of the gospel we have embraced" (Brigham Young to A. Lyman, et al., and Saints in the British Isles, Aug. 2, 1860, Brigham Young Letterbooks, LDS Church Archives). With millennial fervor, Latter-day Saint converts sought to flee the impending woes of a sinful world by gathering "home to Zion," where they could join their American counterparts in preparing for the SECOND COMING OF JESUS CHRIST. This gathering made it possible for the Latter-day Saints to become a dominant economic, political, and religious force in the Great Basin. It reinforced a sense of group identity and shielded them from religious persecution while providing individuals and families with greater economic opportunity.

Most converts were poor; indeed, the majority lacked sufficient funds to emigrate. Individuals and families were encouraged to save systematically, and the few who had surplus funds after emigrating were asked to assist fellow converts. In 1849 the Church organized the PERPETUAL EMIGRATING FUND (PEF) to solicit donations and provide emigrants with loans, the repayment of which would aid others. Such loans were most often made available to individuals with needed skills, to those whose relatives or friends donated to the PEF, or to those who had been faithful Church members for ten years or longer. From 1852 until 1887 the PEF assisted some 26,000 immigrants—more than one-third of the total LDS emigrants from Europe during that period—with at least part of the journey to the mountain West. In the 1850s and 1860s there were three categories of immigrants: the independent, who paid their own way to Utah; "states" or "ordinary" immigrants, who paid only enough to reach a port of entry or other intermediate stopping place in the United States, hoping to earn enough there to finish the journey; and PEF immigrants, assisted by the Perpetual Emigrating Fund. In later years private assistance eclipsed the PEF in the amount of aid rendered. In the 1880s and 1890s, 20 to 50 percent of the immigrants each year received private assistance.

Enthusiasm for emigration was highest during periods of international unrest, with accompanying millennialist expectations of increasing troubles worldwide prior to Jesus' second coming. Thus, in 1855, during the Crimean War, more Latter-day Saints emigrated from Europe than during any other year. That year 4,225 emigrants—about 2.4 percent of all Europeans who migrated in 1855 to the United States—were Latter-day Saints, even though the total number of Church members in Great Britain and on the Continent, from whom the emigrants were drawn, was fewer than 35,000. The American Civil War brought exceptionally high LDS emigration in the years 1861–1865, a time when the general emigration from Europe was relatively low.

Because Church funds, including those of the PEF, were never sufficient to help as many as wished to immigrate, Church leaders on both sides of the Atlantic utilized many approaches. After the 1855 season, when Church and PEF resources were exhausted, donations of Salt Lake City real estate were sold for cash to British arrivals with the proceeds applied to emigration; and the use of handcarts rather than large wagons cut costs for the overland journey from Iowa to Utah. The tragic loss of more than two hundred lives in the two last HANDCART COMPANIES of 1856, because they departed too late and were caught in early snowstorms, grimly underscored the necessity of careful planning and implementation.

While the PEF continued to assist with individual expenses for transatlantic voyages on a limited basis after 1856, most of its aid was applied to the overland portion of the trip. Beginning in 1861 this was made possible by the use of the "Church trains" system for conveying immigrants. Under Brigham Young's direction, oxen and wagons along with teamsters and other personnel from throughout Utah appeared in Salt Lake City as soon as spring grass began to grow along the immigrant trail. The men, for their labors, and the owners of teams and wagons received either credit for TITHING or wages paid in goods from local tithing storehouses. This practice resulted in the Church's tithing system subsidizing the operation heavily: in 1868 teamsters and owners received about $200,000 in tithing credit, while immigrants were charged only $75,000, on credit. It often took immigrants years to pay their indebtedness for emigration, and many failed to complete payment. By 1887, about one-third of the emigrants had paid their debt to the PEF in full, one-third had paid part, and one-third had paid nothing.

After the completion of the transcontinental railroad in 1869, immigrants traveling by steam-powered ships and trains could make the trip from Liverpool, England, to Salt Lake City in just over three weeks. Earlier, the journey by ship and wagon often took nearly six months. Yet advantages in time, comfort, and health were countered by the fact that more cash—a scarce commodity in the pioneer economy (see PIONEER ECONOMY)—was required for the trip. The PEF still provided full passage for more than one hundred emigrants yearly from Europe to Utah in the years 1871–1875 and 1878–1881.

Church personnel at both local and mission levels played important roles in organizing the emigration from Europe. Clerks in each branch (congregation) received deposits to individual emigration savings accounts, which were forwarded to headquarters for a larger area, called a "conference," and then sent on to the mission headquarters. Local leaders sought out potential emigrants who seemed deserving of assistance and forwarded information about them to mission headquarters. Expanding a system dating from 1840–1841, when the QUORUM OF THE TWELVE APOSTLES organized the first emigrant companies (see MISSIONS OF THE TWELVE TO THE BRITISH ISLES), mission publications gave notice of planned departures and costs and provided helpful information such as lists of items passengers should bring. Well in advance of the departure date, conference presidents collected deposits to reserve places on particular vessels. Mission personnel served as passenger agents, thus avoiding middlemen, and used the commission they received for the benefit of poor emigrants or missionaries. Where necessary, they made arrangements for provisions and for cookware and eating utensils. In hectic last-minute efforts they helped hundreds of passengers board ship and obtain their berths. Men traveling with the group, usually returning missionaries, were appointed as presidencies for the ship and were responsible for the conduct and morale of the passengers and for holding religious services. Generally the daily routine involved prayer, washing the decks, cooperative cooking arrangements, and special meetings to discuss problems that arose.

Because the Saints traveled as a Church family under PRIESTHOOD leadership—and with the assistance of an experienced and well-organized system—LDS emigration impressed nonmember observers as orderly and civilized compared with the tumult generally surrounding emigrant ships. One writer noted:

> The ordinary emigrant is exposed to all the chances and misadventures of a heterogeneous, childish, mannerless crowd during the voyage, and to the merciless cupidity of land-sharks the moment he has touched the opposite shore. But the Mormon ship is a Family under strong and accepted discipline, with every provision for comfort, decorum, and internal peace. On his arrival in the New World

the wanderer is received into a confraternity which speeds him onwards with as little hardship and anxiety as the circumstances permit and he is passed on from friend to friend, till he reaches the promised home [*Edinburgh Review*, Jan. 1862, p. 199].

When passengers arrived in America, they were usually met by a Church emigration agent who assisted them with arrangements for transportation to the frontier outfitting point. At the frontier the emigrants remained encamped until all arrangements could be completed for the arduous overland trek (see MORMON PIONEER TRAIL). Before the immigrants arrived, agents purchased teams and wagons or handcarts. During the era of "down and back" Church trains, flour was generally hauled from Salt Lake City—part of it stashed along the trail—and other provisions were purchased by agents near the outfitting point. After 1861, wagon trains sent periodic reports on their progress by telegraph, and, when necessary, relief parties met immigrants en route as they neared the end of the journey.

Immigrant companies were officially welcomed as they arrived at Salt Lake City, where they camped while awaiting assignments. BISHOPS or their representatives then escorted them to the various settlements to which quotas had been assigned.

LDS immigrants, particularly those from northern Europe, were usually assimilated into communities and congregations quickly. New arrivals who did not speak English availed themselves of Church-sponsored publications and activities in their mother tongue, while also attending worship services in English. There was a short-lived effort to produce materials in a phonetic alphabet to ease immigrant learning (see DESERET ALPHABET), but most of the immigrants and virtually all their children became fluent in English. With few exceptions, relatively little sense of ethnic community survived beyond the generation of immigrants themselves. Most descendants of the immigrants who served as missionaries to ancestral lands had to learn the native language during their service.

After the late 1880s, coinciding with a new wave of emigration from central and southern Europe and with negative publicity and ANTIPOLYGAMY LEGISLATION, LDS immigration was frowned upon by many in the United States. The large number of LDS steamship passengers were still assisted with arrangements by Church personnel, but they were instructed to maintain a low profile and did not function visibly as Mormon emigrant companies. By the 1890s the number of Latter-day Saints in Europe had dwindled, and in view of economic conditions in the United States, Church leaders began to discourage emigration—though LDS immigration revived modestly during the following decade. More than 103,000 emigrated in the years 1840–1910, an average of some 2,000 annually. In the years 1911–1946, with two world wars and the Great Depression dampening interest in relocation, LDS emigration declined to an average of only 291 annually. Encouraging the Saints to remain in their native lands and strengthen the Church there—a temporary expedience in the 1890s—eventually became a firmer policy. Leaders obtained more substantial locations for Church meetings in major European cities and promoted a greater sense of permanence.

A resurgence of LDS emigration from Europe took place in the years immediately following World War II; an average of more than 1,000 Latter-day Saints emigrated annually in the years 1947–1953. Beginning in the late 1950s the Church moved to provide its members in Europe and other areas with greater access to opportunities found in the United States, including the TEMPLES, more substantial local meeting places, and local leadership. This reinforced the encouragement to build ZION wherever Saints were found, and emigration from Europe tapered off. The gathering of emigration statistics was discontinued after 1962. By that time approximately 127,000 Latter-day Saints had emigrated from Europe, and thousands more from Canada, the South Pacific, and Mexico, to bring the total to about 150,000 emigrants. The influx of Church members from such areas as Canada and the South Pacific to Utah, California, and Missouri remained at a significant level into the 1970s and 1980s. Additionally, conversions from among other recent immigrants, particularly refugees from Southeast Asia, continued to give the Church in the United States an international flavor. This was also true for other areas of the world, with converts from Africa and the West Indies becoming an important factor in the Church in the British Isles.

From the 1840s on, immigrants made vital contributions to Latter-day Saint life. Immigrant educators, artists, craftsmen, musicians, architects, clerks, and others all enriched life in their adopted land (see SOCIAL AND CULTURAL HISTORY). Immigrants played a particularly significant role in local Church leadership in the nineteenth century. Of 605 bishops and presiding elders in Latter-day Saint congregations in the United States from 1848 to 1890, 40 percent were born outside the United States. Twenty-nine percent were born in the British Isles. Scandinavia, the next richest source of LDS immigrants, accounted for 8 percent. In addition, 29 percent of STAKE PRESIDENTS in the period were born outside the United States, including 23 percent born in the British Isles. Other immigrants have served as General Authorities, including several who served in the FIRST PRESIDENCY.

BIBLIOGRAPHY

Arrington, Leonard J. *Great Basin Kingdom: An Economic History of the Latter-day Saints 1830–1900*, pp. 96–240. Cambridge, 1958.

Larson, Gustive O. *Prelude to the Kingdom: Mormon Desert Conquest: A Chapter in American Cooperative Experience.* Francestown, N.H., 1947.

Mulder, William. *Homeward to Zion: The Mormon Migration from Scandinavia.* Minneapolis, 1957.

Sonne, Conway B. *Saints on the Seas: A Maritime History of Mormon Migration 1830–1890.* Salt Lake City, 1983.

Taylor, P. A. M. *Expectations Westward: The Mormons and the Emigration of Their British Converts in the Nineteenth Century.* London, 1965.

RICHARD L. JENSEN
WILLIAM G. HARTLEY

IMMORTALITY

"Immortality is to live forever in the resurrected state with body and spirit inseparably connected" (*MD*, p. 376). The FALL OF ADAM brought death, and the ATONEMENT OF JESUS CHRIST brought life. Immortality is as broad as the Fall; since all creatures die, all will be given everlasting life (1 Cor. 15:22).

In the Garden of Eden, Adam and Eve were not subject to death until the Fall. When they partook of the forbidden fruit, they were ushered out of God's presence; mortality and its consequent death descended upon them, and subsequently upon all mankind and all other living things.

That humans became mortal was a necessary step in the Lord's eternal PLAN OF SALVATION for his children. The conditions of mortality, however, left mankind subject to death and incapable on its own of reclaiming the dead from the grave. Jesus Christ, the Only Begotten of the Father in the flesh, was the only one capable of redeeming the human family from the effects of the Fall, thus providing for a RESURRECTION of the PHYSICAL BODY.

The individual spirit that inhabits and gives life to the mortal physical body is not subject to the same death that is common to mortality. All spirits are immortal (cf. Alma 42:9; *TPJS*, p. 207; *see also* SOUL; SPIRIT).

The Lord himself died a physical death in order to bring about the resurrection of all the dead and to grant immortality to all mankind. The prophet Lehi said, "Wherefore, how great the importance to make these things known unto the inhabitants of the earth, that they may know that there is no flesh that can dwell in the presence of God, save it be through the merits, and mercy, and grace of the Holy Messiah, who layeth down his life according to the flesh, and taketh it again by the power of the Spirit, that he may bring to pass the resurrection of the dead, being the first that should rise" (2 Ne. 2:8).

During his earthly life, Jesus Christ raised several from the dead; however, they were restored only to mortal life. By his later atonement and resurrection of his physical, tangible body (Luke 24:36–40), Jesus provided the means by which every person will be resurrected to immortal life, with a tangible body of flesh and bones, even as he has. Paul taught, "For as in Adam all die, even so in Christ shall all be made alive" (1 Cor. 15:22), and "When this corruptible shall have put on incorruption, and this mortal shall have put on immortality, then shall be brought to pass the saying that is written, Death is swallowed up in victory" (1 Cor. 15:54; cf. Rom. 6:5).

Immortality is a free gift for all mankind. AMULEK, a Book of Mormon prophet, taught that "this restoration shall come to all, both old and young, both bond and free, both male and female, both the wicked and the righteous; . . . every thing shall be restored to its perfect frame, as it is now, or in the body, . . . that they can die no more; their spirits uniting with their bodies, never to be divided" (Alma 11:44–45). Immortality, or the resurrection from the dead, will be given to all forms of life, for God glorifies himself "by saving all that His hands had made, whether beasts, fowls, fishes or men" (*TPJS*, p. 291; D&C 29:24–25).

Although sometimes used interchangeably, the words "immortality" and "eternal life" are not synonymous. All who obtain eternal life will also have immortality, but not all who receive immortality will have eternal life. The term "eternal life" has reference to the type or quality of life that God has, which is given only to the faithful, and includes much more than living forever. "And thus did I, the Lord God, appoint unto man the days of his probation—that by his natural death he might be raised in immortality unto eternal life, even as many as would believe" (D&C 29:43).

[*See also* Immortality and Eternal Life.]

BIBLIOGRAPHY

Smith, Joseph Fielding. *Doctrines of Salvation*, Vol. 2, pp. 4–13. Salt Lake City, 1955.

Talmage, James E. *AF*, pp. 87–93. Salt Lake City, 1952.

DAN W. ANDERSEN

IMMORTALITY AND ETERNAL LIFE

The Church of Jesus Christ Latter-day Saints teaches that the work and glory of God is to bring to pass both the IMMORTALITY and the ETERNAL LIFE of men and women (Moses 1:39; 2 Ne. 10:23–25). These two conditions in the AFTERLIFE are not necessarily synonymous, though each is given as a consequence of the ATONEMENT OF JESUS CHRIST.

Immortality is to live forever in a resurrected condition without death that was introduced to this world through the FALL OF ADAM AND EVE (2 Ne. 2:22–23). Through Jesus Christ's atonement, all living things will receive a resurrection, the spirit and the flesh uniting never again to be separated, and will live forever in an immortal state (2 Ne. 2:8–9; 9:13; Alma 11:45). Immortality is a free gift from God because of unconditional GRACE, and does not require works of OBEDIENCE. "For as in Adam all die, even so in Christ shall all be made alive" (1 Cor. 15:22).

"Eternal life" is a higher state than immortality alone and means to live forever in a resurrected condition in the presence of God, and to become like God. It likewise is available only through the grace of Jesus Christ and is the greatest of all gifts that God bestows upon his children (D&C 14:7). Eternal life is EXALTATION into the type and quality of life that God lives. Receiving eternal life is conditional, predicated upon obedience to the fulness of gospel law and ORDINANCES (D&C 29:43–44; 130:20–21). It requires voluntary obedience to all of the ordinances and principles of the gospel, beginning with FAITH in Jesus Christ and continuing through BAPTISM, the LAYING ON OF HANDS for the GIFT OF THE HOLY GHOST, and the COVENANTS of the ENDOWMENT and MARRIAGE in the TEMPLE, and of ENDURING TO THE END.

BIBLIOGRAPHY

Smith, Joseph Fielding. *Man, His Origin and Destiny*, pp. 271–72. Salt Lake City, 1954.

LEAUN G. OTTEN

IMPROVEMENT ERA

One of six publications begun as Church auxiliary magazines between 1866 and 1902, the *Improvement Era* (1897–1970) was the official arm of the Young Men's Mutual Improvement Association (YMMIA, which became the YOUNG MEN in 1977). It followed the demise of the CONTRIBUTOR MAGAZINE (1879–1896), an independent journal associated with the YMMIA. Joined officially to the YMMIA, the *Era* immediately became the premier adult periodical of the Church through its General Authority sponsorship and its focus on theology, history, contemporary affairs, and life in the Church. Its name reflected its sponsor's goal to be for the intellectual, moral, and spiritual mutual *improvement* of its readers in a new Church *era* just one year after Utah achieved statehood. The *Era*'s preeminence from 1901 onward for more than half a century was in part due to the participation of the President of the Church as its principal editor; thus, its pages were often used to voice concerns important to Church leadership and to respond to queries concerning Church doctrine and LDS LIFESTYLE. Its circulation of 2,000 in 1897 reached 275,000 when it was succeeded by the ENSIGN in January 1971.

The *Era* soon served more than the YMMIA. It was the publication arm of the Seventies in 1908, of other PRIESTHOOD QUORUMS in 1909, and of Church schools in 1913. It merged with YOUNG WOMAN'S JOURNAL, the publication of the Young Women's Mutual Improvement Association (YWMIA, which became YOUNG WOMEN in 1977) in 1929. By 1936 it had become the arm of the music committee, ward teaching, and other agencies of the Church. Beginning in 1942, the *Era* printed all General Conference addresses (it had previously printed selected addresses).

In 1897 the *Era* had a 5 3/4-by-8 5/8-inch format. Thereafter, it usually contained eighty pages, with photographs printed on stitched-in leaves. In 1908 the paper was upgraded, and the number of photographs was increased. At its 1929 merger, the *Era* changed to an 8-by-10 7/8-inch magazine format, printed its covers in color, and began forty-one years of advertisements for its readers. It also added more general-interest articles. In 1957 the *Era* began publishing anniversary issues with four-color sections, but it did not use four-color printing regularly until 1969. In 1960 it began the section "The Era of Youth," a prelude to the NEW ERA.

The list of editors of the *Era* includes five presidents of the Church: Joseph F. SMITH, Heber J. GRANT, George Albert SMITH, David O. MCKAY, and Joseph Fielding SMITH; two members of the QUORUM OF THE TWELVE APOSTLES: John A. Widtsoe and Richard L. Evans; and two members of the First Council of the SEVENTY: B. H. Roberts and Richard L. Evans. Other editors or managing editors were Edward H. Anderson, Hugh J. Cannon, Harrison R. Merrill, and Doyle L. Green. "The Era of Youth" section was edited by Elder Marion D. Hanks of the Seventy, and Elaine A. Cannon, who later became president of the Young Women (1978–1984).

BIBLIOGRAPHY

Green, Doyle L. "*The Improvement Era*—The Voice of the Church (1897–1970)." *IE* 73 (Nov. 1970):12–20.

JAY M. TODD

INDEPENDENCE, MISSOURI

The tenth Article of Faith of the Church states, "We believe in the literal gathering of Israel and in the restoration of the Ten Tribes; that Zion [the New Jerusalem] will be built upon the American continent." From the Book of Mormon (Ether 13:1–5), early Latter-day Saints realized they had a role in the fulfillment of prophecy and were looking forward to the establishment of the NEW JERUSALEM in America.

Anxious to know exactly where the promised city would be and when it would be built, the

Saints were excited when in 1831 a series of revelations identified Missouri as the general location of the city of Zion, that "Independence is the center place, and a spot for the temple is lying westward, upon a lot which is not far from the courthouse" (D&C 57:1–3; 45:64–66; 48:4–6; 52:1–5, 42–43). Subsequently, Joseph Smith also indicated that the Jackson County area had been the location of the GARDEN OF EDEN.

Independence, Missouri, county seat of Jackson County, was the preparation and departure point in the 1830s and 1840s for trappers, explorers, and pioneers who were going to western America over the Santa Fe, Oregon, and California trails. The Latter-day Saints, however, anticipating permanent residence, purchased land, built homes, prepared their farms, and dedicated a temple site.

After one year of living peacefully in Independence and vicinity, the Saints began to be persecuted by their non-Mormon neighbors. Social, religious, and political differences finally developed into open hostilities, and the Latter-day Saints were driven into neighboring Clay County in 1833, where they petitioned for a peaceful settlement so that they could return to their homes. A settlement never came, but Latter-day Saints still look forward to a time when the city of Zion, the New Jerusalem, will be built in the area of Independence, Missouri.

BIBLIOGRAPHY

Anderson, Richard L. "Jackson County in Early Mormon Descriptions." *Missouri Historical Review* 65 (Apr. 1971):270–93.

Bushman, Richard L. "Mormon Persecutions in Missouri in 1833." *BYU Studies* 3 (Autumn 1960):11–20.

LAMAR C. BERRETT

INDIAN STUDENT PLACEMENT SERVICES

The Indian Student Placement Services was established among NATIVE AMERICANS by the LDS Church in part to fulfill the obligation felt by the Church to help care for the Indians in the Americas (2 Ne. 10:18–19). The program places Indian students in Latter-day Saint homes, where they live while attending the public school of the community during the academic year. Another goal of Indian Student Placement Services, in addition to giving Indian youth better opportunities for education, has been to develop leadership and to promote greater understanding between Indians and non-Indians.

The program started in 1947 in Richfield, Utah, when Helen John, a sixteen-year-old daughter of Navajo beet-field workers, requested permission to stay in Richfield to attend school. As an outgrowth of this request, Golden Buchanan of the Sevier Stake presidency and Miles Jensen, with Elder Spencer W. KIMBALL's support, organized an informal placement program that grew from three students in 1947 to sixty-eight in 1954, with foster homes in four western states.

In July 1954 the program was formalized under Church SOCIAL SERVICES and the Southwest Indian Mission. For the next several years the program grew rapidly, peaking at 4,997 in 1972. The policy for participation was that the natural parents had to request the placement; then foster parents (recommended for the program by their bishop) provided free board, room, and clothing for the Indian children to help them have additional educational, spiritual, and sociocultural experiences. The Indian children, had to be at least eight years of age, baptized members of the Church, and in good health. In 1972 the responsibility for recruiting and screening students for the program was given to local priesthood leaders, and the number of students leveled in the mid and late 1970s to around 2,500 a year.

In the early 1980s several of the Indian tribes from whom many of the placement students had come replaced their boarding schools with dramatically improved education on the reservations. In support of this move, the Church limited Indian Placement Student Services to high school students. New goals emphasized the development and strengthening of LDS family and religious values, with Church Social Services taking responsibility for establishing stronger ties and communication between natural families and foster families. The placement service would introduce young Native Americans to mainstream values and social roles without demanding the abandonment of the old for the new. In 1990 the program served about 500 high school students.

Supporters of the services believe that bicultural experiences have great value. Critics view intervention as an intrusion on the right to be fully Native American, a weakening of cultural pluralism, and a cause of psychological damage. However, empirical studies, even by critics, are ambivalent. One claims that the program has failed to raise achievement and IQ scores of placement students, but notes that placement students read more than their reservation counterparts. A second suggests that students suffer intercultural conflict within their foster families, but expresses surprise that these students function without major symptoms of psychological distress. Still another asserts that the placement experience interferes with the process of identity formation, but acknowledges that the program has done more for the Indian people than any other program to date.

Many theses, dissertations, formal reports, and published articles find that the program has been successful and valuable. Placement students usually come from rural families with stable but limited economic and cultural opportunities. Starting with limited language skills, the students in the placement program come out with less fear of failure, more confidence in their future, and higher academic skills and grades, and a better self-image than their reservation peers. Other studies indicate that placement services graduates are aware of a great variety of occupations open to them and are anxious to continue their education to prepare for them. They typically have come to believe in working hard for future rewards and feel that being Indian does not hold them down. They graduate from high school in larger numbers than non-placement Native Americans, and the college grades of rural placement students are on a par with the grades of urban Indian students.

Most placement students express more pride and interest in Indian culture than do students from Indian boarding schools. That they perceive themselves as truly bicultural, at ease in both societies, is confirmed by their rate of interaction with Indian students as well as with Anglo peers. They also become Church leaders. Most of them are active in the Church, go on missions, and agree with major Church beliefs; many marry in the temple.

Foster parents volunteer for religious reasons and remain in the program to see the child grow and develop emotionally and spiritually. They typically become very attached to their Indian children, maintaining a close relationship with them after graduation from school.

Accusations that the LDS Church used its influence to push children into joining the program prompted the U.S. government in 1977 to commission a study conducted under the auspices of the Interstate Compact Secretariat. Its findings rejected such accusations. In the resulting report, written by Robert E. Leach, Native American parents emphatically stated that they, not the children, decided to apply for placement. These parents typically stated that they were pleased that the program led their children to happiness and a better economic situation while the children still identified with their Indian heritage. This participation, they claimed, also helped the rest of the family to understand and deal more effectively with Anglos. They consistently expressed appreciation to the foster families for caring for their children. Some Indian leaders were intent on limiting the placement of Indian children among Anglos. However, after hearing testimony and examining current research, the committee agreed in 1977 to permit the LDS Indian Student Placement program to continue.

BIBLIOGRAPHY

Bishop, Clarence R. "An Evaluation of the Scholastic Achievement of Selected Indian Students Attending Elementary Public Schools of Utah." Master's thesis, Brigham Young University, 1960.

Chadwick, Bruce A., Stan L. Albrecht, and Howard M. Bahr. "Evaluation of an Indian Student Placement Program." *Social Casework* 67 (Nov. 1986):515–24.

The Church of Jesus Christ of Latter-day Saints Presiding Bishopric, Research and Evaluation Services. *Indian Student Placement Service Evaluation Study.* Salt Lake City, May 1982.

Taylor, Grant H. "A Comparative Study of Former LDS Placement and Non-Placement Navajo Students at Brigham Young University." Ph.D. diss., Brigham Young University, 1981.

GENEVIEVE DEHOYOS

INDIVIDUALITY

It is LDS doctrine that every human being has an eternal identity, existing from the premortal state and continuing forever (Abr. 3:22–23). Moreover, all individuals are responsible for their own choices, and all will stand before the Lord to present an accounting of their lives at the Judgment Day (A of F 2; Moro. 10:27). This, however, does not mean that individuals are autonomous or alone. All individuals are spirit children of God the Father, who organized them into relationships in order to maximize their growth and happiness through loving and serving one another.

LDS teachings make clear that living the gospel of Jesus Christ means voluntarily submitting the self to the will of God. Joseph F. SMITH felt that it shows "a stronger characteristic of individuality" to bring the self into harmony with God than to be separate from him (*JD* 25:245). An individual must voluntarily obey God's will to achieve righteousness (John 7:16), and God's will requires service to others in one's family and community (Matt. 20:26–27). Paradoxically, "he that loseth his life for [Christ's] sake shall find it" (Matt. 10:39); and as David O. MCKAY stated, "A man's duties to himself and to his fellow men are indissolubly connected" (p. 289). The Church cannot force individuals to become one with God and others. That must be done "only by persuasion, by long-suffering, by gentleness and meekness, and by love unfeigned; by kindness" (D&C 121:41–43).

The ultimate objectives of The Church of Jesus Christ of Latter-day Saints are as inclusive and extensive as can be imagined, both individually and collectively—namely, to attain ETERNAL LIFE for all individuals and eternal continuity for families and to maintain a supportive, unified community of Saints on earth who live the fulness of the gospel of Jesus Christ. The scale and profundity of these objectives are equal to the depth of commitment they require. Christ promises righteous men and women that they shall be joint-heirs with him, inheritors of "all that my Father hath" (D&C 84:33–39; Rom. 8:14–18). Having offered the RICHES OF ETERNITY, the Savior may require the faithful to voluntarily sacrifice all their earthly possessions, including life itself, in order "to produce the faith necessary unto life and salvation" (*Lectures on Faith*, Lecture 6, paragraph 7). Latter-day Saints express this principle in a beloved hymn: "I'll go where you want me to go, dear Lord, . . . I'll be what you want me to be" (*Hymns*, p. 270).

Salvation is both an individual and a collective matter. Individuals are punished for their own sins, but the personal choices that foster growth and exaltation necessarily involve other people. The atonement of Jesus Christ is relational: "No man cometh unto the Father, but by me," the Savior said, and people demonstrate their love for him by keeping his commandments (John 14:6, 15). The BAPTISMAL COVENANT is both personal and social: it involves personal willingness to remember Christ always, and it encourages members to "bear one another's burdens" (Mosiah 18:8).

While the singular focus of the Church on achieving its ultimate objectives unifies its members in ways that contrast markedly with organizations having internally competing objectives, there are limits to the diversity in individual beliefs and practices that the Church can tolerate and still achieve its mission (*see* ORTHODOXY, HETERODOXY, AND HERESY). Neither Joseph Smith's oft-quoted statement that "I teach the people correct principles and they govern themselves" (*JD* 10:57–58) nor Lehi's insistence that people are free to choose liberty and eternal life or captivity and death (2 Ne. 2:26–27) means that the Church can ignore internal challenges to its integrity or principles (Matt. 18:17; 2 Thes. 3:14–15; D&C 42:24, 74–93). Severe cases of disruption and violation may be subjected to DISCIPLINARY PROCEDURES and may result in disfellowshipment or even excommunication.

Christ affirms great diversity and individuality in gospel service. Each person has abilities to perform Christlike service that others may not be able to perform. Jesus taught that personal spiritual gifts and talents are to be cultivated and shared: "the best gifts" are given "that all may be profited thereby" (D&C 46:8–12; *see also* GIFTS OF THE SPIRIT).

Organizations may in a measure constrain behavior, and the Church has a constraining influence on individuals insofar as they choose to conform or fulfill the requirements for holding CALLINGS or a TEMPLE RECOMMEND. However, there is ample room for the expression of individuality and appreciation for those who may take a novel approach to the righteous fulfillment of their responsibilities. God counsels his children to use their gifts creatively and intelligently in his service: "It is not meet that I should command in all things; for he that is compelled in all things, the same is a slothful and not a wise servant" (D&C 58:26–28). Moreover, most Church constraints, such as the law of chastity or the directive to avoid addictive substances, are intended to free the individual for a happier life. Voluntarily following Jesus Christ is the ultimate liberty, and sin, the ultimate captivity (John 8:32; 2 Ne. 2:26–27).

Latter-day Saints are taught that they and all the rest of the human family are eternal children of a loving Heavenly Father. Their individuality is priceless and eternal. The recognition that the Church is enriched by a diversity of individual endowments, experiences, and interests always has been fundamental to the LDS faith. The concluding sentence of the Articles of Faith celebrates the diverse individual paths that are part of the righteous life: "If there is anything virtuous, lovely, or of good report or praiseworthy, we seek after these things."

[*See also* Socialization; Unity; Values, Transmission of.]

BIBLIOGRAPHY

Brown, Victor, Jr. "Differences." *Ensign* 8 (July 1978):8–11.

Dahl, Larry E., and Charles D. Tate, Jr., eds. *The Lectures on Faith in Historical Perspective.* Provo, Utah, 1990.

Higbee, Kenneth. "On Doing Your Own Thing." *New Era* 5 (Apr. 1975):18–20.

McKay, David O. "Each Individual Must Work Out His Own Salvation." *Instructor* 96 (1961):289–90.

Packer, Boyd K. *Teach Ye Diligently.* Salt Lake City, 1975.

Talmage, James E. "Practical Religion." *AF,* chap. 24.

HOWARD M. BAHR

INFANT BAPTISM

[*This entry has two parts: the* LDS Perspective *concerning this practice, and the* Early Christian Origins.]

LDS PERSPECTIVE
Children are baptized as members of The Church of Jesus Christ of Latter-day Saints when they reach age eight and receive a bishop's interview to assess their understanding and commitment. This age for baptism was identified by revelation (D&C 68:25, 28). The Church does not baptize infants.

The practice of baptizing infants emerged among Christians in the third century A.D. and was controversial for some time. According to the Book of Mormon, it similarly became an issue and was denounced among the Nephites in the fourth century A.D. When MORMON, a Nephite prophet, inquired of the Lord concerning baptism of little children, he was told that they are incapable of committing sin and that the curse of Adam is removed from them through the ATONEMENT of Christ. Hence little children need neither repentance nor baptism (Moro. 8:8–22). They are to be taught "to pray and walk uprightly" so that by the age of accountability their baptism will be meaningful and effective for their lives.

[*See also* Accountability; Children: Salvation of Children; Fall of Adam; Original Sin.]

BIBLIOGRAPHY

McConkie, Bruce R. "The Salvation of Little Children." *Ensign* 7 (Apr. 1977):3–7.

ROBERT E. PARSONS

EARLY CHRISTIAN ORIGINS
Although the New Testament never mentions infant baptism either to approve or to condemn the practice, many passages therein associate BAPTISM with FAITH in Jesus Christ, REPENTANCE, and forgiveness of SINS, none of which are appropriate requirements for infants (Mark 1:4–5; 16:15–16; Acts 2:37–38; 19:4; 22:16; Rom. 6:1–6; 1 Cor. 6:9–11; Gal. 3:26–27; Col. 2:12–13; Heb. 6:1–6; 10:22; 1 Pet. 3:21).

The assumption that those baptized are committed disciples continues through the second century in Christian literature (*Didache* 7.1; *Shepherd of Hermas:* "Vision" 3.7 and "Mandates" 4.3; *Epistle of Barnabas* 11; Justin, *First Apology* 1.11, 15). The earliest explicit reference to the practice of baptizing infants dates to shortly after A.D. 200 in the writings of Tertullian, a North African theologian who opposed it on the grounds that baptism carries an awesome responsibility and should be delayed until a person is fully committed to living righteously (*De baptismo* 18). A decade later Hippolytus, who would become a schismatic bishop in Rome, wrote a handbook of rules for church organization and practice. Some versions of his *Apostolic Tradition* (21.3–4) refer to baptizing "little ones," who should have an adult relative speak for them if they are unable to do so themselves. However, since Hippolytus prescribed a normative three-year preparatory period of teaching, reading, fasting, and prayer prior to baptism (*Apostolic Tradition* 17), the infant baptism passage has been questioned as a later interpolation.

The first Christian writer to defend infant baptism as an apostolic practice was apparently Origen, the preeminent theologian of the Greek-speaking church, who wrote on the subject around A.D. 240 in Alexandria, Egypt. Origen referred to the frequently asked question of why the church should baptize sinless infants (*Homily on Luke* 14). In response, he argued that baptism takes away the pollution of birth. Origen's *Commentary on Romans* further elaborates this theme, asserting that because of hereditary sin, "the church has a tradition from the apostles to give baptism even to infants" (5.9). However, this passage is suspect because it is found only in a Latin translation by Rufinus, who tended on several occasions to "correct" Origen according to later doctrine. A few years later, Cyprian, bishop of Carthage, addressing the question of the timing of infant baptism, wrote that a child's soul should not be placed in jeopardy of perdition even one day by delaying the grace of baptism (*De peccatorum meritis* 1.34).

Historically, then, infant baptism cannot be demonstrated as beginning before the third century, when it emerged as a topic of extended controversy. Not until Augustine wrote against the Donatists two centuries later was infant baptism established as a universal custom (Jeremias, pp. 94–97; Jewett, p. 16). Thereafter, the practice went largely unquestioned until the Protestant Reformation, when a radical group in Zurich broke with the reformer Zwingli over this and other issues in 1525. These so-called Anabaptists (those who denied the validity of their baptism as infants and were rebaptized as adults) were precursors of the Baptist movement.

BIBLIOGRAPHY

Beasley-Murray, G. R. *Baptism in the New Testament*. London, 1962.

Cullmann, Oscar. *Baptism in the New Testament*, trans. J. Reid. Chicago, 1950.

Jeremias, Joachim. *Infant Baptism in the First Four Centuries*, translated by D. Cairns. Philadelphia, Pa., 1962.

Jewett, Paul K. *Infant Baptism and the Covenant of Grace*. Grand Rapids, Mich., 1978.

KEITH E. NORMAN

INSPIRATION

All humans are entitled to inspiration, which is the influence of the Spirit of the Lord upon their minds and souls (Benson, p. 142). The Lord inspires men and women and calls them "to his holy work in this age and generation, as well as in generations of old" (D&C 20:11). Inspiration from God is essential to understanding spiritual matters. The Prophet Joseph SMITH explained, "If a man learns nothing more than to eat, drink and sleep, and does not comprehend any of the designs of God, the beast comprehends the same things . . . it knows as much as we, unless we are able to comprehend by the inspiration of Almighty God" (*TPJS*, p. 343).

"Inspiration" and "revelation" are sometimes used interchangeably by LDS leaders in explaining the source of prophetic authority. The FIRST PRESIDENCY of the Church said, "Moses wrote the history of the creation, and we believe that he had the inspiration of the Almighty resting upon him. The Prophets who wrote after him were likewise endowed with the Spirit of revelation" (*MFP* 2:232). President Wilford WOODRUFF later noted, "This Church has never been led a day except by revelation. And He will never leave it. It matters not who lives or who dies, or who is called to lead this Church, they have got to lead it by inspiration of Almighty God" (*MFP* 3:225).

Latter-day Saints believe that their efforts can be enhanced and their personal capabilities expanded when they do their best work and at the same time depend upon the Lord "for light and inspiration beyond [their] own natural talents" (Benson, p. 173). Inspiration must be sought and then acted upon when it is received. This quest for inspiration is important in all the affairs of life. President Ezra Taft BENSON's explanation of the necessity of inspiration is as valid in temporal, family, and all other matters as it is in Church concerns: "Inspiration is essential to properly lead (D&C 50:13–14). We must have the spirit of inspiration whether we are teaching (D&C 50:13–14) or administering the affairs of the kingdom (D&C 46:2). If we do our part in preparation and work and have the Spirit of the Lord, we can be led, though we do not know beforehand what needs to be done (1 Ne. 4:6; Alma 17:3). Therefore, we should always pray, especially prior to commencing the work of the Lord (2 Ne. 32:9)" (Benson, p. 433).

Inspiration comes from the Lord and may be received in various ways. It comes from prayer (D&C 63:64), from a personal manifestation of the spirit of the Lord (D&C 20:11), from reading and following the commandments, and from studying and pondering the scriptures. Women and men may also be inspired by good causes, such as protection of home, family, and personal freedoms (Alma 43:45). President Spencer W. KIMBALL explained, "We pray for enlightenment, then go to with all our might and our books and our thoughts and righteousness to get the inspiration" (Kimball, p. 122). Much of the world's fine music, art, and literature can inspire, as can the role models provided by noble people living in the past or present, because "every thing which inviteth and enticeth to do good, and to love God, and to serve him, is inspired of God" (Moro. 7:13).

The fruits of inspiration are many: inspiration from the Lord gives understanding (Job 32:8); those who call upon God may write by the spirit of inspiration (Moses 6:5); and those who believe in the words of the PROPHETS may speak as they are inspired by the GIFT OF THE HOLY GHOST (D&C 20:26). Individuals may be inspired to take specific action, as the Prophet Joseph Smith was inspired to lay the foundation of The Church of Jesus Christ of Latter-day Saints (D&C 21:2,7). The Constitution of the United States "was given by inspiration of God" (MFP 3:12).

When called to specific Church duties, members have the right to receive inspiration from God in fulfilling them. They can also expect their leaders to serve with inspiration. "When you read the Book of Mormon, you know you are reading the truth. Why? Because God directed men to write events as they occurred, and he gave them the wisdom and inspiration to do this" (DS 2:202).

BIBLIOGRAPHY

Benson, Ezra Taft. The Teachings of Ezra Taft Benson. Salt Lake City, 1988.

Kimball, Spencer W. The Teachings of Spencer W. Kimball, ed. Edward L. Kimball. Salt Lake City, 1982.

CAROL L. CLARK

INSTITUTES OF RELIGION

Institutes of religion in The Church of Jesus Christ of Latter-day Saints refer to weekday religious instruction for students attending colleges, universities, and other postsecondary institutions where sufficient LDS students are enrolled. Together with the SEMINARIES for high school students, institutes provide those students an opportunity for organized religious study in connection with their secular studies. The Church funds and administers the institutes of religion as part of its comprehensive CHURCH EDUCATIONAL SYSTEM (CES).

The institute program offers courses in the scriptures and related religious topics such as marriage, Church history, and world religions. Institutes also provide opportunities for students to associate socially, spiritually, and culturally with others who have similar ideals through the Latter-day Saint Student Association (LDSSA), which provides LDS student activities on and off campus.

The Church has established a general regulation that all full-time institute instructors should hold at least a master's degree. A majority hold a doctorate degree. Such degrees are generally not in religion, but in related fields such as education, counseling, or history. The Church expects institute faculty to possess scholarly competence in religion and related fields comparable to that of teachers at adjacent academic institutions, and to be exemplary in all aspects of their lives.

In 1989–1990, there were 317 full-time and several hundred part-time and volunteer instructors in LDS institutes throughout the world, with many full-time instructors serving more than one institute. In the same year, 125,534 students were enrolled in 1,273 institutes serving 1,711 non-LDS college and university campuses internationally.

Historically the rise of public higher education in the United States led to the elimination of religious education from most university and college curriculums. Beginning in 1894, in response to the need for religious education on these campuses, various student organizations were established, including the Roman Catholic Newman Club, full-time Baptist ministries by campus chaplains, the Jewish B'nai B'rith Hillel, and others. LDS leaders addressed the need for weekday religious education for their college students as early as 1912. As the Church's junior colleges closed (see ACADEMIES; SCHOOLS), requests came to establish weekday religious education for LDS students on non-LDS college campuses.

To meet this need, in 1926 the Church initiated a program for LDS students attending the University of Idaho at Moscow, Idaho. University officials welcomed the institute adjacent to the campus. Initially called a college "seminary," the program was renamed the "institute of religion," which established a precedent for subsequent institutes.

In 1935, John A. Widtsoe of the Quorum of the Twelve Apostles outlined the purposes of the institutes of religion:

> During University years students meeting much new knowledge frequently have difficulty, unaided, in reconciling their religious beliefs . . . with their academic studies. . . . LDS Institutes have been established to meet this situation. They offer studies

in religion on the college level, in college terms, dealing with the profound questions which every thinking individual has a right to ask. At the Institute students discuss these questions freely and frankly with the Institute Directors, either in classes or in private consultation ["Why Institutes," *Announcement of the LDS Institutes: 1935–1936, Department of Education, Church of Jesus Christ of Latter-day Saints*].

The Church soon constructed a building adjacent to the University of Idaho that became the headquarters for LDS students at the university. The principle of separation of church and state guided the development of the project and the direction of institute activities. The institute developed a cultural and social activities program providing fellowship for LDS students in the area. This fellowship extended beyond LDS students to faculty and other students on campus.

Institutes in Logan, Utah, at Utah State Agricultural College and in Salt Lake City at the University of Utah soon followed the Moscow institute. Shortly thereafter, the Church established institutes at other universities and colleges in Utah, Arizona, and Washington.

Before there were enough students to establish full-time institute programs on southern California campuses, Deseret Clubs were organized. These became the prototype for small LDS student organizations. These clubs continued until 1971, when the Church formally established the LDSSA as the official LDS student group on university and college campuses.

The first international LDS institute program was established in 1969 in Australia and was soon duplicated in New Zealand and Great Britain. The Church has since established institutes in sixty additional countries. These have become a source of support and training for new Church leadership in those areas.

BIBLIOGRAPHY

Anderson, A. Gary. "A Historical Survey of the Full-Time Institutes of Religion of the Church of Jesus Christ of Latter-day Saints, 1926–1966." Ph.D. diss., Brigham Young University, 1968.

Arrington, Leonard J. "The Founding of the LDS Institutes of Religion." *Dialogue* 2 (Summer 1967):137–47.

Berrett, William E. *A Miracle in Weekday Religious Education.* Salt Lake City, 1988.

STANLEY A. PETERSON

INSTRUCTOR, THE

The *Instructor* was originally published as JUVENILE INSTRUCTOR, from 1866 to 1929. At first a children's magazine, it became the official publication of the SUNDAY SCHOOL of the Church in January 1901. As its pages gradually filled with articles on teaching methods and gospel subjects to be used by the several Church AUXILIARY ORGANIZATIONS, especially the Sunday School, its name was changed to *The Instructor* in November 1929, better to reflect its content.

The Presidents of the Church were identified as editors of the magazine from 1901 through 1970, but coeditors were often largely responsible for its contents.

The Instructor ceased publication in December 1970, when the Church consolidated its English language magazines into three: ENSIGN, for adults; NEW ERA, for youth; FRIEND, for children. Some of the instructional materials for teachers previously published in *The Instructor* are now published in the lesson manuals of the Church.

BIBLIOGRAPHY

McKay, David L. "Goodbye, the Instructor." *Ensign* 1 (Dec. 1970):444–48.

RUEL A. ALLRED

INTELLECTUAL HISTORY

The Church encourages its members to be learned in gospel principles and in every edifying branch of knowledge that supports a life of Christian service. Latter-day Saints value intellectual activity because it can develop and enrich life and faith, beautify the earth and ameliorate mankind's temporal suffering, and further the growth of the kingdom of God on earth. LDS theology takes with utmost seriousness the divine injunction to learn to know, to love, and to serve God with all one's heart, might, mind, and strength (Deut. 6:5; 1 Chr. 28:9; Matt. 22:37; D&C 4:2; cf. John 17:3). In this sense, intellectual activity can be an act of worship.

One of the divinely ordained purposes of life is to gain spiritual and intellectual experience in mind and spirit (*see* REASON AND REVELATION). The Prophet Joseph SMITH taught that "by proving contraries, truth is made manifest" (*HC* 6:248). To "study it out in your mind" is often a prerequisite to heavenly assistance (D&C 9:8), and communication from God may sometimes be recognized by its effect on the mind. Latter-day Saints were enjoined early to seek knowledge out of the best books (D&C 88:118) and to establish schools (*see* SCHOOLS OF THE PROPHETS) for instruction in both sacred and secular matters.

FLOW OF IDEAS. In LDS theology, REVELATION from God to his appointed PROPHETS is the source of DOCTRINE and of "knowledge of the things of God" (*TPJS*, p. 217). Thus, there is no formalized mechanism in the Church for achieving scholarly consensus on theological principles. But there is no doubt of the need for diligent inquiry after truth: Joseph Smith taught that "a man is saved no faster than he gets knowledge" (*TPJS*, p. 217) and that "if a person acquires more knowledge and intelligence in this life through his diligence and obedience than another, he will have so much the advantage in the world to come" (D&C 130:19; *see* EDUCATION: ATTITUDES TOWARD).

The earliest written explorations of LDS beliefs by Church leaders were motivated primarily by missionary activities to teach the gospel. Orson PRATT wrote the two influential series, *The Kingdom of God* (four parts, 1848–1849) and *Divine Authenticity of the Book of Mormon* (six parts, 1850–1851), as well as scientific investigations related to theological speculations. Parley P. PRATT, Orson Spencer, and Lorenzo SNOW also published significant missionary tracts. Parley Pratt's synthetic work *Key to the Science of Theology* captured the free-ranging spirit of LDS thought during the formative years of the Church.

The voluminous output of the missionary press was severely curtailed after 1857 for several reasons; scarce resources were required to bring Saints to Zion and to build TEMPLES. However, the *Journal of Discourses* recorded public addresses of Church leaders, particularly Brigham YOUNG, during this era on topics ranging from agriculture and politics to theology; and presentations of LDS history, doctrine, and philosophy continued in forums ranging from PRAYER CIRCLES to various Church magazines to pioneer lyceums.

With the urbanization of the Church in the twentieth century, Church periodicals, FIRESIDES broadcast from Temple Square, and books published by Church-owned and semi-official presses were widely supplemented by unofficial activities and publications. Pioneer lyceums gave way to various informal activities, including firesides, study groups, or gatherings held in homes. New periodicals, most unsanctioned by the Church and with varying editorial policies (*see* SOCIETIES AND ORGANIZATIONS), investigated issues and ideas too controversial or too academic for the formal Church CURRICULUM. Increasingly in recent years, scholarly publications from university presses, both in Utah and elsewhere, have been written on LDS topics by scholars inside and outside the Church.

INTELLECTUAL PROLOGUE TO THE RESTORATION. Latter-day Saints believe that God prepared the intellectual, political, and spiritual environment prior to the RESTORATION of the gospel through such cultural and religious movements as the Ren-

Orson Pratt (1811–1881), an apostle, was an eloquent preacher and expounder of the gospel. With a scientific background, he shaped positive answers and rational explanations for many religious questions and LDS concepts. Photograph, c. 1878, Charles W. Carter.

aissance and the Reformation, particularly as these were manifested in Puritanism and the English Enlightenment.

The Puritan critique of the Church of England stressed morality for its leaders, education for its members, and a vital relationship between individuals and God. The Puritan ideal of a covenant community imbued with a sense of divine mission sustained their first two generations in America; but by the early eighteenth century, the Puritan movement was shattered by its collision with Enlightenment ideas, in spite of periodic revivals of faith and devotion. Where Puritanism had stressed the magnificence of God and the depravity of fallen man in a sinful world, the Enlightenment emphasized the goodness of man and the beauty of the natural world and linked a natural theology to emerging scientific models.

The conflict between these paradigms polarized American society: Puritan ministers were replaced by patrician aristocrats and lay scientists as leaders of American society. Puritanism continued in a diluted form: Evangelical Methodist and Baptist ministers emerged with new followers after the Great Awakening of 1740. Stressing the "heart" over the "head," these religious movements swept through newly independent America after 1800, while the rationalism of the Enlightenment continued through the Unitarian and Universalist societies.

Joseph Smith grew up in this setting, both directions being represented by his parents. His mother stressed the emotionalism of the revivals to which she regularly took her children. His father, who helped found a Universalist society in Vermont, stressed the rational dimensions of religion. This polarization, in his family and in the larger culture, helped to impel young Joseph to ask God directly for guidance in a "silent grove" in the spring of 1820 (see FIRST VISION). In subsequent visions and revelations, Joseph Smith received knowledge and authority from God to restore the Church of Jesus Christ, whose doctrines and practices are not limited by the former approaches but generate a dynamic interplay between both mind and spirit.

RESTORATION PERIOD (1830–1844). The key intellectual and spiritual figure in the early years of the Church was clearly Joseph Smith. The conceptual framework of the Restoration stems from his prophetic utterances on many key topics (see SMITH, JOSEPH: TEACHINGS OF JOSEPH SMITH). He translated the Book of Mormon; received and published additional revelations; gave doctrinal instructions; provided glimpses into former gospel dispensations; explicated and amended the biblical text in many places throughout the Old and New Testaments (see JOSEPH SMITH TRANSLATION OF THE BIBLE [JST]); and stimulated interest in previously neglected texts (see APOCRYPHA AND PSEUDEPIGRAPHA).

The central focus of Joseph Smith's teaching is the literal and infinite atonement of Jesus Christ and the restoration of the eternal gospel and its ordinances. In this expansive view (popularized under the label of "eternalism" by B. H. Roberts) men and women are eternal beings procreated by a Heavenly Father and Mother (see MOTHER IN HEAVEN), a concept elaborated by Lorenzo Snow and his sister Eliza R. SNOW. Men and women are tested by choices between good and evil in mortal life as preparation for the eternities. The universe, filled with a myriad of worlds inhabited by sons and daughters of God, exists for the purpose of allowing individuals to progress toward becoming gods and goddesses (see GODHOOD). The divine potential in each individual is actualized by voluntarily obeying the FIRST PRINCIPLES OF THE GOSPEL and receiving all the ordinances of salvation, culminating in the ordinances of the temple, a place dedicated as a house of prayer, fasting, faith, and learning, "a house of glory, a house of order, a house of God" (D&C 88:119). Each temple is a meeting place of heaven and earth, where eternal relationships are formed by covenants; it is also a school, where eternal concepts are taught (see TEMPLES: TEMPLE WORSHIP AND ACTIVITY).

COMMUNITY, RENEWED CONSECRATION, AND RESPONSE (1844–1896). The exodus to the Salt Lake Valley and the drive to colonize the Great Basin saw the development of key ideas about economic, political, and social needs in the community and nation. Latter-day Saints rejected the temporal-spiritual separation in politics and economics and viewed the Mormon village as a covenant community based on the concept of gathering. Missionaries taught the gospel to those who would listen; converts gathered out of spiritual Babylon by changing their lives and removing to Utah to build ZION. This literal "gathering of scattered Israel" brought converts into communities that practiced principles of CONSECRATION and

STEWARDSHIP, in social settings hospitable to the making of Saints (*see* ECONOMIC HISTORY OF THE CHURCH).

The LDS economic order, based on the premise that the earth is the Lord's, holds that men are stewards over the property they hold and are responsible for consecrating their time, energy, and talents to the establishment of Zion. Dominion over the earth is not a license to plunder, but a sacred trust to conserve life and protect the environment. LDS cosmology teaches that all living things will be resurrected, that the earth itself has a celestial destiny, and that all people are accountable to God for their earthly stewardship.

Out of this sense of community, combined with living in a barren land, ideals of frugality, cooperation, and equality were nurtured. The earth exists that man "might have in abundance"; poverty exists because some "possess that which is above another" and waste flesh when they have "no need" (D&C 49:19–21). The divine standard mandates temporal and spiritual unity and equality based on individual needs, desires, and varying talents (D&C 78:6). Periodic reformations in the Brigham YOUNG era sought to reach these ideals; analogous concepts motivate the WELFARE programs in the wards of the contemporary Church, now extended well beyond its historic population centers in the western United States.

In the late pioneer period (1869–1896), the Church felt the need to teach its rising generation more systematically than before. In the 1880s, for instance, George Q. Cannon, a member of the First Presidency, published a "Faith-Promoting Series" of journals, biographies, and a periodical, *The Juvenile Instructor*, to instruct young men and women. President Cannon insisted that:

> Latter-day Saints are ardent friends of learning, true seekers after knowledge. They recognize in a good education the best of fortunes; it broadens the mind, creates liberal and noble sentiments, and fits the possessor for a more successful struggle with the obstacles of life. . . . The possession of knowledge is of itself the highest pleasure [*Juvenile Instructor* 27 (1892):210].

Cannon's works filled a significant need, but the fact that these writings addressed primarily the youth of the Church limited their topics and approaches. During this same time President Young established academies throughout LDS-dominated areas. BRIGHAM YOUNG UNIVERSITY, now the largest private university in the United States, began as such an academy in 1875.

President Young had attempted to insulate the LDS community from the influx of non-Mormons after completion of the transcontinental railroad in 1869. This economic move by Brigham Young, focusing on establishing ZCMI and the cooperative movement, reinforced a trend to isolate Church members from outside ideas, especially as persecution intensified. A contemporary reaction to many of Brigham Young's economic policies led some LDS intellectuals to oppose the Church. This group, known as the Godbeites (*see* SCHISMATIC GROUPS), became the prime illustration in Church circles of intellect unchecked that

George Q. Cannon (1827–1901), served in the First Presidency from 1873 to 1901 as counselor to Presidents Brigham Young, John Taylor, Wilford Woodruff and Lorenzo Snow. With his publications aimed mainly at the youth, Cannon was an important bridge between the first generation of Church leaders and late nineteenth-century Church membership. Photographer: Charles Ellis Johnson. Courtesy Rare Books and Manuscripts, Brigham Young University.

rejected prophetic leadership and the larger needs of the LDS community.

Few LDS students journeyed "East" to attend non-Mormon schools before the 1880s, and few LDS authors before 1900 addressed the critical issues being debated in the larger society. An important exception was the issue of women's rights, which found an outlet in the *Woman's Exponent* edited by LDS women.

ENCOUNTER WITH SCHOLARLY SECULARISM (1896–1918). The transformation of Mormon village life began as the first generation of Latter-day Saints started to pursue advanced studies of geology, agricultural science, chemistry, and engineering. Such studies brought the Saints face to face with a secular and skeptical society. James E. Talmage studied geology at Lehigh and Johns Hopkins universities and returned to Utah in 1885 to teach and write about many topics, including evolution and the age of the earth. As president of the University of Utah and later as an apostle, he exerted an enormous influence by systematizing LDS theology in two seminal works, *The Articles of Faith* and *Jesus the Christ*. John A. Widtsoe, later an apostle, studied biochemistry at Harvard and Göttingen; he returned to Utah in 1900 and became president of Utah State University in 1907, playing a pivotal role first in agricultural education and research and later as an educational administrator and writer on intellectual issues facing Church members.

The Mutual Improvement Association (*see* YOUNG MEN; YOUNG WOMEN) chose as its study manual for 1909 Widtsoe's book *Joseph Smith as Scientist*, and the *Improvement Era* frequently ran articles by LDS scientists discussing Latter-day Saint doctrines in light of current scientific theories. Utah universities also began to invite the scholarly luminaries of the day to campus as guest lecturers. However, concerns were raised by the Church's educational administrators when some faculty members advanced evolutionary treatments of the creation accounts in Genesis. By 1911 these concerns led to a policy that temporarily discouraged discussions in Brigham Young University classrooms of such theories.

ADAPTATION AND CONFRONTATION (1918–1945). With worldwide industrialization and the ravages of World War I and the Bolshevik Revolution, agrarian idealism in America and the old order in Europe gave way before new political, economic, and social theories. For both Church leaders and lay members, deeply ingrained concepts of stewardship, cooperation, and individual moral responsibility clashed sharply with the militance of organized labor, the totalitarian excesses of fascism and communism, and the greediness of unregulated capitalism.

The need for teachers in Church schools and institutes of religion swelled to a small stream what had been only a trickle of Latter-day Saints sent "East" for professional training. The "Divinity School" group of Saints at the University of Chicago (see R. Swenson, "Mormons at the University of Chicago Divinity School," *Dialogue* 7 [Summer, 1972]:37–47) drew on their experience of LDS group life to write scholarly articles suggesting answers to the pressing social and economic problems of their day. In this academic setting, these LDS graduate students were also confronted with "higher criticism" of the Bible (*see* BIBLE SCHOLARSHIP), stimulating some to take a moderate, conciliatory approach to scriptural interpretation, analogous to the neo-orthodox movement among Protestant theologians.

During this era, the Church and its members were recognized as a major force in American religious life. The *Encyclopedia Americana* commissioned a lengthy article by Elder B. H. Roberts for the centennial of the Church. Latter-day Saints who were influential outside the Great Basin included Harvey Fletcher in physics, E. E. Erickson in philosophy, J. Reuben Clark, Jr. in international affairs, Franklin S. Harris in agricultural science; and Henry Eyring in chemistry.

URBANIZATION AND GLOBAL MISSION (1945–1990). After World War II, a technocracy based on the positivist view of physical and social sciences dominated the intellectual landscape. Molecular biologists, armed with the tools of physics, seemed to be on the verge of controlling life itself; social scientists, bolstered by mathematics and computers, explained human behavior without reference to man's divine nature.

While existentialist theologians alternately despaired of or embraced the "secular city," LDS leaders again sounded the call to heed revelation as the source of ultimate truth while using science and technology to spread the gospel and alleviate human suffering. LDS emphasis on individual and group guidance through revelation created significant intellectual stresses for the increasing num-

B.H. Roberts (1857–1933), a member of the First Council of Seventy, was one of the most eloquent orators and penetrating writers in the Church's history. An inveterate seeker, he grappled with many historical and scriptural issues as a "defender of the faith." Courtesy Special Collections Department, University of Utah Libraries.

bers of Church members being trained in the professions. A number of scholars wrote cogently to this generation of Latter-day Saint students about the historical, philosophical, and theological foundations of Church doctrines and advocated integrating intellectual pursuits with the spiritual need to love, to serve, and to have faith in Jesus Christ.

The horrors of world war had challenged conventional Christian ideologies. President J. Reuben Clark, Jr., warned that the alliance forged in wartime between science and governments had created a military-industrial complex. Some Church members were troubled by the issues of war and peace in the Korean and Vietnam conflicts and by the quasi-permanent state of war that endangered the world peace on which the missionary work of the Church depended (see WAR AND PEACE).

As mission fields expanded, Zion, "the pure in heart" (D&C 97:21), was gathered into STAKES in locations around the world. President Harold B.

LEE foresaw that the demography and cultural uniformity of the Church would be significantly altered by the immense influx of converts. Scholars and lay leaders in the Church were challenged to differentiate between Church practices derived from fundamental universal gospel principles and those that could be treated as merely cultural practices of members.

The historic LDS affirmation of man as created literally in the image of God—with a Heavenly Mother as well as a Heavenly Father—led to a reinterpretation by Latter-day Saints of many conflicts felt in the larger society about the roles of men and women as individuals and as members of families and the Church. It also produced both a dramatic collision with fundamentalist Protestants and, to some extent, a reconciliation with Catholic and Protestant theologians who have rediscovered such ideas in the theology of the ancient Church.

In the Church, as in society, key roles were played by bureaucratic entities deriving their ex-

James E. Talmage (1862–1933), served as the president of the University of Utah from 1894 to 1897 and as an apostle from 1911 until his death in 1933. A noted geologist, lecturer and author, he was influential in shaping a mainstream statement of LDS teachings consistent with traditional biblical authorities. Courtesy the Utah State Historical Society.

Bruce R. McConkie (1915–1985), an apostle from 1972 to 1985, wrote extensively on Mormon doctrine. He drew heavily upon words of Joseph Smith and latter-day scripture to interpret the Bible and to propound specific answers to gospel questions.

pertise from the study of human behavior. Knowledge of the social sciences, for example, stimulated the founding of a Church Social Services organization, using social science expertise consistent with Church norms. As the Church expands outside the Intermountain West, adapting Church programs to local cultures without sacrificing the essential core of gospel teaching is a matter of increasing urgency. Here the growing worldwide reservoir of LDS professionals is an increasingly valuable asset. This is particularly true in view of the primacy of the family and home as the center of Christ-centered learning and service.

During this period, some turned to engaging metaphors from the Book of Mormon as expressions for LDS thought. In some cases, the symbol of their moral and intellectual response was the iron rod that guided those who obediently held on to revealed truths through the mists of darkness; in other cases the Liahona, a divinely fashioned compass that gave direction in proportion to one's faith, symbolized the faithful search for divine guidance (see 1 Ne. 8, 16; R. Poll, pp. 107–118). In Latter-day Saint life, such approaches are not mutually exclusive.

LDS theology has consistently seen the mind in the service of and as a companion to the spirit. The two remain creatively engaged: The intellect tends to notice problems and to ask questions, while the spirit is drawn toward finding answers and receiving assurance (see Alma 32:21–34); the intellect is often solitary and introspective, while the life of the spirit fosters charitable service and yearns for the collective building of the kingdom of God. Pride is a threat to all: It can cause the intellectual to substitute human judgment for revelation in matters of doctrine and revealed truth or can cause people to "hearken not unto the counsel of God, for they set it aside, supposing they know of themselves" (2 Ne. 9:28; cf. 1 Cor. 2:5–7); pride can also transform faith and trust into overconfidence and dogmatism. The scripture states: "To be learned is good if they hearken unto the counsels of God" (2 Ne. 9:29).

BIBLIOGRAPHY

The history of ideas arises from revealed teachings of the prophets and the ongoing dialogue in which members of the Church seek to understand those teachings, to incorporate them into their daily life, and to teach them to others. Its history is largely unwritten. A useful introduction is Leonard J. Arrington, "The Intellectual Tradition of the Latter-day Saints," *Dialogue* 4 (Spring 1969):13–26. Other important sources include Leonard J. Arrington and Davis Bitton, *The Mormon Experience*, New York, 1979, chaps. 13 and 16; Philip L. Barlow, ed., *A Thoughtful Faith: Essays on Belief by Mormon Scholars*, Centerville, Utah, 1986; Maureen Ursenbach [Beecher], "Three Women and the Life of the Mind," *Utah Historical Quarterly* 43 (Winter 1974):26–40; Lowell L. Bennion, "The Uses of the Mind in Religion," *BYU Studies* 14 (Autumn 1973):47–55; Davis Bitton, "Anti-Intellectualism in Mormon History," *Dialogue* 1 (Autumn 1966):111–34, and response by James B. Allen; Marvin S. Hill, "The Shaping of the Mormon Mind in New England and New York," *BYU Studies* 9 (Spring 1969):351–72; Paul R. Green, comp., *Science and Your Faith in God*, Salt Lake City, 1958 (essays by Henry Eyring, et al.); Duane E. Jeffrey, "Seers, Savants and Evolution: The Uncomfortable Interface," *Dialogue* 8 (Autumn/Winter 1973):41–75; Sterling M. McMurrin, *The Theological Foundations of Mormon Religion*, Salt Lake City, 1965; Hugh W. Nibley, *The World and the Prophets*, in CWHN 3; Erich Robert Paul, *Science, Religion, and Mormon Cosmology*, Urbana, Ill., 1991; Richard D. Poll, "What the Church Means to People Like Me," *Dialogue* 2 (Winter 1967):107–18; Charles S. Peterson, "The Limits of Learning in Pioneer Utah," *Journal of Mormon History* 10 (1983):65–78; John L. Sorenson, "Mormon World View and American Culture," *Dialogue* 8 (Spring 1973):17–29.

RICHARD F. HAGLUND, JR.
DAVID J. WHITTAKER

INTELLIGENCE

According to latter-day scripture, "The glory of God is intelligence, or, in other words, light and truth" (D&C 93:36). Mankind, too, may be glorified by gaining intelligence (D&C 93:28–30). As Christ did not receive a fulness of intelligence at first but continued from "grace to grace" until he received a fulness (D&C 93:11–13, 27–28), so it is with all persons. Whatever principles of intelligence they gain in mortality will rise with them in the Resurrection (D&C 130:18–19).

To gain increased intelligence, individuals must be agents to act for themselves (D&C 93:30), which means that they must be tried and tempted (D&C 29:39), and at the same time, the works of the Lord must be plainly manifest to them (D&C 93:31) so that they will have choice. In PREMORTAL LIFE, men and women were intelligent beings (Abr. 3:21–22) who were given AGENCY by God (Moses 4:3; D&C 29:36). In mortality, they are also given agency by God (D&C 101:78), to gain knowledge of good and evil (Moses 5:11). Intelligence increases as individuals forsake evil and come to the Lord, calling on his name, obeying his voice, and keeping his commandments (D&C 93:1–2, 28, 37). Intelligence is lost through disobedience, hardening of hearts, and clinging to false traditions (Mark 8:21; D&C 93:39).

Intelligence, however defined, is not created or made (D&C 93:29); it is coeternal with God (TPJS, pp. 353–54). Some LDS leaders have interpreted this to mean that intelligent beings—called intelligences—existed before and after they were given spirit bodies in the premortal existence. Others have interpreted it to mean that intelligent beings were organized as spirits out of eternal intelligent matter, that they did not exist as individuals before they were organized as spirit beings in the premortal existence (Abr. 3:22; JD 7:57; 2:124). The Church has taken no official position on this issue.

[See also Intelligences.]

BIBLIOGRAPHY

Roberts, B. H. "Immortality of Man." IE 20 (Apr. 1907):401–423.

DENNIS J. PACKARD

INTELLIGENCES

The word "intelligences" (plural) occurs frequently in LDS literature, having reference to the period of the premortal existence of mankind. The term has received two interpretations by writers within the Church: as the literal spirit children of Heavenly Parents and as individual entities existing prior to their spirit birth. Because latter-day revelation has not clarified the meaning of the term, a more precise interpretation is not possible at present.

The scriptural source for the word "intelligences" is the BOOK OF ABRAHAM 3:21–22. The Lord instructed the patriarch Abraham regarding the premortal experiences of all who have been or ever will be upon the earth. Among those events was the COUNCIL IN HEAVEN, at which the Father's PLAN OF SALVATION for his children was discussed. Abraham wrote of this, "Now the Lord had shown unto me, Abraham, the intelligences that were organized before the world was; . . . for he stood among those that were spirits, and he saw that they were good; and he said unto me: Abraham, thou art one of them" (Abr. 3:22–23). The Prophet Joseph SMITH spoke of intelligences as follows: "God himself, finding he was in the midst of spirits and glory, because he was more intelligent, saw proper to institute laws whereby the rest could have a privilege to advance like himself. The relationship we have with God places us in a situation to advance in knowledge. He has power to institute laws to instruct the weaker intelligences, that they may be exalted with himself, so that they might have one glory upon another, and all that knowledge, power, glory, and intelligence, which is requisite in order to save them" (TPJS, p. 354).

Concerning man's premortal existence, the Lord revealed to Joseph Smith, "Man was also in the beginning with God. Intelligence, or the light of truth, was not created or made, neither indeed can be" (D&C 93:29). "Intelligence," as used here, is singular, and it is not clear from this passage if it refers to individual, conscious identity. As noted, Abraham referred to the spirit offspring of God as organized intelligences, apparently using the word "intelligences" to mean "spirits." Church authorities have indicated that spirit birth was not the beginning. Spencer W. KIMBALL, then a member of the Quorum of the Twelve, wrote, "Our spirit matter was eternal and co-existent with God, but it was organized into spirit bodies by our Heavenly

Father" (*The Miracle of Forgiveness*, p. 5, Salt Lake City, 1969). Marion G. Romney, of the First Presidency, speaking of people's divine origin as children of God, stated, "Through that birth process, self-existing intelligence was organized into individual spirit beings" (*Ensign* 8 [Nov. 1978]:14). Bruce R. McConkie, an apostle, wrote:

Abraham used the name *intelligences* to apply to the spirit children of the Eternal Father. The intelligence or spirit element became intelligences after the spirits were born as individual entities (Abr. 3:22–24). Use of this name designates both the primal element from which the spirit offspring were created and also their inherited capacity to grow in grace, knowledge, power, and intelligence itself, until such intelligences, gaining the fulness of all things, become like their Father, the Supreme Intelligence [*MD*, p. 387].

While the revelations leave no doubt as to the existence of intelligent matter prior to its being organized as spirits, speculation sometimes arises regarding the nature of premortal existence and whether there was individual identity and consciousness prior to birth as a spirit. Some hold that the terms "intelligence" and "intelligences" have reference to a form of prespirit conscious self-existence, which included individual identity, variety, and agency (so reasoned B. H. Roberts, pp. 401–423). Others maintain that while these characteristics, attributes, and conditions are eternal, they essentially came together for each individual at the spirit birth. The question of whether prespirit intelligence had individual identity and consciousness remains unanswered. Elder Joseph Fielding SMITH gave this caution in 1936:

Some of our writers have endeavored to explain what an intelligence is, but to do so is futile, for we have never been given any insight into this matter beyond what the Lord has fragmentarily revealed. We know, however, that there is something called intelligence which always existed. It is the real eternal part of man, which was not created or made. This intelligence combined with the spirit constitutes a spiritual identity or individual [p. 10].

No formal pronouncements have been made by the leading councils of the Church to clarify what additional meanings and attributes may be assigned to the word "intelligences," beyond that which identifies intelligences as spirit children of God.

[*See also* First Estate; Intelligence; Premortal Life; Spirit Body.]

BIBLIOGRAPHY

McConkie, Bruce R. *Mormon Doctrine*, pp. 386–87. Salt Lake City, 1966.

Roberts, B. H. "Immortality of Man." *IE* 10 (Apr. 1907):401–423.

Smith, Joseph Fielding. *Progress of Man*. Salt Lake City, 1936.

PAUL NOLAN HYDE

INTERFAITH RELATIONSHIPS

[*This entry has three articles:*

Christian

Jewish

Other Faiths

The articles focus on the efforts of the Church to relate, assist, understand, and cooperate with other faiths in common social, ethical, and religious quests.]

CHRISTIAN

The Church has never existed in isolation or insulation from other Christian faiths. Its roots and its nurture are in, and remain in, the Christian heritage. But its claim that the heavens have opened anew, that a restoration of the lost radiance and power of the full gospel of Jesus Christ is under way at divine initiative, and its rejection of many long-standing traditions have generated misunderstanding and ill will. In the first generation in the United States, the solidarity of the Latter-day Saints was thought to be inimical to pluralism and at the same time aroused the ire of sectarians. Missionary efforts through personal contact more than through mass media and image making sometimes compounded the problem. In certain times and circumstances, there has been no will, or at least no lasting resolve by either side, for outreach and cooperation.

In three ways these tensions are being reduced:

1. Institutionally. Church officers now participate with leaders of other faiths in Christian interchange. LDS leaders in many countries are welcomed to interfaith devotionals with their Protestant, Catholic, and Orthodox counterparts. This has been in keeping with the precept and example of early Church authorities (*see* TOLERANCE). For mutual support, they likewise meet and organize, across varied lines and programs, for example, the chaplaincies of many na-

tions of the free world, the Boy Scout movement, the National Council of Christians and Jews, and local and international service clubs concerned with social, ethical, and moral issues.

2. Educationally. The Church fosters the largest adult education curriculum in the world. Many of the courses are Bible-related, and some focus on Christian history and institutions. For high school and college-age students, who now exceed half a million, the Church provides similar courses in its seminaries and institutes adjacent to high schools and major universities. Teachers in the Church Educational System are given financial supplements to visit the Holy Land, to study the origins of the three great monotheistic religions, to become familiar with the vocabularies and worldviews of alternative Christian institutions, and to understand and recognize common ground in the lives of the youth they teach. LDS scholars of many disciplines are increasingly involved in the religious studies programs of academic and professional organizations.

The Church has opened its extensive broadcasting facilities to representative programming across the spectrum of Christian groups (see BONNEVILLE INTERNATIONAL; KSL, RADIO). It has also been a major participant in religious broadcasts in the VISN Religious Interfaith Cable Television Network, which represents most major denominations in the United States.

To establish two-way interchange, the Richard L. Evans Chair of Christian Understanding was established at Brigham Young University. Funded and advised by a variety of Christian groups (the initial commitment came from a Presbyterian), this endowment fosters religious studies symposia, lectures, forums, exchange programs, and visiting professorships. It also sponsors interfaith meetings where common as well as controversial theological issues are presented by representatives of each tradition, and where workshops help resolve tensions in an atmosphere of goodwill.

The Religious Studies Center at Brigham Young University produces distinguished volumes utilizing scholars of many faiths who represent interdisciplinary and comparative expertise. Although a literature of disparagement continues both from the left and from the right (see ANTI-MORMONISM), Church leaders continually remind the membership that whatever may be said of those who make a religion of anti-Mormonism, a retaliatory response is neither wise nor Christian.

3. Practically in Christian Humanitarianism. At its best the pattern of LDS life, institutionally and individually, has not been to demand rights but to merit them, not to clamor for fellowship and goodwill but to manifest them and to give energy and time beyond rhetoric. In a major address to regional Church leaders, former President Spencer W. KIMBALL set the tone:

We urge members to do their civic duty and to assume their responsibilities as individual citizens in seeking solutions to the problems which beset our cities and communities.

With our wide ranging mission, so far as mankind is concerned, Church members cannot ignore the many practical problems that require solution if our families are to live in an environment conducive to spirituality.

Where solutions to these practical problems require cooperative action with those not of our faith, members should not be reticent in doing their part in joining and leading in those efforts where they can make an individual contribution to those causes which are consistent with the standards of the Church [Kimball, *Ensign* 8 (May 1978):100].

Examples of recent Church-encouraged projects that reach across different affiliations include cooperative emergency assistance, support for homeless shelters in many cities, and linkage with the work of the Salvation Army. At BYU, students of other faiths are often elected to student offices, and various service clubs strive against intolerance and clannishness. In the same spirit, the Church was among the first to give aid, with other Christian bodies, to disaster areas in such places as China, El Salvador, Nicaragua, Los Angeles, Peru, Armenia, Japan, Iran, Chile, and Greece. Through two special fasts, the Church raised $11 million for the hungry in Africa and Ethiopia, and utilized Catholic services as a delivery system (see HUMANITARIAN SERVICE).

Because so much in contemporary society is dissonant, centrifugal, and divisive, interfaith understanding and mutuality seem indispensable. LDS history suggests that what appear to be intractable political, social, and economic clashes are often, at root, religious. To overcome needless divisions and to heal the wounds of modern life, including the religious life, are not just the commission of Latter-day Saints but of all who take seriously the message and ministry of Jesus Christ. Unless in some there is Christlike concern for all, there is little hope for any.

BIBLIOGRAPHY

Arrington, Leonard. "Historical Development of International Mormonism." University of Alberta, *Religious Studies and Theology* 7 (1) Jan. 1987.

Keller, Roger R. *Reformed Christians and Mormon Christians: Let's Talk.* Ann Arbor, Mich., 1986.

Madsen, Truman G. "Are Christians Mormon?" *BYU Studies* 15 (Autumn 1974):73–94.

RICHARD P. LINDSAY

JEWISH

The chief nexus for interfaith relationships between Jews and Latter-day Saints has been Salt Lake City, Utah. A certain amount of contact has also occurred in the State of Israel as well as in cities in the United States with large Jewish populations, such as Los Angeles and New York. Generally, relations between members of the two groups have been characterized by mutual respect and goodwill. Exceptions include sharp differences between Mormons and some Jews on the issue of the purpose of the Brigham Young University Center for Near Eastern Studies in Jerusalem (dedicated 1989; *see* BRIGHAM YOUNG UNIVERSITY: JERUSALEM CENTER FOR NEAR EASTERN STUDIES). However, a workable relationship prevails.

One of the earliest direct contacts between communities was initiated by Orson Hyde, an LDS apostle, who in 1841 traveled through Europe to reach the Holy Land. With rare exceptions, instead of seeking audience with European Jewish leaders to proselytize them, he warned them of difficulties that they would experience, and urged them to emigrate to Palestine. Orson Hyde continued on to the Holy Land, where, on October 24, 1841, he prayed on the Mount of Olives to "dedicate and consecrate this land . . . for the gathering together of Judah's scattered remnants" (*HC* 4:456–59).

Broader contacts began after 1853 with the arrival of the first Jewish family in Utah. While Jews tended to align themselves politically with non-Mormons, they enjoyed the goodwill of their LDS neighbors. Although some Jewish immigrants into Utah—particularly from eastern Europe and Russia—were ridiculed because of their language and their lack of acquaintance with frontier life, they found no cruelty, no restrictions of movement, and no ugly intolerance. While there were no handouts, charity, or dole, they discovered no restrictions on opportunity among the Latter-day Saints.

In 1900, when Utah Jewish leader Nathan Rosenblatt and his associates decided to build a synagogue for a second congregation, the principal help came from the LDS Church's First Presidency. When the building opened in 1903, Rosenblatt proclaimed his gratitude for the blessing and privilege of living in Utah with the tolerant, understanding men and women of the Mormon faith. He and his associates had always found them to be a people devoted to their own faith, yet a people who respected the Jewish Torah and knew what the noted teacher Hillel meant when he taught, "Do not do to your neighbor what you would not do to yourself."

Brigham Young University in Provo, Utah, regularly offers courses that focus on the religion and history of Jews and Judaism. In addition, Jewish scholars have lectured and taught courses at the university, particularly in recent years. In 1921 President Heber J. GRANT offered clear counsel to Latter-day Saints against anti-Semitism: "There should be no ill-will . . . in the heart of any true Latter-day Saint, toward the Jewish people" (in *Gospel Standards*, Salt Lake City, 1941, p. 147).

An indicator of the reciprocal respect that has existed between Utah Jews and Mormons is the number of Jewish public officials elected to serve the state. These include the state's fourth governor (Simon Bamberger, 1917–1921), a district judge (Herbert M. Schiller, 1933–1939), a mayor of Salt Lake City (Louis Marcus, 1931–1935), and several legislators.

[*See also* World Religions (non-Christian) and Mormonism: Judaism; Zionism.]

BIBLIOGRAPHY

Brooks, Juanita. *History of the Jews in Utah and Idaho.* Salt Lake City, 1973.

Zucker, Louis C. *Mormon and Jew: A Meeting on the American Frontier.* Provo, Utah, 1961.

———. "Utah." *Encyclopaedia Judaica*, Vol. 16, pp. 33–34. Jerusalem, 1972.

———. "A Jew in Zion." *Sunstone* 6 (Sept.–Oct. 1981):35–44.

JOSEPH ROSENBLATT

OTHER FAITHS

In August 1852, while the Church was still struggling to establish itself in the western United States, President Brigham YOUNG issued a bold call for missionaries to go to China, India, Siam (Thailand), and Ceylon (Sri Lanka). The seventeen missionaries who were sent formed some of the earliest contacts that LDS members had with non-Christians (see ASIA, THE CHURCH IN). Because of civil wars, rejection, and language and cultural difficulties, the work in most countries lasted only months; however, work in India continued until 1856. Although some attempts were made in the early twentieth century, the Church did not undertake further significant efforts to establish itself in non-Christian nations, including Asia, until after World War II.

Stimulated by experiences of LDS servicemen in Asia during and after the war, the Church established missions in East Asia at the end of the 1940s. Since then, WARDS and STAKES led by local members have been established in Japan, South Korea, Hong Kong, Taiwan, and the Philippines; temples have been built in all these places except Hong Kong.

In the 1970s and 1980s, the Church expanded into such Southeast Asian nations as Singapore, Thailand, Indonesia, and Malaysia, and in the South Asian nations of India and Sri Lanka. Although small beginnings have been made in some Muslim countries, Church growth in such countries has been limited.

LDS health services programs in the Philippines and refugee assistance in Thailand have been favorably received. High-level contacts with government officials in many countries have elicited a positive response to the values of the Church and its members. Overall, the Church has made consistent efforts to remain sensitive to and abide by local laws and customs, including regulations based on religious sentiment.

Church growth in Africa has principally taken place in the last quarter of the twentieth century, particularly following the 1978 revelation allowing all worthy males to hold the priesthood (see AFRICA, THE CHURCH IN; DOCTRINE AND COVENANTS: OFFICIAL DECLARATION—2). Congregations have been established in several countries, and Church membership is growing rapidly. In recent years, the Church has joined various charitable organizations in sending famine relief to stricken nations on the African continent (see ECONOMIC AID).

In an educational vein, MISSIONARY TRAINING CENTERS teach many foreign languages and courses on the religions and cultures of non-Western countries, and for educational purposes "culturegrams" have been developed that are now used by U.S. government agencies. In addition, courses on world religions are regularly taught in institutions of higher learning. Moreover, symposia on Islam and on the religions of Africa have been hosted at Brigham Young University, with a number of distinguished religious leaders and scholars participating.

In many countries, The Church of Jesus Christ of Latter-day Saints is viewed as an American church. However, Church leaders have strongly emphasized that it is universal, a church for all people everywhere (see WORLD RELIGIONS [NON-CHRISTIAN] AND MORMONISM). A powerful presentation by President Spencer W. KIMBALL in 1974 stressed the responsibility of the Church to share the gospel with all of God's children (*Ensign* 4 [Oct. 1974]:2–14). Consequently, in the last half of the twentieth century the Church has made its most significant efforts to establish itself throughout the world.

Generally the LDS outreach to non-Christians has had a positive, invigorating effect on members of the Church, has strengthened Church membership significantly, and has brought about increased awareness of cultural differences as well as a willingness to work within those differences.

BIBLIOGRAPHY

Palmer, Spencer J. *The Expanding Church*. Salt Lake City, 1978.

———, ed. *Mormons and Muslims*. Provo, Utah, 1983.

SOREN F. COX

INTERNATIONAL GENEALOGICAL INDEX™ (IGI)

The International Genealogical Index™ (IGI) is a vital records index, which at the beginning of 1990 contained more than 147 million names of deceased persons from the 1500s to about 1875. The IGI lists individuals alphabetically according to place of birth/christening or marriage, and clusters similarly spelled surnames under a standard spelling.

The Church publishes the IGI to assist genealogical research and help members determine whether temple ordinances have been performed for deceased ancestors. Countries such as England (47,155,000 entries), Mexico 24,205,000, Germany (18,675,000), the United States (18,660,000), Scotland (10,745,000), and Finland (5,045,000), as well as more than ninety other nations are included.

Available on 9,200 microfiches and on compact disk, the IGI can be searched at the FAMILY HISTORY LIBRARY, Salt Lake City, or at any of the nearly 1,400 LDS FAMILY HISTORY CENTERS located in various parts of the world. Patrons can purchase copies of the microfiche in sets by region, state, or country from the Family History Department, LDS Church Headquarters, Salt Lake City, UT 84150, or copy up to 500 entries to a holding file that can be printed or copied to diskettes for home use.

BIBLIOGRAPHY

Family History Library. *Research Outline: International Genealogical Index* (on microfiche). 1st ed., Aug. 1988, Series IGI, no. 1, 2nd ed., Mar. 1989, Series IGI, no. 5 (compact disk).

GERALD M. HASLAM

INTERNATIONAL MAGAZINES

In 1967 The Church of Jesus Christ of Latter-day Saints began unifying the foreign language magazines that were being independently published to serve its Danish, Dutch, Finnish, French, German, Norwegian, Spanish, and Swedish-speaking missions to give its magazines similar editorial content and a general format. This unification of content greatly reduced redundant staff efforts in the various mission offices and provided Church-approved materials for all issues. The resulting *Unified Magazine* was renamed *International Magazines* in 1974, an umbrella title that in 1990 covered twenty different magazines, each with its own language-specific title. An editorial staff in Salt Lake City chooses materials from the Church's three English publications, *Friend, New Era,* and *Ensign,* that will appeal to international readers of all ages and prepares those and other original articles for international publication.

An English version, *Tambuli,* is prepared in Salt Lake City, and film of the completed layouts, containing both text and art is shipped for local printing in the Philippines. Similar print-ready film is prepared in Salt Lake City for other language editions and is then sent to various printing sites around the world. Some of the translations are prepared in Salt Lake City, but most in the local areas. The various editions contain from eight to sixteen pages of local Church news that is gathered, edited, and printed in the language areas.

The idea of publishing local, foreign-language magazines for Church members started in Wales in 1846, a year before the Mormon Pioneers moved into the Salt Lake Valley. Dan Jones edited and published thirty-two issues of *Prophwyd y Jubili, Neu Seren y Saints* (Prophet of Jubilee, New Star of Saints), filled with doctrinal and historical articles, messages from Church leaders, and replies to attacks from antagonists of the Church. Other magazines followed. The first issues of *Skandinaviens Stjerne* (Scandinavian Star) in Denmark, *l'Etoile du Deseret* (The Star of Deseret) in France, and *Zions Panier* (Zion's Banner) in Germany were all published in 1851. In subsequent years the Church has published magazines in other languages, with the larger number beginning in the twentieth century. In 1990 the Church is increasing the number of its foreign language periodicals.

For a fuller list of Church magazines and newspapers, see Church Periodicals chart in the Appendix.

BIBLIOGRAPHY

Flake, Chad J. *A Mormon Bibliography, 1830–1930.* Salt Lake City, Utah, 1978.

BRIAN K. KELLY

INTERVIEWS

Church leaders conduct a variety of interviews essential to the administration of the Church and the nurturance of members. Interviews of Church members are conducted to determine personal worthiness, approve participation in religious ceremonies and ORDINANCES, assess needs, issue calls to service, listen to members' concerns, receive an accounting of performance in a Church assignment, and record a member's status regarding the payment of TITHING.

Worthiness is required of those who are to serve in Church CALLINGS, represent the Church as missionaries, and attend the temple (*see* TEMPLE RECOMMEND). An interview is used in each of these situations to determine the member's willingness to serve and worthiness to participate. For example, when a person prepares for BAPTISM or an engaged couple seek permission to be married by priesthood authority in the temple, they first answer questions of a Church leader (usually a bishop or stake president) in a confidential worthiness interview regarding their honesty, integrity, moral cleanliness, and overall obedience to the gospel of Jesus Christ.

Church leaders are expected to seek inspiration as they determine worthiness, extend callings, and give counsel to members who are having difficulties. Members may seek an interview for counsel regarding matters of personal anguish, spiritual concerns, moral transgression, marital disharmony, financial welfare, and family functioning. They may come feeling anxious and bearing burdens of guilt. Although Church leaders are not given specific training in the techniques of interviewing, they are encouraged to be supportive and nonthreatening and to create an atmosphere in which the Spirit of the Lord can be present to provide guidance, comfort, and discernment. N. Eldon Tanner, counselor in the First Presidency of the Church, offered the following advice to Church interviewers: "It is important that those we interview realize that they are spirit children of God and that we love them . . . and are interested in their welfare and in helping them succeed in life" (p. 41).

Interviews are also used to issue callings and report service rendered. For example, most adult men and women accept calls to visit specific members of the congregation monthly (*see* HOME TEACHING; VISITING TEACHING) and then discuss these visits in an interview with their supervisor. Members in any calling report on their performance and provide their supervisors with nonconfidential information concerning those they are called to serve (*see* STEWARDSHIP). They report any confidential matters directly to the bishop.

Interviews are regularly scheduled to maintain lines of communication between Church leaders and members. Bishops and their counselors are asked to interview youth twelve to eighteen years of age frequently to encourage obedience to the gospel, the development of talents, the pursuit of education, and preparation for service in the Church and community. These interviews should support family goals and commitments and supplement parental guidance (which often includes appropriate father's and mother's interviews and counsel with their children).

Successful interviews invite unity and build faith. Leaders who conduct worthiness interviews

are to remember that they are "representatives of the Lord and [therefore they] must conduct the interviews as the Lord himself would conduct them" (Tanner, p. 42).

BIBLIOGRAPHY

Dyer, Alvin R. "How Oral Evaluation Can Help Home Teachers Keep Close to the Families They Visit." *IE* 72 (Dec. 1969):18–19.

Tanner, N. Eldon. "The Blessing of Church Interviews." *Ensign* 8 (Nov. 1978):41–42.

LARRY C. FARMER

IOWA, LDS COMMUNITIES IN

[*LDS refugees first settled in southeastern Iowa along the Mississippi River in 1839, after their expulsion from Missouri (see* Missouri Conflict). *The towns of Montrose, Keokuk, and Augusta had numerous LDS settlers. Latter-day Saints established Ambrosia, about three miles west of Montrose; Nashville (now Galland), three miles south of Montrose; and Zarahemla, their principal settlement, immediately west of Montrose. Because of anti-Mormon feelings, questionable land titles, and the desire to live closer to Church headquarters, most members eventually moved across the Mississippi River to Nauvoo, Illinois. See generally* History of the Church: c. 1831–1844.

In 1846, Latter-day Saints moving west from Illinois established way-station settlements at Garden Grove and Mount Pisgah to raise crops for those who would follow. The Mormon Battalion *was recruited first at Mount Pisgah. Also in 1846, numerous temporary settlements were established in the vicinity of Council Bluffs. In 1848 most Latter-day Saints remaining at the Missouri River withdrew from* Winter Quarters, *today part of Omaha, Nebraska, and settled across the river in present-day Council Bluffs, which they called Kanesville. LDS population in Pottawattamie County, Iowa, including Kanesville, may have reached as high as 8,000 in about forty settlements before the massive effort to move them to the Salt Lake Valley in 1852.*

In 1856–1858, Iowa City was the outfitting point for church emigrants, including Handcart Companies. *See* Immigration and Emigration; Mormon Pioneer Trail; *and, more generally,* History of the Church: c. 1844–1877.]

ISAIAH

[*It is the emphasis on Isaiah's words in LDS scripture that necessitates a treatment of his writings under four titles:*

Authorship
Texts in the Book of Mormon
Interpretations in Modern Scripture
Commentaries on Isaiah

The article Authorship *deals with the issue of the single authorship of the book of Isaiah in light of the existence of an Isaiah text possessed by Book of Mormon peoples as early as 600 B.C. The article* Texts in the Book of Mormon *focuses on the question of what can be learned about the history of the text of Isaiah's book from the portions preserved in the Book of Mormon. Many of Isaiah's words that are preserved and commented on in LDS scripture have to do with the latter days, a matter that is taken up in the article* Interpretations in Modern Scripture. *The resulting LDS interest in Isaiah has led to a number of studies that are treated in the article* Commentaries on Isaiah.]

AUTHORSHIP

Of the writings in the Old Testament, the message of Isaiah enjoys high priority among Latter-day Saints. The attraction derives primarily from the extensive use of Isaiah in the Book of Mormon. Secondarily, chapter 11 of Isaiah was quoted to Joseph Smith in a vision in his earliest days as a prophet (JS—H 1:40) and became the subject of a section in the Doctrine and Covenants (D&C 113). In addition, Jesus Christ has given revelations about, and prophets and apostles of the latter days have frequently quoted from and commented upon Isaiah's words when instructing the Saints.

Traditionally, the book of Isaiah has been ascribed to a prophet living in the kingdom of Judah between 740 and 690 B.C. In Germany during the late 1700s, several scholars challenged this view, claiming that chapters 40–66 were written by one or more other individuals as late as 400 B.C. because of the specific references to events that occurred after Isaiah's death. This outlook now permeates many Bible commentaries and has led to the postulation of a second prophetic writer who is commonly called in scholarly literature "Deutero-Isaiah." Indeed, a wide variety of theories regarding the date and authorship of Isaiah now exist. However, LDS belief in revelation and the seership of prophets, along with the quotations from Isaiah in the Book of Mormon and its admonitions to study his writings, have reinforced Latter-day Saints in the traditional view concerning the date and authorship of Isaiah, in the following ways.

First, while some scholars argue that prophets could not see the future and that, therefore, the later chapters of Isaiah must have been written after Isaiah's time (e.g., Isa. 45 concerning Cyrus), Latter-day Saints recognize that prophets can see and prophesy about the future. In chapters 40–66, Isaiah prophesies of the future, just as the apostle John does in Revelation 4–22, and the prophet Nephi$_1$ in 2 Nephi 25–30.

Second, the Book of Mormon prophet Lehi and his family left Jerusalem about 600 B.C. and took with them scriptural writings on plates of brass that contained much of the Old Testament, including Isaiah (1 Ne. 5:13; 19:22–23). Book of Mormon prophets taught from the brass plate records, not only from chapters 1–39, which are usually assigned by scholars to the prophet Isaiah of the eighth century B.C., but also from the later chapters, the so-called Deutero-Isaiah. For example, Isaiah chapters 48–54 are all quoted in the Book of Mormon, with some passages mentioned a number of times (1 Ne. 20–21; 2 Ne. 6:16–8:25; Mosiah 12:21–24; 14; 15:29–31; 3 Ne. 16:18–20; 20:32–45; 22). Hence, the existence of a virtually complete Isaiah text in the late seventh century B.C., as witnessed by the Book of Mormon, negates arguments for later multiple authorship, whether those arguments be historical, theological, or literary.

Finally, other significant witnesses exist for the single authorship of Isaiah, including Jesus Christ in particular (cf. Matt. 13:14–15; 15:7–9; Luke 4:17–19; 3 Ne. 16, 20–22). Indeed, after quoting much from Isaiah 52 (3 Ne. 16:18–20; 20:32–45) and repeating Isaiah 54 in its entirety (3 Ne. 22), the resurrected Jesus Christ admonished his Book of Mormon disciples to study Isaiah's words and then said, "A commandment I give unto you that ye search these things diligently; for great are the words of Isaiah. For surely he spake as touching all things concerning my people which are of the house of Israel" (3 Ne. 23:1–2).

Jewish and Christian traditions from the earliest times have supported the single authorship of Isaiah. The Septuagint, the Dead Sea Scrolls, and other ancient texts also give no hint of multiple authorship. Latter-day Saints accept the words of the risen Jesus that Isaiah was a seer and revelator whose prophecies, as recorded throughout his book, will eventually all be fulfilled (3 Ne. 23:1–3). Particularly from Jesus' attribution of Isaiah 52 and 54 to the ancient prophet have Latter-day Saints concluded that the book of Isaiah is the inspired work of the eighth-century prophet Isaiah, son of Amoz.

BIBLIOGRAPHY

Adams, Larry L., and Alvin C. Rencher. "A Computer Analysis of the Isaiah Authorship Problem." *BYU Studies* 15 (Autumn 1974):95–102.

Anderson, Francis I. "Style and Authorship." *The Tyndale Paper* 21 (June 1976):2.

Gileadi, Avraham. *A Holistic Structure of the Book of Isaiah.* Ph.D. diss., Brigham Young University, 1981.

Kissane, E. J. *The Book of Isaiah,* 2 vols. Dublin, Ireland, 1941, 1943.

Ludlow, Victor L. *Isaiah: Prophet, Seer, and Poet.* Salt Lake City, 1981.

Tvedtnes, John A. "Isaiah Variants in the Book of Mormon." In *Isaiah and the Prophets,* ed. M. Nyman. Provo, Utah, 1984.

Young, Edward J. *Introduction to the Old Testament.* Grand Rapids, Mich., 1949.

VICTOR L. LUDLOW

TEXTS IN THE BOOK OF MORMON

The Isaiah texts quoted in the Book of Mormon are unique. They are the only extant Isaiah texts that have no "original" language source with which the translation can be textually compared. These English texts date to the translation and initial publication of the Book of Mormon (1829).

These Isaiah texts were quoted and paraphrased by many Book of Mormon prophets who had a copy of Isaiah on the PLATES of brass. Attempts to determine the authenticity of those Book of Mormon Isaiah texts by comparing them with Hebrew, Greek, and Latin texts of Isaiah hold interest, but such efforts are moot because the ancient texts behind the Book of Mormon Isaiah translation are not available for study. However, much can be learned by comparing the numerous ancient versions and translations of Isaiah with the Book of Mormon Isaiah texts. Such comparisons result in granting the Book of Mormon Isaiah full recensional status.

The Isaiah materials in the Book of Mormon exhibit many similarities to those in the King James translation of the Bible, which would seem to indicate that both share a Hebrew Masoretic origin. However, many other peculiarities in the Book of Mormon texts point to an origin related to texts similar to those from which the Greek Septuagint and the Latin Vulgate were derived. These peculiar readings are significant enough that they preclude relegating the Book of Mormon Isaiah texts to being a mere copy of the King James Version. The Isaiah texts found in English translation in the Book of Mormon possess a distinctive char-

CHART OF ISAIAH CITATIONS IN THE BOOK OF MORMON

Book of Mormon	Isaiah
1 Ne. 20–21	48–49
1 Ne. 22:6	49:22
1 Ne. 22:8	49:22–23; 29:14
1 Ne. 22:10–11	52:10
2 Ne. 6:6b–7	49:22–23
2 Ne. 6:15	29:6
2 Ne. 6:16–8:25	49:24–52:2
2 Ne. 9:50–51	55:1–2
2 Ne. 12–24	2–14
2 Ne. 25:17 (mixed)	11:11 and 29:14
2 Ne. 26:15–16, 18	29:3–5
2 Ne. 26:25	55:1
2 Ne. 27:2–5	29:6–10
2 Ne. 27:6–9	29:4, 11
2 Ne. 27:15–19	29:11–12
2 Ne. 27:25–35	29:13–24
2 Ne. 28:9b	29:15
2 Ne. 28:14b	29:13b
2 Ne. 28:16a	29:21
2 Ne. 28:30a	28:10, 13
2 Ne. 28:32	9:12–13
2 Ne. 29:1	29:14, 11:11
2 Ne. 30:9, 12–15	11:4–9
Mosiah 12:21–24	52:7–10
Mosiah 14:1–12	53
Mosiah 15:10	53:10
Mosiah 15:14–18	52:7
Mosiah 15:29–31	52:8–10
3 Ne. 16:18–20	52:8–10
3 Ne. 20:32–35	52:8–10
3 Ne. 20:36–46	52:1–3, 6–7, 11–15
3 Ne. 21:8b	52:15b
3 Ne. 21:29	52:12
3 Ne. 22:1b–17	54
Moro. 10:31	52:17; 54:2

acter that indicates a unique textual origin. The important question is not, "Are the Book of Mormon Isaiah texts authentic?" Rather, the issue is, "Do the Book of Mormon Isaiah texts provide clear evidence of variant texts besides those normally acknowledged?" Should they not be considered as valid as, say, the Dead Sea Isaiah texts?

One of the major criticisms of the Book of Mormon Isaiah texts is that they contain parts of what have come to be termed "First Isaiah" and "Deutero-Isaiah" by Bible scholars. It is evident that the Book of Mormon Isaiah texts provide evidence contravening modern theories of multiple authorship of Isaiah's book (*see* ISAIAH: AUTHORSHIP); for if the origins of the Isaiah material in the Book of Mormon are accepted as stated by its authors, then by 600 B.C. the book of Isaiah was essentially as it is today. The chief value of textual criticism, in this case, is to help identify special themes and language patterns, that is, to provide a better understanding of the message, not a determination of authorship. The most viable and certainly the most productive option for determining the origin of the Book of Mormon Isaiah texts is therefore an internal examination.

The Book of Mormon indicates that in "the first year of the reign of Zedekiah, king of Judah" (1 Ne. 1:4) the prophet NEPHI₁ and his brothers retrieved from Jerusalem a "record" written by their ancestors on plates of brass (1 Ne. 3–4), which they carried with them to the Western Hemisphere. Included in the record were prophecies of Isaiah (1 Ne. 19:22–23; cf. 5:13). All of the Isaiah texts in the Book of Mormon are quotations from that record, except perhaps those cited by the risen Jesus (cf. 1 Ne. 16, 21–22). Whether quoting directly or paraphrasing, Book of Mormon prophets were trying to do two things: "persuade [people] to believe in the Lord their Redeemer" (1 Ne. 19:23) and reveal the plans of God for his people, as noted by the prophet Isaiah (e.g., 2 Ne. 25:7; Hel. 8:18–20; 3 Ne. 23:1–2). These features give a singular quality to the Isaiah texts of the Book of Mormon, because it preserves almost exclusively the texts pertaining to salvation and saving principles and ignores Isaiah's historical material. The concerns of Book of Mormon prophets were doctrinal, and passages were utilized to expound their testimonies. Moreover, the passages that concern salvation from the later chapters of Isaiah are presented to show that Jesus was the promised Messiah (cf. Mosiah 13:33–15:31, which cites Isa. 53; 52:7, 8–10). While nineteenth-century biblical scholarship held that the concept of a "saving Messiah" arose after the Babylonian exile (587–538 B.C.) and therefore the later chapters of Isaiah are to be dated to the end of the sixth century or later, the Book of Mormon texts obviously undermine that theory.

Minor changes in the Book of Mormon Isaiah texts have been made since the publication of the work in 1830. These changes in recent editions have attempted to correct early errors in printing and to bring the Isaiah texts of the present edition into "conformity with prepublication manuscripts

and early editions edited by the Prophet Joseph Smith" ("A Brief Explanation About the Book of Mormon," 1981 edition of the Book of Mormon). None of these changes has been substantive.

BIBLIOGRAPHY

Eissfeldt, Otto. *The Old Testament: An Introduction*, pp. 303–346. New York, 1965.

Nibley, Hugh. *Since Cumorah*, pp. 111–34. In *CWHN* 7.

Sperry, Sidney B. *Answers to Book of Mormon Questions*. Salt Lake City, 1967.

Tvedtnes, John A. "The Isaiah Variants in the Book of Mormon." *F.A.R.M.S.* Paper. Provo, Utah, 1981.

LEGRANDE DAVIES

INTERPRETATIONS IN MODERN SCRIPTURE

Isaiah was one of the most important prophetic writers in the Old Testament. The Book of Mormon and the Doctrine and Covenants, modern LDS scriptures, confirm this assessment and contain extensive commentaries on his writings. The Book of Mormon quotes 425 verses and paraphrases many others from the book of Isaiah, taken from the PLATES of brass, a record brought to the Western Hemisphere by the prophet LEHI and his family (c. 600 B.C.). The Book of Mormon quotations from Isaiah are accompanied by the interpretations of Nephite prophets and the resurrected Jesus Christ. The Doctrine and Covenants likewise contains quotations and paraphrases of Isaiah, many illuminating the setting for and relevance of the fulfillment of his prophecies.

THE BOOK OF MORMON. The prophets in the Book of Mormon explicitly praise the writings of Isaiah and provide a thorough commentary thereon. Besides three early NEPHITE prophets, NEPHI₁, JACOB, and ABINADI, who quoted extensively from and explained the meanings of Isaiah, the resurrected Jesus Christ, when he visited the Nephites (A.D. 34), commanded his hearers to "search these things diligently; for great are the words of Isaiah" (3 Ne. 23:1). Most Book of Mormon citations of Isaiah concern two themes: (1) the testimony that Jesus Christ would come into the world to save it (1 Ne. 19:23; cf. 2 Ne. 9:5–12), and (2) pronouncements that even though the Lord would scatter Israel, he would gather and restore them, fulfilling the covenants that he made with Abraham and Israel (2 Ne. 6:5; cf. 9:1–2).

Concerning the house of Israel, Nephi's earliest citation of Isaiah (chaps. 48–49) emphasized two types of scattering: that of large segments of the tribes of Israel, and that of small groups among the nations of the earth (1 Ne. 22:3–5; cf. Isa. 49:1–13). Scattered Israelites of both types would be nursed temporally and spiritually among the GENTILES. The temporal assistance to Israelites would lead to a dependency on Gentiles for survival. The spiritual nursing would come through a "marvelous work" that would gather Israel out of obscurity and darkness and bring them to the knowledge of their Redeemer (1 Ne. 22:6–12).

Nephi presented his longest quotation of Isaiah 2–14 (2 Ne. 12–24) as a third witness of Israel's Redeemer. Nephi, his brother Jacob, and Isaiah had each seen the Redeemer (as the premortal Jesus Christ) face to face (2 Ne. 11:2–3; cf. 2 Ne. 16:1–7). Nephi's own vision (1 Ne. 11:13–20) clarified Isaiah's words pointing to the coming of Christ (cf. 2 Ne. 17:14; 19:6–7 [i.e., Isa. 7:14; 9:6–7]).

Nephi's commentary on Isaiah 2–14 describes what was to happen to the Jews (2 Ne. 25:9–21; cf. Isa. 3:1–15; 5:1–7), to Nephi's own people (2 Ne. 25:22–26:11; cf. Isa. 29:1–4), and among the Gentiles (2 Ne. 26:12–28:32; cf. Isa. 3:16–4:1). Nephi knew by revelation that when the Book of Mormon would come forth among Gentiles, churches would be lifted up in pride and learning, SECRET COMBINATIONS would prevail, and priestcraft would flourish (2 Ne. 26:14–33; cf. Isa. 3:16–4:1; 2 Ne. 13:16–14:1). By contrast, he foresaw that beautiful branches of Israel would be cleansed and grow in both ZION and JERUSALEM and that they would be protected by the Lord (Isa. 4:2–6; 2 Ne. 14:2–6). Expanding Isaiah's prophecy, Nephi prophesied that Gentiles who repented would be numbered with the house of Israel and become heirs of the promised blessings (2 Ne. 30:1–3). He affirmed that his own people would again receive the GOSPEL OF JESUS CHRIST and become a pure and delightsome people (2 Ne. 30:4–6). He foretold the gathering of Jews to Jerusalem, as they would begin to believe in Christ, and also as a delightsome people (2 Ne. 30:7).

The prophet Abinadi (c. 150 B.C.) said that all the prophets had spoken concerning Christ's coming (Mosiah 13:33–35), and he quoted Isaiah 53 as an example (cf. Mosiah 14). In one of the most lucid explanations of the ministry and atonement of Christ, Abinadi explained that chapter 53 of Isaiah underscored that "God himself shall come down among the children of men, and shall redeem his people," and that, because of his redemption, he would stand "betwixt them and justice; having broken the bands of death, taken upon himself their iniquity and their transgressions, . . . and satisfied the demands of [God's] justice" (Mosiah 15:1–9).

During his first visit among Book of Mormon peoples, the resurrected Jesus cited Isaiah 52 and 54 among his principal texts. He declared that when the words of Isaiah were fulfilled, the covenants made to the house of Israel would be fulfilled (3 Ne. 20:11–12). The gospel will be taught to Jews in their scattered locations and, after they accept it, they will return to Jerusalem and teach their own people (3 Ne. 20:29–35; cf. Isa. 52:8–10). Jesus gave his hearers a sign that the restoration of Jews to Jerusalem would indicate that the restoration had already begun among other Israelites in ZION, the Americas (3 Ne. 21:1–7; Isa. 52:1–3, 6–7, 11–12). In a reference to the "marred" servant of Isaiah 52:13–15, he spoke of the servant's "marvelous work." While the marred servant was clearly the mortal Jesus (Mosiah 15:1–9), Isaiah's words form a dual prophecy because the resurrected Jesus said that it also referred to a latter-day servant. Latter-day Saints believe that this servant was the Prophet Joseph Smith, and the marvelous work referred to was the coming forth of the Book of Mormon and the restoration of the gospel (3 Ne. 21:8–11).

While expanding on Isaiah's words, Jesus foretold the building of the NEW JERUSALEM in the Western Hemisphere by a remnant of the house of Israel, assisted by converted Gentiles (3 Ne. 21:22–25; cf. 20:22). The gospel is to be preached among the various groups of the house of Israel, including the Lamanites and the lost tribes (3 Ne. 21:26).

THE DOCTRINE AND COVENANTS. Also a rich source for interpreting and applying the prophecies of Isaiah, the Doctrine and Covenants has over seventy quotations from or paraphrases of Isaiah. Two themes are prevalent: the gospel will be restored, and Israel will be gathered. For example, the "marvelous work and a wonder" (Isa. 29:14) is the coming forth of the Book of Mormon (D&C 6:1); God's "strange act" (Isa. 28:21) refers to the RESTORATION of the Church and its temple ORDINANCES (D&C 95:4); the "good tidings" published "upon the mountains" (Isa. 52:7) consist of the preaching of the gospel to all nations (D&C 19:29); and the restoration of the tribes of Jacob

CHART OF ISAIAH CITATIONS IN THE DOCTRINE AND COVENANTS

The following lists offer a sampling of Isaiah passages that are either quoted, paraphrased, or interpreted in the Doctrine and Covenants.

Isaiah	Doctrine and Covenants
1:2	76:1
1:18	45:10; 50:10–12
1:19	64:34
2:2–3	133:12–13
4:5	45:63–75; 84:5
4:6	115:6
5:1–7	101:43–62
8:16	88:84; 133:72
11:1–5	113:1–4
11:4	19:15
11:10	113:5–6
11:16	133:26–29
13:1	133:14
13:10	29:14; 34:9; 45:42; 88:87; 133:49
13:13	21:6; 35:24
14:12	76:26
24:5	1:15
24:20	49:23; 88:87
25:6	58:8
28:10	98:12; 128:21
28:15, 18	45:31; 5:19; 97:23
28:21	95:4; 101:95
29:14	4:1; 6:1; 11:1; 12:1; 14:1; 18:44; 76:9
33:22	1:13
34:5	38:22
35:1–2	49:24–25; 117:7
35:3	81:5
35:7–10	133:27–33
35:10	45:71; 66:11
40:3	33:10; 45:9; 65:1; 84:28
40:4	88:66
40:5	49:23; 133:22
40:6	101:23 124:7–8
40:31	89:20; 124:99
42:7	128:22
43:11	76:1
45:17	35:25; 38:33
45:23	76:110; 88:104
49:1	1:1
49:2	6:2; 11:2; 12:2; 14:2; 15:2; 16:2; 33:1; 86:9
49:6	86:11
49:22	45:9; 115:5
50:2–3	35:8; 133:66–69
50:11	133:70
51:9–11	101:18
52:1	82:14; 113:7–8
52:2	113:9–10
52:7	19:29; 31:3; 113:10
52:8	39:13; 84:98–99; 133:10
52:10	113:10; 133:3
52:11	38:42; 133:5
52:12	49:27; 58:56; 101:68, 72; 133:15
52:15	101:94
54:2	82:14; 133:9
54:17	71:9; 109:25
55:6	88:62–63
59:17	27:15–18
60:1–4	64:41–42
60:2	112:23
60:22	133:58
61:1	128:22
62:4	133:23–24
62:10	45:9; 115:5
63:1–2	133:46–48
63:3–6	76:107; 88:106; 133:50–52
63:7–9	133:52–53
64:1–2	34:8; 133:40–42
64:3–5	76:10; 133:43–45
65:17	29:23
65:20	63:51; 101:30
65:21–22	101:101
66:1	38:17
66:24	76:44

from among the nations (Isa. 49:6) means the return of scattered Israel to their lands of promise (D&C 133:26–33).

Other themes include the building of the latter-day Zion and her stakes (Isa. 54:1–2; D&C 82:14) as well as the old Jerusalem (Isa. 52:1–2; D&C 113:7–10); verification that Jesus is the only Savior of the world (Isa. 43:11; D&C 76:1); and details of his SECOND COMING (Isa. 63:3–6; 64:1–5; D&C 133:37–52). Finally, many anticipated events are interpreted to be millennial occurrences (Isa. 65; D&C 101:30–31).

BIBLIOGRAPHY

Ludlow, Victor L. *Isaiah: Prophet, Seer, and Poet.* Salt Lake City, 1982.

Nyman, Monte S. *Great Are the Words of Isaiah.* Salt Lake City, 1980.

MONTE S. NYMAN

COMMENTARIES ON ISAIAH

The book of Isaiah is one of the most frequently cited prophetic works within LDS scripture. When the Book of Mormon people left Jerusalem, they carried records on PLATES of brass that contained many Old Testament books predating 600 B.C., including Isaiah. Early in their narratives, NEPHI₁ and his brother, JACOB, quoted extensively from Isaiah. Later, the resurrected Jesus admonished his hearers in the Americas to search the words of Isaiah diligently, for "great are the words of Isaiah" (3 Ne. 23:1).

Latter-day Saints see many of Isaiah's prophecies fulfilled in contemporary events. When the angel Moroni appeared to the Prophet Joseph SMITH on September 21–22, 1823, he quoted Isaiah 11 and said it was "about to be fulfilled" (JS—H 1:40). Isaiah 29 is also seen as a prophecy anticipating the coming forth of the Book of Mormon. Joseph Smith's teachings contain many references to Isaiah, especially about the LAST DAYS before the second coming of Christ. Additionally, Isaiah is often quoted in the Doctrine and Covenants (e.g., 45:10; 50:10–12; 64:34–35; 133), and in some cases interpretations are added (e.g., D&C 113).

Several books written by LDS authors since 1950 have sought to assist Church members and others to understand Isaiah's words. Some of these commentaries addressed a scholarly audience and others were written for general readers.

In 1952 Sidney B. Sperry commented on Isaiah in the first ten chapters of his book *The Voice of Israel's Prophets* (Salt Lake City). Its chief purpose was to offer commentary from an LDS perspective, including Joseph Smith's views, and to analyze the entire book of Isaiah historically and philologically. Sperry included Book of Mormon interpretations of various passages and a discussion of a unified authorship. He also utilized the Septuagint and his mastery of Hebrew to explain and sometimes retranslate passages. Although the earliest such study, it remains a classic of its kind.

In 1982 Avraham Gileadi published *The Apocalyptic Book of Isaiah* (Provo, Utah), a fresh translation of the Hebrew text with interpretive keys for general readers. The book's contributions include his translation and his Jewish-Mormon perspective. In 1988 he published a second volume, *The Book of Isaiah* (Salt Lake City), which included his earlier translation and an enlarged introduction containing four interpretive keys that he derived from the Book of Mormon. This work notes alternate readings in the DEAD SEA SCROLL Isaiah text and the Septuagint.

Two volumes have served as textbooks. In 1980 Monte S. Nyman published *Great Are the Words of Isaiah* (Salt Lake City) as a commentary and study guide. The book's most distinctive contribution is a collection of references to Isaiah from Joseph Smith's writings, the New Testament, the Book of Mormon, the Doctrine and Covenants, and LDS GENERAL AUTHORITIES. In 1982 Victor L. Ludlow authored *Isaiah: Prophet, Seer, and Poet* (Salt Lake City). Important features are his chapter-by-chapter commentary, suggested multiple interpretations of some passages in the text, helpful maps and historical notes, and LDS doctrinal discussions using various translations of the text.

Other books were written for nonscholarly LDS audiences. L. LaMar Adams's *The Living Message of Isaiah* (Salt Lake City, 1981) aimed at helping his readers appreciate Isaiah's prophecies. Its distinctive contribution is its appendix on the apocryphal *Ascension of Isaiah*.

In 1984 W. Cleon Skousen published *Isaiah Speaks to Modern Times* (Salt Lake City) with the intent of assisting an LDS audience to understand Isaiah as one who saw and spoke of the modern era.

Elder Mark E. Petersen is the only General Authority who has written a book on Isaiah, *Isaiah for Today* (Salt Lake City, 1981). His purpose was to help a nonscholarly LDS audience relate Isaiah's prophecies to present-day events.

ANN N. MADSEN

ISHMAEL

Little is known of the Book of Mormon Ishmael. An Ephraimite from Jerusalem (cf. *JD* 23:184), he cooperated in fulfilling God's command (brought to him from the wilderness by Lehi's son) that he, his wife, five daughters, two sons, and their households travel into the wilderness to join the exodus of the prophet LEHI from Jerusalem about 600 B.C. (1 Ne. 7:2–5).

While en route to Lehi's camp, a division arose in which four of Ishmael's children collaborated with LAMAN and Lemuel, the older sons of Lehi, against the others of their party. A reprimand by NEPHI₁, the fourth son of Lehi, provoked them to bind him and threaten to leave him to die. Their hearts were softened toward him only when other members of Ishmael's family pleaded for Nephi's safety (1 Ne. 7:6–21).

After joining with Lehi in the valley of Lemuel, Nephi, his brothers, and ZORAM married the daughters of Ishmael (1 Ne. 16:7). As the journey continued Ishmael died and "was buried in the place which was called Nahom" (16:34). Ishmael's death and the combination of other adversities caused such grieving among his children that they again complained against Lehi and Nephi, repenting only after the voice of the Lord chastened them (16:34–39).

CHRISTINE PURVES BAKER

ISRAEL

[*Four articles are clustered under this entry*:

Overview
Scattering of Israel
Lost Tribes of Israel
Gathering of Israel

The first article is a general introduction of the distinctive LDS concept of Israel. The second article is a review of the scriptural scattering of Israel. The third article treats the scriptural promises of the restoration of the tribes to their homelands. The fourth article constitutes a review of the scriptural promises concerning the latter-day gathering of Israel. They reflect the breadth of interest in the topic among Latter-day Saints and the doctrinal and historical foundations of this interest. Other articles with a related historical component are Abrahamic Covenant; Covenant Israel; Ephraim; Jerusalem; Moses; Promised Land; and Zionism. Articles that incorporate doctrinal aspects of LDS interest are Allegory of Zenos; Law of Adoption; New and Everlasting Covenant; and New Jerusalem.]

OVERVIEW

The name Israel (Hebrew for "God rules" or "God shines") has two particularly distinctive modern applications to Latter-day Saints. First, it refers to members of the Church. Second, it points to modern descendants of ancient Israelite stock, who, because of God's fidelity to ancient covenants made with their forebears, are to become recipients of his blessings in the latter days.

HISTORY OF THE NAME. The name Israel first appears in the Bible as the divinely bestowed second name of Jacob (Gen. 32:28; 35:10). "Sons of Israel" or "children of Israel" initially meant Jacob's sons and their families (Gen. 50:25; Ex. 1:1) and, more distantly, all of Jacob's descendants (e.g., Ex. 1:7, 9). After Jacob's posterity settled in the land of Canaan, the name Israel referred to the league of tribes bound together by a covenant with the Lord (Josh. 24). Later, the united monarchy of Saul, David, and Solomon was known as Israel (e.g., 1 Sam. 9:16; 13:13; 2 Sam. 5:3). After the breach following Solomon's death, the name Israel denoted the northern kingdom (1 Kgs. 11:34–39; 12:3, 16), while the name Judah designated the southern realm (1 Kgs. 12:23, 27). After the northern kingdom fell to the Assyrians in 722 B.C., the name Israel became a spiritual designation for the southern kingdom (e.g., Isa. 5:7; Micah 3:1; Zech. 12:1; 1 Macc. 1:11, 62). The term "Jew" was first applied by outsiders to those living in the kingdom of Judah and first appears in 2 Kings 16:6.

In the New Testament, the name Israel refers to the people of God, not usually in a nationalistic sense but designating those who are, or will be, gathered to Jesus Christ by obeying the word of God (e.g., Matt. 10:6–7; Luke 24:21; John 1:31, 49; Acts 2:22, 36). It also refers to Christ's kingdom (Matt. 27:42; Mark 15:32), into which Gentiles will be grafted as if into an olive tree (Rom. 11:17–21). Two passages in Galatians clearly equate Israel with the early Christian church (Gal. 3:27–29; 6:15–16), and the connection is also affirmed by Jesus' statement that his apostles will judge the tribes of Israel (Matt. 19:28; cf. 1 Ne. 12:9; D&C 29:12).

In the Book of Mormon, several phrases appear with distinctive applications. The phrase "children of Israel" regularly refers back to Jacob's descendants in the Mosaic era, echoing the language of the Exodus account (e.g., Ex. 19:1; 1 Ne. 17:23; Jacob 1:7; Mosiah 7:19; cf. 3 Ne. 29:1–2). God's title Holy One of Israel, drawn from Isaiah (e.g., 48:17; 1 Ne. 20:17), appears in discussions of God's covenants, affirming him to be the faithful God who made covenants with ancient Israel (e.g., 1 Ne. 19:14–17). This title also appears in prophecies concerning God's future "reign in dominion, and might, and power, and great glory" (1 Ne. 22:24–25). The Holy One of Israel is identified as Jesus Christ (2 Ne. 25:29). "House of Israel" refers to the lineal posterity of Jacob and is frequently used in prophetic utterances that have to do with their scattering or latter-day gathering. Moreover,

Book of Mormon people saw themselves as a "remnant" or "branch" of the house of Israel whose descendants would receive the blessings promised to Israel in the latter days (1 Ne. 19:24; 3 Ne. 20:16).

For two major reasons, Latter-day Saints today apply the name Israel to themselves. First, Moses appeared to Joseph SMITH, and Oliver COWDERY in the KIRTLAND TEMPLE on April 3, 1836, and conferred on them the KEYS, or authorization, for "the gathering of Israel" (D&C 110:11; cf. *PWJS*, pp. 145–46). This gathering consists not only in restoring people of Israelite ancestry "to the lands of their inheritance" but also in bringing them "out of obscurity and out of darkness; and they shall know that the Lord is . . . the Mighty One of Israel" (1 Ne. 22:12). This action means bringing them into the Church. Second, Latter-day Saints have often learned from their PATRIARCHAL BLESSINGS that they are literally of the lineage of Israel (D&C 86:8–9), primarily the tribes of EPHRAIM and Manasseh. The Lord has revealed that it is the particular responsibility of Israel to carry the message of the restored gospel to the world, and Ephraim has the responsibility of directing this work (D&C 133:26–34; cf. *TPJS*, p. 163). Those who are not of Israel's lineage become such through adoption at the time of their baptism and reception of the Holy Ghost (*TPJS*, pp. 149–50; Rom. 8:15–17; Gal. 4:5–7; Abr. 2:10; *see also* LAW OF ADOPTION).

LINEAL ISRAEL. Israel's consciousness of lineal distinction was related at least in part to God's formal adoption of it by covenant at the holy mount. "Now therefore, if ye will obey my voice indeed, and keep my covenant, then ye shall be a peculiar treasure unto me above all people . . . and ye shall be unto me a kingdom of priests, and an holy nation" (Ex. 19:5–6). As the chosen people of God, Israel was under a divine obligation to bear the covenant and its promises to others, an obligation established earlier with Abraham and his seed (Abr. 2:9–11; *see also* ABRAHAMIC COVENANT).

The Book of Mormon peoples were literally of Israel. Those who journeyed to the Western Hemisphere from Jerusalem with LEHI around 600 B.C. were descended from JOSEPH OF EGYPT through his sons Manasseh and Ephraim (Alma 10:3; cf. 1 Ne. 5:14–16; *JD* 23:184–85). A second group had links to the royal house of Judah through MULEK, son of Zedekiah (Hel. 6:10; Omni 1:14–16). Several prophecies deal with the eventual restoration of God's covenant among the descendants of these peoples (e.g., 1 Ne. 22:3–12; 3 Ne. 20:22–27; 21:1–7). As a natural corollary, several prophecies focus on the scattering and eventual return of many of the Jews to Jerusalem and the blessings that await them there (e.g., 2 Ne. 6:10–14; 3 Ne. 20:29–46; Ether 13:5). As with other covenants, promises are fulfilled only when people—whether Gentiles or Israelites—obey the commandments of God (e.g., 1 Ne. 14:5–6; 22:17–22).

Today, members of the Church—latter-day Israel, largely Joseph's descendants either by blood or adoption—are to seek out the other descendants of Israel and those who would become Israelites through adoption by baptism. The Prophet Joseph Smith observed that "as the Holy Ghost falls upon one of the literal seed of Abraham, it is calm and serene; . . . while the effect of the Holy Ghost upon a Gentile, is to purge out the old blood, and make him actually of the seed of Abraham. That man that has none of the blood of Abraham (naturally) must have a new creation by the Holy Ghost" (*TPJS*, pp. 149–50; cf. Rom. 6:4; 12:2).

SPIRITUAL ISRAEL. In both ancient and modern times, keeping God's covenants has been the heart of becoming and remaining the people of God (e.g., Ex. 19:5–6; Deut. 4:32–40; D&C 100:15–16). At the physical center of Israel, so to speak, stood the house of God's spiritual blessings, where covenants were made and remade, first the tabernacle in the camp and later the temple in Jerusalem. Almost immediately after giving the Ten Commandments and other terms of the covenant (Ex. 20–23), God gave directions for fashioning the tabernacle (Ex. 24–27), the most sacred structure of Moses' Israel, "that I [God] may dwell among them" (Ex. 25:8). Latter-day Saints have also been commanded by the God of Israel to build temples for worship and for making covenants, so that the lives of men and women will be enriched through eternal family sealings (D&C 110:6–10; cf. *TPJS*, p. 186; *WJS*, p. 212; *see also* TEMPLES).

In the New Testament era Gentiles were offered a broad opportunity to become full partakers of Israel's blessings. While Jesus limited his personal ministry to Israelites (Matt. 15:24; cf. 3 Ne. 15:23) and told the Twelve to proselytize only among Israel (Matt. 10:5), he visited Gentiles in the Decapolis, near Galilee (Matt. 8:28–34), and sent his seventy disciples into areas where there were many Gentiles (Luke 10:1–17). He prophesied that many "shall come from the east and west, and shall sit down with Abraham, and Isaac, and Jacob, in the kingdom of heaven" (Matt. 8:11). John the Baptist proclaimed that "God is able of these stones to raise up children unto Abraham" (Matt. 3:9), evidently referring to the adoption of Gentiles into the house of Israel (*TPJS*, p. 319). Peter learned that the righteous in "every nation" who hearken to God are "accepted with him" (Acts 10:35). Even so, Paul reminded readers to "boast not against the branches" of the tree of Israel when they falter because "all Israel shall be saved" (Rom. 11:18, 26).

The Book of Mormon preserves a prophecy of Joseph of Egypt (2 Ne. 3:5–21) wherein the Lord promised Joseph that "a choice seer will I raise up out of the fruit of thy loins . . . [to bring] them to the knowledge of the covenants which I have made with thy fathers" (2 Ne. 3:7). The "work" of this seer includes bringing forth a record written by Joseph's descendants that will be joined to a record from the tribe of Judah, to bring Israelites "to the knowledge of their fathers in the latter days, and also to the knowledge of my covenants, saith the Lord" (2 Ne. 3:11–12). The record from Joseph's lineage is the Book of Mormon and that from Judah's is the Bible (cf. Ezek. 37:15–23; *see also* BOOK OF MORMON, BIBLICAL PROPHECIES ABOUT). The prophecy states that the seer "shall be called after me [Joseph]; and it shall be after the name of his father. And he shall be like unto me" (2 Ne. 3:15). For Latter-day Saints, this seer is Joseph Smith. Moreover, the Book of Mormon is an instrument for bringing about the restoration of gospel covenants and Israel's gathering. About 600 B.C. the Lord spoke to NEPHI₁ concerning both the Gentiles and Nephi's posterity: "I will manifest myself unto thy seed, that they shall write many things which I shall minister unto them, which shall be plain and precious; . . . behold, these things shall be hid up, to come forth unto the Gentiles, by the gift and power of the Lamb. And in them shall be written my gospel, saith the Lamb" (1 Ne. 13:35–36). On the title page of the Book of Mormon, one finds these words written about A.D. 400 stating the purpose of the work: "Which is to show unto the remnant of the House of Israel what great things the Lord hath done for their fathers; and that they may know the covenants of the Lord, that they are not cast off forever" (*see* BOOK OF MORMON: TITLE PAGE).

The gathering of Israel could not proceed until the restoration of the keys or authorization for this effort. On April 3, 1836 (Passover time), both Moses and Elijah appeared to Joseph Smith and Oliver Cowdery in the Kirtland Temple, Elijah restoring the sealing powers for turning the hearts of the children to the promises made to their ancestors (cf. Mal. 4:5–6; D&C 2:1–3; JS—H 1:38–39) and Moses the keys for gathering Israel (D&C 110:11, 13–16; cf. *TPJS*, pp. 337–38; *PWJS*, pp. 186–87).

LAND OF ISRAEL. While the phrase "land of Israel" is used relatively infrequently in the earlier parts of the Old Testament and is likely the work of a later hand (e.g., 1 Sam. 13:19; 2 Kgs. 5:2), the concept of a definable land given to Israel as an inheritance is at least as old as Abraham (e.g., Gen. 12:7; Abr. 2:6; *see also* PROMISED LAND). Furthermore, it is clear that continued obedience was required for retaining possession of it. For the Lord promised Abraham—with a caution—that his descendants would receive a "land which I will give unto thy seed after thee for an everlasting possession, when they hearken to my voice" (Abr. 2:6; cf. also Lev. 18:25–28; Jer. 16:12–13).

The concept of multiple lands of inheritance is taught in the Book of Mormon. This plurality of territories is joined to the notion of inheritance, as expressed by Isaiah. In most cases, the Book of Mormon writer cites Isaiah about the gathering of Israel to its lands. For instance, Jacob predicted that the house of Israel "shall be gathered home to the lands of their inheritance, and shall be established in all their lands of promise" (2 Ne. 9:2, after quoting Isa. 49:24–52:2; cf. 2 Ne. 6:11; 10:7–8). Significantly, in each instance a spiritual transformation of Israel is to accompany the gathering to lands: "And they shall be brought out of obscurity and out of darkness; and they shall know that the Lord is their Savior and their Redeemer, the Mighty One of Israel" (1 Ne. 22:12). Again, God "has spoken unto the Jews, by the mouth of his holy prophets, even from the beginning [and will continue] . . . until the time comes that they shall be restored to the true church and fold of God" (2 Ne. 9:2; cf. 30:2; 3 Ne. 16:4; 20:13, 31).

The resurrected Jesus stated that there are at least two lands to which descendants of the house of Israel are to be gathered. To hearers of the lineage of Joseph in the Western Hemisphere, he declared that "the Father hath commanded me that I should give unto you this land, for your inheritance" (3 Ne. 20:14; cf. 20:22; Ether 13:6–10). Concerning the Jews, the risen Jesus said, "I will remember the covenant which I have made with my people . . . [that] I would give unto them again the land of their fathers for their inheritance, which is the land of Jerusalem, which is the promised land unto them forever, saith the Father" (3 Ne. 20:29; cf. Ether 13:5, 11). Latter-day scripture indicates that the ten tribes will come first to the Americas, where they will "be crowned with glory, even in Zion" (D&C 133:26–34) and then will inherit the land of their ancestors (3 Ne. 20–21).

STATE OF ISRAEL. LDS leaders have viewed the creation of the modern state of Israel in the Middle East as a consequential world event but not as the complete fulfillment of prophecy. After noting the glory of God's work yet to be done among all branches of Israel and after discussing the redemption promised to Judah, Bruce R. McConkie, an apostle, wrote of the present immigration of a few million Jewish people to the Holy Land, "Is this the latter-day gathering of which the scriptures speak? No! It is not. . . . [It] is nonetheless part of divine plan" of a more complete gathering yet to occur (p. 229).

BIBLIOGRAPHY

Hunter, Howard W. "All Are Alike unto God." *Ensign* 9 (June 1979):72–74.

McConkie, Bruce R. *The Millennial Messiah*, pp. 182–329. Salt Lake City, 1982.

Nelson, Russell M. "Thanks for the Covenant." *Devotional and Fireside Speeches [BYU]*, 1988–89, pp. 53–61. Provo, Utah, 1989.

S. KENT BROWN

SCATTERING OF ISRAEL

The scattering of Israel, as foretold throughout the Bible and the Book of Mormon, is evidence of fulfilled prophecy. On the one hand, Abraham received promises that his children would possess a dwelling place as long as they remained faithful to God's commands (Abr. 2:6); on the other, prophets from Moses on warned that spiritual rebellion would lead to their removal from the promised land (Lev. 18:26–28; 26:21–33). During the divided monarchy, Israelite prophets pled for a re-

turn to neglected covenants to assure the Lord's promised protection (e.g., Hosea 6:1–3; Amos 5:4–9; Isa. 49; 50:1–3; 51–52; Jer. 3:12–19; 18:11). After they rejected prophetic warnings, both Israel and Judah were scattered.

The scattering occurred in three primary phases: (1) the Assyrian captivity of the northern kingdom of ten of the tribes of Israel (c. 722 B.C.); (2) the Babylonian captivity of the kingdom of Judah (c. 587 B.C.); and (3) the destruction of the Judean state and second temple by Rome (A.D. 66–70). While other cases of scattering occurred, these phases accomplished the Lord's purposes of punishing his covenant people by scattering them; but he mercifully made preparation for gathering their descendants in the latter years when they "come to the knowledge of their Redeemer" (2 Ne. 6:8–14).

Numerous references to Israel's scattering appear in scripture. Isaiah, Jeremiah, Ezekiel, NEPHI₁, and others wrote much concerning it (e.g., Isa. 50–53; Jer. 3; 18; Ezek. 6:8–10; 11–12; 36; 2 Ne. 10). Perhaps the most notable of these is the prophecy of ZENOS given "unto the house of Israel" and cited in the Book of Mormon by JACOB, son of LEHI (Jacob 5). In language similar to Isaiah 5:1–7 and echoed in Romans 11:17–24, Zenos compared the history of the house of Israel to an olive tree planted in a vineyard, likening it to a "tame olive tree" that begins to decay. GENTILES, represented in Zenos' allegory as branches from a wild olive tree, were grafted onto the tame tree to preserve its natural fruit. Servants assisted the lord of the vineyard in providing the best conditions for growth—digging, pruning, fertilizing, and finally transplanting, grafting, and pruning. Meanwhile, they planted branches of the mother tree in remote parts of the orchard. In three "visits" to the vineyard (Jacob 5:4, 16, 30), the lord and his servants labored to produce desirable olives that could be stored for "the season, which speedily cometh" (5:76). Finally, the desired fruit appeared, which greatly pleased the lord of the vineyard (5:38–75).

Joseph Fielding SMITH, a modern APOSTLE, summed up this allegory thus: "It records the history of Israel down through the ages, the scattering of the tribes to all parts of the earth; . . . or in other words the mixing of the blood of Israel among the Gentiles by which the great blessings and promises of the Lord to Abraham are fulfilled" (*Answers to Gospel Questions*, Salt Lake City, 1963, Vol. 4, pp. 141–42).

Book of Mormon prophets and the resurrected Savior also spoke of the scattering. Reflecting on his people's situation in a new land, Nephi₁ noted that they were part of scattered Israel that would one day be gathered (1 Ne. 22:3–5, 7–12). Jacob observed, "We have been driven out of the land of our inheritance; but we have been led to a better land" (2 Ne. 10:20–22). The resurrected Jesus told hearers in the Americas that though the prophesied scattering was not yet complete, the promised gathering was certainly forthcoming (3 Ne. 20:11–18, 29–46; 21:1–9, 26–29).

The scattering of Israel interests Latter-day Saints because of the promise of the latter-day gathering, which began in 1829 when the Lord restored the PRIESTHOOD through the Prophet Joseph Smith. Then, on April 3, 1836, Moses appeared and gave the keys, or authorization, of gathering to Joseph Smith and Oliver COWDERY in the Kirtland Temple. Today, commissioned by those with priesthood authority, missionaries gather latter-day Israel back to the covenant, to acceptance of their Redeemer, teaching them in the nations to which their ancestors were long ago dispersed.

BIBLIOGRAPHY

Jackson, Kent P. "Nourished by the Good Word of God." In *Studies in Scripture*, ed. K. Jackson, Vol. 7, pp. 185–95. Salt Lake City, 1987.

Richards, LeGrand. *Israel, Do You Know?* Salt Lake City, 1982.

DOUGLAS A. STEWART

LOST TRIBES OF ISRAEL

Events leading to the separation of the ten tribes of Israel—later known as the ten lost tribes—are linked to the division of the Israelite monarchy (c. 930 B.C.). Following their upstart king, Jeroboam, the northern kingdom of Israel apostatized from COVENANTS they had made with the Lord (1 Kgs. 12:26–30). ISAIAH warned that the Assyrian army would become "the rod of [God's] anger" (Isa. 10:5); the PROPHECY was fulfilled when the Assyrians took most of the people in the northern tribes into captivity (2 Kgs. 17:23). For LATTER-DAY SAINTS, the lost tribes are Israelites other than either the Jewish people or the LAMANITES of the Book of Mormon (2 Ne. 29:13). LDS sources provide some information about their situation and announce that descendants of these lost tribes will be vitally involved in events of the LAST DAYS.

The Lord revealed through Old Testament PROPHETS that the ten tribes would return and receive promised blessings. Isaiah prophesied "that the Lord shall set his hand again . . . to recover the remnant of his people" (Isa. 11:11). JEREMIAH declared that "remnants" would come from "the land of the north" (Jer. 3:18; 16:14–15; cf. 23:7–8; 31:8) and that the Lord would "make a new covenant" with them (Jer. 31:31).

Book of Mormon prophets affirmed that the Lord had not forgotten the ten tribes, and that they are keeping records that will yet be revealed (2 Ne. 29:12–14). When the resurrected Jesus Christ appeared in the Americas, he spoke of being commanded of the Father to minister unto the lost tribes, "for they are not lost unto the Father" (3 Ne. 17:4). Jesus also promised that the Lord's redemptive work in the last days would include "the tribes which have been lost" (3 Ne. 21:26).

For the lost tribes to receive their promised blessings in the last days, priesthood KEYS or authorization had to be restored. On April 3, 1836, MOSES appeared to the Prophet Joseph SMITH and Oliver COWDERY in the KIRTLAND TEMPLE and committed to them the "keys of the gathering of Israel . . . and the leading of the ten tribes from the land of the north" (D&C 110:11). These keys still rest with the PRESIDENT OF THE CHURCH. In time, the ten tribes are to be "crowned with glory . . . by the hands of the servants of the Lord, even the children of Ephraim" (D&C 133:26–34). Elder James E. Talmage also affirmed that "the tribes shall come; they are not lost unto the Lord; they shall be brought forth as hath been predicted" (CR [Oct. 1916]:76). Plainly, according to scripture and teachings of LDS leaders, descendants of the lost tribes—wherever they may be—have continued to receive divine attention and will receive future blessings.

BIBLIOGRAPHY

Smith, Joseph Fielding. *The Way to Perfection*, chap. 20. Salt Lake City, 1968.

Talmage, James E. "The Dispersion of Israel." In *AF*, pp. 314–29.

DAVID L. BOLLIGER

GATHERING OF ISRAEL

Latter-day Saints "believe in the literal gathering of Israel and in the restoration of the Ten Tribes; [and] that Zion (the New Jerusalem) will be built upon the American continent" (A of F 10). In the LDS perspective, gathering Israel in the latter days consists of the following: (1) the spiritual gathering, which includes coming to know that Jesus is the Christ and joining The Church of Jesus Christ of Latter-day Saints; (2) the assembling of Church members to organized STAKES; and (3) the gathering of the descendants of Jacob's twelve sons—including the lost ten tribes (D&C 110:11)—to the lands of their inheritance. These gatherings are necessary because of ancient apostasies that resulted in the dispersion of Israel into all nations (Deut. 4:27; 28:64; Jer. 16:13; Hosea 9:17).

Israelite PROPHETS, foreseeing Israel's scattering, also foretold her gathering in the LAST DAYS (1 Kgs. 22:17; Jer. 31:7–12; 32:37–40; Ezek. 36:24; etc.). According to ISAIAH, Israel will come to know that the Lord is Savior, be gathered again, direct her own affairs, and rebuild JERUSALEM (Isa. 52:1–2; D&C 113:7–10). Anciently, the Lord brought Israel out of Egypt, and Isaiah prophesied a future recovery of Israel from many lands (Isa. 11:11–13; cf. 2 Ne. 6:14; *TPJS*, pp. 14–15; Benson, 1977, pp. 137–38).

The spiritual gathering of Israel through CONVERSION to the restored GOSPEL OF JESUS CHRIST is to be accomplished by the elders of the Church (D&C 133:8) who are set apart and sent out as "fishers" and "hunters" to "hunt them from every mountain, and from every hill, and out of the holes of the rocks" (Jer. 16:16) and to call them to ZION and her stakes (D&C 133:4–9; Isa. 54).

The Book of Mormon and Doctrine and Covenants are seen as tools "to gather out mine elect" from all the earth (Moses 7:62; Benson, *Ensign* 16 [Nov. 1986]:78–80). The risen Jesus declared "that when the words of Isaiah should be fulfilled . . . then is the fulfilling of the covenant" that the Father made to gather Israel (3 Ne. 20:11–13). Further, he proclaimed that the Book of Mormon would come forth as a sign that scattered Israel was about to be gathered (3 Ne. 20–21). NEPHI$_1$ quoted Isaiah 48 and 49, which he regarded as a herald of Israel's future gathering and glory (1 Ne. 20–22).

The priesthood KEYS, or authorization, to gather Israel were restored to the Prophet Joseph SMITH and Oliver COWDERY on April 3, 1836, in the KIRTLAND TEMPLE. "Moses appeared before us, and committed unto us the keys of the gathering of Israel from the four parts of the earth, and the leading of the ten tribes from the land of the north" (D&C 110:11). This authority is now held by the PRESIDENT OF THE CHURCH. That portion of Israel known as the Ten Tribes will yet be led from the north. Their gathering will be accomplished in part as they are converted to the Lord, receive the blessings of the gospel, and return to "the land of their ancient inheritance" (McConkie, 1982, pp. 321, 324–26).

Both the spiritual and the literal characteristics of gathering were emphasized by the Lord in the following interpretation of the PARABLE of the wheat and tares: "I must gather together my people, according to the parable of the wheat and the tares, that the wheat may be secured in the garners to possess eternal life, and be crowned with celestial glory" (D&C 101:65; also 86:7–10). Joseph Smith declared that in all ages the divine purpose of gathering is to build TEMPLES so that the Lord's children can receive the highest ORDINANCES and thereby gain ETERNAL LIFE (*TPJS*, pp. 307–308, 314).

The gathering of Israel continues in the post-earthly SPIRIT WORLD where Christ "organized his forces and appointed messengers . . . and commissioned them to go forth and carry the light of the gospel to them that were in darkness, even to all the spirits of men" so that they too may be gathered (D&C 138:30, 34; cf. 1 Pet. 3:18–19). In the implementation of this gathering, ordinances such as BAPTISM and CONFIRMATION are performed in latter-day temples by Church members on behalf of the dead (cf. 1 Cor. 15:29).

The physical gathering of Israel is a concomitant of the spiritual gathering. The Lord's servants are to unite and "come forth to Zion, or to her stakes, the places of thine appointment" (D&C 109:39). In 1830 the Lord commanded the Saints to gather into "one place" (D&C 29:8), the first place being in OHIO. In July of 1831 he revealed that "the land of Missouri" was "appointed and consecrated for the gathering of the saints" and INDEPENDENCE, MISSOURI, was established as the "center place" (D&C 57:1–3). In 1838, after the Church had expanded, the Lord spoke of "gathering together upon the land of Zion, and upon her stakes" (D&C 115:6; cf. Isa. 54:2–3; D&C 101:21–22).

MISSIONARIES were sent out after the Church was organized (1830) to gather both spiritual and bloodline Israel. In the spirit of gathering, many converts immigrated from the eastern states, Canada, Britain, and Western Europe, first to Ohio, then Missouri, Illinois, and eventually the Great Basin. Between 1840 and 1890, more than eighty thousand converts came from continental Europe and fifty-five thousand from Great Britain (P. A. M. Taylor, *Expectations Westward* [Edinburgh, 1965], p. 144).

At the turn of the century and thereafter, converts were no longer asked to immigrate to America and the West. As Spencer W. KIMBALL reemphasized, converts were to remain in their own lands, where stakes of Zion would be established and temples built, allowing members all the privileges of the gospel in their native countries. He urged the Saints to establish "multiple Zions" and to gather together in their own "culture and nation" (Kimball, pp. 438–40; cf. Palmer, pp. 33–42).

The gathering of Israel includes the LAMANITES. To their ancestors in the Americas, the resurrected Jesus promised: "This people will I establish in this land, unto the fulfilling of the covenant which I made with your father Jacob" (3 Ne. 20:22, 25; 21:1–7).

The gathering of Jews to the state of Israel will continue. Joseph Smith's associates and successors predicted that their initial gathering would be in unbelief (*JD* 4:232; 11:245; 18:64–66; cf. 16:352; 18:225). Elder Bruce R. McConkie calls this a "gathering of the unconverted to Palestine . . . a political gathering" (1982, pp. 229–30). This "preliminary gathering" is to precede Christ's coming to the Jews on the Mount of Olives, when he will personally manifest himself to them (2 Ne. 6:14; cf. Zech. 13:6; D&C 45:48–53; JS—M 1:37).

The land of Canaan was promised to ABRAHAM and his posterity on condition of their RIGHTEOUSNESS (Abr. 2:6), a promise later reiterated to Isaac and Jacob (Gen. 12:7; 26:3; 35:12). Of the descendants of Jacob, the Jews have maintained their identity throughout the ages. As descendants of Abraham, Isaac, and Jacob, the people of Judah are to return to their ancestral lands (D&C 109:64). At the dedication of the Kirtland Temple, Joseph Smith pled with the Lord that "the children of Judah may begin to return to the lands which thou didst give to Abraham, their father" (D&C 109:62–64). Orson HYDE, an early apostle, was called and ordained by Joseph Smith to dedicate Palestine for the return of the Jews. On October 24, 1841, Hyde climbed the Mount of Olives, prayed to "dedicate and consecrate this land . . . for the gathering together of Judah's scattered remnants," and erected a mound of stones to commemorate the event (*HC* 4:456–59).

The Book of Mormon states that the Jews "shall be gathered in from their long dispersion, from the isles of the sea, and from the four parts of the earth" (2 Ne. 10:8; cf. 25:15–17). Moreover, MORMON, editor and compiler of the Book of Mormon, declared that "ye need not any longer hiss, nor spurn, nor make game of the Jews, nor any of the remnant of the house of Israel; for behold, the Lord remembereth his covenant unto them, and he will do unto them according to that which he hath sworn" (3 Ne. 29:8).

[*See also* Zionism.]

BIBLIOGRAPHY

Benson, Ezra Taft. "A Message to Judah from Joseph." *Ensign* 6 (Dec. 1976):67–72.

———. *This Nation Shall Endure.* Salt Lake City, 1977.

Kimball, Spencer W. *The Teachings of Spencer W. Kimball*, ed. Edward L. Kimball. Salt Lake City, 1982.

McConkie, Bruce R. "Come: Let Israel Build Zion." *Ensign* 7 (May 1977):115–18.

———. *The Millennial Messiah: The Second Coming of the Son of Man.* Salt Lake City, 1982.

Palmer, Spencer J. *The Expanding Church.* Salt Lake City, 1978.

Talmage, James E. "The Gathering of Israel." In *AF*, pp. 328–44.

TERRY L. NIEDERHAUSER

ISRAELITES

See: Covenant Israel, Latter-day

JACKSON COUNTY

See: Missouri; LDS Communities in Jackson and Clay Counties

JACOB, SON OF LEHI

Jacob was the fifth son of LEHI and Sariah and the elder of the two sons born during the days of his parents' wilderness tribulation. His birth apparently occurred soon after the family left JERUSALEM (c. 599 B.C.). Jacob's life demonstrated him to be a spiritual leader: He was a defender of the faith, keeper of the sacred records, visionary, doctrinal teacher, expressive writer, and plainspoken servant of Christ.

From birth, Jacob was a child of affliction. As Lehi's firstborn in the wilderness, he never knew the family's earlier life in Jerusalem or indeed any period of sustained family harmony. Rather, he grew up knowing only the hardships of a nomadic life, coupled with deepening dissensions between his two oldest brothers and the rest of the family—conflicts that would erupt into open violence before Jacob was forty years old (2 Ne. 5:34). This bitter family strife, which nearly killed his parents from grief on the sea voyage from the Near East to the Western Hemisphere, deeply distressed young

Jacob as well. Nephi records that Jacob and his younger brother, Joseph, "grieved because of the afflictions of their mother" while on the ship (1 Ne. 18:19). Lehi told young Jacob in a farewell blessing, "Thou hast suffered afflictions and much sorrow, because of the rudeness of thy brethren" (2 Ne. 2:1). Nevertheless, Lehi assured him that God "shall consecrate thine afflictions for thy gain" (2 Ne. 2:2).

Long affliction seems to have rendered Jacob all the more spiritually sensitive, and he became one of the most profound doctrinal teachers in the Book of Mormon. Near the time of his death, he summarized the harsh, melancholic conditions of his life in words of haunting beauty and deep humanity: "Our lives passed away like as it were unto us a dream, we being a lonesome and a solemn people, wanderers, cast out from Jerusalem, born in tribulation, in a wilderness, and hated of our brethren, which caused wars and contentions; wherefore, we did mourn out our days" (Jacob 7:26).

Lehi blessed Jacob to spend his days in the service of God and to live safely with NEPHI₁ (2 Ne. 2:3). From his youth to his death, Jacob indeed labored in the Lord's service (2 Ne. 5:26; Jacob 1:18), working closely with Nephi for many years. Nephi consecrated him a priest and a teacher (Jacob 1:18; 2 Ne. 5:26; 6:2), recorded one of his sermons (2 Ne. 6–10), and gave him a stewardship over the records on the small PLATES and other sacred objects (Jacob 1:2). This latter fact had notable consequences for the Book of Mormon, for all subsequent authors of the small plates were direct descendants of Jacob (see BOOK OF MORMON: BOOK OF ENOS; BOOK OF JAROM; BOOK OF OMNI).

Jacob was a powerful personal witness of the anticipated Redeemer, which was his most prominent theme. Nephi noted that "Jacob also has seen him [the premortal Christ] as I have seen him" (2 Ne. 11:3), and Lehi indicated that it was in his youth that Jacob had beheld the glory of the Lord (2 Ne. 2:4). So firm was Jacob's faith in Christ that Sherem, an anti-Christ, could not shake him by subtle argument, for, declared Jacob, "I truly had seen angels, and they had ministered unto me. And also, I had heard the voice of the Lord speaking unto me in very word, from time to time" (Jacob 7:5; cf. 7:12). Jacob was the first Nephite prophet to reveal that the Savior would be called Christ, having received that information from an angel (2 Ne. 10:3). He characterized his ministry as persuading his people to come unto Christ (Jacob 1:7). Likewise, he explained that he wrote on the plates so that future generations "may know that we knew of Christ, and we had a hope of his glory many hundred years before his coming" (Jacob 4:1–4). (Note: "Christ" is a Greek-English title, equivalent to Hebrew "Messiah," and it means "anointed," that is, divinely appointed as the Savior of mankind.)

A second prominent theme in the book of Jacob is the scattering and subsequent gathering of ISRAEL. Jacob spoke often and longingly of the Lord's promises to scattered Israel. In his first sermon in the Book of Mormon, Jacob quoted and commented extensively on Isaiah 50 about Israel's restoration (2 Ne. 6–8), assuring his people that "the Lord remembereth all them who have been broken off, wherefore he remembereth us also" (2 Ne. 10:22). Likewise, Jacob quoted the words of a prophet named ZENOS, in which God's love for the scattered branches of Israel was depicted through an allegory of the olive trees. "How merciful is our God unto us," exclaimed Jacob as he explained the allegory to his people, "for he remembereth the house of Israel, both roots and branches" (Jacob 6:4).

Jacob employed a unique style, the distinctive features of which are conspicuous in an exhortation in which he condemned the pride, materialism, and unchastity of his people. He began his sermon by confessing his "anxiety" over his people and over his painful duty to rebuke them for their sins (Jacob 2:3). In like fashion, Jacob prefaced his two other discourses by alluding to his "anxiety" (2 Ne. 6:3; Jacob 4:18). No other Book of Mormon prophet so begins a sermon; indeed, half the references to "anxiety" in the Book of Mormon occur in his writing.

Jacob's stylistic stamp is also evident in other features throughout his writings, which are replete with a vivid, intimate vocabulary either unique to him or disproportionally present. Two-thirds of the uses of "grieve" and "tender" (or their derivatives) are attributable to Jacob. Likewise, he is the only Book of Mormon author to use "delicate," "contempt," "lonesome," "sobbings," "dread," and "daggers." He deploys this last term in a metaphor about spiritual anguish: "daggers placed to pierce their souls and wound their delicate minds" (Jacob 2:9). Similarly, Jacob alone uses "wound" in reference to emotions, and never uses it (as do many others) to describe a physical injury. Jacob uses "pierce" or its variants four of nine instances in the Book of Mormon, and he alone uses it in a spiritual sense.

Such stylistic evidence suggests that Jacob lived close to his feelings and was gifted in expressing them. Moreover, the complex consistency of his style, linking as it does widely separated passages from two different books (2 Nephi and Jacob), bears out the portrait of the man that emerges from the narrative. Story, style, and subject matter all reveal Jacob, Lehi's child of tribulation, to have become a sensitive and effective poet-prophet, preacher, writer, and powerful witness of Jesus Christ.

BIBLIOGRAPHY

Matthews, Robert J. "Jacob: Prophet, Theologian, Historian." In *The Book of Mormon: Jacob through Words of Mormon, To Learn With Joy*, ed. M. Nyman and C. Tate, pp. 33–53. Provo, Utah, 1990.

Tanner, John S. "Literary Reflections on Jacob and His Descendants." In *The Book of Mormon: Jacob through Words of Mormon, To Learn With Joy*, ed. M. Nyman and C. Tate, pp. 251–69.

Warner, C. Terry. "Jacob." *Ensign* 6 (Oct. 1976):24–30.

JOHN S. TANNER

JAMES, EPISTLE OF

The Epistle of James has great prominence for Latter-day Saints. They believe that it was composed by James, the brother of the Lord (Gal. 1:19); that it was written to all the house of Israel, but particularly to those in this dispensation or era; and that it directly inspired Joseph SMITH to begin to seek answers from God in prayer. Several teachings from James, including those concerning "pure religion and undefiled," bridling the tongue and controlling anger, the interdependence of faith and works, and blessing the sick, are frequently cited in general conferences and in other Church talks.

That James addresses the lost tribes of ISRAEL (James 1:1) is significant, since Latter-day Saints believe that the ten tribes will be literally gathered in the latter days (A of F 10) and that the tribe of Ephraim, strongly represented in the Church, has the responsibility of carrying the PRIESTHOOD blessings of Abraham, Isaac, Jacob, and Joseph to the ten tribes (cf. D&C 133:20–35). The President of the Church holds the KEYS of the gathering of Israel (cf. D&C 110:11). Since the RESTORATION OF THE GOSPEL through Joseph Smith will effect the gathering, it is notable that Joseph Smith, while reading James 1:5, was deeply moved to prayer, which led to his FIRST VISION in 1820, an event that opened the way for the latter-day gathering of Israel (see ISRAEL: GATHERING OF ISRAEL). James's statement about not doubting also characterized Joseph Smith. Quoting James 1:5–6 and Hebrews 11:6, President David O. MCKAY stated, "In this scripture lies the secret of Joseph Smith's emergence from obscurity to world-wide renown. His belief in God was absolute, his faith in divine guidance unwavering" (IE 65 [Mar. 1962]:149). Many conference talks and presentations apply James 1:5 and Joseph Smith's First Vision to the potentials of prayer in solving life's problems.

Another passage often quoted is James 1:22–24, together with 2:14–18 and 24–26, on the relation between faith and works. Latter-day Saints believe in the "infinite and eternal" power of the ATONEMENT, that it will bring to all mankind an end to the basic effects of the FALL OF ADAM: it automatically forgives the sins of those who are without the law (e.g., children under the age of eight, mentally handicapped, and those who have not known the gospel), provides a universal RESURRECTION (cf. Mosiah 15), and restores mankind back to the presence of God for judgment. However, when individuals willfully rebel against the law that they know, they must repent, be obedient, and prove by their good works that they accept the grace of the Atonement for their personal sins. For such, forgiveness of personal sins through the Atonement is conditional upon their "works," as Latter-day Saints understand the word—faith, repentance, obedience, and serving others in many ways, including performing vicarious temple ordinances (see GRACE).

To underscore the need to serve others, Church leaders often cite James 1:27 on "pure religion and undefiled," relating it to Mosiah 2 in the Book of Mormon, wherein King BENJAMIN exhorts his people to serve selflessly and without concern for the recipient's social or economic status. By so living, people show the pure religion or charity of heart that is manifested in helping others without seeking personal credit. Much of this service is directed toward the young and the elderly, particularly when the traditional support of a nuclear family is not available. Thus, COMPASSIONATE SERVICE becomes a major component of "pure religion and undefiled."

A fourth principle from the Epistle of James appreciated by Latter-day Saints is the admonition to control one's temper and tongue (James 1:26; 3:3–10) and be patient in affliction (James 5). These extensions of the SERMON ON THE MOUNT are principles enunciated frequently by Church leaders.

Of special prominence in Church sermons is James 4:17, regarding sins of omission. Latter-day Saints are encouraged to perform service and good works, and they are reminded that while God judges the intent of the heart, he also requires his people to do every good thing, "for of him unto whom much is given much is required" (D&C 82:3). Further, this scripture is linked with D&C 58:26–29, in which members are encouraged to "be anxiously engaged in a good cause of their own free will."

Latter-day Saints hold a deep and firm belief in healing by faith through blessings by priesthood holders. Concerning this ordinance, D&C 42:43–44 corresponds to James 5:14–16 (see SICK, BLESSING THE). Olive oil is consecrated for the purpose of anointing the sick. Then in the healing ordinance one Melchizedek Priesthood bearer anoints, and another "seals" the anointing through prayer and blesses the sick person as inspired. Many can attest to miracles of healing through faith and the power of the priesthood; they consider them private and sacred. Far from being an "epistle of straw," as Luther called it, the Epistle of James is profound and very relevant for LDS theology.

BIBLIOGRAPHY

Dahl, Larry E. "A String of Gospel Pearls (James)." In *Studies in Scripture*, ed. R. Millett, Vol. 6, pp. 207–224. Salt Lake City, 1987.

McConkie, Bruce R. *Doctrinal New Testament Commentary*, Vol. 3, pp. 243–79. Salt Lake City, 1973.

Swensen, Russel B. *The New Testament: The Acts and the Epistles*, pp. 270–76. Salt Lake City, 1955.

THOMAS W. MACKAY

JAMES THE APOSTLE

James, the son of Zebedee and one of the original apostles of Jesus Christ, played an important part in the restoration of the GOSPEL OF JESUS CHRIST when he and his brother John appeared with Peter as heavenly messengers to the Prophet Joseph SMITH and Oliver COWDERY and conferred on them the MELCHIZEDEK PRIESTHOOD and the apostolic office, including the KEYS, or authority, of presidency. This ordination had been promised as forthcoming by John the Baptist on May 15, 1829, when he bestowed the AARONIC PRIESTHOOD on Joseph Smith and Oliver Cowdery (D&C 13; JS—H 1:68–73). In a revelation dated August 1830, the Lord refers to the restoration of the Melchizedek Priesthood and notes the participation of James: "Peter, and James, and John, whom I have sent unto you, by whom I have ordained you and confirmed you to be apostles, and especial witnesses of my name" (D&C 27:12). In a later epistle to the Church (D&C 128:20), Joseph Smith, reviewing the major events of the restoration, mentions this event and locates its happening near the Susquehanna River between Harmony, Pennsylvania, and Colesville, New York (*see* MELCHIZEDEK PRIESTHOOD: RESTORATION OF).

In the twenty-two references to him in the New Testament, James is never mentioned apart from either his brother John or Peter. In the lists of the apostles, he is always given precedence after Peter except on two occasions when Andrew's name follows Peter's, where it is clear that this order is due to his family connection (Matt. 10:2; Luke 6:14). James' importance is due to his membership in what may be called a presiding council. This idea is borne out by the fact that Peter, James, and John were members of a select circle and were privileged to be present with Jesus on special occasions from which other apostles were excluded, including the raising of the daughter of Jairus (Mark 5:22–23, 35–43), the TRANSFIGURATION on the mountain (Mark 9:2–9), and the agony in GETHSEMANE (Mark 14:32–42).

According to Joseph Smith and later presidents of the Church, James, with Peter and John, received special authority and keys from Jesus, Moses, and Elijah on the MOUNT OF TRANSFIGURATION. This was in addition to other keys received during their ordination as apostles that endowed them with power for their ministry as the

Joseph Smith Seeks Wisdom from the Bible, by Harold T. (Dale) Kilbourn (1970s, oil on canvas, 21″ × 22″). While reading James 1:5, Joseph Smith was inspired to ask God which church was right. Pondering this scripture, Joseph went to pray in a grove of trees near his home. There, God the Father and his son Jesus Christ appeared and instructed him (JS—H 1:11–20).

Presidency of the Twelve and the Church (*HC* 3:386–87; *DS* 2:165).

If their mother, Salome, was a sister of Mary, the mother of Jesus, as is generally believed, then James and John were cousins of Jesus. This may account for Salome's presuming to importune Jesus to grant her sons a special position in his kingdom (Matt. 20:20–23). It may also explain their impetuous zeal against the Samaritan village that denied Jesus' party entry, for which they were called Boanerges ("Sons of Thunder") (Luke 9:52–56; Mark 3:17). James was present with the other apostles in Jerusalem and was a witness of the RESURRECTION of Christ. He was the first of the apostles to be slain, being beheaded by Herod Agrippa I in A.D. 44 (Acts 12:2).

R. DOUGLAS PHILLIPS

JARED

See: Book of Mormon: Book of Ether

JAREDITES

The Jaredites are a people described in the book of Ether (*see* BOOK OF MORMON: BOOK OF ETHER) whose name derives from their first leader, Jared. The Jaredites date to the time of the "great tower" mentioned in the Old Testament (Gen. 11:1–9), which was built in or around Mesopotamia. Led by God, the Jaredites left their homeland for a new land somewhere in the Americas, and there they established a kingdom. They grew to be a numerous population with kings and prophets, and, like the Nephites after them, were eventually annihilated by internecine war evidently sometime between 600 and 300 B.C. Their story was recorded by their last prophet, Ether. Around A.D. 400, the last Nephite survivor, MORONI₂, abridged the record of Ether and appended his summary to the account of the Nephites that had been prepared by his father, MORMON. Although the record is brief, it hints at an epic genre rooted in the ancient Near East.

The Jaredite origin in the Old World probably dates to the third millennium B.C., which due to the scarcity of historical material presents obstacles to the use of comparative literature or archaeology. Parallels with the ancient Near East can only be

described in general forms, and no artifacts or writings identifiable as Jaredite have ever been found outside the Book of Mormon. But while parallels may be nebulous, certain Jaredite terms and names refer to practices, objects, or places in the ancient Near East. Several types, and a few specifics, may be analyzed in order to better understand the Jaredites and their civilization.

The principal theme of the Jaredite story is familiar in the genre of the ancient Near East. God calls a man to lead his people to a new and a promised land. Once settled in the land, the people alternate between stages of good and evil, relying on their king for guidance. When the king is good, the people tend to be good and follow God; when the king is evil, so too are the people. While parallels to the literature of the ancient Near East, especially the Old Testament, are apparent, the Jaredite narrative is unique in that the first leader, Jared, was not the one who received the call from God, but his brother (*see* BROTHER OF JARED). The roles of the two men differ, as do the roles of king and prophet in the Old Testament. From the earliest days after arriving in America, the Jaredites had a monarchical government apparently patterned after Bronze Age Mesopotamian society.

The story of the Jaredites has an epic flavor. Stories of heroes, kings, and princes who perform great deeds dominate the book of Ether. The heroes are great warriors who win decisive battles. Accounts dealing with cycles of life and death, good and evil, prosperity and hardship are the types of things that were done and written about in the epics in the book of Ether and the epics of the ancient Near East (*CWHN* 5:283–443).

The book of Ether begins with a genealogy spanning at least thirty generations, from the final prophet and historian Ether back to Jared. The list is reminiscent of genealogies in Old Testament or king lists common to antiquity. The thirty listed by name are:

Name	Number
Jared	1
Orihah	2
Kib	3
Shule	4
Omer	5
Emer	6
Coriantum	7
Com	8
Heth	9

Name	Number
Shez	10
Riplakish	11
Morianton	12
Kim	13
Levi	14
Corom	15
Kish	16
Lib	17
Hearthom	18
Heth	19
Aaron	20
Amnigaddah	21
Coriantum	22
Com	23
Shiblon(m)	24
Seth	25
Ahah	26
Ethem	27
Moron	28
Coriantor	29
Ether	30

Except for the lengthy accounts concerning the first and the last of these figures, all information about the people in this lineage is found in Ether, chapters 7–11. This dynasty endured for many centuries, always passing directly from father to son, except possibly in the case of Morianton, who was "a descendant of Riplakish," following him by an interval of "many years" (Ether 10:9).

The Jaredites crossed the sea to the New World in eight "barges" in 344 days, driven by currents and winds. Their route is unknown. Perhaps coincidentally, the North Pacific current takes about the same time to cross from Japan to Mexico (Sorenson, p. 111). The question of ancient long-distance sea travel has been much debated, but extensive indications have been found of pre-Columbian transoceanic voyaging (Sorenson and Raish). The Bering land bridge "is no longer recognized as the only scientifically acceptable theory to explain the means and timing of human entry into the New World" (Dixon, p. 27).

The design of the Jaredite barges is unclear. They were built according to instructions given by God. Ether described them as being "light upon the water" like a fowl (Ether 2:16). They were "tight like unto a dish; and the ends thereof were peaked." To allow light and air inside they had some sort of a "hole in the top, and also in the bottom" (Ether 2:17, 20). Ether also compared the barges with Noah's ark (Ether 6:7). Thus it may be relevant that Utnapishtim, the Sumerian Noah in the *Epic of Gilgamesh*, similarly is said to have built his boat with a ceiling and water plugs, and to have waterproofed the entire inside with bitumen. Utnapishtim's story also recounts the raging winds that slammed water into the mountains and people, vividly paralleling the Jaredites' experience of being driven by a furious wind (Ether 6:6).

Stones were made to shine by the touch of God's finger to light these barges. Shining stones are not unique to the book of Ether. One reference to a shining stone in Noah's ark appears in the Jerusalem Talmud, stating that a stone in the ark shone brighter in the night than in the day so that Noah could distinguish the times of day (*Pesachim* I, 1; discussed in *CWHN* 6:337–38, 349). Shining stones were also said to be present in the Syrian temple of the goddess Aphek (see *CWHN* 5:373) and are mentioned several times in the pseudepigraphic *Pseudo-Philo* (e.g., 25:12).

Little original detail remains about the culture of the Jaredite people. Some of them were obviously literate. While their royalty was strictly hereditary, sons sometimes deposed their fathers or were rivals to their brothers. Kings held their opponents in captivity for long periods, entered into SECRET COMBINATIONS, and waged battles. The record indicates that some of these kings were "anointed" (e.g., Ether 6:27; 9:4; 10:10), sat upon beautiful thrones (Ether 10:6), and had concubines (Ether 10:5–6). Their economy was basically agrarian. They were settled people, the ruling lines living most of their long history in a single land called Moron, somewhere near and north of what would later be called the Nephite "narrow neck of land." In some eras, the Jaredites built many cities and buildings (Ether 9:23; 10:5–12). One of their kings "saw the Son of Righteousness" (Ether 9:22). They once fought off a plague of poisonous snakes that came upon the land as a curse (Ether 10:19). At times they mined several ores (e.g. gold, silver, iron, copper) and made metal weapons and tools (Ether 7:9; 10:23–25; see BOOK OF MORMON ECONOMY AND TECHNOLOGY). "Elephants" were useful to them (Ether 9:19). This may refer to the mastodon or mammoth, but it is not possible to date the final disappearance of these animals in the New World. A section in the book of Ether talks of the hunt (10:19–21), a common pattern known in the Near East of the king who is also hunter. In this passage, the Jaredite king Lib designated the land to the south as a hunting preserve. An early Mesopotamian example of a royal hunter is Nimrod, who comes from about the same period as Jared. Other Jaredite parallels are of interest. The dance of Jared's daughter for the life of Omer (Ether 8:10) has been compared with similar incidents from ancient lore (*CWHN* 5:213).

The theophany of the brother of Jared, in which he sees the finger of the Lord, parallels the story of MOSES. The brother of Jared goes up a mountain to pray (Ether 3:1; cf. Ex. 3:1–3); sees the finger of the Lord (Ether 3:6; cf. Ex. 31:18); fears the Lord (also meaning "held in awe"; Ether 3:6; cf. Ex. 3:6); sees the whole spirit body of the Lord (Ether 3:13, 16–18; cf. Ex. 33:11); learns the name of the Lord (Ether 3:14; cf. Ex. 3:14); and, finally, receives a symbol of power and authority (Ether 3:23; cf. Ex. 4:1–5). The unique aspect of the story of the brother of Jared is his extended revelation concerning the nature of God, who appeared to him in a spirit body "like unto flesh and blood" (Ether 3:6).

Some Jaredite prophets were apparently similar to the prophets in biblical Israel. They condemned idolatry and wickedness, and foretold the annihilation of the society and destruction of the people unless they repented. Although some prophets received the protection of the government, most were rejected by the people, and, like Ether, were forced to hide for fear of their lives. Ether's prophecies looked beyond the despair of the final destruction of his people toward the future destiny of the Jaredite land. He foresaw it as the place of "the New Jerusalem, which should come down out of heaven, and the holy sanctuary of the Lord" (Ether 13:3).

The final battle reported by Ether took place at the hill Ramah, the same place where Mormon later buried the sacred Nephite records (Ether 15:11). The war involved two vast armies, and hostilities continued several days until all the soldiers and one of the kings were slain. An exhausted Coriantumr culminated his victory over Shiz by decapitating him. Near Eastern examples of decapitation of enemies are evident in early art and literature, as on the Narmer palette; and decapitation of captured kings is represented in ancient Mesoamerica (Warren, pp. 230–33). Coriantumr was later discovered by the people of Zarahemla (Mulekites), with whom he lived for "nine moons" (Omni 1:21). Ether's plates (historical records), together with the decayed remains from the final

Jaredite battle were later found by a group of lost Nephites who were searching for the city of Zarahemla (Mosiah 8:8–11).

Ether writes of the annihilation of his people, but this was not necessarily an extermination of the entire population. One may assume that many of the commoners were not in the two armies and thus survived after these wars. The Jaredite people were crushed and dispersed, but probably not exterminated, since explicit features of Jaredite culture (especially personal names) were later evident in the Nephite culture (*CWHN* 5:237–41; Sorenson, p. 119).

The similarity between the Jaredite and Nephite histories is striking. But the similarity may be chiefly one of literary convention, which Moroni used to compare the two peoples. Other than possessing similar epic tales of people who were led across the sea to build kingdoms that eventually fell, the underlying cultures were probably quite different; for example, the Jaredite laws and government predate the LAW OF MOSES, and thus their system of justice was different from that of the Israelites and Nephites.

The message drawn by Moroni from the histories of the Jaredites and the Nephites is, however, the same: God revealed himself to both peoples. He gave both a land of promise, where their prosperity was conditioned on righteousness. Both met their demise because of wickedness and secret combinations, and both endings are included in the Book of Mormon to teach this hard-learned lesson. Concerning this, Moroni states: "The Lord worketh not in secret combinations, neither doth he will that man should shed blood, but in all things hath forbidden it, from the beginning of man" (Ether 8:19).

BIBLIOGRAPHY

Hugh Nibley provides material on the Jaredites in *The World of the Jaredites* and *There Were Jaredites*, in Vol. 5 of *CWHN*; see also *CWHN* 6:329–58; reviewed and updated by D. Honey, "Ecological Nomadism Versus Epic Heroism in Ether," *Review of Books on the Book of Mormon* 2 (1990):143–63.

On the epic genre, see H. Munro Chadwick, *The Growth of Literature*, 3 vols. (Cambridge, England, 1932–1940), especially Vol. 1; Samuel Noah Kramer, "New Light on the Early History of the Ancient Near East," *American Journal of Archaeology* 52 (1948):156–64; David M. Knipe, "Epics," in *Encyclopedia of Religion*, Vol. 5, pp. 127–32, and T. G. Panches, "Heroes and Hero-Gods (Babylonian)," in James Hastings, ed., *Encyclopedia of Religion and Ethics*, Vol. 6, pp. 642–46 (New York, 1951).

Concerning kingship in the ancient Near East, see Henri Frankfort, *Kingship and the Gods* (Chicago, 1948). An English translation of the story of Noah's lighted stones may be found in Louis Ginzberg, ed., *The Legends of the Jews*, Vol. 1, pp. 162–63 (Philadelphia, 1937).

On possible ancient connections between the Old World and the New, see John L. Sorenson and Martin H. Raish, *Pre-Columbian Contact with the Americas Across the Oceans: An Annotated Bibliography* (Provo, Utah, 1990). See also Cyrus H. Gordon, *Before Columbus: Links Between the Old World and Ancient America* (New York, 1971); Carroll L. Riley, et al., eds., *Man Across the Sea: Problems of Pre-Columbian Contacts* (Austin, 1971), especially the chapter by Sorenson. See also E. James Dixon, "The Origins of the First Americans," *Archaeology* 38, no. 2 (1985):22–27; Thor Heyerdahl, *Early Man and the Ocean* (Garden City, N.Y., 1979); and Bruce W. Warren, "Secret Combinations, Warfare, and Captive Sacrifice in Mesoamerica and the Book of Mormon," in S. Ricks and W. Hamblin, eds., *Warfare in the Book of Mormon*, pp. 225–36 (Salt Lake City, 1990).

John L. Sorenson, *An Ancient American Setting for the Book of Mormon* (Salt Lake City, 1985), guides the reader through the archaeology of Mesoamerica and proposes possible Jaredite locations in areas occupied at comparable times, during the early and middle preclassic periods in Mexico, which include the Olmec civilization.

MORGAN W. TANNER

JEHOVAH, JESUS CHRIST

The GODHEAD consists of three separate and distinct beings: the Father, Son, and Holy Ghost (D&C 130:22; A of F 1). While some Christians do not equate Jesus Christ and Jehovah in their theologies, biblical passages indicate that relationship, and latter-day scriptures often refer to Jesus Christ, the Son, as Jehovah (e.g., D&C 110:3–4; Moro. 10:34).

The name Jehovah is an anglicized rendering of the tetragrammaton YHWH, a proper noun in biblical Hebrew that identifies God. Following a Jewish tradition that avoided pronouncing God's name, translators of the King James Version rendered almost all occurrences of YHWH as "LORD." Latter-day Saints view many other occurrences of "Lord" as references to Jehovah, both in the New Testament and in LDS scripture.

Since his PREMORTAL LIFE, Jesus Christ has functioned as the constant associate of the Father working under his direction. In 1916 the First Presidency and the Quorum of the Twelve Apostles issued a doctrinal statement on the relationship between the Father and the Son: "Jesus the Son has represented and yet represents Elohim His Father in power and authority. This is true of Christ in His preexistent, antemortal, or unembodied state, in the which He was known as Jehovah; also during His embodiment in the flesh; . . . and since that period in His resurrected state" (*MFP* 5:31–32).

Throughout scripture, several roles of Jehovah-Jesus Christ are specifically identified.

CREATOR. Jehovah as Creator is attested throughout the Old Testament (e.g., Ps. 24:1–2). Speaking to Moses, God said, "Worlds without number have I created; . . . and by the Son I created them, which is mine Only Begotten" (Moses 1:33). John and others acknowledged Jesus as the Word, the Creator: "In the beginning was the Word; . . . all things were made by him; and without him was not any thing made" (John 1:1–3, 14; cf. Eph. 3:9; Col. 1:16). Similarly, the Book of Mormon teaches, "The Lord Omnipotent who reigneth, who was, and is from all eternity to all eternity, shall come down from heaven among the children of men. . . . And he shall be called Jesus Christ, the Son of God, the Father of heaven and earth, the Creator of all things from the beginning" (Mosiah 3:5–8; cf. 2 Ne. 9:5; 3 Ne. 9:15).

LAWGIVER. To Moses, Jehovah identified himself by the title "I AM THAT I AM"—a variation on the verbal root of YHWH (Ex. 3:14). This title was claimed by Jesus in mortality: "Before Abraham was, I am" (John 8:58; cf. John 4:26). After his resurrection, Jesus told hearers in the Americas, "Behold, I am he that gave the law, and I am he who covenanted with my people Israel; therefore, the law in me is fulfilled, for I have come to fulfil the law" (3 Ne. 15:5; cf. Matt. 5:17).

REDEEMER, DELIVERER, AND ADVOCATE. Jehovah delivered the children of Israel from Egypt. Paul taught that this same being would redeem mankind from sin and death (cf. 1 Cor. 10:1–4). This point is made clear in the Book of Mormon: "The God of our fathers, who were led out of Egypt, . . . yea, the God of Abraham . . . yieldeth himself . . . as a man, into the hands of wicked men . . . to be crucified" (1 Ne. 19:10; cf. 2 Ne. 9:1–26; Mosiah 13:33–35). When the Savior appeared to the Prophet Joseph Smith in the Kirtland Temple on April 3, 1836, "his voice was as the sound of the rushing of great waters, even the voice of Jehovah, saying: I am the first and the last; I am he who liveth, I am he who was slain; I am your advocate with the Father" (D&C 110:3–4).

JUDGE. The Book of Mormon prophet Moroni₂ drew attention to "the great Jehovah, the Eternal Judge" (Moro. 10:34), reaffirming what the Psalmist and others had said (e.g., Ps. 9:7–8; Isa. 33:22). Jesus Christ proclaimed that he was the judge: "For the Father . . . hath committed all judgment unto the Son" (John 5:22, 27; cf. Acts 10:42).

IN HIS NAME. In the beginning, men began "to call upon the name of the LORD" (Gen. 4:25, 26; cf. Moses 5:8; 6:4). In Moses's time Jehovah instructed the priests to "put my name upon the children of Israel" (Num. 6:27; cf. Deut. 28:10). Before the coming of Christ, Book of Mormon people took upon themselves his name (Mosiah 5:8–12; Alma 34:38; *see* JESUS CHRIST, TAKING THE NAME OF UPON ONESELF). In all dispensations, the name of Christ is the only name "whereby salvation can come unto the children of men" (Isa. 43:3, 11; Mosiah 3:17; Acts 4:12; cf. Moses 5:7–9).

Divine names and titles, especially in the Bible, are occasionally ambiguous. The distinction between the Father and the Son is sometimes unclear. For example, the Hebrew term ELOHIM—a title usually applied to the Father by Latter-day Saints—often refers to Jehovah in the Bible (e.g., Isa. 12:2). Furthermore, people prayed to Jehovah as if he were the Father. In some cases, ambiguity may be due to the transmission of the text; in others, it may be explained by divine investiture wherein Christ is given the authority of the Father: "Thus the Father placed His name upon the Son; and Jesus Christ spoke and ministered in and through the Father's name; and so far as power, authority, and Godship are concerned His words and acts were and are those of the Father" (*MFP* 5:32).

BIBLIOGRAPHY

Talmage, James E. *JC*, pp. 32–41.

DAVID R. SEELY

JEREMIAH, PROPHECIES OF

The book of Jeremiah presents a number of elements that are significant for Latter-day Saints. Such features range from important doctrinal teachings connected with Jeremiah's call to his prophecies of the latter days. Notably, his work reveals more about him as a person than most other prophetic works do about their authors. Moreover, his definition of a TESTIMONY, hard won through years of persecution, is a classic: The word of God "was in mine heart as a burning fire" (Jer. 20:9).

In calling Jeremiah to be a PROPHET, the Lord explained that he had known Jeremiah and ordained him to be a prophet before his conception and birth (Jer. 1:4–10). LATTER-DAY SAINTS believe this refers to Jeremiah's PREMORTAL LIFE, during which the Lord ordained him and others to special assignments. Though foreordained to be a prophet, Jeremiah was not compelled to serve, and his first reaction was to object (1:6). However, it is apparent that, as Jeremiah exercised his AGENCY, he chose to accept the responsibilities conveyed by his FOREORDINATION and subsequent earthly calling to be a prophet.

A choice feature of Jeremiah's work is his portrait of the Lord's tender responses to people. Although through Jeremiah he denounced the behavior of his people and allowed them to be taken captive, the Lord still affirmed his affection for them. This attribute is seen in the divine laments recorded in Jeremiah 4:19–22, 8:18–9:3, and possibly 10:19–22. In Jeremiah 8:19, for example, the Lord says: "Behold the voice of the cry of the daughter of my people because of them that dwell in a far country: Is not the LORD in Zion? is not her king in her?" The Lord then responds to his own question: "For the hurt of the daughter of my people am I hurt" (8:21).

Another doctrinal contribution is Jeremiah's revelation of the Lord's foreknowledge of future events. Latter-day Saints see in Jeremiah's work evidence that the Lord knows the future and can reveal its relevant dimensions to his prophets. When Jeremiah was first called (627/6 B.C.), the ruling power in the Near East was Assyria. But he accurately predicted that Babylon would become dominant (Jer. 27:2–11), and warned his people that the Babylonian kings would conquer Jerusalem (32:28), take many captive (32:31–32), and then fall to another power (25:12) that would subsequently allow the Jews to return and rebuild Jerusalem (29:10).

Under inspiration, Jeremiah also saw the latter days, referring to them as "the days [to] come" (Jer. 30:3). In those days, he declared, the Lord would establish a "new" and "everlasting covenant" (31:31; 32:40). A significant feature of this new COVENANT would be the divinely authorized gathering of ISRAEL to former inheritances (23:5–8).

An element of interest in Jeremiah's prophetic work is the manner in which he taught object lessons (see TEACHER; TEACHER DEVELOPMENT). For instance, Jeremiah called attention to the impending fall of Jerusalem and captivity of her inhabitants by wearing the yoke of an ox (Jer. 27:2). He showed his faith in the eventual restoration of Israel to her homeland by buying a piece of land (32:1–15). He conveyed some of his messages with parables. In Jeremiah 18:1–10, the Lord inspired him to ask his listeners to observe a potter who had to rework some "marred" clay. He noted that the potter represented the Lord and the marred clay the inhabitants of Jerusalem. So poignantly disturbing was this parable that some of Jeremiah's listeners began to plot against his life (18:18–23). In Jeremiah 24:1–10 he declared that the Lord showed him two baskets of figs, one good and one inedible. The good figs represented those taken captive whom the Lord would "acknowledge." The inedible figs, which the Lord would discard, or have "removed," represented king Zedekiah, his princes, and those Judeans who had fled to Egypt.

Jeremiah and his writings were well respected by his contemporary, LEHI, and later Book of Mormon prophets who possessed a copy of some of Jeremiah's prophecies on the PLATES of brass (cf. 1 Ne. 5:13; 7:14). A later Book of Mormon prophet, NEPHI₂, indicates that Jeremiah had prophesied of the MESSIAH's first coming (Hel. 8:13–20). However, current texts of Jeremiah do not have clear references to this event, underscoring the observation that in the transmission of the biblical text parts may have been lost, or that Lehi may have possessed a fuller version. This is not surprising since ancient evidence both from Dead Sea fragments and from the Septuagint version of Jeremiah suggests that the text of his book has not been well preserved.

The book of Jeremiah presents rich insights into the attributes of God, the nature of prophets and prophecy, and varied teaching techniques. The available text of Jeremiah, however, suggests that scribes or others have allowed some parts that were "plain and precious" (cf. 1 Ne. 13:20–42) to be omitted.

BIBLIOGRAPHY

For Mormon thought on Jeremiah, see Sidney B. Sperry, *The Spirit of the Old Testament* (Salt Lake City, 1970), and S. Kent Brown, "History and Jeremiah's Crisis of Faith," in *Isaiah and the Prophets*, M. Nyman, ed. (Provo, Utah, 1984). For textual transmission, see William J. Adams, Jr., "Some Ways in which the 'Plain and Precious Parts' Became Lost (1 Ne. 13:20–42)," *Newsletter and Proceedings of the Society for Early Historic Archaeology* (No. 159 [July 1985]:1–6), and Ernst Würthwein, *The Text of the Old Testament* (Grand Rapids, Mich., 1979). For current views of Jeremiah, see Alexander Rofé, "Jeremiah, the book of," in *Harper's Bible Dictionary*, ed. P. J. Achtemeier (San Francisco, 1985), and John Bright, *Jeremiah*, The Anchor Bible (Garden City, N.Y., 1965).

WILLIAM J. ADAMS, JR.

JERUSALEM

Latter-day Saints view Jerusalem as a holy city, as do other Christians, Jews, and Muslims. The existence of Jerusalem as a unique holy place stems from at least the time that DAVID captured the city and made it his capital. With Solomon's efforts, the temple stood in Jerusalem as God's dwelling place (1 Kgs. 6). For a millennium, JEHOVAH was worshiped there, and his people looked for redemption in Jerusalem (Luke 2:38). Tradition holds that its former name was Salem (Gen. 14:18; Ps. 76:2), where MELCHIZEDEK reigned and ABRAHAM went to sacrifice Isaac. Later, Jesus Christ died there to atone for the sins of mankind. Concerning Jerusalem's future importance, latter-day scripture affirms biblical prophecies that Jerusalem is to be the scene of important events in the LAST DAYS.

Old Testament prophets spoke of the rise and demise of Jerusalem (e.g., 1 Kgs. 9:3; Micah 3:12). About 600 B.C., the future Book of Mormon prophet LEHI lived in the land of Jerusalem and encountered opposition when he called its inhabitants to repentance and prophesied the coming of the MESSIAH. He and his family were subsequently commanded by the Lord to flee the city, eventually journeying to the Western Hemisphere, where his descendants became two rival Book of Mormon peoples, the NEPHITES and the LAMANITES. Thus, from Jerusalem sprang the Book of Mormon saga.

Jerusalem was the scene of important events in Jesus' ministry. He taught and performed miracles there. No place was more holy to his followers than the temple, which Jesus considered the legitimate sanctuary of God, calling it "my Father's house" (John 2:16) and "my house" (Matt. 21:13). In an upper room of a house in Jerusalem, Jesus celebrated the Passover with his apostles, instituted the SACRAMENT, gave special meaning to the washing of feet, and revealed who would betray him. In GETHSEMANE and on Golgotha, Jesus accomplished the most selfless suffering in history, leading to his atoning sacrifice and resurrection.

Jesus mourned over the city as he recalled its past and envisioned its future (Matt. 23:37–39; Luke 19:41–44; 13:34–35). Like Jesus, Jerusalem would suffer indignities, anguish, and death (JS—M 1:18–22). But as Jesus lives again, so will Jerusalem (Isa. 52:1–2, 9; D&C 109:62). As part of the RESTORATION of all things, the holy city must be restored. The Prophet Joseph SMITH said, "Judah must return, Jerusalem must be rebuilt, and the temple, . . . and all this must be done before the Son of Man will make His appearance" (HC 5:337).

Jerusalem will be restored in its former place, be sanctified, and become a city of holiness, graced with a new temple (Zech. 2:12; 12:6; Ether 13:5, 11; 3 Ne. 20:29–36; D&C 77:15). Elder Orson Hyde, an apostle, journeyed to Jerusalem in 1841 to dedicate the land "for the building up of Jerusalem again . . . and for rearing a Temple in honor of [the Lord's] name" (HC 4:456).

Other events are yet to occur in Jerusalem: a major struggle will yet rage in Jerusalem's streets, that of Armageddon (Zech. 14); an earthquake will divide the Mount of Olives; and the Savior will appear to the Jews (D&C 45:48–53).

Two separate Jerusalems, the old and the new, will serve as headquarters of the millennial KINGDOM OF GOD from which Jesus will rule. Old Jerusalem will be built up by Judah. The NEW JERUSALEM, also to be known as ZION (D&C 45:66–67), will be built up in Jackson County, Missouri, by EPHRAIM, whose descendants largely make up The Church of Jesus Christ of Latter-day Saints. Isaiah foresaw the day when this second Jerusalem or Zion would be established: "For out of Zion shall go forth the law, and the word of the Lord from Jerusalem" (Isa. 2:3; cf. 64:10). MORONI₂, the last Book of Mormon prophet, first described the Jerusalem of old, then quoted the prophecy of Ether that "a New Jerusalem should be built up upon the land, unto the remnant of the seed of Joseph," and finally mentioned the "New Jerusalem, which should come down out of heaven" (Ether 13:3–12). John the Revelator also envisioned this final "Jerusalem, coming down from God out of heaven" (Rev. 21:2, 10). From this new Jerusalem, the city of Zion, God and the Lamb will reign over a celestialized earth (Moses 7:62–63; cf. DS 3:55–79).

This inscribed stone stands in the Orson Hyde Memorial Garden in Jerusalem (dedicated October 24, 1979). The text is repeated in Hebrew, Arabic, and English. The garden, on the slopes of the Mount of Olives across from Mt. Moriah, commemorates Orson Hyde's dedication of Palestine on October 24, 1841. Courtesy LaMar C. Berrett.

BIBLIOGRAPHY

Burton, Alma P. *Toward the New Jerusalem.* Salt Lake City, 1985.

Nibley, Hugh. "Jerusalem: In Early Christianity." In *CWHN*, Vol. 4, pp. 323–54.

D. KELLY OGDEN

JESUS CHRIST

[*This entry consists of twelve articles:*

Overview
Prophecies About Jesus Christ
Firstborn in the Spirit
Only Begotten in the Flesh
Birth of Jesus Christ
Baptism of Jesus Christ
Ministry of Jesus Christ
Crucifixion of Jesus Christ
Resurrection of Jesus Christ
Forty-Day Ministry and other Post-Resurrection Appearances of Jesus Christ
Latter-day Appearances of Jesus Christ
Second Coming of Jesus Christ

These titles are self-explanatory and each emphasizes a major feature about Jesus Christ. The long list of topics illustrates his importance in the doctrines of the Church, and the large amount of information available through the scriptures and the teachings of latter-day prophets.]

OVERVIEW

Jesus Christ is the central figure in the doctrine of The Church of Jesus Christ of Latter-day Saints. The Prophet Joseph SMITH explained that "the fundamental principles of our religion are the testimony of the Apostles and Prophets, concerning Jesus Christ, that He died, was buried, and rose again the third day, and ascended into heaven; and all other things which pertain to our religion are only appendages to it" (*TPJS*, p. 121). Latter-day Saints believe that complete salvation is possible only through the life, death, resurrection, doctrines, and ordinances of Jesus Christ and in no other way.

Christ's relationship to mankind is defined in terms of his divine roles in the three phases of existence—premortal, mortal, and postmortal.

The Lord Jesus Christ, by Del Parson (1983, oil on canvas, 49 cm × 61 cm). Jesus Christ is the literal son of God the Father, Creator of all things from the beginning, and the Redeemer of mankind.

PREMORTAL JESUS. In the PREMORTAL LIFE, Jesus Christ, whose main title was JEHOVAH, was the firstborn spirit child of God the Father and thus the eldest brother and preeminent above all other spirit children of God. In that FIRST ESTATE, he came to be more intelligent than all other spirits, one "like unto God" (Abr. 3:19, 24), and served as the representative of the Father in the creation of "worlds without number" (Heb. 1:1–3; D&C 76:24; Moses 1:33; 7:30). LDS leaders have declared that all REVELATION since the FALL OF ADAM has been by, and through, Jehovah (Jesus Christ) and that whenever the Father has appeared unto man, it has been to introduce and bear record of the Son (JST John 1:19; *DS* 1:27). He was known to Adam, and the patriarchs from Adam to Noah worshiped him in humble reverence. He was the Almighty God of Abraham, Isaac, and Jacob, the God-Lawgiver on Sinai, the Holy One of Israel. Scriptural records affirm that all the prophets from the beginning spoke or wrote of the time when Jehovah would come to earth in the form of man, in the role of a MESSIAH. Peter said, "to him give all the prophets witness" (Acts 2:25–31; 10:43). Jacob taught that "none of the prophets have written, nor prophesied, save they have spoken concerning this Christ" (Jacob 7:11; cf. Mosiah 3:5–10; 13:33; 3 Ne. 20:24).

MORTAL JESUS. Jehovah was born into this life in Bethlehem of Judea and grew up as Jesus of Nazareth. He came in condescension—leaving his station as the Lord Omnipotent to undertake a mission of pain and humiliation, having everlasting consequences for mankind (see 1 Ne. 11; Mosiah 3:5–10; *see also* CONDESCENSION OF GOD). His life was one of moral perfection—he was sinless and completely submissive to the will of the Father (John 5:30; 2 Cor. 5:21; Heb. 4:15; 1 Pet. 2:22; Mosiah 15:2). Jesus is the model and exemplar of all who seek to acquire the divine nature. As taught by Joseph Smith, the Savior "suffered greater sufferings, and was exposed to more powerful contradictions than any man can be." Through all of this, "he kept the law of God, and remained without sin" (*Lectures on Faith*, Lecture 5, paragraph 2). The risen Lord asked the Nephites, "What manner of men ought ye to be? Verily I say unto you, even as I am" (3 Ne. 27:27; cf. 12:48).

Jesus was more, however, than sinlessness, goodness, and love. He was more than a model and teacher, more than the embodiment of compassion. He was able to accomplish his unique ministry—a ministry of reconciliation and salvation—because of who and what he was. President Ezra Taft BENSON stated, "The Church of Jesus Christ of Latter-day Saints proclaims that Jesus Christ is the Son of God in the most literal sense. The body in which He performed His mission in the flesh was fathered by that same Holy Being we worship as God, our Eternal Father. Jesus was not the son of Joseph, nor was He begotten by the Holy Ghost. He is the Son of the Eternal Father!" (Benson, p. 4). From MARY, a mortal woman, Jesus inherited mortality, including the capacity to die. From his exalted Father he inherited immortality, the capacity to live forever. The Savior's dual nature—man and God—enabled him to make an infinite atonement, an accomplishment that no other person, no matter how capable or gifted, could do (cf. Alma 34:9–12). First, he was able, in GETHSEMANE, in some majestic but incomprehensible manner, to assume the burdens and effects of the sins of all mankind and, in doing so, to engage suffering and anguish beyond what a mere mortal could endure (2 Ne. 9:21; Mosiah 3:7; D&C 18:11; 19:16; Taylor, p. 148). Second, he was able to submit to physical death, to willingly lay down his life and then take up his body again in the RESURRECTION (John 5:26; 10:17, 18; 2 Ne. 2:8).

POSTMORTAL JESUS. Latter-day Saints believe that between his death on the cross at Calvary and his resurrection, Jesus' spirit entered the SPIRIT WORLD, a postmortal place of the disembodied, those awaiting and preparing for the reunion of their bodies and spirits. Peter taught that Christ went into this realm to preach to the spirits in prison (1 Pet. 3:18–20; 4:6). A modern revelation explains that Jesus did not go himself among the wicked and disobedient who had rejected the truth. Rather, he ministered to the righteous in PARADISE and organized and empowered them to teach those spirits who remained in darkness under the bondage of sin and ignorance (see D&C 138:29–32). Thus, the Messiah's mission to "preach good tidings unto the meek," to "bind up the brokenhearted, to proclaim liberty to the captives, and the opening of the prison to them that are bound" (Isa. 61:1; Luke 4:18–19) extended after death into the life beyond (see SALVATION OF THE DEAD; SPIRIT PRISON).

Jesus "broke the bands of death"; he was the

Jesus at the Home of Mary and Martha, by Minerva K. Teichert (c. 1935, oil on canvas, 46″ × 70″). Jesus ministered to people of every class and station in life. LDS artist Minerva Teichert shows him here expounding the holy scriptures in the home of two women, Mary and Martha. Mary "sat at Jesus' feet, and heard his word," while her sister "was cumbered about much serving" (Luke 10:39–40). Courtesy Museum of Fine Arts, Brigham Young University.

"first fruits of them that slept" (1 Cor. 15:20; Alma 11:40–41). He rose from the tomb with an immortal, glorified body and initiated the first resurrection or the resurrection of the just, the raising of the righteous dead who had lived from the days of Adam to the time of Christ (Matt. 27:52–53; Mosiah 15:21–25; Hel. 14:25–26; 3 Ne. 23:7–13). Jesus Christ will come again to earth in power and glory. The first resurrection, begun at the time of Christ's resurrection, will resume as the righteous dead from the MERIDIAN OF TIME to his second coming return with him in resurrected and immortal glory. This second advent will also signal the beginning of the MILLENNIUM, a thousand years of earthly peace during which Satan will be bound and have no power over the hearts of those who remain on earth (Rev. 20:1–2; 1 Ne. 22:26). Joseph Smith taught that "Christ and the resurrected Saints will reign over the earth during the thousand years. They will not probably dwell upon the earth [constantly], but will visit it when they please, or when it is necessary to govern it" (*TPJS*, p. 268). During this era, Jesus will reveal himself, and, in the words of Isaiah, "the earth shall be full of the knowledge of the Lord, as the waters cover the sea" (Isa. 11:9; Heb. 2:14).

Jesus Christ is the God of the whole earth and invites all nations and people to come unto him.

His mortal ministry, as described in the New Testament, was primarily among the Jews. Following his death and resurrection he appeared to his "other sheep," groups of scattered Israelites. First, as described in the Book of Mormon, he ministered to the NEPHITES in America. He taught them his gospel and authorized them to officiate in his name. He then visited the lost tribes, the ten northern tribes of Israel, which were scattered at the time of the Assyrian captivity in 721 B.C. (John 10:16; 3 Ne. 15:12–16; 17:4). In addition to the appearances recorded in the Bible and the Book of Mormon, which are ancient scriptural witnesses of the Redeemer, Joseph Smith testified that Jesus Christ, in company with his Eternal Father, appeared to him near Palmyra, New York, in the spring of 1820 to open the DISPENSATION OF THE FULNESS OF TIMES (JS—H 1:1–20; *see* FIRST VISION). On subsequent occasions the risen Savior has visited and revealed himself to his latter-day prophets and continues to direct his latter-day Church and kingdom (*see* JESUS CHRIST: LATTER-DAY APPEARANCES OF).

Latter-day Saints center their worship in, and direct their prayers to, God the Eternal Father. This, as with all things—sermons, testimonies, prayers, and sacraments or ordinances—they do in the name of Jesus Christ (2 Ne. 25:16; Jacob 4:4–5; 3 Ne. 18:19; D&C 20:29; Moses 5:8). The Saints also worship Christ the Son as they acknowledge him as the source of truth and redemption, as the light and life of the world, as the way to the Father (John 14:6; 2 Ne. 25:29; 3 Ne. 11:11). They look to him for deliverance and seek to be like him (see D&C 93:12–20; McConkie, 1978, pp. 568–69). In emphasizing the transforming power of Christ's example, President David O. MCKAY observed that "no man can sincerely resolve to apply to his daily life the teachings of Jesus of Nazareth without sensing a change in his own nature" (*IE* 65 [June 1962]:405).

Jesus Christ brought to pass the bodily resurrection of all who have lived or who will yet live upon the earth (1 Cor. 15:21–22; Alma 11:40–42). Because he overcame the world, all men and women may—by exercising faith in him, trusting in his merits, and receiving his grace—repent of their sins and know the peace of personal purity and spiritual wholeness (John 14:27; Phil. 4:7; 2 Ne. 2:8; 25:23; Enos 1:1–8; Mosiah 4:1–3). Those who have learned to rely on the Lord and lean upon his tender mercies "sing the song of redeeming love" (Alma 5:26). NEPHI₁, the Book of Mormon prophet-leader, exulted, "I glory in my Jesus, for he hath redeemed my soul from hell" (2 Ne. 33:6). "We talk of Christ, we rejoice in Christ, we preach of Christ, we prophesy of Christ, . . . that our children may know to what source they may look for a remission of their sins" (2 Ne. 25:26). A latter-day apostle has written:

> I believe in Christ;
> He stands supreme!
> From him I'll gain my fondest dream;
> And while I strive through grief and pain,
> His voice is heard: Ye shall obtain.
> I believe in Christ; so come what may,
> With him I'll stand in that great day
> When on this earth he comes again
> To rule among the sons of men.
> [Bruce R. McConkie, "I Believe in Christ," no. 134, *Hymns*, 1985]

BIBLIOGRAPHY

Benson, Ezra Taft. *Come Unto Christ*. Salt Lake City, 1983.

Dahl, Larry E., and Charles D. Tate, eds. *The Lectures on Faith in Historical Perspective*. Provo, Utah, 1990.

McConkie, Bruce R. *The Promised Messiah*. Salt Lake City, 1978.

———. *The Mortal Messiah*, 4 vols. Salt Lake City, 1979–1981.

———. *The Millennial Messiah*. Salt Lake City, 1982.

Talmage, James E. *Jesus the Christ*. Salt Lake City, 1972.

Taylor, John. *The Mediation and Atonement of Our Lord and Savior Jesus Christ*. Salt Lake City, 1882.

ROBERT L. MILLET

PROPHECIES ABOUT JESUS CHRIST

Prophecies concerning the birth, mortal ministry, and post-Resurrection ministry of Jesus Christ permeate the Bible. Moreover, the latter-day scriptures used by members of The Church of Jesus Christ of Latter-day Saints—the Book of Mormon, which bears the modern subtitle "Another Testament of Jesus Christ," the Doctrine and Covenants, and the Pearl of Great Price—contain numerous prophetic utterances about the MESSIAH that in general are clearer than those in the Bible. For Latter-day Saints, these four volumes of scripture constitute the principal sources for the prophecies about Jesus' life and mission. This article reviews the prophecies concerning Jesus most often referred to by Latter-day Saints.

The New Testament teaches that the divinity of Jesus Christ was recognized by some during his own lifetime, as well as by God's ancient prophets. For example, Andrew announced to his brother Simon PETER that he had found the Messiah (John 1:41). The Book of Mormon prophets ABINADI and NEPHI₂, son of HELAMAN₂, taught that all of God's prophets, including Moses and Abraham, "have testified of the coming of Christ" (Mosiah 13:33; Hel. 8:16–22; cf. Jacob 4:4).

The scriptures are rich in prophetic detail concerning the birth of Jesus. Isaiah declared, "Behold, a virgin shall conceive, and bear a son, and shall call his name Immanuel" (Isa. 7:14), a passage that Matthew cited as having reference to Jesus (Matt. 1:22–23). Micah poetically pronounced, "Bethlehem Ephratah, though thou be little among the thousands of Judah, yet out of thee shall he come forth unto me that is to be ruler in Israel; whose goings forth have been from of old, from everlasting" (Micah 5:2). Among Book of Mormon people, NEPHI₁ foretold that "even six hundred years from the time that my father [Lehi] left Jerusalem," the Savior would be raised up (1 Ne. 10:4; 19:8). SAMUEL THE LAMANITE (c. 6 B.C.) told a doubting generation of the signs to be given in the Western Hemisphere that would accompany the birth of Christ (Hel. 14:2–8). These included the appearance of a new star and two days and one night without darkness (Hel. 14:4–5).

Some prophecies of the Messiah's birth were fulfilled when the angel of the Lord announced to shepherds near Bethlehem: "Unto you is born this day in the city of David a Saviour, which is Christ the Lord" (Luke 2:11). On the other side of the world, the day before his birth, the Lord announced to his prophet Nephi₃ that he should be of "good cheer; for behold, the time is at hand, and on this night shall the sign be given, and on the morrow come I into the world, to show unto the world that I will fulfill all that which I have caused to be spoken by the mouth of my holy prophets" (3 Ne. 1:13).

Latter-day Saints believe that the mission of Jesus Christ has been known since earliest times. The angel of the Lord declared to Adam that the Son was "the Only Begotten of the Father from the beginning," and that Adam would "be redeemed, and all mankind, even as many as will," if they "repent and call upon God in the name of the Son forevermore" (Moses 5:8–9). The message that Jesus Christ is the Advocate, the Redeemer, and the Intercessor, and that "There is no other way nor means whereby man can be saved, only through the atoning blood of Jesus Christ" (Hel.

5:9), has been repeated by God's representatives in all ages (see Moses 5:14–15; Isa. 53:4–5; Acts 4:12; 2 Ne. 2:9–10; 9:6–7; Mosiah 4:8; 5:8; Alma 11:40; D&C 45:3).

Events of Jesus' mortal life and ministry are found in numerous prophecies. In the JOSEPH SMITH TRANSLATION OF THE BIBLE (JST), an insightful passage states "that Jesus grew up with his brethren, and waxed strong, and waited upon the Lord for the time of his ministry to come . . . [and] needed not that any man should teach him" (JST Matt. 3:24–25). Nephi₁ saw in a vision, and King BENJAMIN learned from an angel, that the Savior would perform healings, cast out devils, and raise the dead (1 Ne. 11:31; Mosiah 3:5–6). According to New Testament writers, Jesus' triumphal ride into Jerusalem on a beast of burden was foreknown by Zechariah (Zech. 9:9; Matt. 21:5; John 12:14–15), as was his betrayal for thirty pieces of silver (Zech. 11:12–13; Matt. 27:9–10). From the angel, King Benjamin learned that blood would come "from every pore, so great shall be his [Jesus'] anguish for the wickedness and the abominations of his people" (Mosiah 3:7). Christ's rejection by his own people was prophesied both by himself and by others (e.g., Ps. 69:8; Mosiah 15:5; 3 Ne. 9:16; John 1:11).

Many years before the event, prophets such as ENOCH and Nephi₁ saw the Lord lifted up on the cross (Moses 7:47, 55; 1 Ne. 11:33). Isaiah prophesied that the suffering servant would make "his grave with the wicked, and with the rich in his death" (Isa. 53:9). The Book of Mormon prophet Abinadi (c. 150 B.C.) associated that passage in Isaiah with Jesus (Mosiah 15), and its fulfillment was recorded by Luke (23:32–33). Matthew tells of the physical disturbances that occurred at the moment Jesus gave up his life (Matt. 27:50–54), events that ZENOS saw in a vision hundreds of years earlier (1 Ne. 19:10–12).

Christ foretold his own death and resurrection when he answered a demand for a sign: "Destroy this temple [physical body], and in three days I will raise it up" (John 2:19). Jesus' eventual victory over death was known by the ancients, for God told Enoch that "righteousness will I send down out of heaven; and truth will I send forth out of the earth, to bear testimony of mine Only Begotten; his resurrection from the dead; yea, and also the resurrection of all men" (Moses 7:62). Later, inspired men in the Americas learned of this event. Nephi₁, JACOB, Benjamin, and Samuel proclaimed the time when Christ "layeth down his life according to the flesh, and taketh it again by the power of the Spirit, that he may bring to pass the resurrection of the dead, being the first that should rise" (2 Ne. 2:8; cf. 1 Ne. 10:11; Mosiah 3:10; Hel. 14:15–17).

Jesus Christ's ministry to the SPIRIT PRISON (1 Pet. 3:18–19) was anticipated by Isaiah when he recorded that "after many days shall [the prisoners gathered in the pit] be visited" (Isa. 24:22). Section 138 of the Doctrine and Covenants records a vision of this event, received by a modern prophet, President Joseph F. SMITH, when he saw "the hosts of the dead, both small and great . . . awaiting the advent of the Son of God into the spirit world, to declare their redemption from the bands of death" (D&C 138:11, 16).

The righteous of earlier ages have looked forward to the second coming of Jesus Christ. Jesus told his disciples to "watch therefore, for ye know neither the day nor the hour wherein the Son of man cometh" (Matt. 25:13; cf. D&C 49:6–7), and indicated that he would come "as a thief" in the night (1 Thess. 5:2; Rev. 3:3; 16:15). He revealed to Joseph Smith that a universal revelation would be given so that "all flesh shall see me together" (D&C 101:23; cf. Isa. 40:5). Isaiah foresaw events of the second coming (Isa. 63–66), as did Daniel, Micah, Zechariah, and Malachi (Dan. 7:13; Micah 1:3; Zech. 12:10; 13:6; Mal. 3:12). When the resurrected Lord appeared among the Nephites, he spoke about his eventual triumphant return to earth, quoting Malachi, chapters 3 and 4 (3 Ne. 24–25).

The Prophet Joseph Smith clarified and added to prophecies of the events surrounding Jesus' second coming, including the RESTORATION of the gospel (D&C 133:36–37), the resurrection of the dead (D&C 88:95–102), the beginning of the Millennium (D&C 43:30–31), and the binding of Satan for a thousand years (D&C 45:55). Both ancient and modern prophets foretold that, at the end of a thousand years of peace, Satan would be loosed and the final battle between good and evil would be waged (Rev. 20:7–8; D&C 43:31). JOHN the Revelator and the ancient prophet ETHER, who both saw in vision all of these events, beheld the renewal of the earth and the establishment of the NEW JERUSALEM (Rev. 21; Ether 13:1–10). This city will have "no need of the sun, neither of the moon, to shine in it: for the glory of God did lighten it, and the Lamb is the light thereof" (Rev. 21:23).

BIBLIOGRAPHY

Jackson, Kent P. "The Beginnings of Christianity in the Book of Mormon." In *The Book of Mormon: The Keystone Scripture*, ed. P. Chessman. Provo, Utah, 1988.

Matthews, Robert J. "The Doctrine of the Atonement—The Revelation of the Gospel to Adam." In *Studies in Scripture*, ed. R. Millet and K. Jackson, Vol. 2, pp. 111–29. Salt Lake City, 1985.

———. *A Bible! A Bible!* Salt Lake City, 1990.

McConkie, Bruce R. *The Promised Messiah.* Salt Lake City, 1978.

———. *The Millennial Messiah.* Salt Lake City, 1982.

GARY LEE WALKER

FIRSTBORN IN THE SPIRIT

Fundamental to the teachings of The Church of Jesus Christ of Latter-day Saints is the concept that all human beings were born as spirit sons and daughters of heavenly parents before any were born as mortals to earthly parents. Latter-day Saints believe that the eldest and firstborn spirit child of God is Jehovah and that it was he who was later born with a physical body to MARY as Jesus Christ. That is, Jehovah of the Old Testament became Jesus Christ of the New Testament when he was born into mortality. The Psalmist refers to the Messiah as the firstborn (Ps. 89:27), and the apostle Paul speaks of Jesus as the "firstborn among many brethren" (Rom. 8:29; cf. Heb. 2:17) and as the "firstborn of every creature" (Col. 1:15). Perhaps the most authoritative statement on the subject is from the Savior himself, who declared to the Prophet Joseph SMITH, "I was in the beginning with the Father, and am the Firstborn" (D&C 93:21; *see also* CHURCH OF THE FIRSTBORN). In 1909 the FIRST PRESIDENCY of the Church declared:

> The Father of Jesus is our Father also. Jesus Himself taught this truth, when He instructed His disciples how to pray: "Our Father which art in heaven," etc. Jesus, however, is the firstborn among all the sons of God—the first begotten in the spirit, and the only begotten in the flesh. He is our elder brother, and we, like Him, are in the image of God. All men and women are in the similitude of the universal Father and Mother, and are literally the sons and daughters of Deity [*MFP* 4:203].

[*See also* "Origin of Man," included in Doctrinal Expositions of the First Presidency in Appendix.]

JERRY C. GILES

ONLY BEGOTTEN IN THE FLESH

Ancient and modern scriptures use the title Only Begotten to emphasize the divine nature of Jesus Christ. Latter-day Saints recognize Jesus as literally the Only Begotten Son of God the Father in the flesh (John 3:16; D&C 93:11; Moses 6:52). This title signifies that Jesus' physical body was the offspring of a mortal mother and of the eternal Father (Luke 1:35, 1 Ne. 11:18). It is LDS doctrine that Jesus Christ is the child of MARY and GOD THE FATHER, "not in violation of natural law but in accordance with a higher manifestation thereof" (JC, p. 81).

The fact of Jesus' being the literal Son of God in the flesh is crucial to the ATONEMENT, which could not have been accomplished by an ordinary man. Because of the FALL OF ADAM, all mankind are subject to physical death and are shut out from the presence of God. The human family is unable to save itself. Divine law required the sacrifice of a sinless, infinite, and eternal being—a God—someone not dominated by the Fall, to redeem mankind from their lost and fallen condition (Alma 34:9–14; cf. 42:15). This price of redemption was more than any mortal person could pay, and included the spiritual sufferings and physical agony in GETHSEMANE (Luke 22:44; Mosiah 3:7; D&C 19:18). To complete the Atonement by physical death and RESURRECTION, it was necessary that Jesus be able to lay down his physical body and also be able to take it up again. He could do this only because he had life in himself, which he inherited from God his Father (John 5:26; 10:17–18). Christ inherited the ability to die from his mortal mother and the power to resurrect himself from his immortal Father. Dying was for him a voluntary, deliberate act for mankind, made possible only because he was the Only Begotten of the Father (D&C 20:18–26).

BIBLIOGRAPHY

McConkie, Bruce R. *The Promised Messiah*, pp. 467–73. Salt Lake City, 1978.

GERALD HANSEN, JR.

BIRTH OF JESUS CHRIST

Latter-day Saint scripture affirms unequivocally that the birth of Jesus Christ was the mortal advent on earth of an actual God, a second and distinct member of the GODHEAD. Adam was assured redemption through the Only Begotten of the Father, and every true prophet had a hope of Christ's glory (Moses 5:6–10; Jacob 4:4).

Biblical prophecies and accounts of Jesus' birth are confirmed and enlarged in latter-day scripture. While Matthew's birth narrative emphasizes Christ's kingship (drawing attention to the magi, King Herod, and Bethlehem, the city of King David) and Luke's account accents Jesus' humility and holiness (mentioning the lowly manger, the shepherds, and the heavenly choirs), the Book of Mormon focuses on his coming as a fulfillment of a loving God's plan that was established from before the foundation of the world.

The time of Jesus' birth, along with the purposes of his mortal ministry, were established in the PREMORTAL LIFE (*see* COUNCIL IN HEAVEN; Moses 4:1–4; 1 Ne. 10:2–4; Mosiah 3:5–10). A detailed vision of the anticipated Savior's birth was recorded by NEPHI₁, a Book of Mormon prophet, shortly after 600 B.C. (1 Ne. 11:7–24). He foresaw a virgin in the city of Nazareth who was carried away in the spirit, and then saw the virgin again with a child in her arms, whom an angel identified as the Son of God. Nephi described Christ's coming as the CONDESCENSION OF GOD, which may be understood in two respects: first, in that God the Father, a perfected and glorified personage of flesh and bones, condescended to become the father of a mortal offspring, born of Mary; and second, in that Jesus (JEHOVAH), the God who created worlds without number (Moses 1:32–33; John 1:1–4, 14; Heb. 1:1–2), willingly submitted himself to all the trials and pains of mortality (Mosiah 3:5–8; MD, p. 155).

For Latter-day Saints, the paternity of Jesus is not obscure. He was the literal, biological son of an immortal, tangible Father and Mary, a mortal woman (*see* VIRGIN BIRTH). Jesus is the only person born who deserves the title "the Only Begotten Son of God" (John 3:16; Benson, p. 3; *see* JESUS CHRIST: ONLY BEGOTTEN IN THE FLESH). He was not the son of the HOLY GHOST; it was only through the Holy Ghost that the power of the Highest overshadowed Mary (Luke 1:35; 1 Ne. 11:19).

The place where the nativity should occur was a point of public controversy in Jesus' day (John 7:40–43). The Book of Mormon prophet ALMA₂, about 83 B.C., foretold that Christ's birthplace would be "at Jerusalem which is the land of our forefathers" (Alma 7:10), referring to the region surrounding the city itself: "Christ was born in a village some six miles from the city of Jerusalem . . . in what we now know the ancients themselves designated as 'the land of Jerusalem'" (*CWHN* 6:102).

The Bible and the Book of Mormon report the appearance of great signs in the Western Hemisphere at the time of the birth of the Messiah for the benefit of the faithful. For example, about 6 B.C. SAMUEL THE LAMANITE prophesied that lights would appear in heaven and that there would be no darkness during the night when Christ was born (Hel. 14:3–7). On the day when Samuel's five-year prophecy was about to expire and the unbelievers were accordingly about to execute those who had believed his words, Samuel's prophecies of the Savior's birth were fulfilled (3 Ne. 1:4–23). In the New World, as in the Old, "angels did appear unto men, wise men, and did declare unto them glad tidings of great joy" (Hel. 16:14).

[*See also* April 6; Book of Mormon Chronology; Christmas.]

BIBLIOGRAPHY

Benson, Ezra Taft. *Come Unto Christ.* Salt Lake City, 1983.

Brown, Raymond E. *The Birth of the Messiah.* Garden City, N.Y., 1977.

McConkie, Bruce R. *The Mortal Messiah*, Vol. 1, pp. 313–66. Salt Lake City, 1981.

ANDREW C. SKINNER

BAPTISM OF JESUS CHRIST

At the commencement of his public ministry, Jesus went from Galilee to the Jordan, where he was baptized by JOHN THE BAPTIST. He did thereby "humble himself before the Father" and witness to him "that he would be obedient to him" (2 Ne. 31:7). For Latter-day Saints this event shows that Jesus by his own example taught that all people must be baptized by immersion by one having AUTHORITY. All persons must also receive the HOLY GHOST in order to obtain the testimony of Jesus (see John 1:32–34; Rev. 1:2; 19:10) and enter into the KINGDOM OF HEAVEN.

Jesus was baptized by immersion by John, who was ordained when eight days old by an angel of God to "make straight the way of the Lord" (D&C 84:28). As Jesus came up out of the water, John saw the heavens open and the spirit of God descending upon Jesus (*see* DOVE, SIGN OF), and the voice of GOD THE FATHER declared to John,

"This is my beloved Son, in whom I am well pleased" (Matt. 3:17). Thereafter John bore record that Jesus was the Son of God (John 1:33–34; D&C 93:15–17). At the baptism of Jesus all three members of the GODHEAD were manifest, thus revealing the separate identities of the Father, the Son, and the Holy Ghost.

Many have wondered why Jesus needed baptism, since he was without SIN. Some have seen this as "an act of simple submissive obedience on the part of the Perfect One" (A. Edersheim, *Life and Times of Jesus the Messiah* [reprinted, Grand Rapids, Mich., 1971], p. 280); others have suggested that Jesus still faced "a possibility of a subtle sin: the sin of shrinking from what might lie ahead" and thus was baptized to fortify himself with "utter consecration" and to express to his nation "the urgency of commitment" (*Interpreter's Bible*, Vol. 8, p. 78).

However, Latter-day Saints understand from the Bible and the Book of Mormon that Jesus was baptized "to fulfill all righteousness," which means that Jesus humbled himself before the Father, witnessed to the Father that he would obey him, and thereby showed mankind the narrowness of the gate leading to ETERNAL LIFE (2 Ne. 31:6–9). In submitting to baptism Jesus "set the example" for all mankind, for if Jesus, being holy, was baptized "to fulfil all righteousness . . . how much more need have we, being unholy, to be baptized?" (2 Ne. 31:5; see also *AF*, chap. 6). Those who follow his example and his gospel with full purpose of heart, with honesty before God, and "with real intent, repenting of [their] sins," are promised that they will receive the BAPTISM OF FIRE AND OF THE HOLY GHOST, and be able to "speak with the tongue of angels, and shout praises" to God (2 Ne. 31:13).

BIBLIOGRAPHY

Farley, S. Brent. "The Baptism and Temptation of Jesus." In *Studies in Scripture*, ed. K. Jackson and R. Millett, Vol. 5, pp. 175–87. Salt Lake City, 1986.

McConkie, Bruce R. *The Mortal Messiah*, Vol. 1, pp. 399–404. Salt Lake City, 1979.

J. PHILIP SCHAELLING

MINISTRY OF JESUS CHRIST

The central role played by Jesus' mortal ministry in Latter-day Saint doctrine and belief is well expressed in Joseph Smith's statement that "the fundamental principles of our religion are the testimony of the Apostles and Prophets, concerning Jesus Christ, that He died, was buried, and rose again the third day, and ascended into heaven; and all other things which pertain to our religion are only appendages to it" (*TPJS*, p. 121; *HC* 3:30).

Latter-day Saints share with many other Christians the acceptance of the four New Testament gospels and Acts 1:1–11 as essentially accurate historical accounts of the earthly ministry of Jesus Christ. While not biblical inerrantists, their confidence in the biblical record is strengthened in two unique ways: First, they believe specific elements of Christ's earthly ministry to have been revealed beforehand to pre-Christian PROPHETS. These REVELATIONS agree with subsequent accounts in the gospels. Second, they believe that the risen Jesus himself has affirmed many details of that biblical account. Thus, the Book of Mormon and other texts of the specifically Latter-day Saint canon are regarded as "proving to the world that the holy scriptures are true" (D&C 20:11; cf. 1 Ne. 13:39).

That God's Son would come to earth and take upon himself a physical body, for example, was foreknown by many prophets (1 Ne. 13:42; Enos 1:8; Mosiah 3:5; Hel. 8:13–22; Ether 3:15–17). The approximate date of his coming was also known (1 Ne. 10:4; 19:8; 2 Ne. 25:19; Hel. 14:2). Several ancient believers were privileged to see him before his mortal advent (2 Ne. 2:4; 11:2; Alma 19:13; Ether 3:14; 9:22; D&C 107:49, 54; Moses 1:2; 7:4; Abr. 2:6–11; cf. Isa. 6:1–3). His name-title, Jesus Christ, (i.e., "Savior Anointed") was known long beforehand, as were the name and virginity of his mother and the place of his birth (1 Ne. 11:13–14, 18–20; 2 Ne. 25:19; Mosiah 3:8; Alma 7:10; Ether 3:14; Moses 6:52, 57; 7:50; cf. Micah 5:2). Ancient prophets foresaw his baptism, predicting even its location and specific details of the mission of JOHN THE BAPTIST (1 Ne. 10:8–10). NEPHI₁ knew that the Savior would call twelve apostles to assist in his ministry (1 Ne. 11:34–36; 12:9; 13:26, 40–41; 14:20, 24, 27), and King Benjamin prophesied of his many miracles (Mosiah 3:5–6). Jesus' atoning death by crucifixion was well known to pre-Christian prophets, who understood that it would be accompanied by three days of darkness preceding his resurrection (1 Ne. 10:11; 11:33; 19:10; 2 Ne. 25:14; Mosiah 3:9–10; Alma 7:11; Hel. 14:14, 20, 27; Moses 7:55). Indeed, sacrificial practices from Adam onward, including the rituals of the law of

Moses, prefigured Christ and, furthermore, were recognized as doing so by many who performed them (Jacob 4:5; Moses 5:5–7).

Later LDS scriptures, including the words of the risen Jesus himself, confirm such details of the New Testament record as the unity of the SERMON ON THE MOUNT (3 Ne. 12–14) and the authenticity of some of his separate sayings (3 Ne. 15:12–24). His pain in the garden of GETHSEMANE is attested (D&C 19:18; cf. Mosiah 3:7), as are his crucifixion (D&C 20:23; 21:9; 35:2; 45:52; 46:13; 53:2), his resurrection on the third day (Morm. 7:5; D&C 18:12; 20:23), and his identity as the long-awaited suffering Savior (3 Ne. 11:10–11). His earthly agonies are said to qualify him as an intercessor between God and man (D&C 45:4; cf. Isa. 53:12). In such texts as Doctrine and Covenants section 7 and the JOSEPH SMITH TRANSLATION OF THE BIBLE (JST), Latter-day Saints believe that they have been granted more complete information on Jesus' Palestinian ministry. (Interestingly, the JST antici-

Christ Calling Peter and Andrew, by James T. Harwood (1928, oil on canvas, 41″ × 51″). An important part of Jesus' ministry was the calling of apostles to lead his Church on earth. Latter-day Saints believe that apostles and prophets form a necessary foundation for Christ's Church.

pates modern scholarly emphasis on the individual character of the New Testament gospels by labeling each one as the "testimony" of its respective author. This same view seems to underlie Doctrine and Covenants 88:141.)

Gospel accounts inform and underscore LDS understanding of the earthly ministry of Jesus, in whom Latter-day Saints see God physically present among his people. Not only did Jesus perform miracles, expressing thereby his power over both demons and natural elements, but he explicitly affirmed his unity of purpose with the Father (John 14:8–10; 17:21) and his identity as the Jehovah of the Old Testament (John 8:56–59). While Moses ascended the mountain to receive the old law, Jesus ascended a mount to proclaim a new one (cf. 3 Ne. 15:4–5). Moses himself was present at the TRANSFIGURATION (Matt. 17:1–8). LDS scriptures further affirm the New Testament gospels' warm portrait of Jesus' compassion for sinners, his concern for the poor, and his love for children. They portray him as a popular teacher who taught with parables, preached in synagogues, confronted hypocrisy, and won the love and admiration of many of his hearers.

Latter-day Saints recall, too, the reaction of Jesus' hearers to the Sermon on the Mount: "For he taught them as one having authority, and not as the scribes" (Matt. 7:29). Just as he did not call upon the power of others to perform miracles, Jesus needed no precedents to justify his teachings. In himself he had power over death—both over the death of others (as in the healing of Lazarus, the daughter of Jairus, and the son of the widow of Nain) and his own death (John 5:26; 10:17–18). Thus, Latter-day Saints join with other Christians in an acceptance of Jesus of Nazareth as their redeemer from death. But he is also the source of PRIESTHOOD authority, who called and empowered ordinary, untrained men to serve him in a newly organized church and, acting for him in his capacity as "the good Shepherd," to "feed his sheep" (John 21:15–17) through both teaching and priesthood ORDINANCES. They reject claims of a dichotomy between the priestly and the prophetic in his ministry. They note that he taught the necessity of baptism and submitted to that requirement himself (John 3:1–5; Matt. 3:15). They recall that he reverenced the temple of his day and expected others to do likewise (Luke 2:41–50; John 2:13–17).

LDS understanding of the role of faith and works in salvation is grounded in the insistence of Jesus that love for him will express itself in OBEDIENCE to his COMMANDMENTS (John 14:15; cf. John 15:14; Matt. 5–7). His call for his followers to be perfect (Matt. 5:48) is rendered plausible by the fact that he overcame the same temptations that beset them (Heb. 4:15–16; Matt. 4:1–11; Luke 4:1–13) and that he suffered for their transgressions (Mosiah 3:7; Isa. 53:3–12). Indeed, Latter-day Saints are informed by their scriptures that it is at least partially because of the experience gained and the empathy achieved during his earthly sojourn that Jesus knows how to minister to the needs of those who trust in him (Alma 7:12; D&C 62:1; 88:6).

BIBLIOGRAPHY

McConkie, Bruce R. *The Mortal Messiah*, 4 vols. Salt Lake City, 1979–1981.

Talmage, James E. *JC*. Salt Lake City, 1915.

Taylor, John. *The Mediation and Atonement of Jesus Christ*. Salt Lake City, 1882; repr. 1964.

DANIEL C. PETERSON

CRUCIFIXION OF JESUS CHRIST

Crucifixion was the form of execution suffered by Jesus Christ on Calvary as the necessary conclusion to his voluntary infinite atoning sacrifice begun in GETHSEMANE (*see* ATONEMENT). Many people supported and followed Jesus, but a small group of influential Judaean leaders, who disagreed with his doctrines and felt threatened by his popularity, succeeded in having the Roman governor, Pontius Pilate, condemn him to death.

LDS scriptures give prophetic witness that crucifixion would be the method of the Savior's death (e.g., 1 Ne. 19:10–13; 2 Ne. 10:3–5; Mosiah 3:9; 15:7; Moses 7:55). Israelites did not crucify. They did hang executed bodies ignominiously "on a tree" for part of a day (Deut. 21:22–23; cf. Acts 5:30), but for crucifixion it was necessary to invoke Roman law and practice.

Crucifixion was a form of execution probably begun by the Persians and used in Egypt and Carthage. The Romans perfected it as a torture designed to produce maximum pain and a slow death. Reserved for the vilest of criminals and rarely administered to Roman citizens, crucifixion was customarily preceded by flogging the back, buttocks, and legs with a short whip consisting of leather thongs with small iron balls or sharp pieces

Palm Sunday, by Robert L. Marshall (1983, oil on canvas, 4′ × 5′). This painting uses dead hanging palms to represent the time when life was gone from the body of Christ and then rose on the third day. It is one of the few LDS paintings to treat the crucifixion theme. The bottom of the painting depicts a sacrament table. Courtesy John W. Welch.

of sheep bone attached. The weakened victim was then made to carry at least a portion of the cross to the site of crucifixion. Romans commonly used large nails to fix the wrists and palms to the cross bar and the feet to the vertical portion of the cross. The nails inflicted terrible pain but caused no immediate life-threatening injury. A person could live in agony for hours or even days. The body's position made breathing difficult since hanging by the arms kept the chest expanded so that exhaling required the active use of the diaphragm. If the sufferer pushed with his feet, he elevated his body, placing the chest in a more natural position and making it easier to breathe. Soldiers sometimes hastened death by breaking the legs of the victim, making it almost impossible to push the body high enough to breathe.

After Jesus had hung on the cross for several hours, he forgave the soldiers who had crucified him (Luke 23:34; JST Luke 23:35) and voluntarily gave up his life (cf. John 10:18), commending his spirit into his Father's hands. The Romans broke the legs of the two who were crucified with Jesus, but believing that he was already dead, they merely thrust a spear into his side (John 19:33–34).

BIBLIOGRAPHY

Edwards, William D.; Wesley J. Gabel; and Floyd E. Hosmer. "On the Physical Death of Jesus Christ." *Journal of the American Medical Association*, 255 (1986):1455–63.

Hengel, Martin. *Crucifixion*. Philadelphia, 1977.

MERRILL C. OAKS

RESURRECTION OF JESUS CHRIST

Latter-day Saints view the resurrection of Jesus Christ as the most glorious event of all time. Having the power to lay down his body and to "take it again" (John 10:18), the Savior conquered death for himself and all mankind (1 Cor. 15:22). LDS faith in the literal and physical resurrection of Jesus is greatly strengthened by ancient and modern testimonies of many witnesses.

The Book of Mormon contains prophecies of the resurrection of Jesus years before the actual event. The prophet Nephi₁ declared, "Behold, they will crucify him; and . . . he shall rise from the dead" (2 Ne. 25:13; also 1 Ne. 19:10). In the Bible Jesus himself prophesied that on "the third day he shall be raised again" (Matt. 17:23).

The third day did come, and Jesus became the "firstfruits of them that slept" (1 Cor. 15:20), his spirit permanently reuniting with his body in a glorified, immortal state. His resurrected body was not subject to pain, disease, or death. It could pass through walls; it could defy the earthly laws of gravity; but it was a tangible "glorious body" (Phil. 3:21) composed of flesh and bones. Jesus said to his disciples, "Behold my hands and my feet, that it is I myself: handle me, and see; for a spirit hath not flesh and bones, as ye see me have" (Luke 24:39). He then ate broiled fish and honeycomb in their presence as a further witness of his corporeal nature.

Latter-day Saints firmly distinguish themselves from those who deny the physical resurrection of Jesus or claim that his divine nature is solely spiritual, with his postmortal appearances being merely temporary physical or mystical manifestations (Nibley, pp. 156–59). They find such doctrine inconsistent with the words of Paul, who

The Doubtful Thomas, by Carl Heinrich Bloch (1834–1890). Thomas, one of the original apostles, kneels at the feet of the resurrected Jesus. The Lord said, "Behold my hands; and reach hither thy hand, and thrust it into my side: and be not faithless, but believing" (John 20:27). Courtesy Frederiksborg Museum, Hillerød, Denmark.

taught that the resurrected Christ "dieth no more" (Rom. 6:9), meaning that his resurrected body would never again be separated from his spirit (James 2:26; Alma 11:45).

In his resurrected state, Jesus retained the prints of nails in his hands and feet as a special manifestation to the world. Such marks, however, are only temporary. After all have confessed that he is the Christ, his resurrected body will, like those of all mankind, be restored to its "proper and perfect frame" (Alma 40:23).

Once resurrected, Jesus "gained the keys . . . to open the graves for all men" (*DS* 1:128), and with those keys he opened the gates of the resurrection: The "graves were opened" and "many saints did arise and appear unto many" (Matt. 27:52; 3 Ne. 23:11).

Christ's resurrection was not hidden. Witnesses of this event were both legion and varied: the women at the tomb (Luke 24:1–10); Mary in the garden (John 20:11–18); ten apostles together (Luke 24:36–43); eleven apostles, including doubting Thomas (John 20:24–29); two disciples on the road to Emmaus (Luke 24:13–24); "above five hundred brethren at once" (1 Cor. 15:6); and Paul on the road to Damascus (Acts 9:3–9). Of all these records, none is more profound than that of his appearance to the Nephites, where, one by one, 2,500 men, women, and children "did see with their eyes and did feel with their hands, and did know of a surety . . . that it was he" (3 Ne. 11:15). To these accounts, Latter-day Saints add modern appearances of the resurrected Lord to Joseph SMITH and others (e.g., JS—H 1:17; D&C 76:22–23).

Jesus Christ will yet appear in the latter days and testify, "These wounds are the wounds with which I was wounded in the house of my friends" (D&C 45:52; cf. Zech. 13:6), visiting all kingdoms over which he is creator (D&C 88:51–61). Honest and credible witnesses of all ages have testified, and will yet testify, as did the angelic messengers of old, "He is risen" (Matt. 28:6).

BIBLIOGRAPHY

Nibley, Hugh W. "Easter and the Prophets." *The World and the Prophets,* in *CWHN* 3:154–62.

Romney, Marion G. "The Resurrection of Jesus." *Ensign* 12 (May 1982):6–9.

TAD R. CALLISTER

FORTY-DAY MINISTRY AND OTHER POST-RESURRECTION APPEARANCES OF JESUS CHRIST

After his RESURRECTION, Jesus spent much of the next forty days with his disciples, "speaking of the things pertaining to the kingdom of God" (Acts 1:3) and opening "their understanding, that they might understand the scriptures," namely, what is "in the law of Moses, and in the prophets, and in the Psalms concerning [him]" (Luke 24:44–45). As part of Jesus' ministry, these forty days are important to Latter-day Saints. In addition, a major section of the Book of Mormon is devoted to his post-resurrection ministry in the Western Hemisphere.

The NEW TESTAMENT mentions the forty-day ministry but provides only limited detail. For example, during this time Jesus appeared to the

Go Ye Therefore, and Teach All Nations, by Grant Romney Clawson, after a work by Harry Anderson (1974; mural, oil on canvas; 16′ × 66′). During his forty-day ministry, the resurrected Jesus instructed his apostles to preach the gospel to all nations (Matt. 28:19–20). The Lord repeated this instruction to Joseph Smith (see D&C 42:58).

Twelve with Thomas present (John 20:26–29), spoke of "things pertaining to the kingdom of God" (Acts 1:3), "and many other signs truly did Jesus in the presence of his disciples, which are not written in this book" (John 20:30). Paul mentions that on one occasion Jesus "was seen of above five hundred brethren at once" (1 Cor. 15:6). Finally, before his ascension Jesus commanded the APOSTLES to go "into all the world, and preach the gospel to every creature" (Mark 16:15–16; cf. Matt. 28:18–20; Luke 24:47–48; John 21:15–17; Acts 1:4–5).

Over forty accounts outside scripture claim to tell what Jesus said and did during his forty-day ministry. Latter-day Saints believe that some of these accounts, like the APOCRYPHA, contain things "therein that are true," but in addition contain "many things . . . that are not true" (D&C 91).

These accounts report the following: Jesus teaches the apostles the gospel they should preach to the world. He tells of a PREMORTAL LIFE and the creation of the world, adding that this life is a probationary state of choosing between good and evil, and that those who choose good might return to the glory of God. He foretells events of the LAST DAYS, including the return of ELIJAH. He also tells the disciples that the primitive church will be perverted after one generation, and teaches them to prepare for tribulation. These apocryphal accounts

state that Christ's resurrection gives his followers hope for their own resurrection in glory. Besides salvation for the living, SALVATION OF THE DEAD is a major theme, as are the ordinances: BAPTISM, the SACRAMENT or eucharist, ordination of the apostles to authority, their being blessed one by one, and an initiation or ENDOWMENT (cf. Luke 24:49; usually called "mysteries"), with an emphasis on GARMENTS, MARRIAGE, and PRAYER CIRCLES. These accounts, usually called secret (Greek, *apokryphon*; Coptic, *hep*), are often connected somehow to the TEMPLE, or compared to the MOUNT OF TRANSFIGURATION. Sometimes the apostles are said to ascend to heaven where they see marvelous things. Whether everything in such accounts is true or not, the actions of the apostles after the post-resurrection visits of Jesus contrast sharply with those before.

Many people dismiss accounts outside the New Testament with the labels apocrypha, pseudepigrapha, fiction, or myth. Some ascribe them to psychological hallucinations that the trauma of Jesus' death brought on the disciples. Others discard such traditions because sects later branded as "heresies" championed them. Most ignore them. Latter-day Saints generally tend to give thoughtful consideration to them, primarily because of the long, detailed account in the Book of Mormon of Christ's post-resurrection ministry among the Nephites and Lamanites "who had been spared" (3 Ne. 11–28).

Many elements found in the Old World forty-day literature also appear in 3 Nephi in the Book of Mormon. This account tells how his Father announced Jesus to some of the surviving Nephites and Lamanites, and how he descended from heaven to the temple at Bountiful to minister to the multitude there for three days. The people "did see with their eyes and did feel with their hands, and did know of a surety and did bear record" that Jesus had risen from the dead (3 Ne. 11:13–17). Jesus chose twelve disciples, gave them authority to perform ordinances, and commanded them to teach all the people (3 Ne. 11:18–41; 18:36–39; 19:4–13; Moro. 2). He declared his doctrine, forbidding disputation about it: "The Father commandeth all men, everywhere, to repent and believe in me. And whoso believeth in me, and is baptized, the same shall be saved" (3 Ne. 11:32–33). Jesus' teachings, including a version of the SERMON ON THE MOUNT very similar to the one contained in the New Testament, comprise "the law and the commandments" for the people (3 Ne. 12:19). Jesus healed their sick, blessed their children, and prayed for the multitude (3 Ne. 17:2–25; 19:5–36). Many were transfigured when ANGELS descended to minister to them (3 Ne. 17:22–25; 19:14–16). Jesus instituted the ordinances of baptism and the sacrament of bread and wine (3 Ne. 11:22–29; 18:1–14, 26–35; 19:10–13; 20:3–9), and taught the multitude how to live their lives free from sin (3 Ne. 18:12–25). He also taught that sin prevents participation in the ordinances, but one is forbidden to attend the synagogue or to repent and come to him (3 Ne. 18:25–33). He described the future in terms of COVENANTS made with the house of Israel, quoting Old Testament prophecies of MOSES (Deut. 18:15–19 = 3 Ne. 20:36–38; Gen. 12:3; 22:18 = 3 Ne. 20:25, 27), ISAIAH (Isa. 52:1–3, 6–8, 9–10, 11–15 = 3 Ne. 20:36–40, 32, 34–35, 41–45; Isa. 52:8–10 = 3 Ne. 16:18–20; Isa. 52:12, 15 = 3 Ne. 21:29, 8; Isa. 54 = 3 Ne. 22), Micah (Micah 4:12–13; 5:8–15 = 3 Ne. 20:18–19, 16–17; 21:12–18), and Habakkuk (Hab. 1:5 = 3 Ne. 21:9), that the remnants of Israel will be gathered when the prophecies of Isaiah begin to be fulfilled and when the remnants begin to believe in Christ, the Book of Mormon itself being a sign of the beginning of these events (3 Ne. 16:4–20; 20:10–23:6; 26:3–5). After inspecting their records, Jesus gave them additional prophecies that

they had not had (Mal. 3–4 = 3 Ne. 24–25), and "did expound all things" to their understanding (3 Ne. 20:10–26:11).

Even more sacred things said and done by Jesus during his three-day visit to the Western Hemisphere were not included in the present record (3 Ne. 26:6–12). His post-resurrection ministries to the people of Nephi and to the Old World disciples were only two of several he performed and of which records were made (3 Ne. 15:11–16:3; cf. D&C 88:51–61; *TPJS*, p. 191). Latter-day Saints hope to prepare themselves to receive the fuller accounts that are yet to come (2 Ne. 29:11–14; D&C 25:9; 101:32–35; 121:26–33; A of F 9).

BIBLIOGRAPHY

Brown, S. Kent, and C. Wilfred Griggs. "The Forty-Day Ministry of Christ." *Ensign* 5 (Aug. 1975):6–11, also in *Studies in Scripture*, ed. K. Jackson, Vol. 6, pp. 12–23. Salt Lake City, 1987.

Nibley, Hugh W. "Evangelium Quadraginta Dierum." *Vigiliae Christianae* 20 (1966):1–24, reprinted in *CWHN* 4:10–44.

For comparisons with the Book of Mormon, see H. Nibley, "Christ Among the Ruins," *Ensign* 13 (June 1983):14–19, in *CWHN* 8:407–34; and *Since Cumorah, CWHN* 7. Specialized studies include H. Nibley, "The Early Christian Prayer Circle," *BYU Studies* 19 (1978):41–78, in *CWHN* 4:45–99.

For the primary sources, see the references in the preceding works; English translations of many are found in Edgar Hennecke and Wilhelm Schneemelcher, *New Testament Apocrypha*, 2 vols., Philadelphia, 1965, and James M. Robinson, *The Nag Hammadi Library*, San Francisco, 1978, rev. ed. 1988.

JOHN GEE

LATTER-DAY APPEARANCES OF JESUS CHRIST

As shown in the New Testament and the Book of Mormon, after his resurrection, Jesus Christ can, and also does, appear to people in this latter-day DISPENSATION OF THE GOSPEL. When these sacred manifestations are for personal instruction, they are not spoken of openly. However, when it is appropriate, the divine communication is made public. It is a principle of the gospel that the Lord Jesus Christ can, and will, manifest himself to his people, including individual members, "in his own time, and in his own way, and according to his own will" (D&C 88:68).

The most important appearance of the Savior in this dispensation occurred when he and the Father came to Joseph SMITH in the spring of 1820. This theophany, commonly called the FIRST

VISION, revealed the separate nature of these two members of the GODHEAD and ushered in the DISPENSATION OF THE FULNESS OF TIMES and the RESTORATION OF ALL THINGS.

In 1832, Jesus Christ again appeared in a vision to Joseph Smith and Sidney RIGDON. Both men saw and conversed with him (D&C 76:14) and also witnessed a vision of the kingdoms to which mankind will be assigned in the life hereafter. The Lord also appeared to Joseph Smith and Oliver COWDERY in April 1836 in the Kirtland Temple shortly after its dedication and manifested his acceptance of this first latter-day temple (D&C 110:1–10).

A revelation pertaining to the salvation of the dead was given to Joseph Smith in an earlier appearance of Jesus Christ and the Father in the Kirtland Temple on January 21, 1836: "The heavens were opened upon us, and I beheld . . . the blazing throne of God, whereon was seated the

Jesus Christ Appearing to Joseph Smith and Oliver Cowdery in the Kirtland Temple, by Gary E. Smith (1980, oil on canvas, 36″ × 42″). Regarding the Savior's appearance in the Kirtland Temple on April 3, 1836, Joseph Smith wrote: "We saw the Lord standing upon the breastwork of the pulpit" (D&C 110:2). Courtesy Blaine T. Hudson.

Father and the Son" (D&C 137:1, 3). Joseph Smith said that visions were given to many in the meeting and that "some of them saw the face of the Savior" (*HC* 2:382).

Joseph Smith also recorded other occasions when Church members beheld the Savior. On March 18, 1833, he wrote of a significant meeting of the SCHOOL OF THE PROPHETS: "Many of the brethren saw a heavenly vision of the Savior, and concourses of angels, and many other things, of which each one has a record of what he saw" (*HC* 1:335). He wrote of a similar experience of Zebedee Coltrin (*HC* 2:387), and on another occasion he reported that "the Savior made His appearance unto some" at a meeting the week after the dedication of the Kirtland Temple (*HC* 2:432).

Appearances of Jesus Christ have not been restricted to the early days of the Church. In 1898 the Savior appeared to Lorenzo SNOW, the fifth President of the Church, and gave him important instructions regarding the Church (*My Kingdom Shall Roll Forth*, pp. 68–70, Salt Lake City, 1980). The sixth President of the Church, Joseph F. SMITH, saw the Savior in a vision in 1918, as recorded in Doctrine and Covenants section 138. This vision showed the Savior's visit to the spirits of the dead while his body was in the tomb between the time of his crucifixion and resurrection. In 1985, Ezra Taft BENSON, the thirteenth President of the Church, said, "Today in Christ's restored church, The Church of Jesus Christ of Latter-day Saints, He is revealing Himself and His will—from the first prophet of the Restoration, even Joseph Smith, to the present" (p. 4).

It is a teaching of latter-day revelation that individual members can have a personal visit from the Savior, and see his face, and receive instruction from him, when they are prepared, and when the Lord chooses to grant such an experience (D&C 93:1; *see* JESUS CHRIST: SECOND COMFORTER).

BIBLIOGRAPHY

Benson, Ezra Taft. "Joy in Christ." *Ensign* 16 (Mar. 1986):4.

JOEL A. FLAKE

SECOND COMING OF JESUS CHRIST

In Jewish and Christian thought there are two basic ways of viewing the coming of the MESSIAH. Some consider promises of a Messiah and a millennial era symbolic of a time when men will finally learn to live in peace and harmony and the world will enter a new age of enlightenment and progress; no one individual nor any one specific event will usher in this age. The Church of Jesus Christ of Latter-day Saints opposes this view and agrees with the many other Jewish and Christian groups who affirm that there is an actual Messiah, that he will come at some future time to the earth, and that only through his coming and the events associated therewith will a millennial age of peace, harmony, and joy begin. Jews look for the first coming of the Messiah; Latter-day Saints and other Christians for the second coming of Jesus Christ.

The SCRIPTURES, both biblical and modern, abundantly testify that the era just preceding the second advent of the Savior will be "perilous" (2 Tim. 3:1) and filled with "tribulation" (Matt. 24:29). At that time "the devil shall have power over his own dominion" (D&C 1:35). The resulting judgments upon the wicked are part of the preparations for the MILLENNIUM.

The righteous as well as the unenlightened will experience these times of tribulation. LDS sources teach that the Lord will gather the righteous together in "holy places" (D&C 101:22), which include ZION and her STAKES (D&C 115:6). These places are described in terms of "peace," "refuge," and "safety for the saints of the Most High God" (D&C 45:66). The promise is that God "will not suffer that the wicked shall destroy the righteous. Wherefore, he will preserve the righteous by his power . . . Wherefore, the righteous need not fear" (1 Ne. 22:16–17).

Attempts to predict the time of the coming of the Messiah are legion in both Jewish and Christian traditions. Latter-day Saints consider the second coming "near, even at the doors" (D&C 110:16). But they also accept the decree of scripture that "the hour and the day [of Christ's coming] no man knoweth, neither the angels in heaven, *nor shall they know until he comes*" (D&C 49:7 [italics added]; cf. Matt. 24:36).

With many other Christians, Mormons believe the second coming will be preceded by the battle of Armageddon and by Christ's appearance on the Mount of Olives (see LAST DAYS). Of this event the Doctrine and Covenants says:

And then shall the Jews look upon me and say: What are these wounds in thine hands and in thy feet? Then shall they know that I am the Lord; for I will say unto them: These wounds are the wounds with which I was wounded in the house of my friends. I am he who was lifted up. I am Jesus that was crucified. I am the Son of God. And then shall they weep because of their iniquities; then shall they lament because they persecuted their king [D&C 45:51–53; cf. Zech. 13:6].

"From that day forward," it has been proclaimed, "the Jews as a nation become holy and their city and sanctuary become holy. There also the Messiah establishes his throne and seat of government" (Clark, p. 258).

Before Christ's coming in glory, "there shall be silence in the heaven for the space of half an hour; and immediately after shall the curtain of heaven be unfolded . . . and the face of the Lord shall be unveiled" (D&C 88:95). This apparently is the time when "all flesh shall see me together" (D&C 101:23; Rev. 1:7).

The Doctrine and Covenants declares that "the earth shall pass away so as by fire" (D&C 43:32). Some have conjectured that this could occur through a nuclear holocaust. Though certain apocalyptic passages may seem to describe the effects of nuclear warfare (e.g., Isa. 34:1–10), a modern REVELATION teaches that the "fire" of the Second Coming is the actual presence of the Savior, a celestial glory comparable to the glory of the sun (D&C 76:70) or a "consuming fire" (Heb. 12:29; cf. Mal. 3:2; 4:1). "So great shall be the glory of his presence that the sun shall hide his face in shame" (D&C 133:49). "The presence of the Lord shall be as the melting fire that burneth, and as the fire which causeth the waters to boil" (D&C 133:41; cf. Isa. 64:2; JS—H 1:37). "Element shall melt with fervent heat" (D&C 101:25) and "the mountains shall flow down at thy presence" (D&C 133:44). The Doctrine and Covenants repeats Isaiah's declaration that "the Lord shall be red in his apparel, and his garments like him that treadeth in the wine-vat" (D&C 133:48; cf. Isa. 63:2).

The apostle PAUL wrote to the Thessalonian Saints that those living on the earth at the time of Christ's appearing would be caught up to meet him (1 Thess. 4:16–17). The Doctrine and Covenants, using similar language, adds that these righteous saints will be "quickened" and will join those "who have slept in their graves," who will also "be caught up to meet him in the midst of the pillar of heaven" (D&C 88:96–97; see RESURRECTION). Christ will descend to earth "in like manner as ye have seen him go into heaven" (Acts 1:11).

With the coming of Christ, the millennial era of peace, harmony, and RIGHTEOUSNESS will begin. Satan will then have "no power over the hearts of the people, for they dwell in righteousness, and the Holy One of Israel reigneth" (1 Ne. 22:26; *see also* MILLENNIUM).

BIBLIOGRAPHY

Clark, James R., comp. "Proclamation of the Twelve." In *Messages of the First Presidency*, Vol. l, p. 258. Salt Lake City, 1965.

Lund, Gerald N. *The Coming of the Lord.* Salt Lake City, 1971.

McConkie, Bruce R. *The Millennial Messiah: The Second Coming of the Son of Man.* Salt Lake City, 1982.

Smith, Joseph Fielding. *The Signs of the Times.* Salt Lake City, 1964.

GERALD N. LUND

JESUS CHRIST, FATHERHOOD AND SONSHIP OF

Latter-day Saint scriptures refer to Jesus Christ as both the Father and the Son. Most notably in the Book of Mormon, Christ introduced himself to the BROTHER OF JARED saying, "I am the Father and the Son" (Ether 3:14); NEPHI₁ referred to the Lamb of God as "the Eternal Father" (1 Ne. 11:21, 1830 ed.), and the prophet ABINADI said that the Messiah would be "the Father . . . and the Son" (Mosiah 15:3). Such usage has been explained in several ways consistent with the fundamental LDS understanding of the Godhead as three distinct beings.

There is no lack of clarity about Christ's sonship. Jesus is the Son of God in at least three ways. First, he is the firstborn spirit child of God the Father and thereby the elder brother of the spirits of all men and women as God the Father, known also by the exalted name-title Elohim, is the father of the spirits of all mankind (Num. 16:22; Heb. 12:9; John 20:17). Thus, when Christ is called the Firstborn (e.g., Rom. 8:29; Col. 1:15; D&C 93:21), Latter-day Saints accept this as a possible reference to Christ's spiritual birth. Second, he is the literal physical son of God, the Only Begotten in the Flesh (e.g., John 1:14; 3:16; 2 Ne. 25:12; Jacob 4:11; D&C 29:42; 93:11; Moses 1:6; 2:26). Third, spiritually he is also a son by virtue of his submission unto the will of the Father (Heb. 5:8).

Jesus Christ is also known by the title of Father. The meaning of scriptures using this nomenclature is not always immediately clear, primarily owing to the fact that Christ and his Father are virtually inseparable in purpose, testimony, glory, and power. In most cases, however, the scriptural usage can be explained in several ways:

Christ is sometimes called Father because of his role as Creator from the beginning (*see* CREATION). Before his mortal birth, and acting under the direction of the Father, Jesus was JEHOVAH, the Lord Omnipotent, through whom God created worlds without number (Moses 1:33; 7:30; John 1:1–3; Heb. 1:2). Because of his creative role, Christ-Jehovah is called "the Father of heaven and earth, the Creator of all things from the beginning" in the Book of Mormon (Mosiah 3:8; see also 2 Ne. 25:16; Alma 11:39; 3 Ne. 9:15). Jesus' role as Creator is similarly attested in the Bible (e.g., John 1:3; Eph. 3:9; Col. 1:16) and the Doctrine and Covenants (e.g., D&C 38:1–3; 45:1; 76:24; 93:9).

Jesus Christ is also known as Father through the spiritual rebirth of mankind (*see* BORN OF GOD). As the foreordained Redeemer, he became the "author of eternal salvation unto all them that obey him" (Heb. 5:9). He is the Savior. No person will come unto the Father except through him and by his name (John 14:6; Acts 4:12; Mosiah 3:17). Those who accept the gospel of Jesus Christ and receive its saving covenantal ordinances, living worthy of its sanctifying and enlightening powers, are "born again" unto Christ and become known as the children of Christ, "his sons and daughters," his "seed" (Mosiah 5:5–8; 15:10–13; 27:25–26; Alma 5:14). Christ thus becomes the Father of their salvation, the Father of life in the Spirit, the Father of the new birth. In a related sense, he is also the Father of all mankind in that the RESURRECTION of the entire human family comes through him (Sperry, p. 35).

Furthermore, Jesus is called Father because of the AUTHORITY God gave him to act for the Father. He explained in Jerusalem: "I can of mine own self do nothing . . . I am come in my Father's name" (John 5:30, 43). An LDS leader has clarified this: "All revelation since the fall has come through Jesus Christ, who is the Jehovah of the Old Testament. . . . The Father has never dealt with man directly and personally since the fall, and he has never appeared except to introduce and bear record of the Son" (*DS* 1:27). Latter-day Saints understand this to mean that, except when introducing the Son, God always acts and speaks to mankind through Jesus Christ. Accordingly, the Father has placed his name upon the Son, authorized and empowered him to speak even in the first person for him, as though he were the Father. An example of this is when the Lord Jehovah (who would later come to earth as Jesus of Nazareth) spoke to Moses: "Moses, my son; . . . thou art in the similitude of mine Only Begotten; and mine Only Begotten is and shall be the Savior" (Moses 1:6). Sometimes the Savior has spoken both as the Father (Elohim) and as the Son (Jesus) in the same revelation (e.g., D&C 29:1 and 42; 49:5 and 28).

In addition, Christ is Father in that he literally inherited attributes and powers from his Father (Elohim). From Mary, his mother, Jesus inherited MORTALITY, the capacity to die. From God, his Father, Jesus inherited IMMORTALITY, the capacity to live forever: "As the Father hath life in himself; so hath he given to the Son to have life in himself" (John 5:26; cf. Hel. 5:11). Christ is "the Father because he was conceived by the power of God" (Mosiah 15:3). "This is a matter of his Eternal Parent investing him with power from on high so that he becomes the Father because he exercises the power of that Eternal Being" (McConkie, p. 371).

Christ is also Father in that he spiritually received all that the Father has. "I am in the Father, and the Father in me, and the Father and I are one—the Father because he gave me of his fulness, and the Son because I was in the world" (D&C 93:3–4).

Other explanations are likewise possible. All persons have multiple roles in life. A man can be a father, son, and brother; a woman can be a mother, daughter, and sister. These titles describe roles or functions at a given time, as well as relationships to others. For Latter-day Saints, this is so with the Christ. He has many names and titles. He ministers as both the Father and the Son. After explaining that the God of Abraham, Isaac, and Jacob would come to earth, take a body, and minister as both Father and Son, Abinadi summarized: "And they are one God, yea, the very Eternal Father of heaven and earth" (Mosiah 15:4; see also Mosiah 7:26–27; D&C 93:14). The Father and the Son, the Spirit and the flesh, the God and the man— these titles, roles, and attributes are blended wondrously in one being, Jesus Christ, in whom "dwelleth all the fulness of the Godhead bodily" (Col. 2:9).

BIBLIOGRAPHY

"'The Father and the Son': A Doctrinal Exposition of the First Presidency and the Twelve," June 30, 1916. In *MFP* 5:26–34. Salt Lake City, 1971.

McConkie, Bruce R. *The Promised Messiah*, chaps. 4, 9, 20. Salt Lake City, 1978.

Smith, Joseph Fielding. *DS* 1:26–34. Salt Lake City, 1954.

Sperry, Sidney B. *Answers to Book of Mormon Questions*, pp. 31–38. Salt Lake City, 1967.

ROBERT L. MILLET

JESUS CHRIST, NAMES AND TITLES OF

Since Jesus Christ is the central focus both in Church devotion and in scripture, he is naturally known under many names and titles, including the following:

JESUS. The Hebrew *yeshua'* or *yehoshua'*, meaning "Jehovah saves," is transliterated into English as the name Joshua. In Greek, it became *Iesous*, thence *Iesus* in Latin and *Jesus* in English. Since Jesus was actually Jehovah performing saving work, his name *yeshua'*, "Jehovah saves," coincides precisely.

MESSIAH. This title comes from the Hebrew *meshiach*, "anointed one." Among the Israelites, prophets, priests and kings were anointed, designating them as rightful successors. Commonly, "messiah" referred to a figure awaited by ISRAEL to be her king. Applied to Jesus, the title retains its full sense of "anointed" prophet, priest, and king.

CHRIST. Greek for Messiah (anointed one) is *Christos*, Christ in English. Thus, "Jesus Christ" joins a name and a title, and means Jesus the Messiah.

SON OF GOD. Jesus was not the son of any mortal man. His biological father was God, the Father. As Son of God, Jesus represents the Father and acts as his agent in all things.

SON OF MAN. From his mother Jesus inherited mortality. Hebrew *ben 'adam* denotes "a son of Adam," that is, any mortal man (Dan. 8:17). Thus, as a son of Adam, Jesus represents Adam's children, acting as their agent with the Father. As both Son of God and Son of Man, Jesus stands between God and man as mediator. With the definite article, *the* Son of Man described an expected apocalyptic heavenly figure, identified with the Messiah (Dan. 7:13). Jesus is the son of the archetypal Man, the perfect heavenly Man, the Eternal Father (Moses 6:57; 7:35). In this sense, "Son of Man" equals "Son of God" and conveys an intentional ambiguity, reflecting both Jesus' mortal and immortal parentage.

SON OF DAVID. Jews expected the Messiah to belong to David's lineage. Prophets had foretold that a son (descendant) of David would restore Israel's kingdom to its former zenith (see Isa. 11:1–9; Jer. 23:5–6). According to Matthew 1:1–16, Jesus was descended from David. "Son of David" refers particularly to Jesus' messiahship in its political aspect as Davidic king.

JEHOVAH. Latter-day Saints believe that Jesus was Jehovah himself, God of Israel, not son of Jehovah (Isa. 41:14; 43:11, 14; Mosiah 3:5; 3 Ne. 11:14; 15:5). The name Jehovah vocalized thus is not found in ancient texts, but is a modern convention. In ancient times, the Hebrew text had no vowels; thus the consonants in God's name were *yhwh*. Jews avoided pronouncing these consonants when reading aloud, substituting *'adonai*, a word meaning "the Lord." Following this practice, King James translators usually rendered *yhwh* as "the LORD." In medieval Hebrew texts, the vowels from *'adonai* were added to the consonants *yhwh* to remind Jewish readers to say *"'adonai."* English translators adopted this convention, creating the artificial form "Jehovah." Latter-day Saints accept Jehovah as a name for the premortal Christ because this is the common English form for *yhwh*.

EL. *'El* is not a name, but is the common noun for God in Hebrew (plural, *'elohim*). Latter-day Saints often use ELOHIM for the Father, allowing a distinction between members of the GODHEAD. Nevertheless, in the Old Testament, El and its cognates, such as Elohim and El Shaddai (God Almighty), usually refer to the premortal Jesus, the god (*'el*) of the Old Testament.

EMMANUEL. Since Jesus was the ancient El, the angel (Matt. 1:23) correctly called his name Emmanuel (Hebrew, *'immanu'el*), meaning El (god) with us.

THE LORD. Since Jews uttered *'adonai* (Lord) instead of the divine name, the Greek Bible (c. 200 B.C.) usually translated *yhwh* as *ho kurios*, "the Lord." Thus, "the Lord," whether *'adonai* or *kurios*, equaled "Jehovah." Not surprisingly, "the Lord" is Jesus' most common title in the New Testament. The confession of the early Church, "Jesus is Lord" could only mean Jesus is Jehovah.

I AM. In Exodus 3:14, Jehovah (Jesus Christ) identified himself as "I AM," perhaps affirming Jesus as the creator who exists independently of his creation. Scholars see connections between this Old Testament title and Jesus' many "I am" statements in the New Testament, for example, "I am the good Shepherd" (John 10:11, 14), or "Before Abraham was I am" (John 8:58).

FATHER. In at least three senses Jesus is Father: (1) he is the creator of the physical universe; (2) he is the Father's agent in everything pertaining to this creation and its inhabitants; and (3) he is Father of all eternal, resurrected human beings. Jesus Christ begets spiritually and gives ETERNAL LIFE to one "born again," who thus becomes Christ's son or daughter (Mosiah 27:25). Moreover, Latter-day Saints call Christ "elder brother." In the premortal context this is correct, for there Jesus was "the Firstborn" of all spirit children of the Father (D&C 93:21). Nevertheless, "Father" best describes Christ's present and future relationship to mortals who have been spiritually reborn.

SECOND COMFORTER. The Holy Ghost, the Comforter, comforts the faithful with the assurance of inheriting the KINGDOM OF GOD. However, through faith in Christ one can receive a *second* comforter, an appearance of Jesus himself, who assures the individual of his or her place in the kingdom. After a witness from the Spirit, the Second Comforter is a personal witness from the risen Lord (John 14:16–23).

SAVIOR. The most sublime of titles, Savior underscores Jesus' role in the divine plan. Both Old and New Testaments specify that the Savior is God (Isa. 45:21–23; Luke 1:47; etc.). Through agony and death suffered for others, Jesus is able to erase imperfections and bestow worthiness, on condition of repentance. Since imperfect beings cannot reside in God's presence (D&C 1:31), Jesus saves believers from their imperfection, their sins, and their worst selves. (See also, above, the definition of his name, "Jesus.")

THE WORD. As words carry the thoughts of one mind to the minds of others, so Jesus communicates the mind and will of the Father to mortals. Moreover, as words are agents for expression, so from the beginning (John 1:1–3) Jesus is the agent for expressing and accomplishing the Father's will. Christ is both the messenger and the message.

ALPHA AND OMEGA. Equivalent to the Old Testament term "the first and the last" (e.g., Isa. 44:6), alpha and omega are the first and last letters of the Greek alphabet. Just as no letters stand before alpha or after omega, so there are no other gods in this creation other than that represented in Jesus Christ. He encompasses all, from beginning to end; he extends beyond all extremities and categories.

ONLY BEGOTTEN. Jesus Christ is the only being begotten by the Father in MORTALITY. His full title is "the Only Begotten of the Father in the flesh." Since Mormons believe all humans were spiritually begotten by the Father before creation, "Only Begotten" is understood as being limited to mortality.

LAMB OF GOD. In the first Passover, a slain lamb's blood was daubed on Israelites' houses to avert the destroyer. In the New Testament, Jesus is understood as a Passover lamb supplied by God, and Passover stands as a type for the death of Jesus, the Lamb of God, whose blood, through BAPTISM and the SACRAMENT of the Lord's Supper, protects Christians from the destroyer, Satan. According to Moses 5:6–8, animal sacrifices were to be "a similitude of the sacrifice of the Only Begotten of the Father."

STEPHEN E. ROBINSON

JESUS CHRIST, SECOND COMFORTER

The term "Second Comforter" refers to Jesus Christ in his role of ministering personally to his faithful followers (John 14:21–23; D&C 93:1; 130:3). Jesus taught his disciples that the Holy Ghost was a comforter (John 14:26), but he also spoke of a second comforter (John 14:16–21). Latter-day Saints have been given additional understanding about the Second Comforter by the Prophet Joseph SMITH:

> After a person has faith in Christ, repents of his sins, and is baptized for the remission of his sins and receives the Holy Ghost (by the laying on of hands), which is the first Comforter, then let him continue to humble himself before God, hungering and thirsting after righteousness, and living by every word of God, and the Lord will soon say unto him, Son, thou shalt be exalted. When the Lord has thoroughly proved him, and finds that the man is determined to serve Him at all hazards, then the man will find his calling and his election made sure, then it will be his privilege to receive the other Com-

forter, which the Lord hath promised the Saints, as is recorded in the testimony of St. John, in the 14th chapter, from the 12th to the 27th verses. . . .

> Now what is this other Comforter? It is no more nor less than the Lord Jesus Christ Himself; . . . when any man obtains this last Comforter, he will have the personage of Jesus Christ to attend him, or appear unto him from time to time, and even He will manifest the Father unto him, and they will take up their abode with him, and the visions of the heavens will be opened unto him, and the Lord will teach him face to face, and he may have a perfect knowledge of the mysteries of the Kingdom of God; and this is the state and place the ancient Saints arrived at when they had such glorious visions—Isaiah, Ezekiel, John upon the Isle of Patmos, St. Paul in the three heavens, and all the Saints who held communion with the general assembly and Church of the First Born [*TPJS*, pp. 150–51].

The Lord has counseled his Saints to "seek his face" (D&C 101:37–38). No sinful person can endure his presence, and hence will not obtain the blessing (D&C 67:10–13; JST Ex. 33:11, 20). In God's wisdom, some faithful individuals are blessed with the Second Comforter while remaining in mortality.

[*See also* Calling and Election; Jesus Christ: Latter-day Appearances of.]

BIBLIOGRAPHY

McConkie, Bruce R. *A New Witness for the Articles of Faith*, pp. 492–99, 549. Salt Lake City, 1985.

THOMAS E. SHERRY

JESUS CHRIST, SOURCES FOR WORDS OF

For followers of Jesus Christ, nothing has more authority or significance than his very words. Called *ipsissima verba* or *logia*, they are not colored by paraphrase or interpretation, but represent his exact instructions, whether spoken by Jesus himself in the first person or by another commissioned by him, speaking in the first person—as if God—through the power of the HOLY GHOST (2 Ne. 32:3; 33:10–11; D&C 1:38; cf. Rev. 19:1–10).

The status given Jesus' words goes back to early Christianity. Much current interest in New Testament APOCRYPHA rests in the hope of recovering authentic sayings of Jesus. For example, in the words of a modern editor, "The Gospel of Thomas is not a 'gospel' in the proper sense. . . . it is no other and no less than a collection of 114 logia, the most extensive collection of sayings of Jesus, or sayings attributed to Jesus, that has yet come down to us independently of the New Testament tradition" (Puech, pp. 284–85).

Some ancient and contemporary sources unique to The Church of Jesus Christ of Latter-day Saints augment the known body of Jesus' words. The Church teaches that Jesus Christ is both the God of the Old Testament and the New Testament. Therefore, it views quotes attributed to God in the Old Testament as *ipsissima verba* of Jesus. For example, God's command to Moses to "stretch out thine hand over the sea, and divide it" is considered to be from Jesus Christ (Ex. 14:16; cf. 1 Cor. 10:1–4). Moreover, when ancient prophets quote God in the first person, such as "I the Lord love judgment, I hate robbery for burnt offering" (Isa. 61:8), these words are reckoned as Jesus' *ipsissima verba* (see JESUS CHRIST: FIRSTBORN IN THE SPIRIT and JESUS CHRIST, NAMES AND TITLES OF).

As the Prophet Joseph SMITH produced under inspiration the JOSEPH SMITH TRANSLATION OF THE BIBLE (JST), many *logia* were recorded. For instance, after Moses broke the first set of tablets with the Ten Commandments, the Lord commanded him to make another. In current Hebrew manuscripts, God says that he will rewrite what was on the first. But in the JST, the Lord adds, "It shall not be according to the first [tablets], for I will take away the priesthood out of their midst; therefore my holy order, and the ordinances thereof, shall not go before them" (JST Ex. 34:11–12; Deut. 10:1–2; cf. D&C 84:18–27).

The JST also adds *logia* to the New Testament. As background to Jesus' illustration of not putting new wine into old bottles, the JST adds, "Then said the Pharisees unto him, Why will ye not receive us with our baptism, seeing we keep the whole law? But Jesus said unto them, Ye keep not the law. If ye had kept the law, ye would have received me, for I am he who gave the law. I receive not you with your baptism, because it profiteth you nothing. For when that which is new is come, the old is ready to be put away" (JST Matt. 9:18–21). Such passages, although not in any extant Greek text, are accepted by Latter-day Saints as true sayings of Jesus.

In addition to accepting biblical scripture, the Church has canonized other scriptures which pre-serve *ipsissima verba* of Jesus Christ: the Pearl of Great Price, the Book of Mormon, and the Doctrine and Covenants.

In the Pearl of Great Price, the BOOK OF MOSES—an excerpt from the JST—preserves the declaration well known among Latter-day Saints, "For behold, this is my work and my glory—to bring to pass the immortality and eternal life of man" (Moses 1:39). The BOOK OF ABRAHAM also contains teachings of Jehovah, or Christ. In chapter 3, Jehovah compares the nature of the universe to the variety of spirits, or intelligences, that inhabit the universe. Recounting God's dealings with people inhabiting the American continent, the Book of Mormon also preserves sayings given to their prophets. In addition to specific words from "the Son" recorded by NEPHI₁ (2 Ne. 31:12, 14) and others (e.g., MORONI₂ in Ether 12:26–28), Jesus' words spoken to the people of the Western Hemisphere soon after his resurrection also appear. Besides a discourse similar to the Sermon on the Mount recorded in Matthew 5–7 (3 Ne. 12–14), the risen Jesus spoke of baptism (3 Ne. 11), the sacrament (chap. 18), the gathering of Israel, and the helping role of the GENTILES (chaps. 16, 20–21).

The Doctrine and Covenants records sayings of Christ directed to people of the contemporary world: "Hearken, O ye people of my church, . . . verily I say: Hearken ye people from afar; and ye that are upon the islands of the sea, listen together," are words spoken in 1831 (D&C 1:1). This volume comprises an extensive collection of the words of Jesus Christ as a VOICE OF WARNING and instruction on how to prepare both the earth and one's own heart for his second coming.

An additional contemporary source for the words of Christ resides in statements of the PRESIDENTS OF THE CHURCH. The Lord has declared that "his word ye shall receive, as if from mine own mouth" (D&C 1:38; 21:5). Thus, whenever the President of the Church speaks officially within his office and CALLING, his words are considered by Latter-day Saints to have the same authority as words of the Lord himself.

[*See also* Jesus Christ in the Scriptures.]

BIBLIOGRAPHY

Millet, Robert L. "The Formation of the Canonical Gospels." In *Apocryphal Writings and the Latter-day Saints*, ed. W. Griggs. Provo, Utah, 1986.

Puech, Henri-Charles. "Gnostic Gospels and Related Documents." In *New Testament Apocrypha*, ed. Edgar Hennecke and Wilhelm Schneemelcher, Vol. 1, pp. 231–362. Philadelphia, 1963.

J. PHILIP SCHAELLING

JESUS CHRIST, TAKING THE NAME OF, UPON ONESELF

It is a doctrine of The Church of Jesus Christ of Latter-day Saints that the only way to obtain salvation is to take the name of Jesus Christ upon oneself. This is categorically stated in several latter-day revelations. Although not specifically stated in the Bible, the concept is implied in Paul's declaration to "put on Christ" (Rom. 13:14; Gal. 3:27); Peter's statement that Jesus Christ is the only name given "among men, whereby we must be saved" (Acts 4:12; Ex. 15:2; 1 Sam. 2:1; Ps. 27:1); and the Lord's instruction to Moses to "put my name upon the children of Israel" (Num. 6:27; cf. Jer. 15:16). The taking of the name of Christ upon oneself in this dispensation begins with being baptized into his Church and keeping the commandments.

The Lord declared to the Prophet Joseph SMITH that all persons desiring a place in the kingdom of the Father must take upon themselves the name of Christ (D&C 18:24–25, 27). Amulek, in the Book of Mormon, counseled the wayward Zoramites to "take upon you the name of Christ" (Alma 34:38). The resurrected Jesus promised, "Whoso taketh upon him my name, and endureth to the end, the same shall be saved at the last day" (3 Ne. 27:5–6; cf. Mosiah 25:23; 26:18). Abraham was told by the Lord, "I will take thee, to put upon thee my name" (Abr. 1:18).

Sacred covenant making is associated with taking the name of Jesus upon oneself. King BENJAMIN said, "There is no other name given whereby salvation cometh; therefore, I would that ye should take upon you the name of Christ, all you that have entered into the covenant with God that ye should be obedient unto the end of your lives" (Mosiah 5:8; cf. 18:8–12; Alma 46:15). The covenants of BAPTISM (D&C 20:37; cf. 2 Ne. 31:13) and of the Lord's Supper (D&C 20:77; Moro. 4:3) require taking the name of Jesus Christ upon oneself. Bruce R. McConkie, a latter-day APOSTLE, stated, "We have taken upon ourselves his name in the waters of baptism. We renew the covenant therein made when we partake of the sacrament

[Lord's Supper]. If we have been born again, we have become the sons and daughters of the Lord Jesus Christ" (McConkie, p. 393).

Dallin H. Oaks, also an apostle, further explained that "we take upon us the name of Christ when we are baptized in his name, when we belong to his Church and profess our belief in him, and when we do the work of his kingdom. There are other meanings as well, deeper meanings that the more mature members of the Church should understand and ponder" (Oaks, p. 80). The "deeper meanings" are identified as inheriting the fulness of God's glory and obtaining EXALTATION in the celestial kingdom (Oaks, pp. 81–83).

BIBLIOGRAPHY
McConkie, Bruce R. "Jesus Christ and Him Crucified." In *BYU Devotional Speeches of the Year*, pp. 391–405. Provo, Utah, 1976.
Oaks, Dallin H. "Taking Upon Us the Name of Jesus Christ," *Ensign* 15 (May 1985):80–83.

PAUL R. WARNER

JESUS CHRIST, TYPES AND SHADOWS OF

Latter-day Saints believe that many events, persons, and objects in the Old Testament and other scriptures were "types" or foreshadowings of Jesus Christ. Jesus taught, for instance, that manna had anticipated him, the true heavenly bread (John 6:30–35), and that Jonah's three days in the fish signified his death and burial (Matt. 12:38–41).

Paul affirmed that the water produced from a rock by Moses pointed to the spiritual nourishment to come through Jesus (Ex. 17:6; 1 Cor. 10:4); furthermore, he asserted that the first Adam prefigured Jesus, the second Adam, who brought life to his spiritual offspring in contrast to Adam who brought death (Rom. 5:12–21; 1 Cor. 15:45). Similarly, the inheritances of Ishmael and Isaac foreshadowed differences between the old covenant and the new (Gal. 4:22–31).

According to Hebrews 7:15, the Messiah came "after the similitude of Melchizedek," (Hebrew, "King of Righteousness") who prefigured the roles of priest and king. The genealogy of Jesus in Matthew 1:2–17 was written to prove that Jesus was both descended from and foreshadowed by David as king over Israel. Some LDS leaders have taught that the lives of many prophets have served as types of Christ (McConkie, pp. 448–53).

Prototypes and intimations can also be found in the symbolism of ancient Israel's sacred ceremonies. For example, the scapegoat and purification rites of the Day of Atonement signify Christ's salvation wrought by suffering and death (Heb. 9:7–14). Further, the Feast of Tabernacles, with its harvest and light associations, teaches of the Messianic reign (2 Bar. 29:4–8; John 8:12).

Book of Mormon passages add impetus to the notion of scriptural types. Amulek observed that "the whole meaning of the [Mosaic] law . . . point[ed] to that great and last sacrifice . . . [of] the Son of God" (Alma 34:14). Moreover, Abraham's offering of Isaac was called a "similitude of God and [the sacrifice of] his Only Begotten Son" (Jacob 4:5). God showed to ancient Israel "many signs, and wonders, and types, and shadows . . . concerning [Christ's] coming" (Mosiah 3:15). The prophet Alma called the LIAHONA a God-given compass, a "type" of Christ, who guides toward eternal life (Alma 37:38–46). In the broad sense, "all things . . . given of God . . . unto man, are the typifying of [Christ]" (2 Ne. 11:4).

The Pearl of Great Price also teaches that all creation bears record of Christ (Moses 6:63). This includes the sun, which points to him, the light of the world (see D&C 88:5–13). Similarly, every revealed ordinance exhibits a symbolic linkage to one element or another of Jesus' ministry. For example, just as the daily sacrifices of Jerusalem's temple foreshadowed Christ's sacrifice (Heb. 7:26–28), so Latter-day Saints see gospel ORDINANCES as pointing to him and to the way back into his presence.

BIBLIOGRAPHY

McConkie, Bruce R. *The Promised Messiah*, pp. 374–453. Salt Lake City, 1978.

Read, Lenet H. "Symbols of the Harvest: Old Testament Holy Days and the Lord's Ministry." *Ensign* (Jan. 1975):32–36.

LENET HADLEY READ

JESUS CHRIST IN THE SCRIPTURES

[*This entry consists of four articles:*

Jesus Christ in the Bible
Jesus Christ in the Book of Mormon
Jesus Christ in the Doctrine and Covenants
Jesus Christ in the Pearl of Great Price

Jesus Christ is the central focus in all scriptures accepted by Latter-day Saints. Jesus Christ in the Bible details how Jesus is seen as the central figure—both in prophecy and in its fulfillment—in the Old and New Testaments. The article Jesus Christ in the Book of Mormon treats the pivotal prophetic interest in Christ manifested in the Book of Mormon, including his post-resurrection appearance to people in the Western Hemisphere. Jesus Christ in the Doctrine and Covenants illuminates the fundamental dominance of the person of Jesus in latter-day revelation. The article Jesus Christ in the Pearl of Great Price summarizes Jesus' place both in ancient prophetic expectation and in its latter-day fruition.]

JESUS CHRIST IN THE BIBLE

Latter-day Saints view Jesus Christ as the central figure of the entire Bible. The Old and New Testaments are divinely inspired records that reveal the mission of Jesus as Creator, God of Israel, Messiah, Son of God, Redeemer, and eternal King. The Bible contains history, doctrinal teachings, and prophecy of future events, with Jesus Christ as the main subject in every category.

The Old Testament contains an account of the Creation, and of the dealings of God with the human family from Adam to about 400 B.C. The promise of a messiah is a generally pervading theme. The New Testament chronicles principal events in the earth life of Jesus the Messiah from his birth through death, resurrection, and ascension into heaven, with a promise that he will return to earth to judge the world and then reign as king. Latter-day Saints identify Jesus as Jehovah, the Creator, the God of Adam, of Abraham, of Moses, and of Israel. Jesus is Jehovah come to earth as the promised Messiah (*see* JEHOVAH, JESUS CHRIST). Hence, the dealings of God with the human family throughout the Old Testament and New Testament periods form a record of the premortal and the mortal Jesus Christ.

THE HISTORICAL JESUS. Latter-day Saints take the biblical message about Jesus literally (*see* JESUS CHRIST: MINISTRY OF). The historical Jesus is the Jesus of the Bible: the Only Begotten Son of God in the flesh, born of the Virgin MARY in Bethlehem, baptized by John the Baptist. He performed a variety of miracles, was a teacher of the gospel who occasionally spoke in parables, and "went about doing good" (Acts 10:38). He chose twelve apostles, organized a church, gathered many followers, and was rejected by the Jewish rulers. His attitudes toward Samaritans, women, political leaders (e.g., Herod, Caesar), ritual law, and prayer were rather revolutionary for his day. He suffered at GETHSEMANE, bled at every pore, was crucified, died, was resurrected from the dead, and subsequently ascended into heaven from the Mount of Olives. Latter-day Saints consider both the historical portion of the record of the life of Jesus, and the prophetic portion, to be accurate. The promises that this same Jesus will come again in glory, in person to judge the world, then reign on the earth as King of Kings, are future realities that are taken literally.

PORTRAYAL OF JESUS THROUGH CEREMONY. Throughout the Bible, the mission of Jesus Christ is portrayed in ceremonies that are types and symbols of actual events. To the Old Testament prophets, animal sacrifices prefigured and typified the coming of Jesus to shed his blood and sacrifice his life for the sins of mankind. Because lambs were frequently offered, Jesus is spoken of in the New Testament as the Lamb of God (John 1:29, 36; cf. 1 Ne. 11:21).

For the animal sacrifice to symbolize Jesus' sacrifice, it had to be from among the firstlings of the flock (meaning the first male born to its mother) without blemish, offered without a bone being broken, and its blood had to be shed. Each of these points had a counterpart in Jesus' life on earth. Even details of the Passover service, requiring the blood of the lamb to be placed on the door post so that the angel of death might pass over that house (Ex. 12:3–24, 46), prefigured the mission and saving power of Jesus, the Lamb of God, who was crucified at the time of the annual Passover celebration. Paul, understanding this symbolism, exclaims, "For even Christ our passover is sacrificed for us" (1 Cor. 5:7).

The LAW OF MOSES is identified by Paul as "our schoolmaster to bring us unto Christ" (Gal. 3:24). To do that, it foreshadowed and typified Christ. When he worked out the Atonement, Christ fulfilled all the law; therefore the law had an end in him, and was replaced by the fulness of the gospel (3 Ne. 9:17; cf. Matt. 5:17–18; Heb. 10:1). LDS understanding of the role of the law of Moses and of other Old Testament ordinances is clearly spoken by the Book of Mormon prophet Nephi about 600 B.C.:

> Behold, my soul delighteth in proving unto my people the truth of the coming of Christ; for, for this end hath the law of Moses been given; and all things which have been given of God from the beginning of the world, unto man, are the typifying of him [2 Ne. 11:4; cf. Jacob 4:5].

When Jesus ate the Passover meal with the Twelve at the Last Supper, he gave them bread representing his flesh, which would be broken, and wine representing his blood, which would be shed. Believers were commanded to partake of this symbolic ceremony often: "This do in remembrance of me" (Luke 22:17–20; cf. 3 Ne. 18:3–13; 20:8–9).

OLD TESTAMENT FORESHADOWINGS. The writers of the four Gospels saw things in the Old Testament that foreshadowed the actual events in Jesus' life. Matthew (1:23) cites Isaiah 7:14: "A virgin shall conceive, and bear a son, and shall call his name Immanuel," a name meaning "God with us." He likewise cites Hosea 11:1, "I . . . called my son out of Egypt" (Matt. 2:15).

John (13:8–11) notes that the betrayal of Jesus by a friend was spoken of in earlier scripture (Ps. 41:9). John (19:24) also cites the dealing of the soldiers for Jesus' robe as a fulfillment of Psalm 22:18, and the sponge with vinegar pressed to Jesus' lips (John 19:28–30) as having been alluded to in Psalm 69:21. John (19:33–36) also notes that Jesus' legs were not broken on the cross, in harmony with Exodus 12:46.

Isaiah prophesied that in Israel a son would be born of the lineage of David, who would be called the "mighty God," the "Prince of Peace" (Isa. 9:6–7). The Messiah's mission as redeemer, suffering for the sins of mankind, is portrayed in Isaiah 53 and 61.

THE GOD OF ISRAEL IS JESUS OF NAZARETH. Revelation to the Prophet Joseph SMITH shows that, beginning with Adam, there have been several gospel DISPENSATIONS on the earth. The prophets in each of these dispensations knew of Christ, taught his gospel (including the ceremonies and ordinances), and held the holy priesthood, which was called "the Holy Priesthood, after the Order of the Son of God" (D&C 107:3; cf. Alma 13:1–16). These ancient prophets not only knew of the future coming of Jesus as the Messiah, but they also knew that the God whom they worshiped, Jehovah, would come to earth and become that Messiah (cf. Mosiah 13:33–35). As noted earlier, in Isaiah 7:14 the name Immanuel identifies Jesus as God. New Testament passages illustrate this concept.

Jesus directed his listeners to search the scriptures, for "they are they which testify of me" (John 5:39). He told the Jewish rulers that Moses "wrote of me" (John 5:45–46; cf. John 1:45; 1 Cor. 10:1–4).

Later he informed them that "Abraham rejoiced to see my day: and he saw it, and was glad" (John 8:56). When asked how he and Abraham could have known each other when their lives on earth were separated by so much time, Jesus replied, "Before Abraham was, I am" (John 8:58). The Greek term here translated "I am" is identical with the Septuagint phrase in Exodus 3:14 that identifies Jehovah as "I AM."

That Jesus' audience understood that he had plainly told them he was none other than Jehovah, also known as I AM, the God of Abraham and of Moses, is evident, for "then took they up stones to cast at him" (John 8:59) because they supposed that he had blasphemed. A further demonstration that they understood Jesus' assertion that he was God come to earth is shown later when they "took up stones again to stone him," and Jesus asked: "For which of [my] works do ye stone me?" Their reply was "for blasphemy; and because that thou, being a man, makest thyself God" (John 10:31–33).

After his resurrection Jesus went through the passages of the Old Testament with his disciples, "beginning at Moses and all the prophets," expounded to them "in all the scriptures the things concerning himself" (Luke 24:27), and showed them "in the law of Moses, and in the prophets, and in the psalms" the prophecies pertaining to his mission (Luke 24:44; see JESUS CHRIST: PROPHECIES ABOUT).

Peter wrote that the ancient prophets "searched diligently" and had the "Spirit of Christ," which "testified beforehand the sufferings of Christ," and that these prophets did "minister [in their day] the things, which are now reported" about Jesus Christ (1 Pet. 1:10–12). And Paul declared that in all his teachings about Jesus, he had said "none other things than those which the prophets and Moses did say should come" (Acts 26:22).

Extensive prophecies that Jesus will come again to the earth as Judge and King are recorded in Matthew (16:27; 24:1–51) and Joseph Smith—Matthew (1:1–55) (see JESUS CHRIST: SECOND COMING OF JESUS CHRIST). Latter-day Saints believe that just as Old Testament foreshadowing and prophecies of Christ were fulfilled in his first coming, so will prophecies of his second coming be literally fulfilled.

CLARIFICATIONS FROM LATTER-DAY REVELATION. The foregoing items from the Bible, coupled with confirmatory and illuminating statements in latter-day revelation, lead members of the Church to see both the Old and the New Testaments as reliable records about the premortal, mortal, postmortal, and future millennial mission of Jesus Christ. Latter-day Saints fully accept the biblical message about Jesus Christ, and, in addition, because of other sacred scriptures that strengthen and supplement the biblical report (see STANDARD WORKS), they appreciate the mission of Jesus in a wider sense than is possible from the Bible alone. For example, Jesus spoke to Jewish hearers about "other sheep," not of the Jews, whom he would visit and who would "hear my voice" (John 10:16). Many have supposed that these were the Gentiles. However, in the Book of Mormon the resurrected Jesus specifically identifies these other sheep as a branch of the house of Israel on the American continent whom he was visiting, personally showing them his body and vocally teaching them his gospel (3 Ne. 15:13–24). The Book of Mormon thus explains a passage about the Savior beyond what the Bible offers, and also enlarges the concept of Jesus' ministry.

Latter-day revelation also provides a deeper appreciation for events that occurred on the MOUNT OF TRANSFIGURATION than is available in the Bible alone. That which the New Testament offers is accepted as historically correct, but incomplete. One learns from latter-day revelation that on the mount, Jesus, Moses, and Elijah gave the keys of the priesthood to Peter, James, and John in fulfillment of the Savior's promise in Matthew 16:19 (TPJS, p. 158). The three apostles also saw a vision of the future glorification of the earth (D&C 63:2–21). These points are lacking in the biblical account. Moses and Elijah (called Elias) "appeared in glory, and spake of [Jesus'] decease which he should accomplish at Jerusalem" (Luke 9:30–31), which shows that they knew him and knew of his mission.

Jesus' ministry is also clarified in other instances in latter-day revelation. John 3:23 suggests that Jesus personally performed baptisms in water, but this is largely negated by John 4:2, which states that it was in fact not Jesus, but his disciples, who performed the baptisms. Through the Joseph Smith Translation of the Bible, the text of John 4:2–3 is clarified to assert that Jesus did indeed perform water baptisms, but not as many as did his disciples. (For other clarifications relating to Jesus' earthly ministry, see JOSEPH SMITH TRANSLATION OF THE BIBLE [JST].) Topics discussed in the latter work include Jesus at the temple at age twelve; his precocious childhood; his temptations in the wilderness; his parables; his ability to redeem little children; and his compassion for people.

BIBLIOGRAPHY

McConkie, Bruce R. *Doctrinal New Testament Commentary*, 3 vols. Salt Lake City, 1965, 1970, 1973.

———. *The Promised Messiah; The Mortal Messiah; The Millennial Messiah*, 6 vols. Salt Lake City, 1978, 1979, 1980, 1981, 1982.

Matthews, Robert J. "A Greater Portrayal of the Master." *Ensign* 13 (Mar. 1983):6–13.

Talmage, James E. *Jesus the Christ*. Salt Lake City, 1963.

ROBERT J. MATTHEWS

JESUS CHRIST IN THE BOOK OF MORMON

The main purpose of the Book of Mormon is to convince all people "that Jesus is the Christ, the Eternal God, manifesting himself unto all nations" (title page). Through the spiritual experiences of its writers, many of whom were prophets and eyewitnesses of Christ's glory, the Book of Mormon communicates clear, personal knowledge that Jesus Christ lives. It explains his mission from the Creation to the Final Judgment, and expresses his pure and atoning love for all mankind.

Sketch of *The Sacrament in the New World*, by Minerva K. Teichert (c. 1952, oil on masonite, 36″ × 48″). After his resurrection, Jesus Christ ministered to a group of people in the Americas. The Book of Mormon records that he taught them, blessed them, and instituted the sacrament among them as a remembrance of the body which he had shown them (3 Ne. 18:1–11). Courtesy Museum of Fine Arts, Brigham Young University.

The Book of Mormon is an intimate scripture. It exhorts each reader "to come unto Christ, and lay hold upon every good gift," mindful that "every good gift cometh of Christ" (Moro. 10:18, 30).

The book is singularly focused. In the words of Nephi₁, "We talk of Christ, we rejoice in Christ, we preach of Christ, we prophesy of Christ" (2 Ne. 25:26). Only by Jesus' sacrifice can the repentant "answer the ends of the law" (2 Ne. 2:7). "There is no other head whereby ye can be made free. There is no other name given whereby salvation cometh" (Mosiah 5:8).

All Book of Mormon prophets proclaimed the same word of Jesus Christ (Jacob 4:5). In visions, public speeches, and personal statements they typically declared (1) that Jesus is the Son of God, the Creator, the Lord God Omnipotent, the Father of heaven and earth, and the Holy One of Israel, (2) who would come and did come down to earth to live as a mortal born of MARY, a virgin, (3) to heal the sick, cast out devils, and suffer temptation, (4) to take upon himself the sins of the world and redeem his people, (5) to be put to death by crucifixion and rise from the dead, (6) to bring to pass the resurrection of all mankind, and (7) to judge all people in the last day according to their works (1 Ne. 11–14; Mosiah 3:5–27; Alma 33:22; *see* CHRISTOLOGY).

The personality and attributes of Jesus are expressed in the Book of Mormon (see Black, pp. 49–64). He is a person who invites, comforts, answers, exhorts, loves, cries, is troubled over the sins of mankind, and is filled with joy. He welcomes all who will come unto him. He patiently pleads with the Father on behalf of all who have become saints through his atoning blood. He is a true and merciful friend. He visits those who believe in him. He heals those who weep at the thought of being separated from him. With hands still bearing the wounds of his death, he touches, is touched, and gives power. He remembers all his covenants and keeps all his promises. He is all-powerful, judging the world and vanquishing the wicked. He is "the light, and the life, and the truth of the world" (Ether 4:12).

Book of Mormon prophets who taught extensively of Christ before his birth include the BROTHER OF JARED (Ether 3); LEHI (1 Ne. 10; 2 Ne. 2); NEPHI₁ (1 Ne. 11, 19; 2 Ne. 25, 31–33); JACOB (2 Ne. 9); ABINADI (Mosiah 13–16); BENJAMIN (Mosiah 3–5); ALMA₂ (Alma 5, 7, 12–13, 33, 36, 42); AMULEK (Alma 34); SAMUEL THE

LAMANITE (Hel. 14); and NEPHI₃ (3 Ne. 1). The apex of the Nephite record is the appearance of the resurrected Lord Jesus Christ to a congregation of 2,500 men, women, and children who had gathered at their temple in the land Bountiful. For three days, Jesus personally ministered among them (3 Ne. 11–28; *see* BOOK OF MORMON: THIRD NEPHI). The Book of Mormon ends with testimonies of Jesus by MORMON (Morm. 7; Moro. 7) and his son MORONI₂ (Ether 4; Moro. 10). Some 101 appellations for Jesus are found in the 3,925 references to Christ in the Book of Mormon's 6,607 verses (Black, pp. 16–30).

In addition to his visitations in 3 Nephi, Jesus appeared to Lehi (1 Ne. 1:9), Nephi₁, Jacob (2 Ne. 11:2–3), King Lamoni (Alma 19:13), Mormon (Morm. 1:15), Moroni₂ (Ether 12:39), and the brother of Jared (Ether 3:14). Each bore personal testimony of Jesus Christ. Many others heard his voice.

From visions and revelations received before he left Jerusalem about 600 B.C., Lehi knew the tender mercies of the promised Messiah. To him the Messiah would be the Redeemer who would restore the fallen, lost, and displaced. In one vision, Lehi read a heavenly book that "manifested plainly of the coming of a Messiah, and also the redemption of the world" (1 Ne. 1:19). This knowledge focused all subsequent Nephite preaching and interpretation on the mission of the Savior. It was also revealed to Lehi that in six hundred years "a prophet would the Lord God raise up among the Jews—even a Messiah, or, in other words, a Savior of the world" (1 Ne. 10:4), the same pleading and merciful servant of whom other prophets had written, including ZENOS in his allegory of the Lord's olive tree representing Israel (Jacob 5). Being "grafted in" to that tree was interpreted by Lehi as "com[ing] to the knowledge of the true Messiah" (1 Ne. 10:14).

From the prophecies of ISAIAH as well as from his own visions, Lehi knew that a prophet would prepare the way of the Lord before his coming (1 Ne. 10:8; cf. Isa. 40:3) and that "after he had baptized the Messiah with water, he should behold and bear record that he had baptized the Lamb of God, who should take away the sins of the world" (1 Ne. 10:10; *see* JOHN THE BAPTIST). Furthermore, Isaiah spoke of the Lord's servant being "despised and rejected, . . . wounded for our transgressions, bruised for our iniquities, . . . brought as a lamb to the slaughter" (Isa. 53:3–7); and Lehi

prophesied that the Jews would slay the Messiah, adding that the Redeemer would rise from the dead (1 Ne. 10:11).

Nephi₁ asked the Lord for a greater understanding of his father's visions, especially for a clearer understanding of the TREE OF LIFE. He acquired a love for the CONDESCENSION OF GOD that would bring the Son of God down to dwell in the flesh, born of a beautiful virgin. Christ's goodness stands in sharp contrast with his rejection and crucifixion (1 Ne. 11:13–33; 19:10; cf. Deut. 21:22). Nephi₁ (who himself knew what it meant to be persecuted for righteousness' sake) referred more than sixty times to the divine offering of this sacrificial Lamb of God (1 Ne. 11:21). As ruler and teacher of his people, Nephi emphasized that they should follow the rule of Christ, the only true Savior who would ever come, the sole source of their life and law, and the only one in whom all things would be fulfilled (2 Ne. 25:16–18, 25–27).

In connection with his calling as a priest and teacher, Jacob, the brother of Nephi₁, expounded on the atonement of Christ. He told how Christ would suffer and die for all mankind so that they might become subject to him through his "infinite atonement," which overcomes the Fall and brings resurrection and incorruptibility (2 Ne. 9:5–14).

Certain terms such as "Messiah" (anointed) and "Lamb of God" were used often by Lehi, Nephi₁ and Jacob as designations for Christ before it was revealed by an angel that the Messiah's "name shall be Jesus Christ, the Son of God" (2 Ne. 25:19; cf. 2 Ne. 10:3; Mosiah 3:8). The name Jesus, like Joshua, derives from the Hebrew root *yasha'*, meaning "to deliver, rescue, or save"; and *christos* is the Greek equivalent of the Hebrew *mashiyach*, meaning "anointed" or "Messiah" (*see* JESUS CHRIST, NAMES AND TITLES OF). Thus, the Nephites used the intimate yet freely spoken name of the mortal Jesus as their name for God, while the ineffable YHWH (*see* JEHOVAH, JESUS CHRIST) appears only twice in the book (2 Ne. 22:2; Moro. 10:34).

Some, such as Sherem, whose cultural roots lay in the monotheistic world of Jerusalem, resisted the worship of the Messiah, alleging that this violated the law of Moses (Ex. 20:3; Jacob 7:7; *see* ANTICHRISTS). Nephi had previously declared that the Father, Son, and Holy Ghost were "one God" (2 Ne. 31:21), but Nephite challengers continued to attack the proposition that Jesus was God, to deny that his atonement could be efficacious in advance of its occurrence, and to argue that there could not be many Gods who were still one God (e.g., Mosiah 17:8; Alma 11:28). Abinadi and others gave inspired explanations (Mosiah 14–16; *see* JESUS CHRIST: FATHERHOOD AND SONSHIP), but until the resurrected Jesus appeared, announced by and praying to the Father, such issues were not firmly put to rest.

About 124 B.C., King BENJAMIN received from an angel a succinct declaration of the atoning mission of Christ (Mosiah 3:2–27). It places central attention on the atoning blood of Christ and corroborates that Jesus would sweat blood from every pore in anguish for his people (Mosiah 3:7; see also Luke 22:43–44; D&C 19:18; Irenaeus, *Against Heresies* 22.2; *see* GETHESEMANE). Christ's blood will atone for the sins of all those who repent or have ignorantly sinned (see Mosiah 3:11, 15, 16, 18). When Benjamin's people passionately cried out in unison for God to "apply the atoning blood of Christ that we may receive forgiveness of our sins" (Mosiah 4:2), Benjamin gave them the name of Christ by covenant, the only name "whereby salvation cometh" (Mosiah 5:7–8).

Alma₂, the judicial and religious defender of the freedom of belief (c. 100–73 B.C.), taught faith in Jesus Christ as the master of personal CONVERSION. Alma had tasted the transforming joy that came when he called upon the name of Jesus Christ for mercy (Alma 36:18), and in his subsequent sermons he described how the "image of God" might be "engraven upon your countenances" (Alma 5:19), and how the word of God is to be planted in each convert's soul, where, if nourished, it will spring up as an everlasting tree of life (Alma 32:40; 33:22–23; for a similar image, see the early Christian *Odes of Solomon* 11:18).

About 30 B.C. a group of Lamanites were converted to Christ when God's light shone and his voice spoke out of an enveloping cloud of darkness (Hel. 5:33–43). Twenty-five years later, a prophet named Samuel the Lamanite foretold that more significant signs of light would appear at the time of Jesus' birth and that massive destruction and darkness would be seen at his death (Hel. 14:2–27). Five years after Samuel, Nephi₃ heard the voice of Jesus declaring that he would come into the world "on the morrow," and the signs of Jesus' birth were seen; thirty-three years and four days after that, all the land heard the voice of Christ speaking through the thick darkness on the Western Hemisphere that accompanied his crucifixion and death (3 Ne. 9).

Within that same year, they saw the resurrected Jesus Christ come down out of heaven (3 Ne. 11:8). The resurrected Christ appeared to a congregation of righteous Nephites at their temple and allowed them to feel the wounds in his hands and feet, and thrust their hands into his side (3 Ne. 11:15). They heard the voice of the Father saying, "Behold my Beloved Son, in whom I am well pleased, in whom I have glorified my name—hear ye him" (3 Ne. 11:7).

For three days, Jesus was with these people. He called and ordained twelve disciples, and taught his gospel of faith, repentance, baptism, and the gift of the Holy Ghost. As the one who had given and fulfilled the law of Moses, he gave the people commandments of obedience, sacrifice of a broken heart, brotherly love and reconciliation, faithfulness to one's spouse, chastity, integrity, charity, and consecration (*see* ENDOWMENT). He taught them to fast and pray, in secret and in their families. He healed their sick, and in the presence of angels and witnesses he blessed the parents and their children. They entered into a sacred covenant with him, and he promised that if they would do his will and keep his commandments they would always have his spirit to be with them (*see* SACRAMENT), would personally know the Lord and would be welcomed into his presence at the last day (3 Ne. 14:21–23; see Welch, pp. 34–83).

As revealed in the Book of Mormon, Jesus wants all people to become like him and their Father in Heaven. Jesus said, "Therefore, what manner of men ought ye to be? Verily I say unto you, even as I am" (3 Ne. 27:27). He invited all, saying, "I would that ye should be perfect even as I, or your Father who is in heaven is perfect" (3 Ne. 12:48). His constant and loving purpose was to make that possible.

BIBLIOGRAPHY

Black, Susan E. *Finding Christ Through the Book of Mormon.* Salt Lake City, 1987.

Charlesworth, James H. "Messianism in the Pseudepigrapha and the Book of Mormon." In *Reflections on Mormonism,* ed. T. Madsen, pp. 99–137. Provo, Utah, 1978.

Roberts, B. H. "Christ in the Book of Mormon." *IE* 27 (1924):188–92.

Scharffs, Stephen. "Unique Insights on Christ from the Book of Mormon." *Ensign* 18 (Dec. 1988):8–13.

Welch, John W. *The Sermon at the Temple and the Sermon on the Mount.* Salt Lake City, 1990.

JOHN W. WELCH

JESUS CHRIST IN THE DOCTRINE AND COVENANTS

The Doctrine and Covenants is a unique collection of revelations and inspired writings bearing witness to the modern world that Jesus Christ lives. Unlike the other STANDARD WORKS of The Church of Jesus Christ of Latter-day Saints, the revelations in the Doctrine and Covenants were received in modern times by latter-day prophets and therefore are not translations of ancient documents. The central figure of the Doctrine and Covenants is indeed Jesus Christ. He identifies himself repeatedly throughout its pages with various titles expressing his Godhood and his redeeming power.

The Doctrine and Covenants presents more than sixty names or titles for Jesus. When referring to himself or his work, the Lord uses at least eighteen descriptive titles, including "Lord" (more than 300 times); "Jesus Christ" (81 times); "Redeemer" (24 times); "Savior" and "Jesus" (19 times each); "Alpha and Omega" and "Only Begotten" (13 times each); "the Beginning and the End" (12 times); "Eternal" (11 times); "Jehovah" (6 times); "Advocate," "Endless," and "Bridegroom" (5 times each); "Lawgiver" and "I AM" (3 times each). These titles invoke special respect for Jesus Christ. "Behold, I am from above . . . I am over all, and in all, and through all . . . and the day cometh that all things shall be subject unto me. Behold, I am Alpha and Omega, even Jesus Christ" (D&C 63:59–60; *see also* JESUS CHRIST, NAMES AND TITLES OF).

Jesus affirms his role as the Creator. "Thus saith the Lord your God, even Jesus Christ, the Great I AM, Alpha and Omega, the beginning and the end, the same which looked upon the wide expanse of eternity, . . . before the world was made . . . I am the same which spake, and the world was made, and all things came by me" (D&C 38:1–3).

A unique reference is made to Jesus as the Son AHMAN. "Ahman" could be an expression in the ADAMIC LANGUAGE (D&C 78:20; 95:17; see also *JD* 2:342). Another unique passage identifies Christ as the Lord of Sabaoth, Hebrew for "hosts"— both of heaven and earth; therefore he is "creator of the first day, the beginning and the end" (D&C 95:7).

In one memorable passage Jesus describes his suffering as the Redeemer of mankind. The autobiographical details expressed here are found nowhere else in scripture: "Which suffering caused myself, even God, the greatest of all, to tremble because of pain, and to bleed at every pore, and to suffer both body and spirit—and would that I might not drink the bitter cup, and shrink" (D&C 19:18). He "suffered these things for all, that they might not suffer if they would repent" (19:16). True to his character, the Savior gives glory and honor to his Father in Heaven: "Nevertheless, glory be to the Father, and I partook and finished my preparations unto the children of men" (D&C 19:19; cf. 78:4). Because he made the sacrifice, Christ can intercede with the Father for the penitent: "I am Christ, and in mine own name, by the virtue of the blood which I have spilt, have I pleaded before the Father for them" (D&C 38:4; cf. 45:1–4).

Jesus refers to himself as the Bridegroom, drawing attention to his parable of the virgins recorded in Matthew 25, when he prophesied of his second coming: "Be faithful, praying always, having your lamps trimmed and burning, and oil with you, that you may be ready at the coming of the Bridegroom" (D&C 33:17).

In modern revelation the Lord also gives comfort: "Be of good cheer, and do not fear, for I the Lord am with you, and will stand by you" (D&C 68:6); and "Be thou humble; and the Lord thy God shall lead thee by the hand, and give thee answer to thy prayers (D&C 112:10). Jesus also warns mankind of the necessity to be humble, stating that "although a man may have many revelations, and have power to do many mighty works, yet if he boasts in his own strength, and sets at naught the counsels of God, and follows after the dictates of his own will and carnal desires, he must fall and incur the vengeance of a just God upon him" (D&C 3:4).

In several sections of the Doctrine and Covenants, the Lord testifies that he is the one who gives scripture through inspiration, and he commands that his words be studied (D&C 1:29; 3:16–20; 11:22; 20:8–9; 84:57). In summary he says, "Search these commandments, for they are true and faithful, and the prophecies and promises which are in them shall all be fulfilled" (D&C 1:37).

The Lord explains perplexing scriptural passages and concepts in the Gospel of John, 1 Corinthians, Revelation, and Isaiah (D&C 7; 77; 86; 113). Scriptural concepts concerning sacred history, priesthood, and patriarchal lineage are emphasized by him in other revelations (D&C 84:6–28; 107:1–14, 40–57). He also restored fragments of lost scriptures (e.g., D&C 7; 93:7–17).

The Lord tells why he gives these revelations to mankind: "I give unto you these sayings that you may understand and know how to worship, and know what you worship, that you may come unto the Father in my name, and in due time receive of his fulness" (D&C 93:19).

The voice of Jesus Christ in the Doctrine and Covenants is the word of the Lord comforting and encouraging his Saints; testifying of his own divinity and sacred mission; warning the world of judgments to come; declaring his majesty and power; and promising forgiveness and mercy to the penitent. Latter-day Saints accept these revelations as latter-day proclamations of the mind and will of the Lord Jesus Christ.

BIBLIOGRAPHY

Maxwell, Neal A. "The Doctrine and Covenants: The Voice of the Lord." *Ensign* 8 (Dec. 1978):4–7.

CLARK V. JOHNSON

JESUS CHRIST IN THE PEARL OF GREAT PRICE

The STANDARD WORK of scripture called the Pearl of Great Price contains selected materials ranging from the time of Adam to the present, including words of Adam, Enoch, Noah, Abraham, Moses, Jesus Christ, and Joseph Smith. It presents some 300 references to Jesus Christ, including such names and titles as Beginning and the End, Beloved Son, Creator, God, Jehovah, Jesus, Jesus Christ, King of Zion, Lord, Lord God, Messiah, Only Begotten, Rock of Heaven, Savior, Son, and Son of Man. A particular contribution is the fact that Jesus Christ has been the focus of every DISPENSATION from Adam to Joseph SMITH.

JESUS THE CREATOR.   Jesus is identified as the Creator under the aegis of God the Father in Moses, chapters 2 and 3. The book of Abraham adds the clarification that Jesus did not act alone but with a council of intelligent spirits, among whom was Abraham (Abr. 3:23).

SATAN'S REBELLION.   In the premortal estate the Father chose Jesus to become the Only Begotten and Redeemer. Satan rebelled against the Father's choice and became the archenemy of Jesus and of all who follow him (Moses 4:1–4; *also see* FIRST ESTATE; WAR IN HEAVEN).

ADAM AND EVE AND THE PLAN OF SALVATION. Adam and Eve (Moses 1:34; 4:26; 5:5–9) were the first to be taught and to accept the Father's PLAN OF SALVATION on this earth. Adam was commanded by God to make an offering of the firstlings of his flocks. After many days, an angel of the Lord asked why he offered sacrifices. When Adam confessed his lack of understanding, the angelic visitor explained, "This thing is a similitude of the sacrifice of the Only Begotten of the Father, which is full of grace and truth. . . . In that day the Holy Ghost fell upon Adam, which beareth record of the Father and the Son, saying: I am the Only Begotten of the Father from the beginning, henceforth and forever, that as thou hast fallen thou mayest be redeemed, and all mankind, even as many as will" (Moses 5:7–9).

The ATONEMENT of Jesus Christ has applied to mankind from the beginning. Adam believed in the coming of Christ, was baptized in his name, and received the GIFT OF THE HOLY GHOST and the priesthood KEYS of a dispensation (Moses 6:51–68; D&C 107:41–42; *see also* ADAM: LDS SOURCES).

ENOCH, A WITNESS OF THE SON OF MAN. Enoch preached faith in Jesus Christ, repentance, baptism, receiving the gift of the Holy Ghost, growing in the knowledge of God, justification, and sanctification, all to be achieved through the atoning blood of Christ (Moses 6:46–62).

Enoch was a prophetic witness of the Lord Jesus Christ and knew that Jesus was the God of the ancient prophets, the Redeemer and Savior, the Son of the "Man of Holiness" who is God the Father. He saw, in vision, the coming of the Savior in the MERIDIAN OF TIME, his crucifixion, and his triumphal ascension unto the Father (Moses 7:47, 53, 55). Enoch the seer (Moses 6:36) saw also the coming of the "Son of Man, in the last days, to dwell on the earth in righteousness for the space of a thousand years" (Moses 7:65).

NOAH, PREACHER OF DELIVERANCE THROUGH CHRIST.   Noah pleaded with the people saying, "Believe and repent of your sins and be baptized in the name of Jesus Christ, the Son of God, even as our fathers, and ye shall receive the Holy Ghost, that ye may have all things made manifest; and if ye do not this, the floods will come in upon you" (Moses 8:24).

ABRAHAM. Abraham was visited by Jehovah (Abr. 1:16) and knew him as the one "like unto God," the Creator, the Son of Man, and the opponent of Satan (Abr. 3:24–28).

MOSES, DELIVERER, AND TYPE OF CHRIST. After Moses had been tried by a confrontation with the devil and had twice stood in the presence of God (Moses 1:2–39), he was told, "And now, Moses, my son, I will speak unto thee concerning this earth upon which thou standest; and thou shalt write the things which I shall speak" (Moses 1:40). Moses was also told that he was in the "similitude" of the Only Begotten, the Savior, who was full of grace and truth (Moses 1:6). When Moses was confronted by the powers of darkness, he called upon God for strength and in the name of the Only Begotten commanded Satan to depart (Moses 1:20–22). Moses served the God of Israel, whom he knew was the Messiah, the Only Begotten, the Savior, and the Creator of "worlds without number" (Moses 1:32–33).

MATTHEW, RECORDER OF THE LORD'S MINISTRY. In a discourse to his disciples three days before his crucifixion, Jesus counseled them on how to survive the forthcoming destruction of Jerusalem and how future disciples should survive a similar devastation to come in the latter days as a prelude to his second coming (Matt. 24). Joseph Smith's translation of that discourse is presented as Joseph Smith—Matthew.

JOSEPH SMITH. The Prophet Joseph Smith learned by divine experience that there are both a Savior, who is Son, and a God who is Father. This he learned in his FIRST VISION when a pillar of light appeared "above the brightness of the sun" and fell upon him. In that light he saw "two Personages, whose brightness and glory defy all description, standing above [him] in the air. One of them spake unto [him], calling [him] by name and said, pointing to the other—This is My Beloved Son. Hear Him!" In this vision, Joseph Smith talked to the Father and to the Lord Jesus Christ (JS—H 1:15–17). The Prophet later wrote, "I had actually seen a light, and in the midst of that light I saw two Personages, and they did in reality speak to me; and though I was hated and persecuted for saying that I had seen a vision, yet it was true (JS—H 1:25).

In the ARTICLES OF FAITH, Joseph Smith declared Jesus' position as a member of the GODHEAD, outlined the first principles of the gospel of Jesus Christ, and affirmed that Christ will come again to reign personally upon the earth.

BIBLIOGRAPHY
Peterson, H. Donl. *The Pearl of Great Price: A History and Commentary*, pp. 20, 74–75. Salt Lake City, 1987.

JAMES R. HARRIS

JEWS

[Articles that deal with the Jews highlight two general areas. The first group treats contacts between Jews and Latter-day Saints: Interfaith Relations, Jewish; Brigham Young University: Jerusalem Center for Near Eastern Studies; World Religions (Non-Christian) and Mormonism: Judaism and Mormonism. Other articles focus only indirectly on Jewish matters but indicate the place that Jews and elements of Judaica hold in LDS doctrine and prophecy: Aaronic Priesthood: Restoration of Aaronic Priesthood; Abraham; Abrahamic Covenant; Circumcision; Covenant Israel; Ephraim; Ezekiel; Gentiles, Fulness of; Hyde, Orson; Isaiah: Interpretation in Modern Scripture; Israel; Jerusalem; Law of Moses; Levitical Priesthood; Melchizedek Priesthood; Moses; New Jerusalem; Old Testament; Restoration of All Things; Sacrifice in Biblical Times; Ten Commandments; Zion; Zionism.]

JOHN, REVELATIONS OF

The apostle John, sometimes referred to as John the Beloved and John the Revelator, and scriptural texts linked to his name are esteemed highly by Latter-day Saints. Modern scripture adds to an understanding of the man and his writings in three important areas: John as a TRANSLATED BEING, an additional record of John, and clarification of the book of Revelation.

JOHN AS TRANSLATED BEING. In April 1829 the Prophet Joseph SMITH received a revelation (D&C 7) that clarified the Savior's statement about John's tarrying on earth until Jesus returned (John 21:22). This revelation teaches that John requested that he receive power over death so that he could bring more souls to Christ (3 Ne. 28:6–11); that the Lord promised him that he could tarry "until I come in my glory"; and that John is a translated being whose state is "as flaming fire and a ministering angel" (D&C 7:1–3, 6).

ADDITIONAL RECORD OF JOHN. In another revelation to Joseph Smith on May 6, 1833, an excerpt of eleven verses appears from what is called the "fulness of the record of John" (D&C 93:7–18). Important similarities exist between these verses and the opening verses of John's gospel (John 1:1–34), but links to the experiences of JOHN THE BAPTIST are also apparent (cf. D&C 93:15; John 1:32–34). Since Doctrine and Covenants 93 mentions only the name John, without annotation, it is unclear whether John the Beloved or John the Baptist is meant (cf. McConkie, 1979, Vol. 1, pp. 426–27).

Whatever the source, these few lines from the "record of John" bear important witness of the Savior, reaffirming that Jesus is the Word, "even the messenger of salvation" (D&C 93:7–8); that he is the light and the redeemer of the world and the spirit of truth (93:9–10); and that he did not receive the fulness at first, but continued "from grace to grace" until he received "all power, both in heaven and on earth" (93:11–17).

BOOK OF REVELATION. Two Book of Mormon passages underscore the importance of the Revelation of John for the latter days. The prophet NEPHI₁ (c. 600 B.C.) saw in vision many future events, but he was forbidden to write them, "for the Lord God hath ordained the apostle of the Lamb of God that he should write them. . . . [And] the name of the apostle of the Lamb was John" (1 Ne. 14:25, 27). Further, speaking of the last days, the Lord said, "Then shall my revelations which I have caused to be written by my servant John be unfolded in the eyes of all the people" (Ether 4:16).

In this connection, three important sources aid the interpretation of the Apocalypse.

1.   Doctrine and Covenants section 77. Received by Joseph Smith while working on the JOSEPH SMITH TRANSLATION OF THE BIBLE (JST), this revelation contains fifteen questions and answers about the book of Revelation. "This Revelation [D&C 77] is not a complete interpretation of the book. It is a *key*. . . . It unlocks the door through which an entrance may be gained, but after the key has been turned, the searcher for treasure must find it for himself" (Smith, p. 478).

2.   The Joseph Smith Translation. In addition to the questions and answers in section 77, Joseph Smith made significant revisions to the text of Revelation in the JST.

3.   Other scriptural and prophetic writings. Much of the Apocalypse is couched in imagery. Both latter-day scripture and the writings of GENERAL AUTHORITIES provide interpretations that help unlock this imagery. Examples include the "rod of iron" as the word of God (Rev. 2:27; cf. 1 Ne. 15:23–24), the "beasts" of chapter 13 as the degenerate kingdoms of the world (*TPJS*, p. 289), and Babylon as the symbol of spiritual wickedness (Rev. 17:5; cf. D&C 133:14).

In brief, the book of Revelation is divided into two major segments—the letters to the seven churches of Asia (chaps. 2–3) and the vision of "things which must be hereafter" (4:1; see chaps. 4–22).

The seven letters written to churches in Asia are important to Christians of all ages. They outline beliefs and practices that the Lord found commendable, as well as those which displeased him. In capsule form, these chapters summarize blessings that await the faithful.

The vision of the future (Rev. 4–22) revolves around a "book," sealed with seven seals, which was in God's hand (5:1–8). According to Doctrine and Covenants section 77, that book represented God's plan for this earth during the seven thousand years of its "temporal existence," each seal representing a thousand years (D&C 77:6–7). "By the seven thousand years of temporal existence is meant the time of the earth's duration from the fall of Adam to the end of time, which will come after the Millennium" (Joseph Fielding Smith, in Smith and Sjodahl, p. 474).

The first five seals highlight, in two or three verses (Rev. 6:1–11), each of the first five thousand years (see also McConkie, 1973, Vol. 3, pp. 476–85). In the sixth seal, representing the sixth millennium, John saw four angels holding the judgments of God (Rev. 7:1; D&C 77:8) and another angel who represented the work of the RESTORATION (Rev. 7:2–3; D&C 77:9–11; McConkie, 1973, Vol. 3, pp. 489–94).

The seventh seal opens in chapter 8. But the prediction of Christ's return does not occur until chapter 19. Thus, a major portion of the book focuses on the time just prior to Jesus' second coming (cf. D&C 77:13). Peter declared that Christ would not come again "until the times of restitution of all things" (Acts 3:21). It is central to this latter-day restitution that angelic ministers (MORONI₂, John the Baptist, Peter, James, John, Moses, etc.) brought back not only the fulness of the everlasting gospel and its KEYS and ORDINANCES but also the "sealing power," which is the power to bind things on earth and have them be binding in heaven (Matt. 16:19; see SEALING). The restoration of the gospel and the power of sealing are important conditions for Christ's coming. During this period three characteristics will prevail: judgments, the kingdom of Christ versus the kingdoms of the world, and the destruction of latter-day Babylon.

As trumpets sound and "vials" of destruction are poured out, one devastating scourge follows another, including vast pollutions, rampant wickedness, and the battle of Armageddon (Rev. 8–11, 16). In the midst of these judgments allowed by God, a voice declares that "the kingdoms of this world are become the kingdoms of our Lord, and of his Christ" (Rev. 11:15). Chapter 12 portrays the Church of Christ and the KINGDOM OF GOD (JST Rev. 12:7; McConkie, 1973, Vol. 3, p. 516). In chapter 13, Satan's kingdoms oppose the Saints and the work of God. Chapter 14 then shows the triumph of Christ's kingdom and what leads to that victory. Christ comes to Mount Zion with his servants (14:1–5), and an angel, having the everlasting gospel to preach to the earth, flies through the heavens (14:6–7). (Verse 6 provides the inspiration for the well-known ANGEL MORONI STATUE placed atop some LDS temples.) Then the fall of Babylon is announced (14:8–11). Like the angel from the east (Rev. 7:2), this angel is interpreted to represent the work of the restoration (McConkie, 1973, Vol. 3, p. 530). It is this work, directed by Christ and his servants, which brings about the eventual destruction of all worldly kingdoms. The fall of Babylon (Rev. 16–18) is so dramatic that all the hosts of heaven spontaneously shout, "Alleluia" (Rev. 19:1–6).

After Christ's coming (Rev. 19:7–21), the vision concludes in quick succession with the Millennium (Rev. 20:1–6), the loosing of Satan for a "little season" (Rev. 20:7–10; D&C 88:111–15), the great Judgment (Rev. 20:11–15), and the celestialization of the earth (Rev. 21:22–5). Thus, the Revelation of John shows that in spite of all of Satan's efforts to the contrary, God's work will triumph and Christ will come again to reign with his Saints for a thousand years during the Millennium and throughout eternity.

BIBLIOGRAPHY

Lund, Gerald N. "Insights from the JST into the Book of Revelation." *The Joseph Smith Translation*, ed. M. Nyman and R. Millet. Provo, Utah, 1985.

McConkie, Bruce R. *Doctrinal New Testament Commentary*, Vol. 3, pp. 476–85, 489–94, 516, 530. Salt Lake City, 1973.

———. "Understanding the Book of Revelation." *Ensign* 5 (Sept. 1975):85–89.

———. *The Mortal Messiah*, Vol. 1, pp. 426–27. Salt Lake City, 1979.

Smith, Hyrum M., and Janne M. Sjodahl. *Doctrine and Covenants Commentary*, rev. ed. Salt Lake City, 1951.

GERALD N. LUND

JOHN THE BAPTIST

John the Baptist was born in Judea about six months before the Savior Jesus Christ. John's primary mortal mission was to prepare the way for, and baptize, Jesus. His later role in restoring the AARONIC PRIESTHOOD in 1829 is particularly significant to Latter-day Saints.

Biblical scholars discern subtle differences in the way each of the four New Testament Gospels presents information about John the Baptist. Mark seems to emphasize how John prefigured Jesus, in that both proclaimed the gospel and then were given over to death. Luke points to personal relationships between John and Jesus, along with important links that the Baptist provides between the Old Testament and the New. Matthew records several ways in which John's ministry parallels that of Jesus, yet at the same time makes it clear that John was subordinate to Jesus, who identifies John as "the Elias who is to come" (cf. Matt. 11:14). The Greek Gospel of John, on the other hand, seems to minimize John's apocalyptic teachings, quotes him as denying that he was that Elias (John 1:21), and never uses the title "the Baptist," apparently in order to emphasize John's role as the first person at that time to know by revelation, and to witness, that Jesus was the son of God (see J. Meier, "John the Baptist in Matthew's Gospel," *Journal of Biblical Literature* 99 [1980]:383–86).

For Latter-day Saints, these nuances are transcended by John's larger roles subsumed within the plan of salvation. For example, his ministry illustrates the concept of the need for a prophet, for "God will do nothing, but he revealeth his secret unto his servants the prophets" (Amos 3:7); he came as a voice of warning, proclaiming the gospel

Baptism of Jesus Christ, Alma B. Wright (mural in the Alberta Temple baptistry, c. 1923). John the Baptist baptized Jesus Christ in the Jordan River. John baptized by immersion, which symbolizes death, burial, and resurrection. Jesus, who was free from sin, obediently set an example for all people to follow.

of repentance, bearing testimony of Jesus Christ, baptizing by immersion, holding divine authority, promising the gift of the Holy Ghost, and enduring to the end, even by suffering martyrdom. He was the Elias who was "to prepare all things" (JST Matt. 11:15), but not the Elias "who was to restore all things" (JST John 1:22, 26).

Both of John's parents were descendants of Aaron: Zacharias was an officiating priest in the temple of Jerusalem, and Elisabeth, of the daughters of Aaron, was a relative of Mary the mother of Jesus (Luke 1:5, 36). His birth was promised by the angel Gabriel (*see* NOAH), who visited Zacharias while he was officiating in the temple. Although Zacharias and Elisabeth had fervently prayed for children, none had been born to them. In their old age, Gabriel's promise was received with some doubt by Zacharias. As a sign, Gabriel struck Zacharias deaf and evidently dumb until the naming of the baby eight days after John's birth, the day John was circumcised according to the law of Moses. Contrary to the custom, by previous direction of Gabriel, the baby was named John instead of Zacharias, after his father. Zacharias gave his son a blessing on this occasion, the words of which are known as the Benedictus in Roman Catholic and Protestant terminology (Luke 1:68–79).

Little is known of John's early life and training. When Mary visited Elisabeth during their pregnancies, John "leaped in her womb" (Luke 1:41). He was "filled with the Holy Ghost from his mother's womb" and "was ordained by the angel of God" when he was eight days old (D&C 84:27–28). Since his parents were elderly, some wonder if he was soon orphaned or associated with religious sects in the Judean desert. Somehow he was carefully reared in gospel principles, for he came forth from the desert preaching repentance (Matt. 3:2)

and was well prepared. He knew his mission and the source of his authority.

Jesus said of him, "Among those that are born of women there is not a greater prophet" (Luke 7:28). John the Baptist was dearly loved by the Savior. John had unusual privileges: none other would proclaim the immediate coming of Jesus; none other would be privileged to baptize the Lamb of God; none other was the legal administrator in the affairs of the kingdom then on the earth and holder of the keys of power. "These three reasons constitute him the greatest prophet born of a woman" (*TPJS*, p. 276).

With these credentials John came forth vigorously preaching repentance and many principles of the gospel in the wilderness of Judea near the river Jordan (Mark 1:4–5). He ate ritually clean foods, locusts (Lev. 11:22), and wild honey; he drank "neither wine nor strong drink" (Luke 1:15); and he wore the traditional clothing of a prophet, camel's hair and a leather girdle (Mark 1:6). He also fasted (Matt. 11:18). He attracted large crowds and came under the increasing condemnation of those Jewish leaders whom he challenged with his preaching.

After a time, the "One mightier than I," even Jesus, approached John and requested baptism (*see* JESUS CHRIST: BAPTISM OF JESUS CHRIST). A humble and meek John initially resisted, declaring that he needed to be baptized by Jesus. Upon Jesus' insistence, John baptized Jesus, following which he witnessed the sign of the dove descending from heaven upon the Christ (John 1:32).

At this juncture John alone seemed to bear the responsibility of spanning two DISPENSATIONS. He was a child of promise whose mission had been prophesied years before by Isaiah, LEHI, and NEPHI₁ (Isa. 40:3; 1 Ne. 10:7–10; 2 Ne. 31:4–8).

John had begun his preaching and baptizing near the river Jordan probably about a year before Jesus began his public ministry. He "had no intention of founding a new sect" (Scobie, p. 131); his calling was to prepare the way for Jesus; and many of his followers became Jesus' closest and earliest disciples. His intense preaching of repentance had deeply angered those in power. He denounced the marriage of Herod Antipas to his brother's wife, Herodias, which clearly violated Jewish law (Lev. 20:21; Josephus, *Antiquities* 18.5.1–2). Herodias wanted John killed, but Herod Antipas had concern for John's popularity with the people. He had John imprisoned (Mark 6:17), somewhat pacifying the Pharisees, as well as Herodias. During all of this, Jesus went to Galilee. While in prison, John sent two of his disciples to Jesus to confirm their faith in the Savior's identity, and Jesus supported and sustained him (Luke 7:24–28). Through shrewd plotting and the beguiling dance of her daughter Salome, Herodias eventually manipulated Herod into having John beheaded.

John the Baptist was among the prophets and saints who were with Christ in his resurrection (D&C 133:55). Approximately eighteen centuries later, on Friday, May 15, 1829, this forerunner of the Savior again appeared, this time as an angel of the Lord preparing the world for the Savior's second coming, and conferred the keys of the Aaronic Priesthood. This occurred when Joseph SMITH and Oliver COWDERY withdrew to a secluded place on the Susquehanna River near Harmony, Pennsylvania, and prayed for instruction. Hardly had they begun when a heavenly messenger appeared, introducing himself as John the Baptist. Placing his hands upon their heads, he conferred upon them the priesthood of Aaron (D&C 13). He then commanded the young men to baptize each other in the nearby Susquehanna River and then lay hands upon each other to reconfer the priesthood that he had bestowed upon them. The messenger promised that the MELCHIZEDEK PRIESTHOOD, or higher priesthood, would be given to them at a future time by the apostles Peter, James, and John (JS—H 1:72).

BIBLIOGRAPHY

Matthews, Robert J. *A Burning Light.* Provo, Utah, 1972.
Scobie, Charles H. *John the Baptist.* Philadelphia, 1964.

LOUI NOVAK

JOHN THE BELOVED

John the Beloved is the author of five New Testament writings—a Gospel, the Revelation (Apocalypse; *see* JOHN, REVELATIONS OF), and three letters. Although the author identifies himself as John in the Revelation (Rev. 1:1, 4, 9), he is known only as "the Elder" in the letters and as "the disciple whom Jesus loved" in the Gospel. Ancient tradition and elements of style have supported the common authorship of these writings, but some argue that "the Beloved" and "the Elder" were two different people.

John emphasizes spiritual qualities in his writings, including some contrasting pairs of qualities that illustrate the two opposing spiritual forces in the world. Examples include light and darkness, love and hate, truth and falsehood, and God and the devil (*see* OPPOSITION). John also emphasizes such ideas as bearing true witness, knowing the Lord, enduring to the end, and being raised up by the Savior.

John and his brother, James, were sons of Zebedee (some feel that Salome was Zebedee's wife, basing their identification on Matt. 27:56 and Mark 15:40), and the men of the family were fishermen at the Sea of Galilee. Their business prospered to the extent that they employed servants (Mark 1:19–20) by the time Jesus called the brothers to the full-time ministry. Although the Gospels of Matthew and Luke list Peter, Andrew, James, and John at the beginning of their lists, Mark and Acts place Peter, James, and John at the beginning of the list of the Twelve. These three apostles were alone with Jesus on special occasions, such as at the raising of Jairus' daughter (Mark 5:37–43), on the Mount of Transfiguration (Matt. 17:1–9), and at Jesus' suffering in the garden of Gethsemane (Matt. 26:37–45). The Prophet Joseph SMITH taught that these three ancient apostles received the KEYS OF THE PRIESTHOOD during the transfiguration experience (*TPJS*, p. 158).

John is usually identified as one of the two disciples of John the Baptist mentioned in the Gospel of John who became disciples of Jesus after his baptism (John 1:35–40). James and John were called Boanerges ("Sons of Thunder") by Jesus, perhaps because of their strong and impulsive personalities. Either they (Mark 10:35–40) or their mother on their behalf (Matt. 20:20–23) asked Jesus to grant them places of honor in his heavenly kingdom. Although rebuked for their ambition, they averred their willingness to share in his trials and suffering, and Jesus affirmed that they would do so.

John describes himself as "leaning on Jesus' bosom" during the Last Supper (John 13:23); later, when Jesus was bound and taken to the high priest, John (who "was known unto the high priest") and Peter followed along (John 18:15). John continued to follow the Savior through the ensuing events and was the only one of the Twelve recorded as being present at the Crucifixion. Jesus asked him to take care of his mother, Mary, and John took her to his own home (John 19:26–27).

Following the resurrection of Christ, Peter and John ran to the tomb when told by Mary Magdalene that the covering stone had been removed. John ran faster and arrived first at the empty tomb (John 20:1–8). Later, the Lord told Peter that John would remain (on earth) until the Lord's second coming (John 21:20–23), giving rise to the early Christian tradition that John did not die. The Prophet Joseph Smith confirmed and corrected that tradition in a revelation that states that John, having been given "power over death," remains on earth "as flaming fire and a ministering angel . . . for those who shall be heirs of salvation" until the Savior returns (D&C 7; *see* TRANSLATED BEINGS). The resurrected Christ also mentioned John's continued earthly ministry during his visit to the people of the Book of Mormon (3 Ne. 28:6–8).

Peter and John appear together in many events of the early chapters of Acts, and some time after James' death (Acts 12:1–2) these two apostles were joined by another James, the "brother of the Lord" (Gal. 1:19), in a presiding responsibility over the Church; James, Peter, and John were the recognized "pillars" (Gal. 2:9).

After Peter's death (traditionally dated about A.D. 67), John would have been the senior and presiding apostle. Many sources state that years later John lived at Ephesus, was exiled to Patmos (c. A.D. 90) by the Emperor Domitian, and returned to Ephesus during the reign of Nerva (A.D. 96–98), Domitian's successor. During his exile to Patmos, John received the Revelation, which he was directed to send with cover letters to seven churches of Asia Minor. The importance of the Revelation to the Latter-day Saints is underscored by the vision of NEPHI₁ in the Book of Mormon, where that prophet was told by an angel not to write all he had seen, for the record of the last days would be made

for the world by John, an apostle of the Lord (1 Ne. 14:18–27; cf. Ether 4:16).

After returning to Ephesus, John wrote the three letters that bear his name in the New Testament. Some think he also wrote his Gospel in Ephesus at this late date, but others date it earlier. Other writings have been ascribed to John, including the apocryphal *Acts of John*, and various versions of the *Apocryphon* [secret writing] *of John*, but none of these has been generally considered an authentic writing of the apostle.

In May–June 1829 the three ancient apostles, Peter, James, and John, appeared to Joseph Smith and Oliver COWDERY, ordained them to the MELCHIZEDEK PRIESTHOOD, and gave to them the same keys they had received on the Mount of Transfiguration (see D&C 27:12–13). Joseph Smith later received a revelation, parts of which paralleled the prologue to the Gospel of John, and was told that "the fulness of John's record" would be given at some future date (D&C 93:6, 18).

BIBLIOGRAPHY

Brown, Raymond E. *The Gospel According to John*, 2 vols. Garden City, N.Y., 1966, 1970.

———. *The Epistles of John.* New York, 1982.

Charles, R. H. *Revelation*, 2 vols. Edinburgh, 1920; rep. 1970.

Ford, J. Massyngberde. *Revelation*. New York, 1975.

Morris, Leon. *Commentary on the Gospel of John.* Grand Rapids, Mich., 1971.

Schnackenburg, Rudolf. *The Gospel According to St. John*, 3 vols. English trans., London, 1968–1982.

C. WILFRED GRIGGS

JOINING THE CHURCH

Converts to The Church of Jesus Christ of Latter-day Saints have various motivations for their initial interest in the Church, and many factors influence them in the conversion process. However, they generally share three common experiences as they seek BAPTISM and membership in the Church. First, most of those interested in joining the Church meet with missionaries for a series of brief lessons on basic LDS beliefs and religious practices. Second, all prospective converts must demonstrate in a prebaptism interview with a Church representative that they are making an informed decision of their own free will and that they willingly fulfill the baptismal requirements. Third, every convert must receive the ORDINANCES of baptism and CONFIRMATION as performed by authorized representatives of the Church and be accepted as a member of the local WARD or BRANCH by the common consent of the members.

LDS converts come from a wide age range and from all socioeconomic groups. Often they have friends or acquaintances who are already members, but sometimes they are located by missionary contacting. They typically have a desire to improve their lives by learning correct gospel principles and by uniting themselves with others having similar needs and attitudes. Thus, the common essential in most conversions to the Church is obtaining a personal conviction that the Church today is authorized by God to teach and administer the gospel of Jesus Christ.

All who are interested in joining the Church must know and understand the responsibilities that Church membership will bring. To this end, they receive a series of lessons from LDS missionaries or from members of the Church. At this stage, prospective converts are called "investigators," because they are investigating or studying the Church. The lessons are called the missionary "discussions," because although they cover standardized topics, missionaries are encouraged to present them in an informal, conversational manner. For example, missionaries typically share their personal experiences and feelings about the topics discussed, and encourage investigators to do likewise, asking questions and giving reactions to LDS teachings. These lessons are usually taught in a home setting, to individuals or to a small group.

The lessons teach the gospel of Jesus Christ, including the nature of the godhead, the PLAN OF SALVATION, keeping the commandments, and living a Christlike life. They also discuss the life and mission of the Prophet Joseph Smith, the coming-forth of the Book of Mormon, the RESTORATION of the PRIESTHOOD, and the importance of following the PROPHETS living today.

Investigators are asked to make various commitments during their course of study, which may last a few weeks or several months, depending on their individual rate of preparation toward baptism. For example, they are challenged and encouraged to engage in daily prayer and scripture study, especially prayerful study of the Book of Mormon. Those who wish to join the Church are urged to begin living an LDS lifestyle. This includes striving for Christlike attitudes and behav-

Eight-year-old boy (standing, center) on his baptismal day, with his parents and extended family, in Logan, Utah, 1987. Joining the Church brings individuals into "the household of God" (Eph. 2:19). Courtesy Craig Law.

ior in all circumstances; attending Church meetings; abstaining from harmful substances, including tobacco, alcoholic beverages, coffee, tea, and drugs; beginning to tithe; living a moral and chaste life (see CHASTITY); and laboring to serve those in need.

In the interview customarily conducted by an authorized Church representative prior to baptism, the interviewer determines the candidate's willingness and worthiness to enter into the baptismal covenant. During this interview, baptismal candidates are asked whether they have a heartfelt TESTIMONY of the fundamental doctrine of the Church. All baptismal candidates also must declare whether they currently keep, and will continue to keep, God's commandments through their lives.

Baptism is required for Church membership. It represents a covenant with God whereby the candidate agrees to follow Christ and live his commandments. The requirements for baptism are described in the Doctrine and Covenants as follows: "All those who humble themselves before God, and desire to be baptized, and come forth with broken hearts and contrite spirits, and witness before the church that they have truly repented of all their sins, and are willing to take upon them the name of Jesus Christ, having a determination to serve him to the end, and truly manifest by their works that they have received of the Spirit of Christ unto the remission of their sins, shall be received by baptism into his church" (D&C 20:37). Baptism symbolizes the washing away of sins as well as a rebirth and the beginning of a new life on earth leading to eternal life with God.

Baptism is followed by confirmation into the Church by the LAYING ON OF HANDS of one holding the MELCHIZEDEK PRIESTHOOD. During this ordinance, the new convert is confirmed a member of the Church and receives the gift of the Holy Ghost. This is typically a momentous and joyous occasion for all involved. Following his confirmation the convert is presented for acceptance by the local membership as a member in full fellowship and embarks on a life of spiritual growth through obedience to the laws of God and activity and service in the Church.

BIBLIOGRAPHY

Rector, Hartman, and Connie Rector. *No More Strangers,* 4 vols. Salt Lake City, 1971–1990.

LINDA A. CHARNEY

JOSEPH OF EGYPT

[*This entry consists of three articles:*

    Joseph, Son of Jacob
    Writings of Joseph
    Seed of Joseph

Latter-day Saint scripture portrays a broader interest in Joseph of Egypt than the Bible does. The article Joseph, Son of Jacob *deals with the resulting wide sweep of LDS interests in Joseph, including the promises of the Lord about the latter-day importance of Joseph's posterity and his ancestral relationship to the Prophet Joseph Smith. The article* Writings of Joseph *treats specifically the matter of the writings of Joseph preserved in LDS scripture. The article* Seed of Joseph *focuses on the ancestral connection between Book of Mormon peoples and Joseph, son of Jacob.*]

JOSEPH, SON OF JACOB

The Book of Mormon prophet NEPHI$_1$ said of Joseph, son of Jacob, "He truly prophesied concerning all his seed. And the prophecies which he wrote, there are not many greater" (2 Ne. 4:2). Latter-day Saints hold Joseph to be a progenitor of a branch of the house of Israel, including certain BOOK OF MORMON PEOPLES about whom he prophesied. Additionally, he is honored as an ancestor of the Prophet Joseph SMITH and many Church

members and as one who prophesied concerning the RESTORATION of the gospel of Jesus Christ through Joseph Smith.

The current Bible text preserves little scripture attributed to Joseph of Egypt. However, some writings of Joseph were recorded on the PLATES of brass, a scriptural record brought to the Western Hemisphere from Jerusalem by the prophet LEHI, and known among the Book of Mormon people. Another prophecy, restored by Joseph Smith, is now found in the JOSEPH SMITH TRANSLATION (JST) Genesis 50. In this text, the ancient Joseph prophesied the bondage of his father's family in Egypt and their eventual deliverance by Moses, and specifically names him and his brother, Aaron. Moses was to deliver Israel from Egypt, have power over the Red Sea, receive commandments from God, and be assisted by Aaron as his spokesman (JST Gen. 50:24, 29, 34–35).

The same source indicates that the Lord visited Joseph, promising him a righteous posterity, a branch of which would be separated from their kindred and taken to a distant country (JST Gen. 50:25–26). According to the Bible, Jacob had already prophesied that Joseph's branches—Ephraim and Manasseh—would inherit the "utmost bound of the everlasting hills" (Gen. 49:26). Moses described the new land of their inheritance as containing riches of both heaven and earth (Deut. 33:13–15). The Book of Mormon records the partial fulfillment of these prophecies with the exodus of the families of Lehi, a descendant of Manasseh (Alma 10:3), and Ishmael, a descendant of Ephraim (JD 23:184), to the western continents. The Book of Mormon is called "the stick of Ephraim" in modern revelation (D&C 27:5) and both "the stick of Ephraim" and "the STICK OF JOSEPH" (Ezek. 37:15–28, esp. verses 16 and 19).

Notwithstanding Israel's anticipated deliverance from Egypt under the leadership of Moses, Joseph of Egypt also foresaw that the Israelites would eventually be scattered. Still he was assured that they would be remembered by the Lord and that he would bring their descendants out of "bondage" in the LAST DAYS. A "choice seer" was to be raised up, a descendant of Joseph, who would bear his name and whose father would also bear the same name. The prophecy stated that this latter-day Joseph would be highly esteemed by Joseph's descendants and would bring them knowledge of their progenitors. Moreover, he would be like both Joseph and Moses. As the ancient Joseph gathered his father's family in Egypt and supplied them with bread during famine, so the latter-day Joseph would gather their descendants from the ends of the earth to feast upon the words of everlasting life. Like Moses, he would bring forth the word of God (the Book of Mormon and other revelations), which would testify of, and sustain, other words of God that had already gone forth (the Bible), thereby confounding false doctrines and laying contentions to rest. As Moses would liberate Israel from Egyptian bondage, the "choice seer" of the last days would liberate them from the bondage of false traditions; as Moses would reveal a new COVENANT and prepare Israel to enter the PROMISED LAND, so his latter-day counterpart would reveal a NEW AND EVER-LASTING COVENANT and prepare modern Israel, the Church, for the day of Christ's millennial reign (JST Gen. 50:24–38; cf. 2 Ne. 3; JST Gen. 48:11).

When Joseph Smith's father, Joseph SMITH, Sr., acting in his office of PATRIARCH, gave his son a PATRIARCHAL BLESSING, he further illuminated what was known to the ancient Joseph.

> I bless thee with the blessings of thy fathers Abraham, Isaac and Jacob; and . . . thy father Joseph, the son of Jacob. Behold, he looked after his posterity in the last days, when they should be scattered and driven by the Gentiles, and wept before the Lord; he sought diligently to know from whence the Son should come who should bring forth the word of the Lord, by which they might be enlightened, and brought back to the true fold, and his eyes beheld thee, my son; . . . and he said, As my blessings are to extend to the utmost bounds of the everlasting hills; as my father's blessing prevailed, over the blessings of his progenitors, and as my branches are to run over the wall, and my seed are to inherit the choice land whereon the Zion of God shall stand in the last days, from among my seed, scattered with the Gentiles, shall a choice Seer arise, whose bowels shall be a fountain of truth, whose loins shall be girded with the girdle of righteousness, whose hands shall be lifted with acceptance before the God of Jacob to turn away his anger from his anointed, whose heart shall meditate great wisdom, whose intelligence shall circumscribe and comprehend the deep things of God, and whose mouth shall utter the law of the just . . . and he shall feed upon the heritage of Jacob his father [*Utah Genealogical and Historical Magazine* 23 (Oct. 1932):175].

A blessing pronounced by Joseph Smith on Oliver COWDERY (Dec. 18, 1833) notes that Joseph of Egypt had seen Oliver in vision and knew of his scribal role in the translation of the Book of Mormon. Oliver was also told that Joseph of Egypt knew that Oliver would be present when the AARONIC PRIESTHOOD, or lesser priesthood, was restored and again when the MELCHIZEDEK PRIESTHOOD, or higher priesthood, was restored by messengers who received it from Jesus during his earthly ministry (Joseph F. Smith, *IE* 7 [Oct. 1904]:943). With the restoration of these priesthoods in 1829 and the publication of the Book of Mormon in 1830, the stage was set for fulfilling Moses' promise that the posterity of Ephraim and Manasseh would "push" or gather scattered Israel from the four quarters of the earth (cf. Deut. 33:17).

BIBLIOGRAPHY

Horton, George A., Jr. "Joseph: A Legacy of Greatness." In *Studies in Scripture*, ed. K. Jackson and R. Millet, Vol. 3, pp. 63–92. Salt Lake City, 1985.

McConkie, Joseph Fielding. *His Name Shall Be Joseph*. Salt Lake City, 1980.

JOSEPH FIELDING MCCONKIE

WRITINGS OF JOSEPH

Certain prophecies of Joseph of Egypt were preserved on brass plates carried by NEPHI₁ from Jerusalem to the Americas in approximately 590 B.C. The Book of Mormon makes available some of these prophecies. Although it is not known when Joseph's prophetic texts were recorded, they are doubtless very ancient. By contrast, the *History of Joseph*, *Prayer of Joseph*, *Testament of Joseph*, and *Joseph and Asenath* are considered to be Hellenistic Jewish writings, dating between 200 B.C. and A.D. 200, and are of unknown authorship (see Charlesworth). Joseph SMITH noted "writings of Joseph" on papyri that he owned (*HC* 2:236).

According to Alma 46:24, Jacob the patriarch saw that part of Joseph's coat would be preserved, symbolizing a remnant of Joseph's seed (cf. *CWHN* 6:211–21). In addition, two similar though not identical texts from Joseph are preserved in 2 Nephi 3 and JST Genesis 50. Both prophesy that Moses will arise, that writings from "the fruit of the loins of Judah shall grow together" with writings of Joseph's descendants, and that a seer named Joseph—whose father would also be named Joseph—would appear in the last days (2 Ne. 3:6–17; JST Gen. 50:24–35; for similar expectations in pseudepigraphic texts, see McConkie). Associates of Joseph Smith saw him as the predicted seer, as did Joseph Smith himself. For instance, President John TAYLOR affirmed:

God called [Joseph Smith] to occupy the position that he did. How long ago? Thousands of years ago . . . Prophets prophesied about his coming, that a man should arise whose name should be Joseph, and that his father's name should be Joseph, and also that he should be a descendant of that Joseph who was sold into Egypt [JD 26:106].

BIBLIOGRAPHY

Charlesworth, James H. *The Old Testament Pseudepigrapha*, 2 vols. Garden City, New York, 1983–1985.

McConkie, Joseph F. "Joseph Smith as Found in Ancient Manuscripts." In *Isaiah and the Prophets*, ed. M. Nyman. Provo, Utah, 1984.

JAMES R. CLARK

SEED OF JOSEPH

The Book of Mormon teaches that Joseph, son of Jacob, "obtained a promise of the Lord" that his seed would become a "righteous branch unto the house of Israel" (2 Ne. 3:5) and that a latter-day descendant also named Joseph would have a role in bringing Joseph's seed and all the house of Israel "unto salvation" (2 Ne. 3:15).

While many of Joseph's posterity were among the ten tribes of Israel taken into captivity about 722 B.C. (2 Kgs. 17:5–6), a few descendants had settled in Jerusalem some 200 years earlier (cf. 2 Chr. 15:9–10). From those came the Book of Mormon leaders LEHI and ISHMAEL, who, about 600 B.C., led their families to the Western Hemisphere. Their descendants were later called "a remnant of the seed of Joseph" (Alma 46:23–24). Lehi reported that Joseph's prophecies concerning his seed included the following: (1) they would become a righteous people; (2) the Messiah would manifest himself to them; (3) a latter-day SEER like Moses, raised up by God from Joseph's seed, would himself be called Joseph (2 Ne. 3:1–25); and (4) the righteous seed of the ancient Joseph who accept the gospel will help in building the NEW JERUSALEM and will participate in events of the LAST DAYS (3 Ne. 20:10–28; 21:2–26).

BIBLIOGRAPHY

Ludlow, Daniel H. *A Companion to Your Study of the Book of Mormon*. Salt Lake City, 1976.

Pratt, Orson. "The Blessings of Joseph." JD 14:7–11.

LIESEL C. MCBRIDE

JOSEPH SMITH—HISTORY

The account called Joseph Smith—History, as it appears in the Pearl of Great Price, tells of the Prophet's experiences from his early years through May 1829. Franklin D. Richards, an early apostle, extracted this part of Joseph SMITH's history from the much longer HISTORY OF THE CHURCH printed in the TIMES AND SEASONS (T&S 3:726), and published the extract in 1851. In the preface of the first edition of the Pearl of Great Price, Richards expressed a hope that this collection of precious truths would increase the members' ability to defend the faith. Joseph Smith—History, the name now given to the historical extract, became canonized scripture to the members of the Church when they accepted the Pearl of Great Price by vote at the October 10, 1880, General Conference (*see* PEARL OF GREAT PRICE: CONTENTS AND PUBLICATION).

This account in the Pearl of Great Price was not the first attempt to record the Prophet's early experiences. From the organization of the Church in 1830, he understood the importance of keeping records but his efforts were hindered by lawsuits, imprisonments, poverty, and mobs. John Whitmer kept a history between 1830 and 1832 that was lost for many years but is now available again, and Oliver COWDERY wrote eight letters about Joseph Smith's early visions that were published in MESSENGER AND ADVOCATE in 1834–1835. Joseph Smith began work on a history between July and November 1832; it opened with the words "A History of the life of Joseph Smith, Jr., an account of his marvilous [sic] experience," and described his early visions. Various clerks and historians made three more beginnings between 1834 and 1836. In the trying years 1837 and 1838, Joseph Smith and the First Presidency worked on the history of the Church, sometimes taking a grammar lesson before the writing sessions. Finally, in June 1839, Joseph undertook the work again. Materials from the previous efforts were assimilated into this new history, which eventually was published in the *Times and Seasons*, beginning March 1, 1842 (T&S 3:706). Joseph Smith—History, as we now have it in the Pearl of Great Price, was part of this 1839 version of the history of the Church.

The history introduces Joseph by giving a brief record of his ancestry and his own birth on December 23, 1805, in the township of Sharon, Windsor County, Vermont, one of eleven children of Joseph Sr. and Lucy Mack Smith. It tells of the religious conditions that led to Joseph Smith's FIRST VISION and describes what he saw and heard when the Father and Son appeared, in a direct, first-person account that makes no effort to adorn the events it relates. Oliver Cowdery, Joseph's close associate in these early years, wrote a much more ornate narrative of the early experiences. Joseph Smith simply described what happened to him, from the First Vision, through the visitation of MORONI₂, the visits to the hill CUMORAH, the translation of the gold plates, and to the visit of John the Baptist to restore the Aaronic Priesthood (*see* AARONIC PRIESTHOOD: RESTORATION).

For many years the Church published Joseph Smith—History as a pamphlet with the title *Joseph Smith's Own Story*. Missionaries carried it to all parts of the world to help explain Joseph Smith's part in the restoration of the gospel in modern times.

BIBLIOGRAPHY

Clark, James R. *Story of the Pearl of Great Price*. Salt Lake City, 1955.

Jessee, Dean C. "The Writing of Joseph Smith's History." *BYU Studies* 11 (1971):439–73.

———. "The Reliability of Joseph Smith's History." *Journal of Mormon History* 3 (1976):23–46.

JOSEPH GRANT STEVENSON

JOSEPH SMITH—MATTHEW

Joseph Smith—Matthew is an extract from the JOSEPH SMITH TRANSLATION OF THE BIBLE (JST), as revealed to the Prophet Joseph SMITH in 1831, and comprises a revision of Jesus' discourse on the Mount of Olives recorded in Matthew 23:39 through chapter 24. First published in Ohio in the mid-1830s as a broadside, Joseph Smith—Matthew was republished in 1851 as part of the original PEARL OF GREAT PRICE (Matthews, p. 52).

On March 7, 1831, Joseph Smith was directed to begin a translation of the New Testament "that ye may be prepared for the things to come" (D&C 45:60–61). In Matthew 24, Jesus foretold the impending destruction of Jerusalem. He also spoke of his own SECOND COMING and the destruction of the wicked.

The following are some of the significant additions and clarifications of Joseph Smith—Matthew to the King James text:

1. Jesus' disciples clearly understood that he would come again in glory "in the clouds of heaven, and all the holy angels with him" (JS—M 1:1).
2. Verses 4–22 of the King James text refer to "things I have spoken unto you concerning the Jews" (JS—M 1:21).
3. Verses 6, 7, and 14 of KJV are repositioned from the early part of the chapter, which deals with the Jews of New Testament times, to the latter part of the chapter, which concerns the second coming.
4. The end of the world is not the end of the earth, but the "destruction of the wicked" (JS—M 1:4, 55).
5. The parable in KJV verse 28 is completed to read, "Wheresoever the carcass is, there will the eagles be gathered together; so likewise shall mine elect be gathered from the four quarters of the earth" (JS—M 1:27).
6. The "abomination of desolation, spoken of by Daniel the prophet," applies both to conditions at the destruction of Jerusalem and to Jesus' second coming (JS—M 1:12, 32).

The plainness and clarity of Joseph Smith—Matthew eliminate much of the confusion that has surrounded Matthew 24. It states that the gospel must be preached in all the world and the elect gathered before the second coming (JS—M 1:31). Finally, the elect will know the signs of the times and will be prepared and preserved during the events of the last days.

BIBLIOGRAPHY

Matthews, Robert J. *"A Plainer Translation": Joseph Smith's Translation of the Bible*. Provo, Utah, 1985.

DAVID T. GILES

JOSEPH SMITH TRANSLATION OF THE BIBLE (JST)

Joseph SMITH, the first PROPHET of The Church of Jesus Christ of Latter-day Saints, made a "new translation" of the Bible, using the text of the King James Version (KJV). This work differs from the KJV in at least 3,410 verses and consists of additions, deletions, rearrangements, and other alterations that cause it to vary not only from the KJV but from other biblical texts. Changes range from minor details to fully reconstituted chapters. This article presents statements by Joseph Smith telling why he made a Bible translation, gives information relating to the development and production of the work, examines a number of the significant variants, and considers some doctrinal results and historical implications.

VIEW OF THE BIBLE. The official position of the Church is stated in its eighth ARTICLE OF FAITH: "We believe the Bible to be the word of God as far as it is translated correctly." The message of the Bible is held to be true, while details of accuracy and completeness are accepted within certain limits. The Prophet Joseph Smith explained: "I believe the Bible as it read when it came from the pen of the original writers. Ignorant translators, careless transcribers, or designing and corrupt priests have committed many errors" (*TPJS*, p. 327). And again, "From sundry revelations which had been received, it was apparent that many points touching the salvation of men, had been taken from the Bible, or lost before it was compiled" (*TPJS*, pp. 9–10).

Joseph Smith often used the words "translated" and "translation," not in the narrow sense alone of rendering a text from one language into another, but in the wider senses of "transmission," having reference to copying, editing, adding to, taking from, rephrasing, and interpreting. This is substantially beyond the usual meaning of "translation." When he said the Bible was not translated correctly, he not only was referring to the difficulties of rendering the Bible into another language but he was also observing that the manuscripts containing the text of the Bible have suffered at the hands of editors, copyists, and revisionists through centuries of transmission. Thus, the available texts of the Bible are neither as complete nor as accurate as when first written.

The Book of Mormon presents an account of a vision in which an angel, looking to the future, describes the Bible as a "record of the Jews" containing writings of "the prophets" and of the "Twelve Apostles of the Lamb." The vision asserts (1) that the ancient authors wrote under the inspiration of the Holy Ghost, (2) that originally their words contained the fulness of the gospel and were plain and easy to understand, but (3) that many things which were plain and precious, and many covenants, would be "taken away" from the original manuscripts; as a result, afterward (4) a great many persons, even with a Bible, would not understand the fulness of the gospel, but (5) the lost material would be restored through "other records" that the Lord would bring forth (1 Ne. 13:21–41). A somewhat parallel statement came to Joseph Smith in June 1830 while he was restoring a revelation received by Moses, declaring that many things would be taken "from the book" which Moses would write, but that the missing information would be restored through another prophet and thus be "had again" among those who believe (Moses 1:41). Latter-day Saints believe that the "other records" referred to include the Book of Mormon, the Doctrine and Covenants, the Pearl of Great Price, the JST, and other records still to come forth, and that the prophet divinely raised up to begin restoring the lost material is Joseph Smith (*see* SCRIPTURES: FORTHCOMING SCRIPTURES). In light of the foregoing statements, it is worth observing that the principal difficulty in the Bible apparently has been omissions. The remaining text may be generally correct in itself, but many important doctrinal items (resulting from the loss of a single word, a verse, a longer passage, or even whole books in some instances) are now missing.

AUTHORITY TO TRANSLATE. The Prophet Joseph Smith claimed a divine appointment to make an inspired rendition or, as he termed it, a "new translation" of the Bible. This appointment can be illustrated by excerpts from his writings. After laboring off and on for ten months on the early chapters of Genesis, Joseph Smith received a revelation from the Lord on March 7, 1831, directing him to begin work on the New Testament: "It shall not be given unto you to know any further concerning this chapter, until the New Testament be translated, and in it all these things shall be made known; wherefore I give unto you that ye may now translate it" (D&C 45:60–61). The manuscript of the JST shows that Joseph Smith began the translation of Matthew the next day. On December 1, 1831, the Prophet entered the following in his journal: "I resumed the translation of the Scriptures, and continued to labor in this branch of my calling with Elder Sidney Rigdon as my scribe" (*HC* 1:238–39). On February 16, 1832, he reported a revelation concerning the RESURRECTION of the dead that includes the following reference to his divine commission to translate: "For while we [Joseph Smith and Sidney Rigdon] were doing the work of translation, which the Lord had appointed unto us, we came to the twenty-ninth verse of the fifth chapter of John" (D&C 76:15). On March 8, 1833, he reported the word of the Lord to him as follows: "And when you have finished the translation of the [Old Testament] prophets, you shall from thenceforth preside over the affairs of the church" (D&C 90:13). On May 6, 1833, Joseph Smith reported the following revelation: "It is my will that you should hasten to translate my scriptures" (D&C 93:53). Although not a complete list, the foregoing items illustrate Joseph Smith's claim to a divine appointment to translate the Old and New Testaments.

PROCEDURE AND TIME FRAME. When he began his work in 1830, Joseph Smith did not have a knowledge of biblical languages. His translation was not done in the usual manner of a scholar, but was a revelatory experience using only an English text. He did not leave a description of the translating process, but it appears that he would read from the KJV and dictate revisions to a scribe.

Joseph Smith was assisted by various scribes. The manuscript shows that Oliver COWDERY was the first, serving between June and October 1830; he recorded an introductory revelation (Moses 1) and the translation of KJV Genesis 1:1 to Genesis 4:18. John Whitmer served second, from October until December 1830, recording the translation of KJV Genesis 4:19 to approximately Genesis 5:20. Sidney RIGDON was next, becoming the main scribe from early December 1830 until the translation was finished on July 2, 1833. He recorded most of the translation from KJV Genesis 5:21 to the end of the Bible, although others recorded small portions.

They used a large edition of the KJV (9 inches by 11 inches by 2½ inches), printed in 1828 by H. and E. Phinney Company of Cooperstown, New York, that included the Old Testament Apocrypha. (A notation on the flyleaf, in what appears to be Joseph Smith's handwriting, states that it had been purchased from the Egbert B. Grandin Bookstore in Palmyra, New York, on October 8, 1829, for $3.75). In this copy of the Phinney Bible are hundreds of pencil and ink notations consisting primarily of checks or crosses marking off passages to be revised. Likewise, a number of italicized words in the KJV text—which usually represent words implicitly understood in the Greek or Hebrew—are lined out. Words of the revision were not writ-

ten on the pages of the Bible itself, but were recorded on sheets of paper and identified by the appropriate citation. The manuscript is written in full from Genesis 1:1 through Genesis 24 and from Matthew 1:1 through John 5, including entire chapters in which there are no corrections. A more rapid and efficient system was eventually used in which only the actual points of revision were written. These sometimes consisted of only one or two words. The markings in the Bible that designate verses to be translated appear only in those portions where the shorter method was used. The manuscript sheets, 17 inches by 14 inches folded to produce surfaces 8½ inches by 14 inches, were once sewn together at the fold in convenient thicknesses. The entire manuscript consists of 477 pages.

The exact date on which the translation was begun is not known, but it is closely associated with the June 1830 revelation that contains an account of visions given to Moses before he composed the book of Genesis (see Moses 1). The work proceeded from June 1830 until July 2, 1833. Genesis 1–17 was translated first, being done between June 1830 and March 7, 1831. On the latter date Joseph Smith received the revelation instructing him to "translate" the New Testament (D&C 45:60–62), which he began at Matthew 1:1. It appears that for a few days the translation may have continued in both Genesis and in Matthew, but the Old Testament was subsequently laid aside, possibly at the end of Genesis 24, in favor of working on the New Testament. The work then proceeded consecutively through the entire New Testament until February 2, 1833. The remainder of the Old Testament (Genesis 25 through Malachi) was then translated, being completed five months later. In response to prayer as to whether he should translate the Apocrypha, Joseph Smith reported a revelation dated March 9, 1833, to the effect that he need not attend to it: "It is mostly translated correctly," though there are some errors and "interpolations by the hands of men" (D&C 91:1–2).

The dates on the JST manuscripts, when compared with dates of related revelations in the Doctrine and Covenants and with dates and events entered in Joseph Smith's personal journal, indicate the movement back and forth between the Old and New Testaments, as explained above, rather than a straight-line progress from Genesis through Revelation. Likewise, the varying styles of handwriting in the manuscript reflect the known coming and going of those who served as scribes. Although the bulk of the translation was accomplished by July 2, 1833, that work represented a preliminary draft. As the manuscript was later reviewed and prepared for publication, further revisions, refinements, and alterations were made.

After Joseph Smith's death in June 1844, the marked Phinney Bible and the 477-page manuscript were kept by his widow, Emma SMITH. She permitted Dr. John M. Bernhisel to examine the materials in the spring of 1845 at NAUVOO, Illinois. Bernhisel later reported that he made a complete copy of the markings in the Bible and an extensive but incomplete copy of the manuscript entries (Matthews, 1975, p. 118). The Bernhisel manuscript is in the Historian's Library of the LDS Church in Salt Lake City, but the location of the Bernhisel marked Bible is not known. Emma Smith gave the Phinney Bible and the original manuscript to a publication committee representing the REORGANIZED CHURCH OF JESUS CHRIST OF LATTER DAY SAINTS (RLDS Church) in 1866. These are now in the custody of the RLDS Church at Independence, Missouri.

PUBLICATION. Although excerpts from the JST were published in Church newspapers and as a broadside tract during the lifetime of Joseph Smith, the entire work was not published in his day, even though he had intended and had expended considerable effort to accomplish it. The distraction of persecution, the demands of Church business, and the lack of financial means prevented him from completing and authorizing a manuscript ready for the press (Matthews, pp. 57–63).

In 1867, after considerable effort and expense, the RLDS Church published a copyrighted edition of the Bible, under the title *Holy Scriptures*, which incorporated the Prophet's translation into the format of a King James text. This was followed by many subsequent printings, all from the same stereotype plates. In 1936 a teacher's edition containing study helps was published by the RLDS Church. At that time a subtitle, "Inspired Version," was added, although the text remained the same as the 1867 edition. In 1944 a "New Corrected Edition" was published by the RLDS Church in which at least 352 verses were amended to correct typographical and judgment errors in the 1867 edition. These corrections were matters of detail, although in a few instances they signifi-

cantly affected the meaning of the passages and brought the printed text into closer harmony with the manuscript. In 1970 a parallel column edition consisting of the Inspired Version and the King James Version was issued by the RLDS Church publishing house.

The Church of Jesus Christ of Latter-day Saints has never published the entire Joseph Smith translation of the Bible. Portions of Genesis and of Matthew, distributed during the time of Joseph Smith in Kirtland and in Nauvoo, are included in the Pearl of Great Price under the title BOOK OF MOSES (JST Gen. 1 through 8:18) and JOSEPH SMITH–MATTHEW (JST Matt. 24). Extensive portions of JST Genesis 1–5 and a single excerpt each from Romans and Hebrews were used in the LECTURES ON FAITH and are still published therein. In 1979 the LDS Church published an edition of the King James Version with hundreds of JST footnotes and a seventeen-page appendix containing JST excerpts (*see* LDS PUBLICATION OF THE BIBLE).

EXTENT OF THE CHANGES. Joseph Smith made extensive corrections and additions to the books of Genesis, Exodus, Psalms, Isaiah, Matthew, Luke, Romans, 1 Corinthians, Galatians, Hebrews, James, 2 Peter, and Revelation. He also made many alterations in the writings of the Old Testament prophets and in Mark, John, Acts, and several of the epistles. He made no changes in Ruth, Ezra, Esther, Ecclesiastes, Lamentations, Obadiah, Micah, Habakkuk, Zephaniah, Haggai, Malachi, Philemon, 2 John, and 3 John. He made some corrections in all other books of the Bible, and rejected the Song of Solomon as not being inspired scripture.

TITLE. Joseph Smith's work with the Bible has been known by various titles. The revelations in the Doctrine and Covenants call it a "translation" (D&C 37:1; 90:13). Joseph Smith called it the "new translation," and it is known by this title in the early literature of the Church. It was published by the RLDS Church under the title "Holy Scriptures," with the later subtitle, "Inspired Version." Many call it an "inspired revision." In 1978 the LDS Church officially labeled it the "Joseph Smith Translation," abbreviated JST.

CONTRIBUTIONS OF THE JST. Assessing the contributions of the JST requires a differentiation between the process and the product. The translation process was revelatory and educational, and was a means of expanding the Prophet Joseph Smith's knowledge and doctrinal awareness (cf. D&C 45:60–61). The contributions, therefore, go beyond the particular biblical text that may have initiated the process. Among the doctrines of the LDS Church that arose from the JST translation process are the building of Zion, patterned after Enoch's city; the age of accountability of children, with baptism at eight years; the extensive revelation about the DEGREES OF GLORY and plural marriage (including celestial, eternal MARRIAGE); and various items of priesthood organization and responsibility. These and other doctrines were often introduced during the translation process and later developed through subsequent revelations now contained in the Doctrine and Covenants. Revelations in the Doctrine and Covenants received during the translation process are sections 76, 77, 86, and 91, and parts of 107 and 132. In this way the JST has affected the spiritual life of every member of the Church, even though most of the members have not known of the JST.

The tangible product—the printed JST—consists of a Bible with thousands of unique corrections, additions, and readings. Although many Latter-day Saints regard this as the most correct version of the Bible now available, and therefore use it as a valuable source for biblical understanding, the wider contribution has probably been the enlightening effect that the process had upon Joseph Smith and the subsequent revelations through him that have shaped Church doctrine and practice. Most of the doctrinal and organizational revelations that have governed the Church, and that are now published in the Doctrine and Covenants, came to Joseph Smith during the period that he was translating the Bible (1830–1833).

Many items in the Doctrine and Covenants relate directly to the process of the JST. These gave direction to the Prophet concerning matters related to the translation, the selection of scribes, when to proceed with the translation, which portions of the Bible to do next, when to lay the work aside for other matters, and other such information, but do not contain *texts* of the JST. This type of related information is seen in the editorial headnotes to sections 35, 71, 76, 77, 86, and 91; and in the text of D&C 9:2; 35:20; 37:1; 41:7; 42:56–58; 45:60–62; 73:3; 76:15–18; 77:1–15; 86:1–11; 93:53; 94:10; 104:58; and 124:89. The Pearl of Great Price presents part of the *product*, and contains two ex-

tracts from the text of the JST, the book of Moses and Joseph Smith—Matthew.

MAIN DOCTRINAL THEMES. Most of the passages revised or added by Joseph Smith are of doctrinal significance. While many individual topics are involved, some main themes are (1) an emphasis in both the Old and New Testaments on the mission and divinity of Jesus Christ; (2) the nature of God; (3) the innocence of CHILDREN; (4) the PLAN OF SALVATION; (5) PREMORTAL LIFE; (6) the holy PRIESTHOOD and credentials of the patriarchs; (7) the ministries of ENOCH and of MELCHIZEDEK; and (8) clarification of ambiguous passages, elimination of some contradictions between biblical texts, and explanations of terms and phrases.

Representative passages of the types of information found only in Joseph Smith's translation of the Bible constitute the remainder of this article.

The purpose of the JST is to provide knowledge not found in other Bibles. Thus it is by nature declarative and informative.

1. Emphasis on Jesus Christ. The JST emphasizes that the gospel of Jesus Christ was taught in the earliest ages of mankind. According to JST Genesis 1–8 (published as Moses 1–8 in the Pearl of Great Price), Adam, Enoch, Noah, and the other patriarchs were preachers of righteousness and taught the gospel of Jesus Christ, including faith, repentance, baptism, and receiving the Holy Ghost.

The JST states that Adam was taught by a heavenly angel to offer animal sacrifice as a type and symbol of the atoning sacrifice that the Son of God would accomplish. He was instructed to do all things in the name of the Son. Adam was taught the gospel, was baptized by immersion, received the Holy Ghost, and was born of the Spirit (Moses 5, 6).

Enoch likewise knew the gospel of Jesus Christ, was ordained to the same priesthood that Adam held, and he taught these principles to others. To Enoch was given a vision that included the spirit world and future events upon the earth from his day to the second coming of Jesus Christ. He presided in a city of righteous people called Zion, which was translated and taken into heaven (Moses 6–7; *see* TRANSLATED BEINGS).

Noah was also a preacher of righteousness, ordained to the same priesthood held by Adam and Enoch, and taught the gospel of Jesus Christ to his contemporaries, including faith in Jesus Christ, baptism, and the reception of the Holy Ghost (Moses 8:12–25).

The New Testament JST portrays a slightly stronger image of Jesus than does the KJV. Examples include the following: In the KJV the wise men ask Herod about the birth of the "King of the Jews" (Matt. 2:2); in the JST they pose a more searching question: "Where is *the child* that is born, *the Messiah* of the Jews?" (JST Matt. 3:2). [JST variants here and hereafter are in italics.] When Herod inquires of the scribes, he is told that it is written that Christ should be born in Bethlehem, "For out of thee shall come a Governor, that shall rule my people Israel" (Matt. 2:6); the JST reads, "for out of thee shall come *the Messiah, who* shall *save* my people Israel" (JST Matt. 3:6).

In the JST a transitional passage without a KJV equivalent is inserted between the end of KJV Matthew chapter 2 and the beginning of Matthew chapter 3:

> *And it came to pass that Jesus grew up with his brethren, and waxed strong, and waited upon the Lord for the time of his ministry to come. And he served under his father, and he spake not as other men, neither could he be taught; for he needed not that any man should teach him. And after many years, the hour of his ministry drew nigh* [JST Matt. 3:24–26].

At age twelve, when Jesus was teaching in the temple, the KJV (Luke 2:46) records that Jesus was "sitting in the midst of the doctors, both hearing them, and asking them questions." The JST reads, "*they were* hearing *him,* and asking *him* questions" (JST Luke 2:46).

The KJV account of Jesus' forty days in the wilderness states that Jesus went there "to be tempted of the devil. And when he had fasted forty days and forty nights, he was afterward an hungered" (Matt. 4:1–2). The JST reads: "Then Jesus was led up of the Spirit, into the wilderness, to be *with God.* And when he had fasted forty days and forty nights, *and had communed with God,* he was afterwards an hungered, *and was left to be tempted of the devil*" (JST Matt. 4:1–2). Luke's record (KJV) says that Jesus was "forty days tempted of the devil" (Luke 4:2). The JST reads, "*And after forty days, the devil came unto him, to tempt him*" (JST Luke 4:2).

The KJV states that "the devil taketh" Jesus to a "pinnacle of the temple" and also to a "high mountain" (Matt. 4:5–8; Luke 4:5–9). The JST says

it was "the Spirit" who transported Jesus to these places (JST Matt. 4:5–8; Luke 4:5–9).

In the KJV John 3:23 states that Jesus performed baptisms, but John 4:2 largely negates Jesus' activity as a baptizer by stating: "Though Jesus himself baptized not, but his disciples." The JST reads, "Though *he himself baptized not so many as his disciples; For he suffered them for an example, preferring one another*" (JST John 4:3–4).

Jesus' parables are touched upon in many JST passages. One of the most important is a statement, presented as the words of Jesus himself, explaining why he used parables to veil the spiritual message when speaking to certain individuals: "Hear another parable; *for unto you that believe not, I speak in parables; that your unrighteousness may be rewarded unto you*" (JST Matt. 21:34).

In Mark 7:22–24 (KJV) Jesus enters a house "and would have no man know it: but he could not be hid." JST Mark 7:22–23 reads, "and would *that no* man *should come unto him. But he could not deny them; for he had compassion upon all men.*"

Luke reports that while Jesus was on the cross, he cried out, "Father, forgive them; for they know not what they do" (KJV Luke 23:34). The JST adds a parenthetical clarification: "*(meaning the soldiers who crucified him)*" (JST Luke 23:35).

2. God's Dealings with Mankind. JST passages bearing on God's dealings with mankind include the following: Genesis 6:6 (KJV) states that "It repented the Lord that he had made man on the earth, and it grieved him at his heart." JST Genesis 8:13 (Moses 8:25) renders this passage thus: "And it repented Noah, and *his heart was pained,* that the Lord had made man on the earth." Exodus 7:3, 13; 9:12; 10:1, 20 (KJV) all state that God will harden Pharaoh's heart. In each of these the JST reads that Pharaoh will harden his own heart:

Isaiah 63:17 (KJV) reads "O Lord, why hast thou made us to err from thy ways, and hardened our heart?" The JST reads, "O Lord, why hast thou suffered us to err, . . . and *to harden* our heart?"

Matthew 6:13 (KJV) reads, "And lead us not into temptation," whereas the JST reads "*suffer us not to be led* into temptation" (JST Matt. 6:14).

3. Innocence of Children. Many passages bear on man's nature in relation to the fall of Adam, his agency, and accountability to God. For instance, concerning the innocence of little children, the JST states that in the days of Adam the Lord re-

vealed that "the Son of God hath atoned for original guilt, wherein the sins of the parents cannot be answered upon the heads of the children, for they are whole from the foundation of the world" (JST Gen. 6:56; Moses 6:54). To Abraham the Lord said, "Children are not accountable before me until they are eight years old" (JST Gen. 17:11). Matthew 18:11 in the KJV states with reference to children: "For the Son of man is come to save that which is lost." The JST adds, "and to call sinners to repentance; but these little ones have no need of repentance, and I will save them."

4. Paul's Writings. The JST offers many clarifications regarding teachings attributed to Paul in the New Testament. Some of these are as follows:

First Corinthians 14:35 (KJV) reports Paul writing "it is a shame for women to speak in the church." The JST reads "for women *to rule* in the church."

Hebrews 6:1 (KJV) reads "Therefore leaving the principles of the doctrine of Christ, let us go on unto perfection." The JST reads *"not* leaving . . . ."

Hebrews 7:3 (KJV) gives the impression that the prophet Melchizedek was "without father, without mother, without descent, having neither beginning of days, nor end of life." The JST states that it was not Melchizedek the man, but his priesthood, that was without lineage or descent, being thus contrasted to the Levitical priesthood.

In 1 Timothy 3:15–16 (KJV) Paul is reported to have written that the church is the "pillar and ground of the truth." In the JST it is Jesus, as God manifested in the flesh, who is the "pillar and ground of the truth."

[*See also* other passages from the JST in the appendices, Vol. 4.]

BIBLIOGRAPHY

Durham, Reed Connell, Jr. "A History of Joseph Smith's Revision of the Bible." Ph.D. diss., Brigham Young University, 1965.

Howard, Richard P. *Restoration Scriptures*. Independence, Mo., 1969.

Matthews, Robert J. *"A Plainer Translation:" Joseph Smith's Translation of the Bible*. Provo, Utah, 1975.

———. *A Bible! A Bible!* Salt Lake City, 1990.

———. "Joseph Smith's Efforts to Publish His Bible Translation." *Ensign* 13 [Jan. 1983]:57–63).

Nyman, Monte S., and Robert L. Millet, eds. *The Joseph Smith Translation*. Provo, Utah, 1985.

ROBERT J. MATTHEWS

JOURNAL OF DISCOURSES

The *Journal of Discourses* was a sixteen-page semi-monthly subscription publication privately printed in Liverpool, England, in 1854–1886. It served as the printed word of The Church of Jesus Christ of Latter-Day Saints, particularly for members who had no access to the Salt Lake City *Deseret News*. While the *Journal* most often published sermons of Church leaders, these speeches were not always considered to be official statements of doctrine. Many different kinds of speeches were printed, including the prayer given at the laying of a cornerstone of the SALT LAKE TEMPLE, a report of a HIGH COUNCIL court decision, a funeral sermon, and a plea for the defendant and the charge to the jury in a murder trial. In all, the collected *Journal of Discourses* contains 1,438 speeches given by fifty-five people, including Presidents of the Church, members of the QUORUM OF THE TWELVE APOSTLES, members of the SEVENTY, and sixteen other speakers. Brigham YOUNG gave 390; John TAYLOR, 162; Orson Pratt, 127; Heber C. KIMBALL, 113; and George Q. Cannon, 111. Twenty-one people gave a single speech, and the rest gave from 2 to 66 speeches. The semimonthly issues have been bound into twenty-six annual volumes and are currently available in a lithograph reprinting "of the original edition."

The origin of the *Journal of Discourses* is tied to George D. Watt, an English convert baptized in 1837 by Heber C. Kimball. Before immigrating to the United States in 1842, Watt learned Pitman shorthand. He used this new skill in his adopted land to record the proceedings of conferences of the Church. He also recorded the trial of the accused murderers of the Prophet Joseph SMITH.

After 1852 Watt transcribed Church conference addresses for the *Deseret News*. But because the *News* was not generally available outside central Utah and because Watt received little pay for his work, he proposed to publish privately and sell sixteen-page semiweekly issues of the *Journal of Discourses* containing selected sermons of the GENERAL AUTHORITIES. The sale of these to the Saints at large would enable Watt to earn a living with his shorthand skill. He was supported in this proposal by Brigham Young, who authorized him to print his sermons.

David W. Evans, also an English convert, an associate editor of the *Deseret News*, and the first violinist in the Salt Lake Theatre Orchestra, succeeded Watt as the main reporter to the *Journal* from 1867 to 1876. Another major reporter was George F. Gibbs, who was born in Wales and was the secretary to the FIRST PRESIDENCY of the Church for fifty-six years. In all, twelve people reported sermons for the *Journal of Discourses*, including one of Brigham Young's daughters, "Miss Julia Young," who reported one of his speeches.

BIBLIOGRAPHY

McConkie, Joseph Fielding, ed. *Journal of Discourses Digest.* Salt Lake City, 1975.

Watt, Ronald G. "Sailing the Old Ship Zion: The Life of George D. Watt." *BYU Studies* 18 (Fall 1977):48–65.

RONALD G. WATT

JOURNALS

Journal writing among the early Latter-day Saints took impetus from a divine charge to the Prophet Joseph SMITH on the day the Church was organized: "There shall be a record kept among you" (D&C 21:1). Although that was an official charge to the Church, individual members took it as a personal charge and began keeping journals. Joseph Smith himself worked regularly with scribes until his death, directing the recording of his daily activities. Much of what is known about the early events of the Church comes from the many personal journals kept by leaders and members.

Careful and complete records served as a protection against opponents of the Church. In instructions to the Quorum of the Twelve in 1835, Joseph Smith urged them to note down the procedures of meetings held, for "the time will come, when, if you neglect to do this thing, you will fall by the hands of unrighteous men. . . . If you will be careful to keep minutes of these things . . . it will be one of the most important records ever seen" (*HC* 2:198–99). Joseph Smith stated that the Saints had been somewhat delinquent in this charge.

In addition to Joseph Smith's comprehensive journal, which he kept with the aid of personal scribes, several early converts began to keep personal diaries, most of them sketchy but some very ambitious. It has been a common practice of missionaries to keep journals of their activities, though most of these early journals tended to be factual

rather than reflective, and followed a quite standard format: the call, travel particulars, names of companions and Church members, lists of letters from home, sightseeing, release, and the return home. A frequent topic of Latter-day Saint journals is the writer's conversion to the Church.

Early journals usually are also quite reportorial, matter-of-fact in tone, sparing in detail, and often repetitive; yet they are valuable for historical reference, if not engaging in content or style, though some passages are eloquent in their plainness. Feelings and introspection are more characteristic of twentieth-century journals. Yet all journals are important resources for FAMILY HISTORY information.

Most Presidents of the Church have kept a journal of some type—either historical or personal, with or without the assistance of a secretary. From the founding of the Church, there was a steady flow of journal writing, the quantity increasing during times of reformation, as in 1856–1857, or when leaders urged the practice of journal keeping. Perhaps best known of the early diarists was Wilford WOODRUFF, who kept a meticulous personal record (including many drawings)—fifteen volumes covering the years 1833–1898. His record is rich in detail and personal insight on many important events in the early Church.

In 1977, in his *Guide to Mormon Diaries & Autobiographies*, Davis Bitton identified and cataloged some 3,000 pieces of LDS autobiographical writing, consisting largely of journals, mostly by men, in repositories throughout the United States, though mainly in the state of Utah. Many more uncataloged journals remain in the possession of individuals and families, and Bitton suggested that his bibliography be updated from time to time.

Twentieth-century LDS journals tend to be longer and more numerous, reflecting increased literacy, more time to write, and greater openness. Both Joseph F. SMITH and Heber J. GRANT, Church presidents from 1901 to 1918 and 1918 to 1945, respectively, left multivolume journal records. LDS journal writing received special stimulus during the presidency of Spencer W. KIMBALL (1973–1985), who himself kept an extensive journal of about eighty volumes. Typical of his many admonitions to Church members is a short remark in the 1977 October General Conference: "A word about personal journals and records: We urge every person in the Church to keep a diary or a

Journal writing has been encouraged since the earliest days of the Church and has been the source of much of what is known about Church history. Many Latter-day Saints today, including children, youth, and adults, regularly record their experiences in personal journals.

journal from youth up, all through his life" ("The Foundations of Righteousness." *Ensign* 7 [Nov. 1977]:4).

Also in recent years, a new reason for journal writing has been voiced: the value of journals as a gift to descendants—a linking of the generations. President Kimball said: "I promise you that if you will keep your journals and records, they will indeed be a source of great inspiration to your families, to your children, your grandchildren, and others, on through the generations. . . . Rich passages . . . will be quoted by your posterity" (p. 61).

Because of the admonitions of scripture and leaders, journal writing, especially in recent decades, has become an integral part of the religious experience of many Latter-day Saints. Parents have been encouraged to write their own personal journals and to help their children begin writing theirs, to make the experience pleasant. President Kimball said in 1980: "Those who keep a personal

journal are more likely to keep the Lord in remembrance in their daily lives" (p. 61).

BIBLIOGRAPHY

Bitton, Davis. *Guide to Mormon Diaries & Autobiographies.* Provo, Utah, 1977.

Forbis, Dianne Dibb. "It's Child's Play: How to Help Your Child Begin a Journal." *Ensign* 7 (Jan. 1977):29.

Kimball, Spencer W. "President Kimball Speaks out on Personal Journals." *Ensign* 10 (Dec. 1980):60–61.

DON E. NORTON
JOANNE LINNABARY

JOY

The Prophet Joseph SMITH declared, "Happiness is the object and design of our existence; and will be the end thereof, if we pursue the path that leads to it" (*TPJS*, p. 255). The concept of true joy to be experienced in this life and in the life to come lies at the core of LDS thought. The Book of Mormon prophet LEHI taught, "Adam fell that men might be; and men are, that they might have joy" (2 Ne. 2:25; cf. Alma 42:8).

Latter-day Saints believe in a PREMORTAL LIFE in which all lived with God, the literal father of the spirits of humankind. Part of God's plan for the growth and progress of his children—the goal of which is to help everyone become as God himself is and to know the joy that he knows—involves a mortal experience. Therein people obtain a physical body, the power of procreation, and an independence and AGENCY that allow experiences of diverse kinds and thereby enhance the powers of self-determination.

In this light, Latter-day Saints view the physical body, the mortal environment, the procreative power, and the freedom of choice as essential elements of joy. Thus, Heavenly Father created this earth and sent his children to it that they might know joy. In this profound sense, joy and happiness arise from combinations of experience, responsibility and service, and pain and grief, along with pleasure and enjoyment. At the center of God's plan to make maximum joy accessible to his children is the ATONEMENT of Christ (2 Ne. 2:10–14, 22–27).

One can identify aspects of joy that are available in this life. First are the simple joys of being aware of and appreciating the gifts of life, the earth, and personal agency (e.g., taste, smell, beauty, music). A second is the joy of using these gifts to create opportunities or to develop relationships (e.g., marriage, parenting, charity). A third is the joy of coming to understand how mortality fits into the divine purpose or plan of the Heavenly Father (see PLAN OF SALVATION). This understanding derives from learning of God's plan for his children's salvation and using it as a framework for comprehending and assimilating life's experiences. Another is the joy of accepting Christ as Savior and feeling his acceptance and approval of one's efforts. This joy is accompanied by the power and beauty of Christ's spirit in one's life. In this connection, the Book of Mormon describes a scene wherein "the spirit of the Lord came upon them, and they were filled with joy, having received a remission of their sins, and having peace of conscience" (Mosiah 4:3; cf. John 15:10–12).

LDS doctrine teaches that joy is obtained only by RIGHTEOUSNESS (Mosiah 4:3, 20). Consequently, Latter-day Saints view God's COMMANDMENTS as loving counsel from a wise Father—a Father whose goal is human happiness. They believe that lives which conform to God's will and are governed by his standards will create the most joyful response to all of life's circumstances, bringing both a fulfillment in life's accomplishments and a sweet resolve in life's sorrows.

BIBLIOGRAPHY

Eyre, Richard M. *The Discovery of Joy*. Salt Lake City, 1974.

———. *Teaching Children Joy*. New York, 1986.

Hanks, Marion D. "Joy Through Christ." *Ensign* 2 (July 1972):104–106.

Romney, Marion G. "Joy and Happiness." *Ensign* 3 (Sept. 1973):2–3.

RICHARD M. EYRE

JUDGMENT

All humankind shall stand before Jesus, "and he shall separate them from one another, as a shepherd divideth his sheep from the goats" (Matt. 25:32). The verb "separate" reflects the Lord's determination of exact boundaries between good and evil, since he "cannot look upon sin with the least degree of allowance" (D&C 1:31). The Greek New Testament word for judgment (*krino*) means to separate or to decide, and refers not only to God's decisions but to those made by man as well (Matt. 7:1–2).

AMULEK warned that this life is the time to prepare to meet God (Alma 34:32). MORTALITY requires basic decisions of a moral and spiritual character, in which individuals are free to choose for themselves yet are accountable to God for their choices. In turn, God will render a perfect and just decision to determine blessings or punishments. In the judgment there will be a perfect restoration of joy for righteous living and of misery for evil (Alma 41:3–5). After death is not the time to repent: "Ye cannot say, when ye are brought to that awful crisis, that I will repent, that I will return to my God; . . . for that same spirit which doth possess your bodies at the time that ye go out of this life . . . will have power to possess your body in that eternal world" (Alma 34:34).

Judgment applies to "the whole human family" (Morm. 3:20; cf. John 5:25–29; *TPJS*, p. 149). Every soul will come before the bar of God through the power of the ATONEMENT and the RESURRECTION (Jacob 6:9). Indeed, as Christ was lifted up on the cross, he will raise all men before him in judgment (3 Ne. 27:14–15; *TPJS*, p. 62). Christ has been given the responsibility for judgment. He taught, "The Father judgeth no man, but has committed all judgment unto the Son" (John 5:22). Others have been given some role in judgment, such as the twelve apostles in Palestine and the twelve disciples among the Nephites as described in the Book of Mormon (Morm. 3:18–19). Individuals will also judge themselves either by having a perfect knowledge of their joy and righteousness or by having a perfect knowledge of their guilt and unrighteousness (2 Ne. 9:14, 46). All have the assurance, however, that final judgment is in the hands of Christ (2 Ne. 9:41).

Three sets of records will be used in judgment: the records kept in heaven, the records kept on earth (D&C 128:6–7), and the records embedded in the consciousness of each individual (*MD*, p. 97; cf. Alma 11:43). Individuals are judged according to their works, thoughts, words, and the desires of their hearts (Alma 12:14; D&C 137:9).

There can be no pretense or hypocrisy in the manner in which people accept and live the gospel (2 Ne. 31:13). The Lord will judge members of the

Church as to whether they have sought to deny themselves all ungodliness (Moro. 10:32) and whether they have served others with their whole soul (D&C 4:3). Other criteria for judgment include their concern for the needs of others, both spiritual and physical, and the use they make of the light and talents that they have been given (D&C 82:2–3). To merit God's approval, everyone must live and serve according to his will (Matt. 7:21–23) and do all things the Lord commands (Abr. 3:26). Yet, since all have sinned and come short of the glory of God (Rom. 3:23), except Jesus only, all are dependent on the Atonement and on repentance to escape the demands of justice (see JUSTICE AND MERCY).

Judgment is an expression of the love of God for his children and is exercised mercifully. Mercy takes into account the variety and differing circumstances of human life. For instance, many of God's expectations are relative to the opportunity that individuals have had to know the gospel. Nevertheless, "mercy cannot rob justice," and those who rebel openly against God merit punishment (Alma 42:25; Mosiah 2:38–39; 2 Pet. 2:9). Although the "Lord's arms of mercy are extended to all" (Alma 5:33), only those who repent have claim on mercy through the Son (Alma 12:33–34). God's judgment reflects the truth that he is "a perfect, just God, and a merciful God also" (Alma 42:15). Eventually all persons will acknowledge that God's judgment is just: "every nation, kindred, tongue, and people shall see eye to eye and shall confess before God that his judgments are just" (Mosiah 16:1).

The principle of judgment was operative in the premortal estate, is continuously operative during mortal life, and will continue in the spirit world and beyond, through resurrection and final judgment. In the premortal state Satan and "a third part" of God's children were denied the opportunity of mortality because they rebelled against God (Abr. 3:24–28; D&C 29:36–38). In mortal life nations and peoples have been destroyed or scattered when they have become ripened in iniquity and the judgments of God have thereby come upon them (1 Ne. 17:37).

Judgment during mortality is a continuous process to assess people's worthiness to participate in the saving ordinances of the gospel and to serve in the Church. This is done by means of interviews with local Church leaders. Priesthood leaders are called upon to judge the deeds of member's who transgress God's commandments to determine their standing in the Church (see DISCIPLINARY COUNCILS). Judgment also occurs at death as individuals are received into the SPIRIT WORLD either in happiness or in misery (Alma 40:9–14).

In LDS doctrine, individual destiny after the final judgment is not limited to either HEAVEN or HELL. Although the wicked will be thrust into hell (D&C 76:106); nevertheless, all humankind (except those who deny the Holy Ghost and become SONS OF PERDITION) will be redeemed when Christ perfects his work (D&C 76:107). Thus, nearly everyone who has lived on the earth will eventually inherit a degree of glory, it being that amount of heavenly bliss and glory that they have the capacity and the qualifications to receive.

Concerning those who die without an opportunity to hear the gospel, the Lord revealed to Joseph SMITH that "all who have died without a knowledge of this gospel, who would have received it if they had been permitted to tarry, shall be heirs of the celestial kingdom of God; also all that shall die henceforth without a knowledge of it, who would have received it with all their hearts, shall be heirs of that kingdom" (D&C 137:7–8). Little children who die also receive the full blessings of salvation (Moro. 8:11, 22). All mankind will be taught the gospel, either on earth or in the spirit world. All necessary ordinances will be performed on the earth vicariously by living proxies in the TEMPLE for those who did not have the opportunity to receive the gospel while in this life, so that they may accept or reject the gospel in the spirit world and be judged on the same basis as those who receive the gospel on earth and remain faithful (1 Pet. 4:6). Such doctrine is not only just; it is also a merciful expression of the pure love of Christ (TPJS, p. 218; Moro. 7:44–47).

[See also Baptism for the Dead; Plan of Salvation; Purpose of Earth Life; Salvation of the Dead; Spiritual Death; Temple Ordinances; Voice of Warning.]

BIBLIOGRAPHY

McConkie, Bruce R. MD, pp. 398–99, 400–408. Salt Lake City, 1966.

Smith, Joseph Fielding, comp. TPJS, pp. 216–23. Salt Lake City, 1938.

DEAN JARMAN

JUDGMENT DAY, FINAL

A purpose of the final judgment is to judge every person, to provide a separation of the faithful from the wicked, and to make available the promised blessings of eternal reward to God's faithful children. Jesus Christ is the judge.

The concept of a final judgment requires that it be deferred until the entire mortal experience is completed. The PLAN OF SALVATION teaches of a partial judgment at the time of death, when the spirit leaves the mortal body and enters the world of spirits (Alma 40:11–14), of another partial judgment at the time of resurrection, when the spirit and the physical body are permanently resurrected and reunited (Alma 11:45); and of a final judgment (Rev. 20:12; D&C 38:5) that will consign individuals to an eternal status (D&C 29:27–29; 3 Ne. 26:4). Thus, this final judgment will take place following the reuniting of body and spirit in the RESURRECTION (Alma 11:44; 12:12). By that time, every person will have been given an opportunity to receive an understanding of the gospel of Jesus Christ (1 Pet. 3:19–20; Luke 4:18; Isa. 42:7).

At the Judgment, each person will be required to give an accounting of the use of his or her moral agency during mortality (D&C 101:78). The final judgment is the final point of eternal accountability for all voluntary actions, words, thoughts, desires, and works of the individual. The full significance of such an accounting cannot be adequately assessed unless it is realized that all judgments granted from the seat of God's justice are of infinite scope and eternal consequence (3 Ne. 26:4; D&C 76:112).

Every person born to mortality will be brought to a final judgment (Morm. 3:18–20). No mortal act, no matter how righteous or wicked, will provide exemption from this judgment.

Each individual is to be judged according to the degree of knowledge and opportunity available during mortal probation (2 Ne. 2:10). On the basis of records kept both on earth and in heaven (Rev. 20:12; 2 Ne. 29:11; D&C 128:7), each individual will be judged according to works, desires, and intent of the heart (Mosiah 4:6; 1 Ne. 15:33; D&C 33:1; 137:7–9; Alma 41:3) and assigned to an eternal kingdom. In this solemn responsibility, the Savior will apply both justice and mercy, such that every individual will know and declare that his or her reward is just (2 Ne. 9:46; Mosiah 27:31). Every soul will recognize that the record presented is true and that the Judgment constitutes a proper decision (Mosiah 16:1; 29:12) at the hand of a loving yet impartial judge (Mosiah 29:12–13; Alma 41:3–7; cf. *TPJS*, p. 218).

Not all, however, will be held equally responsible for personal mortal acts. Speaking of the Judgment, the Prophet Joseph SMITH taught that God "will judge them, 'not according to what they have not, but according to what they have,' those who have lived without law, will be judged without law, and those who have a law, will be judged by that law" (*TPJS*, p. 218).

Each brings his or her own record to this judgment, as stated by Church President John TAYLOR: "Because that record that is written by the man himself in the tablets of his own mind—that record that cannot lie—will in that day be unfolded before God and angels, and those who shall sit as judges" (*JD* 11:79; cf. Alma 41:7). Jesus Christ will be at the judgment bar, for he is the judge of both the living and the dead (Alma 11:44; Moro. 10:34; D&C 76:68).

Others will also participate in the process, but the final judgment rests with Christ. The twelve apostles of the Lamb will judge the righteous among the twelve tribes of Israel (D&C 29:12; Matt. 19:28; 1 Ne. 12:9–10), and the twelve Nephite disciples will judge the Nephites (3 Ne. 27:27). Still other prophets and righteous Saints have been appointed to help judge the works and deeds of their fellow sojourners in mortality (1 Cor. 6:2; Morm. 3:18–20). Thus, "there will be a whole hierarchy of judges who, under Christ, shall judge the righteous. He alone shall issue the decrees of damnation for the wicked" (McConkie, p. 520).

The Lord Jesus Christ earned the right to judge every earthly soul as he ensured the plan of redemption through the Atonement (3 Ne. 27:14–16; Alma 42:23). That this responsibility was explicitly given to the Son by the Father (John 5:22, 27) is attested in the Book of Mormon: "My Father sent me that I might be lifted up upon the cross; . . . that I might draw all men unto me, that as I have been lifted up by men even so should men be lifted up by the Father, to stand before me, to be judged of their works" (3 Ne. 27:14). Evidence of the Father's divine trust is shown in giving Jesus the responsibility of pronouncing eternal judgment on the Father's own children. Christ will judge in accordance with the will of the Father (John 5:30).

The basis of justice carried out at the final judgment lies in the agency granted to mortals so that "every man may be accountable for his own sins in the day of judgment" (D&C 101:78). There would be little value to agency without accountability. Just as Cain was counseled by the Lord, "If thou doest well, shalt thou not be accepted?" (Gen. 4:7), so each person has full option in making moral choices.

As a result of this final judgment, the wicked will be eternally separated from the righteous (D&C 76; Alma 41:5). This separation will be the desired state for both, for neither the wicked nor the righteous could enjoy the constant presence of others so unlike themselves. As stated by Moroni, "Ye would be more miserable to dwell with a holy and just God, under a consciousness of your filthiness before him, than ye would to dwell with the damned souls in hell" (Morm. 9:4). And to the righteous, judgment will bring fulfillment of the promise that "they who have believed in the Holy One of Israel, they who have endured the crosses of the world, and despised the shame of it, they shall inherit the kingdom of God, which was prepared for them from the foundation of the world, and their joy shall be full forever" (2 Ne. 9:18).

BIBLIOGRAPHY

Ludlow, Daniel H., ed. *Latter-Day Prophets Speak*, pp. 50–60. Salt Lake City, 1948.

McConkie, Bruce R. *The Millennial Messiah*. Salt Lake City, 1982.

Young, Brigham. *Discourses of Brigham Young*, ed. John A. Widtsoe, pp. 382–86. Salt Lake City, 1941.

DONALD N. WRIGHT

JUSTICE AND MERCY

Justice and mercy are attributes of deity. They are also eternal principles. The "justice of God" (Alma 41:2; 42:14) is a principle so fundamental that without it, "God would cease to be God" (Alma 42:13). Of equivalent significance is God's mercy, which, broadly, is the ultimate source of all of the blessings of the human race and, specifically, is the principle that allows mankind's redemption. The competing demands of justice's claim for punishment and mercy's claim for forgiveness are reconciled by the unifying power of the ATONEMENT OF JESUS CHRIST.

On one hand, justice rewards righteousness. "And when we obtain any blessing from God, it is by obedience to that law upon which it is predicated" (D&C 130:21, see also D&C 82:10). On the other, justice requires penalties as a consequence of disobedience to the laws of God, for "I the Lord cannot look upon sin with the least degree of allowance" (D&C 1:31). Just as obedience to divine law leads to blessings, justice affixes a punishment to each violation of the Lord's commandments (Alma 42:17–18, 22), and men and women will be "punished for their own sins" (A of F 2). Each person will thus be judged according to his or her works (Rom. 2:5–6; 3 Ne. 27:14; Alma 41:2–6), although the degree of accountability varies according to the extent of each person's knowledge and culpability (2 Ne. 9:25; Mosiah 3:11). Yet the principle of mercy allows the atonement of Jesus Christ to pay the demands of justice on a repentant transgressor's behalf in a way that reconciles the principles of mercy and justice.

Not just any person may invoke mercy on behalf of another: "Now there is not any man that can sacrifice his own blood which will atone for the sins of another . . . therefore there can be nothing which is short of an infinite atonement which will suffice for the sins of the world" (Alma 34:11–12). Jesus Christ alone can achieve such an infinite atonement "once for all" (Hebrews 10:10) because of his nature as the actual son of God in the flesh and because he was himself without sin (*see* ATONEMENT OF JESUS CHRIST; JESUS CHRIST: ONLY BEGOTTEN IN THE FLESH).

Mercy is not extended arbitrarily. To protect individuals from the undeserved effects of sins for which they are not responsible, the Atonement unconditionally paid the penalty for the transgression of Adam and Eve in the Garden of Eden. It pays similarly for sins committed in ignorance (Mosiah 3:11; see also Moses 6:54). However, the Atonement removes the penalty for personal sins for which one is accountable only on the condition of individual repentance.

In this way, the concepts of justice, mercy, and the Atonement retain both a specific integrity and a logically consistent relationship: "The plan of mercy could not be brought about except an atonement should be made; therefore God himself atoneth for the sins of the world, to bring about the plan of mercy, to appease the demands of justice, that God might be a perfect, just God, and merciful God also. . . . But there is a law given, and a punishment affixed, and a repentance granted; which repentance mercy claimeth; otherwise, justice claimeth the creature. . . . For behold, justice exerciseth all his demands, and also mercy claimeth all which is her own; and thus, none but the truly penitent are saved" (Alma 42:13, 15, 22, 24).

Mercy is thus rehabilitative, not retributive or arbitrary. The Lord asks repentance from a transgressor, not to compensate the Savior for paying the debt of justice, but to induce the transgressor to undertake a meaningful process of personal development toward a Christlike nature.

At the same time, mercy depends ultimately on the Lord's extension of unmerited grace. Even though conditioned on repentance for personal sins, mercy is never fully "earned" by its recipients. Repentance is a necessary, but not a sufficient, condition of salvation and exaltation. "For we know that it is by grace that we are saved, after all we can do" (2 Ne. 25:23). The unearned nature of mercy is demonstrated by the Atonement's having unconditionally compensated for the disabilities imposed on mankind by the FALL OF ADAM. Adam and Eve and their posterity were utterly powerless to overcome the physical and spiritual deaths that were introduced by the Fall. Moreover, transgressors do not "pay" fully for their sins through the process of repentance. Even though repentance requires restitution to the extent of one's ability, most forms of restitution are beyond any person's ability to achieve. No matter how complete our repentance, it would all be to no avail without a mediator willing and able to pay our debt to justice, on condition of our repentance. Thus, even with sincere and complete repentance, all are utterly dependent on Jesus Christ.

Through the atonement of Jesus Christ, justice and mercy are interdependent and interactive, demonstrating that God cannot be just without being merciful, nor merciful without being just.

BIBLIOGRAPHY

Hafen, Bruce C. "Justice, Mercy, and Rehabilitation." In *The Broken Heart*, pp. 143–54. Salt Lake City, 1989.

Oaks, Dallin H. "The Atonement and the Principles of Justice and Mercy." Unpublished manuscript, from May 1, 1985, General Authority training meeting.

Roberts, B. H. *The Atonement.* Salt Lake City, 1911.

Taylor, John. *Mediation and Atonement.* Salt Lake City, 1882.

BRUCE C. HAFEN

JUSTIFICATION

Although the word "justify" has several meanings, its main meaning in the latter-day scriptures is inseparably intertwined with the concepts of GRACE (Rom. 3:28; Gal. 2:16; 2 Ne. 2:5; Mosiah 14:11; D&C 20:30; Moses 6:60), FAITH, REPENTANCE, RIGHTEOUSNESS, and SANCTIFICATION.

Justification is a scriptural metaphor drawn from the courts of law: a judge justifies an accused person by declaring or pronouncing that person innocent. Likewise, God may treat a person as being "not guilty" of sin. All mortals individually need to be justified because they fall short of perfect obedience to God, becoming "carnal, sensual, and devilish" through transgression (Moses 5:13; Mosiah 16:3), are "cut off" from God, and are in jeopardy of becoming "miserable forever" (2 Ne. 2:5). In this plight, they of themselves cannot be justified through subsequent obedience to the law and cannot change their own nature to become obedient. Furthermore, they are severed from the source of the divine power that can change, or sanctify, them (2 Ne. 9:5–9).

However, through the ATONEMENT OF JESUS CHRIST, when men, women, or children have faith in Jesus, are truly penitent, call upon his name, and are baptized, they become eligible for the redeeming grace extended through Jesus Christ. In this sense they become justified. This is given as a gift by grace, since fallen man must rely "alone upon the merits of Christ" (1 Ne. 10:6; Moro. 6:4). The faith by which one receives this grace manifests itself in an active determination to follow Christ in all things. It is demonstrated by obedience to the commandments to repent and be baptized, followed by a life of submission, obedience, and service to God and others (2 Ne. 31:16–20; Moro. 8:25–26; *see* GOSPEL OF JESUS CHRIST).

Justification directly opens the way to sanctification by establishing a "right" relationship of mortals with God. Thus, God, without denying justice, can bless them with the sanctifying power of the Holy Ghost (Mosiah 5:1–2; 3 Ne. 27:20). Justification starts the believer on the path toward righteousness.

Because justified, and even sanctified, persons can fall from that state of grace, believers are admonished to "take heed and pray always" (D&C 20:30–33) and to meet together often to fast and partake of the sacrament of the Lord's Supper, thereby renewing and personally reviewing their covenants with God, including baptism and its cleansing effect (Moro. 6:5–6), and to endure to the end (D&C 53:7).

The person whom God justifies has not yet necessarily received the promise of eternal life (*see* HOLY SPIRIT OF PROMISE; JESUS CHRIST: SECOND COMFORTER). To obtain that promise, the justified must continue in the path of faith, wherein nothing can separate the faithful from the love of God.

BIBLIOGRAPHY

Anderson, Richard L. *Understanding Paul.* Salt Lake City, 1983.

Sperry, Sidney B. *Paul's Life and Letters*, pp. 171–78. Salt Lake City, 1955.

COLIN B. DOUGLAS

JUVENILE INSTRUCTOR

The *Juvenile Instructor* began publication in January 1866 and was the first children's magazine published between the Mississippi River and the West Coast of the United States. Its first issue identified its primary audience as the children of The Church of Jesus Christ of Latter-day Saints, and its purpose was to help prepare them for future responsibilities. It was originally published as a 10½-by-15½-inch four-page, three-column, semimonthly publication.

The magazine was initiated, owned, edited, and published by Elder George Q. Cannon until shortly before his death in 1901. During his lifetime he was the general superintendent of the Church's Sunday School, a member of the Quorum of the Twelve Apostles, a Counselor in the First Presidency of the Church, and also a territorial delegate from Utah to the U.S. Congress. The *Juvenile Instructor* published editorials, poetry (some by Eliza R. SNOW), and a monthly column, "Voices from Nature," by Karl G. Maeser (president of Brigham Young Academy, later Brigham Young University). It also printed essays, stories, and biographical sketches that often focused on moral issues or the history of other cultures.

Officially owned and published by the Sunday School from 1901 to 1929, the *Juvenile Instructor* contained important organization and business matters of the Sunday School as well as adult and youth stories and essays. As its interests turned more toward filling the needs of teachers, it became the teachers' magazine of the Church and was renamed *The Instructor* in 1929.

[*See also* Instructor.]

BIBLIOGRAPHY

Green, Doyle L. "The Church and Its Magazines." *Ensign* 1 (Jan. 1971):12–15.

RUEL A. ALLRED

K

KANE, THOMAS L.

A courageous friend of the Latter-day Saints, Thomas Leiper Kane was born in Philadelphia on January 27, 1822. His great-grandfather John Kane (O'Kane) came to America from Ireland before the American Revolution. John's grandson John Kintzing Kane married June Duval Leiper, and they became the parents of Thomas L. Kane.

After completing his college training in Philadelphia in 1840, Thomas studied in England. Returning to America, he studied law under his father's direction and was admitted to the Pennsylvania bar in 1846. Then came a period of service with the U.S. Army, following which he became known as Colonel Kane.

Kane's introduction to the Mormon cause came in his native Philadelphia at a conference in May 1846 held under the direction of Jesse C. Little, presiding elder in the East, who was soliciting support for the Latter-day Saints' WEST-WARD MIGRATION. Colonel Kane gave Little helpful letters of recommendation and later joined him in Washington, D.C., where they called on the secretary of state, secretary of war, and President James K. Polk. As a result of their negotiations, the United States agreed to enlist a battalion of 500 LDS men to serve in the campaign against Mexico (*see* MORMON BATTALION).

Later, after carrying government dispatches to Fort Leavenworth, Kane rejoined Little in the Mormon camp on the Missouri, where he became seriously ill with pulmonary tuberculosis. The Saints nursed him back to health, and during his long convalescence he abandoned plans for a political career and decided to devote himself to helping the Latter-day Saints and other downtrodden people. The Saints later named their principal Iowa settlement Kanesville (present-day COUNCIL BLUFFS) in recognition of his service. Although he was not a member of the Church, Colonel Kane received a PATRIARCHAL BLESSING from the Church's patriarch, John Smith, an uncle of Joseph SMITH. This blessing furnished encouragement, and it also provided a bond with the Saints.

Kane rendered his most significant service by assisting the Saints during the Utah War. Responding to reports from federal officials in Utah, President James Buchanan ordered the UTAH EXPEDITION of 2,500 U.S. Army troops to Utah. Traveling under the alias of Dr. Osborne, supposedly a botanist from Philadelphia, Dr. Kane came to Utah in 1858 and served as a mediator. He succeeded in convincing the newly appointed territorial governor, Alfred Cumming, that the Saints were not in a state of rebellion, and helped arrange a solution to the conflict that avoided a violent confrontation and preserved the peace.

Colonel Kane continued for many years as a friend and political adviser to the Saints. He promoted UTAH STATEHOOD in the nation's capital

Thomas Leiper Kane (1822–1883) was known for his philanthropy. He helped those in prison and was kind to the Quakers. He was a loyal friend to the Latter-day Saints for almost forty years.

throughout the 1850s and defended the Church, its leaders, and its interests at every opportunity. After outstanding service in the Civil War, Kane was promoted to major general. In 1872 he and his wife, Elizabeth, spent the winter in Utah. They traveled throughout the territory and stayed as guests of Brigham YOUNG at his winter home in St. George.

When Brigham Young died in 1877, Kane returned to Utah to express his sorrow and to assure the Church of his continued support. Upon Kane's death in 1883, Church leaders eulogized him for his staunch friendship and assistance. Today the Church helps maintain as a historic site the Thomas L. Kane Memorial Chapel, in Kane, Pennsylvania, where Kane is buried.

BIBLIOGRAPHY

Arrington, Leonard J. "In Honorable Remembrance: Thomas L. Kane's Services to the Mormons." *BYU Studies* 21 (Fall, 1981):389–402.

Cannon, Donald Q. "Thomas L. Kane Meets the Mormons." *BYU Studies* 18 (Fall 1977):126–28.

Kane, Elizabeth [Mrs. Thomas L.]. *Twelve Mormon Homes Visited in Succession on a Journey Through Utah to Arizona*, ed. Everett L. Cooley. Salt Lake City, 1975.

Zobell, Albert L., Jr. *Sentinel in the East: A Biography of Thomas L. Kane.* Salt Lake City, 1965.

DONALD Q. CANNON

KEYS OF THE PRIESTHOOD

The keys of the priesthood refer to the right to exercise power in the name of Jesus Christ or to preside over a priesthood function, quorum, or organizational division of the Church. Keys are necessary to maintain order and to see that the functions of the Church are performed in the proper time, place, and manner. They are given by the laying on of hands in an ordination or setting apart by a person who presides and who holds the appropriate keys at a higher level. Many keys were restored to men on earth by heavenly messengers to the Prophet Joseph SMITH and Oliver COWDERY.

The keys of the kingdom of God on earth are held by the APOSTLES. The PRESIDENT OF THE CHURCH, who is the senior apostle, holds all the keys presently on earth and presides over all the organizational and ordinance work of the Church (D&C 107:8–9, 91–92). He delegates authority by giving the keys of specific offices to others (D&C 124:123). Only presiding priesthood officers (including General Authorities, stake presidents, mission presidents, temple presidents, bishops, branch presidents, and quorum presidents) hold keys pertaining to their respective offices. Latter-day Saints distinguish between holding the priesthood and holding keys to direct the work of the priesthood: one does not receive additional priesthood when one is given keys (Joseph F. Smith, *IE* 4 [Jan. 1901]:230).

The Prophet Joseph Smith taught that "the fundamental principles, government, and doctrine of the Church are vested in the keys of the kingdom" (*TPJS*, p. 21). "The keys have to be brought from heaven whenever the Gospel is sent"; they are revealed to man under the authority of ADAM, for he was the first to be given them when he was given dominion over all things. They have come down through the DISPENSATIONS OF THE GOSPEL to prophets, including NOAH, ABRAHAM, MOSES, ELIJAH; to PETER, JAMES, and JOHN; and to Joseph

ANTHON H. LUND
1910-1918

JOSEPH F. SMITH
1901-1918

CHARLES W. PENROSE
1910-1918

THE FIRST PRESIDENCY
1910-1918

The First Presidency (1910–1918). Left to right: Anthon H. Lund, President Joseph F. Smith, Charles W. Penrose. The keys of the priesthood are held by the apostles; as the senior apostle, the President of the Church exercises all those keys and presides over the Church.

Smith and the designated prophets of the latter days (*HC* 3:385–87). Keys to perform or preside over various priesthood functions were bestowed upon Joseph Smith and Oliver Cowdery by JOHN THE BAPTIST (*see* AARONIC PRIESTHOOD: RESTORATION OF AARONIC PRIESTHOOD), by Peter, James, and John (*see* MELCHIZEDEK PRIESTHOOD: RESTORATION OF MELCHIZEDEK PRIESTHOOD), and by Moses, Elias, and Elijah in the Kirtland Temple (*see* DOCTRINE AND COVENANTS: SECTIONS 109–110).

Many types of keys are mentioned in the scriptures of the Church (see *MD*, pp. 409–13). Jesus Christ holds all the keys. Joseph Smith received the keys pertaining to the RESTORATION OF THE GOSPEL OF JESUS CHRIST (D&C 6:25–28; 28:7; 35:18), and through him the FIRST PRESIDENCY holds the "keys of the kingdom," including the SEALING ordinances (D&C 81:1–2; 90:1–6; 110:16; 128:20; 132:19). Specific mention of certain keys and those who hold them include the following: The QUORUM OF THE TWELVE APOSTLES exercises the keys "to open the door by the proclamation of the gospel of Jesus Christ" in all the world (D&C 107:35; 112:16; 124:128). Adam holds "the keys of salvation under the counsel and direction of the Holy One," and "the keys of the universe" (D&C 78:16; *TPJS*, p. 157); Moses, "the keys of the gathering of Israel" (D&C 110:11); Elias, the keys to bring to pass "the restoration of all things" (D&C 27:6); and Elijah, "the keys of the

power of turning the hearts of the fathers to the children, and the hearts of the children to the fathers" (D&C 27:9). Holders of the Melchizedek Priesthood are said to have "the keys of the Church," "the key of knowledge," and "the keys of all the spiritual blessings of the church" (D&C 42:69; 84:19; 107:18), while belonging to the Aaronic Priesthood are "the keys of the ministering of angels, and of the gospel of repentance, and of baptism by immersion for the remission of sins" (D&C 13:1; 84:26). All these stewardships will eventually be delivered back into the hands of Jesus Christ (*TPJS*, p. 157).

BIBLIOGRAPHY

Durham, G. Homer. "The Keys of the Priesthood." In *Priesthood*, ed. S. Kimball et al. Salt Lake City, 1981.

Nelson, Russell M. "Keys of the Priesthood." *Ensign* 17 (Nov. 1987):36–39.

ALAN K. PARRISH

KIMBALL, HEBER C.

Heber Chase Kimball was First Counselor in the FIRST PRESIDENCY of the Church from December 5, 1847, until his death in 1868. One of the foremost men in the early years of the Church, along with the Prophet Joseph SMITH and Brigham YOUNG, Heber marched in ZION'S CAMP in 1834,

Heber C. Kimball's residence (center) in Salt Lake City in the block northeast of Temple Square. This 1864 photograph also shows the wall around Temple Square (left), the Tithing Office inside Brigham Young's enclosure (right), and Indian tents outside the old city wall (top right). Photographer: C. R. Savage.

was ordained one of the original members of the QUORUM OF THE TWELVE APOSTLES in 1835, and experienced the spiritual manifestations that attended the dedication of the KIRTLAND TEMPLE in 1836. He served two missions to Great Britain, in 1837–1838 and 1839–1841 (see MISSIONS OF THE TWELVE TO THE BRITISH ISLES). Blunt, honest, loyal, and believing, Heber served the struggling Church well when steadfastness was among the most needed qualities. This is reflected in Joseph Smith's saying, "Of the Twelve Apostles chosen in Kirtland, . . . there have been but two [who have not] lifted their heel against me—namely Brigham Young and Heber C. Kimball" (HC 5:412).

Heber C. Kimball was born June 14, 1801, near Sheldon, Vermont, to Solomon F. and Anna Spaulding Kimball. In 1811 the family moved to western New York, where, after scanty schooling, young Heber became a potter. He grew to be a physically impressive man, six feet tall and weighing more than two hundred pounds, barrel-chested, and dark-eyed. He married Vilate Murray in 1822. He, his friend Brigham Young, and their wives joined the Church in 1832, after a two-year period of inquiry, and in 1833 they moved to Church headquarters in KIRTLAND, OHIO.

In 1837 Elder Kimball received an assignment from the Prophet Joseph Smith to lead a group of missionaries to England. As the ship arrived in Liverpool, Kimball leapt ashore, thus becoming the first Latter-day Saint in Europe. His simplicity and spirit suited the men and women who heard him preach, and within a week nine persons sought baptism. On the morning of the baptism, Elder Kimball and his companions reported they experienced an attack by evil spirits, whom they saw distinctly in their room. Calling on God, they received deliverance from the dark power. Through their efforts groups of hundreds of English converts, commencing in 1840, began sailing to the United States to be with the main body of the Church.

After a year Elder Kimball returned to the United States and to Missouri, where the Saints experienced persecution. While Joseph Smith sat imprisoned in the LIBERTY JAIL (Missouri), Heber and Brigham Young organized the removal of approximately 12,000 LDS refugees to Illinois.

When the Prophet Joseph Smith rejoined the Saints in Illinois and established NAUVOO on the Mississippi River, Elder Kimball prepared to return to England. On the appointed day he and

Brigham Young took their leave from sick wives, each with a new baby, and were themselves so ill they had to be lifted into the wagon. Elder Kimball was gone from home for almost two years, until 1841.

Kimball participated in the building of the Nauvoo Temple and received the temple ordinances. Joseph Smith taught him privately that God required him to enter into PLURAL MARRIAGE. After initial resistance, Elder Kimball married Sarah Noon. His anguish at keeping this secret from Vilate ended when she told him that the Lord had shown her that plural marriage was right, and that she accepted his participation in it. Kimball married a total of forty-three women (in many cases a caretaking rather than an intimate relationship), and by seventeen of them he had sixty-five children. He perceived his plural marriages as a religious obligation; Vilate accepted the other wives as sisters. Heber C. Kimball's grandson Spencer W. KIMBALL was President of the Church from 1973 to 1985.

Daguerreotype of Heber C. Kimball (1801–1868). One of the original Quorum of the Twelve Apostles ordained February 14, 1835, he served as first counselor to President Brigham Young from 1847 until 1868. Photograph, c. 1853, attributed to Marsena Cannon.

After Joseph Smith's assassination in 1844, Church leadership was carried forth by the Quorum of the Twelve Apostles under its president, Brigham Young. Elder Kimball stood next in leadership. The Saints soon had to abandon their homes in Nauvoo and flee to the Great Basin.

The brutal trek across Iowa, temporary settlement in Winter Quarters, and the pioneer journey of 1847 to the Great Salt Lake Valley occurred under Brigham Young's supervision, with Kimball as his assistant. In December 1847, at Kanesville (Council Bluffs, Iowa), the First Presidency was organized, with Brigham Young as president and Heber C. Kimball and Willard Richards as his counselors. In summer 1848 President Kimball led one of three large companies of Saints to the Salt Lake Valley, where he established his families and supported them by farming, ranching, milling, freighting, and Church and civic administration.

The organization of Utah Territory in 1850 brought hostile federal appointees, but since the population was predominantly LDS, Church leaders had de facto control of the legislature. Heber served as leader of the legislature. Friction between the federally appointed judges and the Latter-day Saints led to U.S. President James Buchanan's sending federal troops to suppress a supposed "rebellion" of the Mormons. President Kimball helped direct the resistance.

A notably outspoken preacher, President Kimball often urged self-sufficiency, resistance to the corrupting influences of the larger society, and faithfulness to the kingdom of God. He frequently used metaphors from his experience as a potter. He prophesied accurately many times, including a prediction that Parley P. Pratt would go on a mission to Toronto, Canada, and find a people prepared for his message. He likewise prophesied that from there the gospel would spread to England. He correctly predicted that Pratt's invalid wife would bear him a son, even though the couple had been childless for ten years (Whitney, p. 135). He also prophesied to hungry pioneers in early 1849 that "in less than one year there will be plenty of clothes and everything that we shall want sold at less than St. Louis prices" (Kimball, 1981, p. 190). That summer, people traveling to the California gold fields dumped their excess supplies and equipment on the market in Salt Lake City and the prophecy was true.

President Kimball also shouldered special responsibility for the British mission and for all temple ordinances. His journals constitute important sources of Church history.

Heber C. Kimball died June 22, 1868, from the effects of a carriage accident, ending thirty-six years of unexcelled, dependable service to the Church.

BIBLIOGRAPHY

Kimball, Stanley B. *Heber C. Kimball: Mormon Patriarch and Pioneer.* Urbana, Ill., 1981.

———, ed. *On the Potter's Wheel: The Diaries of Heber C. Kimball.* Salt Lake City, 1987.

Whitney, Orson F. *Life of Heber C. Kimball.* Salt Lake City, 1888; 2nd ed., 1945.

EDWARD L. KIMBALL

KIMBALL, SARAH GRANGER

Sarah Melissa Granger Kimball (1818–1898) was founder of the Ladies' Society of Nauvoo, a suffragist, an advocate of women's rights, ward RELIEF SOCIETY president for forty years, and a strong presence in the history of The Church of Jesus Christ of Latter-day Saints for much of the nineteenth century. Described by one of her associates as possessing "the courage to say what she thought," Sarah Kimball labored for the advancement of women, arguing that "education and agitation are our best weapons of warfare" (*Woman's Exponent* 20 [1 May 1892]:159 and 18 [15 Feb. 1890]:139, respectively). Such militancy was tempered, however, by her strong commitment to the Church and her loyalty to its leaders. Indeed, she saw little discrepancy between her devotion to the Church and her dedication to women's rights, since Joseph SMITH's "turning of the key" of power to women in 1842 had, in her view, led to the beginnings of the national women's rights movement.

Born December 29, 1818, in Phelps, New York, to Oliver and Lydia Dibble Granger, Sarah joined the Church and moved with her family to KIRTLAND, OHIO, in 1833 at age fifteen. While she did not detail her own conversion, a dramatic vision of the Book of Mormon prophet MORONI$_2$ experienced by her father made a lasting impression on her. She, however, was never content to live vicariously, either intellectually or spiritually. She was one of the twenty-three women known to have attended Joseph Smith's SCHOOL OF THE PROPHETS in Kirtland, and she later urged the in-

clusion of substantive courses of study in her ward Relief Society, delivered strong addresses expounding doctrine, and spoke in tongues.

Perhaps most significant in her early adulthood was her formation of the Ladies' Society of Nauvoo, the antecedent of the Relief Society. Married at age twenty-one to Hiram Kimball, a wealthy Nauvoo merchant who later converted to the Church, she sought to help build the kingdom of God, which the Saints then saw as embodied in Nauvoo, especially in the temple. She and her seamstress, a Miss (Margaret?) Cook, determined to sew shirts for the temple workmen and subsequently invited other women to join forces with them in a ladies' society. When they approached Joseph Smith for his approval of the society's constitution, written by Eliza R. SNOW, he stated that although the constitution was excellent, the Lord wanted the women organized "under the priesthood after the pattern of the priesthood." According to Sarah Kimball's recollection, Joseph continued, "The Church was never perfectly organized

Sarah Melissa Granger Kimball (1818–1898), founder of a Nauvoo women's group, the precursor of the Relief Society, and president of the Utah Woman Suffrage Association. Photograph c. 1890, C. M. Bell.

until the women were thus organized" (Kimball, p. 51).

In light of her important early involvement with the Relief Society, it is not surprising that Sarah spent much of her life actively engaged in its work. After her 1851 move to Salt Lake City, where she taught school to support her family while her husband recovered from some serious financial losses, she was called in 1857 as president of the Fifteenth Ward Relief Society. She continued in that position until her death in 1898, also serving during twelve of those years as general secretary of the Relief Society under President Eliza R. Snow and later as a vice-president of the organization after its incorporation in 1892.

Sarah Kimball's tenure as ward Relief Society president was noted for its innovation and attention to the complete development of women. Her compassion and charity were legendary, and she organized the women of her ward to provide for the poor and needy. She directed their efforts to fund the first Relief Society hall, which functioned both as a store in which the women sold their items of home manufacture and as a meeting house devoted to secular and sacred education.

During her years of greatest involvement in the Relief Society, Sarah Kimball also became a major force in the suffrage fight as president of the Utah Woman Suffrage Association. Compared by one of her contemporaries to Susan B. Anthony, Sarah Kimball displayed the same courage and forthrightness in contending for women's rights. She argued not only for suffrage but for equal esteem of women with men. Further, many of her sermons spoke of the ultimate and divine equality of "the Father and Mother God" (*Woman's Exponent* 8 [1 July 1879]: 22; *see also* MOTHER IN HEAVEN).

Sarah Kimball died in Salt Lake City on December 1, 1898. A widow for thirty-five years following her husband's death in a steamship explosion while en route to a mission in the Sandwich Islands (Hawaii), she was survived by three sons and one adopted daughter.

BIBLIOGRAPHY

Mulvay, Jill C. "The Liberal Shall Be Blessed: Sarah M. Kimball." *Utah Historical Quarterly* 44 (Summer 1976):205–221.

Kimball, Sarah M. "Auto-Biography." *Woman's Exponent* 12 (Sept. 1, 1883):51.

MARY STOVALL RICHARDS

KIMBALL, SPENCER W.

Spencer Woolley Kimball (1895–1985), twelfth President of The Church of Jesus Christ of Latter-day Saints (1973–1985), came to the Presidency at the age of seventy-eight. Little new had been expected of his administration because of his age and long history of serious health problems, but his personal energy, broad vision, and openness to change produced a dynamic period consistent with the Church's growing awareness of itself as an increasingly international institution. Under his leadership, access to the TEMPLE and the PRIESTHOOD was extended, regardless of race; the number of missionaries greatly increased; administrative innovations significantly changed Church governance; and a burst of temple building occurred. His tenure proved to be one of the

Spencer W. Kimball (c. 1935) was a businessman and stake president in Safford, Arizona, when he was called as a member of the Quorum of the Twelve Apostles in 1943. Courtesy Edward L. Kimball.

most active periods in twentieth-century Church history.

Spencer Woolley Kimball was born March 28, 1895, in Salt Lake City, Utah. His father, Andrew Kimball, was a son of Heber C. Kimball, a counselor to President Brigham YOUNG, and his mother, Olive, was the daughter of Bishop Edwin D. Woolley, Brigham Young's business manager. At that time, Andrew was serving as president of the Indian Territory Mission in what is now Missouri and Oklahoma, overseeing missionary work by correspondence and periodic visits while supporting his family as a traveling dry goods salesman through Utah and southern Idaho.

When Spencer was three, his father received a call from the FIRST PRESIDENCY to move to Thatcher, a Mormon settlement in the Gila Valley of southeastern Arizona, to become president of the St. Joseph STAKE. Andrew earned his living by farming and business while he presided over several thousand Latter-day Saints in the valley and the vast surrounding area.

As a child, Spencer suffered from typhoid fever and facial paralysis and once nearly drowned. Four of his sisters died in childhood, and his mother died when he was eleven. After high school, he served as a missionary in the Central States Mission from 1914 to 1916. During his second year in the mission, he served in the St. Louis area as a supervisor of twenty-five missionaries, all older than himself.

In 1917 he attended the University of Arizona for one semester. He then received an induction notice for army service in World War I. Although expecting to leave any day, he married Camilla Eyring, a school teacher, on November 16, 1917. They eventually had four children: Spencer L., Olive Beth, Andrew E., and Edward L.

Delay in organizing the army contingent from his area resulted in his being deferred, and he obtained work in a bank. When the bank failed in 1923, wiping out the Kimballs' life savings, another bank hired him almost immediately as chief teller. In 1927 he left that bank and, with Joseph W. Greenhalgh, established an insurance and real estate agency in Safford, Arizona. Despite hard times caused by the Great Depression, Kimball said he would set up a peanut stand before he would become another person's employee again. Operating his own business gave him flexibility to attend to Church responsibilities and, with his wife, to engage in many community activities—PTA, library,

elections, city council, Red Cross, Boy Scouts, the local college, and the organization of a radio station. He was selected as statewide leader of the Arizona Rotary Club in 1936.

In the Church, Spencer Kimball served as his father's stake clerk from 1917 until the latter's death in 1924. He then became counselor to the new STAKE PRESIDENT. In 1938, when the St. Joseph Stake was divided, he was called as president of the new Mount Graham Stake, extending 250 miles from Safford, Arizona, where he lived, to El Paso, Texas. As stake president, he supervised Church Welfare Services relief for victims of a major flood in Duncan, Arizona, in 1943.

On July 8, 1943, the First Presidency notified President Kimball of his call to fill a vacancy in the QUORUM OF THE TWELVE APOSTLES. Though he had a slight premonition of the call, he felt shocked, knowing so well his own limitations. With assurance from Camilla and after a long personal struggle, he received spiritual confirmation several days later that the call came from God. He sold his business, moved his family to Salt Lake City, and at the October General Conference in 1943 received the sustaining vote of the Church's membership and was that same day ordained an APOSTLE by President Heber J. GRANT.

For thirty years Kimball served in the Quorum of the Twelve Apostles helping with Church administration, dealing with the personal problems of individuals, visiting stakes and missions, and teaching the gospel of Jesus Christ. In 1946, President George Albert SMITH gave him the responsibility of working with Indians. Soon afterwards, he awoke sensing a horrible enemy, unseen but very real, trying to destroy him. After a struggle, he rebuked the evil spirit and obtained relief. He concluded that perhaps the work he had just begun presented a special threat to the powers of darkness. He publicized the suffering of Navajos during the harsh winter of 1947 and organized relief for them, but concluded that improved roads and education were the keys to long-term improvement. He helped establish the Church's INDIAN STUDENT PLACEMENT SERVICES, under which LDS families with access to good schools took Indian children from the reservations into their homes for the school year on a voluntary basis. The program grew in two decades from one child to nearly 5,000 a year, before improved schools among the Indians reduced the need. He preached vigorously against racial prejudice.

Among other assignments, Elder Kimball also headed the missionary committee. As he traveled about the Church he gave hundreds of twelve-year-old boys a dollar each to begin a mission saving fund. He visited all the missions of Europe in 1955, circled the world in 1960, supervised the Church in South America for four years—where he began missionary work among the Indians of the Andes—and then supervised the missions in Great Britain.

His experience in counseling hundreds of individuals about personal problems, especially sexual immorality, moved him to write *The Miracle of Forgiveness*, a book on the process of REPENTANCE that has been well received among Church members.

Elder Kimball suffered a heart attack in 1948 and throat cancer a few years later. Removal of most of his vocal cords left him with a distinctive weak, raspy voice. In 1972 successful open-heart surgery replaced an obstructed artery and a failing valve. Since he was then age seventy-seven, he considered foregoing the surgery, but President Harold B. LEE said his work was not finished, and he should have the operation.

On December 26, 1973, when President Lee died, Spencer W. Kimball succeeded him. Though already seventy-eight, President Kimball led energetically until 1979, when a cerebral hemorrhage required two brain surgeries. He recovered well, but in mid-1981 a third such operation left him seriously weakened. From that time until his death in 1985, he left active leadership to his counselors, especially President Gordon B. Hinckley. On November 5, 1985, at age ninety, President Kimball died, and was succeeded as Church President by Ezra Taft BENSON. Camilla, notable in her own right, survived to age ninety-two.

Spencer W. Kimball's remarkable resolution and purity of spirit grew from a solid religious background provided by parents and a strong community. In his early teens he met a challenge to read the entire Bible. At age fourteen he taught Sunday School. Given a believing heart, he was serious but not solemn. Short but strong and quick, he enjoyed sports, especially basketball. He played the piano, sang, and all his life was the center of fun and activity. Annually his classmates elected him president of his small high school class. His verbal humor turned to wordplay rather than anecdote, his quick wit usually directed

Elder Kimball was deeply concerned for the Native American people. President George Albert Smith charged him to "watch after the Indians in all the world." Photograph, 1947, Deseret News.

against himself. He often joked about his being short.

He greatly missed his mother and always desired to be a credit to his parents. He hungered for approval. His capacity for hard work as a GENERAL AUTHORITY was legendary. He had the ability to nap for a few minutes and start afresh. Despite his serious illnesses, including typhoid fever, smallpox, two bouts of Bell's palsy, a heart attack and later heart failure, recurring throat cancer, three subdural hematomas, minor strokes, and scores of boils, he never slackened his efforts. He was relatively uncomplaining in suffering and ever grateful for medical help.

Because his formal education ended at marriage, President Kimball feared people might judge the Church negatively because of his inadequacies. He compensated by working doubly hard. In fact, he was well educated by his wide reading. His addresses were carefully prepared, with his own poetic eloquence. A humble man, he felt completely at home with common folk. He expressed

appreciation and love easily and generously. There was no presumptuousness in him; he made no demands. He encouraged publication of a candid biography that portrayed him as an imperfect man striving to meet a divine challenge.

He and Camilla celebrated sixty-eight years of devoted marriage. She was well-spoken, forthright, highly intelligent, and a committed Christian. Ever supportive, she perfectly complemented President Kimball in his calling.

People sometimes perceived him as a strict moralist because of his seriousness in preaching, but he understood individuals' failings. He was the soul of kindness and unfailingly thoughtful. He carried on a massive correspondence, answering children's letters and writing to people he had counseled. He had great compassion for those struggling physically, socially, and spiritually. He expended huge energies trying to improve the conditions of the American Indians. As President and Prophet of the Church, he sought and obtained revelation that Church members of black ancestry could be full participants in all aspects of the Church. Few Church leaders called forth the affection that this unassuming man did.

Many changes resulted from the explosive Church growth during his twelve-year administra-

President Spencer W. Kimball, shown here with his wife Camilla Eyring Kimball at a 1980 Church area conference in Los Angeles, was the President of the Church from 1973 to 1985. Photographer: Jutti Marsh.

tion: from 630 stakes to about 1,500; from organization in 50 countries to 96; and from 3.3 million members to nearly 6 million. At the time of his death, nearly half the Church's membership had known no other president.

Many of the accomplishments of President Kimball's administration came from the effort to cope with this growth, and particularly the expansion into new areas of the globe. He organized the First Quorum of the Seventy (*see* SEVENTY: FIRST QUORUM) to enlarge the number of General Authorities and called as members of that quorum men from Europe, Asia, and South America. The world was divided into areas with a presidency made up of General Authorities in each area (see AREA, AREA PRESIDENCY). He held numerous regional conferences and solemn assemblies. All of this reflected an effort to give the members closer contact with the general Church leadership. To meet leadership needs, additional General Authorities were called for limited terms of approximately five years and others were given emeritus status.

An influential address in 1974 set out his vision of expanded missionary effort. The total number of full-time missionaries increased during President Kimball's administration by more than 50 percent, with many young women and older couples swelling the ranks. The fastest growth of the Church occurred in Latin America and Asia, but the Church also began organized activity in Communist-dominated countries and in sub-Saharan Africa. A center established in Jerusalem under the aegis of Brigham Young University stirred up protest by some orthodox Jews. The fifteen temples in operation when he became President grew to thirty-one around the world at his death, with eleven more under construction or announced. The use of computers to maintain records greatly increased the efficiency of temple work.

All of this activity exemplified his challenge to the Church to "lengthen your stride," and his personal motto was Do It!

Despite all this growth, in his preaching and policies President Kimball emphasized the return of the Church to the simple basics of good living and Church service. He articulated a threefold mission for the Church: to proclaim the gospel, to redeem the dead, and to perfect the Saints. He preached about improved family life, planting gardens, cleaning up yards, maintaining personal journals, and writing family history. Church meetings were compressed into three hours on Sunday to reduce the demands on members and to allow

more time for family activity. Streamlined Church organization was approved for small groups. He urged Church members to give charitable service and backed up his preaching with Church relief for victims of a burst dam in Idaho, an earthquake in Mexico City, and famine in Ethiopia.

Ironically, this peace-loving and kindly man became involved in a number of contentious public issues. First Presidency statements addressed the issues of homosexuality, abortion, and pornography, evincing serious concern about the permissiveness of American society. The First Presidency opposed installation of an MX missile system in the United States and objected doubly because it was projected for the Utah-Nevada desert. Controversy arose over the role of Church historical writing and was accentuated by the purported discovery of significant historical documents by forger Mark Hofmann (*see* FORGERIES OF HISTORICAL DOCUMENTS). The First Presidency endorsed equal rights for women but opposed the Equal Rights Amendment as an improper means to a desirable end. Sensitivity to women's issues resulted in Churchwide meetings for women and for girls, a statuary park in Nauvoo as a monument to women, authorization for women to pray in all meetings, speaking by women leaders in general conference.

No event in the twentieth-century Church matched the excitement attending President Kimball's announcement of receiving a revelation on priesthood in 1978, ending more than a century of limitation on admission of Church members of black African ancestry (*see* BLACKS) to priesthood office and temple ordinances. The announcement made no doctrinal statement, but simply said that the Lord had indicated that the time for change had come. The change was implemented immediately, giving great impetus to missionary work in Africa. The announcement of this revelation was added to the Doctrine and Covenants as Official Declaration—2.

From a man of whom little more than a brief caretaker administration was expected, remarkable achievements came. President Spencer W. Kimball's energetic leadership and willingness to break new ground produced twelve years of unequaled growth and change in the modern Church.

BIBLIOGRAPHY

BYU Studies 25 (Fall 1985):1–166 (issue devoted to articles about Spencer W. Kimball).

Kimball, Edward L., and Andrew E. Kimball, Jr. *Spencer W. Kimball.* Salt Lake City, 1977.

——. *The Story of Spencer W. Kimball: A Short Man, A Long Stride.* Salt Lake City, 1985.

Kimball, Edward L. "The Administration of Spencer W. Kimball." *Sunstone* 11 (Mar. 1987):8–14.

Kimball, Spencer W. *Faith Precedes the Miracle.* Salt Lake City, 1972.

——. *One Silent Sleepless Night.* Salt Lake City, 1975.

——. *The Miracle of Forgiveness.* Salt Lake City, 1969.

——. *The Teachings of Spencer W. Kimball*, Edward L. Kimball, ed. Salt Lake City, 1982.

Miner, Caroline E., and Edward L. Kimball. *Camilla.* Salt Lake City, 1980.

EDWARD L. KIMBALL

KINDERHOOK PLATES

In April 1843 some alleged New World antiquities were presented to Joseph SMITH for his opinion. The six 2 7/8-by-2 1/4-inch bell-shaped brass plates with strange engravings were reported to have been excavated in Kinderhook, Illinois, about seventy miles south of NAUVOO (*HC* 5:372–79). They were shown to Smith because of his claim to have translated the Book of Mormon from ancient GOLD PLATES taken from a New York hill in 1827.

The Kinderhook plates created a stir in Nauvoo; articles appeared in the Church press, an illustrated handbill was published, and some Latter-day Saints even claimed Joseph Smith said he could and would translate them. No translation exists, however, nor does any further comment from him indicating that he considered the plates genuine. After his assassination in June 1844, the incident was largely forgotten. Decades later two of the alleged discoverers announced that the plates were a hoax; an attempt to discredit Smith. By then, however, the Church was headquartered in Utah and little attention was paid to these strange disclosures.

Interest was kindled again in 1920 when the Chicago Historical Society acquired what appeared to be one of the original Kinderhook plates. Later the Chicago plate was subjected to a number of nondestructive tests, with inconclusive results. Then in 1980, the Chicago Historical Society gave permission for destructive tests, which were done at Northwestern University. Examination by a scanning electron microscope, a scanning auger microprobe, and X-ray fluorescence analysis proved conclusively that the plate was one of the

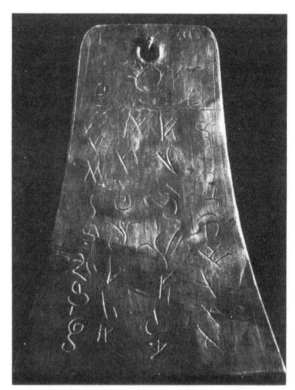

One of the Kinderhook Plates, a forgery used to try to embarrass Joseph Smith. Decorative and Industrial Arts Department, Chicago Historical Society.

Kinderhook six; that it had been engraved, not etched; and that it was of nineteenth-century manufacture. There thus appears no reason to accept the Kinderhook plates as anything but a frontier hoax.

BIBLIOGRAPHY

Kimball, Stanley B. "Kinderhook Plates Brought to Joseph Smith Appear to be a Nineteenth-Century Hoax." *Ensign* 11 (Aug. 1981):66–74.

Ricks, Welby W. "The Kinderhook Plates." *IE* 65 (Sept. 1962):636–37, 656, 658, 660.

STANLEY B. KIMBALL

KINGDOM OF GOD

IN HEAVEN

The kingdom of God in HEAVEN is the place where God lives. It is a CELESTIAL KINGDOM, organized under "the divinely ordained system of government and dominion in all matters, temporal and spiritual" (*JC*, p. 789). It is a purposeful state of existence, composed of intellectual and physical effort. It is a place of perfect order, ETERNAL PROGRESSION, everlasting family, and a fulness of joy.

The Savior taught his disciples to pray, "Our Father which art in heaven, . . . Thy kingdom come. Thy will be done in earth, as it is in heaven" (Matt. 6:9–10). The kingdom of God is set up on the earth to prepare for the kingdom of God in heaven (D&C 65:5–6). The Lord revealed to the Prophet Joseph SMITH that this earth shall be "sanctified from all unrighteousness, that it may be prepared for the celestial glory, . . . that bodies who are of the celestial kingdom may possess it forever and ever" (D&C 88:17–20). When this occurs, this glorified celestial earth will become the kingdom of heaven for the Saints who have lived upon it, and then shall the meek and the righteous inherit it (Matt. 5:5; D&C 88:25–26; 130:9; *TPJS*, p. 181).

The purpose of The Church of Jesus Christ of Latter-day Saints is to help prepare its members to live forever in the kingdom of God in heaven.

GEORGE W. PACE

ON EARTH

The kingdom of God on earth exists wherever the priesthood of God is (*TPJS*, pp. 271–74). At present it is The Church of Jesus Christ of Latter-day Saints. The Church was established by divine authority to prepare its members to live forever in the CELESTIAL KINGDOM or kingdom of God in heaven. Its nature is ecclesiastical and nonpolitical. It "asserts no claim to temporal rule over nations; its scepter of power is that of the Holy Priesthood, to be used in the preaching of the gospel and in administering its ordinances for the salvation of mankind living and dead" (*JC*, p. 788).

The kingdom of God on the earth is the stone, spoken of by Daniel, that in the latter days would roll forth to fill the earth and never be destroyed (Dan. 2:34–45). It is the kingdom that the Savior prayed would come (Matt. 6:10), and he taught us to pray in like manner. In the MERIDIAN OF TIME Jesus set up the kingdom of God on earth, called and ordained apostles and prophets, bestowed the necessary priesthood authority (Matt. 16:19; John 15:16), and charged them with the responsibilities of the Church. After an APOSTASY removed that priesthood from earth, the authority to reestablish the kingdom of God on the earth was given to the

Prophet Joseph Smith by heavenly messengers (*see* RESTORATION OF THE GOSPEL OF JESUS CHRIST). Through Joseph Smith the Lord said:

> The keys of the kingdom of God are committed unto man on the earth, and from thence shall the gospel roll forth unto the ends of the earth, as the stone which is cut out of the mountain without hands shall roll forth, until it has filled the whole earth. . . . Call upon the Lord, that his kingdom may go forth upon the earth, that the inhabitants thereof may receive it, and be prepared for the days to come, in the which the Son of Man shall come down in heaven, clothed in the brightness of his glory, to meet the kingdom of God which is set up on the earth. Wherefore, may the kingdom of God go forth, that the kingdom of heaven may come [D&C 65:2, 5–6].

GEORGE W. PACE

KING FOLLETT DISCOURSE

The King Follett Discourse is the name given to an address the Prophet Joseph SMITH delivered in Nauvoo, Illinois, on April 7, 1844, at a general conference of the Church. It was a commemorative oration for a Church member named King Follett, who had died in an accident on March 9, 1844. The discourse may be one of the Prophet's greatest sermons because of its comprehensive doctrinal teachings. It was his last general conference address, delivered less than three months before he was martyred. Key doctrinal topics in the sermon include the character of God, man's potential to progress in God's likeness, the Creation, and the tie between the living and their progenitors.

Joseph Smith delivered the sermon to several thousand people in a grove west of the Nauvoo Temple in a natural amphitheater, where benches and a rostrum had been placed. He spoke for two hours and fifteen minutes. Four experienced scribes took synoptic notes: Willard Richards, Wilford WOODRUFF, William Clayton, and Thomas Bullock.

The spring of 1844 was a time of tension and turmoil in the Prophet's life. On the one hand, the Church was flourishing in Nauvoo and abroad, construction of the Nauvoo Temple was proceeding apace, and generally men and women were serving in the Church with dedication and effectiveness. On the other hand, apostates, political factions in Illinois and Missouri, and other groups were conspiring against Joseph Smith.

Of the kinship between God and man, Joseph Smith taught, "If men do not comprehend the character of God, they do not comprehend themselves" (*TPJS*, p. 343). "It is the first principle of the Gospel to know for a certainty the Character of God, and to know that we may converse with him as one man converses with another" (*TPJS*, p. 345). Echoing his FIRST VISION, the Prophet taught what he called the "great secret": "If the veil were rent today, and . . . God . . . [were] to make himself visible, . . . if you were to see him today, you would see him like a man in form—like yourselves in all the person, image, and very form as a man" (*TPJS*, p. 345).

Creation, he taught, was not by mere fiat or ex nihilo. God's role was to bring harmony to primal, unorganized elements and to "institute laws" whereby weaker INTELLIGENCES might have the privilege of advancing like himself (*TPJS*, p. 354).

Of man's potential, the Prophet said that even as God is eternal and self-existent, so the intelligence of man is also eternal. The Father has become what he is through eternities of progress. Christ, who did nothing but what he had seen the Father do (cf. John 5:19), followed identical paths and patterns. Since all mankind have a divine Father, they are potential "heirs of God and joint-heirs with Jesus Christ" (*TPJS*, pp. 346–47; cf. Romans 8:17). In this sense, all the children of God are embryonic gods or goddesses. Obedience to the fulness of the gospel is the perfecting process through which they may go "from one small degree to another, and from a small capacity to a great one; from grace to grace, from exaltation to exaltation . . . until [they] arrive at the station of a God" (*TPJS*, pp. 346–47).

On the link between the living and their progenitors, the Prophet asked, "Is there nothing to be done?—no preparation—no salvation for our fathers and friends who have died without having had the opportunity to obey the decrees of the Son of Man?" (*TPJS*, p. 355). He answered, "God hath made a provision that every spirit in the eternal world can be . . . saved unless he has committed [the] unpardonable sin" (*TPJS*, p. 357). He explained these provisions as they apply both in mortality and in the world beyond. To the mourners, the Prophet testified, "We have reason to have the greatest hope and consolations for our dead of any people on the earth; for we have seen them walk worthily in our midst, and seen them sink asleep in the arms of Jesus; and those who have died in the faith are now in the celestial kingdom of God" (*TPJS*, p. 359).

The Prophet indicated some of his concerns: threats on his life, his love of the Saints, the loneliness of leadership ("You never knew my heart"), the wonderment he felt in retrospect ("I don't blame anyone for not believing my history. If I had not experienced what I have, I could not have believed it myself" [*TPJS*, p. 361]). He finished with a plea for peace and invoked God's blessing on the assembly.

BIBLIOGRAPHY

Cannon, Donald Q. "The King Follett Discourse: Joseph Smith's Greatest Sermon in Historical Perspective." *BYU Studies* 18 (Winter 1978):179–92.

———, and Larry E. Dahl, eds. *The Prophet Joseph Smith's King Follett Discourse: A Six-Column Comparison of Original Notes and Amalgamation.* Provo, Utah, 1983.

Hale, Van. "The Doctrinal Impact of the King Follett Discourse." *BYU Studies* 18 (Winter 1978):209–225.

Larson, Stanley. "The King Follett Discourse: A Newly Amalgamated Text." *BYU Studies* 18 (Winter 1978):193–208.

DONALD Q. CANNON

KING JAMES VERSION

See: Bible: King James Version

KIRTLAND ECONOMY

[*This article reports the main facts and points of interest regarding the economic events in Kirtland in the 1830s and the significance of this historical development in the overall growth of the Church.*]

In early 1830, Kirtland, Ohio, was a small rural trading center of approximately 1,000 people, none of whom was LDS (*see* HISTORY OF THE CHURCH: C. 1831–1844). Six years later, it was a bustling community of 3,000, with commercial, mercantile, and small manufacturing firms, and a temple serving the 2,000 Latter-day Saints in the town. Despite its rapid growth and apparent prosperity, within another two years Joseph SMITH departed Kirtland, leaving behind disgruntled creditors, warrants for his arrest, a failed banking experiment, and a divided Mormon population preparing to leave the temple and their homes. By 1840, only 200 Latter-day Saints remained in Kirtland.

The study of the Kirtland economy between 1830 and 1840 continues to generate controversy among historians. One question has to do with the precipitous increases in the land prices between 1832 and 1837. Were they the result of "reckless land speculation" by Joseph Smith and other Church leaders? The average price per acre of land sold in Kirtland rose from approximately $7 in 1832 to $44 in 1837, only to fall back to $17.50 in 1839. These dramatic changes, however, were related to movements in the general price level, trends in the value of land in neighboring communities, and the impact of population growth. Probably between 25 and 40 percent of the change in the nominal price of land was associated with generalized inflation during this period. As much as 84 percent of the remaining change in the real price of land was correlated with the rise and fall in population. Joseph Smith was primarily responsible for the call to gather to Kirtland; naturally, the newcomers needed land. An examination of land transactions reveals nothing in the buying, selling, or subdividing of land that was unusual for a frontier community.

Another question has to do with Joseph Smith's debts. Was his use of credit "irresponsible"? Early studies of the economic difficulties in Kirtland emphasized debts and ignored assets. Actually, Joseph Smith's potential cumulative indebtedness during this period, including all purchases of land and merchandise, totaled a little over $100,000, considerably below earlier estimates by some historians. At least $60,000 of this debt was eventually settled, and probably much more, since the remainder produced no lawsuits and primarily represented debt for land, which would likely have been paid for or the land reclaimed. At the same time, because of the increase in prices, President Smith and his associates held almost $60,000 equity in land. In the environment of rapid population growth from 1830 to 1837, many New York, Buffalo, and Cleveland merchants willingly extended Joseph Smith credit. His position of leadership in an expanding community, the value of his current assets, and the expectation of continued growth made these transactions reasonable at the time.

The financial problems of Church leaders arose from two circumstances. First, their debts were largely in the form of 90-to-180-day notes, while their assets were primarily in nonliquid land. Second, Joseph Smith found it very difficult to demand cash from the sale of land or goods to his followers, many of whom were impoverished by the costly migration to Kirtland. The resulting cash-flow problem, common in frontier communities, could have been alleviated by a bank with the capacity to transfer long-term assets into short-term liquidity.

In the fall of 1836, Joseph Smith and his associates drew up a charter for such a bank, the Kirtland Safety Society. The question of fraud has long hovered over the Society. Its timing was unfortunate. During 1836 and 1837, the Ohio legislature, dominated by the hard-money wing of the Democratic party, refused all applications for bank charters. Within a week of realizing the hopelessness of their request for a charter, Church leaders, probably with legal counsel judging from the language of the document, formed a joint stock company and began issuing notes sometimes stamped "anti-banking" notes.

Because an 1816 Ohio law forbade the issuance of unauthorized money, some have thought that the Kirtland Safety Society notes were illegal. But the definition of what constituted "unauthorized" money remained controversial as late as 1873. Several other commercial institutions in Ohio issued notes or scrip, including the Ohio Railroad Company, which issued almost $100,000 of scrip during the same year as the Kirtland Safety Society. Whigs, soft-money Democrats, and several newspapers encouraged such action in opposition to what they considered the unlawful and unconstitutional behavior of the hard-money majority in the legislature.

Heavy demand for redemption of the Kirtland Safety Society's notes led to the suspension of specie payments within its first month of operation. Thereafter, the notes were backed by land values, rather than specie, and almost immediately its notes circulated at a heavy discount. It was further buffeted by the nationwide banking panic of May 1837, when all Ohio banks suspended specie payment. The tenacious Kirtland bank, or anti-bank, continued its faltering operations until November, when it closed its doors for the last time.

The Kirtland Safety Society's first note issue during January 1837 was probably not for more than $15,000. Subsequent note issues may have totaled as much as $85,000 in face value, but the increasing discounts against these issues probably kept the real value of outstanding notes at about the January level or lower. At the time of the initial issue, paid-in subscriptions were also approximately $15,000. That amount, plus the unusual loyalty of the LDS community and a $3,000 loan from the Bank of Geauga, might have provided resources sufficient for a legally chartered bank in Kirtland to experience modest success.

Whatever might have been, the institution did not have a bank charter and did not survive, thereby adding substantially to Joseph Smith's financial woes. He bought more stock, paid more per share than 85 percent of the other investors, and continued to add his own money to the assets of the bank as late as April 1837, well after it had suspended specie payments. After the banking panic of May, Joseph Smith transferred his interests in the bank and other financial assets to Oliver Granger and Jared Carter, who continued to attempt to settle Joseph's financial obligations as late as 1843.

BIBLIOGRAPHY

Adams, Dale W. "Chartering the Kirtland Bank." *BYU Studies* 23 (Fall 1983):467–82.

Fielding, R. Kent. "The Mormon Economy in Kirtland, Ohio." *Utah Historical Quarterly* 27 (Oct. 1959):331–56.

Hill, Marvin S.; C. Keith Rooker; and Larry T. Wimmer. "The Kirtland Economy Revisited: A Market Critique of Sectarian Economics." *BYU Studies* 17 (Summer 1977):391–475.

Parkin, Max H. "Conflict at Kirtland: A Study of the Nature and Causes of External and Internal Conflict of the Mormons in Ohio Between 1830 and 1838." M.A. thesis, Brigham Young University, 1966.

Sampson, D. Paul, and Larry T. Wimmer. "The Kirtland Safety Society: The Stock Ledger Book and the Bank Failure." *BYU Studies* 12 (Summer 1972):427–36.

LARRY T. WIMMER

KIRTLAND, OHIO

[*This entry presents the history of LDS settlement in Kirtland and gives an idea of what it would have been like to have lived among the Saints in this community in the 1830s.*]

During most of the 1830s there were two gathering places for Latter-day Saints, one in western Missouri and the other in northeastern Ohio. Although more members gathered to the Missouri frontier, Kirtland, Ohio, was the principal administrative headquarters of the Church and the major base for directing missionary work from 1831 until early 1838.

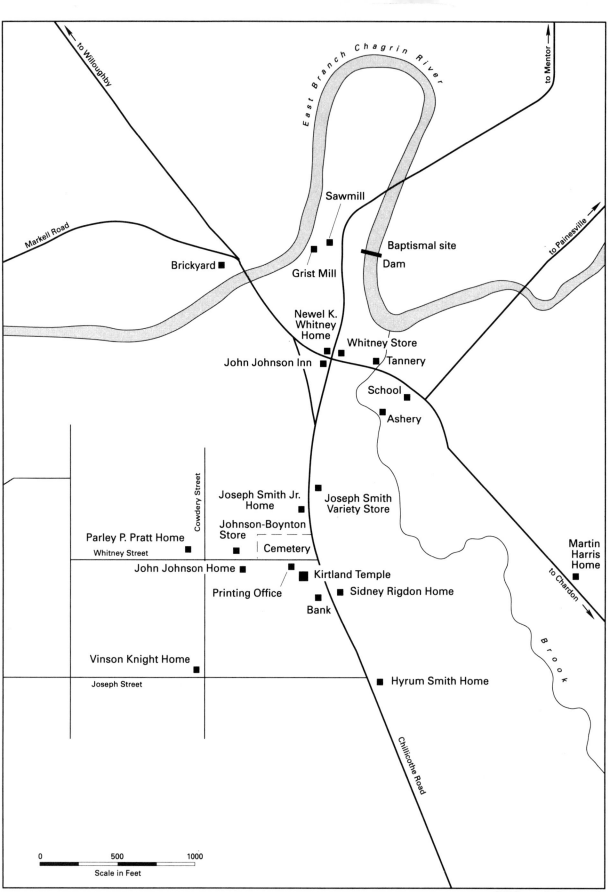

to Willoughby

East Branch Chagrin River

to Mentor

Markell Road

Sawmill

Baptismal site

Dam

to Painesville

Brickyard

Grist Mill

Newel K. Whitney Home

Whitney Store

John Johnson Inn

Tannery

School

Ashery

Cowdery Street

Joseph Smith Jr. Home

Joseph Smith Variety Store

Johnson-Boynton Store

Parley P. Pratt Home

Cemetery

Whitney Street

John Johnson Home

Kirtland Temple

Printing Office

Sidney Rigdon Home

Bank

Martin Harris Home

to Chardon

Vinson Knight Home

Joseph Street

Hyrum Smith Home

Brook

Chillicothe Road

0   500   1000
Scale in Feet

BYU Geography Department

794

Latter-day Saint growth in northeastern Ohio began not long after the Church was organized in 1830. The Church was introduced into Ohio in late October 1830 and within a month gained 135 new members, of whom about 35 lived in Kirtland township (*see* LAMANITE MISSION). Joseph SMITH and his family moved there early in 1831, and in the spring and early summer of that year, other Latter-day Saints, primarily from Ohio and New York, followed. Although the Prophet made two trips to Missouri and lived for a time in nearby Hiram, Ohio, from the summer of 1832 until 1838 the Kirtland area was his primary residence.

The larger part of the first wave of Latter-day Saint settlers in Kirtland moved to Missouri before the end of 1831. The major growth of the LDS population in Kirtland began in 1833. The number rose from approximately 100 in that year to 2,000 in 1838. During the decade preceding the Mormon immigration, the population of the township doubled, increasing from 481 in 1820 to 1,018 in 1830. During the ensuing seven years, primarily as a result of immigration of Latter-day Saints, the population tripled.

Describing conditions in the Kirtland community in the mid-1830s, one contemporary wrote, "They came, men, women, and children, in every conceivable manner, some with horses, oxen, and vehicles rough and rude, while others had walked all or part of the distance. The future 'City of the Saints' appeared like one besieged. Every available house, shop, hut, or barn was filled to its utmost capacity. Even boxes were roughly extemporized and used for shelter until something more permanent could be secured" (*History of Geauga and Lake Counties, Ohio*, p. 248).

The sudden influx of Latter-day Saints to Kirtland had a major impact on the community. One of the visible changes was the increase of small temporary dwellings. Although log and small frame houses dotted the landscape during the first two decades of colonization, larger and more permanent frame and brick structures were erected before 1830. Squatters or renters, comprising half of the population in 1830, lived in small frame houses. As Mormon immigration increased, however, clusters of small unadorned cabins, a throwback to the dwellings of the earliest settlers, ap-

peared primarily in the northwestern section of the township.

Most Latter-day Saints were poorer than the older settlers, partly because the Mormons were recent immigrants. Prior to joining the Church, most members were not transients, nor were they from the lowest economic classes in the East. Many, however, lost economic ground by migrating to Kirtland. Some sold farms in New York or New England for less than the market value, and many left equipment in the East because of the expense of transporting it. All spent a portion of the money derived from such sales on moving their families and supplies westward. The few Saints who moved from Jackson County, Missouri, to Kirtland were also in a difficult economic situation. In the course of their expulsion from that county in 1833, their homes were burned and their property was stolen. On arrival in Kirtland the new settlers faced inflated land values. Since the price of land increased in relation to the growth of population, most newcomers (both Mormon and non-Mormon) could not afford to buy sufficient land to support their families.

After arriving in Kirtland, Latter-day Saints fell further behind economically as a result of contributing labor and scarce resources to Church projects. The Church erected a variety of buildings in Kirtland between the east branch of the Chagrin River and the eastern portion of a plateau that overlooked the river. The principal structure was the KIRTLAND TEMPLE. For almost three years, between the summer of 1833 and the spring of 1836, nearly all members united in building the three-story "House of the Lord" to be used as a meetinghouse and school. While women and girls were carrying on their usual household duties, preparing food for their families, caring for young children, knitting and making clothes, and working in kitchen gardens, they also provided food and clothing for temple workers and drove supply wagons to the temple site. Meanwhile, men and boys worked on farms, cut wood for winter, tanned hides, hunted game, and fished, in addition to hauling stone to the temple site. They also cut, milled, and transported lumber for the construction.

While working on the temple, Latter-day Saints constructed a smaller building to the west

⟵ Kirtland village. Roads, buildings, and properties, 1837.

Cemetery across the street to the north of the Kirtland Temple (1907). Louisa and Thaddeus (the twins born to Joseph and Emma Smith), as well as Jerusha Smith (Hyrum's wife) and Mary Duty Smith (grandmother of the Prophet), are buried in this cemetery. Photographer: George E. Anderson.

that was used as a school, printing establishment, and office building. They also erected a sawmill to assist with their building program, established a tannery and ashery, and constructed shops and stores that provided settlers with merchandise and employment opportunities.

Along with all these sacrifices, many of the men postponed improvement of their standard of living to serve on MISSIONS without pay. During the 1830s, traveling elders preached the gospel throughout the United States and eastern Canada, and Heber C. Kimball led a group of missionaries (many of them from Kirtland) to England in 1837.

While constructing the temple and supporting missionary work, the Kirtland Saints found time for school. Although growing out of their New England culture and impulses in the Ohio environment, the Saints' educational efforts received their greatest impetus from revelations recorded in Kirtland by Joseph Smith. While living in an apartment above the Newel K. WHITNEY STORE, the Prophet received a revelation that declared, "Teach one another words of wisdom; yea, seek ye out of the best books words of wisdom; seek learning, even by study and also by faith" (D&C 88:118; cf. D&C 88:78–79; 93:36).

As a result of this and other divine commands, Joseph Smith in 1833 invited about twenty elders to attend a SCHOOL OF THE PROPHETS. Following the initial sessions of that school, Church leaders and members established a school of the elders, a grammar school, and various private schools, in which adults and youth studied theology, philosophy, government, literature, history, geography, English grammar, penmanship, arithmetic, Latin, Greek, and Hebrew. In 1836 more than one hundred Latter-day Saints commenced studying Hebrew. Women attended and taught school in Kirtland, and studied various subjects with their husbands.

To assist the Latter-day Saints in their educational pursuits and to promote missionary work, Church leaders sponsored a major publishing program in Kirtland beginning in 1834. Within four years, the Saints published a periodical, the *Latter-day Saints' Messenger and Advocate*; a secular and political paper, *Northern Times*; a hymnal (1835); a second edition of the Book of Mormon; and a collection of 102 sections of revelations recorded by Joseph Smith in the first edition of the Doctrine and Covenants (1835), which included the "Lectures on Faith." Historical and doctrinal information that is now included in the JOSEPH SMITH TRANSLATION OF THE BIBLE (JST) and portions of the Pearl of Great Price (book of Moses) were also printed in Missouri and Kirtland during the early 1830s.

In addition to working long hours and studying, Latter-day Saints participated in regular worship services. The first day of the week (Sunday) was observed as the Lord's Day, during which members rested from their daily labors. Meetings were initially held in homes and schools. Following the construction of the Kirtland Temple, meetings were also held there. By the mid-1830s a pattern of Sunday worship had been established. Members attended morning and afternoon services during which they sang, prayed, and listened to sermons delivered by leaders and other members. They generally partook of the Lord's Supper not only during the afternoon meetings but also sometimes during the week in their homes. Confirmations of new members and marriages were also performed on Sunday in the temple and in homes on other days. On the first Thursday of each month, a FAST AND TESTIMONY MEETING was held in the temple, and many of these meetings continued from 10:00 A.M. to 4:00 P.M., with members singing, praying, bearing testimonies, and teaching one another.

During this decade Church members also participated in an unusual pentecostal season. Shortly before and after the dedication of the Kirtland Temple, many Latter-day Saints wrote of seeing visions, speaking in tongues, and receiving the spirit of prophecy. During a series of meetings held between late January and early May 1836, several Latter-day Saints declared that they saw the Savior, and many claimed to have communed with other heavenly messengers. Many also testified that they sang accompanied by a choir of heavenly personages.

Along with their other activities, Latter-day Saints found time for recreation. Hunting, fishing, swimming, sleighing, skating, wrestling, horseback riding, and riding in carriages were among the most popular leisure pursuits. Although children had few toys, they played with balls, marbles, whistles, and homemade dolls (Backman, pp. 275–83).

Some of the non-Mormon residents considered the intrusion of Latter-day Saints into the community a threat to their traditional pattern of living. Some complained that the Mormon practice of living in harmony with revelations recorded by a prophet was hostile to the American spirit of democracy. Residents not only rejected LDS beliefs regarding visions, revelations, and the restoration but also claimed that the Latter-day Saints had increased the poverty of the community and were a political and economic threat. The political competition reached a peak in 1837 when Latter-day Saints were elected to all local township offices except for the office of constable. Prior to that year, only four Latter-day Saints had been elected to a major office, and there had been a tendency for the citizens to reelect the earliest settlers. In addition to gaining control of the local government, Latter-day Saints transformed the township's voting pattern from Whig to Democratic. Since Kirtland was located in a Whig section of Ohio and all townships in Geauga County in the mid-1830s, except Kirtland, supported that party, Whigs in northeastern Ohio united in opposition to the Mormons. Complaints and charges escalated into threats and mob action.

Early in 1838, amid intensifying pressures from outside the Church and apostasy within, accentuated by the demise of the Kirtland Safety Society and the Panic of 1837 (*see* KIRTLAND ECONOMY), the exodus of Latter-day Saints from Kirtland and vicinity began. Joseph Smith, Sidney

Ten-dollar note issued by the Kirtland Safety Society, March 1837, signed by Joseph Smith, Jr., and Sidney Rigdon. Three months later Joseph Smith disassociated himself from this private financial institution, which failed to gain public confidence. It closed in 1837. Some of these notes were later countersigned and validated by Brigham Young and Heber C. Kimball in Salt Lake City. Courtesy Rare Books and Manuscripts, Brigham Young University.

RIGDON, and other leaders fled from mobs in January. Other members gradually followed.

In most instances small groups of less than fifty traveled westward. On July 5, 1838, however, more than 500 members left in a stream of fifty-nine wagons—with twenty-seven tents, ninety-seven horses, twenty-two oxen, sixty-nine cows, and one bull. As this long wagon train, known as Kirtland Camp, moved across the states of Ohio, Indiana, Illinois, and Missouri, spectators gathered to watch the sight. Some gave encouragement, while others jeered and threatened violence. Because of financial problems, many in this group were asked by the leaders to leave the camp, so that only a portion of them reached the Missouri frontier.

By mid-July 1838, more than 1,600 Latter-day Saints in the Kirtland area had reluctantly left the temple, vacated their homes, and headed westward. Only a few Latter-day Saints remained in a neighborhood of predominantly empty cabins, and most of these people moved westward before the mid-1840s.

BIBLIOGRAPHY

Anderson, Karl Ricks. *Joseph Smith's Kirtland: Eyewitness Accounts.* Salt Lake City, 1989.

Backman, Milton V., Jr. *The Heaven's Resound: A History of the Latter-day Saints in Ohio 1830–1838.* Salt Lake City, 1983.

Hill, S. Marvin; Keith Rooker; and Larry T. Wimmer. "The Kirtland Economy Revisited: A Market Critique of Sectarian Economics." *BYU Studies* 17 (Summer 1977):389–475.

History of Geauga and Lake Counties, Ohio. Philadelphia, 1878.

MILTON V. BACKMAN, JR.

KIRTLAND TEMPLE

The divine command that led to the building of the Kirtland Temple was given to the Prophet Joseph SMITH in January 1831 when the Church was beset by poverty and turmoil. At that time, the Saints were to gather to Ohio, where the Lord promised he would endow them "with power from on high" (D&C 38:32; cf. D&C 88:119; 95:3, 8, 11). Thus they began to build the first of the Latter-day Saint TEMPLES.

The Church then consisted of only a few hundred members, men, women, and children who labored together for the temple and contributed, as Eliza R. SNOW wrote, "brain, bone and sinew" and "all living as abstemiously as possible" so that "every cent might be appropriated to the grand object" (Tullidge, p. 82). According to Benjamin F. Johnson, "there was not a scraper and hardly a plow that could be obtained among the Saints," to prepare the ground for the foundation of the temple (Benjamin Johnson, *My Life's Review*, p. 16). Lumber was brought from nearby forests. Stone was hewn from a local quarry.

As the exact patterns of the Tabernacle of Moses and Solomon's temple had been revealed from on high (Ex. 25:9; 1 Chr. 28:11–12), so also were the design, measurements, and functions of the Kirtland Temple revealed. Its interior was to be fifty-five feet wide and sixty-five feet long and have a lower and a higher court. The lower part of the inner court was to be dedicated "for your sacrament offering, and for your preaching, and your fasting, and your praying, and the offering up of your most holy desires unto me, saith your Lord." The higher part of the inner court was to be "dedicated unto me for the school of mine apostles" (D&C 95:13–17).

The cornerstone was laid on July 23, 1833. Brigham YOUNG later explained that the first stone was laid at the southeast corner, the point of greatest light, and at high noon, the time of the greatest sunlight (*JD* 1:133). This was a symbolic reminder that the House of the Lord is a center of light and truth.

The external design of the Kirtland Temple is typical of other contemporary houses of worship at that time, but the arrangement of the interior is unique. On each of the two main floors are two series of four-tiered pulpits, one on the west side, the other on the east. These are symbolic of the offices of the Melchizedek and Aaronic Priesthoods and accommodated their presidencies.

The construction of the temple was abruptly slowed with the call of ZION'S CAMP to Missouri, though many of the women, older men, and the infirm remained in Kirtland. Sidney RIGDON, of the First Presidency, recorded walking the walls of the temple "by night and day and frequently wetting the walls" with his tears, praying for the completion of the temple. At other times the work was slowed because of harassment and threats by enemies of the Church. Elder George A. Smith recalled that sometimes guards attended the temple day and night and worked with a trowel in one hand and a gun in the other.

The women—who, Joseph once remarked, were "first in temple labors"—did spinning, knitting, and sewing so that temple laborers would have clothes to wear. To give the exterior glaze a sparkling appearance, the women contributed glassware to be broken in bits and applied to the plaster. In his dedicatory prayer, Joseph referred to the sacrifice of the Saints: "For thou knowest that we have done this work through great tribulation; and out of our poverty we have given of our substance to build a house to thy name, that the Son of Man might have a place to manifest himself to his people" (D&C 109:5).

An estimated 1,000 people attended the dedication on March 27, 1836. A repeat dedication ceremony was held on March 31. It was a time of great rejoicing. Dedicatory anthems were sung, including "The Spirit of God Like a Fire Is Burning," which was written for the occasion. The sacrament was administered. The inspired dedicatory prayer, filled with Hebraic overtones, became the pattern for all subsequent temple dedications. In it, the Prophet pleaded with the Lord for the visible manifestation of his divine presence (the *Shekhinah*), as in the Tabernacle of Moses, at Solomon's temple, and on the day of Pentecost, "And let thy house be filled as with a rushing mighty wind, with thy glory" (D&C 109:37; cf. Ex. 29:43; 33:9–10; 2 Chr. 7:1–3; Acts 2:1–4). Many recorded the fulfillment

Interior of the Kirtland Temple, facing the Melchizedek Priesthood pulpits. Photograph, 1911, by C. R. Savage Co.

of that prayer. Eliza R. Snow wrote, "The ceremonies of that dedication may be rehearsed, but no mortal language can describe the heavenly manifestations of that memorable day. Angels appeared to some, while a sense of divine presence was realized by all present, and each heart was filled with 'joy inexpressible and full of glory'" (Tullidge, p. 95). After the prayer, the entire congregation rose and, with hands uplifted, shouted hosannas "to God and the Lamb" (see HOSANNA SHOUT).

The climax of the spiritual outpouring occurred on April 3, 1836, when the Savior appeared in the Kirtland Temple to Joseph Smith and Oliver COWDERY and said, "For behold I have accepted this house, and my name shall be here; and I will manifest myself to my people in mercy in this house" (D&C 110:7). Then three other personages of former dispensations, or eras, came and restored KEYS OF THE PRIESTHOOD: Moses restored the keys of the gathering of Israel, Elias restored keys of the GOSPEL OF ABRAHAM, and Elijah restored the keys of SEALING. These keys represent three different aspects of the mission of the Church.

Without the keys restored in the Kirtland Temple, the Latter-day Saints would not have authority to perform the ordinances in their many temples. WASHINGS AND ANOINTINGS had been given in January 1836. After attending to the washing of feet, Joseph assured the quorums that he "had given them all the instruction they needed" to go forth and build up the kingdom of God, having "passed through all the necessary ceremonies" (TPJS, p. 110). These ceremonies were preliminary to the fulness of the ordinances and the tem-

ple endowment later administered in the Nauvoo Temple.

Abandoned by the Saints after severe persecution, the Kirtland Temple was for a time in the hands of dissidents. Today it is owned by the REORGANIZED CHURCH OF JESUS CHRIST OF LATTER DAY SAINTS and is used as a visitors center. It has been recognized as a National Historic Site.

BIBLIOGRAPHY

Anderson, Karl Ricks. *Joseph Smith's Kirtland: Eyewitness Accounts.* Salt Lake City, 1989.

Backman, Milton V., Jr. *The Heavens Resound: A History of the Latter-day Saints in Ohio, 1830–1838.* Salt Lake City, 1983.

Madsen, Truman G. *Joseph Smith, the Prophet,* pp. 67–82. Salt Lake City, 1989.

Tullidge, Edward W. *The Women of Mormondom.* New York, 1877.

KEITH W. PERKINS

KNOWLEDGE

Latter-day Saints believe that certain forms of knowledge are essential for salvation and eternal life (John 17:3). The Prophet Joseph SMITH taught that "a man is saved no faster than he gets knowledge, for if he does not get knowledge, he will be brought into captivity," and thus human beings have a need for "revelation to assist us, and give us knowledge of the things of God" (TPJS, p. 217). One of the purposes of the priesthood, which is the authority to administer the gospel, is to make this saving "knowledge of God" available to all (D&C 84:19). Those who die without a chance to obtain a knowledge of the gospel of Jesus Christ will be given opportunity to receive and accept the gospel in the life after death to become "heirs of the celestial kingdom" (D&C 128:5; 137:7–9; 138:28–34; see SALVATION OF THE DEAD).

Knowledge makes possible moral agency and freedom of choice (John 8:32; 2 Ne. 2:26–27; Hel. 14:30–31; Moro. 7:15–17). Those who receive knowledge are responsible to live in accordance with it. Those who sin after having received knowledge of the truth by revelation bear greater condemnation than those who sin in ignorance (Heb. 10:26–27; 2 Pet. 2:20–21; Mosiah 2:36–39; Alma 24:30), while mercy is extended to those who sin in ignorance, or without knowledge of the truth (Mosiah 3:11; Alma 9:14–17; Hel. 7:23–24).

Knowledge is one of the gifts of the spirit that all people are commanded to seek (1 Cor. 12:8; Moro. 10:9–10; D&C 46:17–18). Knowledge of the truth of the gospel of Christ is conveyed as well as received by the power of the Holy Ghost (Moro. 10:5; 1 Cor. 2:9–16; D&C 50:19–21). Similarly, knowledge of the mysteries of God also comes through personal revelation. Shared knowledge of the things of God is available in the scriptures and other teachings of his prophets.

Knowledge is closely associated in scripture with other virtues such as meekness, long suffering, temperance, patience, godliness, kindness, and charity (2 Pet. 1:5–7; D&C 4:6; 107:30–31; 121:41–42). It is intimately related to truth; genuine knowledge is truth (D&C 93:24). Knowledge is understood to be an active, motivating force rather than simply a passive awareness, or collection of facts. This force is seen, for example, in acts of faith (Alma 32:21–43) and obedience (1 Jn. 2:4). The word "knowledge" is also used to refer to vain or false knowledge, and to the pride that often comes with knowledge based on human learning unaccompanied by righteousness and the spirit and knowledge of God (1 Cor. 8:1–2; 2 Tim. 3:7; 2 Ne. 9:28–29).

All people are encouraged to seek deeply and broadly to gain knowledge of both heavenly and earthly things (D&C 88:77–80). Such knowledge comes by study of the works of others, and also by faith (D&C 88:118). The LDS Church has traditionally encouraged and supported the pursuit of knowledge and education by its members. Knowledge gained through study and also by faith is obtained "line upon line and precept upon precept" (D&C 98:11–12; 128:21). All knowledge gained in this life stays with those who attain it and rises with them in the resurrection, bringing some advantage in the life to come (D&C 130:18–19). The next life holds the promise of "perfect knowledge" or understanding (2 Ne. 9:13–14).

BIBLIOGRAPHY

Reynolds, Noel B. "Reason and Revelation." In *A Thoughtful Faith: Essays on Belief by Mormon Scholars*, ed. P. Barlow, pp. 205–224. Centerville, Utah, 1986.

RICHARD N. WILLIAMS

KSL RADIO

KSL is a clear-channel Salt Lake City radio station, 1160 on the dial. Originally an independent KZN, it went on the air May 6, 1922. The Church bought controlling interest in the station on April 21, 1925.

Earl J. Glade, pioneer broadcaster, was general manager of the station for its first twenty years. He set standards and policies that continue to the present: a strong local and international news service, community and cultural interdependence, and sponsorship of quality-of-life improvements.

In 1932 KSL changed affiliation from NBC to CBS and, in the same year, increased its power to 50,000 watts. The station reaches into all the United States west of the Mississippi and, by occasional "skips," is heard as far away as New Zealand and Norway.

On December 26, 1946, KSL began broadcasting the first FM radio signal in Utah under the call letters of KSL-FM, and on June 1, 1949, KSL Television went on the air. The FM station was sold in 1978. KSL-TV has a survey area that includes seven western states.

In 1961, BONNEVILLE CORPORATION was created to give unified leadership to KSL and other BROADCASTING entities acquired and developed by the Church.

ARCH L. MADSEN

L

LAMAN

Laman was the eldest of six sons of LEHI and Sariah. Lehi was the patriarchal head and prophet at the beginning of the Book of Mormon, and Laman opposed his father and his younger brother NEPHI₁. Unlike the family conflicts in the book of Genesis between Esau and Jacob and between Joseph and his jealous brothers, the hostilities between Laman and Nephi were never quieted or reconciled.

Laman's opposition to the things of God arose from a combination of conflicting spiritual values and a common reaction against the favor he perceived going to a younger brother. The record of Nephi portrays Laman as strong-willed, hardhearted, impulsive, violent, judgmental, and lacking in faith. Though Laman followed his father in their journeyings, he never shared in the spiritual calling that inspired Lehi.

In his rebelliousness, Laman charged that Lehi was a visionary and foolish man (1 Ne. 2:11). Still Lehi continued to exhort him "with all the feeling of a tender parent," even though he feared from what he had seen in a vision that Laman and Lemuel would refuse to come into God's presence (1 Ne. 8:36-37).

Laman objected to leaving Jerusalem and the family's lands, possessions, and security, and to traveling to a new land (1 Ne. 2:11). Throughout their journey he complained of the hardships and was resentful that God had selected Nephi to become "a ruler and a teacher" ahead of him (1 Ne. 2:21–22; 16:36–38). Laman and Lemuel beat Nephi with a rod (1 Ne. 3:28), attempted to leave him tied up in the wilderness to die (1 Ne. 7:16), bound him on board ship, and treated him harshly (1 Ne. 18:11). On various occasions, Laman was rebuked by an angel, chastened by the voice of the Lord, or "shocked" by divine power. Still, he longed for the popular life of Jerusalem even though Lehi had prophesied the city would be destroyed.

Laman was supported in his stance by his wife and children, by Lemuel (the next eldest son) and his family, and by some of the sons of ISHMAEL and their families. Before he died, Lehi left his first blessing with Laman and Lemuel on the condition that they would "hearken unto the voice of Nephi" (2 Ne. 1:28–29), but they so opposed Nephi that he was instructed by God to lead the faithful to settle a new land away from Laman and Lemuel in order to preserve their lives and religious beliefs.

Laman and his followers became the LAMANITES, persistent enemies of the NEPHITES. Stemming from these early personal conflicts, the Lamanites insisted for many generations that Nephi had deprived them of their rights. Thus, the Lamanites taught their children "that they should hate [the Nephites] . . . and do all they could to destroy them" (Mosiah 10:17). When Laman's descendants were converted to faith in Christ, however, they were exemplary in righteousness; and Book of Mormon prophets foretold a noteworthy future for them in the latter days.

BIBLIOGRAPHY

Matthews, Robert J. *Who's Who in the Book of Mormon*. Salt Lake City, 1976.

McConkie, Joseph F., and Robert L. Millet. *Doctrinal Commentary on the Book of Mormon*, Vol. 1. Salt Lake City, 1987.

ALAN K. PARRISH

LAMANITE MISSION OF 1830–1831

The mission to western Missouri in 1830–1831 was important for three reasons: it demonstrated the Church's commitment to preach to the descendants of the LAMANITES of the Book of Mormon; it helped establish a stronghold for the Church in KIRTLAND, OHIO, where the missionaries found numerous unexpected converts; and it ultimately brought Joseph SMITH to Jackson County, Missouri, to lay the foundation of ZION, or the NEW JERUSALEM.

This mission, one of the Church's earliest missionary expeditions, commenced in October 1830 in New York State with the call of Oliver COWDERY, "second elder" in the Church; Peter Whitmer, Jr.; Parley P. PRATT; and Ziba Peterson (D&C 28:8; 32:1–3). It initiated the long continuing Church practice of taking the gospel to NATIVE AMERICANS. The Book of Mormon, in part a record of American Indian origins, prophesies that the Lamanites will assist in building the millennial New Jerusalem (3 Ne. 20-21), to be located in the Western Hemisphere (Ether 13:3–6; cf. D&C 28:9).

In the early 1800s the U.S. government began removing eastern Indians to the American frontier west of all existing states. In May 1830 the U.S. Congress passed the Indian Removal Law, further ensuring that the missionaries' ultimate destination was just west of Independence, Missouri, the last American outpost before "Indian country." To arrive there, the elders traveled on foot from New York, a distance of fifteen hundred miles, in midwinter.

These brethren soon found audiences of white settlers and some Indians. First, at nearby Buffalo, New York, they taught the Catteraugus Indians, who accepted two copies of the Book of Mormon. In northeastern Ohio they preached widely, and their message excited public curiosity. While visiting Mentor, Ohio, Cowdery and Pratt contacted Sidney RIGDON, a dynamic Reformed Baptist minister who was promoting New Testament restorationist beliefs in his congregation and was Pratt's friend and former pastor. They challenged Rigdon to read the Book of Mormon, which he promised to do. Rigdon also allowed the elders to speak in his Mentor church and to his congregation in Kirtland. Positive response to their message was almost immediate. Many members of the congregation, including Rigdon, were baptized. News of their success spread rapidly, sparking intense public feelings and leading to more conversions.

In four weeks in northeastern Ohio, the elders baptized approximately 130 converts, 50 of them from Kirtland. These new members made Kirtland their headquarters. Among the converts were men who would become leaders in the Church: Sidney Rigdon, Frederick G. Williams, Lyman Wight, Newel K. Whitney, Levi Hancock, and John Murdock. Two other prominent men, Edward Partridge and Orson HYDE, joined the Church soon after the missionaries departed. By the end of 1830, membership in Ohio had reached 300, nearly triple the number of members in New York. In December, after learning of the great Ohio harvest, Joseph Smith received a revelation directing the New York Saints to gather to the Kirtland area (D&C 37:1, 3), which most did in 1831.

Joined by Frederick G. Williams, a Kirtland physician, the four missionaries continued west in late November 1830, preaching as they traveled. They visited the Wyandot Indians at Sandusky, Ohio, where their hearers rejoiced over their message. However, during several days at Cincinnati, they were unable to interest other audiences. In late December, the elders took passage down the Ohio River toward St. Louis until encountering ice near Cairo, Illinois, which forced them to walk overland. Thereafter, their journey became increasingly arduous. Because of storms of rare severity, the winter of 1830–1831 is referred to in midwestern annals as "the winter of the deep snow." Food was scarce, and the missionaries were forced to survive on meager rations of frozen bread and pork.

In late January 1831, still in the midst of intense cold, the missionaries arrived at Jackson

Joseph Smith Preaching to the Indians, by William Armitage (late nineteenth century, oil on canvas, 10′ × 16′). In revelations given through the Prophet Joseph Smith in 1830, the Lord appointed several early Church leaders to preach the gospel to the Lamanites. They visited Native Americans in New York, Ohio, and Missouri. Several Native Americans visited Joseph Smith in the early 1840s in Nauvoo, which gave him an opportunity to tell them about the Book of Mormon. Church Museum of History and Art.

County (*see* MISSOURI: LDS COMMUNITIES IN JACKSON AND CLAY COUNTIES). Independence, the county seat, was a ragged and undisciplined frontier village twelve miles from the state's western border. Here the missionaries separated. Whitmer and Peterson set up a tailor shop to earn needed funds, while Cowdery, Pratt, and Williams crossed the state boundary, called by them "the border of the Lamanites," into Indian country. After first contacting the Shawnees, the elders crossed the frozen Kansas River and walked to the Delaware Indian village located about twelve miles west of the Missouri state line.

The Delaware Indians had arrived there only the previous November after a toilsome journey of their own. Because of their present poverty and mistreatment at the hands of whites, the aged Delaware chief, known to the white man as William Anderson Kithtilhund, viewed any Christian missionaries with suspicion. After his initial hesitation, however, Kithtilhund summoned his chiefs into council. For several days, through an interpreter,

Cowdery shared with the receptive Delawares the Book of Mormon account of their ancestors.

Plans to establish a permanent school among the Delawares and to baptize converts were soon interrupted by an order to desist from the federal Indian agent, Richard W. Cummins. After issuing a second warning, he threatened to arrest the elders if they did not leave Indian lands. Pratt believed that the jealousy of the missionaries of other churches and Indian agents precipitated the order. In a letter to William Clark, superintendent of Indian affairs in St. Louis, Cummins indicated that the elders did not possess a certificate authorizing their presence on government Indian lands. Later in Independence, Cowdery wrote the superintendent requesting a license to return to Indian lands, but the request was never granted, and that effectively ended the Lamanite Mission.

From Independence, Oliver Cowdery dispatched Parley P. Pratt to the East to report on the mission while the remaining four missionaries preached to white settlers in Jackson County. In the summer of 1831, Joseph Smith led a group from Kirtland to Jackson County to meet the missionaries. Through revelation the Prophet identified a site a half mile from Independence as the temple lot for the New Jerusalem (D&C 57:1–3).

BIBLIOGRAPHY

Backman, Milton, V., Jr. *The Heavens Resound*, pp. 1–12. Salt Lake City, 1983.

Pratt, Parley P. *Autobiography of Parley Parker Pratt*, pp. 47–58. Salt Lake City, 1938.

MAX H PARKIN

LAMANITES

The name Lamanite refers to an Israelite people spoken of in the Book of Mormon, who were descendants of LEHI and Ishmael, both of whom were descendants of JOSEPH OF EGYPT (1 Ne. 5:14). They were part of the prophet Lehi's colony, which was commanded of the Lord to leave Jerusalem and go to a new promised land (in the Western Hemisphere). The Lamanite peoples in the Book of Mormon during the first 600 years of their history are all linked in some way to LAMAN and Lemuel, Lehi's oldest sons. At times the name refers to "the people of Laman"; at other times it can identify unbelievers and ignore ancestral lines, depending on contextual specifics regarding peoples, time, and place.

LAMANITES IN THE BOOK OF MORMON. After the death of the prophet Lehi (c. 582 B.C.), the colony divided into two main groups, Lamanites and NEPHITES, (2 Ne. 5), each taking the name from their leader. These patronyms later evolved into royal titles (Mosiah 24:3; cf. Jacob 1:11). The Book of Mormon, though a Nephite record, focuses on both Lamanites and Nephites, by means of complex contrasts between the two groups. In the text, other peoples are generally subsumed under one of these two main divisions:

> Now the people which were not Lamanites were Nephites; nevertheless, they were called Nephites, Jacobites, Josephites, Zoramites, Lamanites, Lemuelites, and Ishmaelites. But I, Jacob, shall not hereafter distinguish them by these names, but I shall call them Lamanites that seek to destroy the people of Nephi, and those who are friendly to Nephi I shall call Nephites, or the people of Nephi, according to the reigns of the kings [Jacob 1:13–14].

In the beginning, political and religious disagreements arose between the Lamanites and the Nephites. Subsequently, an increasing cultural differentiation of the Lamanite people from the Nephites seems to have resulted from their different responses to Lehi's religious teachings. Social change quickly took place along many lines. Consequently, the name Lamanite can refer to descendants of Laman and his party; to an incipient nationality based upon an ideology, with its own lineage history and religious beliefs (Mosiah 10:12–17); or to one or more cultures. The Book of Mormon describes several Lamanite cultures and lifestyles, including hunting-gathering (2 Ne. 5:24), commerce (Mosiah 24:7), sedentary herding, a city-state pattern of governance (Alma 17), and nomadism (Alma 22:28). The politicized nature of early Lamanite society is reflected in the way in which dissenters from Nephite society sought refuge among Lamanites, were accepted, and came to identify themselves with them, much as some Lamanites moved in the opposite direction.

Early in the sixth century of Lamanite history (c. 94–80 B.C.), large-scale Lamanite conversions further divided the Lamanite peoples as many embraced the messianic faith in Jesus Christ taught by Nephite missionaries (Alma 17–26). The Lamanite king Lamoni, a vassal; his father, the suzerain king; and many of their subjects accepted the prophesied Christ and rejected their former lifestyles. They took upon themselves a covenant of pacifism, burying their weapons and renouncing warfare, and moved into Nephite territory for their safety (Alma 27:21–26; 43:11–12). This pattern of Lamanite conversion lasted for at least eighty-four years and through several generations (cf. Alma 24:5–6, 15–19, 20–24; 26:31–34; 44:20; Hel. 5:51; 15:9). This major division of Lamanite society had significant political impact: the identity of some of these converts remained Lamanite, but distinct from those who rejected the religion; others chose to be numbered among the Nephites (3 Ne. 2:12, 14–16); and the unconverted Lamanites were strengthened by numerous dissenters from Nephite subgroups (Alma 43:13), some of whom chose explicitly to retain their former identities (3 Ne. 6:3).

After the destructions that occurred at the time of Christ's crucifixion and the subsequent conversions (3 Ne. 11–28), a new society was established in which ethnic as well as economic differences were overcome, and there were no

"Lamanites, nor any manner of -ites; but they were in one, the children of Christ" (4 Ne. 1:17). This situation persisted until almost the end of the second century A.D., when those who rejected the Christian church, regardless of their ancestry, "had revolted from the church and taken upon them the name of Lamanites; therefore there began to be Lamanites again in the land" (4 Ne. 1:20). Divisions increased, so that by A.D. 231 "there arose a people who were called the Nephites, and they were true believers in Christ; and among them there were those who were called by the Lamanites—Jacobites, and Josephites, and Zoramites. . . . and . . . they who rejected the gospel were called Lamanites, and Lemuelites, and Ishmaelites" (4 Ne. 1:36–45).

It had been prophesied that eventually only Lamanite peoples and those who joined them would remain of the original groups (Alma 45:13–14). After the final battles between Lamanites and Nephites, only those who accepted Lamanite rule survived in Book of Mormon lands (Morm. 6:15).

LAMANITES IN EARLY LDS HISTORY. At the beginning of LDS Church history, one reason the Book of Mormon was published was so that it could be taken to the Lamanites (D&C 19:26–27). Within six months of the Church's organization, missionaries were sent to people thought to have Lamanite ancestry (D&C 28:8; 32:2; *see also* LAMANITE MISSION).

[*See also* Book of Mormon Peoples; Indian Student Placement Services; Native Americans.]

BIBLIOGRAPHY

"The Church and Descendants of Book of Mormon Peoples." *Ensign* 5 (Dec. 1975); the entire issue devoted to this topic.

De Hoyos, Arturo. *The Old and the Modern Lamanite.* Provo, Utah, 1970.

Sorenson, John L. *An Ancient American Setting for the Book of Mormon.* Salt Lake City, 1985.

Tyler, S. Lyman. *Modern Results of the Lamanite Dispersion: The Indians of the Americas.* Provo, Utah, 1965.

Widtsoe, John A., and Franklin S. Harris, Jr. *Seven Claims of the Book of Mormon.* Independence, Mo., 1935.

GORDON C. THOMASSON

LAMB OF GOD

See: Jesus Christ: Names and Titles of

LAST DAYS

The term "last days" refers to the current period of time, the preparatory era before the second coming of the Christ. This period is marked by prophetic signs (D&C 45:37–40). "The end of the world" is not the end of the earth, but the end of evil and the triumph of righteousness (JS—H 1:4). At the conclusion of these last days, the Lord Jesus Christ will come again and personally reign upon the renewed "paradisiacal" earth (A of F 10).

During the last days, many marvelous events will occur that are signs that this preparatory period has begun (Isa. 29:14). These include the RESTORATION OF THE GOSPEL OF JESUS CHRIST, the preaching of his gospel among all nations, the coming forth of modern scripture, and the gathering of scattered Israel. The restoration of the gospel before the coming of the Lord (Acts 3:19–21) includes the revealing anew of lost truths, priesthood power, temple worship, and the full organization of the Church of Jesus Christ, including apostles and prophets.

Christ prophesied that his gospel would be preached "in all the world for a witness unto all nations; and then shall the end come" (Matt. 24:1, 4). The Savior also foretold to Enoch that in the last days righteousness would come "down out of heaven," and truth will come "forth out of the earth" to bear testimony of Jesus Christ and of "his resurrection from the dead" (Moses 7:62). The Book of Mormon, Doctrine and Covenants, and Pearl of Great Price have come forth in partial fulfillment of these prophecies. Additional sacred writings are yet to come forth (cf. 2 Ne. 29:13; Ether 4:5–7).

A further sign will be the gathering of Israel. The house of Joseph is to be gathered to the "tops of the mountains" of the Western Hemisphere (Isa. 2:2) and to "stakes" (centers of strength) in many lands (HC 3:390–91). The house of Judah will gather by the millions to Jerusalem and its environs in fulfillment of prophecy (Wilford Woodruff in Ludlow, p. 240; DS 3:257–59). Another gathering will bring the lost tribes of Israel "from the north countries," to join with the house of Joseph (DS 3:306).

In contrast to these preparatory events, the prophecies state that in the last days gross wickedness will cover the earth (2 Tim. 3:1–7). Ancient and modern prophets have written that the world's latter-day inhabitants will "defile the earth" (Isa.

24:5) and become as wicked as Sodom and Gomorrah (Wilford Woodruff in Ludlow, p. 224) and as those of the time of Noah (*DS* 3:20), and that if Jesus "were here to-day, and should preach the same doctrine He did then, they would put Him to death" (*HC* 6:58).

This wickedness will result in wars of unprecedented destruction (George A. Smith, *CR*, Oct. 1946, p. 149), parents and children seeking each other's lives (Mark 13:12; *HC* 3:391), great increases in crime (Wilford Woodruff in Ludlow, p. 228), the destruction of many cities (Brigham YOUNG in Ludlow, p. 223), and a "desolating scourge" that will reach plague proportions (D&C 29:19).

As the end nears, the earth will be in commotion (D&C 45:26; cf. Joel 2:30–32). There will be severe lightnings and thunderings (D&C 87:6). The waves of the sea will heave themselves beyond their bounds (D&C 88:90). The earth will "reel to and fro as a drunken man" (D&C 49:23). A devastating hailstorm will destroy the crops of the earth (D&C 29:16), causing widespread famine (Brigham Young in Ludlow, p. 223). These judgments and wars will ultimately result in the "full end" of all nations (D&C 87:6).

Immediately preceding the Second Coming, unmistakable signs will appear in the heavens. The sun will be darkened, the moon will turn to blood, the stars will fall, and the powers of heaven will be shaken (D&C 45:42). In addition, the rainbow will be taken from the sky (*HC* 6:254). Finally, a great sign will be seen having the appearance of "seven golden lamps set in the heavens representing the various dispensations of God to man" (Wilford Woodruff in Ludlow, pp. 233–34). There will then be silence in heaven for half an hour, and "immediately after shall the curtain of heaven be unfolded as a scroll is unfolded after it is rolled up, and the face of the Lord shall be unveiled" (D&C 88:95).

As the earth becomes increasingly full of violence and immorality, the righteous will be watching the signs of the times and will call upon the Lord and seek to be worthy to abide the day of his coming (Luke 21:36; Acts 2:21). These faithful disciples of the Lord will experience "very little compared with the terrible destruction, the misery and suffering that will overtake the world" (John Taylor in Ludlow, p. 225; Moses 7:61); moreover, the righteous who fall victim to pestilence and to disease will be saved in the kingdom of God (*HC* 4:11).

To escape these judgments, the faithful will obey the commandments (*DS* 3:33–35; Luke 21:36), honor the priesthood (Wilford Woodruff in Ludlow, pp. 235–36), take the Holy Spirit for their guide (D&C 45:57), and stand in holy places (D&C 45:32). As the polarization of the righteous and the wicked increases, the righteous followers of the Savior will be called "Zion" (both the condition of purity of heart and the community of the pure-hearted). A city, Zion (the NEW JERUSALEM), will be established on the American continent and, together with her outlying stakes, will be a place of refuge (*HC* 3:391). And old Jerusalem will become a holy city (Ether 13:5). From these two capital cities of the millennial era, Jesus Christ will personally rule the renewed, paradisiacal world (*see* NEW JERUSALEM).

BIBLIOGRAPHY

Ludlow, Daniel H. *Latter-day Prophets Speak.* Salt Lake City, 1951.

Lund, Gerald N. *The Coming of the Lord.* Salt Lake City, 1971.

GRANT E. BARTON

LAST SUPPER

See: Sacrament

LATTER-DAY SAINTS (LDS)

The Church of Jesus Christ of Latter-day Saints (D&C 115:4) sees itself as a RESTORATION of the original Church of Jesus Christ "of Former-day Saints." Members of the Church in the time of Christ are often referred to as "saints." Actually, the word "saint" predates Christ, and it is used thirty-six times in the Old Testament. It appears sixty-two times in the New Testament. The term "Christian" appears only three times in the New Testament, used by others to identify the followers of Christ. At the time of Christ and the Apostles, the term "saint" was accepted as a proper name for anyone who was a member of the Church, and was not used as a term of special sanctity as in earlier and later traditions. The phrase "latter days" designates the period leading to the LAST DAYS and the series of events that will culminate in the reappearance of Christ to all the world. By referring to themselves as Latter-day Saints, members of the Church reaffirm their historical tie to original

Christians (the Former-day Saints of the New Testament) but differentiate the two time periods. Also, they are striving to become sanctified through obedience to the laws and ordinances of the gospel.

The name unites three themes: (1) the *restoration* theme, since the term has a New Testament origin; (2) the *preparation* theme, since the Saints in the latter days anticipate the coming of Christ; and (3) the *revelation* theme, since the name was received by revelation and recorded in Doctrine and Covenants, section 115.

It is interesting to some that the people of the DEAD SEA SCROLLS also called themselves Latter-day Saints. These individuals believed themselves tied to the PROPHETS and the COVENANT (hence the name Saint) and anticipated the imminent coming of the MESSIAH (hence the term Latter-day).

BIBLIOGRAPHY

Nelson, Russell M. "Thus Shall My Church Be Called." *Ensign* 5 (May 1990):16–18.

Cross, Frank M., Jr. *The Ancient Library of Qumran.* New York, 1961.

ROBERT F. BENNETT

LAW

[*Four different articles treat diverse aspects of LDS beliefs and experience with law. Two of the articles are grouped below:*

Overview

Divine and Eternal Law

The Overview *discusses the LDS concept of law in general and of divine and eternal law in particular.* Divine and Eternal Law *summarizes and describes the references in LDS scripture to the central role of law as pertaining to God.*

The article Nature, Law of *discusses the absence of a developed tradition of moral natural law among Latter-day Saints and describes their limited efforts to provide rational explanations for the laws of nature as described by the natural sciences.* Constitutional Law *summarizes the LDS respect for civil law in general and American constitutional law in particular.*

The experience of Latter-day Saints and the Church in the courts is reported in Legal and Judicial History. *Book of Mormon legal traditions and experience are described in* Book of Mormon, Government and Legal History in. *Regarding LDS views on specific aspects of civil law, see also* Church and State; Civic Duties; Civil Rights; Constitution of the United States of America; Freedom; *and* Politics: Political Teachings. *For information on other law-related topics, see* Justice and Mercy; Law of Moses; *and* Witnesses, Law of. *Commandments and gospel principles are often referred to as "laws"; on these subjects, see such entries as* Commandments; Consecration: Law of Consecration; *and* Obedience.]

OVERVIEW

Three types of laws exist: spiritual or divine laws, laws of nature, and civil laws. Latter-day Saints are deeply and consistently law-oriented, because laws, whether spiritual, physical, or civil, are rules defining existence and guiding action. Through the observance of laws, blessings and rewards are expected, and by the violation of laws, suffering, deprivation, and even punishment will result.

Basic LDS attitudes toward law and jurisprudence are shaped primarily by revelations contained in the Doctrine and Covenants, and by explanations given by the Presidents of the Church. God is, by definition, a god of order: "Behold, mine house is a house of order, saith the Lord God, and not a house of confusion" (D&C 132:8). God and law are inseparable, for if there is no law, there is no sin; and if there is no sin, there is no righteousness, "and if these things are not there is no God" (2 Ne. 2:13). Law emanates from God through Christ. Jesus said, "I am the law, and the light" (3 Ne. 15:9), and God's word is his law (D&C 132:12).

In an 1832 revelation, Joseph SMITH learned that law is a pervasive manifestation of God's light and power: "The light which is in all things . . . is the law by which all things are governed" (D&C 88:12–13). In connection with both spiritual law and natural law, no space or relationship occurs in which law is nonexistent. "There are many kingdoms; for there is no space in the which there is no kingdom; . . . and unto every kingdom is given a law; and unto every law there are certain bounds also and conditions" (D&C 88:37–38).

There are as many laws as there are kingdoms, which reflect greater or lesser light and truth. Some laws are higher, and some are lower. The kingdom of God operates in accordance with higher laws befitting God's exalted station, while the earth and all mortality and other kingdoms belong to lower spheres and therefore operate under different laws. The degree of glory that a person or thing can abide depends on how high a law he, she, or it is able to abide (D&C 88:22–25).

Lower laws are subsumed in higher laws. If people keep the laws of God, they have "no need to break the laws of the land" (D&C 58:21). Similarly, when the law of Moses was fulfilled by Jesus Christ, it was subsumed in him.

Existence is a process of progressively learning to obey higher law. Obeying and conforming to law are understood as a sign of growth, maturity, and understanding, and greater obedience to law produces greater freedom (D&C 98:5) and associated blessings (D&C 130:20–21).

At all levels, the principles of AGENCY and ACCOUNTABILITY are in effect: People may choose which laws to obey or to ignore, but God will hold them accountable and reward them accordingly (D&C 82:4). This is not viewed as a threat; law's purpose is not to force or punish but to guide and provide structure.

In the divine or spiritual sphere, law is not the product of a philosophical or theoretical search for what is right or good. It emanates from deity and is revealed through Jesus Christ and his prophets.

Spiritual laws given by God to mankind are commonly called COMMANDMENTS, which consist variously of prohibitions ("thou shalt not"), requirements ("thou shalt"), and prescriptions ("if a man"). The commandments are uniformly coupled with promised blessings for faithful compliance. Thus, Latter-day Saints describe themselves as covenant people who may be rewarded now, and in the hereafter, for their faithfulness. Many such COVENANTS are bilateral in character; that is, members make personal commitments in a variety of formal ordinances to keep in accord with certain commandments.

Spiritual laws, or God's commandments, are generally understood to have been purposefully decreed by a loving Heavenly Father, who desires to bring to pass the exaltation of his spirit children. Thus, "there is a law, irrevocably decreed in heaven before the foundations of this world, upon which all blessings are predicated" (D&C 130:20). Latter-day Saints believe that God knows or stipulates all types of acts and forbearances required by all individuals in order for them to attain that blessed eternal state of exaltation and that he has revealed these requirements to humankind through his servants. No law given of God is temporal (D&C 29:34).

"Irrevocability" in the foregoing quotation connotes permanence and unchangeability. Since God cannot lie, the commandments and promises contained in his covenants with people will not be revoked, though he can revoke a specific commandment to individuals when they have disobeyed (D&C 56:3–6). The fundamentals are not situational and do not ebb and flow with changing concepts of morality or theology outside the Church. The President of the Church is a prophet of God who receives revelations and inspiration to interpret and apply those basic principles as human circumstances change.

In accordance with the principle of agency, God commands, but he does not compel. No earthly mechanism exists for the enforcement of God's laws. The prophet teaches the members correct principles, and they are expected to govern themselves. Missionary work and education of Church members are carried out so that people may make informed choices. They are taught that making an informed choice results either in a blessing (current or deferred) or an undesirable consequence (current or deferred). Ignorance of the law is considered a legitimate excuse. Because of the atonement of Jesus Christ, repentance is not required of those "who have ignorantly sinned" or "who have died not knowing the will of God concerning them" (Mosiah 3:11), even though failure to abide by the commandment may result in the loss of blessings that would flow from proper conduct. In most cases, violators of divine law can escape the punishment connected with the offense by repentance, the demands of justice having been satisfied by the atonement of Christ in the interest of all (see JUSTICE AND MERCY).

BIBLIOGRAPHY

Firmage, Edwin B., and Christopher L. Blakesley. "J. Reuben Clark, Jr.: Law and International Order." *BYU Studies* 13 (Spring 1973):273–346.

Garrard, LaMar E. "God, Natural Law, and the Doctrine and Covenants." In *Doctrines for Exaltation*, pp. 55–76. Salt Lake City, 1989.

JOHN S. WELCH

DIVINE AND ETERNAL LAW

LDS revelation emphasizes the existence and indispensability of law. The relation of divine law to other species of law has not been given systematic treatment in Mormon thought as it has in traditional Christian theology (e.g., the *Summa Theolo-*

gica of Thomas Aquinas). But distinctive observations about divine law and eternal law may be drawn from Latter-day scriptures and related sources.

Aquinas identified four categories of law: (1) eternal law, which is coextensive with the divine mind and with the overall purpose and plan of God; (2) natural law, which addresses mankind's proper participation in eternal law but is discovered by reason without the assistance of revelation and promulgation; (3) divine positive law, also a part of the eternal law, which pertains to the SACRAMENTS and ORDINANCES necessary to the attainment of mankind's supernatural end made known by revelation; and (4) man-made positive law, which regulates the affairs of mankind not specifically addressed by God's law (e.g., laws that regulate such things as corporations, stocks, bonds, wills, and trusts) or which mandate the natural law with the power of the state.

LDS sources affirm laws roughly corresponding to each of these four types. Unlike traditional Jewish and Christian theologies, which place God outside of, and antecedent to, nature, however, LDS theology places God within nature.

"Divine" laws are instituted by God to govern his creations and kingdoms and to prescribe behavior for his offspring. Such law, in the terms of Acquinas's categories, would be divine positive law (i.e., law existing by virtue of being posited or enacted by God). Some Latter-day Saints believe that "eternal" law is self-existent, unauthored law, which God himself honors and administers as a condition of his perfection and Godhood. It should be noted that the adjectives "divine" and "eternal" do not have fixed usages in writing (*see* TIME AND ETERNITY).

Latter-day scriptures and other sources do not explicitly state that eternal law exists independently or coeternally with God. This characteristic of eternal law is sometimes inferred, however, from two concepts that do have support in scripture and other LDS sources:

1. God is governed (bound) by law. Latter-day scriptures state that "God would cease to be God" if he were to allow mercy to destroy justice, or justice to overpower mercy, or the plan of redemption to be fulfilled on unjust conditions (Alma 42:13). Scriptures further state that "I, the Lord, am bound when ye do what I say" (D&C 82:10),

implying that God by nature and definition—not by any external coercion—is righteous and trustworthy. Some Church writers have said that "[God] himself governs and is governed by law" (*MD*, p. 432) and that "the Lord works in accordance with natural law" (*DS* 2:27). They likewise speak of "higher laws" that account for providence and miracles.

2. Intelligence and truth were not created; they are coeternal with God. "Intelligence, or the light of truth, was not created or made, neither indeed can be. All truth is independent in that sphere in which God has placed it, to act for itself, as all intelligence also; otherwise there is no existence" (D&C 93:29–30). Joseph Smith expanded upon this teaching in his KING FOLLETT DISCOURSE, stating that "we infer that God had materials to organize the world out of chaos. . . . Element had an existence from the time he had. The pure principles of element . . . had no beginning, and can have no end. . . . The mind or the intelligence which man possesses is coeternal with God himself" (*TPJS*, pp. 350–53). If truth and intelligence were not created by God and are coeternal with him, it may be that they are ordered by and function according to eternal laws or principles that are self-existent. This may be implied in Joseph Smith's phrase "laws of eternal and self-existent principles" (*TPJS*, p. 181).

Consistent with the eternal laws, God fashions and decrees laws that operate in the worlds he creates and that set standards of behavior that must be observed in order to obtain the blessing promised upon obedience to that law. Joseph Smith taught that "[God] was the first Author of law, or the principle of it, to mankind" (*TPJS*, p. 56).

Latter-day scriptures emphasize the pervasive nature of divine law: "[God] hath given a law unto all things, by which they move in their times and their seasons" (D&C 88:42). "This is the light of Christ . . . which light proceedeth forth from the presence of God to fill the immensity of space— The light which is in all things, which giveth life to all things, which is the law by which all things are governed, even the power of God who sitteth upon his throne" (D&C 88:7, 12–13).

These same sources suggest, however, that divine law operates within the domain to which it inherently pertains or is assigned by God and, therefore, has limits or bounds: "All kingdoms have a law given; and there are many kingdoms; for there is no space in which there is no kingdom; and there is no kingdom in which there is no space, either a greater or a lesser kingdom. And unto every kingdom is given a law; and unto every law there are certain bounds also and conditions" (D&C 88:36–38).

The above references apparently pertain to descriptive law—that is, the divine law that operates directly upon or through physical and biological orders (see NATURE, LAW OF).

Other laws of God are prescriptive. They address the free will of man, setting forth standards and rules of behavior necessary for salvation and for social harmony. Latter-day Saints embrace such prescriptive commands of God as found in the TEN COMMANDMENTS and the SERMON ON THE MOUNT. Latter-day revelation also confirms that blessings and salvation come through compliance with divine laws: "There is a law, irrevocably decreed in heaven before the foundations of this world, upon which all blessings are predicated—and when we obtain any blessing from God, it is by obedience to that law upon which it is predicated" (D&C 130:20–21). "And they who are not sanctified through the law which I have given unto you, even the law of Christ, must inherit another kingdom, even that of a terrestrial kingdom, or that of a telestial kingdom" (D&C 88:21).

Of these prescriptive laws or commandments of God, LDS teachings tend to emphasize the following characteristics: (1) the extent of the divine laws revealed to mankind may vary from dispensation to dispensation, according to the needs and conditions of mankind as God decrees; (2) they are given through and interpreted by his prophets; (3) they are relatively concise, but "gentle" or benevolent, given to promote the happiness he has designed for his children (*TPJS*, pp. 256–57); and (4) they are efficacious for mankind as God's harmony with eternal law was, and is, efficacious for him, and will bring to pass the exaltation of his righteous children.

BIBLIOGRAPHY

Aquinas, Thomas. *Summa Theologica* 1266–73, trans. the Fathers of the English Dominican Province. London, 1915.

Widtsoe, John A. *A Rational Theology.* Salt Lake City, 1952.

CARL S. HAWKINS

DOUGLAS H. PARKER

LAW OF ADOPTION

The house of Israel in a spiritual and eternal perspective will finally include all who are the true followers of Jesus Christ. Although those of the direct blood lineage of the house of ISRAEL are genealogically the sheep of God's fold, they must fulfill all the spiritual conditions of discipleship. Those not of the blood of Israel can become Israel through adoption (cf. Rom. 8:14; Gal. 3:7, 29; 4:5–7; Matt. 3:9; JST Luke 3:8; Abr. 2:10), through the principles and the ordinances of the gospel: faith in the Lord Jesus Christ; repentance of sins; baptism by water and reception of the HOLY GHOST; and enduring to the end.

In a larger sense, everyone must be adopted into the family of God in order to enjoy the fulness of his blessings in the world to come. As the Only Begotten of the Father in the flesh, Jesus is the only natural HEIR and therefore the only one whose birthright is the kingdom of his Father. If others are to qualify as joint-heirs with Christ in his Father's kingdom, they must be fully adopted by God.

The adoption process is, in the Prophet Joseph SMITH's words, "a new creation by the Holy Ghost" (*TPJS*, p. 150). As summarized in the Doctrine and Covenants, individuals who enter into the COVENANT and "magnify their calling" are "sanctified by the Spirit unto the renewing of their bodies. They become the sons of Moses and of Aaron and the seed of Abraham, and the church and kingdom, and the elect of God" (D&C 84:33–34).

BIBLIOGRAPHY

Irving, Gordon. "The Law of Adoption: One Phase in the Development of Mormon Concept of Salvation, 1830–1900." *BYU Studies* 14 (Spring 1974):291–314.

V. BEN BLOXHAM

LAW OF MOSES

Distinctive views concerning the law of Moses and its relationship to Christ and to the attainment of individual salvation are set forth in the Book of Mormon and Doctrine and Covenants. The Church of Jesus Christ of Latter-day Saints teaches that this law was given by God to MOSES, that it formed part of a peculiar COVENANT of obedience and favor between God and his people, that it symbolized and foreshadowed things to come, and that it was fulfilled in the ATONEMENT OF JESUS CHRIST.

The law of Moses is best understood in a broad sense. It consists of "judgments," "statutes," "ordinances," and "commandments." The Book of Mormon refers to its also including various "performances," "sacrifices," and "burnt offerings." Nowhere in scripture is its full breadth, depth, diversity, and definition made explicit. On such matters, information can be drawn from the Pentateuch itself (the Torah) and from biblical scholarship, but one can only conjecture as to what these terms meant to Book of Mormon writers.

A narrow definition would confine the law of Moses to a body of prohibitions and commands set forth in separate, unrelated literary units within the first five books of the Bible. This view makes it difficult to speak of "biblical law," since these provisions are not drawn together as a unity by the Torah itself. The scattered codes and series include the Covenant Code (Ex. 20:23–23:19), Deuteronomic Law (Deut. 12–26), the Holiness Code (Lev. 17–26), purity laws (Lev. 11–15), festival rituals (Deut. 16), regulations pertaining to sacrifices (Num. 28–29), and the TEN COMMANDMENTS (Ex. 20:2–17; Deut. 5:6–21). While some biblical scholars conclude that "these were once independent units, subsisting in their own right, each having its own purpose and sphere of validity, and having been transmitted individually for its own sake in the first place" (Noth, p. 7), Latter-day Saints generally accept at face value statements in the Bible that attribute authorship to Moses, but the Church has taken no official stand concerning the collection and transmission of these legal texts in the Pentateuch. Scribes and copyists evidently made a few changes after the time of Moses (e.g., compare Moses 1–5 with Gen. 1–6).

Compounding the question of what was meant by the term "law of Moses" in the Book of Mormon is the fact that the "five books of Moses" that the Nephites possessed predated Ezra's redaction and canonization of the Pentateuch (444 B.C.). Quoted passages (e.g., Mosiah 13:12–24), however, indicate that the Nephite laws were substantially similar to the biblical texts that Jews and Christians have today.

As early as the third century A.D., the Jewish view held that the commandments numbered 613. Rabbi Simlai reportedly stated that "613 commandments were revealed to Moses at Sinai, 365 being prohibitions equal in number to the solar days, and 248 being mandates corresponding in number to the limbs [sic] of the human body" (Encyclopedia Judaica 5:760, quoting Talmud Bavli, Makkot 23b). About a third of these commandments have long been obsolete, such as those relating to the tabernacle and the conquest of Canaan. Others were directed to special classes, such as the Nazarites, judges, the king, or the high priest, or to circumstances that would rarely occur. Excluding these, about a hundred apply to the whole people and range from the spiritually sublime to the mundane. Examples of eternally relevant commandments of the law of Moses are the Ten Commandments and those relating to loving God, worshiping God, loving one's neighbor, loving the stranger, giving charity to the poor, dealing honestly, not seeking revenge, and not bearing a grudge. Other commandments cover a kaleidoscope of daily matters, including valuing houses and fields, laws of inheritance, paying wages, agriculture, animal husbandry, and forbidden foods. Jewish scholars classify these as commandments vis-à-vis God and commandments vis-à-vis fellow human beings (Mishnah Yoma 8:9).

Two other definitions should be mentioned. One identifies the law of Moses as coextensive with the Pentateuch. Around the time of Christ, New Testament writers sometimes called the Pentateuch "the law" (Luke 24:44; Gal. 4:21), even though the word "torah" has broader meaning (i.e., "teachings") and the Pentateuch contains poetry and narratives in addition to commandments, and some passages speak to all persons and nations (Gen. 9:1–7). The other defines the law as theologically synonymous with the doctrinal belief, whether mistaken or not, that salvation is dependent upon the keeping of commandments, thus distinguishing the law from grace, which for many Christians eliminates the task of sorting out which Mosaic laws are still in force.

Agreeing in some respects and departing in others from traditional Jewish or Christian views, the main lines of LDS belief about the law of Moses are as follows:

1. Jesus Christ was JEHOVAH, the God of the Old Testament who gave the law to Moses (3 Ne. 15:5; TPJS, p. 276). Jesus, speaking after his atonement and resurrection, stated, "The law is fulfilled that was given unto Moses. Behold, I am he that gave

the law, and I am he who covenanted with my people Israel" (3 Ne. 15:4–9).

2. The entire law was in several senses fulfilled, completed, superseded, and enlivened by Jesus Christ. Jesus said, "In me it hath *all* been fulfilled" (3 Ne. 12:17–18). Its "great and eternal gospel truths" (*MD*, p. 398) are applicable through Jesus Christ in all dispensations as he continues to reveal his will to prophets "like unto Moses" (2 Ne. 3:9–11).

3. Latter-day Saints believe that the law of Moses was issued to the Israelites as a preparatory gospel to be a schoolmaster to bring them to Christ and the fulness of his gospel (Gal. 3:24; cf. Jacob 4:5; Alma 34:14). The authority to act in the name of God is embodied in two priesthoods, the Melchizedek or higher, which embraces all divinely delegated authority and extends to the fulness of the law of the gospel, and Aaronic or lesser, which extends only to lesser things, such as the law of carnal commandments and baptism (D&C 84:26–27). While Moses and his predecessors had the higher PRIESTHOOD and the fulness of the gospel of Christ, both of which were to be given to the children of Israel, "they hardened their hearts and could not endure [God's] presence; therefore, the Lord in his wrath . . . took Moses out of their midst, and the Holy Priesthood also; and the lesser priesthood continued" (D&C 84:23–24; see Heb. 3:16–19; Mosiah 3:14; *TPJS*, p. 60).

4. Book of Mormon people brought the law of Moses with them from Jerusalem. Even though they endeavored to observe it strictly until the coming of Christ (e.g., 2 Ne. 5:10; Alma 30:3), they believed in Christ and knew that salvation did not come by the law alone but by Christ (2 Ne. 25:23–24), and understood that the law would be superseded by the Messiah (Mosiah 13:27–28; 2 Ne. 25:23–25).

5. For Latter-day Saints, all things are given of God to man as types and shadows of the redeeming and atoning acts of Christ (2 Ne. 11:4; Mosiah 13:31). Thus, the law of Moses typified various aspects of the atonement of Christ.

6. Covenant making, promises, and obedience to commandments are part of the fulness of the gospel of Christ: "Through the Atonement of Christ, all mankind may be saved, by obedience to the laws and ordinances of the Gospel" (A of F 3). Both for Latter-day Saints and regarding Jewish observance of the law of Moses, GRACE, FAITH, and WORKS are all essential to salvation: "It is by grace that we are saved, after all we can do" (2 Ne. 25:23). No mortal's obedience to law will ever be perfect. By law alone, no one will be saved. The grace of God makes up the deficit. The Church does not subscribe to a doctrine of free-standing grace unrelated to instructions and expectations required of man. It does have commandments relating to diet (see WORD OF WISDOM), MODESTY, and CHASTITY, as well as many ORDINANCES, such as BAPTISM, LAYING ON OF HANDS, and WASHING AND ANOINTING. If man were perfect, salvation could come on that account; walking in the way of the Lord would be perfectly observed. Since man is mortal and imperfect, God in his love makes known the way his children should walk, and extends grace "after all they can do."

BIBLIOGRAPHY

Daube, David. *Studies in Biblical Law*. New York, 1969.

Falk, Ze'ev. *Hebrew Law in Biblical Times*. Jerusalem, 1964.

Jackson, Kent P. "The Law of Moses and the Atonement of Christ." In *Studies in Scripture*, Vol. 3, pp. 153–72. Salt Lake City, 1985.

Noth, Martin. *The Laws in the Pentateuch and Other Studies*. Edinburgh, 1966.

Patrick, Dale. *Old Testament Law*. Atlanta, 1985.

DOUGLAS H. PARKER
ZE'EV W. FALK

LAWSUITS

Church members are usually inclined to avoid litigation and to find less contentious ways of resolving differences that may arise. This inclination is based primarily upon teachings in the New Testament and the Doctrine and Covenants. The early experience of the Church added powerful reinforcements to scriptural condemnations of litigation. In the 1840s the Prophet Joseph SMITH and other early leaders were obliged to defend themselves repeatedly against false charges. So oppressive were those charges that the Prophet at one time even said that he looked forward to the next life, where people would be reunited with their loved ones and where there "will be no fear of mobs, persecutions, or malicious lawsuits" (*TPJS*, p. 360).

The disparaging view of litigation begins with the Sermon on the Mount. Jesus taught his followers to settle disputes quickly and avoid court proceedings, to "turn the other cheek," and, if an adversary should obtain judgment against them in court to "let him have thy cloak also" (Matt. 5:25–26, 39–40). The apostle Paul condemned the practice that "brother goeth to law with brother, and that before the unbelievers" (1 Cor. 6:6). He counseled the Corinthian Saints to find a wise person from among them to judge the matter and, failing that, to suffer the wrong rather than to take it to legal authorities for a decision (verses 5–7).

More detailed instructions for dealing with offenses are contained in the Doctrine and Covenants, which counsels members to resolve their differences. But it also recognizes that some offenses are violations of criminal law that should be reported to civil authorities, while other categories of offenders should be dealt with by the Church (D&C 42:79–92). Instructions for Church DISCIPLINARY PROCEDURES are detailed (D&C 102:13–23).

When the main body of the Church was established in Utah in the mid-1800s, there was no civil authority, so Church courts exercised jurisdiction over secular as well as religious matters for the next several decades (see COURTS, ECCLESIASTICAL, NINETEENTH CENTURY). However, following the establishment of civil courts, the need for Church courts diminished. They were formally discontinued in 1989 in favor of disciplinary councils.

Church courts never were intended to absolve members from the duty of resolving their disputes by reconciliation and mutual understanding whenever possible. Even when Church courts were available, members were regularly admonished to settle their conflicts by informal means and to avoid litigation. A typical example: "Be reconciled to each other. Do not go to the courts of the Church nor to the courts of the land for litigation. Settle your own troubles and difficulties" (J. F. Smith, *GD*, p. 257).

The preference for forbearance, forgiveness, and informal means of resolution of disputes, both among Church members and with people outside the Church, continues today, as shown by counsel given in a 1988 general conference of the Church: "We live in an environment . . . of litigation and conflict, of suing and countersuing. Even here the powers of healing may be invoked" (G. B. Hinckley, *Ensign* 18 [Nov. 1988]:54).

BIBLIOGRAPHY

Firmage, Edwin B., and Richard C. Mangrum. *Zion in the Courts: A Legal History of the Church of Jesus Christ of Latter-day Saints, 1830–1900.* Urbana, Ill., 1988.

GERALD R. WILLIAMS

LAYING ON OF HANDS

The laying on of hands on the head of an individual as a religious ceremony has served many purposes historically and continues to do so for The Church of Jesus Christ of Latter-day Saints. The most common are the following:

THE SACRIFICIAL CEREMONIES OF ANCIENT ISRAEL. Anciently, in burnt and sin offerings, the offerer laid his hands on the sacrifice prior to its being slain (e.g., Ex. 29:10; Lev. 1:4; 4:4; 2 Chron. 29:23). In the case of the scapegoat, hands were laid on the head, symbolizing transference of the sins of the people to the animal (Lev. 16:21). The hands of the people were laid upon the Levites, and they in turn laid their hands upon the offerings (Num. 8:10–12).

BESTOWAL OF THE GIFT OF THE HOLY GHOST. CONFIRMATION and bestowing of the gift of the Holy Ghost by the laying on of hands follows BAPTISM. The Doctrine and Covenants explains that the one performing the ORDINANCE is acting as proxy for the Lord himself: "I will lay my hand upon you by the hand of my servant Sidney RIGDON, and you shall receive my Spirit, the Holy Ghost, even the Comforter, which shall teach you the peaceable things of the kingdom" (D&C 36:2; cf. Moro. 2:2). This ordinance may be performed only by MELCHIZEDEK PRIESTHOOD holders, not by those of the lesser or AARONIC PRIESTHOOD (D&C 20:58). This explains why JOHN THE BAPTIST, though he performed water baptism, did not bestow the Holy Ghost by the laying on of hands (Matt. 3:11), and it may explain why Philip did not do so for his Samaritan converts (Acts 8:5–17), or Apollos for the Ephesians (Acts 19:6; see also Acts 8:12–20). In Philip's case, he baptized the Samaritans, but PETER and JOHN, who held the higher priesthood, were sent to confer the Holy Ghost, and they laid "their hands on them, and they received the Holy Ghost" (Acts 8:17).

Paul may have referred to this gift when he counseled his companion Timothy to "neglect not the gift that is in thee, which was given thee by prophecy, with the laying on of the hands of the presbytery" (1 Tim. 4:14). On another occasion Paul admonished him to "stir up the gift of God, which is in thee by the putting on of my hands" (2 Tim. 1:6).

BESTOWAL OF THE GIFTS AND RIGHTS OF AN OFFICE. Moses ordained Joshua as his successor by the laying on of hands (Num. 27:18, 23; Deut. 34:9). Jesus' apostles used this procedure in authorizing seven men to manage practical economic matters in the early church (Acts 6:1–6). Paul and Barnabas were ordained to a missionary journey by the laying on of hands of the "prophets and teachers at Antioch" (Acts 13:3).

The BOOK OF MORMON reports that Jesus conferred upon his disciples the power to give the Holy Ghost by laying his hands upon them (3 Ne. 18:37; Moro. 2:3). The Aaronic Priesthood was conferred on the Prophet Joseph SMITH and Oliver COWDERY by the hands of the resurrected John the Baptist (JS—H 1:68–69). All subsequent transmission of AUTHORITY comes from the PRESIDENT OF THE CHURCH by the laying on of hands. A REVELATION on priesthood states: "Wherefore, it must needs be that one be appointed of the High Priesthood to preside over the priesthood, and he shall be called President of the High priesthood of the Church . . . From the same comes the administering of ordinances and blessings upon the church, by the laying on of the hands" (D&C 107:65–67). Accordingly, all men and women are installed in any Church office or CALLING by a SETTING APART by the laying on of hands of those in authority.

HEALING THE SICK. The laying on of hands to heal the sick was a common practice of Jesus (Mark 5:23; 6:5; 16:18; Luke 13:12–13). Luke records that "all they that had any sick with divers diseases brought them unto him; and he laid his hands on every one of them, and healed them" (Luke 4:40). Jesus did not use this method exclusively. Sometimes a touch was sufficient, or his word only. In the case of a man who was deaf and had a speech impediment, Jesus touched his tongue and his ears (Mark 7:33).

Jesus conferred the power of healing on his followers: "And these signs shall follow them that believe . . . they shall lay hands on the sick, and they shall recover" (Mark 16:18). Ananias laid hands on Paul that he might regain his sight (Acts 9:17–18). Paul thus healed the father of Publius in Malta (Acts 28:8). The Lord commanded that this practice should be continued in the Latter-day Church (D&C 42:43–44).

IMPARTING A BLESSING. Blessings in addition to those for health are given by the laying on of hands. Among these are PATRIARCHAL BLESSINGS (as when Jacob blessed Ephraim and Manasseh [Gen. 48:14]), blessings for the Lord's protecting care, blessings for success in the Lord's work, blessings of counsel, and the blessing of children. (Matt. 19:15; Mark 10:13, 16; cf. Acts 8:12–20; Moro. 2:2).

C. KENT DUNFORD

LAY PARTICIPATION AND LEADERSHIP

One of the important defining characteristics of The Church of Jesus Christ of Latter-day Saints is lay participation and leadership. The scope of volunteer service in the Church is extensive, both in the number of people involved and in the amount of their service.

In practice, the building up of the kingdom of God on earth is accomplished by individuals serving in numerous lay assignments, or CALLINGS. They speak in Church meetings and serve as athletic directors, teachers, family history specialists, financial secretaries, children's music directors, and women's and men's organization presidents. The goal of many leaders is to make sure that each member has a calling, reflecting the belief that personal growth comes through service. Millions of people serve in the Church, and that service represents a significant time commitment. In one study, researchers found that on average a BISHOP, the leader of a local WARD (congregation), spends approximately twenty-seven hours weekly in his duties; the president of the RELIEF SOCIETY, or women's organization, thirteen hours; the ward CLERK, eight hours; and so on. As of 1990, there were nearly 50,000 full-time MISSIONARIES contributing one and a half to two years of service. Lay members and leaders are organized and assisted through an extensive Church organization, including a substantial staff of employees located primarily at Church headquarters in Salt Lake City, Utah.

The scriptures indicate that to serve in a priesthood office, a man must be called of God (Heb. 5:4; A of F 5). Likewise, men and women are called, by prophecy and by the laying on of hands, to serve one another in a variety of settings. No Church calling requires extensive formal training. The Lord outlined the requirements of service when speaking about missionary work: "Faith, hope, charity and love, with an eye single to the glory of God, qualify [members] for the work" (D&C 4:5).

Though not formal in nature, training for leadership is provided in a variety of ways. First, and very important, members are given early and repeated opportunities to serve, thereby learning from experience. Beginning at age twelve, young men and women can serve as teachers for children or as members of class presidencies or of youth activities committees. In addition, teacher development courses and in-service lessons assist teachers, and LEADERSHIP TRAINING meetings instruct leaders of various organizations. Manuals and handbooks outline the responsibilities of individuals serving in different organizations at both ward and STAKE levels.

Lay participation and leadership have several implications for the Church and its members. Part of the mission of the Church is to perfect the Saints (Eph. 4:12), to sponsor growth in individual members. Utilizing volunteer members at all levels of the organization may not ensure peak efficiency, but it does provide the experiences and interactions that will help members progress. Volunteer staffing also means that in most of the callings members work part-time and that this service is in addition to regular employment and other responsibilities. This provides the opportunity for learning to SACRIFICE and to balance commitments. In general, members who serve maintain a high level of commitment to the Church, in part because of their awareness that they are responsible for making a contribution and because they take satisfaction from doing so. Because professional training is not required, lay leadership lessens the sense of hierarchy and increases feelings of UNITY. The children's music leader may have more formal education than the bishop. After being released in a few years, that bishop may serve as children's music leader. Opportunities to serve in a variety of callings and to be served by people in different capacities can increase the sense of BROTHERHOOD and SISTERHOOD shared by Church members.

Many callings require men and women to serve as administrators, doing practical tasks to enable the organization to run smoothly. While the role of administrator is a necessary one, it is not the most vital aspect of leadership, which is to minister. Christ's admonition "Feed my sheep" (John 21:15–17) applies to latter-day DISCIPLESHIP. The characteristics of effective spiritual leadership are those that enable individuals to minister to their brothers and sisters in the gospel, including a willingness to seek and follow the counsel of the Lord as manifested through the HOLY GHOST, on one's own behalf and on behalf of those in need of direction. In addition, leaders are to understand the nature of their STEWARDSHIPS and seek to fulfill their responsibilities in meekness and humility. Good leaders understand their roles as servants to others (Matt. 20:27). Thus, doubly benefited, persons gain from leadership experiences through unselfishly serving in a Christlike way and, through such service, come to know the Lord (Mosiah 5:13).

The gospel teaches that this life is a preparatory state for the life to come and that all people are on a course of ETERNAL PROGRESSION. Lay participation plays an important role in that progression by providing opportunities for service and learning. Church callings offer many opportunities to develop practical skills and spiritual qualities that contribute to continued service and fulfillment throughout life. Individuals may hold many different callings over a period of time and sometimes those callings increase in complexity or scope of influence. However, Latter-day Saints are encouraged not to view such changes as promotions. Callings of greater visibility or apparent influence are of no greater importance than humble and unseen service. The progression that is important, to the individual and to the Lord, is not evidenced by the different callings held by a person, but by the increase in Christlike characteristics developed through years of prayerful and thoughtful service. The potential for personal growth and righteous influence is as great for a nursery leader as for a STAKE PRESIDENT.

Latter-day SCRIPTURES encourage widespread participation, declaring that men and women "should be anxiously engaged in a good cause, [doing] many things of their own free will" (D&C 58:27). King Benjamin in the Book of Mormon taught that "when ye are in the service of your fellow beings ye are only in the service of your

God" (Mosiah 2:17). Though he was the Master in all things, Christ stressed his role as servant, setting an example for others to follow (John 13:15). The emphasis on service as a mode of WORSHIP, as a requirement for becoming like Christ, and as a means of establishing the unity that distinguishes the people of God is a major reason for the commitment of the Church and its members to lay participation and leadership.

PAUL H. THOMPSON

LDS BUSINESS COLLEGE

The LDS Business College, located in Salt Lake City, Utah, is a fully-accredited, two-year institution of higher learning owned by the Church, and operated and partially funded through the CHURCH EDUCATIONAL SYSTEM (CES). The 800-plus students receive training for careers in business and industry.

Its forerunner, the Salt Lake Stake Academy, was founded in 1886 under the direction of Karl G. Maeser. Church leaders originally intended to establish the Academy as the Church's leading institution of higher learning, and the name of the school was changed to LDS College in 1889. When Young University (later the Church University) replaced LDS College as the "flagship" of the educational system of the Church, LDS College declined in significance. However, the Church University was closed in 1894, contributing to the subsequent growth of both LDS College and Brigham Young Academy in Provo, later Brigham Young University (1903). An early emphasis on business courses at LDS College led to the creation of a department of business in 1895. When LDS College closed in 1931, the departments of business and music continued to function separately as the LDS Business College and the McCune School of Music.

After a long period in which Church policy required the college to be financially self-sufficient, CES resumed partial funding in 1986. At that time, a project to upgrade programs and facilities was begun. LDS Business College currently offers one- and two-year programs plus short courses and professional seminars in accounting, marketing/management, computer information systems, office administration, health services, fashion merchandising, and interior design. In all courses of study along with imparting information and developing skills, a major emphasis is placed on the importance of morality and ethics in the business profession.

BIBLIOGRAPHY

Quinn, D. Michael. "The Brief Career of Young University at Salt Lake City." *Utah Historical Quarterly* 41 (1973):69–89.

KENNETH H. BEESLEY

LDS FOUNDATION

The LDS Foundation is the department of The Church of Jesus Christ of Latter-day Saints that encourages and facilitates voluntary charitable contributions to the CHURCH EDUCATIONAL SYSTEM and other charities of the Church.

Although it originated in the BRIGHAM YOUNG UNIVERSITY development office, it now operates under the direction of the PRESIDING BISHOPRIC in serving a fuller Churchwide mission. Since 1972 the Foundation has assisted thousands of donors to contribute to the students and programs of Church institutions.

Support is received both from Church members and from individuals who are not members but who recognize the ability of Church institutions to assist humanity. Funding sources include corporations, private foundations, alumni of Church institutions of higher education, and private individuals.

The Foundation employs full-time professionals who help donors prepare contributions in the form of trusts, estates, planned gifts, and cash donations and accounts for all charitable donations to the Church other than the tithes and offerings of members (see TITHING and FINANCIAL CONTRIBUTIONS). Main offices are in Salt Lake City and Provo, Utah.

BIBLIOGRAPHY

Wilkinson, Ernest L., and Leonard J. Arrington, eds. *Brigham Young University: The First One Hundred Years*, Vol. 3, pp. 537–93. Provo, 1976.

DAVID A. WANAMAKER

LDS STUDENT ASSOCIATION

The LDS Student Association (LDSSA) is an organization which sponsors social, religious, and recreational activities for LDS college students and their friends. The organization provides a framework wherein students have access to all phases of the Church that affect their lives during the week.

The purposes of LDSSA are to help college and university students stay closely affiliated with the Church, succeed in their studies, and achieve a balanced educational-social life while on campus; to motivate LDS students to become a powerful influence for good on the campus; to provide meaningful activities that are consistent with Church standards; and to coordinate Church-related activities for college students. These purposes are accomplished under the direction of the priesthood and in cooperation with the institutes of the CHURCH EDUCATIONAL SYSTEM. These student associations create a sense of belonging, an opportunity for leadership, and an expanded circle of friends who share similar values. For some students, LDSSA is the center of their school experience.

LDSSA was established in 1960, and has expanded to every college campus where there is an LDS institute of religion. In 1990, some 290 LDSSA organizations existed within the United States and Canada in post-secondary institutions, including community colleges, universities, and trade and technical schools. Each campus organization operates under the direction of an assigned local stake president who is also the priesthood leader for all LDS affairs on campus. He presides over an executive committee consisting of a student president, vice president(s), a secretary, and an education adviser, who is usually the director of the institute associated with the campus. The student leaders are called, set apart, and serve under the direction of the priesthood leader. The executive committee is the policymaking body for the local student association.

A student president presides over the chapter LDSSA council. The membership includes representatives of all LDS organizations that function on, or are influenced by, the school. These may include LAMBDA DELTA SIGMA sorority and SIGMA GAMMA CHI fraternity, young single adults, married students, campus stakes or wards, and other interest groups. While each of these groups operates as an independent agency, their activities are correlated through the LDSSA council, which strives to meet needs without undue overlap. The type of institution, geographic location, number of LDS students, and the social, cultural, and academic traditions influence how LDSSA is organized and how it functions to meet local and individual student needs.

At the general level of the Church, a governing board is made up of an executive director, presidents of Sigma Gamma Chi and Lambda Delta Sigma, and representatives of the General Authorities, seminaries, and institutes.

ELAINE ANDERSON CANNON

LEADERSHIP TRAINING

The local and general leaders of The Church of Jesus Christ of Latter-day Saints are lay members; they have not received professional training for the ministry (*see* LAY PARTICIPATION AND LEADERSHIP). Instead, Church members prepare to fulfill their callings by personal scripture study, prayer, inspiration, and righteous living; observing other leaders; assuming informal apprenticeships; studying Church-produced handbooks and manuals; participating in leadership training ("in-service") lessons; and accepting counsel and guidance from their presiding officers and from the General Authorities.

The expectation is that all faithful Latter-day Saints are entitled to the inspiration of the Holy Ghost and personal revelation to aid them in meeting the needs of those they teach, counsel, and serve. Reliance on divine guidance makes personal worthiness and Christlike attributes the most important qualifications for all callings in the Church. Attributes qualifying one for the work are "faith, hope, charity and love, with an eye single to the glory of God, . . . virtue, knowledge, temperance, patience, brotherly kindness, godliness, charity, humility, diligence" (D&C 4:5–6).

There are Church handbooks that outline the duties and activities of every leadership position and state the general principles that should apply. These handbooks are prepared by and revised periodically by appointed committees and reviewed by the Correlation Committee.

All Church officers are responsible for training those who serve under them. Leadership training or instructional meetings are held regularly for every group of leaders. For example, members of the First Presidency and the Quorum of the Twelve meet weekly in the Salt Lake Temple for counsel and instruction. These leaders hold training sessions for other General Authorities, who in turn instruct the STAKE PRESIDENTS and other stake leaders under their jurisdiction. Stake officers periodically conduct training sessions for WARD leaders, who in turn instruct other ward officers under their supervision.

Leaders are given virtual autonomy in the performance of their duties and responsibilities. At the same time, they are charged to follow the principles of the gospel and policies of the Church, and they are enjoined to be mindful of service, gentleness, and humility: "Whosoever will be chief among you, let him be your servant" (Matt. 20:27). They are also charged to avoid unrighteous dominion: "No power or influence can or ought to be maintained . . . [except] by persuasion, by long-suffering, by gentleness and meekness, and by love unfeigned" (D&C 121:39–42).

Emphasis is placed on the need for leaders to learn their duties: "Wherefore, now let every man learn his duty, and to act in the office in which he is appointed, in all diligence. . . . He that learns not his duty and shows himself not approved shall not be counted worthy to stand" (D&C 107:99–100).

Leadership training of LDS boys and girls begins at a young age. As children, they observe their parents and other adults serving in a variety of callings. As youth they are called to serve in presidencies in their Aaronic Priesthood, Young Men, Young Women, and seminary organizations. The attempt is made to have all boys and girls hold some kind of leadership position during their teens. Serving missions places many young men and women into a wide variety of leadership positions (e.g., as senior companions, district leaders, zone leaders, and assistants to the mission president). Virtually all Latter-day Saints are asked to serve in the Church in one way or another. In general, the guidelines for leadership are the same for men and women.

For many callings, an unofficial apprenticeship system is followed. Often, a counselor in a PRESIDENCY or another officer in the respective organization will be called as its next president; similarly, a man trained as an assistant clerk may be called as the next clerk. Sometimes, however, one is appointed to a position to which he has had no training, as the BISHOP or stake president follows the impressions of the Spirit in extending calls to service.

Bishops, Relief Society presidents, and other leaders concerned with the welfare of individuals employ many leadership and organizational skills, such as evaluating alternatives, scheduling, delegating, and motivating others. However, all Church leaders are encouraged to focus principally on people, to feed the sheep in the Lord's flock, to know and love the members, to listen, love, and help with personal needs. "It is the leader's duty . . . to teach the member to love—not the leader or teacher, but the truth of the gospel" (D. McKay, IE 71 [Dec. 1968]:108). To do this, leaders are frequently counseled to seek the spiritual gifts of discernment and wisdom (cf. Luke 12:12; D&C 84:85).

In addition to inspiration, leaders may look to others for training or assistance. A leader may confer with his or her own priesthood leader about a problem or need, especially in one's "stewardship review"—a one-on-one session with one's organizational leader. These personal interviews are customarily held four times a year, "for it is required of the Lord, at the hand of every steward, to render an account of his stewardship, both in time and in eternity" (D&C 72:3).

BIBLIOGRAPHY

Barker, Shade R. *Youth Leading Youth*. Salt Lake City, 1987.

Bennion, Lowell L. *Fundamentals of Leadership*. Salt Lake City, 1965.

Lythgoe, Dennis L. *The Sensitive Leader*. Salt Lake City, 1986.

Maxwell, Neal A. *A More Excellent Way*. Salt Lake City, 1967.

Price, Kendall O., and Kent Lloyd. "New Approaches to Church Executive Leadership: Behavioral Science Perspectives." *Dialogue* 2 (Winter 1967):41–49.

WILLIAM G. DYER

LECTURES ON FAITH

Included under the title "Lectures on Faith" in the 1835 edition of the DOCTRINE AND COVENANTS, these seven "lectures on theology" (HC 2:176) were presented to the School for the Elders in the early winter of 1834–1835 in Kirtland, Ohio. The school was organized to help Church leaders and missionaries "[qualify] themselves as messengers of Jesus Christ, to be ready to do His will in carrying glad tidings to all that would open their eyes, ears, and hearts," by being "more perfectly instructed in the great things of God" (*HC* 2:169–70; *see also* SCHOOLS OF THE PROPHETS).

The lectures address three major themes: "first, faith itself—what it is; secondly, the object on which it rests; and thirdly, the effects which flow from it" (Dahl and Tate, p. 31). The first lecture explains what faith is; the second shows how the knowledge of God first came into the world and traces this knowledge from Adam to Abraham; the third and fourth discuss the necessary and unchanging attributes of God; the fifth deals with the nature of GOD THE FATHER, his son JESUS CHRIST, and the HOLY GHOST; the sixth teaches that acquiring faith unto salvation depends on knowing that one's life is pleasing to God, which knowledge can be obtained only by the willingness to sacrifice all earthly things; and the seventh treats the fruits of faith—perspective, power, and ultimately PERFECTION. In the 1835 edition of the Doctrine and Covenants the seven lectures comprised seventy-four pages. The lectures are organized in numbered paragraphs in which principles are stated and supporting scriptures quoted. Appended to the first five lectures are lists of questions and answers restating the principles discussed. These catechisms are about as long as the lectures themselves.

No clear evidence documents who actually wrote the lectures. Recent authorship studies ascribe the wording of the lectures "mainly to Sidney Rigdon," with Joseph Smith substantially involved, and others perhaps having some influence. Joseph Smith's close involvement with the lectures is suggested by Willard Richards's history, which reports that Joseph was "busily engaged" in November in making "preparations for the School for the Elders, wherein they might be more perfectly instructed in the great things of God" (*HC* 2:169–70). The same source indicates that in January 1835 Joseph was engaged in "preparing the lectures on theology for publication" (*HC* 2:180). From these references and other circumstances it seems evident that the lectures were prepared and published with Joseph Smith's approval (Dahl and Tate, pp. 7–10; 16, n. 8).

Until 1921 the "Lectures on Faith" were printed in almost all the English-language editions of the Doctrine and Covenants, and in many, but not all, non-English editions. An introductory statement in the 1921 edition of the Doctrine and Covenants explains that the lectures were deleted because "they were never presented to nor accepted by the Church as being otherwise than theological lectures or lessons" (*see* DOCTRINE AND COVENANTS EDITIONS). The decision may also have been influenced by what many readers have perceived as conflicts between statements about the Godhead in the fifth lecture and certain later revelations (D&C 130; Dahl and Tate, pp. 16–19). Others have found these conflicts to be more apparent than real and have attempted reconciliations (R. Millet, in Dahl and Tate, pp. 221–40).

The "Lectures on Faith" have been published separately from the Doctrine and Covenants for the LDS community four times: in 1840–1843, by Parley P. Pratt in England; in 1940, by compiler N. B. Lundwall in Salt Lake City; in 1985, by Deseret Book Company, Salt Lake City; and in 1990, by the Religious Studies Center at Brigham Young University. They were published separately twice by SCHISMATIC GROUPS: in 1845–1846, by Sidney RIGDON (in Pittsburgh, soon after he left the Church); and in 1952, by the Reorganized Church of Jesus Christ of Latter Day Saints. The Religious Studies Center publication includes a newly edited version of the lectures designed to make the text more readable. It provides textual comparison charts that identify all textual changes that have occurred in various printings of the lectures from 1835 to 1990. It also contains a summary of historical information, a doctrinal discussion of the topic of each lecture, and an extensive bibliography (Dahl and Tate).

Most members of The Church of Jesus Christ of Latter-day Saints are not acquainted with the text of the "Lectures on Faith," though many may recognize excerpts that are occasionally quoted in speeches and writings of leaders and scholars. A sampling of these quotations as printed in the 1990 edited edition follows:

Lecture One

1. Faith [is] the first principle in revealed religion, and the foundation of all righteousness.
9. Faith is the assurance which men have of the existence of things which they have not seen and . . . the principle of action in all intelligent beings.
12. As faith is the moving cause of all action in temporal concerns, so it is in spiritual.
13. But faith is not only the principle of action, but it is also the principle of power in all intelligent beings, whether in heaven or on earth.

15. The principle of power which existed in the bosom of God, by which he framed the worlds, was faith.

Lecture Two

55. Let us here observe that after any members of the human family are made acquainted with the important fact that there is a God who has created and does uphold all things, the extent of their knowledge respecting his character and glory will depend upon their diligence and faithfulness in seeking after him, until, like Enoch, the brother of Jared, and Moses, they shall obtain faith in God and power with him to behold him face to face.

Lecture Three

2–5. Let us here observe that three things are necessary for any rational and intelligent being to exercise faith in God unto life and salvation. First, the idea that he actually exists; Secondly, a *correct* idea of his character, perfections, and attributes; Thirdly, an actual knowledge that the course of life which one is pursuing is according to His will.

Lecture Four

11. Without the knowledge of all things God would not be able to save any portion of his creatures. For it is the knowledge which he has of all things from the beginning to the end that enables him to give that understanding to his creatures by which they are made partakers of eternal life. And if it were not for the idea existing in the minds of men that God has all knowledge, it would be impossible for them to exercise faith in him.

13. It is also necessary that men should have the idea of the existence of the attribute justice in God in order to exercise faith in him unto life and salvation. For without the idea of the existence of the attribute justice in the Deity, men could not have confidence sufficient to place themselves under his guidance and direction. For they would be filled with fear and doubt lest the Judge of all the earth would not do right, and thus fear or doubt existing in the mind would preclude the possibility of the exercise of faith in him for life and salvation. But when the idea of the existence of the attribute justice in the Deity is fairly planted in the mind, it leaves no room for doubt to get into the heart; and the mind is enabled to cast itself upon the Almighty without fear, and without doubt, and with the most unshaken confidence, believing that the Judge of all the earth will do right.

Lecture Five

2. There are two personages who constitute the great, matchless, governing, and supreme power over all things, by whom all things were created and made. . . . They are the Father and the Son: the Father being a personage of spirit, glory, and power, possessing all per-

fection and fulness. The Son, who was in the bosom of the Father, is a personage of tabernacle, made or fashioned like unto man, being in the form and likeness of man, or rather man was formed after his likeness and in his image. He is also the express image and likeness of the personage of the Father, possessing all the fulness of the Father, or the same fulness with the Father; being begotten of him, and ordained from before the foundation of the world to be a propitiation for the sins of all those who should believe on his name. He is called the Son because of the flesh . . . possessing the same mind with the Father, which mind is the Holy Spirit that bears record of the Father and the Son. These three are one; or, in other words, these three constitute the great, matchless, governing and supreme power over all things.

Q & A 15. Do the Father, Son, and Holy Spirit constitute the Godhead? They do.

Lecture Six

2. It is essential for any person to have an actual knowledge that the course of life which he is pursuing is according to the will of God to enable him to have that confidence in God without which no person can obtain eternal life.

4. Such was and always will be the situation of the Saints of God. Unless they have an actual knowledge that the course they are pursuing is according to the will of God, they will grow weary in their minds and faint.

7. Let us here observe that a religion that does not require the sacrifice of all things never has power sufficient to produce the faith necessary unto life and salvation. For from the first existence of man, the faith necessary unto the enjoyment of life and salvation never could be obtained without the sacrifice of all earthly things. It is through this sacrifice, and this only, that God has ordained that men should enjoy eternal life. And it is through the medium of the sacrifice of all earthly things that men do actually know that they are doing the things that are well pleasing in the sight of God.

12. But those who have not made this sacrifice to God do not know that the course which they pursue is well pleasing in his sight. For whatever may be their belief or their opinion, it is a matter of doubt and uncertainty in their mind; and where doubt and uncertainty are, there faith is not, nor can it be. For doubt and faith do not exist in the same person at the same time. So persons whose minds are under doubts and fears cannot have unshaken confidence, and where unshaken confidence is not, there faith is weak. And where faith is weak, the persons will not be able to contend against all the opposition, tribulations, and afflictions which they will have to encounter in order to be heirs of God and joint-heirs with Christ Jesus. But they will grow weary in their minds, and the adversary will have power over them and destroy them.

Lecture Seven

19. All things which pertain to life and godliness are the effects of faith.

20. When faith comes, it brings its train of attendants with it—apostles, prophets, evangelists, pastors, teachers, gifts, wisdom, knowledge, miracles, healings, tongues, interpretation of tongues, etc. All these appear when faith appears on the earth and disappear when it disappears from the earth. For these are the effects of faith and always have attended and always will attend it. For where faith is, there will the knowledge of God be, also, with all things which pertain thereto: revelations, visions, and dreams, as well as every other necessary thing, so the possessors of faith may be perfected and obtain salvation [Dahl and Tate, pp. 31–104].

The Prophet Joseph SMITH, Oliver COWDERY, Sidney RIGDON, and Frederick G. Williams, who compiled the first edition of the Doctrine and Covenants, said in the "Lectures on Faith" preface "that it contains, in short, the leading items of the religion which we have professed to believe," and "we have . . . endeavored to present *our* belief, though in few words, and when we say this, we humbly trust that it is the faith and principles of this society as a body" (Dahl and Tate, pp. 29–30).

Although it is impossible to evaluate the long-term impact of the lectures on LDS belief and teaching, the process of producing the lectures led early Church leaders to articulate and synthesize some of what they had learned from the revelations of the Restoration with the understanding of the Bible that they inherited from American Christianity. Although these lectures have received limited attention from most Latter-day Saints, others have taken them quite seriously and praised their value. LDS scripturalist and apostle Bruce R. McConkie wrote regarding the lectures, "They were not themselves classed as revelations, but in them is to be found some of the best lesson material ever prepared on the Godhead; on the character, perfections, and attributes of God; on faith, miracles, and sacrifice. They can be studied with great profit by all gospel scholars" (*MD*, p. 439). The 1990 republication of the lectures signals the desire of some LDS scholars to stimulate interest in their historical and doctrinal significance for the Church.

BIBLIOGRAPHY

Dahl, Larry E., and Charles D. Tate, eds. *The Lectures on Faith in Historical Perspective*. Provo, Utah, 1990.

Gentry, Leland H. "What of the Lectures on Faith?" *BYU Studies* 19 (Fall 1978):5–19.

Larsen, Wayne A.; Alvin C. Rencher; and Tim Layton. "Who Wrote the Book of Mormon? An Analysis of Wordprints." *BYU Studies* 20 (Spring 1980):249, app. E ("Lectures on Faith"); rev. repr. in *Book of Mormon Authorship*, ed. Noel B. Reynolds, pp. 183–84. Provo, Utah, 1982.

Phipps, Alan J. "The Lectures on Faith: An Authorship Study." Master's thesis, Brigham Young University, 1977.

Van Wagoner, Richard S.; Steven C. Walker; and Allen D. Roberts. "The 'Lectures on Faith': A Case Study in Decanonization." *Dialogue* 20 (Fall 1987):71–77.

LARRY E. DAHL

LEE, HAROLD B.

Harold Bingham Lee (1899–1973) became the eleventh President of The Church of Jesus Christ of Latter-day Saints on July 7, 1972, and served until his death on December 26, 1973. His 538-day tenure was the shortest service by a Church President in history, despite the fact that at age seventy-three President Lee was the youngest person to hold the office initially in nearly forty years. One of his greatest contributions to the Church, the organization of the correlation program, was made when he was still a member of the QUORUM OF THE TWELVE APOSTLES.

President Lee was born on March 28, 1899, in Clifton, Idaho, to Samuel Marion Lee and Louisa Emiline Bingham. He grew up in impoverished, rural conditions, and from childhood he advanced faster than his peers. He started school a year earlier than was the practice in his farming community because he could already write his name and knew the alphabet. As a young boy, he was large for his age, and when his friends were ordained to the priesthood, he became a deacon also, although he was technically not quite old enough for the honor.

In keeping with this pattern, he began his career in education at a young age. He earned a teaching certificate at Albion State Normal School in Idaho, and at seventeen was appointed to be principal of the one-room Silver Star School at Weston, Idaho, teaching twenty to twenty-five pupils, ranging from first to eighth grade. One year later, he was appointed principal of the larger grade school at Oxford, Idaho, where he served for three winters.

These responsibilities prepared him for his call in 1920 to the Western States Mission, headquartered in Denver, Colorado. After nine months

Twenty-two-year-old Harold B. Lee, seated to the right of mission president John M. Knight, served as president of the Denver Conference of the Western States Mission (photo of the Denver Conference, 1921).

he became conference president, presiding over both missionaries and local Church members in Denver. During his two year missionary service, he baptized forty-five converts to the Church.

President Lee was one of the youngest stake presidents in the Church when at thirty-one, he was set apart as president of Pioneer Stake in Salt Lake City. Within a few years, he was faced with the suffering among stake members brought on by the Great Depression. With his counselors, he struggled to save his people from hunger and financial ruin. His ingenuity in helping them obtain basic necessities led to his appointment by the First Presidency in 1935 to organize a welfare program for the entire Church.

In 1932 President Lee was appointed to fill a vacancy in the Salt Lake City Commission and was assigned to direct the Department of Streets and Public Improvements. A year later, he was elected to the same position. For years Utah citizens urged him to run for the governorship or for the U.S. Senate.

Elder Lee was called as a member of the Quorum of the Twelve Apostles on April 6, 1941. As he looked around the council room in the Salt Lake Temple where the quorum held its meetings, Elder Lee, then forty-two, discovered that every man there was at least twenty years his senior. He thought of himself as a seedling among giant red-

woods, causing his tutor and friend J. Reuben Clark, Jr., a counselor in the First Presidency, to refer affectionately to him as the "Kid."

Early in his apostleship, Elder Lee served on a committee to simplify Church organization and functions. For two decades, he studied the subject and prepared proposals. Finally when the time for implementing them came in the 1960s, the CORRELATION program was introduced, with Lee serving as chairman of the Correlation Committee. Correlation emphasized the family and the home, the connection of auxiliary organizations with the priesthood, simplification of the curriculum, the teaching of the scriptures, and restructuring the Church magazines to serve children, youth, and adults better.

In January 1970, Elder Lee was called to serve as a counselor in the First Presidency while concurrently presiding over the Quorum of the Twelve Apostles. He was called to be PRESIDENT OF THE CHURCH after President Joseph Fielding Smith died on July 2, 1972.

Following a long period when age and illness had prevented the previous Church Presidents from traveling, President Lee moved out among the people. He attended area conferences in England, Mexico, and Germany. President Lee also conscientiously and purposefully devoted much time to address youth conferences, to restore the prophetic image to the young members of the Church. He was the first to visit Israel and Palestine as President of the Church.

President Lee possessed a remarkable candidness about himself and the office of President. He talked openly of his feelings about his calling, allowing people to look into his heart. Sensitive spirituality was his greatest leadership quality. He sought answers to prayers for the Saints and boldly labeled the answers revelations. He was a forceful preacher of the gospel. His sermons were always based upon solid scriptural foundations, and yet the lessons were invariably illustrated with poignant and often tender stories of everyday life, appropriate to the day and its challenges. His counsel was practical; for him the most important commandment was the one a person was having difficulty living at the moment.

President Lee's spirituality resulted partly from his personal struggles. He learned to control a fiery temper and a quick, action-oriented disposition that had earlier in his life offended some. In his later years, President Lee was perceived as

Harold B. Lee (photo 1959) became a member of the Quorum of the Twelve Apostles in 1941 and eleventh President of the Church in 1972.

being more gentle in manner, compassionate, gracious, hospitable, and thoughtful of others. He was always a gentleman, impeccably dressed. At age seventy-four he served as though in the prime of life, with a rich, full voice and characteristic vigor. His sudden death on December 26, 1973, from cardiac and lung failure stunned the Church.

President Lee found great pleasure, and also experienced sorrows, in his family. In 1923 he married Fern Lucinda Tanner, whom he first met in the Western States Mission. To them were born two daughters, Maurine and Helen. They had ten grandchildren. Fern died September 24, 1962, and Maurine died shortly thereafter, making this a difficult period in President Lee's life. He married Freda Johanna (Joan) Jensen, an educator, on June 17, 1963.

In the conference meeting in which he was sustained as President of the Church, President Lee characterized his own life: "At times it seemed as though I, too, was like a rough stone rolling down from a high mountainside, being buffeted and polished, I suppose, by experiences, that I,

too, might overcome and become a polished shaft in the quiver of the Almighty" (*CR*, Oct. 1972, p. 20).

BIBLIOGRAPHY

Arrington, Leonard J. "Harold B. Lee." In, *The Presidents of the Church*, ed. Leonard J. Arrington, pp. 342–71. Salt Lake City, 1986.

Goates, L. Brent. *Harold B. Lee, Prophet and Seer*. Salt Lake City, 1985.

———. *He Changed My Life*. Salt Lake City, 1988.

L. BRENT GOATES

LEGAL AND JUDICIAL HISTORY OF THE CHURCH

The Church of Jesus Christ of Latter-day Saints has usually relied upon the law for protection and has honored its judgments in principle and practice. The one significant exception was its resistance to antipolygamy laws before PLURAL MARRIAGE was discontinued in 1890. Obedience to the law of the land is a tenet of LDS belief (*see* POLITICS: POLITICAL TEACHINGS).

Despite this respect for law, nineteenth-century LDS history includes numerous encounters with the law. Peculiarities of doctrine and practice, accompanied by social cohesion that appeared threatening to outsiders, spawned both PERSECUTION and frequent litigation for the Church and its leaders. In western New York, where the Church had its genesis, and in OHIO, where the Prophet Joseph SMITH moved in 1831, evenhanded justice was generally available in the courts. Three times in New York, Joseph Smith was tried and acquitted for "vagrancy" and "disorderly conduct," the charges stemming largely from religious hostility (*see* SMITH, JOSEPH: LEGAL TRIALS). In Ohio the Prophet and other Church leaders used the courts affirmatively to obtain redress against religious persecution. Near the close of the Ohio period, the failure of the Kirtland Safety Society (*see* KIRTLAND ECONOMY), a lending institution, brought a host of lawsuits against individual Church leaders who had sponsored it. The society was engaged in banking activities without a legal charter and collapsed in the wake of bank failures that swept the nation in 1837. Numerous judgments were obtained against Joseph Smith and other principals, some of which they were unable to pay, but anti-Mormon bias appears not to have been a factor in the decisions.

In Missouri, where the Latter-day Saints began to gather in 1831 and where the Prophet went after fleeing Kirtland in January 1838, the courts were less sympathetic. In 1833–1834 the Saints were forcibly expelled from Jackson County and forced into Clay County, Missouri, by mob violence. After resettling in nearby Caldwell and other Missouri counties, they were again driven from their homes in 1838–1839 by armed mobs abetted by the state militia. In neither instance were they able to obtain judicial redress for loss of life and property. Instead, incident to the expulsion from Caldwell County, Joseph Smith and other Church leaders were arrested as instigators of the violence on charges of larceny, arson, and murder. Most of the prisoners, including the Prophet, were later allowed to escape, and they fled to Illinois. Two who reached trial were acquitted for lack of evidence.

In Illinois, for a time, the Saints had a more favorable experience with the law. Courted by Illinois politicians, they obtained a liberal state charter for their city of Nauvoo. Under the NAUVOO CHARTER the local court consisted of the mayor of Nauvoo and the city aldermen, who were also Church leaders. By ordinance, no legal process issued in any other jurisdiction could be served in Nauvoo except by the city marshal, and then only when countersigned by the mayor. The Nauvoo court made extensive use of the writ of habeas corpus to free persons held under arrest warrants issued by courts outside Nauvoo. Joseph Smith was discharged from arrest several times on writs issued by the Nauvoo court; he also obtained habeas relief from the federal district court in Springfield, Illinois. In June 1844 the Prophet accepted the need to stand trial at Carthage, the county seat, on charges arising from the Nauvoo city council's decision to declare the NAUVOO EXPOSITOR (a newly created opposition newspaper) a nuisance and destroy its printing press. While imprisoned in CARTHAGE JAIL awaiting trial, he and his brother Hyrum were killed by a mob. His accused assassins were tried and acquitted. The Illinois legislature repealed the Nauvoo Charter in January 1845, and in early 1846, threatened by mob violence, the Saints began a westward exodus that ultimately led to Utah.

In Utah, local government officials were usually Church leaders, and the territorial legislature

and local judges were drawn almost exclusively from Church membership. When the UTAH TERRITORY was formally organized in 1850, Brigham YOUNG, President of the Church, was appointed territorial governor. A system of ECCLESIASTICAL COURTS was established alongside the territorial courts, and most disputes between Church members were settled there rather than in the civil courts. Except in special circumstances, suing a brother or sister in a civil court constituted "un-Christianlike conduct," for which a penalty of Church disfellowshipment was often imposed. Nonmembers occasionally took their civil claims to

Pleas for Religious Liberty and the Rights of Conscience.

ARGUMENTS

DELIVERED IN THE

SUPREME COURT OF THE UNITED STATES

April 28, 1886, in three cases of

LORENZO SNOW, PLAINTIFF IN ERROR,

v.

THE UNITED STATES,

On Writs of Error to the Supreme Court of Utah Territory.

By GEORGE TICKNOR CURTIS
AND
FRANKLIN S. RICHARDS.

When we compare the strange respect of mankind for liberty with their strange want of respect for it, we might imagine that a man had an indispensable right to do harm to others, and no right at all to please himself without giving pain to any one.

JOHN STUART MILL.

WASHINGTON, D. C.
GIBSON BROS., PRINTERS AND BOOKBINDERS.
1886.

Two appeals to the U.S. Supreme Court by Lorenzo Snow regarding "cohabitation" were dismissed on jurisdictional or procedural grounds. However, Snow's arguments, published in this 1886 document, maintained that his case turned, not on procedure, but on basic religious freedoms and rights of conscience, as had the earlier case of *Reynolds v. United States*. Courtesy John W. Welch.

Church courts as well. The county probate judge was usually a local Church leader, and probate courts were important in the judicial system because the territorial legislature had given them broad jurisdiction in both criminal and civil matters. Congress abolished the general jurisdiction of the probate courts in 1874 as part of the federal campaign against polygamy.

Tension between the Church and the federal government in Utah appeared almost from the beginning. Several federal appointees to the territorial government in 1851, including two of three federal judges, clashed with Church officials and the territorial legislature and quickly left the territory. Their negative reports to the President of the United States and to the public helped lay the foundation for future misunderstanding. The tension reached crisis proportions in 1857 when U.S. President James Buchanan, acting on false reports of a Mormon rebellion, sent an army of 2,500 men to ensure the authority of a new territorial governor, Alfred Cumming of Georgia (*see* UTAH EXPEDITION). The confrontation was resolved without bloodshed, but it signaled a conflict not to be mitigated until after 1890, when the Church officially discontinued the practice of plural marriage and adopted a less intrusive role in the political and economic life of Utah.

Courts and the law, rather than military force, became the means of enforcing Church capitulation to the mandates of the larger secular society. The U.S. Supreme Court, in *Reynolds v. United States* (98 U.S. 145 [1879]), ruled that the First Amendment right to free exercise of religion did not exempt Mormon polygamists from prosecution under the Morrill Anti-Bigamy Act (1862), and this paved the way for even harsher anti-Mormon legislation (*see* ANTIPOLYGAMY LEGISLATION). Unlawful cohabitation, easier to prove than a bigamous marriage, was made a crime in 1882. Other legislation found constitutional by the courts had the effect of excluding Latter-day Saints from territorial juries, denying them the right to vote or hold public office, denying polygamists' children the right of inheritance, and hindering the immigration of Church members from abroad. Church leaders were repeatedly harassed by vexatious lawsuits. Pressure on the Church climaxed when the U.S. Supreme Court, in *The Late Corporation of the Church of Jesus Christ of Latter-day Saints v. United States* (136 U.S. 1 [1890]), upheld provisions of the 1887 Edmunds-Tucker Act that disin-

A trial in Richfield, Territory of Utah. Frontier justice was often rough and arbitrary by modern standards. Courtesy Nelson Wadsworth.

corporated the Church and authorized confiscation of most of its property. On September 24, 1890, President Wilford WOODRUFF, by revelation, issued the MANIFESTO discontinuing the practice of plural marriage. Although a number of property issues remained, the Manifesto spelled the end of the nineteenth-century legal confrontation between the Church and the U.S. government.

In the twentieth century, the Church has avoided conduct that might bring it into conflict with the law of the land. Since the official discontinuance of plural marriage, no Church-sanctioned practices have posed a direct challenge to current legal norms. Disputes over property, business matters, and personal-injury claims have occasionally led to lawsuits, and legal claims sometimes have arisen out of specialized Church operations, such as LDS Social Services and BRIGHAM YOUNG UNIVERSITY. Church activities outside the United States have also produced occasional lawsuits as the Church has expanded internationally. For the most part, this litigation has had little significance for the central mission of the Church or for issues of RELIGIOUS FREEDOM. Compared with other large institutions in modern society, the Church has not been litigious.

A few court actions affecting the Church have had special significance, however. The decision of the U.S. Supreme Court in *Corporation of the Presiding Bishop of The Church of Jesus Christ of Latter-day Saints et al. v. Amos et al.* (483 U.S. 327 [1987]) was a notable affirmation of religious group rights under the U.S. CONSTITUTION. The suit was brought by former employees of the Church-owned Deseret Gymnasium, Beehive Clothing Mills, and Deseret Industries who were discharged for failing to meet religious qualifications for participation in LDS temple worship. The employees alleged religious discrimination in violation of the Civil Rights Act of 1964. In defense, the Church invoked section 702 of the act, which expressly exempts religious organizations from the statutory prohibition of religious discrimination in employment. The lower court found that the section 702 exemption violated the establishment clause of the First Amendment, a constitutional bar to laws having the purpose or primary effect of advancing religion. The Supreme Court unanimously disagreed, holding the statutory exemption to be a permissible governmental accommodation of religion, at least as to nonprofit activities. The *Amos* decision is an important statement of the right of religious organizations to preserve their institutional integrity by maintaining religious qualifications for employees.

In two other establishment clause cases, Church practices were implicated, although the Church was not a party. *Lanner v. Wimmer* (662 F.2d 1349 [10th Cir. 1981]) was a challenge to the Logan, Utah, school district policy of granting released time and high school credit for students attending weekday LDS seminary classes. The court decided that released time was permissible governmental accommodation of religion but that granting of credit was not. The second case, *Foremaster v. City of St. George* (882 F.2d 1485 [10th Cir. 1989]), involved a citizen's objection to the city's subsidization of exterior lighting of the LDS St. George Temple and to the use of a replica of the temple on the St. George city logo. Although St. George claimed it was using the temple to enhance the city's image, the federal appeals court ruled that the city was thereby endorsing the Church in violation of the constitutional rule against establishment of religion.

The Church and its members have helped to define the statutory rights of religious groups through litigation of tax exemption laws in a number of U.S. and foreign jurisdictions. In England the Church's claim to a statutory property tax exemption for its London Temple was ultimately decided by the House of Lords, the highest court of appeal (*Church of Jesus Christ of Latter-day Saints v. Henning*, 2 All E.R. 733 [1963]). The

Lords denied the exemption because the temple, with its restrictive admission requirements, did not qualify under the statute as a place of "public worship." *Henning* has been frequently cited in British cases interpreting the property tax exemption statute. It was cited but not followed in the New Zealand Supreme Court decision of *Church of Jesus Christ of Latter-day Saints Trust Board v. Waipa County Council* (2 N.Z.L.R. 710 [1980]), in which the court, interpreting a New Zealand statute, granted a property tax exemption to the LDS temple in New Zealand. Property tax exemptions for Church property have also been litigated in a number of U.S. states, most commonly in relation to Church welfare farms. Exemption for such property has been denied by courts in Arizona, Idaho, and Oregon, but upheld in South Carolina. In each case, the outcome has turned on the wording of the statute defining the tax exemption.

Of some practical importance for Church members in the United States was the 1990 decision of the U.S. Supreme Court in *Davis v. United States* (110 S.Ct. 2014 [U.S. 1990]). In an income-tax refund suit brought by parents of two former missionaries, the Court held that funds sent directly to missionaries for their support were not deductible as a charitable contribution. To qualify as a charitable deduction, the funds had to be given to the Church itself or else donated through a trust or other legally enforceable arrangement, for the benefit of the Church.

Occasionally other legal actions have been of interest to the Church, even though the Church was not a party and no Church activities were directly at issue. One highly publicized case was the prosecution of Mark Hofmann for two 1985 Utah murder-bombings and various document FORGERIES. The Church was interested because many of the Hofmann forgeries purported to shed new light on the early history of the Church and had been widely accepted as authentic. After a preliminary hearing, the prosecutors accepted a plea bargain mandating life imprisonment. Another widely noted case indirectly affecting the Church arose from an Idaho court challenge to the Equal Rights Amendment (ERA). The Church had taken a strong official stand against the ERA, and proponents of the amendment claimed that U.S. District Judge Marion J. Callister would be biased on the issue because he was a prominent local Church leader. Judge Callister refused to disqualify himself (*Idaho v. Freeman*, 478 F.Supp. 33

[1979], 507 F.Supp 706 [1981]) and subsequently ruled against the ERA on the major issues. On appeal to the U.S. Supreme Court, the case was dismissed as moot because the time for ratification of the ERA had expired (*National Organization for Women, Inc., et al. v. Idaho et al.*, 459 U.S. 809 [1982]).

BIBLIOGRAPHY

Allen, James B., and Glen M. Leonard. *The Story of the Latter-day Saints*. Salt Lake City, 1976.

Burman, Jennifer Mary. "*Corporation of Presiding Bishop v. Amos*: The Supreme Court and Religious Discrimination by Religious Educational Institutions." *Notre Dame Journal of Law, Ethics and Public Policy* 3 (1988):629–62.

Driggs, Kenneth David. "The Mormon Church-State Confrontation in Nineteenth-Century America." *Journal of Church and State* 30 (1988):273–89.

Firmage, Edwin Brown, and Richard Collin Mangrum. *Zion in the Courts: A Legal History of the Church of Jesus Christ of Latter-day Saints, 1830–1900*. Urbana, Ill., 1988.

ROBERT E. RIGGS

LEHI

The patriarch and prophet Lehi led his family from Jerusalem to the western hemisphere about 600 B.C. and was the progenitor of two major Book of Mormon peoples, the NEPHITES and the LAMANITES. His visions and prophecies were concerned chiefly with the pending destruction of Jerusalem, the mortal ministry of the coming Messiah—including the time of his coming and the prophet who would precede him—and future events among his own descendants in the PROMISED LAND. His words provided spiritual guidance to both lines of his posterity during their mutual history (1 Ne. 1, 8, 10; 2 Ne. 1–3). Several of his prophecies concerning his posterity remain to be fulfilled. Although Lehi wrote much, only portions were preserved in the present Book of Mormon from the records of two of his sons NEPHI₁ and JACOB (cf. 1 Ne. 1:16–17; 19:1; Jacob 2:23–34; 3:5; see Brown).

At the time of his first known vision, Lehi lived near Jerusalem, was familiar with "the learning of the Jews," and possessed "gold and silver, and all manner of riches" (1 Ne. 1:2; 3:16). He knew the Egyptian language and was familiar with desert nomadic life. Some scholars have suggested that Lehi was a merchant or smith with ties to Egypt (*CWHN* 5:34–42; 6:58–92).

His life was dramatically changed when he beheld a "pillar of fire" and "saw and heard much" while praying about the predicted fall of Jerusalem (1 Ne. 1:6). In a vision he saw God and a radiant being—accompanied by twelve others—who gave him a book in which he read of the impending destruction of the city and of "the coming of a Messiah, and also the redemption of the world" (1 Ne. 1:19). Like the speeches of his contemporary JEREMIAH, Lehi's warnings to the people of Jerusalem roused strong opposition. Surrounded by growing hatred, he was warned by God that the people sought his life; therefore, he was to flee with his family, consisting of his wife Sariah, his sons LAMAN, Lemuel, Sam, and Nephi, and his daughters (1 Ne. 1:8–2:5).

Sariah once accused her husband of being a "visionary man" in a hard test of her faith (1 Ne. 5:2). The phrase aptly characterizes Lehi, for he dreamed dreams and saw visions through which God guided his family to the promised land. After fleeing Jerusalem, at divine behest Lehi twice sent his sons back: once to obtain written records (containing the holy scriptures, a record of the Jews from the beginning, the law, prophecies, and genealogical records) needed to preserve the family's history, language and religion; and a second time to invite ISHMAEL and his family—including marriageable daughters—to join the exodus (chaps. 3–4, 7).

Through revelation, Lehi instructed his sons where game could be hunted in the wilderness (16:30–31). In this he was assisted by a curious compasslike object (*see* LIAHONA) that operated according to the faith, diligence, and heed they gave it (16:10, 28–29).

One of Lehi's grandest visions was of the tree of life (1 Ne. 8). In a highly symbolic setting, Lehi saw the prospects for his family members measured against the PLAN OF SALVATION. Nephi had the same vision opened to him and gave details and interpretation to what his father had seen (1 Ne. 11–14). Lehi first saw a man dressed in white who led him through a "dark and dreary waste." After traveling many hours, he prayed for divine help, and found himself in a large field where there grew a tree whose fruit was white and desirable (symbolic of God's love). When he urged his family to come and partake, all did so except Laman and Lemuel. Lehi also saw a path, alongside which ran an iron rod (representing God's word) leading to the tree and extending along the bank of a river. Many people pressing forward to reach the path became lost in a mist of darkness (temptations); some reached the tree and partook, only to become ashamed and fall away; others, following the rod of iron, reached the tree and enjoyed the fruit. On the other side of the river Lehi saw a large building (the PRIDE of the world) whose inhabitants ridiculed those eating the fruit. LDS scholars have pointed out that the features of Lehi's dream are quite at home in the desert in which Lehi was traveling (*CWHN* 6:253–64; cf. Griggs; Welch).

Lehi's prophecies concerned the future redemption of Israel. He spoke of the destruction of Jerusalem (587 B.C.), the taking of the Jews to Babylon, and their subsequent return to Jerusalem. He foretold the mission of JOHN THE BAPTIST and the Messiah's coming, death, and RESURRECTION. Finally, Lehi compared Israel's eventual scattering to "an olive-tree, whose branches should be broken off and . . . scattered upon all the face of the earth" (1 Ne. 10:12; cf. ALLEGORY OF ZENOS).

In the wilderness Sariah bore two sons, Jacob and Joseph (1 Ne. 18:7). Apparently the journey was so difficult that she and Lehi aged substantially. During the transoceanic voyage, their grief—caused by the rebellion of their two eldest sons—brought them close to death (18:17–18).

In the New World, Lehi gathered his family before his death to give them final teachings and blessings (2 Ne. 1–4). He taught them that he had received a great promise regarding his descendants and the land they now possessed. This promise was conditioned upon their righteousness: "Inasmuch as ye shall keep my commandments ye shall prosper in the land; but inasmuch as ye will not keep my commandments ye shall be cut off from my presence" (2 Ne. 1:20; cf. Abr. 2:6).

Lehi addressed his son Jacob about the plan of salvation (2 Ne. 2). Instead of using imagery, he explained it plainly and logically. He taught that while all know good from evil, many have fallen short. However, the Messiah has paid the debt if men and women will accept his help with a contrite spirit. He further explained that a fundamental OPPOSITION in all things exists so that people must choose. He reasoned that, as freedom of choice allowed ADAM and EVE to fall, so it permits each to choose between "liberty and eternal life, through the great Mediator of all men, or to choose

captivity and death, according to the captivity and power of the devil" (2 Ne. 2:27).

Before giving his final blessings to others in the family (2 Ne. 4:3–11), Lehi spoke to Joseph, his youngest (2 Ne. 3), mentioning two other Josephs: JOSEPH who was sold into Egypt, and another, of whom the first Joseph had prophesied—Joseph SMITH. He then set forth Joseph Smith's mission of bringing forth the Book of Mormon, prophesying that a "cry from the dust" would summon Lehi's seed (2 Ne. 3:19–25), and he promised the sons and daughters of Laman and Lemuel, "in the end thy seed shall be blessed" (2 Ne. 4:9).

After Lehi's death, family dissentions forced Nephi and others who believed the revelations of God to separate from the group led by the two oldest brothers, causing a rupture in the colony. While Lehi lived, his family stayed together, a demonstration of his leadership abilities.

[*See also* Book of Mormon: First Book of Nephi.]

BIBLIOGRAPHY

Brown, S. Kent. "Lehi's Personal Record: Quest for a Missing Source." *BYU Studies* 24 (Winter 1984):19–42.

Griggs, C. Wilfred. "The Book of Mormon As an Ancient Book." *BYU Studies* 22 (Summer 1982):259–78.

Nibley, Hugh. *Lehi in the Desert, An Approach to the Book of Mormon,* and *Since Cumorah.* In *CWHN,* Vols. 5–7.

Welch, John W. "The Narrative of Zosimus and the Book of Mormon." *BYU Studies* 22 (Summer 1982):311–32.

S. KENT BROWN
TERRENCE L. SZINK

LEVITICAL PRIESTHOOD

Levitical Priesthood is a rarely used term today, and it is sometimes applied to the AARONIC PRIESTHOOD (Heb. 7:11; D&C 107:1, 6, 10). MOSES and his brother AARON belonged to the tribe of Levi. Latter-day revelation indicates that before Moses died, the Melchizedek Priesthood and the higher law of the gospel were withdrawn from the Israelites because of their disobedience. Aaron and his sons were then given a lesser PRIESTHOOD to administer the lesser LAW OF MOSES as priests in Israel (D&C 84:18–28; Ex. 28:1). To assist Aaron and his sons, other worthy male members of the tribe of Levi were also given authority in the lesser priesthood, although they could not be priests. The keys of that priesthood remained with Aaron and his direct posterity (*MD*, pp. 9–10; Widtsoe, pp. 12–17). Hence, the lesser priesthood was called the Aaronic Priesthood, after Aaron, but is sometimes referred to as the Levitical Priesthood because all those who possessed it in ancient times belonged to the tribe of Levi (Num. 3:12–13). In the strict sense the Levitical Priesthood is a lesser part of the Aaronic Priesthood, held among those who were Levites, but not of the family of Aaron. The Doctrine and Covenants states that "there are, in the church, two priesthoods, namely, the Melchizedek and Aaronic, including the Levitical Priesthood" (D&C 107:1). It is anticipated that in the restoration of all things, the sons of Levi will once again function in the Levitical Priesthood on the earth (Mal. 3:2–3).

BIBLIOGRAPHY

Palmer, Lee A. *Aaronic Priesthood Through the Centuries.* Salt Lake City, 1964.

Widtsoe, John A. *Priesthood and Church Government*, rev. ed. Salt Lake City, 1954.

VERDON W. BALLANTYNE

LIAHONA

The Liahona was a compass or director "prepared . . . by the hand of the Lord" for the Book of Mormon prophet LEHI as he and his family traveled in the wilderness (2 Ne. 5:12). It was shown to the Prophet Joseph SMITH and the Three Witnesses in 1829 along with the Book of Mormon plates (D&C 17:1). The Liahona was also understood as a symbol for the words of Christ: "For just as surely as this [Liahona] did bring our fathers, by following its course, to the promised land, shall the words of Christ, if we follow their course, carry us . . . into a far better land of promise" (Alma 37:45).

Described as a ball made of fine brass and "of curious workmanship," it had two spindles, one pointing the direction Lehi's family should travel (1 Ne. 16:10). The term "Liahona" appears only once in the Book of Mormon (Alma 37:38). It was usually referred to as "the ball" (1 Ne. 16:16, 26-27; etc.), "compass" (1 Ne. 18:12; Alma 37:43-44; etc.), or "director" (Mosiah 1:16; cf. D&C 17:1).

Lehi found the Liahona, provided by the Lord (Alma 37:38), outside of his tent door while camp-

Lehi and His People Discover the Liahona, by Arnold Friberg (1951; oil on canvas, 43″ × 61″), in the South Visitors Center, Temple Square, Salt Lake City. While traveling in the wilderness south of Jerusalem, the Book of Mormon prophet Lehi and his family found the Liahona, a compass or director prepared by the Lord.

ing in the wilderness after leaving Jerusalem (1 Ne. 16:10). As his party traveled through the Arabian desert and across the ocean to the PROMISED LAND, one of the spindles pointed the direction to travel. Moreover, the Liahona was a medium through which God communicated with Lehi's family. Written messages occasionally appeared on it, giving them specific directions (1 Ne. 16:26–29).

The instrument worked according to the faith and obedience of Lehi's family. When they lacked faith or disobeyed, it ceased to function. Passed down from generation to generation along with the sacred records, it was stored with the GOLD PLATES.

Liahona is the title of an international Spanish-language magazine published by the Church.

BIBLIOGRAPHY

Nibley, Hugh. *Since Cumorah*. 2nd ed. *CWHN* 7:251–63. Salt Lake City, 1988.

DOUGLAS KENT LUDLOW

LIAHONA THE ELDERS' JOURNAL

The official publication for all the North American missions of the Church from 1907 to 1945 was *Liahona the Elders' Journal*, published in Independence, Missouri. It arose from the merger of *The Elders' Journal*, published by the Southern States Mission from 1903 to 1907, and *The Liahona*, a multimission publication begun by the Central States Mission in Independence on April 6, 1907. Publishing articles of interest to missionaries, people considering membership in the Church, and general members, it helped build a feeling of community among the Saints scattered throughout the North American missions. Thomas C. Romney's *World Religions in the Light of Mormonism* (1946) grew out of articles he first published in the *Liahona*. In its prime, the journal had nearly 20,000 subscribers.

With several missions publishing their own bulletins after World War I and the *Deseret News* introducing the weekly "Church Section" in 1931, *Liahona* subscriptions continually decreased until it ceased publication in 1945.

[*See also* Liahona.]

BIBLIOGRAPHY

Garr, Arnold K. "A History of *Liahona the Elders' Journal*, A Magazine Published for the Mormon Missions of America, 1903–1945." Ph.D. diss., Brigham Young University, 1986.

ARNOLD K. GARR

LIBERTY JAIL

In 1833 a small jail was constructed in Liberty, the seat of Clay County, Missouri. In 1856 the building was abandoned. After a short tenure as an ice house, it fell into disrepair and was finally demolished near the turn of the century. Today, thousands of Latter-day Saints and other tourists visit the partially reconstructed jail and view it as what the LDS historian B. H. Roberts called a "prison temple" because of a notable prisoner it housed: the Prophet Joseph SMITH languished within its four-foot-thick walls from December 1, 1838 until April 6, 1839. Sharing this incarceration were his brother Hyrum (*see* Hyrum SMITH), who served as his second counselor in the presidency of the Church; Sidney RIGDON, his first counselor; and three other brethren—Lyman Wight, Alexander McRae, and Caleb Baldwin.

They were held on a variety of unsubstantiated charges stemming from the "Mormon War" (*see* MISSOURI CONFLICT), which had culminated in their betrayal and the fall of the LDS settlement of Far West, Missouri, a few weeks earlier. As they awaited trial, they suffered severe privation. Confined to the lower level or dungeon portion of the building, they slept on the straw-strewn stone floor with little light and scant protection from the Missouri winter. Alexander McRae described the food they were served as "very coarse, and so filthy that we could not eat it until we were driven to it by hunger" (*CHC* 1:521). He also recorded that several attempts were made to poison them.

Notwithstanding these trying physical conditions, Joseph Smith's greater suffering seemed to come from his anguish for the thousands of Latter-day Saints, including his own family, who were being driven from the state under the executive order of Governor Lilburn W. Boggs calling for the extermination of the Mormons (*see* EXTERMINATION ORDER). In a very long, two-part letter to the Church, written between March 20 and March 25, Joseph cried out, "O God, where art thou? And where is the pavilion that covereth thy hiding place? How long shall thy hand be stayed, and thine eye, yea thy pure eye, behold from the eternal heavens the wrongs of thy people and of thy servants, and thine ear be penetrated with their cries? Yea, O Lord, how long shall they suffer these wrongs and unlawful oppressions?" (D&C 121:1–3).

In answer, he was told to be of good cheer: "My son, peace be unto thy soul; thine adversity and thine afflictions shall be but a small moment; And then, if thou endure it well, God shall exalt thee on high; thou shalt triumph over all thy foes" (D&C 121:7–8). Some of Joseph Smith's most sublime writings are found in this letter. The counsel of the Lord concerning the proper exercise of priesthood authority (D&C 121:33–46) is among the most quoted latter-day scripture. Excerpts from the letter make up sections 121, 122, and 123 of the DOCTRINE AND COVENANTS.

In early April 1839, the prisoners were moved to Daviess County for trial; and then while being taken to Columbia, Boone County, on yet another change of venue, they learned from their captors that, for a variety of reasons, it would be agreeable to the officials if they would escape. With the aid of their guards, the prisoners hastened to join the exiled Latter-day Saints who were gathering in western Illinois.

Today, a commodious visitors center houses Liberty Jail that, in cutaway form, has been partially rebuilt from the original stones.

BIBLIOGRAPHY

Dyer, Alvin R. *The Refiner's Fire.* Salt Lake City, 1968.

Maxwell, Neal A. *But for a Small Moment.* Salt Lake City, 1986.

Roberts, B. H. *CHC*, chap. 38.

LAWRENCE R. FLAKE

LIBRARIES AND ARCHIVES

Latter-day Saints believe that people should document God's dealings with them. Without sacred records, people are destined to "dwindle and perish in unbelief" (1 Ne. 3:13). In one of the first revelations received after the Church was formally organized, the Prophet Joseph SMITH was instructed that "there shall be a record kept among you" (D&C 21:1). This directive, followed a few years later by instruction "to gather up the libelous

Liberty Jail, in Liberty, Missouri, 1888. On top, Church Historian Andrew Jenson; left Joseph S. Black; right, Edward Stevenson. This building, whose outside dimensions are 22 feet square, held Joseph Smith for six months. It was used as a prison until 1856. Photographer: J. T. Hicks.

publications that are afloat" (D&C 123:4), led to the appointment of a succession of Church historians, each charged with keeping an account of the activities of Joseph Smith, his successors, and the Church in general (*see* RECORD KEEPING). Many of these ongoing chronicles, together with the accumulation of day-to-day records of Church enterprises and the papers of Church members, became the foundation of the modern Church Archives in Salt Lake City. The establishment of such archives was accomplished when there were few historical societies and no national or state archives in the United States.

Andrew Jenson, who served as an Assistant Church Historian for fifty years (1891–1941), tirelessly combed LDS communities and foreign missions for records. He wrote histories of hundreds of local wards, branches, missions, and settlements, and established a system for having local leaders produce manuscript histories (quarterly records of Church events and activities). His efforts greatly enriched the Church Archives, and the records have continued to expand with the donations of papers and diaries of many Church members throughout the years. Because of the growth of the Church, minutes of meetings of local congregations are no longer sent to the Archives, and the Manuscript Histories have been replaced by brief annual historical reports.

In the early days of the Church, leaders sought after texts that demonstrated a broad-based learning and cultural understanding. A library was established in Nauvoo in the Seventies Hall that contained many books, including those brought by missionaries who had served abroad. Although the disposition of the Nauvoo library is not known, the Latter-day Saints continued to maintain libraries after they moved west.

Today the main historical library of the Church is maintained and supervised by the Historical Department of the Church in Salt Lake City. It strives to maintain as complete a collection as possible on the Mormon experience throughout the world. It holds a copy of each edition, in each language, of all official Church publications. It attempts to collect all publications in which the Church or the Latter-day Saints are mentioned. It also holds a significant collection of works published by and about SCHISMATIC GROUPS that follow teachings of Joseph Smith or the Book of Mormon.

Perhaps best known of all the LDS Libraries is the FAMILY HISTORY LIBRARY. With approximately 1.6 million reels of microfilm, containing raw genealogical data and copies of published books, as well as a collection of some 200,000 hardcopy volumes, the Family History Library is used by genealogists throughout the world. Its resources are available through a network of over 1,500 local LDS Family History Centers, each staffed by volunteers. Each library has a catalog of the main library's holdings and may order microfilm copies of most of the collection. In addition, the Church operates libraries/media centers in each of its meetinghouses to support the curriculum of the Church's teaching organizations.

Many college and university libraries, as well as other research institutions, hold significant collections on the Mormons and the Church. BRIGHAM YOUNG UNIVERSITY, Utah State University, and the University of Utah all have important Mormon collections. The other colleges and universities in Utah also hold notable materials, as do the Utah State Historical Society, the Daughters of Utah Pioneers Museum, and the Utah State Archives. Outside of Utah, the Library of Congress in Washington, D.C., has collected much published material on the Latter-day Saints. The National Archives has many records documenting the federal government's involvement with the Mormons and the Utah territory. Research collections at Yale University, the New York Public Library, Princeton University, the University of Michigan, the Historical Office of the REORGANIZED CHURCH OF JESUS CHRIST OF LATTER DAY SAINTS, the University of California at Berkeley, and the Huntington Library (San Marino, California), as well as many other libraries throughout the West, can be resources for scholars searching for LDS materials. Indeed, Mormon-related records may be found in any of the hundreds of archives and manuscript libraries throughout the United States.

BIBLIOGRAPHY

Evans, Max J. "A History of the Public Library Movement in Utah." Master's thesis, Utah State University, 1971.

——, and Ronald G. Watt. "Sources for Western History at the Church of Jesus Christ of Latter-day Saints." *Western Historical Quarterly* 8 (July 1977):303–312.

MAX J. EVANS

LIFE AND DEATH, SPIRITUAL

Unlike physical life and death, over which individuals have little control, spiritual life and death are opposite poles between which a choice is required. Latter-day scripture states that all people "are free to choose liberty and eternal life, through the great Mediator of all men, or to choose captivity and death, according to the captivity and power of the devil" (2 Ne. 2:27). This opposition between life and death is viewed as the fundamental dichotomy of all existence.

At one pole is Jesus Christ, who is described throughout the scriptures as light and life (e.g., John 1:4; 3 Ne. 15:9; D&C 10:70). He is the author both of physical life, as the creator of the earth and its life-sustaining sun (D&C 88:7), and of spiritual life, as the giver of eternal life (3 Ne. 15:9). To choose life is to follow him on a path that leads to freedom and eternal life.

Satan, at the opposite pole, is darkness and death (e.g., Rom. 6:23; Alma 15:17; D&C 24:1). He is the author of temporal death, as the one who enticed Adam and Eve to initiate the Fall, and of spiritual death, as the tempter who induces individuals to separate themselves from God through sin. To choose to follow Satan by succumbing to sin and resisting Christ's entreaties to repent is to choose death.

The freedom to choose effectively between life and death is a result of the redemption of Christ (2 Ne. 2:27), and it is God's work and glory "to bring to pass the immortality and eternal life of man" (Moses 1:39).

The scriptures speak of two SPIRITUAL DEATHS. The first has already come upon all humans as a result of the Fall, separating "all mankind . . . from the presence of the Lord" (Hel. 14:16). The second will be experienced by only those who, having once known Christ, willfully deny him and refuse to repent, being thus "cut off again as to things pertaining to righteousness" (Hel. 14:18). Spiritual death does not mean that a person's spirit literally has died (the spirit is immortal), but that one is in "a state of spiritual alienation from God" (Smith, Vol. 1, p. 45), a death "as to things pertaining unto righteousness" (Alma 12:16; 40:26).

Because little children are not capable of sinning (Moro. 8:10–14), the first spiritual death does not begin for an individual on the earth until the age of ACCOUNTABILITY (eight years of age; D&C 68:27). Generally, as individuals mature they begin to recognize the consequences of their acts and become responsible for them (D&C 18:42). Insofar as they do not harmonize behavior with an understanding of truth and goodness, they create a gulf between themselves and God—that is, spiritual death.

The first step toward overcoming this state was taken, paradoxically, before the Fall occurred: in premortal life. All who have been or will be born on this earth chose both physical and spiritual life when as spirit children of God they chose to follow the Father's plan for earth life. After they reach the age of accountability during earth life, they must again choose.

According to LDS understanding, the choice between spiritual life and death is made at the time of BAPTISM and CONFIRMATION, the ordinances that symbolically reconcile a person to God and initiate a lifetime process of spiritual rebirth. Once baptismal covenants are made and the GIFT OF THE HOLY GHOST is conferred and received, the symbolic rebirth must be made actual through the day-to-day struggle to repent and choose life— Christ and righteousness. The choice is not made once and for all, but many times during a lifetime.

Latter-day Saints do not view righteousness simply as a way to avoid an unpleasant AFTERLIFE and gain a heavenly reward. Following Christ is also the path to happiness in mortal life. As people harmonize their lives with God's laws, they are "blessed in all things, both temporal and spiritual" (Mosiah 2:41). In Christ is life abundant (John 10:10); "if thou wilt enter into life, keep the commandments" (Matt. 19:17).

In an everyday sense, choosing life for the Latter-day Saint should include loving and serving others, praying and studying the words of God daily, sharing knowledge of Christ and his plan with others, speaking the truth, remaining chaste before marriage and faithful after marriage, rearing children with patience and love, and being honest in all things. Enjoying such things constitutes the abundant life.

In the postmortal period, "life" again depends upon Christ's ATONEMENT, which overcomes the first spiritual death by making it possible for all men and women to come into God's presence to be judged. At that point, everyone will be judged worthy of a DEGREE OF GLORY and its quality of life except the SONS OF PERDITION. These individuals suffer the second spiritual death for having committed the unpardonable sin, which is denying Christ in the face of full knowledge and truth (D&C 76:30–38; HC 6:314).

[See also Eternal Life; Lifestyle; Opposition; Spiritual Death.]

BIBLIOGRAPHY

Hunter, Howard W. "The Golden Thread of Choice." Ensign 19 (Nov. 1989):17–18.

Smith, Joseph Fielding. DS, 3 vols.

SUE BERGIN

LIFESTYLE

Early Latter-day Saints, who typically gathered into their own communities and shared cultural and religious concepts and experiences, developed a distinctive lifestyle that helped overcome differences in social class or a variety of geographic and religious backgrounds among members of the fledgling Church. The members, mostly former Protestants from New England, New York, Ohio, eastern Canada, the British Isles, and Scandinavia, had compatible Christian and social values, and a shared purpose in building Zion and in creating the culture of their communities. A century and a half later, with more than seven million Latter-day Saints living throughout the world in a multitude of nations and in varied circumstances, the LDS lifestyle continues to be focused on shared personal beliefs and the desires to progress toward exaltation and to build up the kingdom of God on earth.

In the 1940s, more than a century after the Church was established, its one million members were concentrated largely in the western United States. Converts had tended to migrate to join the main body of the Church, and many Utah Church members and leaders were descended from early pioneers. In these circumstances, a concept of LDS lifestyle became clearly defined. Religious observance and participation in Church programs became almost inseparable from other aspects of life in communities comprised largely of Church members. The people with whom one worshiped at Church were also one's neighbors, schoolmates, and associates at work.

This lifestyle, especially in the LDS towns of the rural Intermountain West, was family-oriented and home- and Church-centered. Self-sufficiency through gardening, canning, sewing, and bread-making, and also commitment to hard work, service, duty, thrift, and education were shared cultural patterns and values. The lifestyle, based upon practical considerations, cultural heritage, and family traditions as well as Church teachings, reflected the influence of pioneer agrarian values, the independence and vigor of western frontiersmanship, and New England Puritanism. This lifestyle pervaded LDS society in North America, and even beyond as the Church began to expand rapidly throughout the world in the decades following World War II.

Today, Latter-day Saints make up groups ranging from entire small towns in Utah and surrounding states to small congregations of only a few individuals or families in other areas and countries. Latter-day Saints are now encouraged to build up the Church in their home areas rather than migrate to Utah. Converts retain national and family traditions while adopting the religion and moral teachings and activities of the Church.

While Latter-day Saints throughout the world feel a common spiritual heritage and devotion to their faith, their daily lives may vary considerably. Nevertheless, there are certain shared patterns of LDS lifestyle practiced throughout the world by faithful members regardless of language or cultural differences. These practices identify the members and families as Latter-day Saints and constitute a bond and similarity of values among members— even where there is significant cultural diversity.

A typical day begins and ends with individual and family prayer, and includes scripture study. The WORD OF WISDOM affects a Latter-day Saint's choices in food and drink. Clothing choices are influenced by teachings on modesty. Gospel teachings influence somewhat the choice of an occupation and affect one's conduct while at work, school, and home. Active Church members feel they should be good examples of Jesus Christ's message to their families and all other associates (see MISSIONS). Members' commitment to TITHING and to making other contributions to the Church affects financial decisions. Latter-day Saints who live their religion avoid profanity and entertainment that advocates or encourages immorality. Many members have CALLINGS requiring significant weekly or even daily commitments of time and energy.

Church members are taught that they should establish valuative priorities in order to avoid becoming overwhelmed by the many demands on their time and energies. Important decisions are often made in consultation with one's spouse, parents, or perhaps the entire family, and with the Lord through prayer (cf. D&C 9:8–9). Since there are more opportunities and obligations available than one person can possibly fulfill, Latter-day Saints try to direct their energies by wise individual choices through thought, prayer, consultation with Church leaders, and personal inspiration through the guidance of the HOLY GHOST. Such resources help them decide what is most important at any given time. The influence of Church culture, especially in the United States, is sufficiently strong that even those who become disaffected and no longer participate in LDS religious activities often continue to describe themselves as "cultural Mormons."

Each close-knit community of Saints may have distinctive characteristics, depending upon the area where such Church members live. Ideally, a Church MEETINGHOUSE, whether in a large or small ward, or involving a scattered few members, becomes a second home, a place where one is accepted, loved, helped, and given the opportunity to participate. A sense of belonging, both to the local ward or branch and to the worldwide community of those who have accepted the name of Christ through baptism and are bound to him by covenant, is the foundation of the spiritual and emotional life, as well as the practical daily life, of the Latter-day Saint.

[See also Civic Duties; Community; Enduring to the End; Family Life; Individuality; Joining the Church; Lay Participation and Leadership; "Peculiar" People; Self-sufficiency.]

JAROLDEEN EDWARDS

LIGHT OF CHRIST

The light of Christ refers to the spiritual power that emanates from God to fill the immensity of space and enlightens every man, woman, and child. Other terms sometimes used to denote this same phenomenon are HOLY SPIRIT, "Spirit of the Lord," and "Spirit of Truth," but it is different from the HOLY GHOST. The scriptures are not always precise in the use of such terminology, and several attempts have been made to describe the various aspects of this important manifestation of God's goodness and being.

Jesus Christ is the light and life of the world (John 8:12; 3 Ne. 15:9). This light is described in the Doctrine and Covenants as "the same light that quickeneth your understandings; which light proceedeth forth from the presence of God to fill the immensity of space—the light which is in all things, which giveth life to all things, which is the law by which all things are governed, even the power of God who sitteth upon his throne, who is in the bosom of eternity, who is in the midst of all things (D&C 88:11–13). B. H. Roberts, a seventy, interpreted this to mean that the light of Christ is a creative power, a governing power, a life-giving power, and an "intelligence-inspiring power" (Roberts, 2:7–8).

This light manifests itself in different ways and degrees. In its "less refined existence," wrote Parley P. Pratt, it is visible as sunlight. It is also the refined "intellectual light of our inward and spiritual organs, by which we reason, discern, judge, compare, comprehend, and remember the subjects within our reach." It is revealed as instinct in animals, reason in man, and vision in the prophets (p. 25).

John A. Widtsoe gave this general description of the emanation of God's power: "God is a per-

sonal being of body—a body limited in extent. He cannot, therefore, at a given moment be personally everywhere. . . . By his power, will and word, [he] is everywhere present. . . . The holy spirit permeates all the things of the universe, material and spiritual" (Widtsoe, pp. 68–69).

Since God possesses a fulness of this power and man only a small portion, it becomes a goal of Latter-day Saints to receive more of this light, which for the faithful grows "brighter and brighter until the perfect day" (D&C 50:24). Initially, this "Spirit giveth light to every man that cometh into the world" (D&C 84:46; see also John 1:9; Moro. 7:16). It equips all people with a basic discernment of good and evil, which Latter-day Saints often equate with conscience. By listening to the promptings of the Spirit one is led via faith and baptism to a higher spiritual blessing called the GIFT OF THE HOLY GHOST, "a greater and higher endowment of the same Spirit which enlightens every man that comes into the world" (C. W. Penrose, JD 23:350). Continued progression will eventually lead to a fulness of the Spirit, or glorification in the CELESTIAL KINGDOM.

BIBLIOGRAPHY

Pratt, Parley P. Key to the Science of Theology. Salt Lake City, 1979.

Roberts, B. H. Seventy's Course in Theology, 5 vols. Salt Lake City, 1907–1912; Vol. 3 on the doctrine of deity and Vol. 5 on divine immanence.

Smith, Joseph Fielding. DS, Vol. 1, pp. 49–54.

Widtsoe, John A. A Rational Theology. Salt Lake City, 1915.

C. KENT DUNFORD

LIGHT AND DARKNESS

Many juxtapositions of light and darkness are identifiable in latter-day scripture. Darkness was apparently the primeval condition (Gen. 1:2; Moses 2:2; Abr. 4:2). Light was introduced by the divine word: "Let there be light: and there was light" (Gen. 1:3; Moses 2:3; Abr. 4:3). It was decreed "good" and was divided from the darkness, light being known as "day" and darkness as "night" (Gen. 1:4–5; Moses 2:4–5; Abr. 4:4–5). The account in Abraham adds that "they (the gods) comprehended the light, for it was bright" (Abr. 4:4; see also GODHEAD; CREATION AND CREATION ACCOUNTS).

This primeval contrast figures importantly in the early literature of Mesopotamia, as in the ancient Sumerian epic of King Gilgamesh, also in various pre-Socratic philosophies in Greece, especially the oppositional philosophy of Heraclitus. These usages, like those of scripture, refer to light and darkness as physical phenomena of the environment to be apprehended by the senses. Other meanings, literal and metaphorical, equate light with life, love, goodness, righteousness, godliness, virtue, blessedness, happiness, freedom, sweetness, guiltlessness, spiritual-mindedness, intelligence, wisdom, heaven-sent revelation, and so on. Darkness is associated with things deathly, devilish, infernal, fallen, carnal, wicked, corrupt, intemperate, mournful, miserable, bitter, fettered, benighted, and ultimately ill-fated.

Despite their opposition, light and darkness may be confused. Isaiah speaks of persons who "put darkness for light, and light for darkness" (Isa. 5:20). Further, individuals may prefer darkness to light. John cites Christ's condemnation of those who love darkness rather than light because their deeds are evil, which may induce hatred of light (John 3:19–20).

The proportion of light to darkness within one's body is considered a function of the eye and, specifically, the orientation of the eye. Jesus said in the SERMON ON THE MOUNT, "The light of the body is the eye; if therefore thine eye be single [here the JST adds "to the glory of God"] thy whole body shall be full of light. But if thine eye be evil, thy whole body shall be full of darkness. If therefore the light that is in thee be darkness, how great is that darkness" (Matt. 6:22–23; cf. JST Matt. 6:22). The Doctrine and Covenants explains, "And if your eye be single to my glory, your whole bodies shall be filled with light, and there shall be no darkness in you; and that body which is filled with light comprehendeth all things" (D&C 88:67). And "the day shall come when you shall comprehend even God, being quickened in him and by him" (D&C 88:49).

Christ is a God-appointed source and giver of light, a revealer of God's glory, a banisher of darkness. The apostle Paul wrote, "For God, who commanded the light to shine out of darkness, hath shined in our hearts, to give the light of the knowledge of the glory of God in the face of Jesus Christ" (2 Cor. 4:6). Peter spoke of Christ who "hath called you out of darkness into his marvellous light" (1 Pet. 2:9). The Book of Mormon describes the epiphanous experience of the Lamanite king Lamoni: "The dark veil of unbelief was being cast away from his mind, and the light which did light up his mind, which was the light of the glory of God, which was a marvelous light of his goodness— yea, this light had infused such joy into his soul, the cloud of darkness having been dispelled, that the light of everlasting life was lit up in his soul" (Alma 19:6; cf. Alma 32:35). In modern revelation Christ has reiterated his divine function as "the light which shineth in darkness," which the darkness cannot comprehend nor extinguish (e.g., D&C 6:21; 88:49).

The interplay of these literal and symbolic meanings is perhaps most graphically portrayed in LDS CHRISTOLOGY. On the occasion of his birth in Bethlehem, there was a miraculous interruption of the conventional twenty-four-hour light-dark cycle in the Western Hemisphere; it was, in essence, a celebration of light. The Book of Mormon records that "There was no darkness in all that night, but it was as light as though it was mid-day. . . . The sun did rise in the morning again, according to its proper order; and they knew that it was the day that the Lord should be born, because of the sign which had been given (3 Ne. 1:15, 19). In contrast, at the crucifixion of Christ and for three consecutive days "there was thick darkness upon all the face of the land, insomuch that the inhabitants thereof who had not fallen could feel the vapor of darkness; and there could be no light" (3 Ne. 8:20–23).

The same vividness of contrast between light and darkness is seen in Joseph Smith's experiences (see FIRST VISION).

BIBLIOGRAPHY

Madsen, Truman G. "Man Illumined." In *To the Glory of God*, pp. 121–133, ed. C. Tate. Salt Lake City, 1972.

HAROLD L. MILLER, JR.

LIGHT-MINDEDNESS

Modern scripture deals with "light-mindedness" as trivializing the sacred or making light of sacred things. Latter-day Saints were admonished early in the history of the Church to "trifle not with sacred things" (D&C 6:12; 8:10). At its worst, light-mindedness may become ridicule and then sacrilege and blasphemy—a deliberate irreverence for the things of God.

Divine personages and their names, temple ceremonies, the priesthood and its ordinances, and the saintly life, for example, are intrinsically holy. Other things are holy by association. The Lord has said, "That which cometh from above is sacred, and must be spoken with care, and by constraint of the Spirit" (D&C 63:64). The Saints were warned against "excess of laughter," "light speeches," and "light-mindedness," yet were taught to worship "with a glad heart and a cheerful countenance" (D&C 59:15; 88:121).

In practice, Latter-day Saints distinguish light-mindedness from lightheartedness; the latter is a triumph of the zestful, joyful spirit of the gospel over life's trials. Such cheerfulness and good humor do not preclude, but rather can complement, spirituality. While imprisoned in Liberty Jail, Joseph SMITH wrote that the things of God are only made known to those who exercise "careful and ponderous and solemn thoughts" (HC 3:295); yet he later spoke of himself as "playful and cheerful" (TPJS, p. 307). The Church counsels against a light-minded attitude toward sacred matters but encourages joyfulness in worship and wholesome pleasure in recreation.

BIBLIOGRAPHY

Kimball, Spencer W. We Should Be a Reverent People (pamphlet), pp. 1–5. Salt Lake City, 1976.

WILLIAM L. FILLMORE

LITERATURE, MORMON WRITERS OF

[This entry is made up of five essays:

Drama

Novels

Personal Essays

Poetry

Short Stories

They discuss the development of Mormon literature after Orson F. Whitney's plea for members of the Church to write wholesome, instructive "Home Literature" (1888) to counter the intrusion of the "faithless" literature of the world that was coming into LDS homes. This charge initiated a creative and didactic impulse which continues

as one vein of LDS literature to the present. The resulting stories, plays, and poems on Mormon themes, promoting LDS values and ideals helped build testimony among the youth of the Church.]

DRAMA

Theater has enjoyed a prominent position in the Church from its earliest days in Nauvoo. Thomas A. Lyne, a prominent Philadelphia actor-manager, joined the Church in Nauvoo, and was encouraged by the Prophet Joseph Smith to produce several popular plays. One such was Pizarro, in which Brigham Young played the role of the High Priest. Lyne lifted Nauvoo theater above the amateur level and entertained the Saints with such plays as Shakespeare's Richard III.

While the Church is justifiably proud of its overall support of the arts, the output of drama by LDS writers has been limited and rather late. The first major attempt at an LDS play written and produced by Latter-day Saints was Orestes Utah Bean's dramatic adaptation of B. H. Roberts' 1889 novel, Corianton, A Nephite Story, as Corianton—An Aztec Romance or The Siren and the Prophet. Between 1902 and 1912, it played from San Francisco to New York.

Other playwrights from Utah have achieved national prominence. Harold Orlob wrote musical comedies such as Listen Lester. Otto Harbach wrote many popular plays, including Madam Sherry; Katinka; No No Nanette; High Jinks; The Silent Witness; and Up in Mable's Room. Edwin Milton Royle achieved a national reputation with Friends; The Squaw Man; The Struggle Everlasting; and These Are My People. Despite the prominence of these playwrights, virtually no Latter-day Saints wrote plays with LDS characters or themes until late in the twentieth century.

The 1960s saw something of a flowering of LDS drama by Latter-day Saints about LDS subjects. Clinton F. Larson published a number of serious poetic dramas, several of which were produced, such as Moroni; Mantle of the Prophet; and Mary of Nazareth. Keith Engar's work includes Right Honorable Saint and Montrose Crossing, a thoughtful look at the exodus from Nauvoo. Doug Stewart and Lex de Azevedo's popular musical Saturday's Warrior and its sequel Starchild proved that LDS audiences would support overtly LDS theater with high production values. Predictably, a spate of musicals followed, including Carol Lynn Pearson's My Turn on Earth. Pearson also wrote

The Order Is Love; *The Dance*; and a one-person show, *Mother Wove the Morning*.

James Arrington is an actor/playwright/producer who has become known among Latter-day Saints through touring his one-person production of *Here's Brother Brigham*. He also wrote and produced *Golden*, a one-person portrayal of the wit and wisdom of J. Golden Kimball (1853–1938), of the Seventy. In his *Farley Family Reunion*, Arrington plays all the characters, both male and female. He also collaborated with Tim Slover to produce another one-person show, *Wilford Woodruff: God's Fisherman*, a portrayal of the early years of an apostle and later President of the Church.

For decades Nathan and Ruth Hale wrote and produced plays in southern California, many of LDS theme and for LDS audiences. Since the mid-1980s they have done their work in Utah. Thomas F. Rogers has written a number of dramatic adaptations of nineteenth-century Russian novels, as well as works he describes as "plays of mitigated conscience," some overtly LDS, including *Huebner*; *Fire in the Bones*; *Reunion*; and *Journey to Golgotha*.

Promising younger LDS playwrights include Orson Scott Card (*Stone Tables*, and *Father, Mother, Mother, and Mom*); Robert Elliot (*Fires of the Mind*); Susan Howe (*Burdens of Earth*); Martin Kelly (*And They Shall Be Gathered*); Reed McColm (*Together Again for the First Time*, and *Holding Patterns*); and Tim Slover (*Dreambuilder* and *Scales*).

BIBLIOGRAPHY

Cracroft, Richard H., and Neal E. Lambert, eds. "Drama." In *A Believing People: Literature of the Latter-day Saints*, pp. 403–488. Provo, Utah, 1974.

ROBERT A. NELSON

NOVELS

Until recently, novels written by Latter-day Saints have tended to fall into two disparate categories: "faithful fiction" of the Home Literature tradition, a didactic and cautionary fiction intended primarily to instruct and inspire the youth of the Church; and "faithless fiction" of the Lost Generation tradition, generally a more sophisticated fiction in which dissenting or expatriate Latter-day Saints examine Church members' lives from a position critical of LDS history and tradition, teachings, leadership, and culture. In recent years, an increasing number of LDS writers have crafted novels that affirm their history and tradition and assert an LDS worldview while achieving artistic sophistication and literary craftsmanship.

HOME LITERATURE TRADITION. From the beginnings of the Church (1830) until after 1888, the Latter-day Saints, like many other nineteenth-century literal-minded American religious groups, manifested a deep distrust of fiction. Church leaders considered fiction simply not true, and counseled the Saints to avoid reading it. During the late 1870s and the 1880s, however, young Latter-day Saints, aware of their provincialism and isolation in the Utah Territory, were attracted by the allure of eastern education, sophistication, and lifestyles, and some began to show impatience, indifference, and even rebellion. To counter this tendency, Orson F. Whitney (1855–1931, ordained an apostle in 1906) delivered a landmark sermon, "Home Literature" (*Contributor* 9 [June 1888]:297–302; reprinted in Cracroft and Lambert, pp. 203–207), calling on Latter-day Saints to produce a pure and powerful literature on LDS themes and to promote LDS values among the youth.

Latter-day Saints began writing "faith promoting stories," a didactic literary impulse which continues today. The most important responses to Whitney, himself the author of an epic poem, *Elias* (1904), came from the prolific writing and editing of Susa Young GATES (1856–1933), young women's leader, daughter and confidante of Brigham Young, and founding mother of the Home Literature movement. She published more than thirty poems, forty-five short stories, and three novels, including *John Stevens' Courtship: A Story of the Echo Canyon War* (serialized in *Contributor*, 16–17 [1895–1896]). B. H. Roberts (1857–1933, set apart as one of the presidents of the Seventy in 1888) published the novel *Corianton: A Nephite Story* (serialized in *Contributor* 10 [1889]), based on Book of Mormon characters and events, and later redacted into a drama that played to large audiences in Utah, Chicago, and New York.

The most important author in this tradition is Nephi Anderson (1865–1923), a son of Norwegian converts to the Church, who published ten novels. The most famous and enduring is *Added Upon* (1898, fifty reprintings). Despite its heavy doctrine, light plot, and wooden characters, the book has inspired spinoffs in such late twentieth-century musicals as *Saturday's Warrior* and *My Turn on Earth*.

Anderson demonstrated better than any other LDS novelist to date the possibilities for fiction in Mormon experience, theology, and worldview. His primary purpose was to teach the restored gospel and promote, through telling an exciting story, "the good, pure, and the elevating" in LDS life and beliefs (*IE* 1 [Jan. 1898]:186–88).

LOST GENERATION. Though Home Literature fell into a tedious pattern until taking on a new life in the 1960s, the rise of "Mormondom's Lost Generation" expatriate writers of "faithless fiction" in the 1930s and 1940s set in motion the second important literary impulse in Mormon literature. Five writers of varying accomplishment best illustrate this direction: Paul Drayton Bailey (b. 1906), Samuel Woolley Taylor (b. 1907), Maurine Whipple (b. 1910), Virginia Sorensen (b. 1912), and Vardis Fisher (1895–1968).

Paul Bailey's *For Time and All Eternity* (1964), though flawed, is his finest novel. Samuel Taylor, a son of an apostle and grandson of a President of the Church, is a noted film scenarist. His *Heaven Knows Why* (1948; 1979) is one of the funniest Mormon novels to date. His histories and biographies *Family Kingdom* (1951), *Nightfall at Nauvoo* (1971), and *The Kingdom or Nothing* (1976) are written with such imaginative license that they must be considered quasifictional. Maurine Whipple's *The Giant Joshua* (1941) is considered by many to be the finest Mormon novel. Though a "flawed masterpiece," it is, according to Eugene England, "the *truest* fiction about the pioneer experience" (p. 148). Another Lost Generation novelist, Virginia Sorensen, grew up in Utah, left the Church, married the novelist Alec Waugh (brother of Evelyn), and established herself as a Newbery Award writer of children's books. She is one of the best novelists produced by the LDS culture, and her finest novel, *The Evening and the Morning*, was published in 1949. An earlier novel, *A Little Lower Than the Angels* (1942), was her most popular.

A major novelist among the Lost Generation writers is Vardis Fisher (1895–1968), whose saga, *Children of God: An American Epic* (1939), won the Harper Prize. Fisher grew up in Annis, Idaho, in a devout LDS family, but became disaffected with the Church in his youth. In *Children of God* he returns to his roots and sweeps across LDS history from the First Vision of Joseph Smith of 1820 through the Manifesto of 1890 (after which he feels the Church lost its vitality). While he claims this was his only Mormon novel, several other works have strong autobiographical threads.

The Lost Generation impulse continues to assert itself in such works as Levi S. Peterson's *The Backslider* (1986), Linda Sillitoe's *Sideways To The Sun* (1987), and Judith Freeman's *The Chinchilla Farm* (1989).

CONTEMPORARY HOME LITERATURE. Writers in the revived Home Literature vein borrow from the popular sentimental and genteel tradition to write "faithful" novels teaching Mormon values and beliefs, but often oversimplify human problems and responses to those problems. Aimed primarily at LDS teenagers and young adults, the formula romance is a major literary tool for teaching them how to cope faithfully in a secularized world. Such works include Shirley Sealy's *Beyond This Moment* (1977), Susan Evans McCloud's *Where the Heart Leads* (1979), and Lee Nelson's multi-volume *The Storm Testament* (1982–1990). To date, the most successful and prolific writers for modern Mormon youth have been Jack Weyland and Blaine and Brenton Yorgason. Blaine Yorgason's *Charlie's Monument* (1976), *The Windwalker*, and *Massacre at Salt Creek* (1979) have been regional best sellers, as has their jointly written *The Bishop's Horse Race* (1979). Jack Weyland's *Charly* (1980) and *Sam* (1981) tell faith-promoting stories replete with hope, optimism, and happy endings.

FAITHFUL REALISM. Many late-twentieth-century Mormon writers are both faithful Latter-day Saints and skilled writers. Foremost among these novelists is Orson Scott Card (b. 1951). A native of Orem, Utah, Card has won the Hugo and the Nebula awards, and has established himself as one of America's foremost science fiction and fantasy writers. His science fiction and fantasy have strong LDS undertones, especially his Alvin Maker series *Seventh Son* (1987), *Red Prophet* (1988), and *Prentice Alvin* (1989). His novel *Saints* (1984) is considered by many to be the best Mormon historical novel written since *The Giant Joshua*.

In the same spirit of faithful realism, a number of well-written novels examining the lives of Latter-day Saints have appeared in the last quarter of the twentieth century: Emma Lou Thayne's *Never Past the Gate* (1975), Robert H. Moss's *Nephite Chronicles* (seven novels to date); Douglas

H. Thayer's *Summer Fire* (1983); Donald R. Marshall's *Zinnie Stokes, Zinnie Stokes* (1984); Randall Hall's *Cory Davidson* (1984); Larry E. Morris's *The Edge of the Reservoir* (1988); Chris Heimerdinger's *Tennis Shoes Among the Nephites* (1989); and Gerald Lund's *The Alliance* (1983) and *The Work and the Glory: A Pillar of Light* (1990). These works are encouraging examples of truthful and faithful fictional treatment of the Latter-day Saints.

BIBLIOGRAPHY

Cracroft, Richard H., and Neal E. Lambert, eds. *A Believing People: Literature of the Latter-day Saints.* Salt Lake City, 1974.

England, G. Eugene. "The Dawning of a Brighter Day: Mormon Literature After 150 Years." *BYU Studies* 22 (Spring 1982):131–60.

Geary, Edward A. "Mormondom's Lost Generation: The Novelists of the 1940s." *BYU Studies* 18 (Fall 1977):89–98.

Hunsaker, Kenneth B. "Mormon Novels." In *A Literary History of the American West,* ed. Thomas J. Lyon et al., pp. 849–61. Fort Worth, Texas, 1987.

RICHARD H. CRACROFT

PERSONAL ESSAYS

Growing out of the LDS sermon and partaking of the honest reflection and responsible self-revelation often characteristic of "personal witness" or "testimony," the personal essay has become an important literary form for LDS writers. As essay writers explore personal experiences, draw lessons from them, and apply these lessons to the concerns of the community, they may describe, analyze, and frequently mitigate criticism, pain, and doubt. The result is often a satisfying piece of literature that can serve to entertain and enlighten, and to influence religious and moral conviction.

The personal essay was not a significant literary vehicle among the early Latter-day Saints. While they did keep diaries and write sermons and personal reminiscences, their group struggle for existence left them little time for interest in examining in writing their Church, their beliefs, or their individual differences. By the middle of the twentieth century, however, the Church was essentially at peace with its external surroundings, and a few LDS writers opened the era of the Mormon personal essay. In 1948, BYU English professor P. A. Christensen published his collection *All in a Teacher's Day*; his second collection, *Of a Number of Things*, appeared in 1962. Virginia Sorensen's landmark work, *Where Nothing Is Long Ago: Memories of a Mormon Childhood*, appeared in 1955. This work, usually thought of as fiction, has the point of view and effect on the reader of a personal essay, and it has influenced many recent LDS writers.

Since 1966, when the first issue of *Dialogue: A Journal of Mormon Thought* appeared, LDS personal essays have been published with increasing regularity, in its columns "From the Pulpit" and (since 1971) "Personal Voices," and in such publications as ENSIGN, *Sunstone, BYU Studies, Exponent II, Utah Holiday, BYU Today, This People,* and *Network.*

By the late 1970s, the Mormon personal essay was in full flower, with, for example, Lowell Bennion's collection *The Things That Matter Most* (1978); President Spencer W. KIMBALL's sermon-essays "The False Gods We Worship" (*Ensign,* June 1976) and "Fundamental Principles to Ponder and Live," popularly known as "Don't Kill the Little Birds" (1978), published in *Ensign*; and Hugh Nibley's distinctive, scholarly-personal essays, *Nibley on the Timely and the Timeless* (1978). In the 1980s, three writers directly influenced by Virginia Sorensen published collections that marked the blossoming of the LDS personal essay as a distinct literary genre: Eugene England (*Dialogues with Myself: Personal Essays on Mormon Experience,* 1984, and *Why the Church Is as True as the Gospel,* 1988), Edward Geary (*Goodbye to Poplarhaven: Recollections of a Utah Boyhood,* 1985), and Mary Lythgoe Bradford (*Leaving Home: Personal Essays,* 1987).

The essays of many others writing during this time were collected by Mary Bradford in *Mormon Women Speak: A Collection of Essays* (1982) and *Personal Voices: A Celebration of Dialogue* (1987). Most recently Don Norton has edited *Approaching Zion,* Volume 9 of *The Collected Works of Hugh Nibley* (1989), and Elouise Bell has published *Only When I Laugh* (1990), a collection growing out of her *Network* columns.

BIBLIOGRAPHY

For important evaluations of the Mormon personal essay, see Clifton Jolley, "Mormons and the Beast: In Defense of the Personal Essay," *Dialogue* 11 (Autumn 1978):137–39; Eugene England, "The Dawning of a Brighter Day: Mormon Literature After 150 Years," *BYU Studies* 22 (Spring 1982):131–60; and Mary Lythgoe Bradford, "I, Eye, Aye: A Personal Essay on Personal Essays," *Dialogue* 11 (Summer 1978):81–89, reprinted in her *Personal Voices: A Celebration of Dialogue* (Salt Lake City, 1987).

DONLU DEWITT THAYER

POETRY

Poetry may well be the most essential art. Its uses are numerous. It is most needed in times of urgency and danger, if one may take the quality and amount of poetry written, for example, in times of war as an indication. At such a time the need for poetry is social and communal; it is needed to exhort, to encourage, to unite, to comfort, to state once more those qualities and beliefs which are fundamental to the community from which it springs.

Such benefits were needed from the poems written by early Latter-day Saints. Their community was endangered, its beliefs were called into question, and its leaders were martyred; all this was material for poetry that was confirmatory and, in a sense, repetitive. It repeated, mostly in the form of hymns, and as simply and directly as possible, the truths accepted by the faithful. Such poetry is so much the result of the known situation that it is almost anonymous, balladlike.

Later, when some permanence seemed probable to the community, Mormon poetry became didactic. Its use was still communal, as distinct from the personal use of poetry today—largely a matter between poet and reader—and its purpose was to instruct and to retell, in narrative form, those stories which were peculiar to the traditions of the Church.

There was little room for experiment in such work, nor was there much opportunity for individual lyric poetry in what Orson F. Whitney called Home Literature. It was produced for the promotion and continuation of faith, and necessarily designed for an LDS audience. This is a restriction which contemporary poets have felt increasingly less necessary. As Latter-day Saints have moved away from Utah in larger numbers, established viable communities in many places, and taken more and more positions of authority and importance in the world at large, they have seen more clearly the place they may assume in the general community. This has been at once a liberation and a source of individual concern to poets. That concern is often seen in contemporary poetry. The men and women who write that poetry are very much aware

of what is happening in their art, are sophisticated and adventurous in technique, and completely modern in outlook, yet still need to hold to the clear values and confident virtues of the Church, a complex undertaking in a world and time as doubting as today's.

This has meant that, like the poetry of the English-speaking world in general, a great deal of contemporary LDS poetry is personal, lyric poetry, even if the subject matter is often purely Mormon, or at least clearly composed from an LDS point of view. At the same time, the range of such poetry is much wider. An LDS poet—indeed, an artist in any medium—feels little need now to teach, to speak to an entirely LDS audience, or to use the traditional LDS environments of farm and home.

All this may be clearly recognized in *Harvest*, an anthology of contemporary LDS poetry edited by Eugene England and Dennis Clark. Both men, themselves poets, had realized the importance of changes taking place in LDS poetry as they read the contributions of men and women to such journals as *BYU Studies*, *Dialogue*, *Literature and Belief*, and *Sunstone*.

Naturally, the poets themselves were the first to realize the direction in which their work was heading. Perhaps the first of them to devote his life to poetry, to dedicate serious and full-time effort to his craft, was Clinton F. Larson. Versatile, prolific, and skillful, and with a curious and searching mind, he shows a range of form and material that is unusually wide. Larson is a poet with a distinctive voice, and his influence is less specific than general; he may well have demonstrated to younger writers that the boundaries of their meditations extend farther than they thought, and that their images can be drawn from all aspects of life.

This is not to say that the great subjects of LDS poetry have vanished, but they have changed subtly. *Harvest* contains a surprising number of poems in which an idealized version of the old, simple, pastoral life of earlier years is celebrated. Generally, until the very youngest generation of poets, those who may live in New York or Los Angeles, who have traveled in Peru or China, the imagery is largely drawn from Utah, Idaho or Wyoming. And many poems continue to deal with parents and children, with homes and families. *Harvest* even contains a short section called "Hymns and Songs," which suggests that the very earliest strain of Mormon poetry still exists, old-fashioned as it seems, to call the community to share belief and sing together.

There are, of course, exotic exceptions to this general statement. Arthur Henry King, who came late and from England to the Church, offers quite other traditional virtues in his verse; R. A. Christmas speaks in a wry and memorably different voice. Loretta Randall Sharp has written some stanzas so beautiful and personal ("At Utah Lake" is such a gem) that they transcend such blanket generalizations as this article necessarily contains. The few poems of Bruce Jorgensen are of so steely a delicacy that one could wish from him a more fruitful dedication to his craft.

This last is a concern that might be examined seriously. Of all Utah poets, it may be that May Swenson is best known, and there is little doubt that she has spent her life as a serious poet. It may be time for other Latter-day Saints who write poetry to become poets in effect. It may even be happening. Donnell Hunter, whose verse carries the benign influence of William Stafford, publishes his work and that of others from his little Honeybrook Press in Rexburg, Idaho. Michael R. Collings, a poet represented in *Sunstone* and elsewhere, is about to start *Zarahemla: a magazine of poetry*, which should be a most helpful addition to those LDS journals which already publish poetry. But perhaps most hopeful of all, the very youngest LDS poets are beginning to see their work in national periodicals. In their twenties, most of them pursuing degrees in universities outside Utah or employed in various professions in many states and cities, these LDS poets are putting their poems alongside those of other young writers. Mormon poetry is finding a wider audience.

BIBLIOGRAPHY

Cracroft, Richard H., and Neal E. Lambert, eds. *A Believing People: Literature of the Latter-day Saints.* Salt Lake City, 1974.

England, G. Eugene, and Dennis M. Clark, eds. *Harvest: Contemporary Mormon Poems.* Salt Lake City, 1989.

Lambert, Neal E., and Richard H. Cracroft, eds. *Twenty-two Young Mormon Writers.* Provo, Utah, 1975.

LESLIE NORRIS

SHORT STORIES

The history of the Mormon short story begins with the quasi-official encouragement of all forms of LDS literary expression signaled in Orson F. Whitney's 1888 address "Home Literature." The first generation of "Home Literature" story writers included Susa Young GATES, Augusta Joyce Crocheron, B. H. Roberts, and, most prominently, Josephine Spencer and Nephi Anderson. In "A Plea for Fiction" and "Purpose in Fiction" (1898), Anderson urged the didactic value of "the good, pure, elevating kind" of fiction with "a message to deliver." Anderson's work displays some traits of good "regional" or "local color" fiction, yet none of it is generally read or remembered today. Spencer's stories, also moralistic, are less heavy-handed than Anderson's (characters, not the author, deliver the "message"), and show more skill and attention to craft; seven appeared in her book *The Senator from Utah* (1895).

Into the 1940s, Mormon writers seem to have worked in isolation from the high artistry of Continental, English, and American short-story writers from the 1890s through the 1920s. Despite a leavening of entertainment and humor after 1920, LDS stories largely remained parochial; didactic; thematically and experientially superficial, unreal, or idealized; prescriptive; and artistically weak. One exception might be the stories of Ora Pate Stewart gathered in *Buttermilk and Bran* (1964) but written earlier.

In the 1940s and 1950s there emerged a generation of Mormon "expatriate" writers, born between 1900 and 1930, well read in the Continental and Anglo-American traditions, sometimes trained in literary criticism, and unable to subscribe to the didacticism of "Home Literature." Their stories, though often nourished on the experience and values of growing up in Mormon country, were largely "lost" to an LDS audience. Ray B. West's "The Last of the Grizzly Bears" (1950), Richard Young Thurman's "Not Another Word" (1957), and Jarvis Thurston's "The Cross" (1959) show varying tensions between rejection and nostalgia. Wayne Carver's "With Voice of Joy and Praise" (1965) displays a rich sense of Utah folk culture, especially its humor and its speech. The youngest expatriate, David L. Wright, died before his promise could come to full fruition, but he did publish five stories in literary quarterlies in 1960 and 1961 and saw successful productions of plays based on two of the best, "Speak Ye Tenderly of Kings" (1960) and "A Summer in the Country" (1960, 1976). The oldest expatriate, the novelist Virginia Sorensen, published *Where Nothing Is Long Ago* (1963), likely to remain one of the best collections of Mormon short stories. Finely written, richly nostalgic, yet self-questioning, Sorensen's stories offer insights into the "complex fate" of a Mormon writer removed from, yet deeply attached to, the LDS home place and the community that settled and still inhabits it.

The mid-1960s brought a major expansion in the Mormon short story with the inception of *Dialogue* (1966–) and the revitalization of *BYU Studies* (1967–), which opened outlets to LDS writers in both the "unsponsored" sector and the sponsored. Encouraged by anthologies such as *A Believing People* (1974, 1979), *22 Young Mormon Writers* (1975), the *LDSF* series (1982–), and *Greening Wheat* (1983); by awards and readings offered by the Association for Mormon Letters and other groups; by periodicals such as *Exponent II* (1974–), *Mountainwest* (1975–1981), and *Sunstone* (1975–), and by self-published books and the establishment of independent presses such as Signature Books, the expansion continued exponentially through the 1970s and 1980s. A new generation of writers, most born between 1930 and 1950, is still writing mainly, but not exclusively, for and about Latter-day Saints; yet they are no longer limited by didactic aesthetics, and are thoroughly committed to high standards of literary craft, complexity, and seriousness.

Donald R. Marshall's *The Rummage Sale* (1972, 1985) and *Frost in the Orchard* (1977, 1985) include some of the most various, experimental, multivoiced, and comical Mormon short fiction. "The Sound of Drums" (1972) and "The Wheelbarrow" (1977) examine the "good Mormon" as a sensitive, conscious, committed person who must find a way to love and live in a world that is often obtuse and vulgar.

Douglas H. Thayer's protagonists in *Under the Cottonwoods* (1977, 1983) are driven into perplexity by "perfection"; his craft is severe, his tone seldom humorous, his style deliberate, chiseled, almost mannered. Earlier stories draw on Romantic lyric form in their meditative strategies, and reveal a tense subsurface engagement between Romantic poetics and LDS theology. Thayer's later-published stories in *Mr. Wahlquist in Yellowstone* (1989) explore the seductive American myths of "wilderness" from a perspective implicit in LDS theology.

Gladys Clark Farmer's *Elders and Sisters* (1977) and Bela Petsco's *Nothing Very Important and Other Stories* (1979), both integrated collections, almost novels, deal with the special world of Mormon missionaries in France and in southern California and Arizona. Petsco's book was the first entirely non-Utah-Idaho Mormon fiction.

Eileen Gibbons Kump's *Bread and Milk and Other Stories* (1979) employs a chronological sequence to portray the life of one woman, Amy Taylor Gordon, from age eight (the time of the Edmunds-Tucker Act) to her death many years later, in what may be the finest LDS historical stories yet written. Treating isolation and grace in a peculiarly Mormon way, her stories also suggest that though women submit to masculine will in ways that divide men from women and children from fathers ("Four and Twenty Blackbirds"), they are often humorously resilient ("Sayso or Sense").

Lewis Horne, in Saskatchewan, is geographically expatriated from Utah Mormondom but remains in touch with Latter-day Saint community and family life, as is shown in "Thor Thorsen's Book of Days" (1970). His sometimes "open-ended" stories have appeared widely in American and Canadian literary quarterlies since 1968, have been often cited, and have twice been included in the annual *Best American Short Stories*.

Karen Rosenbaum also experiments with "openness." Her agile, comic voice sounds in "The Joys of Mormonish" (1977) and "Hit the Frolicking, Rippling Brooks" (1978), but she also examines the erosion of simple faith in more somber tones in "The Mustard Seed" (1964) and "Low Tide" (1980).

Stories like those of the older "Home Literature" continue to flourish, represented by Shirley Sealy's professedly didactic *Beauty in Being* (1980) and Jack Weyland's witty teenage and young-adult situation- or problem-comedy stories in the Church youth magazine, *New Era*, collected in *First Day of Forever* (1980), *Punch and Cookies Forever* (1981), and *A Small Light in the Darkness* (1987). Lynne Larson's half-dozen Wyoming stories in *Mountainwest* (1976–1978), straddle the categories of "popular" and "literary"; her best may be "Original Sin" (1978; reprinted in *Greening Wheat*).

Harold K. Moon's collection *Possible Dreams* (1982) is literarily playful, a fact underscored in an introduction and a preface by the author and by the Bivilswiltz, the fantastic protagonist of several fables in the book.

Levi Peterson's *Canyons of Grace* (1982) was the first book of Mormon short stories since Sorensen's to be published outside the LDS circuit; and, in the title story and "The Confessions of Augustine" and "Road to Damascus," the first to deal overtly, in dramatic action, with significant tensions in Mormon theology, especially that between the "obduracy" of "inchoate matter" and the order imposed by divine will. His second collection, *Night Soil* (1990), gives wider play to the rambunctiously comic, folkloric, and tenderly humane elements in Peterson's imagination.

Marden J. Clark's *Morgan Triumphs* (1984) and Sharon M. Hawkinson's *Only Strangers Travel* (1984) are both linked series of stories in the Mormon tradition of "personal history"; like Sorensen, both mix memoir, personal essay, and short story.

Darrell Spencer's *A Woman Packing a Pistol* (1987) shows few overt signs of being the work of a Mormon writer; yet his mostly secular characters "live with the acts of God." Spencer writes postmodern, "open" stories to explore a moral universe that is radically open to personal agency and decision, full of possibility and surprise.

Judith Freeman's well-received *Family Attractions* (1988) includes four Mormon stories: "The Death of a Mormon Elder," "Pretend We're French," "Going Out to Sea," and "Clearfield."

In 1989 and 1990, several excellent collections of Mormon short stories were published: Douglas Thayer's *Mr. Wahlquist in Yellowstone* (1989), Neal Chandler's *Benediction* (1989), Linda Sillitoe's *Windows on the Sea* (1989), Pauline Mortensen's *Back Before the World Turned Nasty* (1989), Phyllis Barber's *The School of Love* (1990), Orson Scott Card's *The Folk of the Fringe* (1990), Levi Peterson's *Night Soil* (1990), and Michael Fillerup's *Visions* (1990).

Including many other writers who have not yet published collections, the Mormon expansion of the short story parallels and is part of a larger American and international renaissance of the genre, though so far it derives more from that renaissance than it contributes to it. Younger LDS writers seem simultaneously critical and loyal in their criticism; they find in Mormonism a sufficiently spacious world, and they locate the conflicts of their stories within that world, even within the parameters of their theology. This source of strength in their fiction makes them valuable, if sometimes disquieting, to the community within which they have chosen to remain.

BIBLIOGRAPHY

Cracroft, Richard H., and Neal E. Lambert. "Fiction." In *A Believing People: Literature of the Latter-day Saints*, pp. 255–306. Provo, Utah, 1974, 1979.

BRUCE W. JORGENSEN

LORD

See: God: Names and Titles; Jesus Christ: Names and Titles of

LORD'S PRAYER

Latter-day Saints regard the Lord's Prayer, which appears twice in the New Testament and once in the Book of Mormon (Matt. 6:9–13; Luke 11:2–4; 3 Ne. 13:9–13), as a guide for all prayer, whether public or private. The three versions teach similar principles but are not identical. The JOSEPH SMITH TRANSLATION (JST) of the Bible clarifies some phrases in the biblical texts.

Luke gives a version of the Lord's Prayer after Jesus was asked by his disciples to "teach us to pray" (Luke 11:1). In the sermons recounted in Matthew and in the Book of Mormon, Jesus introduces the prayer by first cautioning his listeners to avoid "vain repetitions" and to pray "after this manner," indicating that the prayer is meant as a pattern.

All versions of the Lord's Prayer open with the salutation "Our Father," which implies a close and abiding relationship between God and human beings, his spirit children, and sets the pattern of addressing prayers to God the Father.

The salutation is followed by the phrase "hallowed be thy name," which exemplifies respect and a worshipful attitude appropriate to the holy nature of prayer. Then, after expressing hope for the divine kingdom to come, the Savior submits his will to God's with the words "thy will be done in earth, as it is in heaven" (Matt. 6:10), exemplifying another important component of prayer.

After setting a proper context for prayer, Christ makes his first request—for "daily bread." When regarded as a model for prayer, this phrase can be seen as supplication for both temporal necessities and spiritual food. Christ's second request, that God "forgive us our debts, as we forgive our debtors" (Matt. 6:12 and 3 Ne. 13:11), appears in Luke as "forgive us our sins; for we also forgive every one that is indebted to us" (Luke 11:4). An important element in personal prayer is acknowledging and asking forgiveness for one's sins, but always in conjunction with forgiving the offenses of others (cf. D&C 64:10).

The texts then include a phrase that is perhaps the most difficult to understand in most common translations of the Lord's Prayer—"lead us not into temptation," which could be read to imply that God might influence toward evil unless implored to do otherwise. This problem is resolved in the JST, which reads, "And suffer us not to be led into temptation" (JST Matt. 6:14; cf. the Syriac translation; see also James 1:13). Christ's purpose appears to be to inspire mortals to ask daily for God's help as they try to resist evil and to live purely.

In closing the prayer, Christ again acknowledges God's power and glory and then ends with "Amen," as do all LDS prayers. (On the long ending of the Lord's Prayer, cf. Welch, 1990, pp. 157–60).

By praying with their personal heartfelt feelings "after this manner," rather than reciting the Lord's Prayer as a memorized piece, Latter-day Saints seek to find true communion with God the Father, through his Son Jesus Christ.

[See also Sermon on the Mount.]

BIBLIOGRAPHY

Welch, John W. "The Lord's Prayers." Ensign 6 (Jan. 1976): 14–17.

———. The Sermon at the Temple and the Sermon on the Mount. Salt Lake City, 1990.

SUE BERGIN

LORD'S SUPPER

See: Sacrament

LOST SCRIPTURE

Latter-day Saints recognize that many ancient scriptures have been lost. Some contents of these sacred records are known, but much remains obscure. Latter-day Saints look forward to a time when all things revealed from God will be restored and made known again.

The Bible is of inestimable worth; nevertheless, it testifies to its own incompleteness. It mentions sacred works that are no longer available (Josh. 10:13; 1 Kgs. 11:41; 1 Chr. 29:29; Eph. 3:3; Col. 4:16; Jude 1:14–15), and it refers to Old Testament prophecies presently missing (see Matt. 2:23; John 8:56).

Likewise, the Book of Mormon identifies several prophetic writings absent from the Bible, such as words of ZENOS, ZENOCK, NEUM, EZIAS, and JOSEPH OF EGYPT (see also HC 2:236), which were found on the brass PLATES. Their prophecies dealt with the future of Israel and the coming of Jesus Christ. Nephi's brother Jacob stated that all the prophets had testified of Jesus Christ (Jacob 4:4–6; 7:9–11; cf. John 5:39), a fact not readily apparent in the Old Testament as it now exists. The Prophet Joseph SMITH wrote in 1832, "From sundry revelations which had been received, it was apparent that many important points touching the salvation of man, had been taken from the Bible, or lost before it was compiled" (HC 1:245; cf. 1 Ne. 13:26–42). Remedying this, in part, was one of the purposes of the JOSEPH SMITH TRANSLATION OF THE BIBLE (JST).

The Doctrine and Covenants speaks of lost writings of JOHN (D&C 7:1–8; 93:5–18) and refers to a law of dealing with enemies given by God to Abraham, Isaac, Jacob, and Joseph, but not found in the Bible (D&C 98:28–37); the Pearl of Great Price restores a portion of the writings of Abraham, Moses, Enoch, and Adam, especially about the Creation and early history of God's dealings with man. Enoch mentioned an ancient BOOK OF REMEMBRANCE and a genealogy of Adam (Moses 6:5–8, 46), along with now missing blessings and prophecies uttered by Adam and his descendants at the valley of ADAM-ONDI-AHMAN before Adam's death (D&C 107:53–57).

Many Book of Mormon source materials are not now accessible. The GOLD PLATES given to Joseph Smith in 1827 mention a record of LEHI (1 Ne. 1:16–17) and other writings of Nephi₁ (1 Ne. 9:1–6). JACOB, MORMON, and MORONI₂ note that they could scarcely include "the hundredth part" of what could have been written (Jacob 3:13; 3 Ne. 5:8; Ether 15:33). The Lord often commanded the Nephite record keepers not to write or circulate certain things (see 1 Ne. 14:25–28; 3 Ne. 26:11–12), and Joseph Smith was similarly commanded by the Lord not to translate a large sealed portion of the gold plates (D&C 17:6; see also Ether 4:1–7; 5:1–6).

In another, broader sense, much "scripture" was never written down by mortals at all. Whatever God's authorized servants say "when moved upon by the Holy Ghost" is scripture (D&C 68:1–6). If all the acts and words of the Savior had been recorded, John said "the world itself could not contain the books that should be written" (John 20:30–31; 21:25). Also not in written form are myriads of inspired utterances of prophets and apostles and of other men and women filled with the Holy Ghost. Such scripture is not lost to God. "All things are written by the Father," Jesus said (3 Ne. 27:26), and testimonies spoken on earth are recorded in heaven for the angels to look upon (D&C 62:3) and will be recalled at some future day.

BIBLIOGRAPHY

Matthews, Robert J. *A Bible! A Bible!* Salt Lake City, 1990.

McConkie, Joseph Fielding. *Prophets and Prophecy*, pp. 141–54. Salt Lake City, 1988.

ROBERT A. CLOWARD

LOTTERIES

See: Gambling

LOVE

The "pure love of Christ" (Moro. 7:47) is the foundation of true religion. A lawyer once asked Jesus Christ, "Master, which is the great commandment in the law? Jesus said unto him, Thou shalt love the Lord thy God with all thy heart, and with all thy soul, and with all thy mind. This is the first and great commandment. And the second is like unto it. Thou shalt love thy neighbour as thyself. On these two commandments hang all the law and the prophets" (Matt. 22:36–40; cf. Gal. 5:14).

Love is manifest in its perfection in God the Eternal Father and his son Jesus Christ. John declared that "God is love" (1 Jn. 4:8). His love has no portions and no bounds; love given to one does not diminish that given to another. The Father desires to share with his children all that he has—all truth, power, and goodness. He is the Father of all human SPIRITS. He placed human beings upon this earth and provided the plan through which his Only Begotten Son makes it possible for individuals to come back into his presence and receive EXALTATION and ETERNAL LIFE. "For God so loved the world, that he gave his only begotten Son, that whosoever believeth in him should not perish, but have everlasting life" (John 3:16).

Jesus Christ also loved the Father's children, his brothers and sisters, so much that he freely shed his blood and laid down his life to atone for their sins and bring about a universal RESURRECTION. "Greater love hath no man than this, that a man lay down his life for his friends" (John 15:13).

While his death and ATONEMENT were the supreme manifestations of love, his actions during his life in the Holy Land and during his post-resurrection ministry among the NEPHITES in the Western Hemisphere also exemplify this principle. His heart was filled with compassion for the poor and for all who suffered. He healed the sick, raised the dead, fed the hungry, and blessed the children. Then, when his life was ending and he hung in agony on the cross, he besought God to forgive the soldiers who crucified him (JST Luke 23:34[35]).

Within his example are found all the characteristics of what is called in the scriptures charity or "the pure love of Christ" (Moro. 7:47). Love is kind and long-suffering, humble, "seeketh not her own, is not easily provoked, thinketh no evil, and rejoiceth not in iniquity but rejoiceth in the truth, beareth all things, believeth all things, hopeth all things, endureth all things" (Moro. 7:45; cf. 1 Cor. 13:4–7).

To his disciples Jesus said, "A new commandment I give unto you, that ye love one another; as I have loved you, that ye also love one another. By this shall all men know that ye are my disciples, if ye have love one to another" (John 13:34–35).

Human beings show their love to God through obedience to his COMMANDMENTS (2 Jn. 6). Love of God, according to the prophet NEPHI₁ of the Book of Mormon, is "most desirable above all things" (1 Ne. 11:22). According to King BENJAMIN, another Book of Mormon leader, to gain the love of God individuals must put off the natural man, learn to listen to the HOLY GHOST, accept the ATONEMENT OF JESUS CHRIST, and become as children—submissive, meek, humble, patient, and willing to submit to all things, even as a child submits to his father (Mosiah 3:19).

MORMON, another Book of Mormon prophet, declared that the gift of love must be sought: "Pray unto the Father with all the energy of heart," he advised, "that ye may be filled with this love, which he hath bestowed upon all who are true followers of his Son, Jesus Christ" (Moro. 7:48).

Obedience to the first great commandment is not possible without obedience to the second: "If a man say, I love God, and hateth his brother, he is a liar: for he that loveth not his brother whom he hath seen, how can he love God whom he hath not seen? And this commandment have we from him, that he who loveth God love his brother also" (1 Jn. 4:20–21).

As the Savior manifested his love through service, so do human beings. The Saints of God are recognized by the love they show one to another. Love includes kindness, tenderness, understanding, mercy, forgiveness, affection, and ultimately a willingness to sacrifice all that one has, if necessary. The absence of love is a sign of APOSTASY.

Love is particularly important in the family unit. It begins in the home between husband and wife. "Thou shalt love thy wife with all thy heart, and shalt cleave unto her and none else" (D&C 42:22). This encompasses both a spiritual and a physical fidelity. Then, when husbands and wives as parents govern their households by the principle of love, "the same spirit will be sooner or later diffused through every member of [the] family. . . . Love is the only correct governing principle" (Cannon, p. 383). As David O. MCKAY, a latter-day prophet, said, "I picture heaven to be a continuation of the ideal home" (*Gospel Ideals*, Salt Lake City, 1953, p. 490).

Love established in the home then extends out to the neighborhood, the state, the nation, and the world and has the power to bind people together and make them one. "Differences of language, of education, of race and of nationality all disappear. Under its influence, prejudices and animosities vanish" (Cannon, p. 299).

The love of the Saints also includes loving those who are considered adversaries. The Savior taught, "Love your enemies, bless them that curse you, do good to them that hate you, and pray for them who despitefully use you and persecute you; that ye may be the children of your Father who is in heaven; for he maketh his sun to rise on the evil and on the good" (3 Ne. 12:44–45; cf. Matt. 5:44–45).

Love of one's enemies does not extend to love of their wickedness but does extend to efforts to turn them from such actions. It includes respect for their significance and potential as children of God.

Jesus prophesied that in the LAST DAYS evil will have great power and the love of many shall wax cold (Matt. 24:12), but the scriptures also promise great blessings "held in reserve for them that love him" (D&C 138:52).

BIBLIOGRAPHY

Beardall, Douglas, and Jewel Beardall, comps. *The Qualities of Love.* Salt Lake City, 1978.

Cannon, George Q. *Gospel Truth.* Jerreld L. Newquist, comp. Salt Lake City, 1987.

Madsen, Truman G. *Four Essays on Love.* Salt Lake City, 1971.

VIVIAN PAULSEN

LUCIFER

See: Devils

LYMAN, AMY BROWN

Amy Brown Lyman (1872–1959) was the eighth general president of the RELIEF SOCIETY, an author, Utah state legislator, teacher, and social worker. She possessed an active mind, warm personality, good humor, indomitable spirit, and strong desire to serve.

Born in Pleasant Grove, Utah, on February 7, 1872, to pioneers John and Margaret Zimmerman Brown, Amy was a beautiful, popular, and intelligent child, with dark hair and eyes and a joyous zest for living. She attended public school in Pleasant Grove, then the Brigham Young Academy from 1888 to 1890. Her enthusiasm for learning blossomed under Dr. Karl Maeser, with whose family she boarded for several years. She taught at the academy for four years and then in Salt Lake City elementary schools two more years.

On September 9, 1896, she married Richard R. Lyman, a professor of civil engineering at the University of Utah; he later served as a member of

Amy Brown Lyman (1872–1959), eighth president of the Relief Society, served from 1940 to 1945.

the Quorum of the Twelve Apostles for twenty-five years. The Lymans had two children, Wendell Brown and Margaret; they also raised their granddaughter, Amy Kathryn Lyman, after the death of her parents.

Amy continued to develop her talents while raising her family and accompanying her husband on travels for his doctoral studies. She took classes at the University of Utah, the University of Chicago, and Cornell University. While in Chicago, she became interested in social work and spent several days at Hull House, where she met Jane Addams and gained experiences that changed her life. During summers, she studied family welfare work at the University of Colorado, earned a special certificate in social service, and received in-service training at the city and county welfare departments in Denver.

In 1909 she began her long service to the Relief Society, in which she displayed great organizational and leadership skills. She served two years as a general board member, two years as assistant secretary, and fifteen years as general secretary-treasurer. As secretary-treasurer, she brought to the Relief Society office up-to-date practices, introducing the use of secretaries, office machines, and new filing systems; prepared the first uniform record books for ward Relief Societies; and collected all the minutes and historical documents of the Relief Society since its inception in Nauvoo in 1842. For eleven years she served as first counselor in the general presidency, and she also presided over the women's organizations in the European Mission while her husband served as mission president.

Amy Brown Lyman was authorized by President Joseph F. SMITH to organize and promote family welfare work. She established and directed the Relief Society general board's Social Service Department, with its employment bureau and child-placement agency; taught thousands of volunteer Relief Society workers fundamental principles of family welfare; developed extensive health and nurse training programs; and served in public and private welfare agencies through both world wars and the Great Depression of the 1930s.

During this time, she also rendered important service in many civic organizations and in the Utah state legislature (1923–1924), where she sponsored legislation to provide for maternity and infant care. She held offices in the National Council of Women and in 1929 helped establish the Utah State Training School, where she served as a trustee for eleven years.

In January 1940, the centennial year for the Relief Society, Amy Brown Lyman became general president of the Relief Society. In this position she reemphasized the Relief Society's unique position among women's groups in providing opportunities for education and service outside the home. Under her presidency, the Relief Society actively supported the new Church welfare program, especially sponsoring sewing projects to supply Church welfare storehouses and to meet Red Cross needs in World War II.

Amy Brown Lyman experienced much personal tragedy in her life. Besides the early deaths of her son and daughter-in-law, she endured a great ordeal when her husband was released from the Quorum of the Twelve Apostles and subsequently excommunicated from the Church in November 1943. She continued to serve as general president of the Relief Society until she asked to be released in September 1944; the following spring her request was granted. She continued to stand by her husband, who was rebaptized in the Church in 1954.

Her testimony sustained and strengthened her throughout her life. She wrote, "My testimony has been my anchor and my stay, my satisfaction in times of joy and gladness, my comfort in times of discouragement" (Lyman, pp. 160–61). Her vision, wisdom, spirituality, and concern for others made Amy Brown Lyman a fitting president to usher in the Relief Society's second century.

BIBLIOGRAPHY

History of Relief Society 1842-1966. Salt Lake City, 1966.

Lyman, Amy B. *In Retrospect: Autobiography of Amy Brown Lyman.* Salt Lake City, 1945.

Peterson, Janet, and LaRene Gaunt. *Elect Ladies, Presidents of the Relief Society.* Salt Lake City, 1990.

ANN WILLARDSON ENGAR
AMY LYMAN ENGAR

M

MAGAZINES

From the earliest years of the Church, it has sought to build and strengthen the LDS community through a wide variety of periodical publications. Although the early LDS periodicals looked like newspapers (some were called "papers" and carried some news), they mostly printed religious and general interest articles, multipart serials, editorials, sermons, revelations, Christian and Church history, hymns, poems, advertisements, and letters from missionaries. Church magazines have always endeavored "to strengthen the faith of Church members, . . . promulgate the truths of the restored gospel, [and] keep members abreast of current and vital Church policies, programs, and happenings" (*IE* 73 [July 1970]:8). Many LDS missions started their own publications to communicate with and teach their people (*see* INTERNATIONAL MAGAZINES).

Other periodicals were financed, edited, and published independently by members of the Church, and thus technically were not official Church publications. However, some of these journals were brought under the umbrella of the Church AUXILIARIES, and then of the Church. After 1866, many LDS English-language periodicals printed lesson materials and fiction. In 1971, the Church consolidated its English-language periodicals into three new magazines assigned to serve different groups: ENSIGN (adults), NEW ERA (youth, ages twelve to eighteen), and FRIEND (children, to age twelve). *BYU Studies* (1959–) was retained to be published by Brigham Young University for LDS scholars. The chart in Appendix 3 lists the major Church periodicals.

BIBLIOGRAPHY

"Church Publications." *Deseret News 1989–1990 Church Almanac,* pp. 187–91. Salt Lake City, 1989.

Green, Doyle L. "The Church and Its Magazines." *Ensign* 1 (Jan. 1971):12–15.

RICHARD TICE

MAGIC

"Magic" anciently implied something akin to sorcery, and modern definitions retain this sense as well as a host of other meanings that have accrued around the term over many years and from many cultures. On one point there is general agreement: "Magic" suggests the supernatural. Pretending to use the occult when so-called magic tricks are displayed is simply part of the entertainment. When it implies *governing* the forces of nature through supernatural means, however, magic takes on a markedly different character.

Latter-day Saints reject magic as a serious manipulation of nature and are advised to avoid any practice that claims supernatural power apart from the PRIESTHOOD and spiritual gifts of the Church (*see* DEVILS; SATANISM). They are also counseled against using any fortune-telling devices. Both so-called white and black magic can be Satanic.

True miracles are done by the power of Jesus Christ. Devils may be cast out, but only in humility and by fasting, faith, and prayer, and the power of the true priesthood, with no fanfare or public acclaim (cf. Matt. 17:21; D&C 84:66–73). Regarding the DISCERNMENT of true spirits from evil ones, the Prophet Joseph SMITH taught that without the priesthood and "a knowledge of the laws by which spirits are governed," it is impossible to discover the difference between the miracles of Moses and the magicians of the pharaoh or between those of the apostles and Simon the sorcerer (*TPJS*, pp. 202–206). A test of a godly spirit is to discern whether there is "any intelligence communicated" or "the purposes of God developed" (*TPJS*, p. 204).

Ultimately, it is irrelevant to the determination of its sources to note that a so-called miracle is for the good of mankind. The Savior recognized that miracles may come from an evil source: "Many will say to me in that day, Lord, Lord, have we not prophesied in thy name, and in thy name have cast out devils, and in thy name done many wonderful works? And then will I profess unto them, I never knew you: depart from me, ye that work iniquity" (Matt. 7:22–23).

The Lord gave instruction to Israel that the righteous were to call upon him for revelation and to avoid magical devices and incantations that were prevalent among the other ancient nations (Isa. 8:19–20; Ex. 22:18). One danger of preoccupation with forms of magic based on the power of Satan is that it draws people away from the true source of inspiration and makes the worker of magic a servant of the adversary.

The Church holds that no person need unduly fear magic or those who claim magical powers, for magic can have no power over anyone unless the person believes that it can.

BIBLIOGRAPHY

Hinckley, Gordon B. "Lord, Increase Our Faith." *Ensign* 17 (Nov. 1987):52.

McConkie, Bruce R. "Magic." *MD*, pp. 462–63.

Smith, Joseph F. *GD*, pp 375–77.

JANET THOMAS

MAGNIFYING ONE'S CALLING

Magnifying one's calling is a common exhortation among Latter-day Saints. In the OATH AND COVENANT OF THE PRIESTHOOD the promise that "all that [the] Father hath" is given to those who are faithful in obtaining both the Aaronic and Melchizedek priesthoods and "magnifying their calling" (D&C 84:33–39). Paul told the Romans that he magnified his office by teaching the GENTILES (Rom. 11:13). JACOB taught his Book of Mormon people to magnify their CALLINGS (Jacob 1:19; 2:2). And the Lord has given modern admonitions to Latter-day Saints to "magnify" or prepare to "magnify" their callings (D&C 24:3, 9; 66:11; 88:80).

Magnifying one's calling means taking callings seriously, following through responsibly, and realizing the importance of one's efforts. Magnifying one's calling does not mean to enlarge it beyond one's STEWARDSHIP or to make it appear great in the eyes of others, although there is a need to give one's own calling appropriate personal importance.

In Paul's declaration to the Romans that he magnified his office, the Greek verb *doxazo* is used, meaning to make honorable or glorious, the same verb used by New Testament authors to exhort their readers to glorify God (cf. Matt. 5:16; Rom. 15:6). Thus, to magnify a calling means to make it honorable and glorious, even to glorify God through service. Jacob explained that magnifying callings meant that he and his brother Joseph took upon themselves "the responsibility [of] answering the sins of the people upon our own heads if we did not teach them the word of God with all diligence" (Jacob 1:19). The Lord told William E. M'Lellin that if he, M'Lellin, would carry out his assignment fully as explained to him, including obeying the injunction to personal worthiness, he would thereby magnify his office (D&C 66:10–11).

Those who seek to respond to the Lord's admonition to magnify their callings take even the simplest calling seriously as an opportunity to glorify God and serve his children.

BIBLIOGRAPHY

Millet, Robert L. *Magnifying Priesthood Power*. Bountiful, Utah, 1989.

WILLIAM E. EVENSON

MALACHI, PROPHECIES OF

The importance of Malachi's prophecies is reflected in their prominence in nonbiblical LDS scriptures. For example, the resurrected Jesus instructed hearers in the Western Hemisphere (c. A.D. 34) to include Malachi 3 and 4 with their records (3 Ne. 24–25), and references to Malachi's prophecies appear in the DOCTRINE AND COVENANTS and the PEARL OF GREAT PRICE. Those prophecies pertaining to the latter days concern (1) the Lord's latter-day advent; (2) the messenger sent to prepare his way; (3) the sons of Levi and their offering; (4) TITHING; (5) the lot of the wicked; and (6) Elijah's mission. Some of his timeless teachings pertain to such matters as the fatherhood of God and brotherhood of man (Mal. 2:10), the problems of divorce (2:14–16), and problems of immorality (3:5–6).

Malachi prophesied that the Lord would come suddenly to his temple (Mal. 3:1). Latter-day Saints believe that one such appearance occurred in the KIRTLAND TEMPLE when Jesus appeared there in 1836. Other messengers also restored KEYS (D&C 110), making possible the "complete salvation and exaltation of all who are willing to obey the gospel" (Smith 2:47; *see also* JESUS CHRIST: LATTER-DAY APPEARANCES OF).

The "messenger" sent to prepare the way (Mal. 3:1) can refer to all messengers whom God may send to restore blessings and authority lost through apostasy (*see* ELIAS). Most messengers who have assisted in establishing the latter-day kingdom of God have bestowed priesthood powers and keys vital to the authoritative performance of saving ordinances (D&C 1:17–18; 128:20–21).

The Lord promised that he will "purge" the Levites so that they will become worthy to function again (Mal. 3:3). When he has done this, he will direct the restoration of sacrifices (cf. D&C 13). Joseph Smith wrote that the "offering of [animal] sacrifice has ever been connected and forms a part of the duties of the Priesthood. It began with the Priesthood, and will be continued until after the coming of Christ . . . when the [Aaronic] Priesthood is restored with all its authority, power and blessings" (*HC* 4:211).

Malachi emphasizes tithing. Indicting those who have "gone away" by failing to pay tithes and offerings, the Lord promises that if they will return, "I will return" (Mal. 3:7). The principle of tithing, which was practiced as early as Abraham (cf. Gen. 14:20; 28:22), has been renewed in the latter days (D&C 119:4), and blessings are assured for those who give tithes and offerings. The "windows of heaven will be opened," including the pouring out of "revelations" as a reward for such sacrifice (Lee, p. 16).

In the last days, trouble awaits the wicked. "The day cometh, that shall burn as an oven; . . . and all that do wickedly, shall be stubble." They shall be burned, leaving neither "root [ancestors] nor branch [children]" (Mal. 4:1; cf. T. Burton, *IE* 70 [Dec. 1967]:80–82). This burning "is not a figure of speech" (Smith, Vol. 1, p. 238). "It may be . . . that nothing except the power of faith and the authority of the priesthood can save individuals" (McConkie, p. 93). But the "Sun of righteousness" (Mal. 4:2; cf. 3 Ne. 25:2) will bring the healing power of the resurrection and redemption (2 Ne. 25:13), and the righteous will be nourished "as calves of the stall" because of their obedience to the Lord (1 Ne. 22:24).

Malachi's prophecies climax with the mission of Elijah, which receives prominent attention in latter-day sacred writings. During the angel Moroni's visits to Joseph Smith in 1823, he quoted Malachi 4:5–6 with modifications: "Behold, I will reveal unto you the Priesthood, by the hand of Elijah the prophet, before the coming of the great and dreadful day of the Lord. And he shall plant in the hearts of the children the promises made to their fathers. . . . If it were not so, the whole earth would be utterly wasted at his coming" (JS—H 1:38–39). In fulfillment, Elijah appeared to Joseph Smith and Oliver Cowdery in the Kirtland Temple on April 3, 1836 (Passover time), and restored the sealing powers (D&C 110:13–16).

Speaking of Malachi 4:5–6, Joseph Smith asked, "How is [this prophecy] to be fulfilled? The keys are to be delivered, the spirit of Elijah is to come, the Gospel to be established, the Saints of God gathered, Zion built up, and the Saints to come up as saviors on Mount Zion. But how? . . . By building their temples . . . and receiving all the ordinances, baptisms, confirmations, washings, anointings, ordinations and sealing powers upon their heads, in behalf of all their progenitors who are dead, and redeem them; . . . and herein is the chain that binds the hearts of the fathers to the children, and the children to the fathers, which fulfills the mission of Elijah" (*HC* 6:184). If this eternal goal could not be achieved, one of the major purposes of the plan of redemption would fail.

An integral part of this plan is to "further the work of turning the hearts of the children to the fathers by getting . . . sacred family records in order. These records, including especially the 'book containing the records of our dead' (D&C 128:24), are a portion of the 'offering in righteousness' referred to by Malachi (3:3), which we are to present in His holy temple, and without which we shall not abide the day of His coming" (Kimball, pp. 542–43; see also GENEALOGY).

BIBLIOGRAPHY

Kimball, Spencer W. The Teachings of Spencer W. Kimball, ed. Edward L. Kimball. Salt Lake City, 1982.

Lee, Harold B. "The Way to Eternal Life." Ensign 1 (Nov. 1971):9–17.

McConkie, Bruce R. "Stand Independent Above All Other Creatures." Ensign 9 (May 1979):92–94.

Smith, Joseph Fielding. Church History and Modern Revelation, 2 vols. Salt Lake City, 1953.

GEORGE A. HORTON, JR.

MANCHESTER, NEW YORK

See: History of the Church, c. 1820–1831

MAN OF HOLINESS

According to ENOCH's record, Man of Holiness is one NAME OF GOD: "In the language of Adam, Man of Holiness is his name, and the name of his Only Begotten is the Son of Man, even Jesus Christ" (Moses 6:57). God further declared in the revelation to Enoch: "Behold, I am God; Man of Holiness is my name" (Moses 7:35). This name reinforces the observation that GOD THE FATHER is an exalted man of flesh and bones (D&C 130:22), and that every aspect of his character is holy.

In almost a dozen instances, the pre-Christian Nag Hammadi text "Eugnostos the Blessed" uses similar terms—"Immortal Man," "First Man" and "Man"—for the Father (Robinson, pp. 229–31). Another Nag Hammadi tractate, "The Second Treatise of the Great Seth," refers to God as "the Man" and "Man of Greatness" (Robinson, p. 364). Thus, ancient authors likewise seem to have de-fined the Father as a glorified person with a body in whose image man was created.

[See also God the Father: Names and Titles of.]

BIBLIOGRAPHY

Brown, S. Kent. "Man and Son of Man." In The Pearl of Great Price: Revelations From God, ed. H. Donl Peterson and C. Tate. Provo, 1989.

Robinson, James M., ed. The Nag Hammadi Library, 3rd rev. ed. San Francisco, 1988.

GERALD E. JONES

MANIFESTO OF 1890

The Manifesto of 1890 was a proclamation by President Wilford WOODRUFF that the Church had discontinued PLURAL MARRIAGE. It ended a decade of persecution and hardship in which Latter-day Saints tenaciously resisted what they saw as unconstitutional federal attempts to curb polygamy. While the Manifesto is often referred to as a REVELATION, the declaration was actually a press release that followed President Woodruff's revelatory experiences. In this respect, the Manifesto is similar to DOCTRINE AND COVENANTS OFFICIAL DECLARATION—2.

Following the passage of the Edmunds-Tucker Act in 1887, the Church found it difficult to operate as a viable institution (see ANTIPOLYGAMY LEGISLATION). Among other things, this legislation disincorporated the Church, confiscated its properties, and even threatened seizure of its temples. After visiting with priesthood leaders in many settlements, President Woodruff left for San Francisco on September 3, 1890, to meet with prominent businessmen and politicians. He returned to Salt Lake City on September 21, determined to obtain divine confirmation to pursue a course that seemed to be agonizingly more and more clear. As he explained to Church members a year later, the choice was between, on the one hand, continuing to practice plural marriage and thereby losing the temples, "stopping all the ordinances therein," and, on the other, ceasing plural marriage in order to continue performing the essential ordinances for the living and the dead. President Woodruff hastened to add that he had acted only as the Lord directed: "I should have let all the temples go out of our hands; I should have gone to prison myself, and let every other man go there, had not the God of heaven commanded me to do what I do; and when the hour came that I was commanded to do that, it was all clear to me" (*see* Appendix; "Excerpts" accompanying Official Declaration—1).

The final element in President Woodruff's revelatory experience came on the evening of September 23, 1890. The following morning, he reported to some of the General Authorities that he had struggled throughout the night with the Lord regarding the path that should be pursued. "Here is the result," he said, placing a 510-word handwritten manuscript on the table. The document was later edited by George Q. Cannon of the FIRST PRESIDENCY and others to its present 356 words. On October 6, 1890, it was presented to the Latter-day Saints at the General Conference and approved.

While nearly all Church leaders in 1890 regarded the Manifesto as inspired, there were differences among them about its scope and permanence. Some leaders were understandably reluctant to terminate a long-standing practice that was regarded as divinely mandated. As a result, a limited number of plural marriages were performed over the next several years. Not surprisingly, rumors of such marriages soon surfaced, and beginning in January 1904, testimony given in the SMOOT HEARINGS made it clear that plural marriage had not been completely extinguished. The ambiguity was ended in the General Conference of April 1904, when the First Presidency issued the "second manifesto," an emphatic declaration that prohibited plural marriage and proclaimed that offenders would be subject to Church discipline, including excommunication.

The Manifesto of 1890 should be regarded as a pivotal event in the history of The Church of Jesus Christ of Latter-day Saints and of the state of Utah. Not only did it mark the beginning of the end of the official practice of plural marriage, but it also heralded a new age as Latter-day Saints relinquished the isolationist practices of the past and commenced a period of greater accommodation and integration into the fabric of American society (*see* UTAH STATEHOOD).

BIBLIOGRAPHY

Alexander, Thomas G. *Mormonism in Transition*, pp. 3–15. Urbana, Ill., 1986.

Gibbons, Francis M. *Wilford Woodruff*, pp. 353–61. Salt Lake City, 1988.

PAUL H. PETERSON

MANKIND

The Church of Jesus Christ of Latter-day Saints views all descendants of ADAM and EVE as the children of God—not in an abstract or metaphorical sense, but as actual spirit offspring of GOD THE FATHER and a MOTHER IN HEAVEN. This basic premise has profound implications for the LDS understanding of what human beings are, why they are here on earth, and what they can become.

As children of God, men and women have infinite potential (see 2 Ne. 2:20; Heb. 12:9). As a result of their divine heritage, all people carry the inherent capacity and the predisposition to become as their heavenly parents. Latter-day Saints seek to follow the injunction of Christ to be "perfect, even as your Father which is in heaven is perfect" (Matt. 5:48). Their view of each person's relationship with God stresses that life is as a maturing process, a working toward becoming like God, of becoming worthy to be with God (*see* DEIFICATION; EXALTATION; GODHOOD). Mortal life may be only a beginning, but the potential is there.

This view of mankind emphasizes the FAMILY. MARRIAGE is central to the LDS spiritual experience: "Neither is the man without the woman, neither the woman without the man, in the Lord" (1 Cor. 11:11). Marriage is not intended to last for this life only, but for eternity; therefore, Latter-day Saints marry in the TEMPLE for TIME AND ETERNITY. As members of the family of God, Latter-day Saints see the family as the most important arena of life. "No other success," President David O. MCKAY frequently declared, "can compensate for failure in the home" (*Family Home Evening Manual*, "Preface," Salt Lake City, 1966).

The LDS ideal also reaches out toward the universal family of humanity. People with infinite potential have infinite value; all people matter because they are brothers and sisters in the family of God. The LDS perspective affirms the infinite love of God for all mankind, and the essential goodness of human beings and their capacity to improve the world. The conviction that people are responsible for their moral behavior, "agents unto themselves" (D&C 58:28), tends to make Latter-day Saints supporters of political systems that maximize free choices (*see* AGENCY; POLITICS). The intelligence, or inner core of the soul, is seen in LDS theology as self-existent, not created ex nihilo, but having existed always, and thus ultimately responsible for its own decisions and its own destiny as well (*see* INTELLIGENCES).

The vast potential of human beings, as literal spirit children of God, brings to the LDS view of mankind a purposeful and weighty sense of responsibility. Sons and daughters of God have an obligation to develop their divinely given talents, to magnify what God has given them. Latter-day Saints privately, and through the Church, labor to make the most of individuals. They believe that through the ages people are accountable for their responses to God, which determine what they now are and what they will be, and that it is God's work and glory to bring about the exaltation of mankind.

Each human intelligence is born of God as a spirit child, and that spirit child is later born into MORTALITY in a physical body. Spirit is unusually real to the Latter-day Saints, for whom everything that exists has spiritual essence: "All things . . . are spiritual" (D&C 29:34; Moses 3:5). Mortal life thus becomes for Latter-day Saints not only a difficult and risky time, but also a time of infinite opportunities and possibilities, a pivotal step in the eternal process of becoming as wise and good as the heavenly parents.

This sense of possibility and of responsibility tends to make Latter-day Saints strong proponents of all forms of ennobling EDUCATION: "the glory of God is intelligence" (D&C 93:36). In a world fraught with risk and temptation on the one hand and the possibility of godliness on the other, the wise Latter-day Saint will "seek learning, even by study and also by faith" (D&C 88:118).

Thus, the PURPOSE OF EARTH LIFE is to prepare for eternity through learning and experience. In mortal life Latter-day Saints expect TRIALS, challenges, and tests. But the expectation of difficulty in life holds within it the promise of real happiness, of having life "more abundantly" (John 10:10). The Book of Mormon prophet LEHI summarizes the LDS sense of the challenge and reward of this mortal experience made possible by the fortunate FALL OF ADAM: "Adam fell that men might be; and men are, that they might have joy" (2 Ne. 2:25).

BIBLIOGRAPHY

Madsen, Truman G. *Eternal Man*. Salt Lake City, 1966.

Talmage, James E. *The Vitality of Mormonism*. Boston, 1919.

STEVEN C. WALKER

MAN'S SEARCH FOR HAPPINESS

"Man's Search for Happiness" (1964) is a motion picture noted for its skillful blending of aesthetic and spiritual qualities. The film was produced by the Brigham Young University Motion Picture Studio. It is less than fifteen minutes long, yet explores every man's search for meaning in life: the whence, the why, and the whither.

Narrated by Elder Richard L. Evans, longtime announcer of the MORMON TABERNACLE CHOIR broadcasts, the film stresses the gifts of life, freedom, and time, and the blessings of the atonement of Jesus Christ. It is climaxed by a poignant family reunion scene in the life to come.

Over 5 million people saw the film at the Mormon Pavilion in the 1964 New York's World Fair, and over 6.5 million at the Japan World Exposition in 1970. It has since been shown daily at the Temple Square Visitors Center in Salt Lake City and has had special screenings elsewhere. In 1986 the Church commissioned an updated version of the film for worldwide use. The remake retains the original narration by Elder Richard L. Evans.

BIBLIOGRAPHY

Top, Brent L. "Legacy of the Mormon Pavilion." *Ensign* 19 (Oct. 1989):22–28.

PETER N. JOHNSON

MANUSCRIPT, LOST 116 PAGES

The first 116 pages of the original manuscript of Joseph SMITH's translation of the Book of Mormon from the plates of Mormon are commonly known as "the 116 pages" or the "lost manuscript." These foolscap-size pages were hand-written in HARMONY, Pennsylvania, between April and June 14, 1828. Although principally transcribed by Martin HARRIS from dictation by Joseph Smith, some of the pages may also have been transcribed by Joseph's wife, Emma SMITH, or her brother, Reuben Hale.

The pages contained materials "from the Book of Lehi, which was an account abridged from the plates of Lehi, by the hand of Mormon," as Joseph explained in the preface to the first edition of the Book of Mormon (see also *HC* 1:56). LEHI's record is mentioned in 1 Nephi 1:17 and, today, is partially preserved through NEPHI's abridgment of it primarily in 1 Nephi 1-10.

In June 1828 Martin Harris asked Joseph Smith repeatedly to allow him to show the 116 pages to family members to allay their skepticism and criticism of the translation. After prayerful inquiry of the Lord, Joseph Smith twice emphatically denied these requests. As Joseph's 1832 and 1839 histories indicate, a third request received divine permission for Harris to take the 116 manuscript pages to Palmyra, New York. The Prophet required Harris to solemnly covenant that he would show them only to his brother, his parents, his wife, and her sister.

Harris's failure to return to Harmony as promised caused Joseph great anxiety and necessitated a strenuous journey to Manchester. There, a reluctant Harris reported that someone had stolen the manuscript from his home after he had broken his covenant and indiscriminately showed it to persons outside his family. Grief-stricken, Joseph Smith readily shared responsibility for the loss. The most widespread rumor was that Harris' wife, irritated at having earlier been denied a glimpse of the ancient PLATES, had removed the manuscript translation from Martin's unlocked bureau and burned it. Not long afterward, she and Martin separated.

In consequence of this loss and of having wearied the Lord with the requests to let Harris take the pages, Joseph temporarily lost custody of the plates and the URIM AND THUMMIM to the angel MORONI (D&C 3). Lucy Mack SMITH notes also that two-thirds of Harris's crop was oddly destroyed by a dense fog, which she interpreted as a sign of God's displeasure (Smith, p. 132). Following much humble and painful affliction of soul, Joseph Smith again received the plates as well as the Urim and Thummim and his gifts were restored.

Joseph Smith was forbidden by the Lord to retranslate that part of the record previously translated because those who had stolen the manuscript planned to publish it in an altered form to discredit his ability to translate accurately (D&C 10:9–13). Instead, he was to translate the Small Plates of Nephi (1 Nephi–Omni) down to that which he had translated (D&C 10:41). Those plates covered approximately the same period as had the lost manuscript, or four centuries from Lehi to BENJAMIN. Mormon had been so impressed with the choice prophecies and sayings contained in the small plates that he had included them with his own abridgment of Nephite writings when told to by

the Spirit for "a wise purpose" known only to the Lord (W of M 1:7).

The loss of the 116 pages taught Joseph Smith and his associates several lessons: that one should be satisfied with the first answers of the Lord, that keeping one's COVENANTS is a serious matter, that God forgives the repentant in spite of human weakness, and that through his caring foresight and wisdom the Lord fulfills his purposes.

BIBLIOGRAPHY

Bushman, Richard L. *Joseph Smith and the Beginnings of Mormonism*, pp. 89–94. Urbana, Ill., 1984.

Jessee, Dean C., ed. *The Papers of Joseph Smith*, Vol. 1, pp. 9–10, 286–88. Salt Lake City, 1989.

Smith, Lucy Mack. *History of Joseph Smith*, pp. 124–32. Salt Lake City, 1958.

WILLIAM J. CRITCHLOW III

MARRIAGE

[*This entry consists of two articles: The first article,* Social and Behavioral Perspectives, *is an overview of the concept of marriage patterns in LDS society; the second article,* Eternal Marriage, *focuses on distinctive marriage beliefs practiced by members of the LDS Church in their temples. One of the highest religious goals for Latter-day Saints, both male and female, is to be married eternally in an LDS temple and to strive continually to strengthen the bonds of love and righteousness in marriage. Civil marriages are recognized as lawful and beneficial, but they do not continue after death.*]

SOCIAL AND BEHAVIORAL PERSPECTIVES

Marriage is more than a matter of social convention or individual need fulfillment in Latter-day Saint society and lifestyle; it is central to the exaltation of the individual person: "If a man marry a wife by my word, which is my law, and by the new and everlasting covenant, and it is sealed unto them by the Holy Spirit of promise, by him who is anointed, unto whom I have appointed this power and the keys of this priesthood, and . . . [they] abide in my covenant . . . [that marriage] shall be of full force when they are out of the world; . . . then shall they be gods, because they have no end; therefore shall they be from everlasting to everlasting" (D&C 132:19–20). Thus, Latter-day Saints consider it of utmost importance, "1. To marry the right person, in the right place, by the right authority; and 2. To keep the covenant made in connection with this holy and perfect order of matrimony" (*MD*, p. 118).

Central to LDS theology is the belief that men and women existed as spirit offspring of heavenly parents in a PREMORTAL LIFE. Latter-day Saints view life on earth as a time to prepare to meet God (Alma 12:24) and strive toward becoming like him (Matt. 5:48; 3 Ne. 12:48). Becoming like God is dependent to a large extent on entering into "celestial marriage" for "time and all eternity," for eventually all exalted beings shall have entered into this highest PATRIARCHAL ORDER OF THE PRIESTHOOD. Latter-day Saints believe that the marital and family bond can continue in the post-earth life, and indeed is necessary for ETERNAL LIFE, or life in the CELESTIAL KINGDOM with GOD THE FATHER; MOTHER IN HEAVEN; JESUS CHRIST, and other glorified beings.

Given these doctrines, LDS marriages are distinct and different in several aspects from marriages in other denominations, and marriages of faithful Latter-day Saints differ from those of less observant Church members. Research on LDS marriages shows distinctions in four areas: sexual attitudes and behavior, marriage formation, divorce, and gender roles within the marriage.

SEXUAL ATTITUDES AND BEHAVIOR. Because of the importance of the marital bond and family relationships in both this life and the life to come, premarital or extramarital sexual relations are viewed as totally unacceptable. The power of procreation is vital to the entire PLAN OF SALVATION. It is held sacred, to be used "only as the Lord has directed"; as such it is viewed as the "very key" to happiness (Packer, "Why Stay Morally Clean," *Ensign* [July 1972]:113). Studies conducted through the 1970s and 1980s consistently showed that Latter-day Saints have more restrictive attitudes about and are less likely to have participated in premarital sexual intercourse than members of other religious denominations. Active Latter-day Saints also have more conservative attitudes about and are less likely to have engaged in premarital sexual intercourse than those who are less active in the Church (*see* SEXUALITY).

A recent sampling of U.S. households showed Mormons to be significantly less approving of teenagers having sex or of premarital cohabitation than non-Mormons (Heaton et al., 1989). Another study, of over 2,000 adolescents in public high schools in the western United States, showed that

17 percent of the Latter-day Saints had had premarital intercourse compared to 48 percent of the Catholics, 51 percent of those with no religious affiliation, and 67 percent of the Protestants (Heaton, 1988). The difference continues when Church activity is taken into account and active Latter-day Saints are compared to inactive ones. The attitudes and behavior of inactive Mormons are more similar to those of other faiths (religiously active or inactive) than to active Latter-day Saints (Heaton, 1988).

Latter-day Saint attitudes about sex in marriage and frequency of sexual intercourse in marriage are similar to those in other faiths. Although no data exist on the frequency of extramarital sexuality, Latter-day Saints in general are less approving of extramarital sex than other American populations (Heaton et al., 1989).

MARITAL FORMATION. Members of the Church in the United States and Canada are more likely to marry and remarry than Catholics, conservative Protestants, liberal Protestants, or those with no religious affiliation (Heaton and Goodman, 1985). One study of Canadians indicates that Canadian Catholics are three times as likely, Protestants twice as likely, and those without a religious affiliation four times as likely as Latter-day Saints not to have married by age thirty (Heaton, 1988). The most recent national U.S. data show LDS more likely to be currently married and less likely to have never married than other similarly situated Americans (Heaton et al., 1989). Furthermore, the same data show that LDS men marry about one and one-half years earlier than their non-Mormon counterparts, but LDS females marry at about the same age as other females.

Although the findings are not conclusive, it appears that less active Mormons (those not marrying in a TEMPLE) marry at younger ages than those marrying in a temple (Thomas, 1983). Some of this difference may be accounted for by the number of active Latter-day Saint males serving MISSIONS during these early years. Most unmarried young LDS men who go on missions serve from about age nineteen until twenty-one.

Given the necessity of marrying another Latter-day Saint in a temple to achieve the greatest happiness in this life and exaltation in the highest level of the celestial kingdom hereafter, one would expect that Mormons in general, and active Latter-day Saints in particular, would have lower rates of interfaith marriages than members of other faiths or those with no affiliation. What little research has been done on LDS interfaith marriages tends to be based on small, localized samples. It appears, however, that in general (1) Mormon females are more likely to marry outside the Church than are Mormon males; (2) active Mormons are less likely to marry non-Mormons than are less active Mormons; and (3) non-Mormon spouses (especially non-Mormon husbands) are more likely to convert to the Church than Mormons are to convert to a non-Mormon spouse's faith (Barlow, 1977).

DIVORCE. Based on research done in the 1970s and early 1980s, it has been concluded that Latter-day Saints are less likely to divorce than Catholics and Protestants and are far less likely than those with no religious affiliation. A study comparing Mormons in the United States and Canada with Protestants, Catholics, and those with no religious affiliation found that 14 percent of the Mormon men and 19 percent of the women had divorced. Comparable figures among the other groups were 20 percent and 23 percent for Catholic males and females; 24 percent and 31 percent for liberal Protestant males and females; 28 percent and 31 percent for conservative Protestant males and females; and 39 percent for males and 45 percent for females with no religious affiliation (Heaton and Goodman, 1985).

Latter-day Saints married in a temple ceremony are considerably less likely to divorce than those married outside the temple (Thomas, 1983). Among men and women who were married in the temple, 6 percent of the men and 7 percent of the women have been divorced, while among men and women not married in the temple the figures were 28 percent and 33 percent, respectively (Heaton, 1988).

GENDER ROLES. "God established that fathers are to preside in the home. Fathers are to provide, to love, to teach, and to direct. But a mother's role is also God-ordained. Mothers are to conceive, to bear, to nourish, to love, and to train. So declare the revelations" (Benson, p. 2). This statement, made by Church President Ezra Taft BENSON, exemplifies the LDS teaching that men and women have different—but closely intertwined and mutually supporting—roles in the marital and family setting. Research bears out this distinctive emphasis. Mormon males and females tend to be more conservative and traditional in their gender role

attitudes and behavior than members of other faiths (Brinkerhoff and MacKie, 1988; Heaton, 1988; Heaton et al., 1989). LDS males spend about the same amount of time performing household tasks as non-Mormon males, but Mormon females spend significantly more time at such tasks than non-Mormon females. LDS females spend more time performing not only traditional female tasks, but also traditional male tasks (e.g., outdoor tasks, paying bills, and auto maintenance) than do female non-Mormons. These differences in both attitudes and behavior are not viewed negatively by either LDS men or women. They are as likely to be satisfied with their marriages and their roles in marriage as their non-Mormon counterparts (Heaton et al., 1989).

BIBLIOGRAPHY

Bahr, Howard M., and Renata Tonks Forste. "Toward a Social Science of Contemporary Mormondom." *BYU Studies* 26 (1986):73–121.

Barlow, Brent A. "Notes on Mormon Interfaith Marriages." *Family Coordinator* 26 (1977):143–50.

Benson, Ezra Taft. *To the Mothers in Zion.* Salt Lake City, 1987.

Brinkerhoff, Merlin B., and Marlene MacKie. "Religious Sources of Gender Traditionalism." In *The Religion and Family Connection*, ed. D. Thomas. Provo, Utah, 1988.

Heaton, Tim B. "Four C's of the Mormon Family: Chastity, Conjugality, Children, and Chauvinism." In *The Religion and Family Connection*, ed. D. Thomas. Provo, Utah, 1988.

Heaton, Tim B., and Kristin L. Goodman. "Religion and Family Formation." *Review of Religious Research* 26 (1985):343–59.

Heaton, Tim B.; Darwin L. Thomas; and Kristin L. Goodman. "In Search of a Peculiar People: Are Mormon Families Really Different?" Society for the Scientific Study of Religion, Oct. 1989.

Thomas, Darwin L. "Family in the Mormon Experience." In *Families and Religion*, ed. W. D'Antonio and J. Aldous. Beverly Hills, Calif., 1983.

THOMAS B. HOLMAN

ETERNAL MARRIAGE

The principle of eternal marriage and the ordinances implementing it constitute a very distinctive and valuable part of the Church. It involves a ceremony performed in a holy TEMPLE by an officiator endowed with the PRIESTHOOD AUTHORITY to invoke covenants intended to be efficacious for TIME AND ETERNITY. This is a sacred and simple ceremony to unite husband and wife in the bonds of everlasting love and in the hopes of eternity. President Joseph Fielding SMITH taught that such a marriage involves "an eternal principle ordained before the foundation of the world and instituted on this earth before death came into it" (Smith, p. 251), for ADAM and EVE were given in marriage to each other by God in the GARDEN OF EDEN before the Fall (Gen. 2:22–25; Moses 3:22–25). This sacred act of marriage was the crowning act of all creation: "In the day that God created man, in the likeness of God made he him: Male and Female created he them; and blessed them" (Gen. 5:1–2). With his blessing they truly could set the pattern for their descendants thereafter who two by two, a man and a woman, could leave father and mother, cleave to each other, and "be one flesh" (Gen. 2:24). Thus began the great plan of God for the happiness of all his children.

Latter-day Saints believe that life is more secure and more joyous when it is experienced in the sacred relationships of the eternal family. Those who maintain such worthy relationships on earth will live as families in the CELESTIAL KINGDOM following the RESURRECTION. Thus, a person who lives a righteous life in mortality and who has entered into an eternal marriage may look forward to an association in the postmortal world with a worthy spouse, and with those who were earthly children, fathers, mothers, brothers, and sisters. Bruce R. McConkie, an apostle, explained that an eternal family starts with "a husband and a wife,

A couple in 1986 outside the Manila Philippines Temple (dedicated September 1984). Performed only in temples, the ordinance of eternal marriage is intended to create marriage bonds that last for eternity. Courtesy Floyd Holdman.

united in a family unit. It then goes out to our children—the spirits that God gives us to be members of our family—to our grandchildren and so on, to the latest generation. It also reaches back to our parents and our grandparents to the earliest generation" (p. 82). President Brigham YOUNG said that eternal marriage "is the thread which runs from the beginning to the end of the holy Gospel of Salvation—of the Gospel of the Son of God; it is from eternity to eternity" (*Discourses of Brigham Young*, John A. Widtsoe, ed., Salt Lake City, 1971, p. 195).

Even as marriage marks an apex in God's creative processes, so, too, it is for each person the sacred culmination of the covenants and ordinances of the priesthood of God and, indeed, is truly a new and everlasting covenant (D&C 131:2). Eternal marriage is a covenant, a sacred promise that a wife and a husband make with each other and with God, attested to by both mortal witnesses and heavenly angels. Under proper conditions such marriages are sealed by the HOLY SPIRIT OF PROMISE, and the couple, through their faithfulness, can eventually inherit EXALTATION and glory in the celestial kingdom of God (D&C 132:19). The scriptures confirm that eternal marriage, performed by the authority of the priesthood, sealed or affirmed by the Holy Ghost, and sustained by a righteous life, "shall be of full force" after death (D&C 132:19; cf. 1 Cor. 11:11). The phrase "until death do you part" is regarded as a tragic one that predicts the ultimate dissolution of the marriage, and this phase is not stated in the temple marriage ceremony.

The sacred ceremony of temple marriage is conducted in reverence and simplicity, and the occasion is a beautiful and joyous one for Latter-day Saints. The bride and the groom meet with family and friends in a designated sealing room of the temple. The officiator typically greets the couple with a few words of welcome, counsel, and fatherly commendations. He may admonish the couple to treat each other throughout life with the same love and kindness that they feel at this moment, and may add other words of encouragement, with his blessing upon their righteous undertaking. The couple is invited to come forward and kneel facing each other across an altar in the middle of the room. The sealer sometimes directs the attention of all present to the mirrors on opposite walls, reflecting endlessly the images of the couple at the altar, and he may comment on the symbolism. Then the sealer pronounces the simple words of the ceremony, which promise, on condition of obedience, lasting bonds with the potential for eternal joy between these two sealed for eternity. President Ezra Taft BENSON said, "Faithfulness to the marriage covenant brings the fullest joy here and glorious rewards hereafter" (pp. 533–34). At the conclusion of the ceremony, the couple kiss over the altar and may then arise and leave the altar to exchange rings.

Through this ordinance of eternal marriage, men and women commit themselves in pure love to remain true to each other and to God through all eternity. Divorce is discouraged, and couples are taught to confine their intimate affections and sexuality solely to each other. To undertake and honor the covenants of temple marriage require living in ways that contribute to happy and successful family life. A couple's future may include conflicts and even divorce, which when it occurs is often a result of violating temple covenants; but the divorce rate among couples who have been sealed in a temple is very low (see DIVORCE; VITAL STATISTICS).

Eternal marriage is, of course, not just for the blessing, happiness, or benefit of the spouses. It is an act of service, commitment, and love that blesses the next generation. God commanded Adam and Eve to "be fruitful, and multiply, and replenish the earth" (Gen. 1:28). A primary purpose of temple marriage in this life is to grow and mature in sharing God's creative work in raising a family in righteousness. Parents enter into a partnership with God by participating in the PROCREATION of mortal bodies, which house the spirit children of God. At some future time all the worthy sons and daughters of God will be reunited with their Heavenly Parents as one eternal extended family in a state of resurrected glory.

People who live a worthy life but do not marry in the temples, for various reasons beyond their control, which might include not marrying, not having heard the gospel, or not having a temple available so that the marriage could be sealed for eternity, will at some time be given this opportunity (see BAPTISM FOR THE DEAD; SALVATION OF THE DEAD; SEALING). Latter-day Saints believe it is their privilege and duty to perform these sacred ordinances vicariously for deceased progenitors, and for others insofar as possible. Most of the sealing ordinances (temple marriage ceremonies) performed for the deceased are for couples who were married by civil authority in mortality but died without hearing the fulness of the gospel. In this program of vicarious service, men and women meet by appointment in the temple where they stand as proxies for parents, grandparents, or others who have passed into the next world and make the solemn covenants that will reach fruition for all who accept them in the SPIRIT WORLD, to culminate in the day of RESURRECTION.

All leaders of the Church encourage couples to initiate their marriage vows in a holy temple. For those who do not, whether converts to the Church, LDS couples coming to devotion to the Church in later life, or young LDS couples who have married outside the temple and then felt the desire for eternal covenants, temple marriage is a renewal of vows first spoken in a civil marriage ceremony. For those commitments to be honored through eternity, couples must be married by an officiator having the power to bind on earth and in heaven (Matt. 16:19; D&C 124:93). Thus, they must go to a temple, where there are those ordained and appointed to the power to seal covenants for time *and* eternity.

For Latter-day Saints, eternal marriage is an avenue to everlasting joy. Matthew Cowley, an apostle, expressed his conviction that it is "a wonderful thing . . . to kneel at an altar in the temple of God, clasping the hand of one who is to be your companion not only for time, but also for all eternity, and then to have born into that sacred and eternal covenant children for eternity. God is love. Love is eternal. Marriage is the sweetest and most sacred expression of love, therefore, marriage is eternal" (Cowley, p. 444).

BIBLIOGRAPHY

Benson, Ezra Taft. *The Teachings of Ezra Taft Benson.* Salt Lake City, 1988.

Brown, Hugh B. *You and Your Marriage.* Salt Lake City, 1960.

Burton, Theodore M. *God's Greatest Gift.* Salt Lake City, 1976.

Cowley, Matthew. *Matthew Cowley Speaks.* Salt Lake City, 1954.

McConkie, Bruce R. "The Eternal Family Concept." In *Genealogical Devotional Addresses*, pp. 81–93. Second Annual Priesthood Genealogical Research Seminar, Brigham Young University. Provo, Utah, 1967.

Smith, Joseph Fielding. *The Way to Perfection.* Salt Lake City, 1931.

JAMES T. DUKE

MARRIAGE RATES

See: Vital Statistics

MARRIAGE SUPPER OF THE LAMB

According to ancient and modern scripture, Jesus Christ, the bridegroom (Matt. 25:1–13), will host a "marriage supper" at his second coming when he symbolically claims his bride, the faithful members of his Church (Rev. 19:5–9; D&C 109:73–74).

In Jesus' parable of the marriage of the king's son (Matt. 22:1–14), "the king" represents God, and "his son" is Jesus. The guests first "bidden to the wedding," are the house of Israel. Guests invited later from "the highways" are the GENTILES to whom the gospel went after most Jews rejected it in the MERIDIAN OF TIME (*JC*, pp. 536–40).

Latter-day Saints believe that by teaching and exemplifying the gospel of Jesus Christ throughout the world they are extending to all mankind the invitation to come to the marriage feast. "For this cause I have sent you . . . that the earth may know that . . . all nations shall be invited. First, the rich and the learned, the wise and the noble; . . . then shall the poor, the lame, and the blind, and the deaf, come in unto the marriage of the Lamb, and partake of the supper of the Lord" (D&C 58:6–11).

After partaking of the sacrament with his apostles, Jesus said, "I will not drink henceforth of this fruit of the vine, until that day when I drink it new with you in my Father's kingdom" (Matt. 26:29). In latter days, the Lord declared, "The hour cometh that I will drink of the fruit of the vine with you" (D&C 27:5–12). "There is to be a day when . . . those who have kept the faith will be . . . admitted to the marriage feast; . . . they will partake of the fruit of the vine," or the sacramental emblems of Christ's atoning sacrifice, and reign with him on the EARTH (*TPJS*, p. 66).

[*See also* Last Days; Millennium.]

BIBLIOGRAPHY

McConkie, Bruce R. *The Millennial Messiah*, pp. 346–47. Salt Lake City, 1982.

JOHN M. MADSEN

MARTYRDOM OF JOSEPH AND HYRUM SMITH

The violent deaths of the Prophet Joseph SMITH at the age of thirty-eight and his brother Hyrum SMITH (age forty-four), Associate President and PATRIARCH of the Church, dramatically ended the founding period of the LDS Church. On June 27, 1844, they were mobbed and shot while confined at CARTHAGE JAIL in Hancock County, in western Illinois. Climaxing more than two decades of persecution across several states, this event gave them an enduring place as MARTYRS in the hearts of Latter-day Saints.

NAUVOO in 1844, gathering place for the Saints on the Mississippi River, contained elements of both greatness and dissension. Almost overnight, it grew from a village of religious refugees and new converts to the point where it rivaled Chicago as the largest city in Illinois. With Democrats and Whigs both vying for the Mormon vote, Nauvoo was granted one of the most liberal city charters in the state, an independent military force, and a strong judicial system (*see* NAUVOO CHARTER). However, as in Missouri during the 1830s, natural rivalry with older citizens in neighboring towns like Carthage (the county seat) and Warsaw (the next largest port city) turned to jealousy and hatred as Nauvoo's economic and political power grew (*see* NAUVOO ECONOMY; NAUVOO POLITICS).

These tensions coalesced around Joseph Smith. In addition to being prophet and President of the Church, he also served as mayor, commander of the NAUVOO LEGION state militia, justice of the peace, and university chancellor. Non-Mormon fears of this concentration of powers were intensified by the Church's belief in the theocratic union of spiritual, economic, and political matters under the PRIESTHOOD. This and other "unorthodox" doctrines, such as continuing revelation, temple ordinances for the living and the dead, new scripture, and plural marriage, further intensified political and economic rivalries.

Illinois anti-Mormons, perhaps assisted by old enemies from Missouri, joined with a handful of determined Mormon defectors within Nauvoo. Several had held high Church positions and, when excommunicated, fueled efforts to destroy Joseph Smith and the Church.

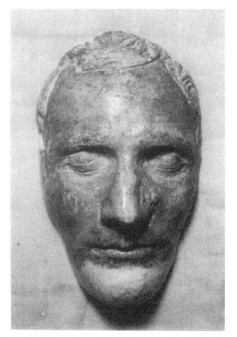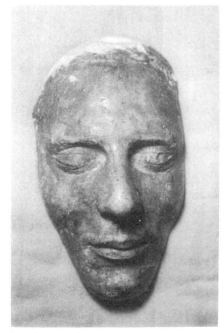

Death masks of Joseph Smith (right) and Hyrum Smith (left; chin reconstructed). From the collection of Wilford C. Wood. Courtesy Nelson Wadsworth.

The Prophet's life and his plans to resettle many of the Saints in the West (*see* WESTWARD MIGRATION) were cut short by a series of explosive confrontations with these conspirators. The igniting spark was the destruction of the defectors' intemperate newspaper, the *Nauvoo Expositor*, as a public nuisance by the Nauvoo city marshal, under orders from Joseph Smith and the city council. Removal of this press came after the first and only issue had vilified Joseph Smith, pledged to cause repeal of the protective Nauvoo charters, and invited mob action against the Saints. Joseph Smith's enemies countered the destroying of the press with criminal charges against him and his brother for inciting a riot. The brothers soon gained release from arrest on a habeas corpus before an LDS tribunal. Then, following the advice of a state circuit court judge, they appeared before a non-Mormon justice in Nauvoo and were exonerated of the charges against them.

However, threats of mob violence increased. In Warsaw and Carthage, newspapers called for extermination of the Mormons. On June 18, Joseph Smith mobilized his troops to protect Nauvoo. When Illinois governor Thomas Ford apparently sided with the opposition and ordered the

Church leaders to stand trial again on the same charges, this time in Carthage, Joseph and Hyrum first considered appealing to U.S. President John Tyler, but then decided instead to cross the Mississippi and escape to the West. Pressured by family and friends who felt abandoned and who believed Joseph to be nearly invincible, he agreed to return and surrender; but he prophesied that he would be going "like a lamb to the slaughter" and would be "murdered in cold blood" (*HC* 6:555, 559). Joseph urged Hyrum to save himself and succeed him as prophet, but Hyrum refused and accompanied his brother to Carthage.

Despite his promises of protection and a fair trial, Governor Ford allowed the Smiths to be imprisoned by their enemies without bail and without a hearing on a wholly new charge of treason for having declared martial law in Nauvoo. Stating that he had to "satisfy the people," the Governor ignored clear warnings of danger and disbanded most of the troops. He then left the hostile Carthage Greys to guard the jail and took the most dependable troops with him to Nauvoo.

During the governor's absence, a mob of between one hundred and two hundred armed men—many of them from the disbanded Warsaw militia—

Hancock County Courthouse, in Carthage, Illinois (c. 1900), the county seat where the assassins of Joseph Smith were tried and found not guilty. Courtesy Rare Books and Manuscripts, Brigham Young University.

gathered in late afternoon, blackened their faces with mud and gunpowder, and then stormed the jail. In less than two minutes, they overcame feigned resistance from the Greys, rushed upstairs, and fired through the closed door. Hyrum, shot first, died instantly. John TAYLOR, an apostle, tried to escape out a window and was shot five times, but survived to later become the Church's third President. Only Willard Richards, another apostle, survived unharmed. Trying to go out the window to deflect attention from the two survivors inside, Joseph Smith was hit in the chest and collarbone with two shots from the open doorway and two more from outside the window. His final words as he fell to the ground outside the jail were, "O Lord, my God!" (HC 6:618). As rumors spread that the Mormons were coming, the mob dispersed.

Several times during his last days Joseph Smith told the Saints that while he had enjoyed God's safekeeping until his mission was fulfilled, he had now completed all that God required of him and could claim no special protection. Early in his career, the Prophet had recorded that the Lord told him, "Even if they do unto you . . . as they have done unto me, blessed are ye, for you shall dwell with me in glory" (D&C 6:30). Church leaders then and now have taught that the shedding of these martyrs' innocent blood was necessary to seal their testimony of the latter-day work that they "might be honored and the wicked might be condemned" (D&C 136:39).

BIBLIOGRAPHY

Esplin, Ronald K. "Joseph Smith's Mission and Timetable: 'God will Protect Me Until My Work Is Done.'" In The Prophet Joseph Smith: Essays on the Life and Mission of Joseph Smith, ed. L. Porter and S. Black, pp. 280–319. Salt Lake City, 1989.

HC 6:519–631, esp. 561–622.

Jessee, Dean C. "Return to Carthage: Writing the History of Joseph Smith's Martyrdom." Journal of Mormon History 8 (1981):3–19.

Madsen, Truman G. Joseph Smith the Prophet, pp. 109–126, 174–83. Salt Lake City, 1989.

Miller, David E., and Della S. Miller. Nauvoo: The City of Joseph, pp. 130–74. Salt Lake City, 1974.

Oaks, Dallin H., and Marvin S. Hill. Carthage Conspiracy: The Trial of the Accused Assassins of Joseph Smith. Urbana, Ill., 1979.

JOSEPH I. BENTLEY

MARTYRS

The term "martyr" (Greek martys, "a witness") in Christianity refers to a person who has suffered death because of his or her Christian witness or commitment and who subsequently has been accorded honors by a church. While Latter-day Saints honor Joseph and Hyrum SMITH as martyrs, they do not venerate them in annual celebrations of their death dates, nor do they view them as heavenly intercessors for mortals.

The ancient use of the term "martyr" involves the legal environment—witnesses testifying in a legal proceeding. The basic idea relates to establishing facts or assertions that concern matters beyond the experience of the listeners. The meaning has reference to objective events or to personal testimonies. However, the usual scriptural use carries the additional meaning of revelation by the Holy Spirit, which would empower a witness to bear inspired testimony of religious truths.

OLD TESTAMENT. In the ancient usage, the name of the Mosaic tabernacle was "tent of testimony" or "tabernacle of witness." The ark within the tabernacle contained the tablets of stone with the Lord's Ten Commandments, Aaron's rod that budded, and a pot of manna. These were tokens of the spiritual power of God.

While most references to "witness" and "testify" carry legal meanings, one sees the additional revelatory sense of a witness in Isaiah's revelation, in which he "saw" the Lord and heard the seraphim cry, gave him an understanding of bearing witness to prophetic matters that are beyond usual human experience (Isa. 6:1–7). Isaiah also recorded a divine commission in which the Lord, the Holy One of Israel, promised to gather his sons and daughters from the ends of the earth. As a result, Israel would come to know the acts of God on their behalf: "Therefore, ye are my witnesses, saith the Lord, that I am God" (Isa. 43:1–12). Though afflicted and hated for their testimony, it would not be in vain: Generations to come would be blessed by it (Isa. 60:14–15). In another instance, the Lord instructed Jeremiah to purchase a plot of land from his cousin. He summoned legal witnesses, paid for the land with silver according to "law and custom," and wondered why he should buy land falling to Babylon. The Lord explained that his purchase of land by a deed foreshadowed that later the people of the city would buy and sell land, a prophetic or spiritual witness of their future return from Babylon (Jer. 32:6–44).

NEW TESTAMENT. The terms "record," "testimony," and "witness" are used more than two hundred times in the New Testament. In speaking to Pilate, Jesus asserted that he had been born into the world to "bear witness unto the truth" (John 18:37; cf. 1 Tim. 6:13). Further, one of Jesus' discourses illuminating the basis of witnessing identified six foundations for a testimony: Jesus himself, John the Baptist, Jesus' own works, the Father, the scriptures, and Moses (John 8:14; cf. 5:32–47). Just prior to his ascension, Jesus explained to the apostles that, after the Holy Ghost had come upon them, they would be "witnesses" to him in Jerusalem and the "uttermost part of the earth" (Acts 1:8). He had warned them they might be hated, afflicted, and killed for his name's sake (Matt. 5:10–12; 24:9). The apostles' association with Jesus during the post-Resurrection ministry satisfied the legal aspect of witnessing, but their testimony of his messianic character would be conferred and confirmed by the Holy Ghost. In a related vein,

one's death could be viewed as a martyrdom for Christ, with eternal rewards to follow, as seen in Revelation 2:8–10; cf. 14:13. Certainly those true to the Savior, and redeemed by him, are his witnesses and are rewarded by him (Rev. 7:13–17).

LATTER-DAY SCRIPTURE. In the Book of Mormon, several persons die and are honored as martyrs. The prophet ABINADI is the most notable example (Mosiah 12:1–17:1). Others include the women and children of Ammonihah who were burned to death for their beliefs (Alma 14:1–10). At the death of those women and children, the prophet ALMA₂ assured his friend AMULEK that "the Lord receiveth them up unto himself, in glory" (Alma 14:11).

The Doctrine and Covenants teaches that "all they who have given their lives for [God's] name shall be crowned" (D&C 101:15) and that the blood of the innocent ascends to God "in testimony" (D&C 109:49; cf. 98:13). In this connection, members of the Church refer to the murder of Joseph and Hyrum Smith as "the martyrdom of Joseph Smith the Prophet, and Hyrum Smith the Patriarch" (D&C 135:1). The Lord spoke through Brigham YOUNG that "it was needful that [Joseph Smith] should seal his testimony with his blood, that he might be honored and the wicked might be condemned" (D&C 136:39; cf. 135).

BIBLIOGRAPHY

Patch, Robert C. "The Spiritual Connotation in the Scriptural Concept of Witness." Ph.D. diss., Brigham Young University, 1964.

Trites, Allison A. *The New Testament Concept of Witness.* Cambridge, 1977.

ROBERT C. PATCH

MARY, MOTHER OF JESUS

Centuries before her birth, Book of Mormon prophets referred to Mary by name in prophecies of her vital mission (Mosiah 3:8). Describing her as "most beautiful and fair above all other virgins" (1 Ne. 11:13–20) and a "precious and chosen vessel" (Alma 7:10), they prophesied that Mary would bear the Son of God and was therefore blessed above all other women. "We cannot but think that the Father would choose the greatest female spirit to be the mother of his Son, even as he chose the male spirit like unto him to be the Savior" (McConkie, p. 327).

Mary's willingness to submit to the will of the Father was noted in the biblical account. When Gabriel announced that she would be the mother of the Savior, Mary was perplexed; yet she did not waiver in her humble OBEDIENCE and FAITH in God. Her response was unadorned: "Behold the handmaid of the Lord; be it unto me according to thy word" (Luke 1:38).

Had Judah been a free nation, Mary could have been recognized as a "princess of royal blood through descent from David" (*JC*, p. 90). Being of that earthly lineage, Jesus was correctly called a descendant of David (*see* JESUS CHRIST IN THE SCRIPTURES: THE BIBLE).

As a faithful Jewish woman, she followed the customs of her day. At least forty-one days after giving birth to her first son, Mary went to the Court of the Women, where she became ceremonially clean in the purification rite, offering two turtledoves or two pigeons at the temple as a sacrifice (Luke 2:22–24). In the years that followed, Mary bore additional children by her earthly husband Joseph (Matt. 1:25; 13:55–56; Mark 6:3). One of them, "James the Lord's brother" (Gal. 1:19), became a Christian leader in Jerusalem.

In the New Testament, Mary is mentioned in conjunction with the accounts of the youthful Jesus teaching in the temple (Luke 2:41–51), his turning the water to wine at Cana (John 2:2–5), his crucifixion (John 19:25–26), and as mourning with the apostles after Jesus' ascension (Acts 1:14).

Doctrinally, Latter-day Saints do not view Mary as the intercessor with her son in behalf of those who pray and they do not pray to her. They affirm the VIRGIN BIRTH but reject the traditions of the IMMACULATE CONCEPTION, of Mary's perpetual virginity, and of her "assumption" (cf. McConkie, p. 327). Mary, like all mortals, returns to the Father only through the atonement of her son Jesus Christ.

BIBLIOGRAPHY

McConkie, Bruce R. *The Mortal Messiah, Book I.* Salt Lake City, 1981.

CAMILLE FRONK

MATERIAL CULTURE

The artifacts of a society are known as its material culture. Latter-day Saints, like all other cultural groups, have altered their physical surroundings to reflect their own worldview. Every object created or modified by members of a group is part of that group's material culture. LDS material culture encompasses a particular constellation of objects, only a few of which are unique. But, taken together, they create what can be identified as a Mormon environment.

In parts of the American West settled heavily by Latter-day Saints in the nineteenth century, the landscape reflects their peculiar approach to town building (*see* COMMUNITY; COLONIZATION). One of the top priorities for early settlers was the establishment of extensive irrigation systems that brought mountain water to every farm. Ditches were dug, and dams of a variety of designs were and still are used to divert water onto a plot of land in a rotating calendar of "water turns." The influence of irrigation can be seen to this day in Mormon-settled areas where green fields, shady, flower-filled yards, and rows of Lombardy poplars mark the landscape, even in the driest desert areas (*see* AGRICULTURE).

A settlement pattern used frequently by Mormon pioneers has become known as the Mormon village (*see* CITY PLANNING; WARD), with homes and businesses situated closely around the central square, streets oriented toward the cardinal directions, and farm lands extending out around this settlement. Farmers left the village to work fields allotted to them by their ecclesiastical leaders. Designs of outbuildings and houses were based on settlers' previous experience or on knowledge gained from neighbors through a process of oral tradition and example (*see* FOLKLORE). Hay was stacked with a "Mormon derrick," a device that can still be seen in several variations although no longer used, in the Mormon-settled West.

The most distinctive Mormon architecture has been in religious buildings: temples, tithing houses, and meetinghouses, for instance. Important LDS symbols, such as the beehive; the sun, moon, and stars; and the all-seeing eye, appear on many of these structures.

Most material objects found in early LDS homes were similar to those found in other American homes. Ethnic origins of the makers often influenced furniture design. Some furniture built by Mormon craftspeople bore cultural symbols similar to those found on buildings. Prior to the coming of the railroad, locally made furniture was distinctive, mostly because it had to be built out of local softwoods rather than eastern hardwoods. Thus, spin-

Emery, Utah, Relief Society quilting, c. 1942–1943. In this project, 104 women spent 3,246 hours in a 75-day period, and made 158 quilts.

dles, legs, and other parts had to be thicker than normal to support the same weight. One item of furniture, a lounge with a section that pulled out to accommodate two sleepers, became known as the "Mormon couch" because of its popularity in Utah.

Today, Latter-day Saints continue to surround themselves with objects typical of their home countries. In addition, an LDS home may contain elements that identify its occupants as practicing Saints. Often, there is a picture of a temple—usually the one where the residents received their endowments or were married. The temple motif may be carried out in other objects, such as quilts and embroidery (see FOLK ART). Photos of family members are often found in profusion, reflecting the cultural and personal emphasis on family.

The Church's emphasis on emergency preparedness, especially home food storage, has caused members to devise methods for creating storage space in homes of limited size. What appears to be a round table covered by a long tablecloth may actually be a large cylindrical container of wheat, beans, or rice. Food practices of the Latter-day Saints, also a part of material culture, often focus on the rotating use of storage foods.

LDS women contribute to their material culture through monthly RELIEF SOCIETY homemaking meetings, where they share recipes, craft ideas, and work methods. Particularly popular are inexpensive projects that transform utilitarian ob-

jects into decorative ones, such as a small kitchen strainer becoming a Christmas reindeer decoration through the application of colored felt shapes. A craft that becomes popular can sweep through homemaking meetings throughout the Church, and eventually may be seen in a majority of LDS homes for a time.

Even after death, material reminders of Latter-day Saints' religious values can be found in their gravestones. Symbols such as clasped hands and doves, while not unique to Mormon culture, evoke images of eternity for Latter-day Saints that are reflective of their beliefs. Modern gravestones often have an image of a temple on one side, with a list of the couple's children on the other, emphasizing again the idea that a good marriage and family are the best measures of a life well lived.

The Church itself contributes to the material culture of its members. It produces or has produced books of scripture, pictures, journals, lesson manuals, videotapes, sacrament trays, Primary bandalos, commemorative jewelry, and other items used by members in practicing their religion. Some, such as printed programs for ward SACRAMENT MEETINGS, are ephemeral, but they are no less part of the material culture.

Today, as the Church spreads throughout the world, it is more difficult to identify specifically LDS objects. The Salt Lake Temple is one symbol that is frequently represented in crafts from many

Navajo pot by Lucy Leuppe McKelvey (1989, fired ceramic). Motifs on this pot include four Book of Mormon brothers (Laman, Lemuel, Sam, and Nephi), gold plates, and serpent designs reminiscent of those associated with the white Aztec god Quetzalcoatl. Some Latter-day Saints believe that Quetzalcoatl mythology derived in part from the resurrected Jesus Christ's visit to the American continent, an event recorded in the Book of Mormon. Church Museum of History and Art.

cultures, including Tongan tapa cloth and Native American beadwork. Some symbols and objects may be universal to all Church members, while others will be localized. A bottle of home-preserved peaches is not unique in itself, but the sense of religious obligation to "put up fruit" and the implications of righteousness attached to the preserver are unique to this culture. All objects identifiable as "Mormon" are expressive of the values of their makers. Latter-day Saints will continue to manipulate their physical environment, mixing their religious values with influences from their ethnic or national cultures to create a landscape that is uniquely their own.

BIBLIOGRAPHY

Brunvand, Jan Harold. *A Guide for Collectors of Folklore in Utah*. Salt Lake City, 1971.

Cannon, Hal. *The Grand Beehive*. Salt Lake City, 1980.

———. *Utah Folk Art: A Catalog of Material Culture*. Provo, Utah, 1980.

Edison, Carol. "Mormon Gravestones: A Folk Expression of Identity and Belief." *Dialogue* 22 (Winter 1989):89–94. Also photos of folk art throughout the issue.

Fife, Austin E., and James M. Fife. "Hay Derricks of the Great Basin and Upper Snake River Valley." *Western Folklore* 10 (1951):320–22; and *Idaho Folklife: Homesteads to Headstones*, ed. Louie Attebery. Salt Lake City, 1985.

"The Tangible Past." *Utah Historical Quarterly* 56 (Fall 1988), special issue edited by Tom Carter.

ELAINE THATCHER

MATERNITY AND CHILD HEALTH CARE

Before professional doctors and nurses assumed primary responsibility for delivering health care, LDS women played a major role in providing maternity and child health care in their communities. Their efforts continued into the twentieth century with the establishment of maternity and children's hospitals and clinics under the sponsorship of the RELIEF SOCIETY and PRIMARY and with some women still serving as midwives in rural areas. The Relief Society also sponsored educational programs to prepare mothers for the delivery and care of infants and children. Concern for the health of mothers and children continues in Relief Society lessons today, and members are advised to seek the best medical care available. Specially trained Church missionaries also assist in programs to improve health care in developing countries.

At the time the Church was established (1830), the methods of many doctors were experimental and often harsh, and women usually did not call upon men for maternity care because it was thought unseemly. When available, midwives often assisted during childbirth. As the Church grew, leaders called and set apart women to serve as midwives. In Nauvoo in the 1840s, the Prophet Joseph SMITH set apart three midwives. After the main body of the Church moved to the Salt Lake Valley, other women were called to serve as midwives both in Salt Lake City and in the outlying settlements. Because midwives were called by priesthood authority, they were accorded trust and respect similar to that given ecclesiastical leaders. They often dispensed herb treatments, passed on by experimentation and word of mouth, and sometimes administered health blessings.

Ward Relief Societies began coordinated health programs in the late 1860s after President Brigham YOUNG assigned two of his plural wives, Eliza R. SNOW and Zina D. H. YOUNG, to promote health-care education among the Saints and to train midwives. In 1873 he asked each ward Relief Society to appoint three women to study nursing and midwifery, and a nursing school was opened for their training.

In the same year, President Young said that the time had come for women to study at medical schools in the East. At least six women responded, earning medical degrees in the 1870s. Most influential among these early doctors were Romania Pratt, Ellis Shipp, and Ellen Ferguson, who set up Utah's earliest professional training programs. Dr. Pratt wrote many articles on health. Dr. Shipp opened the School of Obstetrics and Nursing in Salt Lake City in 1878 and taught two six-month long courses each year, from which more than five hundred students eventually graduated. In 1888 she helped found Utah's first medical journal, the *Salt Lake Sanitarian*. Dr. Ferguson helped initiate plans for the Church-sponsored DESERET HOSPITAL, which opened in 1882 and shortly thereafter became the center for the School of Obstetrics and Nursing.

In 1899 the Salt Lake Stake organized the Relief Society Nursing School to provide nursing training especially for women who lived in rural communities and came to Salt Lake City for instruction. The school continued successfully until 1920.

By 1900 there were at least 34 female and 236 male doctors practicing medicine in Utah (Waters, pp. 108–111). The role of midwives began to diminish, but the Church's concern for maternity and child health care continued.

In 1911 the general presidency and general board of the Primary undertook the establishment of a hospital fund and the endowment of two rooms for children in the LDS Hospital. Primary-sponsored hospital care for children continued, culminating in 1952 in the establishment of the Primary

One of the first graduating classes of nurses stands in front of the Dr. W. H. Groves Latter-day Saints Hospital (c. 1905). Courtesy Utah State Historical Society.

Children's Hospital, which was operated by the Church until 1975, when it was transferred to private ownership (*see* HOSPITALS).

In 1912, following the publication of a Utah State Board of Health report linking many infant deaths to inadequate prenatal and postnatal care (Morrell, p. 197), the Relief Society began an intensive program for educating mothers in health care for infants and children. Local Relief Societies sponsored day-long clinics. Stake Relief Societies in Cottonwood, Utah, and Snowflake, Arizona, established their own maternity hospitals. Clinics and health care for children remained high-priority items for Relief Societies until the mid-1930s, when the federal Social Security Act was passed, subsidizing educational programs, prenatal clinics, and immunization programs.

Today, Relief Society women are encouraged to seek appropriate professional medical care and to participate in nursing and first-aid classes. Relief Society manuals include chapters on health care and nursing. Among the full-time missionaries of the Church are a great many young women (approximately 270 in 1990) with health and teaching backgrounds who, in addition to fulfilling proselytizing responsibilities, are assigned to teach disease prevention, nutrition, and home health care to Church members in developing countries. Like the midwives of the early Church, they devote their time and talents to improving health care in the various communities where they have been called to serve.

BIBLIOGRAPHY

Divett, Robert T. *Medicine and the Mormons.* Bountiful, Utah, 1981.

Morrell, Joseph R. *Utah's Health and You: A History of Utah's Public Health.* Salt Lake City, 1956.

Waters, Christine Croft. "Pioneering Physicians in Utah, 1847–1900." Master's thesis, University of Utah, 1977.

CHRISTINE CROFT WATERS

MATTER

By the end of the eighteenth century, modern scientific methods had begun to provide new insights into the fundamental nature of matter, and these negated the Greek philosophical position of form over matter. This change in scientific thinking was contemporary with the teachings of the Prophet Joseph SMITH in the theological realm. His teachings returned theology to the intimate relationship between God and mankind of early Judeo-Christian writings. These concepts were in contrast to the position that deity is an embodiment of principles and philosophical ideals that transcend in importance the physical realities of matter. Furthermore, the view that matter was created from nothing (ex nihilo), a concept dominating theological and scientific thought for many centuries and still widespread in nineteenth-century thought, lost the support of modern science and was opposed by the gospel restored by Joseph Smith. Modern scientific theories of matter, from Antoine Lavoisier's (1743–1794) to Erwin Schrödinger's (1887–1961), maintain the permanence of matter.

In the twentieth century, atomic theory has embodied a number of fundamental nuclear particles and powerful mathematical theories. Some, falling outside human intuition, account for properties of matter newly discovered in this century. Concepts have led to the development of unified quantum mechanical and quantum dynamic theories for both matter and light. The conservation law of Lavoisier has been extended to include all equivalent forms of matter and energy and still constitutes one of the primary pillars of modern science.

It is significant that the teachings of the restored gospel on the eternal nature of physical matter, along with a parallel in the spiritual realm, embody these conservation principles. These are key statements: "The elements are eternal" (D&C 93:33). "The spirit of man is not a created being; it existed from eternity, and will exist to eternity. Anything created cannot be eternal; and earth, water, etc., had their existence in an elementary state, from eternity" (Joseph Smith, in *HC* 3:387).

Addressing the issue of creation ex nihilo, Joseph Smith asserted in one of his final sermons: "Now, the word create . . . does not mean to create out of nothing; it means to organize; the same as a man would organize materials and build a ship. Hence, we infer that God had materials to organize the world out of chaos—chaotic matter, which is element. . . . Element had an existence from the time [God] had. The pure principles of element are principles which can never be destroyed; they may be organized and reorganized, but not destroyed. They had no beginning and can have no end" (*HC* 6:308–309).

Extending the concept of the eternal nature of matter to the substance of spirit, Joseph Smith revealed, "There is no such thing as immaterial matter. All spirit is matter, but it is more fine or pure, and can only be discerned by purer eyes; we cannot see it; but when our bodies are purified we shall see that it is all matter" (D&C 131:7–8).

Parley P. Pratt, an apostle and close associate of Joseph Smith, wrote, "Matter and spirit are the two great principles of all existence. Everything animate and inanimate is composed of one or the other, or both of these eternal principles. . . . Matter and spirit are of equal duration; both are self-existent, they never began to exist, and they never can be annihilated. . . . Matter as well as spirit is eternal, uncreated, self existing. However infinite the variety of its changes, forms and shapes; . . . eternity is inscribed in indelible characters on every particle" (HC 4:55).

In strict analogy to principles governing physical matter, the revelations to Joseph Smith stress that eternity for spirits also derives from the eternal existence of spiritual matter or elements. The preeminent manifestation of the eternal nature of both physical and spiritual matter is found in the eternal existence of God and ultimately his human children as discrete, indestructible entities. In this unique LDS doctrine, matter in all of its many forms, instead of occupying a subordinate role relative to philosophical paradigms, assumes a sovereign position, along with the principles and laws governing its properties and characteristics.

BIBLIOGRAPHY
Pratt, Parley P. "Eternal Duration of Matter." HC 4:55.

DAVID M. GRANT

MATTHEW, GOSPEL OF

Latter-day Saints consider the Gospel of Matthew as the preeminent introduction to the New Testament. The Gospel of Matthew is reproduced and revised in LDS scripture more than any other biblical text except the Genesis creation account. It is edited throughout in the Prophet Joseph SMITH's inspired revision of the Bible (see JOSEPH SMITH TRANSLATION OF THE BIBLE [JST]), and the edited version of Matthew 24 is reproduced in the Pearl of Great Price (JS—M 1:1–55). The Sermon on the Mount is virtually repeated in the Book of Mormon

by the resurrected Savior to his "other sheep" (John 10:16; 3 Ne. 15:21) in the Western Hemisphere (3 Ne. 12–14); but it is made explicit that it is the poor in spirit who come unto him who are blessed; and it is implied that blessedness comes to all other categories mentioned in the beatitudes by the same means (3 Ne. 12:2–12). The Doctrine and Covenants provides an explanation of the parable of the wheat and the tares in a latter-day context (D&C 86). Each rendition is easily recognized as basically the same sermon. However, the inspired changes are significant to Latter-day Saints, as they often establish or support major points of doctrine.

Latter-day Saints, like many others, equate Levi and Matthew, acknowledging the "publican" apostle as author of the gospel (Matt. 9:9). As a Jew, Matthew saw Christianity as the culmination of Judaism, with Jesus as the promised Messiah. In many details of Jesus' life, Matthew saw fulfillment of Old Testament prophecy (see JESUS CHRIST IN THE SCRIPTURES), and the JST enriches the Matthean theme that all this was done "that it might be fulfilled which was spoken by the prophets" (Matt. 2:23; cf. Millet, 1985, pp. 152–54). Through a royal line, beginning with Abraham, Matthew establishes Jesus' Davidic ancestry (Matt. 1:1–17) and his right to reign as "king of the Jews" (Matt. 27:37); and he relates the nativity story from Joseph's viewpoint (Matt. 1:18–25; Matt. 2:1–25). The Prophet Joseph Smith adds that Jesus grew up with his brethren and waited for his ministry to come, serving under his "father," and "needed not that any man should teach him" (JST Matt. 3:24–25).

Many scriptures note that the Messiah will be "like unto Moses" (Deut. 18:15–19; Moses 1:6; 1 Ne. 22:20–21; Acts 7:37; JS—H 1:40), and in the Matthew account readers see parallels between some of the experiences of Moses and Jesus: There was a sovereign who slew children, a return from Egypt, forty days on a mountain, and the miraculous feeding of multitudes. Most of all, there was an enunciation of divine law by both. The promised similitude, however, may have established expectations in Jewish hearts that Jesus failed to satisfy.

To Latter-day Saints, the Sermon on the Mount is a concise summary of much of Jesus' teaching, emphasizing the spirit of the law and encouraging righteous acts for righteous reasons. They recognize it as a single discourse of Jesus in light of his complete repetition of it among the Nephites (3 Ne. 12–14). Both the JST and 3 Nephi versions include enriching details not found in extent biblical texts, including the setting of the sermon. For example, Jesus directed only his chosen twelve and other selected disciples to take no thought for their life or for the morrow (3 Ne. 13:25) and to teach from house to house, noting that while the world will persecute them, their Heavenly Father will provide for them (JST Matt. 6:2, 25–27). Then he turned to the multitude and warned of unrighteous judgment (3 Ne. 14:1). Latter-day Saints acknowledge the necessity of good judgment and seek to judge righteously (see JST Matt. 7:2; cf. Moro. 7:15–19).

The JST revision of Matthew is replete with subtle but meaningful differences from the King James text. It becomes clear, for instance, that Jesus entered the Judean wilderness primarily to commune with his Father, not merely to be tempted (JST Matt. 4:1–2), and, unswayed by any doubt of his divinity as the One foretold by the prophets, he called his apostles (JST Matt. 4:18). JST Matthew 17:14 introduces a latter-day Elias: "Then the disciples understood that he spake unto them of John the Baptist, and also of another who should come and restore all things, as it is written by the prophets." A doctrinal principle is strengthened when Jesus declares that he came to save the lost, but little children need no repentance (JST Matt. 18:2; 19:13; cf. Moro. 8:5–24).

Latter-day Saints recognize the importance of faith, good works, and ordinances, and do not stress one above the others, as all are essential for salvation. They draw support from Matthew's many references to faith and good works (e.g., Matt. 16:27), and they recognize the ordinances of BAPTISM by immersion (Matt. 3:16; JST Matt. 3:44–45), ORDINATION TO THE PRIESTHOOD (Matt. 10:1), and healing of the sick (Matt. 9:18). In addition, they believe that Jesus established a formal church organization under the supervision of his ordained apostles, and they cite the Matthean text both for Jesus' intent to establish a church (Matt. 16:18) and for the existence of the Church (Matt. 18:17; cf. Millet, 1985, pp. 148–51). At Caesarea Philippi, when Peter declared Christ's divinity (Matt. 16:15), Jesus affirmed that he knew this only through revelation from the Father, noting, "Thou art Peter, and upon this rock I will build my church" (Matt. 16:17–18). While Mormons acknowledge Peter's primacy in the early Church, they quickly point out that Christ's Church—both in Peter's day and in the latter days—was and is

founded upon the rock of revelation and that living prophets still look to that rock for guidance.

BIBLIOGRAPHY

Millet, Robert L. "The JST and the Synoptic Gospels: Literary Style." In *The Joseph Smith Translation*, ed. M. Nyman and R. Millet. .Provo, Utah, 1985.

———. "The Testimony of Matthew." In *Studies in Scripture*, ed. K. Jackson and R. Millet, Vol. 5, pp. 38–60. Salt Lake City, 1986.

WM. REVELL PHILLIPS

MCKAY, DAVID O.

David O. McKay (1873–1970), sustained as the ninth President of The Church of Jesus Christ of Latter-day Saints on April 9, 1951, served as a General Authority for nearly sixty-four years, longer than any other person in Church history. During that time he served as a counselor in the First Presidency for seventeen years and was President for nearly nineteen years. He is remembered for his contributions to education, his exemplary family life, his emphasis on missionary work, his humanitarianism, his practical advice on achieving a happy life, and his participation in civic affairs, and for leading the Church toward increased internationalism.

The third child of David and Jennette Evans McKay, David Oman McKay was born in Huntsville, Utah, on September 8, 1873. While growing up on his father's farm, he faced tragedy and privation much earlier than many children. When he was six, his two older sisters died, and just a year later, his father was called on a two-year mission to his native Scotland. Young David matured quickly when he was left to help his mother care for the farm and the family, which included a younger brother and two younger sisters, one a two-year-old and the other a baby girl born ten days after his father left. The enterprising family, with the help of neighbors, had realized enough profit to surprise their father and husband with a much-needed addition to the house when he returned from his mission.

Young David continued to attend school, work on the farm, and, during the summer, deliver the *Ogden Standard Examiner* to a nearby mining town. He had an insatiable hunger for learning, and during his round trips on horseback, he spent

President David O. McKay (1873–1970), an educator, served in the Quorum of the Twelve or the First Presidency for sixty-three years and nine months, longer than any other General Authority in the history of the Church. Courtesy Utah State Historical Society.

much of the time reading and memorizing passages from the world's great literature that were later to permeate his sermons and writings. He also loved riding horses, swimming, and other sports; dramatics; debate; singing; and playing the piano with the Huntsville town orchestra.

After completing the eighth grade, David enrolled in the Church's Weber Stake Academy in Ogden, Utah. Two years later, he was back in Huntsville as principal of the community school, but after a year he decided that he needed more schooling for a career in teaching and enrolled at the University of Utah. He graduated in June 1897 as class president and valedictorian. The theme of his valedictory address, "An Unsatisfied Appetite for Knowledge Means Progress and Is the State of a Normal Mind," characterized his life.

After graduation Elder McKay accepted a mission call to Great Britain. He arrived in Liverpool on August 25, 1897, and, like his father before him, was soon appointed to preside over the Scottish conference (later known as district). During a special priesthood meeting, he received a powerful spiritual manifestation confirming the truthfulness of the gospel. He had been seeking that confirmation since childhood, and it remained with him throughout his life. In Liverpool in 1899, he discovered a saying that became a lifetime motto. Homesick and discouraged, he noticed over the doorway of an unfinished house an unusual stone arch bearing the inscription "What-E'er Thou Art, Act Well Thy Part." His attitude changed, and that perspective exemplified his life.

He returned home in the fall of 1899 and accepted a teaching position at Weber Stake Academy. On January 2, 1901, he married Emma Ray Riggs in the Salt Lake Temple; they had seven children.

As a teacher, McKay was popular, effective, and deeply concerned that his students absorb more than facts. He believed that teachers must lead students to stretch their minds into the world of ideas. "If you will give your class a thought, even one new thought during your recitation period," he later told other educators, "you will find that they will go away satisfied. But it is your obligation to be prepared to give that new thought" (1953, p. 439). He also believed that teachers must develop in students the moral and ethical values that lead to responsible citizenship. "Teaching is the noblest profession in the world," he proclaimed, for "upon the proper education of youth depend the permanency and purity of the home, the safety and perpetuity of the nation" (1953, p. 436). "True education," he said, "seeks . . . to make men and women not only good mathematicians, proficient linguists, profound scientists, or brilliant literary lights, but also honest men, combined with virtue, temperance, and brotherly love—men and women who prize truth, justice, wisdom, benevolence, and self-control as the choicest acquisitions of a successful life" (1953, p. 441). Teachers must be the exemplars, and he scolded the nation for not recognizing the need to pay for outstanding teachers in the classroom.

In 1902 McKay became the principal of Weber Stake Academy, and he soon instituted a number of progressive and innovative program changes. His Church assignments during these years also centered on education, as he served on the Weber Stake Sunday School board and then as a member of the superintendency (see SUNDAY SCHOOL). He was fully satisfied with what he be-

President McKay (1947) with his horses "Lady" and "Bess." His love of horses began as a boy on the family farm in Huntsville, Utah.

lieved would be a lifelong career in education when in 1906 everything changed: three members of the Quorum of the Twelve Apostles died, and David O. McKay, at age thirty-two, was called to that quorum.

In addition to his new responsibilities, Elder McKay remained active in educational administration. He stayed on as head of Weber Academy until 1908 and then served on its board of trustees until 1922. He was a member of the Board of Regents of the University of Utah in 1921–1922, and in 1940–1941 he was a member of the Board of Trustees of Utah State Agricultural College (later Utah State University). As a General Authority of the Church he became a member of the superintendency of the Church's Sunday School, and from 1918 to 1934 was the superintendent. In 1919 he became the Church's first Commissioner of Education, and in this assignment he had some difficult decisions to make. In 1920 he advised the closing of most Church-owned academies and the establishment of SEMINARIES adjacent to all high schools with sufficient LDS population. Religious instruction would still be given to high school students, but without the expense of full high school programs. A seminary adjacent to Granite High in Salt Lake City had already proved successful, and the new recommendation was quickly put into effect. He also recommended that Brigham Young University adopt a full college curriculum and that the

other five Church colleges (four in Utah and one in Idaho) develop just two-year programs, primarily for training teachers. Within the next ten years, all the Utah colleges except Brigham Young University were transferred to the state.

Elder McKay became the most widely traveled Church leader of his day, an emissary to the growing worldwide Church. In 1920–1921 he toured the missions of the world, stopping at many places never before visited by a General Authority. From 1922 to 1924, he was back in Europe, this time as president of the European Mission (*see* EUROPE). His success there became legendary, as he did much to improve the public image of the Church. He also revitalized missionary work by urging every Latter-day Saint to make a commitment to bring one new member into the Church each year. In later years he became famous for his motto "Every member a missionary," an emphasis that began in Europe in 1923. In addition, he urged the Saints to remain in Europe rather than to emigrate to America, promising them that one day the full program of the Church, including sacred TEMPLES, would be made available in their homelands.

In 1934 President Heber J. GRANT chose David O. McKay to be his Second Counselor in the FIRST PRESIDENCY of the Church. In 1951, the same year that he and Emma Ray celebrated their golden wedding anniversary, he became President of the Church. Tall, still robust despite his seventy-seven years, possessing a full head of wavy white hair, and with eyes that one man characterized as "fiercely tender," David O. McKay looked every bit the prophet his followers revered him to be.

President McKay's administration covered an important period of transition. As he guided the Church into the last half of the twentieth century, he faced critical new challenges connected with numerical growth, international expansion, and a variety of political and social problems related to the rapidly changing world. Church membership nearly tripled, from 1.1 million to 2.8 million; the number of STAKES grew from 184 to 500; the number of missions more than doubled; the missionary force expanded six times; temples were erected in Switzerland, New Zealand, and Great Britain, as well as California; and the Church was established in several new countries. As an experienced leader with both a firm hand and a humanitarian nature, President McKay was admirably suited for the task of moving the Church toward the new internationalism that would characterize the later twentieth century.

In the summer of 1952 he visited nine European countries on what may have been the most significant tour of his career. His announcement that a site had been selected for the erection of a temple just outside Bern, Switzerland, ushered in a new era, symbolizing the establishment of the full program of the Church in nations outside North America. Having temples within traveling distance strengthened the Saints spiritually and encouraged them to remain in their homelands to build up the Church. President McKay dedicated the Swiss Temple in 1955, and soon temples began to dot the world. Smaller and less expensive than previous temples, the new temples introduced design changes and technological innovations (including special films) that made the temple ceremonies available in many languages.

Another step in the maturation of the Church outside North America was the organization of stakes. Having local stakes indicated that the local leaders were experienced enough to assume leadership in place of American mission presidents and that local members, rather than missionaries, could direct Church activities. The first stakes outside North America were organized in Hawaii (1935 and 1955) before President McKay's administration, and the second, in New Zealand (1958). These were followed, during his time as President, by stakes in Australia, England, the Netherlands, Germany, Switzerland, Mexico, Samoa, Scotland, Brazil, Argentina, Guatemala, Uruguay, Tonga, Peru, and Japan.

President McKay's humanitarian impulse, even in controversial areas of Church policy, was demonstrated during a mission tour of South Africa in 1954. There he was reminded of the difficulties involved with the Church's policy of not allowing BLACKS or people with black ancestry to hold the PRIESTHOOD. At that time, to be ordained, members in South Africa had to trace their ancestral lines beyond the continent of Africa because of the high possibility of black ancestry. President McKay listened with great empathy to those whose inability to trace their genealogy kept them from bearing the priesthood, and he felt inspired to modify the policy so that the genealogical test would not apply. It remained for one of his successors, President Spencer W. KIMBALL, to be given the revelation on priesthood in 1978.

Other controversial questions confronted President McKay, one concerning education. In 1954 the continued state support of Utah's junior colleges became a heated political issue. At the urging of Governor J. Bracken Lee and as a money-saving device for the state, the legislature authorized the transfer of Snow, Weber, and Dixie colleges back to the Church. Citizens placed the issue on the ballot as a referendum measure, and President McKay, concerned that the colleges would deteriorate if the state continued to operate them without adequate financing, announced that the Church was willing to take the schools back and operate them on a sound financial basis. In the referendum, however, the people of the state voted against the move.

President McKay made a myriad of far-reaching administrative decisions. As an avid missionary, he approved a new proselytizing plan, A Systematic Program for Teaching the Gospel, and in 1961 he presided over the first world seminar for mission presidents, where the plan was introduced. He promoted the continuing expansion of seminaries, INSTITUTES OF RELIGION, and Church schools in areas where public educational opportunities were limited. Other administrative decisions demonstrated his willingness to innovate as needs

Honored by civic leaders of many faiths in Salt Lake City on December 10, 1962, David O. McKay and his wife Emma Ray were presented with the gift of an organ to be installed in the LDS chapel then under construction in Merthyr Tydfil, Wales, the birthplace of President McKay's mother.

arose. In 1961 he authorized ordaining members of the First Council of the Seventy to the office of high priest, which gave them the right to preside at stake conferences and thus eased the growing administrative burdens of the Quorum of the Twelve, and in 1967 he inaugurated the position of Regional Representative of the Twelve. In 1965 he also took the unusual step of expanding the number of counselors in the First Presidency, as his own ability to function effectively became impaired with age.

President David O. McKay believed that Church leadership also implied civic responsibility. Throughout his career he remained active in public affairs and was frequently asked to head important civic committees. During most of his presidential administration, he held weekly breakfast meetings with the head of the Salt Lake area Chamber of Commerce and the publisher of the *Salt Lake Tribune*, which gave him an opportunity to share concerns with these civic leaders and reach agreements on many areas of mutual interest. Politically, he made every effort to keep the Church nonpartisan and constantly encouraged Church members in the United States to be active in both major political parties. At times, however, he took clear stands on controversial political issues when it was apparent to him that they were also moral issues. His denunciation of communism, for example, was uncompromising, on the grounds of its atheistic nature and its threat to the democratic institutions he valued. In 1969, amid the tense civil rights struggles that were dividing Americans as they had seldom been divided since the Civil War, he authorized the issuing of a strong official statement calling upon Church members everywhere to do their part to see that civil rights for all races were held inviolate.

President McKay kept up a steady pace of travel and administrative work until, in his nineties, his age required him to slow down. On January 18, 1970, at age ninety-six, he died in Salt Lake City.

David O. McKay's values were enunciated in his sermons and writings. His emphasis on education included equal emphasis on good reading. "Good reading is to the intellect what good food is to the body," he observed. "Thoughts, like food, should be properly digested" (1967, p. 53). He was vitally concerned with the family and constantly called upon parents to spend time with their children and to train them in all the virtues of good

President David O. McKay and his friend, movie producer/director Cecil B. DeMille, stand in front of the Los Angeles Temple (c. 1955). Courtesy Frederick G. Williams III.

citizenship. His main religious message concerned the reality of Christ, his atonement and resurrection, and the restoration of the gospel of Christ through the Prophet Joseph Smith. He taught that Christ's gospel was meant to transform the individual and thus change society. The sanctity of the home, kindness, mercy, tolerance, spirituality, love of freedom, the power of prayer, charity, personal integrity—these were the subjects of his sermons and writings.

BIBLIOGRAPHY

Allen, James B. "David O. McKay." In *The Presidents of the Church*, ed. L. Arrington, pp. 274–313. Salt Lake City, 1986.

McKay, David Lawrence. *My Father, David O. McKay*. Salt Lake City, 1989.

McKay, David O. *Gospel Ideals: Selections from the Discourses of David O. McKay*. Salt Lake City, 1953.

———. *Secrets of a Happy Life*, comp. Llewelyn R. McKay. Salt Lake City, 1967.

McKay, Llewelyn R. *Home Memories of President David O. McKay*. Salt Lake City, 1956.

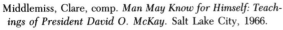

Middlemiss, Clare, comp. *Man May Know for Himself: Teachings of President David O. McKay.* Salt Lake City, 1966.

Morrell, Jeanette McKay. *Highlights in the Life of President David O. McKay.* Salt Lake City, 1967.

Symposium. "President David O. McKay, 1873–1970." *Dialogue* 4 (Winter 1969):47–62.

JAMES B. ALLEN

MEDICAL PRACTICES

At the time the Church was established (1830), medical science was in its infancy. Fundamental mechanisms of disease were just beginning to be understood, and modern diagnostic approaches and notions about infection were only embryonic. Medical treatment for most conditions was ineffective and sometimes harmful. Early Church leaders, including the Prophet Joseph SMITH and President Brigham YOUNG, urged reliance on faith and priesthood blessings and treatment with herbs and mild food. Consistent with advances in medical science and education, Church leaders, including Brigham Young, began about 1870 to rely more on professionally trained physicians than in earlier years. Since that time, Latter-day Saints have been urged by their leaders to take advantage of the best possible medical care along with availing themselves of appropriate priesthood blessings.

In the early nineteenth century, practitioners trained in orthodox medicine relied heavily on bleeding and calomel (mercurous chloride) purges, treatments that were sometimes fatal. Joseph Smith lost his brother Alvin in 1823 when calomel, prescribed for what may have been appendicitis, lodged in his intestines, causing gangrene. This was one of several unfortunate experiences that supported a family inclination against these methods (sometimes called "heroic medicine").

Other practitioners, including Willard Richards, an early member of the Quorum of the Twelve, were trained (most often self-trained) in the Thomsonian system, which used various botanical products, water, and massage. Neither allopathic nor homeopathic in orientation, Thomsonian medicine was perhaps closest to today's naturopathy. While not aggressively dangerous, as were many of the then common practitioners of quackery or some of the orthodox practitioners, most often the Thomsonians could do little more than offer kindness.

In 1831 Joseph Smith received the following revelation regarding health care: "And whosoever among you are sick, and have not faith to be healed, but believe, shall be nourished with all tenderness, with herbs and mild food, and that not by the hand of an enemy. . . . And again, it shall come to pass that he that hath faith in me to be healed, and is not appointed unto death, shall be healed" (D&C 42:43, 48). Many Latter-day Saints from that era recorded remarkable healing experiences following priesthood blessings.

Against this background, Brigham Young, who succeeded Joseph Smith, cautioned Church members against heroic medical care and emphasized reliance on common sense, safe and conservative treatments, and blessings by the priesthood. While critical of both the medical profession and individual practitioners on occasion, he acknowledged their value with fractures and some other conditions.

Medical science advanced rapidly in the latter half of the nineteenth century, and Brigham Young began to rely on physicians for more of his own medical care. During the decade beginning in 1867, he was responsible for sending several of the most gifted young men and women in the Church, among them his nephew Seymour Young, to medical schools in the East. Brigham Young died in 1877 of what his nephew later concluded must have been appendicitis.

Today, many LDS women and men are involved in health care practice and research. Church members, who are advised to seek medical assistance from competent licensed physicians, generally believe that advances in medical science and health care have come though the inspiration of the Lord. They also continue to seek priesthood blessings together with appropriate medical care.

[*See also* Hospitals; Maternity and Child Health Care.]

BIBLIOGRAPHY

Bush, Lester E. "The Mormon Tradition." In *Caring and Curing: Health and Medicine in Western Religious Traditions*, ed. R. Numbers and E. Amundsen, pp. 397–420. New York, 1986.

Divett, Robert T. *Medicine and Mormons: An Introduction to the History of Latter-day Saint Health Care.* Bountiful, Utah, 1981.

CECIL O. SAMUELSON, JR.

MEETINGHOUSE

Meetinghouses for members of The Church of Jesus Christ of Latter-day Saints are often called chapels, but technically the chapel is a special part of the meetinghouse in which worship services are held. In the tradition of the New England meetinghouse, LDS meetinghouses are multipurpose facilities. They developed from a single-room, multiuse building to multiroom complexes.

THE MEETINGHOUSE, 1847–1869. Before 1847 there were few LDS meetinghouses. Soon after the Saints arrived in the Great Basin region in 1847, single-room structures were constructed of indigenous materials in all established communities. Where it was deemed prudent to build forts for the protection of the settlers, such meetinghouses were included within the overall design of the protective enclosure. They had earthen or plank floors, small paned windows, open ceilings, and a roof that could be made from a variety of natural materials. Each served as a chapel, a general meeting facility, and often also a school, making it the focus for the activities of the COMMUNITY or settlement.

The chapel of an LDS meetinghouse (built in 1986). In the foreground are seats for those presiding or speaking at a meeting and for the choir. Not visible to the sides are an organ and piano. At center is the podium, with the sacrament table to the left and a desk for the clerk on the right. The partition at the back opens for additional seating. The simple design of a modern LDS chapel does not include artwork or religious symbols. Courtesy Doug Martin.

Later meetinghouses in this period exhibited a greater sense of style than their earlier counterparts. Classical pediments, bracket motifs, pilasters, small steeples, and inside columns became more frequent. Yet one may not classify these meetinghouses stylistically as Federal, Greek, or Gothic Revival, or as New England variations on English architect Christopher Wren. Rather, the majority remained either eclectic or of a vernacular "high style."

THE MEETINGHOUSE, 1869–1890. More sophisticated designs were developed to accommodate the rapid growth of the Church following the completion of the transcontinental railroad in 1869. Ward needs were met by the construction of halls or chapels of appropriate size with seating benches that faced a raised pulpit area. In some meetinghouses, the floor of the hall was sloped downward toward the pulpit area, and there was a backwall gallery, reached by staircases located at either corner of the hall or by an outside entrance. At times, the gallery extended from the back along the side walls of the meetinghouse. The ceilings were either flat or elliptical depending on the abilities of the artisans. Often, instructional and meeting rooms were placed behind the pulpit area to augment those in the undercroft or basement.

THE MEETINGHOUSE, 1890–1920. Important changes were made in the general design of LDS meetinghouses in the early twentieth century. At first separate halls were built adjacent to many meetinghouses for use in needed cultural and recreational activities of the AUXILIARY ORGANIZATIONS of the Church and for the service activities of the RELIEF SOCIETY. Later modified designs incorporated the separate structures into the overall design of the meetinghouse. The combination of prospering LDS communities, growing numbers of qualified artisans, and a broader knowledge of architectural design led to a greater level of architectural sophistication. Wrenish entrance fronts with associated towers and spires became more frequent. The overall architectural styles of meetinghouses in this period can best be described as Classical, Romanesque/Gothic, and Victorian.

The period between 1890 and 1920 is usually regarded as the most individualistic period in Church architecture. Some of the Church's gifted artisans were sent to study at distinguished educational institutions and brought their knowledge and skills back to Utah. For instance, Joseph Don

Carlos Young, a son of Brigham YOUNG, went to Rennselaer Polytechnical Institute in New York and earned a degree in architecture. Shortly after his return, he was appointed Church architect. One of his responsibilities was to complete the SALT LAKE TEMPLE, which he did in 1893. His virtuosity in architecture soon led him and others to employ distinctive and sometimes exotic variations in style.

The most unique aspect late in this period was the introduction of the "Wrightian style." Derived from the cubic forms of the American modernist Frank Lloyd Wright, it was adapted to LDS meetinghouse architecture by Utah architects Hyrum Pope, Harold W. Burton, and Taylor Woolley (the latter having served as the head of Wright's Detroit office). It became known as the "Mormon style."

THE MEETINGHOUSE AND STANDARD PLANNING, 1920–1990.

Standard planning has characterized LDS architecture since 1920, beginning with Joseph Don Carlos Young in the late years of his work as Church architect. The transformation came in response to Church growth and the need for a more cost effective use of limited Church funds. In the process, attempts were made to arrive at what might be considered an authentic form of LDS architecture. Young devised a plan that structurally joined the previously separate chapel and classrooms with the recreational or cultural hall through a connecting foyer/office/classroom complex. The joining of the two building types created a diversity in ground plans reminiscent of sixteenth- and seventeenth-century English domestic architecture. They became known as "Young's Twins" or the "Colonel's Twins." Most often they were designed in the Colonial style, and soon they became the prominent building type within the Church in the western United States.

During the Depression and war years of the 1930s and 1940s, the Colonial style of the 1920s gave way to a pragmatic or "plain style."

Then in the administration of President David O. MCKAY (1951–1970), a new plan was introduced to replace what had become an impoverished form born of economic necessity. Devised by architect Theodore Pope, the new plan connected the cultural hall to the back of the chapel. A modification of the plan connected two chapels on the opposite ends of a single cultural hall, creating a double-ender or double-chapel design. The latter configuration was intended to reduce land and construc-

Edgemont Stake Center, Provo, Utah (dedicated 1990). LDS meetinghouses contain a chapel and many facilities for religious, social, cultural, and athletic events. Buildings are often shared by two or three congregations. Members are responsible for routine upkeep of the building and grounds. Courtesy Doug Martin.

tion costs where there were larger concentrations of Church members in a small geographic area. Both arrangements allowed for the potential overflow from the chapel to expand into the cultural hall, making both areas more functional and increasing the frequency of use. Classrooms and other meeting areas were attached to or extended around the chapel and cultural hall areas. This concept remains in effect today, though there are differences in outward appearances, interior spatial flow, and room arrangements.

Another concept developed in recent years allows for structural expansion by building additions in regulated phases, to accommodate a small but growing congregation. These later changes stem from events associated with the energy crisis in the 1970s, the rapid growth of the Church, and rising construction costs.

Colonial or classical exterior styles continue to be popular both in America and internationally. Whatever historical or modern motifs are now used, they remain subordinate to the overall standard design concept based on pragmatic functionalism. However, some individualistic plans have been used to conform to special geographic or cultural requirements. Regardless of the resulting style or plan, a Latter-day Saint meetinghouse still serves the same function as the New England meetinghouse—as a multipurpose center for worship and cultural activities.

C. MARK HAMILTON

MEETINGHOUSE LIBRARIES

Meetinghouse libraries in the wards and branches of the Church are provided to assist Latter-day Saints in both learning and teaching the gospel, whether in Church meetings or at home. Instructional materials are indexed to correlate with the Churchwide curriculum and are designed to enrich lives, helping people develop spiritually, emotionally, and intellectually.

An integral part of each meetinghouse, the library ideally contains selected books, pictures, flannel board stories and flannel boards, audiocassettes and players, videocassettes and players, a photocopier, a typewriter, screens, and projectors for the available videocassette tapes, filmstrips, and slides. Additional teaching resources include supplies such as easels, maps, charts, indexes, paper, and chalk. Ward members are allowed access to virtually all library materials for both teaching and home use.

Printed materials in the library typically consist of the standard works, doctrinal works by Church authorities, copies of the current hymnal and children's songbook, current and back issues of Church magazines, copies of current and past lesson manuals for all courses of study, general conference reports, and guide books for self-instruction in genealogical or family history work.

Learning and teaching aids are available for the Bible, Book of Mormon, Doctrine and Covenants, Pearl of Great Price, Church history, Church leaders, FAMILY LIFE, and other resources used in the Church organizations. Many of these materials are prepared under the Church's CORRELATION guidelines.

The librarian and one or more assistants, who are called to the work by the ward BISHOP, instruct members about available items and how to use them. The librarian is normally trained by both the previous librarian and the stake or regional librarian. The librarian orders needed supplies normally from a Church DISTRIBUTION CENTER, planning the order in coordination with ward organization leaders, and subject to an established budget.

Teachers in Church organizations use the library most heavily on worship days. During the week, ward members may draw on library resources for family activities, FAMILY HOME EVENINGS, FIRESIDES, and other occasions.

BETH M. MARLOW

MEETINGS, MAJOR CHURCH

Members of The Church of Jesus Christ of Latter-day Saints are a meeting-going people. When the Church was organized, the instruction was given, "It is expedient that the church meet together often" (D&C 20:75). The pattern for meeting every SUNDAY to pray, speak, and partake of the SACRAMENT or "Lord's Supper" was established immediately, following the Book of Mormon norm (Moro. 6:5–6). The pattern of holding a Church CONFERENCE every three months also began in 1830 (D&C 20:61–62). Since that time other meetings have been added to the Church agenda. The main meetings on Sunday are (1) SACRAMENT MEETING; (2) SUNDAY SCHOOL; and (3) concurrent PRIESTHOOD quorum meetings for men and RELIEF SOCIETY for women, with children under twelve years of age simultaneously attending PRIMARY. Young women meet in their own sessions, while young men of equivalent age are in priesthood meeting.

In addition, families are expected, usually on Monday evening, to meet in their own homes in a FAMILY HOME EVENING, which can include instruction from a Church-prepared manual, an activity, and refreshments. Most families also use this evening as a time to discuss family concerns and make plans for the week. Single Latter-day Saints are encouraged to participate with nearby family groups or in groups of their peers.

Besides the meetings for all members, there are special meetings related to Church CALLINGS. For example, a presidency of three plus a secretary or clerk meet regularly to oversee the many functions of a stake and its wards. Then within each ward are the bishopric, priesthood quorums, Sunday School, Relief Society, Primary, Young

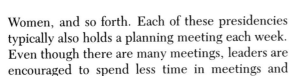

Women, and so forth. Each of these presidencies typically also holds a planning meeting each week. Even though there are many meetings, leaders are encouraged to spend less time in meetings and more time in service.

Most Church meetings are formally organized with hymns, prayers, sermons, lessons, and/or instructions. To involve teenagers and children, many meetings use participative methods such as discussion groups, panels, case studies, and role playing.

In all conferences—ward, stake, regional, and general—Church leaders give presentations of counsel and inspiration. Special meetings are held during the year for the priesthood (e.g., stake and general priesthood meetings), and for the women of the Church (general meeting). There are likewise seminary meetings for participating teenagers attending high school, missionary meetings for those on MISSIONS, and meetings for temple workers, scout leaders, activity directors, nursery teachers, and Sunday School workers. The Latter-day Saint culture flourishes on the principle of meeting together often in order to "be prepared in all things" (D&C 88:80).

In business and planning meetings, there is an attempt to have everyone contribute, but those with official status usually conduct the proceedings and have the most decisive influence. These meeting patterns extend worldwide and are a major part of the cohesiveness that keeps Mormons in touch, involved, acquainted, and united in the common cause of building the KINGDOM OF GOD on earth.

BIBLIOGRAPHY

Allen, James B., and Glen M. Leonard. *The Story of the Latter-day Saints.* Salt Lake City, 1976.

Arrington, Leonard. *Great Basin Kingdom.* Lincoln, Neb., 1966, pp. 28–33.

McKay, David O. *Gospel Ideals,* chap. 11. Salt Lake City, 1975.

WILLIAM G. DYER

MELCHIZEDEK

[*This entry consists of two articles:* LDS Sources, *a discussion of what is known of Melchizedek from Church scripture and revelation, and* Ancient Sources, *a historical view of Melchizedek from ancient writings and traditions.*]

LDS SOURCES

As a king and HIGH PRIEST of the Most High God (Gen. 14:18), Melchizedek holds a place of great honor and respect among Latter-day Saints. An example of righteousness and the namesake of the higher PRIESTHOOD, he represents the scriptural ideal of one who obtains the power of God through FAITH, REPENTANCE, and sacred ORDINANCES, for the purpose of inspiring and blessing his fellow beings.

Melchizedek was evidently a prince by birth, for he became king of Salem (later JERUSALEM— Gen. 14:18; Ps. 76:2), where he reigned "under his father" (Alma 13:18). "Melchizedek was a man of faith, who wrought righteousness; and when a child he feared God, and stopped the mouths of lions, and quenched the violence of fire" (JST Gen. 14:26). Yet the people among whom he lived "waxed strong in iniquity and abomination; yea, they had all gone astray; they were full of all manner of wickedness" (Alma 13:17).

Though living among a wicked people, Melchizedek "exercised mighty faith, and received the office of the high priesthood according to the holy order of God" (Alma 13:18). This priesthood was after the order of the COVENANT that God had made with Enoch (JST Gen. 14:27), and Melchizedek ruled both as king and priest over his people.

As high priest, some of his functions were keeping "the storehouse of God" where the "tithes for the poor" were held (JST Gen. 14:37–38), giving blessings to individuals such as ABRAHAM (JST Gen. 14:18, 25, 37), preaching repentance (Alma 13:18; cf. 5:49), and administering ordinances "after this manner, that thereby the people might look forward on the Son of God . . . for a remission of their sins, that they might enter into the rest of the Lord" (Alma 13:16; JST Gen. 14:17). With extraordinary goodness and power, Melchizedek diligently administered in the office of high priest and "did preach repentance unto his people. And behold, they did repent; and Melchizedek did establish peace in the land in his days" (Alma 13:18). Consequently, Melchizedek became known as "the prince of peace" (JST Gen. 14:33; Heb. 7:1–2; Alma 13:18). "His people wrought righteousness, and obtained heaven" (JST Gen. 14:34). His Hebrew name means "King of Righteousness."

For ALMA₂ and several biblical authors, the order of the priesthood to which Melchizedek was ordained was of prime importance. It was this

This mosaic shows Melchizedek standing behind an altar symbolically receiving the sacrifices of Abel and Abraham. Saint Apollonaire in Classe, Ravenna, Italy (sixth century A.D.). Courtesy John W. Welch.

"order," coupled with faith, that gave Melchizedek the power and knowledge that influenced his people to repent and become worthy to be with God. This order was "after the order of the Son of God; which order came, not by man, nor the will of man; neither by father nor mother; neither by beginning of days nor end of years; but of God" (JST Gen. 14:28; JST Heb. 7:3; Ps. 110:4). It was given to Melchizedek "through the lineage of his fathers, even till Noah," and from Melchizedek to Abraham (D&C 84:14). Those ordained to this order were to "have power, by faith," and, according to "the will of the Son of God," to work miracles. Ultimately, those in this order were "to stand in the presence of God" (JST Gen. 14:30–31). This was accomplished by participating in the ordinances of this order (Alma 13:16; D&C 84:20–22). The result was that "men having this faith, coming up unto this order of God, were translated and taken up into heaven" (JST Gen. 14:32). Accordingly, the Prophet Joseph SMITH taught that the priesthood held by Melchizedek had "the power of 'endless lives'" (TPJS, p. 322; see also ETERNAL LIFE).

So righteous and faithful was Melchizedek in the execution of his high priestly duties that he became a prototype of Jesus Christ (Heb. 7:15). The Book of Mormon prophet Alma said of him, "Now, there were many [high priests] before him, and also there were many afterwards, but none were greater" (Alma 13:19). The Doctrine and Covenants states that Melchizedek was "such a great high priest" that the higher priesthood was called after his name. "Before his day it was called *the Holy Priesthood, after the Order of the Son of God.* But out of respect or reverence to the name of the Supreme Being, to avoid the too-frequent repetition of his name, they, the church, in the ancient days, called that priesthood after Melchizedek, or the Melchizedek Priesthood" (D&C 107:2–4; italics in original).

It was asserted by some early LDS leaders that Melchizedek was Shem, son of Noah (see, e.g., T&S 5:746). Though Shem is also identified as a great high priest (D&C 138:41), it would appear from the Doctrine and Covenants 84:14 that the two might not be the same individual (MD, p. 475), and Jewish sources equating Melchizedek and Shem are late and tendentious.

BIBLIOGRAPHY

Madsen, Ann N. "Melchizedek, the Man and the Tradition." Master's thesis, Brigham Young University, 1975.

Welch, John W. "The Melchizedek Material in Alma 13:13–19." In *By Study and Also by Faith,* ed. J. Lundquist and S. Ricks, Vol. 2, pp. 238–72. Salt Lake City, 1990.

Widtsoe, John A. "Who Was Melchizedek?" *Evidences and Reconciliations,* pp. 231–33. Salt Lake City, 1960.

BRUCE SATTERFIELD

ANCIENT SOURCES

Genesis 14:17–24 reports that Abram ("the Hebrew," 14:3), upon his victorious return from a battle, was met by the king of Sodom ("Bera," 14:2), who was eager to reward Abram for coming to his and his allies' aid. The narrative is interrupted by an enigmatic insertion (14:18–20) featuring "Melchizedek king of Salem," "priest of God Most High" (RSV). Melchizedek "brought out bread and wine" and blessed Abram in the name of God Most High (Hebrew *'el 'elyôn*). Abram then gave Melchizedek a tithe of his booty. This priest-king of Salem has enjoyed a wide range of interpretation among Jewish, Christian, and Gnostic writings, some that brought him up to the heights of heaven, and others—of developing Christian and Jewish orthodoxy—that brought him down to earth again.

The story of Genesis 14 has raised numerous questions. Most modern scholars entertain a possible connection of this Melchizedek with a pre-Israelite kingship and/or priesthood in the Jebusite city of Jerusalem ("Salem") before its conquest by King David (2 Sam. 5:6–10). The incorporation of the story into Judean traditions reflects the interests of the Jerusalem royal ideology.

The only other Old Testament occurrence of the name Melchizedek is found in a royal Jerusalemite psalm, Psalm 110:4. There God ("the Lord") addresses the king thus: "You are a priest for ever after the order of Melchizedek."

Melchizedek occurs in the New Testament only in the Epistle to the Hebrews (5:6–10; 6:20; 7:1–17), where the Old Testament figure is interpreted as a type of the "high priest" of the New Covenant, Jesus Christ. The key passage is Hebrews 7:3, where it is said that Melchizedek "resembles the Son of God." Melchizedek's priesthood, superior to that of the "descendants of Levi" (Heb. 7:5), is a foreshadowing of the priesthood of the Son of God. Hebrews 7:3 becomes the basis for most Christian interpretation of the figure of Melchizedek (Horton, pp. 111, 152, 161–64).

An important witness to pre-Christian Jewish speculation on Melchizedek has surfaced among the Dead Sea Scrolls: 11QMelch. The fragmentary Hebrew text, usually dated to the first century B.C., features Melchizedek as a heavenly end-time redeemer, with attributes of the archangel Michael. He appears in the tenth and final jubilee of world history to rescue the elect, the "men of the lot of Melchizedek" (ii.8), doing battle with Belial and his fellow evil spirits. Melchizedek's triumph is described as a high-priestly act of "expiation" (ii.8; cf. Kobelski, pp. 5–23).

Melchizedek is mentioned by Philo, a first-century Jewish philosopher of Alexandria, in three writings (*Legum Allegoriae* 3.79–82; *De Congressu* 89; *De Abrahamo* 235). Philo interprets the text of Genesis in a Platonic-allegorical fashion, seeing in Melchizedek a reference to the divine Logos, the thought of God in which the pattern of all existing things is conceived and the "image" of God according to which man was created.

Another important text, 2 Enoch, attests to early Jewish interest in the figure of Melchizedek. The date and place of this document are controversial, but recent scholarship places its original Greek version in the first century A.D. in Alexandria (cf. F. I. Andersen's introduction and translation in Charlesworth, Vol. 1, pp. 91–213). In this text (chaps. 71–72), a child is born miraculously to Noah's recently deceased sister-in-law, and the child, marked on his chest with a priestly seal, speaks and praises God. The boy is named Melchizedek by Noah and his brother Nir, whose wife had been posthumously delivered. In a night vision Nir is told of the impending flood; he is also informed that the archangel Michael will bring Melchizedek to paradise, thus enabling him to escape the flood waters. Melchizedek will eventually become the chief of priests among the people, and in the end of days he will be revealed yet another time as the chief priest. In this text, Melchizedek has three different earthly manifestations: born before the Flood, serving in the postdiluvian age as a great priest, and functioning in the end-time as a messianic priest (cf. Gruenewald, pp. 90–92; Delcor, pp. 127–30).

Some of these Jewish interpretations were taken over by Gnostics and are now reflected in some Christian Gnostic texts preserved in Coptic manuscripts of the fourth and fifth centuries (Pearson, 1990). In one fragmentary manuscript, the disciple John asks Jesus to explain what is said about Melchizedek in Hebrews 7:3. Unfortunately, the text breaks off before Jesus' interpretation is given.

A fragmentary text from Nag Hammadi (IX.1: *Melchizedek*; cf. Pearson, 1981, pp. 19–85) contains an apocalypse given by angels to Melchizedek, "priest of God Most High." It is revealed to Melchizedek that he will ultimately reappear as Jesus Christ, Son of God, to do battle with the cosmic forces of darkness. Here one can see influence not only from the Epistle to the Hebrews but also from non-Christian lore.

In the *Second Book of Jeu*, "Zorokothora Melchizedek" is a heavenly priest who presides over a heavenly baptism. No trace of influence from Hebrews is found in this text.

The most developed levels of speculation on Melchizedek, also lacking any influence from Hebrews, are found in *Pistis Sophia*, Book 4, in which Melchizedek plays a key role in the process of purifying human souls for entry into the "Treasury of Light" and transferring them from the domain of the archons, or earthly rulers, to that heavenly region. The younger material in books 1–3 of *Pistis Sophia* develops these ideas further: Melchizedek is a heavenly being who seals the saved souls upon their entry into the realm of light.

The church fathers attest to several heterodox ideas associated with Melchizedek. Hippolytus of Rome (*Refutatio* 7.35–36) and Epiphanius of Salamis (*Panarion* 55) are the most important witnesses to a group of heretics called Melchizedekians. They had a low Christology and exalted Melchizedek as a heavenly power superior to Christ. Others equated Melchizedek with the Holy Spirit (*Panarion* 67), and some "even in the true church" (i.e., not "heretics") naively regarded Melchizedek as the Son of God (*Panarion* 55.7.3). The later view seems also to have been present among the monasteries of Egypt (*Apophthegmata Patrum*, in *Patrologia Graeca* 65.160) and was even defended in a treatise on Melchizedek by a fifth-century resident of the Judean desert, Mark the Hermit (*PG* 65.1117–40). Such views were eventually overcome by teacher-bishops such as Cyril of Alexandria (*PG* 65.160).

On the Jewish side, while early rabbis continued to speculate on Melchizedek's role in scripture (e.g., equating him with Shem, son of Noah; cf. *b. Nedarim* 32b; *Midrash Gen. R.* 44.7; *Targum Ps.-J.* Gen. 14:18), a major stream of rabbinic tradition viewed Melchizedek negatively, a fact that indicates some Jewish sensitivity to the use of Melchizedek traditions by Christians (Gianotto, pp. 172–85).

[*See also* Apocrypha and Pseudepigrapha.]

BIBLIOGRAPHY

Charlesworth, James H. *Old Testament Pseudepigrapha.* Garden City, N.Y., 1983.

Delcor, M. "Melchizedek from Genesis to the Qumran Texts and the Epistle to the Hebrews." *Journal of Jewish Studies* 2 (1971):115–35.

Gianotto, Claudio. *Melchisedek e la sua tipologia.* Supplementi alla Rivista Biblica 12. Brescia, 1984.

Gruenewald, Ithamar. "The Messianic Image of Melchizedek" (in Hebrew). *Mahanayim* 124 (1970):88–98.

Horton, Fred L., Jr. *The Melchizedek Tradition.* Society for New Testament Studies Monograph Series 30. Cambridge, 1976.

Kobelski, Paul J. *Melchizedek and Melchireša'.* Catholic Biblical Quarterly Monograph Series 10. Washington, D.C., 1981.

Pearson, Birger A. "The Figure of Melchizedek in Gnostic Literature." In Pearson, *Gnosticism, Judaism, and Egyptian Christianity.* Studies in Antiquity and Christianity 5. Minneapolis, 1990.

———, ed. *Nag Hammadi Codices IX and X.* Leiden, 1981.

BIRGER A. PEARSON

MELCHIZEDEK PRIESTHOOD

[*This entry consists of two articles*: Powers and Offices in the Melchizedek Priesthood *is a general discussion of the Melchizedek Priesthood, and* Restoration *is a historical treatment of the restoring of this priesthood in this dispensation.*]

POWERS AND OFFICES IN THE MELCHIZEDEK PRIESTHOOD

The Melchizedek Priesthood is the AUTHORITY, responsibility, and power to act in the name of Jesus Christ and to organize and direct part of his work. Through the opportunities of this PRIESTHOOD, men and women in partnership with God can conduct the work of the family and the Church. "It is the duty of this vast body of men holding the holy Priesthood . . . to exert their influence and exercise their power for good among the people of Israel and the people of the world . . . to preach and to work righteousness, both at home and abroad" (Smith, p. 157).

In the words of the Prophet Joseph SMITH, "All Priesthood is Melchizedek, but there are different portions or degrees of it" (*TPJS*, p. 180). Most often, however, the name Melchizedek Priesthood is used in the Church to describe the higher priesthood and its offices. "There are, in the church, two priesthoods, namely, the Melchizedek and Aaronic. . . . The Melchizedek Priesthood holds the right of presidency, and has power and authority over all the offices in the church in all ages of the world, to administer in spiritual things" (D&C 107:1, 8). The Melchizedek Priesthood holds the keys to the kingdom, and "in the ordinances thereof, the power of godliness is manifest" (D&C 84:20).

ORDINATION TO THE MELCHIZEDEK PRIESTHOOD. Every faithful, worthy man in the Church may receive the Melchizedek Priesthood. As with the AARONIC PRIESTHOOD, the Melchizedek Priesthood is conferred on those who have qualified themselves and have been called by those in authority.

Specific standards of worthiness to receive the Melchizedek Priesthood include personal integrity, chastity, obedience to the divine laws of health, and faithful contribution of tithes to the Church. Beyond these traits, it is expected that men will progress in developing attributes of godliness. Like all followers of Christ, they should be faithful, diligent, and amenable to righteous change, learning, and loving: "We can make advancement only upon the principles of eternal truth. In proportion as we become established upon the foundation of these principles which have been revealed from the heavens in the latter days, and determine to accomplish the purposes of the Lord, will we progress, and the Lord will all the more exalt and magnify us" (Smith, p. 141).

The PROPHET and PRESIDENT OF THE CHURCH holds and exercises all of the authority and KEYS of the Melchizedek Priesthood. He delegates to STAKE PRESIDENTS and BISHOPS and others the authority to ordain others to priesthood offices. Conferral of the Melchizedek Priesthood by the LAYING ON OF HANDS must also be approved by the COMMON CONSENT of the priesthood bearers or general membership of the candidate's STAKE or DISTRICT.

After the Melchizedek Priesthood is conferred upon them, all priesthood holders are ordained to an office within the priesthood, usually ELDER. They may later be ordained to the office of HIGH PRIEST or PATRIARCH as their Church CALLINGS require. Those called to be GENERAL AUTHORITIES for the whole Church will be ordained SEVENTIES or APOSTLES. Ordination to an office within the priesthood gives specific responsibilities within the Church.

Finally, a man may be SET APART to carry out an assignment, such as to be president of a quorum of elders, a stake president, or a member of the QUORUM OF THE TWELVE APOSTLES. As appropriate, he will be given the keys of authority necessary to carry out that assignment. This procedure makes it possible for every act performed under priesthood authority to be done at the proper time and place and in the proper way. The authority to direct those specific activities constitutes the keys of the priesthood.

An individual accepts his ordination to the Melchizedek Priesthood by making a covenant in his mind and heart with God (*TPJS*, p. 323; *see also* OATH AND COVENANT OF THE PRIESTHOOD). He covenants to honor, dignify, and learn the duties of his priesthood, to keep the commandments of God, to live by God's counsel, and to walk uprightly and virtuously as he carries out his responsibilities. God promises that if the man keeps his commitments, he will be given eternal life and be exalted in a godly state, inheriting all that the Father has, and will participate with God and the Savior in their continued work (D&C 84:39).

The pulpits in the upper Assembly Hall of the Salt Lake Temple.

FUNCTIONING OF THE MELCHIZEDEK PRIESTHOOD. All who hold the priesthood can use it to benefit others, regardless of their particular Church assignment or priesthood office. For example, in working with their families, men are authorized to carry out their patriarchal responsibilities (*see* FATHERHOOD), including blessing family members. In addition, they are authorized to heal the sick, seek personal knowledge, and give general help and comfort to those whom they contact.

To supervise and carry out priesthood ordinances within the Church, it is necessary to have both the Melchizedek Priesthood and the appropriate keys. For example, to confirm baptized members and bestow the gift of the Holy Ghost upon them, it is necessary to have the power of the Melchizedek Priesthood and to be authorized to use it. In this way, there is order, and the work done on earth is acceptable to the Savior in mortality and in the hereafter (*see* SEALING).

In addition to providing the authority to represent Christ on earth, the Melchizedek Priesthood provides a revelatory channel through which instructions and doctrine from Christ can be made known. Every individual has access to God and the right to receive personal REVELATION pertaining to his or her life and callings, but when revelation concerning principles or the implementation of principles is required for the Church or a priesthood unit of it, God gives this revelation only through appropriate priesthood leaders. The prophet and President of the Church receives revelation for the entire Church. A bishop receives the revelation necessary for leading the WARD. This way of making truth known underscores the right and responsibility of each individual to seek and obtain revelation and at the same time preserves order and harmony by working through the priesthood structure that Christ has set in place.

"The rights of the priesthood are inseparably connected with the powers of heaven; . . . [this power] cannot be controlled nor handled [except] upon the principles of righteousness" (D&C 121:36). One can officiate for God only when administering the work in wisdom and love, in a way consistent with the ways of God. Assignments must be pursued with long-suffering, gentleness, meekness, kindness, love unfeigned, pure knowledge, and charity toward all. In this way, God promises that the "doctrine of the priesthood shall distil upon thy soul as the dews from heaven" (D&C 121:41–45).

Priesthood can be lost as a result of a DISCIPLINARY PROCEDURE for serious sin. When a man is excommunicated, he loses his priesthood. Disfellowshipment or probation may restrict a man from using his priesthood until the repentance process is complete. In addition, "when we undertake to cover our sins, or gratify our pride, our vain ambition, or to exercise control or dominion or compulsion upon the souls of the children of men, in any degree of unrighteousness . . . Amen to the priesthood or the authority of that man" (D&C 121:37).

ANCIENT HISTORY OF THE MELCHIZEDEK PRIESTHOOD. The Melchizedek Priesthood is an eternal priesthood. Before mortality, God delegated authority and responsibility to worthy individuals. This holy priesthood was the means by which that action was taken. After this life, those who have been valiant and have honored their priesthood will continue to bear it and to have the responsibility to use it in serving others.

Adam, the first of the spirit children of God to live on earth, received the holy priesthood, with all its power, authority, and keys. "And thus all things were confirmed unto Adam, by an holy ordinance" (Moses 5:59). This authority was delegated to others in an unbroken chain from one prophet to another. "All the prophets had the Melchizedek Priesthood" (TPJS, p. 181).

Abraham sought the blessings of his fathers and the right to be ordained to the priesthood. Because he had qualified himself for the priesthood, even though his own father had not, Abraham obtained the priesthood from MELCHIZEDEK, the king of Salem and a priest of God (Abr. 1:2–5). Melchizedek met Abraham and blessed him, and Abraham gave him a tenth part of all he had (Heb. 7:1–3). Melchizedek exercised mighty faith and used his priesthood to bring a people practicing iniquity to repentance. None was greater than he (Alma 13:17–19). Originally, the priesthood was known as the "Holy Priesthood, after the Order of the Son of God" (D&C 107:3). To avoid too frequent use of God's name, the Church in ancient days called the priesthood by the name of this noted priesthood leader, Melchizedek (D&C 107:2–4).

Moses received the Melchizedek Priesthood from his father-in-law, Jethro (D&C 84:6). Moses held the Melchizedek Priesthood until he was translated, at which time the keys of the greater priesthood went with him, and what remained with the people was an appendage to the Melchizedek Priesthood called the Aaronic Priesthood, a priesthood with limited authority. After the time of Moses, individual prophets were given the holy priesthood at various times by God, but it was restricted from the general populace.

The Book of Mormon reports that Nephite prophets held the priesthood called after the order of the Son of God, the Melchizedek Priesthood (Alma 13:10). Those who had the authority directed the work of God among the people (Alma 29:13).

The apostles were given the Melchizedek Priesthood by Jesus Christ while he ministered on earth. He gave them authority and responsibility to direct his Church. After Christ left, the apostles continued to officiate for him and conferred the Melchizedek Priesthood on others when it was appropriate (Eph. 4:11–13; Acts 1:22–26; see also ORGANIZATION OF THE CHURCH IN NEW TESTAMENT TIMES). Over time, both the principles and the priesthood authority and keys were lost through APOSTASY.

MODERN HISTORY OF THE MELCHIZEDEK PRIESTHOOD. The Melchizedek Priesthood was given to Joseph Smith and Oliver Cowdery (see below). As directed, they ordained one another first and second elders of the Church on April 6, 1830 (see ELDER). In turn, they conferred the priesthood upon, ordained, and set apart others to offices and callings in the priesthood (*see* ORGANIZATION OF THE CHURCH, 1830). The first bishop was ordained in 1831 to care for the poor and needy and to govern the temporal affairs of the Church. On June 3, 1831, Joseph Smith directed more than twenty men to be ordained to the "high priesthood," as the president of this high priesthood. High priest councils governed the Church until 1834.

In 1835 the Church structure was adjusted to accommodate the additional revelation and increased numbers; PRIESTHOOD QUORUMS made up of men ordained to particular offices were in operation (*see* DOCTRINE AND COVENANTS: SECTION 107). Three PRESIDING HIGH PRIESTS were established as the quorum of the FIRST PRESIDENCY. The Quorum of the Twelve Apostles was a traveling high council directed by the First Presidency. The Seventy were to travel internationally to preach. Stake high councils were established to govern within their stakes, and bishops cared for the temporal concerns of the Church.

It was necessary for additional Melchizedek Priesthood keys to be restored to carry out the higher temple ordinances. Messengers from God brought these keys and instructions on April 3, 1836 (*see* DOCTRINE AND COVENANTS: SECTION 110).

On July 12, 1843, Joseph Smith recorded the revelation concerning eternal marriage relationships, wherein Christ said he would "give unto thee the law of my Holy Priesthood, as was ordained by me and my Father before the world was" (D&C 132:28). He conferred upon Joseph "the keys and power of the priesthood" (D&C 132:45; *see also* PATRIARCHAL ORDER OF THE PRIESTHOOD).

The First Presidency presides over the Melchizedek Priesthood and directs the work of the Church. The Quorum of the Twelve Apostles shares this responsibility according to the keys given to the apostles. In turn, stake presidents supervise the wards and branches of the Church by the authority of the Melchizedek Priesthood and the specific keys given them.

All men who have the Melchizedek Priesthood are members of a priesthood quorum. These quorums are established within geographic boundaries and are made up of a group of men who hold the same office in the priesthood or who are of the same age group and may come to hold that office. Quorums administer the work of the Church as-

signed to them, train members in their priesthood responsibility, and provide opportunities for service and brotherhood for those working toward common goals.

In each stake there is one high priests quorum. The stake president and his counselors serve as the quorum presidency. A high priests group functions in each ward, presided over by a group leader, one or more assistants, and a secretary. An elders quorum, presided over by a president, two counselors, and a secretary, is organized in every ward and independent branch. The stake presidency and high councilors oversee all Melchizedek Priesthood quorum activities in the stake.

BIBLIOGRAPHY

Backman, Milton V., Jr. *The Heavens Resound: A History of the Latter-day Saints in Ohio 1830–1838*, pp. 237–56. Salt Lake City, 1983.

Critchlow, William J., Jr. "Priesthood—Asset or Liability?" *IE* 66 (Dec. 1963):1067–69.

Hartley, William G. "The Priesthood Reform Movement, 1908–1922." *BYU Studies* 13 (Winter 1973):137–56.

Kimball, Spencer W., et al. *Priesthood*. Salt Lake City, 1981.

Smith, Joseph F. *GD*, pp. 136–200.

Widtsoe, John A. *Priesthood and Church Government*, rev. ed. Salt Lake City, 1954.

JAE R. BALLIF

RESTORATION OF MELCHIZEDEK PRIESTHOOD

To act for God in organizing his Church and administering all the ordinances, Joseph SMITH received the Melchizedek Priesthood in the divinely established way. Authority and responsibility for specific assignments are essential (D&C 18:9, 27–32, 35–37; 27:12; *see* KEYS). In addition, Joseph Smith and others received and taught the significance of each ordinance and key. Since no one on earth possessed that authority at the time, the Prophet Joseph Smith and his associate Oliver COWDERY received both instruction and ordination from God and from his messengers.

The Prophet and Oliver Cowdery received the Aaronic Priesthood on May 15, 1829, under the hands of John the Baptist. He informed them that he acted under the direction of Peter, James, and John, who held the keys of the Melchizedek Priesthood, and that that priesthood would be given to them (JS—H 1:72). Although the precise date of this restoration is not known, it is certain

Restoration of the Melchizedek Priesthood, by R. M. Hadi Pranato (1985, Indonesia, dyed fabric batik, 55″ × 31″). This batik by LDS artist R. M. Hadi Pranato of Indonesia portrays Peter, James, and John appearing to the Prophet Joseph Smith and Oliver Cowdery to restore the Melchizedek Priesthood. Church Museum of History and Art.

that it occurred after May 15, 1829, and before August 1830 (D&C 27:12). The documents available and the date of the formal organization of the Church give support to a time of restoration before April 6, 1830. Many students have concluded that late May or early June 1829 is the most probable time frame (*HC* 1:40n–42n; Porter, pp. 5–10).

Sometime before June 14, 1829, the Lord instructed Joseph Smith and Oliver Cowdery concerning their ordination as ELDERS, which is a Melchizedek Priesthood office (*HC* 1:60–61). Furthermore, when Peter, James, and John appeared to Joseph and Oliver, they ordained them also as apostles (D&C 27:12) and committed to them "the keys of the kingdom, and of the dispensation of the fulness of times" (D&C 128:20; cf. 27:13).

Several records document the occurrence and significance of this visitation. An early confirmation of the receipt of apostolic powers is evidenced in an 1829 revelation recorded in the hand of Oliver Cowdery in which the Lord stated, "I command all men every where to repent & I speak unto you even as unto Paul mine apostle for ye are called even with that same calling with which he was called" (Cowdery, 1829; cf. D&C 18:9). In his 1832 history of the Church the Prophet Joseph Smith declared that he had received "the holy Priesthood by the ministering Angels to administer the letter of the Gospel" and that he had been given "a confirmation and reception of the high Priesthood after the holy order of the son of the living God power and ordinance from on high to preach the Gospel in the administration and demonstration of the spirit the Keys of the Kingdom of God conferred upon him and the continuation of the blessings of God to him" (Jessee, p. 3).

Oliver Cowdery on many occasions bore witness that he "was present with Joseph when an holy angel from God came down from heaven and conferred, or restored, the Aaronic Priesthood and . . . was also present with Joseph when the Melchizedek Priesthood was conferred on each other, by the will and commandment of God" (Anderson, p. 22).

Joseph Smith said that Peter, James, and John made their visit "in the wilderness between Harmony, Susquehanna county, and Colesville, Broome county, on the Susquehanna river" (D&C 128:20).

On April 3, 1836, Joseph Smith and Oliver Cowdery knelt in prayer in the KIRTLAND TEMPLE and received another profoundly important vision in which certain Melchizedek Priesthood keys were restored. MOSES appeared and committed the keys of the gathering of Israel. ELIAS gave to them keys of the DISPENSATION of the gospel of Abraham. Finally, ELIJAH stood before them as promised by MALACHI and MORONI and bestowed the keys of SEALING families together (D&C 110:11–16; 2:1–3).

BIBLIOGRAPHY

Anderson, Richard L. "The Second Witness of Priesthood Restoration." *IE* 71 (Sept. 1968):15–24.

Barney, Ronald O. "Priesthood Restoration Narratives in the Early LDS Church." Planned for *BYU Studies* 31 (Summer 1991).

Bushman, Richard L. *Joseph Smith and the Beginnings of Mormonism*. Urbana, Ill., 1984.

Cowdery, Oliver. "Written in the year of our Lord & Savior 1829—A true copy of the articles of the Church of Christ." Ms. 1829. LDS Church Archives. Ms. in handwriting of Oliver Cowdery.

Hartley, William G. "Upon You My Fellow Servants: Restoration of the Priesthood." In *The Prophet Joseph: Essays on the Life and Mission of Joseph Smith*, ed. Larry C. Porter and Susan Easton Black, pp. 49–72. Salt Lake City, 1988.

Jessee, Dean C., ed. *The Papers of Joseph Smith*, Vol. 1. Salt Lake City, 1989.

Porter, Larry C. "Dating the Restoration of the Melchizedek Priesthood." *Ensign* 9 (June 1979):5–10.

JAE R. BALLIF

MEMBERSHIP

Membership in The Church of Jesus Christ of Latter-day Saints is a fulfilling, lifelong undertaking. It begins with the ordinance of BAPTISM, which represents a COVENANT made between the convert and God. By this act, the convert promises to follow Jesus Christ and keep all his commandments in love and righteousness. God, in return, promises the GIFT OF THE HOLY GHOST and the opportunity for ETERNAL LIFE. A newly baptized individual is confirmed a member of the Church by the LAYING ON OF HANDS by a MELCHIZEDEK PRIESTHOOD holder, who also blesses the new member with the gift of the Holy Ghost. This is a gift of spiritual discernment to help and sustain members as they attempt to live Christlike lives.

Figuratively, membership means becoming a member of the body of Christ: Each member is an essential part of the whole, just as the foot, the hand, or the eye is an integral part of the body. Each member serves different purposes and has individual gifts, but each is necessary, and if one suffers, "all the members suffer with it"; they are "many members, yet but one body" (1 Cor. 12:20).

The purpose of such membership is to facilitate fulfillment of one's baptismal covenant and to promote personal and spiritual growth unto the "perfecting of the saints, . . . for the edifying of the body of Christ" (Eph. 4:12). To this end, members participate in many religious activities. These include personal activities (such as prayer, fasting, scripture study, payment of tithing and other offerings; observing wholesome behavioral standards regarding sexual and moral conduct; observing the health principles of the WORD OF WISDOM); family endeavors (such as family prayer and FAMILY HOME EVENING); congregational and community functions (such as attending Sunday meetings, especially SACRAMENT MEETING, where members may partake of the sacrament); and serving faithfully in various CALLINGS (such as acting as a teacher, a clerk, or a musician). Members are encouraged to participate in various welfare projects designed to provide goods and services to needy people. Activity in the Church is considered both a privilege and a duty of membership.

Another important characteristic of membership is proclaiming the gospel (McKay, p. 479). Members fulfill this responsibility in several ways: by serving full-time missions and financially supporting missionaries; by donating several hours per week proselytizing in their own locale as stake or ward missionaries; and by sharing their religion both by word and way of life as opportunities arise during informal daily interactions with others.

Members are also responsible for gathering the names of their ancestors and performing ordinances in the TEMPLE on behalf of those who did not receive them while alive. Once converts have been members for at least a year and have met certain standards of worthiness, they can enter the temple and receive these ordinances personally and thereafter can receive them as proxies for deceased persons.

Membership in the Church is highly valued by Latter-day Saints. It figures prominently in the self-image of faithful members who willingly consecrate and donate as needed of their time, talents, and blessings from God to the building up of the Church of Jesus Christ on this earth.

BIBLIOGRAPHY

McKay, David O. "Closing Address." *IE* 62 (June 1959):479.

LINDA A. CHARNEY

MEMBERSHIP RECORDS

When the Church was organized in 1830, Joseph SMITH was instructed "that a regular list of all the names of the whole church . . . be kept" (D&C 20:82). This revelation was in harmony with other scriptures (cf. Ex. 28:9–12; Num. 1:2; Phil. 4:3; Mosiah 6:1; 26:36; Alma 5:58). Accordingly, each congregation (WARD and BRANCH) kept records thereafter containing the names of all members in the congregation and all blessings, baptisms, confirmations, ordinations, marriages, excommunications, and deaths. Through the years, the Church used several successive ways to keep track of membership information prior to the present electronic automated system. Many improvements have been made in the automated records system, and with rapid growth, reaching more than 7 million members by 1990, the Church is studying ways to reduce and simplify the amount of information being kept. Information concerning Church ordinances (baptism, confirmation, priesthood ordination, etc.) is so important that if the record is lost, the ordinances must be performed again.

In the 1800s, the presiding officer of a congregation would give members who were moving a letter to take to the presiding officer in the new congregation who would then enter that information in his own record book of members. In 1906 the Church formalized the procedure for transferring membership records as members moved from one congregation to another by having the presiding officer send a certificate of membership to the new congregation via the office of the Presiding Bishopric, even though at that time no duplicate or "master" record was kept at central Church offices. There were, however, member censuses taken approximately every five years to update records between 1914 and 1950.

In 1941, membership books were replaced by individual membership record cards, and duplicate records were created for each member. One copy was retained by the congregation, and the other was sent to the Church's master file in Salt Lake City. (Church membership at the time was approximately 890,000.) Each time a baptism, ordination, endowment, or marriage took place, it was recorded on the membership record in the local congregation. All changes were sent to Salt Lake City once a year. When members moved, their membership records were routed through the office of the Presiding Bishopric, and the new address was added to the master record.

The Church conducted a worldwide audit of membership records during 1969 as a forerunner to converting to an automated membership system, which was completed in the United States and Canada in 1975. The Church began decentralization of records that year. The records of all members living outside of the United States and Canada were sent to one of six area offices in which automation began in 1985. All international areas, except Samoa, were using automated systems in 1990. Master records are housed in thirty-five regional offices around the world.

BIBLIOGRAPHY

Membership Records Handbook. Salt Lake City, 1990.

Widtsoe, John A. *Priesthood and Church Government.* Salt Lake City, 1939; rev. ed., 1980.

THOMAS E. BROWN

This membership record from 1856 certifies that Eliza C. Binder, from London, is a member of the Church in good standing. Today membership records preserve vital statistics, including dates of baptism, ordinations, and other ordinances.

MEN, ROLES OF

For men in The Church of Jesus Christ of Latter-day Saints, the ideal example of manhood is Jesus Christ, the Savior of all mankind. There is no substitute. All men must transcend cultural biases and variations when they decide to pattern themselves after the Son of God, who is the complete representative of the Father. LDS men ideally strive to follow Christ by serving family and fellowbeings through love, work, PRIESTHOOD callings, instruction, and example.

The scriptures and the prophets make it clear to Latter-day Saints what the Savior expects of a man. To the Nephites he plainly stated, "For that which ye have seen me do even that shall ye do. . . . Therefore, what manner of men ought ye to be? Verily I say unto you, even as I am" (3 Ne. 27:21, 27). King Benjamin, tutored by an angel, described what has become a characterization of the challenges and potentials of manhood:

For the natural man is an enemy to God, and has been from the fall of Adam, and will be, forever and ever, unless he yields to the enticings of the Holy Spirit, and putteth off the natural man and becometh a saint through the atonement of Christ the Lord, and becometh as a child, submissive, meek, humble, patient, full of love, willing to submit to all things which the Lord seeth fit to inflict upon him, even as a child doth submit to his father [Mosiah 3:19].

PAUL taught about manliness by addressing the husband's role: "Husbands, love your wives, even as Christ also loved the church, and gave himself for it. . . . So ought men to love their wives as their own bodies" (Eph. 5:25, 28). President Brigham YOUNG often expounded on this theme: "Let the father be the head of the family, the master of his own household. And let him treat [the sisters] as an angel would treat them" (JD 4:55). "Set that example before your wives and your children, before your neighbors and this people, that you can say: Follow me, as I follow Christ" (JD 15:229). "I exhort you, masters, fathers, and husbands, to be affectionate and kind to those you preside over" (JD 1:69).

Husbands and fathers are expected to emulate the love of the Savior by teaching, serving, and ministering to their families. It is the man's role to engender and nurture life in benevolent partnership with his wife. It is not the man's role to serve his own selfish interests, declining to marry and to create a family. Obviously, he cannot fulfill his proper role without a loyal wife who is likewise true to her covenants with God.

By ordination to the priesthood, LDS men covenant to magnify their callings and to so live that, after sufficient diligent service to Christ's work, "all that my Father hath shall be given unto [them]" (D&C 84:38; *see also* OATH AND COVENANT OF THE PRIESTHOOD). To receive all that the Father has is to be endowed with the power, knowledge, blessings, and loving responsibilities of eternal fatherhood. With this power, however, comes a sacred obligation to act in love as the Heavenly Father does, never in selfishness or lust.

The duty of men is to acquire knowledge *and* love so that everything they do is right and true, patterned after Jesus Christ, for "this is life eternal, that they might know thee the only true God,

and Jesus Christ, whom thou hast sent" (John 17:3). The Prophet Joseph SMITH taught, "Here, then, is eternal life—to know the only wise and true God; and you have got to learn how to be Gods yourselves . . . namely, by going from one small degree to another, and from a small capacity to a great one; from grace to grace" (*TPJS*, pp. 346–47).

By serving according to the principles of the priesthood, each man should learn how to conduct himself like the Savior, who learned from his Father, for "no power or influence can or ought to be maintained by virtue of the priesthood, only by persuasion, by long-suffering, by gentleness and meekness, and by love unfeigned; by kindness, and pure knowledge, which shall greatly enlarge the soul without hypocrisy, and without guile" (D&C 121:41–42). It is a general responsibility of all men in the Church to serve as HOME TEACHERS; in addition, each will usually hold another calling, such as an Aaronic Priesthood quorum adviser, a scoutmaster or cubmaster, a Sunday School or Primary teacher, an athletic director, musician, activities chairman, clerk, bishop, stake president, or General Authority (*see* PRIESTHOOD OFFICES).

As it is God's work and glory "to bring to pass the immortality and eternal life of man" (Moses 1:39), so it is the responsibility of men to work while in mortality to help other people progress toward eternal life. Work in its broadest sense becomes a mark of a true man: A man is responsible for seeing that he and his family have sufficient means to live and to develop their talents. He is expected to labor to make the place where he and they live as comfortable as possible. He is also to work to bring spiritual order to the household through family prayer, father's blessings, and gospel study, teaching his children that life's proper priorities are gospel centered. He is taught to pray for, and bless, his family members. He shows them by example how to treat a wife—and women in general and children—with utmost respect (cf. Eph. 5:25; 6:4; D&C 42:22; 75:28). The Church encourages husbands to make every possible effort to keep their families intact and, should divorce occur, to strive to influence their children for good and to pay appropriate respect to their mothers, both to make the best of a difficult situation in this life and to prepare for adjustments in the next.

LDS men are exhorted by their leaders to become strong yet mild, to be ambitious to serve yet selfless in order to add to another's eternal growth, and to measure their success by how they nurture others and how they teach and make possible the progress and growth of others rather than use others to feed their own needs. Men, in other words, are expected to become Christlike natural PATRIARCHS, as exemplified by the Father and by the Son, devoid of harshness, domination, or selfishness.

[See also Brotherhood; Fatherhood; Lay Participation and Leadership; Lifestyle; Marriage; Priesthood Quorums; Young Men.]

BIBLIOGRAPHY

Hinckley, Gordon B. "What Will the Church Do for You, a Man?" Ensign 2 (July 1972):71–73.

VICTOR L. BROWN, JR.

MENTAL HEALTH

Recognizing the need for mental health services, The Church of Jesus Christ of Latter-day Saints, like other religious organizations, supports a network of agencies through LDS SOCIAL SERVICES that provides short-term care as needed and offers referral services when more extensive treatment is required. The Church endorses the work of licensed mental health practitioners provided that the suggestions and treatment offered are consistent with Church moral and lifestyle expectations.

Historically some critics have ascribed various mental afflictions of members to the influence of the Church. Today the assertion is sometimes made that as a result of their religion Latter-day Saints have high rates of divorce, drug abuse, depression, and suicide. This is not surprising, since stereotypes are frequently applied to new and different leaders and their followers. Virtually identical defects have been attributed to Jews, Native Americans, Roman Catholics, the Irish, and other groups (Bunker and Bitton; Bromley and Shupe). Research findings, however, show no evidence of unusual mental or social problems among Latter-day Saints.

National statistics show that the state of Utah, which is 70 percent LDS, has lower rates of mental and addictive disorders than U.S. averages. A National Institute of Mental Health report for 1986 ranked Utah as the second-lowest U.S. state in new inpatient admissions to state mental hospitals as a proportion of population. The National Association of State Mental Health Program Directors report for 1986 showed Utah's rate of outpatient mental cases per million population to be lower than that of thirty-six other states. These reports also show lower-than-average rates for alcohol and drug abuse, a finding confirmed in Utah in Demographic Perspective (1986). This report indicates that Utah ranks lowest of all the states in per capita alcohol consumption, and thirty-fifth in alcoholics per 100,000 population. Drug use among adolescents is low compared with national statistics. The overall mortality rate for suicide is slightly above the national average, but slightly below the average for the Rocky Mountain states.

Comparisons of LDS students at Brigham Young University with students at other schools on standard psychological measures, such as the Minnesota Multiphasic Personality Inventory, show more similarities than differences. On accepted indices of mental health, BYU students rank normal. Studies of divorce rates in Utah show that those counties with the highest proportions of LDS have the lowest divorce rates and are significantly below national averages. Studies of depression among BYU students and returned missionaries reveal average or lower levels.

Studies of depression among women in three Utah urban areas show LDS women to be no more or less depressed than their non-Mormon counterparts. For example, using the Beck Depression Inventory, a study of women in the Salt Lake Valley found no differences between LDS women and others (Spendlove, West, and Stanish). Women who were more active in the LDS Church were found to be less depressed than those who were less active, but causal connections to Church activity were inconclusive. Educational level appeared a better predictor of depression scores than religious affiliation: The more educated were less depressed. Responses to a national questionnaire indicated LDS women to be in the middle range on depression when compared with other groups. LDS men had the lowest depression scores of any group (Bergin and Cornwall).

Overall, on average, Latter-day Saints as a group are psychologically normal. They do not manifest unusual rates or kinds of mental disorders, and they do not differ much from national normative samples. In some studies they show less illness, but results may be questioned because of the nature of the population sampled. Statistics for the state of Utah often look better than the national average because of the state's lack of large minority and poverty populations. Other states with similar demographics, such as Wyoming, Idaho, and the Dakotas, manifest similar statistical advantages.

For mainstream, middle class people, denominational affiliation is less relevant to variations in mental health than are such factors as family background, educational level, economic class, marital status, and intrinsic versus extrinsic religious orientation. General findings obscure considerable individual variation because there are diverse ways of being religious. "Intrinsically" religious persons, who hold to personal convictions and do not depend on religion as a crutch, manifest better mental health than the "extrinsically" religious, those who focus on the external trappings of a religious or "righteous" social image. Such variation occurs among Latter-day Saints, as it does among other groups. Thus, the relation between religiosity and pathology is complex. How specific denominations enhance or undermine mental functioning is currently a matter of speculation and controversy.

The LDS culture and lifestyle manifest an interesting combination of possible positive and negative influences for mental functioning. These may cancel each other and create a normal average profile. Some possible negatives include tendencies toward perfectionism and the self-negation that inevitably accompany failure to match unreasonably high expectations. Negative emotions are not readily expressed, and thus conflicts are often difficult to resolve. LDS subcultures are very "group-oriented." Numerous organizations and activities define and reinforce the lifestyle. People "out of step" are easily recognized, and conformity is valued. Individuality and personal self-expression may be inhibited to a degree, while obedience to authority is encouraged.

In theory, these negatives may be balanced by the warmth and social support provided by a cohesive and caring social network, marked by high emphasis on family commitment and active participation in a diverse system of social, religious, athletic, and cultural activities. While members may despair over having "too much to do," they can always find sympathetic peers. Hope is engendered by a positive philosophy of human nature and the eternal potential of human beings.

LDS philosophy is growth-oriented, so there is constant encouragement toward self-improvement. Problems occur when there is not enough

tolerance for human imperfection in the process. When virtues like self-sacrifice, self-control, and hard work are overdone, they can take a toll, but when balanced with honest self-reflection and mutual support, they can be a stimulus for growth.

In establishing itself as an institutional partner in human civilization, the Church has manifested some growth pains. Insecurities that have accompanied being part of a new group are slowly giving way to the securities associated with having arrived as an established entity in the joint enterprise of cultural evolution. As this process has continued, these stresses have given way to a balanced subculture comparable to other mainstream groups.

BIBLIOGRAPHY

Bergin, Allen E., and Marie Cornwall. "Religion and Mental Health: Mormons and Other Groups." Annual Meeting of the Society for the Scientific Study of Religion. Salt Lake City, 1989.

Bromley, David G., and Anson Shupe. "Public Reaction Against New Religious Groups." In *Cults and New Religious Movements*, ed. M. Galanter. Washington, D.C., 1989.

Bunker, Gary L., and Davis Bitton. *The Mormon Graphic Image, 1834–1914*. Salt Lake City, 1983.

Martin, Thomas K.; Tim B. Heaton; and Stephen J. Bahr, eds. *Utah in Demographic Perspective*. Salt Lake City, 1986.

National Institute of Mental Health. *Additions and Resident Patients at End of Year 1986*. Rockville, Md., 1988.

Spendlove, David; Dee West; and William Stanish. "Risk Factors and the Prevalence of Depression in Mormon Women." *Social Science and Medicine* 18 (1984):491–95.

State Mental Health Program Indicators—1986. Alexandria, Va., 1989.

ALLEN E. BERGIN

MERCY

See: Justice and Mercy

MERCY KILLING

See: Death and Dying; Murder; Prolonging Life

MERIDIAN OF TIME

The meridian of time has been defined by one LDS apostle as "the middle or high point of that portion of eternity which is considered to be mortal time" (*MD*, 1966, p. 486). It is the DIS-

PENSATION in which Jesus Christ lived in mortality. The term does not occur in the Bible, but is found in the Doctrine and Covenants (20:26; 39:3) and in the book of Moses (5:57; 6:57, 62; 7:46).

The word "meridian" suggests the middle. According to Old Testament genealogies, from the FALL OF ADAM to the time of Jesus Christ was approximately 4,000 years. It has been nearly 2,000 years since Jesus' birth. The millennial reign will commence "in the beginning of the seventh thousand years" (D&C 77:12). After the MILLENNIUM there will be a "little season," the exact length of which is not revealed, but it could be several hundred years. In the context of these events, the Lord's mortal ministry took place near the meridian, or middle, of mortal time (DS 1:81).

The meridian of time may also be seen as the high point of mortal time. Latter-day revelation shows that all of the ancient prophets looked forward to the Messiah's coming (Jacob 4:4; Mosiah 13:33–35; 15:11). His coming fulfilled their prophecies, and he was prefigured in the LAW OF MOSES (Mosiah 13:29–32) and in ancient ceremonial ordinances (Moses 5:5–8). The meridian of time is the apex of all dispensations because of the birth, ministry, and atonement of Christ. Without him all prophetic writings and utterances would have had no efficacy, and the hopes of mankind today and forever would be but futile desires and yearnings without possibility of fulfillment.

MARSHALL T. BURTON

MESSENGER AND ADVOCATE

The *Latter Day Saints' Messenger and Advocate* was published in Kirtland, Ohio, from October 1834 to September 1837—thirty-six sixteen-page, double-column issues. It succeeded the EVENING AND THE MORNING STAR. The name *Messenger and Advocate* described its purpose: to be the messenger and advocate of The Church of Jesus Christ of Latter-day Saints, thus to help the Saints better understand its doctrines and principles. Main doctrinal contributions came from Joseph SMITH, Sidney RIGDON, Oliver COWDERY, W. W. Phelps, and John Whitmer. Other entries continued articles from the *Star*, a history of the Christian church, letters from missionaries, hymns, news of current Church events such as the building of the Kirtland

Temple and its dedicatory services, editorials, minutes of conferences, summaries of news of the day, marriages, notices, and obituaries.

The last issue of each annual volume contained an index of all twelve issues.

Oliver Cowdery edited the *Messenger and Advocate* from October 1834 to May 1835. He was succeeded by John Whitmer from June 1835 to March 1836, but returned as editor from April 1836 to January 1837. Thereafter, his brother Warren A. Cowdery served from February to September 1837, when publication ceased. Joseph Smith and Sidney Rigdon were listed as publisher for the 1837 February and March issues. In April 1837 the printing office and contents were transferred to William Marks, who was then listed as the publisher.

When Warren A. Cowdery declined further publishing, the *Messenger and Advocate* noted that "a large body of the elders of the church of Latter Day Saints have united and rented the printing establishment" (3:571–72) to publish the *Elders' Journal of The Church of Latter Day Saints*, which ceased publication in Far West, Missouri, in 1838.

BIBLIOGRAPHY

Backman, Milton V., Jr. *The Heavens Resound: A History of the Latter-day Saints in Ohio, 1830–1838*. Salt Lake City, 1983.

J. LEROY CALDWELL

MESSIAH

MESSIAH

Messiah is a Hebrew term signifying "anointed one." The Greek equivalent is *christos*, whence the name Christ. Jesus, the divinely given name of the Savior (Matt. 1:21), derives from the Hebrew *Yeshua* or *Yehoshua* (or Joshua, as it commonly appears in English), from a root meaning "to save." With other Christians, Latter-day Saints agree that implicit in the name Jesus Christ lies the doctrine that he is the Messiah, the Anointed One who saves.

Like the New Testament, the Book of Mormon clearly identifies Jesus as the Messiah (1 Ne. 10:4–17; 2 Ne. 25:16–20; Hel. 8:13–17). It also declares that a knowledge of the Messiah existed "from the beginning of the world" (1 Ne. 12:18;

Mosiah 13:33–35) and prophesies details of his life and mission. For example, the Messiah would appear in a body (1 Ne. 15:13), his name would be Jesus Christ (2 Ne. 25:19; Mosiah 3:8), and he would be baptized as an example of obedience (2 Ne. 31:4–9). Moreover, signs would attend his birth, death, and resurrection (2 Ne. 26:3; Hel. 14:2–8, 20–28). In this connection, he would be slain and rise from the dead, bringing to pass the resurrection (1 Ne. 10:11; 2 Ne. 2:8). At the last day, he is to appear in power and glory (2 Ne. 6:14), to reign as king and lawgiver (D&C 45:59; 1 Tim. 6:14–15).

[See also Jesus Christ, Names and Titles of.]

DAVID B. GALBRAITH

MESSIANIC CONCEPT AND HOPE

It is LDS doctrine that a knowledge of the role of Jesus Christ as the Messiah has been on the earth from the beginning. God taught Adam and Eve about the Messiah who would redeem mankind. Called "Only Begotten" and "Son of Man," even his name Jesus Christ was revealed (Moses 5:7–11; 6:52–57) These are, of course, the anglicized words meaning "Savior Anointed." God also taught ENOCH that the "Messiah, the King of Zion" would die on a cross (Moses 7:53–55).

From other sources it is evident that Hebrew people clearly believed in a redeemer, though characterizations varied. The Bible refers to him through imagery such as "the shepherd, the stone of Israel" (Gen. 49:24), the "tried stone" or "sure foundation" (Isa. 28:16), the "stem of Jesse" and "Branch" (Isa. 11:1; Jer. 33:15–16). He is also called Redeemer, Holy One of Israel, Savior, Lord of Hosts, the First and Last (Isa. 43:1–15; 44:6), and even a servant (Isa. 42:1; 49:3; 50:10; 52:13).

Because biblical prophecy uses the imagery of royalty, some believed that at his first coming the Messiah would save them from political bondage. Jacob foresaw that Shiloh would come, to whom people would gather (Gen. 49:10). Moses prophesied, "There shall come a Star out of Jacob, and a Sceptre shall rise out of Israel" (Num. 24:17). ISAIAH envisioned a child born, "and the government shall be upon his shoulder. . . . Of the increase of . . . peace there shall be no end, upon the throne of David, and upon his kingdom" (Isa. 9:6–7). Micah recorded that from Bethlehem "shall he come forth . . . to be ruler in Israel" (Micah 5:2).

JEREMIAH saw that "a King shall reign . . . and shall execute judgment and justice" (Jer. 23:5). However, such royal prophecies of a king and ruler would find fulfillment in the Messiah's eternal, rather than his mortal, role.

The prophets planted seeds of belief in a Messiah, seeds that would flower during later periods. The DEAD SEA SCROLLS reveal a hope in two Messiahs who would lead a religious revival. Judas Maccabeus' example (d. 160 B.C.), overthrowing the Greeks and reestablishing Jewish independence, spawned hope during the early Roman period (63 B.C.–A.D. 70) that a Messiah would deliver the Jewish nation. Although royalty and battle imagery in the Bible was interpreted to mean political deliverance, those images referred to spiritual salvation. Said Jesus, "My kingdom is not of this world" (John 18:36).

The title Messiah (Hebrew *mashiah*; Greek *christos*) means "anointed one." Among ancient Israelites, persons set apart for God's work were anointed with oil, including prophets, priests, and kings. Jesus, citing a messianic PROPHECY from Isaiah (61:1), told hearers in Nazareth, "The Spirit of the Lord is upon me, because he hath anointed me to preach the gospel, . . . to heal the brokenhearted, to preach deliverance to the captives" (Luke 4:18).

Isaiah described the "servant" as one who would be smitten (Isa. 50:6), even "wounded for our transgressions, . . . bruised for our iniquities," and yet "make intercession for the transgressors" (53:3–5, 12). Zechariah added that he would be wounded in the house of his friends (Zech. 12:10; 13:6–7). New Testament authors also understood that Jesus was to suffer before entering his glory (e.g., Luke 24:26; Acts 3:18).

Throughout his ministry Jesus clearly understood his messiahship (cf. 3 Ne. 15:20–23). For instance, when the Samaritan woman acknowledged, "I know that Messias cometh," Jesus responded, "I that speak unto thee am he" (John 4:25–26). Peter declared, "Thou art the Christ [Messiah]" (Matt. 16:16); and Andrew, Peter's brother, announced, "We have found the Messias" (John 1:41). Even devils are reported to have said, "Thou art Christ the Son of God" (e.g., Luke 4:41).

The biblical portrayal of a mortal Messiah reviled rather than ruling, rejected rather than reigning, is amplified in the Book of Mormon. As its modern subtitle indicates, the Book of Mormon is another testament of Jesus Christ, or Jesus the Messiah. Book of Mormon writers taught that all prophets spoke concerning the Messiah (Jacob 7:11; Mosiah 13:33). In approximately 600 B.C., LEHI taught that "redemption cometh in and through the Holy Messiah. . . . Behold he offereth himself a sacrifice for sin . . . that he may bring to pass the resurrection of the dead" (2 Ne. 2:6–10).

NEPHI₁ wrote that since all are in a fallen state, they must rely on the Messiah, the Redeemer. He learned that the Son of God was willing to come as the Messiah, preach the gospel, serve as an example of righteous living, and be slain for the sins of all (1 Ne. 10:4–6, 11; 11:26–33; 19:9; 2 Ne. 25:11–19; 31:9–16).

King BENJAMIN described how Jesus Christ would come from heaven to dwell in a mortal body, "working mighty miracles, such as healing the sick . . . [and casting] out devils," suffering temptation and fatigue. Even blood would come "from every pore, so great shall be his anguish for the wickedness and the abominations of his people." Saying that he was only a man and that "he hath a devil, [they] shall scourge him, and shall crucify him" (Mosiah 3:5–10).

ALMA₂ said of the Messiah's ministry, "He shall go forth, suffering pains and afflictions and temptations of every kind. . . . And he will take upon him death, that he may loose the bands of death which bind his people; and he will take upon him their infirmities . . . that he may know according to the flesh how to succor his people according to their infirmities" (Alma 7:11–12).

More than five centuries before Christ's birth, JACOB wrote, "For this intent have we written these things, that they may know that we knew of Christ, and we had a hope of his glory many hundred years before his coming; and not only we ourselves had a hope of his glory, but also all the holy prophets which were before us" (Jacob 4:4).

BIBLIOGRAPHY

McConkie, Bruce R. *The Promised Messiah*. Salt Lake City, 1978.

D. KELLY OGDEN

MESSIANIC PROPHECIES IN THE OLD TESTAMENT

See: Jesus Christ: Prophecies About Jesus Christ

METAPHYSICS

Metaphysics is the branch of PHILOSOPHY concerned with the ultimate nature of reality, including those aspects of it, if any, that are unavailable to empirical inquiry. The historical development of metaphysics in Western philosophical thought has been carried out largely by those philosophers and theologians who have aspired more to develop a unified system of ideas than to dwell upon diverse arrays of facts. Especially important to the theologians was the task of bringing abstract philosophical concepts into harmony with the concrete teachings of SCRIPTURE. Their systems differed, but their common goal was to combine philosophy and scripture into a single coherent account of the ultimate nature of things.

TENTATIVENESS. LDS metaphysics stands apart, because the Church has not developed a traditional metaphysical THEOLOGY and does not aspire to one. It has not been much influenced by philosophical thinking. LDS faith springs from two sources, scripture and ongoing RELIGIOUS EXPERIENCE. The absence of any systematic metaphysics of the Church follows from the belief that scripture, as the record of divine REVELATION, may be supplemented by new revelation at any time. A metaphysical system, to be true, must be all-inclusive. But faith in continuing revelation precludes the certainty that such a system exists. Thus, LDS metaphysics remains incomplete, tentative, and unsystematic, subject to revision in the light of things yet to be revealed by God. This tentativeness about metaphysical ideas has saved the Church from the crises that can arise when a religion's beliefs are tied to philosophical ideas which are later abandoned or discredited. The Church's lack of a systematic metaphysical theology has prompted some students of its DOCTRINES who are used to such theology to assert that it has no theology at all, but it would be more accurate to say that its metaphysics and theology are not systematically formulated.

MATTER AND SPIRIT. In the absence of a metaphysical system, the LDS faith still displays some characteristic metaphysical ideas. Latter-day Saints regard MATTER as a fundamental principle of reality and as the primary basis for distinguishing particular beings. The import of this view reveals itself most strikingly in the doctrine concerning the material embodiment of God: "The Father has a body of flesh and bones as tangible as man's; the Son also" (D&C 130:22). This is not to be understood crassly; the matter of exalted bodies is purified, transfigured, and glorified. LDS teachings draw no ultimate contrast between SPIRIT and matter. Indeed, "all spirit is matter, but it is more fine or pure" (D&C 131:7). This position avoids traditional difficulties in explaining the interaction of spirit and body.

The reality of matter implies the reality of space and time. Scripture speaks of the place where God dwells and of "the reckoning of the Lord's time" (Abr. 3:9). So God himself exists within a spatial and temporal environment. In accepting space, time, and matter as constitutive of reality, Latter-day Saints take the everyday world of human experience as a fairly reliable guide to the nature of things. But this acceptance is no dogma, and their belief remains open to the possibility that these three ideas, as presently understood, may be auxiliaries to more fundamental ideas not yet known.

PLURALISM. LDS thought clearly emphasizes the importance of the fundamental plurality of the world, with its continuing novelties, changes, conflicts, and agreements: "For it must needs be, that there is an opposition in all things" (2 Ne. 2:11). The world is not static but dynamic, not completed but still unfolding. This unfinished and future-oriented aspect of things provides the basis for growth and improvement. A monistic world or universe in which all differences are finally absorbed in a higher UNITY is viewed as impossible. The LDS Church has been less inclined than some other religions to regard the world of common experience as an inferior order of that which must be distinguished from a higher and altogether different realm. Heaven itself is regarded as offering the hope of endless progression rather than the ease of final satisfaction.

NATURAL AND SUPERNATURAL. Latter-day Saints see a continuity between the traditional categories of natural and supernatural. They do not deny the distinction, but view it as one of degree, not of kind. God's creative act, for example, is not, as traditionally conceived, a CREATION ex nihilo, but an act of organizing material that already exists (Abr. 3:24). And creation is not a single, unique event, but an ongoing process that continues through the course of time: "And as one earth shall pass away . . . so shall another come" (Moses 1:38).

God acts upon matter within the context of space and time. In comparison with human attributes, God's attributes are supreme and perfect. But the difference between God and mankind remains one of degree. God seeks to provide the guidance and the necessary help for human beings to overcome the differences and become like him. The injunction to be perfect "even as your Father which is in heaven is perfect" (Matt. 5:48) is taken to mean that mankind may indeed become like God by faithfully following his COMMANDMENTS. The principles or laws of goodness that underlie these commandments have their own abiding reality. God exemplifies them but does not arbitrarily create them.

FREEDOM AND PERFECTIBILITY. Nothing is more central to LDS metaphysics than the principle of FREEDOM. The weaknesses of humanity that lead to error and sin are acknowledged. But the claim that human nature is totally depraved is denied. The LDS Church affirms that ideally "men are instructed sufficiently that they know good from evil" and that "men are free according to the flesh, . . . free to choose liberty and eternal life . . . or to choose captivity and death" (2 Ne. 2:5, 27). Human experience has as its final goal the development of virtue and holiness in a world that is not totally the product of God's will. Reality itself poses the challenge to overcome obstacles and achieve greater good. Everyone's life is a response to this challenge.

BIBLIOGRAPHY

Roberts, B. H. *Joseph Smith—Prophet Teacher*. Salt Lake City, 1908.

————. *Comprehensive History of the Church*, 6 vols. Salt Lake City, 1930.

DENNIS RASMUSSEN

MEXICO, PIONEER SETTLEMENTS IN

LDS COLONIZATION in Mexico was planned as a place of refuge from PERSECUTION in the United States and as a springboard for teaching the gospel in Latin America.

In 1875, President Brigham YOUNG sent Daniel W. Jones and others to Mexico to look for possible places to settle. They found the Mexican gov-

Colonia Juárez, Mexico, c. 1900.

ernment anxious for colonization in the sparsely settled areas of northern Chihuahua and Sonora. LDS colonization in Mexico did not begin, however, until after the first severe persecution precipitated by the passage of the 1882 Edmunds Act (*see* ANTIPOLYGAMY LEGISLATION). In 1885, hundreds of families, many of which practiced POLYGAMY, crossed the border into Mexico. In the next several years, seven colonies were founded on the Casas Grandes River and its tributaries in northwestern Chihuahua: Colonia Díaz, Colonia Dublan, Colonia Juárez, and the mountain colonies Cave Valley, Pacheco, García, and Chuichupa. In addition, Latter-day Saints established Colonia Oaxaca and Colonia Morelos on the Bavispe River in northern Sonora.

Hardship marked the early years as land-title problems, hunger, drought, hostile Apache Indians, and such diseases as smallpox and diphtheria challenged the Saints' determination to make the desert valleys their home. With capable leadership they persevered. In addition to local leaders, at one time or another six of the Twelve Apostles of the Church resided in the Mexican colonies.

Most of the settlers had already helped establish colonies in the western United States. With this experience, they imported to Mexico the best varieties of fruit trees for their orchards and selected breeds of cattle and horses. Within ten years, the colony lands were covered with canals, dams, man-made lakes, and irrigated crops. Thriving villages had wide streets lined with maple trees and lilacs and red-brick homes reminiscent of villages where many of the settlers had had their roots. There were stores, mills, and factories. Each community built schools to ensure the acquisition of cultural, literary, and technical skills. Through hard work, the colonists achieved a high degree of self-sufficiency.

On December 8, 1895, the first STAKE in Mexico was formed, with Colonia Juárez as its center and Anthony W. Ivins as stake president. In 1912, during the Mexican Revolution, local Church leaders led a general exodus and abandoned the colonies as the members sought refuge in the United States. Before the revolution, more than 4,000 Latter-day Saints lived in the colonies. Nearly one-fourth later returned and became part of Mexico's revolutionary history, enduring the raids of Pascual Orozco's "Red Flaggers" and American General John J. ("Black Jack") Pershing's search for Pancho Villa.

In 1990, there were again approximately 4,000 Latter-day Saints in the area, about 500 of

Juárez Academy (built 1888).

them descendants of the original pioneers, and the area was still a major supplier of fresh fruits to other parts of Mexico. The Church schools in Mexico are bilingual, with the Juárez Academy a regional center of culture and learning (*see* ACADEMIES). A striking number of Church leaders have roots in the Mexican colonies. The area also produces a high number of Spanish-speaking missionaries and mission presidents, whose work has extended beyond Latin America to Spain and the Spanish-speaking population worldwide.

While visiting Colonia Juárez on November 11, 1989, Carlos Salinas de Gortari, the president of Mexico, commended the LDS colonists in Mexico in these words:

> We appreciate your dedication, honesty, sobriety, and respect for law. You have contributed to the elevation of the regions where you live together, work and labor intensely, and with this you also elevate the level of our nation. You have incorporated new technology, more efficient productive processes, and have shared your knowledge and experience with the rest of your fellow citizens, adding generosity to the characteristics that distinguish you. We know that you are a good people who do

good [transcribed and translated by Guillermo Toscano Arrambí, on file at Juárez Academy].

BIBLIOGRAPHY

Hatch, Nelle Spilsbury. *Colonia Juárez: An Intimate Account of a Mormon Village.* Salt Lake City, 1954.

Johnson, Annie R. *Heartbeats of Colonia Díaz.* Salt Lake City, 1972.

Romney, Thomas Cottam. *The Mormon Colonies in Mexico.* Salt Lake City, 1938.

Tullis, F. LaMond. *Mormons in Mexico: The Dynamics of Faith and Culture.* Logan, Utah, 1987.

SHIRLEY TAYLOR ROBINSON

MEXICO AND CENTRAL AMERICA, THE CHURCH IN

MEXICO

The Church of Jesus Christ of Latter-day Saints first sent missionaries into Mexico in 1875. It had long been a hope of Church leaders to teach the gospel to these descendants of the Book of Mor-

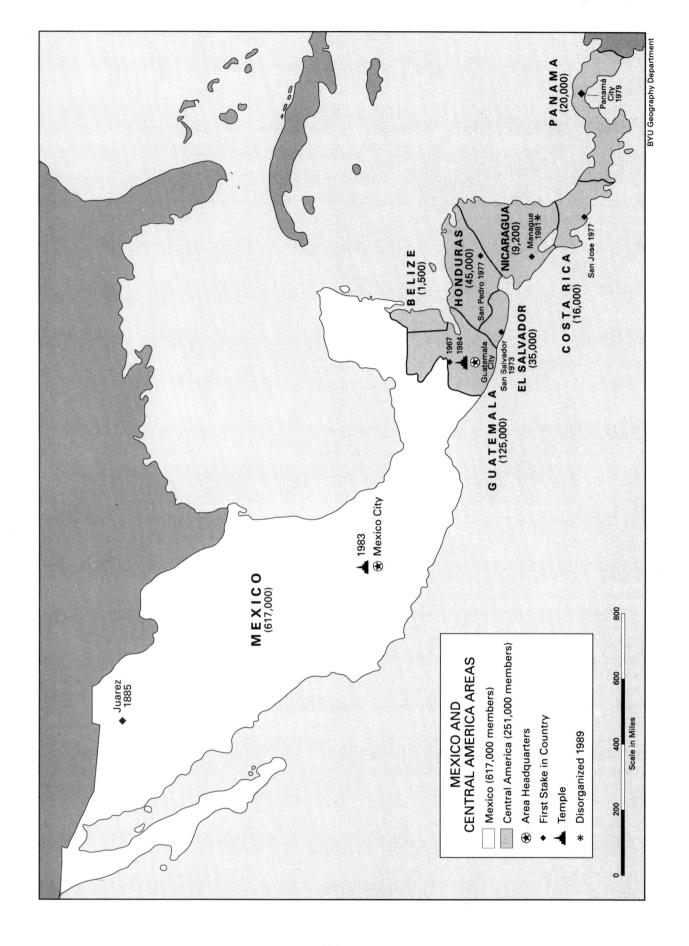

MEXICO AND
CENTRAL AMERICA AREAS

	Mexico (617,000 members)
	Central America (251,000 members)
⊕	Area Headquarters
◆	First Stake in Country
⚒	Temple
✳	Disorganized 1989

Scale in Miles

0   200   400   600   800

MEXICO
(617,000)

Juarez
1885

1983
⚒⊕ Mexico City

GUATEMALA
(125,000)

BELIZE
(1,500)

HONDURAS
(45,000)

San Pedro 1977 ◆

1967
1984
◆
⊕ Guatemala
City

San Salvador
1973

EL SALVADOR
(35,000)

NICARAGUA
(9,200)

Managua
1981 ✳ ◆

COSTA RICA
(16,000)

San Jose 1977 ◆

PANAMA
(20,000)

Panamá
City
1979 ◆

BYU Geography Department

898

mon peoples, and to show them the sacred record of their ancestors. President Brigham YOUNG also looked at Mexico as a possible place of refuge for the Saints in the event of further persecution from the United States government. The Church established colonies in northern Mexico in 1885. Though Church growth in Mexico, and later in Central America, was sporadic and beset with political difficulties, the deep roots of nearly a century began to produce abundantly in the 1970s, so that by the end of 1990 the Church had twenty-seven missions and hundreds of stakes and wards serving approximately a million members in these areas. There are also temples in both Mexico City and Guatemala City.

FIRST MISSIONARIES.   The first LDS missionaries sent to Mexico in 1875 included Daniel W. Jones, his son Wiley, Anthony W. Ivins, James Z. Stewart, and Helaman Pratt. This group was also to scout out good colonizing areas in the southwestern United States and northern Mexico. Though they recorded no baptisms, the missionaries found many possible sites for the Saints to settle, the most promising being in Chihuahua, Mexico.

From Chihuahua the group also mailed a booklet, *Trozos Selectos del Libro de Mormon* (selections of the Book of Mormon), to well-known citizens and government officials. The selections had been translated by Melitón González Trejo and Daniel W. Jones. Meanwhile, a second group of missionaries, called in September 1876, left for Mexico directly following the October general conference. This group was composed of two of the original missionaries, Stewart and Pratt, and four new ones—Stewart's brother Isaac, George Terry, Louis Garff, and Melitón G. Trejo. They separated in Tucson, Arizona, with Pratt and Trejo going south to Hermosillo, Sonora, Mexico, where the first five baptisms in Mexico occurred in 1877. The other four missionaries were not so fortunate as they were driven from the country by the warring Yaqui Indians.

Two of the booklets mailed by the first expedition fell into the hands of two influential citizens who wrote for more information: Ignacio Manuel Altamirano and Dr. Plotino Rhodakanaty (also spelled Rhodacanaty). Dr. Rhodakanaty studied the materials with several of his friends, and when

J. Reuben Clark, Jr., U.S. ambassador to Mexico, with Abel Paez and Isaias Juarez in Mexico (c. 1931–1932).

Elder Moses Thatcher, of the Quorum of the Twelve Apostles, and other missionaries arrived in Mexico City in November 1879, they soon baptized him and his study group. Within a week Thatcher organized the Mexico City branch and appointed Rhodakanaty as branch president, with Silviano Arteaga and Jose Ybarola serving as his counselors.

Thatcher dedicated Mexico for missionary work on January 25, 1880, but because many of the original members left the Church, he rededicated the land and mission on April 6, 1881, from the rim of the volcano Popocatepetl—which has great historical significance to Mexico's Indian people. He formed a second branch that August in Ozumba, a small town nestled at the base of Popocatepetl.

COLONISTS.   By 1885, the U.S. persecution of the Church for polygamy resulted in many Church leaders in the United States going into foreign

The Church of Jesus Christ of Latter-day Saints in Mexico and Central America as of January 1, 1991.

Abel Paez speaking in Mexico in 1946. President George Albert Smith presided at this conference, which rectified issues regarding the leadership of Mexican branches and missions.

countries to find homes for their multiple families, and some of them founded Colonia Juárez in the state of Chihuahua, Mexico. Later colonies were founded at Díaz, Dublán, and also in Pacheco, Oaxaca, Morelos, and San José, Sonora (*see* MEXICO, PIONEER SETTLEMENTS IN).

The American colonists suffered greatly from the political instability in Mexico. Sonora permanently exiled all foreign settlers, and the Chihuahua Saints were evacuated for a time, with the loss of food, possessions, and sometimes lives. However, many of the Saints returned and rebuilt their colonies and had no further trouble.

MISSION CLOSURES (1889–1946). The Mexican Mission was closed in 1889 and the missionaries recalled because of the worsening persecution in the polygamy crisis, but it was reopened in 1901 by Elder John Henry Smith, an apostle, and Presidents Anthony W. Ivins and Henry Eyring from the Juárez Stake. Missionary work continued with lengthy interruptions due to the Mexican Revolution and counterrevolutions (1910–1928).

Elder Rey L. Pratt, of the Seventy, presided over the Mexican Mission from 1907 until his death in 1931, but did not live in Mexico much of that time because the missionaries were often banned. When all foreign missionaries were exiled from 1913 until 1921, President Pratt placed Presidents Isaias Juárez, Abel Paez, and Bernabe Parra, the district presidency, in charge of the Church in

Mexico, and the work of the mission continued under local leadership. Local priesthood brethren also led the Church from 1926 to 1946, when the Mexican government prohibited foreigners from doing religious work in Mexico. Church membership continued to grow.

1946 TO PRESENT. With its rapid growth in Mexico, and noting the need for education among its members there, the Church established thirty-seven schools in Mexico between 1960 and 1974, most of them- elementary schools. The largest, most widely known LDS school in Mexico is its preparatory school, Centro Escolar Benemerito de las Américas, established in 1964.

The Mexican Mission was divided into four missions between 1952 and 1960. In December 1961, Mexico City established its first stake with Harold Brown, an Anglo who was reared in the Mormon colonies, as president. The second stake was organized in 1967 with Agricol Lozano, a native Mexican, as president. On November 9, 1975, Elder Howard W. Hunter, of the Quorum of the Twelve Apostles, organized eleven new stakes in the Mexico City area, among them the Mexico City Zarahemla Stake for the students of Benemerito. From 1976 to 1978 nearly 150 full-time missionaries were called from the membership of this stake. By 1983 Mexico had eight missions, seventy-six stakes, and several hundred thousand members (second only to the United States in membership), and the majority of the missionaries in the country were local Mexicans. Hundreds of the members had been blessed to attend Church schools.

MEXICO CITY TEMPLE. On March 21, 1977, President Spencer W. KIMBALL announced that the Church would build a temple in Mexico City. The Mexico Temple was dedicated on December 2, 1983, by President Gordon B. Hinckley, a counselor in the First Presidency. Its design was a modern adaptation of ancient Mayan architecture, showing respect for the culture and history of Mexico. Harold and Leanore Jespersen Brown were its first president and matron.

CENTRAL AMERICA
The expansion of the Church into Central America is more recent than that of Mexico. The first missionary effort beyond Mexico came in 1941, when John (Juan) O'Donnal, who had grown up in the LDS Mexican colonies, was assigned to Guatemala City by the U.S. Department of Agriculture. He

Mexico City Temple, dedicated 1983. Its exterior is made of white cast stone with ornate adaptations of ancient Mayan designs. Photographer: Eldon Linschoten.

taught the gospel informally in Guatemala for several years and petitioned the Church to send missionaries to what he considered a humble people ready to hear the gospel. In 1947 four missionaries were sent to Guatemala and Costa Rica, as part of the Mexican Mission. On September 7, 1947, the first sacrament meeting was held in Guatemala. Central America was dedicated for preaching the gospel and the Central America Mission was organized on November 16, 1952, by Elder Spencer W. Kimball, then of the Quorum of the Twelve. On August 1, 1965, the Guatemala-El Salvador Mission was divided from the Central American Mission. By 1990 missions had been organized in five Central American countries: Guatemala, Honduras, Panama, El Salvador, and Costa Rica. Guatemala had three missions, and El Salvador opened its second mission in July 1990. In December 1990 the Church had forty-three stakes in Central America.

THE GUATEMALA TEMPLE. While the Mexico City Temple was being built, plans were already being made to build a temple in Guatemala City. Construction of this temple was completed in three years, and it was dedicated in December 1984, one year after the dedication of the Mexico

City Temple. The construction of the temples enables thousands of Mexican and Central American Latter-day Saints to participate regularly in temple ordinances in their own language and without undertaking the long trip to the Arizona Temple in Mesa as they had done before.

In the April 1989 general conference of the Church, the first General Authorities from Mexico

Primary children in Guatemala (c. 1985). Thirty percent of the one million members to join the Church in 1987–1989 came from Mexico and Central America, and another thirty percent from South America.

and Central America were called to the quorums of Seventy: Horacio Tenorio from Mexico and Carlos H. Amado from Guatemala. On April 6, 1991, Jorge A. Rojas of Mexico was also called to the Seventy.

BIBLIOGRAPHY

"Central America: Saints in Six Nations Grow in the Gospel." *Ensign* 7 (Feb. 1977):25–26.

Flake, Gerry R. "Mormons in Mexico: The First 96 Years." *Ensign* 2 (Sept. 1972):20–21.

Gardner, Marvin K. "Taking the Gospel to Their Own People." *Ensign* 18 (Oct. 1988):12–16.

Hansen, Terrence L. "The Church in Central America." *Ensign* 2 (Sept. 1972):40–42.

Lozano, Agrícol. *Historia de la Iglesia en México.* México, D.F., 1980.

Tullis, F. LaMond. *Mormons in Mexico.* Logan, Utah, 1987.

BOANERGES RUBALCAVA

MICHAEL THE ARCHANGEL

See: Adam: LDS Sources; Angels: Archangels

MIDDLE EAST, THE CHURCH IN THE

Political turmoil in the Ottoman empire, two world wars, and restrictions imposed by local governments have challenged the efforts of The Church of Jesus Christ of Latter-day Saints to establish an official presence in the Middle East. Despite these difficulties, the Church has small congregations in several Middle Eastern countries, mostly because of the influx of expatriate (mainly American) Church members working there. Before 1950, Church activities were limited to the Levant (Turkey, Palestine, Lebanon, and Syria), but since then some have also occurred, temporarily at least, in Iran, Egypt, Jordan, Israel, the West Bank, Lebanon, and the Arab countries of the Gulf.

The history of LDS Church activity in the Middle East dates from 1841, when Orson Hyde, an apostle, prayed on the Mount of Olives near Jerusalem for the ingathering of Abraham's children (especially the Jews) to Palestine, for the building up of Jerusalem, and for the rearing of a

temple. LDS missionary work in the Middle East began in 1884, when Jacob Spori opened the Turkish Mission in Constantinople. Branches of the Church, consisting mostly of Armenian and European converts, were eventually established in Aintab, Aleppo, and Haifa, but the mission closed in 1896. It reopened in 1897, but closed again in 1909 because of the increasing political turmoil in the Ottoman empire.

After World War I, the mission was reopened in Aleppo and renamed the Armenian Mission. In 1928 it was headquartered in Haifa, but was closed that December with the sudden death of Joseph Booth, the mission president. It reopened in 1933 as the Palestine-Syrian Mission, but was closed again in 1939 because of World War II. In 1947 the mission was reopened with Badwagan Piranian as president; it was renamed the Near East Mission in 1950 but closed again later that year. From 1950 to 1969, Church activity in the Middle East consisted mostly of small groups scattered in various countries and of a few missionaries from the Swiss Mission assigned to work in Lebanon. In September 1969 a Church group was organized in Jerusalem to accommodate Brigham Young University (BYU) faculty and students involved in a Near Eastern Studies program. Other events there included the organization of the Israel District (1977), the dedication of the Orson Hyde Memorial Garden on the Mount of Olives (1979), and the dedication of the BYU Jerusalem Center for Near Eastern Studies on Mount Scopus (1989).

The Church has established a few congregations in other Middle Eastern countries since 1950 as economic expansion, related mostly to the oil industry, has brought an influx of Western workers to the area. A branch of the Church has been operating in Cairo, Egypt, since 1974. The Iran Tehran Mission was organized in July 1975, the first formal mission in the Middle East since 1950, but it was closed in December 1978 with the worsening political situation between Iran and the United States. In 1989, Jordan became the first Arab country to grant formal recognition to the Church, allowing it to establish the Center for Cultural and Educational Affairs in Amman. The governments in these countries have allowed the Church, along with other non-Muslim groups, to hold services and other activities as long as they are unobtrusive and their members respect Islamic laws and traditions, including the restriction against proselytizing among the Muslim populace.

ISSUES AND CHALLENGES. The manner in which the Church has handled a number of sensitive issues in the Middle East illustrates its capacity to adapt to local needs and customs. Between 1841 and 1950, the most vexing problem for the missionaries was how to deal with the poverty and poor health of the members. The Church attempted to alleviate the suffering of members by teaching them new skills, organizing cooperatives to market goods in Salt Lake City, soliciting clothing and food donations from members in Utah, and arranging for relocation to Europe, Mexico, and the United States. Since 1950 the Church has adjusted to issues of a cultural and political nature. One example is the First Presidency's decision to allow members to hold Sabbath services, customarily reserved for Sunday, on the day of worship designated by local religious tradition: Friday in Muslim countries and Saturday in Israel. The Church has refrained from taking an official stand on the Arab-Israeli question; rather, the position of Church leaders is best revealed by the manner in which they have quietly sought to cultivate good relations and a reputation for impartiality with both Israelis and Palestinians. The following statement by Elder Howard W. Hunter, an apostle, is characteristic of this attitude: "Both the Jews and the Arabs are children of our Father. They are both children of promise, and as a church we do not take sides. We have love for and an interest in each" (pp. 35–36).

The greatest obstacle to Church growth today is the prohibition against proselytizing that prevails in every country in the Middle East. Despite its reputation for vigorous missionary activity in other areas of the world, the Church has observed religious restrictions in the Middle East by making nonproselytizing commitments to government leaders and by issuing strict instructions for members to honor these commitments.

BIBLIOGRAPHY

Baldridge, Steven W. *Grafting In: A History of the Latter-day Saints in the Holy Land.* Murray, Utah, 1989.

Hunter, Howard W. "All Are Alike Unto God." *BYU Speeches of the Year, 1979*, pp. 35–36. Provo, Utah.

Lindsay, Rao H. "A History of the Missionary Activities of The Church of Jesus Christ of Latter-day Saints in the Near East, 1884–1929." Master's thesis, Brigham Young University, 1958.

JAMES A. TORONTO

MILITARY AND THE CHURCH

Although the Church is opposed to war and recognizes that going to war is a very poor alternative in resolving conflicts, tens of thousands of Latter-day Saints have served their countries' armed forces, sometimes even fighting in opposing forces, especially in World War II. The Church considers being loyal citizens to be a duty of its members, irrespective of nationality. Responding to a call for military service is one appropriate manner of fulfilling this duty of citizenship. Latter-day Saints who choose military careers have no restrictions on either their fellowship or their callings in the Church. While any member is free to object to military service because of conscience, Church membership in and of itself is not a justification, and Church leaders have discouraged conscientious objection in every conflict of the twentieth century.

The moral question for Church members is much more one of the spirit than of the uniform. It echoes John the Baptist's counsel to soldiers to avoid violence and extortion, and to be content with their wages (Luke 3:14). The Book of Mormon repeatedly counsels soldiers to abhor the shedding of blood (Alma 44:1–7; 48:14–16, 23; Morm. 4:11–12). However, it also contains principles as to when war may be justified. Concerning the action of the Nephites when they were attacked by the Lamanites, the record states:

> Nevertheless, the Nephites were inspired by a better cause, for they were not fighting for monarchy nor power but they were fighting for their homes and their liberties, their wives and their children, and their all, yea, for their rites of worship and their church.
>
> And they were doing that which they felt was the duty which they owed to their God; for the Lord had said unto them, and also unto their fathers, that: Inasmuch as ye are not guilty of the first offense, neither the second, ye shall not suffer yourselves to be slain by the hands of your enemies.
>
> And again, the Lord has said that: Ye shall defend your families even unto bloodshed. Therefore for this cause were the Nephites contending with the Lamanites, to defend themselves, and their families, and their lands, their country, and their rights, and their religion [Alma 43:45–47].

One of the Church's first significant involvements with a national military was the organization and the march of the MORMON BATTALION. In

Elder Harold B. Lee (front row, standing) and President Hilton A. Robertson of the Japanese Mission, with LDS servicemen at the Chapel in the 8069th AU Compound, Korea, 1954. On this trip, Elder Lee investigated the possibility of opening Korea as a separate mission. Photographer: Jerry Maxwell.

1846, as the Latter-day Saints were beginning their westward migration, they responded to the U.S. Army's request for five hundred volunteers to serve in the conflict with Mexico. The battalion marched from Fort Leavenworth, Kansas, through New Mexico and Arizona into Mexico, and then on to California, without combat. Most of its men then journeyed to join their families in Utah. The relative isolation in Utah provided for very little involvement in the Civil War. The Spanish–American War saw two artillery units mobilized from Utah, with the first LDS chaplain and the first LDS servicemen's worship group organized. Involvement in World War I was similarly based in the activity of Utah soldiers but was far more extensive than in any previous military engagement.

In the period before World War II, President J. Reuben Clark, Jr., counselor in the FIRST PRESIDENCY, vigorously advocated U.S. neutrality, and opposed the maintenance of a standing army with equal vigor when hostilities ceased. However, he was the Church spokesman when it made official declarations encouraging LDS men to respond to their governments' call for military service, despite the fact that these decisions were contrary to his personal viewpoint. In October 1940, he said, "We shall confidently expect that no young man member of the Church will seek to evade his full responsibility" (CR [Oct. 1940]:16). A 1942 First Presidency statement counseled Church members worldwide to be ready to respond to their government's call to military duty and exonerated the members' acts of war: "God . . . will not hold the innocent instrumentalities of the war, our brethren in arms, responsible for the conflict" (MFP 6:159). This statement has been reiterated during each subsequent period of military action.

The Church has always made significant efforts to help its members in the armed forces live by the same moral standards they would uphold at home. The General Servicemen's Committee was organized in 1941 with Elder Harold B. Lee as chairman. Members of the committee had geographical responsibilities, visited military installations, and appointed more than three thousand servicemen as group leaders and assistants. These priesthood leaders facilitated fellowship and organized opportunities for military people who could not meet with ordinary wards and branches to partake of the sacrament of the Lord's Supper. The principle of servicemen's group leadership as a special case of Church organization continues in force. LDS chaplains coordinate their activities with stakes and missions and are authorized to organize groups and call group leaders any time small numbers of LDS service people are put in circumstances that might restrict their access to worship.

The activities of the General Servicemen's Committee (in 1969 it became the Military Relations Committee) ebbed and flowed with the intensity of military conflict. This committee began providing publications specifically for service personnel during World War II. It distributed pocket-sized copies of the Book of Mormon, a hymnal, and a doctrinal compendium, *Principles of the Gospel*, and prepared brochures on military life, sexual morality, missionary opportunities, and the Word of Wisdom. These resources formed the basis of a preservice orientation program instituted during the Vietnam era by the Military Relations Committee. Every stake was provided literature, audiovisual resources, and a curricular outline to help people entering the military prepare for that challenge.

The missionary opportunities in the stresses of military life have proven to be significant, both on a personal and on a national basis. Many military people join the Church, and missionary success in countries such as Japan and Korea has gained momentum from the work of servicemen and women. The membership of the Church commonly prays for service people as a group, much as it does for the missionaries.

Servicemen's conferences are held frequently in Europe and the Far East. An English-speaking servicemen's stake was organized in Europe in 1968, providing members living there the full program of the Church in their native tongue.

BIBLIOGRAPHY

Boone, Joseph F. "The Roles of The Church of Jesus Christ of Latter-day Saints in Relation to the United States Military, 1900–1975." Ph.D. diss., Brigham Young University, 1975.

ROBERT C. OAKS

MILLENARIANISM

While the word "millennium" simply means a thousand years, *the* Millennium is usually understood as a thousand-year period during which Christ will reign on earth. Latter-day Saints from the beginning anticipated the return of Christ and worked to prepare the world for his coming. The Bible mentions the thousand-year period only in Revelation 20:2–7, though many interpreters believe that various Old Testament prophecies, such as Isaiah's vision of the lamb and lion lying down together (Isa. 11), describe that time. "Millenarianism" refers to belief in and the study of the Millennium—how near it is and what life then will be like.

Not surprisingly, Christians have differed on these matters throughout history. Those who take a literal approach to prophecy anticipate a millennial world fundamentally distinct from the present age, an actual return to the paradisiacal conditions that prevailed in the GARDEN OF EDEN. For others, the millennial prophecies are mere metaphors for the better times ahead as the world is gradually Christianized. In nineteenth-century America, the latter interpretation was dominant. Most people believed that religious revivals and foreign missions, not the personal return of Jesus Christ, would be the means of ushering in the Millennium. They defined the Millennium in terms of the spiritual rather than the spiritual and physical transformation of the earth.

The Latter-day Saints rejected this figurative vision of the future. They believed that only the miraculous, divine intervention of Christ could fully destroy wickedness and re-create the New Eden. Mormons then and now literally expect the earth to be "renewed and receive its paradisiacal glory" (A of F 10). The extraordinary biological, geological, and social changes that will make the earth a paradise include the abolishment of infant mortality, the herbivorization of carnivores; the unification of continental landmasses; and the cessation of all enmity, strife, and warfare.

As the revelations unfolded during the early years of the Church, it was learned that Christ and those raised in the first resurrection at the beginning of the Millennium "will not probably dwell upon the earth, but will visit it when they please, or when it is necessary to govern it" (*TPJS*, p. 268). The Saints also came to realize that the destruction of the wicked accompanying Christ's second coming will not remove all unbelievers from the earth. Thus, missionary work will be a major millennial activity. Once the role of temples in the redemption of living and dead became clear, temple work was added to the list of anticipated millennial pursuits.

Since the first century, some Christians have felt that the second coming of Christ was near. Given the numerous revelations to Joseph SMITH and the other dramatic developments of early Church history, many early Latter-day Saints also expected the promised day in their lifetimes. That feeling has been strong at other periods during the subsequent history of the Church, though not as sustained or pervasive as in its earliest years. While affirming the significance of the Millennium, modern Church leaders regularly make calming and qualifying statements as a counterpoint to undue anxiety about its proximity.

BIBLIOGRAPHY

Clouse, Robert G., ed. *The Meaning of the Millennium.* New York, 1974.

Gaustad, Edwin S., ed. *The Rise of Adventism.* New York, 1974.

Underwood, Grant. "The Millenarian World of Early Mormonism." Ph.D. diss., University of California at Los Angeles, 1988.

GRANT UNDERWOOD

MILLENNIAL STAR

The Latter-day Saints' Millennial Star was the official publication of the Church in the BRITISH ISLES from 1840 to 1970. Filled with editorials often written by GENERAL AUTHORITIES and with expositions of the history, DOCTRINE, and organization of the Church, the *Millennial Star* became a literary landmark in the Church. Parley P. Pratt, an APOSTLE of the Church and the first editor of the periodical, outlined its purpose in its first issue, May, 1840, "The *Millennial Star* will stand aloof from the common political and commercial news of the day. Its columns will be devoted to the spread of the fulness of the gospel—the restoration of the ancient principles of Christianity—the gathering of Israel—the rolling forth of the kingdom of God among the nations—the signs of the times— . . . in short, whatever is shown forth indicative of the coming of the 'Son of Man,' and the ushering in of his universal reign on the earth."

That first issue also contained an editorial; extracts of REVELATIONS given to the Prophet Joseph SMITH and published in the United States in the Doctrine and Covenants; challenges to circulars against the Church from other churches; articles on what other religions believe; a report of the CONFERENCE on the Church in Preston, England; current history of the Church in the United States; letters from MISSIONARIES; poetry; and two HYMNS. Subsequent issues of the *Star* (as it was popularly known) followed a similar pattern throughout the years. Some of its poems became the lyrics for Church hymns, such as "Israel, Israel, God Is Calling."

The presidents of the British Mission were always listed as the editors, among whom were five future PRESIDENTS OF THE CHURCH: Wilford WOODRUFF, Joseph F. SMITH, Heber J. GRANT, George Albert SMITH, and David O. MCKAY.

The *Star* was nearly discontinued three times: in 1841 and in 1843 due to lack of subscribers, and a century later during World War II, when all the American missionaries were withdrawn from England. Its pages are an excellent source for the history and development of the Church. Its serial "History of Joseph" was a foundation document for the multivolume *History of the Church*.

The *Millennial Star* was officially retired in 1970, when it was subsumed into the *Ensign*, the current English-language magazine for adults in the Church.

BIBLIOGRAPHY

Hill, James P. "Story of the Star." *Millennial Star* 130:12 (1970):10–13.

STANLEY A. PETERSON

MILLENNIUM

As a generic term, "millennium" connotes any period of 1,000 years' duration. In the Judeo-Christian tradition, however, one such period stands preeminent, namely, that future time when peace and righteousness will prevail under the direct providence of God and his MESSIAH.

The prophet ISAIAH spoke of this time when "they shall beat their swords into plowshares, and their spears into pruninghooks: nation shall not lift up sword against nation, neither shall they learn war any more" (Isa. 2:4). He further declared that the natural fears and enmities within the animal kingdom will cease, that "the wolf also shall dwell with the lamb, and the leopard shall lie down with the kid" (Isa. 11:6–9; cf. D&C 101:26). EZEKIEL prophesied that the EARTH, which lost its pristine character as a result of the FALL OF ADAM (cf. Gen. 3:17–19), will return to its paradisiacal state once again (Ezek. 36:35; cf. A of F 10). For the duration of the Millennium, Satan will be bound (Rev. 20:1–3). In place of the diabolical regime of the "prince of this world" (John 12:31; 14:30; D&C 1:35), the Lord Jesus Christ will dwell personally among the inhabitants of earth, ruling over the KINGDOM OF GOD with the aid of righteous mortals and resurrected Saints from all ages (Isa. 35:2; Dan. 7:14, 27).

Christ taught his disciples to pray to the Father for the kingdom to come when his will would be done on earth as it is in heaven (Matt. 6:10). Jesus declared to them that he would be sent again by the Father at the end of the world for a day of JUDGMENT and an era of paradisiacal glory (cf. Matt. 25:31–46; John 5:22–29; Acts 1:3–8). Some early Christians appear to have anticipated the SECOND COMING OF JESUS CHRIST and the onset of the Millennium as imminent, despite the Savior's caution that none but the Father knew the time of his coming, and despite both angelic and apostolic pronouncements concerning events that must precede the Millennium (cf. Matt. 24; Acts 3:19–21; 2 Thes. 2:1–4). Numerous church leaders in the Post-Apostolic (Patristic) period, such as Justin Martyr of Rome, Papias of Hierapolis, Irenaeus of Lyons, and Lactantius, accepted the notion of a literal millennium following the resurrection of the dead, when a visible and glorious kingdom of Christ would exist on earth. By the late third and fourth centuries, however, church fathers such as Origen (d. c. A.D. 254) and Augustine (d. A.D. 429) had transformed the notion of a literal millennium into an allegorical or figurative one: The millennial reign of peace for them took place in the hearts of individual men and women and began with the outpouring of the Holy Spirit on the day of Pentecost (cf. Acts 2:16–20). From that time until the sixteenth-century PROTESTANT REFORMATION, belief in a literal millennium was regarded as unorthodox by the institutional church. The RESTORATION OF ALL THINGS in this, the DISPENSATION OF THE FULNESS OF TIMES, affirms that Christ will return for a millennial reign of peace. During the Millennium, members of the

Church of Jesus Christ from any era of time will help in the government of the earth under Christ's direction (Dan. 7:27; D&C 103:7; cf. Matt. 5:5).

John the Revelator saw that at the commencement of the Millennium a NEW JERUSALEM would descend to earth from heaven. Traditional Christianity has generally associated this with a renewing of the city where Jesus ministered among the Jews during the meridian of time. However, the revelations given to the Prophet Joseph SMITH show that the New Jerusalem in the Western Hemisphere will coexist with the old Jerusalem, each as a hemispheric capital. From them laws, decrees, and leadership in the kingdom of God will emanate. Thus the nuances found in Isaiah 2:3 that "out of Zion shall go forth the law, and the word of the Lord from Jerusalem" telling of two locations are not redundant or merely rhetorical. According to modern scripture, a New Jerusalem will yet be established within the borders of the state of Missouri in North America (D&C 84:2–4; cf. 57:2–3; A of F 10).

The Millennium symbolizes a sabbatical in human history (cf. D&C 77:12; Moses 7:64), analogous to the role of the weekly SABBATH (cf. Ex. 20:8–11). The millennial period is patterned after the Lord's period of rest following the six creative periods (cf. Gen. 2:1–3).

Life will go on for those on earth: "And they shall build houses, and inhabit them; and they shall plant vineyards, and eat the fruit of them, . . . and mine elect shall long enjoy the work of their hands" (Isa. 65:21–22). Righteous mortal men and women who die after the beginning of the Millennium "shall not sleep . . . in the earth, but shall be changed in the twinkling of an eye" (D&C 101:31), and children born in this era "shall grow up until they become old" (D&C 63:51; Isa. 65:20). The devil will have no "power to tempt any man," being bound because of the righteousness of the earth's inhabitants, and children will grow up without sin (1 Ne. 22:26; D&C 43:30–31; 45:58; 101:28–31). However, those who are wicked will not be resurrected or returned to the earth until after the millennium of righteousness (D&C 76:81, 85).

Whereas numerous temples will already dot the earth prior to the Millennium, their number and distribution will increase during this time, providing places where priesthood ordinances essential to salvation and eternal life can be performed in uninterrupted calm. The work of preaching the gospel of Jesus Christ to all the inhabitants of the earth will continue under his direction. Meanwhile, a similar teaching program will continue among the spirits of those who have departed this life and are waiting the day of their resurrection (D&C 138). While such spirits may hear the gospel of salvation and accept or reject it in the spirit worlds, mortals on earth will perform saving ordinances such as baptism on their behalf (*see* BAPTISM FOR THE DEAD). Conditions of peace and righteousness will prevail during the Millennium to allow this work to proceed until essential ordinances have been made available to every individual who has lived on earth since the time of Adam and Eve (cf. D&C 138).

[*See also* Last Days; New Heaven and New Earth; Time and Eternity.]

BIBLIOGRAPHY

Doxey, Roy W. "The Millennium." *Relief Society Magazine* 54 (Jan. 1967):58–63.

Leonard, Glen M. "Early Saints and the Millennium." *Ensign* 9 (Aug. 1979):43–47.

McConkie, Bruce R. *MD*, pp. 492–501. Salt Lake City, 1966.

PAUL B. PIXTON

MINORITIES

[*In the Book of Mormon, God invites "all to come unto him and partake of his goodness; and he denieth none that come unto him, black and white, bond and free, male and female; and he remembereth the heathen; and all are alike unto God" (2 Ne. 26:33). As LDS missionaries have preached the gospel of Jesus Christ to "every nation, kindred, tongue, and people," people from many ethnic groups from all over the world have accepted baptism and become members of the Church. See* Vital Statistics.

Emphasis has been placed on taking the gospel to the American Indians and to the other peoples of the Americas. See Indian Student Placement Services; Lamanites; Mexico and Central America, The Church in; Native Americans; South America, The Church in.

Substantial LDS populations also exist in the Pacific Islands. See Hawaii, The Church in; Oceania, The Church in; *and* Polynesians.

In 1978 a revelation extended the priesthood to all worthy males. This allowed the priesthood to be held by blacks. See Africa, The Church in; Blacks; Doctrine and Covenants: Official Declaration—2; Priesthood; South America, The Church in: Brazil; *and* West Indies, The Church in.]

MIRACLES

A miracle is a beneficial event brought about through divine power that mortals do not understand and of themselves cannot duplicate. Members of The Church of Jesus Christ of Latter-day Saints believe in the reality of miracles as a consequence of their belief in the existence of God and of his power and goodness.

Just as a shepherd tends his flocks, watches over them, and uses his power to help them, so Jesus Christ used his power and knowledge to help others when he was on earth. For instance, when the supply of wine was exhausted at the marriage feast at Cana, at his mother's request, Jesus miraculously provided wine (John 2:1–10). This act was consistent with his love and compassion, but the means by which he changed the water into wine is not understood, and of themselves people cannot duplicate it. Thus, it is called a miracle. Numerous other examples of the beneficial results of miracles performed by Jesus include the raising from the dead of the widow's son at Naim (Luke 7:11–16), the cleansing of the ten lepers (Luke 17:12–19), and the restoration of the sight of the blind man at Bethsaida (Mark 8:22–26).

Latter-day Saints value miracles because of their beneficial character. As stated in the Book of Mormon, "God has provided a means that man, through faith, might work mighty miracles; therefore he becometh a great benefit to his fellow beings" (Mosiah 8:18). Although God brings about marvelous events to bless humankind, it is known that not every spiritual manifestation necessarily comes from God (*TPJS*, pp. 202–214; Rev. 13:13–14; *see also* SIGN SEEKING).

Faith is considered necessary to bring divine intervention in behalf of those in need. For example, as the Book of Mormon prophet ALMA₂ noted, LEHI and his group of emigrants were given the LIAHONA, a compasslike device to direct their travels toward a new and promised land. "And it did work for them according to their faith in God; therefore, if they had faith to believe that God could cause that those spindles [of the compass] should point the way they should go, behold it was done; therefore they had this miracle, and also many other miracles wrought by the power of God, day by day" (Alma 37:40).

God desires to bless his children, and sometimes does so in ways that require the manifestation of extraordinary power. He is restrained only

Catching Quails, by C. C. A. Christensen (late nineteenth century, tempera on canvas, 6'6" × 9'9"). The last of the Mormons driven from Nauvoo were forced out with few provisions. Many were sick, and some died. On October 9, 1846, many quail flew into camp on the river bank above Montrose, Iowa. Many were caught, cooked, and eaten. To the Saints it was a miracle paralleling a similar incident in ancient Israel (*cf.* Exodus 16:13). Courtesy Museum of Fine Arts, Brigham Young University.

by their lack of faith. Thus, the absence of miracles is evidence of the lack of faith among his children, "for it is by faith that miracles are wrought; and it is by faith that angels appear and minister unto men; wherefore, if these things have ceased wo be unto the children of men, for it is because of unbelief, and all is vain" (Moro. 7:37). "For if there be no faith among the children of men God can do no miracle among them" (Ether 12:12).

When the faithful receive a blessing from God, especially one that requires a manifestation of his extraordinary power, the proper response is gratitude to God for the blessing (D&C 46:32). Manifestations of God's extraordinary power usually come only after faith and do not necessarily create faith (cf. Ether 12:7); it is appropriate, therefore, not to make a public show of such sacred experiences as a demonstration of religious belief. Seeking manifestations of the extraordinary power of the divine for the purpose of coming to believe is rejected as improper sign seeking.

Of the miraculous GIFTS OF THE SPIRIT that come to the righteous, the Lord says, "For verily I say unto you, they are given for the benefit of those who love me and keep all my commandments, and him that seeketh so to do; that all may be benefited that seek or that ask of me, that ask and not for a sign that they may consume it upon their lusts. . . . And all these gifts come from God, for the benefit of the children of God" (D&C 46:9, 26).

A miraculous gift especially valued is the healing of the sick. However, not every faithful soul who ails will be raised, for the Lord has said, "And whosever among you are sick, and have not faith to be healed, but believe, shall be nourished and with all tenderness, with herbs and mild food. . . . And the elders of the church, two or more, shall be called, and shall pray for and lay their hands upon them in my name; and if they die they shall die unto me, and if they live they shall live unto me" (D&C 42:43–44). Thus though the sick may be healed (D&C 46:19), if that does not occur, the sick are nourished by all prudent means, including those available in modern medical science. The ELDERS of the Church perform this ordinance of administering to the sick, as the scriptures prescribe (cf. James 5:14–15; D&C 46:20), and the healing or other blessings are then in accordance with the will of God.

Personal experience with miracles might confirm the faith of the recipients. Further, personal experiences with miracles may give others increased confidence in scriptural accounts of miracles.

Of all the miraculous gifts of God given to his children, the one of greatest benefit is the ATONEMENT OF JESUS CHRIST. By powers and means not understood by mere mortals, Jesus was able to take upon himself the sins of the world and make it possible for anyone by REPENTANCE, to escape the otherwise inescapable suffering of sin and the doom of death, and thereby return to the presence of God. "For behold, I, God, have suffered these things for all, that they might not suffer if they would repent . . . which suffering caused myself, even God, the greatest of all, to tremble because of pain, and to bleed at every pore, and to suffer both body and spirit" (D&C 19:16, 18). The miracle of forgiveness and the marvel of resurrection are supreme indeed.

BIBLIOGRAPHY

Kimball, Spencer W. *Faith Precedes the Miracle*, chap. 1. Salt Lake City, 1972.

PAUL C. HEDENGREN

MISSIONARY, MISSIONARY LIFE

Members of The Church of Jesus Christ of Latter-day Saints accept Jesus' injunction to his ordained disciples, "Go ye therefore, and teach all nations, baptizing them in the name of the Father, and of the Son, and of the Holy Ghost" (Matt. 28:19). They accept, indeed, a reiteration of it in modern times: "Go ye into all the world, preach the gospel to every creature, acting in the authority which I have given you, baptizing in the name of the Father, and of the Son, and of the Holy Ghost" (D&C 68:8). Missionaries consider themselves emissaries of the Lord in proclaiming his message.

WHO ARE CALLED. In the first generation of the Church, married men frequently were called to be missionaries, and they left wives and families for an indeterminate length of time. In recent decades, the majority of missionaries have been young men and women who serve about two years.

Currently, the Church calls as missionaries, on a voluntary, temporary basis, single men from the ages of nineteen to twenty-six, single women twenty-one years and older, and older married couples with no dependent children. Missionary service is coordinated with military service as required.

Missionaries or their families generally cover the major costs of serving a mission. Missionaries called from developing nations may receive needed financial assistance from the general missionary fund of the Church. This assistance covers only basic living costs, as the Church has no paid ministry. No one is paid for missionary service.

As the Church has expanded, more and more missionaries have been called. Approximately 76 percent currently are young men, 18 percent are women, and 7 percent are couples. The number of retired couples accepting calls to serve missions is increasing, with many couples serving more than one mission.

CALLING AND TRAINING. The official missionary call is preceded by an interview, often requested by the prospective missionary, with the ward BISHOP, who assesses the person's worthiness and spiritual preparation. Prolonged formal study to preach the gospel is not required, but LDS parents are expected to prepare their children for missionary service through family scripture study and participation in Church classes and programs. Parents are also encouraged to teach children basic nutrition, health care, and homemaking skills that are essential for missionary service.

When a bishop has approved a missionary candidate, he sends the recommendation to the STAKE PRESIDENT, who also interviews the prospective missionary. When this process is complete, the stake president sends the recommendation to the Missionary Department of the Church. Designated members of the QUORUM OF THE TWELVE APOSTLES suggest a preliminary assignment for each missionary or couple. These assignments are then sent to the FIRST PRESIDENCY of the Church, who confirms or modifies them on the basis of inspiration. These procedures are in keeping with the scriptural admonition that "no man taketh this honour [of ministering in the Church or preaching the gospel in the world] unto himself, but he that is called of God, as was Aaron" (Heb. 5:4). Missionaries may be called to serve in nearby states or countries or anywhere in the world where there is an established mission of the Church. A letter calling the missionary or couple to a specific mission, bearing the signature of the President of the Church, is sent requesting a reply of acceptance or rejection of the call.

The prospective missionary generally is allowed several weeks to prepare before reporting at an appointed date to the nearest Church MISSIONARY TRAINING CENTER (MTC). Often the newly called missionary receives a letter from his assigned MISSION PRESIDENT with specific recommendations for the climate and mission service rules. Missionaries who already are fluent in the language of their assigned mission typically stay in an MTC for three weeks. Otherwise, they receive several weeks of intensive language and cultural training included with their courses in scripture study and methods of teaching the gospel.

Missionaries in an MTC also attend regular inspirational meetings and study classes. One day a week, they may attend a nearby TEMPLE and also write letters and take care of other personal needs. Sundays are devoted to attending regular Church services and studying the gospel.

At an MTC and in the mission field, missionaries are divided into administrative units called zones and districts. Single missionaries are assigned companions of the same gender who are studying the same language or going to the same mission. Married couples, of course, serve as companions to each another. Companionship is one of the most pervasive aspects of missionary life: a missionary never labors alone. The need for harmonious relationships between companions is urgent, and, although it can sometimes be a challenge, it usually leads to lifelong friendships. For missionary couples, it typically leads to an enhanced marriage relationship.

While in an MTC, missionaries begin to experience the meaning and rewards of full-time service to the Lord. The training is intensive. They do not watch television, listen to the radio, or go to places of entertainment. Letters, phone calls home, and nonmission business are limited. Their clothing is conservative business wear with distinctive name tags, except on preparation days or for service projects, physical-fitness activities, or special circumstances. The missionary's time is ac-

counted for on reports submitted to the MTC or mission president; the principle is that one's time as a missionary is dedicated to the Lord.

ENTERING THE MISSION FIELD. When missionaries arrive in their assigned geographic areas, they are welcomed by their mission president and are given a brief orientation in the mission home or headquarters office. Each new single missionary is assigned to be trained by an experienced missionary companion. Missionary couples may be trained by another couple for a short time before they go to their assigned area within the mission.

All single missionaries are asked to follow a daily schedule somewhat as listed below, with variations as suggested by the mission president or as needed according to the customs of the country:

6:30 A.M.	Arise
7:00 A.M.	Study with companion
8:00 A.M.	Breakfast
8:30 A.M.	Personal study
9:30 A.M.	Teaching and contacting
12:00 P.M.	Lunch
1:00 P.M.	Teaching and contacting
5:00 P.M.	Dinner
6:00 P.M.	Teaching and contacting
9:30 P.M.	Plan next day's activities
10:30 P.M.	Retire

Missionary couples may be given considerable latitude with their schedules because they often fill several different assignments, such as helping new converts gain experience in administering a Church unit, serving as guides at VISITORS CENTERS and HISTORIC SITES, or serving as nonproselytizing representatives of the Church in communities that do not allow proselytizing.

If missionaries are serving where they are learning another language, they spend time each day in language study. They also are encouraged to keep journals and exercise regularly. Missionaries spend most of their time finding receptive people and teaching them the restored gospel of Jesus Christ. Frequently they meet with people who have expressed an interest in knowing more about the way of life of their LDS friends and neighbors. Other people develop an interest in the Church and its teachings from media programs, street displays, pamphlets, or from simply seeing missionaries and inquiring about their background and purpose. When missionaries have time between teaching appointments, they often go door to door through a neighborhood asking those at home if they would be interested in learning more about the Church.

Missionaries work closely with local Church members, teaching people in their homes, speaking in ward or branch meetings about the importance of missionary work and on other gospel themes, and participating in social and athletic functions when their duties allow. Ward or branch members are encouraged to invite the missionaries to their homes for a meal as often as they can, to ease the financial burdens and to free their time for missionary work. Church members are often grateful to have the missionaries in their homes as role models for their children, while missionaries appreciate an hour of relaxation, home cooking, and LDS family life. Missionaries also often depend on local members for transportation, repairs on bicycles or other equipment, and advice and encouragement. Often, members of the elders quorum or Relief Society volunteer to serve as companions to male or female missionaries, respectively, so that the two full-time missionaries can split up for an evening and double their effectiveness.

Missionary apartments, while far from luxurious, must meet certain standards for health and safety, minimal space, and furniture. Apartments are rented and often become "missionary apartments" as a succession of missionaries transfer in and out of an area. In some places, Church members have apartments attached to their homes in which they invite missionaries to live. Missionaries travel on foot, by public transportation, by bicycle, or in mission cars, assigned at the mission president's discretion based on the distances missionaries must travel and other circumstances.

Almost every missionary experiences a test of faith and courage. The experience of telling people that one represents Jesus Christ and has a message that will change their lives forever leads to solemn introspection, earnest prayer, and continual study. While some missionaries have already moved through this process, others find that they must spend many hours in prayer and scripture study before they receive a TESTIMONY.

After several months of service, missionaries become proficient in teaching the gospel, and more effective in bearing testimony of its truth. If they are speaking a foreign language, they accommodate to its dialects. As they grow and mature in experience, they may be transferred to different areas in the mission and placed with different companions, or assigned to meet new challenges and work with new people. They may in time become trainers for newly arrived missionaries. One missionary may be called to organize and preside over a branch of the Church. Another may not do formal missionary work but be called to serve the needs of underprivileged people as a welfare worker or to teach English and cultural information to refugees awaiting resettlement. Other missionaries may be placed in charge of the finances or other business of the mission and do direct missionary work only in the evenings. Older missionaries are sometimes called to serve in temples as ordinance workers.

The tasks of a missionary often are traumatic. Missionaries may experience cultural shock, language barriers, health problems, personality adjustments, hostility, and sometimes severe persecution. Yet missionaries are, for the most part, dedicated, enthusiastic, and faithful, and later may describe their service as "the best two years" of their lives to that time. Companions encourage one another, and the missionaries gain a new perspective of themselves, of people, of the place where they serve, and of the gospel. Often missionaries continue their association with a foreign country or language through their choice of a college major or profession.

GOAL OF MISSIONARY WORK. The ultimate goal of missionary work in the Church is to invite all the inhabitants of the earth to come unto Christ, through personal testimony, "by gentleness and meekness, and by love unfeigned" (D&C 121:41). People throughout the world respond differently to the gospel message. Some quickly accept the message and within a few days or weeks request baptism into the Church. For others, it may be more difficult to leave past traditions, overcome social pressure, or break personal habits to conform to gospel standards. Occasionally, political and economic pressures countermand the inclination to conversion. Others simply feel no need for religion. All newly baptized members are accepted into The Church of Jesus Christ of Latter-day Saints as "no more strangers and foreigners, but fellow citizens with the saints, and of the household of God" (Eph. 2:19). Missionaries develop Christlike love for those they teach about the Church and for the people in the area where they serve. They are grateful for those who "hear [the Lord's] voice and harden not their hearts" (D&C 28:7).

BIBLIOGRAPHY

Bishop, Joseph. *The Making of a Missionary.* Salt Lake City, 1982.

SPENCER J. CONDIE

MISSIONARY TRAINING CENTERS

In 1832 a revelation given through the Prophet Joseph SMITH in KIRTLAND, OHIO, directed the elders to tarry and conduct a SOLEMN ASSEMBLY to study the "doctrines of the kingdom," as well as a variety of secular subjects, so that they might "be prepared in all things" to go out and preach to the people (D&C 88:70–81). This initial assembly became the basis for the SCHOOL OF THE PROPHETS with similar purposes, which opened on January 24, 1833. When Church schools were founded in Utah during the latter part of the nineteenth century, they created programs for MISSIONARY training. In 1883 "missionary meetings" were added to the offerings of the Theological Department at Brigham Young Academy, the predecessor to BRIGHAM YOUNG UNIVERSITY in Provo, Utah. Similar programs were inaugurated at Ricks College in Idaho and at the Latter-day Saints University in Salt Lake City.

As missionary training progressed, the FIRST PRESIDENCY approved a Church Missionary Home and Preparatory Training School. A Salt Lake City home was purchased, remodeled, and furnished to accommodate up to ninety-nine missionaries. Inaugurated in 1925, the week-long program for departing missionaries emphasized gospel topics, Church procedures, personal health, and proper manners. This home accommodated the outgoing missionaries until the 1960s, but as the number of missionaries increased, other facilities were needed.

PROGRAM AT BRIGHAM YOUNG UNIVERSITY (BYU). For several years prior to 1960, Church and BYU officials considered the advisability of offering language instruction to missionaries. The occasion to launch this program came when missionaries assigned to Mexico and Argentina experienced lengthy delays in obtaining visas. On December 4, 1961, the Missionary Language Institute (MLI) opened with a class of twenty-nine elders in temporary quarters in a Provo hotel and various BYU buildings. Through classes, leadership meetings, and conferences, missionaries attending the MLI were able to develop facility in Spanish as well as in self-discipline and missionary spirit.

To enhance this program, in 1963 Church leaders gave its director the authority and stature of a MISSION PRESIDENT, and the MLI became known as the Language Training Mission (LTM). Portuguese and German were soon added to its curriculum.

In 1968 Church leaders decided to offer language instruction in all sixteen languages then being used by missionaries. To meet this major challenge, separate LTMs were established at Ricks College to teach Dutch and the Scandinavian languages and at the Church College of Hawaii to teach Polynesian and Oriental languages.

SCOPE BROADENED. The need for missionary training increased with the expansion of the Church. In 1971 over 2,500 missionaries received training at Brigham Young University in classrooms and housing that became increasingly inadequate. In 1973 the Church Missionary Committee approved plans to build a complex in Provo large enough to meet the needs of all language training for missionaries and decided to combine the three existing programs there. By 1976 the first phase was established. This multimillion-dollar complex demonstrated the Church's resolute commitment to missionary work.

Prior to 1978, while foreign-language missionaries were trained at the LTM in Provo, the Missionary Home in Salt Lake City continued to train the English-speaking missionaries. Beginning in 1978, however, all elders, sisters, and couples called from the United States or Canada reported directly to Provo for training, and the name of the facility was changed to Missionary Training Center (MTC) to reflect its more comprehensive program.

ORGANIZATION AND ADMINISTRATION. In the 1980s, the GENERAL AUTHORITIES became more involved in personal direction of missionary training. Although past MTC leaders had customarily handled policies and procedures through BYU, from 1980 on they increasingly reported directly to the Missionary Committee in Salt Lake City.

The internal organization was also at this time restructured to separate ecclesiastical from professional responsibilities. Missionaries were organized into branches whose presidents, called as lay leaders from among Church members in the Provo area, provided needed ecclesiastical authority and service in counseling missionaries and in conducting Sunday meetings. In addition, full-time staff members supervised professional activities such as training and business affairs.

MTC REGIMEN. The MTC is regarded as a mission field. All costs are paid by the missionaries, including board and room, books, and study materials. Every missionary is assigned another new missionary as a companion, and they are together twenty-four hours a day.

The schedule is rigorous. Classes have ten to twelve students who meet in three-hour sessions, morning, afternoon, and evening. Studies include the scriptures, languages, and missionary methodology. Academic responsibilities are balanced by spiritual development and recreational opportunities. Temple attendance and weekly devotional addresses given by visiting General Authorities aid spiritual well-being. Exercise programs promote physical fitness.

The intensive methodology used in foreign-language instruction is based in part on a program developed by the U.S. Army: Trainees learn by listening and repeating. Classroom instructors are usually experienced former missionaries and foreign students from nearby campuses. Linguistic drills are related to the culture, customs, and characteristics of the assigned mission field. In one week basic grammar is learned, and after two weeks a missionary begins to converse, pray, and sing in a new language. In eight weeks, missionaries are reasonably adept in conversation and can teach gospel lessons in a foreign language.

INTERNATIONAL EXPANSION. The Church now operates Area Missionary Training Centers beyond Provo. Previously, missionaries called from outside the United States and Canada typically went directly to the mission field without orientation. Area centers have now been developed to give missionaries from other lands advantages similar to those provided in Provo. The first of these centers was established at São Paulo, Brazil, in 1977. By 1990, thirteen Area MTCs functioned in Latin America, Europe, Asia, and the Pacific. All are adjacent to Latter-day Saint temples.

The goal of the Missionary Training Centers is to provide initial training for full-time missionaries, preparing them to teach more efficiently the restored gospel of Jesus Christ. All programs are continuously evaluated in terms of this objective.

RICHARD O. COWAN

MISSION PRESIDENT

In 1990, some 257 mission presidents, along with their wives, and sometimes families, served in geographical mission areas in more than a hundred nations. The period of service for a mission president is usually three years. In the Church being a mission president is regarded as a challenging and exhilarating spiritual assignment, a link of fellowship with the Master. Calls are issued by the FIRST PRESIDENCY. Both husband and wife are set apart as missionaries by the LAYING ON OF HANDS by an assigned General Authority, often a member of the First Presidency or QUORUM OF THE TWELVE APOSTLES, and receive BLESSINGS and counsel appropriate to their assignment.

The calling is not a regular remunerative position, but interrupts professional employment; whatever financial losses accrue are part of the expected sacrifice. The family involved gives of its time and energies without salary, though there is a modest allowance for living expenses. Men and women from all walks of life and all nationalities and backgrounds serve, called, as it were, "from everywhere to everywhere." Typically, the president is a high priest with extensive prior service in the Church. His wife is likewise experienced in Church leadership and teaching. Their competence in the language and culture of their designated country is enhanced by mission presidents' seminars and training sessions.

A strong legacy of mission presidents permeates Church autobiography and biography, oral tradition, fiction, and folklore. Narratives range from some of flagrant and even life-threatening opposition and martyrdom to sublime accounts of conversions to Christ. It is a common feeling that the Spirit attends missionary work as it does no other.

An important concern of the mission president and his wife is naturally the continued nurture and care of their own children who have come with them. A second concern is the nurture and care of the missionaries, the majority of whom are young, uprooted, often struggling with a new language, and facing new stresses. The mission president trains, counsels, assigns, and gives spiritual support to each missionary, and his wife plays a vital role in training programs and the health, welfare, and safety of each missionary.

A mission is generally assigned from 120 to 250 full-time missionaries, with young men serving two years and young women serving eighteen months. In addition, there are some part-time missionaries and older couples. Older couples generally serve from one year to eighteen months. Single missionaries always labor in same-gender pairs; married couples labor together. Leadership roles are assigned to senior companions, district leaders, and zone leaders. Each mission has a rotating central missionary staff: typically a secretary, recorder-historian, supplies manager, and travel coordinator. Since new missionaries arrive and seasoned missionaries are released each month, training, retraining, and making new assignments and transfers are perpetual tasks.

The mission president, under supervision from Church headquarters, establishes mission rules, study patterns, goals, and discipline. His assignment requires constant travel to zone conferences, which are also testimony meetings, at least every six to eight weeks. The president and his wife have direct contact with the missionaries by phone, mail, and personal visits. They continually foster programs of goodwill, service, and understanding.

At the end of three years, the mission president and his family return home to resume their vocational and regular family lives.

GERALD J. DAY

MISSIONS

The mission of The Church of Jesus Christ of Latter-day Saints is to invite everyone to come to Christ. This includes a mandate to proclaim the GOSPEL OF JESUS CHRIST to every nation, kindred, tongue, and people (cf. Matt. 28:19; Mark 16:15; D&C 42:58). "Therefore, go ye into all the world; and unto whatsoever place ye cannot go ye shall send, that the testimony may go from you into all the world unto every creature" (D&C 84:62). From the earliest days of the Church, missionaries have been called to the nations of the earth to preach that message.

The ultimate destiny of missionary work was envisioned by the Prophet Joseph SMITH in 1842:

Our missionaries are going forth to different nations. . . . The Standard of Truth has been erected; no unhallowed hand can stop the work from progressing; persecutions may rage, mobs may combine, armies may assemble, calumny may defame, but the truth of God will go forth boldly, nobly, and independent, till it has penetrated every continent, visited every clime, swept every country, and sounded in every ear, till the purposes of God shall be accomplished, and the Great Jehovah shall say the work is done [*HC* 4:540].

Two basic types of missions are organized to carry forward the missionary effort: full-time missions and stake missions.

The LDS Church has no paid ministry. The majority of missionaries in the LDS Church are young men between the ages of nineteen and twenty-one who serve on a voluntary basis for approximately two years.

FULL-TIME MISSION. A full-time mission is an ecclesiastical unit of the Church in a designated geographical area. A MISSION PRESIDENT and his wife are called to preside over the mission and supervise from 120 to 250 full-time missionaries. Small missions in newly opened areas begin with fewer missionaries. In areas where STAKES have not yet been established, the mission president also bears ecclesiastical responsibility for all Church members who live within the boundaries of his mission. In areas where stakes have been established, the mission president does not carry this responsibility but is available as a resource to help members advance missionary work. Full-time missions have been organized in nations wherever the Church has official recognition.

STAKE MISSION. A stake mission is organized in each stake of the Church to supplement or extend the resources of the full-time mission in that area. A stake mission president and two counselors preside over the stake mission. Unlike full-time missionaries, stake missionaries serve part-time, mostly in the evenings, and continue to live in their own homes and to fulfill their normal family and occupational responsibilities. They are generally expected to spend ten or more hours a week doing missionary work.

President Spencer W. KIMBALL described missionary work as the lifeblood of the Church. He wrote,

> If there were no converts, the Church would shrivel and die. But perhaps the greatest reason for

Many single women, such as these two in Tonga, 1986, fulfill missions. All single missionaries live and work with a companion of the same sex. Courtesy Floyd Holdman.

missionary work is to give the world its chance to hear and accept the gospel. The scriptures are replete with *commands* and *promises* and *calls* and *rewards* for teaching the gospel. I use the word *command* advisedly, for it seems to be an insistent directive from which we, singly and collectively, cannot escape. Furthermore, the command is clear that not only must all members of His church give missionary service, but we must take the gospel to all the children of our Heavenly Father on this earth [p. 4].

HISTORY OF MISSIONARY WORK. In April 1830, immediately after the Church was organized, the first formal missionary activity began. Samuel H. Smith, a brother of the Prophet Joseph, filled his knapsack with copies of the Book of Mormon and traveled through neighboring towns in upstate New York to acquaint people with the newly published book of scripture. He sold a copy to Phinehas H. Young, who read the book and later joined the Church. The same book came into the hands of Brigham YOUNG and, in conjunction with additional contacts, led to his conversion.

In the fall of 1830, four brethren, Oliver Cowdery, Peter Whitmer, Jr., Parley P. Pratt, and Ziba Peterson, were called to undertake a mission to the western frontier to preach to the Lamanites. They met with several Indian tribes, but their work was hampered by government Indian agents, and their principal success was among the white settlers in Ohio (*see* LAMANITE MISSION). By the end of December 1830, several hundred people had joined the infant Church, including such leaders as Sidney RIGDON and Frederick G. Williams, later named as counselors to Joseph Smith, and Edward Partridge, its first Presiding Bishop.

Through the efforts of several beginning in 1830, missionary work extended into Canada. John TAYLOR, who later became the third President of the Church, was an early convert there in the spring of 1836.

In 1837 Heber C. KIMBALL was called to open the first mission abroad. He and Orson HYDE were set apart to begin the work in the BRITISH ISLES. In that same year, Parley P. PRATT issued his pamphlet *Voice of Warning*, the first tract published for missionary use in the Church. In April 1839, in response to revelation (D&C 118), the Quorum of the Twelve Apostles and others departed for a mission to Great Britain (*see* MISSIONS OF THE TWELVE TO THE BRITISH ISLES). Thousands of converts joined the Church, and great numbers of them emigrated to America during the 1840s and strengthened the Church as it endured dissension within and persecution from without.

By the 1850s, missions had been opened in Chile, France, Germany, Gibraltar, Hawaii, India, Italy, Malta, Scandinavia, South Africa, the South Pacific, and Switzerland. Many of these were discontinued after only a few years; but in the final decades of the nineteenth century, a time when the Church was facing severe persecution and extreme financial difficulties, additional missions were founded in Mexico, Samoa, Tahiti, and Turkey.

In 1901, President Lorenzo SNOW renewed the emphasis on taking the gospel into all the world. Heber J. GRANT of the Quorum of the Twelve Apostles dedicated Japan for the preaching of the gospel. Over the next two years, Francis M. Lyman, also of the Twelve, dedicated the lands of Africa, Finland, France, Greece, Italy, Palestine, Poland, and Russia for missionary work.

In 1920–1921, David O. MCKAY of the Twelve traveled some 56,000 miles in a world survey of Church missions for the FIRST PRESIDENCY. He made stops in the Pacific islands, New Zealand, Australia, Asia, India, Egypt, Palestine, and Europe. While in Asia, he dedicated China for the preaching of the gospel.

In December 1925, Melvin J. Ballard of the Twelve established a mission in South America, with headquarters in Buenos Aires, Argentina, predicting, "The work of the Lord will grow slowly for a time here just as an oak grows slowly from an acorn. It will not shoot up in a day as does the sunflower that grows quickly and then dies. But thousands will join the Church here. It will be divided into more than one mission and will be one of the strongest in the Church. The work here is the smallest that it will ever be. The day will come when the Lamanites in this land will be given a chance. The South American Mission will be a power in the Church" (quoted in *Melvin J. Ballard: . . . Crusader for Righteousness* [Salt Lake City, 1977], p. 84). By 1990, Central and South American converts had emerged as one of the largest segments of the Church.

During President McKay's administration as President of the Church, he instituted a vigorous missionary effort that increased the number of full-time missionaries from 5,000 to 13,000 and soon transformed the Church from an American institution into an international one. Preparation and

Missionaries spend most of their time finding and teaching interested people about the restored gospel of Jesus Christ. As of March 1991, there were 44,000 full-time missionaries serving in 257 missions throughout the world. Courtesy Doug Martin.

training for missionaries were formalized and intensified. The first seminar for mission presidents was held in June 1961. A new teaching plan of six lessons was introduced and his "every member a missionary" program coordinated missionary efforts of Church members. In November 1961 a language training institute was established at Brigham Young University in Provo for missionaries called to Spanish-speaking missions. This institute became the Language Training Mission in 1963 and the MISSIONARY TRAINING CENTER in 1978. During the 1960s and the 1970s, the Church built VISITORS CENTERS at many temple sites and other locations, including major pavilions for the New York World's Fair in 1964–1965 and the expositions in San Antonio, Texas, in 1968; Japan in 1970; and Spokane, Washington, in 1974. A large visitors center was opened on TEMPLE SQUARE in August 1966.

In April 1974, in his first major address as President of the Church, Spencer W. Kimball emphasized that every able, worthy young man should serve a mission. Under his leadership, the missionary force more than doubled in twelve years, and new missions were established in many parts of the world. The June 1978 revelation extending the priesthood to all worthy male members of the Church opened up additional missionary opportunities (*see* DOCTRINE AND COVENANTS: OFFICIAL DECLARATION—2).

Ezra Taft BENSON, who became the thirteenth President of the Church in November 1985, continued to emphasize proclaiming the gospel as an important and basic part of the mission of the Church, emphasizing the role of the Book of Mormon as a necessary and powerful tool.

Changing political conditions throughout the world in the final decades of the twentieth century opened nations previously inaccessible to missionaries—principally in Africa, Asia, and Central and Eastern Europe.

MISSIONARY ORGANIZATION. Under the direction of the First Presidency, the Quorum of the Twelve Apostles is the Missionary Committee of the Church. The members of the Twelve "are called to be the Twelve Apostles, or special witnesses of the name of Christ in all the world, . . . being sent out, holding the keys, to open the door by the proclamation of the gospel of Jesus Christ" (D&C 107:23, 35). The Twelve are assisted in their ministry by the SEVENTY, who "are also called to preach the gospel, and to be especial witnesses unto the Gentiles and in all the world" (D&C 107:25).

The Missionary Department is the staff organization at Church headquarters that assists the Missionary Committee of the Church in providing direction, training, programs, resources, and administrative support to the missions of the Church. Calls to full-time missionaries are processed through the Missionary Department.

A mission president is called by the First Presidency to preside over each mission of the Church, normally for three years (*see* MISSION PRESIDENT). He calls two full-time missionaries as his assistants, and they help him in training and supervising other missionaries. In his stewardship of Church units, the mission president is generally assisted by two local counselors. These counselors help the mission president in training and coordinating with local priesthood leaders and members who live within the stakes and WARDS within the mission area.

CALLS TO MISSIONARY SERVICE. In 1842, Joseph Smith summarized the procedure for calling a person to serve in the Church: "We believe that a man must be called of God, by prophecy, and by the laying on of hands by those who are in author-

Among the full-time missionaries of the Church is a group of young women (approximately 270 in 1990) with health and teaching backgrounds who are assigned to teach disease prevention, nutrition, and home health care to Church members in developing countries in addition to fulfilling proselytizing responsibilities.

ity, to preach the Gospel and administer in the ordinances thereof" (A of F 5).

In the early days of the Church, missionaries were called individually during Church conferences. After the Saints moved to the Salt Lake Valley, the First Presidency announced mission calls at general conferences—often to the surprise of those called. Later, written calls were sent from the office of the President of the Church. The return address on these letters was simply Box B, Salt Lake City, Utah, and for generations of Latter-day Saints, "Box B" became a symbol of the call to serve a mission.

At first, mission calls were issued to anyone, and married men often left their wives and children to serve for an unspecified period of time, ranging from a few weeks to several years. During the latter half of the nineteenth century and the first quarter of the twentieth, wives occasionally accompanied their husbands on missions. The first calls to single women were issued near the end of the nineteenth century.

The ages and terms of service of full-time missionaries have varied over the years, and exceptions are made according to circumstance. In 1990, unmarried men ages nineteen through twenty-five, or occasionally older, were called to serve for twenty-four months. Unmarried women ages twenty-one through thirty-nine were called to serve for eighteen months, and those age forty through sixty-nine were called to serve for twelve months. Married couples normally served for either twelve or eighteen months.

In addition to the traditional tasks of missionaries, couples and sister missionaries may also be given assignments in such areas as leadership training, mission office staff, visitors center staff, public communications, temple work, family history research, health welfare services, education, and other full-time Church service.

MISSIONARY PREPARATION AND TRAINING. Informal missionary training often begins in the homes of Latter-day Saints and continues in the various Church priesthood and AUXILIARY ORGANIZATIONS at the local level. A specific purpose of bearing the AARONIC PRIESTHOOD, designated in the scriptures as the preparatory priesthood (D&C 84:26), is to prepare young men for the responsibilities of the MELCHIZEDEK PRIESTHOOD, including missionary service. Some stakes sponsor missionary-preparation seminars or classes to assist young men and women and older couples in preparing for full-time missions. Brief formal missionary training for those already called is given at local missionary training centers located around the world. Missionaries assigned to missions where they will speak their native language remain at a training center for approximately three weeks. Missionaries who must learn a new language remain for approximately two months (see MISSIONARY TRAINING CENTERS).

On arrival in an assigned field of labor, each missionary receives on-the-job training from a senior companion and other mission leaders. Each missionary pair or married couple spends a portion of each day studying the scriptures, practicing the missionary discussions, and strengthening other missionary skills and attributes. Language study also continues for those who are learning a new language. District meetings held every week and zone conferences held every four to six weeks provide opportunities for missionaries to be instructed, motivated, and further trained by the mission leaders.

MISSIONARY APPROACHES. Historically, missionaries have endeavored to find those who are interested in listening to their message so they can teach them the gospel, baptize those who desire to join the Church, and fellowship new converts as they begin their membership in the Church.

During the first 150 years of the Church, missionary work centered on public meetings and contacting people in their homes: tracting (see below); street meetings; debates; exhibits at fairs, expositions, or shopping malls; FIRESIDES held in public buildings or Church meetinghouses; and "cottage meetings" held in private homes.

Door-to-door contacting is commonly called "tracting" because missionaries in the past often left printed tracts with people as they called on them. As the number and influence of Church members have grown, missionaries have come increasingly to rely on referrals from members to find people to teach. In the latter half of the twentieth century, missionaries have had the benefit of standardized lessons, usually referred to as missionary discussions, to assist them in teaching the gospel.

People who are being taught are invited to become actively involved by reading and studying

In recent years, more and more retired couples have chosen to serve missions together. As of 1991, approximately 1,500 couples were serving on a full-time voluntary basis. In addition to sharing the gospel with nonmembers, many missionary couples have assignments in leadership training, public relations, and family history. Some serve in Church visitors centers or in mission offices. Couples called to work in temples and in Church schools devote full time to these responsibilities and are not involved in proselytizing. Photograph, c. 1980, Deseret News.

on their own, praying about the message they are receiving, attending Church meetings, coming to know Church members, and living the principles of the gospel as they learn them. Full-time and stake missionaries are often assigned specific duties in shepherding new members and helping them become "fellowcitizens with the saints, and of the household of God" (Eph. 2:19).

BIBLIOGRAPHY

Kimball, Spencer W. "It Becometh Every Man." *Ensign* 7 (Oct. 1977):3–7.

DEAN B. CLEVERLY

MISSIONS OF THE TWELVE TO THE BRITISH ISLES

Between 1837 and 1841 there were two apostolic missions to the British Isles. In 1837–1838 Heber C. KIMBALL and Orson HYDE established the first mission, concentrating in the area of Preston and the Ribble Valley. Their efforts saw about 1,500 people baptized into the Church. From 1839 to 1841, nine members of the Quorum of the Twelve Apostles labored in Britain and added another 4,000 converts to the Church. These missions were extremely important. In a relatively short time, the Twelve Apostles established the foundation for the most successful missionary program of the Church in the nineteenth century, organized an extensive emigration program, and established a major publication program. In these activities, they also shared experiences that welded them together as a quorum. The spiritual and administrative dimensions of these missionary experiences prepared the Quorum of the Twelve Apostles to assume their key role in the leadership of the Church following their return to Nauvoo, and especially after the death of the Prophet Joseph SMITH in 1844. These missions were a manifestation of the early LDS recognition of the divine command to take the gospel "into all the world" (D&C 84:61–63; cf. Matt. 28:19) and to "gather" to Zion those who would accept the gospel message. Even as Jesus had commanded his apostles anciently, so had he done with his apostles in the nineteenth century.

THE 1837–1838 MISSION. The Church was barely seven years old when Elders Kimball and

Hyde departed for England in July 1837. The Prophet Joseph Smith had directed men to go on missions from the beginning, and the early missionaries had first concentrated in the smaller hamlets and villages of New England and nearby Canada. By 1836, LDS missionaries were venturing into larger cities. On April 3, 1836, the KEYS of the holy priesthood were bestowed by heavenly messengers upon the Prophet Joseph and Oliver Cowdery in the Kirtland (Ohio) Temple (D&C 110:11–16). These keys included the authority to gather Israel from the four parts of the earth, which is a missionary activity.

In April 1836, Parley P. PRATT, an apostle, was sent to Toronto with a prophetic promise that the fruits of missionary work there would lead to the introduction of the gospel into England (pp. 130–31). Elder Pratt helped to convert, among others, John TAYLOR, Isaac Russell, and Joseph Fielding, all of whom had family contacts in Britain and several of whom accompanied Elders Kimball and Hyde when the Prophet assigned them to go to the British Isles on the first mission.

Elders Kimball and Hyde were in England from July 1837 to April 1838. Landing at Liverpool, they traveled north to Preston, where relatives of the Canadian converts provided various assistance, including a place to preach. Finding ready acceptance of their message, they baptized more than 140 people by October 1837. They moved up the Ribble Valley, finding other audiences, particularly among the textile workers throughout Lancashire. By the time they returned home in April 1838, Church membership had grown to about 1,500 people in Britain, in spite of growing opposition, particularly from local clergy.

THE 1839–1841 MISSION. Dissension and apostasy had arisen among the leading brethren, reflecting the larger troubles of the Church in Ohio and Missouri. Seeking Joseph Smith's counsel in 1837, the Twelve were instructed by revelation to be united (D&C 112), but by 1838, some of the original Quorum of the Twelve did not wholeheartedly support Joseph Smith, and quorum president Thomas B. Marsh weakened the quorum further by his personal apostasy. With the death of David W. PATTEN in 1838, Brigham Young became the senior member of a quorum greatly hampered by defection. The second apostolic mission was also initiated by divine revelation. On July 8, 1838, from the new headquarters at Far West, Missouri, the Prophet Joseph Smith inquired, "Show us thy will, O Lord, concerning the Twelve," and received a revelation that the Twelve Apostles were to leave Far West on April 26, 1839, on a mission "over the great waters" (D&C 118:4). The revelation promised success in their mission and care for their families.

This overseas mission was an opportunity for the Twelve to prove themselves and to take their rightful place next to the First Presidency in leading the Church. The July 8, 1838, revelation gave specific direction, including the naming of four new apostles—John Taylor, John E. Page, Wilford WOODRUFF, and Willard Richards—to fill existing vacancies (D&C 118:6).

Departing in conditions of poverty and illness and trusting in the promises of God that all would be well with them and their families, most of the members of the Twelve made their way in various groups to Liverpool. By April 1840, they were together for the first time as a quorum in a foreign land. On April 14, 1840, in Preston, they ordained Willard Richards an apostle and sustained Brigham Young as "standing president" of their quorum. They held a general conference the next day in which they conducted Church business and further organized the mission. On the 16th they met again as a quorum and further planned their work. On the next day, they separated to various assigned geographical areas: Brigham Young and Willard Richards were to assist Wilford Woodruff with the work he had already begun among the United Brethren in Herefordshire; Heber C. Kimball was to return to the areas of his 1837–1838 missionary successes; Parley P. Pratt was to establish a mission home and publishing concern in Manchester; Orson PRATT was assigned to Scotland, where the work had already begun; John Taylor was to go to Liverpool, Ireland, and the Isle of Man; and George A. Smith was assigned to the area of the Staffordshire potteries. In time, Wilford Woodruff and George A. Smith would extend their work to London.

Under Brigham Young's direction, these apostles diligently supported each other and showed their love for the British people. In their journals and letters to each other they shared the burdens and joy of the hard work they were assigned to do. Truly on their own for the first time, they were forced to depend on the Lord and upon each other for assistance in the challenges they faced. Although they sought the Prophet Joseph's counsel on a variety of items, the distance from him often forced them to make decisions before a response could be received. In all major decisions the Prophet Joseph seems to have approved of their course of action.

In addition to providing leadership to the expanding British Mission, which saw an additional 4,000 converts join the Church by 1841, their efforts had at least three other related consequences: (1) the establishment of a successful emigration program that saw the first converts gathered to Nauvoo, with at least 50,000 members emigrating from the British Isles to America (see PERPETUAL EMIGRATING FUND); (2) the use of Britain as a base for further LDS missionary activity into continental Europe and other countries, such as South Africa, India, and Australia; and (3) the laying of the foundation for extensive LDS publishing in the nineteenth century. The Millennial Star, begun in 1840, became one of the most important LDS periodicals. Later editions of the Book of Mormon and the Doctrine and Covenants followed the text and format of those published by the Quorum of the Twelve Apostles in England. The same is true of the Manchester Hymnal. Also, various pamphlets defending and explaining Church doctrine were issued in regular editions in England. In fact, Liverpool became the LDS book supply depot for most of the nineteenth century.

A major consequence of the 1839–1841 mission was the impact it had on the quorum itself. Beginning in 1841, following the return of the Twelve to Nauvoo, Joseph Smith gave them more direct responsibility in administering the affairs of the Church. They were assigned management of the Church press in Nauvoo, were directed to supervise emigration, were placed on the Nauvoo City Council, and were given direct responsibility over Church finances. They were then brought into closer association with Joseph Smith and entrusted with greater responsibilities in many areas as they took their position as the quorum next to the First Presidency (D&C 107:23–24; 124:127–28).

Perhaps the greatest indication of their true calling as apostles was their vital role of leadership in the Church just before and following Joseph Smith's death in 1844. This mantle of authority, both spiritual and administrative, had been clearly established during the period of their British Mission experience.

BIBLIOGRAPHY

Allen, James B.; Ronald K. Esplin; and David J. Whittaker. *Men with a Mission: The Quorum of the Twelve in Great Britain—1837–1841.* Salt Lake City, 1991.

Bloxham, V. Ben; James R. Moss; and Larry C. Porter, eds. *Truth Will Prevail: The Rise of The Church of Jesus Christ of Latter-day Saints in the British Isles, 1837–1987.* Solihull, England, 1987.

Crawley, Peter, and David J. Whittaker. *Mormon Imprints in Great Britain and the Empire, 1836–1857.* Provo, Utah, 1987.

Esplin, Ronald K. "Joseph, Brigham and the Twelve: A Succession of Continuity." *BYU Studies* 21 (Summer 1981):301–341.

———. "A Preparation for Ascendancy: Brigham Young and the Quorum Experience in England, 1840–41." In "The Emergence of Brigham Young and the Twelve to Mormon Leadership, 1830–1841," pp. 427–98. Ph.D. diss., Brigham Young University, 1981.

———. "A Great Work Done in That Land." *Ensign* 17 (July 1987):20–27.

Evans, Richard L. *A Century of "Mormonism" in Great Britain.* Salt Lake City, 1937.

Jensen, Richard L., and Malcolm R. Thorp, eds. *Mormons in Early Victorian Britain.* Salt Lake City, 1989.

Pratt, Parley P. *The Autobiography of Parley Parker Pratt.* New York, 1874.

Taylor, P. A. M. *Expectations Westward: The Mormons and the Emigration of their British Converts in the Nineteenth Century.* Edinburgh and London, 1965; Ithaca, N.Y., 1966.

Whittaker, David J. "Mormonism in Victorian Britain: A Bibliographic Essay." In *Mormons in Early Victorian Britain,* ed. R. Jensen and M. Thorp, pp. 258–71. Salt Lake City, 1989.

DAVID J. WHITTAKER
JAMES R. MOSS

MISSOURI

[*This entry consists of two articles:*

LDS Communities in Jackson and Clay Counties

LDS Communities in Caldwell and Daviess Counties

The first article identifies the importance of Jackson County, Missouri, in the teachings of the Church and traces LDS history there and in Clay County. The second article discusses how the Missouri State Legislature created Caldwell and Daviess counties especially for the Latter-day Saints to settle in. The Church was driven from Missouri in the winter of 1838–1839, when its lead- *ers were arrested and held for trial and the state militia enforced Governor Boggs's Extermination Order.*]

LDS COMMUNITIES IN JACKSON AND CLAY COUNTIES

LDS interest and settlement in Jackson County, Missouri, came as a direct result of a REVELATION designating it as the location for ZION and the NEW JERUSALEM. Both the Book of Mormon (Ether 13:2–3; 3 Ne. 20:22) and revelations to Joseph Smith (D&C 28:9; 29:7–9; 35:24; 42:9, 35–36, 62; 45:65–71) filled the Latter-day Saints with a zeal to know the time and place for the establishment. Elders from the LAMANITE MISSION had traveled to western Missouri in early 1831, knowing they were near the location of Zion (D&C 28:9). The day after a significant June 1831 conference in Ohio, a revelation directed Joseph SMITH and other Church leaders to go to Missouri, where the land of their inheritance would be revealed (D&C 52:3–5, 42–43).

Three new groups of Saints proceeded to western Missouri in the summer of 1831: Joseph Smith's party of leaders; an entire branch of the Church from COLESVILLE, NEW YORK, who were commanded to relocate in Missouri (D&C 54:8); and thirteen pairs of missionaries who were instructed to preach along the way (D&C 52:7–10, 22–33; 56:5–7). The Prophet's group, traveling by foot, investigated other counties near the western Missouri border before determining that Jackson County was to be their ultimate destination. Their observation of Missouri's frontier communities was in harmony with a general feeling even in the West that the society of western Missouri, composed as it was of recent arrivals who had sought out the frontier to escape society's constraints, was not a model of civilization. "Our reflections were many, coming as we had from a highly cultivated state of society in the east," reads Joseph Smith's official history, "to observe the degradation . . . of a people that were nearly a century behind the times" (*HC* 1:189).

In response to the question "When will Zion be built up in her glory, and where will Thy temple stand?" (*HC* 1:189), the Lord declared, "Wherefore, this is the land of promise, and the place for the city of Zion. . . . The place which is now called Independence is the center place; and the spot for the temple is lying westward, upon a lot which is not far from the court-house" (D&C 57:2–3).

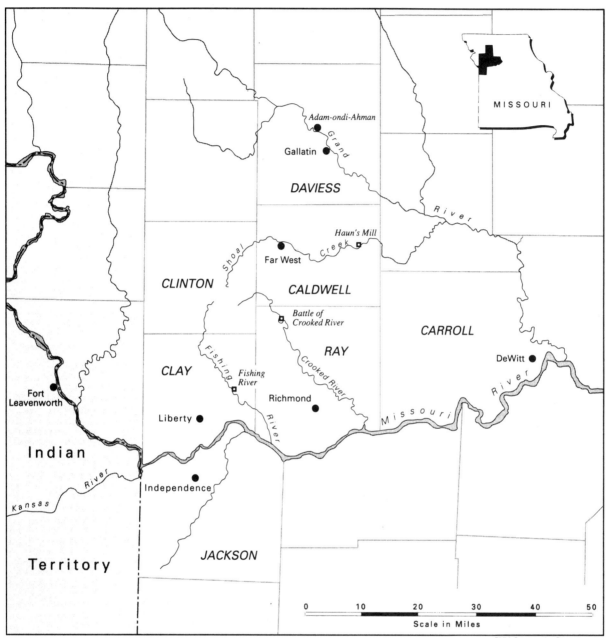

BYU Geography Department

Church history sites in western Missouri, 1831–1839.

In the summer of 1831, Church leaders explored the county, wrote a description of it for future Saints, established the first settlement in Kaw Township (now in Kansas City), dedicated the land for a gathering place, dedicated the temple lot, and conducted a conference for all Saints thus far gathered. The following men were assigned to prominent Church positions in Missouri: Edward Partridge, bishop; A. Sidney Gilbert, financial agent; W. W. Phelps, printer and editor; and Oliver COWDERY, assistant printer and editor. After Joseph Smith returned to Ohio, Bishop Partridge began buying land for the Saints' new inheritances.

LDS settlers who spent the winter of 1831–1832 in Jackson County struggled to cut timber; build ferries, bridges, mills, dams, homes, outbuildings, and fences; and prepare land for cultivation. Even though up to ten families lived in each log cabin, "there was a spirit of peace and union, and love and good will manifested in this little Church in the wilderness" (Pratt, p. 56). Plainly, it was not what Zion was but what it could become that buoyed up the Saints and lifted sagging spirits.

Early in 1832, Gilbert established a Church storehouse and Phelps the printing office. Proceeds from the store were used to buy and develop more land. Phelps began publishing a religious monthly, *The Evening and the Morning Star*, and a secular weekly, *The Upper Missouri Advertiser*; work also proceeded on the BOOK OF COMMANDMENTS, a compilation of revelations that had been received by Joseph Smith, and on a compilation of hymns. Establishing schools also became a high priority. By fall, schools were started in Kaw Township (called the Colesville School) and in Independence near the temple lot. Proper observance of the Lord's Day also received special emphasis (see D&C 59).

The subject that received the most attention was "gathering to Zion." Through the *Star*, Phelps reminded migrating Saints not to gather without adequate preparation, including carrying a recommend from the bishop in Ohio or from three elders. Bishop Partridge assigned land "inheritances" to new arrivals. Some three to four hundred arrived in the spring and summer of 1832, and by November there were 810 Latter-day Saints in Missouri. Up to this time, five settlements had easily absorbed the immigrants: a community in Independence near the temple lot; a branch on the Blue River three miles to the west; the Whitmer Branch three miles farther west; the Colesville Branch in Kaw Township two miles south of the Whitmer Branch; and the Prairie Branch on the Missouri state border. Editorials in the *Star* reflected the Saints' optimism.

The year 1833 brought numerous new challenges to the Church in Jackson County. Some members circumvented appointed leaders and ignored their authority to preside. Others tried to obtain property through means other than the revealed laws. Joseph Smith and Sidney RIGDON had visited the area in the spring of 1832, but now there arose a general concern among Missouri Latter-day Saints that their Prophet should move permanently from Ohio to the new Zion. Additionally, there were petty jealousies, covetousness, and general neglect in keeping the command-ments. None of this helped the newcomers to cope with the worst problem—increasing hostility with the "old settlers" of Jackson County. As the LDS population in the county reached twelve hundred by the summer of 1833, concerns of the local citizens reached fever pitch. It did not help that some members unwisely boasted that nonmembers would be driven from the county.

However, not everything was gloomy in the Jackson County settlements. Solemn assemblies in each branch had brought about a new spirit of humility, diligence, and order to the Church. A school for elders was established on the model of the SCHOOL OF THE PROPHETS in Kirtland, Ohio. Joseph Smith sent a plan for the building-up of the city of Zion and its accompanying temple (*see* CITY PLANNING). The Book of Commandments was nearing completion. But all of this seemed only to increase hostility.

Mob violence broke out against the Saints in late July 1833. The printing press was destroyed, the page sheets of the Book of Commandments were scattered, and Bishop Partridge was tarred and feathered. Under duress, Church leaders signed an agreement to vacate Jackson County (*see* MISSOURI CONFLICT). Church members sought redress from the government, but were granted only sympathy, not help. When the old settlers saw that the Saints intended not to depart immediately but to hold their ground and defend themselves, they resumed acts of violence. After small battles erupted and led to several fatalities, the local militia succeeded in disarming the Mormons and driving them from Jackson County in early November.

Although some Saints fled to Van Buren and Lafayette counties, most found refuge north across the Missouri River in Clay County. The citizens of Liberty, the seat of Clay County, charitably offered shelter, work, and provisions. The refugees moved into abandoned slave cabins, built crude huts, pitched tents, and lived on meager subsistence until spring. Most Clay County citizens were friendly but considered the settlement of the Saints in their midst as only temporary.

To help the Missouri Saints, Joseph Smith arrived in June 1834 at the head of ZION'S CAMP, a paramilitary body of Latter-day Saints from the East. All efforts to achieve either reentry into Jackson County or redress of grievances came to naught. Outright war between Missourians and Mormons seemed imminent. By revelation (D&C

105) Joseph Smith was told to disband the camp because Zion could not yet be redeemed; bloodshed was thereby averted.

Before returning to Ohio, the Prophet established a presidency and high council for the Missouri Saints with David WHITMER as president and W. W. Phelps and John Whitmer as his counselors. Church members began establishing more, permanent residences in Liberty and the surrounding Clay County countryside. They won a reputation for retrenchment and thrift and were generally able to live at peace with their neighbors.

Gradually, however, citizens of Clay became concerned about the permanence of LDS settlements. This concern became acute after the arrival of additional Church members in 1835 and 1836. In June 1836 a public meeting was held at the courthouse in Liberty to discuss objections to the Mormons remaining in the county. The citizens reminded the Saints of their original pledge to leave the county when they were no longer welcome, but promised to control any violence until they left.

Bishop Partridge and W. W. Phelps explored new gathering spots for the Saints in relatively uninhabited territory in northern Missouri, and by early 1837, Church members began moving out of Clay County into the newly created "Mormon county" of Caldwell (*see* MISSOURI: LDS COMMUNITIES IN CALDWELL AND DAVIESS COUNTIES).

BIBLIOGRAPHY

Jennings, Warren A. "Zion Is Fled: The Expulsion of the Mormons from Jackson County, Missouri." Ph.D. diss., University of Florida, 1962.

Parkin, Max H. "A History of the Latter-day Saints in Clay County, Missouri, from 1833 to 1837." Ph.D. diss., Brigham Young University, 1976.

Pratt, Parley P. *Autobiography of Parley Parker Pratt.* Salt Lake City, 1938.

CLARK V. JOHNSON

LDS COMMUNITIES IN CALDWELL AND DAVIESS COUNTIES

The Missouri legislature created Caldwell and Daviess counties in December 1836 in an attempt to resolve "the Mormon problem." After the Latter-day Saints were driven from Jackson County in 1833, they were given temporary refuge in Clay County (*see* MISSOURI: LDS COMMUNITIES IN JACKSON AND CLAY COUNTIES), but three years later, they still lacked a homeland. The small, newly created county of Caldwell in unsettled northern Missouri was to be *their* county; later, they also moved north into Daviess County.

When the Saints sought shelter in Clay County, both they and the local citizens expected their stay to be temporary. Consequently, in the spring of 1836, Bishop Edward Partridge and W. W. Phelps explored potential sites for LDS settlements in northern Ray County, an expansive region commonly known as the Far West, which stretched north to the Iowa border. Most of the territory was prairie covered by tall grass, with timber only along the streams and rivers. They identified suitable sites and the Saints began purchasing land along Shoal Creek in northern Ray County, about thirty miles northwest of Liberty. In the summer of 1836, when Clay County officially requested the Latter-day Saints to leave, Church leaders announced their intent to move to northern Ray.

Ray County residents opposed the plan, however, an opposition made firmer when approximately one hundred families of migrating Saints from Ohio camped on the Crooked River in lower Ray County. Although many of the Saints in the camp were ill and most without funds to purchase either provisions or lands, the local citizens threatened them with violence if they did not leave. Another hundred impoverished LDS families were already traveling toward Missouri. Only after Church leaders assured Ray County officials of their intent to settle uninhabited and generally unwanted prairies to the north and to apply for a new county did opposition wane. Both parties agreed to establish a six-mile buffer zone or a no-man's land where neither Mormons nor non-Mormons would settle.

Early in August 1836, W. W. Phelps and John Whitmer, members of the Missouri stake presidency, located a site for a city on Shoal Creek and called it Far West. It was twelve miles west of Haun's Mill, a small LDS settlement created by Jacob Haun a year earlier. The Saints began gathering near Far West in late summer and fall and soon built numerous smaller settlements.

Alexander W. Doniphan, state legislator and friend to the Saints, introduced a bill in December 1836 to create two new small counties from sparsely settled northern Ray County. Doniphan named the new counties Daviess and Caldwell after two famous Kentucky Indian fighters. Caldwell County, the location of the Far West and Shoal Creek settlements, would be exclusively for Mormons; they would have their own militia and their own representation in the state legislature. Since many considered this segregation of the Latter-day Saints an excellent solution to the Mormon problem, the bill passed and was signed into law December 29, 1836. By early 1837, Missouri Saints were pouring into Caldwell County and began constructing log houses and preparing the soil for spring planting. The standard government rate was $1.25 per acre for unimproved land, and within a year most of the land was claimed and much of it was under cultivation. Civil officers were selected, and as in other counties, a county militia was organized as an arm of the state militia.

Some of the land around Far West was purchased by W. W. Phelps and John Whitmer using nearly $1,500 that had been raised to aid the poverty-stricken incoming Saints. Without consulting other local leaders (*see* HIGH COUNCIL), they developed the land, sold it, and retained some of the profit for themselves, thus creating discord. Conflict festered in Far West throughout 1837 until Joseph SMITH, visiting from Ohio in November, temporarily resolved differences among the leaders. During his visit he also established committees to identify additional settlement sites.

New tension arose among the Saints during the winter, however, when Oliver COWDERY and Frederick G. Williams arrived in Far West from KIRTLAND, OHIO. With Phelps and Whitmer, Cowdery sold Church land in Jackson County, violating a policy that the Saints should retain their claims in Zion (D&C 101:99). The local high council tried the three for disobedience and excommunicated them, along with Williams, who apparently sided with them. As prominent "dissenters," they stirred up trouble among the Saints through the first half of 1838.

In March 1838 Joseph Smith moved the headquarters of the Church to Far West. Other Ohio Saints planned to follow later in the year. That summer, the population in Caldwell County reached five thousand, a large percentage living in Far West, where the Saints had built hundreds of homes, four dry-goods stores, three family grocery stores, several blacksmith shops, two hotels, a printing shop, and a large schoolhouse that doubled as a church and courthouse.

The rapidly increasing LDS population required more new settlements. In mid-May, Joseph Smith led an exploring expedition northward into Daviess County, where a few members had previously settled under a gentleman's agreement with the old settlers. The explorers found a beautiful townsite on the Grand River. While there, the Prophet received a revelation that this was also the site of ADAM-ONDI-AHMAN, mentioned in a revelation three years earlier as the valley where Adam had gathered his righteous posterity "and there bestowed upon them his last blessing" (D&C 107:53; cf. 78:15–16). This news helped confirm the decision to create a stake there and designate the area as a gathering place for Ohio members traveling to Missouri. At a June 28, 1838, conference in the newly laid-out community, affectionately nicknamed Di-Ahman, Joseph Smith's uncle, John Smith, was called as stake president. Throughout the summer of 1838, Latter-day Saints poured into Daviess County, where a plentiful harvest helped provide for the impoverished members of the Kirtland Camp when they arrived in early October. That same spring, the Saints also began to settle in DeWitt, in nearby Carroll County near the confluence of the Grand and Missouri rivers, where they established a steamboat landing from which immigrants could move to the other LDS settlements.

The Saints in northern Missouri industriously planted crops and built log houses throughout the summer, and prospects for peace appeared good. They still hoped for eventual reconciliation with the citizens of Jackson County so that they could return to their center place, but in the meantime they intended to prosper where they were. By revelation, Far West was to become a temple city (D&C 115:7), and the following spring, the Quorum of the Twelve would dedicate the temple site before departing on a mission to Great Britain (D&C 118:4). Revelation in Far West also prescribed the formal name of the Church, "even The Church of Jesus Christ of Latter-day Saints" (D&C 115:4), and established the tithing system, which continues to provide financial stability to the Church and to bless its members (D&C 119, 120).

But new difficulties arose. First, Sidney RIGDON publicly threatened dissenters in his June "Salt Sermon," intimating that they should leave Far West or harm would befall them. News of this threat reinforced anti-Mormon hostility throughout Missouri. Second, LDS militia officer Sampson Avard formed an underground group of vigilantes labeled DANITES. Avard convinced this oathbound group that they operated with the approval of Church leaders and that they were authorized to avenge themselves against the Church's enemies, even by robbery, lying, and violence if necessary. Third, in an inflammatory Independence Day speech, Sidney Rigdon thundered out a declaration of independence from further mob violence. He warned of a war of extermination between Mormons and their enemies if they were further threatened or harassed.

Finally, and perhaps most important, the new LDS settlements in Adam-ondi-Ahman and De-Witt angered other Missourians who thought that the Mormons had agreed to stay in Caldwell County. Church leaders countered that as American citizens they had the right to buy land and live wherever they chose. Soon, depredations occurred, and with mobilization of militias on both sides, the stage was set for war. After violence erupted in October 1838, Governor Lilburn W. Boggs issued his infamous EXTERMINATION ORDER, declaring that all Mormons should be driven from Missouri or be exterminated.

At first, Church members attempted to defend themselves in their respective settlements, but the outlying towns were not defensible. Before all the Saints could gather to safety in fortified Far West, lives were lost in several confrontations, including the HAUN'S MILL MASSACRE, where seventeen LDS men and boys died. The siege of Far West took place during the last three days of October. Joseph Smith and other Church leaders were arrested and incarcerated, several in LIBERTY JAIL, and the Saints were forced to abandon their improved lands to their enemies and leave Missouri (see MISSOURI CONFLICT). Brigham YOUNG and Heber C. KIMBALL, members of the Twelve Apostles who were not imprisoned, and John TAYLOR, who was ordained an apostle in December, led the heroic efforts to relocate the approximately 12,000 Missouri Saints across the Mississippi River into Illinois.

BIBLIOGRAPHY

Gentry, Leland H. "A History of the Latter-day Saints in Northern Missouri from 1836 to 1839." Ph.D. diss., Brigham Young University, 1965.

LeSueur, Stephen C. The 1838 Mormon War in Missouri. Columbia, Mo., 1987.

LELAND H. GENTRY

MISSOURI CONFLICT

Incidents of discord between Latter-day Saints and their neighbors in Missouri from 1831 to 1839 are sometimes known as the Missouri War. In 1838 the tensions that had intermittently produced violence escalated into large-scale conflict that ended with the forced expulsion of the Latter-day Saints from the state.

The first Latter-day Saints entered Missouri in January 1831 as part of the LAMANITE MISSION. These zealous missionaries soon drew the ire of both U.S. Indian agents and local clergy in Independence, the rough-hewn and sometimes disorderly seat of Jackson County and the head of the Santa Fe Trail. Joseph SMITH arrived in July 1831. In August he selected a site for a temple and designated Jackson County as the location of the millennial ZION or NEW JERUSALEM and as the gathering place for the Saints.

That summer more than one hundred Church members arrived in Jackson County from KIRTLAND, OHIO, and from other northern and eastern states; hundreds more soon followed. By the summer of 1833, more than a thousand were grouped into four settlements west of Independence, while others lived in the village itself.

Tension between the Latter-day Saints and their neighbors in frontier Jackson County mounted for several reasons. First, marked cultural differences set them apart. With New England roots, most Saints valued congregational Sabbath worship, education of their children, and refined personal decorum. In contrast, many Jackson County residents had come to the Missouri frontier from other states precisely to avoid such interference in their lives. Many held no schools for their children, and Sunday cockfights attracted more people than church services did. Often hard drinking intensified violent frontier ways. In the opinion of non-LDS county resident John C. McCoy in the Kansas City Journal (Apr. 24, 1881, p. 9), such extreme differences in customs made the two groups "completely unfitted to live together in peace and friendship."

Second, Missourians considered the Latter-day Saints strange and religiously unorthodox. Many LDS Church members aggressively articulated belief in revelation, prophets, the Book of Mormon, spiritual gifts, the Millennium, and the importance of gathering. Some went further and claimed Jackson County land as a sacred inheritance by divine appointment. Even David WHITMER, presiding elder of one branch, thought these boasts excited bitter jealousy. Articles on prophecy and doctrine published in the Church newspaper at Independence, the EVENING AND THE MORNING STAR, added to hard feelings. In addition, local Protestant clergy felt threatened by LDS missionary activity.

Third, because the Saints lived on Church lands and traded entirely with the Church store or blacksmith shops, some original settlers viewed them as economically exclusive, even un-American. Others accused LDS immigrants of pauperism when, because of diminished Church resources, they failed to obtain land.

A fourth volatile issue was the original settlers' fear that Latter-day Saints might provoke battles with either slaves or Indians. They accused the Saints of slave tampering. As transplanted Southerners who valued their right to hold slaves, the settlers erroneously feared that the Saints intended to convert blacks or incite them to revolt. They also correctly asserted that the Latter-day Saints desired to convert Indians and, perhaps, ally themselves with the Indians.

Finally, Missourians feared that continued LDS ingathering would lead to loss of political control. "It requires no gift of prophecy," stated a citizens' committee, "to tell that the day is not far distant when the civil government of the county will be in their hands; when the sheriff, the justices, and the county judges will be Mormons" (HC 1:397). These monumental differences between the Latter-day Saints and the Missourians eventually led to violence.

Vandalism against LDS settlers first occurred in the spring of 1832. Coordinated aggression commenced in July 1833, after the article "Free People of Color" appeared in the *Evening and the Morning Star*. Even though the article was written to curtail trouble, it so outraged local citizens that more than 400 met at the courthouse to demand that the Mormons leave. When the Latter-day Saints refused to negotiate away or abandon lands they legally owned, some citizens formed a mob and destroyed the press and printing house, ransacked the Mormon store, and violently accosted LDS leaders. Bishop Edward Partridge was beaten and tarred and feathered. Meeting three days later, the mob issued an ultimatum: One-half of the Mormons must leave by year's end and the rest by April (1834).

Local Church leaders sought counsel from Joseph Smith at Kirtland and assistance from Missouri Governor Daniel Dunklin. The Prophet urged them to hold their ground, and the governor advised them to seek redress through the courts. They did both. They employed lawyers from Clay County, including Alexander W. Doniphan and David R. Atchison.

Determined to settle the matter decisively, the old settlers mobilized to drive the Mormons out. Renewed violence began on October 31, 1833, with an attack on the Whitmer Branch a few miles west of the Big Blue River, near Independence. The mob demolished houses, whipped the men, and terrorized the women and children. For a week, attacks, beatings, and depredations against the Saints continued. On November 4 a mob again attacked the Whitmer settlement, making its streets a battleground. Two Missourians and one defender died.

The following day men led by Lyman Wight arrived from the Prairie Branch, twelve miles west, to protect members threatened at Independence. Colonel Thomas L. Pitcher then called out the county militia to quell the mob and negotiate a truce with Wight. According to John Corrill, a Church officer at Independence, after the Saints surrendered their arms to the militia, the troops joined the mob in a general assault against them. Some county residents recoiled at this barbarism. John McCoy, whose father rode with the mob, later wrote in the *Kansas City Journal* (Jan. 18, 1885, p. 5) that the Mormons "were unjustly and outrageously maltreated." But neither Colonel Pitcher nor Lieutenant Governor Lilburn W. Boggs, a resident of the county, interfered.

The terrified Saints fled Jackson County in disarray. Most went north, across the Missouri River, and sought refuge in Clay County, whose citizens were generally sympathetic and hospitable. Even there, however, these refugees endured a miserable winter without sufficient shelter, clothing, or food—either in extemporized camps along the river or above the bluffs in abandoned summer slave quarters. By spring, though, industry, better weather, and the aid of Clay County citizens improved their desperate condition.

After the Missouri governor promised militia assistance, about 200 Saints marched from Ohio to Missouri to escort the exiles back to their homes. This paramilitary relief party was known as ZION'S CAMP. But reports of the camp's coming mobilized anti-Mormons throughout Missouri's western counties, and when it arrived in Missouri, it encountered hundreds of armed adversaries. The promised military assistance from the governor was not forthcoming, and the camp disbanded in June 1834 without crossing into Jackson County. The revelation disbanding Zion's Camp declared that, because the Saints had not been blameless and must yet learn much, their anticipated Zion would not be redeemed for "many days" (D&C 105:2–10, 37).

All parties considered the Saints' exile in Clay County to be temporary. Joseph Smith still hoped for the strength to return to Jackson County in the near future. But the Clay County old settlers, fearful of the flood of new LDS arrivals, grew impatient. On the night of June 28, 1836, a Clay County mob, determined to drive the Mormons from the county, commenced to harass and beat them. The following day a convention of leading citizens entreated the Saints to leave the county before the mob struck further. Grateful for the refuge provided by Clay County citizens at a time of deep crisis, Church leaders agreed to move.

An uninhabited area north of Richmond became the new gathering place. Friends of the Saints, including state legislator Alexander W. Doniphan, guided the formation of a new "Mormon county" called Caldwell. By late 1836, with the county seat of Far West surrounded by other settlements, Latter-day Saints streamed into Caldwell County. In early 1838, after experiencing difficulties in Ohio, Joseph Smith arrived at Far West, and the settlement became Church headquarters. Many of the Ohio Saints soon followed. As LDS settlement extended into nearby Daviess and Carroll counties, competition with the old settlers resumed, eventually erupting into conflict.

Internal dissent, the aftermath of problems in Kirtland, also plagued the Church at Far West. Oliver COWDERY, the Missouri stake presidency (David WHITMER, William W. Phelps, and John Whitmer), and three apostles (Luke S. Johnson, Lyman E. Johnson, and William E. McLellin) were all excommunicated. Trying to prevent them from damaging the Church, Sidney RIGDON, a counselor to Joseph Smith, demanded in his June 19 "salt sermon" that the dissenters leave or be punished. Soon after, in a vigorous July 4 address, Rigdon declared the Church's independence from "mobocracy." These two sermons further incensed the public against expanding LDS influence.

Persecutions in Jackson County, Missouri, 1833, by C. C. A. Christensen (1878–1879, tempera on canvas, 6′6″ × 9′9″). Many factors, including cultural and religious differences and the feared loss of political control, led to the violent expulsion of Latter-day Saints from Jackson County, Missouri, in 1833. Homes and barns were demolished, crops destroyed, and families attacked. Courtesy Museum of Fine Arts, Brigham Young University.

Hostilities that began on August 8, 1838, election day, ended a few months later with the expulsion of the Latter-day Saints from the state. At Gallatin, county seat of Daviess County, a fight ensued when Mormons were prevented from voting. Joseph Smith quickly took measures to protect his people in Daviess County, but matters worsened. As false rumors of his efforts and of the election day battle reached surrounding counties, hundreds of self-appointed regulators congregated in Daviess, Caldwell, and Carroll counties. State militia commanded by Major General David R. Atchison worked to keep an uneasy peace.

Fearing that Latter-day Saints, reinforced regularly by new arrivals, would soon control their counties, non-Mormons determined to attack. On October 2, 1838, a mob laid siege to the LDS settlement of DeWitt in Carroll County. The Saints petitioned recently elected Governor Lilburn W. Boggs for protection, only to be told that they must take care of themselves. Atchison's militia, weakened by mutiny and insubordination and lacking the firm support of the governor, failed to quell the mob. After ten days, the DeWitt Saints fled to Far West for safety; some in weakened condition died.

Faced with a heedless governor and an ineffective militia, Latter-day Saints reconsidered their long-standing position of passive defense. Concluding that without civil protection they had to protect themselves, in mid-October LDS leaders mobilized their own state-authorized militias in Caldwell and Daviess counties. These units actively confronted threatening mobs; there may also have been activity by units not strictly part of the militia (see DANITES).

Raiders from Gallatin and Millport in Daviess County harassed the LDS community of ADAM-ONDI-AHMAN. Throughout October both sides engaged in burning, stealing, and intimidation. While clearly acting first in self-defense, some Latter-day Saints nevertheless felt that military measures were excessive. In late October, Thomas B. Marsh and Orson Hyde, both apostles, signed affidavits critical of Mormon actions.

Hostilities escalated into outright warfare. Far West Militia Captain David W. PATTEN, an apostle, pursued a renegade band of Missouri militia overnight to the Crooked River in northern Ray County where, at dawn on October 25, they clashed. Two died on the battlefield, one on each side, and two mortally wounded Saints died soon after, including Patten.

From the Battle of Crooked River, rumors of LDS aggression spread like wildfire. On the strength of these rumors, Governor Boggs issued his infamous EXTERMINATION ORDER on October 27, authorizing the state militia to drive all Mormons from Missouri or exterminate them. Three days later Colonel William O. Jennings launched an unprovoked attacked on an LDS settlement at Haun's Mill, east of Far West, leaving seventeen men and boys dead (see HAUN'S MILL MASSACRE). Survivors joined other refugees fleeing to Far

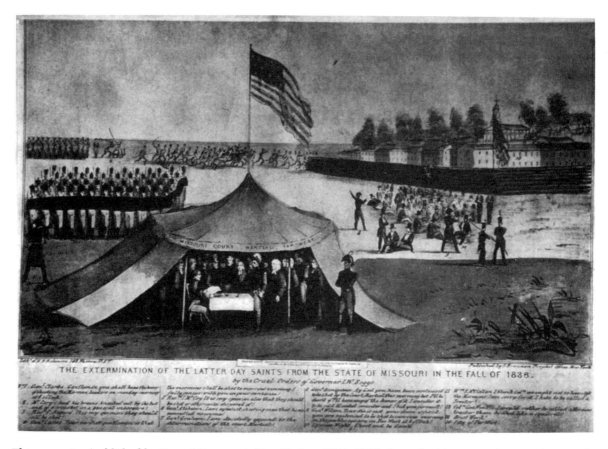

THE EXTERMINATION OF THE LATTER DAY SAINTS FROM THE STATE OF MISSOURI IN THE FALL OF 1838.
by the Cruel Orders of Governor LW. Boggs.

This engraving (published by Samuel Brannan in New York, c. 1844–1845) shows the Missouri militia marching on the LDS settlement of Far West in the fall of 1838. Joseph Smith and other LDS leaders surrendered themselves to a court martial and the inhabitants of the settlement were disarmed. The Saints were then driven from the State.

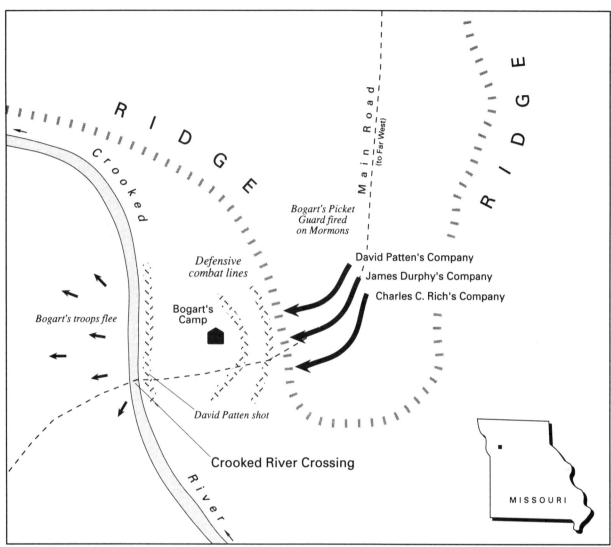

Bogart's Picket Guard fired on Mormons

David Patten's Company
James Durphy's Company
Charles C. Rich's Company

Defensive combat lines

Bogart's troops flee

Bogart's Camp

David Patten shot

Crooked River Crossing

MISSOURI

RIDGE

Crooked

RIDGE

Main Road (to Far West)

River

BYU Geography Department

The Battle of Crooked River, Missouri, October 25, 1838.

West. On October 31, the militia under the command of Major General Samuel D. Lucas laid siege upon Far West.

To avoid bloodshed, Joseph Smith and others agreed to meet with militia leaders, who instead arrested them. A court-martial that evening summarily sentenced Joseph Smith and his associates to be shot, and Lucas ordered Brig. General Alexander Doniphan to execute them at dawn. Doniphan thought the order illegal and heroically refused to carry it out, declaring that he would bring to account anyone who tried to do it. After Far West defenders were disarmed, Missouri at-

tackers committed numerous outrages against women and property; a number of men were shot and at least one was killed.

While Joseph Smith and some of the others were jailed at Independence, in RICHMOND JAIL, and finally in LIBERTY JAIL, the rest of the Latter-day Saints were forced from the state. That winter, under the leadership of Brigham YOUNG, approximately 12,000 suffering Saints fled Missouri, most crossing the Mississippi River into Illinois at Quincy.

Joseph Smith and several others spent five months in jail awaiting trial for alleged murder, treason, arson, and other charges growing out of the fall violence and attempts at defense. For the Prophet, this imprisonment evoked a legacy of strength and revelations from heaven (*see* DOCTRINE AND COVENANTS: SECTIONS 121–23). A trial was never held. On April 15, 1839, while being transported on a change of venue to Boone County, Joseph and his brother Hyrum were allowed to escape to join Saints and their families in Illinois.

BIBLIOGRAPHY

Gentry, Leland H. "A History of the Latter-day Saints in Northern Missouri from 1836 to 1839." Ph.D. diss., Brigham Young University, 1965.

Jennings, Warren A. "Zion Is Fled: The Expulsion of the Mormons from Jackson County, Missouri." Ph.D. diss., University of Florida, 1962.

Johnson, Clark V. *The Missouri Petitions: Documents from the Missouri Conflict, 1833–1838.* Provo, Utah, 1991.

LeSueur, Stephen C. *The 1838 Mormon War in Missouri.* Columbia, Missouri, 1987.

Roberts, B. H. *The Missouri Persecutions.* Salt Lake City, 1900.

MAX H PARKIN

MODESTY

[A quality of mind, heart, and body, modesty is an attitude of humility, decency, and propriety that may be evidenced in thought, language, dress, and behavior. Modesty or immodesty is reflected in almost every aspect of human life. It will be manifest in the "example of the believers, in word, in conversation, in charity, in spirit, in faith, in purity" (1 Tim. 4:12). Articles pertaining to this topic are Chastity; Humility; Lifestyle; Modesty in Dress; Profanity; Reverence; Righteousness.*]*

MODESTY IN DRESS

Latter-day Saints believe that modest dress reflects commitment to a Christlike life and shows respect for self, for fellow beings, and for God. In their homes and in the Church, they are taught that modest dress has a positive effect on both self-esteem and behavior.

According to LDS theology, the body is more than a biological entity; it is a temple that houses an eternal spirit (cf. 1 Cor. 3:16–17). Physical intimacy is reserved for marriage (*see* CHASTITY). Modest dress serves as a physical and spiritual guard against immoral behavior and its inherent physical, emotional, and spiritual harm. Because modesty in dress cannot be reduced to a matter of particular styles, individuals are encouraged to use discretion to determine appropriate dress in varying situations.

Emphasizing the importance of modest dress, President Spencer W. KIMBALL stated, "I am positive that personal grooming and cleanliness, as well as the clothes we wear, can be tremendous factors in the standards we set and follow on the pathway to immortality and eternal life" (1979, p. 3).

BIBLIOGRAPHY

Kimball, Spencer W. *Faith Precedes the Miracle*, pp. 161–68. Salt Lake City, 1972.

———. "On My Honor." *Ensign* 9 (Apr. 1979):3.

MICHELE THOMPSON-HOLBROOK

MORMON

Mormon was a PROPHET, an author, and the last NEPHITE military commander (c. A.D. 310–385). The Book of Mormon bears his name because he was the major abridger–writer of the GOLD PLATES from which it was translated. He was prepared by the experiences of his youth to become a prophet: he was taught "the learning of [his] people," was a "sober child" and "quick to observe," and in his fifteenth year was "visited of the Lord" (Morm. 1:2, 15). At sixteen he became the general of all the Nephite armies and largely succeeded in preserving his people from destruction until A.D. 385, when virtually all of them but his son MORONI$_2$ were destroyed in battles with the LAMANITES (6:8–15; 8:1–3). As keeper of the Nephite records, Mormon abridged the large PLATES of Nephi, bound with them the small plates of Nephi, and added his own short history (W of M 1:1–5; Morm. 1:1). Before his death, he hid the records entrusted to him in the hill CUMORAH, "save it were these few plates which I gave unto my son Moroni" (Morm. 6:6). The Prophet Joseph SMITH received and translated Mormon's abridgment, the small plates of Nephi, and a few other documents, and published them in 1830 as the Book of Mormon.

First and foremost, Mormon was a prophet to his people, urging them to "repent, and be baptized in the name of Jesus, and lay hold upon the gospel of Christ" (Morm. 7:8). He taught that they were "a remnant of the seed of Jacob" (7:10) and could have the blessings of ISRAEL if they would live for them. He also underscored the supporting relationship of the Bible and the Book of Mormon: "For behold, this [record, the Book of Mormon] is written for the intent that ye may believe that [record, the Bible]; and if ye believe that ye will believe this also" (7:9).

Mormon's son MORONI₂ finished the record, including one of Mormon's addresses and two of Mormon's epistles in his own book of Moroni. Mormon's talk on FAITH, HOPE, and CHARITY (Moro. 7) teaches that charity, the greatest of those three virtues, is "the pure LOVE of Christ, and it endureth forever; and whoso is found possessed of it at the last day, it shall be well with him" (7:47). One of Mormon's letters (Moro. 8) condemns INFANT BAPTISM as a practice that denies the ATONEMENT OF JESUS CHRIST, stating "it is solemn mockery before God, that ye should baptize little children" (8:9). Rather, little children need not repent, but "are alive in Christ, even from the foundation of the world" (8:12). In the other epistle (Moro. 9) Mormon notes that the destruction of the Nephites is just retribution for their wickedness, which is so bad that he "cannot recommend them unto God lest he should smite me" (9:21).

As abridger of Nephite records, Mormon had access to a veritable library of engraved documents and was commanded to make an abridgment of the large plates of Nephi so that Lamanites, Jews, and GENTILES of the latter days could know of the Lord's COVENANTS and what he had done for their ancestors and could thereby be convinced that Jesus is the Christ (see BOOK OF MORMON: TITLE PAGE). While making his abridgment, Mormon often noted that he could not include even a hundredth part of the source records (e.g., Hel. 3:14). He regularly sought opportunity to draw spiritual lessons from the course of events experienced by his people. The phrase "and thus we see" frequently introduces one of Mormon's interpretive observations (cf. Hel. 3:27–30). One of the most significant passages from his hand appears in Helaman 12 wherein he offers compelling views about the often vain and fickle character of human nature, especially in response to material prosperity.

As an author, Mormon expressed his feelings, sorrowing at living in a wicked society (Morm. 2:19), and confessing that he had loved and prayed for his people (3:12), but was at last without hope

(5:2). He measured civility by how women and children fared (4:14, 21), seeking to unite them with husbands and fathers even when facing certain doom (6:2, 7). When the last Nephites fell, he penned a poignant lament in their memory (6:16–22).

As general of the Nephite armies (Morm. 2–6), Mormon helped to preserve his people from destruction by the Lamanites for some fifty-eight years, but then began to lose them first to sin and then to death (Morm. 2:11–15). Even so, he taught survivors that they would be spared if they would repent and obey the GOSPEL OF JESUS CHRIST, "but it was in vain; and they did not realize that it was the Lord that had spared them, and granted unto them a chance for repentance" (3:3). At one time the Nephites became so vicious and hardened that Mormon refused to lead them into battle (3:11). But he could not bear to watch them perish, and although he had no hope that they could survive, he relented (5:1) and led them into their last battle from which only he, his son Moroni₂, and a few others survived (8:2–3). Moroni₂ lived to complete his father's record (8:1).

BIBLIOGRAPHY

Holland, Jeffrey R. "Mormon: The Man and the Book." *Ensign* 8 (Mar. 1978):15–18; (Apr. 1978):57–59.

PHYLLIS ANN ROUNDY

MORMON BATTALION

Though it never fought a battle, the Mormon Battalion, a volunteer unit in the 1846 U.S. campaign against Mexico, earned a place in the history of the West. Its men cleared a wagon road from Santa Fe to San Diego and helped secure California as United States territory. Members of the Battalion helped preserve a tenuous peace in southern California before the Treaty of Guadalupe Hidalgo ended hostilities. A wagon road they established between the Gila and the Rio Grande influenced the U.S. government to make the Gadsden Purchase. They also opened wagon roads via Carson and Cajon passes that linked California with Salt Lake City. Some former members of the Battalion eventually participated in the gold discovery and helped stimulate economic development in the Great Basin (see CALIFORNIA, PIONEER SETTLEMENTS IN). These former LDS soldiers ultimately

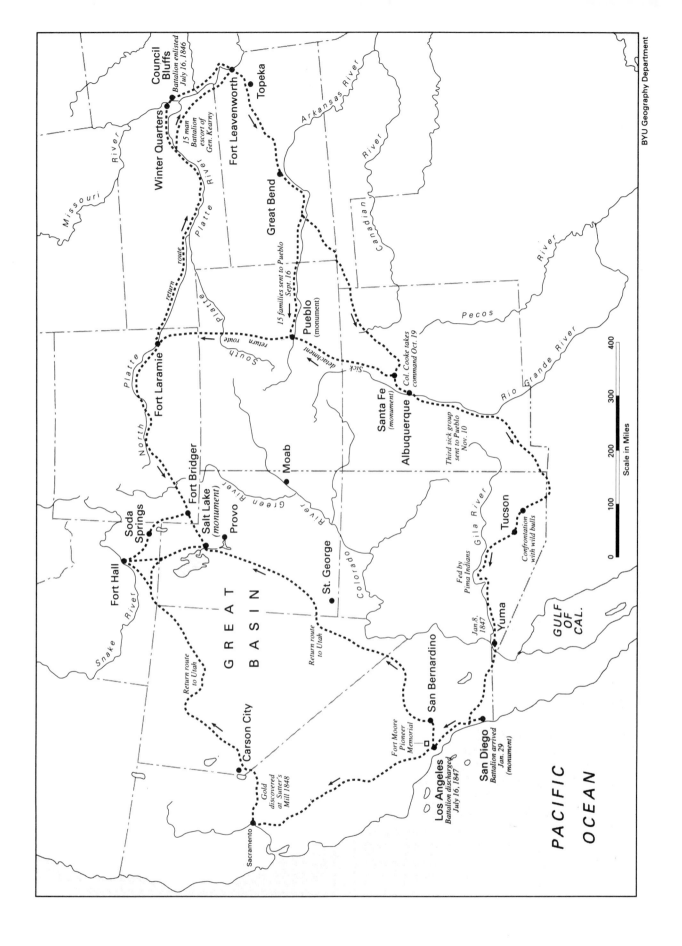

received favorable recognition both from their military commanders and from other non-Mormons for their industriousness and loyalty.

After Brigham YOUNG had determined a timetable for moving west from Winter Quarters early in 1846 (*see* HISTORY OF THE CHURCH: C. 1844–1877; WESTWARD MIGRATION), he instructed Jesse C. Little, president of the Eastern States Mission, to seek government assistance. With the help of Thomas L. KANE, Little explored the matter with Amos Kendall, an influential political adviser, and later directly with U.S. President James K. Polk. After making a decision to send an overland army to California under the command of Stephen W. Kearny, Polk confided in his diary on June 2, 1846: "Col. Kearny was also authorized to receive into service as volunteers a few hundred of the Mormons who are now on their way to California, with a view to conciliate them, attach them to our country, & prevent them from taking part against us" (Polk, p. 109).

President Polk authorized this enlistment despite several concerns. One was the danger of internal conflict because Kearny's fighting regiments were mainly Missouri recruits, and Mormons and Missourians had little respect for each other since the Saints had been forced from the state in 1838–1839 (*see* MISSOURI CONFLICT). Polk also wanted to avoid the possibility that Mormon troops could be the first and possibly only American troops to reach California overland in 1846. The President's confidential orders therefore gave Colonel Kearny almost unlimited authority to deal with such matters.

Kearny dispatched Captain James Allen to raise five hundred volunteers from the LDS camps on the Missouri River. The initial reaction to Allen's call was overwhelmingly negative. Some feared that this call was part of a government conspiracy designed to ascertain their strength and to obstruct or prevent their movement west. The five hundred enlistees would be drawn from the able-bodied men most needed for the trek west, and few saw any potential benefit.

However, by early June Brigham Young realized, after struggling through the rain-soaked quagmires of southern Iowa, that the Saints could not safely reach the Rocky Mountains that year as planned. The proposed enlistment, he recognized, could bring military pay that would be helpful for purchasing supplies; moreover, it would provide for transporting several hundred families to the West, allay fears about LDS loyalty to the United States, and secure the privilege of establishing temporary quarters on Indian land near the Missouri (*see* WINTER QUARTERS).

As a result, Church leaders began vigorously recruiting volunteers from COUNCIL BLUFFS to Mt. Pisgah. Heber C. KIMBALL called the enlistment a great blessing from Heaven, and Brigham Young explained that the soldiers would be mustered out in California, much closer to their new home in the West. Official rolls record an enlistment of 497 volunteers. In addition, as many as 80 women and children marched with the battalion, some of the women serving as paid laundresses.

Brigham Young selected LDS officers for the five companies, and the recruits voted to sustain his selection. The death of Colonel Allen en route to Santa Fe led to conflict: Should leadership fall to Captain Jefferson Hunt, senior Latter-day Saint officer, or to Lieutenant Andrew Jackson Smith of the regular army? Smith led the Battalion to Santa Fe, and the problem was solved when Kearny's new appointee, Philip St. George Cooke, took command.

When it became apparent that some soldiers and most of the families lacked the stamina for the desert march to San Diego, three "sick" detachments, including nearly all the women and children, went to Fort Pueblo, Colorado. Pueblo was an ideal location, partly because it was the temporary home of more than forty Latter-day Saints from Mississippi who had proceeded farther west than the general exodus. Altogether about 275 Latter-day Saints spent an unusually mild winter at Fort Pueblo under the command of Mormon Battalion captain James Brown. The next spring they proceeded to the Salt Lake Valley, arriving July 29, 1847, just five days after Brigham Young's party.

Commander Cooke, meantime, prepared the Battalion for the trek to San Diego. After sending the sick detachments to Pueblo, he reorganized the command staff and acquired provisions, including thirty-seven wagons. He left Santa Fe with 397 soldiers. On the Rio Grande River he sent a final sick detachment to Pueblo, leaving the battalion with approximately 340 men, four officers' wives,

—— Routes traveled by members of the Mormon Battalion, 1846–1847.

and only a few children prepared for the grueling desert march.

After a strenuous desert march, the battalion reached the Pima villages scattered along the Gila River. From there it followed the previously established Gila Trail to the Colorado River, forded the Colorado, then struggled from water hole to water hole along the southern edge of the Imperial Sand Dunes and across the Imperial Valley. Finally, it followed the dry Vallecito Wash to the infamous Box Canyon. As the sidewalls of the wash became too narrow for wagons, the men hewed a route through the rock outcroppings and brought the five remaining wagons into southern California.

The Mormon Battalion's only engagement of the war, the Battle of the Bulls, occurred December 11, 1846, when several of the battalion's hunters opened fire on wild cattle that had stampeded into the rear companies. The toll was ten to fifteen bulls killed, two mules gored to death, three men wounded. When the battalion later neared Tucson, Mexican soldiers and residents chose to flee rather than fight.

After reaching San Diego in January 1847, LDS soldiers were given a variety of garrison responsibilities, with fifteen serving as Kearny's escort back to Fort Leavenworth. After more than 300 were discharged in Los Angeles on July 16, 1847, Captain Hunt led about fifty northward to Monterey. Some of the 300 worked near San Francisco before reuniting for the trip to Salt Lake City. The largest group, about 164 men, met Captain James Brown of the Pueblo detachments on the Truckee River in the Sierra Nevada Mountains on September 7, 1847. Brown was en route to collect his men's pay in San Francisco. Brown brought news of the safe arrival of the PIONEERS in the Salt Lake Valley, along with word that the men were free to work in California or to proceed to Salt Lake City, depending upon their financial circumstances and desire.

While a few went eastward, the majority of the destitute men scattered for odd jobs, including about forty who worked at Sutter's Fort and a few who were at Sutter's Mill when James Marshall discovered gold. Eighty-one men reenlisted as the California Volunteers and performed garrison duty at San Diego. After their discharge in the spring of 1848, these men opened a wagon road via Cajon Pass to Salt Lake City.

Though leaving their families behind was difficult and their desert march arduous, by their sacrifice the men of the Mormon Battalion facilitated the Saints' move to the Salt Lake Valley and helped develop the West.

BIBLIOGRAPHY

Polk, James K. *Polk, the Diary of a President 1845–1849*, ed. Allan Nevins, pp. 108–109. London, 1929.

Tyler, Daniel. *A Concise History of the Mormon Battalion in the Mexican War 1846–1847*. n. p., 1881; Chicago, 1964.

Yurtinus, John F. "A Ram in the Thicket: A History of the Mormon Battalion in the Mexican War." Ph.D. diss., Brigham Young University, 1975.

———. "The Mormon Volunteers: The Recruitment and Service of a Unique Military Company." *Journal of San Diego History* 25 (Summer 1979):242–61.

JOHN F. YURTINUS

MORMON HANDICRAFT

Mormon Handicraft, a consignment store for handwork, including quilts, rugs, dolls, baby clothes, and other handmade items, was founded in 1937 by Louise Y. ROBISON, then general president of the RELIEF SOCIETY. The store was organized as a means of allowing women to supplement their family income during the depression of the 1930s (*History of Relief Society*, p. 115). Mormon Handicraft followed the pattern of earlier women's co-op stores operated by Relief Societies from the mid-1870s to 1912 (*A Centenary of Relief Society*, pp. 83–84).

Operated as a nonprofit organization, the store was originally administered by the Relief Society leaders, who desired "to preserve the skills of our pioneer ancestors and the skills and crafts of the various countries" (*History of Relief Society*, p. 115). General Board member Nellie O. Parker declared, "For the world to beat a path to the door of Mormon Handicraft Shop is our aim; and if Emerson is right, we are confident it will be so when people know of the fineness and skill of the workmanship to be found here" (Parker, p. 417).

An advertising brochure proclaimed, "Rare skill in handicraft from every country has been perpetuated in Utah. . . . This cosmopolitan background, unique for thrift and versatility, has produced a handicraft guild not to be found in any other place in the world. . . . There is quality only hands can produce" (Parker, p. 417). The brochure was distributed in dining and lounge cars of trains coming into Salt Lake City and was placed in a display case in the Hotel Utah lobby. The campaign was successful: On one occasion, Parker reported, after a visit to the store, a buyer for the Altman Company ordered "up-to-the-minute luncheon sets, copper work and oxen-yoke lamps" (Parker, p. 417).

Beginning in 1960, its scope was broadened and Mormon Handicraft became a distribution point for materials and ideas for the Relief Society's homemaking meetings, particularly quilting and other handwork supplies. Through the Homemaking Department of the Relief Society, women learned and practiced homemaking arts. The monthly compassionate service instruction given in Relief Society, where members were taught ways to assist less fortunate Church members, often included the production and distribution of quilts, clothing, and other necessities for the home. Availability of materials and classes was, therefore, welcomed by local Relief Society leaders. The sale of materials also helped maintain the economic viability of Mormon Handicraft.

As the Church grew, the need for a centralized distribution and education point diminished, and the shop as a separate unit was closed in January 1986 (*Church News*, Jan. 26, 1986, p. 12). The store then became a division of DESERET BOOK COMPANY in June 1986. At the time of transfer, Ronald A. Millett, Deseret Book president, affirmed the company's goal of preserving Mormon Handicraft's reputation in both consignment and retail supply operations (*Church News*, June 8, 1986, p. 14).

In 1987, Mormon Handicraft accepted over 9,000 different items made by 1,900 contributors, ages fourteen to ninety-two. Contributors varied from the widow in Salt Lake City who for forty-eight years produced dish towels, stuffed animals, aprons, bibs, and almost ten thousand crocheted heart sachets, to the women in the Philippines who sold elaborate lace-edged handkerchiefs as their sole income source (*Church News*, Mar. 28, 1987, p. 10; *Mormon Handicraft: A Brief History*, p. 5).

BIBLIOGRAPHY

A Centenary of Relief Society, 1842–1942. Salt Lake City, 1942.

History of Relief Society, 1842-1966. Salt Lake City, 1966.

Mormon Handicraft: A Brief History (pamphlet). Salt Lake City, 1987.

Parker, Nellie O. "Mormon Handicraft." *Relief Society Magazine* 26 (June 1939):417.

CAROL L. CLARK

MORMONISM, AN INDEPENDENT INTERPRETATION

One may take two basic approaches to the study of Mormonism as a religion. The first, which involves examination and careful consideration of the claims of Mormonism to be the truth, is a predominantly religious undertaking. Investigators search for answers to the fundamental question of whether The Church of Jesus Christ of Latter-day Saints (or the Reorganized Church of Jesus Christ of Latter Day Saints, as the case may be) is, or is not, the only true Christian church and whether, in fact, the Saints have the only legitimate priesthoods of Jesus Christ (Melchizedek and Aaronic).

The other approach to the study of the Latter-day Saints has as its goal not truth so much as understanding. Scholars—both in and outside the academy—study LDS theology, doctrine, ritual, ecclesiology, organizational structure, and the Mormon experience across time in an effort to determine what sort of movement Mormonism is and where and how it fits into the grand mosaic of world religions.

In addition to all the individuals who became Mormon converts, large numbers of journalists and Gentile clerics mounted explorations of the first sort during the nineteenth and the early part of the twentieth century. Many of the journalists decided that Mormonism was not a religion at all, while most clerics concluded that it was a Christian heresy. As for academic approaches to the topic before the middle of the twentieth century, only a small number of scholars made serious efforts to comprehend where the Latter-day Saints stood among the world's religions.

Some scholarly studies of Mormonism were completed before that time. In an appendix to an article on "Scholarly Studies of Mormonism," Leonard J. Arrington listed thirty-two doctoral dissertations on Mormon history and culture that were completed by 1950 (p. 30). Additionally, almost as soon as professional associations of scholars started to publish articles and proceedings in journal form, articles about the Saints started to appear in professional journals. But despite the serious and systematic study represented in these dissertations and professional articles, only a small number of authors pulled back from their material to attempt a classification of Mormonism within a broad religious context.

This situation changed after World War II when Mormon and non-Mormon scholars alike went beyond intensive studies of such discrete aspects of Mormonism as land settlement patterns, migration, or church–state relations. The results of this new work generally emerged as analyses of Mormonism from the secular perspectives of sociology, and social, cultural, political, and economic history. Then in the 1950s, scholarly taxonomists, working from the viewpoint of the history and sociology of religion, proposed schemes of classification other than the old one of whether or not Mormonism was a Christian heresy.

There were precedents for this study, too. The Scottish historian Robert Baird, who published *Religion in America* (1844), the first systematic description of American Christianity, divided the nation's churches into evangelical and liturgical camps, and included Mormonism in the latter. While essentially correct as far as it went, this obviously superficial analysis reflected the author's concentration on worship forms and ecclesiastical organization and his neglect of essential doctrines. Other students of American religion pictured the LDS movement as an illegitimate hybrid, combining elements of Puritanism, congregationalism, evangelicalism, and the antidenominational Christians (Campbellites) into a deviant variety of Protestantism. In one or another form, this characterization of Mormonism as irregular or aberrant was the standard interpretation that found its way into surveys well past the 1960s (see Handy).

After World War II, religious history—or church history as it was then known—started to change. An increasing number of its practitioners began to approach the study of American religion outside a denominational context and without privileging Protestantism. Disparaging portrayals of Mormonism started to give way among students of American religion. At the same time, with the rise to prominence of social science on the academic scene and a virtual explosion in the number of graduate students pursuing degrees in history, a substantial new contingent of scholars turned their attention to the Latter-day Saints. Rather than debunking Mormonism, they treated the Latter-day Saint movement as a case study from which to generalize about religion and culture—or politics or economics.

Although sharing a similar basic attitude toward Mormonism, the new generation of scholars did not arrive at similar conclusions. The disciplinary approaches and research agendas of the historians and social scientists who worked on Mormonism were so different that their results were not only dissimilar but contradictory. Instead of clarification, they brought confusion. When the distinguished historian Sydney Ahlstrom prepared the text for his *Religious History of the American People* (New Haven, Conn., 1972), he was unable to decide how Mormonism ought to be categorized. "One cannot even be sure," he said, "whether [Mormonism] is a sect, a mystery cult, a new religion, a church, a people, a nation, or an American subculture; indeed, at different times and places it is all of these" (p. 508).

By the time Ahlstrom wrote, a general lack of agreement about Mormonism had replaced the earlier non-Mormon consensus that it was a Christian aberration. In attempting a synthesis, he had to confront a wide array of interpretations and classifications of the movement. Available to him were the works of the scholars who, concentrating on the relationships between the Mormon prophet, his successors, and the Mormon people, tended to argue that the Latter-day Saints are, finally, just one more group over whom a charismatic leader exercised undue control. However carefully written, scholarly treatments in this vein presented conclusions that ultimately coincided with Anthony Hoekema's definition of Mormonism as a cult.

By contrast, the work of those who primarily concerned themselves with LDS beliefs came to agree with William A. Clebsch's classification. Clebsch did not accept the cultic designation. He held that belief in the Church of Jesus Christ as the only true church and in the "restored" LDS Aaronic and Melchizedek priesthoods as the only legitimate priesthoods turned Mormonism into one more "sect to end all sects." Timothy L. Smith described the movement as an idiosyncratic form of primitive Christianity, hence, sectarian.

Taking another tack, Mario De Pillis found in early LDS history a "Search for Authority," and from that reached a much broader conclusion. In 1956, sociologist Will Herberg, in the influential *Protestant-Catholic-Jew*, argued that these three forms of organized religion were the most satisfactory vehicles in America for establishing one's identity within the national culture. De Pillis added Mormonism to Herberg's triad, making it the "fourth major religion . . . generally accepted in American society."

Study of the movement's beginnings in New England and western New York, the celebrated

Mormon trek, and the establishment of an LDS kingdom in the Intermountain West confused the issue further, for geographical circumstance generated the idea that Mormonism is an "American religion" (Thomas J. Yates, "Count Tolstoi and 'The American Religion,'" *IE* 42 [Jan. 1939]:94). This oft-repeated phrase, said to be Count Leo Tolstoi's, was a main idea behind Thomas F. O'Dea's influential sociological study of the Mormons (1957). It was also woven into Klaus Hansen's study of *Mormonism and the American Experience* (1981), and reappeared in R. Laurence Moore's study of *Religious Outsiders and the Making of Americans* (1986).

In the same quarter-century that saw the appearance of enormous numbers of historical and sociological studies of the LDS movement, a new discipline, religious studies, made its way into the American academy. Combining insights from history and sociology as well as anthropology, psychology, theology, and studies of comparative religion, religious studies methodology enabled scholars to study religions without asking about their truthfulness. Significantly, although religionists (the designation increasingly given to scholars in religious studies) address the question of how religion provides an avenue for accomplishing cultural tasks, they do not universally define religion as a product of culture. Central also to this method of studying religion is the distinction between the sacred and the profane (the ordinary, that which is not sacred) and separation of religion into its various dimensions: the mythological, doctrinal, ritual/liturgical, ethical, social/institutional, and experiential.

This new discipline provided students of Mormonism with an additional set of conceptual tools. Approaching Mormonism from this perspective made it possible to see, for instance, that R. Laurence Moore may be correct in his argument that the Mormons were religious outsiders who have moved a long way toward acceptance as insiders in America without concluding that Mormonism is an American religion. Geographical and social locations no more made Mormonism an American religion than the location of Christianity's beginnings in Palestine, Greece, and Rome made Christianity a Palestinian or Graeco-Roman religion.

American culture surely influenced Mormonism. But Fawn McKay Brodie, a biographer of the Prophet Joseph Smith who argued this way, said Mormonism was not simply an American cult or some sort of new subdivision of Christianity. Brodie understood Mormonism to be related to Christianity in much the same way that Christianity is related to Judaism. That insight foreshadowed a religious studies approach. She also saw Mormonism as a product of the creative genius of Joseph Smith, which, in sociological terms, placed Mormonism in the cultic category, one of the older ways of understanding the religion.

A religious studies approach permits an analysis that treats Mormonism as more than the sum of its parts. From this comprehensive viewpoint, any characterization of the movement as the creation of one or two powerful, charismatic figures is seen, at the very least, to be incomplete. The numerous definitions that label the movement as "a sect, a mystery cult, a new religion, a church, a people, a nation, or an American subculture" are also partial. All in all, Mormonism, from the religious studies perspective, is best understood as a new religious tradition. The movement rests on a foundational tripod composed of a prophetic figure, scripture, and experience—Joseph Smith, the Book of Mormon, and the corporate life of the early Saints. By grasping the interaction of these three, one can firmly place Mormonism in the overall sweep of religious history.

Although Smith's role as prophet was established among his first followers before the publication of the Book of Mormon, this mysterious work, claiming to be of ancient origin, supported his prophetic position. It contains statements showing that Joseph Smith's movement would fulfill Old Testament prophecy, making modern Mormonism an extension of ancient Israel. Following on this association, Joseph Smith's own revelations proclaimed the opening of a new dispensation of the fulness of times and the restoration of both the true Church of Jesus Christ and the Aaronic and Melchizedek priesthoods. Together the Book of Mormon and Smith's revelations provided a means for his followers to connect with Christianity's apostolic era and with ancient Israel, while at the same time stirring within them such intense millennial expectations that they came to believe that they were living on the edge of time, in the "winding-up scene."

The revelation for the Saints to gather heightened the power of Smith's message and his place at the head of the movement. It brought his followers together in a place where the Saints could hear the prophet's message with their own ears, see the construction of the House of the Lord, with their own eyes, and participate in the daily activities of a community entirely composed of Saints of the latter days. Whether in New York, Ohio, Missouri, or Illinois, the Mormons' association with their "living prophet" and the routine interaction that occurred among the company of Saints lent such transcendental significance to the events of their everyday lives that Smith and his adherents were collectively ushered into "sacred time." This experience, this conscious living-out of sacred history, was as crucial to the creation of this new tradition as was the initial appearance of the Book of Mormon and the revelations of the Prophet Joseph.

The importance of the revelations should not be underestimated. It was by means of revelation that the Saints came to perceive of their ecclesiastical institution as the Church of Jesus Christ, formed again in a new age, and their community as a communion of Christian Saints called together in a new dispensation. Revelation likewise added to the idea of reformation the much more radical conception of the "restoration of all things." Not only church, priesthood, and primitive *ecclesia* were restored, but also Hebrew patriarchy, a political kingdom developed on a Solomonic model, and "ancient ordinances" (the endowment, baptism for the dead, and marriage for time and eternity). These truly set the Saints apart. The incorporation of these ideas into the movement, first in the political organization of the kingdom of God and afterward in additions to Mormonism's temple ritual and cultural life (through plural marriage) forever separated Mormonism from Catholic and Protestant forms of Christianity.

From that point forward, Mormonism was not merely related to Christianity as Christianity had been related to Judaism, that is, as reformation and consummation; now there was a direct relationship with the Hebrew tradition. Gradually the Christian view of being connected to Israel through adoption, being grafted in, was replaced with a new understanding of the relationship between the Saints and Israel. Acceptance of the LDS gospel came to be regarded as evidence that the blood of Abraham flowed through Mormon veins—evidence that was confirmed through the ritual of the patriarchal blessing in which Saints are informed of their membership of adoption into the family of one of Jacob's sons. Although this belief is, ultimately, a rhetorical construction of blood descent, it gave the Saints an identity as a "chosen

people" that had a powerful impact on their understanding of themselves.

Magnifying as it did the difference between the members of their re-formed Church of Jesus Christ and other Christians, the idea of the restoration of all things was not universally welcomed within the Mormon fellowship. Initially attracted to Mormonism by the emphasis on primitive Christianity, many of Smith's earliest followers felt ambivalent about innovations connecting the movement to ancient times. In Missouri and Illinois there was resistance by some to the creation of a Mormon political kingdom that involved physical as well as psychic separation from non-Mormons.

Growing out of this ambivalence, a rupture divided the movement into two branches after the murder of Joseph Smith in 1844. While the history of The Church of Jesus Christ of Latter-day Saints, headquartered in Salt Lake City, Utah, can be fully comprehended only through the lens of LDS belief in the "restoration of all things," the same is not true of the REORGANIZED CHURCH OF JESUS CHRIST OF LATTER DAY SAINTS, headquartered in Independence, Missouri. Organized again (reorganized) in 1860 when Joseph Smith III, the Mormon prophet's eldest son, accepted the position of president and prophet to the church, this division of Smith's followers rejected the political kingdom of God and many, if not all, the innovations that the first Mormon prophet had introduced under the rubric of the "restoration of all things." Emphasizing the reformation character of the movement, they placed themselves and their church in a much closer relationship to traditional forms of Christianity than did the Saints who followed Brigham Young to the Intermountain West.

In the history of The Church of Jesus Christ of Latter-day Saints and in the distinctive temple beliefs and practices that separate it from the Saints who did not go west, Mormonism is found as a new religious tradition in its purest, most undiluted form. The Utah Latter-day Saints experienced a trek through "the wilderness" and an extended period of residence sequestered in a "land of promise" whose internal political organization and social system were dominated by restoration doctrines. Seclusion within their mountain fastness and a sense of being under siege accelerated the systematizing of their distinctive doctrines as well as the development of a temple-centered culture. These heightened and preserved the Saints' sense of separation and chosenness long after political, social, and economic isolation came to an end.

An advantage of considering Mormonism as a new tradition rather than a church, denomination, sect, or cult is that it clarifies the divisions within the movement. The break following the prophet's death between the Saints who went to the Intermountain West and those who remained in the Midwest cannot really be understood as an ordinary sectarian schism any more than the separation of Christianity into Eastern Orthodoxy and Roman Catholicism or the division of Islam into Sunni and Shi'ite Muslims were sectarian schisms. Within the Mormon tradition, then, there are two divisions, two churches. Because schisms have occurred in both of these divisions, Mormon sects also exist. Mormon fundamentalists, Saints who maintain the practice of plural marriage, are the most visible of such sectarian groups.

Latter-day Saints of all varieties are as certain of their identity as Christians as any Roman Catholic or Evangelical Protestant. But they live in a dispensation all their own. Their particular history, their singular doctrines and ritual practices, and their perception of themselves as a peculiar people do not simply set them apart from other Christians as one more subdivision of that tradition. Mormonism will remain separate and be best understood as a new religious tradition as long as the Saints maintain their belief that their church organization is the original Church of Jesus Christ, restored to them alone in 1830, *and* as long as they maintain the complementary position that in Mormonism is found the restoration of all things.

BIBLIOGRAPHY

Arrington, Leonard J. "Scholarly Studies of Mormonism." *Dialogue* 1 (Spring 1966):15–32.

Clebsch, William A. "Each Sect the Sect to End All Sects." *Dialogue* 1 (Summer 1966):84–89.

De Pillis, Mario. "The Development of Mormon Communitarianism, 1826–1846." Ph.D. diss., Yale University, 1961.

Handy, Robert T. *A History of the Churches in the United States and Canada*, pp. 224–27. New York, 1976.

Hoekema, Anthony A. *Four Major Cults*. Grand Rapids, Mich., 1963. The section on Mormonism was "extensively updated" and published separately by the same press in 1974.

Shipps, Jan. *Mormonism: The Story of a New Religious Tradition*. Urbana, Ill., 1985.

Smith, Timothy L. "The Book of Mormon in a Biblical Culture." *Journal of Mormon History* 7 (1980):3–21.

JAN SHIPPS

MORMONISM, MORMONS

"Mormonism" is an unofficial but common term for The Church of Jesus Christ of Latter-day Saints and the doctrinal, institutional, cultural, and other elements forming its distinctive worldview and independent Christian tradition. "Mormons" is the equivalent term for members of the Church, with "Mormon" being both the singular noun and the adjective.

Over the years these terms and other, less common variants have been widely used (such as "Mormonite" in early decades of the Church), but members prefer the official name revealed by the Savior to the Prophet Joseph SMITH—The Church of Jesus Christ of Latter-day Saints—in order to emphasize the central role of Jesus Christ in their doctrine and worship (D&C 115:3–4). The shortened name that most contemporary members use instead of "Mormonism" is "LDS Church," with "LDS" used in place of "Mormon" and "Latter-day Saints" or "Saints" used instead of "Mormons."

The term "Mormon" derives from the Book of Mormon, published in 1830 and recently subtitled *Another Testament of Jesus Christ*. This book is accepted by the Church as scripture along with the Bible (*see* BIBLE: LDS BELIEF IN THE BIBLE).

Mormonism refers to the divinely inspired doctrine taught by Joseph SMITH and the succeeding leaders of the Church. It views human life as a stage in the eternal progression of intelligent beings who, as God's spirit children, must choose, in thought and deed, whether to accept or reject Christ's gospel, teachings, and covenants (*see* PLAN OF SALVATION). Latter-day Saints see the Church's teachings as true Christianity, restored to earth in its original purity by Christ himself, and thus they frequently refer to the Church, its doctrines, and its priesthood as "restored" (*see* RESTORATION). Basic Church doctrines include belief in a personal God vitally concerned with his children, the divinity of the Savior Jesus Christ and his infinite atonement, the universal need for repentance and baptism by proper authority, continuing revelation through living prophets, the brotherhood and sisterhood of all human beings, the eternal sanctity of marriage and family, and the responsibility to be self-reliant and to help others. Many of the basic beliefs of the LDS Church are succinctly summarized in the thirteen ARTICLES OF FAITH, which serve, among other things, as an outline of the basic doctrines for members of the Church.

A salient characteristic of Church practice is the delegation of specific ecclesiastical responsibilities to every active member of the Church (*see* LAY PARTICIPATION AND LEADERSHIP). This results in a high level of voluntary member activity, commitment, and sense of community. Only men belong to the priesthood; but both women and men share priesthood blessings, and both hold significant leadership and teaching positions, perform missionary and temple work, and participate prominently in most Church meetings. Other notable Church practices include the encouragement of education, thrift, community service, missionary work, genealogical record keeping, and temple worship.

While the Church is clearly conservative on many issues, its central reliance on continuing revelation provides a divinely guided flexibility, especially in areas of practice. Through the living Prophet, changes are effected as revelation is sought and received. Two main practices discontinued over the years are polygamy, officially ended in 1890 (*see* PLURAL MARRIAGE; MANIFESTO OF 1890), and gathering to a central geographical location, largely ended in the 1920s (Allen and Leonard, p. 496–97; *see* IMMIGRATION AND EMIGRATION). At the same time, other practices have been introduced: TITHING, revealed in the 1830s, has been normative since the 1890s; and the complete avoidance of drugs such as tobacco, alcohol, tea, and coffee has been formally required of all active members since the 1920s, nearly a century after first having been revealed (*see* WORD OF WISDOM). FAMILY HOME EVENINGS, introduced in 1915, were widely instituted as a weekly practice in the mid 1960s. Extension of priesthood authority to all worthy male members, regardless of race, was granted in 1978 (*see* DOCTRINE AND COVENANTS: OFFICIAL DECLARATION—2). Latter-day Saints expect that further changes will be made by revelation as the needs of the Church unfold.

Mormonism is not a political ideology. The Church's policy regarding governments allows it to thrive in a wide variety of political contexts around the world. It supports separation of CHURCH AND STATE, respect for duly established law and government, and members' active participation in civic and charitable affairs (D&C 134; *see* POLITICS: POLITICAL TEACHINGS). War is generally condemned, but military service is not forbidden. Well before the 1950s, the Church frequently took positions on political issues, especially some affecting Utah. Since that time, Church leaders have increasingly urged members to decide such questions for themselves and have implemented a policy of Church neutrality toward government, except in instances where political developments clearly impinge on important moral issues or severely restrict members' freedom to practice their religion.

In common speech, the terms "Mormonism" and "Mormon" are not limited to the official teachings or practices of the Church, but often also refer to particular lifestyles, cultural viewpoints, historical events, philosophical outlooks, and artifacts that are characteristic of the broader Latter-day Saint tradition or culture. In most formal settings, however, the Church prefers to avoid the use of these substitute terms wherever possible, to direct attention to the true name of the Church.

BIBLIOGRAPHY

Allen, James B., and Glen M. Leonard. *The Story of the Latter-day Saints.* Salt Lake City, 1976.

Arrington, Leonard J., and Davis Bitton. *The Mormon Experience.* New York, 1979.

The Church of Jesus Christ of Latter-day Saints. *Gospel Principles.* Salt Lake City, 1981.

Richards, LeGrand. *A Marvelous Work and a Wonder.* Salt Lake City, 1988.

Talmage, James E. *AF.* Salt Lake City, 1988.

DONALD K. JARVIS

MORMONISM AND WORLD RELIGIONS

See: World Religions and Mormonism

MORMON PIONEER TRAIL

The approximately 1,300-mile-long trail from NAUVOO, Illinois, to Salt Lake City, Utah, was certified by the National Trails Act of 1986 as a National Historic Trail—officially The Mormon Pioneer National Historic Trail. Contrary to popular belief, however, the famous trail was not a Mormon creation. The Latter-day Saints did very little trail-blazing. They followed territorial roads and Indian trails across Iowa; various segments of the Oregon Trail from the Missouri River to Fort

Bridger in present western Wyoming; and the year-old trail of the ill-fated California-bound Reed–Donner party from Fort Bridger into the valley of the Great Salt Lake.

Although the trail was not blazed by the Latter-day Saints, and parts of it have at times been known as the Council Bluffs Road, the Omaha Road, the Great Platte River Road, or even the North Branch of the Oregon Trail, the entire route is today almost universally known as "The Mormon Trail" because the Latter-day Saints used it for twenty-three years in such large numbers (at least seventy thousand; no one knows just how many), because of the high drama of their "Exodus," and because they developed separate strands or *trails* and wove them into their great *road* (*see* IMMIGRATION-EMIGRATION).

The trail divides into two unequal sections:

1. The approximately 265-mile-long section from Nauvoo on the Mississippi across Iowa to present-day Council Bluffs on the Missouri. This part of the trail was used relatively little: mainly by Latter-day Saints fleeing Illinois in 1846, by some immigrants

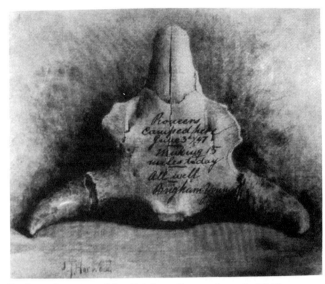

Trail marker, signed by Brigham Young, June 3, 1847. Artist: J. P. Harwood. Courtesy Utah State Historical Society.

"jumping off" from Keokuk, Iowa, in 1853, and in 1856–1857 by seven HANDCART COMPANIES from Iowa City who entered the Mormon Trail at present-day Lewis, Cass County, Iowa. Thousands of other Latter-day Saints crossed Iowa on variants of the 1846 route or on other trails, but all these intersected the trail of 1846 somewhere in western Iowa.

2. The approximately 1,032-mile-long trans-Missouri River segment from present North Omaha (one-time WINTER QUARTERS) and Florence, Nebraska, across Nebraska and Wyoming, into Utah. This part of the trail was used extensively from 1847 until completion of the transcontinental railroad in 1869. As in Iowa, variants evolved, but all LDS immigrants used all or parts of this trans-Missouri trail.

While the 1846–1847 trek from Nauvoo to Salt Lake City is by far the best-known part of the twenty-three-year-long Mormon overland migration, it is only part of the story. Between 1848 and 1868, LDS immigrants traveling west from the Missouri River developed or utilized at least a dozen other points of departure and followed many other trails, such as the Oxbow Trail (1849–1864), the Mormon Grove Trail (1855–1856), and the Nebraska City Cutoff (1864–1866). In one way or another, however, all these trails eventually intersected *the* Mormon Trail. Furthermore, with the

These ruts in stone on the Mormon Trail and Oregon-California Trail are still visible today near Guernsey, Wyoming. Courtesy LaMar C. Berrett.

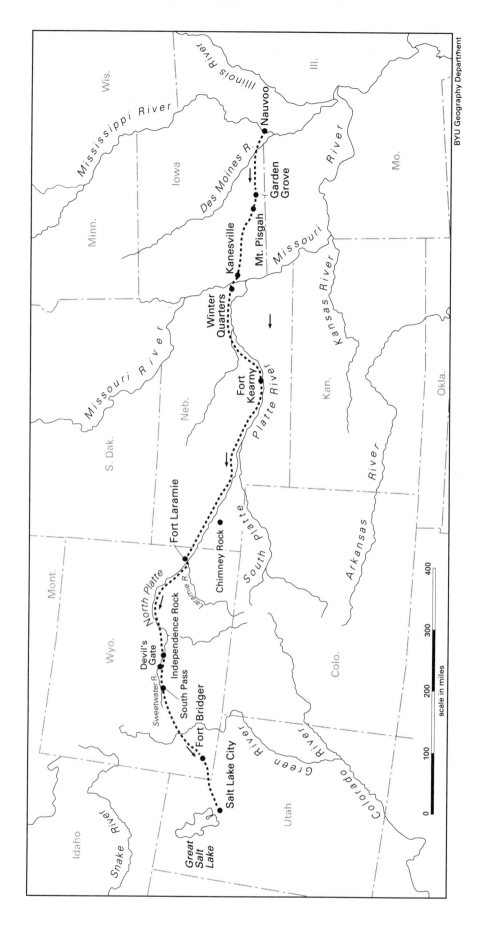

944

Union Pacific Railroad moving west from Omaha beginning in 1865, during 1867–1868 Latter-day Saints took trains from Omaha to four different railheads (North Platte, Nebraska; Julesburg, Colorado; and Laramie and Benton, Wyoming), from which they eventually picked up the Mormon Trail.

Across the monotonous, undifferentiated, rolling central lowlands of Iowa, the Mormon Trail of 1846 generally followed primitive territorial roads as far as Bloomfield, Davis County, and then vague Pottawattamie Indian and trading trails along ridges from one water source to another, always within fifty miles of the present Missouri state line. Today this part of the Mormon Trail is difficult to follow, not because of the terrain but because modern roads seldom parallel it and because the plow has destroyed most vestiges of it.

West of the Missouri River the Saints passed along river valleys, across grasslands, plains, steppes, deserts, and mountains, and through western forests. Topographically, the trail led across the central lowlands and high plains of eastern and central Nebraska, then the upland trough of western Nebraska and eastern Wyoming, through the Wyoming basin and the middle Rocky

Fort Bridger in western Wyoming was an important point on the Mormon Trail. Artist: W. H. Jackson. Courtesy Nelson Wadsworth.

Mountains, and into the desert valleys of the Great Basin.

From the Missouri River, Mormon companies followed the broad, flat valleys of the Loupe and Platte rivers for some six hundred miles to present-day Casper, Wyoming, then the Sweetwater River for about ninety-three miles to South Pass, thence

Pioneer wagon train at the mouth of Echo Canyon, Utah, 1867. Courtesy Utah State University.

←——The Mormon Trail. Nauvoo, Illinois, to Salt Lake City, Utah.

This 1897 reenactment of a Mormon wagon train coming through Echo Canyon celebrates the fiftieth anniversary of the arrival of the first pioneer company in the Salt Lake Valley on July 24, 1847. Photographer: Charles W. Carter. Courtesy Nelson Wadsworth.

along branches of the Sandy River and Blacks Fork to Fort Bridger, finally zigzagging through a series of canyons into the valley of the Great Salt Lake.

In Nebraska, as in Iowa, there is little left today of the Mormon Trail, but modern roads do parallel the old trail closely. In Wyoming, however, with proper maps much of this old trail can still be found because the harsh terrain has held the ruts better and agriculture has obliterated little. In Utah, although modern roads follow the trail closely, very few of the original ruts remain.

BIBLIOGRAPHY

Kimball, Stanley B. *Historic Sites and Markers Along the Mormon and Other Great Western Trails.* Urbana, Ill., 1988.

Kimball, Stanley B., and Hal Knight. *111 Days to Zion.* Salt Lake City, 1978.

Stegner, Wallace. *The Gathering of Zion: The Story of the Mormon Trail.* New York, 1971.

STANLEY B. KIMBALL

MORMONS, IMAGE OF

[*This entry consists of three articles giving a survey of the Mormon image as it has been and is reflected in* The Visual Arts, *in* Film, *and in* Fiction *from the earliest days of the Church to the present.*]

THE VISUAL ARTS

The early history of the Church, especially the uniqueness of its beliefs and practices, influenced the creation of an LDS, or Mormon, image in art. Caricature and cartoon were particularly well suited to the mass market, and Latter-day Saints were a favorite subject. Although some early works conveyed the complexities of the LDS experience, most people developed their image of members of the Church from portrayals that were selective and caricatured. While stereotypical images linger, current depictions of Latter-day Saints, frequently employing works by LDS artists, more accurately reflect the diversity and richness of Mormon life.

By 1860, media depictions had firmly established national stereotypes of Mormonism. During the next decades, negative, stereotyped images of Latter-day Saints appeared regularly in newspapers and magazines such as *Harper's Weekly, Van-*

INCEPTION OF MORMONISM—JOSEPH SMITH'S FIRST VISION.

A non-LDS artist's early graphic image of Mormonism. This etching of Joseph Smith's First Vision appeared in T.B.H. Stenhouse, *The Rocky Mountain Saints* (1873), opposite p. 1. Courtesy Rare Books and Manuscripts, Brigham Young University.

ity Fair, Cosmopolitan, and *Collier's Weekly.* Although some images were humorous, the effect was essentially harmful. Bunker and Bitton explain: "The simple fact is that most of the illustrations treating the Mormons were not low-key or objective; they were cartoons and caricatures with an obvious point of view. And that point of view was, with almost monotonous regularity, negative" (Bunker and Bitton, p. 148).

This negative image developed when the social climate in the United States allowed open hostility toward unpopular religious and ethnic groups. Major themes about Latter-day Saints focused on the public disapproval of the practice of polygamy, the Utah War of 1857–1858, and clashes between U.S. officials and LDS leaders. Although artists created some fresh interpretations as new events transpired, they were usually only variations on established themes.

However, a few artists ignored the stereotypical image of the Latter-day Saints and produced work that conveyed the complexity of the religion and its people. Arthur Boyd Houghton, an artist for the *Graphic,* a British weekly pictorial journal, visited Salt Lake City in 1870 and created a series of drawings featuring the Saints. His scenes of LDS life are rendered with respect and dignity, and reveal his compassion for humble people. Two paintings attributed to Albert Bierstadt and one by Maynard Dixon show thriving LDS settlements, the result of Mormon cultivation of the desert. Enoch Wood Perry, Jr., painted excellent likenesses of Brigham Young and each member of the Quorum of the Twelve Apostles. Photographer William Henry Jackson's pictures and sketches of the West include images of Salt Lake City, Mormon wagon trains, and farm life.

The Latter-day Saints have never lacked for artists and illustrators of their own to tell their story. While graphic artists in the East were generally creating negative, stereotyped images, LDS artists in the West were producing a rich and authentic pictorial record of their experience. The early Mormon experience, including the migration west and pioneer life in Utah, was chronicled by British artist Frederick Piercy and Danish artist C. C. A. Christensen, both converts to the Church (*see* ARTISTS).

In recent years, interest in the portrayal of Mormons as Mormons has diminished in non-LDS media and among non-LDS artists. At the same time, the number of LDS artists, the diversity of their styles, and their interest in conveying LDS themes have all increased. Like the early artists who saw beyond the stereotypical images of their day, these modern artists have succeeded in conveying, at least in some measure, the complexities and richness of the LDS experience, made even more diverse as the Church has grown to include a worldwide membership.

[*See also* Art.]

BIBLIOGRAPHY

Bunker, Gary L., and D. Bitton. *The Mormon Graphic Image, 1834–1914: Cartoons, Caricatures, and Illustrations.* Salt Lake City, 1983.

Gerdts, William H. "Utah." In *Art Across America: Two Centuries of Regional Painting,* Vol. 3, pp. 128–45. New York, 1990.

VIRGIE D. DAY

FILM

From the beginning of the twentieth century until the mid-1930s, the film portrayals of Latter-day Saints were generally negative. First publicly exhibited in the 1890s, commercial motion pictures continued the sensational characterizations depicted in the novels of the period. One of the earliest treatments was Thomas Edison's nickelodeon film *A Trip to Salt Lake City* (1905). More humorous than sinister, the film satirized the problems of a polygamous Mormon husband trying to give his many children a drink of water on a Pullman car bound for the city of the Saints.

More common were films such as *A Mormon Maid* (Lasky-Paramount, 1917), which portrayed the DANITES, stereotyped in earlier fiction as a posse of Missouri Mormon firebrands, as nightriding henchmen costumed like the Ku Klux Klan in D. W. Griffith's *The Birth of A Nation* (1915). Inspired by anti-Mormon novelist Winifred Graham's *The Love Story of a Mormon* (London, 1911), *Trapped by the Mormons* (Pyramid, 1922) brought to the screen a portrayal of a marauding LDS missionary in England preying vampirelike on unwary women. This film capitalized on the unfounded fear that LDS missionaries exploited women left widowed by World War I. A film version of Zane Grey's *Riders of the Purple Sage* (Fox) was released in 1918 and rereleased in 1921 despite protests that its negative depictions of Latter-day Saints and Utah would hinder the state's busi-

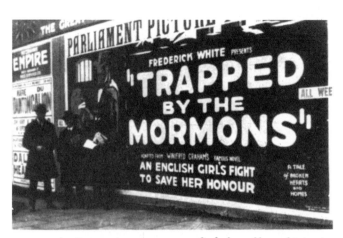

An innocent young woman finds herself caught in the clutches of a Mormon missionary on a billboard advertising the film *Trapped by the Mormons* (England, c. 1922), typical of the sensational image that was given of Mormons in films during the 1920s.

ness development. A sympathetic treatment of the Church was the feature-length historical drama *One Hundred Years of Mormonism* (Utah Moving Pictures Co., 1913).

From 1918 to 1945, approximately thirty anti-Mormon films were released worldwide. In the 1930s, however, the motion picture industry drafted a production code, which, among other things, forbade negative portrayals of religious organizations and their beliefs. In 1938, Twentieth Century Fox informed President Heber J. GRANT that it planned to produce a motion picture based on Vardis Fisher's historical novel *Children of God*. While he privately expressed fears of another negative screen image, partly because Fisher's novel was not fully understanding of the Church and its early leaders, President Grant nevertheless cooperated fully with the studio. The resulting film, *Brigham Young*, released in 1940, although not totally pleasing to Church leaders, was in most respects very positive and reversed almost four decades of negative stereotypes. Met with critical praise, it vividly portrayed the persecutions of Latter-day Saints in Nauvoo during the 1840s, the murder of Joseph SMITH, the trek west to the Great Basin, and the "miracle of the gulls" in 1848. The film showed Latter-day Saints not as the stereotyped wife stealers of earlier films but as industrious pioneers. In a fictional courtroom scene in which Brigham YOUNG defends Joseph Smith, the dialogue depicts the LDS cause as inextricably linked with that of America's founders seeking reli-

gious freedom. Produced at a time when Americans watched with concern the rising persecution of Jews in Hitler's Germany, the film defended the right of Latter-day Saints, or any other minority, to exist in a pluralist nation.

Since the 1940 release of *Brigham Young*, portrayals of Mormon history and culture in Hollywood films and television generally have been limited to humorous episodes dealing with polygamy as in *Wagon Master* (RKO, 1950), *Paint Your Wagon* (Paramount, 1969), *They Call Me Trinity* (West Film, 1971) and *Trinity Is Still My Name* (West Film, 1972), and *The Duchess and the Dirtwater Fox* (Fox, 1976). The only commercial feature-length treatment of Mormons between 1940 and 1990 was *Brigham* (Sunset Films, 1977), a low-budget film covering approximately the same period as *Brigham Young* but lacking the dramatic value of the earlier film.

BIBLIOGRAPHY

D'Arc, James V. "Darryl F. Zanuck's *Brigham Young*: A Film in Context." *BYU Studies* 29 (Winter 1989):5–33.

Nelson, Richard Alan. "A History of Latter-day Saint Screen Portrayals in the Anti-Mormon Film Era, 1905–1936." Master's thesis, Brigham Young University, 1975.

———. "From Antagonism to Acceptance: Mormons and the Silver Screen." *Dialogue* 10 (Spring 1977):58–69.

JAMES V. D'ARC

FICTION

For the first hundred years of LDS history, interest in Latter-day Saints as a subject for popular fiction was remarkably high. Taking its stereotypes from the pseudo-histories and travel narratives that circulated widely, fiction about Mormons emphasized melodramatic characters and fantastic plots full of violence and mystery. Similar patterns continued into the mid-twentieth century, but since then, Latter-day Saints have appeared less frequently and usually only casually in non-Mormon fiction.

Themes of violence and melodrama appeared as early as the 1840s. Typically a beautiful young heroine was said to have escaped or to have been rescued by a heroic "Gentile" and carried from the Mormons and the drunken and lecherous clutches of a polygamous elder or bishop. Frequently the fleeing protagonists were pursued across the continent, sometimes even around the world, by secretive "Danites" or "avenging angels." In these pieces LDS leaders were characterized as scheming, rough, and tyrannical, and the culture as crude and repressive at best, violent and destructive at worst.

By the 1850s, fiction about the Latter-day Saints was almost a genre in itself. Often written by women (especially the wives of ministers) and following the pattern of the more famous *Uncle Tom's Cabin*, these novels and short stories exploited popular ideas, fears, and societal concerns, as in Orvilla S. Belisle's *The Prophets; or, Mormonism Unveiled* (1855) and Metta Victoria Fuller, *Mormon Wives* (1856; published again in 1860 as *Lives of Female Mormons* and republished many times in Europe and translated into several languages).

Each succeeding decade added to the tide of new authors and titles. In the 1880s, for example, more than a score of book-length best sellers came from British and American presses. Even some of the best known writers of the nineteenth century found the topic of Mormonism appealing: Robert Louis Stevenson (*The Dynamiter*, 1885) and Arthur Conan Doyle (*A Study in Scarlet*, 1887) held Mormons up as objects of fear, and Charles Farrer Browne ("Artemus Ward Among the Mormons," 1866) and Mark Twain (*Roughing It*, 1872) treated them as objects of satire and laughter.

In the early twentieth century the same patterns generally continued. Zane Grey (*The Heritage of the Desert*, 1910, and *Riders of the Purple Sage*, 1912) used Latter-day Saints as central figures, and Jack London wrote of the MOUNTAIN MEADOWS MASSACRE in his novel *The Star Rover* (1915). How firmly entrenched the pattern remained even beyond mid-century is illustrated by the images in Irving Wallace's *The Twenty-seventh Wife* (1961) and J. C. Furnas's *The Devil's Rainbow* (1962), which paint Joseph Smith in terms of popular psychosis and caricature Mormon leaders in general. Even the works of more weighty novelists—Vardis Fisher's *Children of God* (1939), for example—follow the old patterns, with a sympathetic protagonist outside the Church struggling against unfavorable, repressive antagonists from within.

Latter-day Saints are not now as popular a subject as they once were for non-Mormon authors, and writers' interest in modern Mormons as Mormons is vastly different from what it was a hundred years ago. While Latter-day Saints may appear occasionally or casually in fiction (e.g., Alan

Mark Twain, who influenced public opinion of Mormons through his humorous accounts in *Roughing It* (1872), sent this postcard, taken in 1870, to Brigham Young in 1872 after Twain's return to New York from the West. Twain presented his kind compliments to "Pres.t Young" and inscribed across the lower border, "Hands off of Brigham!"

Drury's *Advice and Consent*, 1959), they have become both too conventional and too well-known as individuals to be placed easily into alien molds (*see* STEREOTYPING OF MORMONS). While some differences between LDS and non-Mormon culture still persist, these differences now seem to be less exotic or threatening and hence less accessible for exploitation.

BIBLIOGRAPHY

Arrington, Leonard J., and Jon Haupt. "Intolerable Zion: The Image of Mormonism in Nineteenth-Century American Literature." *Western Humanities Review* 22 (Summer 1968):243–60.

——— "The Missouri and Illinois Mormons in Anti-Bellum [*sic*] Fiction." *Dialogue* 5 (Spring 1970):37–50.

Lambert, Neal E. "Saints, Sinners and Scribes: A Look at the Mormons in Fiction." *Utah Historical Quarterly* 36 (Winter 1968):63–76.

NEAL E. LAMBERT

MORMON TABERNACLE CHOIR

The Mormon Tabernacle Choir originated in mid-nineteenth-century Salt Lake City. It consists of 300-plus voices carefully selected from many volunteers. Its members give of their time and talents freely in practices and performances, serving without pay. Probably best known for its weekly radio and TV program of inspirational music and messages, "Music and the Spoken Word," the choir has performed and recorded extensively. It performs regularly in the TABERNACLE on TEMPLE SQUARE and provides music at all general conferences of the Church.

The origins of the Mormon Tabernacle Choir may be found in the desire and commitment of early converts to include appropriate music in both sacred and secular events (*see* MUSIC). The process of collecting hymns for instruction and worship began only four months after the Church was organized in 1830 (*see* HYMNS AND HYMNODY), and a choir was organized as early as 1836 for the dedication of the Kirtland Temple.

As the Latter-day Saints moved west, President Brigham Young included musicians among members even of the advance parties. Consequently, a small choir first sang for a conference in the Salt Lake Valley on August 22, 1847, twenty-nine days after the first party arrived.

Early choirs in the Old Tabernacle (built in 1851) and in the present Tabernacle (completed in 1867) were small and undisciplined by later standards. With the appointment of George Careless as conductor in 1869, the Tabernacle Choir began to flourish. Careless assembled the first large choir, a total of 304 singers, by adding smaller groups from other areas to the eighty-five singers in the Salt Lake Tabernacle Choir for a general conference performance on October 8, 1873. The vision of a choral ensemble to match the size of the Tabernacle was thus born. Early conductors who had prepared the way for Careless included John

Parry (1849–1854), Stephen Goddard (1854–1856), James Smithies (1856–1862), Charles John Thomas (1862–1865), and Robert Sands (1865–1869).

Careless was followed by Ebenezer Beesley (1880–1889), with Thomas C. Griggs, assistant; Evan Stephens (1889–1916), with Horace S. Ensign, assistant; Anthony C. Lund (1916–1935), with B. Cecil Gates and Albert J. Southwick, assistants; J. Spencer Cornwall (1935–1957), with Albert J. Southwick, D. Sterling Wheelwright, John R. Halliday, and Richard P. Condie, assistants; Richard P. Condie (1957–1974), with Jay E. Welch, assistant; Jay E. Welch (1974), with Jerold D. Ottley, assistant; and Jerold D. Ottley (from 1975 onward), with Donald H. Ripplinger, associate conductor.

During his tenure, Evan Stephens increased the size of the choir from about 125 to more than 300, making it the leading musical organization of Salt Lake City. To accommodate this larger size, the choir area of the Tabernacle was redesigned to create the present semicircular tiered seating. Stephens also took the choir to Chicago in 1893 on its first tour out of the state, beginning its now traditional role of emissary for the Church and the region.

Anthony C. Lund brought solid vocal training and a European choral sound to the choir. He excelled in music that required control and subtlety. J. Spencer Cornwall labored to raise the standards of the choir, to improve its sound as an ensemble, and to increase its repertoire from little more than one hundred pieces to almost a thousand. Under his direction the choir was active as a concert organization and released its first long-playing recording, in 1949. Richard P. Condie accelerated the recording activities of the choir and greatly increased its touring schedule. He produced what has been described as "the Tabernacle Choir sound," a large, romantic choral tone, heavy with feeling. Jerold D. Ottley has refined and shaped the traditional tone of the choir into a more flexible, precise, and energetic sound, one capable of expressing the subtleties of the finest choral literature.

Beginning with the installation of the first pipe organ in the Tabernacle in 1867 (*see* TABERNACLE ORGAN), organists have been appointed to assist the choir. Among the finest musicians in the Church, they have also performed recitals, played for church and civic meetings, and composed music (*see* MUSICIANS).

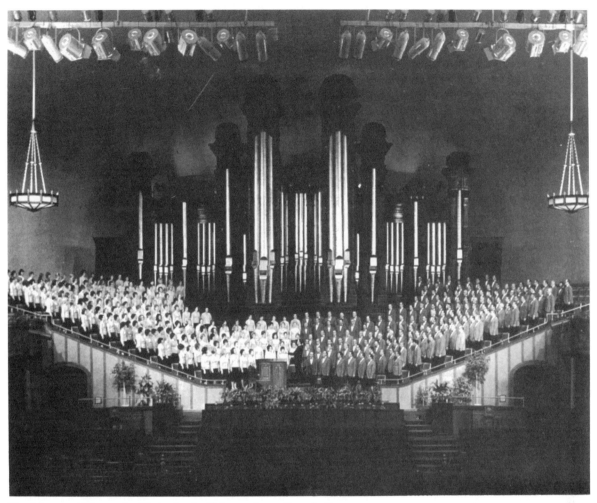

The Mormon Tabernacle Choir, in the Tabernacle on Temple Square.

The choir has profoundly affected music throughout the Church. Its consistently high artistic standard, frequent use of hymns and hymn arrangements, and exemplary service through music continue to inspire, instruct, and encourage Church musicians and the members they serve.

The choir rehearses for two hours every Thursday evening in preparation for its weekly broadcasts and uses Tuesday evenings as needed to prepare for recording sessions, concerts, tours, and general conferences of the Church. A number of choir members have university degrees in music, and many others are professionally trained. All are competent musicians. They include men and women from many walks of life.

The choir has released more than 130 recordings and several films and videotapes. Five of its recordings have achieved "gold record" status.

Most popular has been a 1959 release of "The Battle Hymn of the Republic" with the Philadelphia Orchestra, for which the choir received a Grammy Award.

Many notable personalities, soloists, and conductors have appeared with the choir, including Eugene Ormandy, Jerome Hines, Sherrill Milnes, Marilyn Horne, and Maurice Abravanel.

The choir's first major concert tour culminated in a performance at the World's Columbian Exposition in Chicago in 1893. Subsequent domestic tours have included performances in thirty-two states and the District of Columbia. Tours outside the United States have included Canada, Australia, and sixteen nations in Europe, Asia, South and Central America, the South Pacific, and Scandinavia. The choir has appeared at thirteen world's fairs and expositions, performed at the inauguration of four U.S. presidents, and sung for numerous worldwide telecasts and special events. In his remarks during a broadcast marking the completion of sixty years of weekly broadcasts, U.S. President George Bush called the choir "one of America's greatest treasures." It has become an American institution.

[*See also* Mormon Tabernacle Choir Broadcast ("The Spoken Word").]

BIBLIOGRAPHY

Calman, Charles Jeffrey, and William I. Kaufman. *The Mormon Tabernacle Choir.* New York, 1979.

Petersen, Gerald A. *More Than Music: The Mormon Tabernacle Choir.* Provo, Utah, 1979.

K. NEWELL DAYLEY

MORMON TABERNACLE CHOIR BROADCAST ("THE SPOKEN WORD")

The Mormon Tabernacle Choir Broadcast is the traditional Sunday broadcast of the MORMON TABERNACLE CHOIR. It originates in the SALT LAKE TABERNACLE and is open to the public. Begun in 1929, this weekly performance has become the longest continuously presented nationwide network broadcast in American radio history.

During World War II, the choir broadcasts were aired extensively over Armed Forces Radio Network in Europe and the Far East. Thereafter, local stations extended the broadcast into the Pacific Islands, Australia, and South America. The choir made its television debut in 1962, and the weekly broadcast was relayed to over eight hundred radio and television stations worldwide.

With the sacred hymns and choral works, backed by the TABERNACLE ORGAN, a brief message, the "Spoken Word," is given each Sunday. For forty-one years the voice and the message were those of Richard L. Evans, who during that period was called to be a seventy, then a member of the QUORUM OF THE TWELVE APOSTLES. His messages and delivery attempted to capsulize— usually in less than two minutes—universal principles related to character, human relationships, and the conduct of life. In the spirit of bridge-building, he aimed at both timely and timeless insights. His undergirding message was that the differences that separate people are not nearly as great as the factors that unite them. Selected Spoken Word mes-

Elder Richard L. Evans, the voice of "Music and the Spoken Word" for forty-one years, reads one of the brief messages that accompany each Sunday's broadcast by the Mormon Tabernacle Choir, the longest continuous broadcast in radio history (c. 1953).

sages ran in a weekly syndicated newspaper column circulated nationally and were later published in a series of books. Over two thousand such messages were given before his death in 1971.

Through thousands of broadcasts the opening hymn has remained "Gently Raise the Sacred Strain," and the closing one, "As the Dew from Heaven Distilling," and the signoff phrase is "May peace be with you, this day and always."

[*See also* Mormon Tabernacle Choir; Tabernacle Organ.]

PAUL H. EVANS

MORMON YOUTH SYMPHONY AND CHORUS

The Mormon Youth Symphony and Chorus (often abbreviated MYSC) is an officially sponsored musical organization of the Church. It was organized in 1969 with a primary commission to promote a "greater understanding between all peoples and cultures."

The group is composed of young musicians ages 18 to 33 who have participated in school or community orchestras and choruses. These musicians come from various communities in Utah and rehearse two hours each week.

The MYSC performs approximately thirty times each year, including formal concerts in the TABERNACLE, CONFERENCE appearances, FIRESIDES, tours, broadcasts, and recordings. The programming was changed to the "Boston Pops" format when Conductor Robert C. Bowden received the baton in 1974. Bowden conducts and also composes and arranges much of the music for the groups. Tours have covered the United States. During the Bicentennial celebration of the Constitution in Washington, D.C., the symphony and chorus performed in the Kennedy Center. Many nationally prominent visiting artists have performed with them.

The Mormon Youth Symphony and Chorus has won fourteen national awards for television specials, including two Emmys, two George Washington Awards from the Freedom Foundation, and the Angel Award from Religion in Media. It has also performed for several national and international groups; such presentations have included a television special for the Norwegian Broadcasting Company as well as specials for American Veterans of World War II, Korea, and Vietnam, and for the National League of American Pen Women. The MYSC has eighteen commercial recordings to its credit.

MERRILL BRADSHAW

MORONI, ANGEL

The angel Moroni is the heavenly messenger who first visited the Prophet Joseph SMITH in 1823. As a mortal named MORONI$_2$, he had completed the compilation and writing of the Book of Mormon. He ministered to Joseph Smith as a resurrected being, in keeping with his responsibility for the Book of Mormon, inasmuch as "the keys of the record of the stick of Ephraim" had been committed to him by the Lord (D&C 27:5). Pursuant to this responsibility he first appeared to Joseph Smith on the night of September 21–22, 1823 (JS—H 1:29–49; D&C 128:20), and thereafter counseled with him in several reappearances until the book was

The Angel Moroni, by Cyrus Dallin (1891; cast bronze, gilded; 12′), on the Salt Lake Temple in Salt Lake City. Moroni, a Book of Mormon prophet, returned to earth as a resurrected being and prepared Joseph Smith to receive and translate the gold plates. A symbol of the restoration of the gospel through divine messengers, such statues stand on the top of several LDS temples.

published in 1830. During that time, he instructed Joseph Smith, testified to the Three Witnesses of the Book of Mormon, and otherwise assisted in the work of restoring the gospel.

Because of the angel Moroni's role in restoring the everlasting gospel to be preached to all the world (cf. Rev. 14:6–7; D&C 133:31–39), the Church placed a statue depicting him as a herald of the Restoration atop the Salt Lake Temple, and later on the hill CUMORAH near Palmyra, New York, where anciently he had buried the Book of Mormon plates. Copies of the statue have also been placed atop several other LDS temples.

[*See also* Angel Moroni Statue; Moroni, Visitations of.]

BIBLIOGRAPHY

Peterson, H. Donl. *Moroni: Ancient Prophet, Modern Messenger.* Bountiful, Utah, 1983.

JOSEPH B. ROMNEY

MORONI, VISITATIONS OF

From 1823 to 1829, the angel Moroni$_2$ appeared at least twenty times to Joseph SMITH and others. Those appearances opened the way for the translation and publication of the Book of Mormon and laid the foundation of many of the Church's most characteristic teachings. As a resurrected messenger of God, Moroni told Joseph Smith about the Nephite record on gold plates and taught him concerning the gathering of ISRAEL, the forthcoming visit of ELIJAH, the imminence of the SECOND COMING of Jesus Christ, and the judgments to be poured out on the world prior to that event.

Of Moroni's first appearance on the night of September 21, 1823, Joseph Smith recorded:

> After I had retired to my bed for the night, I betook myself to prayer and supplication to Almighty God for forgiveness of all my sins and follies, and also for a manifestation to me, that I might know of my state and standing before him. . . . While I was thus in the act of calling upon God, I discovered a light appearing in my room, which continued to increase until the room was lighter than at noonday, when immediately a personage appeared at my bedside, standing in the air. . . . He had on a loose robe of most exquisite whiteness. It was a whiteness beyond anything earthly I had ever seen. . . . His hands were naked, and his arms also, a little above the wrist; so, also, were his feet naked, as were his legs, a little above the ankles. His head and neck were also bare. . . . His whole person was glorious beyond description, and his countenance truly like lightning [JS—H 1:29–32].

The angel introduced himself as Moroni, and as he told about the Nephite record, its contents, and the interpreters buried with it, Joseph saw in vision their location in the hill CUMORAH. Moroni warned Joseph not to show the plates or the interpreters to anyone except those whom the Lord designated. Moroni also quoted certain prophecies from the Bible, including Malachi 3–4, Isaiah 11, and Acts 3:22–23.

After the angel left, Joseph lay contemplating this experience, and Moroni returned a second time and repeated verbatim everything he had said in his first visit, adding more detail about the coming judgments, and then returned a third time to repeat his instructions and to warn Joseph that he must put all thoughts of worldly wealth aside and concentrate solely on the translation of the record and the establishment of the kingdom of God.

The Angel Moroni, by Millard F. Malin (1953, cast aluminum, gilded). This statue of Moroni, shown with sculptor, shows the angel carrying the gold plates from which the Book of Mormon was translated and, with trumpet in hand, proclaiming the gospel (see Rev. 14:6). It now stands on top of the Los Angeles Temple. Courtesy Special Collections Department, University of Utah Libraries.

As Moroni left the third time, Joseph said he heard the cock crow, the visitations having occupied the entire night. He arose and went into the fields with his father and his older brother Alvin, but felt tired and feeble. His father, noticing his son's condition, told him to return to the house. As Joseph was climbing over a fence, he fell to the ground unconscious.

The next thing he remembered seeing was Moroni standing over him, repeating his instructions of the night before, adding that Joseph should now tell his father about the visitations. Joseph did so, and his father, assured that the vision came from God, told Joseph to follow the angel's instructions (JS—H 1:46–50).

Joseph Smith then went to the hill and found the place shown him the night before in vision. He uncovered the plates and was about to remove them when Moroni appeared again, counseling Joseph that the time was not yet right. Instead, he instructed Joseph to return to this spot at the same time the following year and that he should continue to do so until the time had come for obtaining the plates (JS—H 1:51–54).

It is reported that during those years Joseph Smith also received visits from Mormon, Nephi, and other "angels of God unfolding the majesty and glory of the events that should transpire in the last days" (*HC* 4:537; cf. *JD* 17:374; Petersen, p. 131). Joseph shared with his family some of his experiences. His mother, Lucy Mack SMITH, recalled, "From this time forth, Joseph continued to receive instructions from the Lord, and we continued to get the children together every evening for the purpose of listening while he gave us a relation of the same. . . . He would describe the ancient inhabitants of this continent, their dress, mode of traveling, and the animals upon which they rode; their cities, their buildings, with every particular; their mode of warfare; and also their religious wor-

The Fourth Appearance of Moroni to Joseph Smith, by Gary E. Smith (1980s, oil on canvas, 36″ × 42″). After seeing the angel Moroni three times the night before in his bedroom, Joseph Smith was so exhausted that he fell while attempting to cross a fence. Again the angel appeared, commanding Joseph to tell his father about the vision. Courtesy Blaine T. Hudson.

ship. This he would do with as much ease, seemingly, as if he had spent his whole life among them" (pp. 82–83).

Moroni temporarily reclaimed the plates and the interpreters after Martin HARRIS had lost the first 116 manuscript pages of the translation. Later, when Joseph Smith moved from Harmony, Pennsylvania, to Fayette, New York, in June 1829, Moroni returned them to him there (Smith, pp. 149–50). Still later, Moroni showed the plates to the Three Witnesses (*HC* 1:54–55), took them after the translation had been completed (JS—H 1:60), and once more returned them briefly to Joseph to show to the Eight Witnesses (*see* BOOK OF MORMON WITNESSES).

In addition to Joseph and the Three Witnesses, Mary Whitmer also saw the angel and talked with him. Mary Whitmer said she was shown the gold plates when she conversed with Moroni (Peterson, pp. 114, 116). Other sources indicate that Moroni appeared also to W. W. Phelps, Heber C. KIMBALL, John TAYLOR, and Oliver Granger (Peterson, pp. 151–52).

BIBLIOGRAPHY

Backman, Milton V., Jr. *Eyewitness Accounts of the Restoration*, rev. ed. Salt Lake City, 1986.

Cheesman, Paul R. *The Keystone of Mormonism*, rev. ed. Provo, Utah, 1988.

Peterson, H. Donl. *Moroni: Ancient Prophet, Modern Messenger*. Bountiful, Utah, 1983.

Smith, Lucy Mack. *History of Joseph Smith*. Preston Nibley, ed. Salt Lake City, 1958.

ELDIN RICKS

MORONI₁

The first Moroni mentioned in the Book of Mormon (died c. 56 B.C.) was twenty-five years old when he was appointed captain of the NEPHITE armies (Alma 43:16). He upheld the liberty of the Nephites against threats posed by invading armies and by "kingmen" who tried to reestablish a monarchy by force after failing to win popular support. Moroni rallied his people for a seven-year struggle by raising "the title of liberty," a banner on which he wrote his reasons for defense, and by having his people covenant to defend their freedom and obey God's commandments (Alma 46:12–13, 20).

The Title of Liberty, maker unknown, Cuna Indian from Panama (mola–cloth appliqué, reverse embroidery and embroidery, 13″ × 15″). In rallying his people to defensive battle, Captain Moroni rent his coat and wrote upon it: "In memory of our God, our religion, and freedom, and our peace, our wives, and our children—and he fastened it upon the end of a pole . . . and he called it the title of liberty" (Alma 46:12–13). Church Museum of History and Art.

Despite many battles, Moroni did not become bloodthirsty. He operated within legal authority, and when he gained advantage over enemies, he offered them freedom if they would lay down their weapons and take an oath not to war again. He introduced new armor and fortifications and sought the direction of a prophet about what his armies should do (Alma 43:23; *see also* BOOK OF MORMON, HISTORY OF WARFARE IN). Five hundred years later, MORMON, the chief editor and compiler of the Book of Mormon, wrote, "If all men had been . . . like unto Moroni, behold, the very powers of hell would have been shaken forever" (Alma 48:17). Mormon even named his son, MORONI₂, after him.

BIBLIOGRAPHY

England, Eugene. "Moroni and His Captains." *Ensign* 7 (Sept. 1977):29–36.

MELVIN J. THORNE

MORONI₂

Moroni₂ is the last prophet and author of the last book in the Book of Mormon. His life spanned the latter part of the fourth century and the early fifth century. He led ten thousand troops in the last battle against the LAMANITES, serving under his father MORMON, who was commander in chief. Prior to the final war, Mormon had abridged the PLATES of Nephi that covered a thousand years of his people's history. He commanded Moroni to conclude the Nephite record by writing "the sad tale of the destruction of [their] people" (Morm. 8:3) and to preserve all the sacred writings (Moro. 9:24).

After Moroni wrote the required postscript to his father's record and prophesied its future discovery (Morm. 8–9), he added an abridgment of ancient Jaredite engravings, a record of a nation that had inhabited the Western Hemisphere for approximately 1,700 years prior to the Nephites' arrival, or perhaps overlapping their arrival (the Book of Ether). "According to the will of the Lord," he then added ten concluding chapters on ORDINANCES, principles, and church practices that he called the Book of Moroni.

Moroni spoke with prophetic assurance of conditions in the LAST DAYS because "Jesus Christ hath shown you unto me, and I know your doing" (Morm. 8:35). With fervor, he proclaimed Christ to be a God of miracles who is the same in all ages unless unbelief causes miracles to cease. He spoke with confidence of the divinity and teachings of Jesus Christ because "I have seen Jesus, and . . . he hath talked with me face to face, . . . even as a man telleth another in mine own language, concerning these things" (Ether 12:39).

Moroni also recorded prophecies of the BROTHER OF JARED, a Jaredite prophet, who helped lead his colony to the New World. These prophecies are "sealed" to come forth at a future day (Ether 4:1–7).

Moroni's last entry in the Book of Mormon was likely written about A.D. 421, thirty-six years after the final battle. He then finished writing the title page of the Book of Mormon and finally buried the Book of Mormon plates to preserve them for a future generation.

Fourteen hundred years later this same Moroni, then a resurrected being "sent from the presence of God," appeared to Joseph Smith, a seventeen-year-old youth, on the night of September 21, 1823, and told him of the sacred records deposited in a stone box in a nearby hill (the hill Cumorah) in what is now Ontario County, New York, within a few miles of Joseph's home in Manchester Township. Moroni appeared to Joseph more than twenty times during the next six years, tutoring him for his calling as a prophet and giving counsel and information concerning the acquisition, translation, and guardianship of the Book of Mormon plates (Joseph Smith—History 1:27–54).

Moroni is frequently identified with the Church because portrayals of him blowing a trumpet, handling the gold plates, or instructing Joseph Smith are commonly displayed—for instance on LDS temple spires, on covers of several printings of the Book of Mormon, and in paintings. A depiction of Moroni with a trumpet is the official emblem on grave markers of American Mormon servicemen.

Moroni is commonly portrayed with a trumpet because of an interpretation of a prophecy of John the Revelator wherein he saw an angel heralding the return of the everlasting gospel to the earth in the last days:

> And I saw another angel fly in the midst of heaven, having the everlasting gospel to preach unto them that dwell on the earth, and to every nation, and kindred, and tongue, and people, saying with a loud voice, Fear God, and give glory to him; for the hour of his judgment is come: and worship him that made heaven, and earth, and the sea, and the fountains of waters [Rev. 14:6–7].

[*See also* Angel Moroni Statue.]

BIBLIOGRAPHY

Peterson, H. Donl. *Moroni: Ancient Prophet, Modern Messenger.* Bountiful, Utah, 1983.

H. DONL PETERSON

MORRILL ACT OF 1862

See: Antipolygamy Legislation

MORTALITY

Mortality is not viewed as a curse by Latter-day Saints, but as an opportunity and an essential stage in progress toward obtaining EXALTATION. The ultimate purpose of the period of mortality from birth to death is to prepare to meet God with a resurrected body of glory (John 5:25–29; Alma 12:24). Death is a temporary separation of the body and the spirit, and, for those who have striven to live in accordance with God's commandments, is not something to be feared: "Fear not even unto death; for in this world your joy is not full, but in me your joy is full" (D&C 101:36; cf. Mosiah 16:7; D&C 42:46).

Although mortality is a temporary stage of life, it is essential for an individual's ETERNAL PROGRESSION for two reasons. First, it is necessary to receive a PHYSICAL BODY. God the Father, in his perfected state, has a body of flesh and bone, as does the Son (Luke 24:36–39; D&C 130:22). Mortal men and women, as the spirit offspring of God, also gain physical bodies in mortality that are indispensable to their progress, and will rise in the RESURRECTION and be perfected (Job 19:25–26; Luke 24:39). Without a physical body one cannot have a fulness of joy.

The Rod and the Veil, by Franz Johansen (1975, cast bronze and resin, 84″ × 99″). "The figure reaching through the veil suggests those in the spirit world concerned about our progress in mortality; the iron rod itself, reaching into both spheres, is the sure guide through mortality upon which all of us, like the slipping boy, must struggle to retain a firm grip" (artist's description). Church Museum of History and Art.

Second, this life is a period of development and probation, a time to overcome temptation or inclinations toward sin and corruption (Mosiah 3:19; see NATURAL MAN). Such inclinations can be given up through REPENTANCE, the ATONEMENT, and AGENCY (Mosiah 5:2). Mortals experience opposites—good and evil, happiness and bitterness, joy and misery—and have the opportunity to live true to the commandments and teachings of God. OPPOSITION is a fundamental feature of mortality, where human actions and choices are made within the possibility of doing wrong, where acceptance of the commandments and teachings of God is done in the face of opposition and temptation. While Latter-day Saints do not believe that perfection is possible in this life, they believe in working toward it in response to the injunction of Jesus Christ to "Be ye therefore perfect" (Matt. 5:48; cf. 3 Ne. 12:48). Through repentance and obedience they try to resist the temptations that beset them.

Inasmuch as mortal existence is a time of learning in order to make the greatest progress, each individual first must accept by faith the validity of God's commandments and teachings, and then through experience gain a knowledge of their truth. People exercise agency in how they live their lives, even as they respond to the Spirit of Christ, which is given to all born into mortality. Thus all have the ability, when given proper instruction, including associations with those who are examples of the light and truth of the gospel of Jesus Christ, to recognize and understand the laws of God (D&C 84:45–46; Moro. 7:16).

To all who are willing and who make the effort, mortality provides a vast opportunity for learning, for overcoming weaknesses, for repenting of wrongdoing, for correcting mistakes, for increasing in wisdom, and for progressing toward God. EVE recognized this when she declared that were it not for her and ADAM's transgression, the human race "never should have known good and evil, and the joy of our redemption, and the eternal life which God giveth unto all the obedient" (Moses 5:11).

[See also Birth; Death and Dying; Evil; Fall of Adam; Joy; Life and Death, Spiritual; Man; Premortal Life; Purpose of Earth Life.]

BIBLIOGRAPHY

Smith, Joseph Fielding. DS 1:56–71.

JAMES P. BELL

MOSES

Few PROPHETS are more revered in ancient and latter-day scripture than Moses, who serves as a model of prophetic leadership not only in the Bible but also in the Book of Mormon, Doctrine and Covenants, and Pearl of Great Price (see Luke 16:29–31; 24:27; 2 Ne. 3:9; D&C 28:2; 103:16; 107:91; Moses 1:41). Modern REVELATION confirms and amplifies the biblical accounts of Moses' intimate association with deity, his role as seer, liberator, lawgiver, and leader of ISRAEL, and his connection with the books of the Pentateuch.

God chose Moses for his earthly mission in PREMORTAL LIFE (TPJS, p. 365). JOSEPH OF EGYPT, son of Jacob, prophesied that the Lord would raise up Moses to deliver Jacob's descendants from Egyptian bondage (2 Ne. 3:9–10; JST Gen. 50:29, 34–35). His preparation for his monumental task began in his youth. Raised in Pharaoh's court, Moses "was learned in all the wisdom of the Egyptians" and became "mighty in words and in deeds" (Acts 7:22). After fleeing from Egypt to Midian (Ex. 2:15), he married Zipporah. His father-in-law, Jethro, ordained him to the MELCHIZEDEK PRIESTHOOD that had come down through generations of prophets (D&C 84:6–17). Known as "priest of Midian" (Ex. 3:1), Jethro descended from Midian, son of ABRAHAM and Keturah (Petersen, pp. 49-50).

Moses not only received instructions directly from God, as the Bible records, but he was also given inspiring revelations concerning God's many creations (Moses 1:4, 33-35) and the earth and its inhabitants (Moses 1:8, 27–28). An account of these VISIONS was revealed to the Prophet Joseph SMITH in June 1830 as part of the JOSEPH SMITH TRANSLATION OF THE BIBLE (JST) and constitutes chapter one of the BOOK OF MOSES in the Pearl of Great Price. For Latter-day Saints, this stands as "the missing introduction not only to Genesis, but to the entire Bible" (Turner, p. 43).

The visions were given to Moses on a high mountain, "the name of which shall not be known among the children of men" (Moses 1:1, 42), after the event at the burning bush and before he led Israel from bondage (Moses 1:17, 26). Hence, they were received separately from the revelations of the Ten Commandments (Ex. 3–4; 19–20). The visions exhibit five themes: the greatness of God in comparison to humans (Moses 1:2–5, 8–11, 35–

38); Jesus Christ as the Only Begotten Son and creator of "worlds without number" (1:32–34); Satan and his opposition to the divine plan (1:12–22); the spiritual stature of Moses (1:6, 25–28, 40–41); and God's purposes (1:30, 31, 39). Moses was able to endure God's presence because he was transfigured, meaning that during the visionary experience God's own glory quickened him (Moses 1:2, 11). He learned that he was created in the similitude of God's Only Begotten Son (Moses 1:6), and was told to write his revelations, even though much of what he recorded would be lost—due to wickedness—until another prophet, like himself, would bring forth his visions to believers of a later day (Moses 1:40–41).

Latter-day scripture attests to Moses' hand in the composition of the Pentateuch (1 Ne. 5:11; 19:23). He had access to, and edited, prior prophetic records, including those of ADAM and ENOCH, which were once apparently included in the works composing the earliest form of the Pentateuch, now found in Moses 2–8 (cf. 1 Ne. 13:20–40).

While in the wilderness, Moses taught the Israelites about the sanctifying power of the Melchizedek Priesthood, "that they might behold the face of God" (D&C 84:23). Unfortunately, they rejected his efforts, and because of their hardened hearts, Moses and the Melchizedek Priesthood were taken from their midst. The lesser or AARONIC PRIESTHOOD remained (D&C 84:24–27).

Moses' ministry extended beyond his mortal lifetime. Along with ELIJAH, he returned to the MOUNT OF TRANSFIGURATION, spoke with Christ, and bestowed certain KEYS of the PRIESTHOOD upon the chief APOSTLES (Matt. 17:1–4; D&C 138:45; HC 3:387). Because he needed a body of flesh and bones to perform this errand and because the RESURRECTION was yet forthcoming, Moses was translated and taken into heaven, like Enoch and Elijah, without experiencing the normal death portrayed in Deuteronomy 34:5–6 (cf. Alma 45:19).

Possessing the keys for gathering Israel (Petersen, p. 186), Moses appeared in the KIRTLAND TEMPLE on April 3, 1836, and conferred those keys on the Prophet Joseph Smith and Oliver COWDERY (D&C 110:11) so that the full authority of the priesthood could operate in this DISPENSATION. Latter-day scripture reminds all priesthood holders of Moses' significance by declaring that those who honor and magnify the priesthood become the adopted sons of Moses (D&C 84:33–34). Moses is also revered by other Christians and by Jews and Moslems.

BIBLIOGRAPHY

Jackson, Kent, and Robert Millet, eds. *Studies in Scripture*, Vol. 3, pp. 93–223. Salt Lake City, 1985.

Petersen, Mark E. *Moses: Man of Miracles*. Salt Lake City, 1977.

Sperry, Sidney B. "The Mission of Moses: Out of Bondage." *Ensign* 3 (Oct. 1973):30–35.

Turner, Rodney. "The Visions of Moses." In *Studies in Scripture*, ed. R. Millet and K. Jackson, Vol. 2, pp. 43–61. Salt Lake City, 1985.

ANDREW C. SKINNER

MOSES, BOOK OF

See: Book of Moses

MOSIAH₁

The first Mosiah mentioned in the Book of Mormon, a king, saved those NEPHITES who "would hearken unto the voice of the Lord" by leading them away from their ancestral home, the land of Nephi, where they were threatened by LAMANITES about 200 B.C. (Omni 1:12). After they had wandered for an unknown period, Mosiah and his group "discovered a people, who were called the people of Zarahemla" (Omni 1:13–14; *see also* BOOK OF MORMON PEOPLES; MULEK). He taught them his language—their language having deteriorated because they lacked written records—and was chosen ruler over both groups (Omni 1:17–19). "By the gift and power of God" he interpreted "engravings" on a stone that the people of Zarahemla had discovered, telling of yet another and earlier migration (Omni 1:20–22; *see also* JAREDITES). Mosiah ruled for about four decades and was succeeded as king by his son BENJAMIN.

BIBLIOGRAPHY

Ludlow, Victor L. "Scribes and Scriptures." In *Studies in Scripture*, ed. K. Jackson, Vol. 7, pp. 196–204. Salt Lake City, 1987.

MELVIN J. THORNE

MOSIAH₂

Mosiah₂ (c. 153–91 B.C.) ruled as a Nephite king during almost thirty-three years of Book of Mormon history. His reign was marked by an innovative separation of religious and civic functions and a popular political reform, reflecting the increased pluralism of Nephite society during this historical period.

Mosiah's people consisted of two groups, Nephites and Mulekites, who had voluntarily united under his grandfather, MOSIAH₁. They appear, to some extent, to have retained their separate identities (Mosiah 25:4). The Mulekites were the more numerous group, but the Nephite leaders were able to rule effectively, relying on COVENANT and commitment rather than force. The people entered into a sacred covenant by which they were promised deliverance and prosperity if they would keep their king's commandments, "or the commandments of God," which he would give them (Mosiah 2:312)—a commitment they honored during all of Mosiah's reign.

Mosiah learned the languages and regard for the sacred records of his ancestors from his father, BENJAMIN, and was a wise and patient man who knew the laws and prophecies contained in the Nephite records (Mosiah 1:2–3). Mosiah became king (c. 124 B.C.) three years before his aged father's death. The coronation, described in detail in Mosiah 1–6, exhibits several features similar to ancient Near Eastern coronations. The account of the coronation also provides valuable information about the religious and political patterns of the time (see BENJAMIN). Mosiah was in his thirtieth year when he began to reign. He walked "in the ways of the Lord," and like his father, he provided for his own temporal needs so that he would not become a burden to his people (Mosiah 6:6–7).

Challenges soon arose for Mosiah. Limhi's people arrived in Zarahemla and had to be assimilated into Nephite society. They brought with them the twenty-four PLATES of Ether, which Mosiah, being a SEER, translated (Mosiah 28:10–19). This Jaredite record revealed an ominous lesson, for wickedness, oppression, and violence had led to the extinction of a people. In contrast, Mosiah promoted righteousness, equality, and harmony in his kingdom. When another group led by ALMA₁ arrived in Zarahemla, Mosiah authorized Alma to organize churches and gave him control over them, including the power to admit members to, or expel members from, that covenant community. The creation of this subgroup comprised of seven churches in Nephite society (Mosiah 25:23) allowed Alma's followers to live as they wished, but it also appears to have sowed seeds of civic tension.

At this time, an opposition group formed. Under a strident leader named Nehor, it rejected Alma's teachings and advocated the creation of a publicly supported priesthood. Mosiah's sons, Ammon, Aaron, Omner, and Himni, together with ALMA₂ and a rising generation that had been too young at the time of Mosiah's coronation to understand the words of King Benjamin (Mosiah 26:1), joined these dissenters. They engaged in systematic religious persecution of the church, wreaking havoc among the Nephite community and with Mosiah's family and reputation. Mosiah dealt with the problem by prohibiting acts of religious persecution (Mosiah 27:2). He also sought divine help through fervent prayer and fasting to reform his sons. Angelic intervention (Mosiah 27:10–32) led to the spiritual transformation of these rebellious souls. Deeming it better soon thereafter to proclaim the gospel than to rule over the kingdom, none of his four sons would accept the Nephite throne.

Under these circumstances and near the end of his life, Mosiah effected a political reform that abolished Nephite kingship. His final speech in 91 B.C. justified righteous monarchs such as his father and himself, but warned against the overriding threats posed by wicked rulers (Mosiah 29:13–21).

In place of kingship, Mosiah created a unique system of judges subject to the voice of the people. From what is known about this legal reform, it appears that each judge was chosen by popular voice, "that every man should have an equal chance"; higher judges judged the lower judges, and a selected body of lower judges judged the higher judges (Mosiah 29:25–29, 38). This law set new precedents by providing that judges should be paid; it also established an Egyptian-style system of measures for exchanging various grains and precious metals (Alma 11:1, 4–19), prohibited all forms of slavery (Alma 27:9), imposed a severe punishment on those who would not pay their debts (Alma 11:2), and granted liberty of belief (Mosiah 29:39; Alma 30:11). The people accepted the law of Mosiah and selected their judges, including Alma₂ as the first chief judge. The equity and justice of this prophet-king won for him the love of his people:

And they did wax strong in love towards Mosiah; yea, they did esteem him more than any other man; for they did not look upon him as a tyrant who was seeking for gain, . . . for he had not exacted riches of them, neither had he delighted in the shedding of blood; but he had established peace in the land, and he had granted unto his people that they should be delivered from all manner of bondage; therefore they did esteem him, yea, exceedingly, beyond measure [Mosiah 29:40].

BIBLIOGRAPHY

"The Coronation of Kings." *F.A.R.M.S. Update*. Provo, Utah, July 1989.

"The Law of Mosiah." *F.A.R.M.S. Update*. Provo, Utah, March 1987.

PAUL RYTTING

MOTHER IN HEAVEN

Latter-day Saints infer from authoritative sources of scripture and modern prophecy that there is a Heavenly Mother as well as a Heavenly Father.

The Church of Jesus Christ of Latter-day Saints rejects the idea found in some religions that the spirits or souls of individual human beings are created ex nihilo. Rather it accepts literally the vital scriptural teaching as worded by Paul: "The Spirit itself beareth witness with our spirit, that we are the children of God." This and other scriptures underscore not only spiritual sibling relationships but heirship with God, and a destiny of joint heirship with Christ (Rom. 8:16–18; cf. Mal. 2:10).

Latter-day Saints believe that all the people of earth who lived or will live are actual spiritual offspring of God the Eternal Father (Num. 16:22; Heb. 12:9). In this perspective, parenthood requires both father and mother, whether for the creation of spirits in the PREMORTAL LIFE or of physical tabernacles on earth. A Heavenly Mother shares parenthood with the Heavenly Father. This concept leads Latter-day Saints to believe that she is like him in glory, perfection, compassion, wisdom, and holiness.

Elohim, the name-title for God, suggests the plural of the Caananite *El* or the Hebrew *Eloah*. It is used in various Hebrew combinations to describe the highest God. It is the majestic title of the ultimate deity. Genesis 1:27 reads, "So God created man in his own image, in the image of God created he him, *male and female* created he them"

(emphasis added), which may be read to mean that "God" is plural.

For Latter-day Saints, the concept of eternal family is more than a firm belief; it governs their way of life. It is the eternal plan of life, stretching from life before through life beyond mortality.

As early as 1839 the Prophet Joseph SMITH taught the concept of an eternal mother, as reported in several accounts from that period. Out of his teaching came a hymn that Latter-day Saints learn, sing, quote, and cherish, "O My Father," by Eliza R. SNOW. President Wilford WOODRUFF called it a REVELATION (Woodruff, p. 62).

In the heav'ns are parents single?
No, the thought makes reason stare!
Truth is reason; truth eternal
Tells me I've a mother there.
When I leave this frail existence,
When I lay this mortal by,
Father, Mother, may I meet you
In your royal courts on high? [Hymn no. 292]

In 1909 the FIRST PRESIDENCY, under Joseph F. SMITH, issued a statement on the origin of man that teaches that "man, as a spirit, was begotten and born of heavenly parents, and reared to maturity in the eternal mansions of the Father," as an "offspring of celestial parentage," and further teaches that "all men and women are in the similitude of the universal Father and Mother, and are literally the sons and daughters of Deity" (Smith, pp. 199–205).

Belief that there is a Mother in Heaven who is a partner with God in creation and procreation is not the same as the heavy emphasis on Mariology in the Roman tradition.

Today the belief in a living Mother in Heaven is implicit in Latter-day Saint thought. Though the scriptures contain only hints, statements from PRESIDENTS OF THE CHURCH over the years indicate that human beings have a Heavenly Mother as well as a Heavenly Father.

BIBLIOGRAPHY

Wilcox, Linda P. "The Mormon Concept of a Mother in Heaven." In *Sisters in Spirit*, ed. Maureen U. Beecher and Lavina F. Anderson. Urbana, Ill., 1987.

Woodruff, Wilford. *The Discourses of Wilford Woodruff*, ed. G. Homer Durham. Salt Lake City, 1968.

ELAINE ANDERSON CANNON

MOTHERHOOD

In an address on the blessings and responsibilities of motherhood, President Ezra Taft BENSON stated: "No more sacred word exists in secular or holy writ than that of mother" (Benson, p. 1). Latter-day Saints revere and respect motherhood, in part because of the mother's role in shaping the FAMILY unit and the individuals within it. President David O. MCKAY taught:

> Motherhood is the greatest potential influence either for good or ill in human life. The mother's image is the first that stamps itself on the unwritten page of the young child's mind. It is her caress that first awakens a sense of security; her kiss, the first realization of affection; her sympathy and tenderness, the first assurance that there is love in the world. . . . This ability and willingness properly to rear children . . . make motherhood the noblest office or calling in the world. . . . She who rears successfully a family of healthy, beautiful sons and daughters . . . deserves the highest honor that man can give, and the choicest blessings of God [McKay, pp. 452–54].

Obviously, the sociological significance of the mother's role is immense: Her relationship with her children and her guidance in their growing years influence the formation of values and attitudes they will carry throughout their lives. But for Latter-day Saints, motherhood has meaning well beyond such sociological significance.

Church doctrine recognizes both a mothering and a fathering role in the spiritual birth and premortal development of each person. In a document issued in 1909, the First Presidency of the Church wrote that "man, as a spirit, was begotten and born of heavenly parents, and reared to maturity in the eternal mansions of the Father," and that "all men and women are in the similitude of the universal Father and Mother, and are literally the sons and daughters of Deity" (Smith, p. 884; *see* MOTHER IN HEAVEN).

Following development in the premortal existence, each of God's spirit children has the opportunity to come to earth and acquire a mortal body that, when resurrected, will be bound with the spirit to form an inseparable, eternal soul. Providing mortal bodies for God's spirit children is a work given to mortal beings, with the greater measure of responsibility falling to mothers, who conceive, sustain, carry, and give birth to children. President Spencer W. KIMBALL said, "Mothers have a

Hawaiian Motherhood, by Avard T. Fairbanks (1917, cast concrete), in front of the Hawaii Temple, Laie, Hawaii. The main figure in this relief sculpture is a Hawaiian mother, holding a giant clam shell and symbolically pouring the love, hope, and care of maternity over her children.

sacred role. They are partners with God. . . . [He] has placed women at the very headwaters of the human stream" (pp. 326–27).

The significance of motherhood continues undiminished following the birth of a child. The long-term stability, security, and peace of a human soul are built in large measure upon the foundation of love, and any individual's ability to give and receive love is rooted strongly in that person's earliest relationships. For most people, that earliest influence is the mother.

She who gives the child life is first and foremost the one to give it a way of life, teaching the child what it should or should not do. She encourages strong character formation as she teaches the child to impose limitations on some of its natural instincts. By her words and actions she teaches her child the regard that should be shown other individuals if that child wishes to be included and loved as a member of the family circle, later as a member of society, and finally as a participating member of the KINGDOM OF GOD.

The ultimate responsibility of a mother, then, is to lead her child lovingly through its personal development and toward its divine destiny. Latter-day Saints believe that if a mother is prayerful and totally committed to such a weighty responsibility, she will receive divine intuitions and spiritual whisperings to aid her in her mothering. Living as a conduit for divine instruction to her child, a mother can greatly enhance its opportunity for joy and EXALTATION. The child who has been mothered in this profound way usually develops a moral conscience, a respect for society, a desire to contribute to the well-being of humankind, and, most important, a love of God and a love for self that will bring everlasting joy and inner peace.

Perhaps the most distinctive Latter-day Saint doctrine regarding motherhood emphasizes the role of a mother after death. The eternal nature of the family unit, when that unit is bound together by priesthood ORDINANCES and temple COVENANTS, guarantees to a faithful LDS mother the privileges, opportunities, and joys of motherhood with her children in a relationship that lasts eternally.

[See also Mother in Israel; Women, Roles of.]

BIBLIOGRAPHY

Benson, Ezra Taft. "To the Mothers in Zion." Salt Lake City, 1987.

Kimball, Spencer W. The Teachings of Spencer W. Kimball, pp. 324–51. Salt Lake City, 1982.

McKay, David O. Gospel Ideals, pp. 452–57. Salt Lake City, 1953.

Smith, Joseph Fielding. "Mothers in Israel." The Relief Society Magazine 57 (Dec. 1970):883–87.

PATRICIA TERRY HOLLAND

MOTHER IN ISRAEL

Every worthy woman who lives a virtuous life and who promotes righteousness in her family and in the Church and her family is entitled both to the designation "mother in Israel" and to the promises given to Sarah and other biblical mothers in Israel (see ABRAHAM; ABRAHAMIC COVENANT; ISRAEL; SARAH). These promises are open to all faithful women who teach others to love the Lord and keep his commandments. The title designates intelligent and faithful support of the Church and its leaders, and historically it has been applied most frequently to leaders among women. It is often found in PATRIARCHAL BLESSINGS and is a title and a promise with more than earthly significance. Motherhood is a God-given role vital to the EXALTATION of a woman and her family.

"Mother in Israel" first appears in the song of Deborah that describes the travail of the people under Jabin, the king of Canaan, until Deborah, a mother in Israel, arose to lead them out of bondage (Judg. 5:2–31; cf. 2 Sam. 20:19).

In Old Testament times, a woman's strength and authority were found in her mothering of faithful children, especially sons. Besides Eve, other outstanding examples of mothers who influenced Old Testament history include Sarah, Rebekah, Leah, Rachel, Hannah, and Naomi. Sarah, of course, figures indispensably in the blessing given to Abraham, and the Lord promised her explicitly that she would be "a mother of nations" (Gen. 17:16). That such a blessing was culturally significant is apparent in the admonition given to Rebekah by her family as she left to marry Isaac: "Be thou the mother of thousands of millions" (Gen. 24:60). Barrenness in biblical culture was often seen as a reproach to a woman and to her family, a matter of sorrow for a woman, and often a matter for sincere prayer to God, but not rejection (e.g., 1 Sam 1:4–8).

In the Christian era, after the death of the apostles, a tradition developed that gave precedent honor to women who offered themselves celibate to religious service. However, as the Protestant reformation emerged, motherhood again became a crowning glory and "the home, not the convent, became the center of woman's highest religious vocation" (Madsen, p. 184).

The expression "mother in Israel" can be found in writings of post-Reformation England and more prominently in Puritan New England. Among Latter-day Saints, who consciously identify with biblical themes and ancient Israel, the appellation appeared early, but was applied infrequently and then only to such outstanding women as Lucy Mack SMITH and Eliza R. SNOW. At the October 1845 general conference of the Church, a year following the deaths of her sons Joseph, Hyrum, and Samuel, Lucy Mack Smith "wished to know of the congregation, whether they considered her a mother in Israel." President Brigham Young put her question to those assembled, who answered with a resounding, "Yes" (CHC, 2:538–39).

In 1916 the *Relief Society Magazine* published a series of articles entitled "Mothers in Israel." One prominent woman honored was Eliza R. Snow. Though childless, she was called a "mother of mothers in Israel" and praised for her leadership among women, for her intelligence, and for her faithful support of the Church and its leaders (Gates, pp. 183–90).

As in New England, the phrase "mother in Israel" appeared in early Utah history in the obituaries of many faithful women who succored the Church and their families. Sometimes they were older women with large families and sometimes notable women in other circumstances. For example, Mary Fielding SMITH had only two children of her own, both young enough when she died that no claim could be made of their future significance, yet at her death, evidently in recognition of her character and commitment, she was called a mother in Israel. A son and a grandson later became Presidents of the Church.

Currently the term is most often found in patriarchal blessings when a woman is promised in substance that she will stand "as a mother in Israel." President Joseph Fielding SMITH said, "To be a mother in Israel in the full gospel sense is the highest reward that can come into the life of a woman" (p. 883). It is a promise open to all faithful sisters who love and serve the Lord and keep his commandments, including those who do not have the opportunity to bear children in this life.

The Book of Mormon recounts the history of 2,000 righteous stripling warriors who were able to accomplish great things and receive great blessings because they believed in what they had "been taught by their mothers" (Alma 56:47–48; 57:21). Modern mothers in Israel also have a responsibility to teach their children—and others whom they are in a position to influence—to love the Lord and keep his commandments. The prophets of this DISPENSATION have consistently stressed the importance of committed motherhood both by those who bear and those who care and have counseled that this is a divinely given role important to the salvation and exaltation of God's children.

[*See also* Motherhood; Women, Roles of.]

BIBLIOGRAPHY

Benson, Ezra Taft. *To the Mothers in Zion.* Salt Lake City, 1987.

Gates, Susa Young. "Mothers in Israel." *Relief Society Magazine* 3 (Jan. 1916):538–39.

———. "The Mothers of Mothers in Israel." *Relief Society Magazine* 3 (Apr. 1916):183–90.

Madsen, Carol Cornwall. "Mothers in Israel: Sarah's Legacy." In *Women of Wisdom and Knowledge*, ed. M. Cornwall and S. Howe, pp. 179–201. Salt Lake City, 1990.

Reynolds, Sydney Smith. "Wife and Mother: A Valid Career Option for the College-Educated Woman." *Ensign* 9 (Oct. 1979):67–70.

Smith, Joseph Fielding. "Mothers in Israel." *Relief Society Magazine* 57 (Dec. 1970):883–86.

SYDNEY SMITH REYNOLDS

MOTION PICTURES, LDS PRODUCTIONS

As early as 1913, when the motion picture industry was in its early stages, leaders of The Church of Jesus Christ of Latter-day Saints expressed an interest in using the film medium: "The moving picture together with all the other modern inventions is to help us carry the Mission of Christ to all the world, and to bring humanity home to the true principles of salvation" (Young, p. 80). With the sanction of President Joseph F. SMITH, Shirley "Shirl" Young Clawson and his brother Chester filmed many Church events and leaders from 1916 to 1929 in black and white and without sound. This era of film production for the Church ended tragically, however, when a fire killed Shirl Clawson and destroyed the studio and many of the films. The Church's next major move into film production began in the 1950s and has resulted in many award-winning items among the programs produced for home, classroom, and missionary use.

In 1946 Wetzel O. "Judge" Whitaker, chief of animation for Walt Disney Studios, invited three members of the QUORUM OF THE TWELVE APOSTLES—Elders Harold B. LEE, Mark E. Petersen, and Matthew Cowley—to tour the Disney Studios in Burbank, California. They were impressed with the potential of motion pictures to teach principles of the gospel. In that same year, wards, stakes, and missions began to be provided with motion picture projectors. Whitaker produced the first two films for the Church on a volunteer basis: *Church Welfare in Action* and *The Lord's Way.*

In January 1953 BRIGHAM YOUNG UNIVERSITY in Provo, Utah, created a department of motion picture production to produce films to be used by the Church and appointed Judge Whitaker as its founding director. The department produced poignant and appealing films such as *Come Back My Son* based on a story from the IMPROVEMENT ERA about reactivating an adult member of the AARONIC PRIESTHOOD. *How Near to the Angels*, the most ambitious LDS film project at that time, was a significant milestone because of its dramatic nature though it was only fifty minutes long. The film had as its theme temple marriage. *A Time for Sowing* showed the effect parents have on the behavior of their children. *Time Pulls the Trigger* looked at the connection between smoking and premature death. *With All Your Heart* showed a relationship between a spiritually sensitive bishop and reverence in Church meetings. *My Brother's Keeper* and *Shannon* dramatized the reclaiming of less active members of the Church. *The Search for Truth* presented the rational observations and testimonies of scientists on the reconciliation of science and religion. *Worth Waiting For* taught that happy marriages are worth preparing for. The most challenging film produced in this first decade of Church film production, and an enduring favorite, was *Windows of Heaven*, a film on blessings through the law of tithing.

MAN'S SEARCH FOR HAPPINESS, the first film written for a non-Mormon audience about the purpose of life, premiered at the 1964 World's Fair in New York City, where it was viewed by five million people. This film was subsequently translated into more languages than any previous Church film, including Afrikaans, Cantonese, Creole, Czech, Danish, Dutch, Esperanto, Finnish, French, French-Canadian, German, Hmong, Italian, Japanese, Korean, Mandarin, Navajo, Norwegian, Portuguese, Quechua, Quiche, Samoan, Serbo-Croatian, Spanish, Swedish, Tagalog, Taiwanese, Thai, Tongan, and Vietnamese. A Japanese version was filmed in Japan and premiered at the 1970 World's Fair Expo there.

No More a Stranger demonstrated the importance of fellowshipping new members in a WARD. *And Should We Die* taught the principle of fasting and prayer. *The Three Witnesses*, a dramatic reenactment of the story of the Three Witnesses to the Book of Mormon, was used widely throughout the Church in teaching this aspect of early Church history. *Meet the Mormons* featured many on-camera, spontaneous interviews and testimonies, and showed the international nature of the Church. It was also translated into many languages. *Where*

Jesus Walked is about the life of Christ and was filmed in the Holy Land.

In addition to the BYU motion picture studio, KSL television has preserved on film many speeches by GENERAL AUTHORITIES and selected specials, such as *Nauvoo*, and *Cumorah, Hill of History*. In 1967 Bonneville Media Communications was organized as a broadcast production facility to help develop a positive media image for the Church and to convey its doctrines and beliefs. Bonneville's direct gospel messages have included *Our Heavenly Father's Plan; Together Forever; What is Real;* and *Labor of Love*. Seasonal gospel films included *Mr. Krueger's Christmas, Nora's Christmas Gift;* an animated version of Henry Van Dyke's *The Other Wise Man;* O. Henry's Easter story *The Last Leaf;* and *Easter Dream*. Radio and television public service announcements broadcast regularly by over 14,000 stations worldwide, called the Homefront Series, are intended to promote family solidarity and to raise awareness of some basic teachings of the Church.

On September 1, 1974, Jesse E. Stay replaced Whitaker as head of the BYU motion picture studio. During Stay's tenure, *Go Ye Into All the World; The First Vision; Restoration of the Priesthood;* and *Morality for Youth* were completed.

On September 1, 1983, Peter N. Johnson replaced Stay and oversaw the production of *Teaching, A Renewed Dedication; Five-Year Retrospective of the Church in Action; Cameos on General Authorities; Teacher, Do You Love Me?; Lamp Unto My Feet; Things of My Soul*, a remake of *Man's Search for Happiness; How Rare a Possession: The Book of Mormon;* and *Called to Serve—* the major Church productions of the 1980s.

In 1991, control of the motion picture studio was transferred from BYU to the Audiovisual Department of the Church.

BIBLIOGRAPHY

Jacobs, David Kent. "The History of Motion Pictures Produced by the Church of Jesus Christ of Latter-day Saints." Master's thesis, Brigham Young University, 1967.

Whitaker, Wetzel O. *Pioneering with Film: A Brief History of Church and Brigham Young University Films*. Provo, Utah, n.d.

Young, Levi Edgar. "'Mormonism' in Picture." *Young Woman's Journal* 24 (Feb. 1913):80.

PETER N. JOHNSON

MOUNTAIN MEADOWS MASSACRE

In September 1990, some two thousand persons gathered in Cedar City, Utah, to effect a reconciliation among those whose ancestors died or participated in what may be considered the most unfortunate incident in the history of the LDS Church, the Mountain Meadows massacre. The massacre occurred between September 7 and 11, 1857, when a group of Mormon settlers in southern Utah joined with nearby Indians in killing all but some of the youngest members of a group of non-Mormon emigrants en route to California.

After years of painstaking research, Juanita Brooks, author of an oft-cited book on the tragedy, concluded, "The complete—the absolute—truth of the affair can probably never be evaluated by any human being; attempts to understand the forces which culminated in it and those which were set into motion by it are all very inadequate at best" (Brooks, p. 223). Yet, as Brooks makes clear, a few elements that helped contribute to the tragedy are evident.

Among these is the fact that a large contingent of United States troops was marching westward toward Utah Territory in the summer of 1857 (see UTAH EXPEDITION). Despite having been the federally appointed territorial governor, Brigham Young was not informed by Washington of the army's purpose and interpreted the move as a re-

John D. Lee seated next to his coffin prior to his execution twenty years after his involvement in the Mountain Meadows Massacre, Utah. From the George Kelly collection, University of Utah. Courtesy Nelson Wadsworth.

newal of the persecution the Latter-day Saints had experienced before their westward hegira. "We are invaded by a hostile force who are evidently assailing us to accomplish our overthrow and destruction," he proclaimed on August 5, 1857. Anticipating an attack, he declared the territory to be under martial law and ordered "[t]hat all the forces in said Territory hold themselves in readiness to march, at a moment's notice, to repel any and all such threatened invasion" (Arrington, p. 254).

Part of Brigham Young's strategy in repelling the approaching army was to enlist local Indian tribes as allies. In an August 4 letter to southern Utah, for example, he urged one Latter-day Saint to "[c]ontinue the conciliatory policy towards the Indians, which I have ever recommended, and seek by works of righteousness to obtain their love and confidence, for they must learn that they have either got to help us or the United States will kill us both" (Brooks, p. 34).

Meanwhile, owing to the lateness of the season, a party of emigrants bound for California elected to take the southern route that passed through Cedar City and thirty-five miles beyond to the Mountain Meadows, which was then an area of springs, bogs, and plentiful grass where travelers frequently stopped to rejuvenate themselves and their stock before braving the harsh desert landscape to the west. Led by John T. Baker and Alexander Fancher, the diverse party consisted of perhaps 120 persons, most of whom left from Arkansas but others of whom joined the company along their journey.

As the Baker-Fancher party traveled from Salt Lake City to the Mountain Meadows, tensions developed between some of the emigrants, on the one hand, and Mormon settlers and their Native American allies, on the other. Spurred by rumors, their own observations, and memories of atrocities some of them had endured in Missouri and Illinois, Mormon residents in and around Cedar City felt compelled to take some action against the emigrant train but ultimately decided to dispatch a rider to Brigham Young seeking his counsel. Leaving September 7, 1857, the messenger made the nearly 300-mile journey in just a little more than three days.

Approximately one hour after his arrival, the messenger was on his way back with a letter from Brigham Young, who said he did not expect the federal soldiers to arrive that fall because of their poor stock. "They cannot get here this season with-

Monument above the site of the Mountain Meadows Massacre, erected September 1990. The monument lists the names of the Arkansas immigrants killed here in 1857 and the names of the children who survived and were returned to relatives in 1859. Courtesy Deseret News.

out we help them," he explained. "So you see that the Lord has answered our prayers and again averted the blow designed for our heads." Responding to the plea for counsel, he added, "In regard to the emigration trains passing through our settlements, we must not interfere with them until they are first notified to keep away. You must not meddle with them. The Indians we expect will do as they please but you should try and preserve good feelings with them" (Brooks, p. 63). The messenger arrived back in Cedar City on September 13.

By that time, however, it was too late, and nearly all the men, women, and children of the Baker-Fancher party lay dead. Besides a few persons who left the party before the attack, only about eighteen small children were spared. Two years later, seventeen of the children were returned to family members in northwestern Arkansas. Two decades after the tragedy, one of the Mormon settlers who were present at the massacre, John D. Lee, was executed by a firing squad at the Mountain Meadows, symbolically carrying to the grave the responsibility for those who "were led to do what none singly would have done under normal conditions, and for which none singly can be held responsible" (Brooks, p. 218).

Yet for more than another century after Lee's death, the community guilt of those who participated in the massacre continued to fester alongside the collective pain of both the children who survived it and the relatives of those who did not. Then in the late 1980s, the descendants of those affected by the tragedy began meeting to bind the wounds and achieve a reconciliation. On September 15, 1990, many of them gathered to dedicate a memorial marker to those who died at the Mountain Meadows.

One speaker at the marker dedication was Judge Roger V. Logan, Jr., of Harrison, Arkansas, a man related to twenty-one of the massacre victims listed on the marker, as well as to five of the children who survived. "I am happy to say that thanks to the work, cooperation and gifts of many of you," he said, "there is now an appropriate monument standing in the place of the emigrants' demise; a monument containing the names of eighty-two persons who died and seventeen who survived and [that] also contains reference to many others who may have been a part of the caravan." As he read the victims' names, he asked all related to them to stand in their honor.

Brigham Young University President Rex E. Lee, a descendant of John D. Lee, also spoke at the memorial service, saying he found little solace in recognizing that similar tragedies had occurred across time and space. "Any attempt to recreate the human dynamics that were at work in southern Utah in the fall of 1857 can only leave us bewildered as to how rational human beings at any time, in any place, under any circumstances could have permitted such a tragedy to occur."

"Fortunately," he added, "full comprehension of the reasons is as unnecessary as it would be impossible. Our task for today is not to look backward, nor to rationalize, nor to engage in any kind of retroactive analysis nor apology. Our focus is not on 1857. It is on 1990. It is on our generation, and on those that are yet to come. And whatever drove the actions of those who came before, ours must be driven by something higher and more noble."

Gordon B. Hinckley, First Counselor in the LDS Church First Presidency, offered the prayer dedicating the new monument. In a talk delivered before the prayer, President Hinckley said he came "not as a descendant of any of the parties involved at Mountain Meadows" but "as a representative of an entire people who have suffered much over what occurred there."

"In our time," he said, "we can read such history as is available, but we really cannot understand nor comprehend that which occurred those tragic and terrible September days in 1857. Rather, we are grateful for the ameliorating influence that has brought us together in a spirit of reconciliation as new generations gather with respect and appreciation one for another. A bridge has been built across a chasm of cankering bitterness. We walk across that bridge and greet one another with a spirit of love, forgiveness, and with hope that there will never be a repetition of anything of the kind." (Excerpts from the talks are all taken from unpublished manuscripts found in the Mountain Meadows Memorial collection, LDS Church Historical Department, Salt Lake City, Utah.)

BIBLIOGRAPHY

Arrington, Leonard J. *Brigham Young, American Moses.* New York, 1985.

Brooks, Juanita. *The Mountain Meadows Massacre.* Revised ed., Norman, Okla., 1991.

CHC 4:139-80.

RONALD K. ESPLIN
RICHARD E. TURLEY, JR.

MOUNT OF TRANSFIGURATION

The Mount of Transfiguration was the scene of a transcendent New Testament event. It has been set in perspective by REVELATIONS to the Prophet Joseph SMITH and portrayed with several related components. First, Jesus conversed with Moses and Elijah, who were then translated beings (Matt. 17:3–4). Second, a transfiguration of Jesus Christ himself occurred there, confirming his divine nature and calling to his three chief apostles: Peter, James, and John (Matt. 17:1–2). Third, those apostles were also temporarily transfigured during that experience (*TPJS*, p. 158). Fourth, in vision those apostles saw the earth in its future transfigured state as the inheritance of the faithful (D&C 63:20–21). Fifth, those same apostles received certain priesthood keys of the kingdom of God, which they utilized during their mortal ministries (*HC* 3:387). Sixth, Moses and Elijah, who were also on the Mount of Transfiguration, also conferred priesthood keys to Joseph Smith and Oliver COWDERY in the Kirtland Temple on April 3, 1836 (D&C 110:11–16).

The experience on the mount no doubt strengthened the Savior as he approached the last months before his atoning sacrifice. Moses and Elijah visited him as he prepared for the infinite sufferings in Gethsemane and the agonies of Golgotha (Luke 9:30–31; *JC*, p. 373).

Jesus' transfiguration before Peter, James, and John made them "eyewitnesses of his majesty" (2 Pet. 1:16). During their visit, the voice of the Father bore record of the Savior's mission, giving assurance to Peter, James, and John of the Father's love and his approval of Jesus (Matt. 17:5–8). Because these apostles would soon constitute the FIRST PRESIDENCY of the early church (MD, pp. 571–572), the event was an unforgettable personal witness of the Father's acknowledgment of Jesus' redemptive mission. John later testified, "We beheld his glory, the glory as of the only begotten of the Father" (John 1:14).

The temporary transfiguration of Peter, James, and John allowed them to hear the voice of the Father and see the transfigured Son (cf. Moses 1:9–11). This extraordinary experience helped prepare them for the coming burden of Church leadership following Jesus' departure from his earthly ministry. Well did Peter declare, "Lord, it is good for us to be here" (Matt. 17:4).

Peter, James, and John also saw the millennial day when the earth will be transfigured, returning it to its condition prior to the FALL OF ADAM (*TPJS*, pp. 12–13; cf. A of F 10). The earth's transfiguration will take place at the time of Christ's second coming (*MD*, pp. 795–96).

The bestowal of priesthood keys on the presiding apostles formed a fifth purpose of the transfiguration. During his ministry, Jesus conferred the MELCHIZEDEK PRIESTHOOD on the twelve, authorizing them to act under his direction (Mark 3:14–15; John 15:16; cf. *JD* 25:207). But with the prospect of his departure, the twelve needed independent authority to direct Church affairs. Fulfilling his promise that Peter would receive the keys of the kingdom (Matt. 16:13–20), Jesus took the chief apostles to the mount, where they received those keys.

After beholding the transfigured Jesus and undergoing transfiguration themselves, the apostles saw Moses and Elijah (and perhaps others; cf. McConkie, p. 400), who had been translated so that they could appear with physical bodies to bestow priesthood keys by the LAYING ON OF HANDS, which made possible, among other things, the preaching of the gospel throughout the world (Matt. 18:19–20) and performing saving ORDINANCES for the living and the dead (cf. 1 Cor. 15:29).

The latter-day fulfillment of some of these events occurred in the Kirtland Temple. The Melchizedek Priesthood and the office and keys of apostleship had been conferred on Joseph Smith and Oliver Cowdery probably in late May or early June 1829 (cf. D&C 27:12), embracing the authority to establish the Church (D&C 128:20). On April 3, 1836, additional keys were given to Joseph and Oliver in the Kirtland Temple by Moses and Elijah—the same ancient ministrants who appeared on the mount—and an additional messenger named ELIAS, who conferred the "dispensation of the gospel of Abraham" (D&C 110:12). The restoration of these keys set in motion the latter-day mission of the Church, including missionary work and all ordinances for the living, as well as redemption of the dead through vicarious ordinance work in temples.

BIBLIOGRAPHY

Haight, David B. "'We Beheld His Glory.'" Ensign 7 (May 1977):7–10.

Matthews, Robert J. "Tradition, Testimony, Transfiguration, and Keys." In *Studies in Scripture*, ed. K. Jackson and R. Millet, Vol. 5, pp. 296–311. Salt Lake City, 1986.

McConkie, Bruce R. *Doctrinal New Testament Commentary*, Vol. 1, pp. 397–404. Salt Lake City, 1965.

DALE C. MOURITSEN

MULEK

Mulek, a Book of Mormon character, son of Zedekiah, escaped the sack of Jerusalem (587 B.C.) and went with others to a place in the Western Hemisphere that they called the land of Mulek (Hel. 6:10). Later a region was named for Zarahemla, a descendant of Mulek (Mosiah 25:2). These people were eventually discovered by Nephite refugees from LAMANITE predations in the south. Mulek is important because he established one of the BOOK OF MORMON PEOPLES and because Bible students have assumed that Nebuchadnezzar executed all of Zedekiah's sons, an observation unsupported by ancient evidence and refuted by the Book of Mormon account of Mulek's survival.

According to the Book of Mormon, the Nephites and "Mulekites" formed a coalition, making Mosiah₂ king over both groups. The Nephites discovered in Mulek's descendants an additional witness concerning the destruction of Jerusalem. The Mulekites were elated to have access to Nephite records, since their own language and traditions had been distorted in the absence of historical documents. The Mulekites lived thenceforth among the Nephites, enjoying separate-but-equal status and ultimately outnumbering the descendants of Nephi (Mosiah 25:1–4, 13).

Ancient Near Eastern sources affirm that during the Babylonian destruction of Jerusalem, Mulek's father, Zedekiah, who was deserted by all who escaped, was captured with members of his family and a few courtiers. Nebuchadnezzar slew Zedekiah's sons and courtiers, put his eyes out, and deported him to Babylon (Josephus, *Antiquities*, 10.8.2). But his daughters, and presumably his wives, stayed at Mizpah until Gedeliah, a former minister with Babylonizing tendencies in Zedekiah's cabinet, was murdered by Ishmael, who then tried to deport the Mizpah colony. When pursued, Ishmael abandoned his captives and fled with eight men to Ammon. The people of Mizpah, including Zedekiah's women, headed for Egypt, fearful of Chaldean reprisals (2 Kgs. 25; Jer. 41–43).

Mulek might have been away when the city fell; perhaps he eluded his captors at Jericho; the women could have hidden him (as Jehoshiba hid her nephew Joash of the royal line earlier [see 2 Kgs. 11:2–4]); he may even have been unborn, although he probably avoided captivity some other way. But nothing in the Bible or other known sources precludes the possibility of his escape from Jerusalem.

Concerning Mulek's existence, the Bible offers important evidence. Mulek is a nickname derived from *melek* (Hebrew, king), a diminutive term of endearment meaning "little king." Its longer form occurs in the Bible as *Malkiyahu* (in English, Malchiah), meaning "Jehovah is king." Malchiah is identified as "the son of Hammelech" in Jeremiah 38:6. But Hammelech is a translator's error, since *ben-hammelek* means "son of the king" and is not a proper name—a fact confirmed by the Septuagint (LXX Jer. 45:6). A fictive paternity thus obscures the lineage of Malchiah as the actual son of Zedekiah. It is also known that names ending in *-yahu* (in English, *-iah*) were common during the late First Temple period, that Zedekiah indeed had a son named Malkiyahu (Aharoni, p. 22), and that the familial forms of *yahu*-names were shorter than their "full" forms. The study of a seal owned by Jeremiah's scribe shows that his full name was Berekyahu (in English, Berechiah), although the biblical text uses only the shorter Baruch (Avigad). This is consistent with viewing the hypocoristic Mulek as the diminutive of Malkiyahu, since *a* is often assimilated to *o* or *u* in the vocalic structure of most Semitic languages. It is therefore possible that the Mulek of the Book of Mormon is "Malchiah, son of the king" mentioned in Jeremiah 38:6.

BIBLIOGRAPHY

Aharoni, Yohanan. "Three Hebrew Ostraca from Arad." *Bulletin of the American Schools of Oriental Research* 197 (Feb. 1970):16–42.

Avigad, Nahman. "Jerahmeel & Baruch." *Biblical Archeologist* 42:2 (Spring 1979):114–18.

"New Information About Mulek, Son of the King." *F.A.R.M.S. Update.* Provo, Utah, 1984.

Rainey, Anson. "The Prince and the Pauper." *Ugarit-Forschungen* 7 (1975):427–32.

H. CURTIS WRIGHT

MURDER

Murder is condemned in latter-day scripture just as it is in the TEN COMMANDMENTS and numerous other passages in both the Old and the New Testament. The Doctrine and Covenants declares that "thou shalt not kill" (D&C 42:18). The murderer "shall not have forgiveness in this world, nor in the world to come" (D&C 42:18).

In LDS doctrine, murder is second in seriousness only to the UNPARDONABLE SIN of blasphemy against the Holy Ghost. And even that sin involves a kind of murderous treachery in that one who previously had obtained an absolute witness of Jesus' divinity (TPJS, p. 358) in effect "crucifies [Christ]" afresh or "assent[s] unto [his] death" (D&C 76:35; 132:27). Thus, murder can be thought of as the archetypal sin, as in the sin of Cain (Gen. 4:6–11, and esp. Moses 5:18–26, 31).

Murder violates the sanctity of life and cuts off the ability of its victims to "work out their destiny" (Benson, p. 355). Moreover, because "man cannot restore life," and restoration or restitution is a necessary step for REPENTANCE, obtaining forgiveness for murder is impossible (Kimball, 1969, p. 129; D&C 42:18–19). Murder wrenches all lives connected to the victim, and ultimately the perpetrator of this crime suffers even more than the victims. "For Cain suffered far more than did Abel, and murder is far more serious to him who commits it than to him who suffers from it" (Kimball, 1982, p. 188).

Secular punishment for killing is to be proved and "dealt with according to the laws of the land" (D&C 42:79). Those who have been convicted of, or have confessed to, homicide cannot be baptized without clearance from the FIRST PRESIDENCY, and excommunication of members guilty of murder is mandatory. Joseph Fielding SMITH, as an apostle, indicated that vicarious temple work should not be done for deceased murderers (DS 2:192).

The Church defines "murder" as the deliberate and unjustified taking of human life. If death is caused by carelessness or by defense of self or others, or if overriding mitigating circumstances prevail (such as deficient mental capacity or state of war), the taking of a human life may be regarded as something other than murder. In making the assessment of a member's guilt or innocence of murder, Church leaders are encouraged to be responsive to inspiration and to submit the facts of the case to the office of the First Presidency for review. In the final analysis, only God, who can discern the thoughts of the heart, can judge whether a particular killing is an unforgivable murder or not.

The Church's concern about murder is both more fundamental and broader than that found in legal definitions. Legal categories of homicide, such as manslaughter or negligent homicide (which typically involve carelessness or mitigating factors), are not necessarily murder, whereas killings involving extremely reckless conduct or "felony murder" may be.

The Church also leaves open the possibility that under some unusual circumstances, standard justifications for killing that would normally relieve the individual from responsibility for murder, such as self-defense or defense of others, may not apply automatically. Wartime military service is considered a mitigating factor, not a justification for indiscriminate killing, thus suggesting that even in warfare one's conduct is measured and weighed by God and is not a matter of license (*MFP* 6:157–61). Only the Lord has the power to give life or to authorize it to be taken. Both the Bible and the Book of Mormon depict situations in which God has commanded the taking of life to accomplish his purposes. Goliath (1 Sam. 17:46–51), the king of Bashan (Deut. 3:3), and Laban (1 Ne. 4:10–18) were slain by servants of God after having been delivered into their hands by the Lord.

A person convicted of murder by a lawful government may be subject to the death penalty. The Church generally has not objected to CAPITAL PUNISHMENT legally and justly administered. Indeed, scriptural records both ancient and modern condone such punishment (Gen. 9:5–6; Ex. 21:12, 23; 2 Ne. 9:35; Alma 1:13–14; D&C 42:19).

With respect to related offenses, the Church distinguishes ABORTION from murder but holds it an extremely grave action, not to be done except in extremely limited circumstances that might include incest or rape, perils to the life or health of the mother, or severe birth defects. As far as has currently been revealed, a person may repent and be forgiven for the sin of abortion.

SUICIDE is regarded as self-murder and a grievous sin if committed by someone in full possession of his or her mental faculties. Because it is possible that a person who takes his or her own life may not be responsible for that action, only God can judge such a matter.

A person who participates in euthanasia—the deliberate, intentional putting to death of a person suffering from incurable conditions or diseases—violates the commandments of God. There is a difference between *allowing* a terminally ill person to die of natural causes and the *initiating* of action that causes someone's death. The application or denial of life-support systems must be decided reverently, usually by competent and responsible family members through prayer and the consultation of competent medical authorities. It is not wrong to ask the Lord, if it be his will, to shorten the physical suffering of a person whose afflictions are terminal and irreversible.

BIBLIOGRAPHY

Benson, Ezra Taft. *Teachings of Ezra Taft Benson.* Salt Lake City, 1988.

Gardiner, Martin R. "Mormonism and Capital Punishment: A Doctrinal Perspective, Past and Present." *Dialogue* 12 (Spring 1979):9–25.

Kimball, Spencer W. *The Miracle of Forgiveness.* Salt Lake City, 1969.

———. *Teachings of Spencer W. Kimball*, ed. Edward L. Kimball. Salt Lake City, 1982.

W. COLE DURHAM, JR.

MUSEUMS, LDS

On April 4, 1984, the Museum of Church History and Art in SALT LAKE CITY, UTAH, was dedicated, culminating over 140 years of effort to erect a building specifically to house LDS Church museum exhibits. Collections of art, artifacts, sculpture, photographs, documents, furniture, tools, clothing, handwork, architectural elements, and portraits represent past and present LDS cultures from around the world unified by a common theology.

One of the first museum references in Church history is from Addison Pratt, who on May 24, 1843, donated "the tooth of a whale, coral, and other curiosities" he had obtained in Polynesia as a young sailor, "as the beginning for a museum in Nauvoo" (*HC* 5:406). On April 7, 1848, paintings by Philo Dibble depicting the MARTYRDOM of Joseph and Hyrum SMITH and Joseph's last address to the NAUVOO LEGION were exhibited to the Brethren in the log tabernacle, Pottawattamie County, Iowa. Dibble was asked to paint scenes from this time in the history of the Church and

The Museum of Church History and Art, west of Temple Square, Salt Lake City (c. 1985). Opened in April 1984, the museum exhibits art, historical artifacts, and other items of Church history from around the world. Photographer: Eldon Linschoten.

display them in "a gallery in Zion" (Wilford Woodruff Journal, 3:340).

A letter from Dibble pleaded for immigrating Saints to bring "glass, nails, oils, paints, etc., to the valley . . . that a museum may be established . . . of the works of nature and art" (*MS* 11 [1849]:11–12). A general epistle to the Church signed by Brigham YOUNG and Willard Richards stated, "We also want all kinds of . . . rare specimens of natural curiosities and works of art that can be gathered and brought to the valley . . . from which, the rising generation can receive instruction; and if the Saints will be diligent . . . we will soon have the best, the most useful and attractive museum on earth" (*MS* 10 [1848]:85).

The first museum in the SALT LAKE VALLEY, established in 1869, was owned by John W. Young, son of Brigham Young. It displayed a variety of curiosities, including geological and live natural specimens indigenous to the region. This Salt Lake City Museum and Menagerie was located in a two-room adobe house behind the west wall of the Lion House. The curator was Guglielmo Giosue Rossetti Sangiovanni, a native of London called "Sangio." In 1871 the Deseret Telegraph needed the property, and, shorn of its "zoo" character, the museum was moved to a top floor of a building opposite the south gate of the temple block. On

September 18, 1878, ownership was transferred to the Church.

Joseph Barfoot, a devoted naturalist, became the second curator, and under his supervision the museum matured scientifically until his death in 1882. Under temporary caretakers and suffering from a lack of funds, the museum then went into decline. To save it, citizens formed the Salt Lake Literary and Scientific Association in 1885 and acquired the property from the Church, renaming it the "Deseret Museum." The association sold the building in which the artifacts were housed in 1890 and moved the collection to the Templeton Building with a new curator, James E. Talmage, appointed in 1891. Twelve years later the association built a three-story building, and again in 1903 the Deseret Museum was moved. J. Reuben Clark, Jr., assisted Dr. Talmage with the exhibits from 1891 to 1903.

In 1903, again being discommoded, the collection was boxed and stored and supervision again transferred to the LDS Church. In 1910 the collection was installed in the new Vermont Building opposite the temple block. William Forsberg assisted Dr. Talmage in creating a number of well-known displays, including the famous selenite crystals taken from a colossal geode found in southern Utah. Specimens taken from these crystals are now found in many prominent museums in the United States and Europe. Due to these farsighted gifts of Dr. Talmage, the Deseret Museum gained membership in the prestigious Museum Association, headquartered in London.

The collection grew as a result of museum exchanges and gifts from MISSIONARIES returning from many lands. Over fourteen thousand items were exhibited; one section brought together by the Daughters of the Utah Pioneers (DUP) told the story of the struggle, survival, and unique life of the LDS COLONIZATION past and present. The DUP established a unit in every community to collect, preserve, and display historical memorabilia to acquaint posterity with the past. A library of two thousand volumes, some rare, was housed in the museum. *The Deseret Evening News,* July 22, 1911, stated: "This museum is one of the most valuable assets the state has among educational institutions." When Dr. Talmage was called to the QUORUM OF THE TWELVE APOSTLES, December 8, 1911, his son, Sterling B. Talmage, was appointed museum curator. To provide a more convenient location for visitors, the Church enlarged the Bureau of Information on TEMPLE SQUARE to hold several exhibits. At this time the collections were divided into categories. Some were transferred to the LDS University Museum and later to BRIGHAM YOUNG UNIVERSITY. The DUP collection was returned to that organization and is now housed in a museum near the state capitol. Many specimens were transferred to the Museum of Natural History at the University of Utah. Items of interest to LDS Church members and visitors were placed on exhibit in the Bureau of Information on Temple Square. In 1976 the museum collection on Temple Square was again boxed and stored, making way for a new VISITORS CENTER and in preparation for the new Church Museum of History and Art.

Many of the original exhibits from the early museums form the nucleus of collections in several prestigious museums. The Museum of Church History and Art, opposite the west gates of Temple Square, maintains exhibits of LDS history and art, from the bas-relief over the entrance of the granite building to the restored 1847 log home of the Duel brothers. The galleries cover 160 years of Church history, spiritual events, art, and artifacts of a people who came west under difficult circumstances and successfully achieved their goal of preserving and promoting their theology in the beautiful, educational, and cultural environment of the Church.

BIBLIOGRAPHY

Johnson, B. F. "Philo Dibble Narrative." In *Faith Promoting Classics*. Salt Lake City, 1880; reprinted, 1968.

Rollins, Kerril Sue. "LDS Artifacts and Art Portray Church History: The New Church Museum." *Ensign* 14 (Apr. 1984):44–53.

Talmage, James E. "The Deseret Museum." *IE* 14 (Sept. 1911):953–82.

Wells, Junius F. "Joseph L. Barfoot." *Contributor* 3 (May 1882):250–52.

FLORENCE SMITH JACOBSEN

MUSIC

Throughout the Church's history, music has permeated the assemblies of the Saints and has energized their pursuit of spiritual and cultural betterment. The diversity of styles in the Church is echoed in the diversity of roles that music plays in LDS life.

As in many churches, congregational hymns open and close most ecclesiastical gatherings. In many LDS meetings instrumental music (most often organ) provides preludes, interludes, and postludes. Choral music is produced by many WARD and STAKE choirs, and the Church's well-known MORMON TABERNACLE CHOIR is heard internationally on the weekly "Music and the Spoken Word" broadcast. Music also brightens most ward and stake social activities, such as cultural nights, parties, pageants, roadshows, dances and dance festivals, as well as family reunions and FAMILY HOME EVENINGS. Music of various styles regularly enhances Church productions designed to educate and proselytize through mass media, including audio and video tapes, films, filmstrips, commercials and programs for radio and television. Amid this diversity of musical endeavors, composers and performers usually follow the cooperative principles of early Mormonism, giving of their talents in anticipation of spiritual rewards—and also for their own enjoyment.

Although American Christian churches historically have held conflicting views on music, a revelation to the Prophet Joseph SMITH in July 1830 (D&C 25) likened "the song of the righteous" to prayer, confirming the propriety of vocal music for worship. With this foundation, the Prophet formed a Church "singing department" in 1835 to teach note reading and vocal technique. In Nauvoo, and later in Utah, musical standards rose as several well-trained British musicians were converted to the Church and immigrated to the United States. These converts helped establish the propriety of instrumental music for worship, a matter not addressed in the 1830 revelation. Although congregational and choral singing clearly prevailed in the Church, instrumental music soon came to accompany it. Wind, brass, and string bands also proliferated in LDS culture, accompanying the military, recreational, and civic exercises of the Saints.

In pioneer Utah several relatively short-lived associations, including the Deseret Musical Association and the Deseret Philharmonic Society, collected musical scores, created a territorial roster of musicians, and disseminated new pedagogical techniques. At the same time, the Saints founded a number of musical businesses that imported instruments and sheet music into the Great Basin in Utah. Meanwhile, Brigham YOUNG sent some of the Church's most skilled musicians, notably C. J.

The Mormon choir, Nottingham, England (1912).

Thomas, on colonizing missions in the 1860s to ensure that the art would flourish even in outlying LDS settlements. From the 1870s through 1920, the Sunday School and other Church auxiliaries gradually assumed leadership in musical training, providing singing lessons and band memberships for young Latter-day Saints as well as publishing a large amount of newly composed music.

Little attempt was made to correlate or standardize LDS musical affairs until 1920, when President Heber J. GRANT appointed a General Music Committee for the Church. Primarily consisting of musicians connected with the Salt Lake Tabernacle, the committee assumed the tasks of evaluating styles of music appropriate to worship, recommending what types of instruments (predominantly the organ) should be played in Church meetings, overseeing the production of hymnals, and fostering musical education. In this last regard, the committee endeavored to train Church musicians in several ways, including hiring professionals to teach in wards and stakes, publishing manuals of choral conducting and organ technique, and issuing music newsletters. Throughout its history, much of the committee's effort went into directing the work of stake and ward music committees. In the 1970s the committee was succeeded by

the Music Department (later Music Division) of the Church.

President Brigham Young set the tone for official LDS statements on music, defining it as a "magic power" that could "fill the air with harmony, and cheer and comfort the hearts of men, and so wonderfully affect the brute creation" (*JD* 1:48). Since his time, General Authorities of the Church have continued to praise music as a soothing influence, a purifier of thought, and a uniter of hearts. The type of music most consistently endorsed has been sacred vocal music prepared especially for LDS worship. LDS composers have written hundreds of hymns and anthems and have created many large-scale, sometimes modernistic sacred works, such as Evan Stephens's "dramatic cantatas" of the 1920s and the numerous oratorios composed since, which usually treat specifically LDS themes, for example, the *Restoration* oratorios of B. Cecil Gates and Merrill Bradshaw, Gates's *Salvation for the Dead*, and Leroy Robertson's *Oratorio from the Book of Mormon*. Moreover, beginning in Brigham Young's day, a strong tradition of theater music has developed among the Saints, one that has fostered the composition of musical scores both for commemorative pageants (e.g., those at Palmyra, New York; Nauvoo, Illinois; and Manti, Utah) and lighter stage works such as the pioneer centennial production *Promised Valley*, and also a host of youth-oriented musicals in the 1970s and 1980s.

A few stylistic issues have surfaced in the twentieth century. Some Church authorities have advised against certain popular styles of music, citing their loudness, their rhythmic intensity, and the indecency of some of their lyrics; members are counseled to be wise in selecting their recreational music. Questions also have been raised over the propriety of using styles of music found outside the hymnal in worship services. Nevertheless, in non-liturgical settings, ethnic religious music thrives and some LDS songwriters have adapted soft rock music for informal religious use. Much of this music has found its way into Church-sponsored songbooks and cassettes and into privately produced recordings for young Latter-day Saints.

The enduring value of much music indigenous to the Church is difficult to predict. On the one hand, the vernacular music often echoes the more ephemeral styles of denominational Christian music. On the other hand, some impressive settings have emerged from the hymnody of the

Children singing in East Berlin (1990). Even though they were substantially cut off from the rest of the Church for many years, members in East Germany maintained one of the highest activity rates in the Church. Courtesy Peggy Jellinghausen.

Church, and some of the larger works manifest a continuing increase in sophistication. Furthermore, the extensive use of worship music borrowed from other Christian traditions unites the Saints to a larger fellowship of believers. Above all, the sheer abundance of music in the Church reveals how untiring are the aesthetic impulses of its members. Whether or not a distinctively LDS style emerges, music of many styles undoubtedly will continue to inspire the Saints.

BIBLIOGRAPHY

Hicks, Michael. *Mormonism and Music: A History.* Urbana, Ill., 1989.

Purdy, William Earl. "Music in Mormon Culture, 1830–1876." Ph.D. diss., Northwestern University, 1960.

Slaughter, Jay L. "The Role of Music in the Mormon Church, School, and Life." Ph.D. diss., Indiana University, 1964.

Some General Recommendations Concerning Music in The Church of Jesus Christ of Latter-day Saints. Salt Lake City, 1950; 2nd ed., 1962.

MICHAEL D. HICKS

Music often plays an important role in LDS family life and in family home evenings.

MUSICIANS

From the early decades of The Church of Jesus Christ of Latter-day Saints, LDS composers, conductors, vocalists, and instrumentalists have helped to shape the Church's distinctive musical heritage. Some of these musicians have made their mark on the larger musical scene, while numerous others have focused their talents for the direct benefit of the Church.

Volunteer musicians—music chairmen, organists, pianists, music directors, choir directors, and Primary music leaders—serve in the Church's weekly worship services. These musicians are called by priesthood leaders and serve without pay in the particular ward or stake in which they live. Contributing time and talents is an expected and rewarding part of Church membership, and both the highly trained musician and the beginner offer

Alexander Schreiner (1901–1987), Salt Lake Tabernacle Organist. Born in Germany, Schreiner came with his family to Utah in 1912. He studied with Tabernacle Organist John J. McClellan and was appointed to the Tabernacle staff in 1924. In 1925 he studied with Charles-Marie Widor and Louis Vierne in Paris, France. From 1930 to 1939 he served as University Organist at UCLA, returning to Salt Lake City during the summers. Until his retirement in 1977 he accompanied the Mormon Tabernacle Choir, toured internationally, and composed music. He was primarily responsible for the present design of the Tabernacle Organ. Courtesy Utah State Historical Society.

their talents as called upon. Wards require from fifteen to twenty-three musicians to fill outlined music positions, with twelve to twenty-four or more needed to sing in the ward choir.

Each ward and stake is responsible for providing the needed training for its own musicians with regard to their Church callings. In addition, since 1978 Brigham Young University has presented an annual Church Music Workshop, where many receive training in music skills.

Converts from the British Isles had a strong influence on MUSIC in the early Church. John Tullidge, an accomplished church musician from Weymouth, England, arrived in Salt Lake Valley in 1863. A singer, composer, arranger, teacher, and music critic, he edited the first Latter-day Saint hymnbook that included both words and music. Other musically trained English converts included C. J. Thomas, David Calder, Ebenezer Beesley, and George Careless. John Parry, born in North Wales, led a choir in Salt Lake City that was the precursor of the MORMON TABERNACLE CHOIR. Evan Stephens, from South Wales, brought the latter choir to wide recognition during his twenty-seven years as conductor (1889–1916).

Many influential Church musicians have been associated with the Tabernacle Choir. Almost half of the musical settings of the hymns in the 1889 Psalmody were composed by directors George Careless, Ebenezer Beesley, and Evan Stephens, or by Joseph J. Daynes, the first Tabernacle organist (from 1867 to 1900). Alexander Schreiner, who served for fifty-three years (1924–1977) as Tabernacle organist, was highly involved with musical affairs of the Church and endeared himself to audiences throughout the world. Other Tabernacle organists to 1989 have included John J. McClellan, Edward P. Kimball, Tracy Y. Cannon, Frank Asper, Wade N. Stephens, Roy M. Darley, Robert Cundick, John Longhurst, Clay Christiansen, and Richard Elliott, with Bonnie Goodliffe and Linda Margetts as associate organists.

During the late nineteenth century many musical performing groups and societies were organized among the Saints (see MUSIC). Behind every such effort was at least one motivated musician and often a supportive Church leader. President Brigham YOUNG often sent such a musician to a particular settlement to promote the instruction and performance of music to enhance pioneer life.

Through the years, many Latter-day Saints have excelled in musical creativity and performance attested by the names in the next three paragraphs. For example, Emma Lucy Gates Bowen, a coloratura soprano, performed widely throughout the United States and Europe. Her brother, B. Cecil Gates, organized the McCune School of Music and Art in Salt Lake City in 1919. Together they formed the Emma Lucy Gates Opera Company in the 1920s.

Currently many accomplished Latter-day Saint musicians are affiliated with institutions of higher learning as composers, conductors, performers, historians, and theorists. Historically these have been concentrated in the music faculties at the University of Utah and, more recently, at Brigham Young University.

BIBLIOGRAPHY

Davidson, Karen Lynn. *Our Latter-day Hymns: The Stories and the Messages*. Salt Lake City, 1988.

Durham, Lowell M. "On Mormon Music and Musicians." *Dialogue* 3 (Summer 1968):19–40.

MICHAEL F. MOODY

MYSTERIES OF GOD

"Mysteries of God" is a scriptural phrase in which the word "mysteries" refers to knowledge about God that is often hidden from mortal understanding. It does not refer to something incomprehensible in principle. Like many people of other religions, Latter-day Saints deem a knowledge of some mysteries to be necessary (D&C 76:5–10), and acquire such knowledge in part through ORDINANCES and in part through REVELATION (cf. *TPJS*, p. 324).

As found both in the Bible and in latter-day scripture, the term "mystery" describes a doctrine revealed only to the faithful but not given to the "world" or to the uninitiated. (Matt. 13:11; 1 Cor. 2:7; Eph. 3:1–7; 1 Ne. 10:11; D&C 42:61, 65).

The terms "mystery," "mysteries," "mystery of God," and "mysteries of Godliness" appear more than a dozen times in the New Testament, always with the sense of something known to God but unknown to humans who have not yet been divinely instructed. Although none of these terms appears in the Old Testament, the word "secrets" in Daniel 2:28 ("But there is a God in heaven that revealeth secrets") and the term "secret" in Amos 3:7 ("Surely the Lord God . . . revealeth his secret

unto his servants the prophets") are equivalent to "mysteries," especially because they are associated with divine revelation (cf. D&C 76:10).

The BOOK OF MORMON prophet NEPHI₁ (c. 570 B.C.) equated the plain and precious truths of the gospel with the mysteries of God, noting that those who were stiff-necked and hard of heart, including some members of his own family, found them difficult to believe. But the faithful accepted such truths willingly, under the heart-softening influence of the HOLY GHOST (1 Ne. 2:11–16; 10:17–22; 15:1–11). Nephi and his followers believed that Jesus Christ would come, that men and women should be baptized and receive the Holy Ghost, and that God speaks to those who inquire, answering their prayers. In fact, Nephi cites his knowledge of these mysteries in the opening statement of his record as part of his qualification to write it (1 Ne. 1:1).

In latter-day scripture the word "mysteries" typically has three interrelated meanings. First, the mysteries consist of significant truths about God and his works. Second, faithful, obedient members of the Church will be given this sacred knowledge through revelation. Finally, those who are not made partakers of this special understanding will not attain the same glory as those who are. Understanding the mysteries of God is a gospel privilege for the reverent who serve God faithfully (D&C 76:1–10; cf. 1 Ne. 10:17–19; Moses 1:5).

The Prophet Joseph SMITH was given the "keys of the mysteries and the revelations" (D&C 28:7; 35:18) in connection with the MELCHIZEDEK PRIESTHOOD (D&C 84:19; 107:18–19). Thus, obtaining the hidden truths is bound up with the power of the Melchizedek Priesthood, "which priesthood administereth the gospel and holdeth the key of the mysteries of the kingdom, even the key of the knowledge of God" (D&C 84:19).

Paradoxically, the term "mystery" encapsulates a dual meaning, both to reveal and to conceal. For the initiated, it designates something believable and understandable. For the nonbeliever its significance is obscure. In other words, the belief and faith of the potential knower determine in great part whether the knowledge is comprehensible or not (Alma 12:9–11).

The knowledge alluded to in the phrases "mysteries of God" or "mysteries of Godliness" may be received in ways other than exclusively verbal. Throughout history, divine knowledge also has been communicated in ceremonies, rites, purifications, and so on. Such is the case in the TEMPLES of the Latter-day Saints, where faithful members of the Church gain knowledge and understanding of heavenly truths as they receive ordinances by COVENANT.

The broad meaning of "Godliness" embraces the state of being like God, of approximating God's nature or qualities. The possibility is suggested in the so-called Law of the Harvest. Just as apple seeds produce apple trees, so the offspring of deity, human beings, when they are fully mature—that is, holy, knowledgeable and virtuous—are like their divine parents.

Jesus' statement in John 17:3, uttered as he petitioned his Father, takes on a more profound meaning in light of the scriptural references to the mysteries of God: "And this is life eternal, that they might know thee the only true God, and Jesus Christ, whom thou hast sent." The "knowing" to which the Savior refers is that higher knowledge often designated "the mysteries of God" or "the mysteries of Godliness."

BIBLIOGRAPHY

Brown, Raymond E. *The Semitic Background of the Term "Mystery" in the New Testament.* Facet Books Biblical Series 21. Philadelphia, 1968.

Welch, John W. "The Calling of a Prophet." In *The Book of Mormon: The Keystone Scripture,* ed. P. Cheesman. Provo, Utah, 1988.

CLARK D. WEBB